DATE DUE

			PRINTED IN U.S.A.

ISBN 0-7876-2871-9

Kevin Hillstrom
Laurie Collier Hillstrom

ENCYCLOPEDIA *of*
Small Business

A-I
VOLUME 1

GALE

DETROIT • LONDON

ENCYCLOPEDIA *of*
Small Business

A-I
VOLUME 1

evin Hillstrom and Laurie Collier Hillstrom, *Editors*

Contributing Authors

Paula M. Ard, Virginia L. Barnstorff, Christopher C. Barry, Laurence Barton, Bradley e Boyd, John Burnett, Robert Buttery, Boyd Childress, Amy Cooper, Raymond A. K. , Richard C. Cuthie, Aldona Cytraus, Louis J. Drapeau, Sina Dubovoy, Art DuRivage, ham Gal, April Dougal Gasbarre, Edmund R. Gray, Susan Bard Hall, Heather Behn Hedden, Tona Henderson, Ned. C. Hill, Ronald M. Horwitz, Cynthia Ianarelli, Frederick C. Ingram, Clint Johnson, Kristin Kahrs, Susan M. Kasuba, Christine M. Kelley, Robert T. Kleiman, Jan Klisz, Michael Knes, David Kucera, John Lawler, Joan Leotta, John G. Maurer, Don Mayer, Bruce Meyer, Dave Mote, Matthew T. Pifer, Richard Rump, Anandi P. Sahu, Susan Salter, John Sarich, Arthur G. Sharp, John Simley, Kathryn Snavely, David Sprinkle, Paulette L. Stenzel, John E. Tropman, Karen Troshynski-Thomas, David E. Upton, David A. Victor, Etan Vlessing, Mark A. Vonderembse, Mark A. White, Roberta H. Winston, Charles Woelfel, Art Wojtowicz, Dave Zemens, and Judith A. Zimmerman

Gale Research Staff

Deborah M. Burek, *Managing Editor*

Eva M. Davis, Linda D. Hall, William H. Harmer, Kelly Hill, Sonya D. Hill, Yolanda A. Johnson, Karin E. Koek, and Julie A. Mitchell, *Contributing Editors*

Mary Beth Trimper, *Production Director*
Evi Seoud, *Assistant Production Manager*
Cindy Baldwin, *Product Design Manager*
Eric Johnson, *Art Director*

Jeff Chapman, *Programmer/Analyst*

While every effort has been made to ensure the reliability of information presented in this publication, Gale Research does not guarantee the accuracy of the data contained herein. Gale accepts no payment for listing; and inclusion in the publication of any organization, agency, institution, publication, service, or individual does not imply endorsement of the editors or the publisher. Errors brought to the attention of the publisher and verified to the satisfaction of the publisher will be corrected in future editions.

Library of Congress Cataloging-in-Publication Data
Hillstrom, Kevin, 1963-
    Encyclopedia of small business / Kevin Hillstrom, Laurie Collier
    Hillstrom
        p. cm.
    Includes bibliographical references and index.
    ISBN 0-7876-1864-0 (set : alk. paper).—ISBN0-7876-2871-9 (vol.
1 : alk. paper).—ISBN 0-7876-2872-7 (vol. 2   : alk. paper)
    1. Small business—Management—Encyclopedia.   2. Small business—
Finance—Encyclopedia.   I. Hillstrom, Laurie Collier, 1965-   .
II. Title.
    HD62.7.H553   1998   98-14862
    658.02'2—dc21   CIP

ISBN 0-7876-1864-0 (set), ISBN 0-7876-2871-9 (V1), ISBN 0-7876-2872-7 (V2)

Printed in the United States of America

CONTENTS

INTRODUCTION AND USER'S GUIDE vii

VOLUME I
Entries Arranged Alphabetically A - I . . . . *1 - 561*

VOLUME II
Entries Arranged Alphabetically J - Z . . . . *563 - 1042*

MASTER INDEX *1045*

Welcome to the *Encyclopedia of Small Business (EOSB)*. The publication of this encyclopedia reflects a recognition of a growing trend, evident across many industries and economic regions, toward entrepreneurship and small business development in North America. Indeed, countless studies indicate that small business enterprises are a vital component of continued economic growth, and both academic research and anecdotal evidence suggest that entrepreneurial ventures will continue to grow in size, number, and importance in the coming years.

The *Encyclopedia of Small Business* serves as a one-stop source for valuable and in-depth information on a wide range of small business topics including:

- Advertising Media on the Web
- Balancing Career and Family
- Business Start-ups
- Employee Compensation
- Family-owned Enterprises
- Financing
- Franchising
- Health Insurance Options
- Home-based Businesses
- International Marketing
- Internet Commerce
- Minority Business Development
- Product Development
- Tax Planning.

In addition, special emphasis is given to how these issues—many of which face businesses of all sizes and in all industries—affect small businesses, from new entrepreneurial ventures to well-established family businesses to rapidly growing enterprises poised for expansion into new markets and emerging industries.

Finally, *EOSB* is written so that it is accessible and relevant to entrepreneurs and small business owners from a variety of backgrounds. Whether the *Encyclopedia's* user is an entrepreneur fresh from the hallways of the corporate world, an established business owner grappling with work force management issues, a veteran freelancer seeking to expand her client base, or a retiring business owner looking to pass his business on to the next generation, *EOSB* contains a great deal of valuable information to help guide the entrepreneur's efforts.

USER'S GUIDE

The *Encyclopedia of Small Business* has been designed for ease of use. The 505 essays are arranged alphabetically by topic in two volumes, with Volume One covering essays beginning with A-I and Volume Two covering essays J-Z. Special features that can be found within individual essays include the following:

- **Bolded Terms** denote words or phrases that are covered in a separate entry in *EOSB*.

- **See Also** references appear at the end of many entries and direct the user to related topics listed within *EOSB* which do not appear within that particular entry.

- **Further Reading** sections are included at the end of most entries. These bibliographic citations point the reader toward additional sources of information on the topic.

The *Encyclopedia of Small Business* also includes a **Master Index**, which can be found at the back of Volume Two. This index contains alphabetical references to the following, as mentioned in *EOSB* entries: important terms in accounting, advertising, finance, human resources, management, product development, and other areas of interest to small business owners; ''see also'' references; names of institutions, organizations, and associations; key government agencies; and relevant legislation. Each index term is followed by volume and page numbers which easily direct the user to both main topics (indicated by **bolded** page numbers) as well as to all secondary reference terms as mentioned above.

ACKNOWLEDGMENTS

The staff at Gale Research would like to thank the following individuals for their advice and suggestions for the generation of the *Encyclopedia's* topic list: Susan Awe, Branch Manager, Jefferson County Public Library—Arvada Branch; JoAnn Kosanke, Business Department Manager, Toledo-Lucas County Public Library; and Jules Mastoff, District Director, Service Corps of Retired Executives (SCORE), Milwaukee Chapter.

COMMENTS AND SUGGESTIONS

Questions, comments, and suggestions regarding the *Encyclopedia of Small Business* are invited and welcomed. Please contact:

Editor
Encyclopedia of Small Business
(Address until September 15, 1998)
Gale Research
835 Penobscot Bldg.
645 Griswold St.
Detroit, MI 48226-4094

(Address after September 15, 1998)
Gale Research
27500 Drake Rd.
Farmington Hills, MI 48331-3535

Toll-free Phone: 800-347-4253
Toll-free FAX: 800-339-3374

A

Absenteeism is the term generally used to refer to unscheduled employee absences from the workplace. Many causes of absenteeism are legitimate—personal illness or family issues, for example—but absenteeism also can often be traced to other factors such as a poor work environment or workers who are not committed to their jobs. If such absences become excessive, they can have a seriously adverse impact on a business's operations and, ultimately, its profitability.

COSTS OF ABSENTEEISM

"Unscheduled absences hurt," wrote M. Michael Markowich in a summary of an article he wrote for the September 1993 issue of *Small Business Reports*. "In fact, they can cost a small company anywhere from $250 to $450 per worker, per year. That includes sick time paid, replacement costs, lost productivity, and delays in meeting customer needs, among other things. Problem is, most sick leave policies foster a 'use it or lose it' mind-set, and employees feel entitled to a certain number of sick days." Markowich went on to note that a survey of 5,000 companies conducted by Commerce Clearing House Inc. (CCH Inc.) found that unscheduled absences cost small businesses $62,636 a year, on average, in lost productivity, sick time, and replacement costs.

Indeed, absenteeism can take a financial toll on a small business (or a multinational company, for that matter) in several different respects. The most obvious cost is in the area of sick leave benefits—provided that the business offers such benefits—but there are

significant hidden costs as well. The *SOHO Guidebook* cites the following as notable hidden cost factors associated with absenteeism:

- Lost **productivity** of the absent employee;
- **Overtime** for other employees to fill in;
- Decreased overall productivity of those employees;
- Any temporary help costs incurred;
- Possible loss of business or dissatisfied customers;
- Problems with employee morale.

Indeed, *Attacking Absenteeism* author Lynn Tylczak contended that excessive absenteeism, if left unchecked, can wear on a company in numerous ways. "[Absenteeism] forces managers to deal with problems of morale, discipline, job dissatisfaction, job stress, team spirit, productivity, turnover, production quality, additional administration, and overhead. To summarize: You don't have an absentee problem. You have a profit problem."

DEVELOPING AN ABSENCE POLICY

Many small business owners do not establish absenteeism policies for their companies. Some owners have only a few employees, and do not feel that it is worth the trouble. Others operate businesses in which "sick pay" is not provided to employees. Workers in such firms thus have a significant incentive to show up for work; if they do not, their paycheck suffers. And others simply feel that absenteeism is not a significant problem, so they see no need to institute new policies or make any changes to the few existing rules that might already be in place. As

Michael W. Mercer wrote in *Turning Your Human Resources Department into a Profit Center,* " 'If it ain't broke, don't fix it.' . . . If absenteeism is not a major problem then an organization would be better off if it did not change its absenteeism policies."

But many small business consultants counsel entrepreneurs and business owners to consider establishing formal written policies that mesh with state and federal laws. Written policies can give employers added legal protection from employees who have been fired or disciplined for excessive absenteeism, provided that those policies explicitly state the allowable number of absences, the consequences of excessive absenteeism, and other relevant aspects of the policy. Moreover, noted *The SOHO Guidebook,* "a formal, detailed policy that addresses absences, tardiness, failure to call in, and leaving early can serve to prevent misconceptions about acceptable behavior, inconsistent discipline, complaints of favoritism, morale problems, and charges of illegal discrimination. General statements that excessive absenteeism will be a cause for discipline may be insufficient and may lead to problems."

Most employees are conscientious workers with good attendance records (or even if they are forced to miss significant amounts of work, the reasons are legitimate). But as Markowich noted, "every company has a small number of abusers—about 3 percent of the workforce—who exploit the system by taking more than their allotted sick time or more days than they actually need. And when they begin calling in sick on too many Monday or Friday mornings, who picks up the slack and handles the extra work? More important, who responds to customer requests?"

To address absenteeism, then, many small businesses that employ workers have established one of two absenteeism policies. The first of these is a traditional absenteeism policy that distinguishes between excused and unexcused absences. Under such policies, employees are provided with a set number of sick days (also sometimes called "personal" days in recognition that employees occasionally need to take time off to attend to personal/family matters) and a set number of vacation days. Workers who are absent from work after exhausting their sick days are required to use vacation days under this system. Absences that take place after both sick and vacation days have been exhausted are subject to disciplinary action. The second policy alternative, commonly known as a "no-fault" system, permits each employee a specified number of absences (either days or "occurrences," in which multiple days of continuous absence are counted as a single occurrence) annually and does not consider the reason for the employee's absence. As with traditional absence policies, once the employee's days have been used up, he or she is subject to disciplinary action.

"USE IT OR LOSE IT" Some companies do not allow employees to carry sick days over from year to year. The benefits and disadvantages of this policy continue to be debated in businesses across the country. Some analysts contend that most employees do not require large numbers of sick days, and that systems that allow carryovers are more likely to be abused by poor employees than appropriately utilized by good employees, who, if struck down by a long-term illness, often have disability alternatives. But Markowich warns that "today, most employees feel entitled to a specified number of sick days. And if they don't take those days, they feel that they are losing a promised benefit. Your company may be inadvertently reinforcing this 'use it or lose it' attitude by establishing policies under which employees 'lose' their sick time if it is not used by the end of the year."

ESTABLISHING A SYSTEM FOR TRACKING ABSENCES

Absenteeism policies are useless if the business does not also implement and maintain an effective system for tracking employee attendance. Some companies are able to track absenteeism through existing payroll systems, but for those who do not have this option, they need to make certain that they put together a system that can: 1) keep an accurate count of individual employee absences; 2) provide the owner with company wide absenteeism totals; 3) calculate the financial impact that these absences have on the business; 4) detect periods when absences are particularly high; and 5) differentiate between various types of absences.

FURTHER READING:

Ceniceros, Roberto. "Written Policies Reduce Risk in Firing Workers Comp Abusers." *Business Insurance.* April 21, 1997.

Keenan, Denis. "Too Much Time Off." *Accountancy.* April 1993.

Markowich, M. Michael. "Attendance Required." *Small Business Reports.* September 1993.

The SOHO Guidebook. CCH Incorporated, 1997.

Mercer, Michael W. *Turning Your Human Resources Department into a Profit Center.* New York: Amacom, 1989.

Tylczak, Lynn. *Attacking Absenteeism: Positive Solutions to an Age-Old Problem.* Menlo Park, CA: Crisp, 1990.

SEE ALSO: Employee Motivation

ACCOUNTING

Accounting has been defined as "the language of business" because it is the basic tool for recording, reporting, and evaluating economic events and transactions that affect business enterprises. Accounting documents all aspects of a business's financial performance, from payroll costs, capital expenditures, and other obligations to sales revenue and owners' equity. An understanding of the financial data contained in accounting documents, then, is regarded as essential to reaching an accurate picture of a business's true financial well-being. Armed with such knowledge, businesses can make appropriate financial and strategic decisions about their future; conversely, incomplete or inaccurate accounting data can cripple a company, no matter its size or orientation. Accounting's importance as a barometer of business health—past, present, and future—and tool of business navigation is reflected in the words of the American Institute of Certified Public Accountants (AICPA), which defined accounting as a ''service activity.'' Accounting, said the AICPA, is intended ''to provide quantitative information, primarily financial in nature, about economic activities that is intended to be useful in making economic decisions—making reasoned choices among alternative courses of action.''

A business's accounting system contains information potentially relevent to a wide range of people. In addition to business owners, who rely on accounting data to gauge their enterprise's financial progress, accounting data can communicate relevant information to investors, creditors, managers, and others who interact with the business in question. As a result, accounting is sometimes divided into two distinct subsets—financial accounting and management accounting—that reflect the different information needs of these end users. Financial accounting is a branch of accounting that provides people outside the business—such as investors or loan officers—with qualitative information regarding an enterprise's economic resources, obligations, financial performance, and cash flow. Management accounting, on the other hand, refers to accounting data used by business owners, supervisors, and other employees of a business to gauge their enterprises's health and operating trends.

GENERALLY ACCEPTED ACCOUNTING PRINCIPLES

Generally accepted accounting principles (GAAP) are the guidelines, rules, and procedures used in recording and reporting accounting information in audited financial statements. Various organizations have influenced the development of modern-day accounting principles. Among these are the American Institute of Certified Public Accountants (AICPA), the Financial Accounting Standards Board (FASB), and the **Securities and Exchange Commission** (SEC). The first two are private sector organizations; the SEC is a federal government agency.

The AICPA played a major role in the development of accounting standards. In 1937 the AICPA created the Committee on Accounting Procedures (CAP), which issued a series of Accounting Research Bulletins (ARB) with the purpose of standardizing accounting practices. This committee was replaced by the Accounting Principles Board (APB) in 1959. The APB maintained the ARB series, but it also began to publish a new set of pronouncements, referred to as Opinions of the Accounting Principles Board. In mid-1973, an independent private board called the Financial Accounting Standards Board (FASB) replaced the APB and assumed responsibility for the issuance of financial accounting standards. The FASB remains the primary determiner of financial accounting standards in the United States. Comprised of seven members who serve full-time and receive compensation for their service, the FASB identifies financial accounting issues, conducts research related to these issues, and is charged with resolving the issues. A super-majority vote (i.e., at least five to two) is required before an addition or change to the Statements of Financial Accounting Standards is issued.

The Financial Accounting Foundation is the parent organization to FASB. The foundation is governed by a 16-member Board of Trustees appointed from the memberships of eight organizations: AICPA, Financial Executives Institute, Institute of Management Accountants, Financial Analysts Federation, American Accounting Association, Securities Industry Association, Government Finance Officers Association, and National Association of State Auditors. A Financial Accounting Standards Advisory Council (approximately 30 members) advises the FASB. In addition, an Emerging Issues Task Force (EITF) was established in 1984 to provide timely guidance to the FASB on new accounting issues.

The Securities and Exchange Commission, an agency of the federal government, has the legal authority to prescribe accounting principles and reporting practices for all companies issuing publicly traded securities. The SEC has seldom used this authority, however, although it has intervened or expressed its views on accounting issues from time to time. U.S. law requires that companies subject to the jurisdiction of the SEC make reports to the SEC giving detailed information about their operations. The SEC has broad powers to require public disclosure in a fair and accurate manner in financial statements and to protect investors. The SEC establishes accounting principles with respect to the information contained within reports it requires of registered companies. These reports include: Form S-X, a registration statement; Form 1O-K, an annual report; Form 1O-Q, a quarterly report of operations; Form S-K, a report used to describe significant events that may affect the company; and Proxy Statements, which are used when management requests the right to vote through proxies for shareholders.

ACCOUNTING SYSTEM

An accounting system is a management information system that is responsible for the collection and processing of data useful to decision-makers in planning and controlling the activities of a business organization. The data processing cycle of an accounting system encompasses the total structure of five activities associated with tracking financial information: collection or recording of data; classification of data; processing (including calculating and summarizing) of data; maintenance or storage of results; and reporting of results. The primary—but not sole—means by which these final results are disseminated to both internal (in-company) and external users such as creditors and investors is the financial statement.

The elements of accounting are the building blocks from which **financial statements** are constructed. According to the Financial Accounting Standards Board (FASB), the primary financial elements that are directly related to measuring performance and the financial position of a business enterprise are as follows:

- **Assets**—probable future economic benefits obtained or controlled by a particular entity as a result of past transactions or events.

- Comprehensive Income—the change in equity (net assets) of an entity during a given period as a result of transactions and other events and circumstances from nonowner sources. Comprehensive income includes all changes in equity during a period except those resulting from investments by owners and distributions to owners.

- Distributions to Owners—decreases in equity (net assets) of a particular enterprise as a result of transferring assets, rendering services, or incurring liabilities to owners.

- Equity—the residual interest in the assets of an entity that remain after deducting liabilities. In a business entity, equity is the ownership interest.

- Expenses—events that expend assets or incur liabilities during a period from delivering or providing goods or services and carrying out other activities that constitute the entity's ongoing major or central operation.

- Gains—increases in equity (net assets) from peripheral or incidental transactions. Gains also come from other transactions, events, and circumstances affecting the entity during a period except those that result from

revenues or investments by owners. Investments by owners are increases in net assets resulting from transfers of valuables from other entities to obtain or increase ownership interests (or equity) in it.

- **Liabilities**—probable future sacrifices of economic benefits arising from present obligations to transfer assets or provide services to other entities in the future as a result of past transactions or events.

- Losses—decreases in equity (net assets) from peripheral or incidental transactions of an entity and from all other transactions, events, and circumstances affecting the entity during a period. Losses do not include equity drops that result from expenses or distributions to owners.

- Revenues—inflows or other enhancements of assets, settlements of liabilities, or a combination of both during a period from delivering or producing goods, rendering services, or conducting other activities that constitute the entity's ongoing major or central operations.

FINANCIAL STATEMENTS

Financial statements are the most comprehensive way of communicating financial information about a business enterprise, and a wide array of users—from investors and creditors to budget directors—use the data it contains to guide their actions and business decisions. Financial statements generally include the following information:

- **Balance sheet** (or statement of financial position)—summarizes the financial position of an accounting entity at a particular point in time as represented by its economic resources (assets), economic obligations (liabilities), and equity.

- **Income statement**—summarizes the results of operations for a given period of time.

- **Cash flow statement**—summarizes the impact of an enterprise's cash flows on its operating, financing, and investing activities over a given period of time.

- Statement of retained earnings—shows the increases and decreases in earnings retained by the company over a given period of time.

- Statement of changes in stockholders' equity—discloses the changes in the separate stockholders' equity account of an entity, including investments by distributions to owners during the period.

Notes to financial statements are considered an integral part of a complete set of financial statements. Notes typically provide additional information at the end of the statement and concern such matters as depreciation and inventory methods used in the statements, details of long-term debt, pensions, leases, income taxes, contingent liabilities, methods of consolidation, and other matters. Significant accounting policies are usually disclosed as the initial note or as a summary preceding the notes to the financial statements.

ACCOUNTING PROFESSION

There are two primary kinds of accountants: private accountants, who are employed by a business enterprise to perform accounting services exclusively for that business, and public accountants, who function as independent experts and perform accounting services for a wide variety of clients. Some public accountants operate their own businesses, while others are employed by accounting firms to attend to the accounting needs of the firm's clients. The largest U.S. accounting firms, commonly referred to as the Big Six, are Arthur Andersen & Co., Coopers & Lybrand, Deloitte and Touche, Ernst & Young, KPMG Peat Marwick, and Price Waterhouse.

A **certified public accountant** (CPA) is an accountant who has 1) fulfilled certain educational and experience requirements established by state law for the practice of public accounting and 2) garnered an acceptable score on a rigorous three-day national examination. Such people become licensed to practice public accounting in a particular state. These licensing requirements are widely credited with maintaining the integrity of the accounting service industry, but in recent years this licensing process has drawn criticism from legislators and others who favor deregulation of the profession. Some segments of the business community have expressed concern that the quality of accounting would suffer if such changes were implemented, and analysts indicate that small businesses without major in-house accounting departments would be particularly impacted.

The American Institute of Certified Public Accountants (AICPA) is the national professional organization of CPAs, but numerous organizations within the accounting profession exist to address the specific needs of various subgroups of accounting professionals. These groups range from the American Accounting Association, an organization composed primarily of accounting educators, to the American Women's Society of Certified Public Accountants.

ACCOUNTING AND THE SMALL BUSINESS OWNER

"A good accountant is the most important outside advisor the small business owner has," according to the *Entrepreneur Magazine Small Business Advisor.* "The services of a lawyer and consultant are vital during specific periods in the development of a small business or in times of trouble, but it is the accountant who, on a continuing basis, has the greatest impact on the ultimate success or failure of a small business."

When starting a business, many entrepreneurs consult an accounting professional to learn about the various tax laws that affect them, and to familiarize themselves with the variety of financial records that they will need to maintain. Such consultations are especially recommended for would-be business owners who: anticipate buying a business or franchise; plan to invest a substantial amount of money in the business; anticipate holding money or property for clients; or plan to incorporate.

If a business owner decides to enlist the services of an accountant to incorporate, he/she should make certain that the accountant has experience dealing with small corporations, for incorporation brings with it a flurry of new financial forms and requirements. A knowledgeable accountant can provide valuable information on various aspects of the start-up phase.

Similarly, when investigating the possible purchase or licensing of a business, a would-be buyer should enlist the assistance of an accountant to look over the financial statements of the licenser-seller. Examination of financial statements and other financial data should enable the accountant to determine whether the business is a viable investment. If a prospective buyer decides not to use an accountant to review the licenser-seller's financial statements, he/she should at least make sure that the financial statements that have been offered have been properly audited (a CPA will not stamp or sign a financial statement that has not been properly audited and certified).

Once in business, the business owner will have to weigh revenue, rate of expansion, capital expenditures, and myriad other factors in deciding whether to secure an in-house accountant, an accounting service, or a year-end accounting and tax preparation service. Sole proprietorships and partnerships are less likely to have need of an accountant; in some cases, they will be able to address their business's modest accounting needs without utilizing outside help. If a business owner declines to seek professional help from an accountant on financial matters, pertinent accounting information can be found in books, seminars, government agencies such as the **U.S. Small Business Administration**, and other sources. Even if a small business owner decides against securing an accountant, however, he/she will find it much easier to attend to the business's accounting requirements if he/she adheres to a few basic **bookkeeping** principles, such as maintaining a strict division betwen personal and business records; maintaining separate accounting systems for all business transactions; establishing separate checking accounts for personal and business; and keeping all business records, such as invoices and receipts.

CHOOSING AN ACCOUNTANT

While some small businesses are able to manage their accounting needs without benefit of in-house accounting personnel or a professional accounting outfit, the majority choose to enlist the help of accounting professionals. There are many factors for the small business owner to consider when seeking an accountant, including personality, services rendered, standing in the business community, and fees.

The nature of the business in question is also a consideration in choosing an accountant. Owners of small businesses who do not anticipate expanding rapidly have little need of a national accounting firm, but business ventures that require investors or call for a public stock offering can benefit from association with a respected, established accounting firm. Many owners of growing companies select an accountant by interviewing several prospective accounting firms and requesting proposals which will, ideally, detail the firm's public offering experience within the industry, describe the accountants who will be handling the account, and estimate fees for auditing and other proposed services.

Finally, a business that utilizes a professional accountant to attend to accounting matters is often better equipped to devote time to other aspects of the enterprise. Time is a precious resource for small businesses and their owners, and according to the *Entrepreneur Magazine Small Business Advisor,* "Accountants help business owners comply with a number of laws and regulations affecting their record-keeping practices. If you spend your time trying to find answers to the many questions that accountants can answer more efficiently, you will not have the time to manage your business properly. Spend your time doing what you do best, and let accountants do what they do best."

The small business owner can, of course, make matters much easier both for his/her company and the accountant by maintaining proper accounting records throughout the year. Well-maintained and complete records of assets, depreciation, income and expense, inventory, and capital gains and losses are all necessary for the accountant to conclude his work; gaps in a business's financial record only add to the account-

ant's time (and to his or her's fee for services rendered).

Such attitudes also reflect an ignorance of the potential management insights that can be gleaned from accurate and complete accounting information. Many small businesses, noted Ian Duncan in *CMA Magazine,* see accounting primarily as a "paperwork burden. It is often delegated to the firm's external accountant, and it is designed primarily to meet government reporting and taxation requirements." But Duncan and many others contend that small firms should recognize that accounting information can be a valuable component of a company's management and decision-making systems, for financial data provide the ultimate indicator of the failure or success of a business's strategic and philosophical direction .

FURTHER READING:

Cornish, Clive G. *Basic Accounting for the Small Business: Simple, Foolproof Techniques for Keeping Your Books Straight and Staying Out of Trouble.* Bellingham, WA: Self-Counsel Press, 1993.

Duncan, Ian D. "Making the Accounting System All That It Can Be." *CMA Magazine.* June 1993, p. 30.

Financial Accounting Standards Board. *Statements of Financial Accounting Concepts.* Irwin, 1987.

Fuller, Charles. *The Entrepreneur Magazine Small Business Advisor.* Wiley, 1995.

Weinstein, Grace W. *The Bottom Line.* New York: NAL Penguin, 1987.

SEE ALSO: Accounts Payable; Accounts Receivable; Accounting Methods

ACCOUNTING METHODS

Accounting methods refer to the basic rules and guidelines under which businesses keep their financial records and prepare their financial reports. There are two main accounting methods used for record-keeping: the cash basis and the accrual basis. Small business owners must decide which method to use depending on the legal form of the business, its sales volume, whether it extends credit to customers, and the tax requirements set forth by the **Internal Revenue Service (IRS).** Some form of record-keeping is required by law and for tax purposes, but the resulting information can also be useful to managers in assessing the company's financial situation and making decisions. It is possible to change accounting methods later, but the process can be complicated. Therefore it is important for small business owners to decide which method to use up front, based on what will be most suitable for their particular business.

CASH VS. ACCRUAL BASIS

Accounting records prepared using the cash basis recognize income and expenses according to real-time cash flow. Income is recorded upon receipt of funds, rather than based upon when it is actually earned, and expenses are recorded as they are paid, rather than as they are actually incurred. Under this accounting method, therefore, it is possible to defer taxable income by delaying billing so that payment is not received in the current year. Likewise, it is possible to accelerate expenses by paying them as soon as the bills are received, in advance of the due date. The cash method offers several advantages: it is simpler than the accrual method; it provides a more accurate picture of cash flow; and income is not subject to taxation until the money is actually received.

Since the recognition of revenues and expenses under the cash method depends upon the timing of various cash receipts and disbursements, however, it can sometimes provide a misleading picture of a company's financial situation. For example, say that a company pays its annual rent of $12,000 in January, rather than paying $1,000 per month for the year. The cash basis would recognize a rent expense for January of $12,000, since that is when the money was paid, and a rent expense of zero for the remainder of the year. Similarly, if the company sold $5,000 worth of merchandise in January, but only collected $1,000 from customers, then only $1,000 would appear as revenue that month, and the remainder of the revenue would be held over until payment was received.

In contrast, the accrual basis makes a greater effort to recognize income and expenses in the period to which they apply, regardless of whether or not money has changed hands. Under this system, revenue is recorded when it is earned, rather than when payment is received, and expenses recorded when they are incurred, rather than when payment is made. For example, say that a contractor performs all of the work required by a contract during the month of May, and presents his client with an invoice on June 1. The contractor would still recognize the income from the contract in May, because that is when it was earned, even though the payment will not be received for some time. The main advantage of the accrual method is that it provides a more accurate picture of how a business is performing over the long-term than the cash method. The main disadvantages are that it is more complex than the cash basis, and that income taxes may be owed on revenue before payment is actually received.

Under generally accepted accounting principles, the accrual basis of accounting is required for all businesses that handle inventory, from small retailers to large manufacturers. It is also required for corporations and partnerships that have gross sales over $5 million per year, though there are exceptions for farming businesses and qualified personal service corporations—such as doctors, lawyers, accountants, and consultants. A business that chooses to use the accrual basis must use it consistently for all financial reporting and for credit purposes. For anyone who runs two or more businesses, however, it is permissible to use different accounting methods for each one.

CHANGING ACCOUNTING METHODS

In some cases, businesses find it desirable to change from one accounting method to another. Changing accounting methods requires formal approval of the IRS, but new guidelines adopted in 1997 make the procedure much easier for businesses. A company wanting to make a change must file Form 3115 and pay a $900 fee. Any company that is not currently under examination by the IRS is permitted to file for approval to make a change. Applications can be made at any time during the tax year, but the IRS recommends filing as early as possible. In considering whether to approve a request for a change in accounting methods, the IRS looks at whether the new method will accurately reflect income and whether it will create or shift profits and losses between businesses.

Changes in accounting methods generally result in adjustments to taxable income, either positive or negative. For example, say a business wants to change from the cash basis to the accrual basis. It has accounts receivable (income earned but not yet received, so not recognized under the cash basis) of $15,000, and accounts payable (expenses incurred but not paid, so not recognized under the cash basis) of $20,000. Thus the change in accounting method would require a negative adjustment to income of $5,000. It is important to note that changing accounting methods does not permanently change the business's long-term taxable income, but only changes the way that income is recognized over time.

If the total amount of the change is less than $25,000, the business can elect to make the entire adjustment during the year of change. Otherwise, the IRS permits the adjustment to be spread out over four tax years. Obviously, most businesses would find it preferable for tax purposes to make a negative adjustment in the current year and spread a positive adjustment over subsequent years. If the accounting change is required by the IRS because the method originally chosen did not clearly reflect income, however, the business must make the resulting adjustment during the current tax year. This provides businesses with an incentive to change accounting methods on their own if they realize that there is a problem.

ACCOUNTS PAYABLE

FURTHER READING:

Ellentuck, Albert B. *Laventhol and Horwath Small Business Tax Planning Guide.* New York: Avon Books, 1988.

The Entrepreneur Magazine Small Business Advisor. New York: Wiley, 1995.

Horngren, Charles T., and Gary L. Sundem. *Introduction to Financial Accounting.* 4th ed. Englewood Cliffs, NJ: Prentice Hall, 1990.

Sherman, W. Richard. ''Requests for Changes in Accounting Methods Made Easier.'' *The Tax Adviser.* October 1997.

SEE ALSO: Accounting; Cash Flow Statements

ACCOUNTS PAYABLE

Accounts payable is the term used to describe the amounts owed by a company to its creditors. It is, along with **accounts receivable**, a major component of a business's cash flow. Aside from materials and supplies from outside vendors, accounts payable might include such expenses as taxes, insurance, rent (or mortgage) payments, utilities, and loan payments and interest.

For the small business owner, where the significance of every overdue payment can often be greatly magnified, it is absolutely essential to deal with the accounts payable side of the business ledger in an effective manner. Bills that are unpaid or addressed in a less than timely manner can snowball into major credit problems, which can easily cripple a business's ability to function.

PLANNING AHEAD

By making informed projections and sensible provisions in advance, the small business can head off many **credit** problems before they get too big. Obligations to creditors, ideally, should be paid off concurrently with the collections of accounts receivable. Payment checks should also be dated no earlier than when the bills are actually due. In addition, many small companies will find that their business fortunes will take on a cyclical character, and they will need to plan for accounts payable obligations accordingly. For instance, a small grocery store that is located near a major factory or mill may experience surges in customer traffic in the day or two immediately following the days in which paychecks are disbursed at that facility. Conversely, the store may see a measurable drop in customer traffic during weeks in which the factory or mill is not distributing paychecks to employees. The canny shop owner will learn to recognize these trends and address the accounts payable portion of his or her business accordingly.

SET PRIORITIES Generally, not all bills will need to be paid at once. Expenses such as payroll, federal, and local taxes, loan installment payments, and obligations to vendors will, in all likelihood, be due at various times of the month, and some—such as taxes—may only be due on a quarterly or annual basis (tax payments should always be made on schedule, even if it means delaying payment to vendors; it is far better to dispute a tax bill after it's been paid than to run the risk of being hit with costly fines). It is important, then, for small business owners to prioritize their accounts payable obligations.

This is especially true for fledgling business owners who are often stretched pretty tightly financially in an enterprise's early years. Entrepreneurs who find themselves struggling to meet their accounts payable obligations have a couple of different options of varying levels of attractiveness. One option is to ''rest'' bills for a short period in order to satisfy short-term cash flow problems. This basically amounts to waiting to pay off debts until the business's financial situation has improved, and there are obvious perils associated with such a stance: delays can strain relations with vendors and other institutions that are owed money, and over-reliance on future good business fortunes can easily launch entrepreneurs down the slippery slope into **bankruptcy**. Another option that is perhaps more palatable is to make partial payments to vendors and other creditors. This good-faith approach shows that an effort is being made to meet financial obligations, and it can help keep interest penalties in check. Partial payments should be set up and agreed to as soon as payment problems are forecast, or as early as possible. It is also a good idea to try to pay off debts to smaller vendors in full whenever possible, unless there's some clear benefit in making installments.

Usually, signs of cash flow problems will start to show up before the vultures begin to circle overhead. One key concern is aged payables. Bills should never be allowed to ''ripen'' more than 45 to 60 days beyond the due date, unless a special payment arrangement has been made with the vendor in advance. At 60 days, a company's credit rating could be jeopardized, and this could make it harder to deal with other vendors in the future.

Outstanding balances can drive interest penalties way up, and this trend is obviously compounded if many bills are overdue at the same time. Such excessive interest payments can seriously damage a business's bottom line. Business owners should keep in mind, however, that it is in the best interest of vendors and other creditors to keep the fledgling business solvent as well. Just about every business has its share of cash flow problems from time to time, something creditors should be quick to realize. Explaining current problems and their planned solutions to creditors can deflect ill feelings and buy more time. Some—

though by no means all—creditors may be willing to waive, or at least reduce, growing interest charges, or make other changes to the payment schedule.

ORGANIZATION It is crucial to the success of a small business that accounts payable be monitored closely. Ideally, this would be supervised by a financial expert (either inside or outside the company) who is not only able to see the company's financial "big picture," but is able to analyze and act upon fluctuations in the company's cash flow. This also requires detailed record keeping of outstanding payables. Reports ought to be checked on a weekly basis, and when payments are made, copies should be filed along with the original invoices and other relevant paperwork. Any hidden costs, such as interest charges, should also be noted in the report. Over a period of time, these reports will start to paint an accurate cash flow picture.

SEE ALSO: Accounting; Cash Management

ACCOUNTS RECEIVABLE

Accounts receivable describes the amount of cash, goods, or services owed to a business by a client or customer. The manner in which the collection of outstanding bills are handled, especially in a small business, can be a pivotal factor in determining a company's profitability. Getting the sale is the first step of the cash flow process, but all the sales in the world are of little use if monetary compensation is not forthcoming. Moreover, when a business has trouble collecting what it is owed, it also often has trouble paying off the bills (**accounts payable**) it owes to others.

MAKING COLLECTIONS Just as there's an art of the sale, there is an art of the collection. In an ideal world, a company's accounts receivable **collections** would coincide with the firm's accounts payable schedule. But there are many outside factors working against timely payments, factors that are often beyond the control of even the most efficient of collection teams. Seasonal demands, vendor shortages, stock market fluctuations, and other economic indicators can all contribute to a client's inability to pay bills in a timely fashion. Recognizing those factors, and learning to make business plans with them in mind, can make a big difference in establishing a solid accounts receivable system for your business.

By looking at receipts from past billing cycles, it is often possible to detect recurring cash flow problems with some clients, and to plan accordingly. Once a bill is at the 60-day overdue mark, it may be a good idea to work out some kind of new payment plan.

Small business owners need to examine clients on a case by case basis, of course. In some instances, the debtor company may simply have an incompetent sales force or accounts payable department, one that needs repeated prodding to cut that check for which you have been waiting. But in other cases, the debtor company may simply need a little more time to make good on its financial obligations. In many cases, it is in the best interests of the creditor company to cut such establishments a little slack. After all, a business that is owed money by a company that files for bankruptcy protection is likely to see very little of it, whereas a well-managed business that is given the chance to grow and prosper can develop into a valued long-term client.

METHODS OF COLLECTING A good way to improve cash flow is to make the entire company aware of the importance of accounts receivable, and to make collections a top priority. Invoice statements for each outstanding account should be reviewed on a regular basis, and a weekly schedule of collection goals should be established. Other tips in the realm of accounts receivable collection include:

- Do not delay in making follow-up calls, especially with clients who have a history of paying late.

- Curb late payment excuses by including a prepaid payment envelope with each invoice.

- Get credit references for new clients, and check them out thoroughly before agreeing to do business with them.

- Know when to let go of a bad account; if a debt has been on the books for so long that the cost of pursuing payment is proving exorbitant, it may be time to consider giving up and moving on (the wisdom of this depends a lot on the amount owed, of course).

- Collection agencies should only be used as a last resort.

ACCOUNTS RECEIVABLE FINANCING

Accounts receivable financing provides cash funding on the strength of a company's outstanding invoices. Instead of buying accounts, lenders use invoices as **collateral** for the loan. Besides benefiting a business in debt, accounts receivable financiers can assume greater risks than traditional lenders, and will also lend to new and vibrant businesses that demonstrate real potential. An accounts receivable lender will also handle other aspects of the account, including collections and deposits, freeing the company to focus on other areas of productivity. However, risks are involved, and agreements can be lengthy and confusing. Before considering this type of financing, a financial advisor should be consulted.

FURTHER READING:

Ayers, Donald, and Timothy Kincaid. "Avoiding Potential Problems when Selling Accounts Receivable." *Healthcare Financial Management.* May 1, 1996.

Fraser, J.A., and A. Murphy. "Getting Paid." *Inc.* June 1, 1990.

SEE ALSO: Accounting; Credit Evaluation and Approval

ADVERTISING AGENCIES

Advertising agencies are full-service businesses which can manage every aspect of an advertising campaign. They vary widely in terms of size and scope, and cater to different kinds of businesses. Some agencies have only one or two major clients whose accounts they manage. Others have hundreds of clients spread throughout the country, and many field offices. In general, an advertising agency will be able to manage an account, provide creative services, and purchase media access for a client.

STRUCTURE OF ADVERTISING AGENCIES

An agency, depending on its size, will likely have different departments which work on the separate aspects of an account. An account manager or the account planning department will coordinate the work of these departments to insure that all the client's needs are met. The departments within a full-service agency will include:

RESEARCH The research department will be able to provide some details about the prospective audience of the final advertising campaign, as well as information about the market for the product being advertised. This should include specific market research which leads to a very focused ad campaign, with advertising directed to the ideal target audience.

CREATIVE SERVICES Advertising agencies employ experts in many creative fields that provide quality, professional services that conform to the standards of the industry. Copywriters provide the text for print ads, and the scripts for television or radio advertising. Graphic designers are responsible for the presentation of print ads, and the art department is responsible for providing the necessary images for whatever format advertisement is decided upon. Some agencies have in-house photographers and printers, while others regularly employ the services of contractors.

The individuals involved in creative services are responsible for developing the advertising platform, which sets the theme and tone of the ad campaign. The

advertising platform should draw upon specific, positive features of the product advertised, and will extrapolate the possible benefits the consumer could expect to receive as a result of using the product. The campaign, through the development of this platform, should prove to be eye-catching, memorable, and in some way unique. The advertising that is remembered by consumers is that which stands out from the rest; it is the advertising agency's (and specifically the creative services department's) responsibility to provide this quality for their clients.

The final advertising provided by an agency should be fully developed and polished. Television commercials should be produced with professionalism; print ads should be attractive, informational, and attention-getting; radio spots should be focused and of high audio quality.

MEDIA-BUYING One of the services provided by advertising agencies is the careful placement of finished advertisements in various media, with an eye toward maximizing the potential audience. The research conducted by the agency will inform any media-buying decisions.

An agency will be able to negotiate the terms of any contracts made for placing ads in any of various media. A full-service agency will deal confidently with television, radio, newspapers, and magazines. Some agencies are also branching into direct mail marketing and point of purchase incentives; some agencies will also place an ad in the local yellow pages or utilize outdoor advertising, or one of the more creative avenues of incidental advertising, such as commercial signs on public buses or subways or on billboards.

The media-buying staff of an advertising agency will draw on specific research done for the client, as well as on past experience with different media. Through this research and careful consideration, the agency will develop a media plan: this should be a fully-realized plan of attack for getting out the client's message. Some factors considered in the development of the media plan include:

Cost Per Thousand: This refers to the cost of an advertisement per one thousand potential customers it reaches. Media-buyers use this method to compare the various media avenues they must choose between. For example, television ads are considerably more expensive than newspaper ads, but they also reach many more people. Cost per thousand is a straightforward way to evaluate how to best spend advertising dollars: if a newspaper ad costs $100 and potentially reaches 2,000 customers, the cost per thousand is $50. If a television ad costs $1000 to produce and place in suitable television spots, and reaches a potential of 40,000 viewers, the cost per thousand is only $25.

Reach: This term is used when discussing the scope of an advertisement. The reach of an ad is the number of households which can safely be assumed will be affected by the client's message. This is usually expressed as a percentage of total households. For example, if there are 1,000 households in a town, and 200 of those households receive the daily paper, the reach of a well-placed newspaper ad could be expressed as 20 percent: one-fifth of the households in the community can be expected to see the advertisement.

Frequency: The frequency of a message refers to how often a household can be expected to be exposed to the client's message. Frequency differs widely between media, and even within the same medium. Newspapers, for example, are read less often on Saturdays, and by many more households (and more thoroughly) on Sundays. Fluctuation like this occurs in all media.

Continuity: The media-buyer will also need to consider the timing of advertisements. Depending on the client's product, the ads can be evenly spread out over the course of a day (for radio or television advertisements), a week (for radio, television, or print advertisements), or a month (radio, television, print, other media). Of course, seasonal realities influence the placement of advertisements as well. Clothing retailers may need to run more advertisements as a new school year approaches, or when new summer merchandise appears. Hardware stores may want to emphasize their wares in the weeks preceding the Christmas holiday. Grocery stores or pharmacies, however, might benefit from more evenly distributed advertising, such as weekly advertisements that emphasize the year-round needs of consumers.

SETTING AN ADVERTISING BUDGET

Deciding on an **advertising budget** is highly subjective, depending on the type of business, the competitive atmosphere, and the available funds. It will also depend on how well established the business is, and what the goal of the advertising is. Trade publications are often good resources to consult in pondering this matter; many provide information on industry standards for advertising budgets.

PRICE STRUCTURES Advertising agencies charge their clients for all the itemized expenses involved in creating finished ads, including hiring outside contractors to complete necessary work. The client should receive invoices for all such expenses. For example, the client may receive an invoice for a television ad which includes a photographer's fee, a recording studio's fee, an actor's fee, and the cost of the film itself. The client will also be charged for the cost of placing the final advertisement in whatever media the agency has chosen (and the client has agreed to, of course).

Beyond these expenses, easily invoiced and itemized for the client, advertising agencies include a charge for their services. This fee pays for the extensive account management, creative services, research, and media placement provided by the agency, all the hidden costs involved in the production of a quality advertising campaign, and profit margin..

When working with a new client, and particularly with a small business, an agency may ask that the client put the agency on a retainer. This retainer will consist of the full advertising budget agreed upon, and will be used to pay all production expenses and media buying costs, as well as provide the agency with its fee. The client should still insist on detailed and accurate invoices for expenses taken from the retainer.

DECIDING TO USE AN AGENCY

Depending upon how important advertising is to the overall health of the particular business, and the amount of resources available for use in advertising, the small business owner should consider whether an investment in the services of advertising agency will yield meaningful benefit.

BENEFITS OF ADVERTISING AGENCIES Advertising agencies provide a valuable resource for any enterprise seeking to increase its customer base or its sales. They bring together professionals with expertise in a wide array of communication fields, and often—though not always—produce polished, quality ads that are well beyond the capacities of the client. Agencies are generally knowledgeable about business strategy and media placement as well. The media-buying experts at an agency will develop a strategic, targeted media plan for their clients, drawing upon years of experience and close relationships with media professionals. This experience and these connections are likely not available to the small business owner, and can be important factors in launching a successful media campaign.

DRAWBACKS OF ADVERTISING AGENCIES One drawback to using an agency, of course, is the added stress of dealing with unfamiliar people and unknown territory. Choosing the right agency will take time, and the process of reaching a satisfactory ad campaign can be a taxing and time-consuming one (especially if the client is vague about his or her desires, or expects a top-dollar campaign at a bargain-basement price). Work will have to be reviewed, changed, and reviewed again. And the account will have to be monitored closely. As with any outside contractor, the small business owner will need to keep careful tabs on what is received for his or her hard-earned dollar.

Cost is another factor that must be weighed carefully by the small business owner. Although advertising agency campaigns are often extremely valuable in terms of shaping **market share**, product recognition, and public image, the small business owner will have to carefully consider the potential benefits against the costs associated with hiring an agency of any size. When deciding whether or not to use an agency, the small business owner should consider whether or not the advertising he or she envisions really requires a team of experts working on it. If the ads will be fairly simple, or if they will be placed only in one media (such as a local newspaper), the owner should probably attempt to create the ads without the aid of an agency. It will be more economical to hire one expert, such as a graphic designer, and to place the ads personally than to hire an agency.

SELECTING AN ADVERTISING AGENCY

Agencies vary widely in their focus. Some cater to only a few large clients, and do not generally accept new accounts. Others have hundreds of clients of varying sizes. It is important for a small business to work with an agency that will be able to devote the time needed to insure a really successful ad campaign. Agencies that maintain a stable of larger companies are unlikely to regard a small business as an important client unless they are convinced that the establishment is destined for big things.

Instead, the agency should ideally be one that is familiar with the specific set of concerns shared by most small businesses. Indeed, it is very important that the advertising agency understand the issues that a small business owner must consider. These include having a limited advertising budget, finding a niche in a community, and establishing a loyal customer base. The agency should have worked in the past for clients in similar situations; it is not imperative, though, that they have other clients which are exactly the same as your business. If the business is a bookstore, for example, and the agency has never promoted a bookstore before, it does not mean they will necessarily be a poor choice to create and manage an advertising campaign. They may have done work for other local retail stores that have faced the same obstacles and challenges.

One of the best ways to choose an agency is the same way you would choose a bank, a doctor, or a housepainter: ask someone you trust who they use. If your friends, neighbors, or fellow business owners have used an agency they were pleased with, it is worth further inquiry. If you see advertising you really like, call up the business and compliment them on their good taste; then ask who prepares their ad copy. The agency-client relationship is very much trust-based, and the creative work they do is subjective. You should work with an agency whose collective personality and creative work make you feel comfortable. These services will cost a considerable amount, and starting off with a firm you feel optimistic about

will help insure your satisfaction throughout the relationship.

During the introductory meeting, the agency will be prepared to show samples of their work. These are called case histories, and they should be relevant to your business. These samples should reflect the agency's understanding of the needs of small business—including who your customer base is—and a working knowledge of the kind of marketing necessary to sell your product. As a potential client, you should feel free to ask many questions concerning the approach of the advertisements, the audience reached by certain media, and what media plans have been developed for businesses similar to yours. An agency, though, should never be asked to do work ''on spec.'' Advertising agencies cannot afford to use their considerable creative resources doing free work for potential clients. The case histories they provide, along with the answers to any questions you may have, should be sufficient to decide whether to give them your business.

Once you have found an agency you feel comfortable with, and have together agreed upon a budget and a timeline for the advertising, the agency will begin producing copy for you to approve. Laying a strong foundation, including asking all the questions you have as they arise, will pave the way for a productive, mutually beneficial relationship.

FURTHER READING:

Business Today, Sixth Edition. New York: McGraw Hill, 1990.

J.K. Lasser Institute. *How to Run a Small Business.* New York: McGraw Hill, 1994.

Peppers, Don. *Life's a Pitch and Then You Buy.* New York: Doubleday, 1995.

Poteet, Howard G. ed. *Making Your Small Business a Success: More Expert Advice from the U.S. Small Business Administration.* Liberty Hall Press, 1991.

Semon, Larry. *''Did You See My Ad?''* Amherst, NH: Brick House Publishing, 1988.

Smith, Jeanette. *The Advertising Kit.* Lexington Books, 1994.

SEE ALSO: Advertising Media; Advertising Strategy

ADVERTISING BUDGET

The advertising budget of a business typically grows out of the marketing goals and objectives of the company, although fiscal realities can play a large part as well, especially for new and/or small business enterprises. As William Cohen stated in *The Entrepreneur and Small Business Problem Solver,* ''in some cases your budget will be established before goals and objectives due to your limited resources. It will be a given, and you may have to modify your goals and objectives. If money is available, you can work the other way around and see how much money it will take to reach the goals and objectives you have established.'' Along with marketing objectives and financial resources, the small business owner also needs to consider the nature of the market, the size and demographics of the target audience, and the position of the advertiser's product or service within it when putting together an advertising budget.

In order to keep the advertising budget in line with promotional and marketing goals, an advertiser should answer several important budget questions:

1) Who is the target consumer? Who is interested in purchasing the advertiser's product or service, and what are the specific **demographics** of this consumer (age, employment, sex, attitudes, etc.)? Often it is useful to compose a consumer profile to give the abstract idea of a ''target consumer'' a face and a personality that can then be used to shape the advertising message.

2) Is the media the advertiser is considering able to reach the target consumer?

3) What is required to get the target consumer to purchase the product? Does the product lend itself to rational or emotional appeals? Which appeals are most likely to persuade the target consumer?

4) What is the relationship between advertising expenditures and the impact of advertising campaigns on product or service purchases? In other words, how much profit is earned for each dollar spent on advertising?

Answering these questions will provide the advertiser with an idea of the market conditions, and, thus, how to advertise within these conditions. Once this analysis of the market situation is complete, an advertiser has to decide how the money to be dedicated to advertising is to be allocated.

BUDGETING METHODS

There are several allocation methods used in developing a budget. The most common are listed below:

- Percentage of Sales method;
- Objective and Task method;
- Competitive Parity method;
- Market Share method;
- Unit Sales method;
- All Available Funds method;
- Affordable method.

It is important to notice that most of these methods are often combined in any number of ways, depending on the situation. Because of this, these methods should not be seen as rigid, but, rather, as building blocks that can be combined, modified, or discarded as necessary. Remember, a business must be flexible—ready to change course, goals, and philosophy when the market and the consumer demand such a change.

PERCENTAGE OF SALES METHOD Due to its simplicity, the percentage of sales method is the most commonly used by small businesses. When using this method an advertiser either takes a percentage of past or anticipated sales and allocates that percentage of the overall budget to advertising. Critics of this method, though, charge that using past sales for figuring the advertising budget is too conservative and that it can stunt growth. However, it might be safer for a small business to use this method if the ownership feels that future returns cannot be safely anticipated. On the other hand, an established business, with well-established profit trends, will tend to use anticipated sales when figuring advertising expenditures. This method can be especially effective if the business compares its sales with those of the competition (if available) when figuring its budget.

OBJECTIVE AND TASK METHOD Because of the importance of objectives in business, the task and objective method is considered by many to make the most sense, and is therefore used by most large businesses. The benefit of this method is that it allows the advertiser to correlate advertising expenditures to overall marketing objectives. This correlation is important because it keeps spending focused on primary business goals.

With this method, a business needs to first establish concrete marketing objectives, which are often articulated in the ''selling proposal,'' and then develop complimentary advertising objectives, which are articulated in the ''positioning statement.'' After these objectives have been established, the advertiser determines how much it will cost to meet them. Of course, fiscal realities need to be figured into this methodology as well. Some objectives (expansion of area market share by 15 percent within a year, for instance) may only be reachable through advertising expenditures that are beyond the capacity of a small business. In such cases, small business owners must scale down their objectives so that they reflect the financial situation under which they are operating.

COMPETITIVE PARITY METHOD While keeping one's own objectives in mind, it is often useful for a business to compare its advertising spending with that of its competitors. The theory here is that if a business is aware of how much its competitors are spending to inform, persuade, and remind (the three general aims of advertising) the consumer of their products and services, then that business can, in order to remain competitive, either spend more, the same, or less on its own advertising. However, as Alexander Hiam and Charles D. Schewe suggested in *The Portable MBA in Marketing*, a business should not assume that its competitors have similar or even comparable objectives. While it is important for small businesses to maintain an awareness of the competition's health and guiding philosophies, it is not always advisable to follow a competitor's course.

MARKET SHARE METHOD Similar to competitive parity, the market share method bases its budgeting strategy on external market trends. With this method a business equates its market share with its advertising expenditures. Critics of this method contend that companies that use **market share** numbers to arrive at an advertising budget are ultimately predicating their advertising on an arbitrary guideline that does not adequately reflect future goals.

UNIT SALES METHOD This method takes the cost of advertising an individual item and multiplies it by the number of units the advertiser wishes to sell.

ALL AVAILABLE FUNDS METHOD This aggressive method involves the allocation of all available profits to advertising purposes. This can be risky for a business of any size, for it means that no money is being used to help the business grow in other ways (purchasing new technologies, expanding work force, etc.). Yet this aggressive approach is sometimes useful when a start-up business is trying to increase consumer awareness of its products or services. However, a business using this approach needs to make sure that its advertising strategy is an effective one, and that funds which could help the business expand are not being wasted.

AFFORDABLE METHOD With this method, advertisers base their budgets on what they can afford. Of course, arriving at a conclusion about what a small business can afford in the realm of advertising is often a difficult task, one that needs to incorporate overall objectives and goals, competition, presence in the market, unit sales, sales trends, operating costs, and other factors.

MEDIA SCHEDULING

Once a business decides how much money it can allocate for advertising, it must then decide where it should spend that money. Certainly the options are many, including print media (newspapers, magazines, direct mail), radio, television (ranging from 30-second ads to 30-minute infomercials), and the Internet. The mix of media that is eventually chosen to carry the business's message is really the heart of the **advertising strategy**.

SELECTING MEDIA The target consumer, the product or service being advertised, and cost are the three main factors that dictate what media vehicles are selected. Additional factors may include overall business objectives, desired geographic coverage, and availability (or lack thereof) of media options.

SCHEDULING CRITERIA As discussed by Hiam and Schewe, there are three general methods advertisers use to schedule advertising: the Continuity, Flighting, and Massed methods

- Continuity—This type of scheduling spreads advertising at a steady level over the entire planning period (often month or year, rarely week), and is most often used when demand for a product is relatively even.

- Flighting—This type of scheduling is used when there are peaks and valleys in product demand. To match this uneven demand a stop-and-go advertising pace is used. Notice that, unlike "massed" scheduling, "flighting" continues to advertise over the entire planning period, but at different levels. Another kind of flighting is the pulse method, which is essentially tied to the pulse or quick spurts experienced in otherwise consistent purchasing trends.

- Massed—This type of scheduling places advertising only during specific periods, and is most often used when demand is seasonal, such as at Christmas or Halloween.

ADVERTISING NEGOTIATIONS AND DISCOUNTS

No matter what allocation method, media, and campaign strategy that advertisers choose, there are still ways small businesses can make their advertising as cost effective as possible. Writing in *The Entrepreneur and Small Business Problem Solver,* author William Cohen put together a helpful list of "special negotiation possibilities and discounts" that can be helpful to small businesses in maximizing their advertising dollar:

- Mail order discounts—Many magazines will offer significant discounts to businesses that use mail order advertising.

- Per Inquiry deals—Television, radio, and magazines sometimes only charge advertisers for advertisements that actually lead to a response or sale.

- Frequency discounts—Some media may offer lower rates to businesses that commit to a certain amount of advertising with them.

- Stand-by rates—Some businesses will buy the right to wait for an opening in a vehicle's broadcasting schedule; this is an option that carries considerable uncertainty, for one never knows when a cancellation or other event will provide them with an opening, but this option often allows advertisers to save between 40-50 percent on usual rates.

- Help if necessary—Under this agreement, a mail order outfit will run an advertiser's ad until that advertiser breaks even.

- Remnants and regional editions—Regional advertising space in magazines is often unsold and can, therefore, be purchased at a reduced rate.

- Barter—Some businesses may be able to offer products and services in return for reduced advertising.

- Seasonal discounts—Many media reduce the cost of advertising with them during certain parts of the year.

- Spread discounts—Some magazines or newspapers may be willing to offer lower rates to advertisers who regularly purchase space for large (two to three page) advertisements.

- An in-house agency—If a business has the expertise, it can develop its own advertising agency and enjoy the discounts that other agencies receive.

- Cost discounts—Some media, especially smaller outfits, are willing to offer discounts to those businesses that pay for their advertising in cash.

RELATIONSHIP OF ADVERTISING TO OTHER PROMOTIONAL TOOLS

Advertising is only part of a larger promotional mix that also includes publicity, **sales promotion**, and **personal selling**. When developing a budget the amount spent on these other tools needs to be considered, and a promotional mix, like a media mix, is necessary to reach as much of the target audience as possible. As Gerald E. Hills stated in "Market Opportunities and Marketing" in *The Portable MBA in Entrepreneurship,* "When business owners think about the four promotion tools, it becomes obvious why promotion managers must use a mix. There are clear trade-offs to be made between the tools."

The choice of promotional tools depends on what the business owner is attempting to communicate to the target audience. Public relations-oriented promotions, for instance, may be more effective at building credibility within a community or market than advertising, which many people see as inherently deceptive. Sales promotion allows the business owner to target both the consumer as well as the retailer, which is often necessary for the business to get its products stocked. Personal selling allows the business owner to get immediate feedback regarding the reception of the business' product. And as Hills pointed out, personal selling allows the business owner "to collect information on competitive products, prices, and service and delivery problems."

FURTHER READING:

Advertising Your Business. Washington: U.S. Small Business Administration, n.a.

Bly, Robert W. *Advertising Manager's Handbook.* Englewood Cliffs, NJ: Prentice Hall, 1993.

Burnett, Leo. *The Leo Burnett Worldwide Advertising Fact Book.* Chicago: Triumph Books, 1994.

Cohen, William. *The Entrepreneur and Small Business Problem Solver.* 2d ed. New York: Wiley, 1990.

Hills, Gerald E. "Market Opportunities and Marketing." *The Portable MBA in Entrepreneurship.* Edited by William D. Bygrave. 2d ed. New York: Wiley, 1997.

SEE ALSO: Advertising Media; Marketing; Public Relations

ADVERTISING MEDIA—AUDIO

The most common audio advertising media is FM radio. Placement of an advertisement on FM radio costs about as much as an advertisement placed in a metropolitan newspaper. However, radio is more dynamic than print alternatives because it allows the advertiser essentially to talk with the consumer. Indeed, many small business consultants believe that an entertaining and informative radio advertising campaign can be a major asset. However, some analysts contend that small business owners should proceed cautiously before deciding to rely exclusively on radio advertising. Indeed, most businesses incorporate a media mix when attempting to sell their products or services, utilizing radio advertising in concert with print and other advertising media. The key for small business owners is to study what types of advertising best suits their products and services and to use that media to spearhead their advertising campaign.

ADVANTAGES Radio stations feature many different programming emphases. These range from music-oriented formats such as country, adult contemporary, classic rock, and alternative rock to news- or talk-oriented formats. Since these different formats attract different demographic segments of the total audience, business owners can take appreciable measures to reach their target audience simply by buying time on appropriate stations. Another major advantage of radio advertising is that it is inexpensive to place and to produce, allowing small business owners to place advertisements on more than one station in a given market. In addition, radio advertising content can be changed quickly to meet changes in the market or to reflect new business objectives. Finally, radio reaches large numbers of commuters, income-generating people who often pay more attention to radio advertising than to other advertising media, especially if they are driving alone.

The costs associated with purchasing radio advertising time reflect this emphasis on reaching the commuter audience. The four time slots, or "dayparts," offered for advertisers by most radio stations are the a.m. drive, daytime, p.m. drive, and evening. The two most expensive—but also most effective advertising slots—are the a.m and p.m. drive times.

DRAWBACKS Although radio advertising is effective, there are drawbacks to consider when deciding on placing and creating a radio spot. Aspects to consider include competitor clutter, the cumulative costs associated with long-term radio spots, and the fleeting nature of a radio message. In addition to these drawback, several other legal and procedural guidelines need to be considered. *Nation's Business* writer Phil Hill provided a rundown of some of these concerns:

1) If celebrity soundalikes are used, make sure a clear disclaimer is included in the advertisement, saying that the soundalikes are not the actual celebrities.

2) If working with a station to create an advertisement always work with a contract.

3) Treat the competition fairly. Federal law mandates that advertisers must accurately depict the competition.

4) Be prepared to run a radio advertisement often. Industry analysts indicate that an advertisement needs to be heard by a consumer on several occasions before it is likely to generate a response.

5) Be cautious about excessive reliance on one station. There may be some instances in which a business's products or services are compatible with only one station (i.e., a dealer in sports paraphernalia may want to limit his or her radio advertising to the lone sports-talk station in town), but small businesses that offer less niche-oriented services or products can dramatically expand the audience they reach if they use more than one station for their audio advertising.

AM RADIO AM radio is a curious anomaly for most young adults who grew up with FM radio, cassettes, and CDs. Yet, AM radio still exists, has a folksy charm, and is listened to by a significant percentage of the population. AM offers alternative programing to the predominantly music formats broadcast on FM stations. AM stations, which suffered serious declines in the 1960s and 1970s, now broadcast talk shows, sporting events, news programs, and traffic and weather reports. In addition, AM radio broadcast can reach remote locations, such as those found in many western states—places that truckers and summer vacationers traverse.

FURTHER READING:

Hill, Phil. "Make Listeners Your Customers." *Nation's Business.* June 1994.

ADVERTISING MEDIA—INFOMERCIALS

Even though they are often considered annoying, infomercials have gained an undeniable reputation for effectiveness that has endeared them to American companies. Infomercials are a type of **direct marketing** (reaching out directly to the individual consumer). Usually thirty minutes long, these extended commercials, which are often hosted by celebrities, typically target a diverse audience from both the lower and upper middle classes. Research over the past decade—the time it has taken for infomercials to become an advertising superpower—has shown that most people who make purchase decisions while watching infomercials are between the ages of 25 and 44.

In the words of Thomas Burke, president of the infomercial division of Saatchi & Saatchi Advertising, infomercials are "the most powerful form of advertising ever created." Given the growth of infomercials and their astounding success it is a claim with significant market support. According to Kevin Whitelaw, writing in *U.S. News & World Report*, infomercials were a $1.5 billion dollar industry in 1995. Much of this success is due to the creativity of infomercial advertisers who use the infomercial's marginality to create a kind of cultural or sub-cultural symbol, giving a voice in the form of purchasing power to the late night and early morning consumer. This consumer tends to be between 25 and 44, and, as pointed out by Brad Edmondson and John Maines in "Victoria the Video Hunter," they are likely to be homemakers, blue-collar workers, and salespeople. This demographic information is an essential component in determining which products are selected for infomercial treatment.

One sign that the legitimacy of infomercials as an effective marketing tool has been recognized in recent years is the growing attention that larger companies have paid to the practice. Whitelaw points out that in

1995 ten percent of infomercials were being produced by big companies, such as Microsoft, Apple, Lexus, Magnavox, Sears, and AT&T. The presence of these newcomers has pushed up the prices of the ad spots on the cable stations which have traditionally carried infomercials, leaving only the very early morning spots (i.e. four a.m) within the budget of most small- and mid-sized businesses. However, with the proliferation of cable and satellite television, and the new respectability that infomercials have gained in recent years, they are still a viable advertising option for small businesses with the right kind of product or service and the creativity to sell it.

Infomercials usually work best with products that are easy to demonstrate, in which an interaction with the viewing audience can be achieved. This interaction is quite often that of teacher to student, in which infomercials become a medium for instruction, teaching people (or supposing to teach) how to better their social lives or their bodies. Such an approach creates a dialogue that the viewer can take part in, which often leads to a viewer inquiry for more information or to a purchase.

Another useful approach is to create a "storymercial," in which the infomercial sells its product by encasing it—and the targeted consumer—within a story. These "storymercials" often look and feel like documentaries in which a family or business-person go about their daily lives aided tremendously by the advertiser's product. Testimonials, or little product specific anecdotes, are similar, both pulling viewers into a world where the product is essential to success and happiness. All in all, these infomercials are attempting to show the consumer how to answer the question "how can this product help me?"

When planning an approach advertisers often consider several criteria, such as how similar products have fared in other markets, time slots, and seasons. Most infomercial producers believe that even small television ratings for an infomercial can translate into strong returns, as Dan Danielson told Edmondson and Maines: "It's not uncommon for an infomercial to register no rating points whatsoever, yet net strong profits."

FURTHER READING:

Edmondson, Brad, and John Maines. "Victoria the Video Hunter." *American Demographics*. June 1993.

McDonald, Marci. "The Dawning of the Infomercial Age." *Maclean's*. September 4, 1995.

Whitelaw, Kevin."Not Just Slicing and Dicing." *U.S. News & World Report*. September 9, 1996.

ADVERTISING MEDIA—PRINT

The two most common print media are newspapers and magazines, but print media also include outdoor billboards, transit posters, the yellow pages, and direct mail. Print media is important because it can reach such a large audience, and the great number of specialized publications enable businesses to focus in on an audience with a specific set of characteristics. Print media are allowed to advertise most anything, such as cigarettes, liquor, and contraceptives; however, many publications will not accept controversial ads.

NEWSPAPERS When deciding upon a newspaper in which to advertise, there are three physical criteria to consider: distribution, size, and audience. Newspapers are either daily or weekly, come in a standard or tabloid size, and reach nearly all of the reading public, which is estimated to be around 85-90 percent of the population. Because of the broad demographic reach of most newspapers it is difficult to target a specific audience; however, newspapers are effective in increasing awareness of a business' products and services in a specific geographical area.

Types of ads placed in newspapers include: display ads, classified ads, public notes, and preprinted inserts. Newspaper ads have some flexibility in their size. For instance, some are small boxes that take up only a small portion of a page, while others might span one or two full pages (the latter, however, are typically only bought by larger corporations). Regardless of this flexibility, newspaper ads can only use limited special effects, such as font size and color. These limitations lead to advertising "clutter" in newspapers because all the ads look very similar. Therefore, advertisers must use original copy and headings to differentiate their ads from their competitors. The quick turnover of newspapers also allows the advertiser to adjust ads to meet new market conditions; however, this turnover means that the same ad may need to be inserted over a significant period of time in order to reach its target audience.

MAGAZINES With magazines an advertiser can focus in on a specific target audience, as the Small Business Administration pointed out in *Advertising Your Business*: "Audiences can be reached by placing ads in magazines which have [a] well-defined geographic, demographic or lifestyle focus." But magazine advertisements often have a lag time of a couple months between the purchase of ad space and the publication of the issue in question. Magazines, then, are sometimes not the optimum option for businesses seeking to target fast-changing market trends.

In addition to the above factors, it is also important to consider the nature of the magazine ad copy. Magazines allow elaborate graphics and colors, which give advertisers more creative options than do newspapers. Also, recent surveys have indicated that informative ads are the most persuasive. Therefore, it is important to include copy and art work that is direct and presents important product information to the consumer, such as how the product works, how it benefits the consumer, and where it can be purchased.

DIRECT MAIL Many consultants feel that **direct mail** is the best way for a small businesses to begin developing awareness in their target consumers. Mailing lists can be generated (even though often difficult to maintain) with the names of those people most likely to purchase the advertiser's products or services. However, direct mail is not always cost effective. According to James W. Taylor, author of *Marketing Planning: A Step by Step Guide,* a direct mailing campaign can cost as much as $1,000 to reach 1,000 people, whereas television can reach a similar number of potential customers at a fraction of that cost. But business experts indicate that direct mail does tend to generate more purchasing responses than does television, and they observe that the products of many small businesses are often more suited to a direct mailing campaign than to indirect, image advertising.

YELLOW PAGES The Small Business Administration stated in ''Advertising Your Business'' that a yellow page ad is often used to ''complement or extend the effects of advertising placed in other media.'' Such an ad has permanence and can be used to target a specific geographic area or community. Essentially, a yellow page ad gives the consumer information needed to make a purchase. Therefore the key information to include in such an ad includes: the products and services available; location; phone number; business hours; special features, such as the acceptable kinds of payment (i.e. credit cards, checks); parking availability; discounts; and delivery policies and emergency services. The best way to arrange this information is in a list, so that the consumer will be able to scan the ad for the desired information.

A major consideration with a yellow page ad is where to place it, which primarily depends on the directory (or category) under which businesses choose to locate their ads. Central to this choice are the products or services that the company wishes to emphasize. The ad copy should compliment the directory, indicating the main products and services for sale, so that the ad will emerge from the similar looking ads that surround it.

OUTDOOR ADVERTISING Outdoor advertising usually comes in two forms: billboards and transit posters. Like yellow page ads, outdoor advertising is usually used to support advertisements placed in other media. Since the prospective consumer often has only fleeting exposure to billboards and transit posters, the advertising copy written for these media needs to be brief with the ability to communicate ideas at a glance; this, of course, requires efficient use of graphics and headings.

FURTHER READING:

Advertising Your Business. Washington: U.S. Small Business Administration, n.a.

Taylor, James W. *Marketing Planning: A Step by Step Guide.* Upper Saddle River, NJ: Prentice Hall, 1997.

ADVERTISING MEDIA—VIDEO

Video advertising can be an effective avenue of reaching an audience, in large measure because of the proliferation of televisions, cable channels, and VCRs in American homes over the past few decades. Video advertising also has the advantage of being free of presentation limitations associated with other advertising media. With video media, an advertiser can combine audio, visual, and textual effects as well as other media in presenting its products or services. Video advertising can be expensive, but there are several video options that can be used effectively by small businesses of modest financial means.

TELEVISION Network television reaches the largest audience of all advertising media. As the Small Business Administration noted in *Advertising Your Business,* most small businesses use ''spot television,'' which is an ad ''placed on one station in one market.'' Placing such a spot ad on one of the national networks can be rather expensive, depending on the size of the audience reached and the demand of the specific time slot desired. In any case, such network television spots are well beyond the financial means of small businesses.

Local television, on the other hand, is much more affordable, and many small business use it to reach local consumers. Local network advertising time is usually purchased as 30-second ''spot announcements,'' which are similar to the network spot ads. The time slots for local ads begin in the early morning and continue up until the network news broadcasts begin. As with network television, the cost for such a spot depends on the size of the audience determined to be watching and the demand for the particular time slot.

Cable and satellite stations offer selectivity, low cost, and flexibility. Since many cable stations, like *ESPN* and the *History Channel*, broadcast specific kinds of programs that appeal to certain demographic groups, a defined audience can be targeted. Spot ads are purchased from either a national cable network or from a local cable station. The cost depends on the cable penetration in the area and the channel's viewership. For example, most infomercials are broadcast on cable stations, such as the *Lifetime Network,* because of the programming flexibility and comparatively low advertising costs. Drawbacks associated with the purchase of advertising time on cable television include fragmentation (which refers to the wide range of viewing options available on cable—and thus the dilution of impact that any one ad may have) and image. The latter factor is primarily associated with local cable stations, which typically have low budgets and viewerships. Moreover, some locally produced cable shows are amateurishly produced and/or feature offensive content.

VIDEO TAPE AND CASSETTES As VCRs and home movies exploded in popularity, video cassettes became a viable advertising option. This viability rests in part on the modest cost associated with producing many business videos. As *Target Market* noted, video companies could produce and distribute a video cassette advertisement for as little as $1.50 per unit in the mid-1990s. These cassettes are often categorized into three general types: promotional videos, demonstration videos, and training videos.

Promotional videos are used to create awareness among both consumers and investors. These kinds of videos can be played on monitors from store show rooms to those in parking garages. They can also be used by salespeople to help with their sales pitches. Demonstration videos can be used in a direct mail or "V-Mail" campaign to introduce consumers to a business's products and services, though the cost associated with such campaigns is usually prohibitive for small enterprises. Finally, videos have become an increasingly popular tool for internal use in the business world. Human resources and sales departments often use videos to educate their employees. Such videos reduce the amount of time experienced staff are required to spend on training their employees. These videos also make sure that the information each employee receives is consistent, communicating agreed upon business objectives.

FURTHER READING:

"Advertising Your Business." Small Business Administration, n.a.

Anderson, Leann. "Show and Tell." *Entrepreneur.* October 1997.

Burnett, Leo. *The Leo Burnett Worldwide Advertising Fact Book.* Chicago: Triumph Books, 1994.

"Video Marketing Gets Attention and Results." *Target Market.* October 1995.

ADVERTISING MEDIA—WORLD WIDE WEB

The invention of the World Wide Web made the Internet a viable advertising vehicle. It is an "open system," and, therefore, potentially available for anyone to use, which gives the Web tremendous reach. The Web allows the combination of sound, graphics, and text at one electronic location, which can be linked to other similar locations by "hyperlinks." The linked multimedia capabilities of the Web center around the creation of "homepages," which are Internet locations that provide information about a chosen subject. These "cyberstores," as they are often called, are used by many small businesses to advertise and sell their products and services. Indeed, a homepage on the World Wide Web gives even the smallest business the ability to compete with large companies. Since small companies can establish an attractive presence on the Internet at relatively modest cost, say industry experts, the medium effectively eliminates the advantages of size and economic power which enable large companies to dominate other advertising media. "Many small-business users see the Internet as a way to increase their marketing power, reduce costs and do more things at once, so they're using it to find ways to do business smarter," remarked one analyst in *Entrepreneur.*

BROWSERS

Small businesses seeking to establish a presence on the World Wide Web need to understand the importance of browsers, such as Netscape and Microsoft's Internet Explorer, to the Web and to Web advertising. These browsers are tools needed to read the HTML (hypertext mark-up language) documents that make up the World Wide Web. These documents are fairly easy to create, and many word processing programs and Web browsers can assist an advertiser in creating one. Since the Web could not exist without these browsers, advertisers needs to understand how they function and how to use them to their advantage. Browsers locate information through search engines, such as Infoseek and Yahoo. Most search engines locate sites that contain a specific set of words, as specified by the logic chosen for the search (i.e. *small business* and *media*). Therefore, businesses need to make sure that their homepages contain words emphasizing their products and services. Browsers also need "plug-ins" to run certain sound and visual effects, so small business owners need to weigh the benefits of such features before adding such extra expenses. After all, many potential customers that find their way to your homepage may not have the necessary "plug-ins" to experience those effects.

HOMEPAGES

In a 1997 *Forbes* article, writer William Davidow pointed out that advertising on the Internet "will be intimately tied to the sales process. Consumers will search out advertising sites when they want to gather information about products and services. They will purchase directly over the network." He and other industry observers note that homepages already function in a fashion similar to an advertisement in the yellow pages. A homepage, then, needs to provide potential consumers with the necessary information (phone numbers, addresses, and product information) for customers to follow through on desired purchases—or at least provide them with enough data to pique their interest and enable them to make a purchase or get additional information via more traditional (i.e., non-electronic) means. Of course, many people using the Internet are comfortable making purchases over the Web itself, so business homepages should also be equipped with the ability to take product orders directly

When developing a homepage, a business needs to consider several relevant aspects of electronic text and presentation. First and foremost, a homepage should be easy to visually and physically navigate. Key to creating an inviting homepage, other than subjective aesthetic concerns, are "hyperlinks," which allow the reader to move vertically through the text. Many experts claim that each level of a homepage should contain text on one topic, which should be clearly indicated by the headings or graphics there. A visually cluttered homepage will be ignored by Web users, who are notorious for quickly moving on to other sites when confronted with confusing or uninteresting homepages.

ADVERTISING BANNERS

Debra Aho Williamson reported in *Advertising Age* that in a recent survey of 6,000 Web users it was found that advertising banners helped increase brand awareness by 5 percent. Advertising banners are multimedia hyperlinks placed on other web pages. Often banners are part of a "link exchange," or cooperative advertising arrangement, in which two businesses with complimentary products and services advertise each other on their respective sites in order to reach a large segment of a given market.

However, some Web advertising agencies claim that few people access homepages through banners, and these agencies are now trying new motion and graphic technologies to make the banners more inviting. One new approach is to turn a banner into a mini homepage where the consumer can make purchases without leaving the current page they are viewing. *PC/Computing* recently published a Web study in which they found that there is "virtually no chance"

that Web users will click on a banner they've seen more than four times. Because of this the editors of *PC/Computing* suggested businesses design a number of different banners for their homepages.

E-MAIL ADVERTISING

The use of direct **electronic mail**, in which businesses send unsolicited mail messages to a list of e-mail accounts, is currently being debated. The practice is currently referred to as SPAMing (even the use of the word SPAM for this practice is under legal scrutiny), and has been received negatively by Web users. To avoid alienating customers, increasing numbers of businesses have supplemented their general customer satisfaction surveys with queries concerning the customer's feelings about being put on a direct mailing list. In this way, businesses are developing lists they can use to keep in touch with the consumers both through traditional mail and e-mail. The key here is that these lists, and the subsequent advertising strategies created around them, be directed at the desires of the consumer, and not only toward the goals of the business.

FURTHER READING:

Davidow, William. "Online Advertisers Must Beware." *Forbes.* April 7, 1997.

Page, Heather. "Surf's Up." *Entrepreneur.* November 1997.

"Web Advertising." *PC/Computing.* February 1997.

Williamson, Debra Aho. "Marketers Spend On Sites, but Not on Ads." *Advertising Age.* April 14, 1997.

SEE ALSO: Internet Commerce; Web Page Design

ADVERTISING STRATEGY

An advertising strategy is a campaign developed to communicate ideas about products and services to potential consumers in the hopes of convincing them to buy those products and services. This strategy, when built in a rational and intelligent manner, will reflect other business considerations (overall budget, brand recognition efforts) and objectives (public image enhancement, market share growth) as well. As *Portable MBA in Marketing* authors Alexander Hiam and Charles D. Schewe stated, a business's advertising strategy "determines the character of the company's public face." Even though a small business has limited capital and is unable to devote as much money to advertising as a large corporation, it can still develop a highly effective advertising campaign. The key is creative and flexible planning, based on an in-depth knowledge of the target consumer and the avenues that can be utilized to reach that consumer.

Today, most advertising strategies focus on achieving three general goals, as the Small Business Administration indicated in *Advertising Your Business:* 1) promote awareness of a business and its product or services; 2) stimulate sales directly and "attract competitors' customers," and 3) establish or modify a business' image. In other words, advertising seeks to *inform, persuade, and remind* the consumer. With these aims in mind, most businesses follow a general process which ties advertising into the other promotional efforts and overall marketing objectives of the business.

STAGES OF ADVERTISING STRATEGY

As a business begins, one of the major goals of advertising must be to generate awareness of the business and its products. Once the business' reputation is established and its products are positioned within the market, the amount of resources used for advertising will decrease as the consumer develops a kind of loyalty to the product. Ideally, this established and ever-growing consumer base will eventually aid the company in its efforts to carry their advertising message out into the market, both through its purchasing actions and its testimonials on behalf of the product or service.

Essential to this rather abstract process is the development of a "positioning statement," as defined by Gerald E. Hills in "Marketing Option and Marketing" in *The Portable MBA in Entrepreneurship*: "A 'positioning statement' explains how a company's product (or service) is differentiated from those of key competitors." With this statement, the business owner turns intellectual objectives into concrete plans. In addition, this statement acts as the foundation for the development of a selling proposal, which is composed of the elements that will make up the advertising message's "copy platform." This platform delineates the images, copy, and art work that the business owner believes will sell the product.

With these concrete objectives, the following elements of the advertising strategy need to be considered: target audience, product concept, communication media, and advertising message. These elements are at the core of an advertising strategy, and are often referred to as the "creative mix." Again, what most advertisers stress from the beginning is clear planning and flexibility. And key to these aims is creativity, and the ability to adapt to new market trends. A rigid advertising strategy often leads to a loss of market share. Therefore, the core elements of the advertising strategy need to mix in a way that allows the message to envelope the target consumer, providing ample opportunity for this consumer to become acquainted with the advertising message.

TARGET CONSUMER The target consumer is a complex combination of persons. It includes the person who ultimately buys the product, as well as those who decide what product will be bought (but don't physically buy it), and those who influence product purchases, such as children, spouse, and friends. In order to identify the target consumer, and the forces acting upon any purchasing decision, it is important to define three general criteria in relation to that consumer, as discussed by the Small Business Administration:

1) **Demographics**—Age, gender, job, income, ethnicity, and hobbies.

2) Behaviors—When considering the consumers' behavior an advertiser needs to examine the consumers' awareness of the business and its competition, the type of vendors and services the consumer currently uses, and the types of appeals that are likely to convince the consumer to give the advertiser's product or service a chance.

3) Needs and Desires—Here an advertiser must determine the consumer needs—both in practical terms and in terms of self-image, etc.—and the kind of pitch/message that will convince the consumer that the advertiser's services or products can fulfill those needs.

PRODUCT CONCEPT The product concept grows out of the guidelines established in the "positioning statement." How the product is positioned within the market will dictate the kind of values the product represents, and thus how the target consumer will receive that product. Therefore, it is important to remember that no product is just itself, but, as Courtland L. Bovee and William F Arens stated in *Contemporary Advertising*, a "bundle of values" that the consumer needs to be able to identify with. Whether couched in presentations that emphasize sex, humor, romance, science, masculinity, or femininity, the consumer must be able to believe in the product's representation.

COMMUNICATION MEDIA The communication media is the means by which the advertising message is transmitted to the consumer. In addition to marketing objectives and budgetary restraints, the characteristics of the target consumer need to be considered as an advertiser decides what media to use. The types of media categories from which advertisers can choose include the following:

- Print—Primarily newspapers (both weekly and daily) and magazines.

- Audio—FM and AM radio.

- Video—Promotional videos, infomercials.

- World Wide Web.

- Direct mail.

- Outdoor advertising—Billboards, advertisements on public transportation (cabs, buses).

After deciding on the medium that is 1) financially in reach, and 2) most likely to reach the target audience, an advertiser needs to schedule the broadcasting of that advertising. The media schedule, as defined by Hills, is "the combination of specific times (for example, by day, week, month) when advertisements are inserted into media vehicles and delivered to target audiences."

ADVERTISING MESSAGE An advertising message is guided by the "advertising or copy platform," which is a combination of the marketing objectives, copy, art, and production values. This combination is best realized after the target consumer has been analyzed, the product concept has been established, and the media and vehicles have been chosen. At this point, the advertising message can be directed at a very concrete audience to achieve very specific goals. Hiam and Schewe listed three major areas that an advertiser should consider when endeavoring to develop an effective "advertising platform":

- What are the product's unique features?

- How do consumers evaluate the product? What is likely to persuade them to purchase the product?

- How do competitors rank in the eyes of the consumer? Are there any weaknesses in their positions? What are their strengths?

Most business consultants recommend employing an **advertising agency** to create the art work and write the copy. However, many small businesses don't have the up-front capital to hire such an agency, and, therefore, need to create their own advertising pieces. When doing this a business owner needs to follow a few important guidelines.

COPY When composing advertising copy it is crucial to remember that the primary aim is to communicate information about the business and its products and services. The "selling proposal" can act as a blueprint here, ensuring that the advertising fits the overall marketing objectives. Many companies utilize a theme or a slogan as the centerpiece of such efforts, emphasizing major attributes of the business's products or services in the process. But as Hiam and Schewe caution, while "something must be used to animate the theme . . . care must be taken not to lose the underlying message in the pursuit of memorable advertising."

When writing the copy, direct language (saying exactly what you mean in a positive, rather than negative manner) has been shown to be the most effective. The theory here is that the less the audience has to interpret, or unravel the message, the easier the message will be to read, understand, and act upon. As Jerry Fisher observed in *Entrepreneur,* "two-syllable phrases like 'free book,' 'fast help,' and 'lose weight' are the kind of advertising messages that don't need to be read to be effective. By that I mean they are so easy for the brain to interpret as a whole thought that they're 'read' in an eye blink rather than as linear verbiage. So for an advertiser trying to get attention in a world awash in advertising images, it makes sense to try this message-in-an-eye-blink route to the public consciousness—be it for a sales slogan or even a product name."

The copy content needs to be clearly written, following conventional grammatical guidelines. Of course, effective headings allow the reader to get a sense of the advertisement's central theme without having to read much of the copy. An advertisement that has "50% Off" in bold black letters is not just easy to read, but it is also easy to understand.

ART WORK AND LAYOUT Small business owners also need to consider the visual rhetoric of the advertisement, which simply means that the entire advertisement, including blank space, should have meaning and logic. Most industry experts recommend that advertisers use short paragraphs, lists, and catchy illustrations and graphics to break up and supplement the text and make the document both visually inviting and easy to understand. Remember, an advertisement has to capture the reader's attention quickly.

ADVERTISING BUDGET The **advertising budget** can be written before or after a business owner has developed the advertising strategy. When to make a budget decision depends on the importance of advertising and the resources available to the business. If, for instance, a business knows that they only have a certain amount of money for advertising then the budget will tend to dictate what advertising is developed and what the overall marketing objectives will be. On the other hand, if a business has the resources available, the advertising strategy can be developed to meet predetermined marketing objectives. For small businesses, it is usually best to put together an advertising budget early in the advertising process.

The following approaches are the most common methods of developing an effective budget. All the methods listed are progressive ones that look to perpetuate growth:

- Percentage of future or past sales

- Competitive approach

- Market share

- All available funds

- The task or objective approach

The easiest approach—and thus the one that is most often used—is the percentage of future or past sales method. Most industry experts recommend basing spending on anticipated sales, in order to ensure growth. But for a small business, where survival may be a bigger concern than growth, basing the advertising budget on past sales is often a more sensible approach to take.

METHODS OF ADVERTISING

Small business owners can choose from two opposite philosophies when preparing their advertising strategy. The first of these, sometimes called the push method, is a stance wherein an advertiser targets retail establishments in order to establish or broaden a market presence, whereas the other option, sometimes called the pull method, targets end-users (consumers). Of course, many businesses employ some hybrid of the two when putting together their advertising strategy.

PUSH METHOD The aim of the push method is to convince retailers, salespersons, or dealers to carry and promote the advertiser's product. This relationship is achieved by offering inducements, such as providing advertising kits to help the retailer sell the product, offering incentives to carry stock, and developing trade promotions.

PULL METHOD The aim of the pull method is to convince the target consumer to try, purchase, and ultimately repurchase the product. This process is achieved by directly appealing to the target consumer with coupons, in-store displays, and sweepstakes.

ANALYZING ADVERTISING RESULTS

Many small businesses are distressingly lax in taking steps to monitor whether their advertising efforts are having the desired effect. Instead, they simply throw a campaign out there and hope for the best, relying on a general sense of company health when determining whether to continue, terminate, or make adjustments to advertising campaigns. These small business owners do not seem to recognize that myriad factors can influence a business's fortunes (regional economic straits, arrival of new competition, seasonal buying fluctuations). The small business owner that does not bother to adequately analyze his or her advertising efforts runs the danger of throwing away a perfectly good advertising strategy (or retaining a dreadful one) if he or she is unable to determine whether business upturns or downturns are due to advertising or some other factor.

The only way to know with any accuracy how your advertising strategy is working is to ask the consumer, the opinions of which can be gathered in several ways. Although many of the tracking alterna-tives are quite specialized, requiring either a large budget or extensive advertising research expertise, even small businesses can take steps to measure the effectiveness of their advertising strategies. The direct response survey is one of the most accurate means of measuring the effectiveness of a company's advertising for the simple reason that it measures actual responses to a business's advertisements. Other inexpensive options, such as use of redeemable coupons, can also prove helpful in determining the effectiveness of an advertising campaign.

ADVERTISING AGENCY

The decision whether or not to use an advertising agency depends both on a company's advertising strategy and its financial resources. An agency has professionals who can organize, create, and place advertising so that it will meet established objectives better than most small businesses can, but of course the expense associated with soliciting such talent is often prohibitive for smaller companies. Still, some small- and mid-sized businesses have found that agencies can be helpful in shaping and monitoring advertising strategies.

Because of their resources and expertise, agencies are useful when a business is planning a broad advertising campaign that will require a large amount of resources. An advertising agency can also help track and analyze the effectiveness of the advertising. Some criteria to consider when choosing an agency include size of the agency, size of their clients (small companies should avoid allying themselves with agencies with a large stable of big corporate clients so that they are not treated as afterthoughts), length of time that the principals have been with the agency, the agency's general advertising philosophy, and the primary nature of the agency's accounts (are they familiar with your industry and the challenges involved in differentiating your company's products or services from others in that industry?).

ADVERTISING LAWS

The **Federal Trade Commission** (FTC) protects consumers from deceptive or misleading advertising. Small business owners should be familiar with the following laws, which pertain to marketing and advertising and are enforced by the Commission:

- Consumer Product Safety Act—Outlines required safety guidelines and prohibits the sale of harmful products.

- Child Protection and Toy Safety Act—Prohibits the sale of toys known to be dangerous.

- Fair Packaging and Labeling Act—Requires that all packaged products contain a label disclosing all ingredients.
- Antitrust Laws—Protects trade and commerce from unlawful restraints, price deception, price fixing, and monopolies.

Many complaints against advertisers center on allegedly deceptive advertisements, so small business consultants urge entrepreneurs and business owners to heed the following general rules of thumb:

1) Avoid writing ads that make false claims or exaggerate the availability of the product or the savings the consumer will enjoy.

2) Avoid running out of advertised sale items. If this does happen, businesses should consider offering ''rain-checks'' so that the consumer can purchase the item later at the same reduced price.

3) Avoid calling a product ''free'' if it has cost closely associated with it. If there are costs associated with the free item they need to be clearly disclosed in the ad.

Since advertising is a complex process, and business law undergoes continual change, business owners should consult an attorney before distributing any advertising.

FURTHER READING:

Adams, Bob. *Adams Streetwise Small Business Start-up*. Holbrook, MA: Adams Media Corporation, 1996.

Advertising Your Business. Small Business Administration, n.a.

Bovee, Courtland L., and William F. Arens. *Contemporary Advertising*. 3d ed. Homewood, IL: Irwin, 1989.

Cohen, William. *The Entrepreneur and Small Business Problem Solver*. 2d ed. New York: John Wiley & Sons, 1990.

Fisher, Jerry. ''Fast Pitch.'' *Entrepreneur*. August 1997.

Hiam, Alexander and Charles D. Schewe. *The Portable MBA in Marketing*. New York: John Wiley & Sons, 1992.

Hills, Gerald E. ''Market Opportunities and Marketing.'' *The Portable MBA in Entrepreneurship*. Edited by William D. Bygrave. 2d ed. New York: John Wiley & Sons, 1997.

Shea, Barbara S., with Jennifer Haupt. *Small Business Legal Guide*. New York: John Wiley & Sons, 1995.

SEE ALSO: Advertising Media; Target Marketing; Product Positioning; Advertising, Evaluation of Results

ADVERTISING, EVALUATION OF RESULTS

Once the small business owner has successfully designed and placed an ad (or had that ad successfully designed and placed by an agency), he or she will be eagerly awaiting the increased sales that advertising promises. While advertising can be an effective means of increasing profitability, measurable increases in sales may not be immediately forthcoming. But if the advertising was well-planned, well-placed, and well-executed, it will likely produce positive results eventually.

CUMULATIVE EFFECTS It is widely accepted among advertising experts that one major benefit of advertising any business is the cumulative effect of the message on consumers. This effect occurs as consumers are repeatedly exposed to advertising which may not have an immediate impact, but becomes familiar and remains in the memory. This message will be recalled when the need arises for the service which was advertised. The consumer, because of the cumulative effects of advertising, will already be familiar with the business's name, as well as the image that it has cultivated through its advertising campaigns. For example, a consumer has heard a carpet cleaning company's ads for months, but until the need arises to have his or her carpets cleaned, there is no reason to contact the company. When that need does arise, however, he or she will already know the name of the company and feel familiar enough with it to engage its services.

CONSISTENCY One trap that advertisers sometimes fall into is that of restlessness or boredom with a long-running campaign. The ownership of a small business may feel a need to change a long-running advertisement simply because of a desire to try a new, more exciting, avenue. There are certainly valid reasons for doing so (stagnant sales, changing competitive dynamics, etc.) at times, but advertising experts discourage businesses from yanking advertisements that continue to be effective for the sake of change. ''If it ain't broke, don't fix it,'' is the guiding principle behind this caution. They note that consumers learn to associate businesses with certain advertisements, design elements, or themes, but that these associations sometimes take time to sink in. Similarly, industry observers counsel small business owners to maintain a level of consistency with the advertising mediums they utilize (provided those mediums are effective, of course).

By choosing an appropriate style and theme, and carefully placing ads in effective media, the small business owner begins to create a lasting foundation for his or her company. Maintaining an advertising campaign in itself advertises the stability, dependability, and tone of a business. If customers are finding the ads useful, then the advertising is working; changing the ads could diminish their effectiveness.

STRATEGIES FOR TRACKING ADVERTISING'S EFFECTIVENESS

But before the advertiser decides to stick with one advertising plan for the next several years, he or she wants to be sure that the advertising is having some effect. Because of the cumulative effect of advertising, this can sometimes be difficult to ascertain; the following are some suggestions for the sometimes vague science of tracking the effectiveness of advertising:

MONITORING SALES FIGURES This strategy involves tracking the changes in sales from a period before the current advertising was used, and then comparing those figures to sales made during the time the advertising is active. One pitfall of this strategy is not choosing a representative time period. One month's worth of sales figures may not be enough to fully gauge the effectiveness of an ad. Ideally, the business owner could compare figures from long periods of sales to exclude changes due to factors other than advertising, such as seasonal fluctuations and holiday sales.

RUNNING A COUPON One satisfyingly concrete way of tracking how many customers were exposed to advertising is to use coupons. These coupons, which will typically provide some sort of discount or other incentive to customers to use them, can be easily tabulated, providing businesses with tangible evidence of the advertising campaign's level of effectiveness. Such measurements, however, are limited to print campaigns. Another version of the coupon, which is effective across media types, is to encourage customers to mention their exposure to an ad in return for a bonus. For example, a radio ad might include the sentence, ''Mention this ad for an additional 5 percent off your purchase!''

SURVEYING CUSTOMERS Perhaps the most accurate and easiest method of tracking the effectiveness of a media campaign is simply asking customers how they were directed to you. You can ask if a customer saw a particular ad, or more generally ask how they came to know about the shop or service. Consumers are generally pleased to be asked for their input, and they can give you first hand accounts of how advertising is effecting your business.

SEE ALSO: Market Research

AFFIRMATIVE ACTION

Affirmative action refers to concrete steps that are taken not only to eliminate discrimination—whether in employment, education, or contracting—but also to attempt to redress the effects of past discrimination. The underlying motive for affirmative action is the Constitutional principle of equal opportunity, which holds that all persons have the right to

equal access to self-development. In other words, persons with equal abilities should have equal opportunities.

Affirmative action programs differ widely in the extent to which they attempt to overturn discrimination. Some programs might simply institute reviews of the hiring process for women, minorities, and other affected groups. Other affirmative action programs might explicitly prefer members of affected groups. In such programs, minimum job requirements are used to create a pool of qualified applicants from which members of affected groups are given preference.

Affirmative action affects small businesses in two main ways. First, it prevents businesses with 15 or more employees from discriminating on the basis of race, color, sex, religion, national origin, and physical capability in practices relating to hiring, compensating, promoting, training, and firing employees. Second, it allows the state and federal governments to favor women-owned and minority-owned businesses when awarding contracts, and to reject bids from businesses that do not make good faith efforts to include minority-owned businesses among their subcontractors.

The interpretation and implementation of affirmative action has been contested since its origins in the 1960s. A central issue of contention was the definition of discriminatory employment practices. As the interpretation of affirmative action evolved, employment practices that were not intentionally discriminatory but that nevertheless had a ''disparate impact'' on affected groups were considered a violation of affirmative action regulations. Another central issue was whether members of affected groups could receive preferential treatment and, if so, the means by which they could be preferred. This issue is sometimes referred to as the debate over quotas. Though affirmative action programs came under heavy attack during the Reagan and Bush administrations, the principles of affirmative action were reaffirmed by the Civil Rights Act of 1991. But in 1997, California's Proposition 209 banned affirmative action in that state. The resulting legal battles, which were expected to reach the U.S. Supreme Court, seemed likely to have wide-reaching effects on affirmative action.

HISTORY OF AFFIRMATIVE ACTION

Affirmative action has its roots in the post-war civil rights movement. In March of 1961, President John F. Kennedy signed Executive Order 10925, which established the President's Commission on Equal Employment Opportunity. The Order stated that contractors doing business with the government ''will take affirmative action to ensure that applicants are employed, and employees are treated during their employment, without regard to their race, creed, color, or national origin.'' The Order did not advocate preferential treatment of affected groups but rather sought to eliminate discrimination in the traditional sense.

The legal status of affirmative action was solidified by the Civil Rights Act of 1964. This landmark legislation prohibited discrimination in voting, public education and accommodations, and employment in firms with more than fifteen employees. Title VII of the Civil Rights Act offered a similar understanding of affirmative action as Executive Order 10925, stating that the Act was not designed ''to grant preferential treatment to any group because of race, color, religion, sex, or national origin.'' The Act's sponsors, Senators Joseph Clark and Clifford Case, emphasized this non-preferential interpretation of affirmative action when they wrote: ''There is no requirement in Title VII that an employer maintain a racial balance in his workforce. On the contrary, any deliberate attempt to maintain a racial balance, whatever such a balance may be, would involve a violation of Title VII, because maintaining such a balance would require an employer to hire or refuse to hire on the basis of race.''

The Civil Rights Act did not provide criminal penalties for employers that discriminated, nor did the civil remedies established by the Act include compensation for pain and suffering or punitive damages. Rather, the Act sought to establish a conciliation process by which victims would be restored to the situation they would have had in the absence of discrimination. To carry out the conciliation process, the Act created a new federal agency as a branch of the U.S. Department of Labor, the **Equal Employment Opportunity Commission** (EEOC). The EEOC acts as a facilitator between plaintiffs and private employers and also pressures violating employers to provide compensation, whether in the form of back pay or restitution. The EEOC also provides legal support for plaintiffs should the plaintiffs pursue their grievances in court.

Two important issues became contested in the wake of the Civil Rights Act of 1964: whether unintentional or structural discrimination constituted violation of the principle of equal opportunity; and the extent to which preferential treatment should be given to affected groups. These issues came to the forefront during the Johnson administration. In a 1965 commencement speech, President Johnson argued that equality of opportunity required more than simply ending discrimination. Rather, he argued for a more active interpretation of affirmative action that would assure ''equality as a result.''

In 1966, the U.S. Department of Labor began collecting employment records with breakdowns by race in order to evaluate hiring practices, overturning earlier policies of the Eisenhower and Kennedy administrations. In 1968, the Office of Federal Contract Compliance issued regulations which required, for the first time, that specific targets be set by which the effects of affirmative action programs could be evaluated. The regulations stated that ''the contractor's program shall provide in detail for specific steps to guarantee equal employment opportunity keyed to the problems and needs of minority groups, including, when there are deficiencies, the development of specific goals and timetables for the prompt achievement of full and equal employment opportunity.'' It was in these regulations and analogous measures by the EEOC that the debate over affirmative action quotas had its origins.

Goals and timetables were established by the U.S. Department of Labor using ''utilization analysis,'' which statistically compared the proportion of employed women and minorities in a firm with the proportion of women and minorities in the regional workforce, deriving a measure of what the Department called ''disparate impact.'' In the absence of discrimination, it was assumed that these proportions would and should be roughly equal. Since these regulations focused on results and not intent, the structural nature of discrimination was officially recognized. In addition, these regulations provided an official and measurable basis for the preferential treatment of affected groups.

In the landmark *Griggs v. Duke Power Co.* case of 1971, the Supreme Court unanimously ruled against Duke's requirement of high school diplomas or IQ tests for those applying for unskilled jobs. The decision held that ''Title VII forbids not only practices adopted with a discriminatory motive, but also practices which, though adopted without discriminatory intent, have a discriminatory effect on minorities and women.'' The ruling provided a legal foundation for cases of ''disparate impact,'' asserting that employers may not use job requirements that adversely affect women and minorities unless required by what it termed ''business necessity.'' (For example, in the case of serious health or safety threats to co-workers or customers.)

The EEOC was strengthened by the Equal Employment Opportunity Act of 1972, which enabled the Commission to file class action suits. Under the Carter administration, the Uniform Guidelines on Employee Selection established the ''four-fifths rule.'' This rule was significant in that it provided an explicit benchmark to determine disparate impact, which had been left vague in earlier U.S. Department of Labor regulations. The four-fifths rule held that firms contracting with the federal government should not be allowed to hire any race, sex, or ethnic group at a rate below four-fifths that of any other group.

Another significant Supreme Court ruling on affirmative action came in a 1978 case, *Regents of the University of California v. Bakke.* Under the University of California at Davis's admission policies, 16 of 100 places were set aside for minority applicants. Allan Bakke was a white applicant who was denied enrollment to Davis's medical school, even though his test scores were higher than the minority students who were admitted. Casting the deciding vote, Justice Lewis Powell held that Bakke should be admitted to the program since Davis's policies constituted a rigid quota, but that, nonetheless, Davis could continue to favor minorities in its admission practices and that it had a "compelling state interest" to attain a diversified educational environment.

The tide favoring affirmative action began to turn in the 1980s during the Reagan and Bush administrations. In his 1980 campaign, Reagan stated, "We must not allow the noble concept of equal opportunity to be distorted into federal guidelines or quotas which require race, ethnicity, or sex—rather than ability and qualifications—to be the principal factor in hiring or education." Through court appointments, hiring and firing decisions, and budget cuts, the Reagan administration sought to end affirmative action as it had evolved since the Johnson administration. Between 1981 and 1983, the budget of the EEOC was cut by 10 percent and the staff by 12 percent. The Office of Federal Contract Compliance was hit harder yet, with budget cuts of 24 percent and staff cuts of 34 percent during these same years.

Two important Supreme Court rulings in the late-1980s also acted to substantially weaken affirmative action. The 1988 case *Watson v. Fort Worth Bank and Trust* overturned the landmark 1971 *Griggs v. Duke Power Co.,* shifting the burden of proof in employment discrimination cases from employers to plaintiffs. In the 1989 case *Wards Cove Packing Company v. Antonio,* the Court ruled that a plaintiff could not simply show disparate impact to prove discrimination, but must demonstrate that a specific employment practice created the existing disparity.

AFFIRMATIVE ACTION IN THE 1990S

In an effort to fight the dramatic rollback of affirmative action, Congress passed the Civil Rights Act of 1991. The Act returned the burden of proof to employers in disparate impact cases, requiring employers to prove that employment practices that resulted in disparate impact were "job related" and "consistent with business necessity." The Act thus overturned the Supreme Court's rulings in *Watson v. Fort Worth Bank and Trust* and *Wards Cove Packing Company v. Antonio.* In addition, the Civil Rights Act of 1991 addressed issues of unlawful harassment and intentional discrimination, allowing minority and fe-

male victims of intentional discrimination to be awarded up to $300,000 in compensatory damages in addition to back pay and restitution.

In 1994, the Federal Communications Commission (FCC) initiated one of the largest affirmative action programs ever. The FCC voted unanimously to set aside 1,000 of 2,000 new radio licenses for small businesses, women, and minorities. These licenses are for businesses serving the rapidly growing number of users of pocket-size telephones, fax machines, pagers, and hand-held computers. Small companies owned by women or minorities could receive up to a 60 percent discount on the cost of these licenses, which federal officials estimated have a total market value of $10 billion. One of the concerns expressed about the FCC ruling is that it will enable the rise of companies that are only nominally headed by women or minorities. This could occur as a result of the acquisition provisions of the ruling, which allow up to 75 percent of the equity and 49.9 percent of the voting stock of a small firm to be acquired by a larger firm, and yet the small firm still qualifies for licensing discounts.

Despite such efforts, the mid-1990s saw affirmative action programs continue to be rolled back by the Republican-controlled U.S. Congress, as well as by state legislatures and court decisions. Critics charged that affirmative action was a form of "reverse discrimination," meaning that by favoring minorities and women it discriminated against white males. In addition, they argued that affirmative action sometimes prevented companies from hiring the best available worker, and in so doing caused resentment toward minority workers on the job.

In 1996, California voters passed Proposition 209, which banned preferential treatment on the basis of gender or race in public employment, education, and contracting in the state. In effect, the measure eliminated affirmative action programs in California, except as necessary to comply with federal law. Although civil rights groups quickly blocked the measure with a court injunction, it took effect in August 1997 when the injunction was overturned on appeal. It was widely believed that if the U.S. Supreme Court upheld Proposition 209, many states would follow California's lead and make dramatic changes to their affirmative action programs.

FURTHER READING:

Green, Kathanne W. *Affirmative Action and Principles of Justice.* San Francisco, CA: Greenwood Press, 1989.

"How to Write an Affirmative Action Plan." *American Demographics.* March 1993.

Lane, Marc J. *Legal Handbook for Small Business.* New York: Amacom, 1989.

Leonard, Jonathan S. "Women and Affirmative Action." *Journal of Economic Perspectives.* Winter 1989.

——. "The Impact of Affirmative Action Regulation and Equal Employment Law on Black Employment." *Journal of Economic Perspectives.* Fall 1990.

Lickson, Charles P. *A Legal Guide for Small Business.* Menlo Park, CA: Crisp Publications, 1994.

Mills, Nicolaus, ed. *Debating Affirmative Action: Race, Gender, Ethnicity, and the Politics of Inclusion.* New York: Dell Publishing, 1994.

Taylor, Bron Raymond. *Affirmative Action at Work: Law, Politics, and Ethics.* Pittsburgh, PA: University of Pittsburgh Press, 1991.

SEE ALSO: Labor Unions and Small Business; Sexual Harassment

AFL-CIO

The AFL-CIO (American Federation of Labor-Congress of Industrial Organizations) is a federation of major autonomous trade unions in the United States and its territories, Canada, and Mexico. Currently the only national labor federation in the United States, the organization is the single most powerful and important voice of American organized labor.

DEVELOPMENT AND CURRENT STRATEGIES The AFL-CIO formed in 1955 as the result of the merger of what were then two competing federations: the American Federation of Labor (AFL) and the Congress of Industrial Organizations (CIO). The AFL was established in the 1880s. Originally comprised almost exclusively of craft unions, the organization was instrumental in securing higher wages, shorter work hours, institution of workers' comp, and safety and child labor laws for union (and eventually non-union) workers in America. The AFL also was able to secure exemption of **labor unions** from antitrust legislation. The most famous of the AFL's early leaders was Samuel Gompers, who is generally viewed as the "father" of the American labor movement.

In the 1930s, however, internal conflict within the AFL triggered a dramatic split within the organization. Craft unionists had long feared that industrial unions might undercut their position, a concern that led many to adopt a stance of fundamental opposition to the formation of industrial unions. But a faction within the group felt that the idea of organizing workers along industry lines (steel, automobile, etc.) was a good one, and their campaigning on behalf of the concept grew so great that they were expelled from the parent body in 1938. Undeterred, these rebellious unions formed their own federation, the Congress of Industrial Organizations. Initially, the competition between the two federations, which chartered competing unions, probably helped the labor movement to grow in the United States. By the 1950s, however, concerns about growing anti-union feelings in the country led the two giant federations to negotiate a merger.

The past 30 years have seen a dramatic reduction in union representation in many American industries, and the fortunes of the AFL-CIO have undergone a corresponding drop during that time. Nonetheless, the organization remains the most powerful voice in the world of U.S. labor, since it ultimately represents about 12.9 million workers (about 80 percent of all unionized workers in the country). And while the number of unions within the group has dropped over the years, the AFL-CIO still boasted 77 member unions in 1997, including most of the nation's leading craft and industrial unions.

In the mid-1990s, many observers contended that the AFL-CIO was showing signs of a renewed sense of activism. James Worsham noted in *Nation's Business,* for instance, that the AFL-CIO had increased its spending on organizing activities from $2.5 million in 1995 to $30 million in 1997. Analysts believe that this level of spending—about one-third of the organization's total annual budget—is indicative of a new level of aggressiveness in reversing union membership trends around the country. Led by John J. Sweeney, who assumed the position of president in 1995, the AFL-CIO has adopted significantly more proactive philosophies in the realms of organizing and striking. "At the same time," wrote Worsham, "Sweeney has overhauled the federation's bureaucracy. He heavily emphasized organizing and increasing labor's numbers with shoe leather and media savvy, and he advocates holding lawmakers strictly accountable for their votes for or against labor's positions." In a review of these initiatives, an executive with the U.S. Chamber of Commerce told Worsham that "the new leadership has energized its rank and file. Organized labor has put its money where its mouth is." Finally, the AFL-CIO has shown an increased interest in grassroots organizing and burnishing the image of unions in communities. As one federation organizer told *Nation's Business,* the AFL-CIO's efforts are aimed at assisting individual unions *and* creating a pro-union climate in communities.

Still, many business analysts believe that the challenge that looms for the AFL-CIO and its member unions is a daunting, if not impossible, one to win. They argue that the AFL-CIO and its membership will have a difficult time halting—let alone reversing—drops in union representation in the United States, given the various elements that have contributed to that drop (growing global competition, declines in traditional "blue-collar" jobs, managerial antipathy toward unions, etc.)

GUIDING PRINCIPLES AND FUNCTIONS The overriding guiding principle of the AFL-CIO is national union autonomy, which means that the federation does not control the affiliates nor dictate their internal policies (though it often tries to influence affiliates).

The federation serves a range of functions. It acts as a lobbying body in the political arena and uses its financial resources in election campaigns. It works to resolve conflicts between affiliated unions, such as disputes between construction craft unions over jurisdiction of different areas of work and disputes between affiliated unions that may be competing in efforts to organize new members. It provides research services to affiliated unions and also helps unions organize new members. The diversity of AFL-CIO standing committees reflects the range of federation functions. These include the Legislative Committee, the Organization and Field Services Committee, the Civil Rights Committee, and the Community Services Committee.

ORGANIZATIONAL STRUCTURE The structure of the AFL-CIO is quite complex, in part because the federation undertakes so many tasks on behalf of its members. The day-to-day business of the federation is handled by its principal officers (president and secretary-treasurer), who confer regularly with an executive council consisting of more than 30 vice presidents, virtually all of whom are drawn from the ranks of the affiliated unions. In addition to the standing committees, the federation has several staff units. There are also several different departments within the federation that serve the specialized needs of different affiliates. An affiliate can choose to associate with those departments relevant to its particular needs, such as the Building Trades Department, the Industrial Union Department, the Metal Trades Department, and the Public Employees Department.

The national AFL-CIO offices are in Washington, D.C. However, there are state-level bodies of the AFL-CIO in all 50 states. These bodies duplicate the federation's national activities at the state level (e.g., lobbying state legislatures and supporting pro-labor candidates in state elections).

FURTHER READING:

Darby, Harrison G., and Margaret R. Bryant. "When Unions Knock, How Should Employers Answer?" *HR Magazine.* July 1997.

"The Future of Unions." *The Economist.* July 1, 1995.

Masters, Marick. *Unions at the Crossroads.* Quorum Books, 1997.

Mills, Daniel Quinn. *Labor-Management Relations.* 5th ed. New York: McGraw-Hill, 1994.

Taylor, B. J., and F. Witney. *Labor Relations Law.* Englewood Cliffs, NJ: Prentice-Hall, 1987.

Worsham, James. "Labor's New Assault." *Nation's Business.* June 1997.

SEE ALSO: Employee Strikes; Labor Unions and Small Business

AIDS IN THE WORKPLACE

Acquired immune deficiency syndrome (AIDS) is a disease that impairs the human immune system and renders it susceptible to infections that would be repelled by a functioning immune system. The terminal stage of the human immuno-deficiency virus (HIV), AIDS is transmitted by contamination of the bloodstream with HIV-infected body fluids, specifically blood, semen, breast milk, and vaginal fluid. The virus is principally spread through vaginal or anal intercourse, by the transfusion of virus-contaminated blood, by the sharing of HIV-infected intravenous needles, or by mothers to fetuses during pregnancy. U.S. Centers for Disease Control (CDC) literature emphasizes that "no additional routes of transmission have been recorded, despite a national sentinel system designed to detect just such an occurrence." AIDS is not spread by casual physical contact, biting insects, or airborne means, and transmission through body fluids such as saliva and tears has never occurred. Once a person becomes infected with HIV, the incubation period averages eight years before AIDS symptoms appear.

As of 1993, the World Health Organization estimated that eight to ten million people worldwide were infected with HIV. The CDC estimated that approximately one million Americans, or one in every 250 people, were infected with HIV at that time. The majority of infected Americans in the early 1990s were between 25 and 44 years old, and members of that age group were most likely to be infected in the future. For the nation's businesses, this meant that 50 percent of the workforce was at risk. In the early 1990s, HIV/AIDS was the third-leading cause of death among 25- to 44-year-olds. An economic analysis by DRI/McGraw-Hill projected that "the potential worldwide economic impact of the worst-case scenario" could equal 1.4 percent of the global gross domestic product annually, "roughly equivalent to the entire economy of Australia or India today." Obviously, the virus carries many legal and ethical implications for businesses.

Given a supportive work environment and early detection, people with HIV and AIDS can continue to be productive members of the workforce. Studies have shown that for half of the people who contract HIV, it takes more than a decade to develop AIDS. With medical treatment, many of them can manage the infection as a chronic, long-term condition, similar to many other medical disorders. The numbers of people with HIV and their extended life expectancy means there will be more employees on the job with HIV in the future. This, in turn, means that most, if not all, businesses will eventually have to deal directly with HIV-infected and AIDS-afflicted employees.

GOVERNMENT AGENCIES AND POLICIES RELATING TO AIDS

The Business Responds to AIDS (BRTA) program was formed in 1992 as a public-private partnership among the CDC, the public health sector, other organizations and agencies, and business and labor to provide workplace education and community services in order to prevent the spread of HIV. The BRTA program assists businesses of all sizes in the creation and implementation of workplace-based HIV and AIDS policies. In addition to education, service, and prevention of the spread of HIV, the program's goals are to prevent discrimination and foster community service and volunteerism both in the workplace and in the community. In order to achieve these goals, the BRTA has developed materials and technical assistance to help businesses form comprehensive HIV and AIDS programs, including training for management and labor leaders and education for employees and their families.

Corporate HIV and AIDS policies and practices should comply with federal, state, and local legislation and **Occupational Safety and Health Administration** (OSHA) guidelines. Federal laws regarding AIDS in the workplace include: the Occupational Safety and Health Act of 1970; the Vocational Rehabilitation Act of 1973 (VRA); the Employee Retirement Income Security Act of 1974 (ERISA); the U.S. Consolidated Omnibus Budget Reconciliation Act of 1986 (COBRA); and the **Americans with Disabilities Act** (ADA) of 1990.

The ADA, which applies to any company with 15 or more employees, forbids discrimination against any employee affected by a disability or chronic disease, including AIDS. It defends people who are infected, people perceived to be at high risk, and relatives and caregivers of people with AIDS in matters ranging from hiring and promotion to resignation and retirement. Basically, employers cannot treat employees who are affected by AIDS any differently than other employees, and they are required to provide appropriate accommodations whenever possible. The ADA does make a slight exception for restaurants, however, in that they are permitted to reassign employees with HIV or AIDS to positions in which they are not required to handle food.

PROACTIVE AIDS POLICIES FOR BUSINESSES

Despite the growing impact of AIDS and AIDS-related illnesses on American businesses, very few companies are aware of their legal obligations to

affected employees or have enacted policies to ensure compliance with the law. In their book *Employee Benefits for Small Business,* Jane White and Bruce Pyenson emphasize that small business owners need to take proactive steps to be prepared to deal with AIDS in the workplace. The owners should educate themselves about AIDS, establish policies to prevent discrimination, and also educate their employees— ideally, before the virus affects an employee, customer, or vendor of the company.

A preemptive AIDS education program can minimize the potential for turnover or loss of productivity when AIDS impacts the small business. White and Pyenson note that educational information should be presented to employees in a number of formats and repeated several times to be effective. AIDS education should stress that HIV cannot be transmitted through the type of contact that ordinarily takes place at work, including handshakes, sharing bathrooms and water fountains, eating in the same cafeteria, or being exposed to coughs and sneezes. HIV-positive individuals may be more susceptible to respiratory diseases that could be contagious, however, so the employer should advise appropriate precautions in that instance. AIDS education should also emphasize actions that can help prevent the spread of HIV. In occupational settings where transmission of the virus is possible, like a hospital, the employer must provide appropriate safety measures. Above all, an education program should promote an atmosphere of compassion and understanding.

White and Pyenson also note that companies should adopt and communicate formal policies and guidelines regarding AIDS in the workplace. First and foremost, the policies should comply with all applicable laws. For example, since HIV-positive people are included within the ADA definition of disabled, they can sue successfully for wrongful termination or discrimination. A small business's hiring and employment policies cannot discriminate against a person with HIV or AIDS as long as he or she is able to perform the job. Mandatory pre-employment screening for HIV is illegal in most states. Once a person with HIV or AIDS becomes an employee, the company is required by law to make reasonable accommodations for their disability, including modifying their duties, giving them time off for medical treatments, allowing them to work at home via computer, or reducing their workload or hours. In addition, the employer is required to maintain the confidentiality of the employee's medical condition. Mere speculation in the workplace that a person has HIV or AIDS can be grounds for libel or slander suits.

Employers and coworkers should strive to approach HIV and AIDS as illnesses, not moral issues. Unfortunately, in spite of the massive public service campaigns of the BRTA and hundreds of agencies across the nation, misinformation has continued to disrupt productivity and cause unnecessary anxiety as the AIDS epidemic progresses through its second decade. In the early 1990s, the Center for Work Performance Problems at the Georgia Institute of Technology reported the results of a survey of 2,000 full time workers that illustrated the scope of workers' fear of AIDS infection from casual contact. Two-thirds of the workers surveyed had reservations about using the same bathroom as co-workers with AIDS; 40 percent were concerned about using the same cafeteria; and over one-third of those surveyed were reluctant to use the same equipment as a co-worker with AIDS. The National Leadership Coalition on AIDS, a consortium of more than 200 businesses, found that two out of three adults still mistakenly believed they could contract the virus by working near, or being touched by, a person with AIDS.

A 1993 *American Management Association Survey on HIV and AIDS-Related Policies* can serve as a "progress report" on AIDS in the workplace. Despite repeated and ongoing prodding from government and private agencies, the survey revealed that most companies continued to assume a reactive, rather than proactive, stance on HIV and AIDS. Three-quarters of the companies surveyed had reviewed their human resources policies, but nearly half determined that a policy change was not necessary. They elected to treat AIDS as another catastrophic illness. Just over half, however, claimed to be prepared with policy provisions, educational materials, and other resources to work with potential cases of HIV infection or AIDS. Only 15 percent had explicit AIDS policies, and 3.3 percent were in the process of formulating them.

FURTHER READING:

Goldbeck, Willis B. "AIDS and the Workplace." *Futurist.* March 1988.

Knotts, Rose, and J. Lynn Johnson. "AIDS in the Workplace: The Pandemic Firms Want to Ignore." *Business Horizons.* July/August 1993.

Pogash, Carol. "Risky Business: Sooner or Later, Everyone Will Deal with AIDS in the Workplace." *Working Woman.* October 1992.

Romano, Catherine. "Experience Drives Corporate AIDS Policies." *Management Review.* December 1993.

Squire, Madelyn C. "The Fear of AIDS: A Just Cause Dilemma?" *Dispute Resolution Journal.* December 1993.

White, Jane, and Bruce Pyenson. *Employee Benefits for Small Business.* Englewood Cliffs, NJ: Prentice-Hall, 1991.

ALIEN EMPLOYEES

Alien employees are those who take positions in U.S. businesses but who are not citizens of the United States. Those individuals who enter the country and secure employment do so by securing employment visas. Employment visas are classified into two categories: immigrant visas and nonimmigrant visas. Immigrant visas are used by aliens who are approved for permanent residency in the United States, while nonimmigrant visas provide for temporary stays in the country of up to seven years.

Alien employees can be a valuable component of a small business owner's work force, but consultants and legal experts note that hiring alien employees will necessitate additional paperwork. As Mary E. Reid wrote in *Small Business Reports,* "determining [immigration] visa categories and adhering to proper procedures can be quite a challenge. . . . All too often, employers are unaware of prospective employees' visa status and of the administrative burden involved in obtaining work authorization. Becoming aware of the constraints of the immigration laws can save valuable time when there's a job waiting to be performed."

IMMIGRANT AND NONIMMIGRANT VISAS Immigrant visas are given to aliens who are granted permanent residency in the United States. These individuals tend to be highly educated persons with experience and skills that are in high demand by companies in the United States. Immigrant visas are most frequently granted for the following employment areas: business executives and managers; notable professors, researchers, and other academics; advanced degree professionals; professionals with bachelor's degrees; investors in new business ventures; and aliens "of exceptional beauty." Skilled and unskilled workers are also sometimes granted immigrant visas.

Nonimmigrant visas, on the other hand, which provide for stays of up to seven years within the U.S., are more frequently bestowed upon aliens working in the following areas: aliens entering the country for business purposes; treaty traders and investors; students engaged in educational pursuits (work authorization is available for practical training after they complete their course of study); registered nurses; temporary agricultural, service, or labor workers; trainees; intracompany transfers; artists and entertainers; athletes; and aliens of "distinguished merit" or "extraordinary ability," especially in such fields as the sciences, education, the arts, business, or athletics.

KEY LEGAL CONSIDERATIONS

The regulatory picture for employing alien workers is ever-changing. In the 1990s alone, the U.S. government passed major laws including the Immigration Act of 1990 and the Illegal Immigration Reform and Immigrant Responsibility Act of 1996 that have had a direct affect on the hiring and work environment for businesses and immigrants alike.

Moreover, these laws are subject to interpretation and new regulations from U.S. agencies such as the U.S. Department of Labor (DOL) and the Immigration and Naturalization Service (INS), which are charged with making sure that companies and individuals obey the nation's laws in this area.

Restrictions on alien hiring can seem ominous or bewildering to small business owners who are unfamiliar with the various requirements. Employers, then, should make sure that they are familiar with the basics of utilizing alien employees in their workplaces. There are a few steps that all small business owners should take when hiring new employees to minimize the likelihood of employing an unauthorized worker and possibly incurring legal penalties.

First, employers should ask all job applicants if they are authorized to work in the United States. "Although it is discriminatory to ask whether applicants are U.S. citizens, your employment application can—and should—ask prospective employees whether they are authorized to work in the United States and if so, under what authority (citizenship or an employment visa)," wrote Reid.

For prospective employees who do have visas, it is sometimes necessary for employers to file appropriate documentation with the INS before the person in question can begin work. Requirements vary considerably from situation to situation, so it is often a good idea for small businesses to secure the services of an attorney with experience in immigration law for guidance. While companies are under no obligation to hire a person who does have the appropriate authorization to work in the United States, they also may not discriminate against an alien authorized to work in America on the basis of his or her citizenship. Given this situation, said Reid, "you [the small business owner] should determine your company's policy of sponsoring work visas and apply it equally to all employees. Having a policy of sponsoring work visas doesn't mean you have to retain an attorney for the employee or pay any visa filing fees. Your only obligation is signing the visa forms and complying with wage and hiring requirements, which can be burdensome."

It is also important for employers to be aware of prevailing wage structures for positions that may be filled by alien workers. Over the past several years, the U.S. government has passed laws in which employers are required to compensate immigrant workers at roughly the same levels that non-aliens in the same positions and in the same geographic region earn. These measures were passed so that alien employees were compensated fairly for their work. Businesses that neglect to meet minimum standards of compensation as laid out in American labor law may be assessed fines and penalties by the DOL. Small

business owners seeking "prevailing wage" information can contact their state's Bureau of Employment Services or secure a wage survey compiled by an authoritative source, such as an employment agency. Reid noted, however, that the DOL has traditionally regarded state employment bureau calculations as the most authoritative sources in this regard.

Small business owners also have to make certain that they file all the appropriate documentation before hiring an alien employee. According to *Small Business Reports,* an alien's visa application can be approved by the INS only after his or her would-be employer has filed the appropriate forms with the DOL. A Labor Certification Application is the most common one for employment-based visa classifications, while Labor Condition Applications are used for professional applicants, such as attorneys and doctors. Presuming the application is approved, the employer may then proceed with the visa application. Visa applications can be filed with the nearest regional INS office. "It's mandatory that you include documentation, such as a diploma, verifying that the employee has the necessary educational requirements and is otherwise qualified for the position," wrote Reid. "The INS will review the visa application and the supporting documents for accuracy. Depending on the type of visa application, the INS review process can take anywhere from one to six months." Finally, small business owners should be aware that Labor Certification and Labor Condition Applications have to be revalidated every two years.

ILLEGAL IMMIGRATION REFORM AND IMMIGRANT RESPONSIBILITY ACT OF 1996 Major immigration legislation added to the body of U.S. employment law is the Illegal Immigration Reform and Immigrant Responsibility Act of 1996. This legislation, which included new sanctions for companies found in violation of alien labor regulations, should be consulted before making any hiring decisions regarding alien workers. Basically, the new law states that American employers have to make sure that all of their employees are eligible to work in the United States when they begin their work. According to *Workforce,* immigration experts recommend that businesses conduct a serious Form I-9 audit to make sure that they are in full compliance with all pertinent immigration laws. Such audits not only help employers meet all legal obligations, but also may be regarded as evidence that they made good-faith attempts to follow employer verification requirements.

ALIEN EMPLOYEES AND AMERICAN CULTURE

Business owners who hire alien employees also may face challenges outside of the legal realm. Managing a culturally diverse work force can be a difficult process at times, although successful integration of people from different cultural and ethnic backgrounds can be a tremendously rewarding experience for a business on a wide range of levels, both socially and economically.

One key to creating a strong multicultural environment in the workplace is anticipating the difficulties that alien employees sometimes have with various aspects of American culture. ''The reality is, the United States is as foreign and strange to international assignees as other countries are to Americans,'' stated Charlene Marmer Solomon in *Workforce*.

FURTHER READING:

Cox, Taylor, Jr. *Cultural Diversity in Organizations.* San Francisco: Berrett-Koehler Publishers, 1993.

Faird, Elashmawia, and Philip Harris. *Multicultural Management.* Houston, TX: Gulf Publishing Company, 1993.

Fernandez, John P. *Managing a Diverse Work Force.* Lexington, MA: Lexington Books, 1991.

Flynn, Gillian. ''It's Time to Update Your Immigration Policies.'' *Workforce.* March 1997.

Kerrigan, Karen. ''Immigration Reform Taking Center Stage.'' *Washington Business Journal.* March 8, 1996.

Reid, Mary E. ''The Paper Chase.'' *Small Business Reports.* February 1993.

Solomon, Charlene Marmer. ''Destination U.S.A.: Incoming Expats Can Find America as Mysterious as the Moon.'' *Workforce.* April 1997.

Thiederman, Sondra. ''Managing the Foreign-Born Work Force: Keys to Effective Cross-Cultural Motivation.'' *Manage.* October 1988.

SEE ALSO: Cross-cultural/International Communication

AMERICANS WITH DISABILITIES ACT (ADA)

The Americans with Disabilities Act (ADA) is a revolutionary piece of legislation designed to protect the civil rights of people who have physical and mental disabilities, in a manner similar to that in which previous civil rights laws have protected people of various races, religions, and ethnic backgrounds. The ADA mandates changes in the way that both private businesses and the government conduct business to ensure that all Americans have full access to and can fully participate in every aspect of society. The ADA requires the removal of barriers that deny individuals with disabilities equal opportunity and access to jobs, public accommodations, government services, public transportation, and telecommunications. The law applies to small companies as well as to large ones, so small business owners must be aware of its provisions and how they affect their companies' employment practices, facilities, and products.

It is estimated that 43 million Americans, or one out of every five, have a disability. As defined in the ADA, the term ''disability'' applies to three categories of individuals: 1) people who have a physical or mental impairment that substantially limits one or more major life activities; 2) people who have a record of an impairment which substantially limits major life activities; and 3) people who may be regarded by others as having such an impairment. The ability of such people to participate in the mainstream of society has gradually increased during the last 30 years as a result of improvements in assistive technology and auxiliary aids and services, as well as expanding requirements for accessibility in newly constructed facilities.

PROVISIONS OF THE ADA

President George Bush signed the ADA into law on July 26, 1990. The legal structure of the ADA is based on the Civil Rights Act of 1964 and the Rehabilitation Act of 1973. The ADA uses concepts of disability, accessibility, and employment which were introduced in the Architectural Barriers Act of 1968 and the Rehabilitation Act of 1973. These two federal laws were the predecessors of the ADA that mandated a level of accessibility in federally funded buildings and programs. The ADA expanded the requirements of accessibility to the new and existing facilities of privately funded companies for the first time.

The ADA consists of five separate parts or titles: Title I relates to employment; Title II concerns public services; Title III pertains to public accommodations and commercial facilities; Title IV refers to telecommunications; and Title V covers miscellaneous other items.

Title 1 of the ADA prohibits discrimination in employment against qualified individuals with disabilities. For companies with 25 or more employees, the requirements became effective on July 26, 1992. For employers with between 15 and 24 workers, the requirements became effective on July 26, 1994.

Title II of the ADA prohibits discrimination in programs, services, or activities of public entities (state and local governments), including public transportation operated by public entities. The provisions of Title II which do not involve public transportation became effective on January 26, 1992.

Title III, pertaining to public accommodations and commercial facilities, requires that private businesses that are open to the public—including restaurants, department stores, convenience stores and specialty shops, and hotels and motels—allow individuals with disabilities to participate equally in the goods and services that they offer. This title also requires that all future construction of commercial facilities, including office buildings, factories, and warehouses, as well as places of public accommodation, be constructed so that the building is accessible to individuals with disabilities.

Title III also mandates modifications in policies, practices, and procedures. Commercial businesses and places of public accomodation are required to provide auxiliary aids and services, and to make accessible transportation available when transportation services are offered. In addition, companies are required to remove architectural and communications barriers and to comply with ADA in any ongoing or new construction. As of January 26, 1992, all fixed-route or on-demand transportation services—such as hotel-to-airport and other shuttle services—must be accessible to the disabled, including persons in wheelchairs.

Title IV of the ADA requires telephone companies to make relay services available for persons with hearing and speech impairments. This will provide equal opportunity for people with this type of disability to use telephone services.

Title V ties the ADA to the Civil Rights Act of 1974 and its amendments. It includes a variety of miscellaneous legal and technical provisions, including one that stipulates that the ADA does not override or limit the remedies, rights, or procedures of any federal, state, or local law which provides greater or equal protection for the rights of individuals with disabilities.

The ADA draws an important distinction between the terms ''reasonable accommodations'' and ''readily achievable.'' ''Reasonable accommodations'' has to do with employees, and no modifications must be undertaken to fulfill this requirement until a qualified individual with a disability has been hired. At that point, ''reasonable accommodations'' must be made unless they impose a significant difficulty or expense. In contrast, ''readily achievable'' has to do with clients or guests and applies to actions that can be accomplished without much difficulty or expense. ''Readily achievable'' modifications must be made in anticipation of a disabled guest's or client's needs, before they ever arrive on the premises.

FURTHER READING:

Allen, Jeffrey G. *Complying with the ADA: A Small Business Guide to Hiring and Employing the Disabled.* New York: John Wiley & Sons, 1993.

The Americans with Disabilities Act—Title II Technical Assistance Manual. Office on the Americans with Disabilities Act, Civil Rights Division, U.S. Department of Justice.

Saimen, John P.S. *Accommodating All Guests: The Americans with Disabilities Act and the Lodging Industry.* American Hotel & Motel Association. Washington: December 1992.

SEE ALSO: Disabled Customers; Employment Practices Liability Insurance

AMORTIZATION

Amortization, an **accounting** concept similar to **depreciation**, is the gradual reduction of the value of an asset or liability by some periodic amount (i.e., via installment payments). In the case of an **asset**, it involves expensing the item over the life of the item—the time period over which it can be used. For a **liability**, the amortization takes place over the time period that the item is repaid or earned. Amortization is essentially a means to allocate categories of assets and liabilities to their pertinent time period.

The key difference between depreciation and amortization is the nature of the items to which the terms apply. The former is generally used in the context of tangible assets, such as buildings, machinery, and equipment. The latter is more commonly associated with intangible assets, such as **copyrights**, **goodwill**, patents, and capitalized costs (e.g. product development costs). On the liability side, amortization is commonly applied to deferred revenue items such as premium income or subscription revenue (wherein cash payments are often received in advance of delivery of goods or services), and therefore must be recognized as income distributed over some future period of time.

Amortization is a means by which accountants apply the period concept in accrual-based financial statements: income and expenses are recorded in the periods affected, rather than when the cash actually changes hands. The importance of spreading transactions across several periods becomes more clear when considering long-lived assets of substantial cost. Just as it would be inappropriate to expense the entire cost of a new facility in the year of its acquisition since its life would extend over many years, it would be wrong to fully expense an intangible asset only in the first year. Intangible assets such as copyrights, patents, and goodwill can be of benefit to a business for many years, so the cost of accruing such assets should be spread over the entire time period that the company is likely to use the asset or generate revenue from it.

The periods over which intangible assets are amortized vary widely, from a few years to as many as 40 years. (The costs incurred with establishing and protecting patent rights, for example, are generally amortized over 17 years.) The general rule is that the asset should be amortized over its useful life. Small business owners should realize, however, that not all assets are consumed by their use or by the passage of time, and thus are not subject to amortization or depreciation. The value of land, for instance, is generally not degraded by time or use (indeed, the value of land assets often increases with time). This applies to intangible assets as well; trademarks can have indefinite lives and can increase in value over time, and thus are not subject to amortization.

The term amortization is also used in connection with **loans**. The amortization of a loan is the rate at which the principal balance will be paid down over time, given the term and interest rate of the note. Shorter note periods will have higher amounts amortized with each payment or period.

SEE ALSO: Intellectual Property; Trademarks and Copyrights

ANGEL INVESTORS

Angel investors are wealthy individuals who provide **capital** to help entrepreneurs and small businesses succeed. They are known as ''angels'' because they often invest in risky, unproven business ventures for which other sources of funds—such as bank loans and formal **venture capital**—are not available. ''Unlike banks, which hold you to stiff rules, offer little guidance, and are reluctant to make loans to start-up companies, angels can act as mentors, providing encouragement, contacts, and cash while staying out of the day-to-day business,'' Ellie Winninghoff wrote in an article for *Working Woman.*

According to David R. Evanson in an article for *Nation's Business,* wealthy private investors provide American small businesses with $10 to $20 billion annually, which ''dwarfs the investment made by traditional venture capital partnerships and offers a viable source of financing for capital hungry entrepreneurs.'' These individuals want to invest in up-and-coming new companies not only to earn money, Evanson suggested, but also to provide a resource that would have been helpful to them in the early stages of their own businesses. In many cases, the investors sit on the boards of the companies they fund and provide valuable, firsthand management advice.

Like other providers of venture capital, angel investors generally tend to invest in private startup companies with a high profit potential. In exchange for their funds, they usually require a percentage of equity ownership of the company and some measure of control over its strategic planning. Due to the highly speculative nature of their investments, angels eventually hope to achieve a high rate of return.

For many entrepreneurs, angels include friends, relatives, acquaintances, and business associates. In

fact, Winninghoff noted that nearly 90 percent of small businesses are started with this type of financial help. Some entrepreneurs gain access to angel investors through venture capital networks—informal organizations that exist specifically to help small businesses connect with potential investors, and visa versa. The networks—which may take the form of computer databases or document clearinghouses—basically provide ''matchmaking'' services between people with good business ideas and people with money to invest.

TYPES OF ANGELS

Although an angel can seem like the answer to a prayer for an entrepreneur who is desperate for capital, it is important to evaluate the person's motives for investing and need for involvement in the day-to-day operations of the business before entering into a deal. ''More and more entrepreneurs are turning to angels,'' Winninghoff noted, but ''many are finding that partners aren't always silent or willing to sit passively on the sidelines. In fact, while they may be brilliant in their own fields, many saviors have little understanding of the entrepreneurial process. Often they invest for the wrong reasons, or with unrealistic expectations.... Knowing how to recruit the right angel and avoid the pitfalls of dealing with him or her can mean the difference between a solid financial foundation and a failing venture.''

In an article for *Entrepreneur,* Evanson and Art Beroff described several basic personality types that tend to characterize angel investors. ''Corporate angels'' are former executives from large companies who have been downsized or have taken early retirement. In many cases, these angels invest in only one company and hope to turn their investment into a paid position. ''Entrepreneurial angels'' are individuals who own and operate their own successful businesses. In many cases, they look to invest in companies that provide some sort of synergy with their own company. They rarely want to take an active role in management, but often can help strengthen a small business in indirect ways.

''Enthusiast angels'' are older, independently wealthy individuals who invest as a hobby. As a result, they tend to invest small amounts in a number of different companies and not become overly involved in any of them. ''Micromanagement angels,'' in contrast, usually invest a large amount in one company and then seek as much control over its operations as possible. ''Professional angels'' are individuals employed in a profession such as law, medicine, or accounting who tend to invest in companies related to their areas of expertise. They may be able to provide services to the company at a reduced fee, but they may also tend to be impatient investors. Evanson and

Beroff stress that understanding the needs of various types of investors can help entrepreneurs to develop positive working relationships.

AVOIDING POTENTIAL PROBLEMS

Regardless of the type of angel a small business owner is able to recruit, there are a number of methods available to help avoid potential problems in the relationship. For example, Winninghoff recommended accentuating the negative when describing the business to a potential investor. Investing in an unproven business or idea always involves risk, and the investor should be told up front that he or she may lose the entire amount invested if the business fails. Most entrepreneurs tend to emphasize the positive aspects of the business opportunity in order to persuade reluctant investors, which may lead to a disintegration of the relationship later if the company cannot achieve its goals.

Winninghoff also suggested that entrepreneurs interview potential investors to be sure that their goals and needs are a good fit with the small business. Some angels may turn into micromanagers—making persistent phone calls, becoming involved in the details, and even issuing ultimatums—if it appears that the business may be in trouble. Other angels may be motivated to invest for hidden, nonfinancial reasons. For example, they may be seeking a job or chance to show off their business skills. It is important to ask questions of potential investors and listen to their answers in order to gauge their needs and interests. Ideally, the angels' investment approach will be compatible with the entrepreneur's needs.

"Entrepreneurs need to keep in mind that partnerships between angels and entrepreneurs are like marriages, involving issues of compatibility and cash," Winninghoff wrote. "Even the best business relationships will need work. In fact, the success of the small business depends on equal parts diplomacy and profit."

FURTHER READING:

Evanson, David R., and Art Beroff. "Heaven Sent: Seeking an Angel Investor? Here's How to Find a Match Made in Heaven." *Entrepreneur.* January 1998.

Evanson, David R. "Venture Capital, Networks Proliferate." *Nation's Business.* September 1996.

Hosmer, LaRue T. *A Venture Capital Primer for Small Business.* Washington, D.C.: U.S. Small Business Administration, 1990.

Schilit, W. Keith. *The Entrepreneur's Guide to Preparing a Winning Business Plan and Raising Venture Capital.* Englewood Cliffs, NJ: Prentice Hall, 1990.

Winninghoff, Ellie. "The Trouble with Angels." *Working Woman.* March 1992.

SEE ALSO: Investor Relations and Reporting; Venture Capital Network

ANNUAL PERCENTAGE RATE

The annual percentage rate (APR) is the effective rate of interest that is charged on an installment loan, such as those provided by banks, retail stores, and other lenders. Since the enactment of the Truth in Lending Act in 1969, lenders have been required to report the APR in boldface type on the first page of all loan contracts. The truth in lending law "requires lenders to disclose in great detail the terms and conditions that apply to consumers when they borrow," according to an article in *United States Banker.* "Its purpose was to allow consumers to shop for credit by comparing the fine print." In the absence of such requirements, it conceivably would be possible for a lender to misrepresent a loan with a 20 percent effective interest rate as a 10 percent loan. However, the APR can be calculated in different ways and can sometimes cause rather than eliminate confusion.

LOANS AND INTEREST RATES

A loan is the purchase of the present use of money with the promise to repay the amount in the future according to a pre-arranged schedule and at a specified rate of interest. Loan contracts formally spell out the terms and obligations between the lender and borrower. **Loans** are by far the most common type of **debt financing** used by small businesses. The **interest rate** charged on the borrowed funds reflects the level of risk that the lender undertakes by providing the money. For example, a lender might charge a startup company a higher interest rate than it would a company that had shown a profit for several years. The interest rate also tends to be higher on smaller loans, since lenders must be able to cover the fixed costs involved in making the loans.

The lowest interest rate charged by lenders—which is offered only to firms that qualify on the basis of their size and financial strength—is known as the prime rate. All other types of loans feature interest rates that are scaled upward from the prime rate. Interest rates vary greatly over time, depending on the policies set forth by the Federal Reserve Board as well as prevailing economic conditions in the nation. For all but the simplest of loans, the nominal or stated rate of interest may differ from the annual percentage rate or effective rate of interest. These differences occur because loans take many forms and cover various time periods. The effect of compounding and the addition of fees may also affect the APR of a loan.

CALCULATING THE APR

The effective rate of interest on a loan can be defined as the total interest paid divided by the amount of money received. For simple interest loans—in which the borrower receives the face value of the loan and repays the principal plus interest at maturity—the effective rate and the nominal rate are usually the same. As an example, say that a small business owner borrows $10,000 at 12 percent for 1 year. The effective rate would thus be $1,200 / $10,000 = 12 percent, the same as the stated rate.

But the effective rate would be slightly different for a discount interest loan—in which the interest is deducted in advance, so the borrower actually receives less than the face value. Using the same example, the small business owner would pay the $1,200 interest up front and receive $8,800 upon signing the loan contract. In this case, the effective interest rate would be $1,200 / $8,800 = 13.64 percent.

The most problematic differences between the nominal and effective rates of interest occur with installment loans. In this type of loan, the interest is calculated based on the nominal rate and added back in to get the face value of the loan. The loan amount is then repaid in equal installments during the loan period. Using the same example, the small business owner would sign for a loan with a face value of $11,200 and would receive $10,000. Since the loan is repaid in monthly installments, however, the business owner would not actually have use of the full loan amount over the course of the year. Instead, assuming 12 equal installments, the business owner would actually have average usable funds from the loan of $5,000. The effective rate of the loan is thus $1,200 / $5,000 = 24 percent, twice the stated rate of the loan.

True APR calculations should also include any up-front fees or penalties that are applied to a loan. These amounts are totaled and added to the interest figure. In the case of mortgage loans, such charges can be significant. They might include a mortgage insurance premium, points, lost interest earnings on escrow accounts, and prepayment penalties, for example.

FURTHER READING:

Brigham, Eugene F. *Fundamentals of Financial Management.* 5th ed. Chicago, IL: Dryden Press, 1989.

Buch, Joshua. "The Full Cost of a Home Mortgage Loan Revisited: Recalculation of APR, Using Variables That Are Usually Omitted from the Calculation." *Real Estate Review.* Fall 1996.

Eaglesham, Jean. "APRs Daze and Confuse." *Financial Times.* April 16, 1997.

Heath, Gibson. *Doing Business with Banks: A Common Sense Guide for Small Business Borrowers.* Lakewood, CO: DBA/ USA Press, 1991.

"Preparing for Truth in Savings." *United States Banker.* November 1992.

Rabianski, Joseph S., and James D. Vernor. "The Full Cost of a Home Mortgage Loan." *Real Estate Review.* Summer 1992.

Schulz, Matt. "Bankers Seek Way to Ease Lending Disclosure Rules to Eliminate Confusion." *American Banker.* February 22, 1996.

ANNUAL REPORTS

Annual reports are formal **financial statements** that are published yearly and sent to company stockholders and various other interested parties. The reports assess the year's operations and discuss the companies' view of the upcoming year and the companies' place and prospects in their industries. Both for-profit and not-for-profit organizations produce annual reports.

Annual reports are a **Securities and Exchange Commission** (SEC) requirement for businesses owned by the public. Companies meet this requirement, however, in many ways. At its most basic, an annual report includes:

- General description of the industry or industries in which the company is involved.

- Audited statements of income, financial position, and cash flow and notes to the statements providing details for various line items.

- A management's discussion and analysis (MD&A) of the business's financial condition and the results that the company has posted over the previous two years.

- A brief description of the company's business in the most recent year.

- Information related to the company's various business segments.

- Listing of the company's directors and executive officers, as well as their principal occupations, and, if a director, the principal business of the company that employs him or her.

- Market price of the company's stock and dividends paid.

Some companies provide only this minimum amount of information. Annual reports of this type usually are only a few pages in length and produced in an inexpensive fashion. The final product often closely resembles a photocopied document. For these companies, the primary purpose of an annual report is simply to meet legal requirements.

ANNUAL REPORT AS MARKETING TOOL

Many other companies, however, view their annual report as a potential effective marketing tool to disseminate their perspective on company fortunes, and large companies devote large sums of money to making their annual reports as attractive and informative as possible. In such instances the annual report becomes a forum through which a company can relate, influence, preach, opine, and discuss any number of issues and topics. Since annual reports, then, are inevitably colored by management perspectives, *Newsweek*'s Robert J. Samuelson noted that they warrant a degree of skepticism from readers. "Their messages are selective (bad news drops to footnotes, if possible) and their tone is upbeat (few companies admit to bleak prospects or befuddled management). Still, they can instruct and entertain. . . . [Even] the boilerplate rhetoric is revealing; it illuminates prevailing management philosophy."

An opening "Letter to Shareholders" often sets the tone of annual reports prepared for publicly held companies. The contents of such letters typically focus on topics such as the past year's results, strategies, market conditions, significant business events, new management and directors, and company initiatives. The chairman of the board of directors, the chief executive officer, the president, the chief operating officer or a combination of these four usually sign the letter on behalf of company management. Some of these letters may run a dozen or more pages and include photographs of the CEO in different poses (some even expound on topics that, while perhaps of only tangential interest to stockholders and other readers, are of importance to the CEO). More often, however, these letters are significantly shorter, amounting to a few pages or less.

Annual reports usually advance a theme or concept that has been embraced by company management and/or its marketing wings. Catch phrases such as "Poised for the Twenty-first Century" or "Meeting the Realities of the Nineties" can unify a company's annual report message. In addition, particular events or economic conditions of a given year may be incorporated into the themes advanced in an annual report. Companies also use milestone anniversaries—including industry as well as company anniversaries—in their annual reports. Promoting a long, successful track record is often appealing to shareholders and various audiences, for it connotes reliability and quality. Still other companies have developed a tried-and-true format that they use year after year with little change except updating the data. Whatever the theme, concept, or format, Wall Street will consider the most successful reports ones that clearly delineate a company's strategies for profitable growth.

TARGET AUDIENCES FOR ANNUAL REPORTS

Current shareholders and potential investors remain the primary audiences for annual reports. Employees (who today are also likely to be shareholders), customers, suppliers, community leaders, and the community-at-large, however, are also targeted audiences.

EMPLOYEES The annual report serves many purposes with employees. It often relates the company's goals. Employee innovation, quality, teamwork, and commitment are all critical to achieving company goals, so it is essential that employees and management share the same focus.

An annual report is also a vehicle for relating the company's successes—a new contract, a new product, cost-saving initiatives, new applications of products, expansions into new geographies—all of which have an impact on its work force. Seeing a successful project or initiative profiled in the annual report gives reinforcement to the employees responsible for the success.

The annual report can help increase employee understanding of the different parts of the company. Many manufacturing locations are in remote areas, and an employee's understanding of the company often does not go beyond the facility where he or she works. An annual report can be a source for learning about each of a company's product lines, its operating locations, and who is leading the various operations. The annual report can show employees how they fit into the "big picture."

Employees also are often shareholders. So, like other shareholders, these employees can use the annual report to help gauge their investment in the company. In this case, they also realize that the work they are doing in making products or providing a service is having an impact on how Wall Street values the company's stock.

CUSTOMERS Customers want to work with quality suppliers of goods and services, and an annual report can help a company promote its image with customers. Publishing management positions such as the company's mission and core values is one idea. Describing company initiatives such as projects to improve manufacturing processes, reduce costs, create quality, or enhance service can also illustrate a company's customer orientation. Finally, the annual report can also show the company's financial strength. Customers are reducing their number of suppliers, and one evaluation criterion is financial strength. They want committed and capable suppliers that are going to be around for the long term.

SUPPLIERS A company's abilities to meet its customers' requirements will be seriously compromised if it is saddled with inept or undependable suppliers. Successful companies today quickly weed out such companies. By highlighting internal measurements of quality, innovation, and commitment, annual reports can send an implicit message to suppliers about the company's expectations of those enterprises with which it does business. Sometimes an annual report will even offer a profile of a supplier that the company has found exemplary. Such a profile serve two purposes. First, it rewards the supplier for its work and serves to further cement their business relationship. Second, it provides the company's other suppliers with a better understanding of the level of service desired (and the rewards that can be reaped from such service).

THE COMMUNITY Companies invariably pay a great deal of attention to their reputation in the community or communities in which they operate. Most companies are very sensitive to how they are perceived in the community, for their reputations as corporate citizens can have a decisive impact on bottom line financial figures. A company would much rather be known for its sponsorship of a benefit charity event than for poisoning a river, whatever its other attributes. Annual reports, then, can be invaluable tools in burnishing a company's public image. Many annual reports discuss community initiatives undertaken by the company, including community renovation projects, charitable contributions, volunteer efforts, and programs to help protect the environment. The objective is to present the company as a proactive member of the community.

This sort of publicity also can be valuable when a company is making plans to move into a new community. Companies seek warm welcomes in new communities (including tax breaks and other incentives). Communities will woo a company perceived as a ''good'' corporate citizen more zealously than one that is not. The good corporate citizen also will receive less resistance from local interest groups. The company's annual report will be one document that all affected parties will pore over in evaluating the business.

READING AN ANNUAL REPORT

People read annual reports for widely different purposes and at dramatically different levels. Generalizations, however, are difficult. The stockholder with five shares might be as careful and discriminating a reader of an annual report as the financial analyst representing a firm owning one million shares.

It may require an MBA to understand all the details buried in an annual report's footnotes. Nevertheless, a good understanding of a company is possible by focusing on some key sections of the report.

COMPANY DESCRIPTION Most companies will include a description of their business segments that includes products and markets served. Formats vary from a separate fold-out descriptive section to a few words on the inside front cover. A review of this section provides readers with at least a basic understanding of what the company does.

THE LETTER Whether contained under the heading of Letter to Shareholders, Chairman's Message, or some other banner, the typical executive message can often provide some informative data on the company's fortunes during the previous year and its prospects for the future, though readers should always bear in mind that it is invariably in the executive's best interests to maintain a fundamentally upbeat tone, no matter how troubled the company may be.

MANAGEMENT'S DISCUSSION AND ANALYSIS This section can be dry and is often bursting with accounting jargon, but the MD&A nonetheless provides, in fairly succinct form, an overview of the company's performance over the previous three years. It makes a comparison of the most recent year with the year previous, and then compares this latter year with the year previous to it. It discusses sales, manufacturing income and margin, operating income, and net income, as well as the principal factors that influenced business trends. Other portions discuss capital expenditures, cash flow, changes in working capital, and anything ''special'' that happened during the years under examination. The MD&A is also supposed to be forward-looking, discussing anything the company may be aware of that could negatively or positively affect results. An MD&A can be written at all different levels of comprehension, but with even a little accounting understanding, the reader can get valuable insights.

FINANCIAL SUMMARY Most companies will include either a five-, six-, ten-, or eleven-year summary of financial data. Sales, income, dividends paid, shareholders' equity, number of employees, and many other balance sheet items are included in this summary. This section summarizes key data from the statements of income, financial position, and cash flow for a number of years.

MANAGEMENT/DIRECTORS A page or more of an annual report will list the management of the company and its board of directors, including their backgrounds and business experience.

INVESTOR INFORMATION There almost always is a page that lists the company's address and phone number, the stock transfer agent, dividend and stock price information, and the next annual meeting date. This information is helpful for anyone wanting additional data on the company or more information about stock ownership.

PACKAGING THE ANNUAL REPORT

For most companies, large or small, the financial information and the corporate message are the most important aspects of an annual report. Many companies also want to be sure, however, that their targeted audiences are going to read and understand the message. This is less essential for privately owned businesses that do not need to impress or soothe investors, but they too recognize that disseminating a dry, monotonous report is not in the company's best interests. At the same time, turning the message over to a designer who is more intent on creating a visual, aesthetic monument than providing readers with easily found and coherent information is likely to have a similar negative effect.

The challenge for producers of annual reports is to disseminate pertinent information in a comprehensible fashion while simultaneously communicating the company's theme and/or message. Many annual report readers spend very little time looking through a report, so the challenge is a substantial one. Thus, annual reports have in recent years become quite reminiscent of advertisements in their reliance on bold graphics and splashy colors. Indeed, in many ways the annual report serves as an advertisement for the company, a reality that is reflected in the fact that leading business magazines now present awards to company reports deemed to be of particular merit. Of course, the personality of the company—and perhaps most importantly, the industry in which it operates—will go a long way toward dictating the design format of the annual report. The owner of a manufacturer of hospital equipment is far less likely to present a visually dramatic annual report to the public than are the owners of a chain of suntanning salons. The key is choosing a design that will best convey the company's message.

SUMMARY ANNUAL REPORTS

Few major trends have jarred the tradition of annual reports, but one is the "summary annual report." In 1987, the SEC eased its annual reporting requirements. It allowed companies to produce a summary annual report, rather than the traditional report with audited statements and footnotes. Public disclosure of financial information was still required, but with the new rulings, filing a Form 10-K—provided it contained this information and included audited financial data and other required material within a company's proxy statement (another SEC-mandated document for shareholders)—met SEC requirements. Promoters of the summary annual report see it as a way to make the annual report a true marketing publication without the cumbersome, detailed financial data. Financial data is still included, but in a condensed form in a supporting role. Since its

use was approved, however, the summary annual report has not gained widespread support.

In some respects, annual reports are like fashions. Certain techniques, formats, and designs are popular for a few years and then new ideas displace the old. Several years later, the old ideas are back in vogue again. Other formats are "classic," never seeming to go out of style or lose their power. A key to a successful annual report is not getting caught up in a trend, and instead deciding what works best for conveying the message.

FURTHER READING:

"Financial World Annual Report Competition Winners." *Financial World.* November 18, 1996.

Fulkerson, Jennifer. "How Investors Use Annual Reports." *American Demographics.* May 1996.

Samuelson, Robert J. "Close to the Lunatic Edge: Corporate Annual Reports Often Tell Us More Than Their Authors Know or Intend." *Newsweek.* April 21, 1997.

SEE ALSO: Community Relations; Corporate Image

ANNUITIES

An annuity is a type of financial product that combines the tax-deferred savings and investment properties of retirement accounts with the guaranteed-income aspects of insurance. "Basically, an annuity is an interest-bearing contract, typically issued by an insurance company to help you save for and fund your retirement," Mel Poteshman explained in an article for the *Los Angeles Business Journal.* "Annuities are sometimes described as the flip side of life insurance. Whereas life insurance is designed to provide financial protection against dying too soon, annuities provide a hedge against outliving your retirement savings," Stephen Blakely noted in an article for *Nation's Business.* "While life insurance is designed to create principal, an annuity is designed ultimately to liquidate principal that has been created, typically in regular payments over a number of years."

Annuities can be purchased from insurance providers, banks, mutual fund companies, stockbrokers, and other financial institutions. They come in several different forms, including immediate and deferred annuities, and fixed and variable annuities. Each form has different properties and involves different costs. Although the money placed in an annuity is first subject to taxation at the same rate as ordinary income, it is then invested and allowed to grow tax-deferred until it is withdrawn. Distribution is flexible and can take the form of a lump sum, a systematic payout over a specified period, or a guaranteed income spread over the remainder of a person's life. In most cases annuities are a long-term investment vehicle, since the costs involved make it necessary to hold an annuity for a number of years in order to reap financial benefits. Because of their flexibility, annuities can be a good choice for small business owners in planning for their own retirement or in providing an extra reward or incentive for valued employees.

Thanks to the surge in the stock market, sales of variable annuities increased more than 58 percent over a three-year period to reach $74 billion in 1996. In addition, according to Blakely, they were projected to nearly double again by the year 2000. Although annuities have become extremely popular in recent years, they are still the subject of heated debate among investment advisors. "The devices work something like this: You put in as much cash as you want at one end, then watch the gears mesh, the wheels whir, and—presto!—out from the other end comes a great deal more money," as Karen Hube described annuities in *Money.* "But unfortunately, for most investors the annuity machine—part investment, part insurance—doesn't work nearly as well as promised."

TYPES OF ANNUITIES

There are several different types of annuities available, each with different properties and costs. "It is important to understand the various types of annuities on the market today to determine if and how they fit into your retirement investment portfolio and to identify the risks that may be involved," Poteshman noted. The two basic forms that annuities take are immediate and deferred.

An immediate annuity, as the name suggests, begins providing payouts at once. Payouts may continue either for a specific period or for life, depending on the contract terms. Immediate annuities—which are generally purchased with a one-time deposit, with a minimum of around $10,000—are not very common. They tend to appeal to people who wish to roll over a lump-sum amount from a pension or inheritance and begin drawing income from it. The immediate annuity would be preferable to a regular bank account because the principal grows more quickly through investment and because the amount and duration of payouts are guaranteed by contract. In contrast, deferred annuities delay payouts until a specific future date. The principal amount is invested and allowed to grow tax-deferred over time. More common than immediate annuities, deferred annuities tend to appeal to people who want a tax-deferred investment vehicle in order to save for retirement.

There are also two basic types of deferred annuity: fixed and variable. Fixed annuities provide a guaranteed **interest rate** over a certain period, usually between one and five years. In this way, fixed annu-

ities are comparable to certificates of deposit (CDs) and bonds, with the main benefit that the sponsor guarantees the return of the principal. Fixed annuities generally offer a slightly higher interest rate than CDs and bonds (the average rate was 6 percent in mid-1997), while the risk is also slightly higher. In addition, like other types of annuities, the principal is allowed to grow tax-deferred until it is withdrawn.

On the other hand, the more popular variable annuities offer an interest rate that changes based on the value of the underlying investment. Purchasers of variable annuities can usually choose from a range of stock, bond, and money market funds for investment purposes in order to diversify their portfolios and manage risk. Some of these funds are created and managed specifically for the annuity, while others are similar to those that may be purchased directly from mutual fund companies. The minimum investment usually ranges from $500 to $5,000, depending on the sponsor, and the investments (or subaccounts) usually feature varying levels of risk from aggressive growth to conservative fixed income. In most cases, the annuity principal can be transferred from one investment to another without being subject to taxation. Variable annuities are subject to market fluctuations, however, and investors also must accept a slight risk of losing their principal if the sponsor company encounters financial difficulties.

FEATURES OF ANNUITIES

Variable annuities have a number of features that differentiate them from common retirement accounts, such as **401(k)s** and **individual retirement accounts (IRAs)**, and from common equity investments, such as mutual funds. One of the main points of differentiation involves tax deferral. Unlike 401(k)s or IRAs, variable annuities are funded with after-tax money—meaning that contributions are subject to taxation at the same rate as ordinary income prior to being placed in the annuity. In contrast, individuals are allowed to make contributions to the other types of retirement accounts using pre-tax dollars. "That is why financial specialists generally advise people first to maximize contributions to 401(k) plans and IRAs (when eligible) before considering annuities," according to Blakely. On the plus side, there is no limit on the amount that an individual may contribute to a variable annuity, while contributions to the other types of accounts are limited by the federal government. Unlike the dividends and capital gains that accrue to mutual funds which are taxable in the year they are received, the money invested in annuities is allowed to grow tax free until it is withdrawn.

Another feature that differentiates variable annuities from other types of financial products is the death benefit. Most annuity contracts include a clause guaranteeing that the investor's heirs will receive either the full amount of principal invested or the current market value of the contract, whichever is greater, in the event that the investor dies before receiving full distribution of the assets. However, any earnings are taxable for the heirs. Although this provision is unlikely to be needed given the strong growth of long-term investments in recent years, it is nonetheless a key provision of annuities.

Another benefit of variable annuities is that they offer greater withdrawal flexibility than other retirement accounts. Investors are able to customize the distribution of their assets in a number of ways, ranging from a lump-sum payment to a guaranteed lifetime income. Some limitations do apply, however. The federal government imposes a ten percent penalty on withdrawals taken before age 59½, for example. But contributors to variable annuities are not required to begin taking distributions until age 85, whereas contributors to IRAs and 401(k)s are required to begin taking distributions by age 70½.

COSTS ASSOCIATED WITH ANNUITIES

In exchange for the various features offered by annuities, investors must pay a number of costs. Many of the costs are due to the insurance aspects of annuities, although they vary among different sponsors. One common type of cost associated with annuities is the insurance cost, which averages 1.25 percent and pays for the guaranteed death benefit in addition to the insurance agent's commission. Also, there are usually management fees, averaging one percent, which compensate the sponsor for taking care of the investments and generating reports. Many annuities also charge administrative or contract fees ranging from $25 to $40 per year.

One of the most problematic costs of annuities, in the eyes of their critics, is the surrender charge for early removal of the principal. In most cases, this fee begins at around 7 percent but then phases out over time. However, the surrender fee is charged in addition to the 10 percent government penalty for early withdrawal if the investor is under age 59½. "The effect is that you are essentially trapped in the product," Hube noted.

All of the costs associated with annuities detract somewhat from their attractiveness as a financial product. According to Blakely, the combined costs make the average variable annuity quite a bit more expensive, at 2.01 percent of invested assets annually, than the average mutual fund, at 1.24 percent of assets. The costs also mean that there are no quick profits associated with annuities; instead, they must be held as a long-term investment. "All the fees so erode your returns that it can take as long as 17 years for the benefits of tax deferral to kick in and outweigh the expenses," Hube stated. "If you can afford to put money away for a period that lasts longer than some marriages, then variable annuities can make sense."

DISTRIBUTION OPTIONS

On the positive side, investors in annuities have a number of options for receiving the distribution of their funds. The three most common forms of distribution—all of which have various costs deducted—are lump sum, lifetime income, and systematic payout. Some investors who have contributed to a variable annuity over many years may elect to make a lump-sum withdrawal. The main drawback to this approach is that all the taxes are due immediately. Other investors may decide upon a systematic payout of the accumulated assets over a specified time period. In this approach, the investor can determine the amount of payments as well as the intervals at which payments will be received. Finally, some investors choose the option of receiving a guaranteed lifetime income. This option is the most expensive for the investor, and does not provide any money for heirs, but the sponsor of the annuity must continue to make payouts even if the investor outlives his or her assets. A similar distribution arrangement is joint-and-last-survivor, which is an annuity that keeps providing income as long as one person in a couple is alive.

ADVANTAGES AND DISADVANTAGES

Annuities are rather complex financial products, and as such they have become the subject of considerable debate among financial planning experts. As mentioned earlier, many experts claim that the special features of annuities are not great enough to make up for their cost as compared to other investment options. As a result, financial advisors commonly suggest that individuals maximize their contributions to IRAs, 401(k)s, or other pre-tax retirement accounts before considering annuities. Some experts also prefer mutual funds tied to a stock market index to annuities, because such funds typically cost less and often provide a more favorable tax situation. Contributions to annuities are taxed at same rate as ordinary income, for instance, while long-term capital gains from stock investments are taxed at a special, lower rate—usually 20 percent. Still other financial advisors note that, given the costs involved, annuities require a very long-term financial commitment in order to provide benefits. It may not be possible for some individuals to tie up funds for the 17 to 20 years it takes to prosper from the purchase of an annuity.

Despite the drawbacks, however, annuities can be beneficial for individuals in a number of different situations. For example, annuities provide an extra source of income and an added margin of safety for individuals who have contributed the limit allowed under other retirement savings options. In addition, some kinds of annuities can be valuable for individuals who want to protect their assets from creditors in the event of bankruptcy. An annuity can provide a good shelter for a retirement nest egg for someone in a risky profession, such as medicine. Annuities are also recommended for people who plan to spend the principal during their lifetime rather than leaving it for their heirs. Finally, annuities may be more beneficial for individuals who expect that their tax bracket will be 28 percent or lower at the time they begin making withdrawals.

Annuities may also hold a great deal of appeal for small businesses. For example, annuities can be used as a retirement savings plan on top of a 401(k). They can be structured in various ways to reward key employees for meeting company goals. In addition, annuities can provide a nice counterpart to life insurance, since the longer the investor lives, the better an annuity will turn out to be as an investment. Finally, some annuities allow investors to take out loans against the principal without paying penalties for early withdrawal. Overall, some financial experts claim that annuities are actually worth more than comparable investments because of such features as the death benefit, guaranteed lifetime income, and investment services. "The big negative [with annuities] is that it's an expensive way to get investment service and a guarantee," financial analyst A. Michael Lipper told Blakely. "But the safety factor is important, especially for a lot of small companies that want to guarantee their workers there will be something there for their retirement."

A small business owner thinking about setting up an annuity should consider all options, look carefully at both the costs and the returns, and be prepared to put money away for many years. It is also important to shop around for the best possible product and sponsor before committing funds. "Before investing in an annuity, make sure the insurance company that will sponsor the contract is financially healthy. Also, find out from the sponsoring company the interest rates that have been paid out over the last five to ten years and how interest rate changes are calculated. This will give you an idea of the annuity's overall performance and help you identify the annuity that provides the best long-range financial security," Poteshman wrote. Finally, Hube noted that investors should never put an annuity into another tax-sheltered account, like an IRA, because the tax shelter then becomes redundant and the investor will be paying large annuity fees for nothing.

FURTHER READING:

Blakely, Stephen. "What You Need to Know about Annuities." *Nation's Business.* November 1997.

Goode, Robin Wright. "Tax-Free Investing: Whether Fixed or Variable, Annuities May Be Just the Thing for Your Portfolio." *Black Enterprise.* August 1996.

Guthrie, Jonathan. "Choose Right—Or Lose Plenty." *Financial Times.* March 23, 1996.

Hube, Karen. "The Annuity Machine: Will It Reward You?" *Money.* June 1997.

Poteshman, Mel. "Annuities Can Help Build Sizeable Retirement Nest Egg, Reduce Taxes." *Los Angeles Business Journal.* September 23, 1996.

Streiff, Thomas. "Assessing Annuity's Role in Asset Allocation Plan." *National Underwriter and Life.* May 6, 1996.

SEE ALSO: Retirement Planning

APPRENTICESHIP PROGRAMS

Apprenticeship programs are occupational training programs that combine on-the-job work experience with technical or classroom study and are designed to develop useful job skills in individuals entering the work force. These programs, which are designed to address the need for better trained entry-level workers and to help young people make the transition from school to the work world, can also serve as a good source of labor for businesses of all shapes and sizes.

Many U.S. industries maintain thriving apprenticeship programs. Many of these programs can be found in the skilled trades and crafts, notably in occupations related to the construction industry. Indeed, in many states apprenticeship programs are required to obtain occupational licensing or certification. Although the United States does not currently maintain a national apprenticeship program, in the mid-1990s, 27 states regulated apprenticeship programs within their borders. The U.S. Department of Labor, Bureau of Apprenticeship and Training, maintains a registry of apprenticeship programs and the occupations that are covered throughout the country.

Apprenticeship programs may be sponsored by employers, a group of employers, or a union. Trade and other nonprofit organizations also sponsor apprenticeship programs within certain industries. Unions and employers often form joint apprenticeship committees to administer the programs. Such committees are concerned with determining an industry's particular needs and developing standards for the apprenticeship programs. Apprenticeship programs are usually registered with the federal or state government to ensure that the programs meet standards relating to job duties, instruction, wages, and safety and health conditions.

Individuals who are interested in entering an apprenticeship program must meet certain qualifications. Because of child labor laws in the United States, most apprenticeship programs in the United States require applicants to be at least 16 or 18 years of age. While some states have apprenticeship programs for high school juniors and seniors, most apprenticeship programs require a high school diploma. Other requirements relate to aptitude and physical condition.

Once an individual has been accepted into an apprenticeship program, he or she usually signs an agreement with the program's sponsor. The agreement covers such matters as the sponsor's compliance with the program's standards and the apprentice's performance of the required work and completion of the necessary studies. While enrolled in the program the apprentice works under the supervision of a fully qualified journeyperson as a paid, full-time employee. Apprentices are usually paid about half of what a journeyperson makes, and also receive relevant instruction outside of regular working hours, either in a classroom or through at-home study. The program may last from one to six years, depending on the occupation and other requirements. Certification is usually granted upon successful completion of an apprenticeship program.

In recent years, growing numbers of economists and industry experts have called for the establishment of some type of national apprenticeship program in the United States. Supporters contend that such a program, which would provide apprenticeship training and job skills certification at the national level, would help to reduce the wage gap between college graduates and those who do not attend college, and would produce better-trained entry-level workers.

FURTHER READING:

Gitter, Robert J. ''Apprenticeship-Trained Workers: United States and Great Britain.'' *Monthly Labor Review.* April 1994.

Glazer, Nathan. ''A Human Capital Policy for the Cities.'' *Public Interest.* Summer 1993.

Kiester, Edwin. ''Germany Prepares Kids for Good Jobs; We Were Preparing Ours for Wendy's.'' *Smithsonian.* March 1993.

Szabo, Joan C. ''Training Workers for Tomorrow.'' *Nation's Business.* March 1993.

SEE ALSO: Business Education; Training and Development

ARBITRATION AND MEDIATION

Arbitration and mediation are integral parts of the American business landscape today. Arbitration is the procedure by which parties agree to submit their disputes to an independent neutral third party, known as an arbitrator. Although there are several types of arbitration, labor arbitration is the dispute resolution procedure used in labor relations. Mediation also involves the active participation of a neutral third party whose role is to facilitate the dispute resolution process and to suggest solutions to resolve disputes. The term conciliation is often used interchangeably with mediation, but conciliation generally refers to the third party who brings the disputing parties together. While the mediator *suggests* possible solutions to the disputing parties, the arbitrator makes a final decision on the labor dispute which is *binding* on the parties.

Collective bargaining agreements detail the rights of labor, the responsibilities of management, and the ultimate relationship between the two. Nearly all of these collective bargaining agreements provide for arbitration as the final step in dispute resolution. Arbitration can represent either all employees covered by the agreement or a specific individual on one side and management concerns on the other. Arbitration holds advantages over both strikes and litigation as a means of resolving disputes. Even the U.S. Supreme Court has determined that arbitration is the preferred method of resolution in reaching a workable solution to labor problems.

ARBITRATION ASSOCIATIONS AND ORGANIZATIONS There are several U.S. organizations and agencies that are directly involved in arbitration and arbitration issues. These include the National Academy of Arbitrators (NAA), the American Arbitration Association (AAA), and the Federal Mediation Conciliation Service (FMCS). The NAA was founded in 1947 as a non-profit organization to foster high standards for arbitration and arbitrators and to promote the process. The NAA works to attain these objectives through seminars, annual conferences, and educational programs. The non-profit AAA offers its services for voluntary arbitration as part of its mandate to promote the use of arbitration in all fields. The FMCS, meanwhile, maintains a roster from which arbitrators can be selected and champions procedures and guidelines designed to enhance the arbitration process.

THE ARBITRATION PROCESS The arbitration process involves an arbitrator and representatives of both sides involved in the disagreement. The arbitrator is either a permanent arbitrator, an independent arbitrator selected by the two parties to resolve a particular grievance, or an arbitrator selected through the procedures of the AAA or FMCS. A board of arbitrators can also be used in a hearing.

After the arbitrator is selected, both sides are given the opportunity to present their perspectives on the issue or issues in dispute. These presentations include testimony and evidence that are provided in much the same way as a court proceeding, although formal rules of evidence do not apply. Upon completion of the arbitration hearing, the arbitrator reviews the evidence, testimony, and the collective bargaining agreement, considers principles of arbitration, and makes a decision. The arbitrator's decision is generally rendered within 60 days, but unless it is so specified in the arbitration clause of the contract between the two parties, arbitrations are not binding on either party. If the contract does include a binding arbitration clause, then the decision must be taken to court to establish it as a legally enforceable judgement.

When all parties agree, is submitted for possible publication by one of several commercial publishers, either the Bureau of National Affairs (*Labor Arbitration Reports*), the Commerce Clearing House (*Labor Arbitration Awards*), or other sources. Fewer than 10 percent of these decisions are published.

OTHER TYPES OF ARBITRATION Other forms of labor arbitration include the following:

1) Compulsory arbitration is a dispute resolution which is required by law. Widely accepted in Australia and New Zealand, compulsory arbitration was practiced by the National War Labor Board during World War II. This is a binding process.

2) Expedited arbitration is a process intended to speed up (and save money on) the arbitration process with an informal hearing. Under this process, decisions are generally rendered within five days. It was first used in 1971 in settling disputes in the steel industry.

3) Interest arbitration is the use of an arbitrator or arbitrator board to render a binding decision in resolving a dispute over new contract terms.

4) Final offer selection arbitration is an interest arbitration process in which the arbitrator or arbitrator board selects either the union or management proposal to the solution. There can be no compromised decisions. This process is also termed either-or arbitration.

5) Tripartite arbitration is a process wherein a three-member panel of arbitrators is used to reach a decision. Both labor and management select an arbitrator and the third is selected by the other two arbitrators or the parties to the dispute as a neutral participant.

MEDIATION In contrast to arbitration, mediation is a process whereby the parties involved have to solve the dispute themselves. Rather than dictating a solution to the dispute between labor and management, the mediator suggests various proposals to help the two parties reach a mutually agreeable solution. In mediation, the various needs of the conflicting sides of an issue are identified, and ideas and concepts are exchanged until a viable solution is proposed by either of the parties or

the mediator. Rarely does the mediator exert pressure on either party to accept a solution. Instead, the mediator's role is to encourage communication and compromise in order to resolve the dispute.

In labor disputes, the terms "grievance mediation" and "preventive mediation" are commonly used. Grievance mediation is an attempt to ward off arbitration through a course of fact-finding that is ultimately aimed at promoting dialogue between the two parties. Preventive mediation dates to the Taft-Hartley Act (1947) and is an FMCS program intended to avoid deeper divisions between labor and management over labor issues. Also termed technical assistance, the program encompasses training, education, consultation, and analysis of union-management disputes.

FURTHER READING:

Elkouri, Frank and Edna Asper. *How Arbitration Works*. Washington: Bureau of National Affairs, 1985.

Kagel, Sam and Kathy Kelly. *The Anatomy of Mediation: What Makes it Work*. Washington: Bureau of National Affairs, 1989.

SEE ALSO: Employee Strikes; Labor Unions; Negotiation

ARTICLES OF INCORPORATION

For small businesses that decide to incorporate, one of the first steps they must take is filing the articles of incorporation (sometimes called certificates of incorporation, articles of association, or charters) at a Secretary of State's Office or with the **U.S. Department of Commerce**. A company can file in the state in which it does business or in any other state of its choosing. In the past, businesses were often advised to incorporate in Delaware because of its simple and advantageous corporate laws. More recently, though, there is less agreement on the subject. Many other states have reformed their tax codes in order to keep businesses at home, thus muting the advantages previously associated with incorporating in Delaware.

In most states, the Secretary of State can provide blank forms. These differ from state to state, but they are fairly straightforward and only require you to fill in the blanks. In a few states, no forms are available, and you will have to draw up the articles of incorporation from scratch. You may prepare the articles of incorporation on your own (there are many guides available, some of which are specifically created for a certain state and include sample forms), or you may hire a lawyer to do this for you. But even if you take on the task yourself, it may be a good idea to ask a lawyer to look over the form.

Generally, the articles of incorporation include the following sections:

- Corporate Name.

- Initial agent (sometimes called a registered agent or resident agent) and office—This is usually the corporate president or one of the directors. In any case, this is the contact person to whom all legal notices and official mailings will be sent.

- Purpose for which the Corporation is organized—In most states, this section does not need to be filled in. It will already contain a statement to the effect that the Corporation can do anything that's legal for a corporation to do in that state. If you have to fill it in yourself, it is best to leave the language as general as possible. That way, if you later change the nature of your business, you will not need to amend the articles of incorporation.

- The Duration of the Company—This is usually listed as perpetual.

- Authorized Shares, Issued Shares, and Classification of Stock—The amount of information about authorized or issued shares required in this section varies by state. You may be asked to list the total number of shares authorized to be issued, the number of shares actually issued, the class of stock (common, preferred or both), the value per share, or the consideration received for the shares.

- Directors of the Corporation and their Addresses

- Name(s) and Address(es) of Incorporator(s)—This section should list the name of those individuals who have performed the incorporation and prepared the articles of incorporation (attorneys, directors, or owners).

- Estimated Property and Gross Revenue—This section, which is optional in some states, may include an estimate of the business's property value and the estimated gross amount of business which will be transacted during the following year.

Once the form is complete, it should be mailed to the Secretary of State or Department of Commerce in the state in which the business will operate. Any fees that are due should be sent along at this time as well. Each state has a filing fee, and there are usually other fees such as a franchise tax (usually based on your capitalization), a fee for designating a registered agent, or an organization tax based on the number and value of stock. These fees vary dramatically from state to state.

When the articles of incorporation are returned to the business owner after being accepted by the Secretary of State, they will probably need to be filed with the Recorder of Deeds in the county where the corporation's home office is located. The articles of incorporation, now the company's charter, then become public record.

FURTHER READING:

Diamond, Michael R. and Julie L. Williams. *How to Incorporate: A Handbook for Entrepreneurs and Professionals.* 3rd ed. New York: John Wiley & Sons, 1996.

Steingold, Fred S. *The Legal Guide for Starting and Running a Small Business.* Second Edition. Berkeley, CA: Nolo Press, 1995.

Williams, Phillip G. *Small Business Incorporation Series* (with guides for incorporating in Illinois, Ohio, Michigan, Indiana, and Missouri). Oak Park, IL: P. Gaines Co., 1993.

SEE ALSO: Incorporation

ASSEMBLY LINE METHODS

An assembly line is a production arrangement of workers and equipment in which the product that is being assembled passes consecutively from operation to operation, with each station adding to the work of previous stations, until the product is completed. Assembly line methods were originally introduced to increase factory **productivity** and efficiency by reducing the cost and manufacturing time required to produce a finished product. Current advances in assembly line methods have been introduced with the same basic objectives: to increase throughput, or the number of products produced in a given period of time, and to save money. While assembly line methods apply primarily to manufacturing processes, business experts have also been known to apply its principles to other areas of business, from product development to management.

The introduction of the assembly line to American manufacturing floors in the early part of this century revolutionized myriad industries and fundamentally transformed the character of business throughout the nation, as production periods shortened, equipment costs accelerated, and labor and management alike endeavored to keep up with the changes. Today, using modern assembly line methods, manufacturing has become a highly refined process in which value is added to parts along the line. Increasingly, assembly line manufacturing is characterized by concurrent processes—multiple parallel activities that feed into a final assembly stage. These processes require a well planned flow of materials and the development of an advanced materials and supply infrastructure.

Just-in-time (JIT) manufacturing methods have been developed to reduce the cost of carrying parts and supplies as **inventory**. Under a JIT system, manufacturing plants carry only one or a few days' worth of inventory in the plant, relying on **suppliers** to provide parts and materials on an as needed basis. Future developments in this area may call for suppliers to establish operations within the manufacturing facility itself to provide for a more efficient supply of materials and parts.

VARIATIONS IN ASSEMBLY LINE METHODOLOGIES
The passage of years have brought numerous variations in assembly line methodologies. These new wrinkles can be traced back not only to general improvements in technology and planning, but to factors that are unique to each company or industry. Capital limitations, for example, can have a big impact on a small business's blueprint for introducing or improving assembly line production methods, while changes in international competition, operating regulations, and availability of materials can all influence the assembly line of entire industries. Following are brief descriptions of assembly line methods that are currently enjoying some degree of popularity in the manufacturing world.

- Modular Assembly—This is an advanced assembly line method that is designed to improve throughput by increasing the efficiency of parallel subassembly lines feeding into the final assembly line. As applied to automobile manufacturing, modular assembly would involve assembling separate modules—chassis, interior, body—on their own assembly lines, then joining them together on a final assembly line.

- Cell Manufacturing—This production methodology that has evolved out of increased ability of machines to perform multiple tasks. Cell operators can handle three or four tasks, and robots are used for such operations as materials handling and welding. Cells of machines can be run by one operator or a multi-person work cell. In these machine cells it is possible to link older machines with newer ones, thus reducing the amount of investment required for new machinery.

- Team Production—Team-oriented production is another development in assembly line methods. Where workers used to work at one- or two-person work stations and perform repetitive tasks, now teams of workers can follow a job down the assembly line

through its final quality checks. The team production approach has been hailed by supporters as one that creates greater worker involvement in and knowledge of the entire manufacturing process.

As new assembly line methods are introduced into manufacturing processes, business managers look at the techniques for possible application to other areas of business. New methods all share the common goal of improving throughput by reducing the amount of time individual workers and their machines spend on specific tasks. By reducing the amount of time required to produce an item, assembly line methods have made it possible to produce more with less.

ASSETS

Assets are anything of value that is owned by a company, whether fully paid for or not. These range from cash, **inventory**, and other ''current assets'' to real estate, equipment, and other ''fixed assets.'' Intangible items of value to a company, such as exclusive use contracts, **copyrights**, and patents, are also regarded as assets.

CURRENT ASSETS

Also known as soft or liquid assets, current assets include cash, government securities, marketable securities, notes receivable, **accounts receivable**, inventories, raw materials, prepaid expenses, and any other item that could be converted to cash in the normal course of business within one year.

Cash is, of course, the most liquid of assets. But in business circles, the definition of cash is expanded beyond currency (coins and paper money) to include checks, drafts, and money orders; the balance in any company checking account (provided there are no restrictions attached to the account); and even less liquid assets that are nonetheless commonly regarded as cash equivalents. These include **certificates of deposit** (CDs) with maturities of less than a year, **money market instruments**, and Treasury bills.

For many small businesses, cash comprises the bulk of its current assets. It can, after all be quickly and easily converted into needed goods or services. But the very ease with which it can be used makes it attractive for disreputable people both within and without the business, so small business owners need to make sure that they take the appropriate precautions when handling such assets. Consultants often recommend that their clients take out insurance policies to protect themselves from financial losses as a result of employee theft or error; this practice is commonly known as "bonding."

Companies can take other steps as well to protect this most important of their assets. "In both receipts and disbursements, systems and procedures based on separation of functions help prevent manipulation of cash by individuals in the company," noted Joseph Peter Simini in *Balance Sheet Basics for Nonfinancial Managers.* "Independent reconciliation of company cash accounts are wise forms of insurance against cash loss. A petty cash fund is a practical way to provide for small outlays. While small businesses may not be able to institute the elaborate systems used in larger enterprises, cash control is important even in smaller companies."

Accounts receivable is another important part of many companies' current assets package. These assets are sums owed to the company for services or goods rendered. Inventories are important current assets as well, particularly for business firms engaged in manufacturing and merchandising. Simini defined inventories as "assets that a business has acquired either for sale or for use in the manufacture of goods for sale." Inventories typically held by merchandisers include finished goods ready for sale or resale, while the inventories of manufacturing establishments can include raw materials, supplies used in manufacture, partially completed work, and finished goods.

FIXED ASSETS

Also known as hard assets, fixed assets include real estate, physical plant and facilities, leasehold improvements, equipment (from office equipment to heavy operating machinery), vehicles, fixtures, and other assets that can reasonably be assumed to have a life expectancy of several years. It is recognized, however, that most fixed assets—although not land—will lose value over time. This is known as **depreciation**, and is typically figured into a business's various financial documents (the expense of real estate purchases can also be depreciated when figuring taxes). Small business consultants note, however, that this depreciation can be figured by several different formulas. The smart business owner will take the time to figure out which formula is most advantageous for his or her company.

Fixed assets are among the most important assets that a company holds, for they represent major investments of financial resources. Indeed, fixed assets usually comprise the majority of a business's total assets. Intelligent allocation of resources to meet a business's land, facility, and large equipment needs can bring it assets that will serve as cornerstones of successful operation for years to come. Conversely, a company saddled with ill-considered or substandard fixed assets will find it much more difficult to be successful. This

is especially true for small businesses, which have a smaller margin of error. "Decisions about acquisition and management of long-lived assets are part of virtually every business, and these decisions can set the stage for future success—or failure," remarked Simini. "Because inflation is a fact of life in the present-day business world, a company that invests in a quality long-lived asset will gain a distinct competitive advantage in years to come." He notes that competing firms that enter the field in future years will often be forced to pay higher initial prices and higher financing costs for the same type of asset. "Thus the company that invests today can expect to enjoy a cash flow bonus later on. And this advantage becomes even greater once the asset is fully paid for. In many cases, for example, a company's ownership of a fully paid-for plant has made the difference between victory and defeat in a competitive business environment."

Fixed assets are also very important to small business owners because they are one of the things that are examined most closely by prospective lenders. When a bank or other lending institution is approached by an entrepreneur or small business owner who is seeking a **loan** to establish or expand a company's operations, loaning agents will always undertake a close study of the prospective borrower's hard assets, since they usually are a decisive indicator of the business's financial health and obligations.

When examining a business's fixed assets, lenders are typically most concerned with the following factors: 1) The type, age, and condition of equipment and facilities; 2) The depreciation schedules for those assets; 3) The nature of the company's mortgage and lease arrangements; and 4) Likely future fixed asset expenditures.

RISKY VS. RISKLESS ASSETS

The monetary flow that a business owner receives from an asset can vary because of many different factors. When comparing the value of various assets, then, the monetary flow or an asset is an important consideration, especially relative to the asset's value or price. "A risky asset provides a monetary flow that is at least in part random," wrote Robert S. Pindyck and Daniel L. Rubinfeld in *Microeconomics.* "In other words, the monetary flow is not known with certainty in advance. A share of General Motors stock is an obvious example of a risky asset—one cannot know whether the price of the stock will rise or fall over time." But Pindyck and Rubinfeld hasten to add the assets other than stock holdings can also carry a certain amount of risk. An apartment building owner, for example, "cannot know how much land values will rise or fall, whether the building will be fully rented all the time, or even whether the tenants will pay their rent promptly." A "riskless" asset, on the other hand, is one that features a known level of monetary flow to its owner. Bank savings accounts, certificates of deposit (CDS), and Treasury bills all qualify as riskless assets because the monetary flow of the asset to the owner is known. Finally, the ''return'' on an asset—whether risky or riskless—is the total monetary reward it yields as a fraction of its price.

ASSET UTILIZATION RATIOS

As Lawrence W. Tuller explained in *Finance for Non-Financial Managers and Small Business Owners,* an asset utilization ratio is a **financial ratio** that measures the speed at which a business is able to turn assets into sales, and hence cash. But he also warns small business owners not to overreact to a single asset utilization ratio; instead, entrepreneurs and other business managers should study several such ratios before drawing any broad conclusions about the health of the business in question, and even then, many other business aspects need to be factored in. As Tuller wrote, ''the speed with which inventory turns this year may be a relevant measure for evaluating purchasing and production personnel, but it has little meaning in the broader scope of analyzing the health of a business.'' Still, he notes, asset utilization ratios can be valuable: ''A trend might show that inventory turns are slowing, which could indicate an increase in obsolete goods, slowing sales, or errors in recording transactions.''

The four primary asset utilization ratios, as recounted by Tuller, are: 1) Receivables turnover, which studies the number of times that receivable balances are collected annually; 2) Inventory turnover, which is determined by dividing the annual cost of sales by the average inventory at both the beginning and the end of the period being studied; 3) Fixed asset turnover; and 4) Total asset turnover. Asset turnover ratios, remarked Tuller, ''measure the efficiency with which a company uses its assets to generate sales; the higher the turnover, the more efficient the company.'' He noted, however, that fixed asset turnover ratios are not particularly useful to compute if the company under examination does not have a significant amount of hard assets.

FURTHER READING:

DeThomas, Art. *Financing Your Small Business: Techniques for Planning, Acquiring & Managing Debt.* Grants Pass, OR: Oasis Press, 1992.

Financing for the Small Business. Washington: U.S. Small Business Administration, n.a.

Harrison, W. T., Jr., and C. T. Horngren. *Financial Accounting.* 2d ed. Upper Saddle River, NJ: Prentice Hall, 1995.

Pindyck, Robert S., and Daniel L. Rubinfeld. *Microeconomics.* 2d ed. New York: Macmillan, 1992.

Simini, Joseph Peter. *Balance Sheet Basics for Nonfinancial Managers.* New York: Wiley, 1990.

Tuller, Lawrence W. *Finance for Non-Financial Managers and Small Business Owners.* Adams Media, 1997.

SEE ALSO: Liabilities

ASSUMPTIONS

An assumption is a statement that is presumed to be true without concrete evidence to support it. In the business world, assumptions are used in a wide variety of situations to enable companies to plan and make decisions in the face of uncertainty. Perhaps the most common use of assumptions is in the **accounting** function, which uses assumptions to facilitate financial measurement and reporting.

According to Glenn A. Welsch, Robert N. Anthony, and Daniel G. Short in their book *Fundamentals of Financial Accounting,* there are four basic, underlying assumptions in accounting: the separate-entity assumption, the continuity or going concern assumption, the time-period assumption, and the unit-of-measure assumption. The separate-entity assumption holds that the particular business entity being measured is distinct and separate from similar and related entities for accounting purposes. The continuity or going-concern assumption holds that the entity will not cease operations or liquidate its assets during the accounting period. The time-period assumption holds that accounting reports are applied to short time periods, usually one year. Finally, the unit-of-measure assumption holds that the U.S. dollar is the common denominator or measuring stick for all accounting measurements taken for American companies.

In addition to these underlying accounting assumptions, there are also a number of smaller assumptions that are commonly made in certain calculations. For example, companies must make several assumptions in computing the value of pension and medical benefits that will be provided to retirees in the future. These funds—which are built up over time and held as investments until needed, but are actually owed to employees at some future point—are reported by companies as assets and liabilities on their financial statements. The assumptions made by a company help determine the monetary amounts that are reported, and thus may affect the company's current reported earnings and tax liability.

In the case of pensions that are provided to employees following retirement, companies must make assumptions regarding the likely rate of wage inflation and the discount rate to be applied to projected future payments. Similarly, the calculation of health care benefits provided to retirees includes assumptions about the discount rate and medical cost trend rate, as

AUTOMATION

well as demographic assumptions such as the employee turnover rate, the average age of employees at retirement, and the percentage of married retirees. Changing one of these assumptions can have a marked effect on a company's results. For example, increasing the discount rate reduces the present value of the company's liabilities and the amount of annual contributions that must be made to fund the retirement accounts, and therefore increases the company's current earnings.

In fact, as Peggie R. Elgin reported in an article for *Corporate Cashflow Magazine,* companies may be able to reduce their liabilities for retirement benefits by as much as 15 percent simply by changing their accounting assumptions. It is important to note, however, that companies must be able to justify any changes they choose to make. Some legitimate reasons for changing assumptions might include changes in the economy or in company policies, inflation in health care costs, trends in the use of medical services, or technological advances in medicine. Given the possibilities for increasing reported earnings or reducing taxes, experts recommend that companies review their accounting assumptions every few years to see whether making a change would be beneficial.

FURTHER READING:

Elgin, Peggie R. "Fine-Tuning FAS 106 Assumptions Can Help Balance Sheet." *Corporate Cashflow Magazine.* March 1994.

Welsch, Glenn A., Robert N. Anthony, and Daniel G. Short. *Fundamentals of Financial Accounting.* 4th ed. Homewood, IL: Irwin, 1984.

SEE ALSO: Accounting Methods

AUTOMATION

Automation refers to the use of computers and other automated machinery for the execution of business-related tasks. Automated machinery may range from simple sensing devices to robots and other sophisticated equipment. Automation of operations may range from the automation of a single operation to the automation of an entire factory.

There are many different reasons to automate. Increased **productivity** is normally the major reason for many companies desiring a competitive advantage. Automation also offers low operational variability. Variability is directly related to quality and productivity. Other reasons to automate include the presence of a hazardous working environment and the high cost of human labor. Decisions associated with automation are usually associated with some or all of these economic and social considerations. For small

business owners, weighing the pros and cons of automation can be a daunting task. But consultants contend that it is an issue that should not be put off. "We are creating a new ball game," wrote Perry Pascarella in *Industry Week.* "Failure to take a strategic look at where the organization wants to go and then capitalizing on the new technologies available will hand death-dealing advantages to competitors—traditional and unexpected ones."

TYPES OF AUTOMATION

Automation is most prevalent in manufacturing industries. In recent years, the manufacturing field has witnessed the development of major automation alternatives. Some of these major automation alternatives include:

- Information technology (IT);
- Computer-aided manufacturing (CAM);
- Numerically controlled (NC) equipment;
- Robots;
- Flexible manufacturing systems (FMS);
- Computer integrated manufacturing (CIM).

Information technology (IT) encompasses a broad spectrum of computer technologies used to create, store, retrieve, and disseminate information.

Computer-aided manufacturing (CAM) refers to the use of computers in the different functions of production planning and control. Computer-aided manufacturing includes the use of numerically controlled machines, robots, and other automated systems for the manufacture of products. Computer-aided manufacturing also includes computer-aided process planning (CAPP), group technology (GT), production scheduling, and manufacturing flow analysis. Computer-aided process planning (CAPP) means the use of computers to generate process plans for the manufacture of different products. Group technology (GT) is a manufacturing philosophy that aims at grouping different products and creating different manufacturing cells for the manufacture of each group.

Numerically controlled (NC) machines are programmed versions of machine tools that execute in operational sequence on parts or products. Individual machines may have their own computers for that purpose; such tools are commonly referred to as computerized numerical controlled (CNC) machines. In other cases, many machines may share the same computer; these are called direct numerical controlled machines.

Robots are automated equipment that may execute different tasks that are normally handled by a human operator. In manufacturing, robots are used to handle a wide range of tasks, including assembly, welding, painting, loading and unloading of heavy or hazardous materials, inspection and testing, and finishing operations.

Flexible manufacturing systems (FMS) are comprehensive systems that may include numerically controlled machine tools, robots, and automated material handling systems in the manufacture of similar products or components using different routings among the machines.

A computer-integrated manufacturing (CIM) system is one in which many manufacturing functions are linked through an integrated computer network. These manufacturing or manufacturing-related functions include production planning and control, shop floor control, quality control, computer-aided manufacturing, computer-aided design, purchasing, marketing, and other functions. The objective of a computer-integrated manufacturing system is to allow changes in product design, to reduce costs, and to optimize production requirements.

AUTOMATION AND THE SMALL BUSINESS OWNER

Understanding and making use of automation-oriented strategic alternatives is essential for manufacturing firms of all shapes and sizes, but it is particularly important for smaller companies who often enjoy inherent advantages in terms of operational nimbleness. But experts note that whatever your company's size, automation of production processes is no longer sufficient in many industries. "The computer, in its hardened and non-hardened forms, has made it possible to control manufacturing more precisely and to assemble more quickly, factors which have increased competition and forced companies to move faster in today's market," wrote Leslie C. Jasany in *Automation.* "But now, with the aid of the computer, companies will have to move to the next logical step in automation—the automatic analysis of data into information which empowers employees to immediately use that information to control and run the factory as if they were running their own business." Indeed, industry analyst Scott Flaig proclaimed to Jasany that "automation of information is clearly where the opportunity is, not in automation of labor. The work that is being done now in advanced manufacturing is work to manage and control the process, not the automation of the added-value aspect of the process."

Small business owners face challenges in several distinct areas as they prepare their enterprises for the technology-oriented environment in which the vast majority of them will operate. Three primary issues are employee training, management philosophy, and financial issues.

EMPLOYEE TRAINING Many business owners and managers operate under the assumption that acquisition of fancy automated production equipment or data processing systems will instantaneously bring about measurable improvements in company performance. But as countless consultants and industry experts have noted, even if these systems eliminate work previously done by employees, they ultimately function in accordance with the instructions and guidance of other employees, and if those latter workers receive inadequate training in system operation, the business will not be successful. All too often, wrote Lura K. Romei in *Modern Office Technology,* "the information specialists who designed the software and installed the systems say that the employees are either unfamiliar with technology or unwilling to learn. The employees' side is that they were not instructed in how to use the system, or that the system is so sophisticated that it is unsuited to the tasks at hand. All the managers see are systems that are not doing the job, and senior management wonders why all that money was spent for systems that are not being used." An essential key to automation success for small business owners, then, is to establish a quality education program for employees, and to establish a framework in which workers can provide input on the positive and negative aspects of new automation technology. As John Hawley commented in *Quality Progress,* the applications of automation technology may be growing, but the human factor still remains paramount in determining organizational effectiveness.

MANAGEMENT PHILOSOPHY Many productive business automation systems, whether in the realm of manufacturing or data processing, call for a high degree of decision-making responsibility on the part of those who operate the systems. As both processes and equipment become more automatically controlled, claimed Jasany, "employees will be watching them to make sure they stay in control, and fine tune the process as need. These enabler tools are changing the employee's job from one of adding touch labor to products to one of monitoring and supervising an entire process." But many organizations are reluctant to empower employees to this degree, either because of legitimate concerns about worker capabilities or a simple inability to relinquish power. In the former instance, training and/or workforce additions may be necessary; in the latter, management needs to recognize that such practices ultimately hinder the effectiveness of the company. "The people aspect, the education, the training, the empowerment is now the management issue," Flaig told Jasany. "Management is confronted today with the decision as to whether or not they will give up perceived power, whether they will make knowledge workers of these employees."

FINANCIAL ISSUES It is essential for small businesses to anticipate and plan for the various ways in which new automation systems can impact on bottom-line financial figures. Factors that need to be weighed include tax laws, long-term budgeting, and current financial health.

Depreciation tax laws for software and hardware are complex, which lead many consultants to recommend that business owners use appropriate accounting assistance in investigating their impact. Budgeting for automation costs can be complex as well, but as with tax matters, business owners are encouraged to educate themselves. By doing so, wrote *Best's Review*'s Janice L. Scites, "you can ensure that you are investing your money wisely and can bring some predictability to your financial planning. With the shortened life of most new technology, especially at the desktop, it is critical that you plan on annually reinvesting in your technology. Spikes in spending can be difficult to manage and can wreak havoc with your budgets. You'll also need to decide what is an appropriate level of spending for your company, or for yourself if it's a personal decision. Arriving at that affordable spending level requires a strategic look at your company to assess how vital a contributor technology is to the success of your business."

Scites notes that "hardware decisions are generally complex, with long-term implications" in such areas as stream of payments, maintenance costs, and additional support expenses. But she adds that business owners can reduce risks by "having a clear understanding of business plans, establishing a sound technology architecture, selecting hardware in the context of this architecture, building strong vendor alliances, and adopting standard software interfaces."

Once new automation systems are in operation, business owners and managers should closely monitor financial performance for clues about their impact on operations. "Unused technology or underused technology is a big tipoff that something is wrong," wrote Romei. "Many ideas for applications with few in actual operation is another. Watch for cost overruns on new systems, and look out when new systems are brought in predictably late."

The accelerating pace of automation in various areas of business can be dizzying. As James Pinto observed in *Automation,* "technology is causing ever faster movement, with cost variations and fluctuations that defy even contemporary financial tracking." It will be a challenge for small businesses to keep pace—or stay ahead—of such changes, but the forward-thinking business owner will plan ahead, both strategically and financially, to ensure that the increasingly automated world of business does not leave him or her behind.

FURTHER READING:

Bradbury, Danny. "Through the Looking Glass." *Computing.* April 3, 1997.

Cernadas, Al. "Softening Automation's Impact." *Journal of Commerce and Commercial.* August 24, 1992.

Hawley, John K. "Automation Doesn't Automatically Solve Problems." *Quality Progress.* May 1996.

Hitomi, K. *Manufacturing Systems Engineering.* London: Taylor and Francis, 1979.

Jasany, Leslie C. "Knowledge (and Power) to the People." *Automation.* July 1990.

Partch, Ken. "The Coming Impact of Information Technology." *Supermarket Business.* February 1997.

Pascarella, Perry. "Unlearn the 'Truths' About Automation." *Industry Week.* May 26, 1986.

Pinto, James J. "If It Ain't Broke—Fix It Anyway!" *Automation.* September 1991.

Romei, Lura K. "Take a Nice, Easy Backswing and Then Just Follow Through." *Modern Office Technology.* October 1987.

Scites, Janice L. "How Can I Successfully Budget for Automation?" *Best's Review—Life-Health Insurance Edition.* May 1995.

Stasko, Linda. "Computers Alone are Not Always a Solution." *Machine Design.* September 28, 1995.

SEE ALSO: Computer-Aided Design; Robotics; Training and Development

LEASING AUTOMOBILES

Leasing an automobile is an alternative to purchasing that usually enables consumers to pay lower up-front costs and make affordable monthly payments. At the end of the lease period, however, the consumer does not own the vehicle. Instead, consumers opting for automobile leasing arrangements pay for the use and depreciation of the vehicle over the duration of the lease. Purchasing a vehicle for cash is usually the most cost-effective option, followed by financing a purchase and then leasing, but it depends to a large extent on the individual consumer's situation. In many cases, leasing enables people to drive a more expensive car or to pay a lower amount per month than they would under a purchase arrangement. Leasing can be an attractive option for small business owners because of the tax deductibility of lease payments on cars used for business purposes. In recent years, many special lease deals have been established with small business owners in mind.

BUY OR LEASE?

The decision of whether to buy or lease an automobile depends upon a number of factors. First, it depends upon how long the consumer tends to keep cars before obtaining new ones. Leasing tends to make more sense when the consumer changes cars every four years or less, because then monthly car payments are a basic part of his or her budget. Second, the buy-or-lease decision depends upon the amount of annual mileage the consumer tends to put on cars. Leasing is not a good idea for consumers who drive many miles annually, since most leases limit mileage to 12,000 per year and charge a high fee for excess mileage. However, many car dealers allow consumers to purchase extra miles at a reduced rate at the time the lease is signed. Finally, the decision depends upon the consumer's budget. Leasing is a good way for people on a limited budget to minimize up-front costs, since they are usually required to pay a down payment consisting only of the first month's lease rate plus a security deposit.

It is also important to note, however, that there can be hidden costs associated with leasing. For example, many dealers charge a variety of lease-end fees. A disposition fee of several hundred dollars is common for consumers who do not wish to purchase the car, in addition to charges for extra wear and tear. Some dealers also establish maintenance rules for leased vehicles and charge fees when consumers fail to perform the required maintenance. In some cases, there are higher liability insurance requirements for leased vehicles than for those acquired through a purchase arrangement, which also costs consumers more money. Finally, most dealers include a premature termination clause in the lease contract and charge consumers a disposition fee, the car's residual value, and the remaining lease payments to end the lease early.

''Before you decide how to acquire your next car, consider whether you'd rather save money in the long run or enjoy the lower current expenses or more luxurious model that leasing can deliver,'' Roger B. Hill wrote in an article for *Medical Economics*. ''Though there's no litmus test to determine whether leasing or buying is best for you, a thorough understanding of how leasing works can make your decision easier—and financially sound.''

HOW AUTOMOBILE LEASES WORK

Like financed purchases, automobile leases require consumers to make monthly payments. Rather than covering the principal and interest on a loan, however, these payments cover the use and depreciation of the car over the lease period. According to Hill, the amount of the payment is calculated using the purchase price (capitalized cost) of the vehicle, its expected residual value (cost less expected depreciation) at the end of the lease, a fraction of the going interest rate (called the leasing factor), and applicable taxes.

The first step in calculating the monthly payment is to determine the monthly lease rate. This rate is equal to the capitalized cost, plus the residual value, multiplied by the leasing factor. For example, a $20,000 car with a residual value of $15,000 and leasing factor of .00375 (1/24th of a 9 percent interest rate) would have a monthly lease rate of $131. The next step is to find the monthly cost of depreciation on the vehicle by subtracting the residual value from the capitalized cost, then dividing by the number of months in the lease. For example, $5,000 / 24 months would give a monthly cost of depreciation of $208. Finally, the monthly lease rate can be calculated by adding the monthly lease rate, the monthly cost of depreciation, and applicable taxes. In this case, $131 plus $208 equals a monthly payment of $339 plus tax.

A closed-end lease—the most common kind—means that the dealer assumes the risk that the car's residual value will be lower than expected at the end of the lease period. In this type of lease, the consumer can either buy the car for the residual value or walk away. In contrast, an open-end lease means that the consumer assumes the risk that the residual value will be lower than expected, and must make up the difference if that is the case. In exchange for accepting greater risk, the consumer usually makes lower payments in this type of lease. In general, two- or three-year leases tend to be the most cost effective for consumers. Shorter leases do not justify the added taxes, while longer leases mean that the car will require too many repairs.

TAX BENEFITS OF LEASING

Leasing rather than buying an automobile often holds some tax benefits for small businesses. ''Leasing may beat buying when it comes to tax benefits. Under current law, the interest you pay on a car loan is usually not deductible. However, when you lease, the finance charges are included in the monthly payment,'' Donald J. Korn wrote in *Black Enterprise*. ''If you get to deduct three-quarters of your lease payment, you're actually deducting three-quarters of the interest as well.''

Small business owners can deduct a percentage of their automobile lease payments—as well as fuel, maintenance, and insurance costs—from their federal income taxes. To calculate the deduction on a leased vehicle, a small business owner would use the actual-expense approach. This approach adds up all the costs of operating the car for a year and multiplies that total by the percentage of the annual mileage that was attributable to business purposes. For example, a small business owner who paid a total of $3,000 in operating costs and drove a total of 15,000 miles, only 1,500 of which were business-related, would gain a deduction of $3,000 × .10 or $300. It is necessary to maintain an accurate log of business mileage and associated automobile expenses in order to support the deduction.

The mileage deduction is a better deal for self-employed people than for those who work for large companies. Self-employed persons merely report the total expense on Schedule C with their other business expenses. Employees, on the other hand, must report the expense on Schedule A with their other miscellaneous itemized deductions; the deduction is only allowed for the amount by which the expense exceeds 2 percent of their adjusted gross income. It is also important to note that commuting to and from work is considered personal rather than business mileage for employees. All of the tax rules are outlined in IRS Publication 917, Business Use of a Car.

FURTHER READING:

Barron, James. "Lease or Buy? It's More Than a Matter of Money." *New York Times.* October 16, 1997.

Coulombe, Charles A. "Little Fleet: A New Approach to Leasing Lets Small Businesses Zoom into High Gear." *Success.* October 1997.

Hill, Roger B. "Should You Lease Your Next Car?" *Medical Economics.* October 14, 1996.

Jaworski, Robert M. "Car Leasing Developments: A Roadmap for Bankers." *Banking Law Journal.* September 1997.

Kaye, Steven D. "Lease Is More." *U.S. News and World Report.* April 7, 1997.

Korn, Donald J. "Lessees: Drive Hard for Every Tax Break." *Black Enterprise.* December 1996.

SEE ALSO: Tax-deductible Business Expenses

B

BALANCE SHEET

A balance sheet is a financial report that provides a summary of a business's position at a given point in time, including its **assets** (economic resources), its **liabilities** (financial debts or obligations), and its total or **net worth**. "A balance sheet does not aim to depict ongoing company activities," wrote Joseph Peter Simini in *Balance Sheet Basics for Nonfinancial Managers.* "It is not a movie but a freeze-frame. Its purpose is to depict the dollar value of various components of a business at a moment in time." Balance sheets are also sometimes referred to as statements of financial position or statements of financial condition.

Balance sheets are typically presented in two different forms. In the report form, asset accounts are listed first, with the liability and owners' equity accounts listed in sequential order directly below the assets. In the account form, the balance sheet is organized in a horizontal manner, with the asset accounts listed on the left side and the liabilities and owners' equity accounts listed on the right side. The term "balance sheet" originates from this latter form, for when the left and right sides have been completed, they should have equal dollar amounts—in other words, they must balance.

CONTENTS OF THE BALANCE SHEET

Most of the contents of a business's balance sheet are classified under one of three categories: assets, liabilities, and owners' equity. Some balance sheets, though, also include a "notes" section wherein relevant information that does not fit under any of the above accounting categories is included. Information that might be included in the notes section would include mentions of pending lawsuits that might impact future liabilities or changes in the business's accounting practices.

ASSETS Assets are items owned by the business, whether fully paid for or not. These items can range from cash—the most liquid of all assets—to inventories, equipment, patents, and deposits held by other businesses. Assets are further categorized into the following classifications: current assets, fixed assets, and miscellaneous or other assets. As David H. Bangs Jr. related in *Finance: Mastering Your Small Business,* "the list of assets starts with cash and ends with the least liquid fixed assets, those that are the hardest to turn into cash. For instance, if you have an item labeled 'good will' on your balance sheet, you'll have to sell the business itself to turn that particular asset into cash."

Current assets include cash, government securities, marketable securities, notes receivable, accounts receivable, inventories, prepaid expenses, and any other item that could be converted to cash in the normal course of business within one year. Fixed assets, meanwhile, include real estate, physical plant, leasehold improvements, equipment (from office equipment to heavy operating machinery), vehicles, fixtures, and other assets that can reasonably be assumed to have a life expectancy of several years. It is recognized, however, that most fixed assets—although not land—will lose value over time. This is known as **depreciation**. When determining a company's fixed assets, then, a business owner needs to make certain that depreciation is figured into the final value of his or her fixed assets. The net fixed asset value of a company's holdings is calculated as the net of cost minus accumulated depreciation. Finally, businesses often have assets that are less tangible than securities, inventory, or high-speed printers. These are classified as ''other assets'' and include such intangible assets as patents, trademarks, and **copyrights**, notes receivable from officers or employees, and contracts that call for them to serve as exclusive providers of goods or services to a client. Writing in *Finance for Non-Financial Managers and Small Business Owners,* Lawrence W. Tuller defined intangible assets as ''any expenditure that adds value to the company but cannot be touched or held.''

LIABILITIES Liabilities, on the other hand, are the business's obligations to other entities as a result of past transactions or events. These entities range from employees (who have provided work in exchange for salary) to investors (who have provided loans in exchange for the value of that loan plus interest) to other companies (who have supplied goods or services in exchange for agreed-upon compensation). Liabilities are typically divided into two categories: short-term or current liabilities and long-term liabilities.

Liabilities that qualify for inclusion under the short-term or current designation include all those that are due and payable within one year. These include obligations in the areas of accounts payable, taxes payable, notes payable, accrued expenses (such as wages, salaries, withholding taxes, and FICA taxes) and other expenses that are supposed to be paid off over the next year. Such obligations include the portion of long-term debt that is scheduled to be paid off during the course of the coming year. Long-term liabilities are those debts to lenders, mortgage holders, and other creditors that will take more than one year to pay off.

OWNERS' EQUITY Once a business has determined its assets and liabilities, it can then determine owners' equity, the book value of the business's assets once all liabilities have been deducted. Owners' equity, which is also sometimes called stockholders' equity, is in essence the net worth of the company.

BALANCE SHEETS AND SMALL BUSINESSES

A comprehensive, accurate balance sheet can be a valuable tool for the small business owner or entrepreneur seeking to gain a full understanding of his or her operation. Studying current assets and current liabilities, for instance, can reveal significant information about a company's short-term strength, wrote Simini. ''If current liabilities exceed current assets, the business may have difficulty meeting its payment obligations within the year. In fact, some experts feel that in a well-run company current assets should be approximately double current liabilities.'' Indeed, balance sheets—if produced on a monthly or quarterly basis and compared with earlier statements—can provide entrepreneurs and small business owners with valuable information on operating trends and areas of developing strength or weakness. ''By analyzing a succession of balance sheets and income statements, managers and owners can spot both problems and opportunities,'' noted Simini. ''Could the company make more profitable use of its assets? Does inventory turnover indicate the most efficient possible use of inventory in sales? How does the company's administrative expense compare to that of its competition? For the experienced and well-informed reader, then, the balance sheet can be an immensely useful aid in an analysis of the company's overall financial picture.''

Given the balance sheet's value in providing an overview of a company's financial standing at a given point in time, it is understandably one of the primary financial documents demanded by prospective lenders, investors, and business clients. Small business owners, then, need to recognize that the investment of time necessary in compiling balance sheets (which is minimal in most instances because of the proliferation of business software available on the market) is well worth it.

FURTHER READING:

Bangs, David H., Jr., with Robert Gruber. *Finance: Mastering Your Small Business.* Chicago, IL: Upstart, 1996.

Simini, Joseph Peter. *Balance Sheet Basics for Nonfinancial Managers.* New York: Wiley, 1990.

SEE ALSO: Financial Statements; Income Statements

BANKRUPTCY

Bankruptcy is a legal proceeding, guided by federal law, designed to address situations wherein a debtor—either an individual or a business—has accumulated debts so great that the individual or business is unable to pay them off. It is designed to distribute those assets held by the debtor as equitably as possible among creditors. Most of the time it also frees the debtor or ''bankrupt'' from further liability, but there are exceptions to this. Bankruptcy proceedings may be initiated either by the debtor—a voluntary process—or by creditors—an involuntary process.

''The Bankruptcy Code is a world of its own,'' wrote Lawrence Tuller in *Getting Out: A Step-by-Step Guide to Selling a Business or Professional Practice.* ''A completely separate set of laws come into play under which a business or an individual must perform. State and federal laws that we all live by from day-today are not applicable. New laws, mysterious to all except the bankruptcy lawyers, concerning contracts, wages, debtor/creditor relations, individual rights, and so on, go into effect.'' For this reason, business consultants commonly urge their clients—whether debtor or creditor—to secure legal help in all instances in which bankruptcy comes into play.

CHAPTER 7 BANKRUPTCY

Individuals may file either Chapter 7 or Chapter 13 bankruptcy. Under Chapter 7 bankruptcy law, all of the debtor's assets—including any unincorporated businesses that he or she owns—are totally liquidated. In such cases, the federal bankruptcy court hearing the case is provided with a full listing of all the debtor's assets and liabilities. The court then undertakes the process of dividing those assets among the various creditors. Unpaid taxes are given top priority, and secured creditors are generally the next entities to be considered. In many instances, all of the debtor's assets have been exhausted by the time the court turns to the claims of unsecured creditors. The decision to go the Chapter 7 route is ultimately, as Tuller noted, an admission that ''you have really given up, with no hope for the continuation of your company.'' Since Chapter 7 bankruptcies are so final, they are only initiated by the owners in extreme circumstances. In fact, Chapter 7 actions are usually filed by creditors.

CHAPTER 13 BANKRUPTCY

A far less severe bankruptcy option for individuals whose straits are not quite so hopeless is Chapter 13. Under Chapter 13 bankruptcy laws, debtors turn over their finances to the court, which subsequently allocates funds and payment plans at its discretion. As with Chapter 7 bankruptcy cases, unsecured creditors are least likely to be compensated for their losses.

CHAPTER 11 BANKRUPTCY

The Chapter 11 bankruptcy option is open to incorporated businesses who still hope to recover from their financial difficulties. As Tuller noted, ''with even a glimmer of hope for recovery . . . filing under Chapter 11, which allows the company to reorganize, keep going, and eventually negotiate a settlement with creditors, is certainly preferable to a liquidation under Chapter 7.''

Companies generally turn to Chapter 11 protection after they are no longer able to pay their creditors, but in some instances, businesses have been known to act proactively in anticipation of future liabilities. Once a company has filed under Chapter 11, its creditors are notified that they cannot press suits for repayment (though secured creditors may ask the court for a ''hardship'' exemption from the general debt freeze

that is imposed). Creditors are, however, permitted to appear before the court to discuss their claims and provide data on the debtor's ability to reorganize. In addition, unsecured creditors may appoint representatives to negotiate a settlement with the debtor company. Finally, creditors who feel that the debtor company's financial straits are due to mismanagement or fraud may ask the court to appoint an examiner to look into such possibilities.

In the meantime, the company continues with its day-to-day operations, though major expenditures must first meet the approval of the presiding judge. Negotiations with creditors continue as well, and once a reorganization agreement has finally been hammered out—a process that sometimes takes several years—creditors may find themselves unable to secure even half of what they are owed. The reorganization plan, which is subject to the approval of the court and a majority of creditors, then becomes the blueprint for the company's future.

''Chapter 11 laws exist to protect the company, pure and simple,'' commented Tuller. ''The individual has no rights, the unsecured creditors have few rights, and the secured bank creditors have substantial rights. The court places the company's interests first, secured creditors second, and leaves the rest to fend for themselves, including the owner.''

SMALL BUSINESS CREDITORS

Small businesses that find themselves unable to collect on money owed them because of bankruptcy proceedings often have few options with which to protect themselves. There are instances, however—usually when the debtor is engaged in questionable or fraudulent business activities—when small business creditors do have additional legal options. In situations where the debtor has incurred debt only a short time before filing before bankruptcy, creditors can sometimes obtain judgments that put added pressure on the debtor to make good on that liability. In addition, noted the *Entrepreneur Magazine Small Business Advisor,* ''the law provides for a '60-day preference' rule. This rule is designed to prevent debtors from paying off their friends right before they file bankruptcy while leaving others stiffed. The 60-day rule allows the court to set aside any payments made up to 60 days before the actual filing of bankruptcy. Creditors who have been paid must return the money to the bankruptcy court for it to be placed in the pot. Business owners should keep in close contact with their ongoing customers so that they will have a good enough relationship to know far in advance to avoid being caught up in this rule.'' Indeed, small business owners in particular should always be watching for clients/customers who show signs of being in financial distress. If such indications become present, the owner needs to determine 1) the depth of that distress, and 2) whether his or her small business can withstand the likely financial repercussions if that client/customer declares bankruptcy.

Finally, advisors typically counsel small business creditors to file confirmations of debt with the court even if it seems highly unlikely that they will ever be compensated. This filing allows creditors to write off the bad debts on their taxes.

FURTHER READING:

Boshkoff, Douglas. *Bankruptcy and Creditor's Rights.* Josephson-Kluwer, 1986.

The Entrepreneur Magazine Small Business Advisor. New York: John Wiley, 1995.

Jackson, Thomas. *The Logic and Limits of Bankruptcy Law.* Cambridge, MA: Harvard University Press, 1986.

Tuller, Lawrence W. *Getting Out: A Step-by-Step Guide to Selling a Business or Professional Practice.* Liberty Hall, 1990.

SEE ALSO: Business Failure and Dissolution

BANKS AND BANKING

A bank is an institution that provides financial services to consumers, businesses, and governments. One major type of bank is the commercial bank, which has fewer restrictions on its services than other types of banks. Commercial banks profit by taking deposits from customers, for which they typically pay a relatively low rate of interest, and lending the deposits to borrowers at a higher rate of interest. These borrowers may be individuals purchasing homes, cars, and other things or they may be businesses financing working **capital** needs, equipment purchases, etc. Banks may also generate revenue from services such as asset management, investment sales, and mortgage loan maintenance.

In addition to commercial banks, major types of banks include savings banks, trust companies, and central banks. Savings banks are similar to commercial banks but they are geared toward serving individuals rather than businesses. They take deposits primarily from individuals, and their investment activity is limited by the federal government to specific noncommercial investments, such as home mortgage loans. Trust companies act as trustees, managing assets that they transfer between two parties according to the wishes of the trustor. Trust services are often offered by departments of commercial banks. Central banks are usually government-controlled institutions that serve regulatory and monetary management roles. Among other activities, central banks may issue their nation's currency, help to determine interest rates,

collect and disburse government resources, and issue and redeem government debt.

Savings banks, savings and loan associations (S&Ls), and credit unions are known as thrift institutions. Like commercial banks, thrifts are depository institutions and are distinguished from nondepository institutions such as investment banks, insurance companies, and pension funds. S&Ls traditionally have taken savings, time, and demand deposits as their primary liability, and made most of their income from loaning deposits out as mortgages. Credit unions are financial cooperatives designed exclusively for the purposes of serving their members, or "owners." Credit unions are nonprofit financial institutions and are generally as concerned with community involvement as with profits. One of the main differences between credit unions and banks relates to the fees that they charge. Banks typically charge higher fees for such items as stop-payment orders, below minimum balances, and check bouncing, as these fees help to increase the bottom line for banks. Credit unions are typically more forgiving concerning service fees. They provide a lower cost, "friendly" savings investment option, while still maintaining competitive interest rates as well as a wide variety of financial services for their members.

COMMERCIAL BANK ORGANIZATION

Most commercial banks are operated as corporate holding companies, which may own one or several banks. Because of regulatory constraints, banks that are not associated with holding companies must operate under restrictions that often put them at a disadvantage compared with other financial institutions. Holding companies are often used as vehicles to circumvent legal restrictions and to raise capital by otherwise unavailable means. For instance, many banks can indirectly operate branches in other states by organizing their entity as a holding company. Banks are also able to enter, and often effectively compete in, related industries through holding company subsidiaries. In addition, holding companies are able to raise capital using methods from which banks are restricted, such as issuing commercial paper. Multibank holding companies may also create various economies of scale related to advertising, bookkeeping, and reporting, among other business functions.

Commercial banking in the United States has been characterized by: 1) a proliferation of competition from other financial service industries, such as mutual funds and leasing companies; 2) the growth of multibank holding companies; and 3) new technology that has changed the way that banks conduct business. The first two developments are closely related. Indeed, as new types of financial institutions have emerged to meet specialized needs, banks have increasingly turned to the holding company structure to increase their competitiveness. In addition, a number of laws passed since the 1960s have favored the multibank holding company format. As a result the U.S. banking industry had become highly concentrated in the hands of bank holding companies by the early 1990s. By 1993, in fact, the approximately 1,000 U.S. multibank holding companies controlled more than 90 percent of the entire banking industry's assets. Furthermore, the top 100 multibank corporations accounted for a full 80 percent of all bank assets.

Electronic information technology, the third major factor in the recent evolution of banking, is evidenced most visibly by the proliferation of electronic transactions. Electronic fund transfer systems, automated teller machines (ATMs), and computerized home-banking services all combined to transform the way that banks conduct business. By the mid-1990s, there were nearly 100,000 ATMs operating in the United States—far surpassing the number of bank branches—and an additional 200,000 worldwide. Such technological gains have served to reduce labor demands and intensify the trend toward larger and more centralized banking organizations. They have also diminished the role that banks have traditionally played as personal financial service organizations. Finally, electronic systems have made possible nationwide, and even globally, banking systems with nearly instant information access.

BANKS AND SMALL BUSINESSES

Small business is the fastest-growing segment of the American business economy. As a result, more and more commercial banks are creating special products and programs designed to attract small business customers. It is vitally important for entrepreneurs and small business owners to develop a comfortable, productive relationship with a bank in order to meet their current and future financing needs. Ideally, Gibson Heath indicated in his book *Doing Business with Banks,* a banker should be part of a small business owner's team of outside advisors that also includes an attorney, an accountant, an insurance agent, and other specialty consultants. The banker's role on that team is to assist with the business's overall financial needs, from savings, checking, and retirement accounts to employee benefit plans, loans, and investments.

Before selecting a bank and establishing a relationship, an entrepreneur should take steps to understand his or her current financial needs and plan for future ones. It may be helpful to examine the business's current position, immediate monetary needs, level of credit worthiness, and ability to repay loans. It is also important to look at the company's future direction and determine when it is most likely to require infusions of cash. When establishing or chang-

ing a banking relationship, Heath recommended that a small business owner also review the information that the bank would be likely to want for its decision-making purposes (i.e., the business plan, balance sheet, income statement, cash flow projections, tax returns, and owner's personal financial information).

There are a number of factors a small business owner should consider when selecting a bank, including its accessibility, compatibility, lending limit, loan approval process, general services provided, and fees charged. Heath encouraged small business owners to write down the elements of a banking relationship that are most important to them before approaching different banks. Later, after meeting with several bankers, the business owner can review the list and evaluate the banks against them. Perhaps the best way to approach banks is to obtain referrals to business representatives or loan officers at three to five banks. This approach aids the small business owner by providing a recommendation or association from a known customer, and also by providing the name of a specific banker to talk to. The company's accountant, business advisors, and professional contacts will most likely be good sources of referrals.

The next step in forming a positive banking relationship is to arrange for a preliminary interview at each bank to get a feel for their personnel and services. It may be helpful to bring a brief summary of the business and a list of questions. The small business owner should also expect to answer the bankers' questions—including general information about business, its financial condition, and its banking needs—that are designed to evaluate the small business as a potential client. After all the face-to-face meetings have taken place, the small business owner should compare each bank to the list of preferred criteria, and consult with his or her business advisors as needed. It is important to notify all the candidates once a decision has been made.

Ideally, a small business's banking relationship should feature open communication. Heath suggested scheduling semiannual or quarterly appointments to keep the banker updated on the business's condition, as well as to give the banker an opportunity to update the small business owner on new services. The banker can be a good source of information about financing, organization, and record keeping. He or she may also be able to provide the small business owner with referrals to other business professionals, special seminars or programs, and networking opportunities. An important part of maintaining a good working relationship with a bank involves notifying the banker in advance of problems and seek help in solving them. Since the bank participates in the formation and growth of a small business through loans and lines of credit, it should be considered a partner.

FURTHER READING:

Heath, Gibson. *Doing Business with Banks: A Common Sense Guide for Small Business Borrowers.* Denver: DBA/USA Press, 1991.

Kamerschen, David R. *Money and Banking.* Cincinnati: South-Western, 1988.

McClellan, Hassell H. *Managing One Bank Holding Companies.* New York: Praeger, 1981.

SEE ALSO: Loans; Venture Capital

BAR CODING

Bar coding is an automatic identification technology that allows data to be collected rapidly and extremely accurately. Because of these attributes, bar coding has been used for a wide range of applications in almost every aspect of business. In the early 1990s, a variety of different types of bar-code encoding schemes, or symbologies, were developed to fulfill specific needs in specific industries. Several of these symbologies grew into de facto standards that have become universally used throughout most industries.

Bar codes provide a simple method of encoding text information that can be easily read by inexpensive electronic readers called scanners. A bar code consists of a series of parallel, adjacent bars and spaces. Predefined bar and space patterns, or symbologies, are used to code character data into a printed symbol. Bar codes might be considered a printed version of the Morse code, with narrow bars representing dots and wide bars representing dashes.

A bar-code reading device decodes a bar code by scanning a light source across it and measuring the intensity of the light reflected back to the device. Bar-code scanners come with different resolutions to enable them to read differently-sized bar codes. The pattern of reflected light produces an electronic signal that exactly matches the printed bar-code pattern and is easily decoded into the original data by inexpensive electronic circuits. Because of the design of most bar-code symbologies, scanning a bar code from right to left or from left to right makes no difference. The basic structure of a bar code consists of a leading and trailing quiet zone, a start pattern, one or more data characters, one or two optional check characters, and a stop pattern.

First utilized in supermarkets and libraries, bar coding has grown over the years to have applications in many fields. In combination with a record-tracking system (composed of a symbology, a scanner, decoding software, and labels), bar coding is an important tool in advanced file-room and record-center environments, allowing for speedier, more accurate data entry, improved document tracking, and increased productivity at lower cost.

Bar-code technology has proven virtually 100 percent accurate, because the symbologies eliminated the human factors that could often lead to inaccuracies in keyboard data entry. Moreover, bar codes have to pass a series of tests before the symbol can be decoded. The encoded data can also be structured in order to minimize data entry. In addition, bar-code scanner operation can be learned in approximately ten minutes.

APPLICATIONS OF BAR CODING

The technology of bar-code scanning is used widely in retail stores for basic functions, including price verification and inventory control. Hundreds of new applications, however, are under development. Other major users include the U.S. Postal Service, which applies the technology to route letters to their correct ZIP codes and to track packages (along with competitors United Parcel Service and Fed Ex); publishing companies, which use bar coding to identify newspapers, magazines, and books and to keep records of sales; libraries, which utilize the technology for inventory and charging-out of materials; airlines, which enhance bar coding to allow the preparation of shipping labels as well as the tracing and monitoring of cargoes by shippers and freight-forwarding agents; automobile manufacturers, who track the cars they ship by using an automated identification system based on bar codes appearing on the windshields of automobiles; and banks, which are testing a bar-code-based computerized check-processing system to track the movement of bar-coded courier bags of checks between a bank's branches and its operating centers.

TYPES OF BAR CODES

UNIVERSAL PRODUCT CODES Universal Product Codes (UPCs) are used principally for retail purposes. UPC-A, a 12-digit numeric symbology used in retail applications, consists of 11 data digits and 1 check digit. The first digit is a number-system digit that usually represents the type of product being identified. The next 5 digits are a manufacturer's code, and the following 5 digits are used to identify a specific product. UPCs are also emblazoned on manufacturers' coupons, with the last 3 of the second set of 5 digits sometimes indicating the monetary value of the cash-off. When the vendor coupon is scanned, the amount of the cents-off is automatically deducted from the customer's bill, and misredemption is mitigated. Assigned to specific products and manufacturers by the **Uniform Code Council** (UCC), UPC numbers may be applied for by contacting the UCC.

UPC-E, a smaller, 6-digit UPC symbology for number system 0, is often used for small retail items. UPC-E is also called ''zero-suppressed'' because UPC-E compresses a normal 12-digit UPC-A code into a 6-digit code by ''suppressing'' the number system digit—trailing zeros in the manufacturer's code, and leading zeros in the product identification part of the bar code. A seventh check digit is encoded into a parity pattern for the 6 main digits. Thus, UPC-E may be uncompressed into a standard UPC-A 12-digit number. Both UPC-A and UPC-E allow for a supplemental two- or five-digit number to be appended to the main bar-code symbol. Designed for use on publications and periodicals, the supplemental code is simply a small additional bar code placed on the right side of a standard UPC symbol, which provides more precise product identification.

PDF417 Forging a path beyond that traveled by UPCs, Symbol Technologies in 1992 unveiled a new ''smart'' bar code. Not only does it identify the product, it also gives information about its source, destination, and proper handling. Whereas the ordinary bar code is one-dimensional, linear, and may contain 20 to 30 symbols per inch, the new bar code is two-dimensional and uses height and width to convey information. One small square of the new bar code may contain data equal in amount to a 20-foot strip of the old. T.A.L. Enterprises' high-density, two-dimensional bar-code symbology is called PDF417 and essentially consists of a stacked set of smaller bar codes. PDF stands for Portable Data File because the symbology can encode as many as 2,725 data characters in a single bar code. The complete specification for PDF417 provides many encoding options, including data compaction, error detection and correction, and variable size and aspect ratio symbols. Software analysts believe that the development of national standards for the technology will provide the impetus for its acceptance by industries.

EANS AND EAN SUPPLEMENTALS A European version of the UPC, the European Article Number (EAN) system (known as JAN in Japan), uses the same size requirements and a similar encoding scheme as for UPC codes. EAN-8 encodes 8 numeric digits consisting of 2 country code digits, 5 data digits, and 1 check digit. EAN-13 is the European version of UPC-A, differing only insofar as it encodes a 13th digit into the parity pattern of the left 6 digits of a normal UPC-A symbol. This 13th digit, in combination with the 12th digit, defines two flag characters that represent a country code. Both EAN-8 and EAN-13 allow for a supplemental two- or five-digit number to be appended to the main bar-code system. Designed for use on publications and periodicals, EAN Supplemental is simply a small additional bar code appended to the right side of a standard EAN symbol. EAN bar-code numbers are assigned to specific products and manufacturers by an organization called ICOF located in Brussels, Belgium.

EAN-13 is adopted as the standard in the publishing industry for encoding the International Standard Book Number (ISBN) on books. An ISBN bar code is simply an EAN-13 symbol consisting of the ISBN number preceded by the digits 978. Thus, the supplemental message in an ISBN bar code is simply the retail price of the book preceded by the digit 5. For example, if the ISBN number were 1-23456-789-2 and the price of the book were $22.95, then one would enter 978123456789 as the bar-code message and 52295 as the supplemental message.

In 1992, a controversy arose between booksellers and drug and grocery stores over the use of UPC and Bookland EANs on the backs of books. While most booksellers' systems were adjusted to EANs, drug stores and supermarkets used UPCs. At a March 1993 meeting of the Book Industry Systems Advisory Committee, a compromise was worked out wherein both Bookland EANs and UPCs would be placed on mass-market paperback books beginning in 1994. In November of 1993, the Association of American Publishers decided to keep UPCs on the back covers of mass-market paperback books and put EANs on the front covers, since most of these books were sold through drug and grocery stores rather than book stores. Booksellers objected to the decision, but a change to EANs on the back covers would have involved a $10 million expenditure.

CODE 39 The Normal Code 39 is a variable-length symbology that can encode the 43 alphabetic and numeric characters. The most popular symbology in the nonretail world, Code 39 is used extensively in manufacturing, military, and health applications. Each Code 39 bar code is framed by a start/stop character represented by an asterisk (*). Code 39 allows for a check character in cases where data security is important. Consequently, the health-care industry adopted the use of this check character for health-care administration purposes. Another feature of Code 39 allows for concatenation (linkage) of two or more bar codes. A Full ASCII version of Code 39 is also available.

POSTAL SERVICE BAR CODES Used by the U.S. Postal Service to encode ZIP code information for automatic mail sorting by ZIP code, POSTNET (Postal Numeric Encoding Technique) is able to represent a five-digit ZIP Code (32 bars), a nine-digit ZIP + 4 Code (52 bars), or an eleven-digit Delivery Point Code (62 bars). Unlike other bar codes, POSTNET features data encoded in the height of the bars instead of in the width of the bars and spaces. As a result, most standard bar-code readers cannot decipher POSTNET. Chosen by the U.S. Postal Service in 1976 because it was extremely easy to print on almost any type of printer and was very easy to be modified,

POSTNET is a fixed-dimension symbology, in that the height, width, and spacing of all bars has to fit within exact tolerances. The symbology is called a "clocked" bar code because the lower portion may be used as a standard "clock" and the reader does not require a completely steady scan for accurate results.

FIM (Facing Identification Mark) patterns are another type of bar code used by the U.S. Postal Service in automated mail processing. Utilized for automatic facing and canceling of mail which does not contain a stamp or meter imprint (business-reply mail, penalty mail, etc.), FIMs also provide a means of separating business- and courtesy-reply mail from other letters. The FIM pattern is placed in the upper right corner of the piece of mail, along the top edge, and two inches in from the right edge of letters and cards.

OTHER BAR CODES Other bar codes widely used in the mid-1990s include the codabar, the Interleaved 2 of 5, the Discrete 2 of 5, Code 93, Code 128, and EAN/UCC 128. Commonly used in libraries, blood banks, and the air-parcel business, the codabar is a variable-length symbology that allows encoding of 20 characters. The Interleaved 2 of 5 is a high-density, variable-length, numeric-only symbology that encodes digit pairs in an interleaved manner, with the odd-position digits encoded in the bars and the even-position digits encoded in the spaces. Discrete 2 of 5, very similar to Interleaved 2 of 5, is a variable-length numeric symbology which encodes data only in the bars. Code 93, a variable-length symbology that can encode the complete 128 ASCII character set, was developed as an enhancement to the Code 39 symbology by providing a slightly higher character density than does Code 39. Code 93 also incorporates two check digits as an added measure of security. While Code 93 is considered more robust than Code 39, it has never enjoyed the same popularity as the latter. Code 128, a variable-length high-density alphanumeric symbology, contains 106 different bit and space patterns. The EAN/UCC 128 symbology, designed primarily for use in product-identification applications, is a variation of the original Code 128 symbology.

THE FUTURE OF BAR CODING

In today's business world, bar coding is everywhere. Consumers encounter the ubiquitous black-and-white stripes on everything from retail packaging to rental cars. In fact, bar coding has become a basic requirement for tracking any type of inventory. But bar coding remains most prevalent in the retail arena, where UPC symbols are required to appear on all items and to be 99 percent scanable on the first try.

Retailers now use bar codes as part of complicated electronic **point-of-sale (POS) systems** that provide them with the ability to capture a wide variety of inventory data on a continuous basis. For example, a seller of health and beauty aids can scan the bar codes on merchandise as it leaves the store and transmit that data via an **Electronic Data Interchange** (EDI) system to its main suppliers, who can then replenish the store's inventory automatically as needed. Internally, the health and beauty aids retailer can study the point-of-sale data to determine more effective ways of marketing and merchandising its offerings.

As the use of bar coding has become increasingly popular in a wide variety of business settings, the technology involved in scanning bar codes and interpreting bar-code data has improved significantly as well. Bar-code scanners have become more affordable and more portable. In fact, some previously hand-held scanners have taken the form of special gloves, with the scanner imbedded in a fingertip. In addition, a vast array of software is now available to help small businesses create and print their own bar-code labels. Most such software packages are easy to use and support several common bar-code symbologies.

FURTHER READING:

Alpert, Mark. "Building a Better Bar Code." *Fortune.* June 15, 1992.

Betts, Mitch. "IS Must Get a Handle on Bar Coding: Business Opportunities Missed As Management Fails to Take Technology Leadership Role." *Computerworld.* September 9, 1991.

"Big Bad Bar Code: Two-Dimensional Bar Codes and Advances in Data Collection Technology Promise to Deliver More Operational Data to Decision Makers." *Computerworld.* May 25, 1992.

"Does It Mean 'Toothpaste' or 'Rat Poison'?" *Fortune.* February 17, 1997.

"Expanded Bar Code Makes Grade." *Supermarket News.* February 7, 1994.

Fales, James F. "Can You Really Bank on Bar-Coded Data?" *Industrial Engineering.* October 1992.

Filipczak, Bob. "Bar Coding: Not Just for Groceries Anymore." *Training.* December 1992.

Mark, Teri J. "Decoding the Bar Code." *Records Management Quarterly.* January 1994.

Reese, K. M. "Checking the Accuracy of Identification Numbers." *Chemical and Engineering News.* January 25, 1993.

Reitter, Chuck. "Bar-Code Benefits Outlined for NPCA Panel." *American Paint & Coatings Journal.* March 22, 1993.

Rice, Judy. "Two-Dimensional Data Matrix Symbology. . . . A Future Alternative to Bar Coding?" *Food Processing.* June 1992.

Sadhwani, Arjan T., and Thomas Tyson. "Does Your Firm Need Bar Coding?" *Management Accounting (USA).* April 1990.

Seideman, Tony. "BC Labels Turn High-Tech." *Distribution.* January 1993.

Sharp, Kevin R. "Packing a Page of Info into Two Inches: Two-Dimensional Bar Codes Are Emerging as a Way to Get More Data into a Small Space." *Computerworld.* May 25, 1992.

Snell, Ned. ''Bar Codes Break Out: Once You Learn What Bar Codes Do Today, You May Find Uses You Never Thought of Before.'' *Datamation.* April 1, 1992.

Verity, John W. ''Goodbye, Bar Codes, Hello, Buttons.'' *Business Week.* May 18, 1992.

BARRIERS TO MARKET ENTRY

Barriers to market entry include a number of different factors that restrict the ability of new competitors to enter and begin operating in a given industry. For example, an industry may require new entrants to make large investments in capital equipment, or existing firms may have earned strong customer loyalties that may be difficult for new entrants to overcome. The ease of entry into an industry in just one aspect of an industry analysis; the others include the power held by suppliers and buyers, the existing competitors and the nature of competition, and the degree to which similar products or services can act as substitutes for those provided by the industry. It is important for small business owners to understand all of these critical industry factors in order to compete effectively and make good strategic decisions.

''Understanding your industry and anticipating its future trends and directions gives you the knowledge you need to react and control your portion of that industry,'' Kenneth J. Cook explained in his book *The AMA Complete Guide to Strategic Planning for Small Business.* ''Since both you and your competitors are in the same industry, the key is in finding the differing abilities between you and the competition in dealing with the industry forces that impact you. If you can identify abilities you have that are superior to competitors, you can use that ability to establish a competitive advantage.''

The ease of entry into an industry is important because it determines the likelihood that a company will face new competitors. In industries that are easy to enter, sources of competitive advantage tend to wane quickly. On the other hand, in industries that are difficult to enter, sources of competitive advantage last longer, and firms also tend to benefit from having a constant set of competitors. The ease of entry into an industry depends upon two factors: the reaction of existing competitors to new entrants; and the barriers to market entry that prevail in the industry. Existing competitors are most likely to react strongly against new entrants when there is a history of such behavior, when the competitors have invested substantial resources in the industry, and when the industry is characterized by slow growth.

In his landmark book *Competitive Strategy: Techniques for Analyzing Industries and Competitors,*

Michael E. Porter identified six major sources of barriers to market entry:

1) **Economies of scale**—Economies of scale occur when the unit cost of a product declines as production volume increases. When existing competitors in an industry have achieved economies of scale, it acts as a barrier by forcing new entrants to either compete on a large scale or accept a cost disadvantage in order to compete on a small scale. There are also a number of other cost advantages held by existing competitors that act as barriers to market entry when they cannot be duplicated by new entrants—such as proprietary technology, favorable locations, government subsidies, good access to raw materials, and experience and learning curves.

2) Product differentiation—In many markets and industries, established competitors have gained customer loyalty and brand identification through their long-standing advertising and customer service efforts. This creates a barrier to market entry by forcing new entrants to spend time and money to differentiate their products in the marketplace and overcome these loyalties.

3) Capital requirements—Another type of barrier to market entry occurs when new entrants are required to invest large financial resources in order to compete in an industry. For example, certain industries may require capital investments in inventories or production facilities. Capital requirements form a particularly strong barrier when the capital is required for risky investments like research and development.

4) Switching costs—A switching cost refers to a one-time cost that is incurred by a buyer as a result of switching from one supplier's product to another's. Some examples of switching costs include retraining employees, purchasing support equipment, enlisting technical assistance, and redesigning products. High switching costs form an effective entry barrier by forcing new entrants to provide potential customers with incentives to adopt their products.

5) Access to channels of distribution—In many industries, established competitors control the logical channels of distribution through long-standing relationships. In order to persuade distribution channels to accept a new product, new entrants often must provide incentives in the form of price discounts, promotions, and cooperative adver-

tising. Such expenditures act as a barrier by reducing the profitability of new entrants.

6) Government policy—Government policies can limit or prevent new competitors from entering industries through licensing requirements, limits on access to raw materials, pollution standards, and product testing regulations.

It is important to note that barriers to market entry can change over time as an industry matures, or as a result of strategic decisions made by existing competitors. In addition, entry barriers should never be considered insurmountable obstacles. Some small businesses are likely to possess the resources and skills that will allow them to overcome entry barriers more easily and cheaply than others. "Low entry and exit barriers reduce the risk in entering a new market, and may make the opportunity more attractive financially," Glen L. Urban and Steven H. Star explained in their book *Advanced Marketing Strategy.* But "in many cases, we would be better off selecting market opportunities with high entry barriers (despite the greater risk and investment required) so that we can enjoy the advantage of fewer potential entrants."

FURTHER READING:

Cook, Kenneth J. *The AMA Complete Guide to Strategic Planning for Small Business.* Chicago, IL: American Marketing Association, 1995.

Geroski, Paul A. "Keeping Out the Competition." *Financial Times.* February 23, 1996.

Porter, Michael E. *Competitive Strategy: Techniques for Analyzing Industries and Competitors.* New York: Free Press, 1980.

Urban, Glen L., and Steven H. Star. *Advanced Marketing Strategy.* Englewood Cliffs, NJ: Prentice Hall, 1991.

SEE ALSO: Competitive Analysis; Emerging Markets; Market Research

BARTERING

Bartering is the exchange of goods and services among businesses. This practice may be undertaken by single businesses, but in recent years many companies that choose to barter have joined organized bartering networks that offer memberships to firms in a variety of industries.

The popularity of bartering has surged over the past several years. Indeed, after making its first appearance in the modern U.S. economy in the late 1970s, its modest rate of growth suddenly accelerated in the late 1980s and early 1990s. In 1993 alone, North American firms traded more than $6 billion in goods and services, according to the International Reciprocal Trade Association (IRTA), and by 1996 it was estimated that North American companies were bartering approximately $7.6 billion on an annual basis. The IRTA, which is a bartering information clearinghouse that also seeks to establish standards of ethical bartering conduct, estimates that commercial bartering is growing at better than ten percent a year. Both large and small companies have contributed to this growth. Companies of all sizes have been attracted to its capacity for putting excess **inventory** and resources to good use, while small businesses in particular have embraced its usefulness as a viable cash alternative to cover basic expenditures in such areas as **business travel**, facility maintenance and/or improvements, **marketing**, and a whole host of other areas. "When it's properly done," one entrepreneur told *Small Business Reports,* "barter gives smaller businesses the clout of a much larger company."

ORGANIZED BARTERING NETWORKS

According to *Black Enterprise,* approximately 600 bartering organizations in the United States oversaw markets in the mid-1990s. About 100 of these are trade companies or brokers that exchange goods and services on behalf of their mostly multinational clientele. But the other 500 bartering organizations are tailored so that its members may trade goods and services with one another. "Members must list a good or service for trade," explained Carolyn M. Brown in *Black Enterprise.* "In return, those businesses receive trade credit based on the dollar value of the product or service offered. A business uses its trade credits to purchase goods or services offered by other members." Once a transaction takes place, "the seller's account is credited and the buyer's account is debited," added *Small Business Reports* contributor Susan Groenwald. "The exchange helps promote members' products and services through brokers (who act as an outside sales force for members), publications such as a barter directory and monthly classified ads listing specific items that client have to sell. Many barter networks also have reciprocal agreements with networks in other cities, allowing members to trade with even more businesses."

Most observers agree that these networks can provide small business owners with potentially valuable options when it comes time to 1) pay debts during "cash-crunch" periods, and 2) collect from clients who are undergoing their own financial difficulties. But practitioners also contend that it helps a company's bottom line even when everybody's financial situation is stable.

JOINING A NETWORK Since organized bartering networks conduct a variety of administrative and record keeping tasks on behalf of their members, they require businesses to pay for their membership. These costs can take a variety of forms, including commissions (often 10 to 15 percent of the value of each transaction), one-time fees, annual fees (some networks charge no annual fee, while others may charge several hundred dollars), maintenance fees, or some combination thereof. Entrepreneurs who are intrigued with the idea of joining a bartering network, however, should be aware that pursuing such a course of action is likely to be a waste of time if his or her company is on shaky financial ground or is less than committed to providing top services or goods. Some networks will reject applicants whose solvency is in question, and even companies that are accepted should anticipate being closely monitored during their first few transactions. "We watch the first couple of trades very carefully," one bartering broker told *San Diego Business Journal.* "The newer the members, the closer we watch them." Some networks also assign established members to serve as mentors of sorts for new members.

NETWORKING WITHIN THE NETWORK "Bartering through an organized network is inherently more flexible than using cash because the network facilitates trade transactions among all its business members," stated Groenwald. Indeed, these networks are devoted to keeping members in touch with one another and facilitating transactions for the simple reason that they are reliant on trades for their very existence. Many networks are adept at keeping the lines of communication—and thus the lines of bartering—open between their members. In addition to directories, newsletters, and the like, many networks sponsor membership gatherings in which representatives from various businesses can meet and talk. These "mixers" enable small business owners to establish valuable contacts and, in many cases, make transactions that benefit both themselves and other network members. "For weeks after [mixers], the vouchers triple," one network executive told *San Diego Business Journal.* "Deals are being done." Members of the barter network community also note that these face-to-face encounters tend to keep businesses focused on ensuring that they uphold their end of the bargain in barter agreements. A network member who provides substandard service to a fellow member will find that negative publicity can travel quickly in mixer settings.

ADDITIONAL NETWORK SERVICES In addition to serving as a facilitator of bartering transactions, barter networks usually provide a range of ancillary services to their members. In addition to providing record keeping on all transactions that go through the organization, most networks will provide regular statements (monthly, quarterly, annual) to members, and provide them with necessary tax forms and information. (Participating companies should be aware that barter income is treated like regular income by the IRS, and it is taxable in the year that it is credited; of course, this status also means that it is tax-deductible for business expenses.

ADVANTAGES AND DISADVANTAGES OF BARTERING

Bartering has been hailed as a potentially valuable new addition to the strategic arsenal of small business owners for several reasons. Groenwald offered five major areas in which bartering can be useful to the ambitious entrepreneur:

Perks and Bonuses—Small business enterprises are often strapped for cash when it comes to providing bonuses or perks to their employees, but Groenwald noted that with barter exchanges, companies may use their barter credits to buy "morale-boosting items." In addition, "some companies have worked out a system with their barter network that allows employees to choose their own rewards." Under such arrangements, business owners set up "sub-accounts" for individual employees to which barter credits owned by the business can be transferred. Employees thus have the opportunity to spend those credits anywhere in the exchange as they see fit. "Remember, though, that barter bonuses and incentives, like their traditional counterparts, are subject to payroll and federal and state withholding taxes," she added.

Business Travel—Increasing numbers of small business owners are using bartering as a way to cut down on costs associated with business travel, especially as the number of lodging facilities engaged in bartering practices continues to grow.

Debt **Collections**—Groenwald noted that small businesses often depend on prompt debt collection to maintain their very viability, "yet using an attorney or commercial service for collections takes both time and money, and writing off the debt is a no-win situation." Instead, she pointed out that many small business owners have begun to offer debtors the option of paying in merchandise or services, which are subsequently sold on the barter network with the credit going to the small business that would otherwise have been unable to collect anything. "In effect, the trade credits are equal to receiving the original debt in cash," wrote Groenwald. She admitted that some of this value would be sacrificed to network transaction fees, but that small businesses would still come out much farther ahead than they would if they turned to a collection service or attorney.

Line of **Credit**—Bartering networks can also serve as an alternative to more traditional means of financing for small businesses. "With this financing strategy, the barter network advances a set amount of trade dollars to your company against its projected future sales," said Groenwald. "Generally, the barter network [will] determine the trade-dollar amount your company is likely to earn back in a one-year period and base the advance on that amount." In addition, Groenwald pointed out that the interest that is charged on the line of credit may be paid in trade.

Closing Sales—"If you need an extra edge to clinch a cash sale," wrote Groenwald, "consider accepting part of the payment in barter. This option can make your company more appealing than competitors because the transaction will cost your customer less out-of-pocket cash."

Analysts do admit, however, that there are drawbacks associated with bartering as well. Some businesses that participate in bartering may find that the range of products or services available do not fully address their needs, or they may not be available when they are needed. Finally, as mentioned above, providing shoddy service or materials to clients or other network members will likely result in a drop in community and/or industry reputation, which is something that small business owners should avoid at all costs.

FURTHER READING:

Briggins, Angela. "When Barter is Better." *Management Review.* February 1996.

Broderick, Pat. " 'Let's Make a Deal' is the Slogan for These Firms: Merchants Exchange Brings Order to Old Practice of Bartering." *San Diego Business Journal.* June 23, 1997.

Brown, Carolyn M. "Bartering for Business: Business Owners Short on Cash Trade Goods and Services." *Black Enterprise.* April 1996.

Green, Paula L. "The Booming Barter Business." *Journal of Commerce and Commercial.* April 1, 1997.

Groenwald, Susan. "Creative Trends in Trade." *Small Business Reports.* October 1994.

SEE ALSO: Networking

BENCHMARKING

Benchmarking is the practice of identifying another business that is the best, or one of the best, in its class, and learning as much as possible from it. The term was popularized in the 1980s by Xerox Corporation's Robert Camp, who wrote the first major book on the subject, *Benchmarking: The Search for Industry Best Practices that Lead to Superior Performance.*

Benchmarking is a business strategy that is used primarily by manufacturers, although it is applicable to other business activities as well. While it may involve learning from one's competitors, benchmarking is more focused and narrowly defined than **competitive analysis**. Competitive analysis can be used in conjunction with benchmarking to identify gaps and provide strategic direction; however, benchmarking itself measures specific performance gaps between a company and its competitors.

Benchmarking is used when there is a clearly defined gap between a company and its competitors that must be overcome in order to remain competitive. For example, the Xerox Corporation benchmarked Japanese manufacturers who were able to sell a copier for the same amount it cost Xerox to build one. Benchmarking may focus on products, manufacturing processes, management practices, and/or overall corporate direction. It is often focused on learning from one's direct competitors. Benchmarking can lead to improved performance by studying general business practices that are not industry specific (generic benchmarking), specific business or manufacturing functions (functional benchmarking), general industry characteristics (industry benchmarking), strategies in general (tactical benchmarking), or the numerical characteristics of specific products or processes (performance benchmarking). As a result of its benchmarking in Japan, Xerox Corporation eventually developed a completely new copying process by creatively improving on the concepts it had learned from its chief competitors.

Benchmarking involves some measure of cooperation between two companies who become benchmarking partners. Xerox Corporation has pioneered benchmarking and often serves as a benchmarking partner for other companies interested in learning from it. After a company chooses a competitor to study, information is exchanged between the two companies through a series of on-site visits by teams representing each partner. These cross-functional benchmarking teams contain representatives from different functional areas of each company, including management. At the on-site visits, teams representing the two partners determine such issues as the focus for discussion, proprietary issues, the agenda, and who the participants will be.

Once the period of study and information exchange is completed, the benchmarking team issues an action plan and presents it to management for approval. The study and plan provide evidence that a top company is doing things in a better way and that the benchmarking company can implement similar changes to become more competitive. The action plan sets objectives and provides a road map for achieving those goals. It also spells out the necessary capital investment.

In the 1990s benchmarking was still relatively new to most companies. But Xerox Corporation established the International Benchmarking Clearinghouse in Houston to help educate other companies to its benefits. Small companies as well as large corporations can use benchmarking techniques to improve their performance by learning from other companies in their field.

FURTHER READING:

Camp, Robert. *Benchmarking: The Search for Industry Best Practices that Lead to Superior Performance.* Quality Resources, 1989.

BETTER BUSINESS BUREAUS

Better Business Bureaus (BBBs) are private nonprofit organizations that collect and report information to help consumers make informed decisions when dealing with businesses or charitable organizations. The BBB is not a government or law enforcement agency; it does not have the power to collect money, administer sanctions, or impose other penalties against companies or individuals that engage in poor business practices. But its ability to disseminate a company's operating track record make it a force to be reckoned with. Faced with the prospect of losing customers because of unfavorable BBB rankings, companies have a significant incentive to adhere to proper business practices and address customer complaints. In addition to their information-gathering activities, local BBBs also provide mediation services when disputes arise between customers and businesses, promote ethical business standards, maintain standards for truthful advertising, and share pertinent information (about possible fraudulent activity, etc.) with local and national law enforcement agencies. BBBs are licensed by the Council of Better Business Bureaus (CBBB) and governed by their own local boards of directors. By the mid-1990s more than 180 Better Business Bureau offices operated in the United States, Canada, and Puerto Rico.

BBB MEMBERSHIP

Each Better Business Bureau is independently supported by businesses that operate within their designated service area. BBBs receive their operating funds from the membership dues that are paid by business and professional groups in those service areas. Companies that become members of their local Better Business Bureau receive several benefits in return. These usually include: 1) membership identification on the company's place of business; 2) access to all BBB publications, programs, and services; 3) right to participate in BBB training programs in such areas as arbitration, customer service, and mediation; 4) affiliation with other member businesses.

But the BBB maintains certain standards for membership to ensure that the organization's integrity remains unquestioned. Companies with bad track records are not accepted, and companies that do become members have to adhere to certain rules. For example, BBB members must respond to consumer complaints presented by the BBB; if they do not do so, they lose their membership. In addition, it should be noted that the BBB attaches a number of conditions to ensure that companies do not join simply for the purpose of trumpeting their membership. BBBs do not endorse or recommend businesses or what they sell. Moreover,

they do not allow members to advertise their membership, because the public could conceivably reach the erroneous conclusion that such advertising means that the BBB is endorsing the member's business. In addition, BBB membership dues are not tax deductible for federal income tax purposes, though they may be tax deductible as an ordinary and necessary business expense. Finally, the CBBB has noted that membership does not confer any advantages when complaints arise: "The BBB's integrity is on the line every time we review and process a complaint. If a Bureau were to favor members over non-members in a complaint, such action would destroy our most valuable asset—the public trust that we have held for over 80 years."

BBB REPORTS

According to its own literature, "the BBB reports on a firm's marketplace practices. It does not report either individual or business credit information. BBB reliability reports contain information about the nature of the business, its principal officers, a three-year summary of any complaints processed, and any government action involving the company's marketplace practices. Most Bureaus will also report a company's BBB membership in its public report and note whether it participates in any special BBB programs to improve customer satisfaction."

In addition, a branch of the Council of Better Business Bureaus known as the Philanthropic Advisory Service maintains information on various charitable organizations. These reports, which are maintained by the national Council but updated by local BBBs, cover all sorts of charitable and other **nonprofit organizations**. Information typically included in these reports includes the group's background, its current programs (if any), the structure of its governing body, its tax-exempt status, its fund raising practices, its financial standing, and notification as to whether the organization complies with the CBBB's "Standards for Charitable Solicitations."

These reliability reports can be invaluable to both individual and business customers who want to make sure that they are conducting business with an ethical company. The BBB cautions, however, that it does not maintain reports on every business operating in a given area. The reasons for this vary. In some cases, the business is relatively new. In other instances, the company may simply operate in such a manner that customers see no reason to file a complaint.

FURTHER READING:

"BBB History and Traditions." Better Business Bureau Consumer Information Series, n.d.

"Frequently Asked Questions About the Better Business Bureau." Better Business Bureau Consumer Information Series, n.d.

''What is a Better Business Bureau.'' Better Business Bureau Consumer Information Series, n.d.

SEE ALSO: Business Ethics

BONDS

Bonds are debt instruments issued by corporations and a variety of government entities to raise money to purchase assets and finance deficits. In effect the bond issuer borrows money from the bond purchaser and agrees to pay interest at an established rate over a fixed period of time. The ''loan,'' or face value of the bond, is repaid at the end of the bond's term when it matures. The bond serves as a contract between the two parties, with stipulations regarding the obligations of the bond issuer to the bondholder. While shareholders are considered owners of a corporation, bondholders are among its creditors. A company's stock is part of its equity, while bonds are part of its debt. If the bond issuer is a corporation, bondholders have a prior claim against the corporation's assets and earnings to that of the corporation's shareholders.

BOND CLASSIFICATIONS There are many classifications of bonds. Within the United States there are government or civil bonds that are issued by the federal government, individual states, and municipalities, and corporate bonds that are issued by corporations. The international bond market includes bonds issued by international bodies, governments of other countries, and companies based in other countries.

Bonds may also be classified according to the reason for issuing them, such as school bonds, airport bonds, equipment bonds, or general improvement bonds. Bonds may be secured or unsecured, which refers to whether or not the bondholder has a specific claim against the assets of the bond issuer. Bonds also vary in terms of principal and interest payments, and they may be registered or unregistered. Unregistered bonds are also known as bearer bonds.

BOND COMPONENTS Regardless of classification, all bonds share certain features. Bonds are a form of **contract**, and the rights of investors as well as the obligations of the issuer are usually set forth in what is known as a bond indenture. Most bonds are issued for a specified length of time, usually from one to 30 years, and are called term bonds. At the end of the term the bond reaches maturity, and all liabilities that have not been paid off before maturity must be paid to the bondholder. Bonds are usually categorized as short-term (1 to 5 years), intermediate-term (5 to 12 years), and long-term (more than 12 years). Short-term bonds are often referred to as notes, while those with terms of less than 12 months are called money market instruments.

All bonds pay interest to their holders. The nominal or coupon **interest rate** is the rate shown on the bond that the issuer has agreed to pay. If the bond has been sold or purchased for more than the face amount, then it is said to have been sold at a premium and the effective interest rate becomes less than the coupon rate. That is, the bond purchaser will actually earn less than the coupon rate because more than the face amount was paid for the bond. Similarly, if the bond is sold for less than the face amount, it is sold at a discount and the effective interest rate is more than the coupon rate.

Bond interest is usually paid twice a year, but there are several variations as to how bond interest is paid. Zero-coupon bonds pay all of the interest at maturity, for example. The interest a bond pays may be fixed or floating. That is, it may yield a specified interest rate for its entire term, or the interest rate may be adjusted periodically.

Bonds that are callable are those that can be called in, or redeemed, by the bond issuer. Since bond issuers typically call in such bonds when interest rates are lower than the bond is paying, callable bonds usually yield higher rates of return than bonds that are not callable. On the other hand, convertible bonds are usually issued at lower rates of return. A convertible bond is one that gives the bondholder the option of converting the bond into another type of investment, usually some form of stock in the company.

Domestic corporate and government bonds are assigned credit ratings by five agencies recognized by the **Securities and Exchange Commission**, with Standard & Poor's and Moody's Investor Service being the two dominant rating agencies. Other agencies provide similar ratings for bonds in other countries. Bond ratings are based on such factors as the creditworthiness of the issuer, the issuer's past record of interest and/or dividend payments, and the nature of the assets or revenues that will be applied to repayment. Bond ratings range from AAA, the highest rating, to C. A D rating indicates the issuer is already in default. Bonds with lower ratings carry a higher risk of default and consequently usually pay a higher interest rate. Bonds with low ratings are also known as junk bonds.

SEE ALSO: Debt Financing

BOOKKEEPING

Bookkeeping is that aspect of **accounting** that is concerned with the mechanics of keeping accounts, ledgers, and journals, including posting entries and taking trial balances. Bookkeeping provides the necessary support for such accounting functions as the preparation of **financial statements**, cost reports, and **tax returns**.

Bookkeeping involves keeping track of a business's financial transactions and making entries to specific accounts using the debit and credit system. Each entry represents a different business transaction. Every accounting system has a chart of accounts that lists actual accounts as well as account categories. There is usually at least one account for every item on a company's balance sheet and income statement. For example, there might be an account for utilities, and this account might be broken down further into electricity, water, and gas. In theory, there is no limit to the number of accounts that can be created, although the total number of accounts is usually determined by management's need for information.

The process of bookkeeping involves four basic steps: 1) analyzing financial transactions and assigning them to specific accounts; 2) writing original journal entries that credit and debit the appropriate accounts; 3) posting entries to ledger accounts; and 4) adjusting entries at the end of each accounting period. Bookkeeping is based on two basic principles. One is that every debit must have an equal credit. The second, that all accounts must balance, follows from the first.

Bookkeeping entries are made in a journal, which is a chronological record of all transactions. Journal entries are typically made into a computer from paper documents that contain information about the transaction to be recorded. Journal entries can be made from invoices, purchase orders, sales receipts, and similar documents, which are usually kept on file for a specified length of time. For example, the journal entry for a transaction involving a cash payment for a new stapler might debit the cash account by the amount paid and credit the office supplies account for the value of the stapler.

Journal entries assign each transaction to a specific account and record changes in those accounts using debits and credits. Information contained in the journal entries is then posted to ledger accounts. A ledger is a collection of related accounts and may be called an Accounts Payable Ledger, Accounts Receivable Ledger, or a General Ledger, for example. Posting is the process by which account balances in the appropriate ledger are changed. While account balances may be recorded and computed periodically, the only time account balances are changed in the ledger is when a journal entry indicates such a change is necessary. Information that appears chronologically in the journal becomes reclassified and summarized in the ledger on an account-by-account basis.

Bookkeepers may take trial balances occasionally to ensure that the journal entries have been posted accurately to every account. A trial balance simply means that totals are taken of all of the debit balances and credit balances in the ledger accounts. The debit and credit balances should match; if they do not, then one or more errors have been made and must be found.

Other aspects of bookkeeping include making adjusting entries that modify account balances so that they more accurately reflect the actual situation at the end of an accounting period. Adjusting entries usually involves unrecorded costs and revenues associated with continuous transactions, or costs and revenues that must be apportioned among two or more accounting periods.

Another bookkeeping procedure involves closing accounts. Most companies have temporary revenue and expense accounts that are used to provide information for the company's income statement. These accounts are periodically closed to owners' equity to determine the profit or loss associated with all revenue and expense transactions. An account called Income Summary (or Profit and Loss) is created to show the net income or loss for a particular accounting period. Closing entries means reducing the balance of the temporary accounts to zero, while debiting or crediting the income summary account.

Good bookkeeping is particularly important to small businesses, since they can rarely afford to waste money. Bookkeeping enables the small business owner to support expenditures made for the business in order to claim all available tax credits and deductions. It also provides detailed, accurate, and timely records that can prove invaluable to management decision-making, or in the event of an audit.

FURTHER READING:

The Entrepreneur Magazine Small Business Advisor. New York: Wiley, 1995.

Myers, Randy. ''Pay the Piper Only What's Due.'' *Nation's Business.* March 1994.

BRAINSTORMING

Brainstorming is a group problem-solving technique that is intended to help members develop innovative new approaches to a problem in an unthreatening environment. Developed by A. F. Osborne in 1941, brainstorming in its most basic form involves stimulating all the members of a group to express a variety of ideas, which are built upon and recorded for future reference. Critical judgment of the ideas is reserved until later in the process, when the ideas are evaluated, combined, improved, and changed until the group reaches a final resolution of the problem. Brainstorming can be particularly useful in providing creative solutions to problems that have defied traditional problem-solving methods, as well as in such applications as new product development.

There are three critical factors that determine the success of a brainstorming effort. First, the group must strive to produce a large quantity of ideas, as this increases the likelihood that they will happen upon the best possible solution. Second, the group must be certain to withhold judgement of the ideas as they are expressed, since the negative thinking of one group member can make others less willing to participate and thus derail the whole process. Third, the group leader must create a positive environment for the brainstorming session and channel the creative energies of all the members in the same direction.

In his book *Thinkertoys,* Michael Michalko outlined a series of steps that should be followed in setting up a brainstorming session.

1) Select the problem to be addressed, defining it as specifically as possible.

2) Choose participants for the group. Ideally, the group should consist of six to twelve participants from diverse areas of the company, including non-experts as well as experts. They should be flexible thinkers and independent personalities. They should also have a positive attitude about the brainstorming process, as well as a genuine desire to improve the performance of the company. It may be helpful to include one member who has the power to make decisions about the problem being addressed, as long as that person understands the brainstorming process. Everyone present should be a participant—guests and onlookers should be discouraged.

3) Choose a suitable environment. Brainstorming requires a comfortable, unthreatening environment to work effectively. Many companies use off-site locations.

4) Select a group leader. This person should have strong interpersonal skills as well as a good understanding of the process. The leader's duties include planning the meeting ahead of time, preparing and distributing an agenda, employing various creativity techniques to get members' ideas flowing, and keeping the group focused on the problem at hand. If the discussion should become stagnant—perhaps because members have trouble overcoming their disciplined ways of viewing the problem—it is the group leader's job to get it moving. One possible technique is temporarily to move the focus of the discussion into unrelated areas by asking a series of abstract questions, like "What shocks people?," and having members free-associate based upon their responses.

5) Select someone to record all the ideas generated by the group, possibly on large wall sheets or a chalkboard. Sometimes it is helpful to record the flow of ideas in graphic form rather than creating a linear list.

After the brainstorming portion of the meeting has been completed, the leader or group should arrange all the ideas into related categories to prioritize and evaluate them. Michalko suggests creating three lists: ideas of immediate usefulness, ideas deserving further exploration, and ideas representing new approaches to the problem. These lists can be manipulated by the group in order to settle on the best solution. After the conclusion of the meeting, it may be helpful to send participants a copy of the idea lists to keep them thinking about the problem. The group leader may ask members to report back later on ideas they considered worthy of action, and to offer any ideas they might have about implementation.

There are a number of variations on the basic theme of brainstorming. In brainwriting, the members of a group write their ideas down on paper and then exchange their lists with others. When group members expand upon each other's ideas in this way, it frequently leads to innovative new approaches. Another possibility is to brainstorm via a bulletin board, which can be hung in a central office location or posted on a computer network. The bulletin board centers upon a basic topic or question, and people are encouraged to read others' responses and add their own. One benefit of this approach is that it keeps the problem at the forefront of people's minds. Finally, it is also possible to perform solo brainstorming. In this approach, a person writes down at least one idea per day on an index card. Eventually he or she can look at all the cards, shuffle them around, and combine the ideas.

FURTHER READING:

Michalko, Michael. *Thinkertoys: A Handbook of Business Creativity for the 90s.* Berkeley, CA: Ten Speed Press, 1991.

SEE ALSO: Innovation

BRANDS AND BRAND NAMES

A brand is a name, symbol, or other feature that distinguishes a seller's goods or services in the marketplace. More than 500,000 brands are registered globally with pertinent regulatory bodies in different countries. Brands serve their owners by allowing them to cultivate customer recognition of, and loyalty toward, their offerings. Brands also serve the consumer by supplying information about the quality, origin, and value of goods and services. Without brands to guide buying decisions, the free market would become a confusing, faceless crowd of consumables. An established and respected brand can be the most valuable asset a company possesses.

Brands have been used since ancient times. For example, people burned singular designs into the skin of their livestock to prove ownership, while potters and silversmiths marked their wares with initials or other personal tags. But it is only since the second half of the nineteenth century that branding evolved into an advanced marketing tool. The industrial revolution, new communication systems, and improved modes of transporting goods made it both easier and more necessary for companies to advertise brands over larger regions. As manufacturers gained access to national markets, numerous brand names were born that would achieve legendary U.S. and global status. Proctor and Gamble, Kraft, Heinz, Coca-Cola, Kodak, and Sears were a few of the initial brands that would become common household names by the mid-1900s. Before long, legal systems were devised to recognize and protect brand names, and branding was extended to services—such as car repair—as well as products. Thus the brand concept moved into the forefront of modern advertising strategy.

THE BRAND CONCEPT

A brand is backed by an intangible agreement between a consumer and the company selling the products or services under the brand name. A consumer who prefers a particular brand basically agrees to select that brand over others based primarily on the brand's reputation. The consumer may stray from the brand occasionally because of price, accessibility, or other factors, but some degree of allegiance will exist until a different brand gains acceptance by, and then preference with, the buyer. Until that time, however, the consumer will reward the brand owner with dollars, almost assuring future cash flows to the company. The buyer may even pay a higher price for the goods or services because of his commitment, or passive agreement, to buy the brand.

In return for his brand loyalty, the company essentially assures the buyer that the product will confer the benefits associated with, and expected from, the brand. Those numerous benefits may be both explicit and subtle. For example, the buyer of a Mercedes-Benz automobile may expect extremely high quality, durability, and performance. But he will also likely

expect to receive emotional benefits related to public perception of his wealth or social status. If Mercedes licenses its nameplate to a manufacturer of cheap economy cars or supplies an automobile that begins deteriorating after only a few years, the buyer will probably feel that the agreement has been breached. The value of the brand, Mercedes-Benz, will be reduced in the mind of that buyer and possibly others who become aware of the breach.

There are two major categories of brands: manufacturer and dealer. Manufacturer brands, such as Ford, are owned by the producer or service provider. The best-known of these brands are held by large corporations that sell multiple products or services affiliated with the brand. Dealer brands, like Die-Hard batteries, are usually owned by a middleman, such as a wholesaler or retailer. These brand names often are applied to the products of smaller manufacturers that make a distribution arrangement with the middleman rather than trying to establish a brand of their own. Manufacturers or service providers may sell their offerings under their own brands, a dealer brand, or as a combination of the two types, which is called a mixed brand. Under the latter arrangement, part of the goods are sold under the manufacturer's brand and part are sold under the dealer brand.

SELECTING BRAND NAMES

Brand names are very important for small businesses, as they provide potential customers with information about the product and help them form an immediate impression about the company. A well-chosen brand name can set a small business's product apart from those of competitors and communicate a message regarding the firm's marketing position or corporate personality. When preparing to enter a market with a product or service, an entrepreneur must decide whether to establish a brand and, if so, what name to use.

Experts claim that successful branding is most likely when the product is easy to identify, provides the best value for the price, is widely available, and has strong enough demand to make the branding effort profitable. Branding is also recommended in situations where obtaining favorable display space or locations on store shelves will significantly influence sales of the product. Finally, a successful branding effort requires economies of scale, meaning that costs should decrease and profits should increase as more units of the product are made.

After deciding to establish a brand, a small business faces the task of selecting a brand name. An entrepreneur might decide to consult an advertising agency, design house, or marketing firm that specializes in naming, or to come up with a name on their own. A good brand name should be short and simple;

easy to spell, pronounce, and remember; pronounceable in only one way; suggestive of the product's benefits; adaptable to packaging and labeling needs or to any advertising medium; not offensive or negative; not likely to become dated; and legally available for use.

In order to create a brand name for a product without the help of experts, a small business owner should begin by examining names already in use in the market and evaluating their effectiveness. The next step is to identify three to five attributes that make the product special and should help influence buyers to choose it over the competition. It may also be helpful to identify three to five company personality traits—such as friendly, innovative, or economical—that customers might appreciate in relation to the product. Then the small business owner should make a list of all the words and phrases that come to mind for each attribute or personality trait that has been identified. If the brand name is to include the type of product or service being offered, it is important to consider whether the phrases on the list fit well with these terms. The next step is to think about how the phrases on the list would look on a sign or on a product package, including possible visual images and typefaces that could be used to enhance their appearance.

Next, the entrepreneur should narrow down the list with the help of a few friends. It may be helpful to say the possible names aloud, thinking about how they would sound if they were used by a receptionist answering a telephone or by a customer requesting a product from a store. It is also important to consider whether the names will stand the test of time as the business grows, or whether they include an in-joke that may become dated. Once the list has been narrowed down to between ten and fifteen candidates, then the possibilities should be tested for impact on at least thirty strangers, perhaps through a focus group or survey. The opinions of people who may be potential customers should be given the most weight.

Finally, once the top few choices have been identified, the entrepreneur can find out whether they are available for use—or are already being used by another business—by conducting a trademark search. This search can be performed by advertising or marketing firms, or by some attorneys, for a fee. Alternatively, the small business owner can simply send in a formal request for a trademark and wait to see whether it is approved. The request must be sent to the state patent and trademark office, and also to the federal office if the business will be conducting interstate commerce. In order for a trademark to be approved, it must be available and distinctive, and it must depart from a mere description of the product.

BRAND STRATEGY

In order to benefit from the consumer relationship allowed by branding, a company must painstakingly strive to earn brand loyalty. The company must gain name recognition for its product, get the consumer to actually try its brand, and then convince him that the brand is acceptable. Only after those triumphs can the company hope to secure some degree of preference for its brand. Indeed, name awareness is the most critical factor in achieving success. Companies may spend vast sums of money and effort just to attain recognition of a new brand. To penetrate a market with established brands, moreover, they may resort to giving a branded product away for free just to get people to try it. Even if the product outperforms its competitors, however, consumers may adhere to their traditional buying patterns simply because of their comfort with those competitive products.

An easier way to quickly establish a brand is to be the first company to offer a product or service. But there are also simpler methods of penetrating existing niches, namely product line extension and brand franchise extension. Product line extension entails the use of an established brand name on a new, related product. For example, the Wonder Bread name could be applied to a whole-wheat bread to penetrate that market. Brand franchise extension refers to the application of an old brand to a completely new product line. For example, Coca-Cola could elect to apply its name to a line of candy products. One of the risks of brand and product extensions is that the name will be diluted or damaged by the new product.

Besides offering ways to enter new markets, product line and brand franchise extension are two ways in which a company can capitalize on a brand's ''equity,'' or its intangible value. Three major uses of brand equity include family branding, individual branding, and combination branding. Family branding entails using a brand for an entire product mix. The Kraft brand, for example, is used on a large number of dairy products and other food items. Individual branding occurs when the name is applied to a single product, such as Budweiser beer. Combination branding means that individual brand names are associated with a company name. For example, General Motors markets a variety of brands associated with the GM name.

Once a company establishes brand loyalty, it must constantly work to maintain its presence with consistent quality and competitive responses to new market entrants and existing competitors. The science of sustaining and increasing brand loyalty and maximizing brand equity is called ''brand management.'' Large companies often hire brand managers whose sole purpose is to foster and promote an individual brand. In many ways, the job of a brand manager in a large company is similar to that of an entrepreneur who seeks to enter and maintain a presence in a market with a branded product or service.

LEGAL ASPECTS

By legal definition, a brand is a trademark (or service mark for brands associated with services). Trademarks may be protected by virtue of their original use. Most U.S. trademarks are registered with the federal government through the Patent and Trademark Office of the **U.S. Department of Commerce**. Federal trademark registration helps to secure protection related to exclusive use, although additional measures may be necessary to achieve complete exclusivity. The Lanham Act of 1946 established U.S. regulations for registering brand names and marks, which are protected for 20 years from the date of registration. Various international agreements protect trademarks from abuse in foreign countries.

Trademarks have suffered from infringement and counterfeiting since their inception. The U.S. government, in fact, does not police trademark infringement, but leaves that task to registrants. In the late 1980s approximately $7 billion worth of ''gray market'' goods, or imported branded goods that bypass the brand owner, were shipped into the United States annually. The trade of brand-counterfeited goods, such as falsely branded automobile parts, is a major hurdle for many brand owners. Besides depriving the brand owner of potential sales and profits, counterfeiters can destroy consumer confidence in a brand by selling inferior-quality products under its name.

FURTHER READING:

Buzzell, Robert D. and John A. Quelch. *Multinational Marketing Management.* Reading, MA: Addison-Wesley, 1988.

Schoell, William F., and Joseph P. Guiltinan. *Marketing: Contemporary Concepts and Practices,* 5th ed. Needham, MA: Allyn and Bacon, 1992.

SEE ALSO: Marketing; Trademarks and Copyrights

BREAK-EVEN ANALYSIS

Break-even analysis is used in cost **accounting** and capital budgeting to evaluate projects or product lines in terms of their volume and profitability relationship. At its simplest, the tool is used as its name suggests: to determine the volume at which a company's costs will exactly equal its revenues, therefore resulting in net income of zero, or the ''break-even'' point. Perhaps more useful than this simple determination, however, is the understanding gained through such analysis of the variable and fixed nature of certain costs. Break-even analysis forces the small business owner to research, quantify, and categorize the company's **costs** into fixed and variable groups.

''Understanding what it takes to break even is critical to making any business profitable,'' Kevin D. Thompson stated in an article for *Black Enterprise.* ''Incorporating accurate and thorough break-even analysis as a routine part of your financial planning will keep you abreast of how your business is really faring. Determining how much business is needed to keep the door open will help improve your cash-flow management and your bottom line.''

The basic formula for break-even analysis is as follows:

$$BEQ = \frac{FC}{P - VC}$$

Where BEQ = Break-even quantity
FC = Total fixed costs
P = Average price per unit, and
VC = Variable costs per unit.

Fixed expenses include rent, equipment leases, insurance, interest on borrowed funds, and administrative salaries—costs that do not tend to vary based on sales volume. Variable expenses, on the other hand, include direct labor, raw materials, sales commissions, and delivery expenses—costs that tend to fluctuate with the level of sales. A key component of break-even analysis is the contribution margin, which can be defined as a product or service's price (P) minus variable costs (VC) per unit sold. The contribution margin concept is grounded in incremental or marginal analysis; its focus is the extra revenue and costs that will be incurred with the next additional unit.

The first step in determining the level of sales needed for a small business to break even is to compute the contribution margin, by subtracting the variable costs per unit from the selling price. For example, if P is $30 and VC are $20, the contribution margin is $10. The next step is to divide the total annual fixed costs by the contribution margin. For example, a company with FC of $50,000 and a contribution margin of $10 would need to sell 5,000 units to break even. This number can easily be converted to the dollars of revenue the company would need to break even for the year. Simply multiply the break-even point in units by the average selling price per unit. In this case, a BEQ of 5,000 units multiplied by a P of $30 per unit yields break-even revenue of $150,000.

Break-even analysis has numerous potential applications for small businesses. For example, it can help managers assess the effect of changing prices, sales volume, and costs on profits. It can also help small business owners make decisions regarding whether to expand their operations or hire new employees. Break-even analysis would also be useful in the following situation: a small business owner is skeptical of her marketing manager's projection for sales of 15,000 units of a new product, and wants to know what minimum quantity of units must be sold to avoid losing money, assuming a selling price of $25, fixed costs of $100,000, and variable costs of $15. The equation tells her that these parameters will require a break-even volume of 10,000 units; fewer than that level yields losses, more than that level yields profits. This perspective of analysis may be employed where the analyst is highly confident of the estimates for price and costs, but feels less certain about the assessment of market demand. In this case, the small business owner might be interested in how low sales could fall below the marketing manager's forecast without causing an embarrassment at year-end reporting time.

Another scenario may involve the question of how to manufacture a product, in terms of the nature of operations and how they will affect fixed costs. Here, a small business owner may have a good handle on the quantity expected, the likely selling price, and the variable costs involved, but be undecided about how to structure the new operation. If the volume is expected to be 10,000 units, at a selling price of $5 and variable costs of $3.50, the break-even equation tells him that fixed costs can be no greater than $15,000.

"The bottom line is that, especially for small businesses, the margins for error are much too narrow to make business decisions on gut instinct alone," Thompson concluded. "Every idea, whether it is the introduction of a new product line, the opening of branch offices, or the hiring of additional staff, must be tested through basic business analysis."

FURTHER READING:

Dennis, Michael C. "What Credit Managers Should Know about Break-Even Analysis." *Business Credit.* February 1995.

Hilton, Ronald W. *Managerial Accounting.* New York: McGraw-Hill, 1991.

"Numbers You Should Know to Keep in Touch with Your Business." *Profit-Building Strategies for Business Owners.* May 1993.

Thompson, Kevin D. "Business Management: Planning for Profit." *Black Enterprise.* April 1993.

SEE ALSO: Budgets and Budgeting

BUDGETS AND BUDGETING

A budget is a comprehensive, formal plan that estimates the probable expenditures and income for an organization over a specific period. Budgeting describes the overall process of preparing and using a budget. Since budgets are such valuable tools for planning and control of finances, budgeting affects nearly every type of organization—from governments and large corporations to small businesses—as well as families and individuals. A small business generally engages in budgeting to determine the most efficient and effective strategies for making money and expanding its asset base. Budgeting can help a company use its limited financial and human resources in a manner which best exploits existing business opportunities.

Intelligent budgeting incorporates good business judgment in the review and analysis of past trends and data pertinent to the business. This information assists a company in decisions relating to the type of business organization needed, the amount of money to be invested, the type and number of employees to hire, and the marketing strategies required. In budgeting, a company usually devises both long-term and short-term plans to help implement its strategies and to conduct ongoing evaluations of its performance. Although budgeting can be time-consuming and costly for small businesses, it can also provide a variety of benefits, including an increased awareness of costs, a coordination of efforts toward company goals, improved communication, and a framework for performance evaluation.

PLANNING FOR PROFIT AND WEALTH

The idea behind any profitable commercial enterprise lies in employing resources to exploit various business opportunities. If the profits are consistent, a company may purchase more assets and, therefore, expand its base of wealth. To do this effectively, a company undertakes the budgeting process to assess the business opportunities available to it, the keys to successfully exploiting these opportunities, the strategies the historical data support as most likely to succeed, and the goals and objectives the company must establish. The company must also plan long-term strategies which define its overall effort in building **market share**, increasing revenues, and decreasing **costs**; short-term strategies to increase profits, control costs, and invest for the future; control mechanisms incorporating performance evaluations and good business judgment; and control mechanisms for making modifications in the above strategies when and where necessary.

Although opportunities initially find their impetus in the business judgment of company leaders, a company expresses its assessment of them and formulates its strategies in quantifiable terms, such as: the volume of units which the company expects it can sell, the percentage of market share the volume of units represents, the dollars of revenues it will receive from these sales, and the dollars of profit it will earn. Likewise, a company outlines its long-term goals and specifies its short-range plans in quantifiable terms which detail how it expects to accomplish its goals: the dollars the company will spend in selling the units; the dollar costs of producing the units; the dollar costs of administering the company's operations; the dollars the company will invest in expanding and upgrading facilities and equipment; the flow of dollars into the company coffers; and the financial position, expressed in dollars, at specific points in the future.

FINANCIAL FORECASTS AND BUDGETS

Financial **forecasting** efforts are designed to project where the company wants to be in three, five, or ten years. It quantifies future sales, expenses, and earnings according to certain assumptions adopted by the company. The company then considers how changes in the business climate would affect the outcomes projected. It presents this analysis in the pro forma statement, which displays, over a time continuum, a comparison of the financial plan to ''best case'' and ''worst case'' scenarios. The pro forma statement acts as a guide for meeting goals and objectives, as well as an evaluative tool for assessing progress and profitability.

Through forecasting a company attempts to determine whether and to what degree its long-range plans are feasible. This discipline incorporates two interrelated functions: long-term planning based on realistic goals and objectives and a prognosis of the various conditions that possibly will affect these goals and objectives; and short-term planning and budgeting, which provide details about the distribution of income and expenses and a control mechanism for evaluating performance. Forecasting is a process for maximizing the profitable use of business assets in relation to: the analyses of all the latest relevant information by tested and logically sound statistical and econometric techniques; the interpretation and application of these analyses into future scenarios; and the calculation of reasonable probabilities based on sound business judgment.

Future projections for extended periods, although necessary and prudent, suffer from a multitude of unknowns: inflation, supply fluctuations, demand variations, credit shortages, employee qualifications, regulatory changes, management turnover, and the like. To increase control over operations, a company narrows its focus to forecasting attainable results over the short-term. These short-term forecasts, called budgets, are formal, comprehensive plans that quantify the expected operations of the organization over a specific future period. While a company may make few modifications to its forecast, for instance, in the

first three years, the company constructs individual budgets for each year.

A budget describes the expected month-to-month route a company will take in achieving its goals. It summarizes the expected outcomes of production and marketing efforts, and provides management benchmarks against which to compare actual outcomes. A budget acts as a control mechanism by pointing out soft spots in the planning process and/or in the execution of the plans. Consequently, a budget, used as an evaluative tool, augments a company's ability to more quickly react and make necessary alterations.

PRINCIPLES AND PROCEDURES FOR SUCCESSFUL BUDGETING

To be successful, budgets should be prepared in accordance with the following principles:

REALISTIC AND QUANTIFIABLE In a world of limited resources, a company must ration its own resources by setting goals and objectives which are reasonably attainable. Realism engenders loyalty and commitment among employees, motivating them to their highest performance. In addition, wide discrepancies, caused by unrealistic projections, have a negative effect on the credit worthiness of a company and may dissuade lenders. A company evaluates each potential activity to determine those that will result in the most appropriate resource allocation. A company accomplishes this through the quantification of the costs and benefits of the activities.

HISTORICAL The budget reflects a clear understanding of past results and a keen sense of expected future changes. While past results cannot be a perfect predictor, they flag important events and benchmarks.

PERIOD SPECIFIC The budget period must be of reasonable length. The shorter the period, the greater the need for detail and control mechanisms. The length of the budget period dictates the time limitations for introducing effective modifications. Although plans and projects differ in length and scope, a company formulates each of its budgets on a 12-month basis.

STANDARDIZED To facilitate the budget process, managers should use standardized forms, formulas, and research techniques. This increases the efficiency and consistency of the input and the quality of the planning. Computer-aided accounting, analyzing, and reporting not only furnish managers with comprehensive, current, ''real time'' results, but also afford them the flexibility to test new models, and to include relevant and high-powered charts and tables with relatively little effort.

INCLUSIVE Efficient companies decentralize the budget process down to the smallest logical level of responsibility. Those responsible for the results take part in the development of their budgets and learn how their activities are interrelated with the other segments of the company. Each has a hand in creating a budget and setting its goals. Participants from the various organizational segments meet to exchange ideas and objectives, to discover new ideas, and to minimize redundancies and counterproductive programs. In this way, those accountable buy into the process, cooperate more, work harder, and therefore have more potential for success.

SUCCESSIVELY REVIEWED Decentralization does not exclude the thorough review of budget proposals at successive management levels. Management review assures a proper fit within the overall "master budget."

FORMALLY ADOPTED AND DISSEMINATED Top management formally adopts the budgets and communicates their decisions to the responsible personnel. When top management has assembled the master budget and formally accepted it as the operating plan for the company, it distributes it in a timely manner.

FREQUENTLY EVALUATED Responsible parties use the master budget and their own department budgets for information and guidance. On a regular basis, according to a schedule and in a standardized manner, they compare actual results with their budgets. For an annual budget, managers usually report monthly, quarterly, and semi-annually. Since considerable detail is needed, the accountant plays a vital role in the reporting function. A company uses a well-designed budget program as an effective mechanism for forecasting realizable results over a specific period, planning and coordinating its various operations, and controlling the implementation of the budget plans.

FUNCTIONS AND BENEFITS OF BUDGETING

Budgeting has two primary functions: planning and control. The planning process expresses all the ideas and plans in quantifiable terms. Careful planning in the initial stages creates the framework for control, which a company initiates when it includes each department in the budgeting process, standardizes procedures, defines lines of responsibility, establishes performance criteria, and sets up timetables. The careful planning and control of a budget benefit a company in many ways, including:

ENHANCING MANAGERIAL PERSPECTIVE In recent years the pace and complexity of business have outpaced the ability to manage by "the seat of one's pants." On a day-to-day basis, most managers focus their attention on routine problems. However, in preparing the budget, managers are compelled to consider all aspects of a company's internal activities.

The act of making estimates about future economic conditions, and about the company's ability to respond to them, forces managers to synthesize the external economic environment with their internal goals and objectives.

FLAGGING POTENTIAL PROBLEMS Because the budget is a blueprint and road map, it alerts managers to variations from expectations which are a cause for concern. When a flag is raised, managers can revise their immediate plans to change a product mix, revamp an advertising campaign, or borrow money to cover cash shortfalls.

COORDINATING ACTIVITIES Preparation of a budget assumes the inclusion and coordination of the activities of the various segments within a business. The budgeting process demonstrates to managers the interconnectedness of their activities.

EVALUATING PERFORMANCE Budgets provide management with established criteria for quick and easy performance evaluations. Managers may increase activities in one area where results are well beyond exceptions. In other instances, managers may need to reorganize activities whose outcomes demonstrate a consistent pattern of inefficiency.

REFINING THE HISTORICAL VIEW The importance of clear and detailed historical data cannot be overstated. Yet the budgeting process cannot allow the historical perspective to become crystallized. Managers need to distill the lessons of the most current results and filter them through their historical perspective. The need for a flexible and relevant historical perspective warrants its vigilant revision and expansion as conditions and experience warrant.

CLASSIFICATIONS AND TYPES OF BUDGETS

The budgeting process is sequential in nature, i.e., each budget hinges on a previous budget, so that no budget can be constructed without the data from the preceding budget. Budgets may be broadly classified according to how a company makes and uses its money. Different budgets may be used for different applications. Some budgets deal with sources of income from sales, interest, dividend income, and other sources. Others detail the sources of expenditures such as labor, materials, interest payments, taxes, and insurance. Additional types of budgets are concerned with investing funds for capital expenditures such as plant and equipment; and some budgets predict the amounts of funds a company will have at the end of a period.

A company cannot use only one type of budget to accommodate all its operations. Therefore, it chooses from among the following budget types.

The *fixed budget*, often called a *static* budget, is not subject to change or alteration during the budget period. A company "fixes" budgets in at least two circumstances:

1) The cost of a budgeted activity shows little or no change when the volume of production fluctuates within an expected range of values. For example, a 10 percent increase in production has little or no impact on administrative expenses.

2) The volume of production remains steady or follows a tight, pre-set schedule during the budget period. A company may fix its production volume in response to an all inclusive contract; or, it may produce stock goods.

The *variable* or *flexible budget* is called a *dynamic* budget. It is an effective evaluative tool for a company that frequently experiences variations in sales volume which strongly affect the level of production. In these circumstances a company initially constructs a series of budgets for a range of production volumes which it can reasonably and profitably meet.

After careful analysis of each element of the production process, managers are able to determine overhead costs that will not change (fixed) within the anticipated range, overhead costs that will change (variable) as volume changes, and those overhead costs which vary to some extent, but not proportionately (semi-variable) within the predicted range.

The *combination budget* recognizes that most production activities combine both fixed and variable budgets within its master budget. For example, an increase in the volume of sales may have no impact on sales expenses while it will increase production costs.

The *continuous budget* adds a new period (month) to the budget as the current period comes to a close. Under the fiscal year approach, the budget year becomes shorter as the year progresses. However, the continuous method forces managers to review and assess the budget estimates for a never-ending 12-month cycle.

The *operating budget* gathers the projected results of the operating decisions made by a company to exploit available business opportunities. In the final analysis, the operating budget presents a projected (pro forma) income statement which displays how much money the company expects to make. This net income demonstrates the degree to which management is able to respond to the market in supplying the right product at an attractive price, with a profit to the company.

The operating budget consists of a number of parts which detail the company's plans on how to capture revenues, provide adequate supply, control costs, and organize the labor force. These parts are: sales budget, production budget, direct materials budget, direct labor budget, factory overhead budget, selling and administrative expense budget, and pro forma income statement.

The operating budget and the *financial budget* are the two main components of a company's *master budget*. The financial budget consists of the capital expenditure budget, the cash budget, and the budgeted balance sheet. Much of the information in the financial budget is drawn from the operating budget, and then all of the information is consolidated into the master budget.

PREPARATION OF THE MASTER BUDGET

The master budget aggregates all business activities into one comprehensive plan. It is not a single document, but the compilation of many interrelated budgets which together summarize an organization's business activities for the coming year. To achieve the maximum results, budgets must be tailor-made to fit the particular needs of a business. Standardization of the process facilitates comparison and aggregation even of mixed products and industries.

Preparation of the master budget is a sequential process which starts with the sales budget. The sales budget predicts the number of units a company expects to sell. From this information, a company determines how many units it must produce. Subsequently, it calculates how much it will spend to produce the required number of units. Finally, it aggregates the foregoing to estimate its profitability.

From the level of projected profits, the company decides whether to reinvest the funds in the business or to make alternative investments. The company summarizes the predicted results of its plans in a balance sheet which demonstrates how profits will have affected the company's assets (wealth).

THE SALES FORECAST AND BUDGET The sales organization has the primary responsibility of preparing the **sales forecast**. Since the sales forecast is the starting point in constructing the sales budget, the input and involvement of other managers is important. First, those responsible for directing the overall effort of budgeting and planning contribute leadership, coordination, and legitimacy to the resulting forecast. Second, in order to introduce new products or to repackage existing lines, the sales managers need to elicit the cooperation of the production and the design departments. Finally, the sales team must get the support of the top executives for their plan.

The sales forecast is prerequisite to devising the sales budget, on which a company can reasonably schedule production, and to budgeting revenues and variable costs. The sales budget, also called the revenue budget, is the preliminary step in preparing the master budget. After a company has estimated the range of sales it may experience, it calculates projected revenues by multiplying the number of units by their sales price.

The sales budget includes items such as: sales expressed in both the number of units and the dollars of revenue; adjustments to sales revenues for allowances made and goods returned; salaries and benefits of the sales force; delivery and setup costs; supplies and other expenses supporting sales; advertising costs; and the distribution of receipt of payments for goods sold. Included in the sales budget is a projection of the distribution of payments for goods sold. Management forecasts the timing of receipts based on a number of considerations: the ability of the sales force to encourage customers to pay on time; the impact of credit sales, which stretch the collection period; delays in payment due to deteriorating economic and market conditions; the ability of the company to make deliveries on time; and the quality of the service and technical staffs.

THE ENDING INVENTORY BUDGET The *ending inventory budget* presents the dollar value and the number of units a company wishes to have in inventory at the end of the period. From this budget, a company computes its cost of goods sold for the budgeted income statement. It also projects the dollar value of the ending materials and finished-goods inventory, which eventually will appear on the budgeted balance sheet. Since inventories comprise a major portion of current assets, the ending inventory budget is essential for the construction of the budgeted financial statement.

THE PRODUCTION BUDGET After it budgets sales, a company examines how many units it has on hand and how many it wants at year-end. From this it calculates the number of units needed to be produced during the upcoming period. The company adjusts the level of production to account for the difference between total projected sales and the number of units currently in inventory (the beginning inventory), in the process of being finished (work in process inventory), and finished goods on hand (the ending inventory). To calculate total production requirements, a company adds projected sales to ending inventory and subtracts the beginning inventory from that sum.

THE DIRECT-MATERIALS BUDGET With the estimated level of production in hand, the company constructs a direct-materials budget to determine the amount of additional materials needed to meet the projected production levels. A company displays this information in two tables. The first table presents the number of units to be purchased and the dollar cost for these purchases. The second table is a schedule of the expected cash distributions to suppliers of materials.

Purchases are contingent on the expected usage of materials and current inventory levels. The formula for the calculation for materials purchases is: Materials to Be Purchased for Production = Units of Materials to Be Used + Units Desired in Ending Inventory − Units of Material in Beginning Inventory. Purchase costs are simply calculated as: Materials Purchase Costs = Unit of Materials to Be Purchased × Unit Price.

A company uses the planning of a direct-materials budget to determine the adequacy of their storage space, to institute or refine Just-in-Time (JIT) inventory systems, to review the ability of vendors to supply materials in the quantities desired, and to schedule material purchases concomitant with the flow of funds into the company.

THE DIRECT-LABOR BUDGET Once a company has determined the number of units of production, it calculates the number of direct-labor hours needed in the direct labor budget. A company states this budget in the number of units and the total dollar costs. A company may sort and display labor-hours using parameters such as: the type of operation, the types of employees used, and the cost centers involved.

THE PRODUCTION OVERHEAD BUDGET A company generally includes all costs, other than materials and direct labor, in the production overhead budget. Because of the diverse and complex nature of business, production overhead contains numerous items. Some of the more common ones include:

1) Indirect materials—factory supplies which are used in the process but are not an integral part of the final product, such as parts for machines and safety devices for the workers; or materials which are an integral part of the final product but are difficult to assign to specific products, for example, adhesives, wire, and nails.

2) Indirect labor costs—supervisors' salaries and salaries of maintenance, medical, and security personnel.

3) Plant occupancy costs—rent or depreciation on buildings, insurance on buildings, property taxes on land and buildings, maintenance and repairs on buildings, and utilities.

4) Machinery and equipment costs—rent or depreciation on machinery, insurance and property taxes on machinery, and maintenance and repairs on machinery.

5) Cost of compliance with federal, state, and local regulations—meeting safety requirements, disposal of hazardous waste materials, and control over factory emissions (meeting class air standards).

BUDGET OF COST OF GOODS SOLD At this point the company has projected the number of units it expects to sell and has calculated all the costs associated with the production of those units. The company will sell some units from the preceding period's inventory, others will be goods previously in process, and the remainder will be produced. After deciding the most likely mix of units, the company constructs the budget of the cost of goods sold by multiplying the number of units by their production costs.

ADMINISTRATIVE EXPENSE BUDGET In the administrative expense budget the company presents how much it expects to spend in support of the production and sales efforts. The major expenses accounted for in the administrative budget are: officers' salaries; office salaries; employee benefits for administrative employees; payroll taxes for administrative employees; office supplies and other office expenses supporting administration; losses from uncollectible accounts; research and development costs; mortgage payments, bond interest, and property taxes; and consulting and professional services.

Generally, these expenses vary little or not at all for changes in the production volume which fall within the budgeted range. Therefore, the administrative budget is a fixed budget. However, there are some expenses which can be adjusted during the period in response to changing market conditions. A company may easily adjust some costs, such as consulting services, R&D, and advertising, because they are discretionary costs. Discretionary costs are partially or fully avoidable if their impact on sales and production is minimal. A company cannot avoid such costs as mortgage payments, bond interest, and property taxes if it wishes to stay in production into the next period. These committed costs are contractual obligations to third parties who have an interest in the company's success. Finally, a company has variable costs, which it adjusts in light of cash flow and sales demand. These costs include such items as supplies, utilities, and the purchase of office equipment.

BUDGETED INCOME STATEMENT A budgeted income statement combines all the preceding budgets to show expected revenues and expenses. To arrive at the net income for the period, the company includes estimates of sales returns and allowances, interest income, bond interest expense, the required provision for income taxes, and a number of nonoperating income and expenses, such as dividends received, interest earned, nonoperating property rental income, and other such items. Net income is a key figure in the profit plan for it reflects how a company commits the majority of its talent, time, and resources.

FINANCIAL BUDGET

The financial budget contains projections for cash and other balance sheet items—assets and liabilities. It also includes the capital expenditure budget. It presents a company's plans for financing its operating and capital investment activities. The capital expenditure budget relates to purchases of plant, property, or equipment with a useful life of more than one year. On the other hand, the cash budget, the budgeted balance sheet, and the budgeted statement of cash flows deal with activities expected to end within the 12-month budget period.

THE CAPITAL EXPENDITURES BUDGET A company engages in capital budgeting to identify, evaluate, plan, and finance major investment projects through which it converts cash (short-term assets) into long-term assets. A company uses these new assets, such as computers, robotics, and modern production facilities, to improve productivity, increase market share, and bolster profits. A company purchases these new assets as alternatives to holding cash because it believes that, over the long-term, these assets will increase the wealth of the business more rapidly than cash balances. Therefore, the capital expenditures budget is crucial to the overall budget process.

Capital budgeting seeks to make decisions in the present which determine, to a large degree, how successful a company will be in achieving its goals and objectives in the years ahead. Capital budgeting differs from the other financial budgets in that they require relatively large commitments of resources, extend beyond the 12-month planning horizon of the other financial budgets, involve greater operating risks, increase financial risk by adding long-term liabilities, and require clear policy decisions that are in full agreement with the company's goals. For the most part, a company makes its decisions about investments by the profits it can expect and by the amount of funds available for capital outlays. A company assesses each project according to its necessity and potential profitability using a variety of analytical methods.

THE CASH BUDGET In the cash budget a company estimates all expected cash flows for the budget period by stating the cash available at the beginning of the period, adding cash from sales and other earned income to arrive at the total cash available, and then subtracting the projected disbursements for payables, prepayments, interest and notes payable, income tax, etc.

The cash budget is an indication of the company's liquidity, or ability to meet its current obligations, and therefore is a very useful tool for effective management. Although profits drive liquidity, they do not necessarily have a high correlation. Often when profits increase, collectibles increase at a greater rate. As a result, liquidity may increase very little or not at all, making the financing of expansion difficult and the need for short-term credit necessary.

Managers optimize cash balances by having adequate cash to meet liquidity needs, and by investing the excess until needed. Since liquidity is of paramount importance, a company prepares and revises the cash budget with greater frequency than other budgets. For example, weekly cash budgets are common in an era of tight money, slow growth, or high interest rates.

THE BUDGETED BALANCE SHEET A company derives the budgeted balance sheet, often referred to as the budgeted statement of financial position, from changing the beginning account balances to reflect the operating, capital expenditure, and cash budgets. (Since a company prepares the budgeted balance sheet before the end of the current period, it uses an estimated beginning balance sheet.)

The budgeted balance sheet is a statement of the assets and liabilities the company expects to have at the end of the period. The budgeted balance sheet is more than a collection of residual balances resulting from the foregoing budget estimates. During the budgeting process, management ascertains the desirability of projected balances and account relationships. The outcomes of this level of review may require management to reconsider plans which seemed reasonable earlier in the process.

BUDGETED STATEMENT OF CASH FLOWS The final phase of the master plan is the budgeted statement of cash flows. This statement anticipates the timing of the flow of cash revenues into the business from all resources, and the outflow of cash in the form of payables, interest expense, tax liabilities, dividends, capital expenditures, and the like.

The statement of cash flows includes:

- The amount of cash the company will receive from all sources, including nonoperating items, creditors, and the sale of stocks and assets. The company includes only those credit sales for which it expects to receive at least partial payment.

- The amount of cash the company will pay out for all activities, including dividend payments, taxes, and bond interest expense.

- The amount of cash the company will net from its operating activities and investments.

The net amount is a clear measure of the ability of the business to generate funds in excess of cash outflows for the period. If anticipated cash is less than projected expenses, management may decide to increase credit lines or to revise its plans. Note that net cash flow is not the same as net income or profit. Net income and profit factor in depreciation and nonoperating gains and losses which are not cash generating items.

SUMMARY

Budgeting is the process of planning and controlling the utilization of assets in business activities. It is a formal, comprehensive process which covers every detail of sales, operations, and finance, thereby providing management with performance guidelines. Through budgeting, management determines the most profitable use of limited resources. Used wisely, the budgeting process increases management's ability to more efficiently and effectively deploy resources, and to introduce modifications to the plan in a timely manner.

FURTHER READING:

Ameiss, Albert P., and Nicholas A. Kargas. *Accountant's Desk Handbook*. Englewood Cliffs, NJ: Prentice-Hall, 1980.

Brock, Horace R., Charles E. Palmer, and Billie M. Cunningham. *Accounting Principles and Applications*. 5th ed. New York: McGraw-Hill, 1986.

Livingstone, John Leslie. *The Portable MBA in Finance and Accounting*. New York: Wiley, 1992.

Meigs, Robert F., and Walter B. Meigs. *Accounting: The Basis for Business Decisions*. 8th ed. New York: McGraw-Hill, 1990.

SEE ALSO: Business Planning

BUSINESS APPRAISERS

Appraisers are agents who establish the value of businesses, personal property, **intellectual property** (such as patents, **trademarks and copyrights**), and real estate through a process known as valuation or appraisal. The demand for valuation of business enterprises has increased in the last several years in many industry sectors for a variety of reasons, including the rise in corporate restructuring, rising incidences of litigation (such as divorce, in which value and possession of closely held businesses may be hotly contested), changing employee-compensation packages, continued purchases of existing businesses, and the proliferation of **employee stock ownership plans (ESOPs)**, which require annual appraisals of value. As David Burke noted in *Business Journal—Portland,* ''since an ESOP is tax deductible, valuation is one of the most important aspects of an ESOP company. It has to be valued properly to satisfy the IRS. If a stock were overvalued, the IRS would say the tax deduction is too large and would disallow part of it, and in some cases the agency might disallow the entire ESOP.'' Indeed, the dramatic surge in popularity of ESOP plans accounts for a significant portion of the increase in appraisal/valuation activity across the American business landscape.

PROBLEMS IN THE BUSINESS APPRAISAL INDUSTRY Many business owners and valuation experts contend that the business appraisal industry faces a number of significant problems as it enters the latter part of the 1990s, and that such difficulties inevitably have an impact on small and large businesses that solicit the services of its membership. Geoffrey Richards, writing in *National Real Estate Investor,* offered a bleak—and somewhat representative—assessment of the situation: ''Low certification standards have allowed a glut of inexperienced appraisers into the field, knocking the bottom out of the fee structure [for the industry] and leaving clients questioning the opinions they are buying. Changes made by federal regulatory agencies to improve the quality of work in the appraisal industry may have had the opposite affect, by flooding the industry with appraisers and reducing the amount of work available for them.''

Analysts further observed that while the ''glut'' in appraisers was first felt in the single-family housing real estate market, it triggered an inevitable spill into the commercial market. As a result, observers have reported instances in which inexperienced or otherwise less-than-ideal appraisers have pushed out qualified appraisers who become frustrated with dropping fee rates and rising operating costs.

FINDING A QUALIFIED APPRAISER But while the business appraisal industry is a troubled one in some respects, consultants hasten to add that many qualified appraisers do exist, and that they can be of valuable service to small business owners who take the trouble to investigate the merits of various appraisers. Keys to finding a good appraiser include the following:

- Network—As one tax and estate-planning attorney told *Inc.,* ''Ask around, and then ask around some more. Talk to people in your geographical area, even if their businesses aren't just like yours; talk to people with similar businesses, even if they're not in your geographical area. Appraisal is a fraternity, and once you know who's in the fraternity, who's respected, you'll know who to go to. And, very importantly, if the reason you're looking for a valuation has anything to do with taxes, or is likely to somewhere down the line, find out who's respected by the Internal Revenue Service— who do they use to do their valuation work?''

- Look for experience and education— Appraisers with significant experience and a

good educational background (MBA or CPA) are far preferable to those who are limited in either area. Moreover, some analysts believe that the appraisal industry is moving towards increased specialization (office buildings, hotels, professional practices, retail outlets, etc.); if possible, find an appraiser who is familiar with your business area.

- Recognize that valuations vary from client to client—Appraisals of business can vary significantly in terms of their cost, both in terms of time and money. Learn about standard fees imposed on business that most resemble yours in terms of size, health, and situation. ''The vicissitudes of most projects—the standard ESOP valuation being an exception—often make it impossible to charge on a flat-fee basis, or even give a responsible estimate of hourlies,'' warned Nell Margolis in *Inc.*

- Find a licensed appraiser—The relative ease with which people are able to secure certification in the appraisal business has drawn fire, but it does establish a ground floor of presumed competence.

FURTHER READING:

Burke, David. ''Business Valuation: New Complexities of Business Appraisal Field Keeping Portland-Based Company Alive.'' *Business Journal—Portland.* September 28, 1987.

Margolis, Nell. ''Something of Value.'' *Inc.* January 1986.

Richards, Geoffrey. ''Appraisers Feel New Regulations Have Diluted Quality of Work.'' *National Real Estate Investor.* June 1995.

Semanik, Michael K., and John H. Wade. *The Complete Guide to Selling a Business.* New York: Amacom, 1994.

Tuller, Lawrence W. *Getting Out: A Step-by-Step Guide to Selling a Business or Professional Practice.* Liberty Hall, 1990.

Yegge, Wilbur M. *A Basic Guide to Buying and Selling a Company.* New York: Wiley, 1996.

BUSINESS ASSOCIATIONS

Business associations are membership organizations engaged in promoting the business interests of their members. These associations typically perform activities that would be unduly costly or time-consuming for an individual company to perform by itself, including lobbying, information gathering, research, and setting industry standards. Association spokespeople contend that by combining their voices under one banner, companies are able to establish a strong and unified presence and effectively protect their shared interests. As U.S. Television Association president Roy Neel told *America's Network,* "national associations have enormous political credibility as representing an entire industry." Leading business associations in the United States in the 1990s included the U.S. Chamber of Commerce, the National Restaurant Association, the National Retail Federation, and the National Manufacturers Association, but there are tens of thousands more that operate at local, state, regional, and national levels all over America.

SMALL BUSINESSES AND ASSOCIATIONS Large firms have long been active participants in business associations, using the organization to advance their goals in a wide range of areas, from regulatory issues to research to industry image improvement. But smaller companies can benefit from association memberships as well, provided they find an organization that adequately reflects their priorities and needs, which may be dramatically different from those of big corporations. For example, a small business owner may value an association that provides education, peer contact, and networking opportunities more than one that is focusing its resources on eliminating an OSHA regulation that pertains primarily to large companies.

"All too often," wrote Robert Davis in *Black Enterprise,* "contact-hungry entrepreneurs and professionals join networking organizations before investigating them thoroughly. Does this sound familiar? You hastily join an organization, only to discover later that it's disorganized, poorly attended and moreover, doesn't meet your needs." Davis counsels small business owners to "avoid wasting your time, money, and energy on the wrong organizations" by following several steps. Davis recommends that before entrepreneurs and small business owners begin shopping around for an association, they should first compile a chart of specific business and personal goals, as well as a list of talents that they have that would be welcomed by an association. As Los Angeles-area businessman Paul R. Hammons told Davis, "If you can bring something to an organization to help build its membership, you could reap benefits in the long run by means of positive imaging and business promotion."

In addition, small business owners should undertake a serious information-gathering effort before committing to an association. People considering an association should first request a brochure or information packet on the group that adequately covers its background, philosophy, structure, services, and affiliations, then request a meeting with an association representative or attend an organization meeting or event to get more detailed information. Davis also recommends that business owners talk to current and former members of the association being considered, including both recommended members and those who do not enjoy that recognition. "Ask them about the level of commitment needed for worthwhile member-

ship. Also ask them to compare the benefits they have received from this organization with benefits received from other groups."

Association membership can be a positive development for a small business, but all associations are not created equal. In addition, some associations may simply be too much of a reach. "Joining a good organization can become a bad investment if you can't make the time to attend meetings or take an active role, or if the group's financial requirements are beyond your means," warned Davis. "Whether or not you decide to join the group(s) you investigate, you'll have a head start on expanding your network and developing relationships."

FURTHER READING:

Bovet, Susan Fry. "Leading Companies Turn to Trade Associations for Lobbying." *Public Relations Journal.* August-September 1994.

Bowers, Heidi. "Associations Advance America." *Association Management.* April 1990.

Davis, Robert. "Look Before You Leap." *Black Enterprise.* September 1992.

Eby, Deborah. "Who Needs Associations?" *America's Network.* December 1, 1995.

Jarratt, Jennifer, et al. "Focusing on the Future." *Association Management.* January 1995.

Stybel, Laurence J., and Maryanne Peabody. "Association Membership: A Strategic Perspective." *Compensation & Benefits Management.* Autumn 1995.

BUSINESS BROKERS

Business brokers act as intermediaries between buyers and sellers of a business. They may represent either party in the transaction, and do not take possession of goods or property, or deal on their own account. Brokers differ from dealers in that the latter transact on their own account and may have a vested interest in the transaction. Brokers fill the important marketing function of bringing buyers and sellers together and helping them negotiate mutually beneficial agreements. In addition, they facilitate transactions by providing expertise and advice.

Indeed, brokers supply numerous benefits to both buyers and sellers. For example, sellers benefit because they do not have to spend time and money searching for buyers. Qualified brokers have access to people that are in the market to purchase a company, and they know how to attract and screen potential buyers much more quickly than do typical business owners. The broker may also be able to help the seller place an accurate value on his enterprise, devise a strategy to transfer ownership over time, address necessary paperwork, and overcome legal hurdles related to taxes.

The buyer also benefits from the broker's access to business buying and selling channels. A buyer that goes to a broker may be able to find a business that suits his abilities, wants, and financial situation much more quickly than he would working independently. Moreover, good business brokers will not accept businesses that are overpriced, shady, or otherwise fatally flawed, thus saving buyers the legwork of finding this out for themselves (good brokerage firms turn down as many as half of the businesses that they are asked to sell). In addition to screening, the broker can help the buyer determine what he or she can afford and may be able to assist in arranging financing to purchase the business. And, as with sellers, business brokers can provide help with licenses, permits, and other paperwork. In addition, it is the broker's duty to ensure that the interests of the buyer (and the seller) are protected by any **contracts** or agreements relating to the sale.

All of these services can be of great value to business buyers and sellers, but perhaps none is as valuable as the broker's status as a buffer between the two sides. The skilled business broker will diplomatically field and address sensitive questions and concerns that, were they delivered directly between the buyer and seller, might damage or ruin the prospects for a transaction. Brokers that can address the concerns of one side without ruffling the feathers of the other are invaluable to the negotiating process.

For their services, brokers typically receive in compensation a percentage of the total value of the transaction. The fee may be paid by the buyer, seller, or both parties, depending on the nature of the transaction. Commissions vary widely, usually depending on the size of the transaction and the level of service provided by the broker.

THE BROKERAGE PROCESS

Although it is a broker's chief function, bringing buyer and seller together is often the easiest part of his/her job. Indeed, actually closing the transaction is often a complicated process, colored by a spectrum of factors that are unique to each situation. For instance, the seller of a business often views the enterprise as his or her ''baby,'' and subsequently place a value on it that may be greater than its actual worth. Similarly, a buyer may fail to appreciate the amount of work involved in building a business to a certain point. Other major factors that can complicate an agent's task include financing, which can become very complicated, and problems related to employees and/or clients of the business being sold.

As Susan Pravda and Gabor Garai observed in *Mergers and Acquisitions,* the process of securing an agreement typically is a multi-faceted one. Once a business broker brings an interested buyer and seller together, he or she often attempts to set a target for completion of the transaction. This is usually accomplished by means of a letter of intent in which the buyer and seller agree to move toward a deal. The importance of the letter of intent is that it serves as a framework around which to structure negotiations. The letter also reduces ambiguity and misunderstanding, and ensures that both parties are serious about pursuing the transaction. Finally, establishing a deadline through a letter of intent helps to keep the buyer and seller focused on the big issues, rather than on minor details that can drag the deal out for months on end or kill the sale.

After setting a target date, the broker's next task is to close the nearly inevitable price gap between what the seller wants and what the buyer is willing to pay. A wide range of considerations have to be taken into account here (value of inventory, value of accounts receivables, value of community goodwill, inclusion or exclusion of equipment in final purchase price, tax issues for both buyer and seller, etc.). Another possible obstacle to a sale that often crops up around this time is ''seller's remorse.'' Seller's remorse commonly occurs during the latter stages of negotiations, when the seller suddenly realizes that he is relinquishing control of the company that has been a cornerstone of his life (and often the life of his entire family) for many years. Seller's remorse can kill the deal if the broker fails to confront it early in the negotiations by assuaging the seller's particular fears or concerns.

After the framework for an agreement has been reached, the business brokering process moves on to due diligence, wherein various legal technicalities which could thwart an otherwise legal arrangement are identified and addressed. For example, the buyer might want to ensure that he or she was procuring the legal rights to all patents held by the firm. It is the broker's job to facilitate due diligence to protect parties on both sides of the deal.

In the final stage, the broker helps the buyer and seller iron out and sign a final contract. This stage is the one most likely to entail the use of attorneys on both sides, even for smaller transactions. The best way for the broker to reduce the chance that the deal will fail at this critical juncture is to try to address all questions and concerns in the letter of intent and due diligence stages. Despite his best efforts, one or both parties may employ brinkmanship tactics that threaten to scrap the entire deal, such as significantly raising the asking price or demanding that some new contingency be added to the agreement. At this point, the broker's expertise as mediator and peacemaker is key to ensuring that the transaction goes through.

BUSINESS BROKERS AND THE ENTREPRENEUR

Business brokers can be invaluable to both buyers and sellers of small businesses, but the quality of these agents can vary tremendously. Business brokerage firms have traditionally been a notoriously unregulated group, and while there have been some improvements in this regard in recent years, complaints about incompetence and/or questionable business practices are still fairly commonplace. Whether an entrepreneur is looking to start a business through a purchase or sell an existing business to start on a new idea, then, it is important for him or her to take steps to ensure that they secure the services of a skilled and qualified broker.

There are, of course, certain basic areas of information that any buyer or seller should secure when shopping for a business broker. "When you're looking for a broker to help you buy or sell a business, ask about the broker's level of experience and pursuit of continuing education," counseled *Nation's Business*. "When getting references, ask for the names of not only buyers and sellers but also attorneys, accountants, and commercial bankers." Another basic aspect of an agent's operation that should be checked is its exclusivity policy (some brokers will list businesses only if they can do so exclusively, a requirement that limits its visibility). But there are other steps that can be taken as well, as business executive Shannon P. Pratt told *Inc.* magazine. For example, a broker's record of sales as a proportion of total listings can provide significant insight into his or her abilities. Brokers who are unable to deliver sales on more than 50 percent of listings on the market for six months to a year should probably be avoided. "A broker who can document a successful track record of sales to listings is preferable to one that can't," said Pratt.

Other recommendations that Pratt gave to *Inc.* included the following:

- Determine how often the broker's listing price corresponds to the eventual sales price—"I'd be much more favorably inclined to work with a brokerage if its average selling price is withing at least 20 percent of the average listing price," remarked Pratt.

- Inquire about the broker's affiliation with highly regarded industry groups, like the International Business Brokers Association, which maintains rigid standards for its members.

- Inquire whether the broker specializes in specific geographic regions or industries—A broker who has primarily dealt with manufacturing firms may not be the best choice to help a business owner sell his or her restaurant.

- Look for tell-tale signs of unethical or incompetent behavior—Does the broker accept bogus listings (those that are listed at ridiculously inflated prices or owned by owners uncertain of their desire to sell)? Has the agent prematurely leaked private information about your company to potential buyers? Is the broker favorably adjusting a company's income statement to an excessive degree? Unfortunately, these signs often become apparent only after a buyer or seller has established a relationship with the agent. In such cases, business experts counsel entrepreneurs to sever all ties and move on to another broker or method of purchase/sale.

FURTHER READING:

Bianchi, Alessandra. "The American Dream Revisited: Why You Won't Sell Your Business," *Inc.* August 1992.

Coleman, Bob. *Guide to Business Start-Ups.* New York: Entrepreneur Magazine Group, 1993.

Garai, Gabor, and Susan Pravda. "The Critical Line Between Dealmakers and Deal Breakers," *Mergers and Acquisitions.* March/April 1994.

Maynard, Roberta. "Business Brokers." *Nation's Business.* July 1997.

Rosenbloom, Joe, III. "Brokers for Hire." *Inc.* March 1987.

SEE ALSO: Buying an Existing Business; Mergers and Acquisitions; Selling a Business

BUSINESS CYCLE

A business cycle is a sequence of economic activity in a nation's economy that is typically characterized by four phases—recession, recovery, growth, and decline—that repeat themselves over time. Economists note, however, that complete business cycles vary in length. The duration of business cycles can be anywhere from about two to twelve years, with most cycles averaging about six years in length. In addition, some business analysts have appropriated the business cycle model and terminology to study and explain fluctuations in business inventory and other individual elements of corporate operations. But the term "business cycle" is still primarily associated with larger (regional, national, or industrywide) business trends.

STAGES OF A BUSINESS CYCLE

RECESSION A recession—also sometimes referred to as a trough—is a period of reduced economic activity in which levels of buying, selling, production, and employment typically diminish. This is the most unwelcome stage of the business cycle for business owners and consumers alike. A particularly severe recession is known as a depression.

RECOVERY Also known as an upturn, the recovery stage of the business cycle is the point at which the economy "troughs" out and starts working its way up to better financial footing.

GROWTH Economic growth is in essence a period of sustained expansion. Hallmarks of this part of the business cycle include increased consumer confidence, which translates into higher levels of business activity. Because the economy tends to operate at or near full capacity during periods of prosperity, growth periods are also generally accompanied by inflationary pressures.

DECLINE Also referred to as a contraction or downturn, a decline basically marks the end of the period of growth in the business cycle. Declines are characterized by decreased levels of consumer purchases (especially of durable goods) and, subsequently, reduced production by businesses.

FACTORS THAT SHAPE BUSINESS CYCLES

For centuries, economists in both the United States and Europe regarded economic downturns as "diseases" that had to be treated; it followed, then, that economies characterized by growth and affluence were regarded as "healthy" economies. By the end of the 19th century, however, many economists had begun to recognize that economies were cyclical by their very nature, and studies increasingly turned to determining which factors were primarily responsible for shaping the direction and disposition of national, regional, and industry-specific economies. Today, economists, corporate executives, and business owners cite several factors as particularly important in shaping the complexion of business environments.

VOLATILITY OF INVESTMENT SPENDING Variations in investment spending is one of the important factors in business cycles. Investment spending is considered the most volatile component of the aggregate or total demand (it varies much more from year to year than the largest component of the aggregate demand, the consumption spending), and empirical studies by economists have revealed that the volatility of the investment component is an important factor in explaining business cycles in the United States. According to these studies, increases in investment spur a subsequent increase in aggregate demand, leading to economic expansion. Decreases in investment have the opposite effect. Indeed, economists can point to several points in American history in which the importance of investment spending was made quite evident. The Great Depression, for instance, was caused by a collapse in investment spending in the aftermath

of the stock market crash of 1929. Similarly, prosperity of the late 1950s was attributed to a capital goods boom.

There are several reasons for the volatility that can often be seen in investment spending. One generic reason is the pace at which investment accelerates in response to upward trends in sales. This linkage, which is called the acceleration principle by economists, can be briefly explained as follows. Suppose a firm is operating at full capacity. When sales of its goods increase, output will have to be increased by increasing plant capacity through further investment. As a result, changes in sales result in magnified percentage changes in investment expenditures. This accelerates the pace of economic expansion, which generates greater income in the economy, leading to further increases in sales. Thus, once the expansion starts, the pace of investment spending accelerates. In more concrete terms, the response of the investment spending is related to the *rate* at which sales are increasing. In general, if an increase in sales is expanding, investment spending rises, and if an increase in sales has peaked and is beginning to slow, investment spending falls. Thus, the pace of investment spending is influenced by changes in the rate of sales.

MOMENTUM Many economists cite a certain "follow-the-leader" mentality in consumer spending. In situations where consumer confidence is high and people adopt more free-spending habits, other customers are deemed to be more likely to increase their spending as well. Conversely, downturns in spending tend to be imitated as well.

TECHNOLOGICAL INNOVATIONS Technological innovations can have an acute impact on business cycles. Indeed, technological breakthroughs in communication, transportation, manufacturing, and other operational areas can have a ripple effect throughout an industry or an economy. Technological innovations may relate to production and use of a new product or production of an existing product using a new process. The video imaging and personal computer industries, for instance, have undergone immense technological innovations in recent years, and the latter industry in particular has had a pronounced impact on the business operations of countless organizations. However, technological innovations—and consequent increases in investment—take place at irregular intervals. Fluctuating investments, due to variations in the pace of technological innovations, lead to business fluctuations in the economy.

There are many reasons why the pace of technological innovations varies. Major innovations do not occur every day. Nor do they take place at a constant rate. Chance factors greatly influence the timing of major innovations, as well as the number of innovations in a particular year. Economists consider the variations in technological innovations as random (with no systematic pattern). Thus, irregularity in the pace of innovations in new products or processes becomes a source of business fluctuations.

VARIATIONS IN INVENTORIES Variations in inventories—expansion and contraction in the level of inventories of goods kept by businesses—also generate business cycles. Inventories are the stocks of goods firms keep on hand to meet demand for their products. How do variations in the level of inventories trigger changes in a business cycle? Usually, during a business downturn, firms let their inventories decline. As inventories are cut down considerably, businesses ultimately find themselves short of inventories. As a result, they start increasing inventory levels by producing output greater than sales, leading to an economic expansion. This expansion continues as long as the rate of increase in sales holds up and producers continue to increase inventories at the preceding rate. However, as the rate of increase in sales slows, firms begin to cut back on their **inventory** accumulation. The subsequent reduction in inventory investment dampens the economic expansion, and eventually causes an economic downturn. The process then repeats itself all over again. It should be noted that while variations in inventory levels produce business cycles, the resulting business cycles are not really long. The business cycles generated by fluctuations in inventories are called *minor* or *short* business cycles. These periods, which usually last about two to four years, are sometimes also called inventory cycles.

FLUCTUATIONS IN GOVERNMENT SPENDING Variations in government spending are yet another source of business fluctuations. This may appear to be an unlikely source, as the government is widely considered to be a stabilizing force in the economy rather than a source of economic fluctuations or instability. Nevertheless, government spending has been a major destabilizing force on several occasions, especially during and after wars. Government spending increased by an enormous amount during World War II, leading to an economic expansion that continued for several years after the war. Government spending also increased, though to a smaller extent compared to World War II, during the Korean and Vietnam wars. These also led to economic expansions. However, government spending not only contributes to economic expansions, but economic contractions as well. In fact, the recession of 1953-54 was caused by the reduction in government spending after the Korean War ended. More recently, the end of the Cold War resulted in a reduction in defense spending by the United States that had a pronounced impact on certain defense-dependent industries and geographic regions.

POLITICALLY GENERATED BUSINESS CYCLES Many economists have hypothesized that business cy-

cles are the result of the politically motivated use of macroeconomic policies (monetary and fiscal policies) that are designed to serve the interest of politicians running for re-election. The theory of political business cycles is predicated on the belief that elected officials (the president, members of congress, governors, etc.) have a tendency to engineer expansionary macroeconomic policies in order to aid their re-election efforts.

MONETARY POLICIES Variations in the nation's monetary policies, independent of changes induced by political pressures, are an important influence in business cycles as well. Use of fiscal policy—increased government spending and/or tax cuts—is the most common way of boosting aggregate demand, causing an economic expansion. Moreover, the decisions of the Federal Reserve, which controls interest rates, can have a dramatic impact on consumer and investor confidence as well.

FLUCTUATIONS IN EXPORTS AND IMPORTS The difference between exports and imports is the net foreign demand for goods and services, also called net exports. Because net exports are a component of the aggregate demand in the economy, variations in exports and imports can lead to business fluctuations as well. There are many reasons for variations in exports and imports over time. Growth in the gross domestic product of an economy is the most important determinant of its demand for imported goods—as people's incomes grow, their appetite for additional goods and services, including goods produced abroad, increases. The opposite holds when foreign economies are growing—growth in incomes in foreign countries also leads to an increased demand for imported goods by the residents of these countries. This, in turn, causes U.S. exports to grow. The United States economy is quite huge. The net foreign demand for the U.S. goods and services has been negative for some years. Because of the size of the U.S. economy, the net foreign demand is not considered a major source of business cycles. However, this is quite often a source of business cycles in export-dependent smaller economies. Currency exchange rates can also have a dramatic impact on international trade—and hence, domestic business cycles—as well.

KEYS TO SUCCESSFUL BUSINESS CYCLE MANAGEMENT

Small business owners can take several steps to help ensure that their establishments weather business cycles with a minimum of uncertainty and damage. "The concept of cycle management may be relatively new," wrote Matthew Gallagher in *Chemical Marketing Reporter,* "but it already has many adherents who agree that strategies that work at the bottom of a cycle need to be adopted as much as ones that work at the top of a cycle. While there will be no definitive formula for every company, the approaches generally stress a long-term view which focuses on a firm's key strengths and encourages it to plan with greater discretion at all times. Essentially, businesses are operating toward operating on a more even keel.''

Specific tips for managing business cycle downturns include the following:

- Flexibility—According to Gallagher, ''part of growth management is a flexible business plan that allows for development times that span the entire cycle and includes alternative recession-resistant funding structures.''

- Long-Term Planning—Consultants encourage small businesses to adopt a moderate stance in their long-range forecasting.

- Attention to Customers—This can be an especially important factor for businesses seeking to emerge from an economic downturn. ''Staying close to the customers is a tough discipline to maintain in good times, but it is especially crucial coming out of bad times,'' stated Arthur Daltas in *Industry Week*. ''Your customer is the best test of when your own upturn will arrive. Customers, especially industrial and commercial ones, can give you early indications of their interest in placing large orders in coming months.''

- Objectivity—Small business owners need to maintain a high level of objectivity when riding business cycles. Operational decisions based on hopes and desires rather than a sober examination of the facts can devastate a business, especially in economic down periods.

- Study—''Timing any action for an upturn is tricky, and the consequences of being early or late are serious,'' said Daltas. ''For example, expanding a sales force when the markets don't materialize not only places big demands on working capital, but also makes it hard to sustain the motivation of the salespeople. If the force is improved too late, the cost is decreased market share or decreased quality of the customer base. How does the company strike the right balance between being early or late? Listening to economists, politicians, and media to get a sense of what is happening is useful, but it is unwise to rely solely on their sources. The best route is to avoid trying to predict the upturn. Instead, listen to your customers and know your own response-time requirements.''

FURTHER READING:

Daltas, Arthur J. ''Manage Now for the Upturn.'' *Industry Week.* May 4, 1992.

Gallagher, Matthew. ''An Even Keel.'' *Chemical Marketing Reporter.* July 24, 1995.

Gordon, Robert J. *Macroeconomics.* 6th ed. New York: Harper-Collins, 1993.

Hartwig, Robert P. ''Riding the Economic Cycles: How Growth and Recession Affect Workers' Compensation.'' *Compensation and Benefits Review.* May/June 1997.

Mansfield, Edwin. *Principles of Macroeconomics.* 7th ed. New York: W.W. Norton, 1992.

Wilson, Robert A. ''Where Were You When the Cycle Died?'' *Pulp and Paper.* February 1997.

SEE ALSO: Government Procurement

BUSINESS EDUCATION

Business education is a term that encompasses a number of methods used to teach students the fundamentals of business practices. These methods range from formal educational degree programs, such as the Master of Business Administration (MBA), to school-to-work opportunity systems or cooperative education. Business education programs are designed to instill the basic theories of management and production. The main goals of business education programs are to teach the processes of decision making; the philosophy, theory, and psychology of management; practical applications; and business start-up and operational procedures.

TYPES OF BUSINESS EDUCATION PROGRAMS

Traditional academic business education programs include college courses that teach students the fundamentals of management, marketing, ethics, accounting, and other relevant topics. Students can earn degrees ranging from an Associate to a Ph.D (Doctor of Philosophy) in business administration. Some programs may consist of classwork only, while others—such as tech-prep and cooperative education programs, **internships**, and school-to-work opportunities—combine academics with on-the-job training.

A tech-prep program is a four-year planned sequence of study for a technical field which students begin in their junior year of high school. The program extends through either two years of college in occupational education, or a minimum two-year apprenticeship. Students who complete the program earn either certificates or Associate degrees. Nationally, there are over 800 partnerships between high schools and two-year postsecondary high schools that offer tech-prep programs.

Cooperative education (co-op) is a program which offers students a combination of college courses and work experience related to their majors. Co-op programs are available in a wide range of business disciplines, e.g., information systems, accounting, and sales. Participants enroll in a postsecondary educational program while employed in a related job. Most co-op participants are paid by their employers. The co-op program provides students with the work experience they need to obtain full-time employment after graduation. More than 1,000 postsecondary educational institutions and 50,000 employers participate in co-op programs throughout the United States.

Internships are related closely to co-op programs. The main difference, however, is that those who participate in internship programs are not paid, as internships are designed specifically to provide participants with work experience. Often, interns will complete the program separately from their academic setting, rather than combining the two.

School-to-work opportunity programs focus on career awareness for students. They provide participants with work mastery certificates and furnish them with links to technical colleges. In these programs, all participants have jobs, apprenticeships, or further schooling after finishing high school.

Career academies are occupationally focused high schools that contain "schools within schools." Primarily, they train high school juniors and seniors in such areas as environmental technology, applied electrical science, horticulture, and engineering. In addition to these schools, there are also privately operated business schools that grant certificates to students who complete their programs.

All of these types of business education programs provide participants with career paths for high-skill technical and professional occupations by formally linking secondary and postsecondary education, and by integrating academic and occupational learning. Students who complete such programs gain an advantage over people who concentrate solely on the academic part of business education. Whichever route students use to acquire a basic knowledge of business skills and principles, there exist ample opportunities to prepare them for business careers.

ENTREPRENEURS AND THE MBA

In the past, many entrepreneurs viewed the Master of Business Administration (MBA) degree as unnecessary to small business success, and some believed that it stifled the creativity that allowed small businesses to develop and grow. Most entrepreneurs counted on their energy, work experience, industry knowledge, and business connections rather than on their formal business education. But in recent years, increasing numbers of entrepreneurs have chosen to pursue an MBA degree. Jay Finegan, writing in *Inc.,* suggested two reasons for this change. First, today's business world often requires small companies to compete for the same customers as much larger, professionally managed corporations. Second, entrepreneurs are finding that even their smaller competitors are likely to be run by MBAs, as more downsized executives decide to start their own companies.

When they face the fact that their competitors' business training might offer them an advantage, many entrepreneurs choose to pursue an MBA in order to even the playing field. The MBA degree offers entrepreneurs a set of sophisticated management tools that can be brought to bear on the challenges of running a small business. According to Finegan, some of these tools include economic analysis, marketing savvy, strategic planning, and negotiating skills. In addition, a business education might help small business owners to broaden their viewpoints and see the "big picture" surrounding their business or industry. While attending school, some entrepreneurs might even be able to enlist the help of their classmates or professors with specific company problems.

Yet another reason for the increase in entrepreneurs pursuing MBA degrees is that most such programs have become more practical in recent years. In addition to teaching theory, MBA programs are increasingly emphasizing teamwork, hands-on experience, and cross-disciplinary thinking. This approach makes the MBA much more applicable to the entrepreneur's interests and experience.

FOCUS ON BUSINESS EDUCATION

There is a growing focus on business education programs in the United States. This new emphasis reflects the fact that the United States is one of the few industrialized nations without an organized, comprehensive system to help young people prepare for careers and enter the workforce. Due to the increasing demands of a highly competitive global economy, employers have had difficulty finding workers with the academic, analytical, and technical skills they require. In recognition of this fact, the United States government has attempted to promote business education across the educational spectrum.

In 1993, the federal government passed the School-to-Work Opportunities Act to establish a national framework for broadening the educational, career, and economic opportunities for youth through partnerships among businesses, schools, community-based organizations, and state and local governments.

In 1994, the government provided $100 million to fund the included programs. At least $90 million of the money was used for grants to states and local communities, including grants to partnerships in urban and rural high poverty areas. President Clinton requested $300 million for fiscal year 1995, at least 90 percent of which was earmarked for grants. The new emphasis on business education in the United States will place the nation's business owners in a stronger competitive position in the global economy, which will benefit the entire country in the long run.

FURTHER READING:

Finegan, Jay. "Too Cool for School: For Generations, Entrepreneurs Have Loathed Everything about the MBA. So Why Are So Many Now Going Back to Get One?" *Inc.* October 1996.

Lynton, Ernest A. *The Missing Connection Between Business and the Universities.* Macmillan, 1984.

Rion, Michael. *The Responsible Manager.* New York: Harper and Row, 1989.

Ryder, Kenneth G., and James W. Wilson. *Cooperative Education in a New Era.* San Francisco, CA: Jossey-Bass Publishers, 1987.

Sharp, Arthur G., and Elizabeth O. Sharp. *The Business-Education Partnership.* Morrisville, PA: International Information Associates, 1992.

SEE ALSO: Apprenticeship Programs; Training and Development

BUSINESS ETHICS

Most people involved in business—whether functioning as a small business owner, employee, or chief executive officer of a multinational company—eventually face ethical or moral dilemmas in the workplace. Such dilemmas are usually complex, for they force the person making the decision to weigh the benefits that various business decisions impart on individuals (including him or herself) and groups with the negative repercussions that those same decisions usually have on other individuals or groups. LaRue Hosmer, a business ethics expert who teaches at the University of Michigan, observed that reaching a "right" or "just" conclusion when faced with moral problems can be a bewildering and vexing proposition. But he contended that businesspeople are likely to reach and act on morally appropriate decisions if they do not lose sight of the fundamental issue of fairness. Those who get sidetracked by issues of profitability and legality, however, in gauging the morality of a business decision, often reach ethically skewed choices. As has been proven time and again in the business world, the legality of a course of action may be utterly irrelevant to its "rightness." In addition, any discussion of business ethics is a subjective one, for everyone brings different concepts of ethical behavior to the table. These moral standards are shaped by all sorts of things, from home environment to religious upbringing to cultural traditions.

In recent years, the issue of business ethics has garnered increased attention. Corporate research and watchdog groups such as the Ethics Resource Center and the Council on Economic Priorities point out that the number of corporations that engage in ethics training and initiate socially responsive programs has increased dramatically over the course of the past two decades, and that courses on business ethics have proliferated in America's business schools during that time as well. But observers have also noted that over that same period of time, the business world saw numerous instances of stock price pumping through corporate **downsizing**, punitive actions against "whistleblowers," and other practices that point to a still-prevalent emphasis on the bottom line over all other considerations.

COMPETITIVE PRESSURES ON ETHICAL PRINCIPLES

American society places a great emphasis on success, which in and of itself is not a bad thing. It is perfectly justifiable to want to make full use of one's talents and provide for oneself and one's family. People involved in the world of business, however, almost inevitably face situations in which advancement—whether in position, influence, or financial stature—can be gained, but only by hurting other individuals or groups. Small business owners are confronted with these choices even more often than other people of the business world because of the greater degree of autonomy in decision-making that they often enjoy. Moreover, the ethical decisions of small business owners are likely to impact far greater numbers of people than are the ethical decisions of that business owner's employees. Very often, an employee's ethical choices (to claim credit for the work done by another, to falsify number of hours worked, etc.) have an impact on a relatively small number of people, usually co-workers or his or her employer. The ethical choices of business owners, however—whether to use inferior materials in preparing goods for customers, whether to place employees in a poor HMO, whether to lay off a dozen workers because of personal financial needs, etc.—often have far more wide-ranging repercussions.

Indeed, the pressure to make morally compromised choices on behalf of the company you lead can be quite powerful, whether the enterprise is a lone clothing store or a regional chain of record stores. As Mary Scott observed in the *Utne Reader,* "companies that go public, are sold to outside investors, merge with other businesses, and feel the increased competition of businesses based less on values increasingly face an unnerving conflict between their social values and their bottom line.''

Some business analysts contend that American businesses—and their leaders—are more prone to ignore ethics as a part of a decisionmaking process than ever before. Even some ''good citizen'' efforts undertaken by businesses are dismissed as evidence of increased marketing savvy rather than demonstrations of true devotion to ethical business standards. Other critics of modern American business practices grant that good citizen efforts, while laudable, are all too often aberrations. As David Korten wrote in the May/June 1996 issue of *Business Ethics,* ''all this focus on measures like recycling, cleaning up emissions, contributing to local charities, or providing day care sounds noble, but it's little more than fiddling at the margins of a deeply dysfunctional system.'' Korten insists that the current widespread emphasis on maximizing financial returns to shareholders—an emphasis that starts with multinational companies but filters down to smaller enterprises as well—makes it ''all but impossible to manage for social responsibility.''

Some economists and ethicists even contend that such emphases on profitability are, in and of themselves, evidence of a set of ethical principles. Economist Milton Friedman criticized those who insisted that executives and business owners had a social responsibility beyond serving the interests or their stockholders or members, saying that such views showed ''a fundamental misconception of the character and nature of a free economy. In such an economy, there is one and only one social responsibility of business—to use its resources and engage in activities designed to increase its profits, so long as it stays within the rules of the game, which is to say, engages in open and free competition, without deception of fraud.'' Some observers even argue that this pursuit of financial gain ultimately serves the larger community, albeit unintentionally. Economist James McKie wrote that ''the primary goal and motivating force for business organizations is profit. The firm attempts to make as large a profit as it can. . . . Profits are kept to reasonable or appropriate levels by market competition, which leads the firm pursuing its own self-interest to an end that is not part of its conscious intention: enhancement of the public welfare.'' Others, of course, vigorously dispute such interpretations of capitalism and corporate duties as an outright abdication of responsibility for actions undertaken in pursuit of the best possible bottom line. Such philosophies, they argue, provide people with a veneer of ethical cover to engage in everything from ruthless downsizing to environmental degradation to misleading advertising.

ORGANIZATIONAL PRESSURES Organizational pressures can further complicate ethics issues, especially for employees of larger firms. The small busi-

ness owner can often do a great deal to shape the ethical environment in which his or her employees work (and the ethical rules under which the business itself operates), but the responsibility for imposing ethical standards in larger organizations often becomes more diffuse. But both large and small businesses sometimes impose operating systems that make it more tempting for workers to engage in acts that are questionable or wrong. As Hosmer pointed out, a business may employ an incentive system for its sales force that is so heavily commission-oriented that salespeople feel greater pressure to make bribes, or a corporate control system may be so fixated on cost controls that production managers find it impossible to fulfill orders without using inferior materials or cutting corners on workmanship. Indeed, Hosmer observed that perhaps the most powerful organizational pressure that can be placed on an employee is the pressure to do the ''wrong'' thing for the alleged good of the company. In such instances, the employee is presented with a choice between career and morality.

PERSONAL PRESSURES Of course, many people in business also find themselves at crossroads wherein the ethical road is clearly marked, but see at a glance that the other road looks far more inviting because of its promises of professional or financial advancement. ''It is not difficult to discern right from wrong, but grasping the difference is only a first step,'' wrote business executive William R. Holland in *Industry Week.* ''There must be the will, the inner discipline, the strength, and the character to do the right thing, regardless of the cost. Doing the wrong thing is to disregard the rights of others and inflict harm or grief on them.''

ESTABLISHING AND MAINTAINING ETHICAL STANDARDS OF BEHAVIOR IN A SMALL BUSINESS

Entrepreneurs and small business owners wield great influence in determining the ethical philosophies of their business enterprises. Employees often follow the lead of the owner in executing their duties and attending to their responsibilities, so it is incumbent on the owner to establish a work environment that embraces moral standards of behavior. There are exceptions to this, of course; dishonest and unethical employees sometimes work in otherwise ethical companies, just as honest and ethical workers can be found in organizations that routinely engage in duplicitous and selfish activities. But a business owner or manager who wishes to establish an ethical mind set in his or her company can help the cause by being proactive.

Business experts and ethicists alike point to a number of actions that owners and managers can take to help steer their company down the path of ethical operations. Establishing a statement of organizational values, for example, can provide employees—and the company as a whole—with a specific framework of expected behavior. Expressions of shared values can help unite people within a company. Indeed, they can provide employees, business associates, and the larger community alike with a consistent portrait of the company's operating principles—why it exists, what it believes, and how it intends to act to make sure that its activities dovetail with its professed beliefs. Active reviews of strategic plans and objectives can also be undertaken to make certain that they are not in conflict with the company's basic ethical standards. In addition, business owners and managers should review standard operating procedures and performance measurements within the company to ensure that they are not structured in a way that encourages unethical behavior. As Ben & Jerry's Ice Cream founders Ben Cohen and Jerry Greenfield stated, "a values-led business seeks to maximize its impact by integrating socially beneficial actions into as many of its day-to-day activities as possible. In order to do that, values must lead and be right up there in a company's mission statement, strategy and operating plan."

Finally, and most importantly, business owners and managers lead by example. If a business owner treats employees, customers, and competitors in a fair and honest manner—and suitably penalizes those who do not perform in a similar fashion—he or she is far more likely to have an ethical work force of which he or she can be proud. "It is perfectly possible to make a decent living without compromising the integrity of the company or the individual," wrote business executive William R. Holland. "Quite apart from the issue of rightness and wrongness, the fact is that ethical behavior in business serves the individual and the enterprise much better in the long run."

Indeed, some business owners and managers argue that ethical companies have an advantage over their competitors. Said Cohen and Greenfield, "consumers are used to buying products despite how they feel about the companies that sell them. But a values-led company earns the kind of customer loyalty most corporations only dream of—because it appeals to its customers on the basis of more than a product. . . . They like how doing business with [a values-led company] makes them feel."

For more information on ethical and socially responsible ways of doing business, contact the Social Ventures Network (1388 Sutter St., No. 1010, San Francisco, CA 94109), an organization devoted to helping entrepreneurs interested in ethics, or Business for Social Responsibility (1030 15 St. NW, Washington, DC 20005), a group that promotes ethical business practices.

FURTHER READING:

Boroughs, Don L. "The Bottom Line on Ethics." *U.S. News and World Report.* March 20, 1995.

Cohen, Ben, and Jerry Greenfield. *Ben & Jerry's Double Dip: Lead With Your Values and Make Money, Too.* New York: Simon and Schuster, 1997.

Holland, William R. "Ethics in a Plain Manilla Envelope: Simple Guidelines for Doing Business Honestly." *Industry Week.* March 18, 1996.

Lynn, Jacqueline. "A Matter of Principle." *Entrepreneur.* August 1995.

Reder, Alan. *In Pursuit of Principle and Profit: Business Success Through Social Responsibility.* G.P. Putnam's Sons, 1994.

Rokeach, Milton. *The Nature of Human Values.* New York: Free Press, 1973.

Roleff, Tamara, ed. *Business Ethics.* San Diego, CA: Greenhaven, 1996.

Scott, Mary. "Bottom-Line Blues: Is Ethical Business Only a Dream?" *Utne Reader.* January-February 1997.

"The Uncommon Good." *Economist.* August 19, 1995.

BUSINESS EXPANSION

All successful small business startups eventually face the issue of handling business expansion or growth. Business expansion is a stage of a company's life that is fraught with both opportunities and perils. On the one hand, business growth often carries with it a corresponding increase in financial fortunes for owners and employees alike, and expansion in and of itself is usually seen as a validation of the entrepreneur's initial business startup idea, and of his or her subsequent efforts to bring that vision to fruition. But as Andrew J. Sherman observed in *The Complete Guide to Running and Growing Your Business,* business expansion also presents the small business owner with myriad issues that have to be addressed: "Growth causes a variety of changes, all of which present different managerial, legal, and financial challenges. Growth means that new employees will be hired who will be looking to the top management of the company for leadership. Growth means that the company's management will become less and less centralized, and this may raise the levels of internal politics, protectionism, and dissension over what goals and projects the company should pursue. Growth means that **market share** will expand, calling for new strategies for dealing with larger competitors. Growth also means that additional **capital** will be required, creating new responsibilities to shareholders, investors, and institutional lenders. Thus, growth brings with it a variety of changes in the company's structure, needs, and objectives." Given these realities, Sherman stated that "the need of the organization to grow must be tempered by the need to understand that meaningful, long-term, profitable growth is a by-product of effective management and planning.''

METHODS OF GROWTH

Small businesses can expand their operations by pursuing any number of avenues. The most commonplace methods by which small companies increase their business are incremental in character, i.e., increasing product inventory or services rendered without making wholesale changes to facilities or other operational components. But usually, after some period of time, businesses that have the capacity and desire to grow will find that other options should be studied. Common routes of small business expansion include:

- Growth through acquisition of another existing business (almost always smaller in size)

- Offering franchise ownership to other entrepreneurs via a **franchising** strategy

- Licensing of **intellectual property** to third parties

- Establishment of business agreements with distributorships and/or dealerships

- Pursuing new marketing routes (such as catalogs)

- Joining industry cooperatives to achieve savings in certain common areas of operation, including advertising and purchasing

- Public stock offerings

- **Employee stock ownership plans**.

Of course, none of the above options should be pursued until the business's owners have laid the necessary groundwork. ''The growth process begins with an honest assessment of strengths and weaknesses,'' wrote Erick Koshner in *Human Resource Planning.* ''Given those skills, the organization then identifies the key markets or types of future market opportunities the company is likely to capture. This, of course, raises another set of issues about how to best develop the structures and processes that will further enhance the organization's core capabilities. Once these structures and processes are identified and the long range planning completed, the business has a view of where it will be in three to five years and agreement on key strategies for building future business.''

EXPANSION ISSUES

Whatever method a company chooses to utilize to expand—and whatever guiding strategy it chooses to employ—its owners will likely face a combination of potentially vexing issues as they try to grow their business in a smooth and productive manner. ''Ex-

panding a company doesn't just mean grappling with the same problems on a larger scale,'' wrote Sharon Nelton in *Nation's Business.* ''It means understanding, adjusting to, and managing a whole new set of challenges—in essence, a very different business. A growth spurt can produce a company that's much more complex—one that needs much more sophisticated management and an infrastructure that it probably never had.''

GROWING TOO FAST This is a common malady that strikes ambitious and talented entrepreneurs who have built themselves a thriving business. Success is wonderful, of course, but too heavy a dose of it can sometimes overwhelm the ill-prepared business owner. ''Companies growing at hyper-speed sometimes pay a steep price for their success,'' confirmed *Ingram's* contributor Bonar Menninger. ''According to management experts, controlling fast-track growth and the problems that come with it can be one of the most daunting tasks an entrepreneur will face.'' This problem most often strikes on the operational end of a business. Demand for a product will outpace production capacity, for example. In such instances, the business often finds that its physical needs have outgrown its present facilities but that its lease agreement or other unanticipated factors hinder its ability to address the problem. ''You may sign a five-year lease for a building, and 18 months later you're busting at the seams,'' one executive told Menninger. ''We had to move three times in five years. When we signed our latest lease, we signed a three-year deal. It's a little more expensive, but we can bail if we have to.'' In other cases, a business may undergo a period of feverish expansion into previously untapped markets, only to find that securing a meaningful share of that market brings them unacceptably low profit margins. Effective research and long range planning can do a lot to relieve the problems often associated with rapid business expansion.

RECORDKEEPING AND OTHER INFRASTRUCTURE NEEDS It is essential for small businesses that are undergoing expansion to establish or update systems for monitoring cash flow, tracking inventories and deliveries, managing finances, tracking human resources information, and myriad other aspects of the rapidly expanding business operation. As one business owner told *Nation's Business,* ''if you double the size of the company, the number of bills you have goes up by a factor of six.'' Many software programs currently available in the marketplace can help small businesses implement systems designed to address these **recordkeeping** requirements. In addition, growing enterprises often have to invest in more sophisticated **communication systems** in order to provide adequate support to various business operations.

EXPANSION CAPITAL Small businesses experiencing growth often require additional financing. Finding expansion capital can be a frustrating experience for the ill-prepared entrepreneur, but for those who plan ahead, it can be far less painful. "When financing your expansion efforts, heed the advice of entrepreneurs who came before you and plan ahead," counseled the *Entrepreneur Magazine Guide to Raising Money*. "Revise your business plan on a yearly basis (even more frequently if possible), and generate marketing plans to complement your business plan. These strategic planning tools not only help you define goals and objectives, they also provide you with the time frame upon which to build your financial projections. . . . [This knowledge] will also allow you to shop for a loan *before* you need it, instead of when you need it. By giving yourself the luxury to shop the type of financing available and the terms being offered, you will be able to arrange a better deal for yourself—and you won't have to take whatever is available."

PERSONNEL ISSUES Menninger noted that "according to experts, the most common kinds of problems facing fast-growing companies are people issues. Whether it's hiring the right person for a particular task, managing a diverse and growing collection of employees or keeping newcomers motivated, problems associated with personnel are often complex and many times overlooked in the mad scramble to stay ahead."

Growing companies will almost always have to hire new personnel to meet the demands associated with new production, new marketing campaigns, and new recordkeeping and administrative requirements. Careful hiring practices are always essential, but they are even more so when a business is engaged in a sensitive period of expansion. As one consultant told *Ingram's,* "too often, companies spend all their energy on marketing and production plans and ignore developing similar roadmaps for their personnel needs."

Business expansion also brings with it increased opportunities for staff members who were a part of the business in its early days. The entrepreneur who recognizes these opportunities and delegates responsibilities appropriately can go far toward satisfying the desires of employees who want to grow in both personal and professional capacities. But small business owners also need to recognize that business growth often triggers the departure of workers who are either unable or unwilling to adjust to the changing business environment. Indeed, some employees prefer the more relaxed, family-type atmosphere that is prevalent at many small business establishments to the more business-like environment that often accompanies periods of growth. Entrepreneurs who pursue a course of ambitious expansion may find that some of their most valuable and well-liked employees decide to instead take a different path with their lives. In addition, Nelton pointed out that "some employees

may not be able to grow with the company. You may have to let them go, despite their intense loyalty and the fact that they have been with the company since its inception. This will be painful."

CUSTOMER SERVICE Good **customer service** is often a significant factor in small business success, but ironically it is also one of the first things that tends to fall by the wayside when business growth takes on a hectic flavor. "When the workload increases tremendously, there's a feeling of being overwhelmed," one small business owner admitted to Menninger. "And sometimes you have a hard time getting back to clients in a timely fashion. So the very customer service that caused your growth in the first place becomes difficult to sustain."

DISAGREEMENTS AMONG OWNERSHIP On many occasions, ownership arrangements that functioned fairly effectively during the early stages of a company's life can become increasingly problematic as business issues become more complex and divergent philosophies emerge. For example, Sherman noted that in many growing enterprises that were founded by two or more people, "one or more of the cofounders are unable to keep pace with the level of sophistication or business acumen that the company now requires. Such a cofounder is no longer making a significant contribution to the business and in essence has become 'obsolete.' It's even harder when the obsolete partner is a close friend or family member: In this case, you need to ask: Will the obsolete cofounder's ego allow for a position of diminished responsibility? Can our overhead continue to keep him or her on staff?" More commonly, however, "the cofounders are all gradually moving in different strategic directions, with different visions and plans for the course the company should take and the markets it should enter," wrote Sherman. "At this point, communication is strained and difficult, since each partner has his or her own ideas about where the company should be heading." In such instances, it usually requires the departure of one or more partners to establish a unified direction for the growing company.

FAMILY ISSUES Embarking on a strategy of aggressive business expansion typically entails an extensive sacrifice of time—and often of money—on the part of the owner(s). But as Sherman noted, "many growing companies, especially those founded by younger entrepreneurs, are established at a time when all of the cofounders are either unmarried or in the early stages of a marriage. As the size of the company grows, so does the size of the cofounders' family. Cofounders with young children may feel pressure to spend more time at home, but their absence will significantly cut their ability to make a continuous, valuable contribution to the company's growth." Entrepreneurs pondering a strategy of business growth, then, need to decide whether they are willing to make the sacrifices that such initiatives often require.

METAMORPHOSIS OF COMPANY CULTURE As companies grow, entrepreneurs often find it increasingly difficult for them to keep the business grounded on the bedrock values that were instituted in its early days. Owners are ultimately the people that are most responsible for communicating those values to employees, but as staff increases, markets grow, and deadlines proliferate, that responsibility often falls by the wayside and one day, the business owner suddenly realizes that the prevailing culture at his or her company is far different than the one that he instituted—and enjoyed—just a few short years ago. Entrepreneurs need to make sure that they stay attentive to their obligations and role in shaping **corporate culture**.

CHANGING ROLE OF OWNER ''In the early years, from the time you start a business until it stabilizes, your role [as small business owner] is probably hands-on,'' said Nelton. ''You have few employees; you're doing lots of things yourself. But when a company experiences its first real surge of growth, it's time for your to change what you do. You need to become a CEO—that is, the leader, the strategic thinker, and the planner—and to delegate day-to-day operations to others.''

Moreover, as businesses grow in size they often encounter problems that increasingly require the experience and knowledge of outside people. Entrepreneurs guiding growing businesses have to be willing to solicit the expertise of accounting and legal experts where necessary, and they have to recognize their shortcomings in other areas that assume increased importance with business expansion.

CHOOSING NOT TO GROW

Finally, some small business owners choose not to expand their operations even though they have ample opportunity to do so. ''For many small business people, the greatest satisfactions in owning a business, which often include working closely with customers and employees, inevitably diminish as the business growths and the owner's role changes,'' indicated *Nation's Business* contributor Michael Barrier. ''Many entrepreneurs would rather limit growth than give up those satisfactions.'' Other successful small business owners, meanwhile, simply prefer to avoid the headaches that inevitably occur with increases in staff size, etc.

Entrepreneurs looking to limit the pace of their business's growth need to consider the ramifications of various expansion options. For example, a small business owner may decide that he or she needs an infusion of capital. But entrepreneurs who decide to secure that capital by making a public stock offering are in essence relinquishing any claim on pursuing a course of slow growth. After all, stockholders expect to see growth in the value of their stock, and that growth is predicated on upward trends in market share, sales revenue, and other factors. Robert Tomasko, author of *Go for Growth,* indicated that business owners should make certain that they and their staffs are poised to handle the pressure associated with pleasing stockholders. He pointed out that while stock offerings are an excellent way of underlining ambitious growth plans, they can put nightmarish pressure on small business owners who place greater emphasis on a relaxed business environment, improving current products or services, travel, and/or time with family.

Analysts rush to point out, however, that the entrepreneur who chooses to pursue a philosophy of limited or slow growth is not necessarily adopting a course of management in which he or she allows the business to slowly atrophy. ''Limiting growth doesn't mean refusing to change,'' said Barrier. ''In fact, the right changes can be crucial for profitability. A store's product mix may change radically over the years even if the store itself remains the same size.'' Indeed, almost all companies have introduced technological innovations, for example, into their internal operations, whether they are in the midst of tremendous growth or operating at the same basic size from year to year.

Finally, the methodologies that small business owners can employ to limit expansion vary from industry to industry. Management experts point out, for instance, that small service businesses (carpentry outfits, dressmakers, housepainters, swimming pool cleaning services, for example) can often restrict growth by simply turning down new business, provided that they have a sufficiently reliable stable of clients already in place. Other small businesses can limit growth by raising the prices on their goods and services. This method of reining in growth needs to be studied carefully before implementation, because the firm does not want to lose too much business. But analysts contend that for many niche industries, this option not only limits growth but increases profits on the company's existing workload.

Experts warn, however, that strategies of limited expansion are not practical in many of today's highly competitive industry sectors. As one executive in the high-technology industry pointed out to *Nation's Business,* fast-growing companies in high-tech typically obliterate companies that do not grow as quickly: ''They'll get big, their manufacturing costs will drop, they'll have three times as many R&D [research and development] people fighting against you.'' Other businesses that operate in industries in which a dominant company is eating up big chunks of marketshare likewise can not afford to pursue policies of limited growth. Quite the opposite, in fact; such small businesses often have to aggressively investigate possible new areas of expansion in order to survive.

FURTHER READING:

Barrier, Michael. ''Can You Stay Small Forever?'' *Nation's Business.* October 1996.

Chaneski, Wayne S. ''Discovering Those Business Growth Opportunities.'' *Modern Machine Shop.* June 1996.

Churchill, Neil. ''The Six Key Phases of Company Growth.'' *Financial Times.* January 20, 1997.

Dugas, Christine. ''. . . And Manage Your Money Carefully.'' *Working Woman.* May 1997.

Entrepreneur Magazine Guide to Raising Money. New York: John Wiley & Sons, 1998.

Henkoff, Ronald. ''Growing Your Company: Five Ways to Do It Right!'' *Fortune.* November 25, 1996.

Killian, William P. ''Importance of Corporate Growth: It's Not Just for Computer Firms.'' *Air Conditioning, Heating & Refrigeration News.* November 25, 1996.

Koshner, Erick L. ''A Market-Focused and Customer-Driven Approach to Growth.'' *Human Resource Planning.* June 1997.

Kotkin, Joel, and Leslie Brokaw. ''The Great American Revival: While the Pundits Debate How to Restore U.S. Industrial Competitiveness, Thousands of Small, Flexible, Market-Driven Manufacturers are Already Doing It.'' *Inc.* February 1988.

Krajanowski, David. ''Maturing Businesses Must Keep Their Focus on Profit.'' *Los Angeles Business Journal.* August 4, 1997.

Menninger, Bonar. ''Fast-Track Growth.'' *Ingram's.* July 1997.

Nelton, Sharon. ''Coming to Grips With Growth.'' *Nation's Business.* February 1998.

Sherman, Andrew J. *The Complete Guide to Running and Growing Your Business.* New York: Times Business, 1997.

Stolze, William J. *Start Up Financing: An Entrepreneur's Guide to Financing a New or Growing Business.* Franklin Lakes, NJ: Career Press, 1997.

Tomasko, Robert. *Go for Growth.* New York: John Wiley & Sons, 1996.

SEE ALSO: Buying an Existing Business; Career and Family; Employee Hiring; Entrepreneurship; Work Force

BUSINESS FAILURE AND DISSOLUTION

Business failure is defined as the closing of a business that results in financial loss for at least one of the business's creditors. An associated term, business dissolution, refers to the formal termination or closure of a business as well, but with dissolution, financial loss (for the business owners or for the business's creditors) is not necessarily a part of the equation.

All entrepreneurs who decide to establish their own business face the possibility of failure, and a good deal of ''popular wisdom'' holds that failure is not only possible but probable for the small business owner seeking to launch his or her own enterprise (it has long been said that four out of five new businesses fail within five years of their establishment, for instance). But current studies indicate that such gloomy forecasts often present a false picture of entrepreneurial realities. Indeed, many business experts that the majority of small business owners are actually successful with their ventures. ''Outright failures of small businesses are in fact remarkably rare,'' contended *Nation's Business,* ''if failure is defined, reasonably enough, as a business closing that results in losses to creditors because the firm files for bankruptcy or because it simply closes its doors without paying its debts. In 1988, for instance, 63,000 businesses of all sizes filed for bankruptcy, and an additional 57,000 failures were recorded. But these were mere drops in the bucket when measured against 20 million or more active businesses.'' Other studies, meanwhile, have found that more than 50 percent of small businesses remain in existence even after several years of operation.

DISTINGUISHING BETWEEN BUSINESS FAILURES AND BUSINESS DISSOLUTIONS

Business experts who study the gap between actual rates of business failure and the popular perception of those rates often blame it on a general misunderstanding of the nature of business dissolutions. ''The confusion comes in mixing up business failures with business dissolutions,'' *Nation's Business* flatly stated. ''Lots of small companies go out of business for reasons that probably shouldn't be called 'failure'—the owner may have gotten bored, for instance, may be disappointed with the returns, or may simply want to try a greener pasture. If an entrepreneur closes one business and starts another one that is more successful, that's more reason for celebration than concern.'' Bruce D. Phillips, a director with the Small Business Administration's office of economic research, even told *Nation's Business* that studies indicate that there may be four to eight times as many dissolutions as there are outright business failures.

REASONS FOR BUSINESS FAILURE

Nonetheless, thousands of small business ventures do fail every year in America. ''The looming prospect of business failure can announce itself in many ways,'' remarked Michael Barrier in *Nation's Business.* ''You let yourself get a little too dependent on one big customer, and it suddenly goes out of business. You never miss a payment to your bank, but for some reason it gets nervous and shuts down your revolving line of credit. You dominate a comfortable niche market for years, but then a big competitor starts shouldering its way in.'' These developments—as well as myriad others—can have a debilitating impact on an operation, as many small business surveys will attest. Chief reasons for business failure cited within such surveys include the following:

POOR PLANNING Ultimately, many small businesses fail because of fundamental shortcomings in their **business planning**. Planning begins with finding the right business and is integral to every aspect of business operations, including selecting a site, deciding on financing, anticipating work force needs, budgeting, and managing company growth. Planning that is grounded in realistic expectations and accurate, current information is an invaluable asset. Conversely, planning that is based on hopes and hearsay can cripple or destroy even a good business idea in fairly short order.

POORLY CONCEIVED OR UNDERCAPITALIZED GROWTH "Every business owner wants to grow his or her business, but expanding with no infrastructure in place makes a business ripe for failure," wrote Tonia Shakespeare in *Black Enterprise*. "You can incur tremendous losses when you expand outside your core market. Not only is the physical aspect of expansion costly but there are different buying habits in different geographical locations. If you venture into an area outside your home turf, you had better prepare by doing a lot of research."

CASH FLOW DIFFICULTIES Poor cash flow kills thousands of small businesses every year. "Most business owners don't realize how much money it takes to run a business," wrote Shakespeare. "Understand what it takes to get a revolving line of credit before you start your business. It's always easier to get money when you don't need it, so don't wait until you're desperate. Develop your business plan using conservative projections and don't be overly optimistic." Shakespeare warned that profitable, fast-growing businesses can also run into cash crunches that can ultimately lead to bankruptcy. "That's why ongoing cash-flow analysis—tracking the money coming in and going out of the business—is a must."

REFUSAL OR INABILITY TO REIN IN FLAWED BUSINESS STRATEGIES Some business owners simply refuse to admit when they are wrong. Many small businesses can recover from ill-conceived business initiatives if they are recognized and halted before too much damage is done. But all too often, business owners and managers stubbornly stick with strategies that are doomed to failure, rationalizing that the initiative will begin paying off next month or next quarter. And before they know it, their business is gone, dragged down by poor planning and inordinate pride. Writing in *Management Today,* Robert Heller characterized this tendency thusly: "Top management sets its sights on some grand but imperfectly conceived objective, launches an incompetent plan of action, pours in cash rather than control when the action misfires, and ignores all the adverse evidence until the disaster strikes."

DETERIORATION IN CUSTOMER BASE This can happen for any number of reasons, including poor service, high prices, and new competitors. "Pay heed to increased customer complaints and decreased customer traffic," counseled Shakespeare. "Management experts agree that the costs of keeping a customer is a lot cheaper than the cost of getting a new one." Making improvements in marketing, inventory, customer service, and work force personnel can all do a great deal to halt deterioration in customer relations.

INATTENTION TO WARNING SIGNS Most small business failures do not come out of the blue. Certainly, business failures that result from catastrophic natural disasters or the sudden death of a key business member can not be anticipated, but most businesses expire as a result of more mundane factors. Basic financial tools such as balance sheets and financial statements can be very helpful tools in helping business owners diagnose what is ailing their company. The numbers contained in those documents often provide ample warning of poor cash-flow management, inventory problems, excessive debt, undercapitalization, or untrustworthy customers, but the business owner has to take the time to look (or take the time to hire an accountant to look) or the warning signs may go unheeded until it is too late.

Other reasons often given for small business failures include the following:

- Inattentive and/or indecisive management
- Micromanagement
- Poor control of production costs
- Poor control of product or service quality
- Underpricing of goods or services sold
- Inadequate staff training
- Loss of key employees or business partners, either to extended absence or another company
- Deteriorating morale within the company
- Overreliance on one customer
- Inadequate financing
- Inadequate insurance
- Inadequate tax planning
- Failure to promote and maintain a good public image in the community and/or marketplace
- Poor control of inventory
- Poor relationships with suppliers/vendors
- Poor employees

- Inadequate or subpar professional assistance (accountants, attorneys, etc.)

- Competition

- Failure to anticipate marketplace trends and developments

- Poor budgeting decisions

- Extending too much credit

- Inattention to financial indications of company health

- Flawed or discarded business plan

- Excessive reliance on credit.

BANKRUPTCY

Bankruptcy is a legal proceeding, guided by federal law, designed to address situations wherein a debtor—either an individual or a business—has accumulated debts so great that the individual or business is unable to pay them off. It is designed to distribute those assets held by the debtor as equitably as possible among creditors. Bankruptcy proceedings may be initiated either by the debtor—a voluntary process—or by creditors—an involuntary process.

CHAPTER 7 BANKRUPTCY Individuals are allowed to file for bankruptcy under either Chapter 7 or Chapter 13 law. Under Chapter 7 bankruptcy law, all of the debtor's assets—including any unincorporated businesses that he or she owns—are totally liquidated, and the assets are divided by a bankruptcy court among the individual's creditors. Writing in *Getting Out: A Step-by-Step Guide to Selling a Business or Professional Practice,* Lawrence Tuller characterized Chapter 7 bankruptcy as essentially an admission that the business owner has given up hope of saving the company.

CHAPTER 13 BANKRUPTCY This is a less severe bankruptcy option for individuals. Under the laws of Chapter 13 bankruptcy, debtors turn over their finances to the court, which distributes funds and payment plans at its discretion.

CHAPTER 11 BANKRUPTCY Chapter 11 bankruptcy law is designed to provide businesses with the opportunity to restructure their finances and debt obligations so that they can continue to operate. Companies usually turn to Chapter 11 protection after they are no longer able to pay their creditors, but in some instances, businesses have been known to act proactively in anticipation of future liabilities.

RECOVERING FROM BUSINESS FAILURE

Business failure can be a demoralizing event in a person's life. But observers are quick to point out that people who experience business failure can still go on to lead rewarding professional lives, either as part of another company or—down the line—with another entrepreneurial venture.

In an interview with *Black Enterprise,* Stanford University business professor H. Irving Grousbeck recommended that business owners recovering from a business failure go to work for another small company for a while if possible: "Try to run the operation, and in two to three years start your business again. If you try to restart your business right away, you may have trouble attracting investors. Investors will logically ask what is different now from when you failed."

Most importantly, though, people who have suffered through business failure should take the time to honestly examine the reasons for the failure. Was your marketing plan flawed? Did you underestimate the amount of time it would take to become profitable? Did your manufacturing processes compromise product quality? Was your family fully committed to supporting the endeavor? Did you pay enough attention to work force training issues? Small business consultants strongly encourage entrepreneurs to seek out the opinion of others—industry experts, area businesspeople, loan officers, investors, family members, etc.—when taking on this task, for their perspectives can be invaluable in helping you to establish a successful business on your next attempt.

FURTHER READING:

Barrier, Michael. "Back From the Brink." *Nation's Business.* September 1995.

Bowles, Erskine. "Good News." *Entrepreneur.* February 1994.

Collins, James C., and Jerry I. Porras. *Built to Last: Successful Habits of Visionary Companies.* New York: HarperBusiness, 1994.

Cook, Robert J. "Famous Last Words: 24 Quick and Easy Ways to Kill Your Business." *Entrepreneur,* June 1994.

Delaney, Kevin J. *Strategic Bankruptcy: How Corporations and Creditors Use Chapter 11 to Their Advantage.* University of California Press, 1992.

Doran, Kenneth. *Personal Bankruptcy and Debt Adjustment.* New York: Random House, 1991.

Heller, Robert. "Managements That Lost Control." *Management Today.* October 1995.

"The Most Dangerous Game?" *Nation's Business.* September 1995.

Schuchman, Matthew L., and Jerry S. White. *The Art of the Turnaround: How to Rescue Your Troubled Business from Creditors, Predators, and Competitors.* Amacom, 1995.

Shakespeare, Tonia. "Warning Signs That Your Business is Failing." *Black Enterprise.* November 1996.

Tuller, Lawrence W. *Getting Out: A Step-by-Step Guide to Selling a Business or Professional Practice.* Liberty Hall, 1990.

SEE ALSO: Cash Flow Statements; Customer Retention; Strategy; Undercapitalization

The term "business hours" refers to the "open" and "closed" schedule that every business decides upon for its operations. Small and large businesses adhere to a wide range of business hours, depending on many factors, including target customer expectations and demands, technology, and seasonal fluctuations in business. One relatively recent development in this realm has been the dramatic growth of businesses that have expanded their hours of operation in recognition of America's so-called round the clock economy. "A growing number of small business owners . . . are recognizing that the traditional eight- or 10-hour workday and the five-day business week have become remnants of the past," explained Dale D. Buss in *Nation's Business*. "The marketplace has shifted into what some observers call '24-x-7'—a milieu in which early mornings, evenings, nights, and weekends are regarded as seamless phases of a new, never-ending business stretch. . . . The around-the-clock economy now influences nearly every type and size of business. It is providing a launching point for some trailblazing entrepreneurs, tempting opportunistic owners of existing companies, and forcing still other small business owners to adapt—or lose ground."

PRINCIPAL DETERMINANTS OF BUSINESS HOURS
Business owners and consultants point to several factors that are particularly important in determining what hours a business establishment will keep. Perhaps the single greatest consideration is the market or audience that the business is trying to reach. A nightclub that targets young, single professionals in search of after-work socializing opportunities, for example, is likely to maintain hours that are quite different than those established by a bakery that specializes in doughnuts, bagels, and other traditional breakfast fare. Similarly, companies that are primarily involved in providing goods or services to other firms will almost certainly establish hours that are most conducive to meeting those needs without inconveniencing their clients. "We have to align our work with the needs of our corporate customers," one executive confirmed in an interview with *Nation's Business*.

But there are many other factors at work as well, including the following:

- Non-traditional lifestyles—Increasing numbers of customers, and especially retail customers, keep non-traditional work hours themselves. Some work overtime, while others are employed on a part-time basis or work two or even three jobs to support their families. These potential customers will likely be lost to stores that do not keep extended hours. Moreover, some consumers simply prefer to shop late at night to avoid long checkout lines and hassles associated with busy aisle ways and parking lots.

- Seasonal considerations—Some businesses are highly seasonal in nature. Retail establishments based in regions that are highly dependent on tourist dollars, for example, often scale back their hours (or even close entirely) during the off-season.

- Technology—The emergence of e-mail, fax machines, cellular phones, and other trappings of the modern business world has accelerated the pace of the entire commercial environment in the U.S. and around the world, in part because they have made it so easy for people and businesses to communicate with one another, no matter the time of day.

- Competitive pressures—Analysts point out that simple economics have played a large part in the surge in expanded business hours for many companies. "The ceaseless search for efficiencies and the high cost of adding capacity are compelling many small companies to squeeze more out of existing facilities by adding second and third shifts," said Buss.

Members of the business community agree that for many companies, hours of operation are likely to continue to expand, as demands for convenience on the part of both individual and corporate customers do not appear likely to abate any time soon. But small business owners should make sure that they lay the appropriate groundwork for an expansion of operating hours before committing to it. Thorny issues will almost inevitably crop up, whether they take the form of logistical worries about restocking shelves in the presence of customers or difficulties in finding employees to work that fledgling second shift. But the business owner who takes the time to study these issues in advance will be much better equipped to handle them in an effective fashion than the owner who tackles each issue as it rears its head.

FURTHER READING:

Buss, Dale D. "A Wake-Up Call for Companies." *Nation's Business*. March 1998.

Flohr, Diane. "More on Business Hours." *Gifts & Decorative Accessories*. August 1991.

Fredericks, Alan. "Convenience Shopping." *Travel Weekly*. March 30, 1995.

Rubel, Chad. "Longer Closing Hours are Here to Stay." *Marketing News*. January 2, 1995.

Sebastian, Pamela. "Open 24-Hours? All-Night Business may be a Trend, but Some Suburbs Shudder." *Wall Street Journal.* September 25, 1997.

Weeks, Linton. "In U.S., Nighttime is the Right Time: 24-Hour Businesses are Making Odd Hours Ideal for Doing Errands." *Washington Post.* July 20, 1997.

SEE ALSO: Customer Service; Target Markets

BUSINESS INCUBATORS

Business incubators are business assistance programs that provide entrepreneurs with an inexpensive start-up environment and a range of administrative, consulting, and networking services. In essence these programs—which may be managed by economic development agencies, local governments, for-profit businesses, or colleges and universities—serve as "homes for new companies," wrote Richard Steffens in *Planning.* "They offer low-cost space, shared equipment, and the comradeship of fellow entrepreneurs. An incubator usually houses about a dozen tenants, who stay two to three years, then 'graduate' to commercial space. At their best, incubators help new firms create jobs and revive communities." Indeed, statistics indicate that incubator firms have a significantly greater chance of survival than do other start-up businesses.

DEVELOPMENT OF INCUBATORS

The incubator program is a relatively new concept. Although early incubator models were instituted in the Northeast in the late 1950s and early 1960s, programs similar to today's versions did not arrive on the scene until the 1970s and early 1980s. The 1990s saw a surge in incubator creation, and the level of success that many programs have enjoyed have further encouraged organizations to launch their own models. As Dinah Adkins, executive director of the National Business Incubation Association (NBIA), indicated to writer Tracey Rosenthal for *Business First of Buffalo,* the excitement over what incubators can do for small businesses has not diminished over the years, but has instead grown as more and more companies graduate from the programs into enduring self-sufficiency.

By the mid-1990s well over 500 incubators were operating around the United States, with many regions reporting that they expected continued growth through the rest of the decade. (The National Business Incubation Association estimated that U.S. incubators were opening at the rate of one per week). This trend has been traced to a wide variety of factors, including increased **entrepreneurship**, corporate **downsizing**, new technologies, increased involvement of educational institutions in technology transfer, and economic globalization. Of those incubators in existence in the mid-1990s, nearly 70 percent were maintained by economic development agencies (about 40 percent percent) or local government agencies (about 30 percent), who used the concept to boost regional economic growth or blunt the impact of big lay-offs and other bad economic news; the remainder were operated by universities and colleges or for-profit businesses. The incubator concept has been popular in a variety of geographic regions, from rural areas to urban settings. Indeed, urban-based incubators made up more than 60 percent of the total in the country in the mid-1990s, while suburbs accounted for only about 12 percent of the total number.

ADVANTAGES OF INCUBATORS

Given the myriad advantages associated with membership in an incubator program, small business consultants often counsel their clients to at least investigate the possibility of securing a spot in one. Strengths of incubators include the following:

SHARED BASIC OPERATING COSTS Tenants in a business incubator share a wide range of overhead costs, including utilities, office equipment, computer services, conference rooms, laboratories, and receptionist services. In addition, basic rent costs are usually below normal for the region in which the fledgling business is operating, which allows entrepreneurs to realize additional savings. It is worth noting, however, that incubators do not allow tenants to remain in the program forever; most lease agreements at incubator facilities run for three years, with some programs offering one or two one-year renewal options.

CONSULTING AND ADMINISTRATIVE ASSISTANCE Incubator managers and staff members can often provide insightful advice and/or information on a broad spectrum of business issues, from marketing to workplace issues to securing financing for business expansion. Small business owners should remember that the people that are responsible for overseeing the incubator program are usually quite knowledgeable about various aspects of the business world. They are a resource that should be fully utilized.

ACCESS TO CAPITAL Many business incubators can provide entrepreneurs with "access to the kind of early-stage capital that emerging companies desperately need," wrote *Entrepreneur*'s David R. Evanson. "According to a recent survey of [National Business Incubation Association] members, 83 percent of incubator owners and directors provide access to seed capital. Seventy-six percent provide assistance with obtaining federal grants, 74 percent assist with preparing financial proposals, 60 percent can help obtain royalty financing, and 57 percent can lend a hand in obtaining purchase-order financing.''

LEGITIMACY IN THE COMMUNITY Many entrepreneurs have stated that their start-up businesses receive an instant injection of legitimacy among both vendors and customers when they are accepted into a business incubator program. ''The fact that a business has been accepted into an incubator offers due diligence value to potential investors,'' Adkins told *Entrepreneur*. ''They have already passed an important litmus test by simply being there.'' Entrepreneurs agree with this assessment. ''In the early years, the incubator was absolutely critical,'' concurred one business owner in an interview with Rosenthal. ''Once you reach a certain point, you don't need that credibility. The value of it diminishes over time.''

UNIVERSALITY OF INCUBATOR CONCEPT One of the key advantages of incubators is that the concept works in all size communities, in both urban or rural areas, and in a substantial array of industries. As Richard Steffens observed in *Planning*, ''a particular strength of an incubator is its ability to aid companies that fulfill specific needs: technology transfer, revitalizing neighborhoods, creating minority jobs, among others.'' In many cases, the incubator naturally takes on some of the characteristics of the community in which it is located. For example, rural-based incubators may launch companies based on the agriculture present in the area. But whether based in a small town in the Midwest or a large urban area on the West Coast, proponents of incubator programs contend that the small business people in the community would know more about how to start and operate such businesses than major corporations that focus on mass production.

COMRADESHIP OF FELLOW ENTREPRENEURS Many small business owners that have launched successful ventures from incubators cite the presence of fellow entrepreneurs as a key element in their success. They note that by gathering entrepreneurs together under one roof, incubators create a dynamic wherein business owners can 1) provide encouragement to one another in their endeavors; 2) share information on business-related subjects; and 3) establish networks of communication that can serve them well for years to come. ''Incubators provide psychological support for entrepreneurs, who are far more likely to persist as a result,'' stated Steffens. ''This support is, perhaps, the incubator's unique place in economic development.''

FACTORS TO WEIGH IN CHOOSING AN INCUBATOR

Many incubators have been pivotal in nourishing small businesses to the point where they can make it on their own. But observers note that the programs are not fool-proof. Some small businesses fail despite their membership in such programs, and incubators themselves sometimes fold, crippled by any number of factors. ''According to many incubator managers, the most common causes of failure are lack of sustained funding, lack of tenants, and inexperienced management,'' wrote Steffens. ''A poorly run incubator or an underfinanced one will go under, as will any other small business.'' Entrepreneurs, then, need to recognize that some incubators are better suited to meet their needs than others. Considerations to weigh when choosing an incubator include the following:

- Is It a True Incubator?—Some office building owners falsely advertise themselves as incubators in order to lure tenants. Entrepreneurs need to study the details of each offer to determine whether such claims are legitimate.

- Length of Operation—''Incubators take time,'' said Steffens. ''To get funding, incubator promoters and managers tend to promise all things to all people. Then, if early results are not promising, the supporters often panic. One manager told me that creation of an incubator typically takes two years from concept to opening, then two more years from opening to full occupancy.''

- Incubator Leadership—Many analysts contend that entrepreneurs can learn a great deal about the fundamental quality of an incubator program simply by studying the program's leadership. Is the incubator managed by people with backgrounds in business, or by general college or agency administrators? Can the managers provide long-term business plans that show how they intend to guide the incubator to financial independence? As Steffens commented, ''It's up to the planner to make sure that the incubator is part of an overall development scheme, that there is space nearby for companies that outgrow the incubator, and that there are opportunities for interaction between the entrepreneurs, university faculty and students, and local professionals.''

- Location—Does the incubator's setting adequately address your fledgling company's needs in terms of target market, transportation, competition, and future growth plans?

- Financing—Is the incubator's financial base a reliable one, or is it on shaky ground?

LOCATING AN INCUBATOR

Entrepreneurs interested in exploring the incubator concept can request information from several sources, including the **U.S. Small Business Administration**, area economic development agencies, area educational institutions, or the National Business Incubation Association (One President St., Athens, Ohio 4570, 614-593-4331).

Would-be small business owners should have a complete **business plan** in hand before applying for entrance into an incubator program. Most incubators maintain a stringent screening process to ensure that their resources are put to the best possible use.

FURTHER READING:

Brandt, Ellen. "Incubators: A Safe Haven for New Business." *Journal of Property Management.* January-February 1991.

Doescher, William F. "Hatching Young Companies." *D & B Reports.* July-August 1988.

Evanson, David R. "Fertile Ground." *Entrepreneur.* August 1997.

Fry, Fred L. "The Role of Incubators in Small Business Planning." *American Journal of Small Business.* Summer 1987.

Rosenthal, Tracey. "Business Incubators Give Fledglings Warm Place to Grow." *Business First of Buffalo.* January 2, 1995.

Steffens, Richard. "What the Incubators Have Hatched: An Assessment of a Much-Used Economic Development Tool." *Planning.* May 1992.

BUSINESS INFORMATION

Business information encompasses a broad spectrum of sources that people involved in the world of commerce can turn to for data on and discussion of business-related subjects. These sources, which can range from daily newspapers and nationally distributed financial magazines to professional associates, colleagues, and social contacts, can be invaluable in helping small business owners to tackle various aspects of operations, such as marketing, product forecasting, and competitive analysis.

Writing in his book *Business Information: How to Find It, How to Use It,* Michael R. Lavin commented that business information is of tremendous value in two fundamental aspects of operations: problem solving and strategic planning: "Information can be used to evaluate the marketplace by surveying changing tastes and needs, monitoring buyers' intentions and attitudes, and assessing the characteristics of the market. Information is critical in keeping tabs on the competition by watching new product developments, shifts in market share, individual company performance, and overall industry trends. Intelligence helps managers anticipate legal and political changes, and monitor economic conditions in the United States and abroad. In short, intelligence can provide answers

to two key business questions: How am I doing? and Where am I headed?"

Business analysts cite two primary sources of business information: external information, in which documentation is made available to the public from a third party; and internal information, which consists of data created for the sole use of the company that produces it, such as personnel files, trade secrets, and minutes of board meetings.

EXTERNAL BUSINESS INFORMATION

External information comes in a variety of forms—from printed material to broadcast reports to online dissemination.

PRINT INFORMATION The category of print covers not only a vast array of books and periodicals, but also includes microfilm and microfiche, newsletters, and other subcategories. State and federal government reports also fit into this category; indeed, Lavin described the U.S. Government Printing Office as "the largest publisher in the free world; its products can be purchased by mail, telephone or through GPO bookstores in major cities."

Perhaps the most accessible documents in the print category are books and periodicals. Certainly business owners have a wide array of book titles to choose from, many of which find their way onto the shelves of public, business, and university libraries every year. In addition to books that provide general reference information on human resources management, start-up financing, product development, establishing a home-based business, and a plethora of other topics of interest to small business owners, the publishing industry has seen a surge of books that tackle more philosophical issues, such as balancing work and family life, establishing healthy personal interactions with co-workers and employees, the nature of entrepreneurialism, and many others.

Many other small business owners, meanwhile, get a considerable amount of their business information from print sources. As with books, entrepreneurs and established business owners (as well as corporate executives, human resource managers, and nearly every other category of person involved in business) can turn to a variety of periodical sources, each with their own target niche. Some magazines and newspapers, such as *Business Week* and *Wall Street Journal,* provide general interest coverage, while others (*Forbes, Fortune, Inc.*) provide more of an emphasis on subjects of interest to investors and executives in large firms. Still others—most notably *Entrepreneur, Small Business Start-Ups,* and *Nation's Business* (published by the U.S. Chamber of Commerce)—publish information specifically targeted at small business owners. These magazines can provide entrepreneurs with helpful information on every aspect of operations, from creating a good business plan to determining which computer system is most appropriate for your enterprise.

Then there are the trade journals, an enormous subsection of print aimed at a very select audience. These trade journals, which typically provide narrow coverage of specific industries (journals targeted at owners of bakeries, amusement parks, real estate businesses, grocery stores, and a variety of other businesses can all be found), often contain valuable industry-specific information. Another subcategory of the specialized print category is the material published through business research services and associations such as Commerce Clearing House, the Bureau of National Affairs, and Dun & Bradstreet.

Finally, both government agencies and educational institutions publish a wide variety of pamphlets, brochures, and newsletters on a range of issues of interest to small business owners and would-be entrepreneurs. While government brochures and reports have long been a favored source of business information—in some measure because many of these documents are available free of charge—consultants indicate that valuable studies and reports compiled by educational institutions are often underutilized by large and small companies alike.

TELEVISION AND RADIO MEDIA This source of business information is perhaps the least helpful of the various external sources available to small business owners. Programs devoted to general investment strategies and the changing fortunes of large companies can be found, of course, but the broad-based nature of broadcasting makes it difficult, if not impossible, to launch programs aimed at narrow niche audiences (like dental instrument manufacturers or accounting firms, for example).

ONLINE INFORMATION The phenomenon of online information is burgeoning as much as computers are themselves. ''The power of the computer to store, organize and disseminate vast amounts of information has truly revolutionized business publishing,'' noted Lavin. ''Large online systems can help overcome the incredible fragmentation of published information. Many online vendors offer global search capabilities, allowing access to the contents of dozens of databases simultaneously, the equivalent of reading dozens of different reference books at the same time.'' Many of these databases offer information that is pertinent to the activities of small business owners. As Ying Xu and Ken Ryan observed in *Business Forum,* the Internet includes data on demographics and markets, economics and business, finance and banking, international trade, foreign statistics, economic trends, investment information, and government regulations and laws. This information is provided by Internet

news groups, online versions of newspapers and magazines, and trade associations. In addition, ''many colleges, universities, libraries, research groups, and public bodies make information freely available to anyone with an Internet connection,'' stated Robert Fabian in *CMA—The Management Accounting Magazine.* ''Often, the motivation is to make information available to people within the institution. But it can be less costly to provide general access than to screen access.'' He also noted that ''increasingly, governments are publishing information on the Internet and insisting that organizations they fund also publish on the Internet. It's a practical way to move towards open government, and does make information, which is paid for by the taxpayers, far more accessible to those taxpayers (and any others with Internet access). The range of available information is impressive.''

CD-ROM INFORMATION CD-ROM (compact disc read only memory) is a popular alternative to online services. As the name implies, CD-ROM is not so much an interactive system; in usage it is close to traditional print. In fact, CD-ROM versions of such print staples as the *Oxford English Dictionary* are now commonly available. Business applications for CD-ROM include corporate directories such as Dun & Bradstreet's *Million Dollar Disk* and demographic statistics such as Slater Hall Information Products' *Population Statistics.* An advantages of CD-ROM over online services is the amount of data that can be stored. The primary drawback associated with business CD-ROM products is the absence of current information, although many publishers of CD-ROM products offer updates on an annual—or even more frequent—basis.

OTHER SOURCES OF BUSINESS INFORMATION

External sources of business information can be invaluable in helping a small business owner or entrepreneur determine appropriate courses of action and plan for the future. But researchers note that members of the business community often rely on personal contact for a great deal of their information. ''Common experience and the result of numerous research studies show quite clearly that managers, and indeed all seekers of information, frequently prefer personal and informal contacts and sources to published documents and formal sources generally,'' wrote David Kaye in *Management Decision.* ''The reasons are well understood. A knowledgeable friend or colleague will often provide, not only the facts requested, but also advice, encouragement, and moral support. He or she may be able to evaluate the information supplied, indicate the best choice where there are options, relate the information to the enquirer's needs and situation, and support the enquirer's action or decision. Many such personal contacts will of course be found within the manager's own organization, which is for many people the prime source of facts, knowledge, and expertise. . . . Any organization is a complex information processing system in which actions and decisions are underpinned by an array of oral and written instructions, reports, regulations, information, and advice. Accordingly, many managers seldom look beyond the organization's boundaries in their search for information.'' Business analysts note, however, that companies that do rely exclusively on internal information sources run the risk of 1) remaining uninformed about important trends in the larger industry—including new products/services and competitor moves—until it is too late to respond effectively; and 2) receiving skewed information from employees whose goals and opinions may not exactly coincide with the best interests of the business.

FURTHER READING:

Daniells, Lorna M. *Business Information Sources.* Berkeley: University of California Press, 1993.

Fabian, Robert. ''Business Information and the Internet,'' *CMA—The Management Accounting Magazine.* November 1994.

Kadlecek, James M. ''Information: The Resource of Enterprise.'' *Economic Development Review.* Winter 1995.

Kaye, David. *Information and Business: An Introduction.* London: Library Association, 1991.

Kaye, David. ''Sources of Information, Formal and Informal.'' *Management Decision.* September 1995.

Lavin, Michael. *Business Information: How to Find It, How to Use It.* 2nd ed. Phoenix, AZ: Oryx Press, 1992.

Ying Xu and Ken Ryan. ''Business Travelers on the Infobahn: Fee Vs. Free Access to Internet Business Resources.'' *Business Forum.* Summer-Fall 1995.

SEE ALSO: Business Literature; Business Press

BUSINESS INSURANCE

Business insurance is a **risk management** tool that enables businesses to transfer the risk of a loss to an insurance company. By paying a relatively small premium to the insurance company, the business can protect itself against the possibility of sustaining a much larger financial loss. All businesses need to insure against risks—such as fire, theft, natural disaster, legal liability, automobile accidents, and the death or disability of key employees—but it is especially important for small businesses. Oftentimes, the life savings of the small business owner are tied up in the company, so the owner must take steps to protect his or her family from the financial consequences of events that could disrupt operations, reduce profits, or even cause the business to go bankrupt.

Many large corporations employ a full-time risk management expert to identify and develop strategies to deal with the risks faced by the firm, but small business owners usually must take responsibility for risk management themselves. Though it is possible to avoid, reduce, or assume some risks, very few companies can afford to protect themselves fully without purchasing insurance. But according to *Nation's Business,* 50 percent of small businesses are either not adequately insured or not insured at all. ''Some of it's the entrepreneurial spirit—the last thing they think of is covering risk. Some of it's money—they can't afford the premium,'' noted Sean Mooney of the Insurance Information Institute. ''But if a disaster occurs, they're out of business.'' Insurance can help a small business be successful by reducing the uncertainties under which it operates. It places the economic burden of risk elsewhere so that managers can focus their attention on running the business. In addition, the premiums paid for many types of insurance are considered tax deductible business expenses.

COMMON TYPES OF LOSSES AND INSURANCE

The first step for small business owners thinking of purchasing insurance is to identify their company's main areas of exposure to risk. A risk analysis survey or questionnaire, available through many insurance companies and agents, can be a useful tool in this process. Next, the business owner can evaluate the probability of each risk and determine the potential severity of the loss associated with it. Armed with this information, the owner can decide which risks to insure against and the amount of coverage needed. According to the Small Business Administration, the most common types of risks encountered by small businesses involve: property losses; legal liability for property, products, or services; the injury, illness, disability, or death of key employees; and the interruption of business operations and income due to the occurrence of these other losses. Each category of loss can be managed with a corresponding type of insurance.

PROPERTY The types of property losses that can befall a small business include theft, physical damage, and loss of use. Losses from theft can result from the criminal activity of outsiders, as in the case of burglary, or from the illegal activities of employees, including fraud, embezzlement, and forgery. Physical damage can occur due to fire, severe weather, accidents, or vandalism. In analyzing the risk of physical property damage, it is important for the small business owner to consider the potential for damage to the contents of a building as well as to the structure itself. For example, a manufacturing company might lose expensive raw materials in a fire, a retail store might lose valuable inventory in a flood, and any type of business could lose important records to computer vandalism. Although loss of use of property usually results from another covered event, in some instances it can occur without actual physical damage to the property. For example, an office building may be closed for several days due to a gas leak, or a restaurant may be shut down by a health inspector for unsanitary practices.

In insuring against property losses, experts recommend that small business owners purchase a comprehensive policy that will cover them against all risks, rather than just the ones specifically mentioned in the policy. Comprehensive property insurance policies help small business owners avoid gaps in coverage and the expense of duplicating coverage, plus they usually allow for quicker settlements of claims. Still, additional insurance may be needed to adequately cover a specific calamity that is particularly likely in the business's geographic area—such as a hurricane in Florida or an earthquake in California. Experts also recommend that business owners purchase a policy that covers the full replacement cost of materials and equipment in order to protect themselves against inflation.

Small businesses may be able to improve their property insurance rates by implementing a variety of safety measures and programs. For example, installing locks, alarm systems, sprinkler systems, and smoke vents may help lower premiums. In addition, some companies can improve their rates by joining a highly protected risk (HPR) classification that is preferred by insurers. The HPR designation is based on stringent property protection programs and involves routine compliance checks.

LEGAL LIABILITY A small business's legal liability usually comes in two forms: general liability and **product liability**. General liability covers business-related injuries to employees, customers, or vendors, on the company premises or off, that occur due to the company's negligence. Product liability covers problems that occur due to defective merchandise or inadequately performed services. In both the manufacturing and retail sectors, a company is legally responsible for knowing if a product is defective. This responsibility lasts long after the product leaves the company's control, and the fact that a product met all known safety standards at the time it was sold has proven to be a poor defense. Even in the service sector, the service provider may be held liable under certain circumstances—for example, if a repair later causes an injury, or if a poorly prepared tax return leads to an IRS audit.

Whether the determination of the company's liability results from a court decision, a legal statute, or a violation of the terms of a contract, litigation can be time consuming and expensive. Basic liability insurance is available to protect small businesses against the costs associated with these and other sources of liability. A comprehensive general liability policy, which is recommended for nearly every sort of business, covers accidents and injuries that may occur on the company's premises, or off the premises when they involve a company employee. Such policies generally cover the medical expenses, attorney fees, and court fees associated with the liability. These policies do not, however, cover product liability or automobile accidents. A separate policy can cover product liability, though producers of some types of products—such as children's toys or food products—may find it difficult or expensive to obtain coverage.

WORKERS' COMPENSATION A special category of liability coverage pertains to **workers' compensation**. This type of insurance is mandatory in most states and provides medical and disability coverage for all job-related injuries to employees, whether they occur on company property or not. A few states provide workers' compensation through state-run funds, and companies simply pay a mandatory premium per employee, depending on their line of business. Other states allow private insurers to compete for companies' workers' compensation dollars. Another option available to some businesses is self-insurance, in which the company creates a special reserve fund to use in case a workers' compensation claim is filed against it. In effect, these companies assume the risk themselves rather than transferring it to an insurer. A company's workers' compensation rates depend on its line of business and accident record. The best way to reduce rates is to reduce the risk of employee injuries by improving safety standards.

COMPANY VEHICLE Company vehicles must be insured, just like vehicles that are intended for personal use. Automobile insurance is usually handled separately from other property and liability coverage. Experts recommend that business owners be sure to list all employees on the insurance policies for company vehicles. In order to determine needed coverage and obtain the most favorable rates, small businesses can consult an insurance watchdog agency.

KEY PERSON LOSS Small businesses tend to depend on a few key people, some of whom are likely to be owners or partners, to keep operations running smoothly. Even though it is unpleasant to think about the possibility of a key employee becoming disabled or dying, it is important to prepare so that the business may survive and the tax implications may be minimized. In the case of a partnership, the business is formally dissolved when one partner dies. In the case of a corporation, the death of a major stockholder can throw the business into disarray. In the absence of a specific agreement, the person's estate or heirs may choose to vote the shares or sell them. This uncertainty could undermine the company's management, impair its credit, cause the flight of customers, and damage employee morale.

Small businesses can protect themselves against the loss of a key person in a number of ways. One is to institute a buy-sell agreement, which gives the surviving partner or stockholders the right to purchase the deceased person's portion of the business. Another way a business can protect itself is by purchasing a key person insurance policy. This type of insurance can provide an ill or disabled person with a source of income, and can facilitate financial arrangements so that the business can continue operations in his or her absence. Partnership insurance basically involves each partner acting as beneficiary of a life insurance policy taken on the other partner. In this way, the surviving partner is protected against a financial loss when the business ends. Similarly, corporate plans can ensure the continuity of the business under the same management, and possibly fund a repurchase of stock, if a major stockholder dies.

LIFE AND HEALTH Some experts claim that—since the most valuable asset in many businesses is the employees—insuring employee welfare is a vital form of coverage. Group life and health insurance are common methods companies use to provide for employee welfare. This type of coverage falls under the category of **employee benefits**, along with disability and retirement income. It can help small businesses compete with larger ones to attract and retain qualified employees. **Life insurance** is generally inexpensive and is often packaged with health insurance for a small additional fee. Specialized plans are available to provide survivors with income upon an employee's death. Other plans can protect the firm against financial losses due to the death or disability of a key employee. It is important to note, however, that when the company is named as beneficiary of a life insurance policy taken on an employee, the cost is not tax deductible for the business.

In recent years, many health insurance providers have begun offering affordable plans for small businesses. In some states, businesses are required to provide health insurance if they employ more than five workers. The type of coverage a business needs depends upon its work force. For example, a company with a work force consisting primarily of married people with dependent children will need more comprehensive coverage than a company with a mostly unmarried, childless work force. Many insurance companies offer computer models that enable small businesses to determine the most economical insurance plan given the previous year's health care expenses. Another option that can reduce premiums is pooling insurance with other small businesses through trade associations or other organizations.

The two basic health insurance options are fee-for-service arrangements and managed care plans. In a fee-for-service arrangement, employees can go to the hospital or doctor of their choice. The plan reimburses costs at a set rate—for example, the insurance company might pay 80 percent and the company or employee might pay 20 percent—for all medically necessary services. This type of plan has declined in popularity during the 1990s in favor of managed care plans. These plans, the most common of which are run by **Health Maintenance Organizations (HMOs) and Preferred Provider Organizations (PPOs)**, require participants to use an approved network of doctors and hospitals. They pay the health care providers a predetermined price for each covered service. The employee may have a deductible and a small co-pay amount. It is important to note that a company that employs more than twenty people and provides group health insurance to its employees is obliged to offer an employee who leaves the company the option to continue that coverage for a certain period of time at his or her own expense under the terms of the Consolidated Omnibus Budget Reconciliation Act (COBRA).

BUSINESS INTERRUPTION Though property, liability, and other types of insurance can provide businesses with protection against specific risks, most policies do not cover the indirect costs associated with losses. When a small business suffers a loss, as in the case of property damage in a fire, it may be forced to shut down for some time or move to a temporary location. A typical property damage policy will cover the cost to repair or replace buildings and equipment, but it will not cover the loss of income the business is likely to experience during its downtime. The business thus may be forced to tap cash reserves in order to pay expenses that continue—such as taxes, salaries, loan payments, etc.—even when the company has no income. In addition, the company may face extra expenses in a crisis, such as employee overtime or rent on a temporary location. **Business interruption insurance** (also known as business income protection, profit protection, or out-of-business coverage) provides a company with the difference between its normal income and its income during a forced shutdown. The prior year's records or tax returns are usually used to determine the payment amount.

BUSINESS OPPORTUNITY PLANS A wide variety of specialized insurance packages that cover a custom combination of risks are available to small businesses. One popular option is a Business Opportunity Plan or BOP, which acts as a starting point for many small businesses that require insurance. A BOP provides basic property coverage for computers and other office equipment, plus liability protection for work-related accidents. In some cases, a BOP might also include business interruption coverage that will maintain the company's income stream for up to a year if a catastrophe disrupts business. Many BOPs also offer optional coverage against power failures and mechanical breakdowns, liability for workplace practices (including discrimination, sexual harassment, and compliance with the Americans with Disabilities Act), professional liability, and other risks.

Many people who work out of their homes assume that their homeowner's insurance will cover them against property and liability losses. But in reality, a typical homeowner's policy is not sufficient to cover business equipment and liability. In fact, most homeowner's insurance limits the amount paid for the loss of electronic equipment to $2,500, and it will not cover the business's liability if a client trips and falls on the property. Additional protection is required, although it may be possible to add a rider to the homeowner's policy for business equipment and liability.

PROFESSIONAL ASSISTANCE WITH INSURANCE NEEDS

A small business owner involved in risk management should 1) identify the risks faced by the company; 2) seek ways to reduce or eliminate the risks; 3) decide which risks the business can assume; 4) determine which risks should be transferred to an insurance company; and 5) shop around for the best insurance coverage for the money. Obtaining the assistance of a professional insurance agent with all of these steps is highly recommended. To gain the most benefit from a relationship with an insurance agent or broker, experts recommend that business owners write down their needs and expectations ahead of time, avoid withholding information, check the credentials of the agents and their firms, obtain competitive bids, and keep careful records of coverages and losses.

Insurance agents are usually work independently and may select among the offerings of a variety of different insurance companies. They may be able to offer expertise on the regulations that apply in the small business's home state and tailor a policy to meet the unique needs of a particular business. Many large insurance companies have also begun to focus on the needs of small businesses. These companies offer the advantage of being able to provide legal assistance with liability claims, rehabilitation programs for injured workers, and inspection of facilities for safety. Experts recommend that a small business owner select an insurance professional who offers experience working with small businesses, a knowledge of the particular industry, and an ability to provide needed coverage at a competitive price.

Other helpful hints for small business owners include covering the largest area of exposure first, then adding other coverage as the budget permits; selecting the largest affordable deductible in order to save money on premiums; and reviewing costs and coverages periodically or whenever the company's location or situation changes. Experts also warn small business owners against self-insurance. Although it may be tempting to simply keep some funds in reserve in case problems occur, the pool of funds needed to provide adequate coverage is extremely large—well beyond the capacity of most small businesses. In contrast, insurance premiums are relatively small, and their cost is often offset by a tax deduction.

FURTHER READING:

Anastasio, Susan. *Small Business Insurance and Risk Management Guide.* Washington: U.S. Small Business Administration, n.d.

Blakely, Stephen. "Finding Coverage for Small Offices." *Nation's Business.* June 1997.

Bury, Don. *The Buyer's Guide to Business Insurance.* Grants Pass, OR: Oasis Press, 1994.

Janecek, Lenore. *Health Insurance: A Guide for Artists, Consultants, Entrepreneurs, and Other Self-Employed.* New York: Allworth Press, 1993.

Lynn, Jacquelyn. "A Quick Guide to Insurance." *Entrepreneur.* June 1997.

McIntyre, William Stokes. *101 Ways to Cut Your Business Insurance Costs without Sacrificing Protection.* New York: McGraw-Hill, 1988.

Williams, C. Arthur Jr., and Richard M. Heins. *Risk Management and Insurance.* New York: McGraw-Hill, 1989.

SEE ALSO: Disability Insurance; Employment Practices Insurance; Health Insurance Options

BUSINESS INTERRUPTION INSURANCE

Business interruption insurance (also known as business income protection, profit protection, or out-of-business coverage) is a type of policy that provides a company with funds to make up the difference between its normal income and its income during a forced shutdown. Businesses can be forced to cease or limit operations due to an accident or injury that causes the disability of an owner or key employee, a legal liability claim, or a property loss—which might result from a fire, natural disaster, theft, or vandalism. Self-employed persons and small business owners are particularly vulnerable to the loss of income associated with forced shutdowns. Entrepreneurs often invest a great deal of personal funds in their businesses, and the businesses are often unable to continue operations without their involvement.

Though property, liability, disability, and other types of insurance can provide businesses with protection against specific risks, most policies do not cover the indirect costs associated with losses. When a small business suffers a loss, as in the case of property damage in a fire, it may be forced to shut down for some time or move to a temporary location. A typical property damage policy will cover the cost to repair or replace buildings and equipment, but it will not cover the loss of income the business is likely to experience during its downtime. The business thus may be forced to tap cash reserves in order to pay expenses that continue—such as taxes, salaries, loan payments, etc.—even when the company has no income. In addition, the company may face extra expenses in a crisis, such as employee **overtime** or rent on a temporary location.

Business interruption insurance steps in to fill the gaps in ordinary property or disability coverage. In most cases, this type of policy pays the business's ongoing expenses—such as rent, electricity, phone, heat, water, taxes, mortgage, and maintenance—plus compensates the owners or shareholders for lost revenues during a forced shutdown. Some policies also cover employees' salaries. In general, the benefits paid under a business interruption insurance policy are taxed as business income, but the policy premiums are tax deductible. The tax status depends on the type of policy and is subject to change, however, so small business owners should consult with their legal or accounting advisors to gain the maximum tax advantages.

Many business interruption policies tend to become a bit technical, particularly in determining the amount of the benefit paid for lost income. Since it can often be difficult to predict the future profitability of a firm—particularly a relatively small or new one—the payment may be based on the prior year's results. This information may come from the company's own records or from its tax returns. In either case, maintaining a second copy of important records in off-site storage can help facilitate claims. If a business operated at a loss during the previous year, then most policies only compensate the owner for fixed expenses. Business interruption coverage can be tailored to the needs of a specific business. For example, some policies feature special provisions that reimburse lost income until the company is able to resume normal operations, rather than when it is able to reopen in a makeshift fashion. Other provisions are available to cover businesses with seasonal income fluctuations.

Business interruption insurance can also provide a small business with income protection in the event an accident or injury causes the disability of an owner or key employee. This type of policy is usually combined with basic individual disability coverage. Basic disability benefits generally begin one month to one year after the onset of the disability, can last between two years and the remainder of the person's life, and pay between 60 and 70 percent of the individual's usual income during the period when he or she is unable to work. Though this type of policy is important to help an owner or key employee cover living expenses, additional benefits—in the form of a business interruption insurance policy—are often needed to keep the business running in his or her absence.

Variations of this type of disability policy are available to protect small business owners who lose revenues because of a partial disability, to pay the salary of a professional replacement hired to perform the duties of a sole proprietor during a total disability, and to provide funds for remaining partners to purchase the portion of a partnership held by a person with a permanent disability.

FURTHER READING:

Anastasio, Susan. *Small Business Insurance and Risk Management Guide.* U.S. Small Business Administration, n.d.

Blakely, Stephen. ''Finding Coverage for Small Offices.'' *Nation's Business.* June 1997.

Bury, Don. *The Buyer's Guide to Business Insurance.* Grants Pass, OR: Oasis Press, 1994.

Janecek, Lenore. *Health Insurance: A Guide for Artists, Consultants, Entrepreneurs, and Other Self-Employed.* New York: Allworth Press, 1993.

Lynn, Jacquelyn. ''A Quick Guide to Insurance.'' *Entrepreneur.* June 1997.

White, Jane, and Bruce Pyenson. *Employee Benefits for Small Business.* Upper Saddle River, NJ: Prentice-Hall, 1991.

SEE ALSO: Business Insurance; Disability Insurance; Risk Management

BUSINESS LITERATURE

The term ''business literature'' encompasses the broad range of written materials that companies use to market their goods and services. Examples of business literature, then, include publications as disparate as product catalogs, service brochures, and promotional newsletters. The content of such literature can differ dramatically, depending on the goals of the company distributing the material. Ultimately, however, business literature generally falls under the umbrella of the firm's marketing and public relations efforts.

Business literature that is intelligently shaped and effectively disseminated can be a valuable tool for companies, and this is especially true of small businesses, which often have fewer resources and thus need to make certain that every marketing initiative they do launch has a positive impact. Conversely, small business owners who fritter away valuable time, money, and other resources on uninspired—or downright poor—business literature creations may feel the negative repercussions even more acutely than larger companies. Business consultants, then, counsel entrepreneurs and other business owners to adhere to several fundamental guidelines when creating and distributing business literature. Herta A. Murphy and Herbert W. Hildebrandt, for example, noted in *Effective Business Communications* that effective business communication efforts require that businesses go through the following steps before creating their message:

- Know the purpose of the message
- Analyze the target audience
- Choose which ideas should be included
- Collect facts to support those ideas
- Organize the message.

NEWSLETTERS Along with service brochures and product catalogs, newsletters are among the most commonly used and effective means of disseminating information about a company. But unlike brochures and catalogs, which by their very nature are primarily concerned with delivering basic facts of content, price, etc., to potential clients and customers, the content of many newsletters is more amorphous. Some newsletters emphasize industry news and information, while others are basically extended advertisements. Many small business experts recommend a blending of the two. "When properly executed, a customer newsletter can become a vital element of the marketing mix," wrote Elaine Floyd in *Small Business Reports*. "It enables you to reach both existing and prospective customers, a crucial factor in maintaining your company's long-term viability. And it provides a cost-effective way to give customers the details they need to make purchasing decisions. Simply by providing this information, you can generate sales that more than pay for the cost of the project." Floyd pointed out that good newsletters can provide business owners with an avenue with which to send a uniform message that reinforces other marketing tools, like trade shows and brochures. But unlike those other marketing tools, "the newsletter is not a strictly promotional tool. It provides value to readers by blending marketing copy with the credible content of an editorial product."

According to some experts, some small business owners unnecessarily limit the effectiveness of their newsletters by shaping and disseminating it for too narrow an audience. Certainly, customers are vital to any company's success, and their information needs and interests should be a central factor in putting together any business newsletter. But as Floyd noted, the promotional power of the newsletter also depends on the strength of the mailing list, which "should include

nearly everyone with whom your company interacts—customers and prospects, suppliers, employees, the editors of all important industry publications, and any company from which you get referrals."

Of course, even a newsletter that is sensibly distributed will have little impact if its content is lackluster. As Floyd indicated, "even if you're convinced that a newsletter is a great marketing tool, you need to ensure that its content appeals to your target audience." One way to do so, she suggested, is to supplement information on the company's products, services, and business initiatives with current industry news, such as calendars of upcoming events and reprints or summaries of regulatory developments, management techniques, and industry trends. Other companies, meanwhile, have taken to including information on the firm's history in their newsletters. A company's story, wrote *Inc.* Contributor Edward O. Welles, "can be much more powerful than any marketing pitch. In a perilous economy, a story can serve as a competitive tool that defines a company's sense of self and its place. . . . Stories that reflect a recognition of the truth that drives a business can retain their vitality, even as the market evolves."

Another way to ensure newsletter effectiveness is make certain that appropriate personnel within the company have input into its content. Marketing managers and salespeople should be involved in determining content to ensure that the newsletter is coordinated with other marketing efforts, and good writers should be enlisted to polish the final product. If the company does not have talented writers on staff, it should investigate hiring a freelance editor or newsletter service to ensure quality. For as many consultants state, it is better for a small business to forego production of a newsletter than to produce one that makes it look bad.

FURTHER READING:

Floyd, Elaine. "The Printed Word." *Small Business Reports.* April 1992.

Murphy, Herta A., and Herbert W. Hildebrandt. *Effective Business Communications.* 6th ed. New York: McGraw-Hill, 1991.

Welles, Edward O. "Why Every Company Needs a Story." *Inc.* May 1996.

SEE ALSO: Business Information

BUSINESS NAME

A business name is any name, other than that of the owner, under which a company conducts business. One of the first decisions entrepreneurs must make when starting a new business involves coming up with an appropriate and marketable business name. Although some entrepreneurs simply conduct business under their own names, most opt to create a distinctive business name that provides a good fit with the aims of their companies. However, it is important to choose a name that will not be confused with that of another business and that will not infringe on another business's rights. The procedures that businesses use to register and protect their names depend to a large extent on the way they are organized.

Entrepreneurs organizing as a corporation, **limited liability company**, or limited **partnership** are creating a distinct entity when they form their businesses. The entity comes into existence through filing a charter with the state in which it will operate. At this point, the state checks to see if the name chosen for the new business will be ''confusingly similar'' to that of an entity already registered in the state. Even if the state gives the business clearance to use the name, that does not necessarily mean that no other business is using or can use it. A similar business may be using the name in another state, for example, or a sole proprietorship or partnership (which are not usually required to register their names with the state) may be using. To avoid this situation, entrepreneurs can check a variety of databases that include the names used by a wide range of entities. These databases appear in many business libraries, and most attorneys have access to them as well.

Although **sole proprietorships** and partnerships are not usually required to file charters with the state in which they operate, they are subject to certain rules if they plan to do business under any name besides the owner's. The procedures for registering a ''fictitious name'' for a sole proprietorship or partnership vary by state. In some cases, the small business owner simply fills out a form—known as a ''doing business as'' form or DBA—available at its city or county offices, has the form notarized, and pays a registration fee ranging from $10 to $100. In other cases, the small business owner is required to print a legal notice announcing the fictitious name in a local newspaper. Perhaps the easiest way for the owner of a sole proprietorship or partnership to determine the appropriate procedure is to call his or her bank and inquire whether it requires registration of the business name to open a commercial account. It is important to note that corporations, as distinct entities, do not have to file a DBA unless they plan to do business under a name other than the corporate name for some reason. The documents of incorporation and the charter filed with the state serve the same purpose as a DBA.

Businesses can protect their names in a number of different ways. One option involves filing the name, along with any associated logo or slogan, with the trademark (or servicemark in the case of a service business) registry of any state in which it will do business. Although the protection is limited—because

state registration can be preempted by federal registration—it does provide valuable evidence of prior use of the name in that state. Federal registration with the U.S. **Patent and Trademark Office** is the strongest protection available for a business name. Federal registration prevents any person or business from using the name in the future within a relevant class of goods. However, people or businesses who have established rights through prior use of the name are usually allowed to continue to use it. Federal protection for a business name is generally difficult to obtain. It will ordinarily be denied if the name is already in use or if it is deemed too generic—applying to a class of goods rather than a specific product. In most cases, however, small businesses can obtain a comfortable level of protection by registering their names according to the procedures set forth by their home state.

FURTHER READING:

Mandel, Richard P. ''Legal and Tax Issues.'' In *The Portable MBA in Entrepreneurship*. William D. Bygrave, ed. New York: Wiley, 1997.

The Entrepreneur Magazine Small Business Advisor. New York: Wiley, 1995.

BUSINESS PLAN

A company's business plan is one of its most important documents. It can be used by managers and executives for internal planning. It can be used as the basis for loan applications from banks and other lenders. It can be used to persuade investors that a company is a good investment. For start-up ventures, the process of preparing a business plan serves as a road map to the future by making entrepreneurs and business owners think through their strategies, evaluate their basic business concepts, recognize their business's limitations, and avoid a variety of mistakes.

Virtually every business needs a business plan. Lack of proper planning is one of the most often cited reasons for business failures. Business plans help companies identify their goals and objectives and provide them with tactics and strategies to reach those goals. They are not historical documents; rather, they embody a set of management decisions about necessary steps for the business to reach its objectives and perform in accordance with its capabilities.

SITUATIONS THAT REQUIRE A BUSINESS PLAN

Business plans have several major uses. These include internal planning and forecasting, obtaining funding for ongoing operations or expansion, planned

mergers and acquisitions, divestiture and spin-offs, and restructuring or reorganizing. While business plans have elements common to all uses, most business plans are tailored according to their specific use and intended audience.

When used for internal planning, business plans can provide a blueprint for the operation of an entire company. A company's performance and progress can be measured against planned goals involving sales, expenditures, time frame, and strategic direction. Business plans also help an entrepreneur or business manager identify and focus on potential problem areas, both inside and outside the company. Once potentially troublesome areas have been identified, proposed solutions and contingency plans can be incorporated into the business plan. Business plans also cover such areas as marketing opportunities and future financing requirements that require management attention. In some instances—such as scenarios in which an entrepreneur decides to turn a favorite hobby into a home-based business enterprise—the business plan can be a simple document of one or two pages. A business proposal of significant complexity and financial importance, however, should include a far more comprehensive plan. A tool and die manufacturer looking for investors to expand production capacity, for example, will in all likelihood need to compose a business plan of greater depth and detail than will a computer enthusiast who decides to launch a desktop publishing business out of his/her home.

Ideally, everyone in the company will use the information contained in the company's business plan, whether to set performance targets, guide decision-making with regard to ongoing operations, or assess personnel performance in terms of the their ability to meet objectives set forth in the business plan. In addition, workers who are informed about the business plan can evaluate and adjust their own performance in terms of company objectives and expectations.

Business plans can also be used in the restructuring or reorganization of a business. In such cases, business plans describe actions that need to be taken in order to restore profitability or reach other goals. Necessary operational changes are identified in the plan, along with corresponding reductions in expenses. Desired performance and operational objectives are delineated, often with corresponding changes in production equipment, work force, and certain products and/or services.

Banks and other lenders use business plans to evaluate a company's ability to handle more debt and, in some cases, equity financing. The business plan documents the company's cash flow requirements and provides a detailed description of its assets, capitalization, and projected financial performance. It provides potential lenders and investors with verifiable facts about a company's performance so that risks can be accurately identified and evaluated.

Finally, the business plan is the primary source of information for potential purchasers of a company or one of its divisions or product lines. As with outside lenders and investors, business plans prepared for potential buyers provide them with verifiable facts and projections about the company's performance. The business plan must communicate the basic business premise or concept of the company, present its strengths as well as weaknesses, and provide indications of the company's long-term viability. When a company is attempting to sell off a division or product line, the business plan defines the new business entity.

PREPARING THE BUSINESS PLAN

The process of preparing and developing a business plan is an interactive one that involves every functional area of a company. Successful business plans are usually the result of team effort, in which all employees provide input based on their special areas of expertise and technical skill. Business owners and managers provide overall support for the planning process as well as general guidelines and feedback on the plan as it is being developed.

Some companies make the planning process an ongoing one. In other cases, such as for a business acquisition, it may be necessary to prepare a business plan on short notice. The process can be expedited by determining what information is needed from each area of a company. Participants can then meet to complete only those plan components that are needed immediately. During the planning process, it is usually desirable to encourage teamwork, especially across functional lines. When people work together to collect and analyze data, they are far more likely to be able to arrive at objectives that are consistent with one another.

A few basic steps can be identified in the planning process. The first step is to organize the process by identifying who will be involved, determining the basic scope of the plan, and establishing a time frame within which the plan is to be completed. Company leaders not only communicate their support for the planning process, they also define the responsibilities of each party involved. Work plans that supplement the general timetable are helpful in meeting deadlines associated with the planning process.

Once the planning process has been fully organized, participants can begin the process of assessment. Internal evaluations include identification of strengths and weaknesses of all areas of the business. In addition, it is generally useful to assess and evaluate such external factors as the general economy, competition, relevant technologies, trends, and other circumstances outside the control of the company that can affect its performance or fundamental health.

Setting goals and defining strategies are the next key steps in the planning process. Using the assessment and evaluation of internal and external factors, fundamental goals for the business are developed. Pertinent areas to be studied include the company's competitive philosophy, its market focus, and its customer service philosophy. Specific performance and operational strategies are then established, based on these goals.

After strategies and goals have been defined, they are translated into specific plans and programs. These plans and programs determine how a company's resources will be managed in order to implement its strategies and achieve its goals. Specific areas that require their own plans and programs include the overall organization of the company, sales and marketing, products and production, and finance. Finally, these specific plans are assembled into the completed business plan.

ELEMENTS OF A BUSINESS PLAN

Business plans must include authoritative, factual data, usually obtained from a wide range of sources. The plans must be written in a consistent and realistic manner. Contradictions or inconsistencies within a business plan create doubts in the minds of its readers. Problems and risks associated with the business should be described rather than avoided, then used as the basis for presenting thoughtful solutions and contingency plans. Business plans can be tailored to the needs and interests of specific audiences by emphasizing or presenting differently certain categories of information in different versions of the plan.

Business plans contain a number of specific elements as well as certain general characteristics. These include a general description of the company and its products or services, an executive summary, management and organizational charts, sales and marketing plans, financial plans, and production plans. They describe the general direction of a company in terms of its underlying philosophy, goals, and objectives. Business plans explain specific steps and actions that will be taken as well as their rationale. That is, they not only tell how a company will achieve its strategic objectives, they also tell why specific decisions have been made. Anticipated problems and the company's response to them are usually included. In effect, business plans are a set of management decisions about how the company will proceed along a specified course of action, with justifications for those decisions. Listed below are brief descriptions of the major elements found in business plans.

EXECUTIVE SUMMARY This is usually a two- to five-page summary of the entire business plan. It is an important part of the plan, in that it is designed to capture the reader's attention and create an interest in the company. It usually includes the company's mission statement and summarizes its competitive advantages, sales and profit projections, financial requirements, plans to repay lenders or investors, and the amount of financing requested.

DESCRIPTION OF BUSINESS The business description includes not only a profile of the company, but also a picture of the industry in which the company operates. Every business operates within a specific context that affects its growth potential. The description of a company's operating environment may cover new products and developments in the industry, trends and outlook for the industry, and overall economic trends.

The intent of the company profile, meanwhile, is to provide readers with a description of unique features that give the company an edge in the environment in which it competes. A brief company history reveals how specific products and services were developed, while descriptions of pertinent contracts and agreements should also be mentioned (information on contracts and legal agreements may also be included in an appendix to the business plan). Other topics covered include operational procedures and research and development.

DESCRIPTION OF PRODUCTS AND/OR SERVICES The goal of this section is to differentiate a company's products or services from those of the competition. It describes specific customer needs that are uniquely met by the firm's products or services. Product features are translated into customer benefits. Product life cycles and their effects on sales and marketing can be described. The company's plans for a new generation of products or services may also be included in this section.

DESCRIPTION OF MANAGEMENT AND ORGANIZATIONAL STRUCTURE The quality of a company's management team can be the most important aspect of a business plan. This section presents the strengths of the company's management team by highlighting relevant experience, achievements, and past performance. Key areas include management's ability to provide planning, organizational skills, and leadership. This section also contains information about the company's ownership and work force. It may present an existing or planned organizational structure that will accomplish the goals set forth in the business plan. Specific management and control systems are often described as well.

MARKET ANALYSIS A thorough **market analysis** serves as the basis for a company's sales and marketing plans. The analysis generally covers the company's competition, customers, products, and market acceptance. The **competitive analysis** details the competition's strengths and weaknesses, providing a basis for discovering market opportunities. A customer analysis provides a picture of who buys and uses the company's products or services. This section of the business plan highlights how the company's products or services satisfy previously unfulfilled market needs. It also includes evidence of market acceptance of the company's unique products or services.

SALES AND MARKETING PLAN The marketing plan delineates the methods and activities that will be employed to reach the company's revenue goals. This section describes the company's customer base, products or services, and marketing and sales programs. The latter is supported by conclusions drawn from the market analysis. Different revenue outcomes may be presented to allow for contingency planning in the areas of finance and production.

PRODUCTION PLAN A production plan is usually included if the business is involved in manufacturing a product. Based on the sales and marketing plan, the production plan covers production options that are available to produce a desired mix of products. The production plan contains information that allows for budgeting for such costs as labor and materials. In non-manufacturing companies, this section would cover new service development.

FINANCIAL PLAN This section covers the financing and cash flow requirements implicit in other areas of the business plan. It contains projections of income, expenses, and cash flow, as well as descriptions of budgeting and financial controls. Financial projections must be supported by verifiable facts, such as sales figures or market research. Monthly figures are generally given for the first two years, followed by annual figures for the next three to eight years. If the business plan is written for investors or lenders, the amount of financing required may be included here or in a separate section.

IMPLEMENTATION SCHEDULE This section provides key dates pertaining to finance, marketing, and production. It indicates when specific financing is needed, when specific aspects of a particular marketing campaign will take place, and delivery dates based on production schedules.

CONTINGENCY PLANS This section defines problems and challenges that the company may face and outlines contingency plans for overcoming obstacles that might arise. Specific topics that may be explored are competitive responses, areas of weakness or vulnerability, legal constraints, staffing, and continuity of leadership.

OTHER DETAILS Most business plans include a table of contents and a cover sheet containing basic information about the company. An appendix may include a variety of documentation that supports different sections of the business plan. Among the items that may be found in an appendix are footnotes from the main plan, biographies, graphs and charts, copies of contracts and agreements, and references.

TAILORING THE BUSINESS PLAN TO SPECIFIC AUDIENCES

Business plans are organized to address major concerns and interests of their intended audience. They are commonly tailored to a specific audience by emphasizing aspects that directly relate to the interests of the reader. For example, a business plan written to obtain a loan for ongoing operations would address the major concerns of potential lenders.

BANKS, INVESTORS, AND OTHER SOURCES OF FUNDING Business plans are frequently written to obtain additional funding. Start-up capital may be needed for a new venture, or the company may require additional working capital for ongoing operations. New capital may be needed to acquire assets for expansion, or equity financing may be needed to support a company's long-range growth.

Potential lenders of debt or equity financing are usually concerned with minimizing their risks and maximizing the return on their investment. It is important, then, when composing a business plan to this audience, to make a strong financial presentation and provide adequate documentation of projected revenue and costs. Areas to be stressed in the business plan include the predictability of the company's cash flow, how well cash flow will cover debt servicing, the reasons additional funding is needed, strengths of the company's financial management, assets used to collateralize debt, and the capital and ownership structure of the company. In addition, business plans written to obtain funding for expansion provide details on the overall scope of the market and profit potential. Such plans typically enumerate the return on investment for equity investors.

POTENTIAL BUYERS Potential buyers are generally interested in such factors as the basic business concept underlying the company, its long-term viability, and its strategic position within its industry. They also look for strengths and weaknesses in the company's basic functional components and its management team. Business plans written for this audience stress the company's strengths and include contingency plans designed to overcome weaknesses, challenges, and other possible developments.

Other factors that might be emphasized in a business plan written for potential buyers are the company's ability to improve profitability and market share, the company's competitive edge, the company's potential to take advantage of opportunities in related industries, managerial and technical skills within the company, and the company's financial capacity.

PARTIES INTERESTED IN REORGANIZATION OR RE-STRUCTURING Business plans written for a company reorganization may be tailored for a variety of readers, including internal management, outside creditors, or new owners. Such a plan sets forth the necessary action designed to reorganize or restructure the company to achieve greater profitability or production capacity. The business plan identifies operational changes that need to be made in different functional areas of the company. It also establishes performance and operational measures against which the functional areas of the company are evaluated.

The audience for this type of business plan is interested in such factors as the timing and sequence of specific changes, and the operational and financial impact of restructuring efforts. The business plan provides details on the new functional organization, as well as key personnel and their responsibilities. Transitional plans are typically furnished, and operating and financial goals are defined.

INTERNAL USERS Business plans written primarily for use within the company generally stress the benefits that will result from implementation of the plan. These may include improved and more consistent performance, improved coordination and consistency among various segments of the company, greater ability to measure performance, empowerment of the work force, and a better motivated and educated work force. The plan provides a comprehensive framework and direction for ongoing operations.

Business plans written for internal use typically identify the company's strengths and weaknesses, potential problems, and emerging issues. They set forth performance standards on which expectations will be based, and clearly delineate goals and objectives to allow for coordination and better communication between all company areas.

BUSINESS PLANS AS PLANNING DOCUMENTS

Business plans are not historical documents about a company's past performance. Rather, they are planning documents that provide information to decision-makers who can help the company achieve its goals and objectives. These decision-makers may be the company's own managers and executives, or they may be sources of capital or potential buyers. Regardless of the intended audience, all business plans address the fundamental strategic issues facing a busi-

ness. They provide verifiable data and projections covering marketing and sales; production, service, and quality; product development; organization and management structure; and financial requirements.

FURTHER READING:

Attard, Janet. *The Home Office and Small Business Answer Book.* New York: Henry Holt, 1993.

Covello, Joseph A., and Brian J. Hazelgren. *The Complete Book of Business Plans.* Naperville, IL: Sourcebooks Trade, 1994.

Kravitt, Gregory I. *Creating a Winning Business Plan.* Probus, 1993.

Massarella, Gregory J. et al. *How to Prepare a Results-Driven Business Plan.* New York: Amacom, 1993.

Pinson, Linda. *Anatomy of a Business Plan.* 2d ed. Enterprise Dearborn, 1993.

SEE ALSO: Budgets and Budgeting; Business Planning; Strategy

BUSINESS PLANNING

Business planning, also known as strategic or long-range planning, is a management-directed process that is intended to determine a desired future state for a business entity and to define overall strategies for accomplishing it. Through planning, management decides what objectives to pursue during a future period, and what actions to undertake to achieve those objectives.

Successful business planning requires concentrated time and effort in a systematic approach that involves: assessing the present situation; anticipating future profitability and market conditions; determining objectives and goals; outlining a course of action; and analyzing the financial implications of these actions. From an array of alternatives, management distills a broad set of interrelated choices to form its long-term strategy. This strategy is implemented through the annual budgeting process, in which detailed, short-term plans are formulated to guide day-to-day activities in order to attain the company's long-term objectives and goals.

For entrepreneurs and small business owners, the first step in successful business planning involves creating a formal **business plan**, of the type commonly used to attract investors and secure bank loans. Careful preparation of this document forces a small business owner to examine his or her own goals as well as the market conditions in which the business operates. It also includes a detailed financial analysis, a look at current staffing levels and future needs, and information about management's expertise. "All the elements can be folded together to formulate a strategic plan that focuses on where you want your company to be in the long run, and how you plan to get there,'' Vince Maietta wrote in *The Business Journal*. ''That also helps entrepreneurs focus on the strengths and weaknesses of the firm, as well as opportunities and threats.''

The use of formal business planning has increased significantly over the past few decades. The increase in the use of formal long-range plans reflects a number of significant factors:

- Competitors engage in long-range planning.

- Global economic expansion is a long-range effort.

- Taxing authorities and investors require more detailed reports about future prospects and annual performance.

- Investors assess risk/reward according to long-range plans and expectations.

- Availability of computers and sophisticated mathematical models add to the potential and precision of long-range planning.

- Expenditures for research and development increased dramatically, resulting in the need for longer planning horizons and huge investments in capital equipment.

- Steady economic growth has made longer-term planning more realistic.

BENEFITS OF PLANNING

Planning provides a means for actively involving personnel from all areas of the business enterprise in the management of the organization. Company-wide participation improves the quality of the plans. Employee involvement enhances their overall understanding of the organization's objectives and goals. The employees' knowledge of the broad plan and awareness of the expected outcomes for their responsibility centers minimizes friction between departments, sections, and individuals. Involvement in planning fosters a greater personal commitment to the plan and to the organization. These positive attitudes improve overall organizational morale and loyalty.

Managerial performance also benefits from planning. Planning focuses the energies and activities of managers in the utilization of scarce resources in a competitive and demanding marketplace. Able to clearly identify goals and objectives, managers perform better, are more productive, and their operations are more profitable. In addition, planning is a mental exercise from which managers attain experience and knowledge. It prepares them for the rigors of the marketplace by forcing them to think in a future- and contingency-oriented manner.

THE PLANNING HORIZON

Basically, there are two timetables for planning. The first is long range, extending beyond one year and normally less than five or ten years. Often called the strategic plan or investment plan, it establishes the objectives and goals from which short-range plans are made. Long-range plans support the organizational purpose by providing clear statements of where the organization is going.

The second is short-range, covering a period of up to one year. Short-range plans are derived from an in-depth evaluation of the long-range plan. The annual budget is a quantified expression of the enterprise's plans for the fiscal year. It generally is divided into quarters, and is used to guide and control day-to-day activities. It is often called the tactical plan because it sets priorities, in the near term, for the long-range plans through the allocation of resources to specific activities.

TYPES OF PLANS

In addition to differentiation by planning horizon, plans are often classified by the business function they provide. All functional plans emanate from the strategic plan and define themselves in the tactical plans. Four common functional plans are:

1) Sales and marketing: for developing new products and services, and for devising marketing plans to sell in the present and in the future.

2) Production: for producing the desired product and services within the plan period.

3) Financial: for meeting the financing needs and providing for capital expenditures.

4) Personnel: for organizing and training human resources.

Each functional plan is interrelated and interdependent. For example, the financial plan deals with moneys resulting from production and sales. Well-trained and efficient personnel meet production schedules. Motivated salespersons successfully market products.

Two other types of plans are strategic plans and tactical plans. Strategic plans cover a relatively long period and affect every part of the organization by defining its purposes and objectives and the means of attaining them. Tactical plans focus on the functional strategies through the annual budget. The annual budget is a compilation of many smaller budgets of the individual responsibility centers. Therefore, tactical plans deal with the micro-organizational aspects, while strategic plans take a macro-view.

STEPS IN THE PLANNING PROCESS

The planning process is directly related to organizational considerations, management style, maturity of the organization, and employee professionalism. These factors vary among industries and even among similar companies. Yet all management, when applying a scientific method to planning, perform similar steps. The time spent on each step will vary by company. Completion of each step, however, is prerequisite to successful planning. The main steps in the planning process are:

- Conducting a self-audit to determine capabilities and unique qualities

- Evaluating the business environment for possible risks and rewards

- Setting objectives that give direction

- Establishing goals that quantify objectives and time-frames

- Forecasting market conditions that affect goals and objectives

- Stating actions and resources needed to accomplish goals

- Evaluating proposed actions and selecting the most appropriate ones

- Instituting procedures to control the implementation and execution of the plan.

THE SELF-AUDIT In order to create an effective overall plan, management must first know the functional qualities of the organization and what business opportunities it has the ability to exploit. Management conducts a self-audit to evaluate all factors relevant to the organization's internal workings and structure.

A functional audit explores such factors as: sales and marketing (competitive position, market share and position, quality and service); production (operational strategies, productivity, use and condition of equipment and facilities, maintenance costs); financial (capital structure, financial resources, credit facilities, investments, cash flow, working capital, net worth, profitability, debt service); and personnel (quantity and quality of employees, organizational structure, decision making policies and procedures).

THE BUSINESS ENVIRONMENT Management surveys the factors that exist independently of the enterprise but which it must consider for profitable advantage. Management also evaluates the relationships among departments in order to coordinate their activities. Some general areas of the external environment considered by management include: demographic changes (sex, age, absolute numbers, location, movement, ethnicity); economic conditions (employment level, regional performance, sex, age, wage levels, spending patterns, consumer debt); government fiscal policy and regulations (level of spending and entitlements, war and peace, tax policies, environmental regulations); labor supply (age, sex, education, cultural factors, work ethics, training); competition (market penetration and position, market share, commodity or niche product); and vendors (financial soundness, quality and quantity of product, research and development capabilities, alternatives, foreign, domestic, just-in-time capabilities).

SETTING OBJECTIVES AND ESTABLISHING GOALS
The setting of objectives is a decision-making process that reflects the aims of the entire organization. Generally, it begins at the top with a clear statement of the organization's purpose. If well communicated and clearly defined throughout the company, this statement becomes the basis for short-range objectives in the annual budget.

Management articulates the overall goals throughout the organization in order to coordinate all business activities efficiently and effectively. It does this by: formulating and distributing a clear, concise statement of the central purpose of the business; leading in the formulation of long-range organizational goals; coordinating the activities of each department and division in developing derivative objectives; ensuring that each subdivision participates in the budget process; directing the establishment of short-term objectives through constructing the annual budget; and evaluating actual results on the basis of the plans.

The organization must know why it exists and how its current business can be profitable in the future. Successful businesses define themselves according to customer needs and satisfaction with products and services. Management identifies the customers, their buying preferences, product sophistication, geographical locations, and market level. Analyzing this data in relation to the expected business environment, management determines the future market potential, the economic variables affecting this market, potential changes in buying habits, and unmet needs existing now and those to groom in the future.

In order to synchronize interdepartmental planning with overall plans, management reviews each department's objectives to ensure that they are subordinate to the objectives of the next higher level. Management quantifies objectives by establishing goals that are: specific and concrete, measurable, time-specific, realistic and attainable, open to modification, and flexible in their adaptation.

Because goals are objective-oriented, management generally lists them together. Some examples of goals might include:

1) Profitability. Profit objectives state performance in terms of profits, earnings, return on investments, etc. A goal might call for an

annual increase in profits of 15 percent for each of the next five years.

2) Human resources. This broad topic includes training, deployment, benefits, work issues, and qualifications. In an architectural consulting firm, management might have a goal of in-house CAD training for a specified number of hours in order to reach a certain level of competence.

3) Customer service. Management can look at improvements in customer service by stating the number of hours or the percentage of complaints it seeks to reduce. The cost or cost savings are stated in dollar terms. If the business sells service contracts for its products, sales goals can be calculated in percentage and dollar increases by type and level of contract.

4) Social responsibility. Management may desire to increase volunteerism or contributions to community efforts. It would calculate the number of hours or dollars within a given time frame.

FORECASTING MARKET CONDITIONS Forecasting methods and levels of sophistication vary greatly. Each portends to assess future events or situations that will affect either positively or negatively the business's efforts. Managers prepare forecasts to determine the type and level of demand for products currently produced or that can be produced. Management analyzes a broad spectrum of economic, demographic, political, and financial data for indications of growing and profitable markets.

Forecasting involves the collection and analysis of hard data, and their interpretation by managers with proven business judgment. Individual departments such as sales, and divisions such as manufacturing, also engage in forecasting. Sales forecasting is essential to setting production volume. Production forecasting determines the materials, labor, and machines needed.

STATING ACTIONS AND RESOURCES REQUIRED With the objectives and forecasts in place, management decides what actions and resources are necessary in order to bring the forecast in line with the objectives. The basic steps management plans to take in order to reach an objective are its strategies. Strategies exist at different levels in an organization and are classified according to the level at which they allocate resources. The overall strategy outlines how to pursue objectives in light of the expected business environment and the business's own capabilities. From the overall strategy, managers develop a number of more specific strategies.

1) Corporate strategies address what business(es) an organization will conduct and how it will allocate its aggregate resources, such as finances, personnel, and capital assets. These are long-term in nature.

2) Growth strategies describe how management plans to expand sales, product line, employees, capacity, and so forth. Especially necessary for dynamic markets where product life cycles are short, growth strategies can be a) in the expansion of the current business line, b) in vertical integration of suppliers and end-users, and c) in diversifying into a different line of business.

3) Stability strategies reflect a management satisfied with the present course of action and determined to maintain the status quo. Successful in environments changing very slowly, this strategy does not preclude working toward operational efficiencies and productivity increases.

4) Defensive strategies, or retrenchment, are necessary to reduce overall exposure and activity. Defensive strategies are used to reverse negative trends in profitability by decreasing costs and turning around the business operations; to divest part or all of a business to raise cash; and to liquidate an entire company for an acceptable profit.

5) Business strategies focus on sales and production schemes designed to enhance competition and increase profits.

6) Functional strategies deal with finance, marketing, personnel, organization, etc. These are expressed in the annual budget and address day-to-day operations.

EVALUATING PROPOSED PLANS Management undertakes a complete review and evaluation of the proposed strategies to determine their feasibility and desirability. Some evaluations call for the application of good judgment—the use of common sense. Others use sophisticated and complex mathematical models.

ASSESSING ALTERNATIVE STRATEGIC PLANS Because of the financial implications inherent in the allocation of resources, management approaches the evaluation of strategic alternatives and plans using comprehensive profit planning and control. Management quantifies the relevant strategies in pro forma statements that demonstrate the possible future financial impact of the various courses of action available. Some examples of pro forma statements are: budgets, income statements, balance sheets, and cash flow statements.

The competing strategic long-range plans constitute simulation models that are quite useful in evaluating the financial effects of the different alternatives under consideration. Based on different sets of assumptions regarding the interaction of the company with the outside world, these plans propose various scenarios of sales, production costs, profitability, and viability. Generally categorized as normal (expected results), above normal (best case), and below normal (worst case), the competing plans project possible outcomes at input/output levels within specified operating ranges attainable within the fiscal year.

Management selects courses of action relative to pricing policy, advertising campaigns, capital expenditure programs, available financing, R&D, and so forth based on the overall **return on investment (ROI)** objective, the growth objective, and other dominant objectives. In choosing between alternative plans, management considers:

- Volume of sales likely attainable

- Volume of production currently sustainable

- Size and abilities of the sales forces

- Quality and quantity of distribution channels

- Competitors' activities and products

- Pace and likelihood of technological advances

- Changes in consumer demand

- Costs and time horizon of implementing changes

- Capital required by the plan

- Ability of current employees to execute proposed plans.

CONTROLLING THE PLAN THROUGH THE ANNUAL BUDGET Control of the business entity is essentially a managerial and supervisory function. Control consists of those actions necessary to assure that the company's resources and operations are focused on attaining established objectives, goals, and plans. Control compares actual performance to predetermined standards and takes action when necessary to correct variances from the standards. Exercised continuously, control flags potential problems so that crises may be prevented. It also standardizes the quality and quantity of output, and provides managers with objective information about employee performance.

In recent years some of these functions have been assigned to the point of action, the lowest level at which decisions are made. This is possible because management carefully grooms and motivates employees through all levels to accept the organization's way of conducting business.

The planning process provides for two types of control mechanisms: feedforward, which provides a basis for control at the point of action (the decision point); and feedback, which provides a basis for measuring the effectiveness of control after implementation. Management's role is to feedforward a futuristic vision of where the company is going and how it is to get there, and to make purposeful decisions coordinating and directing employee activities. Effective management control results from leading people by force of personality and through persuasion; providing and maintaining proper training, planning, and resources; and improving quality and results through evaluation and feedback.

Effective management means goal attainment. In a profit-making business or any income generating endeavor, success is measured in dollars and dollar-derivative percentages. The comparison of actual results to budget expectations becomes a formalized, routine process that measures performance against predetermined objectives, plans, and standards; communicates results to appropriate personnel; analyzes variations from the plans in order to determine the underlying causes; corrects deficiencies and maximizes successes; chooses and implements the most promising alternatives; implements follow-up to appraise the effectiveness of corrective actions; and solicits and encourages feedback to improve ongoing and future operations.

SUMMARY

Business planning is more than simply forecasting future events and activities. Planning is a rigorous, formal, intellectual, and standardized process. Planning is a dynamic, complex decision-making process where management evaluates its ability to manipulate controllable factors and to respond to uncontrollable factors in an environment of uncertainty.

Management evaluates and compares different possible courses of action it believes will be profitable. It employs a number of analytical tools and personnel, especially in accounting, to prepare the appropriate data, make forecasts, construct plans, evaluate competing plans, make revisions, choose a course of action, and implement that course of action. After implementation managerial control consists of efforts to prevent unwanted variances from planned outcomes, to record events and their results, and to take action in response to this information.

FURTHER READING:

Black, Homer A., John E. Champion, and Gibbes U. Miller. *Accounting in Business Decisions: Theory, Method, and Use.* 3rd ed. Englewood Cliffs, NJ: Prentice Hall, 1973.

Cyert, Richard M. ''Positioning the Organization.'' *Interfaces.* March-April 1994.

Ewing, David W. *Long-Range Planning for Management*. New York: Harper & Row, 1972.

Hiam, Alexander. ''Strategic Planning Unbound.'' *Journal of Business Strategy*. March-April 1993.

Maietta, Vince. ''Business Plans Map Your Growth.'' *The Business Journal*. March 14, 1997.

Shillinglaw, Gordon, and Philip E. Meyer. *Accounting: A Management Approach*. Chicago, IL: Irwin, 1983.

Steiner, George A. *Strategic Planning: What Every Manager Must Know*. New York: Free Press, 1979.

Taylor, Bernard. ''The Return of Strategic Planning: Once More with Feeling.'' *Long Range Planning*. June 1997.

Welsch, Glenn A. *Budgeting: Profit Planning and Control*. Englewood Cliffs, NJ: Prentice Hall, 1976.

SEE ALSO: Budgets and Budgeting

BUSINESS PRESS

The business press is a major source of news about governmental regulation, corporate taxes, job leads, industry sales, and even investment leads, since the business press frequently covers emerging business trends before they are noticed by the general mass media. The business press provides in-depth news features about individual companies and the issues facing various industries. It examines how business really operates and how it should operate. While business management books can take years to move from idea to the bookstore, the business press tackles the same issues on a monthly, or sometimes weekly basis.

The business press covers a variety of media. It can include the business section of the daily newspaper and the weekly business tabloid found in most cities. It also includes national daily, weekly, and monthly general business newspapers and magazines like the *Wall Street Journal*, *Business Week*, *Fortune*, and *Forbes*. Some of the major national publications relating specifically to small businesses include *Entrepreneur* and *Nation's Business*. In addition to print media, today's business press has expanded to the point that business news aficionados can watch cable television programs reporting live on what is happening in the stock market.

Trade magazines make up the biggest category of the business press. Each industry has at least one magazine covering it. There are literally thousands of magazines dealing with the day-to-day business intricacies of nearly every conceivable business. No matter how small or new an industry is, there is—or soon will be—a trade magazine or newsletter that covers it.

Besides its importance for helping company owners and managers keep abreast of what is hap-

pening in their industry, the business press also offers many marketing and public relations opportunities. Many businesses selling only to other businesses use the trade press to promote their products and services through advertising and news exposure. While the mass media is busy selling consumer products, like deodorant and gasoline, over the television airwaves, the business press is selling industry-specific products through advertising that is usually more detailed and informative.

This focus also allows companies to get more detailed news coverage than they could expect from newspapers written for the average consumer and taxpayer. The trade press focuses on industry issues, new technology and how to use it, and new products. What newspapers may consider mundane information coming from a local company could be big product news worthy of extensive coverage in the trade press.

TYPES OF BUSINESS PUBLICATIONS

Two types of business publications are found on a local level in most medium to large cities. There is the local daily newspaper's business section, plus a weekly business tabloid covering the companies in that locale. Besides general news concentrating on the major employers in the city, both publications usually feature local business columnists, management-level new hires and promotions, times of meetings of business clubs, and coverage of how local company stocks are doing. The tabloids—usually owned either by a chain specializing in this type of publication or by a newspaper syndicate—will run special sections focusing editorial and advertising on special topics, such as the environment or health care. These business tabloids offer good opportunities for business people to get local coverage through public relations efforts if they can demonstrate how their companies are having an impact on the community.

Many states also have at least one magazine covering the companies based in that state. Frequently owned by a larger news organization, the state business magazine concentrates on features and regular in-depth articles on the state's economy. Most publish an annual economic outlook for the state, a subject usually too big and of little interest to local newspapers and regional tabloids. Because the numbers of companies to cover are so broad, public relations opportunities are usually limited to ''pitching'' editors on the reasons why the magazine should run even a small feature on a particular business.

National business publications usually take in the big picture, looking at the largest and most innovative companies. One exception is the *Wall Street Journal*'s front page feature that focuses on quirky, sometimes small, business efforts or unusual social trends. *Inc.* is a national monthly magazine that tries to accomplish two tasks—reporting on medium-sized businesses, and helping readers build their businesses by following the suggestions of the magazine. *Entrepreneur* and *Nation's Business,* similarly, are national monthly magazines covering trends and topics specifically relating to small businesses. Public relations opportunities on the national level are tough, since editors are inundated with requests to feature "unique" companies that rarely are all that different from each other.

TRADE PUBLICATIONS

The best public relations opportunities and sources for information on running a better business are found in the trade press. Thousands of trade magazines, and an even larger number of subscription-only newsletters, cover only news pertinent to their industries. New product sections sometimes offer color photographs and detailed tests of the products by the magazine's staff. New hire sections and classified ads show where job openings are all over the nation. Many trade magazines have a legislative action section that covers state and national regulatory news that would never be carried in the local newspaper because of its specialization. Most trade publications feature detailed, researched "how to do it better" stories or interviews with industry experts.

The trade press can be very receptive to public relations pitches if the news is important in the industry and if the company making the pitch is willing to cooperate with the magazine's editors and writers. The company seeking the publicity must be as open as possible with the magazine and go beyond the press release that probably started the media contact. While trade magazines have more respect for the press release than most newspapers or national business magazines, few trades will print a release announcing "an amazing new discovery" without any investigation.

FURTHER READING:

Gale Directory of Publications and Broadcast Media. Detroit, MI: Gale Research Inc. 1994.

Saltz, Linda Citroen. "How to Get Your News Releases Published." *Journal of Accountancy.* November 1996.

Soderberg, Norman R. *Public Relations for the Entrepreneur and the Growing Business.* Hinsdale, IL: Probus, 1986.

Zacek, Judith. "Using the Media: No News Isn't Good News." *Travel Weekly.* July 20, 1995.

BUSINESS PROPOSALS

Business proposals are documents that attempt to persuade targeted clients to buy a particular service or product. These documents, which are used in acade-mia and government as well as business and industry, may range from relatively short (a few pages) proposals to "formal" documents of 50 or more pages. Many business proposals—and especially those proffered by startup businesses seeking to obtain new clients and business—are unsolicited (those that are created at the request of the prospective client are known as "**request for proposals**"). Given the fact that many business proposals have not been formally requested by the recipient, businesses that put these documents together have to make sure that they create a final product that will grab the attention of the prospective client in a positive way. As Tom Sant wrote in *Small Business Reports,* "whether you're selling products, services, ideas or projects, you need a proposal to persuade clients that whatever you're selling is the best solution to their business problems. In short, a proposal is a selling tool."

ELEMENTS OF THE BUSINESS PROPOSAL Business proposals are sometimes lumped in the same category as **competitive bids**, but other analysts point out that proposals—and especially unsolicited proposals, whether aimed at convincing a publisher to publish your new book idea or convincing an investor to take a look at a potential new business site—are essentially designed to pique the interest of the prospective client, and often do not get into the nuts and bolts of compensation, time frame, and other matters. Competitive bids, on the other hand, provide detailed information on all aspects of the proposed business arrangement.

Standard elements of basic business proposals include the following (although, depending on the degree of formality of the proposal, not all parts are always necessary) :

- Cover Letter—This should provide an overview of your proposal as well as an introduction, if necessary, in which you include a brief synopsis of your company's background and qualifications.

- Title Page—This part typically includes the name of you and your company, the name of the person or company to whom the proposal is submitted, and the date of submission. "Some titles are one line long, occasionally two," commented Herta A. Murphy and Herbert W. Hildebrandt in *Effective Business Communications.* "Some even include a colon—followed by words to clarify the thought. Clarity and comprehensiveness are dual criteria for a good proposal title."

- Table of Contents—While usually not necessary for shorter proposals, these are sometimes used for big, formal proposals (such as request for proposals).

- Executive Summary—This is the portion of the proposal where you make your case for a business arrangement. "This is the most important part of your proposal," said Sant. "It's the section that will be read by every decision maker. Make sure it's easy to read. Avoid technical jargon and technical details. Focus on organizational issues and benefits, and keep it short."

- Body/Procedures Section—This is the section in which you place technical details and explanations, as well as information on price, implementation schedules, logistical and support issues, documentation, and training. Legal experts note that if the proposal is accepted, it can become a legally binding document. For this reason, and because of the length of time that is usually necessary to produce this section, writers of unsolicited proposals may wish to hold off on preparing this section unless the targeted person or company expresses interest in the basic proposal.

WRITING A SUCCESSFUL PROPOSAL Writing a successful proposal requires both salesmanship and fundamental communication skills. "Basically, proposals—like other reports—should be factual, objective, logical, well written," said Murphy and Hildebrandt. "They should also be persuasive. All proposals should present facts honestly to justify the requested expenditure to be paid by the reader's organization to the writer's firm or to an individual for solving a problem or altering a procedure." In addition, many business communication experts counsel their clients to arrange their proposal in such a way as to emphasize persuasive arguments at the beginning and the conclusion of the proposal, which often are the most remembered sections of any presentation.

Ultimately, however, it is commonly believed that the likelihood of garnering new business via business proposals, whether solicited or not, lies with anticipating the priorities of the targeted firm or individual. As Colette Nassutti observed in *Outlook,* an essential ingredient of successful proposals is the proposal writer's ability to understand the prospective client's circumstances, requirements, and business objectives. Sant agreed, pointing out that "a focus on cost is advantageous if your client is experiencing a period of decline," while "advanced, automated solutions will appeal to growing companies." Proposals aimed at companies that are well-known for attention to quality, advertising image, or quick product development can be structured accordingly as well.

FURTHER READING:

Bhasin, Roberta. "Evaluating Proposals." *Pulp & Paper.* December 1997.

Chairez, Becky Chavarria. "Tackling Business Proposals." *Dallas Business Journal.* November 17, 1995.

Fulscher, Richard J. "A No-Fail Recipe: Winning Business Proposals." *Journal of Property Management.* January-February 1996.

Murphy, Herta A., and Herbert W. Hildebrandt. *Effective Business Communications.* 6th ed. New York: McGraw-Hill, 1991.

Nassutti, Colette. "Art and Science of Proposals." *Outlook.* Fall 1993.

Sant, Tom. "Persuasive Business Proposals." *Small Business Reports.* January 1993.

Urban, Glen L., and Steven H. Star. *Advanced Marketing Strategy: Phenomena, Analysis, and Decisions.* Englewood Cliffs, NJ: Prentice Hall, 1991.

BUSINESS SITE SELECTION

For a small business, the site from where it operates can be pivotal in its success or failure. Indeed, business location is an essential component for many larger companies as well. Site selection can spell the difference between financial success and failure in all sorts of businesses, including retail, service, wholesale, and manufacturing efforts. In fact, studies conducted by the Small Business Administration (SBA) and other organizations indicate that poor location is one of the primary causes of business failure in America. Conversely, a good business location can be enormously beneficial to a small firm. As Fred I Weber Jr. remarked in *Locating or Relocating Your Business,* "sometimes a business that might otherwise be only marginal makes a good profit because of an excellent location. On the other hand, a poor location can often drag down a good business. It can affect sales adversely and help decrease the company's profit by adding to its cost."

LOCATION NEEDS OF VARIOUS BUSINESS TYPES

Each of the above-mentioned business types—retail, service, wholesale, and manufacturing—have different site needs that need to be considered when settling upon a location for starting or relocating a business.

RETAIL BUSINESSES The success of retail establishments is often predicated to a large degree on their location. "Real estate professionals are fond of saying that the three most important factors in choosing a business space are location, location, and location," wrote Fred S. Steingold in *Legal Guide for Starting and Running a Small Business.* "For certain types of retail stores and restaurants, this may be true. For example, a sandwich shop requires a location with a high volume of foot traffic. Or maybe you'll benefit if you're near other businesses that are similar to yours; restaurants often like to locate in a restaurant district.''

Since location is so important to most retail operations, small business retailers often have to make significant expenditures to secure a good site on which to operate. Property owners that offer land or buildings or office space for lease or sale in already-thriving retail areas know that they can command a higher price because of the volume and quality of business that the location will bring to the company.

SERVICE BUSINESSES Many service-oriented businesses also need to operate in "high traffic" regions, but there are exceptions to this. Most home-based business owners, for example, package their talents in service-oriented businesses (software development, freelance writing, home improvement, etc.). Others, such as pest control services or landscaping services, secure the majority of their customers through the Yellow Pages, etc., and thus do not need to worry as much about their location (although location can become a problem because of other factors; for example, a service business that has to travel great distances to take care of the majority of its customers might consider relocating closer to its primary customer base). Still other service-oriented businesses, of course, rely to a great degree on their location. Dry cleaners, hair salons, and other businesses can not afford to locate themselves on the outskirts of a business district. Many of their customers frequent their business precisely because of the convenience of their location; if that benefit dries up, so too do the customers.

WHOLESALE BUSINESSES Whereas the primary consideration for retailers and some service businesses is to locate themselves in high traffic areas—hence the ubiquity of such businesses in shopping centers and malls—the major location concern of wholesalers is to find a site that has good shipping and receiving facilities and close proximity to transportation routes. Zoning laws are also a consideration. Most communities maintain **zoning ordinances** that restrict where wholesalers can set up their businesses.

MANUFACTURING BUSINESSES As with wholesalers, businesses engaged in manufacturing usually have limited site location options because of local zoning laws. But manufacturers generally do not lack for options when the time comes to build or relocate a facility. Most communities have any number of sites to choose from. The key is to select the land or building that will be most beneficial to the company in the long run. "Several factors must be considered when locating or relocating a small plant," wrote Weber. "Among them are the company's market, the

available labor force, transportation, raw materials, and available buildings or building sites. . . . Perhaps the most important consideration in any location is *being able to satisfy your market. . . .* Your plant must be located with convenient access to all of your customers, present and potential, and the customers must have convenient access to you.'' Weber then went on to explain how a poor location choice can adversely impact another important part of the business—the labor force. "Some areas do not always have an adequate group of people to draw on," he said. "If you find the present supply of labor inadequate or marginal, consider whether or not the living conditions of the area are conducive to attracting new people. Certain climates have constant appeal. In other areas, the climate makes it difficult for employers to attract people whom their companies need. Unskilled people, in generally, will move more readily than skilled people. Skilled people, particularly professionals, may not move unless they find amenities they consider important.'' In addition, wages can vary widely from area to area. Finally, the small manufacturer needs to weigh such factors as transportation costs, raw materials cost and accessibility, and community attitudes before committing to a given site.

BUILDING OPTIONS

Small business have a number of different choices when it comes time to decide on a facility. The type of facility most often embraced by retail and many service establishments is the shopping center. The shopping center, which houses a variety of different stores (often including well-known chain stores), can take several different forms, but the best known of these is the mall. Indeed, many malls around the country have reached enormous proportions. These establishments provide their tenants with large numbers of potential customers and professional marketing and maintenance services, but in return, tenants often pay high rent and additional fees (to cover maintenance costs, etc.) Many other small businesses, meanwhile, are located in smaller shopping centers that are sometimes known as strip malls or neighborhood shopping centers. These centers, which rely on a smaller customer base than their mega-mall cousins, are typically anchored by one or two large supermarkets or discount stores. The rest of the stores are usually small retail or service establishments of one type or another. The rent at strip malls is generally much less than it is at major malls, but of course, the level of traffic is generally not as high either. The small business owner who wishes to establish his or her store in a shopping center must carefully weigh the financial advantages and pitfalls of each of these options before moving forward. Other retailers or service businesses prefer to set up their businesses in freestanding locations. Restaurants, for instance, often choose to set up their business in a lone building, attracted by the lower fixed rent and relaxed operating regulations that often accompany such arrangements.

Another facility option for the small business is the business park or office building. Indeed, many professionals (doctors, architects, attorneys) choose this option, attracted by the professional image that such trappings often convey and the ability to share maintenance costs with other tenants. Some service businesses also operate from these facilities, especially if their primary clientele are other businesses. As the editors of the *Entrepreneur Magazine Small Business Advisor* noted, "most managers in corporations prefer to deal with professional organizations. To compete with other companies vying for the same business, you must portray your business as one that is just as competent and professional. This takes on greater significance if your clients will be coming to your office on a regular basis."

OTHER FACTORS IN BUSINESS SITE SELECTION

There are myriad factors that need to be evaluated when deciding where to locate a business. Settling on a site that is both convenient and comfortable for the company's primary customers is, of course, vital, but that is only one piece of the site selection puzzle. These considerations include:

- Will projected revenues cover the total costs of leasing or purchasing the site?

- Will ancillary costs associated with business establishment or relocation (purchase and/or transportation of equipment, computer wiring requirements, etc.) be prohibitive?

- Will it be possible to secure lenders to help cover costs associated with moving into the new business site?

- Are there restrictive ordinances that will unduly interfere with business operations?

- Is the facility itself in good condition (including both exterior and interior), and does it meet layout requirements? If not, how expensive will refurbishment be?

- Are the grounds (landscaping, light fixtures, drainage, storage facilities) in good condition?

- If sharing costs of maintenance/housekeeping services, do other tenants view services favorably?

- How secure is the facility?

- Is the site large enough for your business?

- Can the site accommodate future growth?

- Are nearby business establishments successful, and are they likely to attract customers to your business?

- Are regional competitors successful?

- Does the site provide for adequate parking and access for customers?

- Might the area surrounding the facility (neighboring lots, parking facilities, buildings) undergo a dramatic change because of sale and/or construction?

- What sort of advertising expenditures (if any, in the case of malls, etc.) will be necessary?

- What sort of leasehold improvements (if any) will be necessary?

- Will customer service be interrupted by a relocation? If so, for how long?

- Will major system changes (addition or subtraction of equipment or processes) be necessary?

- What impact will the business site have on workforce needs?

- Should the choice of facility reflect changes in the industry or market in which you are operating?

- Are there any existing or proposed government regulations that could change the value of the facility?

- What is the climate as far as business taxation is concerned?

- Are important suppliers located nearby?

OWNERSHIP VS. LEASING

Whether starting up a new business or moving an already established one, small business owners are faced with the question of whether to lease or purchase the land and/or facility that they choose as the site for their company. Most small businesses operate under lease arrangements—indeed, many small business owners do not have the necessary capital to buy the facility where they will operate—but some do choose to go the purchase route, swayed by the following advantages:

- Increased sense of permanence and credibility in the marketplace.

- Property taxes and interest payments are tax-deductible.

- Facility improvements increase the value of the business's property rather than the landlord's property.

- Increased net worth through appreciation of both the business and the facility (including land and buildings).

- No forfeiture of asset at the end of term.

- Ability to liquidate (lessors often have far less freedom in this area).

Of course, there are also factors associated with ownership that either convince small business owners to stick with lease agreements or preclude the possibility of them even pursuing the idea. These include:

- Risk that value of the land and/or facilities will actually go down over time because of business trends (a neighboring anchor store goes bankrupt) or regional events (a flood, massive layoffs).

- Financial risks associated with purchasing are greater, and put a greater financial drain on small establishments that often have other needs (purchasing typically requires greater initial capital investment and entails higher monthly costs).

- Property can be claimed by creditors as an asset if the business goes bankrupt.

For these and other reasons, many small business owners continue to lease rather than purchase the facilities that they conduct their business in. However, the numbers of entrepreneurs and small companies that have become property owners has risen in recent years. As Jeff Keller remarked in *BC Business,* "growing numbers of small businesses are becoming property owners, rather than renters, largely because interest rates have declined and strata-title developments (office, retail and industrial space sold on a condominium-like basis where individual unit holders share common maintenance expenses) have made ownership more affordable." In addition, both private and public lenders have proven more amenable to bankrolling such acquisitions in recent years. Finally, recent years have seen bargains in the commercial real estate market that businesses have snapped up.

Of course, a business owner's decision to lease does not necessarily close the door forever on ownership of the facility. Some landlords are willing to provide lessors with an option to purchase the property at a later time. For additional information on leasing, consult the *Small Business Encyclopedia*'s "Leasing Property" entry.

PLANNING FOR THE FUTURE

An important factor that small business owners need to consider when weighing various business location alternatives is the site's ability to address the company's future needs. "You should keep in mind the danger of putting off relocating because you 'can't

afford it now,' " warned Weber. "Some owner-managers find that, as time goes by and their competitive positions worsen, they can afford relocating even less. They learn the hard way that if a company stays too long in a location it can die in that location." Even a company that is performing satisfactorily can benefit from regular reviews of the pros and cons of its location. "What about technological improvements?" wrote Weber. "Have you ever thought that, if you move, you could take advantage of the technological improvements that have come along in your industry since your present facility was built? If your facility has become a competitive liability because of such innovations, moving to another building may be the most economical way to become competitive again."

Most business consultants counsel their clients to do two things to avoid getting stuck with an inadequate business facility and/or location: 1) plan for the future; and 2) pay attention to the tell-tale signs that are often buried in the business's balance sheet. "Facility costs are a normal everyday concern," wrote Wadman Daly in *Relocating Your Workplace,* "but their relationship to other operating and overhead expenses can alter gradually in ways that, once perceived, suggest a facility change. Rent, operating expense, maintenance, taxes and insurance, etc., should be monitored as a percent of one or more preferred productivity measures to serve as a good indicator of the need for facility change."

SOURCES TO CONSULT WHEN SELECTING A BUSINESS SITE

Local assistance in selecting a site for a new business can usually be found from a number of sources. These include local utilities, some of which have departments designed to provide help in this area; local **Chambers of Commerce**; banks and insurance agencies; real estate agents who specialize in commercial and industrial property; and state agencies. More informal networking with members of the local business community can also provide both leads and warnings about various regional properties.

FURTHER READING:

Ady, Robert M. "Discussion: How to Select an Ideal Business Site." *New England Economic Review.* March-April 1997.

Binder, Stephen. *Corporate Facility Planning.* New York: McGraw-Hill, 1989.

Cronin, Michael P. "Temporary Offices with All the Frills." *Inc.* April 1992.

Daly, Wadman. *Relocating Your Workplace: A User's Guide to Acquiring and Preparing Business Facilities.* Menlo Park, CA: Crisp Publications, n.d.

The Entrepreneur Magazine Small Business Advisor. Wiley, 1995.

Keller, Jeff. ''Be Your Own Landlord: Why Even Small Businesses are Deciding to Buy Rather than Rent.'' *BC Business.* December 1995.

Rappoport, James E., Robert F. Cushman, and Karen Daroff, eds. *Office Planning and Design Desk Reference.* Wiley, 1992.

Schriner, Jim. ''Picking Your Neighborhood.'' *Industry Week.* July 3, 1995.

Steinberg, Brian. ''Green Acres: Why Some Entrepreneurs are Saying 'Goodbye, City Life.' '' *Entrepreneur.* October 1997.

Steingold, Fred S. *Legal Guide for Starting and Running a Small Business.* 3d ed. Berkeley, CA: Nolo Press, 1997.

Weber, Fred I., Jr. *Locating or Relocating Your Business.* Washington: U.S. Small Business Administration, n.d.

SEE ALSO: Leasing Property; Relocation; Zoning Ordinances

BUSINESS TRAVEL

Business travel is a significant expense for companies of all shapes and sizes. Indeed, business observers cite travel costs as one of the largest expenditure areas for many companies, along with payroll, data processing, and a few others. Certainly, several American industries rely on business travelers for their continued existence (business travelers account for more than 50 percent of airline revenues in the U.S., for example). But while business travel is commonly associated with huge corporations, many small businesses rely on the practice as well to make sales, keep in contact with vendors, market their products or services, and keep up with industry trends (via **trade shows**, conventions, etc.). Unfortunately, many small- and mid-sized businesses find it more difficult to find good travel deals, for as Marcia Kaplan observed in *The Business Journal,* ''as in so many other areas, small businesses take a backseat to their larger counterparts when it comes to travel deals.'' Still, travel experts say that small business owners can triumph over this inequitable state of affairs if they are sufficiently motivated. They agree that making intelligent choices in the realm of business travel can be a major factor for small businesses hoping to curb spending without sacrificing in other business areas.

''Many small companies simply assume they are not entitled to discounts and thus are ignorant of what's available to them,'' wrote Kaplan. ''However, with planning and judicious use of travel agencies and special corporate cards, small firms can achieve cost savings.''

HOTELS

Several factors are typically taken into account when a hotel is selected for business travel. Convenience of location (proximity to client, field office, or airport), quality of room, and quality of service are all major considerations. But price is often the paramount consideration, especially if other elements of the hotel—location, etc.—are acceptable.

Small businesses can pursue a couple different strategies to cut down on lodging expenses. Writing in *Nation's Business,* Peter Weaver noted that ''you can sometimes cut one-half off quoted room rates by getting your reservations through a hotel broker. Hotels often designate 10 to 15 percent of their rooms to be sold by brokers at deeply discounted rates because these specialized travel companies can guarantee the hotels business in the low season and can bring in new customers all year. . . . Hotel brokers generally find the biggest discounts among the largest chains in major metropolitan areas and resort spots. But you can often get even lower rates by staying at budget hotels.'' In addition, surveys and studies indicate that small business owners are often able to cut their lodging expenses by negotiating discounts of as much as 30 percent if they provide a large volume of business to a particular hotel.

AIR TRAVEL

Small businesses can save huge amounts of money on air fare if they are able to plan trips in advance. This is not always possible, of course, and there may be instances in which the company may simply have to bite the bullet and pay full price for a short-notice trip. As travel expert Ed Perkins told Weaver, ''You always pay top dollar to the airlines by making your plans, or changing them, at the last minute.'' But Weaver noted that according to experts, companies can cut as much as 50 percent of their airline expenses through judicious timing of out-of-town meeting dates. Tuesdays and Wednesdays are cited as particularly good travel days for obtaining discount fares, and savings can also be realized by choosing mid-day or evening flights rather than early morning or later afternoon flights.

''If your destination is served by major airlines as well as lower-cost carriers, there may be deep discounts on fares, particularly at certain times,'' stated Weaver, who noted that lower-cost carriers usually maintain their status as the cheapest alternative in such instances. ''Sometimes, though, it pays to pick the major airline's discounted fare over a low-cost airline's offering,'' he added. ''You might want to build frequent-flyer points with the major airlines rather than with a smaller carrier that you seldom use. Or you might prefer a major airline's amenities—such as a full meal instead of a bag of peanuts.''

Other tactics that can be used by small business to cut their air travel expenses include the following: 1) If a company's business requires regular travel (a minimum of 40 flights a month on the same airline) between the same two cities, it may be able to secure a "city-pair" discount of up to 10 percent; 2) Business travelers who choose flights that include stops in a carrier's "hub city" can sometimes secure discounts; 3) Some airports have greater levels of competition—and hence, a greater likelihood of discounted fares—than others. Some metropolitan areas of the eastern United States support two airports within an hour's drive of one another, which gives business travelers an opportunity to explore this possibility.

CAR RENTALS

As with other aspects of business travel, advance planning in securing car rentals can help reduce costs, sometimes by significant amounts. In addition to making advance reservations, business travelers should use discount coupons from travel agents, membership organizations, or airline frequent-flyer clubs when securing a rental car.

TRAVEL AGENTS

As is the case with larger corporations, many smaller businesses choose to handle their travel needs by securing a travel agent. Travel agencies can be invaluable to a small business, for they are able to provide savings to the company while simultaneously freeing up company resources to attend to the operations of the business itself. Indeed, travel agencies have become an integral part of the American business landscape. They sell more than 80 percent of all domestic airline tickets, and more than 90 percent of all international airline tickets.

Many travel agencies belong to larger groups that commonly pool their reservations together so that their smaller clients can enjoy the same discounts and upgrades as their larger corporate customers. These discounts and upgrades are likely to be more sizable with lodging and car rentals than with air travel. A less visible benefit of securing an outside travel agency for your company's business travel needs is that they are often equipped to manage a company's entire travel-related billing and accounting systems. Ancillary services offered by some travel agencies include weekly billing analysis, spreadsheets indicating expenses and itineraries, and "frequent traveler worksheets" that provide basic preference information (class of service, seat location, special meals) on all people that travel on behalf of the company. But Kaplan noted that dealing with travel agencies sometimes requires larger payouts in the area of ancillary fees than in past years. "Many agencies now impose fees for ticket delivery, ticket re-issue, and date changes, which they used to absorb. These fees also apply to ally companies, regardless of size."

Experts recommend that small businesses weigh the following factors when deciding on a travel agency:

Rates—Are the agency's rates comparable with those of competitors offering similar services? What are its policies regarding travel cancellations, etc.? What services are included in their packages?

Competence—A travel agency that is less expensive than others may actually cost your business large sums of money if its level of service is lacking. Experts counsel small businesses to shop around and find out who other successful businesses in the community depend on for their travel needs.

Technological investment—Automated reservations and ticketing systems are essential in today's business travel environment. An agency that is not adequately equipped in this area will not be able to give its clients the best possible service.

Dependability—While duration of existence is not always a true indicator of reliability or competence, it can be generally said that operations that have established a track record of dependable service in the community are preferable to those that have not done so. Analysts also note that agencies often have varying levels of involvement with corporate clients. Agencies that secure more than 40 to 50 percent of their business from corporate clients may be better equipped to serve your company's needs than one that receives most of its business from vacationers.

Continuous service—Does the agency have the ability to provide service to company representatives on an "around-the-clock" basis? Travel agencies maintain the same operating hours as most other businesses do, but some also provide clients with the ability to contact them at other times to provide help with hotel or airline arrangements in the event of a missed connection, etc.

TRAVEL DEDUCTIONS

Provided that the representative of the firm incurs his or her costs while engaged in "company business," many costs of business travel can be deducted for tax purposes. Travel deductions are permitted for the cost of transportation, whether by automobile, train, bus, or plane; lodging; meals; and other miscellaneous costs such as baggage fees, facsimile calls, dry cleaning, tips, and public transportation (bus service, taxicab service). Business travelers should note, however, that these miscellaneous deductions are only permitted if the person in question stays overnight.

Deduction rules for travel to foreign countries is somewhat more complicated, especially for self-employed business owners and major shareholders of small corporation. While many deductions still apply, the **Internal Revenue Service (IRS)** does have some additional stipulations; contact the agency for more information.

FURTHER READING:

Cohen, Amon. "How to Ease the Burden." *The Financial Times.* June 23, 1997.

Dix, Sally. "Hanging Pigs, Angry Cats, and Fake Plants: Loving, Hating, and Copying with Business Travel." *Internal Auditor.* June 1997.

Jordan, Archie. "Family Considerations While on the Road." *American Salesman.* February 1997.

Kaplan, Marcia. "In the Clouds as on Land, Small Companies Hold Little Clout." *The Business Journal.* August 21, 1995.

Miller, Lisa. "Why Business Travel is Such Hard Work." *Wall Street Journal.* October 30, 1996.

Morris, Hal. "It Pays to Review Travel Coverage." *Nation's Business.* September 1997.

Ward, Angela. "Planes, Trains, and Automobiles . . ." *Acquisitions Monthly.* November 1996.

Weaver, Peter. "Cutting Costs Before Takeoff." *Nation's Business.* November 1997.

SEE ALSO: Expense Accounts; Tax Deductible Business Expenses

BUYING AN EXISTING BUSINESS

The decision to buy a business is an extremely important one, for such an acquisition almost inevitably brings significant changes in the buyer's financial situation and personal life. Such purchases, then, should not be made before first thoroughly investigating all aspects of the business under consideration and the impact that ownership of that enterprise would likely have on his or her personal and professional life.

Even before beginning the search for an appropriate existing business, would-be buyers are encouraged to honestly assess the level of commitment and resources that they are willing to bring to bear to make a new business endeavor a successful one. Small business experts encourage potential business buyers to frankly ponder the levels of time and energy that they can devote to a new enterprise. Are the number of hours available sufficient given the work involved? Does the business require a higher level of exertion than you are prepared to expend? Experts also encourage potential business buyers to canvass their families about their attitudes regarding the sacrifices—both financial and personal—that are sometimes necessary to move an acquired business forward. In addition, buyers should investigate whether the nature of the business will be a rewarding one for them. What are their motives in pursuing a business purchase? What criteria are being used to search for one? Finally, potential buyers should determine the level of financial commitment that they are willing to make to the new business (and the level of financial assistance that they are likely to be able to secure, if needed). If, after a thorough assessment of these factors, the would-be buyer is still in the market for a business, he or she can proceed.

EVALUATING BUSINESSES

"The first step a buyer must take in evaluating a business for sale is that of reviewing its history and the way it operates," wrote John A. Johansen in the SBA's *How to Buy or Sell a Business.* "It is important to learn how the business was started, how its mission may have changed since its inception and what past events have occurred to shape its current form. A buyer should understand the business's methods of acquiring and serving its customers and how the functions of sales, marketing, finance and operations interrelate." Much of this information—and all-important data on the company's fundamental financial health—can be gleaned through an examination of the enterprises's **financial statements** and operations documents. Johansen pointed to several areas of the business's **balance sheet** that should be thoroughly looked over when evaluating a company:

- **Accounts Receivable**—can provide information to buyers on diversification of customer accounts (or lack thereof), accounts that are overdue or in dispute, accounts that have been pledged as collateral, and the company's credit policies.

- **Accounts Payable**—as with Accounts Receivable, can provide information on diversification and status of accounts; can also help buyers identify undisclosed or contingent liabilities.

- **Inventory**—can provide buyers with information on the size, age, and condition of the inventory, the method of inventory valuation, the process by which damaged inventory is valued, and other data on current owner inventory methods.

- Real Estate—these records can help buyers establish the condition and market value of all buildings and lands that are part of the business, and can be valuable in assessing whether to secure the services of an appraiser; also provides information on various aspects of maintenance, including business relationships and costs.

- Marketable Securities—can aid buyers in determining the value and status (restricted or pledged) of any marketable securities.

- Machinery/Equipment—schedules of machinery and equipment owned or leased by the company can provide potential buyers with information on 1) condition, age, and maintenance needs of equipment and machinery; and 2) those items that are used to adhere to local, state, or federal regulatory requirements, and whether existing machinery is sufficient to meet those requirements.

- Accrued Liabilities—schedules of accrued liabilities inform buyers about the business's accounting mechanisms for unpaid wages, accrued vacation pay and sick leave, payroll taxes due and payable, and accrued federal taxes, among other accruals.

- Notes Payable and Mortgages Payable—can help buyers identify causes of debt, determine terms and payment schedules of those debts (and whether they are assumable); also delineates whether a change in ownership would accelerate the note or mortgage or trigger a prepayment penalty.

Problems in any of these areas can help prospective buyers decide whether to secure the services of an appraiser.

The balance sheet, though, is only one of myriad aspects that need to be thoroughly evaluated by buyers. Other areas of the business that should be examined include its **financial ratios**, **income statements**, rental or lease arrangements, employees, station in the marketplace, and other legal issues (ranging from status of patents to current level of adherence to legal requirements).

INCOME STATEMENTS Profit and loss statements provide vital information on the business's recent financial history and potential for future success. Experts commonly advise would-be buyers to examine income statements from the previous three to five years, and to substantiate the data contained therein via the company's tax returns. Johansen cautioned, though, that the business's earning power "is a function of more than bottom line profits or losses. The owner's salary and fringe benefits, non-cash expenses, and non-recurring expenses should also be calculated."

FINANCIAL RATIOS Information contained in the company's income statements and balance sheet can be used to figure important financial ratios that can provide insights into the company's fiscal well-being. Important financial ratios include current ratio, accounts receivable turnover, inventory turnover, and sales/accounts receivable.

LEASE ARRANGEMENTS Any examination of a business is woefully incomplete without also checking on the business's lease or rental obligations. All such agreements should be closely studied to learn not only about the length of the contract, but other matters as well. For example, some landlords include a "percent of sales" clause in their leases which require commercial tenants to pay them an additional fee over and above their rent (some also call for additional fees for common area maintenance, etc.). Other lease agreements include option periods and/or demolition clauses. Lease contracts also detail maintenance parameters (will the landlord fix the air conditioning, or will you foot the bill?) and conditions—if any—under which the lease can be assumed or extended by a new owner.

EMPLOYEES A business's work force can be among its most attractive assets. Conversely, it can also be a problem area. Key information that should be analyzed when looking at a company's personnel include job descriptions and current compensation (including benefits) for each employee, skill levels, and morale. In settings where unions are present (or imminent), buyers need to inform themselves about current contracts and management-union relations. Finally, buyers that are pondering acquiring a business in an industry with which they are unfamiliar need to determine whether they will be able to retain key personnel after a purchase is made.

MARKETPLACE STATUS Potential buyers should find out not only about the targeted company's market standing—including market share, competitive advantages, and geographic strength—but also about the strengths and weaknesses of its competitors.

LEGAL ISSUES Diligent buyers will make certain that they are well-informed about a company's legal situation, from its standing with the IRS to its vulnerability to litigation. Would-be owners should determine if any lawsuits against the company have been filed or are pending. They should also ensure that the company is meeting OSHA and EPA requirements, and that the business is in compliance with state registration and local zoning requirements. **Articles of incorporation**, bylaws, **partnership agreements**, supplier contracts, and franchise agreements should also be carefully reviewed if applicable.

NEGOTIATING A PURCHASE PRICE

Once a buyer has located a suitable business—usually through newspaper advertisements, industry contacts, or intermediaries (business brokers or merger and acquisition consultants)—undertaken the appropriate research into the enterprise's strengths and weaknesses, and determined what sort of business organization (partnership, sole proprietorship, corporation) will be most advantageous in terms of taxes and other issues, he or she must then go about the process of negotiating a purchase price with the seller.

Buyers and sellers of corporations often lock horns when the time comes to decide whether the acquisition will be a stock sale or an asset sale. The choice has ramifications for both parties in terms of both taxes and legal liability for past operations. Under the terms of a stock sale, the seller receives an agreed-upon price for his or her shares in the company, and after ownership of those stocks has been transferred, the buyer steps in and operates the still-running business. In this kind of purchase, the buyer receives both company assets and company liabilities. This arrangement is popular with sellers because of its tax advantages. The sale of stock qualifies as a capital gain, and it enables the seller to avoid double taxation, since sale proceeds flow directly to the seller without passing through the corporation. In addition, a stock sale frees the seller from any future legal action that might be leveled against the company. Lawsuits and claims against the company become the sole responsibility of the new stock owner(s).

Partnerships and sole proprietorships, meanwhile, *must* change hands via asset sale arrangements, since stocks are nonexistent under these forms of business. Under asset sale agreements, the seller hands over business equipment, inventory, trademarks and patents, trade names, ''goodwill,'' and other assets for an agreed-upon price. The seller then uses the money to pay off any debts; the remainder is his or her profit. Asset transactions are favored by buyers for two big reasons. First, the transaction sometimes allows the buyer to claim larger depreciation deductions on his or her taxes. Second, an asset sale provides the buyer with greater protection from unknown or undisclosed liabilities—such as lawsuits or problems with income taxes or payroll withholding taxes—incurred by the previous owner. Given the dramatically different impact that asset and stock transactions have on both the buying and selling parties, it is hardly surprising that **negotiations** on this issue can become arduous. ''This subject usually deserves a fair amount of negotiating time and, if there is radical disagreement, it can be a deal breaker,'' warned Lawrence Tuller in *Getting Out: A Step-by-Step Guide to Selling a Business or Professional Practice.*

As buyers enter into negotiations with sellers, they should make it clear that they expect the seller to provide asked-for information in a timely and detailed manner. ''Whatever the results of [the] negotiation,'' wrote Tuller in *Buying In: A Complete Guide to Acquiring a Business or Professional Practice,* ''be very careful to make the agreement contingent on satisfactory completion of a thorough and complete investigation of the company's records, facilities, people, and markets. Ordinarily the seller doesn't object to this proviso. He knows what skeletons will come out during detailed due diligence and, if he has been honest, realizes there won't be any major surprises. If, on the other hand, he insists on a firm Offer to Purchase at the conclusion of this first round of negotiations, there is something important he hasn't revealed and you better back off fast.'' In return, sellers often ask prospective buyers to sign confidentiality agreements in which they promise not to divulge any information about the business to anyone other than immediate advisors. Sellers also sometimes ask for would-be buyers to provide personal financial statements so that they do not waste time with people who do not have the financial wherewithal to make a serious offer.

If a buyer is still interested in acquiring the business in question after negotiating the above issues and securing a reliable valuation of the business, he or she can proceed with an opening offer. This can take the form of a **letter of intent** (which is generally non-binding) or a purchase and sale agreement (which is usually legally binding). Both kinds of offers will typically include the following:

- Total compensation offered, including breakdown (size of security deposit, down payment, seller-financed debt, bank debt);
- Warranties of clear and marketable title;
- Detailed list of all liabilities and assets to be purchased;
- Assurances of the validity and assumability of contracts (if applicable);
- Tax liability limitations;
- Operating condition of all equipment and machinery at time of purchase;
- Stipulations allowing buyer to adjust the purchase price in the event that: 1) undisclosed liabilities come due after settlement, and 2) actual inventory purchased does not match amount specified in sale agreement;
- Provisions that the business passes any and all necessary inspections;
- Provisions that final sale is contingent on verification of financial statements, license and lease transfers;
- Provisions that final sale is contingent on obtaining financing for purchase;
- Restrictions on business operations until final settlement;
- Non-competition and advisory clauses (these are sometimes arranged in a separate document);
- Allocation of purchase price;
- Date for settlement.

Business buyers are encouraged to secure the services of professionals during this process. Attorneys, accountants, consultants, and SBA counselors can all provide valuable assistance to people interested in acquiring a business.

FINANCING

Whether the buyer and seller ultimately agree to an installment sale, a leveraged buyout, a stock exchange, or an earn-out to transfer ownership of the company (see the entry ''Selling a Business'' for descriptions of these options), the sale cannot proceed if the buyer is unable to secure adequate financing.

Most small businesses are acquired by buyers who finance a considerable portion of the purchase price themselves. Even so, the buyer must still make sure that he or she has enough money for a down payment and the business's capital requirements. Sometimes, then, buyers are forced to secure financing from outside sources. Johansen noted that ''to grant such financing, an institutional lender is almost certain to require personal collateral for the loan as well as a compendium of financial and operating data of the business to be acquired. It is rare indeed to be granted a loan to purchase a smaller, privately-held business when the loan is secured only be the assets of the business. The most attractive types of personal collateral from the lender's point of view are real estate, marketable securities and cash value of life insurance.'' Lending institutions like banks and consumer finance companies are more open to borrowers involved in purchasing larger companies, but even in these instances, the institutions often ask buyers to put up the company's inventory, machinery, real estate, and accounts receivable as collateral. As Johansen observed, ''it is rare for a privately-held business to be acquired without leveraging the business's assets in some manner, pledging them as collateral for a loan made either by the owner of the business or an outside lender.'' Sensible buyers in need of outside financing will make certain that they approach potential lenders with a comprehensive and well-considered **loan proposal** (including a good **business plan**).

CLOSING THE DEAL

Closings are generally done either via an escrow settlement or via an attorney performs settlement. In an escrow settlement, the money to be deposited, the bill of sale, and other relevant documents are placed with a neutral third party known as an escrow agent until all conditions of sale have been met. After that, the escrow agent disburses the held documents and funds in accordance with the terms of the contract.

In an attorney performs settlement, meanwhile, an attorney—acting on behalf of both buyer or seller, or for the buyer—draws up a contract and acts as an escrow agent until all stipulated conditions of sale have been met. Whereas escrow settlements do not require the buyer and the seller to get together to sign the final documents, attorney performs settlements do include this step.

Several documents are required to complete the transaction between business seller and business buyer. The purchase and sale agreement is the most important of these, but other documents often used in closings include the escrow agreement; bill of sale; promissory note; security agreement; settlement sheet; financing statement; and employment agreement.

FURTHER READING:

Johansen, John A. *How to Buy or Sell a Business.* Washington: U.S. Small Business Administration, n.a.

Klueger, Robert F. *Buying and Selling a Business.* Wiley, 1988.

Tuller, Lawrence W. *Buying In: A Complete Guide to Acquiring a Business or Professional Practice.* Liberty Hall, 1990.

Tuller, Lawrence W. *Getting Out: A Step-by-Step Guide to Selling a Business or Professional Practice.* Liberty Hall, 1990.

Yegge, Wilbur M. *A Basic Guide for Buying and Selling a Company.* Wiley, 1996.

SEE ALSO: Business Brokers; Choosing a Small Business; Franchising; Selling a Business; Valuation

C

C CORPORATION

When a small business incorporates, it is automatically a C corporation, also called a regular corporation. The most basic characteristic of the corporation is that it is legally viewed as an individual entity, separate from its owners, who are now shareholders. This means that when the corporation is sued, shareholders are only liable to the extent of their investments in the corporation. Their personal assets are not on the line, as they would be if the business was a **partnership** or **sole proprietorship**. Any debts that the corporation may acquire are also viewed as the corporation's responsibility. In other words, once the business is incorporated, shareholders are protected by the corporate veil, or limited liability.

Because the corporation is a separate entity, it is also viewed as an individual taxpayer by the Internal Revenue Service. As a result, corporations are subject to **double taxation**, which means that the profits are taxed once on the corporate level and a second time when they are distributed as dividends to the shareholders. (If a business is eligible, it may elect **S corporation** status to avoid this negative characteristic of C corporations.)

ADVANTAGES

LIMITED LIABILITY Most small businesses that consider incorporating do so for the limited liability that corporate status affords. The greatest fear of the sole proprietor or partner—that their life's savings could be jeopardized by a law suit against their business or by sudden overwhelming debts—disappears once the business becomes a corporation. Although the shareholders are liable up to the amount they have invested in the corporation, their personal assets cannot be touched. Rather than purchase expensive liability insurance, then, many small business owners choose to incorporate to protect themselves.

RAISING CAPITAL It can be much easier for a corporation to raise capital than it is for a partnership or sole proprietorship, because the corporation has stocks to sell. Investors can be lured with the prospect of dividends if the corporation makes a profit, avoiding the necessity of taking out loans and paying high interest rates in order to secure capital.

ATTRACTING TOP-NOTCH EMPLOYEES Corporations may find it easier to attract the best employees, who may be lured by stock options and fringe benefits.

FRINGE BENEFITS One advantage C corporations have over unincorporated businesses and S corporations is that they may deduct fringe benefits (such as group term life insurance, health and disability insurance, death benefits payments to $5,000, and employee medical expenses not paid by insurance) as a business expense. In addition, shareholder-employees are also exempt from paying taxes on the fringe benefits they receive. To be eligible for this tax break, though, the corporation must not design a plan that benefits only the shareholders/owners. A good portion of the employees (usually 70 percent) must also be able to take advantage of the benefits. For many small businesses, the expense of providing fringe benefits for all employees is too expensive, so the tax break may not be considered an advantage.

CONTINUANCE OF EXISTENCE Transfer of stock or death of an owner does not alter the corporation, which exists perpetually, regardless of owners, until it is dissolved. While this is usually considered an advantage, Fred Steingold argues in *The Legal Guide for Starting and Running a Small Business* that, in reality, "You don't need to incorporate to ensure that your business will continue after your death. A sole proprietor can use a living trust or will to transfer the business to heirs. Partners frequently have insurance-funded buy-sell agreements that allow the remaining partners to continue the business."

DISADVANTAGES

DOUBLE TAXATION After they deduct all business expenses, such as salaries, fringe benefits, and interest payments, C corporations pay a tax on their profits at the corporate level. If any of those profits are distributed as dividends to the shareholders, those individuals must also pay a tax on the money when they file their personal tax returns. For companies that expect to reinvest much of the profits back into the business, double taxation may not affect them enough to be a serious drawback. In the case of the small business, most if not all of the company's profits are used to pay salaries and fringe benefits, which are deductible, and double taxation may be avoided because no money is left over for distributing dividends

BUREAUCRACY AND EXPENSE Corporations are governed by state and federal statutes, which means that they have to abide by sometimes intricate corporate laws. Therefore, lawyers and tax preparers will need to be hired, and regular stockholder and board of directors meetings will have to be held, and detailed minutes of those meetings must be taken. All of the corporation's actions must be approved by the directors, who can limit the ability of the corporation to take quick action on pressing matters. Corporations have to pay fees, which vary by state, when they file the **articles of incorporation**. And in order to bring up a case in small claims court, the corporation is required to be represented by a lawyer, whereas sole proprietors or partners can represent themselves. In addition, if the corporation does interstate business, it is subject to taxes in other states.

RULES GOVERNING DIVIDEND DISTRIBUTION A corporation's profits are divided on the basis of stockholdings, whereas a partnership may divide its profits on the basis of capital investment or employment in the firm. In other words, if a stockholder owns ten percent of the corporation's stock, she may only receive ten percent of the profits. However, if that same person was a partner in an unincorporated firm to which she had contributed ten percent of the company's capital, she might be eligible to receive more than ten percent of the business's profits if such an agreement had been made with the other partners. Strict rules, though, govern the way corporations di-

vide their profits, even to the point, in some states, of determining how much can be distributed in dividends. Usually, all past operations must be paid for before a dividend can be declared by the corporation's directors. If this is not done, and the corporation's financial stability is put in jeopardy by the payment of dividends, the directors can, in most states, be held personally liable to creditors.

STRUCTURE OF A CORPORATION

In small businesses, the owners often hold more than one or all of the following positions, which are required of all corporations:

SHAREHOLDERS They own the company's stock and are responsible for electing the directors, amending the bylaws and articles of incorporation, and approving major actions taken by the corporation like mergers and the sale of corporate assets. They alone are allowed to dissolve the corporation.

DIRECTORS They manage the corporation and are responsible for issuing stock, electing officers, and making the corporation's major decisions.

OFFICERS The corporation must have a president, secretary, and treasurer. These officers are responsible for making the day-to-day decisions that govern the corporation's operation.

EMPLOYEES They receive a salary in return for their work for the corporation.

FINANCING A CORPORATION

EQUITY This is cash, property, or services exchanged for stock in the company. Generally, each stock is equivalent to one dollar of investment. If the small business owner is planning to exchange property to the corporation for stock, then a tax advisor should be consulted; if the property has appreciated, taxes may be due on the exchange.

DEBT This is money lent by banks or shareholders. In the former case, a personal guarantee by the corporation's principals is usually required, which makes an exception to the limited liability rule. The owner of a corporation who personally guarantees a loan is also personally responsible for paying it back if the corporation goes under. Many corporations have preferred to fund the corporation with shareholder money in exchange for promissory notes because unlike dividends, the repayment of debts is not taxable. The Internal Revenue Service monitors such debt closely, though, to make sure it is not excessive and that adequate interest is paid.

PAYING C CORPORATION TAXES

After the C corporation deducts all business expenses, such as salaries, fringe benefits, and interest payments, it pays a tax on its profits at the corporate level. Then dividends may be distributed to the shareholders, who must pay a tax on the money when they file their personal tax returns. In the case of the small business, though, double taxation may not be a consideration, because most, if not all of the company's profits go to pay salaries and fringe benefits, which are deductible, and no money is left over for distributing dividends. To avoid double taxation, corporations often pay their shareholder-employees higher salaries. But the IRS looks out for this trick and often audits corporations, claiming that executive salaries are not "reasonable" compensation. To prevent this charge, then, the corporation should consider the duties performed, the experience and/or special abilities of the employee, and how much other corporations pay for similar positions before determining "reasonable" compensation. In *How to Run a Small Business*, the J. K. Lasser Institute also advises that a corporation keep salaries somewhat consistent: "Fluctuating salaries, high salaries in high earning years and low salaries in lean years, will attract a review of salary payments by the Internal Revenue Service. A charge might be made, for example, that the high salary payments were in fact dividend payments."

RUNNING A CORPORATION

Once a small business has been incorporated, the day-to-day management of business affairs should not be that much different than it was beforehand. It is important, though, that the business is treated like a corporation. The courts have been known on occasion to overlook a business's corporate status and find the shareholders/owners liable because the business was run as if it were still a sole proprietorship or partnership. Simply filing the articles of incorporation does not guarantee limited liability. In order to maintain corporate status in the law's eyes, these guidelines should be followed:

ACT LIKE A CORPORATION Before doing business, stock certificates should be issued to all stockholders, and a corporate record book should be established to hold the articles of incorporation, records of stock holdings, the corporation's bylaws, and the minutes of board and shareholder meetings. In addition, such meetings should be held regularly (once a year is the minimum requirement). In this way, the corporation can record all important actions taken and show that such actions were approved by a vote. It is also important to treat the corporation like the separate entity it is by keeping personal and corporate accounts separate. Whereas a small business owner may have previously used one account to pay the company's accounts and personal expenses, as a corporate shareholder, he now needs to receive a regular salary from the corporation, deposit it in a separate account, and pay his personal expenses from that account. In all respects, the corporation and owner must be treated as distinct individuals. Fred Steingold advises "document all transactions as if you were strangers. If the corporation leases property to you, sign a lease." In addition, the corporation's full name (which should indicate the company's corporate status through use of "Inc." or an equivalent) must be used on all correspondence, stationary, advertising, phone listings, and signs.

ACT LIKE A CORPORATE OFFICER When the corporation's owner signs her name to checks, contracts, or correspondence for the corporation, she must always indicate that she is the president to show that she is not acting on her own but as an agent of the corporation.

ADEQUATE CAPITAL INVESTMENT AND INSURANCE COVERAGE It is important to protect the corporation against failure due to debts and lawsuits. In other words, simply trying to protect the owners' assets by becoming a corporation and neglecting to fortify the business can be viewed as reason to disregard a business's corporate status in a lawsuit. Therefore, enough capital should be invested in the corporation to handle all business activities. Likewise, if business activities pose a risk to employees or customers and reasonably priced insurance is available to protect against such risks, such coverage should be secured.

FURTHER READING:

The Entrepreneur Magazine Small Business Advisor. New York: John Wiley & Sons, 1995.

Handmaker, Stuart A. *Choosing a Legal Structure for Your Business*. Upper Saddle River, NJ: Prentice Hall, 1997.

J.K. Lasser Institute. *How to Run a Small Business*. New York: McGraw-Hill, 1994.

Selecting the Legal Structure for Your Business Washington: U.S. Small Business Administration. n.a.

Steingold, Fred S. *The Legal Guide for Starting and Running a Small Business*. 2d ed. Berkeley, CA: Nolo Press, 1995.

SEE ALSO: Debt Financing; Equity Financing; Incorporation

CAPITAL

Capital, in the most basic terms, is money. All businesses must have capital in order to purchase assets and maintain their operations. Business capital comes in two main forms: debt and equity. Debt refers to loans and other types of credit that must be repaid in the future, usually with interest. In contrast, equity generally does not involve a direct obligation to repay the funds. Instead, equity investors receive an ownership position which usually takes the form of stock in the company.

The capital formation process describes the various means through which capital is transferred from people who save money to businesses that require funds. Such transfers may take place directly, meaning that a business sells its stocks or bonds directly to savers who provide the business with capital in exchange. Transfers of capital may also take place indirectly through an investment banking house or through a financial intermediary, such as a bank, mutual fund, or insurance company. In the case of an indirect transfer using an investment bank, the business sells securities to the bank, which in turn sells them to savers. In other words, the capital simply flows through the investment bank. In the case of an indirect transfer using a financial intermediary, however, a new form of capital is actually created. The intermediary bank or mutual fund receives capital from savers and issues its own securities in exchange. Then the intermediary uses the capital to purchase stocks or bonds from businesses.

THE COST OF CAPITAL

"Capital is a necessary factor of production and, like any other factor, it has a cost," according to Eugene F. Brigham in his book *Fundamentals of Financial Management.* In the case of debt capital, the cost is the interest rate that the firm must pay in order to borrow funds. For equity capital, the cost is the returns that must be paid to investors in the form of dividends and capital gains. Since the amount of capital available is often limited, it is allocated among various businesses on the basis of price. "Firms with the most profitable investment opportunities are willing and able to pay the most for capital, so they tend to attract it away from inefficient firms or from those whose products are not in demand," Brigham explained. But "the federal government has agencies which help individuals or groups, as stipulated by Congress, to obtain credit on favorable terms. Among those eligible for this kind of assistance are small businesses, certain minorities, and firms willing to build plants in areas with high unemployment."

As a rule, the cost of capital for small businesses tends to be higher than it is for large, established businesses. Given the higher risk involved, both debt and equity providers charge a higher price for their funds. "A number of researchers have observed that portfolios of small-firm stocks have earned consistently higher average returns than those of large-firm stocks; this is called the 'small-firm effect,'" Brigham wrote. "In reality, it is bad news for the small firm; what the small-firm effect means is that the capital market demands higher returns on stocks of small firms than on otherwise similar stocks of large

firms. Therefore, the cost of equity capital is higher for small firms." The cost of capital for a company is "a weighted average of the returns that investors expect from the various debt and equity securities issued by the firm," according to Richard A. Brealey and Stewart C. Myers in their book *Principles of Corporate Finance.*

CAPITAL STRUCTURE

Since capital is expensive for small businesses, it is particularly important for small business owners to determine a target capital structure for their firms. The capital structure concerns the proportion of capital that is obtained through debt and equity. There are tradeoffs involved: using debt capital increases the risk associated with the firm's earnings, which tends to decrease the firm's stock prices. At the same time, however, debt can lead to a higher expected rate of return, which tends to increase a firm's stock price. As Brigham explained, "The optimal capital structure is the one that strikes a balance between risk and return and thereby maximizes the price of the stock and simultaneously minimizes the cost of capital."

Capital structure decisions depend upon several factors. One is the firm's business risk—the risk pertaining to the line of business in which the company is involved. Firms in risky industries, such as high technology, have lower optimal debt levels than other firms. Another factor in determining capital structure involves a firm's tax position. Since the interest paid on debt is tax deductible, using debt tends to be more advantageous for companies that are subject to a high tax rate and are not able to shelter much of their income from taxation.

A third important factor is a firm's financial flexibility, or its ability to raise capital under less than ideal conditions. Companies that are able to maintain a strong **balance sheet** will generally be able to obtain funds under more reasonable terms than other companies during an economic downturn. Brigham recommended that all firms maintain a reserve borrowing capacity to protect themselves for the future. In general, companies that tend to have stable sales levels, assets that make good collateral for loans, and a high growth rate can use debt more heavily than other companies. On the other hand, companies that have conservative management, high profitability, or poor credit ratings may wish to rely on equity capital instead.

SOURCES OF CAPITAL

DEBT CAPITAL Small businesses can obtain debt capital from a number of different sources. These sources can be broken down into two general categories, private and public sources. Private sources of debt financing, according to W. Keith Schilit in *The Entrepreneur's Guide to Preparing a Winning Business Plan and Raising Venture Capital,* include friends and relatives, banks, credit unions, consumer finance companies, commercial finance companies, trade credit, insurance companies, factor companies, and leasing companies. Public sources of **debt financing** include a number of loan programs provided by the state and federal governments to support small businesses.

There are many types of debt financing available to small businesses—including private placement of bonds, convertible debentures, industrial development bonds, and **leveraged buyouts**—but by far the most common type of debt financing is a regular loan. **Loans** can be classified as long-term (with a maturity longer than one year), short-term (with a maturity shorter than two years), or a credit line (for more immediate borrowing needs). They can be endorsed by co-signers, guaranteed by the government, or secured by **collateral**—such as real estate, **accounts receivable**, **inventory**, savings, **life insurance**, **stocks** and **bonds**, or the item purchased with the loan.

When evaluating a small business for a loan, Jennifer Lindsey wrote in her book *The Entrepreneur's Guide to Capital,* lenders ideally like to see a two-year operating history, a stable management group, a desirable niche in the industry, a growth in market share, a strong cash flow, and an ability to obtain short-term financing from other sources as a supplement to the loan. Most lenders will require a small business owner to prepare a loan proposal or complete a loan application. The lender will then evaluate the request by considering a variety of factors. For example, the lender will examine the small business's credit rating and look for evidence of its ability to repay the loan, in the form of past earnings or income projections. The lender will also inquire into the amount of equity in the business, as well as whether management has sufficient experience and competence to run the business effectively. Finally, the lender will try to ascertain whether the small business can provide a reasonable amount of collateral to secure the loan.

EQUITY CAPITAL Equity capital for small businesses is also available from a wide variety of sources. Some possible sources of **equity financing** include the entrepreneur's friends and family, private investors (from the family physician to groups of local business owners to wealthy entrepreneurs known as ''angels''), employees, customers and suppliers, former employers, venture capital firms, investment banking firms, insurance companies, large corporations, and government-backed **Small Business Investment Companies (SBICs)**.

There are two primary methods that small businesses use to obtain equity financing: the private placement of stock with investors or venture capital firms; and public stock offerings. Private placement is simpler and more common for young companies or startup firms. Although the private placement of stock still involves compliance with several federal and state securities laws, it does not require formal registration with Securities and Exchange Commission. The main requirements for private placement of stock are that the company cannot advertise the offering and must make the transaction directly with the purchaser.

In contrast, public stock offerings entail a lengthy and expensive registration process. In fact, the costs associated with a public stock offering can account for more than 20 percent of the amount of capital raised. As a result, public stock offerings are generally a better option for mature companies than for startup firms. Public stock offerings may offer advantages in terms of maintaining control of a small business, however, by spreading ownership over a diverse group of investors rather than concentrating it in the hands of a venture capital firm.

FURTHER READING:

Brealey, Richard A., and Stewart C. Myers. *Principles of Corporate Finance.* 4th ed. New York: McGraw-Hill, 1991.

Brigham, Eugene F. *Fundamentals of Financial Management.* 5th ed. Chicago, IL: Dryden Press, 1989.

Hovey, Juan. ''A Source of Funds in Search of Work.'' *Nation's Business.* September 1997.

Lindsey, Jennifer. *The Entrepreneur's Guide to Capital.* Chicago, IL: Probus, 1986.

Schilit, W. Keith. *The Entrepreneur's Guide to Preparing a Winning Business Plan and Raising Venture Capital.* Englewood Cliffs, NJ: Prentice Hall, 1990.

SEE ALSO: Banks and Banking; Private Placement of Securities; Venture Capital

CAPITAL GAIN/LOSS

A capital gain or loss results from the sale, trade, or exchange of a capital asset. Simply stated, when the resulting transaction nets an amount lower than the original purchase value, or basis, of the capital asset, a capital loss occurs. When the resulting transaction nets an amount greater than the basis, a capital gain occurs. Capital gain/loss can either be short-term (when the transaction is completed within one year) or long-term (when the transaction is completed in more than one year). The period is determined from the day after acquisition to the day of disposal. Capital gain/loss is a concept that affects small business owners in a number of ways—from the decisions they must make regarding their personal property and investments, to the attractiveness of their businesses to outside investors. The factors relevant to capital gain/loss are the capital asset, the transactional event, and time.

The subject of capital gain/loss causes much debate in government and economic circles. The current philosophy centers on the benefits and efficiencies of capital accumulation and utilization. To encourage capital formation and investment, the federal tax codes tax capital gains at lower rates than ordinary income. In 1997, the maximum tax rate on a long-term capital gain was lowered from 28 percent to 20 percent (compared to maximum income tax rates of 39.6 percent). A lower capital gains tax is supposed to encourage people to sell stock and other assets, which increases the government's tax revenues. In the past, it has also had a beneficial effect on investment in small businesses, as it tends to provide investors with income via an appreciation in stock price (which is taxed as a capital gain) rather than via dividends (which are taxed as ordinary income).

CAPITAL ASSETS

Everything one owns for personal use, pleasure, or investment is a capital asset. These include: securities, a residence, household furnishings, a personal car, coin and stamp collections, gems and jewelry, and precious metals. Since property held for personal use is considered a capital asset, the sale or exchange of that property at a price above the basis thus results in a capital gain, which is taxable. If one incurs a loss on that property from a sale or exchange, however, the loss cannot be deducted unless it resulted from a personal casualty loss, such as fire, flood, or hurricane. Other types of property and investments also have some irregularities in their treatment as capital gains or losses for tax purposes.

INVESTMENT PROPERTY, COLLECTIBLES, PRECIOUS METALS, AND GEMS All investment property is also considered a capital asset. Therefore, any gain or loss is generally a capital gain or loss, but only when it is realized—that is, upon completion of the transaction. For example, a person who owns stock in a growing technology company may see the price of that stock appreciate considerably over time. For a gain to be realized, however, the investor must actually sell shares at a market price higher than their original purchase price (or lower, in the case of a capital loss). Section 1244 of the federal revenue code treats losses on certain small business stocks differently. If a loss is realized, the investor can deduct the amount as an ordinary loss, while he or she must report any gain as a capital gain.

SALE OF A HOME The sale of a personal residence enjoys special tax treatment in order to minimize the impact of long-term inflation, and to accommodate the changing lifestyle needs of persons 55 and over. For most people, a residence is the largest asset they own. While some appreciation is expected, residences are not primarily used as investment vehicles. Inflation may cause the value of a home to increase substantially while the constant-dollar value may increase very little. In addition, the growth in family size may encourage a family to step up to a larger home. To minimize the impact of inflation and to subsidize the purchase of new homes, the tax code does not require reporting a capital gain if the individual purchases a more expensive house within two years. For individuals age 55 and over who are downsizing (perhaps due to an "empty nest"), the code allows a once-in-a-lifetime exclusion of $125,000 of realized gain if the owners lived in that home three years out of the previous five.

DETERMINING THE BASIS

Capital gain/loss is calculated on the cost basis, which is the amount of cash and debt obligation used to pay for a property, along with the fair market value of other property or services the purchaser provided in the transaction. The purchase price of a property may also include the following charges and fees, which are added to the basis to arrive at the adjusted basis:

1) Sales tax.

2) Freight charges.

3) Installment and testing fees.

4) Excise taxes.

5) Legal and accounting fees that are capitalized rather than expensed.

6) Revenue stamps.

7) Recording fees.

8) Real estate taxes where applicable.

9) Settlement fees in real estate transactions.

The basis may be increased by the value of capital improvements, assessments for site improvements (such as the public infrastructure), and the restoration of damaged property. A basis is reduced by transactional events that recoup part of the original purchase price through tax savings, tax credits, and other transactions. These include **depreciation**, nontaxable corporate distributions, various environmental and energy credits, reimbursed casualty or theft losses, and the sale of an easement. After adjusting the basis for these various factors, the individual subtracts the adjusted basis from the net proceeds of the sale to determine gain/loss.

NET GAIN OR LOSS

To calculate the net gain/loss, the individual first determines the long-term gain/loss and short-term gain/loss separately. The net short-term gain/loss is the difference between short-term gains and short-term losses. Likewise, this difference on a long-term basis is the net long-term gain/loss. If the individual's total capital gain is more than the total capital loss, the excess is taxable generally at the same rate as the ordinary income. However, the part of the capital gain which is the same amount as the net capital gain is taxed only at the capital gains tax rate, maximum 20 percent. If the individual's capital losses are more than the total capital gains, the excess is deductible up to $3,000 per year from ordinary income. The remaining loss is carried forward and deducted at a rate up to $3,000 until the entire capital loss is written off.

FURTHER READING:

Internal Revenue Service. *Tax Guide for Small Business*. Washington: Department of the Treasury, 1995.

Kadlec, Daniel. "Capital Gain = Market Pain?" *Time*. August 18, 1997.

SEE ALSO: Capital; Tax Planning

CAREER AND FAMILY

Over the last several decades, American society has undergone significant changes in its attitudes toward balancing work and family life. These attitudes have been influenced by changing demographics; a dramatic increase in the percentage of women who choose to work in non-household related areas; rising costs in the realm of housing, transportation, clothing, and food; changing societal and personal priorities; and a host of other factors. Today, both employer and employee are grappling with the challenges of balancing career and family obligations and desires in a more visible way than ever before. The American media simultaneously extoll the virtues of those who excel in the business world and lament the impact that such ambition allegedly can have on the psychological health of the individual, his or her partner, and their children. This concern with the issue of career/family balance is reflected in the barrage of media attention that accompanies any small trend in this area, whether it be an upturn in professional women who leave work behind to wholly concentrate on motherhood or a general society-wide movement toward simplification of life, which is typically characterized as symbolic of an increased emphasis on family happiness/growth at the expense of career development.

Indeed, the debate over what constitutes an appropriate balance between family and career is livelier than ever. For example, proponents of recent trends toward attitudes that are typically characterized as "family-friendly" laud the decisions of those who choose less time-consuming careers or institute flexible work rules to increase family time. Others, though, resent the assumption that is sometimes made that people who are ambitious and driven in their chosen profession, and thus spend significant amounts of time involved in such endeavors, must have their priorities screwed up. For example, Joseph Nocera wrote in *Fortune* that "without question, it's unhealthy to be so consumed by work that the kids feel abandoned. But there is also something unhealthy about so sanctifying family time that we diminish the importance of work. Yet that is precisely the judgment our culture now renders on a regular basis." Nocera went on to critique the widespread assumption that "no matter what's going on at the office, it can't be more important than coaching your kid's basketball team. Well, sometimes it isn't, and sometimes it is. Sometimes other people's jobs are at stake, or a crisis has to be averted. Sometimes you need to accomplish something in your work for the sheer satisfaction of it, and sometimes that means staying late or working on weekends. Why should it be such a sin to admit this out loud?"

For the small business owner, achieving a reasonable balance between work and family obligations can be a particularly daunting task. The challenge of striking this appropriate balance can be especially acute for **women entrepreneurs**, who, despite tremendous changes in societal acceptance of their right to make their mark in the business world, still face disapproval in some quarters for making such a choice.

For both men and women, the demands of establishing and maintaining a profitable business are numerous and time-consuming in most instances. After all, it is the entrepreneur who is ultimately responsible for realizing his or her vision of the business, and who has typically invested a great deal of time, thought, and energy into nourishing that vision. The small business owner is often the chief decision maker within the business, and is oftentimes the primary producer of the company's goods and/or services as well. This latter element is particularly true of smaller businesses, whether the enterprise is concerned with silk screening, freelance writing, portrait photography, carpentry, or some other area of endeavor. But life partners and children have needs as well, and successful entrepreneurs and family counselors alike warn that a person who establishes a profitable business is likely to find that his or her victory is a hollow one if his or her relationship with a partner or child is irreparably damaged in the process. "Balancing home and career is the greatest juggling act of all," wrote

Marian Thomas in *Balancing Career and Family*. "It requires practice, concentration and a great deal of self-confidence. And, just like a juggler, if you try to juggle too many balls at once, you're bound to drop one of them. In order to have it all you have to make sacrifices. There is no easy way around it. You have to decide what your goals are and set priorities. You have to decide what is most important to you and your family and build your life around that."

Finally, small business owners have to recognize the career/family issue is one that impacts on employees as well. Indeed, "family-friendly" policies have proliferated in many industries in recent years, as various sectors respond to general societal perceptions that the work/family balance had become unevenly weighted toward work over the past few decades. In many cases, it has become essential for small business owners to recognize the changing expectations of their employees in this area.

ESTABLISHING AN APPROPRIATE WORK/ FAMILY BALANCE FOR EMPLOYEES

Increasingly, small businesses have shown an interest in helping their work forces manage the challenges of addressing both work and family obligations. Their ability to do so is dictated somewhat by financial health, workload, competitive pressures, and a host of other factors, but many small business owners have come to the conclusion that workplaces that insist on long hours from their employees may be sacrificing long-term health for short-term gains. "Many experts in the field of management have argued that family-responsive policies and programs will be necessary to attract and retain needed employees and to build competitive advantages," wrote Teresa Joyce Covin and Christina C. Brush in *Review of Business*. "Research also suggests that conflicts between work and family are related to decreased productivity, lost work time, job dissatisfaction, increased health risks for employed parents, poorer performance of the parenting role, absenteeism, poor morale, reduced life satisfaction, and depression. While work-family conflict is commonly viewed as a women's problem, more companies are beginning to recognize that both men and women feel the impact of work-family conflicts."

There are several steps that small business owners can take to help employees manage their obligations both in the office and at home. "A number of external, structural innovations help people immeasurably in balancing work and family," stated Deborah Lee in *Having It All/Having Enough: How to Create a Career/Family Balance that Works for You*. These include "flexible work schedule, the availability of part-time work that is taken seriously and is respected by employers, the option of working at home or bring-

ing a child to work. However, these options won't help much unless people also adjust their attitudes about work and unless employers adjust their expectations about what people can produce. A part-time schedule doesn't help if it contains a full-time equivalent workload or penalties such as loss of health benefits or loss of advancement opportunities." Of course, some small business owners contend that a person who takes on a part-time schedule does not warrant the same consideration for advancement as does a full-time employee, and that providing health benefits to all part-time employees puts the business at an unacceptable competitive disadvantage. Each individual business faces challenges and considerations that are unique; thus, each business owner has to decide for him or herself what family-friendly policies (and attitudes) can be put in place.

BALANCING WORK AND FAMILY IN HOME-BASED BUSINESSES

Owners of **home-based businesses** face unique challenges in the realm of achieving a desired work/ family balance. Whereas small business owners who commute to their place of business every day are usually freed from child-rearing responsibilities for the duration of their time there, entrepreneurs who work out of their home often have to devise methods in which they can both attend to the needs of their business and provide adequate attention to their children. Researchers and homebased business owners tout several steps that can be taken to assist entrepreneurs in meeting these twin challenges.

- Establish a family-friendly business—This sounds simple but in reality, all homebased businesses are not created equal. Some may provide a parent with significant freedom in structuring business around his or her children's schedule, while others may not provide nearly the same level of flexibility.

- Communicate with spouse and/or others— Establishing and maintaining a home-based business requires changes in the routines of all family members, not just the entrepreneur. Changes in travel schedules, household chore allocation, and other areas of family life may all need to be made. The key to making sure that such changes are made with a minimum of disruption and/or resentment is open, honest communication.

- Make maximum use of free time— Homebased entrepreneurs can dramatically increase their productivity—and keep a lid on feelings of frustration—by scheduling demanding and/or important work obligations for times when child supervision obligations are minimal. Nap times, pre-school sessions, extracurricular programs, etc. can all provide parents with valuable windows of opportunity to attend to vital work-related matters.

- Prioritize and establish a daily schedule—Business owners who work out of their home should avoid falling into a routine in which tasks—both family- and work-related—are addressed in a haphazard, "as they come up" fashion. Instead, they should try to establish a daily or weekly schedule. Work discipline can be difficult to maintain at home even without children; their presence further compounds the challenge.

- Establish an office area that is physically removed from the rest of the house—People who attempt to take care of work while situated in the heart of a child's play area are apt to experience high levels of frustration. Instead, homebased entrepreneurs should consider establishing an office in a separate area that includes all necessary equipment to conduct business. Moreover, children should be taught to respect the importance of that area. Another option which may be more popular with parents of toddlers and young children is to create a "child-friendly" office with a corner that is set aside for their needs.

- Communicate the importance of your work to children—Roberts noted that homebased entrepreneurs should make a special effort to educate their children about the importance of the work they are doing. She counseled parents to "share your victories, challenges and rewards as often as possible. If your children feel like they're a part of what you're doing, they'll be much more supportive than if they see your business as something that's just taking you away from them."

- Enjoy your family—Many homebased business owners create such a situation for themselves for the express purpose of spending greater time with their mates or children, yet find themselves feeling frustrated with the demands on time and energy that those people inevitably make during the course of every day. Counselors urge homebased entrepreneurs not to lose sight of why they made the decision to operate out of the home in the first place.

FURTHER READING:

Barnett, Rosalind C., and Caryl Rivers. "The Myth of the Miserable Working Woman." *Working Woman*. February 1992.

Covin, Teresa Joyce, and Christina C. Brush. "Attitudes Toward Work-Family Issues: The Human Resource Professional Perspective." *Review of Business*. Winter 1993.

Friedman, Dana, and Ellen Galinsky. *Work and Family Trends*. New York: Families and Work Institute, 1991.

Lee, Deborah. *Having It All/Having Enough: How to Create a Career/Family Balance that Works for You*. New York: Amacom, 1997.

Levine, James A., and Todd L. Pittinsky. *Working Fathers: New Strategies for Balancing Work and Family*. 1997.

Marks, John. "Time Out: Plagued by Stress, a Growing Number of People Say They Think Time is Becoming More Precious than Money and They're Trying to Slow Down." *U.S. News & World Report*. December 11, 1995.

Murray, Katherine. *The Working Parents' Handbook: How to Succeed at Work, Raise Your Kids, Maintain a Home, and Still Have Time for You*. Indianapolis, IN: Park Avenue, 1996.

Nocera, Joseph. "Oh, Quit Whining and Get Back to Work!" *Fortune*. March 17, 1997.

Roberts, Lisa. *How to Raise a Family and a Career Under One Roof*. Brookhaven Press, 1996.

Rose, Karol L. "Assessing Work/Family Needs." *Compensation and Benefits Management*. Summer 1995.

Shellenbarger, Sue. "Work-Family Issues Go Way Beyond Missed Ball Games." *Wall Street Journal*. May 28, 1997.

Thomas, Marian. *Balancing Career and Family: Overcoming the Superwoman Syndrome*. Shawnee Mission, KS: National Seminars, 1991.

SEE ALSO: Child Care; Flexible Work Programs

CAREER PLANNING AND CHANGING

A change in career, whether initiated voluntarily or involuntarily, can be a time of significant anxiety. Even if one is excited about future career plans, a certain degree of apprehension is perfectly natural. If you have been forced out of a job—either because of outright dismissal, painful realizations about professional prospects in the position you had previously held, or simply burnout—these feelings of anxiety are apt to be even more profound. But a change in career can also be a time of great opportunity and personal freedom. The casting off of old ways can be a liberating experience, for it frees people to consider a variety of professional and personal avenues that were previously closed to them because of their previous work attachments. Some choose to return to school to pursue courses of study that can lead into whole new careers, while others use their skills and experience to take a position similar to their previous one, but in a fresh environment. Many others, however—and especially those who have voluntarily changed their career path—choose to join the ever-growing ranks of small business owners in America.

The decision to launch a small business is one that should not be arrived at in hasty or haphazard fashion. Indeed, any entrepreneur faces obstacles that have to be addressed, whether those obstacles take the form of capital shortfalls, tough competition, problems with location, management issues, or arriving at a satisfactory balance of work and family time. Those who neglect to investigate or anticipate these barriers to business success are far more likely to flounder. Conversely, the well-prepared, realistic entrepreneur who take the time to lay the groundwork for his or her business initiative is significantly more likely to be ultimately successful in his or her endeavor. ''Give yourself every chance to succeed,'' wrote the editors of *How to Run a Small Business*. ''Successful entrepreneurs, aware of the various chances for failure in a new venture, work hard to shift the odds in their favor by thorough investigation at the outset. The person destined for failure is the one who is carried into a business on the euphoria of going it alone without doing the essential preparatory work.''

LAYING THE GROUNDWORK FOR A NEW BUSINESS

People launch their own businesses for all sorts of reasons. Some are weary of the corporate settings in which they have previously labored, and hunger for an opportunity to exercise greater control over their lives. Some want to make greater use of their skills and education, while others envision entrepeneurship/ small business ownership as a path to a different lifestyle. Finally, many people start new business enterprises in hopes of improving their financial circumstances.

But before beginning a new business, economic and entrepeneurial analysts recommend that the prospective small business owner take time to honestly assess not only the viability of their business idea, but the level of motivation, talent, money and other resources that they can bring to bear to best ensure that their enterprise succeeds. For example, the would-be entrepeneur needs to frankly consider a number of aspects of his or her own personality before embarking on a small business venture. These issues include: assessing how you like to spend your time; determining how compatible your skills and interests are with the proposed business; deciding how much money your are willing or able to invest in a new business enterprise; deciding how much debt you are willing to accrue in establishing a new business; defining how many hours you are willing to invest in the business on a week-in, week-out basis; determining if that allotment of time will be sufficient to make your business a success; and assessing the level of support you can expect to receive from your family and other important people in your life. It is important to be realistic in considering these issues; a decision to start a new business that is built on a foundation of best-

case scenarios or unrealistic hopes is almost certainly doomed to struggle and ultimately fail.

In addition, one needs to ponder the following questions about the proposed venture itself:

- What services or products will you offer?
- How much time will be required?
- What economic trends are evident in the industry in which you propose to enter?
- Who are your likely competitors, and how well entrenched are they?
- How can you wrest business away from those competitors?
- Where will you locate your business?
- What equipment or supplies will you need to start your business?
- How many employees will you need?
- What will be your start-up costs?
- How will you finance your business?
- How will you market your products or services?
- What demographic group (or groups) do you intend to target with your business?
- How long will it likely take for your business to become profitable?
- Who will you seek to target as customers/ clients of your products/ services?
- What legal structure will you choose for your enterprise?
- What kinds of insurance will you need to secure for your company?
- How will your business's legal and financial needs be addressed?

Each of the above factors has its own complexities and qualities that need to be fully researched and considered. Cursory consideration of any of these factors, warn business experts, is simply unacceptable in preparing to launch a business. For instance, a prospective small business owner might include rent (including first-month rent, final-month rent, and security deposits), employee payroll (including benefits), equipment costs, inventory requirements, insurance, and leasehold improvements in calculating start-up costs for his or her business. But if the prospective entrepeneur neglects to include such financial factors as product/service marketing costs, licensing costs, pre-opening payroll costs (for painters, builders, etc.), and attorney and/or accountant fees, then that person is entering the small business world with insufficient data, which can disable a business from the very beginning.

BUYING A BUSINESS

Another option for the would-be entrepreneur who wishes to go into business for him or herself is to investigate buying an already established business. This option has a number of significant advantages. The financial investment, while it can be substantial if one is seeking to buy a profitable business, is easier to determine, since equipment is already in place and employee work force, location, equipment costs, and other aspects of the business have already been established. In addition, whatever financing is needed is often easier to obtain when creditors see that the money is intended for purchasing an already successful business. Moreover, if the business has been successful, one can realize a return on investment much more quickly than the small business owner who starts from scratch. Finally, purchasing a successful business generally gives the entrepreneur an established client or customer base and working relationships with suppliers. Of course, there are dangers associated with purchasing a business as well; eroding market share, employees unhappy with the change in ownership, business debt (as a result of overexpansion, for instance), outdated inventory systems, and changes in the competitive environment such as the arrival of a new competitor in the area are all factors that have to be weighed when considering the purchase of an established business. As always, though, the prospective buyer can avoid many of these pitfalls by first undertaking a thorough investigation of the business and the trends in the industry of which it is a part.

FRANCHISE OPPORTUNITIES

People seeking to establish their own business can also look into **franchising** opportunities. A franchising opportunity allows the business owner to offer goods or services under the trademark of a franchiser, often a large corporation. The entrepreneur does not enjoy the same level of freedom in determining the character and direction of his or her enterprise under this arrangement, and securing franchise rights is typically an expensive proposition. In addition, royalty fees, in which the franchisee pays a certain percentage of revenue (as much as 15 percent) to franchisers, are a standard part of franchisee arrangements in many industries. Nonetheless, franchisees also receive several weighty benefits. These include instant name recognition, a proven marketing plan, and attractive odds of success (According to the *1991 Franchisees Owners Survey* conducted by Arthur Anderson, for example, more than 96 percent of units owned by franchisees are still in business after five years). Indeed, franchising has emerged as an explosive component in America's overall economic growth in recent years. Franchise stores account for more than one-third of all retail sales in America, for example, and many business analysts note that this trend shows no sign of slowing.

As countless businessmen, financial experts, and academics have long observed, no new business venture is guaranteed to succeed. The marketing strategies of competitors, changes in the legal landscape, and personal issues such as health and family can all change quickly, and all can have a dramatic impact on your business. But by embarking on an honest and comprehensive course of research and planning, an entrepreneur will be far better equipped to prepare a **business plan** that will maximize the likelihood of making a new enterprise a successful one.

SOURCES TO CONSULT WHEN PONDERING A CAREER CHANGE

There are many valuable information sources readily available to individuals pondering the pros and cons of establishing a business or changing careers. Perhaps the most plentiful source of information—and one of the least inexpensive—is the United States government. Many branches of the U.S. government publish large quantities of information of interest to the small business owner or prospective entrepreneur. The weekly *Official Gazette of the U.S. Patent Office,* for instance, offers particularly helpful information to the entrepreneur who hopes to establish a business based on a new product idea.

The **U.S. Small Business Administration** (SBA) is the most important of the government agencies for the prospective small business owner. It maintains several programs that offer services in the realms of training, counseling, research, and other assistance to the small business community. These include Small Business Development Centers (SBDCs), the Service Corps of Retired Executives (SCORE), Business Information Centers (BICs), Small Business Technology Transfer programs (SBTT), and Small Business Investment Companies (SBICs). The latter program is specifically designed to fund new companies, while the SBTT program concentrates on providing assistance to technology-oriented enterprises, especially at the start-up phase of business.

Other sources of information include state economic development agencies, municipal chambers of commerce, trade shows, fellow entrepreneurs, and small business or trade associations, such as the Center for Entrepeneurial Management (180 Varick St., New York, NY 10014, 212-633-0060), the Small Business Network (10451 Millrun Circle, Suite 400, Owensville, MD 21117, 410-581-1373) and the Small Business Service Bureau (554 Main St., Worcester, MA 01601, 508-756-3513). Finally, as small businesses—home-based and otherwise—assume ever greater importance and influence in both the domestic and international economies, a massive body of literature devoted to attracting the entrepreneur and small business owner has emerged in recent years. In addition to the large number of books that have been published on various aspects of small business ownership, many periodicals devoted to small business issues can be found at your local bookstore, including *The Business Owner, Entrepreneur, Journal of Small Business Management,* and the U.S. Chamber of Commerce's *Nation's Business.*

FURTHER READING:

Breidenbach, Monica E. *Career Development.* Upper Saddle River, NJ: Prentice Hall, 1989.

J. K. Lasser Institute. *How to Run a Small Business.* New York: McGraw-Hill, Inc., 1994.

Jackson, Tom. *Not Just Another Job: How to Invent a Career that Works for You—Now and in the Future.* New York: Times Books, 1992.

Moreau, Daniel. *Kiplinger's Take Charge of Your Career.* Washington: Kiplinger Books, 1990.

Pines, Ayala, and Elliot Aronson. *Career Burnout: Causes and Cures.* New York: Free Press, 1988.

Powell, C. Randall. *Career Planning Today.* Kendall/ Hunt Publishing Co., 1990.

SEE ALSO: Buying an Existing Business; Entrepreneurship; Self-Assessment

CARIBBEAN BASIN INITIATIVE

The Caribbean Basin Initiative (CBI) is a broad program providing the duty-free entry of merchandise from designated beneficiary countries or territories. It, along with the Andean Trade Preferences Act (ATPA), stands as the second-most preferential trade program enacted by the United States, after the **North American Free Trade Agreement (NAFTA)**.

CBI was first enacted by the United States as the Caribbean Basin Economic Recovery Act. It first came into being on January 1, 1984, and currently has no expiration date. Under its precepts, duty-free treatment was extended to nearly all products imported from the beneficiary Caribbean Basin countries (with exceptions), provided the countries maintain certain standards in such areas as intellectual property, investment, and labor rights/conditions. The only products that did not qualify for the CBI program were textile and apparel, petroleum, canned tuna, footwear, some leather goods, and some watches and watch parts. In the latter part of the 1980s, CBI was hailed by large corporations and free trade proponents as an advantageous tool in buttressing Caribbean economies and improving corporate performance (larger U.S. companies took advantage of CBI to relocate certain manufacturing operations in beneficiary countries).

In 1990 the CBI was revised through legislation called the Caribbean Basin Economic Recovery Act II (CBI II). Basically, the 1990 legislation tweaked the original legislation in several ways, Most importantly, it made CBI a permanent program. It also stipulated that articles that are the growth, product, or manufacture of Puerto Rico and which are subsequently processed in a CBI-beneficiary country may received duty-free status when brought into the U.S., provided that 1) they are imported directly from a beneficiary country into the U.S.; 2) the routing through the beneficiary country results in an advancement in the good's value or condition; and 3) all materials added to the good are a product of the U.S. or a CBI nation. Finally, the 1990 program established that goods assembled or processed in whole from U.S. components in a beneficiary country may be entered into the United States free of duty.

The Caribbean Basin Initiative received renewed attention in the early 1990s, as the U.S. government grappled with NAFTA. The 1993 adoption of NAFTA, which established a free trade zone between Mexico, the U.S., and Canada, prompted a call for renewed study of CBI, since NAFTA had suddenly created a tariff disadvantage for Caribbean facilities hoping to export to the United States. Many of these facilities were owned by U.S. companies, who warned that they would consider shifting their operations to Mexico if changes were not made to CBI to put the Caribbean nations on an equal trade footing with America's southern neighbor. Given the interests of large manufacturers, it was perhaps inevitable that major U.S. industry groups (the American Apparel Manufacturers Association, the American Textile Manufacturers Institute, the United States Apparel Industry Council, the National Cotton Council, etc.) would launch lobbying campaigns to urge approval of extending NAFTA-like tariff treatment to all Caribbean-produced products. For their part, the more than two dozen Caribbean nations impacted by CBI lent their voices to the cause as well, urging the United States to extend ''trade parity'' to them.

Proponents of broadening CBI, however, ran into concerted opposition from labor groups, who raised concerns about U.S. job and wage losses, and some business sectors. Domestic textile makers, for instance, which are typically smaller in size than their multinational brethren, vehemently opposed proposals to upgrade CBI, arguing that such a move would put many of them out of business. Indeed, a change to provide NAFTA-like rights to CBI nations is regarded as more beneficial to larger businesses with overseas facilities than smaller companies that manufacture exclusively on U.S. soil.

The push to extend the boundaries of CBI to NAFTA-size dimensions stalled through the mid 1990s, and in late 1997 the pro-CBI contingent suffered a significant setback when the Clinton Administration proved unable to secure a continuation of its "Fast Track" Trade Negotiation Authority. This inability was due at least in part to unhappiness in some U.S. quarters with NAFTA's impact on job security in some American industry sectors and dissatisfaction with levels of adherence to work and environmental standards. Nonetheless, proponents of CBI parity are hopeful that they will be able to push through the necessary legislation in the next few years.

FURTHER READING:

Barrett, Joyce. "CBI Advocate: Parity Hangs on Fast-Track." *WWD.* May 23, 1997.

"Clinton's Budget: Pro-CBI, Anti-Sweatshop." *WWD.* March 20, 1996.

Guide to the Caribbean Basin Initiative. International Trade Administration, 1994.

Hogan, Bill. "Caribbean Basin Initiative II—Boom or Bust?" *D & B Reports.* January-February 1991.

Maggs, John. "Caribbean Parity Bill Still Shaky." *Journal of Commerce and Commercial.* December 4, 1995.

Millman, Joel. "It's Working." *Forbes.* February 19, 1990.

SEE ALSO: Exporting; Labor Unions

CASH CONVERSION CYCLE

The cash conversion cycle (CCC) is a key measurement of small business liquidity. The cycle is in essence the length of time between cash payment for purchase of resalable goods and the collections of **accounts receivable** from the sale of such goods to customers; as such, it focuses on the length of time that funds are tied up in the cycle. Large business firms tend to have shorter CCC periods than do small retail businesses, but the latter can take a couple of different steps to reduce the length of their cash conversion cycles, including reducing inventories or receivables conversions. CCC length is also inversely related to organizational cash flows, and a significant positive relationship exists between CCCs and current and quick ratios.

Effective management of the cash conversion cycle is imperative for small business owners. Indeed, it is cited by economists and business consultants as one of the truest measurements of business health available to entrepreneurs, especially during periods of growth. "Some of the traditional tools designed to provide a measure of overall guidance can become unstable at high rates of growth," explained John Costa in *Outlook.* "Others are more dangerous still; they provide the wrong signal at crucial points of working capital buildup. For example, the current and quick ratios are popular with companies and their

bankers. In a period when collections have slowed, asset turns have become sluggish and vendors have not extended terms beyond previously agreed limits, the current ratio would probably look good." At the same time, the quick ratio may even show improvement or remain steady, even though the company is actually in substantial need of working capital. This happens, suggested Costa, because of the balance-sheet-oriented limitations of current and quick ratios. "These quick and dirty ratios fall short of what a rapidly changing, dynamic company needs," he stated flatly.

Instead of the above, potentially misleading measurements, small business owners should consider using cash conversion cycles, which, according to Costa usually provide a more accurate reading of working **capital** pressure on cash flows. "The objective is to keep your CCC as low as possible," he explained. "At a minimum, you should strive to maintain a constant CCC during periods of rapid sales growth. Unless inventory, credit, or vendor policies change, rapid growth should not cause the CCC to increase. . . . Because the CCC is related to asset turnover, it is more dynamic and therefore more accurate. What's more, it is easy to calculate" and explain to key staffers.

FURTHER READING:

Belt, Brian. "The Trend of the Cash Conversion Cycle and Its Components." *Akron Business and Economic Review.* Fall 1985.

Costa, John. "Challenging Growth: How to Keep Your Company's Rapid Expansion on Track." *Outlook.* September 1997.

Gentry, James A., R. Vaidyanathan, and Hei Wai Lee. "A Weighted Cash Conversion Cycle." *Financial Management.* Spring 1990.

Hilton, Ronald W. *Managerial Accounting.* New York: McGraw-Hill, 1991.

Moss, Jimmy D., and Bert Stine. "Cash Conversion Cycle and Firm Size: A Study of Retail Firms." *Managerial Finance.* December 1993.

CASH FLOW STATEMENT

A cash flow statement is a financial report that describes the source of a company's cash and how it was spent over a specified time period. Because of the varied accrual accounting methods companies may employ, it is possible for a company to show profits while not having enough cash to sustain operations. A cash flow statement neutralizes the impact of the accrual entries on the other financial statements. It also categorizes the sources and uses of cash to provide the reader with an understanding of the amount of cash a company generates and uses in its operations, as opposed to the amount of cash provided by sources outside the company, such as borrowed funds or funds from stockholders. The cash flow statement also tells the reader how much money was spent for items that do not appear on the **income statement**, such as loan repayments, long-term asset purchases, and payment of cash dividends.

In November 1987, the Financial Accounting Standards Board (FASB) adopted Statement of Financial Accounting Standards No. 95—Statement of Cash Flows. FASB 95 requires that a full set of financial statements include a cash flow statement as the fourth required financial statement (along with a balance sheet, income statement, and statement of retained earnings). This statement also established standards for cash flow reporting.

FORMATS AND REQUIREMENTS FOR THE CASH FLOW STATEMENT

FASB 95 requires that a statement of cash flows classify cash receipts and payments according to whether they stem from operating, investing, or financing activities. It also provides that the statement of cash flows may be prepared under either the direct or indirect method, and provides illustrative examples for the preparation of statements of cash flows under both these methods.

CLASSIFICATIONS OF CASH RECEIPTS AND PAYMENTS At the beginning of a company's life cycle, a person or group of people come up with a marvelous idea for a new company. The initial money comes from the owners, or could be borrowed. This is how the new company is "financed." The money owners put into the company, or money the company borrows, is classified as a financing activity. Generally, any item that is classified on the balance sheet as either a long-term liability or an equity is a candidate for classification as a financing activity.

The owners or managers of the business use the initial funds to buy equipment or other assets they need to run the business. In other words, they invest it. The purchase of property, plant, equipment, and other productive assets is classified as an investing activity. Sometimes a company has enough cash of its own that it can lend money to another enterprise. This, too, can be classified as an investing activity. Generally, any item that is classified on the balance sheet as a long-term asset is a candidate for classification as an investing activity.

Now the company can start doing business. It has procured the funds and purchased the equipment and other assets it needs to operate. It starts to sell merchandise or services and making payments for rent, supplies, taxes, and all of the other costs of doing business. All of the cash inflows and outflows associated with doing the work for which the company was established is classified as an operating activity. In general, if an activity appears on the company's income statement, it is a candidate for the operating section of the cash flow statement.

ACCRUAL AND ITS EFFECT ON FINANCIAL STATEMENTS Generally accepted accounting principles (GAAP) require that financial statements are prepared on the accrual basis. For example, revenues that were earned during an accounting period may not have been collected during that period, and appear on the balance sheet as accounts receivable. Similarly, some of the collections of that period may have been from sales made in prior periods. Cash may have been collected in a period prior to the services rendered or goods delivered, resulting in deferred recognition of the revenue. This would appear on the balance sheet as unearned revenue.

Sometimes goods or services are paid for prior to the period in which the benefit is matched to revenue (recognized). This results in a deferred expense, or a prepaid expense. Items such as insurance premiums that are paid in advance of the coverage period are classified as prepaid. Sometimes goods or services are received and used by the company before they are paid for, such as telephone service or merchandise inventory. These items are called accrued expenses, or payables, and are recognized on the income statement as an expense before the cash flow occurs. When buildings or equipment are purchased for cash, the cash flow precedes the recognition of the expense by many years. The expense is recognized over the life of the asset as depreciation. One of the main benefits of the cash flow statement is that it removes the effect of any such accruals or deferrals.

METHODS OF PREPARING THE CASH FLOW STATEMENT FASB 95 allows the preparer a choice of the direct or the indirect method of cash flow statement presentation. The operating section of a cash flow statement prepared using either method converts the income statement from the accrual to the cash basis, and reclassifies any activity not directly associated with the basic business activity of the firm. The difference lies in the presentation of the information.

Companies that use the direct method are required, at a minimum, to report separately the following classes of operating cash receipts and payments:

Receipts:

1) Cash collected from customers

2) Interest and dividends received

3) Other operating cash receipts, if any.

Payments:

1) Cash paid to employees and suppliers of goods or services

2) Interest paid

3) Income taxes paid

4) Other operating cash payments, if any.

Companies are encouraged to provide further breakdown of operating cash receipts and payments that they consider meaningful.

Companies using either method to prepare the cash flow statement are required to disclose separately changes in inventory, receivables, and payables to reconcile net income (the result of the income statement) to net cash flow from operating activities. In addition, interest paid (net of amount capitalized) and income taxes paid must be disclosed elsewhere in the financial statements or accompanying notes. An acceptable alternative presentation of the indirect method is to report net cash flow from operating activities as a single line item in the statement of cash flows and to present the reconciliation details elsewhere in the financial statements.

The reconciliation of the operating section of a cash flow statement using the indirect method always begins with net income or loss, and is followed by a section entitled Adjustments to reconcile net income to net cash provided by operating activities.

Regardless of whether the direct or the indirect method is used, the operating section of the cash flow statement ends with net cash provided (used) by operating activities. This is the most important line item on the cash flow statement. A company has to generate enough cash from operations to sustain its business activity. If a company continually needs to borrow or obtain additional investor capitalization to survive, the company's long-term existence is in jeopardy.

The presentation of the investing and financing sections is the same regardless of the whether the statement is prepared using the direct or indirect method. The final section of the cash flow statement is always a reconciliation of the net increase or decrease in cash for the period for which the statement is prepared with the beginning and ending balances in cash for the period.

ANALYZING AND CLASSIFYING COMMON TRANSACTIONS

Transactions on the balance sheet also must be analyzed and converted from the accrual to the cash basis in preparation of the cash flow statement. Every balance sheet account reflects specific activity. There are only a few distinctive transactions that affect each account. Following are examples of some of the common transactions affecting balance sheet items.

Accounts receivable increases when the company sells merchandise or does a service on credit, and decreases when the customer pays its bill. Accounts receivable is associated with the income statement account Sales or Revenue. The change in accounts receivable or the cash collected from customers is classified as an operating activity.

Inventory increases when the company buys merchandise for resale or use in its manufacturing process, and decreases when the merchandise is sold. Inventory is associated with the income statement account Cost of Goods Sold. The change in inventory or the cash paid for inventory purchases is classified as an operating activity.

Prepaid insurance increases when the company pays insurance premiums covering future periods and decreases when the time period of coverage expires. Prepaid insurance is associated with the income statement account Insurance Expense. The change in prepaids or the amount paid for insurance is classified as an operating activity.

The land, building, and equipment accounts increase when the company purchases additional assets and decrease when the assets are sold. The only time the income statement is affected is when the asset is sold at a price higher or lower than book value, at which time a gain or loss on sale of assets appears on the income statement. The amount of cash used or received from the purchase or sale of such assets is classified as an investing activity. The gain or loss is classified as an adjustment in the operating section on a cash flow statement prepared using the indirect method.

Accumulated **depreciation** increases as the building and equipment depreciates and decreases when building and equipment is sold. Accumulated depreciation is associated with depreciation expense on the income statement. Depreciation expense does not appear on a cash flow statement presented using the direct method. Depreciation expense is added back to net income on a cash flow statement presented using the indirect method, since the depreciation caused net income to decrease during the period but did not affect cash.

Goodwill increases when the parent company acquires a subsidiary for more than the fair market value of its net assets. Goodwill amortizes over a time period not to exceed 40 years. Goodwill is associated with amortization expense on the income statement. Amortization expense appears in the operating section of a cash flow statement prepared using the indirect method. Amortization expense does not appear on a cash flow statement prepared using the direct method.

Notes payable increases when the company borrows money, and decreases when the company repays the funds borrowed. Since only the principal appears on the balance sheet, there is no impact on the income statement for repaying the principal component of the note. Notes payable appear in the financing section of a cash flow section.

Premiums and discounts on **bonds** are amortized through bond interest expense. There is no cash flow associated with the amortization of bond discounts or premiums. Therefore, there will always be an adjustment in the operating section of the cash flow statement prepared using the indirect method for premium or discount amortization. Premium or discount amortization will not appear on a cash flow statement prepared using the direct method.

Common **stocks** and preferred stocks with their associated paid in capital accounts increase when additional stock is sold to investors, and decrease when stock is retired. There is no income statement impact for stock transactions. The cash flow associated with stock sales and repurchases appears in the financing section.

Retained earnings increases when the company earns profit and decreases when the company suffers a loss or declares dividends. The profit or loss appears as the first line of the operating section of the cash flow statement. The dividends appear in the financing section when they are paid.

CASH INFLOWS OR RECEIPTS When preparing the cash flow statement using the direct method, the cash collected from customers may be found by analyzing accounts receivable, as follows: Beginning balance of accounts receivable, plus sales for the period (from the income statement), less ending balance of accounts receivable, equals cash received from customers. This is an extremely simplified formula, and does not take into account written off receivables or other noncash adjustments to customer accounts. If there is no accounts receivable on the balance sheet, the company does a cash business and cash collected from customers will equal sales or revenue on the income statement.

If the cash flow statement is prepared using the indirect method, the adjustment to net income may be found in a similar manner. If the cash received from customers is more than the sales shown on the income statement, causing accounts receivable to decrease, the difference is added to net income. If cash received from customers is less than the sales shown on the income statement, causing accounts receivable to increase, the difference is subtracted from net income.

The amounts borrowed during the period may be found by analyzing the liability accounts. The amounts received from investors during the period may be found by doing a similar analysis on the Equity Accounts. Both of these types of transactions will be classified as financing activities.

If any land, buildings, or equipment were sold during the period, the information will be found in the Land, Building, and Equipment Accounts and their associated accumulated depreciation. One simple way to properly categorize the transaction is to reconstruct the journal entry. For example, assume that equipment that had cost $8,000 and had accumulated depreciation of $6,000 was sold during the period for $2,500. The journal entry for this transaction would have been:

Cash	2,500
Accumulated depreciation	6,000
Equipment	8,000
Gain on sale of equipment	500

The cash received from the sale of the equipment is classified as an investing activity. If the statement is prepared using the direct method, no other part of the journal entry is used. If the statement is prepared using the indirect method, the gain on sale of equipment is subtracted from net income. When the gain was recorded, net income increased. However, since the company is not in the business of buying and selling equipment, the gain needs to be subtracted from net income to arrive at the adjusted total related only to the proceeds from the company's direct business activities. If the sale had resulted in a loss, the loss is added back to net income.

CASH PAYMENTS Cash payments are found using similar methods to those used for finding cash received. Cash payments for the purchase of inventory are found by analyzing accounts payable. The following formula can be used to find the cash paid for inventory purchases: beginning balance of accounts payable, plus inventory purchases during the period, less ending balance of accounts payable, equals payments made for inventory during the period. This is a simplified formula and does not take into account any noncash adjustments.

If the cash paid for inventory is greater than the inventory purchased during the period, the difference between the amount purchased and the amount paid is deducted from net income if preparing the cash flow statement using the indirect method. If cash paid for inventory is less than the inventory purchased during the period, the difference between the amount purchased and the amount paid is added to net income if preparing the cash flow statement using the indirect method. Cash payments for land, building, and equipment purchases, repayments of loans, purchases of treasury stock, and payment of dividends may be found by performing similar analysis on the appropriate accounts.

SIGNIFICANT NONCASH TRANSACTIONS Noncash transactions are not to be incorporated in the statement of cash flows. Examples of these types of transactions include conversion of bonds to stock and the acquisition of assets by assuming liabilities. If there are only a few such transactions, it may be convenient to include them on the same page as the statement of cash flows, in a separate schedule at the bottom of the statement. Otherwise, the transactions may be reported elsewhere in the financial statements, clearly referenced to the statement of cash flows.

Other events that are generally not reported in conjunction with the statement of cash flows include stock dividends, stock splits, and appropriation of retained earnings. These items are generally reported in conjunction with the statement of retained earnings or schedules and notes pertaining to changes in capital accounts.

FURTHER READING:

Kieso & Weygandt. *Intermediate Accounting.* 7th ed. New York: Wiley, 1992.

Livingstone, John Leslie. *The Portable MBA in Finance and Accounting.* New York: Wiley, 1992.

"Official Releases, Statement of Financial Accounting Standards No. 95—Statement of Cash Flows." *Journal of Accountancy.* February 1988.

CASH MANAGEMENT

Cash management is a broad area having to do with the collection, concentration, and disbursement of cash. It encompasses measuring a company's level of liquidity, managing its cash balance, and making short-term investments. In some ways, managing cash flow could be considered the most important job of business managers. If at any time a company fails to pay an obligation when it is due because of the lack of cash, the company is insolvent. Insolvency is the primary reason firms go bankrupt. Obviously, the prospect of such a dire consequence compels companies to manage their cash with care. Moreover, efficient cash management means more than just preventing bankruptcy. It improves the profitability and reduces the risk to which the firm is exposed.

Cash management is particularly important for new and growing businesses. As Jeffrey P. Davidson and Charles W. Dean indicated in their book *Cash Traps,* cash flow can be a problem even when a small business is swamped with work, offers a superior product to its customers, and enjoys a sterling reputation in its industry. Companies suffering from cash flow problems have no no margin of safety in case of unanticipated expenses. They also may experience trouble in finding the funds for innovation or expansion. Eventually, as a small business's cash flow situation worsens, the owner may begin to dread the time for quarterly tax payments or to find himself or herself fielding angry calls from creditors. Finally, after poor

cash flow makes it difficult to hire and retain good employees, the small business is likely to fail.

It is only natural that expenses are incurred in the production of goods or the provision of services. In most cases, a business incurs such expenses before the corresponding payment is received from customers. When cash suddenly becomes available in abundance, there is also a natural tendency to spend it rather than holding some in reserve for lean times that may occur later. The key to successful cash management, therefore, lies in creating projections, monitoring collections and disbursements, and following budgets in order to remain solvent.

CASH COLLECTION AND DISBURSEMENT

Cash collection systems aim to reduce the time it takes to collect the cash that is owed to a firm (for example, from its customers). Some of the sources of time delays are mail float, processing float, and bank float. Obviously, an envelope mailed by a customer containing payment to a supplier firm does not arrive at its destination instantly. Likewise, the payment is not processed and deposited into a bank account the moment it is received by the supplier firm. And finally, when the payment is deposited in the bank account oftentimes the bank does not give immediate availability to the funds. These three "floats" are time delays that add up quickly, requiring the firm in the meantime to find other sources of cash to pay its bills.

Cash management attempts to decrease the time delays involved in collection at the lowest cost. A collection receipt point closer to the customer—perhaps with an outside third-party vendor, such as a lock box, to receive, process, and deposit the payment (check)—is one way to speed up the collection. The effectiveness of this method would depend upon where the customers were located; how much and how often they paid; the bank they remitted checks from; the collection sites the firm had (their own or through a third-party vendor); the costs of processing payments; the time delays involved for mail, processing, and banking; and the prevailing interest rate that can be earned on excess funds.

Once the money has been collected, most firms then proceed to concentrate the cash into one center. The rationale for such a move is to have complete control of the cash and to provide greater investment opportunities with larger sums of money available as surplus. There are numerous mechanisms that can be employed to concentrate the cash, such as wire transfers, automated clearinghouse (ACH) transfers, and checks. The tradeoff is between cost and time.

Disbursement is the opposite of collection. Here, the firm strives to slow down payments. It wants to increase mail delays and bank delays whenever possible, in order to keep more cash on hand for other uses. However, the firm has no control over processing delays.

THE OPTIMAL CASH BALANCE

Another aspect of cash management is knowing a company's optimal cash balance. There are a number of methods that try to determine this magical cash balance, which is the precise amount needed to minimize costs yet provide adequate liquidity to ensure bills are paid on time (hopefully with something left over for emergency purposes). One of the first steps in managing the cash balance is measuring liquidity, or the amount of money on hand to meet current obligations. There are numerous ways to measure this, including: the Cash to Total Assets ratio, the Current ratio (current assets divided by current liabilities), the Quick ratio (current assets less inventory, divided by current liabilities), and the Net Liquid Balance (cash plus marketable securities less short-term notes payable, divided by total assets). The higher the number generated by the liquidity measure, the greater the liquidity—and vice versa. However, there is a trade-off between liquidity and profitability which discourages firms from having excessive liquidity.

MODELS FOR CASH MANAGEMENT

To help companies to manage cash on a day-to-day basis in actual dollars and cents, a number of cash management models exist. These include the Baumol model, the Miller-Orr model, and the Stone model.

The Baumol model is similar to the Economic Order Quantity (EOQ). Mathematically, it can be stated as $C = (2FS/i)1/2$, where C is the optimal amount of cash to be acquired when reaching a threshold balance, F is the fixed cost of acquiring the cash (C) amount, S is the amount of cash spent during a time interval, and i is the interest rate expressed in the same time interval as S. One shortcoming of this model is that it only accommodates a net cash outflow situation as opposed to both inflows and outflows. Also, the cash outflow is at a constant rate, with no variation.

The Miller-Orr model rectifies some of the deficiencies of the Baumol model by accommodating a fluctuating cash flow stream that can be either inflow or outflow. The Miller-Orr model has an upper limit (U) and lower limit (L). When there is too much cash and U is reached, cash is taken out (to buy short-term securities to earn interest) such that the cash balance goes to a return point (R). Otherwise, if there is too little cash and L is reached, cash is deposited (from the short-term investments) to replenish the balance to R. The equations of the Miller-Orr Model are: $R = (3fs2/4i)1/3$, and $U = 3R$, where R is the return point,

f is the fixed cost for each transaction to withdraw or deposit cash, s2 is the variance of the cash flows, i is the interest rate per same time period as s2, and U is the upper limit. L is determined by other means; for example, compensating balance requirement, minimum balance to avoid bank service charges on checking account, or zero.

The Stone model is somewhat similar to the Miller-Orr model insofar as it uses control limits. However, it incorporates a look-ahead forecast of cash flows when an upper or lower limit is hit to take into account the possibility that the surplus or deficit of cash may naturally correct itself. If the upper control limit is reached but is to be followed by cash outflow days that would bring the cash balance down to an acceptable level, then nothing is done. If instead the surplus cash would substantially remain that way, then cash is withdrawn to get the cash balance to a predetermined return point. Of course, if cash was in short supply and the lower control limit was reached, the opposite would apply. In this way the Stone model takes into consideration the cash flow forecast.

The goals of these models are to ensure adequate amounts of cash on hand for bill payments and to minimize transaction costs in acquiring cash when deficiencies exist and in disposing of cash when a surplus arises. These models assume some cash flow pattern as a given, leaving the task of cash collection, concentration, and disbursement to other methods.

RELATED SHORT-TERM INVESTMENT DECISIONS

A key cash management problem becomes which money market instruments to select to place the temporary excess funds (including how much money and for how long). This short-term investment decision necessitates the analysis of return (need to annualize returns in order to compare) and liquidity. Only short-term investments meet the liquidity test, as long-duration instruments expose the investor to too much interest rate risk. In addition, federal government obligations are popular due to the absence of default risk and ease of resale in the secondary market. Nonetheless, there are numerous money market securities available with varying characteristics from many types of issuers.

FURTHER READING:

Davidson, Jeffrey P., and Charles W. Dean. *Cash Traps: Small Business Secrets for Reducing Costs and Improving Cash Flow.* New York: Wiley, 1992.

Emery, Gary W. ''Measuring Short-Term Liquidity.'' *Journal of Cash Management.* July/August, 1984.

Hill, Ned C. and William L. Sartoris. *Short-Term Financial Management.* New York: Macmillan, 1992.

Shulman, Joel S. and Raymond A. K. Cox. "An Integrative Approach to Working Capital Management." *Journal of Cash Management*. November/December 1985.

CENSUS DATA

Census data are numerical facts collected by the government on a regular basis relating to population, geographic trends, and the economy. Census data are used in a multitude of different ways. While the decennial population count is by far the biggest census that the U.S. Bureau of the Census undertakes, it also does thousands of other censuses—some annually, others monthly—to track changes in American society. This data is used to allocate government resources and determine regional representation in the U.S. Congress. The U.S. Economic Survey, another type of census which comes out every five years, is particularly helpful to small business owners. This data can help entrepreneurs evaluate business opportunities, consumer preferences, and competitive strategies, as well as locate the best geographic sites for new businesses.

The original mandate to perform a national population census every ten years is contained in the U.S. Constitution. In 1880, Congress streamlined the census process by establishing a separate Census Office in the U.S. Department of the Interior. The Census Bureau has been compiling ever greater numbers of censuses since it was first established. Every conceivable aspect of business, industry, and commerce is documented either monthly, annually, biannually, or quinquennially in the form of census surveys and polls, averaging 2,000 per year. Some of the census data are published in the form of one- or two-page reports; others are compiled annually into the *Statistical Abstract of the United States*. A recent innovation has been the Census Bureau's geographic database, TIGER (Topologically Integrated Geographic Encoding and Referencing), which provides a block-by-block population survey of the United States, including every bridge, stream, road, and tunnel. TIGER is available on CD-ROM as well as on the Internet, and many local libraries make it available to the general public.

In short, billions of facts are churned out by the Census Bureau annually. Approximately 40,000 different federal, state, and local government agencies and business entities rely on these facts. The decennial population census guides the reapportionment of seats in the U.S. House of Representatives, as well as in state, county, and municipal legislatures. Major cities also are vitally interested in the census data, since the population figures determine the amount of federal aid they receive. The census data also detail the amount of spending by state and local governments.

USEFULNESS OF DATA TO SMALL BUSINESSES

Virtually every business, industry, and service uses (or could benefit from using) census data. Entrepreneurs and self-employed persons can turn to the Census Bureau's popular publication *Taking Care of Business: A Guide to Census Bureau Data for Small Businesses* to find information to aid in decision-making. For a business catering to an ethnic minority, the census provides the population figure, location, and incomes for that ethnic group. For example, a restaurant in Los Angeles was able to contact the Census Bureau to find out the number of residents from the Deep South residing in the city, in order to determine how many ham hocks the restaurant should order. Companies can plot their future marketing strategies more effectively when they discover that the 1990 census indicates that by 2050, America's elderly—over 85 years of age—will have increased sixfold. Census data can also tell a household appliance service business the percentage of homes that use gas for heating and cooking.

Many businesses and manufacturers rely heavily on the five year U.S. Economic Survey, which is compiled from the results of questionnaires sent to 3.5 million companies. This data can help small business owners evaluate business opportunities, consumer preferences, market share, and competitive strategies, as well as enable them to locate the best geographic sites for new business and distribution routes for their products. It can also provide strong clues as to how to advertise products or target direct mail more effectively. The Economic Survey has become so detailed and complex in recent years that the Census Bureau issues a special reference book to guide the researcher through the data. But the information is available in a number of other forms. For example, the Census Bureau cooperates with the U.S. Small Business Administration to provide statistics for a range of publications and helps organize business seminars and workshops throughout the country. In addition, numerous private research firms offer their own census data "packages," complete with a user-friendly electronic format and their own projections. Many newspapers and magazines also cite social or economic data from current Census Bureau surveys.

Despite the utility and profit derived from using or marketing census data, there have nearly always been controversies surrounding the Census Bureau and the data it gives out. Because census data are vital in determining the amount of federal aid to cities, and whether or not to expand low income housing and other social programs, the Census Bureau has faced dozens of lawsuits alleging undercounting of minorities. The matter of privacy has also continually perplexed census efforts. While the pressure on the Bureau to provide increasingly detailed information has increased over the years, so has resistance to the "prying" nature of census questionnaires on the part of the public—from businesses to private individuals. Although the Bureau has been mandated to keep all of its information confidential since 1929, the computerization of government records has cast public doubt on the "leakproof" nature of census information. Finally, the demands for more diversified data have sizably increased the budget of the Census Bureau. To the dismay of many small businesses, the Bureau has responded with plans to scale back its survey activities, especially those involving small geographic areas. This means that responsibility for collecting census and other sorts of data may increasingly fall upon the private sector, especially universities and research firms.

FURTHER READING:

Anderson, Margo. *The American Census: A Social History.* New Haven, CT: Yale University Press, 1988.

Dodd, Don. *Historical Statistics of the States of the United States: Two Centuries of the Census, 1790-1990.* Greenwood Press, 1993.

Halacy, D.S. *Census: 190 Years of Counting America.* Elsevier/Nelson Books, 1980.

Myers, Dowell. *Analysis with Local Census Data: Portraits of Change.* San Diego, CA: Academic Press, 1992.

SEE ALSO: Demographics

CERTIFICATES OF DEPOSIT

Certificates of deposit (CDs) are certificates issued by a federally chartered bank against deposited funds that earn a specified return for a definite period of time. They are one of several types of interest-bearing "time deposits" offered by banks. An individual or company lends the bank a certain amount of money for a fixed period of time, and in exchange the bank agrees to repay the money with specified interest at the end of the time period. The certificate constitutes the bank's agreement to repay the loan. The maturity rates on CDs range from 30 days to six months or longer, and the amount of the face value can vary greatly as well. There is usually a penalty for early withdrawal of funds, but some types of CDs can be sold to another investor if the original purchaser needs access to the money before the maturity date.

Large denomination (jumbo) CDs of $100,000 or more are generally negotiable and pay higher interest than smaller denominations. However, such certificates are insured by the FDIC only up to $100,000. There are also eurodollar CDs, which are negotiable certificates issued against U.S. dollar obligations in a foreign branch of a domestic bank. Brokerage firms have a nationwide pool of bank CDs and receive a fee for selling them. Since brokers deal in large sums, brokered CDs generally pay higher interest rates and offer greater liquidity than CDs purchased directly from a bank.

NEW CD VARIATIONS

In the past, CDs—with their low risk and guaranteed interest rates—were considered the investment of choice by many retirees. "The old retirement plan was fairly simple," Bruce Andriatch explained in an article for *Business First of Buffalo*. "Take all your money, buy a bunch of certificates of deposit, and live off the interest." In recent years, however, the interest rate on regular CDs has declined so that it may not even keep up with the rate of inflation. As a result, investors sought alternatives that would provide greater returns along while maintaining a reasonable level of security.

In response to this trend, many banks began offering variations on the basic CD with special features designed to appeal to the needs of different investors. One popular option is an equity-linked CD, which guarantees the return of principal while paying a return at maturity that is based on the stock market index, rather than on a simple interest rate. Equity-linked CDs are generally sold as five-year coupon notes and charge fees averaging around 4 percent. "Equity-linked CDs are recommended as an investment product for retirees who want more equity exposure," according to Charles Baubonis, Gary Gastineau, and Dave Purcell in an article for *American Banker*.

Other variations on the basic CD are intended to provide investors with greater flexibility to make deposits and early withdrawals. Although most of these products have a higher level of risk than basic CDs, some investors find the tradeoff worthwhile. For example, some banks offer adjustable-rate CDs that increase or decrease the applicable interest rate depending on changes in the market rate. Other banks allow investors to add to their starting balance over the first year or more, and to make a one-time, penalty-free withdrawal of up to half of their funds. There are also health care CDs, which pay a slightly lower interest rate but allow investors to withdraw their money without penalty if they experience a financial hardship related to injury or illness. Finally, naked CDs are arranged similar to basic CDs but are more risky because they do not include federal deposit insurance coverage. In exchange for the increased risk, investors can receive a significantly higher return. Of course, it is important to assess the health of a financial institution offering naked CDs before investing.

"So how can you tell whether buying an exotic CD makes sense?" Debra Potter wrote in Medical Economics. "Before you bypass higher yields in favor of frills, make certain that those frills are really useful. You are, in effect, paying for them. And take on only as much risk as you can comfortably live with. CDs, long regarded as bastions of safety, should never keep you awake at night."

FURTHER READING:

Andriatch, Bruce. "Cracking Open the Nest Egg; Retirement Incentives Pushing Workers to Rethink Golden Years." *Business First of Buffalo*. January 10, 1994.

Baubonis, Charles, Gary Gastineau, and Dave Purcell. "Equity-Linked CDs Balance Risk and Return." *American Banker*. December 29, 1993.

Black, Pam. "CDs That Try a Little Harder." *Business Week*, September 5, 1994.

Brealey, Richard A., and Stewart C. Myers. *Principles of Corporate Finance*. 4th ed. New York: McGraw-Hill, 1991.

Dunnan, Nancy. *Dunn and Bradstreet Guide to Your Investments*. 1991.

Munn, Glen G., I. Garcia, and Charles J. Woelfel. *Encyclopedia of Banking and Finance*. 9th ed. Salem Press, 1991.

Potter, Debra. "Are the New CDs Right for You?" *Medical Economics*. July 24, 1995.

CERTIFIED LENDERS

Certified lenders are banking institutions that qualify for inclusion in a streamlined lending program maintained by the **U.S. Small Business Administration**. Certified lenders are institutions that have been heavily involved in regular SBA loan-guaranty processing and have met other criteria stipulated by the SBA. When a lender is approved as a SBA certified lender, its applications are given priority by the U.S. Small Business Administration. The lender receives a partial delegation of authority and is given a three-day turnaround by the SBA on the loan applications (they also have the option of using regular SBA loan processing). By the mid-1990s, more than 1,500 banks qualified as certified SBA lenders. These institutions accounted for nearly a third of all SBA business loan guarantees.

Lending institutions can become a part of the SBA's Certified Lender Program (CLP) in one of two ways: 1) It may make a request to an SBA field office for consideration for the program; or 2) An SBA field office may nominate the lender. SBA district directors approve and renew a lender's status as part of the CLP. Primary considerations in determining whether the lender will qualify include:

- Whether the applicant has the ability to process, close, service, and liquidate **loans**.

- Whether the applicant has a good performance history with the SBA (i.e., has it submitted complete and accurate loan guarantee application packages in the past?).

- Whether the applicant has an acceptable SBA purchase rate.

- Whether the applicant seems able to work amicably with the local SBA office.

If a lending institution makes an application for inclusion in the CLP, only to be turned down, it may make an appeal to the SBA's Assistant Administrator, Financial Assistance, whose decision is final.

According to the U.S. Small Business Administration, the AA/FA may suspend or revoke CLP status upon written notice providing the reasons at least 10 business days prior to the effective date of the suspension or revocation. Lending institutions may lose their status for a variety of reasons, including poor loan performance record; failure to make the required number of loans; violations of applicable statutes, regulations, or published SBA policies.

In recent years, the exact parameters of the SBA's CLP system have come under increased study. In 1996, for instance, legislation was drafted that would have required banks to make eight SBA loans a year for two consecutive years to qualify as certified lenders (the requirement for rural banks, which do not serve as many small businesses, would have been relaxed somewhat, but still would have required them to make four SBA loans a year for two years). That language was changed, however, so that institutions that are deemed to have "substantial experience" in making SBA loans would also be able to qualify or continue to be recognized as certified lenders.

PREFERRED LENDERS Similar to certified lenders are preferred lenders. Banks that qualify as preferred lenders are among the best SBA lenders and enjoy full delegation of lending authority in exchange for a lower rate of guaranty. In other words, they do not have to run an SBA loan past the SBA before approving it. This lending authority has to be renewed every two years, and the lender's portfolio is examined by the SBA on an annual basis. Preferred lenders are also required to employ two SBA-trained loan officers. Preferred loans accounts for about ten percent of all SBA loans.

FURTHER READING:

Heath, Gibson. *Doing Business with Banks: A Common Sense Guide for Small Business Borrowers*. Denver, CO: DBA/USA Press, 1991.

Kamerschen, David R. *Money and Banking*. Cincinnati, OH: South-Western, 1988.

Olaya, Phil. ''House Committee Eases Plan That Would Have Excluded 800 Banks from SBA Program.'' *American Banker*. July 23, 1996.

SEE ALSO: Banks and Banking; U.S. Small Business Administration Guaranteed Loans

CERTIFIED PUBLIC ACCOUNTANTS

The first laws regulating Certified Public Accountancy were enacted in New York in the 1890s. One hundred years later, Certified Public Accountants (CPAs) are representatives of one branch of a profession which has many different fields and specializations. With accounting practices spanning governments and other institutions, the accounting field has expanded exponentially

Unlike large corporate enterprises, small business owners may not need continuous accounting services. Still, small business owners need to ensure that their enterprise operates in accordance with the complexities of modern finance, and that their understanding of the business's financial situation is sufficient to ensure sound business decisions. Many entrepreneurs and business owners turn to CPAs for help in these areas. For a small business, financial mismanagement can spell failure, so choosing and using the services of a CPA are critical to business success.

QUALIFICATIONS

The CPA has a comprehensive educational background. Each candidate must attend a four-year program in accounting at an accredited institution. There is also the potential for a national requirement of a fifth year of education, though this has not yet been passed. A CPA must also pass a standard test for competency in the field. The CPA Exam covers four main areas: Law and Professional Responsibility; Auditing Procedures; Accounting and Reporting (taxation and accounting); and Financial Accounting and Reporting. This exam is administered in every state by the State Board of Accounting.

Individual State Boards also set up state regulations for professional licensing standards. This often means that CPAs are required to have professional experience. Each state has requirements that are peculiar to the state, so small business owners should contact their State Board of Accounting if they have any question about a CPA's qualifications.

There are several organizations for CPAs which also provide information and educate the public on the role of the CPA. The major national organization is the American Institute of Certified Public Accountants (AICPA). Its goals are to provide members with resources and information and to promote public awareness about the CPA profession. The AICPA sets a code of professional standards which serve as guidelines for CPAs in conduct and professional responsibility.

SERVICES

CPAs provide financial services to the general public—which can encompass both private citizens and business enterprises—rather than to one single company. They can act individually or as members of a public accounting firm. A CPA may provide service in one or more areas in which they have been trained, including the following:

- Financial Planning—A CPA may analyze assets, income, and spending in order to give a person a clear picture of their financial status. This can be done on an individual basis (retirement planning or investment planning) or on the business level (preparation of pension plans and business investments).

- Tax Preparation—A CPA can be a valuable resources to entrepreneurs seeking help in unraveling various tax codes and their impact on business. This function includes areas such as tax regulation compliance, consultation, and planning and representation.

- Management Advisory Services—Small business owners may need advice on anything from how to file for a business loan to the preparation of a budget. A CPA can help, educating businesses in preparing **financial statements**, budgets, strategic planning, and other financial matters.

- Accounting and Auditing—This involves verification of a company's accounting processes, documentation, and data to be certain it conforms to accounting principles. In this function, the CPA makes sure that financial statements are in order.

CPAs often specialize in specific areas of the accounting practice, such as auditing and accounting, tax law, or management advisory. They may also specialize in certain industry areas, such as retail, health care, or restaurant businesses.

ENTREPRENEURS AND THE CPA

Entrepreneurs seeking a CPA should look for the following:

- Reasonable Prices—Most CPAs charge competitive rates, but it makes sense to check pricing to be sure that the CPA is not charging rates exorbitantly higher than others in the field. It is always advisable to request a letter from the firm or individual CPA that explicitly states the CPA's fee or billing rate. This letter may also specify the billing and payment methods.

- Good Reputation—Does the CPA come well recommended? Integrity is something people discuss when talking about people who work with financial information. Listening to other business owners can provide valuable information in making your own choices.

- Flexibility and Adaptability—Can the CPA's business or firm fit your needs? Some CPAs provide only auditing or tax services, while others offer a host of financial planning, retirement, pension, and other services. A business should choose a CPA who can continue to provide services as its needs change.

In addition, entrepreneurs should prepare to do some footwork to make the relationship a valuable one. The business owner should be prepared to keep accurate records, including invoices, payments, and amounts spent on business-related expenses. A little bookkeeping goes a long way to improving the service a CPA can provide.

FURTHER READING:

Causey, Denzil. *Duties and Liabilities of Public Accountants*. Dow Jones Irwin, 1982.

Fox, Jack. *Starting and Building Your Own Accounting Business*. New York: John Wiley and Sons, 1984.

Miranti, Paul. "The Birth of a Profession," *The CPA Journal*. April 1996.

Rosenberg, Martin. *Opportunities in Accounting*. Lincolnwood, IL: VGM Career Horizons, 1983.

Shapiro, Leslie. "Future Services of Accountants—an AICPA Perspective," *National Public Accountant*, January/February 1997.

Weinstein, Grace. *The Bottom Line: Inside Accounting Today*. New American Library, 1987.

SEE ALSO: Accounting; Tax Planning

CHAMBERS OF COMMERCE

A chamber of commerce is a voluntary association whose membership is comprised of companies, civic leaders, and individual business people. Its members seek to promote the interests of business, typically in a broad-based way. Chambers of commerce exist on municipal, state, regional, national, and even international levels. Today, chambers of commerce—sometimes called boards of trade or commercial associations—can be found in most of the world's industrialized countries.

In the United States, the first chamber of commerce was created in 1768 in New York City. Its stated objectives encompassed "encouraging commerce, supporting industry, adjusting disputes relative to trade and navigation, and producing such laws and regulations as may be found necessary for the benefit of trade in general." Soon other chambers of commerce formed in other major cities. Arising in quick succession during the 19th century, chambers of commerce spread throughout the country and today number in the thousands.

At the local level, chambers of commerce strive to develop and publicize business opportunities in their communities, as well as work for the betterment of local schools and other community institutions. Local chambers of commerce offer a range of programs and services to their members, including information and advice on timely business matters, opportunities for networking, and a variety of publications. Local chambers of commerce also provide their members with numerous forums—task forces, committees, special events, and so on—in which to express their specific views and concerns, whether pertaining to the challenges facing small businesses or to the issues surrounding international commerce. Depending on their geographic settings, local chambers of commerce can be small or large in terms of their membership and scope of activities. The Greater Boston Chamber of Commerce, for instance, has 2,000 members, 80 percent of which are small businesses.

At the national level, chambers of commerce function as a unified voice for their affiliates. The Chamber of Commerce of the United States, for example, counts some 185,000 companies, affiliate chambers of commerce, and trade and professional associations among its members. Through them, it represents five million business organizations and individuals. Founded as a national federation in 1912 and headquartered in Washington, D.C., the national chamber was instrumental in persuading the federal government to institute a national budget and in gaining passage of the Federal Reserve Act. Its chief aims are to: promote economy in government, cut taxes, and devise an equitable tax system; improve labor relations; increase production, develop new markets, and provide more jobs; raise educational levels; build better cities; and keep organized business strong and increasingly effective.

To carry out its mission, the national chamber maintains a staff of 1,500 and engages in a broad spectrum of activities, ranging from informing and counseling its members on key government developments to conducting policy studies and issuing reports, bulletins, booklets, and the monthly magazine *Nation's Business*. In addition, the national chamber maintains a vigorous stance in making its policies and members' viewpoints known to federal agency personnel, members of Congress, and other public officials. Augmenting the national chamber are four regional offices and 50 foreign-based American chambers of commerce.

At the global level is the International Chamber of Commerce, founded in 1920. This organization constitutes an international federation of business organizations and individuals and as such serves as a powerful voice for business interests worldwide. It holds the highest-ranking status afforded to organizations the United Nations calls on in a consultative capacity. It also operates a prominent court of arbitration to settle international business disputes; utilizes teams of experts to formulate solutions to problems in such areas as communications, law, and financial relations; and issues a quarterly publication entitled *World Trade*. Headquartered in Paris, the International Chamber of Commerce functions as a vital mechanism for articulating global business concerns to world opinion leaders and the public at large.

Junior chambers of commerce, known as the Jaycees, also originated in the 1920s. These associations, evolving from the larger chamber of commerce movement, are composed of young businesspeople in their twenties and thirties. Prevalent throughout the United States and in many other countries as well, junior chambers of commerce principally devote their energies to projects of community improvement. For further information on the Chamber of Commerce of the United States, write the organization at 1615 H Street NW, Washington, DC 20062.

FURTHER READING:

"Chamber of Commerce of the United States." *Collier's Encyclopedia*. Collier, Inc.

Foundation for Public Affairs Staff. *Public Interest Profiles*. Washington: Congressional Quarterly.

SEE ALSO: Business Associations

CHARITABLE GIVING

Many small business owners engage in charitable giving, either as private individuals or in their corporate capacity. This charitable giving can take many forms, including **corporate sponsorship** of local charitable events, donations of excess **inventory**, and sustained philanthropy in one or more areas through the establishment of a formal foundation or council.

Whatever form the charitable giving takes, experts and entrepreneurs agree that such activity can have a beneficial impact on the company as well as the charities and institutions it supports.

CONTRIBUTIONS OF GOODS AND SERVICES

Charitable giving by small businesses most often takes the form of contributions of goods and, less often, services. Indeed, many companies have made donations of obsolete, excess, erroneously packaged or slow-moving inventory. The bottom-line advantages of such donations are considerable for small companies. "Not only can you get rid of that inventory and free up warehouse space, but you also can get a hefty tax deduction—often, more than your production costs—and at the same time help a not-for-profit organization," wrote Marsha Bertrand in *Nation's Business*. Indeed, some companies that donate goods to charitable causes can reap tax deductions that equal the cost of producing those goods plus half the difference between that cost and the fair market value of those goods. The amount of the deduction for which companies are eligible will vary with their legal status. **Partnerships**, **S corporations**, and **sole proprietorships** will only be able to claim deductions amounting to the production cost of the donated goods, but for **C corporations**, the deduction can be two times the production cost.

Bertrand and others point out, however, that the donated goods will entitle businesses to a deduction only if they meet requirements laid out in the Internal Revenue Service's tax code. For instance, the donor business will qualify for a deduction only if it hands over its goods to a qualified **non-profit organization**. Moreover, products that are donated must be targeted at helping disadvantaged or otherwise legitimate groups, such as children, the needy, and people who are ill. Finally, donated goods must be handed over unconditionally; the donor business is not allowed to receive compensation in any form for its largess. Despite these restrictions, analysts and companies that have established charitable giving programs agree that making such donations can have a potent positive impact for the participating business. "Besides the tax deduction and the reduction in inventory-carrying costs, companies realize tremendous public relations benefits," pointed out an executive with Second Harvest, one of America's leading charitable organizations, in an interview with *Nation's Business*.

Many businesses that choose to direct their excess inventory toward philanthropic targets have come to realize that there are a number of agencies that can help them in this task. In addition to non-profit organizations themselves, which typically try to make the donation process as easy as possible for donor companies, companies interested in handing over goods can enlist the help of organizations known as exchanges. These organizations serve as middlemen, accepting products from companies and then distributing them to various deserving charitable groups. "In addition to finding an outlet for your goods, exchanges supply you with the proper tax documentation, handle distribution, and ensure that the recipient qualifies under the tax code," stated Bertrand.

ORGANIZED GIVING IN SMALL FAMILY ENTERPRISES

Business experts agree that charitable giving is an activity that, when considered by small **family-owned businesses**, is particularly rife with both opportunities and challenges. The chief pitfall of charitable giving by members of family businesses is lack of communication. As Henry Welt observed in *Small Business Reports,* "Charity may begin at home, but when it makes its way into the family business, a common problem occurs: Each family member writes out checks at random, and no one keeps an eye on the big picture. Mom's giving to the cancer society, Dad to the police athletic league, and the children to Greenpeace. When you tally up the total donations for the year, you find a lack of direction and consistency in your family's support of charitable causes." Welt thus encourages owners of family businesses to organize their charitable giving in a cohesive way that can benefit both deserving non-profit organizations and the business itself: "With a strategic plan in place . . . your family can actively choose the charities that support both business and personal goals."

ORGANIZING A STRATEGY FOR PHILANTHROPIC GIVING There is no one organized giving plan that all family-owned businesses should adhere to. Indeed, small and mid-sized family businesses utilize a broad range of charitable strategies, many of which are tremendously effective despite their differences in emphasis, direction, and execution. But most successful giving programs share a common characteristic that is also a hallmark of success in the business arena: proper research and planning. Family businesses seeking to establish a program of charitable giving need to recognize that such policies are predicated on three major issues—choice of charities, size of donations, and the vehicle that will be used to execute donations.

CHOICE OF CHARITY OR CHARITIES Some family businesses choose to provide financial support only to causes that are personally important to family members, regardless of their influence on the business or industry in which the family is involved. Other families, meanwhile, may choose to steer their charitable giving toward areas that also impact on the family business. "A publisher that chooses to support literacy causes, for example, can publicize that connection and boost its image in the minds of consumers," explained Welt. "A paper manufacturer that supports environmental and deforestation causes can create good will in the community."

Of course, many families will discover that agreeing on the primary recipients of a charitable giving program is no easy matter. Some family members may be enthusiastic supporters of a non-profit organization, only to find to their dismay that other members are lukewarm or even hostile to that organization's goals and mission. In such instances, consultants urge individuals not to adopt an intransigent position or engage in "tit-for-tat" negotiations in which approval of a charity is withheld until family members agree to provide financial support to a cause to which they may not be enamored. There are plenty of charities out there upon which everyone should be able to agree. And Weld noted that in instances where disagreements break down along generational lines, "another option is to create a three- to five-year plan in which the causes favored by one generation give way over time to those favored by another."

DECIDING HOW MUCH TO GIVE The size of charitable donations that family-owned businesses give is, of course, directly linked to the size and fortunes of the family business. A family-owned lumber business with several locations and a host of reliable corporate clients is obviously going to be able to make larger donations, if they are so inclined, than are the owners of a single sporting goods store. But no matter what the sum total of donations is, family members should make sure that they arrive at the total together and in an informed fashion. That is, organized giving totals should be arrived at with an eye toward the business's current financial standing and its future business plans and prospects. A company poised on the brink of a major expansion effort, for example, may adopt a more modest strategy of organized giving than would a mature business helmed by owners who have decided to devote more time to raising children or other personal matters.

Another consideration that members of family-owned businesses need to weigh is their allocation of time to charities. Certain individuals may be enthusiastic supporters of a charity, giving considerable amounts of time and talent to the organization in order to advance its work. Such selflessness is laudable, but it can also give rise to resentments among fellow family members if they begin to feel like they are taking on an unfair share of the company's workload as a result. For this reason, family members should make sure that they communicate the needs of the business as well as the charity to one another through regular meetings. Of course, sometimes a business may find that extensive involvement in charitable work can also pay dividends for the company. ''Hands-on involvement not only demonstrates a tangible commitment [to the charity's work], but also allows you to network with others in the business community,'' said Welt.

CHOOSING A VEHICLE FOR GIVING Many family-owned businesses choose to establish a philanthropic foundation to guide its charitable activities. This is especially true of families that own larger businesses that can afford to make donations of considerable size. ''If you plan to donate more than $250,000, there are advantages to setting up a foundation, which is a legal entity recognized under state law and by the IRS as a non-profit corporation,'' said Welt. ''Although subject to somewhat complex rules, all contributions to the foundation generally are tax-deductible, whether they're made by family members or by non-family members who support the foundation's goals. A foundation also allows you to accumulate contributions over time—tax-free—to donate to your chosen causes. That might allow you to build up principal for, say, an on-going school scholarship.'' Before committing to a foundation, however, small business owners should consider the various restrictions that apply (foundations are required by law to distribute a minimum of five percent of their net worth to charities every year, for example) and the legal and accounting fees associated with running it.

Another option that some family businesses pursue is the formation of a charitable council. ''Like individuals, the council can give tax-deductible donations to charities,'' observed Welt. ''However, because councils are not recognized by or accountable to the IRS, there is no opportunity to accumulate principal tax-free, and contributors do not receive a tax break on any direct contributions to the council's funds.''

FURTHER READING:

Benson, Benjamin. *Your Family Business.* Irwin, 1990.

Bertrand, Marsha. ''Donations for Deductions.'' *Nation's Business.* January 1996.

Hise, Phaedra. ''Charity Begins at Home.'' *Inc.* April 1993.

''How It May Help Your Business to Sponsor Charitable Events.'' *Profit-Building Strategies for Business Owners.* July 1987.

Jaffe, Dennis. *Working with the Ones You Love.* Conari, 1990.

Stern, Linda. ''Generous to a Fault.'' *Small Business Reports.* August 1992.

Welt, Henry. ''All in the Charity.'' *Small Business Reports.* August 1994.

SEE ALSO: Community Relations; Corporate Image

CHILD CARE

Child care has emerged as an important issue for both employers and employees over the past 30 years. Indeed, a mid-1990s U.S. Department of Labor study observed that, during that period,

''America has become a society in which everyone is expected to work—including women with young children. But many of society's institutions were designed during an era of male breadwinners and female homemakers. What is needed is a . . . reform of the institutions and policies that govern the workplace to ensure that women can participate fully in the economy and that men and women have the time and resources to invest in their children.'' Researchers, child care experts, and working parents have been heartened by the success that some businesses have experienced in their efforts to assist their employees in this area, but the consensus remains that many child care arrangements are inadequate for working parents. Moreover, Katherine Smith pointed out in *Folio* that another societal trend has exacerbated the problem even more: ''The proliferation of single parents creates the additional burden of your employees not having partners to rely on to take over in a crisis situation.'' The child care problem is particularly acute in certain industries; studies indicate that working women in professional occupations (typified by high levels of education and salary) are two or three times more likely to receive child care benefits from their employers than are women who work in service, production, and agricultural occupations. Researchers hasten to point out, however, that the child care environment has ample room for improvement in nearly all industry sectors.

Child care problems have repercussions for employers as well; analysts have pointed out that problems with child care can be significant drain on worker **productivity**, and in some cases can even result in the permanent loss of valued employees. According to some experts, small businesses are particularly vulnerable to such losses, since they often do not have the financial resources to install the on-site child care centers that have proven beneficial to some innovative larger companies. But observers contend that small business enterprises have a variety of options at their disposal to help their employees deal with the child care issue.

Of course, the first priority for working parents is ensuring that their children are placed in a child care environment that protects them and attends to their physical and emotional needs. ''Working parents may differ in family situations and child care needs, but they all immediately voice the same concern,'' confirmed *Personnel* contributor Bob Smith. ''Parents want their children to be cared for in a safe environment, shielded from the potential dangers and abuses that the media often expose in graphic and horrifying detail. When parents believe their children are safe in another person's care, they feel a sense of relief, the lifting of a burden so prevalent among today's career mothers and fathers.'' But Smith noted that while safety is the paramount issue in selecting a child care provider, ''they also look at other tangible quality factors such as cleanliness, licensing, staff certification, and curriculum. But parental concerns go beyond the immediate classroom surroundings. Many parents said that they expected day care to be a practical learning experience for their youngsters.'' Unfortunately, the state of professional child care in the United States all too often leaves much to be desired. As David Whitman remarked in *U.S. News & World Report,* ''the warped dynamic of the child-care market is all too plain: There are too many parents chasing too few day-care openings in settings where there is too much turnover of providers who receive too little training and pay.'' This state of affairs naturally serves to further exacerbate the concerns of working parents seeking to juggle home and office responsibilities.

INTERGENERATIONAL CARE Changing demographics in the United States have created a situation wherein increasing numbers of working people find themselves dividing their time, energy, and financial resources between two sets of care demands. On one end lie small children, while on the other can be found elderly parents. This phenomenon has given rise to the still modest but growing success of so-called ''intergenerational care'' centers, in which working parents who also have obligations to care for their own parents can place both categories of dependents in a single facility. Most experts expect that, given the continued rise in participation by women in the work place—and the track record of success enjoyed by intergenerational care programs in hospitals, nursing homes, and child care centers—the concept of intergenerational care will continue to increase in popularity in the business world. In fact, some studies indicate that demographic trends practically ensure the continued growth of intergenerational care facilities. A study in the early 1990s by the National Council on Aging, for example, determined that approximately 40 percent of the American work force was providing care for both children and elders. Given all of these considerations, observers believe that businesses looking to provide some measure of child care assistance to their employees will factor the elder care issue into their analysis of options with increasing frequency. ''Companies that aren't doing anything at all probably could not envision doing on-site intergenerational care, or even **elder care**,'' admitted one executive—whose company opened an intergenerational care facility for its employees—in an interview

with *HR Focus.* ''But we're finding that companies that are either planning or thinking about on-site child care now are rethinking their space [to accommodate elder care in the future].''

BENEFITS OF CHILD CARE FOR EMPLOYERS Discussions of child care nearly always center on the desired benefits of such programs for working parents and their children. But analysts note that employers can also reap significant benefits from good child care arrangements, and they argue that if business leaders—whether CEOs of large companies or small business owners—were more aware of these benefits, they would be more likely to take an active role in helping their workers secure good child care (and elder care, to a lesser extent).

Indeed, many researchers insist that employers lose significant amounts of productivity from employees who are grappling with child care difficulties. These workers spend sometimes large amounts of company time on the issue (calling about possible providers, checking on the well-being of sick children, etc.), may fall victim to tardiness, and typically miss several days of work each year due to child care situations. Indeed, studies conducted in the early 1990s indicated that one out of three sick days taken by a working parent is actually due to child-related illnesses that preclude the child's presence at school or their usual day-care provider, and that other child-care problems can siphon off another seven or eight days of employee attendance on an annual basis. Some businesses, meanwhile, allow parents to occasionally bring their children to work with them when child care plans fall through. In some business environments, this may not result in dramatic reductions in productivity, but in other settings—such as office environments—this can result in significant productivity downturns for both the parent (who has to divide his or her time between work and child supervision) and co-workers, who are often distracted by the presence of the youngster. Finally, some businesses permanently lose valuable workers who decide, after having a child, that the expenses and hassles associated with day care make returning to the workplace a questionable strategy.

Given the above factors, small and large businesses alike should investigate ways in which they can help their employees secure acceptable child care arrangements. By doing so, they may well reap increased benefits in the realm of worker productivity and retention. In addition, they are likely to find that having a program of child care assistance in place can be a tremendous boon in recruiting efforts. Moreover, they may also find that providing such help is not nearly as expensive as they believed, since the provision of child care assistance is tax-deductible to employers. ''From a company standpoint, assisting your employees with their child care needs is good business," summarized Smith. "Child care saves a company more money than any other employee benefit. It allows a company to recruit employees more effectively, improves turnover, reduces absenteeism, and increases the productivity of employees."

RESEARCHING EMPLOYEES' CHILD CARE NEEDS

Prior to settling on a methodology by which to help working parents in their employ, businesses should first do some research to learn which alternatives will do the best job of meeting the needs of both the company and its workers. *HR Focus* contributor Karen Matthes wrote that before doing anything else, "employers should take a close look at their organizations and determine what their corporate goals are, what type of corporate culture exists, and how much money they're willing to spend." A child care plan that flouts any of these considerations will almost certainly perform inadequately or fail.

Employers should then consider disseminating a questionnaire or find some other means of assessing the needs and desires of their work force. In addition, business owners and managers should take a good look at the demographic make-up of their employee roster. After all, a company that employs relatively few people under the age of 40 is far less likely to need a comprehensive child care assistance plan that is a business that employs large numbers of women under the age of 35. "Ask how many would be involved in some kind of child care arrangement, the ages of their children and their current arrangements for having those children taken care of," one management consultant told *Nation's Business.* Employee impressions of various child care options and the amounts they are willing to contribute to employer-assisted child care programs should also be solicited.

From there, said Matthes, businesses should investigate the community in which they operate: "Companies should check out what programs the surrounding communities already have to offer, as well as determine both the resources and barriers to starting new ones." As one executive told *HR Focus,* "It doesn't make sense to reinvent the wheel. If there's already really good existing services in the community, take advantage of them or subsidize them. Work with the community to build the infrastructure."

CHILD CARE ASSISTANCE OPTIONS FOR SMALL BUSINESSES

In the past, business enterprises have associated child care almost exclusively in terms of on-site centers, which have been viewed as excessively expensive to build and operate. But proponents of such facilities contend that those opinions are based partly on misconceptions. In addition, child care experts and business consultants alike point to several other options that may be viable for employers, including those of small size. These options include company consortiums, outside referral services, salary reduction plans, and reimbursement plans.

ON-SITE FACILITIES Providing on-site child care facilities is the most expensive option for businesses. It requires significant up-front costs and in some cases increased operating costs in such areas as payroll (states have various guidelines on the necessary qualifications of day care facility managers/professionals, which may necessitate hiring new personnel), utilities, and liability insurance (although companies in some areas may be able to avoid increases in this area). But this option also usually provides the greatest peace of mind to employees, who can visit their children during lunch breaks, etc., and dramatically reduces logistics complications that workers face with off-site facilities (routine drop-offs and pick-ups, picking up kids who are sick, for example). Moreover, the presence of an on-site day care facility is a terrific attraction to prospective employees. And as mentioned above, the expense of establishing an on-site facility can be deducted from taxes. Nonetheless, as of the mid-1990s, most of these arrangements have been established by larger companies with healthy bottom lines rather than smaller businesses with more modest assets.

CONSORTIUMS Consortiums are among the most popular child care alternatives for small businesses with limited resources that nonetheless want to assist their workers in securing good care for their youngsters. Katherine Smith of *Folio* described this option as a "pooling of resources among companies in your area for employees with the same needs. This will create a day-care center that is run not by your company, but by a day-care provider." By combining forces, companies can realize significant cost savings while also meeting the child care needs of their employees. They simply pay for a certain number of slots and make the openings available to their employees (unused slots are usually made available to parents who are employed outside the consortium). Smith cautioned, though, that to be successful, "a consortium needs a committed individual to act as the motivator. . . . A prime mover is needed to make sure that the dollar projections are accurate and realistic, and to ensure that the companies involved will be protected from liability, that each is contributing its fair share, and that state and federal regulations are being met."

OUTSIDE REFERRALS Companies that pursue this option contract with an outside agency to provide their employees with community day care information. This information includes rates, locations, and openings at various licensed facilities. According to

Smith, some agencies also sponsor seminars designed to help parents select facilities, babysitters, and in-home day care providers. "These options," said Smith, "offer flexibility for parents who can select the day-care provider situation that's best for them and their children." Providing outside referrals is a relatively inexpensive option for businesses.

SALARY REDUCTION PLANS A favorite of business owners, who like its minimal expense, salary reduction plans call for the establishment of a flexible spending account that permits employees to reduce their pre-tax incomes by a specified amount and place that money in an account that is used to reimburse them for child care expenses. "The benefit of this plan is that the employees get a tax break and the company ends up spending very little," said Smith. "Social Security and federal unemployment insurance taxes are not paid on these dollars. The downside may be in the kinds of receipts that you will need to prove your deductions. Many private day care providers do not report their income to the IRS, and are therefore reluctant to provide your employees with receipts."

REIMBURSEMENT PLANS Under these plans, tax-deductible payments are either paid directly to the child care provider or to the working parents by the company. This option is easy to put in place and manage.

In addition to these child-care assistance options, business owners can institute other policies that can have a beneficial impact on their employees' ability to balance work and family responsibilities. Flextime, job sharing, work-at-home options, and extended maternity or paternal leaves have all been touted as policies that can be helpful to working parents.

FURTHER READING:

Bonfield, Phyllis K. "Working Solutions for Working Parents." *Management World.* February 1986.

Dilks, Carol, and Nancy L. Croft. "Child Care: Your Baby?" *Nation's Business.* December 1986.

"Few Employers Provide Direct Childcare Help." *IRS Employment Trends.* September 15, 1997.

Leveen-Sher, Margery. "Flexibility is the Key to Small Business Benefits." *Washington Business Journal.* February 16, 1996.

Matthes, Karen. "A Coming of Age for Intergenerational Care." *HR Focus.* June 1993.

Olmstead, Barney, and Suzanne Smith. *Creating a Flexible Workplace: How to Select and Manage Alternative Work Options.* AMACOM.

Reece, Barry L., and Rhonda Brandt. *Effective Human Relations in Organizations.* Boston, MA: Houghton Mifflin, 1993.

Sandroff, Ronni. "Helping Your Company Become Family-Friendly." *Working Woman.* November 1989.

Smith, Bob. "On the Outside Looking In: What Parents Want From Childcare." *Personnel.* September 1991.

Smith, Katherine. "Child Care: Not only the Employee Benefits." *Folio: the Magazine for Magazine Management.* November 1989.

Thiede Thomas, Linda, and James E. Thomas. "The ABCs of Child Care: Building Blocks of Competitive Advantage." *Sloan Management Review.* Winter 1990.

Vaeth, Elizabeth. "Child Care Presents Challenge, Expense for Working Parents." *Atlanta Business Chronicle.* September 6, 1996.

Whitman, David. "Waiting for Mary Poppins." *U.S. News & World Report.* November 24, 1997.

SEE ALSO: Career and Family

CHOOSING A SMALL BUSINESS

The individual who decides to establish his or her own small business stands on the cusp of an exciting and potentially rewarding period of life, but also faces a number of decisions that will likely have a considerable impact not only on the ultimate success of his or her entrepreneurial venture, but also the very character of the individual's life. Of these decisions, perhaps none is more significant than choosing the type of small business that they will establish and maintain.

Factors that should be considered before choosing a small business are myriad, ranging from financial and family issues to those of personal fulfillment and work background. Most consultants, though, recommend that before embarking on an entrepreneurial venture, would-be small business owners start by taking the time to examine their personal strengths and weaknesses, a seemingly fundamental step that, amazingly enough, is sometimes given short shrift in the decision-making process.

Yet a self-examination of positive and negative attributes is of little use to the prospective entrepreneur if he or she rationalizes or discounts negative qualities and overstates positive qualities. Honesty is essential, for after all, these good and bad qualities are going to be the foundation of your business. It is better to find out that the base is insufficiently strong to support your enterprise before you begin building rather than after. The list should be a comprehensive one, including both personal and professional attributes. But whereas the personal attributes will tend to cover such issues as your ability to get along with others, your level of self-motivation, your talent for written and oral communication, your temperament, your organizational abilities, and your capacity for forcefully dealing with unpleasant people (customers, employees, and vendors), professional attributes should grade your level of expertise in various business areas that you will need to attend to (or at least have some familiarity, should you decide to hire someone to take care of it), such as bookkeeping, marketing/advertising, sales, financial planning, project management, research, and computers/technology. Once a would-be entrepreneur has taken the time to list his or her attributes, her or she will be able to glean not only what qualities they already have, but also what areas need shoring up (via training, or assistance from employees). As countless entrepreneurs and researchers can attest, the strengths and weaknesses of the establishment's owner are, more often than not, reflected in the business itself.

In addition, such an exercise allows the prospective entrepreneur to match his or her personality "with a business whose personality is compatible," commented James Halloran in *The Right Fit: The Entrepreneur's Guide to Finding the Perfect Business.* "A business's *personality* is that center (product, service, or activity) that directs the behavior of the business activity. If there is a mutual attraction between what you enjoy and the business personality, it will greatly enhance your chances for success. In other words, doing what you like to do will allow you to work closer to your potential."

Of course, some people are not well suited, either in terms of skills or temperament, to run any kind of small business. Successful small business owners are often characterized by self-confidence, energy, and creativity; those who lack some or all of these qualities should think long and hard before launching a business enterprise. Indeed, confidence, determination, and creativity are perhaps the most important personal characteristics necessary for success. Of these, Halloran indicated in *Why Entrepreneurs Fail: Avoid the 20 Fatal Pitfalls Of Running Your Business* that self-confidence was perhaps the "the most important characteristic an entrepreneur must have . . . because there will be days when everything will go wrong. The confident entrepreneur will go to bed on these nights with the attitude that tomorrow will be a better day. You will also need confidence to be an effective decision maker. As a small business owner, there is no buck passing."

WEIGHING THE ALTERNATIVES

Rhonda M. Abrams, author of *The Successful Business Plan: Secrets and Strategies,* commented that "typically, entrepreneurs get their original business inspiration from one of four sources: 1) previous work experience; 2) education or training; 3) hobbies, talents, or other personal interests; or 4) recognition of an unanswered need. Occasionally, the impetus will come from the business experience of a relative or friend." Whatever the inspiration, potential small business owners need to consider a broad spectrum of factors when choosing whether or not to follow that inspiration and start a new business.

OBJECTIVES People establish businesses for themselves for a wide variety of reasons. Some entrepreneurs simply tire of being a cog in a larger business enterprise and pine for greater independence, while others are determined to carve out a life for themselves in which they can make a living doing something that they already love to do in their spare time. And, of course, many people take the small business ownership plunge in hopes of improving their financial fortunes or creating a more compatible lifestyle for themselves. "Wealth, independence, creativity, self fulfillment, status, contribution to society, choice of life style are commonly listed goals," summarized Halloran in *The Right Fit.* But he warned that "what you want from a business might well conflict with your career anchor [the set of interests, motives, and skills that have historically defined your career choices] and your values. Someone with a true creative anchor does not necessarily achieve monetary success. Artists must have realistic expectations and must often choose between creativity and wealth. The person who wishes to have evenings free to spend with friends or family will find that expectation does not equate with the goal of opening a restaurant. Therefore, it is important for you to state your needs and then to make sure the expectations from your areas of interest match them."

RISK ASSESSMENT Once a prospective entrepreneur has taken stock of his or her personal and professional talents and areas of interest, consideration of compatible small business options can begin. But even after the entrepreneur has settled on a business idea that seems like an ideal match, a diligent period of risk assessment should be undertaken. After all, starting a new business usually has significant repercussions in various areas of the entrepreneur's life (and the lives of the entrepreneur's family members).

Factors that need to be studied, then, include the following:

- Financial Situation—This is usually the single most important factor to consider. Not only do would-be entrepreneurs need to assess their current financial standing, they also need to undertake a comprehensive examination of business start-up costs (including initial operating expenses) and likely—not hoped for—business financial fortunes in the first few years of operation. Quantitative financial analysis is a must.

- Impact on Friends and Family—Family members and friends can often provide valuable insights into the pros and cons of various new business proposals. "Small business owners need a support group to explore their ideas with," wrote Halloran in *Why Entrepreneurs Fail.* "If you can't get support, particularly from family, it might be a fatal flaw. Because owning a business is so engrossing, it is not fair to your family to proceed without their support. You will need their understanding and involvement if you expect to realize your goals."

- Market for Business's Products or Services—Would-be entrepreneurs need to research the potential market for their business, and the various steps needed to reach and expand on that audience.

- Industry Health and State of Competition—"Your business does not operate in a vacuum," stated Abrams. "Generally, your company is subject to the same conditions that affect your overall industry. If consumer spending declines and retail industries as a whole suffer, there's a good chance your neighborhood boutique will also experience poor sales. As you develop your plan, you need to respond to the industry-wide factors that will affect your own company's performance. While it is certainly possible to make money in an industry that is experiencing hard times, you can only do so if you make a conscious effort to position your company appropriately." In addition, start-up businesses often find that raising capital is a considerably more difficult task if the business is in a struggling business sector. **Industry analysis**, then, is a vital component of business success.

- Choice of Partners and/or Managers—Selecting partners and/or key personnel for your new business venture is a task that is both fraught with peril and bursting with possibility. The addition of a talented, enthusiastic business partner or experienced, trustworthy management staff can help get your business off to a sound, promising start; conversely, taking on an unreliable partner because you have chosen to enter a business that requires a big up-front investment can put a swift end to entrepreneurial dreams.

- **Franchising** Option—Many entrepreneurs choose to make their first venture into the world of small business ownership with a franchise. "The ever-growing franchise market offers opportunities in all areas of the small business spectrum," confirmed Halloran. "Although they are more expensive to enter and you will lose a certain degree of your independence, the good ones have a track record to be of great support to the owner."

Prospective small business owners also need to take precautions to make sure that they are basing their decision to open a new business or buy an existing one on sound business criteria rather than emotionalism, which often strikes hardest during periods of personal stress. For example, some consultants and researchers warn would-be entrepreneurs of the hazards of making huge career decisions during a divorce. Others, such as Halloran, writing in *Why Entrepreneurs Fail,* note that "losing a job can often be the worse scenario for opening a new business. The potential owner has just gone through an exhausting psychological experience and is not prepared to make the necessary and difficult decisions in an objective manner." Finally, there are others who, tantalized by best-case scenarios of wealth and independence, become trapped in businesses that they never should have launched or for which they did not adequately prepare.

FURTHER READING:

Abrams, Rhonda M. *The Successful Business Plan: Secrets and Strategies.* Rev. ed. Grants Pass, OR: Oasis Press, 1993.

Bangs, David H., Jr. *The Start Up Guide: A One Year Plan for Entrepreneurs.* Upstart Publishing, 1989.

Burstiner, Irving. *The Small Business Handbook: A Comprehensive Guide to Starting and Running Your Own Business.* Prentice Hall, 1989.

Halloran, James W. *The Right Fit: The Entrepreneur's Guide to Finding the Perfect Business.* Blue Ridge Summit, PA: Liberty House, 1989.

Halloran, James W. *Why Entrepreneurs Fail: Avoiding the 20 Fatal Pitfalls of Running Your Business.* Blue Ridge Summit, PA: Liberty House, 1991.

Levitt, Mortimer. *How to Start Your Own Business Without Losing Your Shirt: Secrets of the Artful Entrepreneur.* New York: Macmillan, 1988.

SEE ALSO: Career and Family; Entrepreneurship

CLOSELY HELD CORPORATIONS

Closely held firms are those in which a small group of shareholders control the operating and managerial policies of the firm. Over 90 percent of all businesses in the United States are closely held. These firms differ from most publicly traded firms in which ownership is widely disbursed and the firm is administered by professional managers. Most—but not all—closely held firms are also **family-owned businesses**. Family businesses may be defined as those companies where the link between the family and the business has a mutual influence on company policy and on the interests and objectives of the family. Families control the operating policies at many large, publicly traded companies. In many of these firms, families remain dominant by holding senior management positions, seats on the board, and preferential voting privileges even though their shareholdings are significantly less than 50 percent.

VALUATION ISSUES One of the major concerns associated with closely held firms is the determination of their value. This uncertainty is largely due to the fact that shares of a closely held business are owned by a small number of stockholders, and often by members of a family. Because there is no established market for the shares, it is difficult to establish the value of the shares in an estate or gift tax situation.

In preparing a **valuation** report, the major guidelines to be followed are contained in **Internal Revenue Service** guidelines. According to the IRS, the proper estimate of value should be based on the price at which a property would change hands between a willing buyer and a willing seller, with neither party under any compulsion to buy or sell and with all relevant facts available to both parties (the fair market value standard). The IRS provides valuation criteria for closely held businesses that are generally accepted by appraisers and the courts. The criteria include the history of the business, economic outlook, book value, earning capacity, dividend-paying capacity, **goodwill** and other intangibles, past sales of company stock, and stock of comparable businesses.

Without a marketplace that reflects the price arrived at by both buyer and seller, the security prices of a closely held firm must be set by calculation, comparison, and the use of financial ratios. Valuation techniques that have evolved fall into three principal categories: (1) market (price-earnings) methods; (2) cash flow methods; and (3) book value (balance sheet) methods. Another area of concern when addressing valuation issues is the notion of discounts for minority interests and lack of marketability.

BUY/SELL AGREEMENTS It is important to have detailed plans and procedures for the sale or transfer of stock at the time of the death, disability, or retirement of a shareholder in a closely held firm. Without such procedures, the departure of one major shareholder could also signal the end of a business. Buy/sell agreements spell out the terms governing sale of company stock to an outsider and thus protect control of the company. In many instances, these agreements allow co-owners to buy out heirs or other shareholders in the event of death or disability. In order to be considered valid for estate tax purposes, a stock buy-sell agreement must meet several conditions, including a "full and adequate consideration" provision. **Life insurance** is generally used to provide the funds to purchase the shares of a closely held company if one of the owners dies.

There are two basic types of buy-sell agreements: cross-purchase agreements and redemption agreements. With a cross-purchase agreement, the owner separately purchases a policy on the other owner(s). With a redemption agreement, the corporation is obligated to redeem the stock at a price set in the agreement if any of the business owners die. Typically, the buy/sell agreements are funded with life insurance; the life insurance proceeds provide the necessary funds for the purchase of the business.

The prolonged disability of a principal can also present serious difficulties for closely held firms. A long-term disability buy-sell agreement can provide a cushion to protect the disabled principal's interests during recovery. The first step in implementing such an agreement is to determine how long the company should be without the disabled partner's services before a buyout is activated. It is recommended that an actual buyout of ownership interest be postponed at least 12 months but not more than 24 months after the infirmity occurs.

FURTHER READING:

Klaris, Raynor J. "Valuing the Family Business." *Trusts & Estates*. February 1990.

Owens, Thomas. "Buy-Sell Agreements." *Small Business Reports*. January 1991.

Ward, John L., and Craig E. Aronoff. "Two 'Laws' for Family Businesses." *Nation's Business*. February 1993.

COLLATERAL

Collateral is an item that is pledged to guarantee repayment of a loan. Collateral items are often of significant value—property and equipment are often used as collateral—but the range varies considerably, depending on the lending institution and variables in the borrower's situation. Collateral only comes into play when a company needs to make a secured loan. Unlike unsecured loans, in which a borrower is able to get a loan solely on the strength of its credit reputation, secured loans require borrowing companies to put up at least a portion of their assets as additional assurance that the loan will be repaid. Many start-up businesses turn to collateral-based loans to get their start.

TYPES OF COLLATERAL Many different types of collateral arrangements can be made by companies, whether they are experiencing a financial crunch or making plans for expansion. Common types of collateral include the following:

1) Purchase Money Security Interest (PMSI)—
Also known as a chattel mortgage, this option allows the borrower to secure a loan by

borrowing against the value of the equipment being purchased.

2) Real Estate—Businesses that utilize real estate as collateral are generally requesting long-term loans of significant size (the company has plenty of other collateral options for smaller loans). The size of the loan under this arrangement is predicated in large measure on the market and foreclosure value of the property, as well as the amount of insurance coverage that the company has taken out on it.

3) Endorser—Under this form of collateral, a company secures a loan by convincing another person to sign a note that backs up the promises of the borrower. "This endorser is then liable for the note," stated Mark Van Note in *ABCs of Borrowing*. "If the borrower fails to pay, the bank expects the endorser to pay. Sometimes the endorser may also be asked to pledge assets." A guarantor loan security is similar to the endorser arrangement, except that the guarantor is not required to post collateral.

4) Warehouse Receipts—Another option for borrowers is to put up a portion of their warehouse commodities as collateral. Van Note explained that with warehouse receipts, "the receipt is usually delivered directly to the bank and shows that the merchandise has either been placed in a public warehouse or has been left on your premises under the control of one of your employees who is bonded. Such loans are generally made on staple or standard merchandise that can be readily marketed. The typical loan is for a percentage of the cost of the merchandise."

5) Display Merchandise—This method of borrowing, which is also sometimes referred to as "floor planning," is similar to warehouse **inventory**. Under this plan, **display merchandise** such as furniture, automobiles, boats, large appliances, and electronic equipment can be used to secure loans.

6) Inventory—This encompasses all the various assets (merchandise, property, equipment, etc.) owned by the borrowing business that could be liquidated to repay the loan.

7) Accounts Receivable—As Van Note remarked, "many banks lend money against accounts receivable; in effect, counting on your customers to pay your loan. The bank may take accounts receivable on a notification or nonnotification plan. Under the notification plan, the purchaser of the goods is informed by the bank that the account has been assigned and is asked to make payments directly to the bank. Under the nonnotification plan, customers continue to pay you and you pay the bank." Under this collateral agreement, lenders sometimes advance up to 80 percent of the value of the receivables once the goods are shipped.

8) Savings Account—Savings accounts (and certificates of deposit) can be used as collateral.

9) Stocks and Bonds—Publicly held companies have the option of offering **stocks** and **bonds** within the company as security.

10) Life Insurance—Some lenders are willing to accept the cash value of a **life insurance** policy as collateral on a loan.

FURTHER READING:

Brealey, Richard A., and Stewart C. Myers. *Principles of Corporate Finance.* 4th ed. New York: McGraw-Hill, 1991.

Financing for the Small Business. Washington: U.S. Small Business Administration, n.a.

Pickle, Hal B., and Royce L. Abrahamson. *Small Business Management.* 5th ed. New York: John Wiley & Sons, 1990.

Van Note, Mark. *ABCs of Borrowing.* Washington: U.S. Small Business Administration, n.a.

SEE ALSO: Loans; Venture Capital

COLLECTIONS

Collections refer to the efforts small businesses must make to obtain payment from customers for purchases that have been made on **credit**. Most customers will simply pay the amount due on their accounts upon receipt of an invoice. In some cases, however, the amount of a sale or debt exceeds a customer's ability or willingness to pay. The small business then must make a special effort to collect the money owed. In his book *A Practical Guide to Credit and Collections,* George O. Bancroft noted that an effective collection program "must be an integral part of the total sales process. The main objective of the collection program must be to develop customer relations and recover the company's delinquent receivables as quickly and economically as possible, while encouraging the formerly delinquent customer to patronize the company with future good business— business that is paid within the credit terms."

Like the procedures for granting credit to customers, a small business's collection procedures should be outlined in a company manual. The central message of the collection program should be consistent with the company's overall goals. Ideally, the collection process should follow a well-ordered progression, so that each step builds upon the last in a timely fashion. It also should be friendly and professional, offering customers an opportunity to respond in a positive manner. In order for a collections program to meet these criteria, good record-keeping is essential.

ELEMENTS OF THE COLLECTIONS PROCESS

Bancroft outlined four elements of a collections program: paper notices, telephone notices, personal visits, and assignment of accounts to collections specialists. The first approach to try when a customer's credit account becomes overdue is sending paper notices. These include a first past-due notice, a second past-due notice, a notice that further purchases will be on a cash-on-delivery (COD) basis until the balance is paid on the account, a letter informing the customer that the account has been turned over to an attorney or collection agency, and a letter reinstating the previous credit terms after the balance has been paid. These letters should be sent at specific, predetermined intervals for most ordinary delinquent accounts.

Telephone notices are used regularly for ''special'' accounts, such as large corporations, hospitals, schools, and government agencies. In many cases it seems inappropriate for a small business to send regular past-due letters to such customers. Using the telephone can help the small business owner to understand the circumstances surrounding the customer's failure to pay and to make arrangements that will fit the needs of both parties. It is important to avoid using the telephone in such a manner that the customer feels harassed, however.

Personal visits to a customer may be used to verify their location, review records, or give personalized attention to an account. Of course, the selection of different collection methods depends on some extent to the amount of money that is outstanding on the account. Less expensive paper procedures may be most appropriate for small sums, while more expensive personal visits may be warranted for large sums. Throughout all of these steps, Bancroft emphasized that the small business owner should assume the best of the customer and offer them a way to save face while motivating them to take action on the delinquent account.

As a final step in the collection process, it may be necessary to assign delinquent accounts to an outside collection agency or an attorney that handles collections. Most small businesses have no need and cannot afford to maintain a great deal of collections expertise in-house, so these collections professionals can take over after the small business exhausts its resources

and abilities to obtain payment. A general rule is to hire a professional when an account has been delinquent for over 90 days with no action by the customer. Even with professional help, some debts will inevitably be uncollectible due to bankruptcy, customers that ''skip'' (move without notice), or the expense required to collect them.

COLLECTION APPROACHES

Experts recommend that small business owners view all but the most persistent collection problems as an opportunity to help a customer resolve a situation. In many cases, nonpayment of a credit account by a customer is due to a temporary problem—such as illness, divorce, or unexpected business losses—and a supportive approach will enable the customer to continue to patronize the small business in the future. As a result, the first attempt to collect a delinquent account should always be gentle and low-key, with an eye toward preserving the business relationship.

Customers that are honest and cooperative when dealing with a past-due account should be treated with patience. Ideally, they will be able to make a token payment and set up a schedule for repaying the full amount owed. Customers that seem reluctant but are not particularly uncooperative should be prodded gently at first, then treated with increasing firmness over time. In these cases, it may be necessary to make a definite plan for repayment of the debt and get collateral or other reassurance. Customers that make no effort to repay money owed, or even actively try to avoid paying, may require a somewhat more aggressive approach.

But small business owners should be aware that the law has become fairly stringent about collection methods. For example, it is illegal to make continual phone calls, to use bad language, to threaten repossession when in fact the article cannot be repossessed, or to threaten to damage a customer's credit report or have their wages garnished. It is also illegal to discuss a customer's collection problem in public. Overall, small business owners should consult an attorney before using any aggressive approaches to collecting delinquent accounts.

FURTHER READING:

Bancroft, George O. *A Practical Guide to Credit and Collection.* New York: American Management Association, 1989.

Bond, Cecil J. *Credit and Collections for Your Small Business.* Blue Summit, PA: Liberty House, 1989.

J. K. Lasser Institute. *How to Run a Small Business.* New York: McGraw-Hill, 1989.

SEE ALSO: Credit Evaluation and Approval; Customer Retention; Customer Service

COMMUNICATION SYSTEMS

Communication systems are the various processes, both formal and informal, by which information is passed between the managers and employees within a business, or between the business itself and outsiders. Communication—whether written, verbal, nonverbal, visual, or electronic—has a significant impact on the way business is conducted. The basic process of communication begins when a fact or idea is observed by one person. That person (the sender) may decide to translate the observation into a message, and then transmit the message through some communication medium to another person (the receiver). The receiver then must interpret the message and provide feedback to the sender indicating that the message has been understood and appropriate action taken.

The goal of any form of communication is to promote complete understanding of a message. But breakdowns in communication can occur at any step in the process. Business managers need to understand and eliminate the common obstacles that prevent effective communication. Some of the causes of communication problems in business settings include: differing expectations and perceptions; selectivity (the tendency for individuals to pick and choose what they retain when they receive a message from another person); and distractions (such as ringing telephones, scheduled meetings, and unfinished reports).

According to Herta A. Murphy and Herbert W. Hildebrandt in their book *Effective Business Communications,* good communication should be complete, concise, clear, concrete, correct, considerate, and courteous. More specifically, this means that communication should: answer basic questions like who, what, when, where; be relevant and not overly wordy; focus on the receiver and his or her interests; use specific facts and figures and active verbs; use a conversational tone for readability; include examples and visual aids when needed; be tactful and good natured; and be accurate and nondiscriminatory.

Unclear, inaccurate, or inconsiderate business communication can waste valuable time, alienate employees or customers, and destroy goodwill toward management or the overall business. ''Your jobs, promotions, and professional reputation often depend on the success or failure of your written and oral communication,'' Murphy and Hildebrandt noted. ''Especially if your career requires mainly mental rather than manual labor, your progress will be strongly influenced by how effectively you communicate your knowledge, proposals, and ideas to others who need or should receive them.''

HISTORY OF BUSINESS COMMUNICATIONS

In the early years of corporate America, business managers operated on a strict basis of top-down communications. Whatever the boss or owner of the company said was the law. In most cases, strategies for doing everything from selling product to dealing with employees would be discussed behind closed doors. Once those decisions were made by managers, lower-level employees were expected to put them into effect. Employees had little input; they did as they were told or found work elsewhere. Such management attitudes, particularly when they applied to worker safety issues in such places as coal and steel mines, led to the growth of **labor unions**. If nothing else, unions had the power in many cases to slow or shut down production until management listened to demands.

In reaction to union demands, corporations eventually set up communication systems where rank and file members could speak their minds through union representatives. Although the unions provided the impetus for corporate managers to implement such systems, managers eventually realized that employees could have meaningful input into solving company problems. When presented with the opportunity to contribute, many employees jumped at the chance. This sort of feedback came to be called bottom-up communication.

In today's business environment, most corporations encourage employees to take an active role in the company. Employees who notice ways to improve production are encouraged, and usually rewarded, for passing those ideas on to managers. Employees who submit ideas that withstand intense study can be rewarded with a percentage of the savings to the company. Employees who are harassed on the job are strongly encouraged to report such harassment as far up the chain of management as necessary to stop it. Regular employee meetings are held where the lowest-level employee can stand up and ask the highest-level manager a direct question with the full expectation that a direct answer will be offered in return.

Business managers have also developed a method of monitoring how the company is running while meeting employees halfway. Sometimes called ''management by walking around,'' this method of communication calls for top managers to get out of their offices and see what is happening at the level where the work is performed. Instead of simply reading reports from subordinates, business owners visit factories or service centers, observe employees on the job, and ask their opinions. Although the practice is both praised and denigrated regularly by business management experts, this form of communications does serve to keep the boss in touch.

PREPARING EFFECTIVE MESSAGES

Perhaps the most important part of business communication is taking the time to prepare an effective and understandable message. According to Murphy and Hildebrandt, the first step is to know the main purpose of the message. For example, a message to a supplier might have the purpose of obtaining a replacement for a defective part. The next step is to analyze the audience so that the message can be adapted to fit their views and needs. It may be helpful to picture the recipient and think about which areas of the message they might find positive or negative, interesting or boring, pleasing or displeasing. After that, the sender must choose the ideas to include and collect all the necessary facts. The next step involves organizing the message, since a poorly organized message will fail to elicit the required response. It may be helpful to prepare an outline beforehand, paying particular attention to the beginning and ending portions. Some examples of ways to organize messages include: a direct organization, which may be used for a request or to relate good news; or an indirect organization, which may be used to persuade or to relate bad news. Finally, before transmitting the message it is important to edit and proofread.

COMMUNICATION MEDIA

There are two main media used for communication: written and oral. "If your message requires an immediate answer, an oral channel may be the better choice," Murphy and Hildebrandt stated. "But if the message contains complicated details and figures or if its subject requires filing for future reference, a written communication is necessary." Written communication systems that might be used within a business include memos, reports, bulletins, job descriptions, posters, employee manuals, and electronic mail. Outside of the business, examples of written communication might include letters, reports, proposals, telegrams, faxes, postcards, contracts, advertisements, brochures, and news releases. Internally, businesspeople might communicate orally through staff meetings, personal discussions, presentations, telephone calls, or the informal employee grapevine. Oral communication with those outside of the business might take the form of face to face meetings, telephone calls, speeches, teleconferences, or videoconferences. In addition to written and oral communication, individuals may also communicate through nonverbal means. Each of these types of communication is described below.

WRITTEN COMMUNICATION Written communication is very common in business situations, so it is important for small business owners and managers to develop effective written communication skills. The basic principles of written communication are similar to those for overall communication, such as determining the purpose for writing, analyzing the audience, organizing the message, and proofreading. Since written communication does not usually receive immediate feedback, it is particularly important when using this medium to use simple words and short sentences, and to avoid technical jargon and cliches.

Some of the most important business uses of written communications involve persuading the receiver to take some action, such as invest funds in a small business or agree to purchase a product or service. Persuasive letters have a special organization. According to Murphy and Hildebrandt, they should: 1) attract favorable attention from the reader; 2) arouse interest; 3) convince the reader and create desire; and 4) describe the action the reader should take. When the purpose of the letter is to make a sale, it is also important to include facts about the product and a clear central selling point. Above all, it is important that any type of written communication that originates from a business create or enhance goodwill.

ORAL COMMUNICATION Small business owners and managers are frequently called upon to make presentations, conduct interviews, or lead meetings, so **oral communication** skills are another important area for development. Presentations might be made to employees for training purposes, or to potential customers for sales purposes. In either case, good presentation techniques can generate interest and create confidence. Interviewing skills might be needed for hiring new employees, conducting performance appraisals, or doing market research. Meetings or conferences can be important tools for relating to employees or to interested parties outside of the organization in order to solve problems or set goals.

The same principles that apply to other forms of oral communication also apply to telephone calling. It is important to plan business calls by determining the purpose, considering the audience (including the best time to call), and deciding the ideas to be included and the questions to be asked. When answering the telephone in a business setting, it is important to answer promptly and to state your name and department in a clear, pleasant voice. Communication over the telephone can create impressions that are vital to small business success.

An often overlooked element of oral communication is listening. Good listening skills can be vital in finding a solution to grievances or even in making sales calls. Listening involves showing an interest in the speaker, concentrating on the message, and asking questions to ensure understanding. It helps to be prepared for the discussion, to avoid arguing or interrupting, to take notes as needed, and to summarize the speaker's statements.

NONVERBAL COMMUNICATION Nonverbal communication—such as facial expressions, gestures, posture, and tone of voice—can aid in the successful interpretation of a message. "Sometimes nonverbal messages contradict the verbal; often they express true feelings more accurately than the spoken or written language," Murphy and Hildebrandt noted. In fact, studies have shown that between 60 and 90 percent of a message's effect may come from nonverbal clues. Therefore, small business owners and managers should also be aware of the nonverbal clues in their own behavior and develop the skill of reading nonverbal forms of communication in the behavior of others.

There are three main elements of nonverbal communication: appearance, body language, and sound. The appearance of both the speaker and the surroundings are vital in oral communications, while the appearance of written communications can either convey importance or cause a letter to be thrown out as junk mail. Body language, and particularly facial expressions, can provide important information that may not be contained in the verbal portion of the communication. Finally, the tone, rate, and volume of a speaker's voice can convey different meanings, as can sounds like laughing, throat clearing, or humming.

COMMUNICATIONS TECHNOLOGIES

Although the form and content of business communications has remained fairly constant in recent years, technology has improved the way management and employees keep in touch with each other. Almost all companies have some regular method of keeping in touch with employees through bulletin boards, newsletters, or magazines. Larger, more technically proficient and geographically spread out companies may also use corporate-produced television shows, or copy-only messages transmitted by closed circuit television. Some companies distribute electronic mail (E-mail) newsletters or messages, which can be instantly transmitted and placed in every computer wired into the company's network.

Bulletin boards are one of the oldest forms of corporate communications. In the early days, bulletin boards were frequently the only communication that management had with employees. Everything from demands for longer hours to the announcement of new plant openings would be announced on the boards. Today, bulletin boards are not always found in businesses. Some companies use them for nothing more important than posting legal requirements such as wage and hour rates. Other companies try to make bulletin boards a force for employee recognition and information. The challenge all companies face with bulletin boards is that they fade in the consciousness of employees who get used to seeing them every day.

Unless the information is changed regularly and presented in an attractive way, employees can ignore it.

Company newsletters and magazines try to address the inability of management to speak to each employee personally. These forms of written communication explain management policies, announce new products or initiatives, answer questions, and provide each employee with a reminder of what the company is all about. The increased availability and simplicity of desktop publishing systems has made newsletters and magazines an option even for small businesses.

In the meantime, closed-circuit, satellite, and videotape-based television have become popular with some larger corporations. Some corporations have spent millions of dollars in developing a television presence that would be difficult to distinguish from the quality produced by regular television networks. Television is immediate and can quickly grab the attention of employees. For example, a CEO who had to make an emergency announcement to employees could do so within minutes over a television system, while a newsletter or magazine takes weeks to produce.

The latest and fastest growing method of corporate communications is electronic mail. **E-mail** is instantaneous and is available to anyone with a computer terminal. E-mail can be customized to be sent to an individual or to a group of people with a common interest, such as the members of a committee or task force. It can help internally with scheduling, as well as with exposing managers to employee comments and complaints. E-mail can also be used to communicate with people external to the organization, as can other electronic tools like Internet home pages.

INFORMAL COMMUNICATIONS

Informal methods of communication, such as rumors and "the company grapevine," can be outside of management's control. The grapevine is a bottom-up form of communication in which employees try to understand what is happening around them when there is no official word from management. When management is silent, employees fill the void with guesses about what is happening. Although there is no way the grapevine can be stopped, it can be influenced. When dealing with questions that cannot, or should not, be answered, managers should take the initiative before negative rumors get started. If it is obvious to employees that the company will soon undergo major changes, for example, management should confirm that it will. Employees should be informed that management recognizes they have legitimate concerns, which will be addressed when possible. If official talk would damage the company, that should be made clear to the employees.

THE IMPORTANCE OF GOOD COMMUNICATION

All forms of communication, even the lack of it, can have a significant impact on business dealings. A stiffly-worded, official-sounding memo to employees telling them not to talk to the press about impending litigation could be interpreted as admitting that the company did something wrong. Management's repeated "no comments" to employees and the press on a rumored merger may launch dozens of informal discussions about company suitors, how much the company will sell for, and how many employees will be laid off.

In order to avoid the negative effects of such scenarios, small business owners should make it a practice to communicate as much and as often as possible. They should think twice before eliminating the company newsletter as a cost saving measure, keep bulletin boards up-to-date, and hold meetings in which employees can ask questions of management. In addition, they should develop their skills so that all business communications are easily understandable. Management terms and jargon, stiff or flowery language may contribute to the impression among employees that management is talking down to them. It is also helpful to obtain and analyze feedback. Asking employees what they think of communication efforts, which methods are most effective, and whether they want more information can open valuable channels of communication.

FURTHER READING:

Golen, Steven. *Effective Business Communication.* Washington: U.S. Small Business Administration, 1989.

Murphy, Herta A., and Herbert W. Hildebrandt. *Effective Business Communications.* 6th ed. New York: McGraw-Hill, 1991.

Townsend, Robert. *Up the Organization.* New York: Knopf, 1984.

COMMUNITY DEVELOPMENT CORPORATIONS

Community development corporations (CDCs) are locally based organizations that work to help the residents of impoverished areas to improve their quality of life. Such organizations exist in virtually all major urban areas of the United States today. CDCs provide residents with a variety of benefits, including housing, day care for children, nursing home care for the elderly, employment opportunities, job training, and health care facilities. Some CDCs act as part-owners of vital businesses within their neighborhoods, like supermarkets and shopping centers, while others assist residents in starting their own small businesses.

"Community development corporations function somewhat like private developers but are governed by the community," Gustav Spohn explained in an article for the *San Diego Business Journal.* "Their boards of directors are typically composed of community residents together with experts who advise them on the technical aspects of fund-raising and development projects. They depend heavily on government and private philanthropic funds, which in turn leverage financing from banks and other investors. Their goal is not to turn a profit but to generate economic renewal in poor communities."

As recently as a decade ago, CDCs were being dismissed as small-time players unable to make a real contribution to solving urban problems. Banks were rarely willing to provide them with financing or any other assistance. But today CDCs are viewed as "key components of public strategies to fight poverty in cities across the country," according to Spohn. Nearly every major bank in the country is now actively involved in community development in at least one city. "CDCs are the driving force in most reviving poor places because they refurbish housing, restore enterprise to ruined commercial districts, and make life unpleasant for those standing in the way of progress, from junkies to zoning bureaucrats," Harrison Rainie wrote in an article for *U.S. News and World Report.*

Although CDCs have had an increasing impact on the fight to reclaim urban neighborhoods, they are still the subject of some skepticism. Some critics believe that CDCs cannot operate on a large-enough scale to overcome a 40-year lack of investment in the inner cities. Others believe that community improvement efforts in impoverished neighborhoods are pointless, claiming that residents will simply choose to leave as soon as they are able to raise their incomes to a certain level. Finally, some people worry that CDCs—which receive major funding from the federal government through the Community Development Block Grant and other programs—will not be able to remain effective in the face of inevitable budget cuts.

In his article, Spohn outlined some of the functions of a successful CDC. First, it must make local residents feel that they have an investment in the neighborhood. Second, it must serve a mediating role between the differing interests of various neighborhood groups. Third, it must not polarize the interests of the community and the interests of government and outside private-sector institutions. Finally, it must continually battle the forces that act to return the inner cities to a state of disorder. Overall, CDCs can have a significant impact on the communities they serve. "Nationally there's a feeling that nothing can work in the cities—they have no hope—that there's nothing the society can do," Roland Anglin of the Ford Foundation told Spohn. "It's not true. There is a movement there. There is a structure there in inner cities. There is a strategy that can help."

FURTHER READING:

Rainie, Harrison. "The Lessons of Banana Kelly: Community Development Corporations Help to Revive Inner Cities." *U.S. News and World Report.* June 5, 1995.

Riggin, Leslie J.C., Patrick G. Grasso, and Mary L. Westcott. "A Framework for Evaluating Housing and Community Development Partnership Projects." *Public Administration Review.* January-February 1992.

Sower, James, and James Vitarello. "CDCs—Little Known or Understood Development Tool." *Nation's Cities Weekly.* May 11, 1987.

Spohn, Gustav. "Engines for Rebuilding Communities Make Headway." *San Diego Business Journal.* June 16, 1997.

SEE ALSO: Empowerment Zones

COMMUNITY RELATIONS

Community relations refers to the various methods companies use to establish and maintain a mutually beneficial relationship with the communities in which they operate. The underlying principal of community relations is that when a company accepts its civic responsibility and takes an active interest in the well-being of its community, then it gains a number of long-term benefits in terms of community support, loyalty, and good will.

A comprehensive, ongoing community relations program can help virtually any organization achieve visibility as a good community citizen. Organizations are recognized as good community citizens when they support programs that improve the quality of life in their community, including crime prevention, employment, environmental programs, clean-up and beautification, **recycling**, and restoration. Some other examples of ongoing programs might include scholarship programs, urban renewal projects, performing arts programs, social and educational programs, children's activities, community organizations, and construction projects. On a more limited scale, small businesses might achieve community visibility and engender good will by sponsoring local sports teams or other events. Support may be financial or take the form of employee participation.

Good community relations programs offer small businesses a wide variety of benefits. For instance, they give employees a reason to be proud of the company, which increases loyalty and may help to reduce labor and production costs. Furthermore, a company with happy employees and a good reputation in the community is likely to attract highly qualified new employees. A small company also might generate new business through the contacts and leads it generates in its community relations activities. Such contacts might also make it easier for the company to obtain financing for expansion, find promising new locations, or gain favorable treatment in terms of taxes, ordinances, or utilities. Good community relations can also be beneficial in times of crisis, such as a fire or a plant closing, by rallying the community around the affected business.

TYPES OF COMMUNITY RELATIONS PROGRAMS

According to Norman R. Soderberg in his book *Public Relations for the Entrepreneur and the Growing Business,* small businesses can become involved in their communities in any number of ways. Some recommended routes toward increasing community involvement include: taking an active interest in community problems; sponsoring youth activities; participating in local government; joining business and service groups; purchasing materials and supplies from local companies; encouraging community education and culture; making offices or other facilities available to community organizations; supporting local charity drives; and taking part in civic activities.

Soderberg discusses a number of specific programs designed to increase a small business's visibility and prestige within a community. For example, the company might volunteer to develop a civic program, like a charity drive or auction. In addition, the small business owner, or another company representative, could give talks before the local chamber of commerce or civic association. The company could also invite community groups to tour its plant or offices, or could make its facilities available to such groups for meetings or events. Alternatively, the company could prepare an informational videotape about its products, services, employment policies, and overall mission and make this resource available to the community. Informational brochures and newsletters might also be distributed to civic and government leaders. Another way to improve community relations might be to beautify the company's surroundings with a fountain, sculpture, or garden, so that it becomes a local landmark. Whichever types of community relations programs are used, it is important to keep the media informed about the company's activities.

Soderberg stresses that for a small business, community relations should involve more than just an annual contribution to the United Way. Instead, the small business owner should become personally involved in the effort, and should encourage employees to participate as well. A company's employees should try to represent it well in all their interactions—from practicing good manners on the road while driving company vehicles to treating customers and even visiting salespeople with courtesy. In order to motivate employees to be good company representatives, small business owners should take whatever steps are needed to boost morale. These might include maintaining an open-door policy, setting up a complaint box, or recognizing employees who are helping the community.

FURTHER READING:

Soderberg, Norman R. *Public Relations for the Entrepreneur and the Growing Business.* Hinsdale, IL: Probus, 1986.

Stodder, Gayle Sato. "Civic Duties." *Entrepreneur.* November 1997.

Young, Davis. *Building Your Company's Good Name.* New York: Amacom, 1996.

SEE ALSO: Charitable Giving; Corporate Image; Corporate Sponsorship; Public Relations

COMP TIME

Comp Time, or Compensatory Time, is an alternate way of rewarding **overtime** work. Instead of paying an hourly employee time-and-a-half for work done over the time allotted in the normal work week, employers would allow an hour and a half of time off for each hour of overtime worked. This time could be used in emergencies, or scheduled for personal use. Comp time should not be confused with "flex-time." Flex-time allows employees to schedule their regular working hours in a way that accommodates their personal preferences and family commitments. Comp time strictly refers to compensation for overtime work.

Comp time programs are heavily restricted by federal regulations, so that employees are not unfairly prevented from receiving financial compensation. Business owners who violate existing regulations are subject to heavy fines. But there is a movement on a national level to amend the Fair Labor Standards Act to include a program of comp time that would safeguard the rights of both business owners and their employees.

THE CURRENT DEBATE Two bills concerned with the issue of comp time went before Congress at the end of 1997: the Working Families Flexibility Act and the Family Friendly Workplace Act. Both bills would provide for a system of comp time in which employers offer one and a half hours of paid time off for each hour of overtime worked. Both would require the employer to pay the employee the dollar amount of comp time accrued but not used at the end of the year,

or within being given thirty days notice by the worker. Both bills allow that any time over 80 hours accrued by an employee could be converted to the corresponding dollar amount by the employer, and paid to the employee at the employer's discretion.

THE POLITICAL ARGUMENTS FOR COMP TIME The movement to pass the comp time legislation is led largely by Republicans. As the names of the two bills suggest, a major benefit of comp time is the freedom it allows employees to schedule their work around family commitments. Parents and those with sick or elderly family members in particular are valuing time off from work, as well as flexible work schedules, even above higher pay.

THE POLITICAL ARGUMENTS AGAINST COMP TIME Some Democrats and the **AFL-CIO** are contesting the bills. Primary reasons for contesting the use of comp time are questions over the actual scheduling of time off, and whether employees will be free to choose either comp time or payment in return for overtime work. Those opposing the bills suggest that employees in practice will not be allowed to freely schedule the use of their comp time, but will be restricted by employers. This would result in an option that is much less valuable to employees, limiting the prospect of "emergency" time, and restricting time off at certain points during the year. Concerns have also been expressed over possible pressure from businesses on employees to accept comp time over monetary compensation for overtime work, and whether voluntary overtime could be offered only in exchange for comp time.

COMP TIME IN SMALL BUSINESSES Some business experts believe that employers who do not offer large benefits packages, significant vacation time, or paid time off should seriously consider offering comp time as a kind of perk for employees. These observers contend that comp time can be a sensitive (and economical) way of rewarding employees for extra help at crunch times, especially since many workers have come to value time off even more than increased pay.

But small businesses, which may not be in a position to offer employees elaborate benefits, may also not be able to support a comp time system. Whether the system is regimented or informal, the small business may not be able to afford the lost productivity and additional paperwork involved in keeping track of comp time accrued and taken. There may also arise scheduling problems, especially for very small businesses that rely on only a few employees for their entire function. If a business is necessarily inflexible when it comes to scheduling time off, comp time may not be a valid alternative to regular overtime compensation.

FURTHER READING:

Barlas, Stephen, ''Timely Decision.'' *Entrepreneur.* July 1997.

Boyett, Joseph H., and Henry P. Conn, *Workplace 2000.* New York: Penguin, 1991.

''Comp Time Legislation,'' *Entrepreneur.* December 1997.

Employees: How to Find and Pay Them. Washington: U.S. Small Business Administration, n.a.

SEE ALSO: Employee Compensation; Employee Reward Systems

COMPETITIVE ANALYSIS

Competitive analysis is the practice of analyzing the competitive environment in which your business operates (or wishes to operate), including strengths and weaknesses of the businesses with which you compete, strengths and weaknesses of your own company, demographics and desires of marketplace customers, strategies that can improve your position in the marketplace, impediments that prevent you from entering new markets, and barriers that you can erect to prevent others from eroding your market share.

Competitive analysis has long been a cornerstone of overall competitive strategy for multinational conglomerates and ''mom and pop'' stores alike. Moreover, business experts note that competitive analysis transcends industry areas; indeed, the practice is deeply relevant to all industries. For example, *Folio* contributor Bruce Sheiman provided a synopsis of the importance of competitive analysis to the magazine industry that is fairly representative: ''First, it is critical to discover whether a competitor is encroaching on your proposed magazine's editorial or market franchise—or, indeed, whether a competitor renders your magazine idea superfluous. Second, competition helps to define a magazine's market position. I've seen business plans stating that the proposed magazine would have no competition. This is naive. Every magazine has competition—and needs competition. Third, competitive magazines give you benchmarks. By studying your competitors, you can learn much about developing your magazine's editorial, circulation, and advertising strategies. And you can determine your revenue and profitability prospects.'' Competitive analysis is of similar importance to muffler shops, office furniture manufacturers, photofinishing laboratories, and countless other industries as well.

Despite this, however, business experts say that while established businesses commonly practice competitive analysis on a regular basis, new businesses too often are derelict in this area. ''Every business has competition,'' wrote Rhonda Abrams in *The Successful Business Plan: Secrets and Strategies.* ''Those currently operating a company are all too aware of the many competitors for a customer's dollar. But many people new to business—excited about their concept and motivated by a perceived opening in the market—tend to underestimate the actual extent of competition and fail to properly assess the impact of that competition on their business.''

ELEMENTS OF COMPETITIVE ANALYSIS

There are several important elements of competitive analysis, each of which need to be carefully studied if one hopes to transform competitive analysis activities into business profitability. Major aspects of competitive analysis include the following:

DEFINING COMPETITORS ''The first step [in competitive analysis] is to define your universe of competitors,'' wrote Sheiman, who warned that both unduly broad definitions and excessively narrow definitions of competition can compromise the effectiveness of competitive analysis. Some businesses may offer products or services that largely mirror those offered by your own company, while others may only dispense one or two products/services that compete with your company's offerings. The business conducting the competitive analysis has to decide whether latter examples of competition are incidental or whether they present a potential threat (either now or in the future) to the business's financial well-being. Consultants and business experts also recommend that small business owners scan the horizon for *potential* as well as current competitors. As *Management Review*'s Oren Harari stated, ''the gumption of entrepreneurs coupled with the 24-hour electronic flows of capital they can access worldwide means that competitors suddenly turn up out of nowhere, and traditional barriers to entry in any business fall like bricks in an earthquake.''

ANALYSIS OF COMPETITOR STRENGTHS AND WEAKNESSES Once a company's universe of competitors has been defined and identified, it can start on the process of identifying the strengths and weaknesses of those competitors. Abrams cautioned that many small business owners are tempted to place undue weight on the quality of the product or service they offer (or plan to offer, in the case of new businesses). This may be a comforting thought, admitted Abrams, but it betrays a fundamental misunderstanding of how business works: ''The objective features of your product or service may be a relatively small part of the competitive picture. In fact, all the components of customer preference, including price, service, and location, are only half of the competitive analysis. The other half of the equation is examining the internal strength of your competitors' companies. In the long run, companies with significant financial resources, highly motivated or creative personnel, and other operational assets will prove to be tough, enduring competition.''

There are two main questions that cut to the heart of this element of competitive analysis: What key advantages does the competing business possess in the realms of production management, marketing, service reputation, and other aspects of business operation? What key vulnerabilities does the competing business have in these same areas?

Of course, examination of a competitor's strengths and weaknesses also requires separating important advantages (intense customer loyalty, for instance) and disadvantages (reputation as a polluter) from unimportant advantages (a larger parking lot, perhaps) and disadvantages (older forklift machinery). Writing in his book *Developing Business Strategies,* David Aaker suggested that business owners should concentrate their analysis efforts in four major areas:

- Studying the reasons behind the successes— and failures—of competitive firms

- Major issues that motivate customers

- Major component costs

- Barriers to mobility within the industry.

The Entrepreneur Magazine Small Business Advisor contended that ''an analysis of strong performers should reveal the causes behind such a successful track record. This analysis, in conjunction with an examination of unsuccessful companies and the reasons behind their failure, should provide a good idea of just what key assets and skills are needed for success within a given industry and market segment.''

ANALYSIS OF INTERNAL STRENGTHS AND WEAKNESSES Another important element of competitive analysis is determining what your own company's strengths and weaknesses are. What aspects of the company's operation convey an advantage in the marketplace? Is your sales force composed of bright, ambitious individuals? Does your company have an advanced inventory management system in place? Do you have an employee with a talent for advertising and/or marketing? Once a company has determined its strengths, it can go about the process of utilizing those strengths to improve its position in the marketplace. Conversely, an examination of internal weaknesses (uninspired product presentation, recalcitrant work force, bad physical location, etc.) should spur initiatives designed to address those shortcomings.

ANALYSIS OF CUSTOMER NEEDS AND WANTS Learning about customer needs and wants is an important part of competitive analysis as well. Customer priorities should become your business's priorities. In addition, small businesses should take care that they not limit their study to priorities that are already mani-

fested in the marketplace. Indeed, new product development and new innovations in service are essential to business success in any industry. Business owners and managers need to learn to study—and thus anticipate—future customer needs and wants as well those needs and wants that are currently evident.

STUDYING IMPEDIMENTS TO MARKET FOR YOU AND YOUR COMPETITION Businesses seeking to enter new markets typically have to grapple with several different barriers. Some of these can be surmounted without inordinate difficulty, while others may be so imposing that they preclude launching a campaign (for the time being, at least). Abrams cited several common barriers to entry for new competition:

- Patents—These provide some protection for new products or processes.

- High start-up costs—In many cases, this barrier is the most daunting one for small businesses.

- Knowledge—Lack of technical, manufacturing, marketing, or engineering expertise can all be a significant obstacle to successful market entry.

- Market saturation—It is a basic reality that it is more difficult to carve out a niche in a crowded market than it is to establish a presence in a market marked by relatively light competition.

''Realistically, few barriers to entry last very long, particularly in newer industries,'' concluded Abrams. ''Even patents do not provide nearly as much protection as is generally assumed. Thus, you need to realistically project the period of time by which new competitors will breach these barriers.''

BUILDING STRATEGIC PLANS TO IMPROVE MARKETPLACE POSITION Once a small business owner has attended to the above requirements of competitive analysis, he or she can proceed with the final element of the practice: building a strategic plan that reflects the findings. Strategic plans should touch on all areas of a business's operations, including production of goods and/or services, distribution of those goods and/or services, pricing of goods and/or services, and marketing of goods and/or services. After all, all of these areas ultimately have an impact on basic financial health.

CRITICISMS OF COMPETITIVE ANALYSIS

While the practice of competitive analysis is generally recognized as an important component of long-term business success, some voices do offer cautions about flawed competitive analysis practices. They note that competitive analyses that are incomplete or based on incorrect data can lead businesses to construct faulty business strategies. Experts have also pointed out that traditional competitive analysis has become more complex and potentially time-consuming, since so many businesses offer diversified products and services. Still others contend that excessive preoccupation with keeping pace with the strategies, products, and services of other competitors can result in atrophy in internal originality of production and design.

Other observers, meanwhile, argue that judging your company's performance *strictly* on the basis of how you are performing against chief competitors can retard your business's profitability and lead to a false sense of security. "As long as we appear to be doing better than someone else, we can feel that we must be doing well, so we don't need to change," wrote James R. Lucas in *Fatal Illusions*. "These illusions can begin when we compare ourselves with our own past performance . . . or with the performance of other organizations. The companies we're comparing ourselves to may *all* be performing at lower levels than the market requires. They may *all* be doing it wrong. Since every organization is unique, another company's solutions may not apply to us. . . . If we've grown at an annual rate of 15 percent compared with an industry average of 5 percent, we may be wildly successful—unless a new competitor from an unexpected direction or unrelated industry finds a way to deliver our service at 60 percent of our cost."

Finally, some experts contend that preoccupation with competitive analysis too often leads companies to spend too little time looking ahead. "Effective strategy formulation and implementation relies on concepts like uniqueness, differentiation and standing out in a very, very crowded marketplace. Ineffective strategy formulation and implementation relies on concepts like imitation, caution and blending in with the rest of the pack. Competitive analysis does a great job in fostering the latter," wrote Oren Harari in *Management Review*. "I have no problems in performing a quick, occasional scan of what today's competitors are doing. That is just plain prudent management. . . . The problem is that executives can easily wind up sinking big resources and becoming hypnotized into tracking the movements of today's solutions for yesterday's customers." Harari contended that "traditional competitor analysis is often short-sighted in depth, range, and possibility. . . . If you're spending a lot of valuable time tracking your competitors' movements, you're not only running in circles, but you're probably paying too much attention to the wrong guys. It's the folks that you can't track—the ones that don't exist yet either as competitors, or even as companies—who are your real problems. That's because they're not worrying about tracking you. They're moving ahead with new offerings, redefining and reinventing the marketplace as they go along."

FURTHER READING:

Aaker, David A. *Developing Business Strategies.* 2d ed. New York: John Wiley and Sons, 1988.

Abrams, Rhonda M. *The Successful Business Plan: Secrets and Strategies.* Rev. ed. Grants Pass, OR: Oasis Press, 1993.

The Entrepreneur Magazine Small Business Advisor. New York: John Wiley and Sons, 1995.

Harari, Oren. "The Hypnotic Danger of Competitive Analysis." *Management Review.* August 1994.

Lucas, James R. *Fatal Illusions.* New York: Amacom, 1997.

Oster, Sharon M. *Modern Competitive Analysis.* 2d ed. 1995.

Sheiman, Bruce. "Boost Your New Title with Competitive Analysis." *Folio: The Magazine for Magazine Management.* September 1, 1994.

Zahra, Shaker A. "Unethical Practices in Competitive Analysis: Patterns, Causes, and Effects." *Journal of Business Ethics.* January 1994.

Zahra, Shaker A., and Sherry S. Chaples. "Blind Spots in Competitive Analysis." *The Academy of Management Executive.* May 1993.

SEE ALSO: Benchmarking; Market Analysis; Strategy

COMPETITIVE BIDS

Competitive bids are offers extended by businesses in which they detail proposed compensation that they will receive in exchange for executing a specific task or tasks. These tasks can range from providing a service for a set period of time to manufacturing and transporting a certain quantity of goods or materials. Competitive bidding differs from other pricing strategies in that with bid pricing, a specific price is put forth for each possible job rather than a generic price that applies to all customers. "The big problem in bid pricing," wrote E. Jerome McCarthy and William D. Perreault Jr. in *Basic Marketing*, "is estimating all the costs that will apply to each job. This may sound easy, but a complicated bid may involve thousands of cost components. Further, management must include an overhead charge and a charge for profit. Competition must be considered when adding in overhead and profit. Usually, the customer will get several bids and accept the lowest one. So unthinking addition of 'typical' overhead and profit rates should be avoided. Some bidders use the same overhead and profit rates on all jobs—regardless of competition—and then are surprised when they don't get some jobs." In addition, small business owners should take precautions to ensure that, in their rush to secure business, they do not make bids that do not provide them with adequate profits. While an occasion unprofitable job may be necessary—to establish inroads with a specific customer or in a specific industry niche, for instance—a steady diet of such work can irrevocably damage a business.

Competitive bidding is an especially common practice with government buyers, many of whom have instituted mandatory bidding procedures. Government buyers are typically required to accept the lowest bid that they receive, but it is important to note that low bids can often be disregarded if they are judged to be lacking in meeting minimum job specifications.

SMALL BUSINESS AND PRIVATE-SECTOR PROCUREMENT

"Most small-company owners chalk up the time and energy spent bidding on customer contracts to the cost of getting new business," wrote Stephanie Gruner in *Inc.*, even though some customers may simply be using the small business to push down the price demands of already established vendors. Given this reality, there are several steps that small business owners can take to 1) improve their chances of securing a contract, and 2) minimize loss of time and energy on the competitive bidding process. "Ask for information," wrote Gruner. "Most companies won't share confidential data, but it doesn't hurt to ask for specifics, such as current costs. The way the customer handles your requests will also tell you whether the company seriously wants to work with you." Gruner also counseled small business operators to try and establish contact with a variety of people within the targeted company. Making contacts with several people within an organization can be valuable not only for information-gathering purposes, but also because, as Gruner put it, "one might become your advocate."

Another key to success in competitive bidding is simply recognizing long-term trends, both in your company's industry and in the larger world of commerce. For example, writer Matthew S. Scott pointed out in *Black Enterprise* in 1995 that many entrepreneurial ventures have the potential to reap huge benefits from the ever-expanding telecommunications industry. "The key to linking up with the billions of dollars in procurement contracts that will potentially become available over the next decade is to remember that the information superhighway is still under construction. . . . Over the next decade, these high-tech telecommunications firms will spend billions of dollars to develop the new technologies and information transmission systems that will make up the infrastructure of the information superhighway. So, considering the type of small business you own, if you can help the telecommunications giants build these new systems quickly, and in a cost-efficient manner, you can benefit from the coming golden age of telecommunications."

Other business experts indicate that a spectrum of business trends are also increasing the importance of competitive bidding in ensuring small business success. One of the most dramatic of these trends is the one toward increased **outsourcing** by companies of all sizes. As responsibilities that were previously attended to in-house continue to be shipped outside, opportunities for establishing your company as a valued producer of goods and/or services will also increase.

Scott discussed several steps that small business firms should take when preparing to make a competitive bid on a project: 1) Contact the company's procurement officer and enquire whether or not the company has a current (or possible future) need for the type of services or products that your company provides. 2) If you are a minority or woman business owner, check to see if the company has any minority- or women-owned business programs in place. Also, if you represent a minority-owned business, be prepared to secure minority certification from a regional chamber of commerce or the National Minority Supplier Development Council. 3) Request a information package on the procurement process that is in place at the company. This package, stated Scott, "will contain a supplier capability information form, which routinely asks for information about your product or service, references, financial viability, and past track record. Fill out the forms and send them back." Of course, the exact nature of these forms will vary from industry to industry; a company seeking to outsource three months of copyediting work will likely require somewhat different information than a company that is looking for a new supplier of electronic parts. 4) Once the above-mentioned supplier capability information form has been completed and returned to the company, Scott noted that "your small business may be referred to different buyers within the agency or to different corporate offices throughout the country. Your company may also be placed on a data base that these buyers have access to." 5) Adopt a proactive business stance. Many successful businesses that secure work through the bidding process remain aggressive—though not unduly so—even after taking care of all the necessary paperwork. "Don't rely on the buyers to offer contracts to you," cautioned Scott. "It is up to the small business owner to sell his business as an asset to each company or agency. That means calling constantly to inquire about opportunities, and showing real evidence that your company can do the job. . . . You must be persistent. It may take months or years to win a contract."

NEGOTIATED BIDS

Not all competitive bidding situations end with the customer's acceptance of one of the bids offered. In some instances, a subsequent negotiation step may take place. "Some buying situations (including much government buying) require the use of bids—and the purchasing agent must take the lowest bid," said McCarthy and Perreault. "In other cases, however, the customer asks for bids and then singles out the company that submits the *most attractive* bid—not necessarily the lowest—for further bargaining. The list price or bidding price the seller would like to charge is sometimes only the *starting point* for discussions with individual customers. What a customer will buy—if the customer buys at all—depends on the negotiated price, a price set based on bargaining between the buyer and seller.'' McCarthy and Perreault go on to note that negotiated pricing, like simple bid pricing, ''is most common in situations where the marketing mix is adjusted for each customer—so bargaining may involve the whole marketing mix, not just the price level.''

FURTHER READING:

Chlon, Christopher J. ''Competitive Bids: Saving Money on Supplies.'' *Ceramics Monthly.* February 1990.

Gruner, Stephanie. ''Bid to Win.'' *Inc.* October 1996.

Ho, Rodney. ''Federal Procurement Rule Changes Streamline Bidding Process.'' *Wall Street Journal.* October 14, 1997.

Markus, Edward. ''Low Bid Alternatives Earning Respect.'' *American City and County.* August 1997.

McCarthy, E. Jerome, and William D. Perreault, Jr. *Basic Marketing: A Managerial Approach.* 10th ed. Homewood, IL: Irwin, 1990.

Roberts, Kenneth, and Nancy Smith. ''Design-Build Contracts Under State and Local Procurement Laws.'' *Public Contract Law Journal.* Summer 1996.

Schotter, Andrew. ''Bad and Good News About the Sealed-Bid Mechanism: Some Experimental Results.'' *American Economic Review.* May 1990.

Scott, Matthew S. ''Tapping into the Telecommunications Industry: One of the Nation's Hottest Industries Looks Like a Gold Mine for Small Businesses Seeking Procurement Opportunities.'' *Black Enterprise.* February 1995.

Urban, Glen L., and Steven H. Star. *Advanced Marketing Strategy: Phenomena, Analysis, and Decisions.* Englewood Cliffs, NJ: Prentice Hall, 1991.

SEE ALSO: Business Proposals; Government Procurement

COMPUTER-AIDED DESIGN AND COMPUTER-AIDED MANUFACTURING

Computer-aided design (CAD) involves creating computer models defined by geometrical parameters. These models typically appear on a computer monitor as a three-dimensional representation of a part or a system of parts, which can be readily altered by changing relevant parameters. CAD systems enable designers to view objects under a wide variety of representations and to test these objects by simulating real-world conditions.

Computer-aided manufacturing (CAM) uses geometrical design data to control automated machinery. CAM systems are associated with computer numeri-

cal control (CNC) or direct numerical control (DNC) systems. These systems differ from older forms of numerical control (NC) in that geometrical data is encoded mechanically. Since both CAD and CAM use computer-based methods for encoding geometrical data, it is possible for the processes of design and manufacture to be highly integrated. Computer-aided design and manufacturing systems are commonly referred to as CAD/CAM.

THE ORIGINS OF CAD/CAM

CAD had its origins in three separate sources, which also serve to highlight the basic operations that CAD systems provide. The first source of CAD resulted from attempts to automate the drafting process. These developments were pioneered by the General Motors Research Laboratories in the early 1960s. One of the important time-saving advantages of computer modeling over traditional drafting methods is that the former can be quickly corrected or manipulated by changing a model's parameters. The second source of CAD was in the testing of designs by simulation. The use of computer modeling to test products was pioneered by high-tech industries like aerospace and semiconductors. The third source of CAD development resulted from efforts to facilitate the flow from the design process to the manufacturing process using numerical control (NC) technologies, which enjoyed widespread use in many applications by the mid-1960s. It was this source that resulted in the linkage between CAD and CAM. One of the most important trends in CAD/CAM technologies is the ever-tighter integration between the design and manufacturing stages of CAD/CAM-based production processes.

Numerical Control (NC) of automated machinery was developed in the early 1950s and thus preceded the use of computerized control by several years. Like CAM, NC technologies made use of codified geometrical data to control the operations of a machine. The data was encoded by punch holes on a paper tape that was fed through a reader, essentially the same mechanism as that found on a player piano. Once the control tape was produced, it offered a reliable means to replace the skilled machinists that had previously operated such machines. From the firm's point of view, the drawback of the old NC technologies was the difficulty in converting the design for a three-dimensional object into holes on a tape. This required the services of a tape encoding specialist. Since this specialist was required to work without any significant visual feedback, work was essentially trial and error and could only be tested in the actual production process. The tape encoder had to account for a large number of variables, including optimal feed rates and cutting speeds, the angle at which the tool should contact the part, and so on. Given the considerable time and expense involved in NC technologies, it was only economically viable when a large number of parts were to be produced.

The development of CAD and CAM and particularly the linkage between the two overcame these problems by enabling the design and manufacture of a part to be undertaken using the same system of encoding geometrical data. This eliminated the need for a tape encoding specialist and greatly shortened the time between design and manufacture. CAD/CAM thus greatly expanded the scope of production processes for which automated machinery could be economically used. Just as important, CAD/CAM gave the designer much more direct control over the production process, creating the possibility of completely integrated design and manufacturing processes.

The rapid growth in the use of CAD/CAM technologies after the early 1970s was made possible by the development of mass-produced silicon chips and the microprocessor, resulting in more readily affordable computers. As the price of computers continued to decline and their processing power improved, the use of CAD/CAM broadened from large firms using large-scale mass production techniques (the automobile industry, for instance) to firms of all sizes. The scope of operations to which CAD/CAM was applied broadened as well. In addition to parts-shaping by traditional machine tool processes such as stamping, drilling, milling, and grinding, CAD/CAM has come to be used by firms involved in producing consumer electronics, electronic components, and molded plastics. Computers are also used to control a number of manufacturing processes that are not defined as CAM because the control data are not based on geometrical parameters. An example of this would be at a chemical processing plant.

Using CAD, it is possible to simulate in three dimensions the movement of a part through a production process. This process can simulate feed rates, angles and speeds of machine tools, the position of part-holding clamps, as well as range and other constraints limiting the operations of a machine. The continuing development of the simulation of various manufacturing processes is one of the key means by which CAD and CAM systems are becoming increasingly integrated. CAD/CAM systems also facilitate communication among those involved in design, manufacturing, and other processes. This is of particular importance when one firm contracts another to either design or produce a component.

ADVANTAGES AND DISADVANTAGES

Modeling with CAD systems offers a number of advantages over traditional drafting methods that use rulers, squares, and compasses. For example, designs can be altered without erasing and redrawing. CAD

systems also offer "zoom" features analogous to a camera lens, whereby a designer can magnify certain elements of a model to facilitate inspection. Computer models are typically three dimensional and can be rotated on any axis, much as one could rotate an actual three dimensional model in one's hand, enabling the designer to gain a fuller sense of the object. CAD systems also lend themselves to modeling cutaway drawings, in which the internal shape of a part is revealed, and to illustrating the spatial relationships among a system of parts.

To understand CAD it is also useful to understand what CAD cannot do. CAD systems have no means of comprehending real-world concepts, such as the nature of the object being designed or the function that object will serve. CAD systems function by their capacity to codify geometrical concepts. Thus the design process using CAD involves transferring a designer's idea into a formal geometrical model. In this sense, existing CAD systems cannot actually design anything.

In their 1993 volume *CADCAM: From Principles to Practice*, McMahon and Browne summarize limitations of existing CAD/CAM systems as follows: "There is a widespread view that CAD is not yet adequate as an *aid* to the designer in generating a design. CAD is considered to concentrate rather too much on providing means of representing the final form of the design, whereas designers also need a continual stream of advice and information to assist in decision making.... The tasks of CAD systems of the future are therefore to represent a wider variety of a design's properties, in terms that are familiar to engineers, and of a company's organization and equipment that influence design." Some of these limitations of CAD were addressed by the development of the Parametric Technology Corporation's Pro/ENGINEER software, which provides the designer with a number of geometrical building blocks on which to base designs.

Other limitations to CAD are being addressed by research and development in the field of expert systems. This field derived from research done on artificial intelligence. One example of an expert system involves incorporating information about the nature of materials—their weight, tensile strength, flexibility, and so on—into CAD software. By including this and other information, the CAD system could then "know" what an expert engineer knows when that engineer creates a design. The system could then mimic the engineer's thought pattern and actually "create" a design. Expert systems might involve the implementation of more abstract principles, such as the nature of gravity and friction, or the function and relation of commonly used parts, such as levers or nuts and bolts. Expert systems might also come to change the way data is stored and retrieved in CAD/

CAM systems, supplanting the hierarchical system with one that offers greater flexibility.

One of the key areas of development in CAD technologies is the simulation of performance. Among the most common types of simulation are testing for response to stress and modeling the process by which a part might be manufactured or the dynamic relationships among a system of parts. In stress tests, model surfaces are shown by a grid or mesh, that distort as the part comes under simulated physical or thermal stress. Dynamics tests function as a complement or substitute for building working prototypes. The ease with which a part's specifications can be changed facilitates the development of optimal dynamic efficiencies both as regards the functioning of a system of parts and the manufacture of any given part. Simulation is also used in electronic design automation, in which simulated flow of current through a circuit enables the rapid testing of various component configurations.

The processes of design and manufacture are, in some sense, conceptually separable. Yet the design process must be undertaken with an understanding of the nature of the production process. It is necessary, for example, for a designer to know the properties of the materials with which the part might be built, the various techniques by which the part might be shaped, and the scale of production that is economically viable. The conceptual overlap between design and manufacture is suggestive of the potential benefits of CAD and CAM and the reason they are generally considered together as a system.

THE FUTURE OF CAD/CAM

Recent technical developments have addressed all aspects of CAD/CAM systems. The use of personal computers and the Microsoft Corp.'s Windows software emerged as an alternative to older mainframe- and workstation-based systems. The greater viability of personal computers for CAD/CAM applications results from their ever-increasing processing power. An important trend is toward the standardization of software, so that different packages can readily share data. Standards have been established for some time regarding data exchange and graphics, and the X Windows System and Microsoft's Windows are becoming established as industry standards for user interfaces. An increasing number of software producers based their products on Windows in the mid-1990s. For electronic design automation software, the trend toward standardization was facilitated by the standards put forth by Computer Framework Initiative Inc. in the early 1990s. Other improvements in software include greater sophistication of visual representation, such as the replacement of three dimensional by solid modeling, in which objects are represented in

a more fully defined manner. Improvements have also been made in the greater integration of modeling and testing applications.

FURTHER READING:

Bedworth, D.D., M.R. Henderson, and P.M. Wolfe. *Computer-Integrated Design and Manufacture*. New York: McGraw-Hill, 1991.

"The CAD/CAM Claims Come True After All." *Machine Design*. October 22, 1992.

"CAD/CAM Spells Big Market." *Computing Canada*. October 13, 1992.

McMahon, Chris, and Jimmie Browne. *CADCAM: From Principles to Practice*. Menlo Park, CA: Addison-Wesley Publishing Co., 1993.

Medland, A.J., and Piers Burnett. *CAD/CAM in Practice: A Manager's Guide to Understanding and Using CAD/CAM*. New York: Wiley, 1986.

Mortenson, M.E. *Geometric Modelling*. New York: Wiley, 1985.

Oshuga, S. "Toward Intelligent CAD Systems." *Computer-Aided Design*. 21(5).

Taylor, D.L. *Computer-Aided Design*. Menlo Park, CA: Addison-Wesley, 1992.

SEE ALSO: Computers and Computer Systems

COMPUTER APPLICATIONS

Finding computer applications for various aspects of a company's operations has, in recent years, become an increasingly vital task of many small business owners. Indeed, computers are an integral part of the business landscape today, in part because they can be an effective tool in so many different aspects of a business's daily operations. Computer systems are now relied on for a broad spectrum of duties, including bookkeeping, business communications, product design, manufacturing, inventory control, and marketing. Indeed, a 1997 survey conducted by *Sales & Management* magazine indicated that 85 percent of respondents felt that technology was increasing the efficiency of its sales force, while another 62 percent concluded that it was helping them increase their sales.

SMALL BUSINESS AND COMPUTER USE

Entrepreneurs and other small business owners utilize today's rapidly changing computer technology in many different realms of operation:

BOOKKEEPING Computer systems are heavily utilized for a variety of **accounting** functions, including employee payroll; cash flow analysis; job costing; tracking of vendor and customer payments and debts; federal, state, and local taxes; and other expenses and revenues that impact on the business's fiscal health. Small business owners use computers for **bookkeeping** more than for any other purpose, and software programs designed to help even inexperienced business owners with their bookkeeping have proliferated on the marketplace in recent years as a result.

BUSINESS COMMUNICATIONS The introduction of computer faxes and especially **electronic mail** (''e-mail'') systems has revolutionized the way that businesses communicate with one another. Moreover, e-mail has significantly altered how employees within the same company interact with one another. The savings, both in time and money, that have been realized through the use of this computer technology have been considerable. E-mail, for instance, not only enables users to save significant sums of money that would otherwise go to long-distance telephone and delivery charges, but also speeds up the process of information delivery. Computer faxes, meanwhile, also enable businesses to ''save, labor, office supplies, and long-distance phone charges'' that are associated with regular fax machines, noted Sandi Smith in the *Journal of Accountancy.* ''The savings: You don't have to make a paper copy, go to the fax machine, wait to be sure the pages don't jam—and if they do, resend. The cost of sending a fax via computer is a fraction of the cost of sending a machine fax.''

PRODUCT DESIGN Product design is one of the most popular computer applications in the business world today. Computer-aided design(CAD) involves creating computer models of products that are ultimately transformed into reality. CAD systems enable designers to view objects under a wide variety of representations and to test these objects by simulating real-world conditions.

MANUFACTURING Computer-aided manufacturing(CAM), meanwhile, uses geometrical design data to control automated machinery and other production processes. Since both CAD and CAM use computer-based methods for encoding geometrical data, it is possible for the processes of design and manufacture to be highly integrated. Computer-aided design and manufacturing systems are commonly referred to as CAD/CAM.

In recent years, technological advances have triggered fundamental changes in many CAD/CAM systems. Whereas CAD/CAM applications used to be limited to older mainframe and workstation-based systems, advances in personal computers and software programs have spurred a dramatic upsurge in their use among small business owners, who are now better able to afford the technology. The greater viability of personal computers for CAD/CAM applications results from their ever-increasing processing power. An important trend is toward the standardization of software, so that different packages can readily share data. Standards have been in place for some time regarding data exchange and graphics, user interfaces are rapidly going the same route. In the realm of electronic design automation software, a similar trend toward standardization has also been underway. Other improvements in software include greater sophistication of visual representation and greater integration of modeling and testing applications.

INVENTORY CONTROL Small businesses are increasingly using computers to track all aspects of their **inventory**, including warehousing, ordering, receiving, and distribution. In addition, many computer systems maintain programs that integrate inventory control needs with other aspects of the business's operations, which helps the company perform in a cohesive and intelligent manner as it negotiates the various obstacles of the business world.

MARKETING Computer applications for **marketing** have surged in recent years. Whereas computer applications for other business needs have been a part of the picture for a decade or two now, the widespread use of computers to shape a company's marketing strategies and campaigns is a relatively new development. ''Firms . . . are gathering tremendous amounts of information about customers, markets, and industries by using an array of relatively inexpensive software and computerized databases,'' wrote Tim McCollum in *Nation's Business.* ''These resources can help entrepreneurs increase their effectiveness in targeting markets, cultivating leads, and closing sales. . . . Whether it's called database marketing, smart marketing, or target selling, it boils down to using technology to delivery information that can boost sales.''

Many consultants and business experts contend that it is particularly important for small business enterprises to make maximum use of this still-developing computer technology. Small business entities typically have fewer clients than do larger firms, which makes the search for new customers an essential component of future success. As analyst Martha Rogers noted in *Nation's Business,* information technologies like business and customer databases and sales force automation systems can be effective tools for small business owners looking to develop profitable and lasting relationships with customers. Indeed, smaller firms often need good customer information simply to keep pace with larger competitors.

Of course, reliable customer information is a major key to any effective marketing campaign. Consequently, database service providers such as Dun & Bradstreet Information Services (DBIS) and American Business Information Inc. (ABI) have become enormously popular with businesses of varying shapes and sizes. "These businesses," wrote McCollum, "have accumulated vast amounts of data on companies throughout the United States and Canada. Customers can buy the records on firms in specific locations or industries or of certain sizes or sales volumes. The databases make it easy to generate lists of potential customers for direct mail or telemarketing campaigns." In addition, DBIS, ABI, and other companies that provide similar services have made their information available via CD-ROMs (with regular updates). Another favorite site for finding business leads is the expanding group of CD-ROM products that provide business and residential telephone listings for various geographic regions of the United States.

Ultimately, however, *Nation's Business* magazine noted that although computers can be a valuable marketing resource for small firms, "technology itself won't boost sales. . . . For sales to climb, information must be carefully integrated into a total marketing strategy." The magazine thus made the following recommendations to companies looking to apply computer resources to marketing efforts:

- Build a database of customers and prospective customers, and update it regularly.

- Decide what marketing information is needed, and establish a plan to obtain it.

- Use demographic and geographic data to put together a profile of current customer base, which can then be used to identify potential new markets.

- Use data to identify long-term interests and buying habits of clients.

- Involve sales force (if any) in introduction of new technologies; "If salespeople don't think the automated system will benefit them, they won't use it."

- Share information throughout the company.

- Use computer resources to personalize and coordinate direct mailings and other campaigns.

- Arrange so that pertinent customer information is available to those who need it.

FACTORS TO WEIGH WHEN CONSIDERING NEW COMPUTER APPLICATIONS

Many small business owners have embraced computers as a potent new weapon in their arsenal. But despite their usefulness in dealing with a wide variety of business tasks, the pros and cons of various computer systems need to be carefully weighed before making the investment. Missteps in this area, after all, can cripple a company's finances and productivity.

Personal computers currently comprise the bulk of most small companies' information technology costs, and most small companies are perfectly capable of determining whether they can afford the initial expense of purchasing PCs for bookkeeping, marketing, or other purposes. But consultants and experienced small business owners contend that small firms need to recognize that the initial price tag of a new computer(s) is only a part—and sometimes only a small part—of the total cost of ownership (sometimes known as the TCO). Technical support costs and various administrative and labor costs associated with managing and developing policies for computer resources all need to be considered when pondering computer applications for different business areas. But as Heather Page observed in *Entrepreneur,* perhaps the single biggest hidden cost associated with adding computers to the workplace is euphemistically known as "user operations." Page defines user operations as "those things that all employees do while sitting in front of a PC that sap their time, indirectly costing you money in lost productivity. These activities include time spent on PC management tasks, such as installing software, creating and moving files, and learning new technology," as well as time that may be wasted on soliciting PC advice from other employees or attending to personal business. Moreover, Page noted that there are myriad supplementary costs associated with PCs, such as printer ink, paper, and software upgrades.

Page subsequently suggested that small business owners take the time to fully consider the advantages and drawbacks of various computer applications before making a big investment in PCs and other computer equipment. "Buy new technology because it enables you to do something you couldn't do before or because it gives your business added flexibility or a competitive edge. In fact, the best solutions may not be the cheapest. Consider the case of the notebook computer. True, they're much more expensive to implement than desktop computers. But the high initial costs often pale in comparison to the benefits companies receive: added flexibility and increased productivity."

FURTHER READING:

Colombo, George. *Sales Force Automation.* New York: McGraw-Hill, 1996.

Greiner, Lynn. "Small Business: Managing Your Systems." *CMA - The Management Accounting Magazine.* September 1996.

Hensley, Richard. "Owner Quandary: How Much to Spend on New Technology?" *Cincinnati Business Courier.* March 3, 1997.

Massey, Tom K. Jr. "Computers in Small Business: A Case of Under-Utilization." *American Journal of Small Business.* Fall 1986.

McCollum, Tim. "High Tech Marketing Hits the Target." *Nation's Business.* June 1997.

Page, Heather. "What Price PC?" *Entrepreneur.* October 1997.

"Productivity: Lost in Cyberspace." *The Economist.* September 13, 1997.

Smith, Sandi. "The Smart Way to Invest in Computers." *Journal of Accountancy.* May 1997.

SEE ALSO: Computer-Aided Design (CAD) and Computer-Aided Manufacturing (CAM); Communication Systems; Computers and Computer Systems; Inventory Control Systems; Product Development

COMPUTER CRIMES

Computer crimes encompass unauthorized or illegal activities perpetrated via computer as well as the theft of computers and other technological hardware. As firms of all sizes, industrial orientation, and geographic location increasingly rely on computers to operate, concerns about computer crime have also risen, in part because the practice appears to be thriving despite the concerted efforts of both the law enforcement and business communities. But computer experts and business consultants alike note that both international corporations and modest family-owned businesses can do a great deal to neutralize computer viruses and other manifestations of computer crime.

Many analysts believe, however, that small business owners are less likely to take steps to address the threat of computer crime than are larger firms. Indeed, many small businesses admit that they are passive about the threat because of costs associated with implementing safeguards and the perception that computer "hackers" and other threats are far more likely to pick on bigger companies. But as Tim McCollum flatly stated in *Nation's Business,* "companies increasingly are falling prey to hackers, computer thieves, software viruses, and, in particular, unauthorized and often illegal activities by their own employees. In fact, chances are that sooner or later most companies will become victims of high-tech crime . . . [and] when computer criminals strike, small-business victims can suffer relatively more than large corporations, whose bottom lines are more resistant to damage from any single theft of equipment or information."

Indeed, McCollum pointed out that computer crime statistics in the United States in the mid-1990s are sobering. In 1997, for instance, a study commissioned by the Federal Bureau of Investigation (FBI) indicated that 75 percent of business respondents—which included companies of all sizes and orienta-

tions—said that they had been victimized by at least one computer-related crime in the previous year. These crimes ranged from problems of epidemic proportions (such as virus infection, which was mentioned by 65 percent of victims) to less prevalent but still serious problems like financial fraud (12 percent), sabotage (11 percent), and network break-ins (8 percent). Of those companies that attached a dollar figure to their losses as a result of computer crime, the average loss was more than $400,000. Other experts offer similarly grim evaluations of the hardware theft problem. A computer-insurance company in Ohio called Safeware, for instance, estimated that American businesses lost $1.4 billion in 1996 to the theft of computers.

THE BIRTH OF "HACKING"

Early use of the term "hacker" was applied to computer hobbyists who spent their spare time creating video games and other basic computer programs. However, this term acquired a negative connotation in the 1980s when computer experts illegally accessed several high-profile databanks. Databases at the Los Alamos National Laboratory (a center of nuclear weapons research) and the Sloan-Kettering Cancer Center in New York City were among their targets. The introduction of relatively inexpensive personal computers and modems helped make this pastime affordable; the use of regular telephone lines as accessways made it possible. Over time, the designation "hacker" came to be associated with programmers and disseminators of computer viruses, and the public perception of hackers continues to be one of lone computer experts with a taste for mischief or mayhem. But "hacking" has come to encompass a wide range of other computer crimes as well, many of them primarily grounded in efforts to make money. Indeed, the vital information kept in computers has made them a target for corporate espionage, fraud, and embezzlement efforts.

INTERNAL AND EXTERNAL THREATS

As criminologist and computer-insurance executive Ron Hale indicated to McCollum, one of the most unsettling facts about computer crime is that the greatest threat to information security for small businesses is their employees. As McCollum noted, "a company's employees typically have access to its personal computers and computer networks, and often they know precisely what business information is valuable and where to find it." The reasons for these betrayals are many, ranging from workplace dissatisfaction to financial or family difficulties.

Computer crimes perpetrated by outsiders are a major threat too, of course, but whereas employees often abscond with sensitive information or attempt to benefit financially when engaging in illegal activities, outsiders are more likely to engage in behavior that is simply destructive (i.e., computer viruses). Some security experts believe that the continued threat of outside ''hackers'' is due at least in part to the growing number of employees who engage in ''telecommuting'' via modem and the swelling ranks of company networks hooked to the Internet. These connections can be used to infiltrate computer systems. The damage wreaked by outside intruders can be significant and wide-ranging, as Scott Charney, chief of the U.S. Justice Department's section on computer crime, told *Nation's Business.* Charney remarked that while many companies never find out that information has been stolen, other businesses are heavily damaged by the incursion. Yet many companies do not report thefts and other security breaches that they do discover because they fear that the publicity will result in a loss of prestige and/or business.

VIRUSES The most common outside threat to a business's computer network is the virus. Indeed, the National Computer Security Association (NCSA) estimated that in 1996, two out of three U.S. companies were affected by one or more of the estimated 16,000 computer viruses that were floating around the country at that time. ''Viruses infect your machine by attaching themselves to programs, files, and start-up instructions,'' wrote Cassandra Cavanah in *Entrepreneur.* ''There are two main types of computer viruses: macro and binary. Macro viruses are written to attack a specific program. . . . Binary viruses are either actual programs designed to attack your data or attach themselves to program files to do similar destruction. Binary viruses are the ones to be concerned with; they can reformat your hard drive, wipe out data and stop your operating system from working. The best way to fight these bugs is to avoid them—but in today's word of Internet downloads and e-mail file exchanges, this is an impossible task.'' Luckily for small business owners, a wide variety of anti-virus software programs are available at computer stores and the Internet (the latter can be downloaded).

SECURITY MEASURES

Computer security is concerned with preventing information stored in or used by computers from being altered, stolen, or used to commit crimes. The field includes the protection of electronic funds transfers, proprietary information (product designs, client lists, etc.), computer programs, and other communications, as well as the prevention of computer viruses. It can be difficult to place a dollar value on these assets, especially when such factors as potential loss of reputation or liability issues are considered. In some cases (e.g., military and hospital applications) there is a potential for loss of life due to misplaced or destroyed data; this cannot be adequately conveyed by risk analysis formulas. The question most companies face, then, is not whether to practice computer security measures, but how much time and effort to invest. Fortunately, companies looking to protect themselves from computer crime can choose from a broad range of security options. Some of these measures are specifically designed to counter internal threats, while others are shaped to stop outside dangers. Some are relatively inexpensive to put in place, while others require significant outlays of money. But many security experts believe that the single greatest defense that any business can bring to bear is simply a mindset in which issues of security are of paramount concern. ''Firewalls, security scanners, antivirus software, and other types of security technology aren't enough to prevent high-tech crime,'' said *Nation's Business.* ''Real prevention begins by formulating a company security policy that details—among other matters— what information is valuable and how to protect it.''

PROTECTION FROM INTERNAL THREATS Whereas big corporations typically have entire departments devoted to computer system management, small businesses often do not have such a luxury. ''In a small business, the system administrator could be anyone from a secretary to the CEO,'' wrote Lynn Greiner in *CMA - The Management Accounting Magazine.* ''Whoever it is, you can almost guarantee it'll be a busy person who has the duties tacked on to his or her job description. And you can also almost guarantee that this unlucky soul will have few if any resources, and probably no training to help with the burden of keeping the corporate systems running. Fortunately, the technology has advanced to a level that allows administrators to ensure the stability and security of their computer systems, without spending too much time or money.''

Common-sense measures that can be taken by managers and/or system administrators to minimize the danger of internal tampering with computer systems include the following:

- Notify employees that their use of the company's personal computers, computer networks, and Internet connections will be monitored. Then do it.

- Physical access to computers can be limited in various ways, including imposition of passwords; magnetic card readers; and biometrics, which verifies the user's identity through matching patterns in hand geometry, signature or keystroke dynamics, neural networks (the pattern of nerves in the face), DNA fingerprinting, retinal imaging, or voice recognition. More traditional site control methods such as sign-in logs and security badges can also be useful.

- Classify information based on its importance, assigning security clearances to employees as needed.

- Eliminate nonessential modems that could be used to transmit information.

- Monitor activities of employees who keep odd hours at the office.

- Make certain that the company's hiring process includes extensive background checks, especially in cases where the employee would be handling sensitive information.

- Stress the importance of confidential passwords to employees.

PROTECTION FROM EXTERNAL THREATS Small businesses also need to gird themselves against outside intruders. "As with employee crime, the best protection against attacks by outsiders are matters of common sense," said McCollum. "Companies can buy a technological barricade called a firewall and position it between their internal networks and external ones, but hackers often can get in anyway because the firewall hardware and software are poorly configured or are not activated. One way to avoid these problems is to pay outside experts to carry out these complex configuration and installation chores." Of course, good firewalls tend to be expensive (some cost $20,000 or more), but lower cost alternatives have made their way into the marketplace in recent years.

The single greatest scourge from the outside is, of course, the computer virus. But business owners can do much to minimize the threat from viruses by heeding the following basic steps:

- Install and use anti-virus software programs that scan PCS, computer networks, CD-ROMs, tape drives, diskettes, and Internet material, and destroy viruses when found.

- Update anti-virus programs on a regular basis.

- Ensure that all individual computers are equipped with anti-virus programs.

- Forbid employees from putting programs on their office computers without company approval.

- Make sure that the company has a regular policy of backing up (copying) important files and storing them in a safe place, so that the impact of corrupted files is minimized. Having a source of clean (i.e., uninfected by viruses) backup copies for data files and programs is as important as it is elementary.

HARDWARE THEFT

Although computer viruses and other high-tech threats cause the most dread within the business community, the most common type of computer crime actually involves the theft of computer hardware. Unfortunately, employees are often the culprits with this type of crime as well, especially if they work shifts after business hours. Other losses are attributed to outsiders who abscond with computers through elementary breaking-and-entering means. Security experts, though, say that companies can do a lot to cut down on such losses simply by maintaining accurate and up-to-date equipment inventories; locking up hardware that is not in use; locking computers and monitors to desks; and attaching electronic tags to computers. The latter device emits a radio-frequency signal that can activate video cameras or set off alarms when the computer is removed from the premises. Finally, companies should make sure that they purchase adequate insurance.

Business travelers, meanwhile, need to keep a close eye on their notebook and desktop computers, which are highly coveted by thieves. Indeed, the allure of these portable computers is so great that thieves sometimes work in teams to get their hands on them. Airports and hotels are favorite haunts of thieves looking to make off with these valuable items. Security experts thus counsel business travelers to be especially vigilant in high traffic areas, to carry computer serial numbers separately from the hardware, and to consider installing locks, alarms, or tracing software.

NON-CRIMINAL SECURITY THREATS

Of course, not all threats to computer well-being come from parties with criminal intent, however. Savvy small business owners will make sure that their computers—including data as well as hardware—are protected from environmental disaster (power surges, floods, blizzards, fires, etc.) and operator incompetence alike.

Any computer security program should include elements that reflect an understanding of the basic environmental conditions a computer requires in order to operate properly. Ensuring that the system receives adequate power is paramount. Drops in voltage or blackouts can occur due to utility switching problems, stormy weather, or other difficulties at the utility company. In such instances, computers may lose unsaved data or fall victim to "disk crashes." Computer systems can also be endangered by sharp increases in voltage, known as "spikes," which can seriously damage hardware. A variety of voltage regulators, surge protectors, grounding techniques, and filters exist to combat these problems. In the 1990s, intense activity centered on the development of uninterruptible power systems that use storage batteries to ensure a smooth transition between power sources in the event of power failure. Local area networks as well as individual computers can be protected by these devices.

Fire is another important threat to computer systems. Their susceptibility to fire damage is exacerbated by the flammability of paper supplies likely to be stored in close proximity. Plastics used in the manufacture of computers can produce explosive gases when exposed to high temperatures. Moreover, common fire prevention measures such as water sprinklers can further damage computers, especially if the computers are under active power. The use of fire-resistant construction materials, fire walls, vent closure systems, etc., are standard ways to mitigate the threat of fire. Carbon dioxide and Halon 1211 gas extinguishers are suitable for use near electronic equipment because they do not leave a residue.

Other physical security concerns include protection against excessive heat, humidity, and water, which can be introduced by flooding, burst pipes, and other unfortunate developments. Of course, computers and other electronic equipment also suffer damage from less dramatic sources, such as spilled coffee, airborne particles, and cigarette smoke, so coverings made of plastics and other materials have become standard in many firms that rely on computers. But these safeguards will be of little use in the face of more serious situations. Organizations vitally dependent on data processing facilities should prepare contingency plans for disasters such as hurricanes, earthquakes, or blizzards. Ideally, backup facilities should be located far enough away so that they will not be damaged along with the original system in the event of catastrophe.

FURTHER READING:

Avolio, Frederick M. ''Building Internet Firewalls,'' *Business Communications Review*. January 1994.

Belsie, Laurent. ''Firewalls Help Protect Internet From Attack of the Hackers,'' *Christian Science Monitor*. April 29, 1994.

Cavanah, Cassandra. ''Get the Bugs Out: Cure Your Computer's Ills with Anti-Virus Software.'' *Entrepreneur*. September 1997.

DeMaio, Harry B. *Information Protection and Other Unnatural Acts*. New York: Amacom.

''Develop a Company Policy.'' *Nation's Business*. November 1997.

Greiner, Lynn. ''Small Business: Managing Your System.'' *CMA - The Management Accounting Magazine*. September 1996.

McCollum, Tim. ''Computer Crime: The Era of Electronic Innocence is Over.'' *Nation's Business*. November 1997.

Merrick, Bill. ''Electronic Funds Transfer: Biometrics, Neural Networks Poised to Fight Fraud,'' *Credit Union Magazine*. November 1993.

Shain, Michael. ''Security Issues with Enterprise Multimedia,'' *Computers & Security*. February 1994.

Steffora, Ann, and Martin Cheek. ''Hacking Goes Legit,'' *Industry Week*. February 7, 1994.

''Toll Fraud: Ways to Reduce Your Business' Vulnerability,'' *Managing Office Technology*. February 1994.

SEE ALSO: Business Travel; Computers and Computer Systems; Disaster Planning; Employee Theft

COMPUTERS AND COMPUTER SYSTEMS

A computer is a programmable device that can automatically perform a sequence of calculations or other operations on data without human aid. It can store, retrieve, and process data according to internal instructions. A computer may be either digital, analog, or hybrid, although most in operation today are digital. Digital computers express variables as numbers, usually in the binary system. They are used for general purposes, whereas analog computers are built for specific tasks, typically scientific or technical. The term ''computer'' is usually synonymous with digital computer, and computers for business are exclusively digital.

ELEMENTS OF THE COMPUTER SYSTEM

The core, computing part of a computer is its central processing unit (CPU), or processor. It comprises an arithmetic-logic unit to carry out calculations, main memory to temporarily store data for processing, and a control unit to control the transfer of data between memory, input and output sources, and the arithmetic-logic unit. A computer is not fully functional without various peripheral devices, however. These are typically connected to a computer through cables, although some may be built into the same unit with the CPU. These include devices for the input of data, such as keyboards, mice, trackballs, scanners, light pens, modems, magnetic strip card readers, and microphones, as well as items for the output of data, such as monitors, printers, plotters, loudspeakers, earphones, and modems. In addition to these input/output devices, other types of peripherals include computer data storage devices for auxiliary memory storage, where data is saved even when the computer is turned off. These devices most often are magnetic tape drives, magnetic disk drives, or optical disk drives.

Finally, for a digital computer to function automatically, it requires programs, or sets of instructions written in computer-readable code. To be distinguished from the physical or hardware components of a computer, programs are collectively referred to as software.

A computer *system*, therefore, is a computer combined with peripheral equipment and software so that it can perform desired functions. Often the terms ''computer'' and ''computer system'' are used interchangeably, especially when peripheral devices are built into the same unit as the computer or when a system is sold and installed as a package. The term ''computer system,'' however, may also refer to a configuration of hardware and software designed for a specific purpose, such as a manufacturing control system, a library automation system, or an accounting system. Or it may refer to a network of multiple computers linked together so that they can share software, data, and peripheral equipment.

Computers tend to be categorized by size and power, although advancements in computers' processing power have blurred the distinctions between traditional categories. Power and speed are influenced by the size of a computer's internal storage units, called words, which determine the amount of data it can process at once and is measured in bits (binary digits). Computer speed is also determined by its clock speed, which is measured in megahertz. Additionally, the amount of main memory a computer has, which is measured in bytes (or more precisely, kilobytes, megabytes, or gigabytes) of RAM (random access memory), plays a role in determining how much data it can process. The amount of memory that auxiliary storage devices can hold also determines the capabilities of a computer system.

THE MINICOMPUTER

Generally, minicomputers can perform the same functions as mainframe computers, although they have less storage capacity, processing power, and speed. Minicomputers may be small enough to sit on a desktop, but typically are the size of a small cabinet and stand on the floor. Minicomputer systems range in size from single-user units to those which can support several hundred terminals, and their prices range between $15,000 and $250,000. The class of minicomputers having the fastest processing speeds, similar to those of small-scale mainframes, are called superminis. Minicomputers became predominant in the 1970s by serving a broad range of businesses. The most widely used minicomputer line in the 1980s was the DEC VAX, starting with the VAX-11/780 in 1977, a 32-bit computer which runs DEC's proprietary VMS operating system. The IBM AS/400, introduced in 1988, was one of the more popular minicomputers for small business in the early 1990s. Recently, the term ''midrange'' has begun to replace that of minicomputer, to differentiate the medium-sized computer from the even smaller microcomputer.

THE MICROCOMPUTER

The development of the microprocessor, a CPU on a single integrated-circuit chip, enabled the development of affordable single-user microcomputers for the first time. The slow processing power of the early mi-

crocomputers, however, made them attractive only to hobbyists and not to the business market. In 1977, however, the personal computer industry got under way with the introduction of off-the-shelf home computers from three separate manufacturers: the Commodore PET, the Apple, and Radio Shack's TRS-80. These were each 8-bit computers that had a maximum of 64 kilobytes of memory and used only floppy disks, instead of an internal hard disk, for data storage. Popular home computers at the beginning of the 1980s included the Commodore 64 and Commodore 128, the Apple II, and the Atari 500. CP/M was the dominant operating system of microcomputers in the early 1980s.

The term ''personal computer'' (PC) was coined by IBM with the launch of its PC in 1981. This model became an instant success and set the standard for the microcomputer industry. Hence the term PC is often used specifically to designate microcomputers that are ''compatible'' with the IBM PC line, although it may also be synonymous with any microcomputer. Actually, an ''IBM-compatible PC'' means a microcomputer that has a chip compatible with the Intel 80x86 chip and is capable of running the DOS operating system and therefore can run the same applications software. By the late 1980s, DOS had overtaken CP/M as the dominant operating system for personal computers of any manufacturer.

Apple's Macintosh line, introduced in 1984, is the leading personal computer make that does not use DOS; it instead uses Apple's own proprietary operating system, MacOS. MacOS made the Macintosh very popular because of its excellent graphical user interface. However, Apple did not begin licensing MacOS to other computer manufacturers until 1994. Beginning with Windows 3.0, the graphical user interface that Microsoft developed for the PC, increasing numbers of software applications were written for the DOS/Windows platform. Thus DOS continued to hold the largest share of the personal computer operating system market well into the 1990s. The Macintosh, meanwhile, remained dominant in desktop publishing and graphics applications.

In addition to IBM and Apple, leading manufacturers of personal computers in the 1990s included Compaq, AST Research, NEC, Gateway, and Dell. Personal computers, which today range in price from a few hundred dollars to several thousand dollars, usually fit on a single desktop. Since they are designed for single users, personal computers typically come with at least a monitor, keyboard, and disk or tape drive. Hard disks for auxiliary data storage only became standard on personal computers in the later 1980s.

By the early 1990s personal computers had become the fastest-growing category of computers. This was largely due to the adoption of their use in businesses of all sizes. The availability of these small, inexpensive computers brought computer technology to even the smallest of enterprises. Minicomputers or midranges, meanwhile, still remained widely used in business in the 1990s, although UNIX workstations have made significant inroads in their marketshare during that time. Workstations are a class of microcomputers that combine the processing power and speeds of lower-end midranges with the size of personal computers.

The workstation was first introduced by Apollo Computer in 1980. However, it was Sun Microsystems, founded only in 1982, that soon dominated the new industry segment by producing affordable computers from standard off-the-shelf parts and using a form of the versatile, commonly used operating system, UNIX. Workstation performance was further enhanced with the adoption of a microprocessor based on reduced instruction set computing (RISC), first developed by IBM in 1986. Sun introduced its first workstation based on RISC, called the SPARCstation, in 1989. Soon, other workstation manufacturers, such as Hewlett-Packard, were also providing computers which had RISC-based microprocessors and ran UNIX. Thus, it was not only the increased power at a low price that made workstations more attractive than midranges, but also the greater compatibility among the computers of different workstation manufacturers.

Workstations are used most often in graphic design, engineering, or manufacturing operations, where the processing power to handle sophisticated computer-aided design and manufacturing software and graphics is needed, yet individual engineers or designers require their own computers instead of sharing a midrange. By the early 1990s networked workstations began to replace midranges to a certain extent in general business usage as well.

PORTABLE COMPUTERS

The most recent category of microcomputer to enter the business world is the portable computer. These small and light—but increasingly powerful—computers are commonly known as laptop or notebook computers. Laptop computers have the same power as desktop personal computers, but are built more compactly and use flat screen monitors, usually using liquid crystal display, that fold down to form a slim unit that fits in a briefcase and usually weigh under 15 pounds. A notebook computer is one that weighs under 6 pounds and may or may not have a full-size keyboard. A pocket computer is a hand held calculator-size computer. A personal digital assistant is a pocket computer that uses a pen and tablet for input, has a fax/modem card, and is combined with the capabilities of a cellular telephone for remote data communications. Portable computers are increasingly popular among businesspeople who travel, such as executives or sales representatives.

BUSINESS USAGE OF COMPUTERS

Computers are used in government, industry, nonprofit and nongovernmental organizations, and in the home, but their impact has been greatest in business and industry. The competitive nature of business has created demands spurring continuous advancements in computer technology and systems design. Meanwhile, the declining prices of computer systems and their increasing power and utility has led more and more enterprises to invest in computer systems for an ever widening range of business functions. Today, computers are used to process data in all aspects of a business enterprise: product design and development, manufacturing, inventory control and distribution, quality control, sales and marketing, service data, accounting, and personnel management. They are also used in businesses of all sizes and in all industry segments, including manufacturing, wholesale, retail, services, mining, agriculture, transportation, and communications.

The most common business uses of a computer system are for database management, financial management and accounting, and word processing. Companies use **database management systems** to keep track of changing information in databases on such subjects as clients, vendors, employees, inventory, supplies, product orders, and service requests. Financial and accounting systems are used for a variety of mathematical calculations on large volumes of numeric data, whether in the basic functions of financial service companies or in the accounting activities of firms. Computers equipped with spreadsheet or database management software, meanwhile, are used by accounts payable, accounts receivable, and payroll departments to process and tabulate financial data and analyze their cash flow situations. Finally, word processing is ubiquitous and is used to create a wide range of documents, including internal memos, correspondence with outside entities, public relations materials, and products (in publishing, advertising, and other industries).

Databases may also be used to help make strategic decisions through the use of software based on artificial intelligence, or the use of logic. A database system may include—in addition to records and statistics of products, services, clients, etc.—information about past human experience within a specific field. This is referred to as a knowledge base. Examples of expert system usage include business forecasting activities such as investment analysis, financial planning, insurance underwriting, and fraud risk prediction. Expert systems are also used in activities associated with regulatory compliance, contract bidding, complex production control, customer support, and training.

COMPUTER SYSTEMS AND SMALL BUSINESS

For most small businesses, jumping into the world of computers is a competitive requirement. Indeed, a mid-1990s survey conducted by National Small Business United and Arthur Andersen's Enterprise Group indicated that approximately 86 percent of America's small- and mid-sized companies had computers, and that 50 percent of companies indicated that all office-based employees were equipped with computers. Moreover, this reliance on computers is accelerating, driven by advances in computer performance and various business applications associated with the Internet.

But computer system purchases can be daunting for entrepreneurs and established business owners alike. After all, small business enterprises typically have less margin for error than their big business brethren. Given this reality, it is very important for owners and managers to make wise choices when choosing and maintaining computers and computer systems. Four major areas that business owners and managers need to consider when weighing computer options are: 1) your company's overall business strategy; 2) the needs of your customers; 3) the needs of your workforce; and 3) the technology's total cost of ownership (TCO).

COMPANY STRATEGY ''It is common to view computer systems technology as a stand-alone entity when, in fact, it should be regarded as one of the larger-scale and more widely-used business tools,'' wrote Richard Hensley in *Cincinnati Business Courier*. ''[Computer systems technology is] a tool that is critical for achieving the overall corporate **strategy**. . . . Although it may well exist in the owner's mind, many small and mid-sized companies have no detailed written system strategy. It is not surprising then, that many of the systems technology implementation decisions are more reactive than they are strategically based. Competitive pressures, the need to catch up to the marketplace, and internal growth tend to force buying decisions.'' Instead, system purchasing decisions should be used proactively as an opportunity to evaluate overall strategies and assess the effectiveness of current operational processes.

CUSTOMER NEEDS Business owners also need to ensure that their chosen computer system meets the needs of customers. Is ongoing communication with clients a critical component of your business? If so, then your system should be equipped with features that allow you and your client to communicate via computer in a timely and effective fashion. Does your business's health hinge on processing customer orders and generating invoices? If so, make sure your system can easily handle such requirements?

WORKFORCE NEEDS Whether introducing a new computer system or making changes to an existing system, businesses inevitably change the ways in which their employees work, and this factor must be taken into consideration. ''It is not unusual to experience some resistance from employees who are reluctant to accept departure from the status quo,'' said Hensley. ''Such resistance can often be greatly reduced by involving the affected employees in the development of, or modification to, the system. They can provide practical information on what works well within the current system and what doesn't. Once the changes have been implemented, establish a training program and support structure for all users. This will maximize the benefits of the system and better equip employees to achieve the results expected from the change.'' In addition, companies need to make sure that computer technology is distributed in an intelligent fashion. Computers should be allocated according to need, not ranking.

TOTAL COST OF OWNERSHIP Many small businesses neglect to consider the accumulated costs associated with various computer systems when making their hardware decisions. In addition to original price tag, companies need to weigh hidden information technology costs associated with the purchase. These costs, known as total cost of ownership (TCO), include technical support, administrative costs, wasteful user operations, and supplementary expenses (printer ink and paper costs, electricity, etc.). Another factor that should be considered is the equipment's useful life. After all, as Hensley noted, ''to assure the capability to produce relevant information, technology systems require scheduled investments.'' Business owners that ignore this reality do so at their peril, suggest experts. ''When it comes to cutting costs, one of your first instincts may be to hold on to your PCS as long as you can, thinking the less money you spend on new technology, the better,'' wrote Heather Page in *Entrepreneur*. Actually, though, such reasoning ultimately raises business costs. ''Having several generations of hardware, software and operating systems increases the complexity of your PC environment, thus increasing your costs,'' explained Page. ''Not only do you have to maintain technical expertise in older technologies, but you also have to find ways for older equipment to work with the new technologies and develop all your custom applications to support multiple environments.''

RECENT TRENDS IN COMPUTER SYSTEMS

OPEN SYSTEMS The most significant trend in computer systems has been increased compatibility of computer hardware and software from different manufacturers. In the past, all components of a computer system originated from the same manufacturer. There were no industry-wide standards. As a result, printers, monitors, and other peripheral equipment from one manufacturer would not operate when matched with the computer of another manufacturer. More significantly, software could only run on the specific computer brand for which it was designed. Today, however, ''open systems,'' wherein various equipment from different manufacturers can be matched together, is common. Open systems are especially popular among small business owners because they allow enterprises to upgrade or expand their computer systems more easily and cheaply. Open systems provide business owners with more buying options, enable them to minimize expenses of employee retraining on new systems, and give them greater freedom to share computer files with outside clients or vendors.

NETWORKING Another major trend in computer systems is the networking of multiple computers so that they can share data and peripheral equipment. Computers on a network are physically linked by cables and use network software in conjunction with the operating system software. Depending on the hardware and software used, different types of computers may be put on the same network. This may involve computers of different sizes—such as mainframes, midranges, and microcomputers—or computers and peripherals of different manufacturers, which the trend toward open systems has facilitated. **Local area networks (LANs)** link computers within a limited geographical area, while **Wide area networks (WANs)** connect computers in different geographic regions. Networks may have various architectures which determine whether computers on the network can act independently. A commonly used system architecture is client-server, whereby a server computer is designated as the one storing and processing data and is accessed by multiple users each at a client computer.

LANs have transformed how employees within an organization use computers. In organizations where employees formerly accessed midrange computer through ''dumb'' terminals, these employees now typically have more capabilities. These users have their own personal computer at their desks, but are still able to access needed data from a midrange or other server through the network. Whereas smaller businesses typically favor LANs, WANs are often used by companies with multiple facilities located over a wide geographic area. After all, under a WAN system, a company's databases can be accessed at headquarters in one city, at a manufacturing plant in other city, and at sales offices in other locations.

CD-ROM A relatively new form of data storage medium that has made a significant impact on business computer systems is CD-ROM (compact disc read-only memory). CD-ROMs store data optically instead of magnetically and therefore can hold over 600 megabytes of data, instead of the 1.44 megabytes held by the typical high-density 3-1/2-inch floppy diskette. A corresponding peripheral device, a CD-ROM drive, is required for a computer to read CD-ROMs.

Due to their capacity to hold large volumes of data, one of the most practical applications of CD-ROMs has been the publishing of indexes or directories on a single disc that would otherwise require multiple volumes of printed text; the data can then be searched by a database management program. For business applications, this may involve directories of companies, products, or patents, as well as indexes of business literature. Another emerging business application of CD-ROM production can be found in the marketing of software, since a single CD-ROM can hold dozens of software packages.

MULTIMEDIA Closely associated with the trend toward CD-ROM use are multimedia computer systems, which emerged at the beginning of the 1990s. A multimedia system has a user interface that supplements text and graphics with sound and video capabilities. Sound, graphics, and video data require a great deal of data storage space, so such multimedia software relies on the storage capacity of CD-ROM technology.

FURTHER READING:

Anderson, Ronald E., and David R. Sullivan. *The World of Computing*. Boston: Houghton Mifflin Company, 1988.

Codkind, Alan. ''Automating The Business Process.'' *CMA - The Management Accounting Magazine*. October 1993.

Hensley, Richard. ''Owner Quandary: How Much to Spend on New Technology?'' *Cincinnati Business Courier*. March 3, 1997.

''Is It New? Or Is It Hype?'' *Nation's Business*. August 1993.

Massey, Tom K. Jr. ''Computers in Small Business: A Case of Under-Utilization.'' *American Journal of Small Business*.

Page, Heather. ''What Price PC?'' *Entrepreneur*. October 1997.

''Productivity: Lost in Cyberspace.'' *The Economist*. September 13, 1997.

''Small Firm's Usage Patterns.'' *Nation's Business*. August 1993.

Smith, Sandi. ''The Smart Way to Invest in Computers.'' *Journal of Accountancy*. May 1997.

CONSTRUCTION

Many successful small businesses eventually decide to expand their operations by either purchasing, leasing, or building a new facility. In some instances, the business in question relocates its entire operation in the new facility, while in other cases, the business may use the new facility to house excess inventory, maintain equipment, relieve office overcrowding, or open a new store.

For those companies that decide to expand via new construction, the experience can be an unsettling one, full of uncertainties. In fact, relatively few start-up businesses choose construction as their mode of entry due to the higher costs associated with it and the greater length of time involved from the breaking ground stage to the day when the establishment opens its doors for business. Small- and mid-sized businesses, however, are far more likely to have the financial wherewithal to launch a new construction project; such firms have a proven track record—which can help them with financing—and already productive operations that bring in revenue that can be used to defray the costs of construction. Owners of these businesses, however, should fully weigh the advantages and disadvantages of construction before moving forward. As the J. K. Lasser Institute indicated in *How to Run a Small Business,* "building has the advantage of giving you the space and arrangements which meet your needs, providing you know specifically and objectively what the needs are. The obvious disadvantages are the delay in occupancy while land acquisition, design work, and building are going on, and the cost of overruns and mistakes caused by forecasting errors and planning oversights."

Certainly, there are risks associated with construction. But for small- and mid-sized business owners that choose this method of expansion and/or growth—and plan wisely both before, during, and after the construction phase—it can also mark the beginning of a bright new chapter in the company's history. As Dave Pelland stated in *Risk Management,* "constructing or renovating a corporate facility can mark an important crossroads in the development of a growing company. Constructed properly, the new facility can allow the company to generate additional revenue, reduce expenses, or increase efficiency."

SECURING A BUILDING CONTRACTOR Pelland noted that small business owners seeking to secure a good building contractor should concentrate on three factors:

- The contractor's reputation in the community.
- The financial condition of the contractor.
- The status of currently uncompleted jobs by the contractor.

Warning signs can take many forms when examining the above issues. Is the contractor known for subcontracting out large percentages of the total construction work? Does the contractor have a history of

clashes with subcontractors? How long has the contractor done business in the area? What percentage of jobs does he complete on schedule? Does his previous work experience adequately match the sort of renovation or construction that your company needs? Does the contractor have a backlog of projects that could hurt his ability to match your timetable? What sort of references can he provide? The answers to all of these questions can be either reassuring or cause for further investigation. In either case, the key is to make sure that you ask them. Pelland and other analysts note that one way in which small business owners can learn the answers to some of these questions is by requiring bidding contractors to submit a surety bond, which is basically a three-party contract between the contractor, the project owner, and the underwriting surety company. Surety companies, noted Pelland, will make an extensive review of the construction company before issuing such a bond. In addition, if the contractor signs the bond, he is basically guaranteeing his ability to complete the project on which he is bidding.

MONITORING THE CONSTRUCTION PROCESS "After the bidding process is completed," said Pelland, "the successful contractor should be asked to provide a performance bond, which guarantees that the project's contractual provisions will be carried out, and a payment bond, which certifies that suppliers and subcontractors will be paid." Ensuring that the contractor and all of his subcontractors have adequate insurance (workers' comp, general and umbrella liability, equipment, builders' risk, etc.) to address problems is another key to attaining piece of mind for the small business owner. Finally, the project owner needs to make sure that he or she continuously monitors the performance of the contractor.

FURTHER READING:

J. K. Lasser Institute. *How to Run a Small Business.* 7th ed. New York: McGraw-Hill, 1994.

Malpas, William. "Management: Minimizing Construction Risks." *Progressive Architecture.* June 1990.

Pelland, Dave. "Creating Buildings, Not Problems: Managing Construction Risk Effectively." *Risk Management.* November 1996.

Weiss, Howard J., and Mark E. Gershon. *Production and Operations Management.* Boston: Allyn and Bacon, 1989.

SEE ALSO: Business Growth; Renovation

CONSTRUCTIVE DISCHARGE

The term "constructive discharge" describes a situation in which an employee is forced to quit a job because the employer has made working conditions intolerable. Working conditions may be considered intolerable if, for example, the employee is discriminated against or harassed, or if he or she suffers a negative change in pay, benefits, or workload for reasons that are not performance-related. In most cases, an employee who voluntarily leaves a company—as opposed to one whose employment is terminated by the company against his or her will—is not entitled to unemployment benefits and loses the right to sue the company for wrongful termination. But the law recognizes constructive discharge as an exception to this rule.

''In an increasing number of cases, employees are quitting their jobs, filing wrongful discharge suits against their former employers, and—here's the kicker—coming out a winner,'' J.D. Thorne wrote in an article for *Small Business Reports.* ''The courts have reasoned in these cases that the employers made the workers' jobs so unbearable that they would rather quit than suffer more abuse. Being compelled to quit was much the same as being unfairly discharged. This claim, commonly known as constructive discharge, essentially excuses the employee from being the one to sever the employment relationship.''

LEGAL STANDARDS AND APPLICABLE PENALTIES

In order to sue successfully on the basis of constructive discharge, an employee must prove in court that the working conditions he or she experienced were intolerable. The legal standard for intolerable working conditions requires that an objective, reasonable person in the same position would also choose to quit. In addition, the employee must prove that the intolerable conditions were directly attributable to the employer.

According to Thorne, some of the most common problems cited by employees in constructive discharge complaints include a loss of pay or benefits, an abnormal increase or decrease in workload, or discrimination under the **Americans with Disabilities Act**, equal employment opportunity laws, or unfair labor practice statutes. Constructive discharge suits may also be triggered when an employer is abusive toward an employee, particularly when that employee is a member of a protected class by virtue of gender, race, or age. Improper disciplinary actions can also be cause for a constructive discharge complaint, although employers can criticize employees' job performance and deny benefits for reasons that are business related.

In recent years, as the number of legal actions related to constructive discharge have increased, some states have strengthened the burden of proof for employees. Rather than simply proving that working conditions were intolerable, some employees now must also show that the employer knew about the poor conditions and could have remedied the situation. ''Unless an employee can prove that you deliberately made working conditions so intolerable that the worker was forced to quit, then a court probably won't find the company guilty of constructive discharge,'' Thorne explained.

Some states also require employees to notify their employer of the problem and give them a fair chance to fix it. The idea behind such measures is to make it unnecessary for employees to quit in order to see their problems resolved, as well as to prevent employers from being blind sided by employees who quit and then sue for wrongful discharge. In Arizona, for example, employees must provide 15 days' written notice of their intention to quit for cause. The employer then has that time to make necessary changes in working conditions. If the employee is not satisfied with the employer's response and still decides to quit, then he or she is entitled to file suit for constructive discharge. The Arizona law does provide an exception, however, for employees who encounter working conditions so serious that they must leave the company immediately.

The penalties a company can face if a former employee sues successfully for constructive discharge can be severe. As Thorne noted, the usual penalties include both back pay (the amount of wages the employee would have been paid had they continued working for the company up until the time of the lawsuit) and front pay (an amount based on the employee's remaining work years and the expected length of time it will take him or her to find a similar job), as well as reimbursement of attorney fees. There may also be monetary damages, compensatory damages for pain and suffering or mental distress, and punitive damages of up to $300,000 in some discrimination cases. Employees who win constructive discharge cases are usually not reinstated, however, because it would be counterproductive to return them to an intolerable working environment.

HOW TO AVOID CONSTRUCTIVE DISCHARGE LAWSUITS

Thorne outlined a number of steps small business owners can take to strengthen their defenses against charges of constructive discharge. One suggestion is to implement a formal complaint system. In addition to giving the company a chance to rectify problems before they lead to lawsuits, complaint systems make it appear as if a disgruntled employee had another option available besides quitting. Another recommendation is to establish and follow company guidelines for informing employees of performance problems and taking disciplinary action. In this way, employees cannot claim that changes in working conditions were discriminatory or were made for non-business reasons.

Another important suggestion for small business owners is never to change the conditions of employment in order to get employees to resign rather than having to fire them—even in cases where termination may cost the company money for unemployment benefits. Some managers may find it tempting to take steps to make the employee want to leave the company rather than going through the formal dismissal process. Instead, companies should always follow their standard procedures for discipline and termination. It may also be helpful to request a letter of resignation from employees who quit voluntarily and keep it on file as evidence of their reasons for leaving the company. Finally, exit interviews should be made mandatory for all employees who leave the company. The exit interview gives management an opportunity to iron out differences with employees who quit with hard feelings toward the company.

Perhaps the best policies a small business can follow to avoid being sued for constructive discharge, however, are to promote fair management practices and create a favorable working environment. ''The best advice, as always, is to play it straight with employees,'' Thorne wrote. ''There's no substitute for allowing them to air grievances, correcting problems with working conditions, and disciplining them fairly for unsatisfactory work.''

FURTHER READING:

Mesritz, George D. ''Constructive Discharge and Employer Intent: Are the Courts Split over a Distinction without a Difference?'' *Employee Relations Law Journal.* Spring 1996.

Thorne, J.D. ''Who Says Quitters Never Win?'' *Small Business Reports.* October 1994.

Turco, Frank. ''Law Expected to Put Employee Suits to Rest.'' *Phoenix Business Journal.* June 13, 1997.

SEE ALSO: Employee Rights; Employee Termination; Legal Advice and Services; Liabilities

CONSULTANTS

A consultant is an individual who possesses special knowledge or skills and provides that expertise to a client for a fee. Consultants help all sorts of businesses find and implement solutions to a wide variety of problems, including those related to business start-up, marketing, manufacturing, strategy, organization structure, environmental compliance, health and safety, technology, and communications. Some consultants are self-employed, independent contractors who offer specialized skills in a certain field; other consultants work for large consulting firms, such as Anderson Consulting or Gemini Consulting, that offer expertise in a wide range of business areas; and still other consultants hail from academia.

The consulting industry has grown rapidly since its origins in the 1960s. In fact, the market research firm Gartner Group Inc. found that U.S. companies spent $11.4 billion on consultants in 1994, and predicted that this amount would nearly double by year 2000. Several factors have contributed to the growth of consulting in the 1990s. First, as a result of the trend toward corporate **downsizing**, many companies have found that they lack the internal manpower to complete all necessary tasks. Second, the complexity of today's business climate—as a result of deregulation, globalization, and technology advancements—has outpaced many companies' level of expertise. Finally, consultants provide a way for companies to get special projects done without adding employees to the payroll.

The decision to hire a consultant is not one that a small business should take lightly. Consultants can be very expensive, although their expertise can prove invaluable. The small business owner must first decide whether the situation facing the company requires the input of a consultant. If it does, then advance preparation should be done to ensure a successful consulting experience. The small business owner is then ready to find and negotiate a contract with the right consultant. An important part of this process is understanding the ways in which consultants charge for their services. Hopefully, after completing the consulting process, the small business will emerge with a successfully implemented solution to its problem.

DECIDING WHETHER TO USE A CONSULTANT

In deciding whether or not to hire a consultant, the small business owner should consider the nature of the problem, the reasons why internal resources cannot be used to solve it, and the possible advantages a consultant could offer. In his book *How to Select and Manage Consultants,* Howard Shenson describes several situations in which a consultant's services are likely to be required. When a small business needs specialized expertise, talents, or skills that do not exist internally, or needs technical assistance on a temporary basis, then it may want to consider hiring a consultant. Likewise, hiring a consultant might be appropriate when the small business needs an objective, frank opinion on a problem. A consultant might also be able to help a small business that is having problems with cash flow, the availability of funds, or in acquiring resources. Political or organizational problems, regulatory problems, and training needs are some other areas in which a small business might benefit from the use of a consultant. A small business should not hire a consultant simply in order to have someone else implement unpopular decisions

MAKING THE CONSULTING EXPERIENCE WORK

Once the decision has been made to enlist the help of a consultant, there are several steps the small business owner can take in advance to increase the likelihood that the consulting experience will be successful. First and foremost, the company's managers should define the problem they need the consultant to address. Using probing questions to go beyond superficial symptoms to underlying causes, the managers should attempt to state the problem in writing. Next, they should define the expected results of the consulting experience. The objectives the managers come up with should be clear, realistic, and measurable.

Another important step in preparing for a successful consulting experience is to communicate with employees. The small business owner should explain the problem fully and honestly, in as positive terms as possible, and ask employees for their understanding and cooperation. When employees feel surprised or threatened, they may hamper the consultant's efforts by withholding information or not providing honest opinions. It is also helpful to gather all important company documents relating to the problem in order to make them available to the consultant. The consultant's job will be easier if they have ample information about both the company and the problem at hand.

Once the consulting project begins, there are several other steps a small business owner can take to help ensure its success. For example, it is important to manage the project from the top in order to give it the visibility and priority it deserves. The small business owner should appoint a liaison to assist the consultant in gathering information, and should receive regular progress reports about the project. In the implementation stage, the small business owner should adequately staff the project and empower those involved to make any necessary changes.

HOW TO SELECT A CONSULTANT

Selecting the right consultant for the company and the type of problem at hand is a vital part of the process. The first step is to assemble a list of candidates by getting recommendations from people in the same line of business, contacting consulting associations or consultant brokers that represent the same industry, or reviewing advertisements in trade or professional journals. Several library reference books, such as Gale Research's *Consultants and Consulting Organizations Directory,* provide contact information for consultants in a variety of fields. It is important to avoid selecting a consultant based upon a current

management fad; instead, the decision should be based upon the company's particular needs.

The next step is to determine, based on the nature of the problem, what type of consultant is needed. An advisory consultant analyzes the problem and turns recommendations over to the client, but is not involved in implementation of the solution. In contrast, an operational consultant remains on hand to assist the client in proper implementation, or in some cases handles the implementation without the client's assistance. Part-time consultants are generally employed full-time within their field of expertise—marketing, for example—but also offer their services to other companies on the side. They usually charge less money than full-time consultants, but they also cannot devote their undivided time and energy to the client.

Process consultants are skills-oriented generalists. With expertise in one or more technical areas, these consultants can apply their skills to any industry or organization. In contrast, functional consultants apply their skills to a particular environment; for example, a hospital facilities planner would concentrate on consulting to hospitals, rather than to other types of businesses that require facilities planning. Another distinction between consultants is based on the size of their operation. Consultants can work for large firms, small firms, or even independently. Large firms offer greater resources, but also have higher overhead and thus charge higher fees. Small firms or independent consultants may offer more attentive service, but may not have access to the precise type of talent that is required. Finally, consultants can be academically or commercially based. In general, academic consultants may be most helpful with problems requiring research or a background in theory, while commercial consultants may be able offer more practical experience.

Once a small business owner has determined what type of consultant would be best suited to handle the company's problem and assembled a list of candidates, the next step is to interview the candidates. Some of the traits to consider include experience with the company or industry, availability, knowledge of the problem at hand, communication skills, flexibility, and compatibility. Since consultants are usually required to work within the corporate culture, often in times of crisis, it is important that their style is compatible with that of the firm.

After discussing the problem in detail with the leading candidates, the small business owner may opt to ask each consultant to submit a written proposal to aid in the selection process. In some cases, the contents of these proposals may convince the small business owner that the problem could be better handled using in-house resources. After deciding to hire a specific consultant, the small business owner should ask that consultant to draw up a **contract**, or at least a formal letter, confirming their arrangements. It is important to note that the contract should be based on negotiations between the two parties, so the small business owner may wish to add, delete, or clarify the information included. There are several peripheral issues that the small business owner may want to address in the contract, including the consultant's proposed methods of handling conflicts of interest, subcontractors, insurance/liability, expenses, confidentiality, and nonperformance.

HOW CONSULTANTS CHARGE CLIENTS

According to Stenson, all consultants use the same basic formula to determine the fees charged for their services, but clients are asked to pay these fees in a wide variety of ways. All consultants' fees are based on a daily billing rate, which reflects the value they place on one day's labor plus expected overhead expenses. In some cases, this daily billing rate—multiplied by the amount of time the consultant spends on the project—is the amount the company actually pays. But other consultants may estimate the amount of time needed and quote the client a fixed fee. Other consultants may provide a bracket quotation, or a range within which the total fee will fall. Another way in which consultants charge clients is a monthly retainer, which covers all the necessary services for that month. Finally, some consultants—especially in high-technology fields—charge on the basis of the company's performance.

THE CONSULTING PROCESS

The consulting process begins when the client company decides to enlist the services of a consultant. The consultant then analyzes the company's problem and provides recommendations about how to fix it. Small business owners should avoid the temptation to blindly follow a consultant's recommendations; instead, they should seek to understand the diagnosis and be prepared to negotiate any necessary changes. As Stenson notes, the consulting process should not be ''mysterious or unusual,'' but rather a ''mutually beneficial business arrangement between consultant and client.'' Finally, after implementing the consultant's recommendations, the client company should formally evaluate the success of the consulting experience so that those lessons can be applied to future problems.

FURTHER READING:

Grassell, Milt. ''Getting Help from Consultants.'' *Supervision.* September 1992.

Hathaway, Donald B. ''Consultants: If Necessary.'' *CMA—The Management Accounting Magazine.* May 1990.

McCune, Jenny C. ''The Consultant Quandary.'' *Management Review.* October 1995.

Salmon, Bill, and Nate Rosenblatt. *The Complete Book of Consulting.* Ridgefield, CT: Round Lake Publishing, 1995.

Shenson, Howard L. *How to Select and Manage Consultants.* Lexington Books, 1990.

SEE ALSO: Consulting

CONSULTING

Consulting is the business of providing advice to clients for a fee in order to help them solve a particular problem or range of problems within a certain area of business. Consulting services are provided by consultants, a majority of whom have gained their expertise from previous employment. Some consultants work for large consulting firms, such as Anderson Consulting or Gemini Consulting, that offer expertise in a wide range of business areas; other consultants hail from academia and assist companies with problems relating to research or theory; and still other consultants are self-employed, independent contractors who offer specialized skills in a certain field. For example, a former stock broker might become a financial consultant; a computer scientist might become a computer consultant; a former employee in a non-profit organization might open a business as a fund-raising consultant; and an accountant might become a tax consultant.

Expertise alone, however, does not make someone a consultant—at least not a full-time one. To be a consultant requires applying that expertise to practical problem solving. Consulting, moreover, is a business, so it also requires marketing skills and the ability to reach out and establish job contacts. Personality also plays a role in consulting success. In general, the kind of people who can put the needs and interests of clients before their own, who are not condescending, and who are unfailingly courteous and patient have the best chance at success. A small minority of consultants work as internal consultants for one firm, usually a very large one. The majority, however, work independently and with no partners, often from their own homes, or run their own small consulting firms.

Consultants constitute a growing number (as yet undetermined, since there are no licensing requirements for consultants) of the self-employed. This growth began in the early 1990s, when the trend toward corporate downsizing left many skilled professionals without jobs. According to the American Consultants League, the consulting field grew by over 400,000 men and women between 1993 and 1994, approximately 150,000 of whom had lost their jobs. The vast majority of these new entrepreneurs were found to be between the ages of 35 and 55, and many of them were former mid-level managers.

According to the American Consultants League, the failure rate for first time consulting businesses is extremely high—91 percent in the first year. Those who do succeed, however, usually earn as much if not more than they did in their former employment. Reasons for failure often involve a combination of such factors as poor initial planning, careless marketing of one's business, and intense competition. The successful consultants are usually those who find a market niche for themselves through research, intensive marketing, and locale. Charging the right fee and avoiding falling into the trap of ''free'' consulting (for instance, when a client whose contract with a consultant has ended insists upon additional ''feedback'' or ''follow up'') requires business sense. Consulting fees can vary from almost nothing to several thousand dollars per assignment, depending on the assignment, market conditions, and the minimal rate for that type of work.

Since the vast majority of consultants are self-employed professional business people, consulting typically is a business that involves long hours and much pressure. Consultants must study their fields of expertise continuously to keep abreast of developments. To the millions of entrepreneurs who enter the consulting profession, however, the attraction and challenge of creative, independent work performed in a comfortable environment outweigh the difficulties. And while competition is great, the number of large firms that dominate this profession are few. While some consulting fields have become saturated—such as the computer and environmental fields—there are always new trends emerging. For instance, with the unexpected fall of communism, the demand for eastern European specialists and ''free market'' consultants skyrocketed. As the need for business information grows and changes, and the demand for consultants should continue to escalate.

TYPES OF CONSULTANTS

Consultants help all sorts of businesses find and implement solutions to a wide variety of problems, including those related to business start-up, marketing, manufacturing, strategy, organization structure, environmental compliance, health and safety, technology, and communications. In addition to size of the operation and field of specialty, consultants can be categorized in a number of other ways. For example, an advisory consultant analyzes the problem and turns recommendations over to the client, but is not involved in implementation of the solution. In contrast, an operational consultant remains on hand to assist the client in proper implementation, or in some cases handles the implementation without the client's assistance.

Part-time consultants are generally employed full-time within their field of expertise—marketing, for example—but also offer their services to other companies on the side. Although they are not usually able to charge as much money as full-time consultants, they also are not expected to devote their undivided time and energy to the client. Process consultants are skills-oriented generalists. With expertise in one or more technical areas, these consultants can apply their skills to any industry or organization. In contrast, functional consultants apply their skills to a particular environment; for example, a hospital facilities planner would concentrate on consulting to hospitals, rather than to other types of businesses that require facilities planning.

ESTABLISHING A CONSULTING BUSINESS

START-UP An entrepreneur starting up a consulting business must go through many of the same processes as those starting other types of businesses. The first step should be completing an honest assessment of skills. The aspiring consultant should identify both content skills—the technical expertise that clients will be willing to pay for—and process skills—the qualities that would enable someone to run a successful consulting business. Some of the most important process skills include communication, problem-solving, and interpersonal skills. In addition, independent consultants must have the ability to manage, market, and grow their own businesses. In *The Complete Book of Consulting,* Bill Salmon and Nate Rosenblatt recommend that new consultants make a list of all their relevant skills and qualities, and then work from that list to create a short mission statement to guide their consulting business.

Like other entrepreneurs, consultants also must determine the most appropriate structure, location, and name for their businesses. The form or structure of the business depends upon the new consultant's tax situation, willingness to assume liability, and interest in taking on partners. A consultant who operates as a sole proprietorship, for example, is taxed as individual and holds all personal and business liability. In a partnership of two or more consultants, each partner is taxed as an individual and shares in the liability. A consultant who organizes as a corporation enjoys limited liability (to the value corporate assets), and the business is taxed as a separate entity. Preparing a detailed **business plan** can help aspiring consultants to think about how their business should be financed, where it should be positioned in relation to its competition, and what its most effective forms of marketing might be.

SETTING FEES However interesting or fulfilling it may be, most consultants ultimately view their work as a money-making venture. To avoid confusion, each service the consultant performs should have a clearly defined fee. But deciding how much to charge for various services can be a challenge for a new consultant. As Salmon and Rosenblatt explain, the first step should be examining the costs relating to the consulting business itself. In addition to direct costs—expenses that can be directly attributed to a specific project and thus billed to the client in question—the consultant must also consider indirect costs—overhead expenses associated with running the business. Some common indirect costs include rent, utilities, insurance, office supplies and equipment, marketing costs, postage, automobile expenses, accounting or legal fees, dues to professional associations, and entertainment. The next step in developing a fee structure is to determine the cost of the consultant's labor. Some new consultants might use their previous salary as a starting point, or the salary of a comparable position. The most important factor to consider is whether the figure reflects the market value of the consultant's skills and experience.

Finally, the estimates of indirect costs and labor should be converted to daily values, taking any expected non-working days into consideration (including vacations, administrative time, business development time, and downtime). For example, a consultant hoping to earn $100,000 over the course of a year, expecting to pay $30,000 in indirect costs, and planning to perform 200 days of billable work would have a daily rate of $100,000 + $30,000 / 200, or $650 per day. This does not take a **profit margin** into account, which can range from 10 to 30 percent of daily expenses. A consultant's daily rate only provides a starting point for determining his or her fees for various types of services. The fee also depends on the kind of assignment, the prevailing rate in the industry or marketplace, the client's budget, and whether the consultant may need to establish a relationship with a new client or develop a reputation in a new industry. In addition, a consultant's fees may be structured in a number of ways. Some consultants charge by the hour, for example, while others charge a fixed price for specific services, receive a monthly retainer, or are paid on a contingency basis.

MARKETING Potential clients cannot take advantage of a consultant's services if they are unaware of them. Therefore, in order to remain in business, new consultants must be able to market their services effectively. Salmon and Rosenblatt recommend that consultants use a variety of direct and indirect marketing techniques to gain clients and grow their businesses. One possible direct marketing technique is **telemarketing**, which involves calling potential clients on the telephone. Telemarketing is most effective if the consultant making the call is armed with knowledge about the company ahead of time, uses a prepared script, describes the benefits he or she offers, and mentions successful projects with other clients.

In some cases, telemarketing can be augmented with a **direct mail** marketing campaign. Although direct mail can be expensive, it is flexible and allows responses to be tracked. Experts suggest increasing the success rate of direct mail campaigns by making them specific, easy to read and understand, and aesthetically pleasing, and by including testimonials and business reply cards. Other possible **direct marketing** methods for consulting businesses include magazine and newspaper advertisements, association directories, **networking**, and referrals from other clients.

Indirect marketing techniques, while less likely to lead to immediate client relationships, are invaluable in helping new consultants increase their name recognition and credibility over the long term. Giving seminars, speaking before groups, joining professional associations, and writing articles or books are all good ways for consultants to build their reputations as sought-after experts in a given field. Another important means of publicizing a new business is through news releases, which can be sent to local media or trade journals to announce client relationships, successful projects, upcoming seminars, or other important happenings related to the business.

EVALUATING CONSULTING OPPORTUNITIES New consultants may be tempted to jump at any business opportunity that comes along. But Salmon and Rosenblatt recommend that consultants gather information about the client in order to make an informed decision about pursuing a consulting opportunity. This process, called qualifying the client, involves considering the nature, scope, and urgency of the project, as well as the client's budget. It is also helpful to find out about the client's desired outcomes and decision-making process. In addition, it may be useful to know whether the client has had successful experiences with consultants in the past, and what they feel the major obstacles to success would be for the project under consideration. A face-to-face interview and a formal **request for proposal** are the two main tools companies use in selecting consultants. Consultants can use these tools as a way to find out more about their clients, as well.

PROPOSALS AND CONTRACTS Proposals are an important part of the consulting business. Sometimes proposals serve to introduce consultants and their services to prospective clients, while other times proposals serve to finalize the arrangements between a consultant and a client. In this way, Salmon and Rosenblatt note, proposals often serve as sales tools and project planning documents at the same time. Prospective clients may request a formal proposal in order to compare several possible consultants, make decisions related to budgets or scheduling, or simply to collect ideas about how to solve a particular problem using in-house resources. Though companies sometimes ask for proposals and then do not end up hiring a consultant, companies that make a habit of such behavior are simply looking for "free consulting." Most experienced consultants try to discern the motives of potential clients ahead of time in order to avoid committing excessive time and resources to "free consulting."

Prior to submitting a proposal, a consultant needs to gather information about the company and its problem from interviews and outside sources. When writing a proposal, it is important for a consultant to demonstrate a strong understanding of the client's needs, describe his or her own ability to meet those needs, and detail a plan of action toward that end. As Salmon and Rosenblatt explain, many successful consulting proposals are divided into three sections: the introduction, the methodology section, and the timing and cost section. The introduction provides an overview of the proposal, and should be used to demonstrate the consultant's understanding of the client's needs and desired outcomes. The methodology section is the main part of the proposal, and specifies the actions the consultant plans to take in order to provide a focused solution to the client's problem. It may also be helpful for the consultant to mention any unique services or expertise he or she can offer, in order to differentiate the proposal from those submitted by other consultants. The timing and cost section provides a realistic and specific fee structure and schedule for completion of the project. In addition, the consultant may wish to outline what effect, if any, the consulting process will have on the client's internal resources.

As Salmon and Rosenblatt note, the proposal should be submitted as part of a package that also includes a cover letter and any necessary attachments. The cover letter, which should only be one page in length, describes the contents of the package, highlights important areas of the proposal—including how it may differ from what the client expected—and explains what the consultant would like to happen next. Some possible attachments that could be added to the proposal package include: a biographical sketch of the consultant, outlining academic and work experiences, membership in professional associations, books or articles published, and awards or recognition received; a description of the consulting firm's history and philosophy; a list of current and former clients, especially those relating to the prospective client's industry or type of project; and anything else that may help the client in the decision-making process.

Proposals should be written in a conversational tone, without excessive use of technical jargon, and with the prospective client's needs in mind. The consultant may benefit from keeping in touch with the client while writing the proposal, as this helps avoid misunderstandings or incomplete information. If the consultant receives the assignment, the proposal then serves as the basis for a formal contract. Although some clients may simply sign the proposal to authorize the consultant to begin work, many consultants prefer to clarify the arrangements in a separate document. At a minimum, the contract should outline the scope of the project, the consultant's fees, and the proposed time frame. There are several other issues that the consultant may wish to address, including conflicts of interest, subcontractors, insurance/liability, expenses, confidentiality, and cancellation.

FURTHER READING:

Block, Peter. *Flawless Consulting.* Pfeiffer, 1981.

Karlson, David. *Marketing Your Consulting or Professional Services.* Menlo Park, CA: Crisp Publications, 1988.

Kelley, Robert E. *Consulting, The Complete Guide to a Profitable Career.* New York: Charles Scribner's Sons, 1986 [revised].

Salmon, Bill, and Nate Rosenblatt. *The Complete Book of Consulting.* Ridgefield, CT: Round Lake Publishing, 1995.

Shenson, Howard L., and Ted Nicholas. *The Complete Guide to Consulting Success.* Chicago, IL: Upstart Publishing, 1993.

Weiss, Alan. *Million Dollar Consulting: The Professional's Guide to Growing a Practice.* New York: McGraw-Hill, 1992.

SEE ALSO: Business Proposals; Consultants

CONSUMER ADVOCACY

Consumer advocacy refers to actions taken by individuals or groups to promote and protect the interests of the buying public. Historically, consumer advocates have assumed a somewhat adversarial role in exposing unfair business practices or unsafe products that threaten the welfare of the general public. Consumer advocates use tactics like publicity, boycotts, letter-writing campaigns, and lawsuits to raise awareness of issues affecting consumers and to counteract the financial and political power of the organizations they target. Since even large businesses can be visibly wounded when their mistreatment of consumers or other constituencies arouses the ire of consumer advocacy organizations, it should be obvious to small business owners that they can ill-afford to engage in business practices that could draw the attention of consumer advocates.

Periods of vocal consumer advocacy around the turn of the twentieth century and in the late 1960s have left a legacy of federal legislation and agencies intended to protect consumers in the United States. The rights of consumers have expanded to include product safety, the legitimacy of advertising claims, the satisfactory resolution of grievances, and a say in government decisions. In the early days of industry, companies could afford to ignore consumers' wishes because there was so much demand for their goods and services. As a result, they were often able to command high prices for products of poor quality. The earliest consumer advocates to point out such abuses were called "muckrakers," and their revelations of underhanded business practices spurred the creation of several federal agencies and a flurry of legislation designed to curb some of the most serious abuses. At the same time, increased competition began to provide consumers with more choices among a variety of products of higher quality. Still, some notable cases of corporations neglecting the public welfare for their own gain continued, and corporate influence in American politics enabled many businesses to resist calls for reform in advertising, worker or consumer safety, and pollution control.

This situation led to the consumer movement of the 1960s. One of the country's most outspoken and controversial consumer advocates, lawyer Ralph Nader, came to the forefront during this time. Nader's effective and well-publicized denunciations of the American automobile industry included class-action lawsuits and calls for recalls of allegedly defective products, and many of his actions served as a tactical model for future advocacy organizations.

The efforts of Nader and other activists led to the formation of several federal agencies designed to protect consumer interests. The U.S. Office of Consumer Affairs, created in 1971, investigates and resolves consumer complaints, conducts consumer surveys, and disseminates product information to the public. The **Consumer Product Safety Commission**, formed in 1973, sets national standards for product safety and testing procedures, coordinates product recalls, and ensures that companies respond to valid consumer complaints. Other government agencies that benefit consumers include the **Better Business Bureau** and state consumer agencies. The Consumer Federation of America is the largest consumer advocacy group in the United States, consisting of about 220 member organizations. The International Organization of Consumers Unions, based in the Netherlands, actively promotes consumer interests on a global scale. In the 1990s, the widespread use of home computers advanced consumer advocacy by making it easier for citizens to gather information and make their views known.

FURTHER READING:

"A Consumer Warning on New Ripoffs," *Money*. March 1992, p. 34.

Cook, Gareth G. "The Case for (Some) Regulation," *Washington Monthly*. March 1995, p. 34.

Hamburg, Joan. "From Refunds to Ripoffs: Your Consumer Problems Solved," *Family Circle*. February 1, 1994, p. 134.

"Is Lawsuit Reform Good for Consumers?," *Consumer Reports*. May 1995, p. 312.

Kemper, Vicki. "A Citizen for All Seasons," *Common Cause Magazine*. Spring 1995, p. 12.

Mayer, Robert N. *The Consumer Movement: Guardians of the Marketplace*. Boston: Twayne, 1989.

Stingley, Ruth Nauss. "It Pays to Complain," *Reader's Digest*. October 1993, p. 116.

SEE ALSO: Product Liability

CONSUMER PRICE INDEX

The Consumer Price Index (CPI), sometimes called the cost-of-living index, measures the average change in prices that typical American wage earners pay for basic goods and services, such as food, clothing, shelter, transportation, and medical care. It is expressed as a percentage of the cost of the same goods and services in a base period. For example, using the years 1982 to 1984 as a base period with a value of 100, the CPI for April 1995 was 151.9, meaning that prices had increased by an average of 51.9 percent over time. The CPI is often used to measure **inflation**, so it is closely monitored by government policymakers and by individuals whose wages vary with the purchasing power of money. The practice of indexing wages to the CPI is known as a cost-of-living adjustment (COLA). The term "cost of living" is often applied to the numerical result of the CPI. Loosely defined, it refers to the average cost to an individual of purchasing the various goods and services needed to maintain a reasonable living standard.

The U.S. Bureau of Labor Statistics (BLS) began calculating the CPI in 1917, and over the years it has become an important economic statistic. The CPI is calculated monthly and is usually reported within the first two weeks of the following month. In order to calculate the CPI, the BLS surveys about 24,000 households to find out where families shop regularly and what types of goods and services they purchase. It then contacts about 21,000 retail businesses in 85 major metropolitan areas to obtain prices for 90,000 items. All of this information is combined in the CPI, which represents the average price of a "market basket" of goods and services. The BLS tries to incorporate any new developments in the market by changing 20 percent of the retail outlets and items in its survey every year on a rotating basis.

A separate CPI is calculated for different income levels, geographical areas, and types of goods and services. For example, the CPI-U is calculated for all urban households, which includes about 80 percent of the U.S. population. In contrast, the CPI-W measures average price increases for the 32 percent of Americans who derive their primary income as wage earners or clerical workers. The BLS also publishes a CPI for each of seven major categories of items: food and beverages, housing, apparel, transportation, medical care, entertainment, and other goods and services. In addition, it compiles individual indexes for 200 different items and combined indexes for 120 smaller categories of items. Separate CPI measurements are also released for four major geographical regions of the United States—Northeast, North Central, South, and West—as well as 29 large metropolitan areas.

The CPI influences the American economy in several ways. A high annual percentage increase in the CPI reflects a high rate of inflation. The Federal Reserve Board, which controls the nation's money supply, often reacts to such increases by raising **interest rates**. This makes it more expensive for individuals and businesses to borrow money, which usually slows spending, encourages saving, and helps to curb inflation in the economy. The CPI also determines the percentage of annual increase or decrease in income for many Americans. For example, COLA formulas based on the CPI are built into many employment contracts. The federal government also uses the CPI to adjust Social Security and disability benefits, to determine the income level at which people become eligible for assistance, and to establish tax brackets. In addition, the CPI is often used to compare prices for certain goods within a set of years, and to calculate constant dollar values for two points in time.

Some economists believe that the CPI overstates actual increases in the cost of living by 1 percent or more annually. They generally attribute the discrepancy to some combination of the following four factors: improvements in the quality of goods; the introduction of new goods; substitution by consumers of different goods or retail outlets; and the difficulty of measuring the prices consumers actually pay for goods.

FURTHER READING:

''Cost-of-Living Lesson.'' *American Demographics.* December 1994.

Darnay, Arsen J., ed. *American Cost of Living Survey.* Chicago, IL: American Marketing Association, 1994.

Epstein, Gene. ''Economic Beat: Increases in Consumer Prices May Be Less Than Meet the Eye.'' *Barron's.* September 19, 1994.

Money Income of Households, Families, and Persons in the United States Washington: U.S. Bureau of the Census, 1994.

Reinsdorf, Marshall. ''The Effect of Price Dispersion on Cost of Living Indexes.'' *International Economic Review.* February 1994.

Wynne, Mark A., and Fiona D. Sigalla. ''The Consumer Price Index.'' *Economic Review* (Federal Reserve Bank of Dallas). Second Quarter 1994.

CONSUMER PRODUCT SAFETY COMMISSION

The Consumer Product Safety Commission (CPSC) was established in 1972 with the passage of the Consumer Product Safety Act. The primary responsibility of the CPSC is to protect the public from unreasonable risks of injury that could occur during the use of consumer products. The CPSC also promotes the evaluation of consumer products for potential hazards, establishes uniform safety standards for consumer products, eases conflicting state and local regulations concerned with consumer safety, works to recall hazardous products from the marketplace, and selectively conducts research on potentially hazardous products. The CPSC promotes the development of voluntary safety standards and under certain circumstances has the authority to issue and enforce standards and ban unsafe products. In all its activities the CPSC strives to work closely with private consumer groups, industry, the media, and agencies of various state and local governments.

Although the CPSC is an independent federal regulatory agency it does not have jurisdiction over all consumer products. Safety standards for trucks, automobiles, and motorcycles are set by the U.S. Department of Transportation; drugs and cosmetics are handled by the U.S. Food and Drug Administration; and alcohol, tobacco, and firearms fall under the authority of the U.S. Department of the Treasury. Nevertheless, approximately 15,000 types of consumer products are regulated by the CPSC.

Early federal consumer safety legislation dealt primarily with foods, drugs, and cosmetics. The Federal Food and Drugs Act of 1906 (also known as the Wiley Pure Food and Drug Act) forbade the adulteration and fraudulent misbranding of foods and drugs sold through interstate commerce. Other early consumer legislation included the Meat Inspection Act of 1907 (amended in 1967 by the Wholesome Meat Act). In 1933 legislation was introduced to strengthen the Federal Food and Drugs Act of 1906. This legislation mandated the standardized labeling of food products, required that manufacturers prove drugs are safe for the purpose for which they are sold, and established a pre-market clearance procedure for new drug products. Many drug companies opposed this bill; they were joined by much of the nation's print media, which feared the loss of corporate advertising revenue. After a five-year battle in Congress, however, the bill was passed in 1938 as the Food, Drug, and Cosmetic Act. Amendments to the bill in 1962 established biennial factory inspections, disclosure through labeling of dangerous side effects, FDA approval of all new drugs, FDA power to remove dangerous drugs from the market, and the requirement that a manufacturer prove that its drugs are not only safe but also effective for its stated purpose.

The scope of federal consumer safety legislation broadened throughout the 1950s and 1960s. The Flammable Fabrics Act of 1953 established safety standards for fabrics used in clothing. The Refrigerator Safety Act of 1956 required that refrigerator doors have inside release mechanisms. The 1962 National Traffic and Motor Vehicle Safety Act established federal jurisdiction over motor vehicle safety, while the 1965 Federal Cigarette Labeling and Advertising Act required the infamous ''Caution: Cigarette Smoking May Be Hazardous to Your Health'' label. Other pre-1972 consumer product safety legislation included the Radiation Control for Health and Safety Act of 1968, which dealt with radiation emission levels of electronic products, and the Poison Prevention Packaging Act of 1970, which established packaging standards to protect children from potentially hazardous substances.

In 1967 the National Commission on Product Safety was established. It was believed that federal consumer safety legislation was not effective enough because it took a piecemeal approach, targeting only specific products for regulation. Supporters of the commission contended that the government needed to establish legislative authority over broad categories of potentially hazardous goods and products. The National Commission on Product Safety was charged with identifying these broad categories of potentially hazardous goods and evaluating existing legal and voluntary methods for securing consumer product safety. The commission subsequently found that ''the exposure of consumers to unreasonable product hazards is excessive by any standards of measurement.'' The commission also asserted that even though consumers must take some responsibility for their own safety, industry must also assume responsibility for the design and manufacturing of safe consumer products.

On the basis of their inquiry the commission recommended the creation of an independent federal regulatory agency and a presidential appointee to the commission to serve as a consumer advocate before the new agency. The commission also recommended that the new agency have the authority to issue safety regulations and standards. Thus, the Consumer Product Safety Commission was created in 1972.

The CPSC consists of five commissioners, each appointed by the president of the United States with the advice and consent of Congress. One of the commissioners is appointed chairman. The CPSC is headquartered in Bethesda, Maryland, with regional offices in Chicago, New York, and San Francisco and field offices in various cities across the country. The CPSC also maintains a toll-free Consumer Product Safety Hotline (1-800-638-CPSC).

SEE ALSO: Consumer Advocacy; Product Liability

Contracts are vital to society because they facilitate cooperation and trust. Rather than relying on fear of reprisal or the hope of reciprocity to get others to meet their obligations, people can enlist other people to pursue common purposes by submitting to contracts that are backed by impartial authority. Without contracts and their supporting institutions, promises would be much more vulnerable to ill will, misunderstanding, forgetfulness, and other human flaws. Indeed, contracts allow people that have never even met to reach agreements, such as lending/borrowing money to buy a house, that they would never consider making outside of a legal framework. Discussed below are characteristics and types of contracts.

CONTRACT ELEMENTS

By its most basic definition, a contract is a legally enforceable promise. It differs from a simple verbal promise in that either party may ask the state to force the other party to honor its promise. To distinguish contracts from other types of promises and agreements, courts have established basic elements that are necessary for a contract to exist. A contract may be legally defined as a voluntary, legal, written agreement made by persons with the proper capacity. It should include: 1) an offer; 2) an acceptance; and 3) consideration, or an exchange of value. There are legal exceptions to most of these conditions, and all of them are subject to interpretation in the courts. Furthermore, some contracts do not meet these requirements, such as implied contracts and those created under promissory estoppel, both of which are discussed later.

Contracts not entered into voluntarily are voidable. For example, a company might tell a supplier that it was considering ending their business relationship if, within the next ten minutes, the supplier did not sign a contract to provide materials at a certain cost. If the supplier signed the agreement, it might be able to convince the courts that it did so under duress or undue influence, and therefore was not bound by its terms. In general, contracts created under duress, undue influences, fraud, and misrepresentation are voidable by the injured party.

Contracts are also void if they involve a promise that is illegal or violates public policy. For instance, a contract regarding the sale of illegal drugs is unenforceable. Likewise, contracts that are legal but are not in the public interest may be rendered null. For example, a contract in which a company requires a customer to pay an extremely high rate of interest on borrowed funds could be deemed invalid by the courts. Similarly, a retail company that required an employee to sign an agreement that he would never work for another retailer would likely not be able to enforce the contract because it had unreasonable restrictions or imposed undue hardship on the worker.

Contracts do not have to be written to be enforceable in court. In fact, most oral contracts are legally enforceable. However, they are obviously much more difficult to prove. Furthermore, most states have adopted "statutes of frauds," which specify certain types of contracts that must be in writing. Examples of contracts that typically fall under the statues of frauds include agreements related to the sale of real estate, contracts for the sale of goods above $500, and contracts in which one person agrees to perform the obligation of another person. Such contracts need not be overly long or involved. In fact, a simple memo or receipt may satisfy all legal requirements. There are exceptions in this area, however. For instance, when one party will suffer serious losses as a result of reliance on an oral agreement, the statute of frauds may be waived (see promissory estoppel below).

An otherwise acceptable contract may also be voided if one (or both) of the parties making the agreement does not have the mental or legal capacity to do so. Obviously, a mentally retarded individual or a child could not be bound by a contract. But a contract signed by a person exceeding his authority to make an agreement may also be voided.

In addition to being voluntary, legal, written, and made by persons with proper capacity, contracts usually must possess three basic components: an offer, an acceptance, and consideration. An offer is a promise to perform an act conditioned on a return promise of performance by another party. It is recognized by a specific proposal communicated to another party. Once a legal offer has been made, the offering party is bound to its terms if the other party accepts. Therefore, the offering party must clearly indicate whether the proposal is an offer or some other communique, such as an invitation to negotiate. The offering party, however, may stipulate certain terms of acceptance, such as time limits, and even withdraw the offer before the other party accepts.

Acceptance, the second basic requirement for the existence of a contract, is legally defined as "a manifestation of assent to the terms [of the offer] made by the offeree in the manner invited or required by the offer." As with offers and offerors, the courts look for an intent to contract on the part of the acceptor. The difference is that the offeror may stipulate terms of acceptance with which the other party must comply. If the offeree attempts to change the terms of the offer in any way, a rejection is implied and the response is considered a counteroffer, which the original offeror may reject or counter. As with most rules regarding

contracts, exceptions exist. For example, the Uniform Commercial Code includes a "Battle of the Forms" provision whereby an offeree may imply acceptance under certain circumstances even if it changes or alters the offer.

Even if an offer is accepted, it must be consummated by consideration for a legally enforceable contract to exist. Consideration entails doing something that you were not previously bound to do outside of the agreement. In other words, promisees must pay the price (consideration) that they agreed to pay the promisor in order to gain the right to enforce the promisor's obligation.

The requirement of consideration serves an important purpose. It protects the promisor from being liable for granting, or relying on, gratuitous promises. For example, suppose that a person told her roommate that she would always pay the entire rent for their apartment. If she later changed her mind, she could not be held liable for the rent because she had neither asked for, nor received, anything in exchange for the promise. Had the other roommate promised to clean the apartment in exchange for the roommate's promise to pay the rent, an enforceable contract would exist (assuming other requirements were met).

CONTRACT TYPES

The two primary categories of contracts are "unilateral" and "bilateral." In a unilateral contract only one party promises something. For instance, if a car dealer tells a customer, "I will give you that car if you give me $15,000," he has made an offer for a unilateral contract—the contract will only be created if the customer accepts the offer by paying the $15,000. If the dealer says, "I will promise to give you the car if you promise to pay me $15,000," a bilateral contract has been proposed because both parties must make a promise. The concept of unilateral contracts is important because it has been used by courts to hold a party liable for a promise even when consideration was not given by the other party. For instance, an employer may be liable for providing pension benefits that it promised to an employee, even if the worker gave no promise and did nothing in return.

Contracts may also be classified as "express" or "implied." Express contracts are those in which both parties have explicitly stated the terms of their bargain, either orally or in writing, at the time that the contract was created. In contrast, implied contracts result from surrounding facts and circumstances that suggest an agreement. For instance, when a person takes a car to a repair shop he expects the shop to exercise reasonable care and good faith in fixing the car and charging for repairs. Likewise, the shop expects the customer to pay for its services. Although no formal agreement is created, an implied contract exists.

In addition to express and implied contracts are "quasi-contracts," which arise from unique circumstances. Quasi-contracts are obligations imposed by law to avoid injustice. For instance, suppose that a man hires a woman to paint his house. By accident, she paints the wrong house. The owner of the house knows that she is painting it by mistake but, happy to have a free paint job, says nothing. The painter would likely be able to collect something from the homeowner because he knowingly was "unjustly enriched" at her expense. Had she painted his house while he was on vacation he would be under no obligation to her.

Contracts may also be categorized as valid, unenforceable, voidable, and void. Valid contracts are simply those that meet all legal requirements. Unenforceable contracts are those that meet the basic requirements but fail to fulfill some other law. For instance, if a state has special requirements for contracts related to lending money, failure to comply could make the contract unenforceable. Voidable contracts occur when one or both parties have a legal right to cancel their obligations. A contract entered into under duress, for example, would be voidable at the request of the injured party. Void contracts are those that fail to meet basic criteria, and are therefore not contracts at all. An illegal contract, for example, is void.

A separate type of contract, and one which overtly exemplifies the trend away from strict interpretation and toward fairness, is created by promissory estoppel. Under the theory of promissory estoppel, a party can rely on a promise made by another party despite the nonexistence of a formal, or even implied, contract. Promissory estoppel can be evoked if allowing a promisor to claim freedom from liability because of a lack of consideration (or some other contractual element) would result in injustice. Suppose that a business owner promised an employee that he would eventually give her the business if she worked there until he (the owner) retired. Then, after 20 years of faithful service by the employee, the owner decides to give the business to his son-in-law. The owner could be "estopped" from claiming in court that a true contract did not exist, because the worker relied on the owner's promise.

CONTRACTS AND SMALL BUSINESSES

"Business relationships are not a matter of trust. People change and circumstances change," attorney Charles Melville wrote in an article for *Agency Sales Magazine.* "Written agreements, negotiated up front, are really the practical and low cost answer. As people and circumstances change, the agreement should be reevaluated to make sure that it still reflects the intentions of the parties." Contracts are a necessary part of all sorts of small business transactions—office and equipment leases, bank loan agreements, employment contracts, independent contractor agreements, supplier and customer contracts, agreements for professional services, and product warranties, to name a few. Even the process of writing a contract can be helpful, because it forces the parties to think through contingencies and decide in advance how to handle them. Small business owners should be careful of the standard legal terminology that appears in some types of contracts. It is important to understand and agree with all aspects of a contract before signing it. "No matter how small the print is, it's still part of the contract," Martin A. Goldberg wrote in an article for *Medical Economics.* "Understand what you're signing, or don't sign it."

FURTHER READING:

Business Law and the Regulatory Environment. 8th ed. Chicago, IL: Irwin, 1992.

Fried, Charles. *Contract as Promise: A Theory of Contractual Obligation.* Boston, MA: Harvard University Press, 1981.

Goldberg, Martin A. "Watch Out for Traps in That 'Standard' Contract." *Medical Economics.* August 17, 1992.

Melville, Charles. "It's Not a Matter of Trust...." *Agency Sales Magazine.* May 1995.

Metzger, Michael B., et al. *Business Law and the Regulatory Environment: Concepts and Cases.* Chicago, IL: Irwin, 1992.

Wincor, Richard. *Contracts in Plain English.* New York: McGraw-Hill, 1976.

Winn, Steven L. "All Contracts Are Not Created Equal." *Business Credit.* March 1995.

COOPERATIVE ADVERTISING

Cooperative advertising, simply put, is the sharing of the cost for locally-placed advertising between the retailer or wholesaler and the manufacturer. Many manufacturers have a set amount of cooperative advertising funds available per year, distributed as opportunities for collaboration arise. Manufacturers report, however, that much of this money goes unspent, as relatively few retailers and wholesalers pursue cooperative agreements.

Cooperative advertising can be a very powerful tool for the small business owner, especially one with limited means to support the kind of advertising campaign which can be vital to the survival and success of a business enterprise. The added funds from such a cooperative agreement can improve the quality of advertising or broaden the breadth of its distribution. It can create important links between products and the small wholesaler or retailer who handles the product for the manufacturer. Above all, it can attract customers loyal to a certain product to a vendor whose name had not before been associated with that product.

BUSINESS NICHES AND COOPERATIVE ADVERTISING

Any small business that deals with the products of a major manufacturer (tennis shoes, perfume, ice cream, propane, computers, etc.) and engages in national—as opposed to local—advertising can benefit from cooperative advertising ventures. These terms can be deceptive, because frequently national advertising is done through local media. But there do exist clear differences between local and national advertising.

Local advertising refers strictly to the advertisement of local shops and services that are not available nationwide or over large regional areas. Small businesses that would engage solely in local advertising, for example, would be small groceries and specialty stores, or small service providers which are not linked to any national chain, such as a local dry cleaner.

National advertising, on the other hand, is advertising that focuses on nationally recognized and available goods and services. Most brand-name items would fall into this category: automobiles and machinery, designer clothes and jewelry, some services. But the actual advertisements are likely to be run only locally, to draw attention to the local provider of these national goods and services—the small dealership, for example, which sells John Deere tractors. It is with this type of advertising that the small business owner can seek a cooperative agreement with a national manufacturer.

BENEFITS TO THE SMALL BUSINESS OWNER

The biggest benefit of cooperative advertising, of course, is that such arrangements can dramatically cut advertising costs. Manufacturers will sometimes provide anywhere from 50 to 100 percent of the cost of placing local ads. These corporate advertising dollars can make it possible for small businesses to establish a far stronger presence in the community than would otherwise be possible.

Another benefit that sometimes results from such agreements is valuable creative and media-buying guidance. Some large manufacturers will provide help for the small business owner in refining the look and message of the advertisement, and in effectively placing the ad in a mutually beneficial way.

Finally, cooperative advertising can lend an air of legitimacy to small business enterprises. Small companies that are able to link their name with that of a nationally recognized product or service should work

hard to maintain such ties, particularly if the product or service in question already has strong user loyalty.

BENEFITS TO THE MANUFACTURER

Cooperative advertising also benefits manufacturers and service providers. Enlisting small business allies diminishes the cost of advertising for these larger companies, especially if they encourage cooperative advertising arrangements in several communities. In addition, just as local businesses can benefit from associations with established national corporations, these large manufacturers and service providers may also enjoy benefits associated with having their products or services aligned with leading businesses in a given community. For example, a designer brand of clothing may benefit from cooperative advertising with an exclusive neighborhood boutique: the personality of the shop itself will reflect positively on the product.

DRAWBACKS TO COOPERATIVE ADVERTISING

The small business owner must be careful that he or she completely understands the commitment involved when seeking a cooperative advertising agreement. Many manufacturers demand a certain style of advertising, or a high level of quality that may be difficult for a struggling business to achieve. There may be hidden requirements which must be met, or limits on the kind of advertising which can be funded by manufacturers' dollars. The specific demands involved in an advertising cooperation will vary widely between manufacturers; business consultants recommend that small business owners consult an attorney before signing any such agreements.

SEE ALSO: Advertising Budget; Advertising Strategy; Small Business/Large Business Relationships

COPYRIGHT

Copyright is a kind of protection offered by the laws of the United States to the authors of ''original works of authorship,'' including literary, musical, dramatic, artistic, and other intellectual works. Copyright law thus protects a wide variety of creative compositions, including books, magazine articles, songs (both lyrics and music), plays (and any accompanying music), choreography, photographs, drawings, sculptures, and films and other audiovisual works. This protection is extended to both published and unpublished works. Copyright experts note that the definition of ''intellectual works'' should be interpreted quite broadly in this regard. For example, computer software programs can be registered as "literary works," and maps and architectural blueprints can be registered as "pictorial, graphic, and sculptural works."

Once the author or creator of an intellectual work secures a copyright for that work, he or she has exclusive rights to do whatever he or she wishes with it. The owner can distribute copies of it for sale; transfer ownership via sale, lease, rental, or lending; prepare derivative works based on the copyrighted work; or provide public displays or performances of the work.

Several categories of material are generally not eligible for copyright protection. These include ideas, methods, concepts, principles, titles, names, slogans, familiar symbols or designs, listings of ingredients or contents, coloring, and variations of typographic ornamentation. Other material not eligible for copyright include works consisting entirely of information that is common property and contains no original authorship (standard calendars, height and weight charts, tables taken from public documents) and works that, in the words of the Copyright Office, "have not been fixed in a tangible form of expression." Examples of the latter include improvisational performances or choreographic works that have not been written or recorded.

CORNERSTONES OF COPYRIGHT LAW

The basic philosophy underlying American copyright law can be found in Article 1, Section 8 of the Constitution, which stipulates that "Congress shall have Power . . . To promote the Progress of Science and useful Arts, by securing for limited Times to Authors and Inventors the exclusive Right to their respective Writings and Discoveries." The sentiments embodied in this proclamation were given added legal heft in 1909 and 1976, years that saw major copyright legislation become law.

A major change in American copyright law came in the late 1970s, as Congress passed new laws addressing the length and character of copyright protection. (Bills that would further strengthen copyright protections for authors of intellectual works have been introduced in the 105th Congress as well). As a result of that legislation, which took effect on January 1, 1978, all works created on or after that date automatically receives legal protection from the moment of its creation (before then a work did not receive copyright protection until it had been published or registered with the Copyright Office). The new legislation expanded the duration of copyright protection as well. It provided authors with legal protection that ordinarily lasts for the entire life of the author, plus an additional 50 years after the author's death. In the case of "joint works" (works created by two or more authors under circumstances that were not "for hire"), the copyright protection lasts for 50 years after the last surviving author's death. For works made for hire, anonymous works, and pseudonymous works (unless the author's identity is revealed in Copyright Office records), the copyright on the work in question last for 75 years from publication or 100 years from creation, whichever is shorter. Creative works that came into being prior to January 1, 1978, but had not yet been published or registered by that date are given similar protection under the terms of the statute.

Copyright protection is somewhat different for works originally created and published or registered prior to January 1, 1978. For works created during this period, authors could secure copyright protection for 28 years, with an option to renew that protection for another 28 years as the initial term expired. The new copyright law extended the length of that second term from 28 years to 47 years, thus making pre-1978 works eligible for a total of 75 years of copyright protection. In addition, a 1992 amendment to the Copyright Act of 1976 automatically extended the term of copyrights obtained from January 1, 1964, through December 31, 1977, to the full renewal limit of 47 years.

American copyright law underwent another change in 1989, when copyright notices on copyrighted material become optional. Prior to March 1, 1989, copyright notices had been mandatory on all published works; any works not carrying a copyright notice risked loss of copyright protection. After March 1, 1989, however, that notice was no longer required—though it was still highly recommended—because works created after that date were automatically copyrighted the moment they were presented in a fixed form (generally print, audio, or video).

Despite the changes that have taken place in American copyright rules over the past 200 years, in many respects copyright protection has always been—and continues to be—fairly simple. "Basically, copyright law says that if you create something and express it in a fixed and tangible form, you own it," wrote William Rodarmor in *Newmedia*. "Ownership means you can pretty much control what other people do with it. The two major exceptions are material in the public domain and so-called "fair use."

PUBLIC DOMAIN Once the term of a copyright (or a patent) expires, it is said to become a part of the "public domain." In essence, this means that it becomes community property that anyone can use. Photographs, magazine articles, and books are among the most common public domain materials used today.

Another potentially valuable source of public domain material is works produced by the United States government. While state and local governments often copyright their documents, reports, and other publications, the federal government does not do so.

FAIR USE Perhaps no other aspect of copyright law concerns writers, publishers, multimedia developers, graphic artists, and others as much as the issue of "fair use." As Rodarmor stated in *Newmedia,* "fair use is a tricky doctrine and a trap for the unwary." Fair use concerns the use of copyrighted material without securing the explicit permission of the copyright holder. Even copyright experts admit that the rules regarding fair use are kind of hazy, but they basically boil down to the following questions:

- Is the excerpted material intended for news reporting, critical commentary, scholarship, research, or teaching purposes? (Scholars, teachers, critics, and commentators have greater leeway in using copyrighted material, provided that they are using it for scholarly/educational purposes rather than for commercial use, and provided that they attribute the material.)

- Is the excerpted material appearing in a primarily commercial work?

- What is the nature of the copyrighted work?

- What percentage of the copyrighted work is being excerpted? (Publishers generally require writers to err on the side of caution; no full-proof formula to determine what is acceptable currently exists.)

- What effect could use of the copyrighted material have on the potential market for or value of the copyrighted work?

Adherence to fair use guidelines and other aspects of copyright law is particularly important for entrepreneurs/small business owners engaged in activities that lead them to deal with copyrighted works. Both freelancers and those who employ freelancers need to understand what is and is not acceptable in this realm. For instance, lawsuits that charge small business owners with copyright infringement can be quite costly. Indeed, even if the owner is found not guilty, the legal costs of mounting a defense are often considerable. Of course, securing adequate permissions rights through licensing, etc., puts more of a burden on small businesses and entrepreneurs as well, since their financial resources are not as great as those of bigger companies. Rodarmor, for example, noted that small multimedia developers hoping to enter into commercial markets face sometimes daunting realities in this regard: "Companies like Time Warner and Sony can afford platoons of savvy lawyers to acquire content for their own multimedia projects and to protect the content they own, but the legal costs of acquiring rights to video, audio, photographs, and text may swamp the small developers."

WORK FOR HIRE AND COPYRIGHT

In situations where a work—a software program, an essay, a mural, an advertising design, or other intellectual work—has been produced for someone who is working for someone else, the copyright for the work may belong to the person or business that arranged to have the work done, rather than the creator of the work itself. Such arrangements are known as work for hire. Copyright law defines "work for hire" as either: 1) a work prepared by an employee within the scope of his or her employment, or 2) a work specially ordered or commissioned for use as a contribution to a collective work, as a part of a motion picture or other audiovisual work, as a translation, as a supplementary work, as a compilation, as an instructional text, as a test, as answer material for a test, or as an atlas, provided that the parties involved expressly agree in a written contract signed by both of them that the work shall be considered a work made for hire. Indeed, **contracts** that specifically define copyright ownership for work performed are essential, especially for small business owners who contract work out to freelancers. In an article entitled "Copyright Rules to Live By," Rodarmor urged small business owners to "put your employment contracts in writing—even with your friends (maybe especially with your friends). When using freelancers, the contract must state that the project is work for hire or that the freelancer grants you all the rights you need and it belongs to you. If not, you may discover that your former buddies (and some forgotten freelancer in Wisconsin) are all joint owners of your new CD-ROM." In addition, he notes, distributors are typically very wary of products that do not have exclusive licenses.

COPYRIGHT NOTICE

Although attaching a formal notice of copyright to a work is no longer required by law (it was required prior to March 1, 1989), it is still a good idea. "Use of the notice is recommended because it informs the public that the work is protected by copyright, identifies the copyright owner, and shows the year of first publication," stated the Copyright Office. "Furthermore, in the event that a work is infringed, if the work carries a proper notice, the court will not allow a defendant to claim 'innocent infringement'—that is, that he or she did not realize that the work is protected. (A successful innocent infringement claim may result in a reduction in damages that the copyright owner would otherwise receive.)"

According to the Copyright Office, forms of notice vary for different kinds of intellectual works. For books, articles, sheet music, architectural plans, designs, and other kinds of "visually perceptible"

COPYRIGHT

works, copyright notice should contain all of the following three elements:

1) The copyright symbol (the letter ''C'' in a circle) or the word ''Copyright,'' or the abbreviation ''Copr.''

2) The year of first publication of the work (in cases where the work is a compilation or derivation that incorporates previously published material, the year date of first publication of the compilation or derivation is acceptable). The year date may be omitted in instances where a pictorial, graphic, or sculptural work, with accompany text (if any) is reproduced in or on greeting cards, postcards, stationery, jewelry, dolls, toys, or any useful article.

3) The name of the owner of copyright in the work, or an abbreviation by which the name can be recognized, or a generally known alternative designation of the owner.

For works that are fixed through audio means—cassette tapes, CDs, books-on-tape, etc.—the requirements for copyright notice are somewhat different. Copyright notice for these types of works should contain all of the following:

1) The sound recording copyright symbol (the letter ''P'' in a circle).

2) The year of first publication of the sound recording.

3) The name of the owner of copyright in the sound recording, or an abbreviation by which the name can be recognized, or a generally known alternative designation of the owner. In addition, if the producer of the recording is named on the label or containers of the work, and if no other name appears in conjunction with the notice, the producer's name shall be considered a part of the notice.

Notice of copyright can also be extended to unpublished works. Finally, when affixing notice of copyright to intellectual works of any kind, it is important to make sure that the notice is plainly visible.

COPYRIGHT REGISTRATION

Registration of copyrighted material may be made at any time during the life of the copyright. It is no longer required under American copyright law, but there are advantages associated with taking such a step.

- Registration establishes a public record of the copyright claim.

- Certificates of registration are required if the copyright owner wants to file an infringement suit.

- Registration establishes *prima facie* evidence in court of the validity of the copyright and of the facts stated in the certificate in instances where the registration is made within five years of original publication.

- Registrations made within three months of the work's publication—or prior to any infringement of the work—entitle the copyright owner to statutory damages and coverage of attorney's fees in court; otherwise, only an award of actual damages and profits is available to the copyright holder.

- Registration gives the copyright owner additional protection against the importation of infringing copies.

To register a copyright, the Copyright Office must receive a properly completed application form, a nonrefundable filing fee for each work that is being registered, and a nonreturnable copy of the work that is being registered. There are variations to the above rules depending on the kind of work that is being registered, so registration seekers should contact the Office beforehand to get a full rundown on what is required for their particular work. The Copyright Office uses a variety of forms for the various intellectual works that people register; copyright owners need to make sure that they use the correct one. Form TX, for example, covers published and unpublished non-dramatic literary works such as board game instructions, computer programs, and books, while Form VA is intended for use in registering published and unpublished visual works such as photographs, sculptures, and architectural designs.

All applications and materials related to copyright registration should be addressed to the Register of Copyrights, Copyright Office, Library of Congress, Washington, DC 20559-6000. In the future, however, many copyright registrations are expected to be executed electronically. The Copyright Office is developing a system known as CORDS (Copyright Office Electronic Registration and Deposit System) to give copyright owners such an option.

INTERNATIONAL COPYRIGHT PROTECTION

As the Copyright Office itself admits, ''there is no such thing as an 'international copyright' that will automatically protect an author's writings throughout the entire world. Protection against unauthorized use in a particular country depends, basically, on the national laws of that country. However, most countries do offer protection to foreign works under certain conditions, and these conditions have been greatly simplified by international copyright treaties and conventions.''

The two major copyright treaties to which the United States belongs are the Universal Copyright Convention (UCC) and the Berne Convention for the Protection of Literary and Artistic Works. The United States was actually a founding member of the UCC, which came into being in September 1955. Under the rules of the UCC, a work by a citizen or resident of a member nation or a work first published in a member nation may claim protection.

The Berne Convention, meanwhile, was first established more than a century ago, in 1886. The central feature of the Berne Convention is the automatic copyright protection that it extends to all citizens of member nations. If a country is a signatory to the Berne Convention, it must extend to nationals of other member nations the same copyright protection and copyright restrictions afforded to its own citizens. The United States joined the Berne Convention—which is regarded as the wellspring of most other national and international copyright regulations—in 1989, becoming its 77th member.

COPYRIGHT OFFICE

The Copyright Office is one of the most important service departments operated by the Library of Congress. It is also an exceedingly busy one; in fiscal year 1994 alone, it registered more than 520,000 claims to copyright. All correspondence intended for the Office should be addressed to the Register of Copyrights, Copyright Office, Library of Congress, Washington, DC 20559-6000.

FURTHER READING:

Copyright Basics From the U.S. Copyright Office. Washington: Copyright Office, n.d.

Field, Thomas. *Avoiding Patent, Trademark and Copyright Problems.* Washington: U.S.Small Business Administration, 1992.

Fishman, Stephen. *The Software Developer's Legal Guide.* Berkeley, CA: Nolo Press, 1994.

Levy, Richard C. *The Inventor's Desktop Companion.* Detroit, MI: Visible Ink, 1995.

Porter, Vincent. *Beyond the Berne Convention: Copyright, Broadcasting and the Single European Market.* John Libbey, 1991.

Rodarmor, William. "Copyright Rules to Live By." *Newmedia.* September 1993.

Rodarmor, William. "Rights of Passage." *Newmedia.* September 1993.

SEE ALSO: Free-lance Employment/Independent Contractors; Intellectual Property; Inventions and Patents; Trademarks

CORPORATE CULTURE

Corporate culture refers to the shared values, attitudes, standards, and beliefs that characterize members of an organization and define its nature. Corporate culture is rooted in an organization's goals, strategies, structure, and approaches to labor. Every company has a culture, though not every culture is beneficial in helping a company reach its goals. A healthy corporate culture is one in which employees are encouraged to work together to ensure the success of the overall business. Developing and maintaining a healthy corporate culture can be particularly problematic for entrepreneurs, as the authoritarian practices that helped establish a small business often must be exchanged for participatory management strategies that allow it to grow.

AN INCREASING EMPHASIS ON CULTURE

Since the 1980s, several factors have led American businesses to evaluate corporate culture alongside such traditional ''hard'' measures of corporate health as assets, revenues, profits, and shareholder return. One such factor is the transition from a manufacturing-based to a service-based economy, with the corresponding shift in emphasis from the quality of a material product to the quality of business relationships. Another factor is the need for American businesses to compete in a global marketplace against international rivals whose corporate cultures are distinct but demonstrably effective. A related factor is the need for creative adaption to rapid technological advances in the marketplace. The rash of acquisitions and mergers associated with the 1980s also drew attention to the often intractable aspects of organizational culture that may facilitate or impede corporate assimilation.

Corporate culture affects many areas of a firm's operations. One broad area of corporate culture involves corporate citizenship—the company's relationship to the larger environment. In this area, a company's culture helps determine its overall ethics and attitude toward public service. A second broad area of corporate culture involves human resource management. A company's culture affects a variety of **human resource policies** and practices, including the nature of interaction between managers and employees, the responsiveness to diversity issues in the work place, and the availability of flextime and telecommuting options, safety and training programs, and health and recreation facilities. In a smoothly functioning organization, all such policies and practices foster an internally consistent corporate culture.

CULTURE IN SMALL BUSINESSES

Culture can be a particularly important consideration for small businesses. A healthy company culture may increase employees' commitment and productivity, while an unhealthy culture may inhibit a company's growth or even contribute to business failure. Many entrepreneurs, when they first start a new business, quite naturally tend to take on a great deal of responsibility themselves. As the company grows and adds employees, however, the authoritarian management style that the small business owner used successfully in a very small company can become detrimental. Instead of attempting to retain control over all aspects of the business, as consultant Morty Lefcoe told *Nation's Business,* the small business owner should strive to "get everybody else in the organization to do your job, while you create an environment so that they can do it."

In a healthy culture, employees view themselves as part of a team and gain satisfaction from helping the overall company succeed. When employees sense that they are contributing to a group effort, their level of commitment and productivity, and thus the quality of the company's products or services, are likely to improve. In contrast, employees in an unhealthy culture tend to view themselves as individuals, distinct from the company, and focus upon their own needs. They only perform the most basic requirements of their jobs, and their main satisfaction comes from simply collecting a paycheck.

Since every company is different, there are many ways to develop a culture that works. Writing in *Nation's Business,* Michael Barrier identified several main principles that small business owners should consider in order to create a healthy corporate culture: 1) the main support for the culture should come from the top; 2) a candidate's fit with the culture should be a factor in hiring; and 3) two-way communication—discussing problems realistically and enlisting employees' help in solving them—is vital in maintaining a healthy culture. Once a participatory and engaging culture has been established, it can help propel a small business ahead of its competition.

On the other hand, problems with the corporate culture can play a major role in small business failures. When employees only perform the tasks necessary to their own jobs, rather than putting out extra effort on behalf of the overall business, productivity declines and growth comes to a halt. Unfortunately, many entrepreneurs tend to ignore the developing cultures within their businesses until it is too late to make needed changes.

In an article for *Entrepreneur,* Robert McGarvey outlined some warning signs of trouble with the company culture, including: increased turnover; difficulty in hiring talented people; employees arriving at work and leaving for home right on time; low attendance at company events; a lack of honest communication and understanding of the company mission; an "us-versus-them" mentality between employees and management; and declining quality and customer satisfaction. A small business exhibiting one or more of these warning signs should consider whether the problems stem from the company culture. If so, the small business owner should take any steps necessary to improve the culture, including reaffirming the company's mission and goals and establishing a more open relationship with employees.

FURTHER READING:

Barrier, Michael. "Building a Healthy Company Culture." *Nation's Business.* September 1997.

Hindle, Tim. *Field Guide to Strategy.* Boston: Harvard Business/The Economist Reference Series, 1994.

McGarvey, Robert. "Culture Clash." *Entrepreneur.* November 1997.

Phegan, Barry. *Developing Your Company Culture: The Joy of Leadership.* Reno, NV: Context Press, 1996.

SEE ALSO: Employee Hiring; Employee Motivation

CORPORATE IMAGE

Corporate image, or reputation, describes the manner in which a company, its activities, and its products or services are perceived by outsiders. In the competitive business climate of the 1990s, many businesses actively work to create and communicate a positive corporate image to their customers, shareholders, the financial community, and the general public. A company that mismanages, or even just ignores, its image is likely to encounter a variety of problems. "Reputation problems grow like weeds in a garden," Davis Young wrote in his book *Building Your Company's Good Name.* "Direct and indirect costs escalate geometrically."

Some of the warning signs that a business might have an image problem include high employee turnover, the disappearance of major customers, a drop in stock value, and poor relationships with vendors or government officials. If an image problem is left unaddressed, a company might find many of its costs of doing business rising dramatically, including the costs of product development, sales support, employee wages, and shareholder dividends. In addition, since the majority of consumers base their purchase decisions at least partly on trust, current and future sales levels are likely to suffer as well.

In businesses of all sizes, it is vital that managers be aware of the importance of creating and maintaining a strong image, and that they also make employees aware of it. Corporate image begins within the offices of a company's managers. It should be based on the development of good company policies, rather than on controlling the damage caused by bad company policies. Young recommends that business owners and managers take the following steps toward improving their companies' image: focus on the firm's long-term reputation; base actions on substantive policies; insist on candor in all business dealings; and uphold the stakeholders' right to know. After all, he notes, a good corporate image can take years to build and only moments to destroy.

IMPORTANCE OF CORPORATE IMAGE

Several factors have contributed to the increasing importance of corporate image in recent years. For example, the business climate in the United States has become one of environmental complexity and change, and consequently corporations have been forced to significantly alter their strategies to better compete and survive. Mergers, acquisitions, and divestitures represent a major dimension of corporate change over the past several decades. The acceleration of **product life cycles** is another vital dimension of the turbulent business environment. Nowhere is this more evident than in the electronics industry. Personal computers can become outmoded in the period of a year. In the audio segment of the market, tapes replaced records and, in turn, were replaced by compact discs, which may in the future be superseded by digital audio tapes. Companies with strong corporate images, such as Sony and JVC, obviously have an advantage in such fluid markets. Their names add value to their products by reducing uncertainty in the eyes of distributors, retailers, and consumers.

Deregulation has been a critical factor in increasing the importance of corporate image in many industries. For instance, as a result of the court-ordered breakup, AT&T had to develop a new strategy and a more aggressive, marketing-oriented culture to adjust to its new realities. Concurrently, the telecommunications giant adopted a new logo and initiated a communication program to help convey its new identity. Globalization has been still another catalyst in the rise of corporate image programs, as companies have sought ways to spread their reputations to distant markets. A related factor is that as a corporation expands its operations internationally, or even domestically, through acquisitions, there is a danger that its geographically dispersed business units will project dissimilar or contrary images to the detriment of corporate synergy.

A final factor stimulating the current interest in corporate image is society's growing expectation that corporations be socially responsible. Many of today's

consumers consider the environmental and social image of firms in making their purchasing decisions. Companies such as Ben and Jerry's and The Body Shop have built their reputations around this idea and consequently have grown very rapidly.

THEORY OF CORPORATE IMAGE

In the process of managing corporate image, the fundamental variables are: corporate identity, corporate communication, corporate image, and feedback. Corporate identity is the reality of the corporation—the unique, individual personality of the company that differentiates it from other companies. Corporate communication is the aggregate of sources, messages, and media by which the corporation conveys its uniqueness or brand to its various audiences. Corporate image is in the eye of the beholder—the impression of the overall corporation held by its several audiences.

The objective in managing corporate image is to communicate the company's identity to those audiences or constituencies that are important to the firm, in such a way that they develop and maintain a favorable view of the company. This process involves fashioning a positive identity, communicating this identity to significant audiences, and obtaining feedback from the audiences to be sure that the message is interpreted positively. An unsatisfactory image can be improved by modifying corporate communication, re-shaping the corporate identity, or both.

CORPORATE IDENTITY Corporate identity—the reality and uniqueness of the organization—may be broken down into four component parts: corporate strategy, corporate culture, organizational design, and operations. **Strategy** is the overall plan that determines the company's product/market scope and the policies and programs it chooses to compete in its chosen markets. **Corporate culture** is the shared values and beliefs that the organization's members hold in common as they relate to each other, their jobs, and the organization. It defines what the firm's personnel believe is important and unimportant, and explains to a large degree why the organization behaves the way it does.

Organizational design refers to the fundamental choices top managers make in developing the pattern of organizational relationships. It encompasses issues such as whether basic tasks should be organized by function or product division, the company's overall configuration, the degree of decentralization, the number of staff personnel, the design of jobs, and the internal systems and procedures. Operations, the fourth and final component of corporate identity, is the aggregate of activities the firm engages in to effect its strategy. These activities become part of the reality of the corporation and can influence its identity in a wide variety of ways.

CORPORATE IMAGE Corporate image is the reputation of the firm with the various audiences that are important to it. These groups that have a stake in the company are known as stakeholders. Stakeholders are affected by the actions of the company and, in turn, their actions can affect the company. Consequently, its image in the eyes of its stakeholders is important to the company. The principal stakeholders with which most large corporations must be concerned are: customers, distributors and retailers, financial institutions and analysts, shareholders, government regulatory agencies, social action organizations, the general public, and employees.

The image that stakeholders have of the company will influence their willingness to either provide or withhold support. Thus, if customers develop a negative perception of a company or its products, its sales and profits assuredly will decline. The company's shareholders are another critical group because they ultimately give or withhold their approval of management's decisions through their proxies. Government regulatory agencies, another important set of stakeholders, are required by law to monitor and regulate firms for specific, publicly defined purposes. Nevertheless, these agencies have considerable discretion in how they interpret and apply the law. Where they have a positive perception of the firm, they are likely to be much less censorious.

Social action organizations represent still another set of stakeholders. To the extent a corporation projects a negative image in the particular area of concern of a social action group, it likely will be targeted for criticism and harassment by that group. A strong positive image with the general public can be beneficial to the firm. For example, research suggests that a superior corporate image is a consequential factor in attracting a high quality workforce. Current employees represent the internal constituency that a firm must consider when communicating corporate identity. It is widely believed that a positive image in the eyes of employees is a prime causal factor of high morale and productivity. Additionally, it should be noted that employees play a large role in representing the company to its external stakeholders.

Obviously, each of the various stakeholder groups is likely to have a somewhat different perception of the corporation because each is concerned primarily with a different facet of its operation. Thus, consumers are principally interested in the price, quality, and reliability of the company's products and services. Financial institutions are concerned with financial structure and performance. Employees are mainly concerned with wages, working conditions, and personnel policies. Logically, then, a company

should tailor its communication to each stakeholder group individually to engage the special concerns of that group.

However, maintaining a consistent image among the several stakeholder groups is also vital. Although it is prudent to stress different facets of the firm's identity to its various publics, the firm should avoid projecting an inconsistent image, because the concerns and memberships of different stakeholder groups often overlap. For instance, the financial community and the shareholders would have many of the same financial and strategic concerns about the company. In fact, many shareholders rely heavily on the advice of experts from financial institutions. Similarly, both employees and the general public have an interest in the overall prestige of the firm and the reputation of its products. A social action group's criticism, whether economically effective or not, is bound to influence some customers and affect the company's public reputation. A regulatory agency such as OSHA would focus narrowly on the firm's safety record and policies, but the company's employees and their labor unions also have a stake in these matters.

CORPORATE COMMUNICATION Corporate communication provides the link between corporate identity and corporate image. It should be defined in the broadest possible sense, because companies communicate identities in many different ways. Communication can include almost anything the company does, from the way telephones are answered to the involvement of company employees in community affairs. Some of the principal sources of corporate communication include nomenclature, graphics, formal statements, architecture, and interactions and events.

Nomenclature refers to the names used to identify the corporation, its divisions, and its products. In recent years, many firms have changed their corporate names to communicate a major change in identity. Graphics refers to the overall visual presentation of the organization. A company's graphic communication system should dictate the design of its literature, signs, and stationery. It involves coordinating the style of the typeface, photography, illustrations, layout, and coloring in all the company's graphics. The logo is the heart of the graphic communication system, and can be changed subtly over time to reflect an evolving corporate identity. The key point is that the company's nomenclature and visual presentation must appropriately communicate its identity.

Formal statements made by a company include mission statements, credos, codes of ethics, annual reports, advertising copy, and company slogans. Company slogans—such as Avis's "We Try Harder" or Prudential's "Get a Piece of the Rock"—can be a particularly potent means of communicating an image to stakeholders. Even architecture, the design of corporate buildings and the interior layout of offices and factories, can reveal much about a company. A series of closed office doors suggests a very different culture from a large, open room with desks in full sight of each other.

Every interaction a company employee has with a stakeholder, and every event related to a company, communicates something about the firm's identity. This underlines the importance of training and motivating employees to project a positive image of the company. Though many managers think of planned events, such as open houses or anniversary celebrations, as a communication tool, few realize that unexpected events can also affect corporate image. A company's reaction to unexpected events such as consumer complaints, a lawsuit, or a takeover attempt can play a prominent role in its projected image.

In fact, times of crisis are perhaps when managing a company's image becomes most important. Young outlines some of the major steps in maintaining a business's solid reputation during a crisis. First, he suggests that management be the first to break the bad news. This allows the company to explain the problem in its own way and present possible solutions, and to avoid later being accused of a cover-up. Second, he recommends understanding the concerns that are being expressed, as well as the feelings of fear or anger those concerns may generate in customers. Whether or not the problem can be solved, it is important not to trivialize the concerns of stakeholders. Third, he suggests that a company in crisis attempt to remain customer-friendly by providing complete and accurate information in reassuring language, and avoiding jargon. Fourth, Young recommends that companies in crisis employ long-term thinking, which will enable them to focus on the effect the problem will have on the corporate image rather than the current bottom line. Finally, he suggests that "when you are wrong, say so." Admitting an error and apologizing for it engenders trust, while other reactions usually have the opposite effect.

FEEDBACK Feedback is essential to the management of corporate image. Managers need accurate information on stakeholder perceptions if they are to make sound decisions. Ideally, feedback should be continuous. As a practical matter, continuous feedback can be elicited from salespeople, public relations executives, finance managers, and other employees who routinely interact with stakeholders. Based on such input, modifications may be made in the company's communication methods or, if warranted, a formal study of the corporate image may be initiated. In addition to systematically utilizing internal sources, it is prudent to conduct formal studies of the corporate image on a regular basis. Formal studies are typically performed by identity/image consultants using in-depth, one-on-one and group interviews as their chief research tools. This type of comprehensive outside review would normally include an analysis of the corporate identity, an appraisal of the firm's image in the eyes of its stakeholders, and an evaluation of the efficacy of its corporate communications. The consultant's recommendations might run from making slight alterations in the corporate communication program to a re-shaping of the company's identity.

CONCLUSION

The objective of any serious corporate image program is to communicate an accurate and positive image of a company to its stakeholders. To accomplish this goal, senior management must discern, through valid feedback, the image being projected to its stakeholders. These executives must also comprehend the true corporate identity along with the efficacy and potential of the company's system of communication with the stakeholders. The concept is simple, but its implementation can be profoundly challenging. The firms that master this challenge, in all likelihood, will be the ones that survive and prosper in today's dynamic business environment.

FURTHER READING:

Balmer, John M.T. "Building Societies: Change, Strategy and Corporate Identity." *Journal of General Management.* Winter 1991.

——. "The BBC's Corporate Identity: Myth, Paradox, and Reality." *Journal of General Management.* Spring 1994.

Garbett, Thomas. *How to Build a Corporation's Identity and Project Its Image.* Lexington Books, 1988.

Gray, Edmund R., and Larry R. Smeltzer. "Corporate Image—An Integral Part of Strategy." *Sloan Management Review.* Summer 1985.

Gray, Edmund R., and Larry R. Smeltzer. "Planning a Face-Lift: Implementing a Corporate Image Program." *Journal of Business Strategy.* Summer 1987.

Ind, Nicholas. *Corporate Image.* Kogan Page, 1992.

Margulies, W.P. "Make the Most of Your Corporate Identity." *Harvard Business Review.* July-August 1977.

Olins, Wally. *Corporate Identity: Making Business Strategy Visible through Design.* Boston, MA: Harvard Business School Press, 1990.

Soderberg, Norman R. *Public Relations for the Entrepreneur and Growing Business.* Hinsdale, IL: Probus, 1986.

Young, Davis. *Building Your Company's Good Name: How to Create and Project the Reputation Your Organization Wants and Deserves.* New York: Amacom, 1996.

SEE ALSO: Community Relations; Crisis Management; Public Relations

Corporate logos are symbols, usually designed for easy recognition, that are used to represent companies. Indeed, logos are a ubiquitous presence on a wide range of materials distributed or maintained by companies, including store signs, business cards, major equipment, stationery, marketing materials, packaging, uniforms, etc. Effective company logos have been cited as important elements in building **corporate image**. Conversely, many marketing experts believe that poorly conceived or unattractive logos can have a negative impact on a business's appeal, and ultimately its place in the marketplace.

As small business owners and CEOs of major multinational firms alike are aware, corporate image is an important factor in business success. Companies that are thought of as innovative, smart, or stable in the marketplace have achieved that status in part because of the way in which they present themselves to clients and competitors alike. Corporate logos are one of the tools that businesses have at their disposal in shaping that image. As Anne McGregor Parsons argued in *Colorado Business Magazine,* corporate logos are potentially valuable visual symbols because they can express both the personality and the mission of a company.

ISSUES IN CORPORATE LOGO CREATION Business consultants, entrepreneurs, and designers that specialize in logo creation all agree that several factors have to be weighed when creating a logo for a company:

1) Desired Image—This is far and away the most important consideration, and it can be of even greater importance to business start ups that may not have the financial wherewithal to recover from early slips in logo choice and other marketing areas. Entrepreneurs seeking to make or update a logo, then, should make sure that specific business objectives, target markets, and competitor image are all factored into the logo's creation. For example, a new microbrewery would probably be more inclined to go with a creative, bold logo that features a stylized image of its product than would an independent insurance agency, which would place greater value on logo characteristics that connote stability and trustworthiness.

2) Industry—Many companies sport logos that reflect the industry in which they operate. Providing such associations often makes it easier to attract prime customers.

3) Cost—Creating a logo, or updating an existing logo, "can be an expensive proposi-

tion,'' wrote McGregor Parsons, "affecting a company's entire range of visual communications from business cards to truck fleets.'' Opinions vary about the financial emphasis that start ups and established small businesses should place on logos and slogans. "Much attention is given in emerging enterprises to logo types and slogans,'' wrote Robert T. Davis and F. Gordon Smith in *Marketing in Emerging Companies,* but they contended that "it is good advice not to spend too much time or money initially on attempting to create the distinctive logo or slogan. Unfortunately, many young companies feel that this is vital and devote precious resources to turning out a 'clever' graphic or slogan, which they later regret.'' Davis and Smith counsel entrepreneurs to hold off on making heavy investments in logo creation and implementation until the start up is on its feet and able to help with associated costs. Other consultants and experienced small business owners, however, believe that a visually interesting logo can not only attract much needed attention to fledgling businesses, but can also present businesses with opportunities to make additional sales, by making available clothing, gear, and other merchandise in which the logo is prominently featured. This phenomenon has been most evident on the national stage, as athletic shoe manufacturers and professional sports teams have proven quite adept at selling such wares to customers, but it can also be seen with local logos that are deemed trendy by young consumers.

4) Impact on Current Customers—Owners of established businesses who are considering changing their logo should weigh the potential negative impact that such a switch could have on existing clients/customers. As Raymond Snoddy observed in *Marketing,* redesigning familiar corporate logos can be disturbing to customers who have established a certain comfort level with the old logo.

5) Longevity—Entrepreneurs should beware of using logos that are overly reliant on passing fads or marketing gimmicks. "Communications cost a lot of money for a company, so they need to have the greatest longevity that they can,'' one logo designer told *Colorado Business Magazine.* "That's why we try to focus on timeless, classic design [when making logos], leaving the trendier things to the more short-term tactical type of advertising media.'' Another designer

agreed, remarking that a logo ''must stand the test of time.''

6) Distinctive—Experts urge business owners not to use gimmicky logos, but they also tout the benefits of logos that are unique in some fashion. Not only do such logos enjoy a certain level of legal protection from infringement, they also catch the eye of the customer.

7) Flexible—Logo designs should be made so that they can be used on a wide variety of promotional materials, from billboards and the sides of trucks to letterheads and shirt insignias.

FURTHER READING:

Davis, Robert T., and F. Gordon Smith. *Marketing in Emerging Companies.* Reading, MA: Addison-Wesley, 1985.

Debelak, Don. *Total Marketing: Capturing Customers with Marketing Plans That Work.* Homewood, IL: Dow Jones-Irwin, 1989.

Love, Kenneth D., and Kenneth J. Roberts. ''Your Company's Identity Crisis.'' *Management Review.* October 1997.

McGregor Parsons, Anne. ''Making Your Mark.'' *Colorado Business Magazine.* August 1994.

Snoddy, Raymond. ''Familiarity with Design Kills Off Shock of the New.'' *Marketing.* October 23, 1997.

Ten Kate, Nancy. ''Graphic Design for the Bottom Line.'' *American Demographics.* April 1994.

Underwood, Elaine. ''Proper I.D.: With Brand Values Under Increasing Attack, Companies are Keener Than Ever to Devise Memorable, Meaningful Corporate Identities.'' *Brandweek.* August 8, 1994.

SEE ALSO: Marketing

CORPORATE SPONSORSHIP

Corporate sponsorship—also known as event marketing or cause marketing (in the case of sponsorship of nonprofit or charitable events)—is a relatively new form of advertising in which companies pay to be associated with certain events. Corporate sponsorship has been growing rapidly in recent years; in fact, its growth has taken place at a faster rate than the growth in overall corporate advertising. In North America, for example, the total spent on corporate sponsorship increased from less than $1 billion in 1985 to $5.4 billion in 1996, and was expected to reach $6.8 billion in 1998. Part of the increase is attributable to the number of small and medium-sized firms that are becoming involved, according to Paula Moore of the *Denver Business Journal.* ''Not long ago, only large entities . . . could afford 'cause marketing' as a means of building **goodwill** and boosting revenue,'' she

wrote. ''Sponsorship can offer a quick and efficient way for a low-profile company to make a big splash,'' Deni Kasrel added in an article for the *Philadelphia Business Journal.*

Corporate sponsorship can offer a number of potential benefits for small businesses, from increasing consumer awareness of product and service offerings to enhancing the company's image in the community. ''Companies that want to get closer to target customers and generate product awareness,'' Heidi Jacobs wrote in an article for *Small Business Reports,* ''have discovered the benefits of event marketing, or sponsoring special events to reach a particular market segment. Typical examples include cultural and sports-related events, fairs, and street festivals.'' On a larger scale, event marketing might include sponsorship of college football bowl games (i.e., the Carquest Sugar Bowl) and the Olympic Games, as well as special television productions (i.e., the Hallmark Hall of Fame movie).

In addition to the advertising and promotion aspects of corporate sponsorship, it also provides benefits in the realm of **community relations**. A comprehensive, ongoing community relations program—including event sponsorship—can help virtually any organization achieve visibility as a good community citizen. Organizations are recognized as good community citizens when they support programs that improve the quality of life in their community, including crime prevention, employment, environmental programs, clean-up and beautification, recycling, and restoration. Some other examples of ongoing programs might include scholarship programs, urban renewal projects, performing arts programs, social and educational programs, children's activities, community organizations, and construction projects. Small businesses might achieve community visibility and engender goodwill by sponsoring local sports teams or other events.

Good community relations programs give employees a reason to be proud of the company, which increases loyalty and may help to reduce labor and production costs. Furthermore, a company with happy employees and a good reputation in the community is likely to attract highly qualified new employees. A small company also might generate new business through the contacts and leads it generates in its community relations activities. Such contacts might also make it easier for the company to obtain financing for expansion, find promising new locations, or gain favorable treatment in terms of taxes, ordinances, or utilities. Good community relations can also be beneficial in times of crisis, such as a fire or a plant closing, by rallying the community around the affected business.

Event sponsorship, in particular, is an attractive option because it provides a business with access to various audiences, including employees, business decision makers, and government regulators as well as consumers. It can be an especially good **marketing** tool for companies that participate in international trade, because sponsorship transcends language and cultural barriers. Many marketers feel that corporate sponsorship is superior to other methods because it allows for an immediate customer response to new product offerings. Events provide business managers with an opportunity to come face to face with their customers. They also provide customers with an opportunity to try a company's products out firsthand. By comparison, marketing research tools like focus groups can be expensive and may not target the right people, while market questionnaires or surveys generally do not give potential customers a chance to try the product.

Corporate sponsorship also provides marketers with a unique opportunity to position their products in the marketplace. With corporate sponsorship—unlike conventional marketing techniques—the company, the product, and the event or cause being sponsored tend to become linked in consumers' minds. "By sponsoring an event or providing a budget for an event's broadcast, a sponsor can generate audience awareness while simultaneously creating associations of the event's values in people's minds," Tony Meenaghan explained in an article for the *Sloan Management Review.* "The event generates the audience while concurrently sending a message to that audience about the event's values.... Each sponsorship property or vehicle has certain associated images in the consumer's mind that transfer to the sponsor."

Given this tendency for consumers to associate sponsors with events, it is important for sponsoring companies to choose events that fit well with the image of their products. A cigarette company should not choose to sponsor an American Cancer Society benefit, for example. It is also best, whenever possible, to choose events where potential customers can see and sample the company's products. For instance, a manufacturer of sports drinks might want to sponsor a marathon.

Even when there is a good fit between sponsor and event, however, it is still vital for a company to promote the event and its involvement in order to gain benefits. After all, sponsorship is a form of **advertising**, even when it is of a nonprofit venture or charitable event. "Some smaller companies," Moore noted, "are more reticent about profiting from niceness." Possible ways to promote events sponsorship include billboards, print and broadcast advertisements, and direct mail. Sponsoring companies may also find it helpful to issue press releases about the event to the media, as well as to contribute articles and editorials to publications that reach the target audience. Marketers of consumer products may also engage in joint promotions with retailers, such as coupons and tie-ins.

The fees involved in event marketing can range from a few hundred dollars to hundreds of thousands of dollars, depending on the scale of the event and the level of the sponsor's involvement. In addition to the cost of staging the event itself, there are also associated advertising, publicity, and administrative costs to consider. Many small businesses choose to begin as a co-sponsor of an existing event, which allows them to take advantage of the other sponsors' experience. It may also be possible for a small business to underwrite a new event and share advertising costs with a co-sponsor. Some businesses find it difficult to justify the expense of corporate sponsorship because it can be difficult to gauge the results in monetary terms. But it is often possible to conduct before and after interviews with attendees of the event, or to give away coupons and then track redemption rates. Some businesses also attempt to gauge the success of an event by providing a toll-free telephone number for attendees to call for more information about their products or services. With the growing popularity of corporate sponsorship, many market research firms are now equipped to aid businesses in the selection, implementation, and evaluation of sponsorship opportunities.

AMBUSH MARKETING

The benefits provided by corporate sponsorship can be decreased significantly by competitive tactics known as "ambush marketing," which occurs when competitors take steps to deflect an event audience's attention away from the sponsor and toward themselves. According to Meenaghan, some of the tactics used in ambush marketing include sponsoring the media coverage of an event rather than the event itself, sponsoring a subcategory of an event, sponsoring individual athletes or teams involved in an event, or planning advertising to coincide with the event. For example, the Wendy's hamburger chain featured U.S. Olympic figure skater Kristi Yamaguchi in its advertising during the 1992 Olympic Games, while its rival McDonald's was the official sponsor of U.S. team's involvement.

"An ambush marketer can associate with a major event without large-scale investment in securing rights and thereby fulfill brand awareness and image objectives at low cost—benefits usually available only to the official sponsor," Meenaghan noted. "It also generates goodwill, which is a consumer's natural reaction to support for an activity of which he or she approves. At the very least, it creates consumer confusion, thereby denying the legitimate sponsor clear recognition for its sponsorship role." Meenaghan claimed that ambush marketing "simultaneously reduces the effectiveness of the sponsor's message while undermining the quality and value of the sponsorship opportunity that the event owner is selling.'' Although the practice is considered unethical by paid sponsors and event owners, others consider it a normal part of competitive advertising.

Meenaghan outlined several preemptive measures corporate sponsors can take to reduce the chances of being hit with ambush marketing. He suggested that sponsor companies try to anticipate competitive promotions and establish those specific rights with the event owner, identify related avenues for promotion and block them, and seek legal remedies when their sponsorship rights are infringed upon. But perhaps the most effective way for sponsor companies to reduce the effectiveness of ambush marketing tactics is to promote their involvement effectively.

FURTHER READING:

Bond, Cathy. ''The Stage Management Art.'' *Marketing.* October 27, 1994.

Dwek, Robert. ''Compassionate Commitment with Cash.'' *Marketing.* February 18, 1993.

Fry, Andy. ''Sponsors Play to Win.'' *Marketing.* August 7, 1997.

Jacobs, Heidi. ''Taking It to the Street.'' *Small Business Reports.* January 1994.

Kasrel, Deni. ''Corporate Sponsorship Grows.'' *Philadelphia Business Journal.* May 2, 1997.

Meenaghan, Tony. ''Ambush Marketing—A Threat to Corporate Sponsorship.'' *Sloan Management Review.* Fall 1996.

Miles, Louella. ''Results Service.'' *Marketing.* July 6, 1995.

Moore, Paula. ''Companies Unearth a Gold Mine of Goodwill: Using Generosity as a Marketing Strategy.'' *Denver Business Journal.* August 22, 1997.

SEE ALSO: Corporate Image

COST-BENEFIT ANALYSIS

Cost-benefit analysis is the exercise of evaluating an action's consequences by weighing the pluses, or benefits, against the minuses, or costs. Whether performed formally or informally, cost-benefit analysis is the fundamental assessment behind virtually every business decision, due to the simple fact that business managers do not want to spend money unless the resulting benefits are expected to exceed the costs. As companies increasingly seek to cut costs and improve productivity, cost-benefit analysis has become a valuable tool for evaluating a wide range of business opportunities, such as major purchases, organizational changes, and expansions. In recent years, the use of cost-benefit analysis has expanded beyond the business world. For example, it forms the basis for the federal government's enforcement of environmental regulations.

Some examples of the types of business decisions that may be facilitated by cost-benefit analysis include whether or not to add employees, introduce a new technology, purchase equipment, change vendors, implement new procedures, and remodel or relocate facilities. In evaluating such opportunities, managers can justify their decisions by applying cost-benefit analysis. This type of analysis can identify the hard dollar savings (actual, quantitative savings), soft dollar savings (less tangible, qualitative savings, as in management time or facility space), and cost avoidance (the elimination of a future cost, like overtime or equipment leasing) associated with the opportunity.

Although its name seems simple, there is often a degree of complexity, and subjectivity, to the actual implementation of cost-benefit analysis. This is because not all costs or benefits are obvious at first. Take, for example, a situation in which a company is trying to decide if it should make or buy a certain subcomponent of a larger assembly it manufactures. A quick review of the accounting numbers may suggest that the cost to manufacture the component, at $5 per piece, can easily be beat by an outside vendor who will sell it to the company for only $4. But there are several other factors that need to be considered and quantified (if possible):

1) When production of a subcomponent is contracted to an outside vendor, the company's own factory will become less utilized, and therefore its fixed overhead costs have less components over which to be spread. As a result, other parts it continues to manufacture may show an increase in costs, consuming some or possibly all of the apparent gain.

2) The labor force may be concerned about outsourcing of work to which they feel an entitlement. Resulting morale problems and labor unrest could quickly cost the company far more than it expected to save.

3) The consequences of a loss of control over the subcomponent must be weighed. Once the part is outsourced, the company no longer has direct control over the quality, timeliness, or reliability of the product delivered.

4) Unforeseen benefits may be attained. For example, the newly freed factory space may be deployed in a more productive manner, enabling the company to make more of the main assembly or even another product altogether.

This list is not meant to be comprehensive, but rather illustrative of the ripple effect that occurs in real business decision settings. The cost-benefit analyst needs to be cognizant of the subtle interactions of other events with the action under consideration in order to fully evaluate its impact.

A formal cost-benefit analysis is a multi-step process which includes a preliminary survey, a **feasibility study**, and a final report. At the conclusion of each step, the party responsible for performing the analysis can decide whether continuing on to the next step is warranted. The preliminary survey is an initial evaluation that involves gathering information on both the opportunity and the existing situation. The feasibility study involves completing the information gathering as needed and evaluating the data to gauge the short- and long-term impact of the opportunity. Finally, the formal cost-benefit analysis report should provide decision makers with all the pertinent information they need to take appropriate action on the opportunity. It should include an executive summary and introduction; information about the scope, purpose, and methodology of the study; recommendations, along with factual justification; and factors concerning implementation.

Capital budgeting has at its core the tool of cost-benefit analysis; it merely extends the basic form into a multi-period analysis, with consideration of the time value of money. In this context, a new product, venture, or investment is evaluated on a start-to-finish basis, with care taken to capture all the impacts on the company, both cost and benefits. When these inputs and outputs are quantified by year, they can then be discounted to present value to determine the net present value of the opportunity at the time of the decision.

FURTHER READING:

Brealey, Richard A. and Stewart C. Myers. *Principles of Corporate Finance*, 4th ed. New York: McGraw-Hill, 1991.

Dmytrenko, April L. "Cost-Benefit Analysis." *Records Management Quarterly.* January 1997.

Horngren, Charles T. and Gary L. Sundem. *Introduction to Management Accounting.* Upper Saddle River, NJ: Prentice-Hall, 1990.

SEE ALSO: Decision-Making

COST CONTROL AND REDUCTION

Cost control and reduction refers to the efforts business managers make to monitor, evaluate, and trim expenditures. These efforts might be part of a formal, company-wide program or might be informal in nature and limited to a single individual or department. In either case, however, cost control is a particularly important area of focus for small businesses, which often have limited amounts of time and money. "In a small business, you are so busy serving your customers, you tend to get lackadaisical about what you're buying," business owner John Clark noted in *Jane Applegate's Strategies for Small Business Success.* Even seemingly insignificant expenditures—for such items as **office supplies**, telephone bills, or overnight delivery services—can add up for small businesses. On the plus side, these minor expenditures can often provide sources of cost savings.

PLANNING AND CONTROL

Cost control refers to management's effort to influence the actions of individuals who are responsible for performing tasks, incurring costs, and generating revenues. First managers plan the way they want people to perform, then they implement procedures to determine whether actual performance complies with these plans. Cost control is a continuous process that begins with the annual budget. As the fiscal year progresses, management compares actual results to those projected in the budget and incorporates into the new plan the lessons learned from its evaluation of current operations. Through the budget process and accounting controls, management establishes overall company objectives, defines the centers of responsibility, determines specific objectives for each responsibility center, and designs procedures and standards for reporting and evaluation.

A budget segments the business into its components, or centers, where the responsible party initiates and controls action. *Responsibility centers* represent applicable organizational units, functions, departments, and divisions. Generally a single individual heads the responsibility center exercising substantial, if not complete, control over the activities of people or processes within the center. *Cost centers* are accountable only for expenses. *Revenue centers* primarily generate revenue. *Profit centers* accept responsibility for both revenue and expenses. The use of responsibility centers allows management to design control reports and pinpoint accountability. A budget also sets standards to indicate the level of activity expected from each responsible person or decision unit, and the amount of resources that a responsible party should use in achieving that level of activity.

The planning process, then, provides for two types of control mechanisms: feedforward, which provides a basis for control at the point of action (the decision point); and feedback, which provides a basis for measuring the effectiveness of control after implementation. Management's role is to feedforward a futuristic vision of where the company is going and how it is to get there, and to make clear decisions coordinating and directing employee activities. Management also oversees the development of procedures to collect, record, and evaluate feedback.

CONTROL REPORTS

Control reports are informational reports that tell management about a company's activities. Control reports are only for internal use, and therefore management directs the accounting department to develop tailor-made reporting formats. Accounting provides management with a format designed to detect variations that need investigating. In addition, management also refers to conventional reports such as the income statement and balance sheet, and to external reports on the general economy and the specific industry.

Control reports need to provide an adequate amount of information so that management may determine the reasons for any cost variances from the original budget. A good control report highlights significant information by focusing management's attention on those items in which actual performance significantly differs from the standard.

Managers perform effectively when they attain the goals and objectives set by the budget. With respect to profits, managers succeed by the degree to which revenues continually exceed expenses. In applying the following simple formula, Net Profit = Revenue − Expenses, managers realize that they exercise more control over expenses than they do over revenues. While they cannot predict the timing and volume of actual sales, they can determine the utilization rate of most of their resources; that is, they can influence the cost side. Hence, the evaluation of management's performance and the company's operations is cost control.

STANDARDS

For cost control purposes, a budget provides standard costs. As management constructs budgets, it lays out a road map to guide its efforts. It states a number of assumptions about the relationships and interaction among the economy, market dynamics, the abilities of its sales force, and its capacity to provide the proper quantity and quality of products demanded. An examination of the details of the budget calculations and assumptions reveals that management expects operations to produce the required amount of units within a certain cost range. Management bases its expectations and projections on the best historical and current information, as well as its best business judgment.

For example, when calculating budget expenses, management's review of the historic and current data might strongly suggest that the production of 1,000 units of a certain luxury item will cost $100,000, or $100 per unit. In addition, management might determine that the sales force will expend about $80,000 to sell the 1,000 units. This is a sales expenditure of $80 per unit. With total expenditures of $180, management sets the selling price of $500 for this luxury item. At the close of a month, management compares the actual results of that month to the standard costs to determine the degree and direction of any variance. The purpose for analyzing variances is to identify areas where costs need containment.

In the above illustration, accounting indicates to management that the sales force sold 100 units for a gross revenue of $50,000. Accounting's data also shows that the sales force spent $7,000 that month, and that production incurred $12,000 in expenses. While revenue was on target, actual sales expense came in less than the projected, with a per unit cost of $70. This is a *favorable* variance. But production expenses registered an *unfavorable* variance since actual expenditures exceeded those projected. The company produced units at $120 per item, $20 more than projected. This variance of 20 percent significantly differs from the standard costs of $100 and would likely cause management to take corrective action. As part of the control function, management compares actual performance to predetermined standards and makes changes when necessary to correct variances from the standards. The preparation of budgets and control reports, and the resulting analysis of variances from performance standards, give managers an idea of where to focus their attention to achieve cost reductions.

COST CUTTING FOR SMALL BUSINESSES

A variety of techniques can be employed to help a small business cut its costs. One method of cost reduction available to small businesses is hiring an outside analyst or consultant. These individuals may be independent consultants or accountants who analyze costs as a special service to their clients. They generally undertake an in-depth, objective review of a company's expenditures and make recommendations about where costs can be better controlled or reduced. Some expense-reduction analysts charge a basic, up-front fee, while others collect a percentage of the savings that accrue to the company as a result of their work. Still others contract with specific vendors and then pool the orders of their client companies to obtain a discount. Some of the potential benefits of using a consultant include saving time for the small business owner, raising awareness of costs in the company, and negotiating more favorable contracts with vendors and suppliers.

In his book *One Hundred Ways to Prosper in Today's Economy,* Barry Schimel suggested a variety of simple ways for small business owners to reduce costs, including printing or photocopying on both sides of the paper whenever possible, locking the office supply cabinet to prevent employee theft, and canceling insurance on unused equipment and vehicles. Schimel went on to outline an internal cost-cutting program that small business owners can apply. He recommended that small business owners set aside time to review several months' worth of checks and invoices and make a detailed list of all their monthly expenses. Then they should decide upon a few areas that might benefit from comparison-shopping for better prices. If the small business owner is not inclined to undertake the comparison-shopping personally, a responsible employee can be assigned to the task.

It may be helpful to compare the prices in office-supply catalogs to those offered by local stores, and to purchase supplies in bulk at a discount if possible. Some small businesses are able to form purchasing cooperatives with other small businesses in order to buy in larger quantities and negotiate better prices. After comparing the various options available and finding the lowest prices, Schimel suggested that small business owners take those numbers back to their original vendors and ask them to meet the lowest price. Many vendors are willing to do so in order to avoid losing business.

Despite the importance of cost control to small businesses, and the potential for cost savings, Schimel still warned small business owners that cost reduction alone cannot guarantee success. ''You can't cost-cut your way to prosperity,'' he stated. ''To improve profits, you also need more sales and adequate margins.''

FURTHER READING:

Ameiss, Albert P., and Nicholas A. Kargas. *Accountant's Desk Handbook*. Englewood Cliffs, NJ: Prentice-Hall, 1977.

Applegate, Jane. *Jane Applegate's Strategies for Small Business Success*. New York: Plume, 1995.

Dopuch, Nicholas, Jacob G. Birnberg, and Joel Demski. *Cost Accounting: Accounting Data for Management's Decisions*. New York: Harcourt Brace Jovanovich, 1974.

Meigs, Robert F., and Walter B. Meigs. *Accounting: The Basis for Business Decisions*. 8th ed. New York: McGraw-Hill, 1990.

Neuner, John J., and Edward B. Deakin. *Cost Accounting: Principles and Practices*. Homewood, IL: Irwin, 1977.

Schimel, Barry. *One Hundred Ways to Prosper in Today's Economy*. Herndon, VA: Acropolis Books, 1994.

SEE ALSO: Budgets and Budgeting

COST SHARING

Cost sharing is a process wherein two or more organizations work together to secure savings in one or more areas of business operations. Such partnerships may also be pursued to realize other business advantages—increased marketplace exposure, access to technology —but cost savings are usually a central component of these arrangements. Cost-sharing partnerships can be implemented in any number of operating areas, from marketing to transportation to research and development. It is a favorite tool of many small business enterprises that have limited financial resources.

Relatively few cost-sharing arrangements have been implemented for the actual manufacture of goods or execution of services. Instead, the majority of cost-sharing plans are in the area of **marketing** and **advertising**. ''Today's direct marketing partnerships achieve impressive cost-benefit results,'' stated Myron Gould in *Direct Marketing*. He cited three primary advantages associated with cost-sharing partnerships in this operational area:

- They enable marketers to address the competitive challenges of the rising cost of direct marketing essentials such as postage and paper.

- They help marketers reduce direct mail expenses because costs are shared.

- Their effectiveness is enhanced by the development of technology tools and media outlet alternatives.

Gould cited the latter factor as particularly important for businesses seeking to engage in effective cost-sharing. ''Computers have transformed [the marketing] industry and given birth to partnership opportunities. Today's computer-driven partnerships empower us to target qualified recipients and segment lists as never before. Many of our alternative direct marketing programs have traditionally taken a broadcast approach—reaching broadly defined segments. Now, partnerships offer qualified segmentation, targeting narrower, clearly defined lifestyle and demographic segments. Technical advances in imprinting and inserting also offer enhanced ability to customize the package and the offer.''

FINDING A COST-SHARING PARTNER

''There are no rules, standards, or boundaries that should restrict your vision when seeking a partner. Rather, shared goals should guide your 'vision quest,' '' wrote Gould. ''Partnership can be formed in the profit and nonprofit sectors, in the same or different industries, within different divisions of the same company, and in similar market segments/demographics in non-competitive industries.''

Many small business owners seek out allies for the exclusive purpose of registering savings in their operating costs. This is a perfectly legitimate course of action, but entrepreneurs should make certain that the final agreement is a fair one that explicitly delineates the terms of the agreement. Indeed, written partnership agreements that define each partner's spending obligations should be insisted upon, for in addition to discussing cost-sharing matters, these documents can also provide details on agreed-upon procedures and work flow, parameters for responsibilities, and mechanisms to measure results both during and after the project. As Gould observed, carefully crafted proposals "will help you mitigate concerns about loss of control and structuring the partnership for mutual benefit. When a partnership fulfills the consumers' needs with a new, exciting, or value-added offer or program, risks are minimized for all involved."

In addition to ensuring that cost-sharing agreements are sufficiently documented, small business owners should weigh possible other benefits associated with partner alternatives when making their decision. Gould noted, for example, that a larger company might be able to provide a small business with valuable access to technology and training, while a smaller business might be blessed with a much-coveted contemporary market image. Ideally, a small business owner will be able to find a partner who not only can help him or her secure savings in one or more aspects of business operations, but also provide additional benefits.

COST-SHARING ARRANGEMENTS AND THE INTERNAL REVENUE SERVICE

The **Internal Revenue Service** maintains certain rules concerning how cost-sharing agreements within business groups should allocate costs. According to the IRS, a cost-sharing arrangement is defined as an agreement under which costs to develop intangibles are shared in proportion to reasonably anticipated benefits that each entity will reap. According to *The Tax Advisor*'s Adrian J. W. Dicker, such arrangements must include two or more participants; provide a method to calculate each controlled participant's share of intangible development costs, based on factors that can reasonably be expected to reflect each participant's share of anticipated benefits; provide for adjustments to the controlled participant's shares of intangible development costs to account for changes in economic conditions and the business operations and practices of the participants; and be recorded in an up-to-date document that provides detailed information on specifics of the arrangement. Dicker noted that the IRS also established a "safe harbor" for actual benefits that diverge from estimates, but only if the difference is less than 20 percent: "In allocating intangible development costs under a cost-sharing agreement, it is necessary to project the participant's share of anticipated benefits. That share is then compared to the participant's allocated share of the total costs. If these shares are not equal, the Service has the power to make adjustments. Benefits would include not only additional income generated but also costs saved by the use of the intangible. Timing of costs and benefits can be adjusted using discounting."

Finally, Dicker pointed out that businesses that take part in a cost-sharing agreement are required to make a buy-in payment if the partnership calls for any transfer of intangible property. These buy-in payments can take the form of lump sums, installment payments, or royalty payments. "Similarly, if a participants' shares change or a participant withdraws," wrote Dicker, "there are deemed disposals and acquisitions requiring buy-in or buy-out payments."

FURTHER READING:

Clift, Vicki. "Small Firms Benefit From a Promotional Partner." *Marketing News.* September 23, 1996.

Dicker, Adrian J. W. "Final Cost-Sharing Regulations." *Tax Advisor.* May 1996.

Dodge, William G., Julie Joy, Tim Seitz, and Alan Shapiro. "Amendments to Final Cost Sharing Regs. Add a Few More Pieces to the Intangibles Puzzle." *Journal of Taxation.* October 1996.

Fitzgerald, Kevin R. "Proprietary Information—Should Suppliers Share It?" *Purchasing.* October 3, 1996.

Gould, Myron. "Partnering for Profit—How to Achieve Impressive Cost-Benefit Results." *Direct Marketing.* February 1997.

Solomon, Stephen D. "When You've Exhausted Cost-Cutting Measures: Sharing the Costs." *Inc.* December 1989.

COSTS

Costs are the necessary expenditures that must be made in order to run a business. Every factor of production has a cost associated with it: labor, fixed **assets**, and **capital**, for example. The cost of labor used in the production of goods and services is measured in terms of wages. The cost of a fixed asset used in production is measured in terms of depreciation. The cost of capital used to purchase fixed assets is measured in terms of the interest expense associated with raising the capital.

Businesses are vitally interested in measuring their costs. Many types of costs are observable and easily quantifiable. In such cases there is a direct relationship between cost of input and quantity of output. Other types of costs must be estimated or allocated. That is, the relationship between costs of input and units of output may not be directly observable or quantifiable. In the delivery of professional services, for example, the quality of the output is usually more significant than the quantity, and output cannot simply be measured in terms of the number of patients treated or students taught. In such instances where qualitative factors play an important role in measuring output, there is no direct relationship between costs incurred and output achieved.

DIFFERENT WAYS TO CATEGORIZE COSTS

Costs can have different relationships to output. Costs also are used in different business applications, such as financial accounting, cost accounting, budgeting, capital budgeting, and valuation. Consequently, there are different ways of categorizing costs according to their relationship to output as well as according to the context in which they are used. Following this summary of the different types of costs are some examples of how costs are used in different business applications.

FIXED AND VARIABLE COSTS The two basic types of costs incurred by businesses are fixed and variable. Fixed costs do not vary with output, while variable costs do. Fixed costs are sometimes called overhead costs. They are incurred whether a firm manufactures 100 widgets or 1,000 widgets. In preparing a budget, fixed costs may include rent, depreciation, and supervisors' salaries. Manufacturing overhead may include such items as property taxes and insurance. These fixed costs remain constant in spite of changes in output.

Variable costs, on the other hand, fluctuate in direct proportion to changes in output. Labor and material costs are typical variable costs that increase as the volume of production increases. It takes more labor and material to produce more output, so the cost of labor and material varies in direct proportion to the volume of output. The direct proportionality of variable costs to level of output may break down with very small and very large production runs.

In addition, some costs are considered mixed costs. That is, they contain elements of fixed and variable costs. In some cases the cost of supervision and inspection are considered mixed costs.

DIRECT AND INDIRECT COSTS Direct costs are similar to variable costs. They can be directly attributed to the production of output. The system of valuing inventories called direct costing is also known as variable costing. Under this accounting system only those costs that vary directly with the volume of production are charged to products as they are manufactured. The value of inventory is the sum of direct material, direct labor, and all variable manufacturing costs.

Indirect costs, on the other hand, are similar to fixed costs. They are not directly related to the volume of output. Indirect costs in a manufacturing plant may include supervisors' salaries, indirect labor, factory supplies used, taxes, utilities, depreciation on building and equipment, factory rent, tools expense, and patent expense. These indirect costs are sometimes referred to as manufacturing overhead.

Under the accounting system known as full costing or absorption costing, all of the indirect costs in manufacturing overhead as well as direct costs are included in determining the cost of inventory. They are considered part of the cost of the products being manufactured.

PRODUCT AND PERIOD COSTS The concepts of product and period costs are similar to direct and indirect costs. Product costs are those that the firm's accounting system associates directly with output and that are used to value inventory. Under a direct or variable cost accounting system, only direct or variable costs are charged to production. Indirect costs such as property taxes, insurance, depreciation on plant and equipment, and salaries of supervisors are considered period costs. Period costs are charged as expenses to the current period. Under direct costing, period costs are not viewed as costs of the products being manufactured, so they are not associated with valuing inventories.

If the firm uses a full cost accounting system, however, then all manufacturing costs—including fixed manufacturing overhead costs and variable costs—become product costs. They are considered part of the cost of manufacturing and are charged against inventory.

OTHER TYPES OF COSTS These are the basic types of costs as they are used in different accounting systems. In addition, other types of costs are used in different business contexts. In budgeting it is useful to identify controllable and uncontrollable costs. This simply means that managers with budgetary responsibility should not be held accountable for costs they cannot control.

Financial managers often use the concepts of out-of-pocket costs and sunk costs when evaluating the financial merits of specific proposals. Out-of-pocket costs are those that require the use of current resources, usually cash. Sunk costs have already been incurred. In evaluating whether or not to increase production, for example, financial managers may take into account the sunk costs associated with tools and machinery as well as the out-of-pocket costs associated with adding more material and labor.

Financial planning also utilizes the concepts of incremental, opportunity, and imputed costs. Incremental costs are those associated with switching from one level of activity or course of action to another. Incremental costs represent the difference between two alternatives. Opportunity costs represent the sacrifice that is made when the means of production are used for one task rather than another, or when capital is used for one investment rather than another. Nothing can be produced or invested without incurring an opportunity cost. By making one investment or production decision using limited resources, one necessarily forgoes the opportunity to use those resources for a different purpose. Consequently, opportunity costs are not usually factored into investment and production decisions involving resource allocation.

Imputed costs are costs that are not actually incurred, but are associated with internal transactions. When work in process is transferred from one department to another within an organization, a method of transfer pricing may be needed for budgetary reasons. Although there is no actual purchase or sale of goods and materials, the receiving department may be charged with imputed costs for the work it has received. When a company rents itself a building that it could have rented to an outside party, the rent may be considered an imputed cost.

BUSINESS APPLICATIONS USE DIFFERENT TYPES OF COSTS

Costs as a business concept are useful in measuring performance and determining profitability. What follows are brief discussions of some business applications in which costs play an important role.

FINANCIAL ACCOUNTING One of the major objectives of financial **accounting** is to determine the periodic income of the business. In manufacturing firms a major component of the income statement is the cost of goods sold (COGS). COGS is that part of the cost of inventory that can be considered an expense of the period because the goods were sold. It appears as an expense on the firm's periodic income statement. COGS is calculated as beginning inventory plus net purchases minus ending inventory.

Depreciation is another cost that becomes a periodic expense on the income statement. Every asset is initially valued at its cost. Accountants charge the cost of the asset to depreciation expense over the useful life of the asset. This cost allocation approach attempts to match costs with revenues and is more reliable than attempting to periodically determine the fair market value of the asset.

In financial accounting, costs represent assets rather than expenses. Costs only become expenses when they are charged against current income. Costs may be allocated as expenses against income over time, as in the case of depreciation, or they may be charged as expenses when revenue is generated, as in the case of COGS.

COST ACCOUNTING Cost accounting, also sometimes known as management accounting, provides appropriate cost information for budgeting systems and management decision making. Using the principles of general accounting, cost accounting records and determines costs associated with various functions of the business. This data is used by management to improve operations and make them more efficient, economical, and profitable.

Two major systems can be used to record the costs of manufactured products. They are known as job costing and process costing. A job cost system, or job order cost system, collects costs for each physically identifiable job or batch of work as it moves through the manufacturing facility and disregards the accounting period in which the work is done. With a process cost system, on the other hand, costs are collected for all of the products worked on during a specific accounting period. Unit costs are then determined by dividing the total costs by the number of units worked on during the period. Process cost systems are most appropriate for continuous operations, when like products are produced, or when several departments cooperate and participate in one or more operations. Job costing, on the other hand, is used when labor is a chief element of cost, when diversified lines or unlike products are manufactured, or when products are built to customer specifications.

When costs are easily observable and quantifiable, cost standards are usually developed. Also known as engineered standards, they are developed for each physical input at each step of the production process. At that point an engineered cost per unit of production can be determined. By documenting variable costs and fairly allocating fixed costs to different departments, a cost accounting system can provide management with the accountability and cost controls it needs to improve operations.

BUDGETING SYSTEMS Budgeting systems rely on accurate cost accounting systems. Using cost data collected by the business's cost accounting system, budgets can be developed for each department at different levels of output. Different units within the business can be designated cost centers, profit centers, or departments. Budgets are then used as a management tool to measure performance, among other things. Performance is measured by the extent to which actual figures deviate from budgeted amounts.

In using budgets as measures of performance, it is important to distinguish between controllable and uncontrollable costs. Managers should not be held accountable for costs they cannot control. In the short run, fixed costs can rarely be controlled. Consequently, a typical budget statement will show sales revenue as forecast and the variable costs associated with that level of production. The difference between sales revenue and variable costs is the contribution margin. Fixed costs are then deducted from the contribution margin to obtain a figure for operating income. Managers and departments are then evaluated on the basis of costs and those elements of production they are expected to control.

COST OF CAPITAL Capital budgeting and other business decisions—such as lease-buy decisions, bond refunding, and working capital policies—require estimates of a company's cost of capital. Capital budgeting decisions revolve around deciding whether or not to purchase a particular capital asset. Such decisions are based on an estimate of the net present value of future revenues that would be generated by a particular capital asset. An important factor in such decisions is the company's cost of capital.

Cost of capital is a percentage that represents the interest rate the company would pay for the funds being raised. Each capital component— debt, equity, and retained earnings—has its own cost. Each type of debt or equity also has a different cost. While a particular purchase or project may be funded by only one kind of capital, companies are likely to use a weighted average cost of capital when making financial decisions. Such practice takes into account the fact that the company is an ongoing concern that will need to raise capital at different rates in the future as well as at the present rate.

OTHER APPLICATIONS Costs are sometimes used in the valuation of assets that are being bought or sold. Buyers and sellers may agree that the value of an asset can be determined by estimating the costs associated with building or creating an asset that could perform similar functions and provide similar benefits as the existing asset. Using the cost approach to value an asset contrasts with the income approach, which attempts to identify the present value of the revenues the asset is expected to generate.

Finally, costs are used in making **pricing** decisions. Manufacturing firms refer to the ratio between prices and costs as their markup, which represents the difference between the selling price and the direct cost of the goods being sold. For retailers and wholesalers, the gross margin is the difference between their invoice cost and their selling price. While costs form the basis for pricing decisions, they are only a starting point, with market conditions and other factors usually determining the most profitable price.

FURTHER READING:

Hilton, Ronald W. *Managerial Accounting.* New York: McGraw-Hill, 1991.

Horngren, Charles T., and Gary L. Sundem. *Introduction to Financial Accounting.* 4th ed. Englewood Cliffs, NJ: Prentice Hall, 1990.

Welsch, Glenn A., Robert N. Anthony, and Daniel G. Short. *Fundamentals of Financial Accounting.* 4th ed. Homewood, IL: Irwin, 1984.

SEE ALSO: Cost Control and Reduction; Fixed and Variable Expenses; Financial Analysis

COUPONS

Coupons are certificates that provide consumers with discounts on goods or services when they are redeemed with retailers or manufacturers. Offered mainly by retailers and manufacturers as **sales promotion** tools to accomplish specific sales and marketing goals, they are very popular with small business owners because they are so inexpensive to disseminate and because of their historical effectiveness. Consumers are attracted to coupons because they offer immediate value and savings, but in recent years the proliferation of coupon distribution programs have produced a decided excess in the marketplace. This flood of coupon offers, commonly known as ''coupon clutter,'' has resulted in falling redemption rates. Only an estimated 1.8 percent of all coupons distributed in the United States in 1993 were redeemed by consumers.

ADVANTAGES AND DISADVANTAGES Like other sales promotion tools, coupons have their advantages as well as their problems. On the plus side, they have the advantage of passing along savings directly to consumers, as opposed to trade allowances given to retailers by producers. Consumers perceive coupons as a temporary special offer rather than a price reduction, so the withdrawal of coupons usually does not have an adverse effect on sales. In addition, coupons often create added traffic for retailers, who have the option of doubling or even tripling the value of manufacturers' coupons at their own expense to create even more store traffic. Moreover, retailers often receive additional compensation from manufacturers for handling the coupons.

Critics of coupon-oriented sales promotions, however, argue that coupon clutter has dramatically lessened their effectiveness. They question whether coupons actually generate incremental business from new users, pointing out that the increased quantity of distributed coupons has been paralleled by falling redemption rates. In addition, excessive coupon distribution also increases the likelihood of fraud and misredemption. Coupons that are issued for established brands, say critics, tend to be redeemed primarily by loyal users who would have purchased the product without a coupon.

COUPON OBJECTIVES Coupons may be issued to serve a variety of different strategic marketing objectives. One use is to encourage consumers to try new products; coupons have historically been fairly efficient at getting consumers to try new products by reducing the risk of trying something new. Coupons are also issued to convert trial users into regular customers, such as when a product sample includes a cents-off coupon. In addition, coupons can be used to convince consumers to make purchases of new sizes, flavors, or forms of an established product.

Other objectives served by issuing coupons include building retail distribution and support, moving out-of-balance inventories, targeting different markets, cushioning price increases, and enhancing other promotional efforts with coupon add-ons. Coupons are frequently used by manufacturers because of competitive pressure. When used offensively against the competition, coupons are issued to get users of a competitive product to try a new brand. When used defensively, manufacturers provide coupons to current users to keep them from purchasing a competing brand.

COUPON DISTRIBUTION There are several ways in which small businesses can distribute coupons, including **direct mail**, in-store or central location, print media, in-pack and on-pack, and through retailer advertising. Because of its targeted distribution, coupons sent by direct mail offer higher redemption rates than coupons distributed by print media—an estimated 4.3 percent in 1991. Freestanding inserts (FSIs) in newspapers, which accounted for more than four-fifths of all coupon distribution in the early 1990s, are generally regarded as more effective than other coupon distribution methods. Perhaps the most popular coupon distribution method for small businesses, however, is the coupon mailer. This is a strategy wherein a group of retail businesses in a community send out a mailing of individual coupons together; consumers within the community thus receive a variety of coupons for area businesses in one envelope. Sometimes the mailing will consist of an actual booklet of coupons for participating businesses, but most are sent out in ''loose-leaf'' fashion. Many business communities house businesses that specialize in putting such coupon mailers together. These companies charge a fee for their production and distribution services.

SEE ALSO: Direct Marketing

CREDIT

Credit is a transaction between two parties in which one, acting as creditor or lender, supplies the other, the debtor or borrower, with money, goods, services, or securities in return for the promise of future payment. As a financial transaction, credit is the purchase of the present use of money with the promise to pay in the future according to a pre-arranged schedule and at a specified cost

defined by the interest rate. In modern economies, the use of credit is pervasive and the volume

enormous. Electronic transfer technology moves vast amounts of **capital** instantaneously around the globe irrespective of geopolitical demarcations.

In a production economy, credit bridges the time gap between the commencement of production and the final sale of goods in the marketplace. In order to pay labor and secure materials from

vendors, the producer secures a constant source of credit to fund production expenses, i.e., working capital. The promise or expectation of continued economic growth motivates the

producer to expand production facilities, increase labor, and purchase additional materials. These create a need for long-term financing.

To accumulate adequate reserves from which to lend large sums of money, banks and insurance companies act as intermediaries between those with excess reserves and those in need of financing. These institutions collect excess money (short term assets) through deposits and redirect it through loans into capital (long term) assets.

REASONS FOR PURCHASING CREDIT

In a production economy, credit is widely available and extensively used. Because credit includes a promise to pay, the credit purchaser accepts a certain amount of financial and personal risk. These points summarize the reasons for purchasing credit:

1) The lack of liquidity prevents profitable investments at advantageous times.

2) Favorable borrowing costs make it less expensive to borrow in the present than in the future. Borrowers may have expectations of rising rates, tight credit supplies, growing inflation, and decreasing economic activity. Conversely, profit expectations may be sufficiently favorable to justify present investments that require financing.

3) Tax incentives, which expense or deduct some interest costs, decrease the cost of borrowing and assist in capital formation.

USES FOR CREDIT

A debtor accepts the risks of borrowing to secure something of value, whether perceived or real, profitable or neutral. Borrowing extends one's purchasing power and ability to invest in capital assets to build wealth. But credit is not only used to produce wealth; credit may be necessitated by psychological and cultural factors as well. The following are some of the most common reasons for using credit:

Enjoyment. Credit has come to finance the enhancement of one's life style or quality of life through activities and purchases for enjoyment. Activities "profitable" to one's well being may translate into a more productive economic life. Enjoyment includes the financing of a boat, an education, a vacation, a health club membership, or a retreat.

Utilitarian consumption. With the introduction of credit cards in the 1950s and the increase of home equity debt in the 1980s, the financing of daily consumption has greatly expanded. In fact, consumer credit in 1990 was four times that of 1975. Much of this debt was for convenience purchases, consumer goods, and services with a life of less than one year.

Profit and wealth building. The profit incentive plays an important role in the accumulation of capital assets and in wealth building not only for companies—which increase profits through the introduction of capital improvements that must be financed over the long-term—but also for individuals. Home buyers use a similar rationale when buying a house. They expect the purchase of a certain house in a certain location to be more "profitable" than renting or purchasing another house elsewhere.

PROMISE TO PAY

The credit contract defines the terms of the agreement between lender and borrower. The terms of the contract delineate the borrower's obligation to repay the principal according to a schedule and at a specified cost or interest rate. The lender reserves the right to require **collateral** to secure a loan and to enforce payment through the courts.

The lender may levy a small charge for originating or participating in a loan placement. This charge, measured in percentage points, covers administrative costs. This immediate cash infusion decreases the costs of the loan to the lender, thereby reducing the risk. The lender may also require the borrower to provide protection against nonpayment or default by securing insurance, by establishing a repayment fund, or by assigning collateral assets.

A promissory note is an unconditional written promise to pay money at a specified time or on demand. The maker of the note is primarily liable for settlement. No collateral is required. A lien agreement, however, holds property as security for payment of debt. A specific lien identifies a specific property, as in a mortgage. A general lien has no specific assignment.

CREDIT TERMS

The terms of the credit contract deal with the repayment schedule, interest rate, necessity of collateral, and debt retirement.

REPAYMENT SCHEDULES Credit contracts vary in maturity. Short-term debt is from overnight to less than one year. Long-term debt is more than one year, up to 30 or 40 years. Payments may be required at the end of the contract or at set intervals, usually on a monthly basis. The payment generally comprises two parts: a portion of the outstanding principal and the interest costs. With the passage of time, the principal amount of the loan is amortized, or repaid little by little, until completely retired. As the principal balance diminishes, the interest on the remaining balance also declines. Interest paid on loans does not pay down the principal. The borrower pays interest on the principal loan amount and is expected to retire the principal at the end of the contract through a balloon payment or through refinancing.

Revolving credit has no fixed date for retirement. The lender provides a maximum line of credit and expects monthly payment according to an amortization schedule. The borrower decides the degree to which to use the line of credit. The borrower may increase debt anytime the outstanding amount is below the maximum credit line. The borrower may retire the debt at will, or may continue a cycle of paying down and increasing the debt.

INTEREST RATES Interest is the cost of purchasing the use of money, i.e., borrowing. The **interest rate** charged by lending institutions must be sufficient to cover operating costs, administrative costs, and an acceptable rate of return. Interest rates may be fixed for the term of the loan, or adjusted to reflect changing market conditions. A credit contract may adjust rates daily, annually, or at intervals of three, five, and ten years.

COLLATERAL Assets pledged as security against loan loss are known as collateral. Credit backed by collateral is secured. The asset purchased by the loan often serves as the only collateral. In other cases the borrower puts other assets, including cash, aside as collateral. Real estate or land collateralizes mortgages.

Unsecured debt relies on the earning power of the borrower. A debenture is a written acknowledgment of a debt similar to a promissory note in that it is unsecured, relying only on the full faith and credit of the issuer. Corporations often issue debentures as bonds. With no collateral, these debentures are subordinate to mortgages.

A bond is a contract held in trust obligating a borrower to repay a sum of money. A debenture bond is unsecured, while a mortgage bond holds specific property in lien. A bond may contain safety measures to provide for repayment. An indenture is a legal document specifying the terms of a bond issue, including the principal, maturity date, interest rates, any qualifications and duties of the trustees, and the rights and obligations of the issuers and holders. Corporations and government entities issue **bonds** in a form attractive to both public and private investors.

DEBT RETIREMENT Overnight funds are lent among banks to temporarily lift their reserves to mandated levels.

A special commitment is a single purpose loan with a maturity of less than one year. Its purpose is to cover cash shortages resulting from a one-time increase in current assets, such as a special inventory purchase, an unexpected increase in accounts payable, or a need for interim financing.

Trade credit is extended by a vendor who allows the purchaser up to three months to settle a bill. In the past it was common practice for vendors to discount trade bills by one or two percentage points as an incentive for quick payment. A seasonal line of credit of less than one year is used to finance inventory purchases or production. The successful sale of inventory repays the line of credit. A permanent working capital loan provides a business with financing from one to five years during times when cash flow from earnings does not coincide with the timing or volume of expenditures. Creditors expect future earnings to be sufficient to retire the loan.

Commercial papers are short-term, unsecured notes issued by corporations in a form that can be traded in the public money market. Commercial paper finances inventory and production needs. A letter of credit (''l/c'') is a financing instrument that acts more like credit money than a loan. An l/c is used to facilitate a transaction, especially in trade, by guaranteeing payment at a future date. Unlike a loan, which invokes two primary parties, an l/c involves three: the bank, the customer, and the beneficiary. The bank issues, based on its own credibility, an l/c on behalf of its customer, promising to pay the beneficiary upon satisfactory completion of some predetermined conditions. A bank's acceptance is another short-term trade financing vehicle. A bank issues a time draft promising to pay on or after a future date on behalf of its customer. The bank rests its guarantee on the expectation that its customer will collect payment for goods previously sold.

Term loans finance the purchase of furniture, fixtures, vehicles, and plant and office equipment. Maturity generally runs more than one year and less than five. A large equipment purchase may have longer terms, matched to its useful production life. Mortgage loans are used to purchase real estate and are secured by the asset itself. Mortgages generally run 10 to 40 years. When creditors provide a mortgage to finance the purchase of a property without retiring an existing mortgage, they wrap the new mortgage around the existing debt. The interest payment of the wraparound mortgage pays the debt service of the underlying mortgage.

Treasury bills are short-term debt instruments of the U.S. government issued weekly and on a discounted basis with the full face value due on maturity. T-bill maturities range from 91 to 359 days and are issued in denominations of $10,000. Treasury notes are intermediate-term debt instruments ranging in maturity from one to ten years. Issued at par, full face value, in denominations of $5,000 and $10,000, T-notes pay interest semiannually. Treasury bonds are long-term debt instruments. Issued at par values of $1,000 and up, T-bonds pay interest semiannually, and may have call dates (retirement) prior to maturity.

CREDIT WORTHINESS

The granting of credit depends on the confidence the lender has in the borrower's credit worthiness. Generally defined as a debtor's ability to pay, credit worthiness is one of many factors defining a lender's credit policies. Creditors and lenders utilize a number of financial tools to evaluate the credit worthiness of a potential borrower. Much of the evaluation relies on analyzing the borrower's balance sheet, cash flow statements, inventory turnover rates, debt structure, management performance, and market conditions. Creditors favor borrowers who generate net earnings in excess of debt obligations and contingencies that may arise. Following are some of the factors lenders consider when evaluating an individual or business that is seeking credit:

Credit worthiness. A history of trustworthiness, a moral character, and expectations of continued performance demonstrate a debtor's ability to pay. Creditors give more favorable terms to those with high credit ratings via lower point structures and interest costs.

Size of debt burden. Creditors seek borrowers whose earning power exceeds the demands of the payment schedule. The size of the debt is necessarily limited by the available resources. Creditors prefer to maintain a safe ratio of debt to capital.

Loan size. Creditors prefer large loans because the administrative costs decrease proportionately to the size of the loan. However, legal and practical limitations recognize the need to spread the risk either by making a larger number of loans, or by having other lenders participate. Participating lenders must have adequate resources to entertain large loan applications. In addition, the borrower must have the capacity to ingest a large sum of money.

Frequency of borrowing. Customers who are frequent borrowers establish a reputation which directly affects their ability to secure debt at advantageous terms.

Length of commitment. Lenders accept additional risk as the time horizon increases. To cover some of the risk, lenders charge higher interest rates for longer term loans.

Social community considerations. Lenders may accept an unusual level of risk because of the social good resulting from the use of the loan. Examples might include banks participating in low income housing projects or business incubator programs.

INTEREST RATES AND RISK

Lenders use both subjective and objective guidelines to evaluate risk and to establish: a) a general rate structure reflective of market conditions; and b) borrower-specific terms based on individual credit analysis. To be profitable, lenders charge **interest rates** that cover perceived risks as well as the costs of doing business. The risks calculated into the interest rate include the following:

Opportunity cost risk. The lender fixes interest costs at a level sufficient to justify making a loan in the present rather than waiting for more advantageous terms in the future. The lender focuses on a desired rate of return rather than the credit worthiness of the borrower.

Credit risk or repayment risk. The borrower may not be able to make scheduled payments nor repay the debt at all. The greater the credit risk, the higher the interest rate. Creditors charge lower interest rates to those with the highest credit ratings, and those who are the most able to pay. In other words, those least able to pay find themselves paying the highest rates.

Interest rate risk and prepayment risk. These risks arise when the payment or prepayment of outstanding debt does not match the terms and pricing of current debt, thus exposing the lender to a ''mismatch'' in the costs of doing business and the terms of lending.

Inflation risk. Inflation decreases the purchasing power of money. Lenders anticipate these losses with higher interest rates.

Currency risk. International trade and money markets may devalue the currency, decreasing its purchasing power abroad even during times of low inflationary expectations at home. Since currency devaluation heightens inflationary expectations in a global economy, interest rates rise.

FINANCIAL INTERMEDIATION

Financial intermediation is the process of channeling funds from financial sectors with excesses to those with deficiencies. The primary suppliers of funds are households, businesses, and governments. They are also the primary borrowers. Financial intermediaries, such as banks, finance companies, and insurance companies, collect excess funds from these sectors and redistribute them in the form of credit. Financial intermediaries accumulate reserves of funds through investment and savings instruments.

Banks provide savings and checking accounts, certificates of deposit, and other time accounts for customers willing to loan the bank their funds for the payment of interest. Insurance companies gather funds through various investments and through the collecting of premiums. Banks, finance, and insurance companies also raise cash by selling equity positions or borrowing money from private or public investors. Pension funds utilize available funds from participant contributions and from investment earnings. Federally sponsored credit intermediaries capitalize themselves in a manner similar to banks.

Financial intermediation provides an efficient and practical method of redistributing purchasing power to qualified borrowers. Banks aggregate many small deposits to finance a single family home mortgage, for example. Finance companies break large pools of cash down to sizes appropriate for the purchase of an automobile. The pooling of funds from many sources and the distribution of credit to a large number of creditors spreads the risks.

Managers of financial intermediaries also reduce risk by qualifying borrowers, thereby funneling funds into creditworthy situations. Furthermore, financial intermediation increases liquidity in the system, acting as a buffer against cash shortages resulting from unexpected increases in deposit withdrawals.

CREDIT SECURITIZATION

Credit securitization is one of the most recent and important developments in financing and capital formation. Underwriters of financial investments gather together a large number of outstanding credit instruments and other receivables, and repackage them in the form of securities which, to the layperson, are similar to closed-end mutual funds. Underwriters sort the credit instruments into homogeneous groups by maturity, purpose, interest rates, and so forth, and market participation in the cash flow generated by the debt instruments backing these securities. Hence the term ''asset backed securities.''

In many instances the underlying debt is mortgages, secured by real estate, and guaranteed by some agency or insurance company. For example, an underwriter may place into securitization only mortgages guaranteed by the Veterans Administration of maturities no less than 20 years, with interest rates of not less than 9 percent, and with a cumulative principal (face) value of $10 million. The underwriter sells shares in this pool of mortgages to the public. Other credit instruments securitized are commercial mortgages, auto loans, credit card receivables, and trade receivables.

Credit securitization supports the viability of financial intermediaries by: a) spreading the risk over a broader range of investors who purchase the securities; and b) increasing liquidity through an immediate cash infusion for the securitized debt. This process is also helpful to investors and borrowers alike. The large volume and efficiency of the system puts downward pressure on interest rates. The pooling of loans into large, homogeneous securities facilitates the actuarial and financial analyses of their risks.

Investors may participate in a portion of the cash flow generated by the interest and/or principal payments made by borrowers of the underlying debt. Investor participation may be limited to the cash flow of a set number of years, or to a portion of the principal when the underlying debt is retired. Investors also choose to participate at a point suitable to their risk/reward ratio. Thus, investors have the opportunity to derive different benefits from one package of credit instruments.

FURTHER READING:

The Federal Reserve System: Purposes & Functions. Washington, D.C.: Board of Governors of the Federal Reserve System, 1984.

Guttman, Robert. *How Credit-Money Shapes the Economy: The United States in a Global System.* M.E. Sharpe, 1994.

Heath, Gibson. *Doing Business with Banks: A Common Sense Guide for Small Business Borrowers.* Denver, CO: DBA/USA Press, 1991.

McNeil, Jane H., and Edward T. O'Leary. *Introduction to Commercial Lending.* American Bankers Association, 1983.

Rosenthal, James A., and Juan M. Ocampo. *Securitization of Credit: Inside the New Technology of Finance.* New York: Wiley, 1988.

Wray, L. Randall. *Money and Credit in Capitalist Economies: The Endogenous Money Approach.* Edward Elgar, 1990.

SEE ALSO: Credit Evaluation and Approval

CREDIT CARD FINANCING

Increasing numbers of entrepreneurs have turned to credit cards to finance their business ventures in recent years. Often, these credit cards were originally secured for personal use, but credit card issuers are targeting business owners for corporate cards as well. "Credit cards are one of the most overlooked resources for obtaining start-up capital," said the *Entrepreneur Magazine Guide to Raising Money.* "The downside is that most charge perilously high interest rates; but it is a way to get several thousand dollars

quickly without the hassle of dealing with paperwork."

Studies indicate that use of credit cards for small business purposes has surged dramatically in recent years. An estimated 15 to 20 percent of small businesses utilized personal credit cards for financing in the early 1990s, but that percentage had just about doubled by 1997. In fact, a 1997

Survey of Small and Mid-Sized Companies indicated that 34 percent of its respondents used credit-card financing to start or expand their businesses. The majority of these cards are for personal accounts, though credit card companies are making an effort to convert these holders to corporate accounts in many cases. According to *Inc.,* "credit-card issuers are no longer turning a blind eye to the use of personal cards for business purchases. Instead, they're aggressively pursuing small business owners in the hopes of selling them on corporate credit cards." The reasons for this new emphasis are fairly straightforward: annual fees are more common on corporate cards, corporate cards make it easier to establish long-term relationships with customers, and issuers can charge extra fees for multiple cards for a single account.

The reasons for the increase in credit card financing vary. Surely the single biggest factor is the explosion in overall credit card use. Consumer credit card issuers sent out approximately 2.5 billion applications in 1997 alone, and an estimated 450 million cards are currently in use in America (a nation that has a population of only 270 million). In addition, consumer credit limits increased by about 25 percent in 1997 over the previous year. But there are other reasons for the growing use of plastic by entrepreneurs. For one thing, many entrepreneurs contend that large banks habitually steer businesses that are looking for less than $10,000 to consumer loan departments. In addition, entrepreneurs commonly blame their use of credit cards on the reluctance of banks to provide loans. Moreover, using personal or corporate credit cards allows small business owners to skirt the bureaucratic paperwork associated with obtaining loans from banks or the U.S. Small Business Administration (SBA). Also, stories of entrepreneurial success that started with the use of credit card financing have proliferated in the business press in recent years, providing further encouragement to business owners weighing whether or not to take the plunge.

Once a small business owner begins using credit cards to pay off business expenses, he or she also may find that other benefits accrue. Accomplished managers of credit can use credit cards to stretch their payment periods, and many entrepreneurs have reaped hefty frequent-flier points through credit card use.

Nonetheless, *Inc.* contributor Phaedra Hise noted that "using credit cards is a riskier-than-usual way to finance your company. You have that huge bill to face every month, instead of several smaller ones that can be juggled. Once you max out, you can't pay your bills anymore. And the interest payments on carrying a balance can make a grown entrepreneur cry. . . . It's a short hop from weakness to bankruptcy. We talked to dozens of successful entrepreneurs who grew their businesses on credit cards, and every one had seen comrades choke and die on the stuff.'' And strictly speaking, using personal credit cards for business purposes violates the term of the consumer-cardholder credit agreement. Given these realities, even entrepreneurs who have parlayed their credit cards into business success caution fellow business owners to exhaust other financing options before turning to credit card financing.

If a small business owner does decide to use credit cards to finance a start up or expansion, Hise stated that they need to recognize that ''the real secret to credit card financing isn't just to juggle the cards and make the payments on time. It's this: parlay those personal credit cards into corporate-credit *history*. First, make the credit cards part of your financial plan. (Keep personal and business charges on separate cards.) Second, stick to it. Third, impress a bank with your financial management of the cards and earn a credit line.''

FURTHER READING:

Entrepreneur Magazine Guide to Raising Money. New York: John Wiley & Sons, 1998.

Hise, Phaedra. ''Don't Start a Business Without One.'' *Inc.* February 1998.

Meece, Mickey. ''20% of Small Businesses Obtain Financing Via Personal Credit Card.'' *American Banker.* February 13, 1996.

Mukherjee, Sougata. ''Credit Card Financing on Increase: Less Reliance on Banks, Study Shows.'' *Puget Sound Business Journal.* October 3, 1997.

Mukherjee, Sougata. ''Credit Cards Financing Many Small Businesses.'' *Washington Business Journal.* September 26, 1997.

Stolze, William J. *Start Up Financing: An Entrepreneur's Guide to Financing a New or Growing Business.* Franklin Lakes, NJ: Career Press, 1997.

Survey of Small and Mid-Sized Companies. Enterprise Group/ National Small Business United, 1997.

CREDIT EVALUATION AND APPROVAL

Credit evaluation and approval is the process a business or an individual must go through to become eligible for a loan or to pay for goods and services over an extended period. It also refers to the process businesses or lenders undertake when evaluating a request for credit. Granting credit approval depends on the willingness of the creditor to lend money in the current economy and that same lender's assessment of the ability and willingness of the borrower to return the money or pay for the goods obtained—plus interest—in a timely fashion. Typically, small businesses must seek credit approval to obtain funds from lenders, investors, and vendors, and also grant credit approval to their customers.

EVALUATING CREDIT WORTHINESS

In general, the granting of **credit** depends on the confidence the lender has in the borrower's credit worthiness. Credit worthiness—which encompasses the borrower's ability and willingness to pay—is one of many factors defining a lender's credit policies. Creditors and lenders utilize a number of financial tools to evaluate the credit worthiness of a potential borrower. When both lender and borrower are businesses, much of the evaluation relies on analyzing the borrower's balance sheet, cash flow statements, inventory turnover rates, debt structure, management performance, and market conditions. Creditors favor borrowers who generate net earnings in excess of debt obligations and any contingencies that may arise. Following are some of the factors lenders consider when evaluating an individual or business that is seeking credit:

Credit worthiness. A history of trustworthiness, a moral character, and expectations of continued performance demonstrate a debtor's ability to pay. Creditors give more favorable terms to those with high credit ratings via lower point structures and interest costs.

Size of debt burden. Creditors seek borrowers whose earning power exceeds the demands of the payment schedule. The size of the debt is necessarily limited by the available resources. Creditors prefer to maintain a safe ratio of debt to capital.

Loan size. Creditors prefer large **loans** because the administrative costs decrease proportionately to the size of the loan. However, legal and practical limitations recognize the need to spread the risk either by making a larger number of loans, or by having other lenders participate. Participating lenders must have adequate resources to entertain large loan applications. In addition, the borrower must have the capacity to ingest a large sum of money.

Frequency of borrowing. Customers who are frequent borrowers establish a reputation which directly impacts on their ability to secure debt at advantageous terms.

Length of commitment. Lenders accept additional risk as the time horizon increases. To cover some of the risk, lenders charge higher interest rates for longer term loans.

Social and community considerations. Lenders may accept an unusual level of risk because of the social good resulting from the use of the loan. Examples might include banks participating in low income housing projects or business incubator programs.

OBTAINING CREDIT APPROVAL FROM LENDERS

Many small business must rely on loans or other forms of credit to finance day-to-day purchases or long-term investments in facilities and equipment. Credit is one of the foundations of the American economy, and small businesses often must obtain credit in order to compete. To establish credentials for any credit approval process, from short-term loans to equity funding, a small business needs to have a business plan and a good credit history. The company must be able to show that it can repay the loan at the established interest rate. It must also demonstrate that the outlook for its type of business supports planned future projects and the reasons for borrowing.

In applying for credit, small business owners should realize that potential creditors—whether banks, vendors, or investors—will seek to evaluate both their ability and willingness to pay the amount owed. This means that the creditor will examine the character of the borrower as well as his or her ability to run a successful business. Creditors will also look at the size of the loan needed, the company's purpose in obtaining funds, and the means of repayment. Ideally, lenders evaluating a small business for credit approval like to see up-to-date books and business records, a large customer base, a history of prompt payment of obligations, and adequate insurance coverage.

According to Gibson Heath in his book *Doing Business with Banks: A Common Sense Guide for Small Business Borrowers,* many lenders compare a small business borrower's strengths and weaknesses when considering granting credit. Factors that are commonly considered to be strengths include profitability, good cash flow, the availability of collateral, professional contracts for sales and services, solid accounting practices, and good personal credit for the owners. On the other hand, factors that are considered weaknesses include past due taxes, poor bookkeeping practices, a history of slow payment to creditors, a lack of profitability, and being in business for less than three years.

The process of granting loans to businesses is regulated by the **Federal Trade Commission (FTC)** to ensure fairness and guarantee nondiscrimination and disclosure of all aspects of the process. The Small Business Administration (SBA) publishes a series of pamphlets and other information designed to assist businesses in obtaining loans. These publications advise businesses on a range of credit approval topics, including describing assets, preparing a business plan, and determining what questions to expect and how to prepare responses to those questions.

GRANTING CREDIT APPROVAL TO CUSTOMERS

Credit approval is also something that a small business is likely to provide for its customers, whether those customers are primarily individual consumers or other businesses. The process by which a small business grants credit to individuals is governed by a series of laws administered by the Federal Trade Commission that guarantee nondiscrimination and other benefits. These laws include the Equal Credit Opportunity Act, Fair Credit Reporting Act, Truth in Lending Act, and Fair Debt Collection Practices Act.

Experts recommend that small businesses develop credit policies that are consistent with overall company goals. In other words, a company's approach toward extending credit should be as conservative as its approach toward other business activities. While granting credit to customers can offer a small business a number of advantages, and in fact may be necessary for companies to increase sales and do volume business, it also involves risks. Some of the disadvantages of providing customers with credit include increasing the cost of operations and tying up capital that could be used elsewhere. There is also the risk of incurring losses due to nonpayment, and of eroding cash flow to an extent that requires borrowing. But granting credit does offer the advantage of creating a strong base of regular customers. In addition, credit applications provide important information about these customers that can be used in mailing lists and promotional activities. In the retail trade, furthermore, credit purchasers have proven to be less concerned with prices and inclined to buy more goods at one time.

When developing credit policies, small businesses must consider the cost involved in granting credit and the impact allowing credit purchases will have on cash flow. Before beginning to grant credit to customers, companies need to be sure that they can maintain enough working capital to pay operating expenses while carrying accounts receivable. If a small business does decide to grant credit, it should not merely adopt the policies that are typical of its industry. Blindly using the same credit policies as competitors does not offer a small business any advantage, and can even prove harmful if the company's situation is atypical. Instead, George O. Bancroft wrote in his *Practical Guide to Credit and Collec-*

tions, small businesses should develop an overall credit policy in accordance with its goals. This policy should be outlined in a company credit and collections procedures manual, along with detailed procedures for investigating potential credit customers and making the decision about whether to grant credit. The manual should also include standard credit application forms, acceptance and rejection letters, and other documents.

The decision about whether to grant credit to a certain customer must be evaluated on a case-by-case basis. The small business needs to gather and evaluate financial information, decide whether to grant credit and if so how much, and communicate the decision to the customer in a timely manner. At a minimum, the information gathered about a credit applicant should include their name and address, Social Security number (for individuals), bank and/or trade references, employment and income information (for individuals), and financial statements (for companies). The goal is to form an assessment of the character, reputation, financial situation, and collateral circumstances of the applicant.

CREDIT PROGRAMS FOR BUSINESS CUSTOMERS

There are many avenues available to small businesses for gathering information about credit applicants. In the case of business customers, a small business's sales force can often collect trade references and financial statements from potential customers. The small business can also contact local attorneys to find out about liens, claims, or actions pending against the applicant, and can hire independent accountants to verify financial information. An analysis of a company's debts, assets, and investments can provide a solid picture of its credit worthiness, particularly when the data is compared to a composite of companies of similar size in similar industries. It is important to note that all information gathered in the credit approval process should be held strictly confidential.

CREDIT PROGRAMS FOR INDIVIDUAL CONSUMERS

Consumer credit bureaus can provide a useful resource for small businesses in evaluating the credit worthiness of individual customers. These bureaus maintain records of consumers' experiences with banks, retailers, doctors, hospitals, finance companies, automobile dealers, etc. They are able to provide this information in the form of a computerized credit report, often with a weighted score. Still, credit bureau reports do have some potential for error, so small businesses should not necessarily use them as the only source of consumer credit information. It is also important to note that credit granted to consumers is subject to the federal Truth in Lending Law, as well as a number of other federal statutes.

Many small businesses, particularly in the retail trade, choose to participate in major credit card plans.

Allowing customers to pay with credit cards offers businesses a number of advantages. Since most large retailers provide this service to customers, accepting credit cards may help a small business to compete and to gain customers. In addition, customers are often tempted to spend more when they do not have to pay cash. The convenience of credit card purchases may also attract new business from travelers who do not wish to carry large sums of cash. Finally, credit card programs enable small businesses to receive payment more quickly than they could with an individual credit account system. The main disadvantage to participating in credit card plans is cost, which may include card reading and verification machinery, fees, and a percentage of sales. Credit cards also make it easier for customers to return merchandise or refuse to pay for items with which they are dissatisfied.

Another common type of consumer credit is an installment plan, which is commonly offered by sellers of durable goods such as furniture or appliances. After credit approval, the customer makes a down payment and takes delivery of the merchandise, then makes monthly payments to pay off the balance. The down payment should always be large enough to make the purchaser feel like an owner rather than a renter, and the payments should be timed so that the item is paid off at a faster rate than it is likely to depreciate from use. The merchandise acts as collateral and can be repossessed in the case of nonpayment. Although installment plans can tie up a small business's capital for a relatively long period of time, it is possible to transfer such contracts to a sales finance company for cash.

FURTHER READING:

Bancroft, George O. *A Practical Guide to Credit and Collection.* New York: American Management Association, 1989.

Bond, Cecil J. *Credit and Collections for Your Small Business.* Blue Summit, PA: Liberty House, 1989.

Dawson, George M. *Borrowing for Your Business: Winning the Battle for the Banker's ''Yes.''* Dover, NH: Upstart Publishing, 1991.

A Guide to Building a Better Credit Record. Washington, D.C.: U.S. Federal Trade Commission, n.d.

Heath, Gibson. *Doing Business with Banks: A Common Sense Guide for Small Business Borrowers.* Denver, CO: DBA/USA Press, 1991.

Hosmer, LaRue T. *A Venture Capital Primer for Small Business.* Washington, D.C.: U.S. Small Business Administration, 1990.

J.K. Lasser Institute. *How to Run a Small Business.* 6th ed. New York: McGraw-Hill, 1989.

Picker, Ida. ''The Ratings Game.'' *Institutional Investor.* August 1991.

Van Note, Mark. *The ABCs of Borrowing.* Washington, D.C.: U.S. Small Business Administration, 1990.

CRISIS MANAGEMENT

Crisis management is a business plan-of-action that is implemented quickly when a negative situation occurs. The Institute for Crisis Management defines a business crisis as a problem that: 1) disrupts the way an organization conducts business, and 2) attracts significant news media coverage and/or public scrutiny. Typically, these crises have the capacity to visit negative financial, legal, political, or governmental repercussions on the company, especially if they are not dealt with in a prompt and effective manner.

Over the past several years, high-profile public relations disasters (environmental disasters, various product recalls, product tampering incidents) have thrown an intense spotlight on the issue of crisis management. Indeed, as companies have witnessed the damage that poor crisis management can wreak on business fortunes, a growing percentage of firms have intensified their efforts to put effective crisis management strategies in place.

Hundreds of potential threats exist for every organization. Corporate crises can take the form of plant fires, loss of competitive secrets, workplace violence, product defects, embezzlement and extortion, industrial accidents, sabotage, and natural disasters. Any of these events—as well as numerous others—can cause an immediate and prolonged financial loss to a company, require an intensive communications effort directed to investors, employees, consumers and other entities, and may present a series of regulatory, community relations and competitive challenges. To assess whether a particular company has a higher exposure than others to categories of crisis, a company may employ a risk or crisis manager who may prepare statistical models, review industry data, or work with consultants to understand how one or more crises could affect the organization. Once this process of risk assessment is completed, many companies design a Crisis Management Plan (CMP) to determine how negative events can be avoided or reduced in scope. But business consultants and public relations experts counsel *all* companies to put CMPs in place, no matter how remote such threats seem. In fact, many businesses are able to secure lower insurance premiums if they have written crisis management procedures in place.

SUDDEN CRISIS AND SMOLDERING CRISIS

Robert B. Irvine, president of the Institute for Crisis Management, noted in *Communication World* that the Institute characterizes most business crises in two ways: sudden or smoldering. "We define a sud-

den crisis as a disruption in the company's business that occurs without warning and is likely to generate news coverage," he said. Examples of such events include business-related accidents, natural disasters, sudden death or disability of a key person, or workplace violence. Smoldering crises, meanwhile, are defined by the Institute as "any serious business problem that is not generally known within or without the company, which may generate negative news coverage if or when it goes 'public' and could result in more than U.S.$250,000 in fines, penalties, legal damage awards, unbudgeted expenses, and other costs." Examples of smoldering business crises include indications of significant regulatory action, government investigations, customer allegations, and media investigations. According to Irvine, while companies need to make sure that they prepare as best they can for sudden crises, it is often the slow-burning smoldering crisis that causes the most damage to a company's image and bottom line. "You really need to be focused on the less dramatic, more complicated, and ultimately more costly smoldering crises that are likely to be brewing in your business. The problem is that these smoldering crises often are the result of management decisions, or indecisions. They may be caused be shortcuts to win contracts, questionable actions by top producers or someone who has had an unblemished record with your organization and is close to retirement. In short, they often are tough to detect and then to resolve because they directly or indirectly involve management decisions, and management has a tough time admitting errors because it reflects on their egos and abilities."

SMALL BUSINESSES AND CRISIS MANAGEMENT

"A good image is a terrible thing to lose!" noted Bill Patterson in *Public Relations Journal.* "It has been said that 30 years of hard work can be destroyed in just 30 seconds." This grim truth is especially evident among small businesses that are rocked by crises, since they are less likely to have the deep financial pockets to weather unpleasant public relations developments. After all, business crises often throw multiple financial blows at companies. Diminished sales as a result of unfavorable publicity, and boycotts are the most widely recognized of these blows, but others can have a significant cumulative impact as well. Added expenses often come knocking in the areas of increased insurance premiums, recall/collection programs, reimbursements, attorneys' fees, and the need to retrieve lost customers through additional advertising.

But business consultants and public relations professionals agree that small business enterprises can do a lot to minimize the damage done by sudden flare-ups of bad news, provided they adhere to several fundamental rules of behavior.

PREPARATION BEFORE THE CRISIS Small businesses that are faced with public relations crises are far more likely to escape relatively unscathed if they can bring two weapons to bear: 1) a solid record as a good citizen, and 2) an already established crisis management strategy.

"Before the crisis, it is important to build **good will** and good relations on a daily basis," said media consultant Virgil Scudder in an interview with *Communication World.* "The way you are treated in a crisis, by the media and the public, will be determined in part by what they think of you at the beginning of the crisis situation." Writing in *Public Relations Journal,* Bill Patterson offered a similar assessment of the importance of building a "reservoir of good will" in the community: "The most important rule in defending, preserving, or enhancing a reputation is that you work at it all year long, regardless of whether or not a crisis strikes."

The other vital component of crisis management preparation is the creation of an intelligent and forceful **strategy** for dealing with various crises if they do occur. "For many executives, a crisis is something that happens to someone else," wrote Patterson. "It is a distant thought that can quickly be relegated to the back of the mind, replaced by concern for profit and productivity." But business owners and managers who choose to put off assembling a CMP do so at significant risk. Indeed, the hours and days immediately following the eruption of a crisis are often the most important in shaping public perception of the event. A company that has a good CMP in place is far more likely to make good use of this time than one that is forced into a pattern of response by on-the-spot improvisation, or one that offers little response at all in the hopes that the whole mess will just go away.

RESPONDING DURING THE CRISIS When a crisis does erupt, prompt and proactive communication should be a cornerstone of any crisis containment strategy. As Stephanie Smith and Kim Hunter pointed out in *Communication World,* "in the throes of a crisis, effective communication is crucial to a favorable public perception. Actions taken by a communicator during the first moments of a crisis can affect perceptions of an individual or company well after the crisis is resolved."

In order to ensure that your company's perspective is heard, it is vital that you do all you can to make sure that your message is accurately presented to any media providing coverage of the crisis. "Perception is truth," wrote Patterson. "And, even though most executives don't like it, the media establishes the perception of your organization. So, in this new public relations discipline of reputation management, deal-

ing with the media in an organized, aggressive, and timely fashion is mandatory." In addition, Scudder suggested that effective interaction with various media—radio, newspaper, television—is often predicated on realizing that representatives of those media outlets are not infallible. "There are two things you should not assume on the part of any journalist," he said. "Knowledge and perspective. Do not assume they know the facts. Tell them the facts. And if they know the facts, do not assume they know what the facts add up to."

Effective communication with media, then, is an essential element of any CMP. But consultants offer other tips as well. Following are a list of other actions that small businesses should take when confronted with a crisis management situation:

1) Be open and honest with media and customers alike—Such a stance may well garner sympathy with customers and consumers, particularly if the crisis is one over which the company has little control, such as malicious product tampering. "Take the perspective of the people who are out there," said Scudder. "Be candid, be truthful, and give people what they want to know."

2) React quickly—Scudder noted that a company's actions in the early stages of a crisis "will determine how the coverage of the client and the crisis goes and whether you are perceived as good guys who had an accident or bad guys."

3) Utilize only one spokesperson—Consultants can cite countless instances in which companies faced with a business crisis compounded their problems by using multiple spokespeople who gave conflicting statements. "Only one story must come from the company, and it must always be consistent," commented Patterson. "When you have several people talking to the media during a crisis, several versions of what happened usually end up in the various media. This confuses the public, often leading them to believe what you are saying is untrue."

4) Arm yourself with the facts—Companies can hurt themselves terribly when they make public statements based on incomplete knowledge of events.

5) Stay on message—Engaging in speculation and/or rambling discourses does not help your company's cause. Spokespeople should be candid without being unduly negative.

6) Do not lie or mislead the media, the public, or investigating agencies—The discovery of

one single lie casts every statement that your company makes into doubt.

7) Establish and maintain contact with other important groups—Depending on the nature of the crisis, communication with employee, industry, and community groups can be a valuable part of a crisis response plan. Is the crisis likely to have an affect on the company's labor union or general work force? If so, arrange a meeting with representatives so they can be kept informed and ask questions, and so you can get your message across. Is your company faced with an embarrassing allegation of racial discrimination or harassment? Perhaps a meeting with local religious and/or civil leaders would help (provided, of course, that your company signals a genuine interest in hearing their thoughts, so that they do not view the meeting as a cynical public relations ploy). Are your company's production processes arousing the ire of local civic or environmental groups (and the growing interest of local media)? Arranging a meeting in which they could register their concerns might relieve the situation somewhat (again, provided that your company shows a genuine interest in hearing them out and responding to legitimate concerns).

FURTHER READING:

Barton, Laurence. *Crisis In Organizations: Managing And Communicating In The Heat of Chaos.* SouthWestern Publishing, 1993.

Bryan, Jerry L. ''The Coming Revolution in Issues Management: Elevate and Simplify.'' *Communication World.* July 15, 1997.

Clark, Susan. ''Don't Walk Away . . .'' *Super Marketing.* June 16, 1995.

Irvine, Robert B. ''What's a Crisis, Anyway?'' *Communication World.* July 15, 1997.

Patterson, Bill. ''Crises Impact on Reputation Management.'' *Public Relations Journal.* November 1993.

Peak, Martha H. ''The Alaskan Oil Spill: Lessons in Crisis Management.'' *Management Review.* April 1990.

Smith, Stephanie, and Kim Hunter. ''Virgil Scudder Tackles Crisis Tactics.'' *Communication World.* February 1997.

SEE ALSO: Disaster Planning

CROSS-CULTURAL/INTERNATIONAL COMMUNICATION

Business is not conducted in an identical fashion from culture to culture. Consequently, business relations are enhanced when managerial, sales, and technical personnel are trained to be aware of areas likely to create communication difficulties and conflict across cultures. Similarly, international communication is strengthened when businesspeople can anticipate areas of commonality. Finally, business in general is enhanced when people from different cultures find new approaches to old problems, creating solutions by combining cultural perspectives and learning to see issues from the viewpoint of others.

ETHNOCENTRISM Problems in business communication conducted across cultures often arise when participants from one culture are unable to understand culturally determined differences in communication practices, traditions, and thought processing. At the most fundamental level, problems may occur when one or more of the people involved clings to an ethnocentric view of how to conduct business. Ethnocentrism is the belief that one's own cultural group is somehow innately superior to others.

It is easy to say that ethnocentrism only affects the bigoted or those ignorant of other cultures, and so is unlikely to be a major factor in one's own business communication. Yet difficulties due to a misunderstanding of elements in cross-cultural communication may affect even enlightened people. Ethnocentrism is deceptive precisely because members of any culture perceive their own behavior as logical, since that behavior works for them. People tend to accept the values of the culture around them as absolute values. Since each culture has its own set of values, often quite divergent from those values held in other cultures, the concept of proper and improper, foolish and wise, and even right and wrong become blurred. In international business, questions arise regarding what is proper by which culture's values, what is wise by which culture's view of the world, and what is right by whose standards.

Since no one individual is likely to recognize the subtle forms of ethnocentrism that shape who he or she is, international business practitioners must be especially careful in conducting business communication across cultures. It is necessary to try to rise above culturally imbued ways of viewing the world. To do this, one needs to understand how the perception of a given message changes depending on the culturally determined viewpoint of those communicating.

FACTORS AFFECTING CROSS-CULTURAL BUSINESS COMMUNICATION

The communication process in international business settings are filtered through a range of variables, each of which can color perceptions on the part of both parties. These include language, environment, technology, social organization, social history and mores, conceptions of authority, and nonverbal communication behavior.

By assessing in advance the roles these variables play in business communication, one can improve one's ability to convey messages and conduct business with individuals in a wide range of cultures.

LANGUAGE

Among the most often cited barriers to conflict-free cross-cultural business communication is the use of different languages. It is difficult to underestimate the importance that an understanding of linguistic differences plays in international business communication. Given this reality, business consultants counsel clients to take the necessary steps to enlist the services of a good translator. Language failures between cultures typically fall into three categories: 1) gross translation problems; 2) subtle distinctions from language to language; and 3) culturally-based variations among speakers of the same language.

Gross translation errors, though frequent, may be less likely to cause conflict between parties than other language difficulties for two reasons. Indeed, the nonsensical nature of many gross translation errors often raise warning flags that are hard to miss. The parties can then backtrack and revisit the communication area that prompted the error. Even if they are easily detected in most cases, however, gross translation errors waste time and wear on the patience of the parties involved. Additionally, for some, such errors imply a form of disrespect for the party into whose language the message is translated.

The subtle shadings that are often crucial to business negotiations are also weakened when the parties do not share a similar control of the same language. Indeed, misunderstandings may arise because of dialectical differences within the same language. When other parties with full control over the language with whom the nonnative speaker communicates assume that knowledge of this distinction exists, conflict deriving from misunderstanding is likely.

Attitudes toward accents and dialects also create barriers in international business communication. The view that a particular accent suggests loyalty or familiarity to a nation or region is widespread in many languages. The use of Parisian French in Quebec, of Mexican Spanish in Spain, or subcontinental Indian English in the United States are all noticeable, and may suggest a lack of familiarity, even if the user is fluent. More importantly, regional ties or tensions in such nations as Italy, France, or Germany among others can be suggested by the dialect a native speaker uses.

Finally, national prejudices and class distinctions are often reinforced thorough sociolinguistics—the social patterning of language. For example, due to regional prejudice and racism certain accents in the United States associated with urban areas, rural regions, or minorities may reinforce negative stereotypes in areas like business ability, education level, or intelligence. Similarly, some cultures use sociolinguistics to differentiate one economic class from another. Thus, in England, distinct accents are associated with the aristocracy and the middle and lower classes. These distinctions are often unknown by foreigners.

ENVIRONMENT AND TECHNOLOGY

The ways in which people use the resources available to them may vary considerably from culture to culture. Culturally-ingrained biases regarding the natural and technological environment can create communication barriers.

ISSUES OF ENVIRONMENT Many environmental factors can have a heavy influence on the development and character of cultures. Indeed, climate, topography, population size and density, and the relative availability of natural resources all contribute to the history and current conditions of individual nations or regions. After all, notions of transportation and logistics, settlement, and territorial organization are affected by topography and climate. For example, a mountainous country with an abundance of natural waterways will almost certainly develop different dominant modes of transportation than a dry, land-locked region marked by relatively flat terrain. Whereas the first nation would undoubtedly develop shipping-oriented transportation methods, the latter would concentrate on roadways, railroads, and other surface-oriented options.

Population size and density and the availability of natural resources influence each nation's view toward export or domestic markets as well. Nations with large domestic markets and plentiful natural resources, for example, are likely to view some industries quite differently than regions with that have only one (or none) of those characteristics.

ISSUES OF TECHNOLOGY Some businesspeople fail to modify their cross-cultural communications to accommodate environmental differences because of inflexibility toward culturally learned views of technology. Indeed, cultures have widely divergent views of technology and its role in the world. In *control cultures,* such as those in much of Europe and North America, technology is customarily viewed as an innately positive means for controlling the environment. In *subjugation cultures,* such as those of central Africa and southwestern Asia, the existing environment is viewed as innately positive, and technology is viewed with some skepticism. In *harmonization cultures,* such as those common in many Native American cultures and some East Asian nations, a balance is attempted between the use of technology and the existing environment. In these cultures, neither technology nor the environment are innately good and members of such cultures see themselves as part of the environment in which they live, being neither subject to it nor master of it. Of course, it is dangerous to over-generalize about the guiding philosophies of societies as well. For example, while the United States may historically be viewed as a control culture that holds that technology is a positive that improves society, there are certainly a sizable number of voices within that culture that do not subscribe to that point of view.

SOCIAL ORGANIZATION AND HISTORY

Social organization, as it affects the workplace, is often culturally determined. One must take care not to assume that the view held in one's own culture is universal on such issues as nepotism and kinship ties, educational values, class structure and social mobility, job status and economic stratification, religious ties, political affiliation, gender differences, racism and other prejudices, attitudes toward work, and recreational or work institutions.

All of these areas have far-reaching implications for business practice. Choosing employees based on résumés, for example, is considered a primary means of selection in the United States, Canada, and much of northern Europe—all nations with comparatively weak concepts of familial relationships and kinship ties. In these cultures, nepotism is seen as subjective and likely to protect less qualified workers through familial intervention. By contrast, it would seem anywhere from mildly to highly inappropriate to suggest to members of many Arabic, central African, Latin American, or southern European cultures to skip over hiring relatives to hire a stranger. For people in these cultures, nepotism both fulfills personal obligations and ensures a predictable level of trust and accountability. The fact that a stranger appears to be better qualified based on a superior resume and a relatively brief interview would not necessarily affect that belief. Similarly, the nature of praise and employee motivation can be socially determined, for different cultures have settled upon a wide array of employee reward systems, each of which reflect the social histories and values of those cultures.

Finally, it is often difficult to rid business communication of a judgmental bias when social organization varies markedly. For example, those from the United States may find it difficult to remain neutral on cultural class structures that do not reflect American values of equality. For instance, the socially determined inferior role of women in much of the Islamic world, or of lower castes in India—to name just two—may puzzle or anger Western citizens. Nevertheless, if the Western businessperson cannot eliminate the attendant condemnation from his or her business communication, then he or she cannot expect to function effectively in that society. An individual may personally believe that a country's social system is inefficient or incorrect. Nevertheless, in the way that individual conducts business on a daily basis, it is necessary to work within the restraints of that culture to succeed. One may choose not to do business with people from such a culture, but one cannot easily impose one's own values on them and expect to succeed in the business arena.

CONCEPTIONS OF AUTHORITY

Different cultures often view the distribution of authority in their society differently. Geert Hofstede, the Dutch international business researcher, has called this dimension of cultural variation ''power distance,'' defining this as ''the extent to which a society accepts the fact that power in institutions and organizations is distributed unequally.''

Views of authority in a given society affects communication in the business environment significantly, since it shapes the view of how a message will be received based on the relative status or rank of the message's sender to its receiver. In other words, conceptions of authority influence the forms that managerial and other business communications take. In working with cultures such as Israel and Sweden, which have a relatively decentralized authority conception or small ''power distance,'' one might anticipate greater acceptance of a participative communication management model than in cultures such as France and Belgium, which generally make less use of participative management models, relying instead on authority-based decision making.

NONVERBAL COMMUNICATION

Among the most markedly varying dimensions of intercultural communication is **nonverbal communication**. Knowledge of a culture conveyed through what a person says represents only a portion of what that person has communicated. Indeed, body language, clothing choices, eye contact, touching behavior, and conceptions of personal space all communicate information, no matter what the culture. A prudent business person will take the time to learn what the prevailing attitudes are in such areas before conducting businesses in an unfamiliar culture (or with a representative of that culture).

SMALL BUSINESS AND INTERNATIONAL COMMUNICATION

As business has turned more and more to an integrated world market to meet its needs, the difficulties of communicating at a global level have become increasingly widespread. Lack of understanding deriving from ethnocentrism or ignorance of culturally based assumptions erroneously believed to be universal can readily escalate to unproductive conflict among people of differing cultural orientation. Still, in an increasingly competitive world economy, it is harder for the successful business venture to conduct business exclusively within the safe confines of a single domestic business environment. Consequently, the need for dealing with intercultural differences and cross-cultural communication barriers has grown as well.

Small business owners and representatives face a sometimes dizzying array of communication considerations when they decide to move into the international arena, but most issues can be satisfactorily addressed by respectfulness toward all people you meet and research on current business etiquette, cultural and customer sensitivities, current events, and relevant history.

FURTHER READING:

Chan-Herur, K. C. *Communicating with Customers Around the World: A Practical Guide to Effective Cross-Cultural Business Communication.* San Francisco, CA: AuMonde International, 1994.

Hall, Edward T. *The Dance of Life: The Other Dimension of Time.* Garden City, NY: Anchor Press/Doubleday, 1984.

Hall, Edward T. *The Silent Language.* Greenwich, CT: Fawcett Publications, 1959.

Hofstede, Geert. *Culture's Consequences: International Differences in Work-Related Values.* Beverly Hills, CA: Sage Publications, 1984.

Hofstede, Geert. *Cultures and Organizations: Software of the Mind.* London: McGraw-Hill, 1991.

Ricks, David A. *Big Business Blunders: Mistakes in Multinational Marketing.* Homewood, IL: Dow-Jones Irwin, 1983.

Victor, David A. *International Business Communication.* New York: Harper Collins, 1992.

SEE ALSO: Corporate Culture; International Marketing; Multicultural Work Force

CROSS-FUNCTIONAL TEAMS

The most simple definition of cross-functional teams (or CFTs) is teams that are made up of people from different functional areas within a company—marketing, engineering, sales, and human resources, for example. These teams take many forms, but they are most often set up as working groups that are designed to make decisions at a lower level than is customary in a given company. They can be either a company's primary form of **organization structure**, or they can exist in addition to the company's main hierarchical structure.

Cross-functional teams have become more popular in recent years for three primary reasons: they improve coordination and integration, span organizational boundaries, and reduce the production cycle time in new product development. Bringing people together from different disciplines can improve problem solving and lead to more thorough decision making. They foster a spirit of cooperation that can make it easier to achieve customer satisfaction and corporate goals at the same time.

Cross-functional teams are not new. Northwestern Mutual Life insurance company pioneered their use in the 1950s when the CEO of the company brought together people from the financial, investment, actuarial, and other departments to study the impact that computers would have on the business world. As a result of that first CFT, Northwestern was among the first companies in the country to create an information systems department that gave the company a large competitive advantage as computers gained in popularity. The company now relies on cross-functional teams in almost every facet of its organization. Based on success stories like this one, CFTs slowly grew in popularity throughout the 1960s and 1970s before exploding in popularity in the 1980s, when faster production time and increased organizational performance became critical in almost every industry.

Cross-functional teams are similar to conventional work teams, but they differ in several important ways. First, they are usually composed of members who have competing loyalties and obligations to their primary subunit within the company (for example, a marketing person serving on a cross-functional team has strong ties to his or her home department that may conflict with the role he or she is being asked to play on the CFT). Second, in companies where CFTs are being used on a part-time basis as opposed to a permanent organizational structure, they are often temporary groups organized for one important purpose, which means group members are often under considerable pressure. On these temporary teams, the early development of stable and effective group interaction is imperative. Finally, CFTs are often held to higher performance standards than conventional teams. Not only are they expected to perform a task or produce a product, but they are also expected to reduce cycle time, create knowledge about the CFT process, and disseminate that knowledge throughout the organization.

For cross-functional teams to succeed, several factors have been identified that are imperative:

- Team members must be open-minded and highly motivated.

- Team members must come from the correct functional areas.

- A strong team leader with excellent communication skills and a position of authority is needed.

- The team must have both the authority and the accountability to accomplish the mission it has been given.

- Management must provide adequate resources and support for the team, both moral and financial.

- Adequate communications must exist.

Without these elements, any cross-functional team will be fighting an uphill battle to succeed.

CROSS-FUNCTIONAL TEAMS AND NEW PRODUCT DEVELOPMENT

Many businesses have been able to use cross-functional teams to reduce the cycle time in new product development. As a result, CFTs have become a common tool in new product development at many companies, especially those in industries in which rapid change and innovation are the norm. CFTs have shown the flexibility to adapt to changing market needs and the ability to more quickly develop innovative products.

In the past, new product development invariably meant gathering data sequentially from a number of departments before a new product was given the green light. First, the idea would be conceptualized. Then, it would be handed off to the marketing department, which would conduct market research to see if the product was viable. The product might then be passed on to the sales department, which would be asked to create a sales estimate. From there, the idea would move on to engineering or manufacturing, which would determine the costs to produce the product. Finally, with all those numbers gathered over the course of months, or even years, the product would move to an executive committee which would either approve or kill the project. By that time, market conditions sometimes had shifted sufficiently to render the product obsolete.

Cross-functional teams eliminate the ''throw it over the wall'' mentality that passes a product from department to department. Instead, each of the functional areas would have a representative on the new product team. Team members would learn of the new product at the same time and would begin working on estimates together. If part of the product simply could not be manufactured cheaply enough, the team member from that area could immediately sit down with the engineering representative and come up with a new production method. The two of them could then meet with the marketing and sales team members and discuss new ways to position the product on the market. The result, say proponents, is a vastly improved product that is manufactured and released to the market in far less time than was achieved using traditional methods.

ESTABLISHING A CROSS-FUNCTIONAL TEAM

SET GOALS When CFTs are first convened, conflict may result. There is a good chance that some of the members of the new team have bumped heads in the past when their functional areas clashed over a project. Additionally, some CFT members may think that their area of specialty is the most important on the team and thus assume an inflated sense of value to the team. Finally, since CFTs often bring together people who have vastly different ranks in the organizational hierarchy, there can be power plays by members who are high-ranking employees off the team but are actually less important stakeholders on the team. Those high-ranking team members may try to assert authority over the team in a situation when they should be deferring to lower-ranking team members.

The best way to solve these conflicts is to set clear goals for the team. It is important to start with a general goal, such as improving quality, but more specific goals should be set almost immediately to give the group a common bond and to ensure that everyone is working together towards the goal. Goals are easier to establish if research has been conducted by someone in the organization before the team is convened. This allows the team to jump right into goal-setting and problem-solving without getting bogged down in background research.

When setting goals, it is important to clearly define the problem that needs to be solved, not the solution that needs to be achieved. If the desired solution is held up as the outcome, then the group's focus becomes too narrow—the range of options is narrowed to fit that solution before the team even begins its work. Also, when setting goals, the team should determine if there are operating limits that it faces. For example, are there time or budget limitations that have to be considered? Are there some solutions that have been deemed undesirable by the company's officers? The team must recognize these limitations and work around them if it hopes to be successful in reaching its goal.

The final thing to do when goal-setting will identify key interdependencies on the team—does one team member have to finish his or her part of the project before another team member can get started? It is essential to know these sequential steps before a team gets too deep into its project.

WORK WITH KEY STAKEHOLDERS Stakeholders are those who stand to benefit or lose from the work of the team. Every stakeholder should be represented on the team, and it is these stakeholders who can make or break the team. For example, if a key department head does not believe that the team is needed, he or she can withhold his or her best employees from participating on the team, thus depriving the team of resources. Or, that department head can choose to ignore the work of the team, conducting business as usual because the team threatens his or her traditional role in the company. It is up to the business ownership, management, and key CFT members to make all stakeholders understand the importance of the team and its purpose and priorities.

Customers, whether internal or external, are also stakeholders. Teams should spend the maximum allowable time interacting with customers to learn their needs and what outcomes they expect from the team. Some CFTs find it works best if one person is named to act as customer liaison because it makes it easier for customers to provide the team with feedback and it allows the team to have one person go through training in client management skills. Other businesses have had success in letting customers either join the team or attend team meetings as an observer.

When identifying stakeholders, determine what level of representation each group needs on the team. Some groups will need permanent members, others may only need to participate in certain areas of the project. Communicate with all stakeholders and anyone else in the company who is affected by the team's work. Do not spring surprises—this will make people resistant to the work that the team is trying to achieve. Communication steps should be decided upon upfront and planned as carefully as any other part of the project.

Northwestern Mutual Life, one of the leaders in CFTs, has expanded the stakeholder idea. When it used to create a CFT, Northwestern followed the traditional model and appointed only those people whose roles were crucial to the process at hand. That is no longer the case. Now, Northwestern is experimenting with appointing one person to each CFT who is not a stakeholder at all. Colleen Stenholt, director of human resources at Northwestern, was quoted in *Getting Results* magazine as saying that ''One of our goals is to break out of the box, and the stakeholders are the people who built the box.'' She went on to note that outsiders are desirable because they are not locked into an established way of thinking and are often thus able to bring a fresh perspective to a problem.

DEAL WITH TEAM CONFLICT Because of the reasons mentioned above under goal-setting, and for many other reasons, CFTs often face conflict situations. This is especially true of cross-functional teams that are relatively new. Business owners and managers should be aware, however, that important steps can be taken to manage and reduce conflict, including:

- Providing all team members with conflict resolution training. Conflicts can have value if managed properly, so improving team members' listening and consensus-building skills is necessary.

- Make sure that the company's human resources personnel are involved in the team-building process to help teach facilitation and group dynamics skills.

- Disregard the rank or perceived status of each group member and have standards in place that put value on what every team member brings to the CFT.

- Co-locate the team members. Putting team members together on an everyday basis strengthens communication and breaks down barriers.

CROSS-FUNCTIONAL TEAMS AND SMALL BUSINESS

Many people think that cross-functional teams are only successful in large companies. Conventional wisdom dictates that small companies are probably already operating cross-functionally out of necessity—i.e., the company is so small that people have to perform multiple tasks and work together with everyone else in the company. While that may be true in start-up operations, it is certainly not true of the majority of small businesses. Most small operations have to weigh the pros and cons just like their larger counterparts when deciding whether or not to use CFTs. Those that have chosen to adopt CFTs have been largely pleased with the results.

For example, *Getting Results* magazine documented the use of CFTs by Reprint Management Services of Lancaster, Pennsylvania, a small company with fewer than 30 employees. The owner of the business originally arranged his company into functional units, but found that he had an odd assortment of employees left over who did not fit into any of the existing teams. As a result, he created a permanent cross-functional team to handle special projects at the company. The results were immediate and impressive. He claimed that since adopting the cross-functional team concept:

- Employees in support roles are more concerned with profits and ways to increase sales. They now realize that the more the company succeeds, the more they benefit directly.

- People communicate more openly and are more helpful to each other. There is a far greater sense of teamwork instead of each person looking our for number one.

- Employees' problem-solving skills have improved dramatically, and it is easier to build consensus for a given solution.

- People are more likely to speak out and point out problems. Before the CFT, people were more likely to be passive and quiet, reasoning that the problem was not their responsibility.

- People recognize that there is strength in diversity—that not everyone has to agree on an issue. They know they are being understood, but that some people may still choose to disagree with them, and that such differences are acceptable.

Staff members have also benefitted from the CFT arrangement. Employees now understand the different processes that occur throughout the organization and understand the interrelationships between different functional areas. Instead of looking only at their one "silo" of operations, employees now see the big picture. Indeed, according to CFT supporters, participating employees often improve their interpersonal and problem-solving skills, which make them better employees and makes them more attractive on the job market should they choose to pursue other opportunities. Finally, proponents say that employees are less likely to become bored with their own job when they are given the opportunity to learn new skills on the CFT.

COMPENSATION AND CROSS-FUNCTIONAL TEAMS

The overall goal of cross-functional teams is increased organizational profits through teamwork. As a result, companies have had to develop new **employee compensation** systems to reward members of cross-functional teams. One example of this is team incentive pay. Instead of individual merit increases, team members instead earn rewards based on overall team performance. The incentive pool is funded by increased profits and new business that are created as a result of using teams. The amount of compensation that can be earned in the team incentive model is actually far greater than that which can be obtained in the standard individual merit pay system.

Another system that has proven popular in organizations that utilize CFTs is the system called Pay for Applied Services (PAS). Under this system, employees who learn and apply new skills have their base pay increased. In addition, performance bonuses are available if their teams and the company perform better than expected. PAS works this way: employees identify their "primary service," i.e., their basic job skill or title. This primary service determines the person's entry-level salary. A salary range is deter-

mined for all people who provide that primary service, ranging from entry-level to maximum based on experience and performance. Employees can increase their salary the traditional way, by gaining increases within their service range, or they can learn new services and qualify for bonuses or increases. In addition to individual increases, employees can earn team incentive bonuses that total up to 10 percent of base pay. Team incentives are paid out once per year.

DRAWBACKS TO CROSS-FUNCTIONAL TEAMS

Cross-functional teams have become an integral part of the business landscape in many industries in recent years. Observers point out, however, that their use can have unintended drawbacks if companies are not watchful.

For example, analysts note that CFTs can actually limit the professional growth of team members because they have a narrow focus on one area. One company profiled in *Nation's Business* found that after two years of serving on the same team, team members were becoming bored and were learning only about the clients or the business categories handled by their team. The solution? Once or twice every year, team members were reorganized into new teams so that they could learn new skills. As a result of the new team environment, revenue-per-employee rose 70 percent, while clients reported in questionnaires that the company's performance met or exceeded their goals 97 percent of the time. Ninety-two percent of clients rated the company better than the competition when it came to service.

Some companies try to hand off projects to CFTs that are simply too large in scope and are essentially doomed to failure from the start. Such large projects lack the focus needed for CFT success, and trying to make such a project work in that environment can sour an entire organization on using CFTs for other projects. Another sure pitfall is to establish a CFT without imposing either project deadlines or interim reporting deadlines. Without a sense of urgency to complete a project, the project will almost certainly stall and fail.

Converting employees to a new compensation system when CFTs are implemented can be difficult as well. When team incentives replace individual merit increases, team members often complain, even though more money can be earned in the team-based system. Employees often feel that they have very little control over whether or not the company's profits actually increase, therefore they have no control over earning a raise. Additionally, many employees balk at giving up their own merit increase for the sake of the team. They may see the team plan as a way to demand more from teams than from individuals without giving anything back in return.

FURTHER READING:

Andrews, Katherine Zoe. "Cross-Functional Teams: Are they Always the Right Move?" *Harvard Business Review*. November-December 1995.

Chaudron, David. "Organizational Development: How to Improve Cross-Functional Teams." *HR Focus*. August 1995.

Hendricks, Mark. "Golden Rules: Top Management Strategies of the Past 20 Years—And What Still Works." *Entrepreneur*. May 1997.

Hultman, Kenneth E. "The 10 Commandments of Team Leadership (Training 101: It's a Team Effort)." *Training & Development*. February 1998.

Kezsbom, Deborah S. "Making a Team Work: Techniques for Building Successful Cross-Functional Teams." *Industrial Engineering*. January 1995.

Leshner, Martin. "Targeting Work Culture Leads to Winning Teams." *Best's Review—Property-Casualty Insurance Edition*. February 1996.

McCartney, Laton. "A Team Effort." *Information Week*. December 18, 1995.

McNerney, Donald J. "Compensation Case Study: Rewarding Team Performance and Individual Skillbuilding." *HR Focus*. January 1995.

Maynard, Roberta. "A Client-Centered Firm's Lesson in Team Work." *Nation's Business*. March 1997.

Parker, Glenn M. "Cross-Functional Teams." *Small Business Reports*. October 1994.

Proehl, Rebecca A. "Cross-Functional Teams: A Panacea or Just Another Headache?" *Supervision*. July 1996.

"Recipe for Success: Cross-Functional Teams + Project Management Skills." *Getting Results*. October 1996.

Sharf, Stephan. "Teams Aren't the End-All: Is Management Abdicating Its Responsibilities?" *Ward's Auto World*. January 1998.

Swamidass, Paul M., and Dayne M. Aldridge. "Ten Rules for Timely Task Completion in Cross-Functional Teams." *Research-Technology Management*. July-August 1996.

SEE ALSO: Product Life Cycle; Training and Development

CROSS-TRAINING

Cross-training involves teaching an employee who was hired to perform one job function the skills required to perform other job functions. "Simply put, cross-trained employees become skilled at tasks outside the usual parameters of their jobs," Lynda Rogerson noted in an article for *Small Business Reports*. "Cross-trained workers might focus their efforts on one process. Or, you could set up a systematic job-rotation plan and train workers to become proficient in a variety of functions."

Cross-training offers a wide variety of benefits for small businesses. For example, a well-designed program can help reduce **costs**, improve employee morale, reduce turnover, and increase **productivity**. It can also give a company greater scheduling flexibility, and may even lead to operational improvements. Perhaps the most important benefit to companies that implement cross-training programs, however, is greater job satisfaction among employees. Cross-training demonstrates that the company has faith in employees' abilities and wants to provide them with opportunities for career growth. In an age when companies are always trying to accomplish more work with fewer workers, anything that helps to motivate and retain employees can be worthwhile. "Cross-trained employees usually feel that their jobs have been enriched, and they often suggest creative and cost-effective improvements," Rogerson noted. "Cross-training can lead to productivity gains that help you stay competitive."

For small businesses with limited manpower and resources, cross-training can also enable operations to continue if a key employee becomes ill or requires a leave of absence. "The serious illness of a key executive in a small company can spell disaster for the firm—unless that person has trained others to conduct operations smoothly during an extended absence," Thomas Love wrote in an article for *Nation's Business*. "While you could always hire a temporary worker to replace an employee, that may not be the best solution if the job requires technical skill or an in-depth knowledge of your operations," Rogerson added.

The ability of cross-trained employees to fill in during absences, vacations, and peak demand periods can reduce the costs involved in hiring and training temporary workers or new employees. "By cross-training, a person on staff already knows and can perform the needed job functions," Brian Gill explained in an article for *American Printer*. "Recruiting costs also can be reduced since cross-training supplies the company with internally qualified applicants who are ready and willing to move into a new position. Being able to promote qualified candidates internally also will reduce overall orientation costs. Although external hiring cannot be completely eliminated, cross-training will decrease the need to look outside."

Cross-training can also improve the overall work atmosphere in a small business, which may in turn improve the bottom line. Employees are a valuable asset in small businesses, which often must maintain only a bare-bones staff in order to remain competitive. This makes it even more important to make maximum use of employees' skills and talents. "Investing in on-the-job training clearly proves that individual career growth is a valuable and necessary part of the company's overall growth," Gill wrote. "If employees believe they have the potential to improve within the company, they will be more willing to learn new skills. Employees will be more productive and loyal, and overall morale will improve.''

IMPLEMENTING A CROSS-TRAINING PROGRAM

To be effective, a cross-training program must be carefully planned and organized. It cannot be implemented during a crisis. There are a number of decisions that a company must make before the program can get started. For example, it is important to decide who will be eligible for training, whether the training will be mandatory or voluntary, whether the training will be restricted within job classifications or open to other classifications, and whether it will be administered internally or externally. Prior to implementation, Gill noted, it might be helpful to set up a task force of consisting of both management and employees to research the pros and cons of cross-training for the business, assess the feasibility of setting up a program, work out the implementation issues, and set up a realistic schedule for each position.

Rogerson suggested that small business owners begin by having each different area or department draw up a list of functions and tasks that are necessary to its day-to-day operations. Then the various tasks can be prioritized to decide which should be included in the cross-training program. "This helps match employees to the functions and tasks that need cross-training coverage," she explained. "Be sure to have each employee review these lists to identify the functions/tasks they already know how to do, those they would like to learn, and those they would be willing to learn if necessary. That way, you can consider both competence and interest in the matching process.''

Rather than simply training one employee to perform another one's job—which would not really solve the problem if the first employee experienced a long absence—it may be better to train several employees in various components of the first one's job so that they can all pitch in as needed. Training can take place through an on-the-job buddy system, or supervisors can be asked to conduct all the training. It is important to note that those selected as trainers may need to receive instruction in how to teach others. Rogerson noted that adult learning courses are available at many community colleges or through training organizations. Finally, cross-trained employees must be given the time they need to absorb the new information. Their workload should be reduced both during the training and during later practice sessions so that they will not feel as if they are being penalized for participating in the program. It may also be helpful to evaluate newly trained employees' progress on a regular basis.

SUCCESS FACTORS

One of the most important factors in the success of any cross-training initiative is gaining the full support of top management. "To be truly dedicated to cross-training, the traditional idea of one job per person must be replaced with a broader definition," Gill explained. It is also vital to involve employees who are already performing the job in the training process. "Employees will be able to share their thoughts and opinions on how to properly train others for the same job," according to Gill. Besides making employees feel included, involving them in training will help prevent them from feeling like their job may be in jeopardy. "It is extremely important to communicate to employees that cross-training is not a management scheme designed to eliminate jobs and that it is a benefit to both the individual employee and the company," Gill stated.

Creating a successful cross-training program is not necessarily easy, and small business owners should expect to encounter some resistance from employees. One way to help ease acceptance of such a program is to address compensation issues ahead of time. Companies must be willing to compensate employees for increasing their skills. In some cases, instituting pay-for-skill or pay-for-knowledge programs may help encourage people to participate. It may also be helpful to promote people who learn new skills to a new grade in a graded-pay system, or to attach a dollar value to specific skills and then pay employees for the time they spend cross-training on a higher-paying skill. Employees must be made to feel that their efforts are being recognized for a cross-training program to be successful.

In her article, Rogerson outlined several potential pitfalls that companies need to avoid in order to implement a successful cross-training initiative. One of the major pitfalls is trying to establish a program without taking a systematic approach. Some other potential pitfalls include failure to include employees in planning the program, trying to coerce the participation of reluctant employees, assuming that employees are familiar with the techniques needed to train others, penalizing employees who take part in cross-training by not reducing their workload accordingly, and not recognizing the value of new skills with appropriate changes in compensation.

FURTHER READING:

Craig, Robert L., ed. *Training and Development Handbook: A Guide to Human Resource Development.* New York: McGraw-Hill, 1987.

Fryer, Bronwyn. "Find and Nurture Employees." *Working Woman.* May 1997.

Gill, Brian. "Cross-Training Can Be a Win-Win Plan." *American Printer.* October 1997.

Goldstein, Irwin L., ed. *Training and Development in Organizations.* San Francisco, CA: Jossey-Bass, 1989.

Love, Thomas. "Keeping the Business Going When an Executive Is Absent." *Nation's Business.* March 1998.

Maurer, Rick. "Options in Work Force Planning." *Supervision.* May 1997.

Rogerson, Lynda. "Cover Your Bases." *Small Business Reports.* July 1993.

SEE ALSO: Corporate Culture; Employee Reward Systems; Training and Development

CUSTOMER RETENTION

Customer retention refers to the percentage of customer relationships that, once established, a small business is able to maintain on a long-term basis. It is a major contributing factor in the net growth rate of small businesses. For example, a company that increases its number of new customers by 20 percent in a year but retains only 85 percent of its existing customers will have a net growth rate of only five percent (20 percent increase less 15 percent decrease). But the company could triple that rate by retaining 95 percent of its clients.

"Of course, growth is just one of the benefits experienced by companies with superior retention rates," William A. Sherden explained in an article for *Small Business Reports.* "Your profits also should improve considerably when customers stay on board for longer periods of time. The cost of acquiring customers and putting them on the books generally runs two to four times the annual cost of serving existing customers. So the longer you keep customers, the more years over which these one-time costs can be spread."

A variety of strategies are available to small business owners seeking to improve their customer retention rates. Of course, the most basic tools for retaining customers are providing superior product and service quality. High quality products and services minimize the problems experienced by customers and create **goodwill** toward the company, which in turn increases customers' resistance to competitors' overtures. However, it is important that small business owners not blindly seek to improve their customer retention rate. Instead, they must make sure that they are targeting and retaining the right customers—the ones who generate high profits. "In short, customer retention should never be a stand-alone program, but rather part of a comprehensive process to create market ownership," Sherden wrote.

According to Sherden, the first step in establishing a customer retention program is to create a time line of a typical customer relationship, outlining all the key events and interactions that occur between the first contact with and the eventual loss of the customer. The next step is to analyze the company's trends in losing customers. Customer defections may be related to price increases or to a certain point in the relationship life cycle, for example. Finally, small business owners can use the information gathered to identify warning signs of customer loss and develop retention programs to counteract it.

One basic customer retention strategy available to small business owners involves focusing on employee retention and satisfaction. A company with a high turnover rate may not be able to maintain strong personal relationships with its customers. Even if relationships are established, the customer may decide to take his or her business to a new company when their contact person leaves. At the very least, high turnover creates a negative environment and reduces the quality of service provided to customers. In order to reduce turnover, it is important to provide employees with career development opportunities and high degrees of involvement in the business.

Another possible strategy for retaining customers involves institutionalizing customer relationships. Rather than just providing contact with individual employees, a small business can provide value to customers through the entire company. For example, it could send newsletters or provide training programs in order to become a source of information and education for customers. It may also be possible to establish membership cards or frequent-buyer programs as direct incentives for customer retention.

Some companies may be able to use electronic links to improve the service they provide to customers. For example, e-mail connections could be used to provide updates on the status of accounts, electronic order systems could be used to simplify reordering and reduce costs, and online services could be used to provide general information.

Sherden noted that customer retention programs are particularly important in volatile industries—those characterized by fluctuating prices and product values. In this situation, superior service may discourage but not prevent customer defections. Some strategies that may be useful to companies in volatile industries include providing stable prices over the customer life cycle, basing prices on the overall cost and profitability of the customer relationship, and cross-selling additional products and services. All of these strategies are intended to minimize the changes and problems customers experience, thus making them want to maintain the business relationship.

FURTHER READING:

McCarthy, E. Jerome, and William D. Perrault, Jr. *Basic Marketing: A Managerial Approach.* 10th ed. Homewood, IL: Irwin, 1990.

Sherden, William A. "The Tools of Retention." *Small Business Reports*. November 1994.

SEE ALSO: Business Expansion; Customer Service; Market Share; Pricing

CUSTOMER SERVICE

The term "customer service" encompasses a variety of techniques used by businesses to ensure the satisfaction of a customer, from friendly and attentive staff to prompt response when confronted with product defects. Successful small business owners often cite this factor as one of the most important in establishing and maintaining a prosperous company. "A cascade of beneficial effects can result when a small business cultivates customer loyalty," wrote Michael Barrier in *Nation's Business*. "That pattern holds in all kinds of small businesses—those that sell to other businesses as well as those that sell to consumer." Indeed, some business experts contend that quality customer service can be a more important factor in ensuring company success in some industries than promotion, advertising, and other marketing efforts. "Customer service is a great business advantage," wrote *Canadian Manager*'s John Tschohl. "When you have several competitors in a field and one of them courts customers with service and the others don't, it's the customer-oriented company that pulls ahead. Customers buy more. They return to buy again. And the feed the positive word-of-mouth grapevine about the quality service company." Business owners who make customer service a central guiding principle in their business, then, are far more likely to succeed than those who are indifferent to such practices. As one thriving entrepreneur told Tschohl, "You can't lose sight of the fact that customers come first. No matter what the product . . . you must always please the customer. If you don't, they can find someone nicer and more accommodating to take their business."

DEVELOPING A CUSTOMER-ORIENTED COMPANY CULTURE

"Good customer service rests on three pillars: the right employees, sound practices, and training," wrote George Paajanen in *Discount Store News*. "Like a three-legged stool, your customer service efforts will be shaky if they rest on only one of the pillars."

EMPLOYEES Many business observers contend that the most critical facet of ensuring good customer service lies in simply hiring personable and responsible employees. "The good news is that pre-employment screening tests can enhance the interviewing process by helping employers measure the skills and characteristics needed for success in customer service jobs,"

said Paajanen. "There are a variety of valid tests available, and consistently hiring people who score higher on them will ensure that you select employees who will represent your business to customers in a positive light." In addition, business owners are urged to make sure that they adequately inform potential employees of any customer-relations obligations that they might have. This is typically accomplished through training programs.

TRAINING Employee training is an important component of customer service. Customer service principles should be put in writing, and it should be made clear that all employees are expected to be familiar with them and be prepared to live up to them. Small business owners also need to recognize that customer service training should be extended to all employees who interact with clients, not just those in high profile sales positions. Service technicians, for example, often regularly interact with customers, but all too often they receive little or no customer service training. "More companies are asking their technicians to fill gaps in sales efforts and to repair communication breakdowns," noted Roberta Maynard in *Nation's Business*. "Some companies are cultivating their technicians' abilities to clarify customer needs and identify and capitalize on sales opportunities. . . . Some managers are giving technicians greater authority to do what it takes to keep customers happy, such as occasionally not charging for a service call or a part."

SOUND PRACTICES Finally, businesses need to make sure that they work hard to ensure customer satisfaction on a daily basis. Customer service should be ingrained in the company, commented one entrepreneur in an interview with Barrier: "It has to be part of the organization's mission and vision, right from Day One. Then the rest tends to be simple—it carries over to your products, your advertising, your staffing, and everything else."

INSTILLING CUSTOMER LOYALTY

Business experts cite several tangible steps that small business owners can take to ensure that they provide top-notch service to their customers. These include:

- Erection of quality support systems— Companies armed with tangible, easily understood guidelines for establishing and maintaining quality customer service will go far toward satisfying clients.

- Communication with customers—Communication with customers can often be accomplished more easily by smaller businesses than larger companies that are often slowed by layers of bureaucracy. Methods of communication can include telephone calls, postcards, newsletters, and surveys as well as face-to-face conversation. Such interactions can guide small businesses both in meeting current concerns of customers and in anticipating future issues. And while such steps are perhaps most helpful when dealing with regular customers, consultants counsel business owners who specialize in making big-ticket sales to try and maintain communications with their customers as well. Such customers may not make a purchase every month, noted Frederick F. Reichheld, author of *The Loyalty Effect,* but those purchases that they do make carry a lot of weight. Reichheld notes that big-ticket purchases typically have a fair amount of service and financing associated with them, both of which provide small businesses with opportunities to nourish their relationship with the customer. In addition, consultants observe that communication with ex-customers can be helpful as well. "A defecting customer may offer a reason that points to a potentially serious problem [within your company]," wrote Carrier.

- Communication with front-line employees—Employees who are kept appraised of changes in company products and services are far more likely to be able to satisfy customers than those who are armed with outdated or incomplete information.

- Retention of employees—Many customers establish a certain comfort level over time with individual employees—a salesman, a project coordinator, etc.—and these relationships should be valued and nurtured by the small business owner. "Each customer has special needs," observed Carrier, "and the longer that employee and customer work together, the more easily those needs can be met. Companies that want long-term relationships with their customers need equally healthy relationships with their employees. In particular, they must encourage employee involvement."

- Invest in technology that aids customer service—Small businesses should choose voice mail systems that make it easy for customers to contact the person or department that they wish to reach. Technology systems can also help small businesses gather information about their customers.

- Cultivate an atmosphere of courtesy—Small gestures such as friendly smiles, use of the customer's first name, and minor favors can have a disproportionate impact on the way

that a business is viewed. "Remember that small kindnesses can carry a lot of weight," said Carrier.

- Address mistakes promptly and honorably—No business is infallible. Errors inevitably occur within any business framework, and sooner or later a customer is apt to be impacted. But business experts contend that in many instances, these incidents can actually help strengthen the bond between a company and its customers. "In the normal course of a business relationship, the depth of a vendor's commitment will not be put to the test," wrote Carrier, "but a serious mistake will reveal quickly just how trustworthy that vendor is."

- Avoid equating price with customer service—Many small businesses find it difficult to compete with larger, high-volume competitors, in the realm of price, but most analysts insist that this reality should not be construed as a failure in the realm of customer service. Moreover, most experts indicate that many small businesses can triumph over price differences, provided that they are relatively minor, by putting an extra emphasis on service. "For some customers, of course, price is all that matters," admitted Carrier. "Those are customers you probably can live without."

- Create a user-friendly physical environment—Writing in *Entrepreneur,* Jay Conrad Levinson counseled small business owners to "design your company's physical layout for efficiency, clarity of signage, lighting, accessibility for the disabled and simplicity. Everything should be easy to find."

Any one of these traits might not be enough to sway a customer into beginning a long-term relationship with a company. But combined with one another, they can be a potent attraction to other businesses and consumers alike. As Thomas A. Stewart remarked in *Fortune,* "customer satisfaction—deep satisfaction, the kind that creates loyalty—isn't likely to result from one big thing. . . . A customer's decision to be loyal or to defect is instead the sum of many small encounters with your company."

CUTTING TIES WITH BAD CUSTOMERS

Although smart entrepreneurs and business managers recognize that customer service is an important element in ensuring company success, it is a reality of life that a small percentage of customers are simply incapable of being satisfied with the service they receive. Small business owners are generally averse to letting any customers go, but consultants contend that some clients can simply become more trouble than they are worth for any number or reasons. The solution to determining whether a business owner should sever ties with a problematic customer, observed *Nation's Business,* ''may lie in defining the word 'customer' properly: Someone who costs you money isn't a customer but rather a liability.''

Entrepreneur's Jacquelyn Lynn listed several scenarios in which consultants recommend that small businesses consider ending their relationship with a troublesome client. Client attitudes and actions that should prompt an honest assessment include:

- Lack of respect or appreciation for the small business owner's work.

- Excessive demands, either on company or individual staff members.

- Unreasonable expectations in terms of monetary arrangements for work or good provided.

- Proclivity for imposing difficult or unrealistic deadlines.

- Tendency to pay bills late (or not at all).

- Treats company as a commodity that can be discarded as soon as it ceases to be useful to the client.

Lynn noted that, in some instances, honest communication with the client can salvage a deteriorating relationship, but this does not always work. ''If your attempts to make the relationship a mutually productive one don't work,'' said Lynn, ''it may be time to move on and focus on more profitable clients or prospective clients. Calculate what you will lose in gross revenue, and decide if you business can stand the financial hit.'' If the business is able to withstand the loss of revenue, move forward to terminate the relationship in a professional manner. If not, then the company's leadership needs to develop a strategy to expand existing business relationships or garner new clients so that the company can sever relations with the offending customer down the line.

FURTHER READING:

Barrier, Michael. ''Ties that Bind.'' *Nation's Business.* August 1997.

''Customers You Want to Lose.'' *Nation's Business.* August 1997.

Friedman, J. Roger. ''Quality Service is the Key to Earning Repeat Customers.'' *Nation's Restaurant News.* September 1, 1997.

Levinson, Jay Conrad. ''Taking Care: 17 Ways to Show Your Customers You Care.'' *Entrepreneur.* October 1997.

Lynn, Jacquelyn. ''Good Riddance.'' *Entrepreneur.* October 1997.

Maynard, Roberta. ''Are Your Technicians Customer-Friendly?'' *Nation's Business.* August 1997.

Paajanen, George. ''Customer Service: Training, Sound Practices, and the Right Employee.'' *Discount Store News.* September 15, 1997.

Reichheld, Frederick F. *The Loyalty Effect.* Boston, MA: Harvard Business School Press.

Stewart, Thomas A. ''A Satisfied Customer Isn't Enough.'' *Fortune.* July 21, 1997.

Tschohl, John. ''How to Succeed in Business by Really Trying.'' *Canadian Manager.* Spring 1997.

Weinstein, Steve. ''Rethinking Customer Service.'' *Progressive Grocer.* May 1995.

Wiersema, Fred. *Customer Intimacy.* Knowledge Exchange.

Wilhelm, Wayne, and Bill Rossello. ''The Care and Feeding of Customers.'' *Management Review.* March 1997.

SEE ALSO: Customer Retention; Difficult Customers; Employee Hiring; Training and Development

D

DATA BASE MANAGEMENT SYSTEMS

Database management is simply maintaining records of any type—customer lists, vendor histories, or addresses, for example—using computer software known as a database management system. As Anne Kerven said in *Colorado Business Magazine,* ''database management means the transferring of file cabinet contents to an electronic file.'' Out of that simple statement has sprung a multimillion dollar computer software industry and a thriving database management consulting niche. Almost every company has records of one type or another to maintain, which means that almost every company is affected by database management systems (DBMS).

Databases can range in size from a few hundred addresses maintained on a user's hard drive to hundreds of terabytes of data maintained on huge corporate mainframe computers. One of the benefits of using a database management system, however, is that even if the data is vast and is stored on a remote mainframe, end-users throughout a company can access the data from their desktop using computer networking technology. Reports that in the past had to be requested days or even weeks in advance and created by computer technicians can be generated in minutes by the average user with today's database management systems.

The most common type of system is the relational database management system (RDBMS). It is found in almost every company data center. An RDBMS sorts data into unique fields and allows users to retrieve that data by each field and by linking fields between related records. Relational databases can sort the fielded data any number of ways and generate reports in a matter of minutes. Data can often be output in any form the end-user desires. In addition, an RDBMS can serve as the front-end program that brings data together from several individual databases and produces data tables that combine the information from the various databases.

Database management technology is improving every year, however, and relational data bases are starting to be replaced by more sophisticated database management systems. This movement was spurred in large part by companies that realized they had more than simple records to maintain—they had complicated files, sounds and images, brochures, photographs, time-series inputs, and 3-D coordinates—all of which could be more easily maintained if they were organized and stored in a database. In response to this growing need, software developers have created new object-oriented database management systems (OODBMS) and object-relational database management systems (ORDBMS).

It is expected that ORDBMS will become the most popular system because the need to store disparate types of information is growing. An example of the type of data that might be stored in an object-relation system is a human resources file on an employee. In the past, the database record might have only included text information about the employee—birth date, address, starting date, etc. With an object-relational system, the record could also include the employee's photo or voice sample. Or, a company could maintain geospatial information that would allow it to query the database to locate all employees who made more than $50,000 and lived within 10 miles of the company's location.

SELECTING A SYSTEM FOR A SMALL BUSINESS

For small business owners who are entertaining thoughts about purchasing a database management system, experts say that the first thing to do is determine what they hope to get out of the system—what type of reports do they need, etc. Once the output is known, it is easier to know what type of database is needed, what information will be gathered, and what fields will be created. It is a good idea to start small—such as with a mailing list—to get used to the software. Once the first database is mastered, it is easy to set up additional ones for order tracking, inventory, or other purposes.

Most databases are one of two types—transactional or warehouse. Transactional databases are easier to build and are ideal for tracking simple things, such as the availability of a product or part. Warehouse databases collect company data of any type, such as sales histories or hiring statistics, and produce reports that can identify trends or group information in new and relevant ways. Small businesses use both types of databases.

Once system needs and database type are identified, the next step is to select the right software for the job. An experienced, computer savvy user may be able to study the available software packages and choose the appropriate tool. If not, or if the job appears complex, it is best to locate a consultant to assist in system selection and development.

The simpler the system the better. ''If you can buy off-the-shelf, that's fantastic because it's less expensive,'' said Larry Skaff, owner of Junction Software Services, in *Colorado Business Magazine.* ''But it will have tradeoffs. If they don't do business exactly the way that database is written, can they live with that?''

For small businesses that have even more extensive database needs, **consultants** and computer professionals will undoubtedly be needed. Consultants will charge anywhere from $50 to $200 per hour to create a custom database, and this can turn into a time-consuming project.

MAINTAINING A DATABASE MANAGEMENT SYSTEM

One of the most important and most often forgotten facts about databases—no matter how good the software is, no matter how expensive the computers are—is that databases are only as good as the data put into them. Information must be loaded into the system via data entry work or some other form of input, and it is up to the business owner or manager of information systems to make sure that records are accurate and kept up-to-date.

Letting records slip from time to time may seem like a small thing, but especially for a small business enterprises, poor database maintenance can reflect poorly on the business and make clients think twice about doing business there. Database managers estimate that more than half of small businesses do not maintain their databases once they are created. Examples of the kinds of mistakes that can occur include failing to bill an account, mailing literature to someone who is deceased, or indicating that there is plenty of a particular product in stock when in fact the supply was exhausted weeks ago. Such situations can give rise to business disasters for owners of small businesses.

Writing in *Colorado Business Magazine,* Anne Kerven outlined some of the other common maintenance mistakes that are made:

- Collecting too much or too little data. Collecting too much information slows down the system, clutters screens with unnecessary fields, and inflates the costs of gathering data. Recording too little data can render the database worthless for compiling reports that can help the business grow; instead, money spent on inputting the little data that is there is wasted.

- Poorly conceived data fields. The most common mistake is putting too much information in one field—the computer can only sort by field, not by what is in the field. The best rule of thumb is to put each unique record element—ZIP code, phone number, fax number, address—in its own searchable field.

- Try to avoid using personal names as the key identifier of a record or as a link between records. Instead, use numbers, assigning a unique number to each record. Personal names cause problems when two or more people have the same name; additionally, if the name is not entered exactly the same way every time it is used as a link—a middle initial is included in one instance and left out in another, for example—the records will not link properly.

- Check the database integrity at least once a month. Corrupted links or other problems can creep in over time. Utility programs are available for this function.

- Back up information and store it in a separate location, preferably someplace that is fireproof and waterproof.

- Set strict standards that must be followed whenever data is input into the system to ensure consistency. This is especially important if multiple departments will be adding data to the system.

- Periodically clean the database out, weeding out records that are inactive or no longer relevant. If you do not want to lose those records permanently, create an archive database and move the records into that file.

COMMON USES OF DATABASE MANAGEMENT SYSTEMS

As discussed, database management systems store company information and allow users to easily retrieve that information. But what does that mean in the business world? How exactly are database management systems being put to use so that companies get the most bang for their buck? Currently, there are two primary uses that are gaining in popularity—data marts and data warehouses, and the use of DBMS together with a company's Internet site or intranet.

DATA MARTS AND DATA WAREHOUSES Data marts and data warehouses refer to the information repositories that companies create with their database management software. Data marts are simply smaller versions of data warehouses, storing information on a department-by-department basis. Data warehouses are huge, centralized databases that unify information across an entire company. These huge databases can be used to improve customer service, profitability measurement, and product sales.

Data marts gained popularity before data warehouses. They were seen as a way for departments to achieve one of their main goals—getting information into the hands of all their users quickly and at the same time. However, as DBMS technology improves and larger databases become possible, the flaws in using data marts are being exposed. Data marts do not unify data across an organization—in fact, they can fragment it because every department might be doing things a little differently. Each department's data becomes an island that yields different answers to the same query.

That is not to say that data marts *cannot* work, however. They can, *if* they are built *after* a main data warehouse is built. Most people think it is better to start small with data marts and build up to the big data warehouse, but many experts contend that the opposite is true. If the data marts are built first, then fragmented data held in uniquely structured databases that cannot be accessed by all employees are created.

Instead, small business owners should build the warehouse first. Look at the types of information that are gathered in each department around the company and select the key data from each area. Use this as the starting point for the warehouse. Do not try to build an all-purpose warehouse right from the start. Do what

makes sense, then add historical data and other information as time goes by. If information is simply gathered and stored with no allowance made for cross-departmental analysis, then the warehouse is useless. Those considering building a database should understand that if, upon examination, the current processes a company uses do not allow for such cross-departmental analysis, then fundamental changes will have to be made to those processes if the warehouse is to work. This is an extremely significant point that too many managers or business owners do not understand when they decide to build a warehouse.

Small businesses also have to make sure that end-users from every department are actively involved in the design of the data warehouse. Without that type of feedback, the database may turn out to be useless because it does not store the right type of information, or it stores it in the wrong way. Those end-users involved in the design can learn how to use the system first and then serve as trainers in their department. Once the main warehouse is built, it then becomes easy for each department to build its own data marts by pulling out the fields from the main database that it needs.

The initial costs of building a data warehouse are high—software, hardware, and consulting fees add up quickly. However, most businesses, from supermarkets to banks, are finding that having a data warehouse is a competitive necessity. One example of how data warehouses are being used is a practice called "data mining." Data mining is the technique of creating statistical and predictive models of the real world based on patterns that are discovered as a result of complex queries performed on the huge amounts of data stored in a warehouse. When data mining is done right, it can produce amazing results, spotting trends before they happen or identifying new sales prospects, for instance. When done incorrectly, however, data mining can produce false correlations and misleading results. Companies should not rely too heavily on data mining and should ensure that they hire professionals who fully understand statistical analysis to perform the task.

DATABASE MANAGEMENT AND THE INTERNET OR INTRANETS

Data warehouses started out as internal projects, but now they are being seen as the next logical step on the Internet. As one analyst told *InfoWorld*, "in about two years, 80 percent of queries will be run across the Web." Companies that need to gather data from customers and pass information down the line to business customers are finding it beneficial to make their data warehouse available over the World Wide Web. This means that either HTML or Java-based client servers need to be created to allow Web users to search the database. If the company desires to gather information on customers, it might make the warehouse available to the public over the Web. If the main purpose is to pass information on to business customers, then the company will make the warehouse available as part of its corporate intranet, which is available only to selected individuals.

As of early 1998, only basic queries could be run easily over the Web, but observers note that the situation was changing rapidly. Each of the major database management systems companies was scrambling to enable their databases to work closely with Web servers. Using new technology known as online analytical processing (OLAP), high-level, intricate queries of data warehouses will be possible. At the same time, consumers looking to data mine corporate information should be able to run simple queries.

There are risks associated with making such huge amounts of data available over the Web. Security is the paramount issue, since opening data warehouses to users around the world means that internal systems are exposed to outside interference or hacking. A second issue is the drain on system resources that unlimited access to the data warehouses would cause. Popular databases visited and searched by large numbers of users would need extremely powerful servers to keep up with demand. The servers would have to ensure that the employees and clients of a company would not be hindered by the excess traffic on the system. Finally, there is the issue of cost. As with any new technology, opening databases to the Web costs money. In addition to development costs associated with creating the search engines and OLAP tools, businesses will also have to weigh the cost of the powerful servers needed to meet the increased demand for information.

FURTHER READING:

Alur, Nagraj, and Judith R. Davis. "How to Improve RDBMSes." *Byte.* April 1997.

Atre, Shaku. "Achieving Unity of Data." *Computerworld.* September 15, 1997.

Barthel, Matt. "Data Warehousing: It's Happening Today But Don't Count on Benefits by Tomorrow." *American Banker.* August 20, 1997.

Coy, Peter. "He Who Mines Data May Strike Fool's Gold." *Business Week.* June 16, 1997.

Cummer, Lawrence. "IT World Getting Excited about Object Databases." *Computing Canada.* January 26, 1998.

Greenberg, Ilan. "Move to 'Net and Intranets Causing Warehouse Boom." *InfoWorld.* May 12, 1997.

"The Info Depot: Data Warehouses Have the Potential to Manage the Industry's Information Overload." *Supermarket News.* September 15, 1997.

Kerven, Anne. "Database Management Keys." *Colorado Business Magazine.* March 1997.

——. "Keep Files Clean." *Colorado Business Magazine.* April 1997.

Mullins, Craig S. "Openness Complicates Database Management." *Computing Canada.* January 26, 1998.

Schultz, Beth. "Warehousing Data Web Style." *Network World.* July 21, 1997.

Stedman, Craig. "Data Vaults Unlocked." *Computerworld.* June 2, 1997.

Taschek, John. "The Truth About Marts and Warehouses." *PC Week.* July 14, 1997.

VanDuyvenvoorde, David. "Being Objective about RDBMS." *Computing Canada.* October 14, 1997.

Walera, Edward J., and Charlie Button. "Using a Supply Usage Relational Database to Reduce Costs." *Healthcare Financial Management.* September 1997.

Weldon, Jay-Louise. "RDBMSes Get a Makeover." *Byte.* April 1997.

SEE ALSO: Computers and Computer Systems

DEBT FINANCING

Debt financing is a strategy that involves borrowing money from a lender or investor with the understanding that the full amount will be repaid in the future, usually with interest. In contrast, **equity financing**—in which investors receive partial ownership in the company in exchange for their funds—does not have to be repaid. In most cases, debt financing does not include any provision for ownership of the company (although some types of debt are convertible to stock). Instead, small businesses that employ debt financing accept a direct obligation to repay the funds within a certain period of time. The interest rate charged on the borrowed funds reflects the level of risk that the lender undertakes by providing the money. For example, a lender might charge a startup company a higher interest rate than it would a company that had shown a profit for several years. Since lenders are paid off before owners in the event of business liquidation, debt financing entails less risk than equity financing and thus usually commands a lower return.

Though there are several possible methods of debt financing available to small businesses—including private placement of bonds, convertible debentures, industrial development bonds, and leveraged buyouts—by far the most common type of debt financing is a regular loan. **Loans** can be classified as long-term (with a maturity longer than one year), short-term (with a maturity shorter than two years), or a credit line (for more immediate borrowing needs). They can be endorsed by co-signers, guaranteed by the government, or secured by collateral—such as real estate, accounts receivable, inventory, savings, life insurance, stocks and bonds, or the item purchased with the loan.

When evaluating a small business for a loan, Jennifer Lindsey wrote in her book *The Entrepreneur's Guide to Capital,* lenders ideally like to see a two-year operating history, a stable management group, a desirable niche in the industry, a growth in market share, a strong cash flow, and an ability to obtain short-term financing from other sources as a supplement to the loan. Most lenders will require a small business owner to prepare a loan proposal or complete a loan application. The lender will then evaluate the request by considering a variety of factors. For example, the lender will examine the small business's credit rating and look for evidence of its ability to repay the loan, in the form of past earnings or income projections. The lender will also inquire into the amount of equity in the business, as well as whether management has sufficient experience and competence to run the business effectively. Finally, the lender will try to ascertain whether the small business can provide a reasonable amount of collateral to secure the loan.

ADVANTAGES AND DISADVANTAGES OF DEBT FINANCING

Experts indicate that debt financing can be a useful strategy, particularly for companies with good credit and a stable history of revenues, earnings, and cash flow. But small business owners should think carefully before committing to debt financing in order to avoid cash flow problems and reduced flexibility. In general, a combination of debt financing and equity financing is considered most desirable for small businesses. In the Small Business Administration publication *Financing for the Small Business,* Brian Hamilton listed several factors entrepreneurs should consider when choosing between debt and equity financing. First, the entrepreneur must consider how much ownership and control he or she is willing to give up, not only at present but also in future financing rounds. Second, the entrepreneur should decide how leveraged the company can comfortably be, or its optimal ratio of debt to equity. Third, the entrepreneur should determine what types of financing are available to the company, given its stage of development and **capital** needs, and compare the requirements of the different types. Finally, as a practical consideration, the entrepreneur should ascertain whether or not the company is in a position to make set monthly payments on a loan.

No matter what type of financing is chosen, careful planning is necessary to secure it. The entrepreneur should assess the business's financial needs, and then estimate what percentage of the total funds must be obtained from outside sources. A formal business plan, complete with cash flow projections, is an important tool in both planning for and obtaining financing. Lindsey noted that small businesses should choose debt financing when federal interest rates are low, they have a good credit history or property to use as collateral, and they expect future growth in earnings as well as in the overall industry.

Like other types of financing available to small businesses, debt financing has both advantages and disadvantages. The primary advantage of debt financing is that it allows the founders to retain ownership and control of the company. In contrast to equity financing, the entrepreneurs are able to make key strategic decisions and also to keep and reinvest more company profits. Another advantage of debt financing is that it provides small business owners with a greater degree of financial freedom than equity financing. Debt obligations are limited to the loan repayment period, after which the lender has no further claim on the business, whereas equity investors' claim does not end until their stock is sold. Furthermore, a debt that is paid on time can enhance a small business's credit rating and make it easier to obtain various types of financing in the future. Debt financing is also easy to administer, as it generally lacks the complex reporting requirements that accompany some forms of equity financing. Finally, debt financing tends to be less expensive for small businesses over the long term, though more expensive over the short term, than equity financing.

The main disadvantage of debt financing is that it requires a small business to make regular monthly payments of principal and interest. Very young companies often experience shortages in cash flow that may make such regular payments difficult. Most lenders provide severe penalties for late or missed payments, which may include charging late fees, taking possession of collateral, or calling the loan due early. Failure to make payments on a loan, even temporarily, can adversely affect a small business's credit rating and its ability to obtain future financing. Another disadvantage associated with debt financing is that its availability is often limited to established businesses. Since lenders primarily seek security for their funds, it can be difficult for unproven businesses to obtain loans. Finally, the amount of money small businesses may be able to obtain via debt financing is likely to be limited, so they may need to use other sources of financing as well.

SOURCES OF DEBT FINANCING

Small businesses can obtain debt financing from a number of different sources. These sources can be broken down into two general categories, private and public. Private sources of debt financing, according to W. Keith Schilit in *The Entrepreneur's Guide to Preparing a Winning Business Plan and Raising Venture Capital,* include friends and relatives, banks, credit unions, consumer finance companies, commercial finance companies, trade credit, insurance companies, factor companies, and leasing companies. Public sources of debt financing include a number of loan programs provided by the state and federal governments to support small businesses.

PRIVATE SOURCES Many entrepreneurs begin their enterprises by borrowing money from friends and relatives. The main advantage of this type of arrangement is that friends and relatives are likely to provide more flexible terms of repayment than banks or other lenders. In addition, these investors may be more willing to invest in an unproven business idea, based upon their personal knowledge and relationship with the entrepreneur, than other lenders. A related disadvantage, however, is that friends and relatives who loan money to help establish a small business may try to become involved in its management. Experts recommend that small business owners create a formal agreement with such investors to help avoid future misunderstandings.

Banks are the sources that most people immediately think of for debt financing. There are many different types of banks, although in general they exist to accept deposits and make loans. Most banks tend to be fairly risk averse and proceed cautiously when making loans. As a result, it may be difficult for a young business to obtain this sort of financing. Commercial banks usually have more experience in making business loans than do regular savings banks. It may be helpful to review the differences among banks before choosing one as the target of a loan request. Credit unions are another common source of business loans. Since these financial institutions are intended to aid the members of a group—such as employees of a company or members of a labor union—they often provide funds more readily and under more favorable terms than banks. However, the amount of money that may be borrowed through a credit union is usually not as large as that available from other financial institutions.

Finance companies are another option for small business loans. Although they generally charge higher interest rates than banks and credit unions, they also are able to approve more requests for loans. Most loans obtained through finance companies are secured by a specific asset as collateral, and that asset can be seized if the entrepreneur defaults on the loan. Consumer finance companies make small loans against personal assets and provide an option for individuals with poor credit ratings. Commercial finance companies provide small businesses with loans for inventory and equipment purchases and are a good resource for manufacturing enterprises. Insurance companies often make commercial loans as a way of reinvesting their income. They usually provide payment terms and interest rates comparable to a commercial bank, but require a business to have more assets available as collateral.

Trade credit is another common form of debt financing. Whenever a supplier allows a small business to delay payment on the products or services it purchases, the small business has obtained trade credit from that supplier. Trade credit is readily available to most small businesses, if not immediately then certainly after a few orders. But the payment terms may differ between suppliers, so it may be helpful to compare or negotiate for the best terms. A small business's customers may also be interested in offering a form of trade credit—for example, by paying in advance for delivery of products they will need on a future date—in order to establish a good relationship with a new supplier.

Factor companies help small businesses to free up cash on a timely basis by purchasing their accounts receivable. Rather than waiting for customers to pay invoices, the small business can receive payment for sales immediately. Factor companies can either provide recourse financing, in which the small business is ultimately responsible if its customers do not pay, and nonrecourse financing, in which the factor company bears that risk. Although **factoring** can be a useful source of funds for existing businesses, they are not an option for startups that do not have accounts receivable.

Leasing companies can also help small businesses to free up cash by renting various types of equipment instead of making large capital expenditures to purchase it. Equipment leases usually involve only a small monthly payment, plus they may enable a small business to upgrade its equipment quickly and easily.

Entrepreneurs and owners of startup businesses often must resort to personal debt in order to fund their enterprises. Some entrepreneurs choose to arrange their initial investment in the business as a loan, with a specific repayment period and interest rate. The entrepreneur then uses the proceeds of the business to repay himself or herself over time. Other small business owners borrow the cash value of their personal life insurance policies to provide funds for their business. These funds are usually available at a relatively low interest rate. Still other entrepreneurs borrow money against the equity in their personal residences to cover business expenses. Mortgage loans can be risky, since the home is used as collateral, but they are a common source of funds for small business owners. Finally, some fledgling business people use personal credit cards as a source of business financing. Credit card companies charge high interest rates, which increases the risk of piling up additional debt, but they can make cash available quickly.

PUBLIC SOURCES The state and federal governments sponsor a wide variety of programs that provide funding to promote the formation and growth of small businesses. Many of these programs are handled by the **U.S. Small Business Administration (SBA)** and involve debt financing. The SBA helps small businesses obtain funds from banks and other lenders by guaranteeing loans up to $500,000, to a maximum of 70-90 percent of the loan value, for 2.75 percentage points above the prime lending rate. In order to qualify for an SBA guaranteed loan, an entrepreneur must first be turned down for a loan through regular channels. He or she must also demonstrate good character and a reasonable ability to run a successful business and repay a loan. SBA guaranteed loan funds can be used for business expansion or for purchases of inventory, equipment, and real estate. In addition to guaranteeing loans provided by other lenders, the SBA offers direct loans of up to $150,000, as well as seasonal loans, handicapped assistance loans, disaster loans, and pollution control financing.

Small Business Investment Companies (SBICs) are government-backed firms that make direct loans or equity investments in small businesses. SBICs tend to be less risk-averse than banks, so funds are more likely to be available for startup companies. Another advantage is that SBICs are often able to provide technical assistance to small business borrowers.

The Economic Development Commission (EDC), a branch of the **U.S. Department of Commerce**, makes loans to small businesses that provide jobs in economically disadvantaged regions. Small businesses hoping to qualify for EDC loans must meet a number of conditions.

Overall, debt financing can be a valuable option for small businesses that require cash to begin or expand their operations. But experts warn that carrying too much debt can cause a small business to encounter severe cash flow problems. Instead, it is best to use a combination of different forms of financing to spread the risk and facilitate future funding efforts. Planning is essential for entrepreneurs seeking loans and other types of debt financing. It may take time and persistence for an entrepreneur to convince a lender of the value of his or her business ideas and plans. With so many possible sources of debt financing, it is important for small business owners to find a lender with whom they can develop a comfortable working relationship. Forming a good relationship may help the entrepreneur negotiate favorable interest rates and fees, which can make a big difference in the final cost of the debt financing.

FURTHER READING:

Hamilton, Brian. *Financing for the Small Business.* Washington, D.C.: U.S. Small Business Administration, 1990.

Heath, Gibson. *Doing Business with Banks: A Common Sense Guide for Small Business Borrowers.* Lakewood, CO: DBA/USA Press, 1991.

Lindsey, Jennifer. *The Entrepreneur's Guide to Capital.* Chicago: Probus, 1986.

Schilit, W. Keith. *The Entrepreneur's Guide to Preparing a Winning Business Plan and Raising Venture Capital.* Englewood Cliffs, NJ: Prentice Hall, 1990.

Silver, A. David. *Up Front Financing: The Entrepreneur's Guide.* New York: Wiley, 1982.

Timmons, Jeffrey A. *Planning and Financing the New Venture.* Brick House Publishing Company, 1990.

Van Note, Mark. *ABCs of Borrowing.* Washington, D.C.: U.S. Small Business Administration, 1990.

DECISION MAKING

Decision making is a vital component of small business success. Decisions that are based on a foundation of knowledge and sound reasoning can lead the company into long-term prosperity; conversely, decisions that are made on the basis of flawed logic, emotionalism, or incomplete information can quickly put a small business out of commission (indeed, bad decisions can cripple even big, capital-rich corporations over time). All businesspeople recognize the painful necessity of choice. Furthermore, making these choices must be done in a timely fashion, for as most people recognize, indecision is in essence a choice in and of itself—a choice to take no action. Ultimately, what drives business success is the quality of decisions, and their implementation. Good decisions mean good business.

The concept of decision making has a long history; choosing among alternatives has always been a part of life. But sustained research attention to business decision making has developed only in recent years. Contemporary advances in the field include progress in such elements of decision making as the problem context; the processes of problem finding, problem solving, and legitimation; and procedural and technical aids.

THE ELEMENTS OF DECISION MAKING

THE PROBLEM CONTEXT All decisions are about problems, and problems shape context at three levels. The *macrocontext* draws attention to global issues (exchange rates, for example), national concerns (the cultural orientations toward decision processes of different countries), and provincial and state laws and cultures within nations. The *mesocontext* attends to organizational cultures and structure. The *microcontext* addresses the immediate decision environment—the organization's employees, board, or office.

Decision processes differ from company to company. But all companies need to take these three context levels into consideration when a decision needs to be made. Fortunately, economical ways to obtain this information are available and keep the cost of preparing for decision making from becoming prohibitive.

PROBLEM FINDING AND AGENDA SETTING To be a problem, an issue must be identified as problematic and of consequence. An important difficulty in decision making is failure to act until one is too close to the decision point—when information and options are greatly limited. Organizations usually work in a "reactive" mode. Problems are "found" only after the issue has begun to have a negative impact on the business. Nevertheless, processes of environmental scanning and strategic planning are designed (though they do not often work well) to perform problem reconnaissance to alert business people to problems that will need attention down the line. Proactivity can be a great strength in decision making, but it requires a decision intelligence process that is absent from many organizations.

Moreover, problem identification is of limited use if the business is slow to heed or resolve the issue. Once a problem has been identified, information is needed about the problem and potential actions to be taken. Unfortunately, small business owners and other key decision makers too often rely on information sources that "edit" the data—either intentionally or unintentionally—in possibly misleading fashion. Information from business managers and other employees, vendors, and customers alike has to be regarded with a discerning eye.

Another kind of information reflects the array and priority of solution preferences. What is selected as possible or not possible, acceptable or unacceptable, negotiable or non-negotiable depends upon the culture of the firm itself and its environment.

A third area of information involves determining the possible scope and impact the problem and its consequent decision might have. Knowledge about impact may alter the decision preferences. To some extent, knowledge about scope dictates who will need to be involved in the decision process.

PROBLEM SOLVING

Problem solving—also sometimes referred to as problem management—can be divided into two parts—process and decision.

The process of problem solving is predicated on the existence of a system designed to address issues as they crop up. In many organizations, there does not seem to be a system. In such businesses, owners, executives, and managers are seemingly content to operate with an ultimately fatalistic philosophy—what happens, happens. Business experts contend that such an attitude is simply unacceptable, especially for smaller businesses that wish to expand, let alone survive.

The second part of the problem management equation is the decision, or choice, itself. Several sets of elements need to be considered in looking at the decision process. One set refers to the rationales used for decisions. Others emphasize the setting, the scope and level of the decision, and the use of procedural and technical aids.

RATIONALES Organizational decision makers have adopted a variety of styles in their decision making processes. For example, some business leaders embrace processes wherein every conceivable response to an issue is examined before settling on a final response, while others adopt more flexible philosophies. The legitimacy of each style varies in accordance with individual business realities in realms such as market competitiveness, business owner personality, and acuteness of the problem.

SETTINGS Certainly, some entrepreneurs/owners make business decisions without a significant amount of input or feedback from others. Home-based business owners without any employees, for example, are likely to take a far different approach to problem-solving than will business owners who have dozens of employees and/or several distinct internal departments. The latter owners will be much more likely to include findings of meetings, task forces, and other information gathering efforts in their decision making process. Of course, even a business owner who has no partners or employees may find it useful to seek information from outside sources (accountants, fellow businesspeople, attorneys, etc.) before making important business decisions. "Since the owner makes all the key decisions for the small business, he or she is responsible for its success or failure," wrote David Karlson in *Avoiding Mistakes in Your Small Business.* "Marketing and finance are two of several areas in which small business owners frequently lack sufficient experience, since they previously worked as specialists for other people before they started their own businesses. As a result, they generally do not have the experience needed to make well-informed decisions in the areas with which they are unfamiliar. The demands of running and growing a small business will soon expose any achilles heel in a president/owner. It is best to find out your weaknesses early, so you can develop expertise or get help in these areas."

SCOPE AND LEVEL Finally, attention must be paid to the problem's scope and organizational level. Problems of large scope need to be dealt with by top levels of the organization. Similarly, problems of smaller scope can be handled by lower levels of the organization. This is a failing of many organizations, large and small. Typically, top level groups spend much too much time deciding low-level, low-impact problems, while at the same time avoiding problems of high importance and organizational impact.

PROCEDURAL AND TECHNICAL AIDS In recent years, a number of procedural and technical aids have been developed to help business managers in their decision making processes. Most of these have taken the form of software programs that guide individuals or groups through the various elements of the decision making process in a wide variety of operational areas (budgeting, marketing, inventory control, etc.).

OUTCOME Whatever decision making process is utilized, those involved in making the decision need to make sure that a decision has actually been made. All too often, in meetings and other settings in which multiple individuals provide input into possible problem responses, those meetings adjourn in at atmosphere of uncertainty. Participants in decision making meetings are sometimes unsure about various facets of the decision arrived at. Some meeting participants, for example, may leave a meeting still unsure about how the agreed-upon response to a problem is going to be implemented, while others may not even be sure what the agreed-upon response is. Indeed, business researchers indicate that on many occasions, meeting participants leave a meeting with fundamentally different understandings of what took place. It is up to the small business owner to make sure that all participants in the decision making process fully understand all aspects of the final decision and next steps.

IMPLEMENTATION The final step in the decision making process is the implementation of the decision. This is an extremely important element of decision making; after all, the benefits associated with even the most intelligent decision can be severely compromised if implementation is slow or flawed.

DEFINING THE QUALITY OF DECISIONS

Decisions are a product, and decision makers need to look at those products and ask if they are of high quality. If undertaken in a serious and effective manner, dissection of past and present decisions can be an important contributor to total process improvement efforts.

One method of decision analysis is to review a business decision and grade it on an A to F scale. These grades can be defined as follows:

- ''A'' decision—one in which all stakeholders come out ahead, though they do not necessarily benefit equally.

- ''B'' decision—includes both positive and negative aspects, but ultimately results in advancing the organization's health.

- ''C'' decision—this common result is basically a standoff, in which the decision may help some elements of a business, but hurt other areas.

- ''D'' decision—one in which the negative ramifications of the decision outweigh the positive results. For example, a manufacturer may introduce a new product line that increases total sales by 5 percent, but also increases operating costs (raw material purchases, transportation and storage costs, marketing expenses, etc.) by four times that amount.

- ''F'' decision—these are decisions that are outright disasters for the business.

This method relies on judgement calls by the examining individual or group, and different people inevitably have different opinions about the impact of various policy or strategic decisions that are made. But if the examining parties approach this exercise honestly, they can, in some cases, gain interesting insights into the strengths and weaknesses of their decision making processes.

FACTORS IN POOR DECISION MAKING

Why do decisions go wrong? Several factors are commonly cited by business experts, including the following: limited organizational capacity; limited information; the costliness of analysis; interdependencies between fact and value; the openness of the system(s) to be analyzed; and the diversity of forms on which business decisions actually arise. Moreover, time constraints, personal distractions, low levels of decision making skill, conflict over business goals, and interpersonal factors can have a deleterious affect on the decision making capacities of a small (or large) business.

A second category of difficulties is captured in a number of common pitfalls of the decision procedure. One such pitfall is '' decision avoidance psychosis,'' which occurs when organizations put off making decisions that need to be made until the very last minute. One form of this is the ''non-decision.'' In such instances, it may appear that a decision has been made, when in reality one has not. Over time this pattern of nondecision can lead to the ''boiled-frog phenomenon,'' as described by Noel Tichy and Mary Ann Devanna in their book *The Transformational Leader*. This phenomenon takes its name from an experiment in which one puts a frog in a beaker filled with water, and slowly heats the water over a burner. The frog boils to death. Why does it not leave? The answer seems to be that the incremental increase in temperature is not enough to cause action. This ''just noticeable'' or ''barely noticable'' difference phenomenon is an important source of nondecision in organizations. Members see things pretty much as they were, and thus wrongly conclude that there is no need to act.

A second problem is decision randomness. This process was outlined in the well-known paper "A Garbage Can Model of Organizational Choice" by M. James Cohen, G. March and J. Olsen. The authors argued that organizations have four roles or vectors: problem knowers (people who know the difficulties the organization faces); solution providers (people who can provide solutions but do not know the problems); resource controllers (people who do not know problems and do not have solutions but control the allocation of people and money in the organization); and a group of "decision makers looking for work." For effective decision making, all these elements must be in the same room at the same time. In reality, the authors contended, most organizations combine them at random, as if tossing them into a garbage can.

Decision drift is another malady that can strike at a business with potentially crippling results. This term, also sometimes known as the Abilene Paradox in recognition of a model of this behavior, refers to group actions that take place under the impression that the action is the will of the majority, when in reality, there never really was a decision to take that action.

Decision coercion, also known as **groupthink**, is another common decision problem. In this flawed decision making process, decisions are actually coerced by figures in power. This phenomenon can most commonly be seen in instances where a business owner or top executive creates an atmosphere where objections or concerns to a decision favored by the owner/executive are apt to be viewed unfavorably. Only later, in the hallway, when the real discussion occurs, do the problems associated with the decided-on course of action surface.

IMPROVING DECISION MAKING

Small business owners and managers can take several steps to improve the decision making process at their establishments.

- Improve the setting—Organizing better meetings (focused agenda, clear questions, current and detailed information, necessary personnel) can be a very helpful step. Avoid the garbage can; get the relevant people in the same room at the same time. Pay attention to planning and seek closure.

- Use logical techniques—Decision making is a simple process when approached in a logical and purposeful manner. Small businesses that are able to perceive the problem, gather and present data, intelligently discuss the data, and implement the decision without succumbing to emotionalism are apt to make good decisions that will help the business prosper in the present and in the future.

- Enlist decision aids—Groupware and decision software might be helpful, as well as steps to improve one's meeting processes. Specific attention to the structure of the decision system might yield useful results.

- Evaluate decisions and decision making patterns—Evaluation tends to focus the attention, and make individuals and teams more sensitive to what they are actually doing in their decision making tasks. Evaluation is especially helpful in today's business environment because of the interdependency of individuals and departments in executing tasks and addressing goals.

- Determine appropriate levels of decision making—Business enterprises need to make sure that operational decisions are being made at the right level. Keys to avoiding micromanagement and other decision making pitfalls include: giving problems their proper level of importance and context; addressing problems in an appropriate time frame; and establishing and shifting decision criteria in accordance with business goals.

Decision making is at the heart of business operations. High quality decision making is essential for businesses to thrive and prosper. Unfortunately, the decision process is hard to pin down and understand and often receives far less attention than it deserves. Small business owners need to remember that the future of one's business is written in the decisions of today.

FURTHER READING:

Cohen, M. James, G. March, and J. Olsen. "A Garbage Can Model of Organizational Choice." *Administrative Science Quarterly*. March 1972.

Daft, Richard. *Organization Theory and Design*, 4th ed. West Publishing, 1992.

Dawson, Roger. *The Confident Decision Maker*. New York: William Morrow, 1993.

Graham, John R. "Avoiding Dumb and Dumber Business Decisions: Why Even the Experts Make Mistakes." *American Salesman*. April 1997.

Harvey, Jerry B. "The Abilene Paradox." *Organizational Dynamics*. Summer 1974.

Janis, I. *Crucial Decisions*. The Free Press, 1989.

Janis, I. *Groupthink: Psychological Studies of Policy Decisions and Fiascoes*. New York: Houghton Mifflin, 1983.

Jay, Antony. "How To Run A Meeting." *Harvard Business Review*. March/April 1976.

Karlson, David. *Avoiding Mistakes in Your Small Business*. Crisp, 1994.

Plous, S. *The Psychology of Judgement and Decision Making*. Philadelphia: Temple University Press, 1993.

Roe, Amy. "One of the Most Ticklish Jobs is Decision Making." *The Business Journal*. June 2, 1997.

Thurow, Lester. *The Management Challenge*. MIT Press, 1986.

Tichy, Noel, and Mary Ann Devanna. *The Transformational Leader*. New York: Wiley, 1986.

Tropman, John E. ''The Decision Group.'' *Human Systems Management*. Vol. 3, 1982.

Tropman, John E., and Gersh Morningstar. *Entrepreneurial Systems for the 1990s*. Quorum Books, 1989.

DECISION SUPPORT SYSTEMS

From a very elementary viewpoint, decision support systems are a set of manual or computer-based tools that assist in some decision-making activity. In today's business environment, however, decision support systems (DSS) are commonly understood to be computerized **management information systems** designed to help business owners, executives, and managers resolve complicated business problems and/or questions. Good decision support systems can help business people perform a wide variety of functions, including cash flow analysis, concept ranking, multistage forecasting, product performance improvement, and resource allocation analysis. Previously regarded as primarily a tool for big companies, DSS has in recent years come to be recognized as a potentially valuable tool for small business enterprises as well.

THE STRUCTURE OF DECISIONS

In order to discuss the support of decisions and what DSS tools can or should do, it is necessary to have a perspective on the nature of the decision process and the various requirements of supporting it. One way of looking at a decision is in terms of its key components. The first component is the data collected by a decision maker to be used in making the decision. The second component is the process selected by the decision maker to combine this data. Finally, there is an evaluation or learning component that compares decisions and examines them to see if there is a need to change either the data being used or the process that combines the data. These components of a decision interact with the characteristics of the decision that is being made.

STRUCTURED DECISIONS Many analysts categorize decisions according to the degree of structure involved in the decision-making activity. Business analysts describe a structured decision as one in which all three components of a decision—the data, process, and evaluation—are determined. Since structured decisions are made on a regular basis in business environments, it makes sense to place a comparatively rigid framework around the decision and the people making it.

Structured decision support systems may simply use a checklist or form to ensure that all necessary data is collected and that the decision making process is not skewed by the absence of necessary data. If the choice is also to support the procedural or process component of the decision, then it is quite possible to develop a program either as part of the checklist or form. In fact, for structured decisions it is also possible and desirable to develop computer programs that collect and combine the data, thus giving the process a high degree of consistency or structure. When there is a desire to make a decision more structured, the support system for that decision is designed to ensure consistency. Many firms that hire individuals without a great deal of experience provide them with detailed guidelines on their decision making activities and support them by giving them little flexibility. One interesting consequence of making a decision more structured is that the liability for inappropriate decisions is shifted from individual decision makers to the firm.

UNSTRUCTURED DECISIONS At the other end of the continuum are unstructured decisions. While these decisions have the same components as structured ones—data, process, and evaluation—there is little agreement on their nature. With unstructured decisions, for example, each decision maker may use different data and processes to reach a conclusion. In addition, because of the nature of the decision there may only a limited number of people within the organization that are even qualified to evaluate the decision.

Generally, unstructured decisions are made in instances in which all elements of the business environment—customer expectations, competitor response, cost of securing raw materials, etc.—are not completely understood (new product and marketing strategy decisions commonly fit into this category). Unstructured decision systems typically focus on the individual or team that will make the decision. These decision makers are usually entrusted with decisions that are unstructured because of their experience or expertise, and therefore it is their individual ability that is of value. One approach to support systems in this area is to construct a program that simulates the process used by a particular individual. In essence, these systems—commonly referred to as ''expert systems''—prompt the user with a series of questions regarding a decision situation. ''Once the expert system has sufficient information about the decision scenario, it uses an inference engine which draws upon a data base of expertise in this decision area to provide the manager with the best possible alternative for the problem,'' explained Jatinder N. D. Gupta and Thomas M. Harris in the *Journal of Systems Management*. ''The purported advantage of this decision aid is that it allows the manager the use of the collective knowledge of experts in this decision realm. Some of the current DSS applications have included long-range and strategic planning policy setting, new product planning, market planning, cash flow management, operational planning and budgeting, and portfolio management.''

Another approach is to monitor and document the process that was used so that the decision maker(s) can readily review what has already been examined and concluded. An even more novel approach used to support these decisions is to provide environments that are specially designed to give these decision makers an atmosphere that is conducive to their particular tastes. The key to support of unstructured decisions is to understand the role that experience and expertise play in the decision and to allow for individual approaches.

SEMI-STRUCTURED DECISIONS In the middle of the continuum are semi-structured decisions, and this is where most of what are considered to be true decision support systems are focused. Decisions of this type are characterized as having some agreement on the data, process, and/or evaluation to be used, but are also typified by efforts to retain some level of human judgement in the decision making process. An initial step in analyzing which support system is required is to understand where the limitations of the decision maker may be manifested, i.e., will it be in the data acquisition portion, the process component, or in the evaluation of outcomes.

Grappling with the latter two types of decisions—unstructured and semi-structured—can be particularly problematic for small businesses, which often have limited technological or work force resources. As Gupta and Harris indicated, ''many decision situations faced by executives in small business are one-of-a-kind, one-shot occurrences requiring specifically tailored solution approaches without the benefit of any previously available rules or procedures. This unstructured or semi-structured nature of these decisions situations aggravates the problem of limited resources and staff expertise available to a small business executive to analyze important decisions appropriately. Faced with this difficulty, an executive in a small business must seek tools and techniques that do not demand too much of his time and resources and are useful to make his life easier.'' Subsequently, small businesses have increasingly turned to DSS to provide them with assistance in business guidance and management.

KEY DSS FUNCTIONS

Gupta and Harris observed that DSS is predicated on the effective performance of three functions: information management, data quantification, and model manipulation. They note ''information management refers to the storage, retrieval, and reporting of information in a structured format convenient to the user.

Data quantification is the process by which large amounts of information are condensed and analytically manipulated into a few core indicators that extract the essence of data. Model manipulation refers to the construction and resolution of various scenarios to answer 'what if' questions. It includes the processes of model formulation, alternatives generation and solution of the proposed models, often through the use of several operations research/management science approaches.''

Small businesses can implement a DSS for as little as $2,000 (more sophisticated systems might cost four or five times that amount), but entrepreneurs and owners of established enterprises are urged to make certain that their business needs a DSS before buying the various computer systems and software necessary to create one. ''In order to ensure selection of the most appropriate and most beneficial DSS,'' said Gupta and Harris, ''a small business executive must determine the following: 1) if the business needs a DSS; 2) what DSS functions are desired to serve the needs of the business; and 3) if a DSS is warranted, what specific decision support software will serve business needs most effectively and efficiently.'' Another key consideration, say some observers, is whether the business's key personnel will ensure that the necessary time and effort is spent to incorporate DSS into the establishment's operations. After all, even the best decision support system is of little use if the business does not possess the training and knowledge necessary to use it effectively.

Some small businesses, of course, have no need of a DSS. But for those business owners who are guiding a complex operation, a decision support system can be a valuable tool. If, after careful study of questions of DSS utility, the small business owner decides that DSS can help his or her company, the necessary investment can be made, and the key managers of the business can begin the process of developing their own DSS applications using available spreadsheet software.

DSS SOFTWARE ''In the 1990s spreadsheets have come of age,'' commented Chris Parkinson in *CMA— The Management Accounting Magazine.* ''Functionality is much improved and they have greatly increased the size of model they can address. They have been helped by significant developments in PC technology, particularly the introduction of Microsoft Windows (tm) for IBM-type PCs, the easy-to-use graphical user interface (GUI).'' This increase in power and functionality, say researchers, has dramatically improved their performance in the realm of decision support modeling.

''A myriad of available software packages can establish DSS capabilities on a microcomputer, giving any number of variations of applications in a system,'' wrote Gupta and Harris. "These packages are truly interactive systems easily used by individuals with little experience in computers and analytical methods. [In addition], a new genre of software that specifically aims at personal decision making for the manager has been developed. Many statistical analysis software packages are now available which enable the manager to perform nearly any conceivable statistical test. Similarly, several management science techniques are now available as software packages that a small business executive can use rather easily."

DSS UNCERTAINTIES AND LIMITATIONS

While decision support systems have been embraced by small business operators in a wide range of industries in recent years, entrepreneurs, programmers, and business consultants all agree that such systems are not perfect.

LEVEL OF "USER-FRIENDLINESS" Some observers contend that although decision support systems have become much more user-friendly in recent years, it remains an issue, especially for small business operations that do not have significant resources in terms of technological knowledge. "[The current technology] is not intuitive enough," stated one business manager in an interview with *Supermarket News*. "To a management person who is not highly computer literate, none of the stuff we do is intuitive enough. That kind of person needs a technology mentor to help them, or the tool will sit idle or underutilized. Related to that is the issue of user-friendliness, which I would say is the biggest challenge in decision-support today."

HARD-TO-QUANTIFY FACTORS Another limitation that decision makers confront has to do with combining or processing the information that they obtain. In many cases these limitations are due to the number of mathematical calculations required. For instance, a manufacturer pondering the introduction of a new product cannot do so without first deciding on a price for the product. In order to make this decision, the effect of different variables (including price) on demand for the product and the subsequent profit must be evaluated. The manufacturer's perceptions of the demand for the product can be captured in a mathematical formula that portrays the relationship between profit, price, and other variables considered important. Once the relationships have been expressed, the decision maker may now want to change the values for different variables and see what the effect on profits would be. The ability to save mathematical relationships and then obtain results for different values is a feature of many decision support systems. This is called "what-if" analysis, and today's spreadsheet software packages are fully equipped to support this decision-making activity. Of course, additional factors must be taken into consideration when making

business decisions. Hard-to-quantify factors such as future interest rates, new legislation, and hunches about product shelf life may all be considered. So even though the calculations may indicate that a certain demand for the product will be achieved at a certain price, the decision maker must use his or her judgment in making the final decision.

If the decision maker simply follows the output of a process model, then the decision is being moved toward the structured end of the continuum. In certain corporate environments, it may be easier for the decision maker to follow the prescriptions of the DSS; users of support systems are usually aware of the risks associated with certain choices. If decision makers feel that there is more risk associated with exercising judgment and opposing the suggestion of the DSS than there is in simply supporting the process, the DSS is moving the decision more toward the unstructured end of the spectrum. Therefore, the way in which a DSS will be used must be considered within the decision-making environment.

PROCESSING MODEL LIMITATIONS Another problem with the use of support systems that perform calculations is that the user/decision maker may not be fully aware of the limitations or assumptions of the particular processing model. There may be instances in which the decision maker has an idea of the information that is desired, but not necessarily the best way to get that information. This problem may be seen in the use of statistical analysis to support a decision. Most statistical packages provide a variety of tests and will perform them on whatever data is presented, regardless of whether it is appropriate. This problem has been recognized by designers of support systems and has resulted in the development of DSS that support the choice of the type of analysis—but, as with other features, the user must understand the choices and their implications.

FURTHER READING:

Arinze, Bay, and Snehamay Banerjee. "A Framework for Effective Data Collection, Usage, and Maintenance of DSS." *Information and Management*. May 1992.

Chaudhry, Sohail S., Linda Salchenberger, and Mahdi Beheshtian. "A Small Business Inventory DSS: Design, Development, and Implementation Issues." *Computers & Operations Research*. January 1996.

Cohen, Morris A., Jehoshua Eliashberg, and Tech H. Ho. "An Anatomy of a Decision-Support System for Developing and Launching Line Extensions." *Journal of Marketing Research*. February 1997.

Gupta, Jatinder N. D., and Thomas M. Harris. "Decision Support Systems for Small Business." *Journal of Systems Management*. February 1989.

Kimball, Ralph, and Kevin Strahlo. "Why Decision Support Fails and How to Fix It." *Datamation*. June 1, 1994.

Kuang-Chian, Chen. ''Developing Decisions Support Systems for Small Business Management: A Case Study.'' *Business Management.* July 1989.

Laudon, Kenneth C., and Jane Price Laudon. *Management Information Systems: A Contemporary Perspective.* 2d ed. New York: Macmillan, 1991.

Muller-Boling, Detlef, and Susanne Kirchhoff. ''Expert Systems for Decision Support in Business Start-Ups.'' *Journal of Small Business Management.* April 1991.

Parkinson, Chris. ''What If? Decision Shaping Systems.'' *CMA—The Management Accounting Magazine.* March 1995.

Raggad, Bel G. ''Decision Support System: Use It or Skip It.'' *Industrial Management and Data Systems.* January 1997.

Raymond, Louis, and Francois Bergeron. ''Personal DSS Success in Small Enterprises.'' *Information and Management.* May 1992.

Schmall, Karen E. ''Variation in Success of Implementation of a Decision Support/Finite Scheduling System.'' *Production and Inventory Management Journal.* Winter 1996.

SEE ALSO: Computers and Computers Systems; Decision Making

DELEGATION

Delegation is the practice of turning over work-related tasks and/or authority to employees or subordinates. Small business owners often have difficulty with delegation for a variety of reasons, from concerns about the abilities of subordinates to long-standing ''hands-on'' management habits (a common characteristic of successful entrepreneurs). Indeed, ''businesses founded on the creative talents of the owner often struggle with [delegation] because the success of the enterprise depends on the owner's style,'' wrote Linda Formichelli in *Nation's Business.* But small business consultants warn that owners that do not learn to delegate responsibilities and tasks often end up stunting their company's growth.

THE NEED FOR EFFECTIVE DELEGATION PRACTICES ''Many managers think of delegation as a task—an activity to be carried out and forgotten. In reality, delegation is a process that makes up a critical component of successful management,'' wrote Janet Houser Carter in *Supervisory Management.* ''To get work done with and through others, a manager must regularly give authority to his or her staffers. This shows staffers that the manager has faith in their abilities—which is what makes delegation such a powerful motivational tool.''

A propensity for micromanagement—or nano-management, as it is sometimes called when applied to a small business firm—can have a deleterious impact on a company in a variety of ways. Moreover, many analysts contend that a lack of delegation can be particularly detrimental to the fortunes of smaller businesses. ''In small, entrepreneurial companies, micromanagement by one person—typically the owner—can be especially growth-inhibiting because it can have a proportionately larger sweep through the firm than micro-management by one executive in a large company,'' wrote Formichelli. Business consultants thus counsel their clients to practice sensible delegation of tasks to their employees—even in instances where they might not do as good a job initially. ''Employees can't learn unfamiliar tasks if they never get the chance to learn and practice them,'' noted Carter. ''In the short term, it may make sense to do it yourself; over the long term, however, you save more time by showing others how to do the job.''

Of course, not all tasks or responsibilities should be delegated to employees. Small business owners need to take care of basic strategic and planning issues themselves, and other management duties—conflict resolution, performance evaluations, etc.—should be delegated judiciously.

Business experts cite a number of specific problems that are often associated with companies that do not effectively delegate. These include:

- Poor employee morale—An inability or refusal to delegate can have a corrosive impact on the morale of good employees that want to contribute their talents to the business in a meaningful way. ''The front-line victims of nanomanagement are, undeniably, employees,'' said Formichelli. ''Their room for advancement becomes restricted because the owner won't relinquish responsibilities,'' and the resentment that employees feel when they are not trusted to do their jobs can eventually trigger high turnover.

- Burnout—Even the most talented, ambitious, and energetic entrepreneurs are apt to run out of gas if they insist on tackling all major aspects of a company's operation. Some small business owners can manage all or most important tasks for the early life of a company. Indeed, some small businesses—especially single-person enterprises like freelance graphics design or editorial services—may be able to handle all significant aspects of a company's operation for years on end. But for the vast majority of small and mid-sized businesses enjoying a measure of growth, owners sooner or later must face the reality that they cannot undertake all duties and responsibilities.

- Misallocation of Personal Resources—Small business owners and entrepreneurs who do not delegate often run the risk of using too much of their time on routine tasks and not enough time on vital aspects of the company's future, such as strategic planning, long-range budgeting, and marketing campaigns.

- Damage to Company Image—Business owners who do not empower their employees, insisting instead on attending to all relevant aspects of his or her business themselves, run the risk of inadvertently suggesting to customers and vendors that the company's workforce is not competent and/or trustworthy.

- Damage to Company Health—This should be the bottom-line consideration of all entrepreneurs running their own business. If micromanagement is slowing processing of work orders, hindering development of new marketing efforts, or otherwise causing bottlenecks in any areas of a company's operation, then it may be eating away at the company's fundamental financial well-being.

Small business owners are encouraged to evaluate whether they are perhaps falling into the trap of micromanagement. Consultants and entrepreneurs cite the following as major warning signs:

- Taking work home in the evening or working long hours of overtime;

- Failure to give important tasks the amount of attention that they warrant;

- Basic company documents (like business plans) are not updated for long periods;

- Excessive amounts of time spent going over work already completed by employees;

- Completing important tasks with little time to spare (or a day or two late);

- Spending inordinate amounts of time on relatively unimportant or routine jobs;

- Vacations assume mythic status;

- Unhappy employees;

- Unhappy family members.

KEYS TO EFFECTIVE DELEGATION Effective delegation is ultimately predicated on ensuring that the company's workforce is sufficiently talented and motivated to take on the responsibilities that are delegated to them. "New entrepreneurs often have difficulty figuring out what kind of workers to hire," remarked Formichelli. "If the wrong people are hired, they require more training and supervision, which invites nanomanagement." Sound hiring practices and adequate training are thus universally regarded as major factors in establishing a healthy system of delegation. Once those aspects have been addressed, there are other considerations that can be studied as well. These include:

- Work Environment—Establish a positive work environment where employees are not paralyzed by fear of failure or dismissive of tasks that they think are beneath them. Owners and managers need to emphasize tools of motivation and communication to nourish employee enthusiasm.

- Review Responsibilities—Business owners and managers need to objectively examine which tasks that they have previously taken care of can be delegated to others. "Reserve for yourself those tasks which require the experience, skill, and training which only you possess," wrote W.H. Weiss in the *Supervisor's Standard Reference Handbook.*

- Established Policies—Detailed manuals of policies and procedures can go far toward eliminating the uncertainties that hamstring some delegation efforts.

- Plan for Delegation—A company that is armed with a strong, clear vision of its future—and the role that its employees will play in that future—is far more likely to be successful than the business that does not plan ahead. "Delegation should be a planned process, not an act of desperation" that takes place only when things become hectic, wrote Carter.

- Communication—"Be clear and concise when delegating," said Weiss. "Right from the beginning you must clarify what decisions you are delegating and what you are reserving for yourself. Delegating fails when the person to whom you have delegated a task fails to perform it or makes a decision beyond the scope of authority granted." Conversely, delegation can also fail if the business owner hands off a responsibility, but does not give his or her employee the necessary level of authority to execute that responsibility. In addition, small business owners should make sure that they keep lines of communication open at all times. "Employees need to be reassured that the manager will be there to offer assistance or clarification, and that mistakes during the learning period are to be expected," said Carter. "Mistakes should be viewed as opportunities to teach, not punish."

Ultimately, small business owners need to recognize that delegation can help a business grow and prosper, and that good employees, when used intelligently, can be a significant advantage in the marketplace. "The manager who wants to learn to delegate more should remember this distinction," wrote Thomas S. Bateman and Carl P. Zeithaml in *Manage-*

ment: Function and Strategy. "If you are not delegating, you are merely doing things; the more you delegate, the more you are truly *building* and *managing* an organization."

FURTHER READING:

Bateman, Thomas S., and Carl P. Zeithaml. *Management: Function and Strategy.* Hinsdale, IL: Richard D. Irwin, 1990.

Carter, Janet Houser. "Minimizing the Risks from Delegation." *Supervisory Management.* February 1993.

Formichelli, Linda. "Letting Go of the Details." *Nation's Business.* November 1997.

Roberts, Gary, Gary Seldon, and Carlotta Roberts. *Human Resources Management.* Washington: U.S. Small Business Administration, n.a.

Weiss, W.H. *Supervisor's Standard Reference Handbook.* 2d ed. Englewood Cliffs, NJ: Prentice-Hall, 1988.

SEE ALSO: Employee Hiring; Employee Motivation

DELIVERY SERVICES

Regardless of the nature of their business, all business owners find it necessary and convenient to make use of delivery services. At one time, the United States Postal Service provided virtually all mail and package delivery in the United States. From mailing a single letter to shipping just-in-time manufacturing products, today's business owner has a number of choices when it comes to delivery services. Moreover, these options are relatively inexpensive, due to the fierce competition that characterizes the industry. As a matter of fact, delivery services have become so competitive that overnight and same day delivery services have been the norm since 1995.

Indeed, as United Parcel Service vice president Peter Fredo told *Brandweek,* "It's no longer an issue of overnight, but rather what time of day." In addition to the industry standard overnight delivery, most of the major players in the delivery industry offer some type of program that guarantees same-day delivery. Federal Express and United Parcel Service began just this type of program in 1995. However, competitor DHL Worldwide Express had been offering same-day service for six years. In addition to large fleets of delivery trucks, several delivery services have also become operators of large fleets of aircraft.

TECHNOLOGICAL ADVANCES IN PACKAGE DELIVERY As competition for delivery dollars has increased, so has the technological advances and innovations offered by delivery companies. "Technology has become the key basis of differentiation," one Federal Express executive told *Brandweek.* These technological advances show themselves in all facets of company operations. Specialized, company-owned aircraft that can land and take off in severe weather ensure that next day deliveries adhere to schedules. Sophisticated customer service operations and package tracking software allow the customer to be instantly apprised of the location and status of the package shipped.

One of the most popular advances in delivery technology was the advent of desktop software packages that allow customers to order deliveries and then track those deliveries to the doorstep of the receiving party. An added enhancement to these software packages is Internet web sites set up by each of the major delivery companies. By checking a delivery service's web site, the customer can find information on all relevant shipment data, including rates, drop off and pick up times, and tips on economical ordering and packaging.

KEEPING COSTS LOW

Each of the major delivery services offers several delivery plan options. When it is not necessary to have a package delivered overnight, economical two- or three-day delivery plans may be the best bet. As *Purchasing* magazine noted, cost-conscious customers have found that second- and third-day services offer a time-definite guarantee, yet are a fraction of the cost of next day services. Certainly, in today's fast-paced business environment, overnight delivery will remain popular with small and large businesses alike. Indeed, *Purchasing* reported that demand for overnight services increased by 9 percent in 1996. However, the magazine noted that demand for second day service enjoyed an increase of more than 7 percent in the same year.

According to *Black Enterprise* magazine, business owners can save money on their next-day delivery costs by shopping around, and by following the simple tips listed below:

1) Address the package correctly. Incorrectly addressed packages incur added charges.

2) Drop off the package at the carrier site. Discounts are offered by many major services if they are dropped off at the company site.

3) If next-day delivery is really not necessary, use a more economical delivery plan.

4) Use the smallest box possible to ship the package. Some services charge fees based upon package size as well as the weight of the package.

5) Seek alternatives to overnight delivery. For example, companies can fax documents for a fraction of the cost of personal delivery.

MAJOR AMERICAN DELIVERY SERVICES The United States supports a number of major national and regional delivery services. Foremost among these are the United Parcel Service (55 Glendale Pkwy., NE, Atlanta, GA 30328, 404-828-6000), Federal Express (2005 Corporate Ave., Memphis, TN 38194-1854, 901-369-3600),

Airborne Express (3101 Western Ave., Seattle, WA 98111, 206-285-4600), and DHL Airways, Inc. (333 Twin Dolphin Dr., Redwood City, CA 94065, 415-593-7474).

FURTHER READING:

Brown, Ann. "Saving on Next-Day Delivery: The Right Mailing Service Can Reduce Your Office Expenses." *Black Enterprise.* December 1996.

Coleman, Lisa. "Overnight isn't Fast Enough." *Brandweek*, July 31, 1995.

Minahan, Tim. "Putting the Express Back in Package Express." *Purchasing*, February 13, 1997.

Rice, Marc. "Competition Fierce in Complex Business of Delivering Packages." *Marketing News*, May 22, 1995.

SEE ALSO: Postal Costs

DEMOGRAPHICS

Demographics are the statistical characteristics of human populations, such as age or income, that are used by businesses to identify markets for their goods and services. For the businessperson, identifying the demographic groups that will be most interested in your product can mean the difference between success and failure. This is especially critical for the small businessperson who might have less room for error than larger companies.

Demographics are used to identify who your customers are (now and in the future), where they live, and how likely they are to purchase the product you are selling. By studying your customers and potential customers through demographics, one can identify changing needs in the marketplace and adjust to them.

Basic demographic analysis is used for two reasons: to identify population characteristics in order to determine just who your potential customer is and to serve as a means of locating geographic areas where the largest number of potential customers live. For example, if you were interested in selling a new denture cream, it is likely that you would want to identify the counties or cities in the United States that had the largest concentration of elderly consumers. Once you identified those areas, you would want to know more about the elderly people who lived in those counties: What are their buying habits? How

many wear dentures? How many are on a fixed income? These are the types of questions that demographics can help answer.

MASS MARKETING

Until recent years, most companies used demographic information, but only in the broadest possible way. The most common method of selling was mass marketing—trying to reach the most people possible via the media—primarily television, radio, and newspapers. Finding the people who were most likely to purchase the product was not the point—spreading the word about the product to as many people as possible was. The result of this "shotgun" approach to selling was fairly obvious. Companies were spending enormous amounts of money to reach audiences with no guarantees that anyone in that audience wanted to buy the products that were being pitched to them. For example, a prime time television advertisement for a sports car would reach some of the people who were most likely to buy such a car (young men, for instance) but it would also reach millions and millions of people who had absolutely no interest in the car.

Today's companies, however, have realized that such methodologies might not be the most cost-efficient means of selling a product. But if mass marketing worked for so long, why is it coming under fire now? There are several answers that explain the demise of mass marketing. First, the past three decades have been the most tumultuous in recent memory, ushering in tremendous social, political, and technological changes. Lifestyles have changed dramatically as a result of the rising divorce rate and the subsequent increase in single-parent households, increased participation by women in the labor force, and other societal changes. Women have far more control over household purchasing decisions than ever before. Technology, especially the Internet, has changed the way people interact and purchase products. In addition, the sheer number of products available for purchase has exploded—consumers have literally dozens of products to choose from in almost every product category.

Perhaps the most important change though has been in the ethnic makeup of the United States. Even with immigration restrictions, the U.S. is still the melting pot of the world. It is estimated that by the early part of the next century, Caucasians will be a minority in the United States. The Latin American and Asian populations in the United States are experiencing particularly explosive growth at this time.

BUILDING A CUSTOMER PROFILE

As mass marketing's appeal begins to fade, it is being replaced by target marketing. Target marketing means knowing as much as possible about your current and potential customers and reaching them through very specialized advertising or marketing campaigns. Demographic data is the cornerstone of target marketing. Information is now readily available in computerized formats that make it easy to know a tremendous amount about consumers, from the national level right down to the neighborhood or block level.

The first question to ask when relying on **target markets** is: Is a product to be sold to a household or an individual? Products such as refrigerators, stoves, and dinette sets are sold to a household (a household might need only one of such products), while products such as shoes and toothbrushes are sold to individuals (each individual who lives in a household needs those products). Households can be broken down as "family" households and "nonfamily" households. The younger the person, the more likely they are to live in a nonfamily household (such as with a roommate, friend, or significant other). Everyone in the U.S., with the exception of the homeless, live in a household or something known as "group quarters." Group quarters covers such diverse living spaces as nursing homes, prisons, and college dormitories. With the exception of dormitories, most group quarters are considered to be unimportant marketing targets.

Once that question has been answered, a company can use demographics to compile a "customer profile" of their target audience. Factors that should be considered in the profile include:

- Ethnic background. It is important to make a distinction between ethnicity and race. The term "Hispanic," for example, refers to an ethnic group, not a race of people.

- Income. In general, income tends to increase with age as people obtain better-paying jobs and receive promotions. Married couples often have a higher income because both partners usually work. Income is recorded by the U.S. Census Bureau in a number of ways, each with different ramifications for marketers. Income is defined as all money and public assistance that is earned before taxes and union dues are taken out. Personal income is money plus noncash benefits such as food stamps. Disposable income is the money that is left after taxes are taken out, and discretionary income is the amount of money left after taxes are paid and necessities such as food and shelter are paid for. It is often this last type of income that marketers are most interested in. Income can be reported for households or individuals.

- Education. This is an increasingly important demographic factor as technology becomes more important to day-to-day living. Gener-

ally, the more education a person has, the greater the income they earn, thus the more money they have to purchase products. Education is most often measured by level of schooling completed. As a rule, college-educated people are among the most desirable consumer groups, but studies show that they also tend to be the least brand loyal. This means a business may have to work harder to reach and keep those customers.

Any of those key elements of a customer profile are readily available from companies that repackage and sell U.S. Census Bureau data. Most common is something called a cluster system, which is also known as a geodemographic segmentation system. Cluster systems measure concrete data, such as age, income, and actual purchase decisions and combine them to create profiles of individuals and households. When used in conjunction with business mapping systems that link demographic data to geographic areas (as specific as the household level, but more commonly by ZIP Codes or other market areas), cluster systems are a powerful marketing tool.

Psychographics, by comparison, measure less tangible items, such as a person's attitudes and lifestyle, and his or her openness to technology or to trying new products. The results of both cluster systems and psychographic surveys must be considered to develop a truly accurate customer profile.

Demographic information can be used to create a snapshot of a customer base as it currently exists, but to use the same information to make educated guesses about the future, population trends must be studied. This can mean the population of the United States, which is fairly easy to project, right down to a particular neighborhood, which is far more difficult to project. Studying past population trends can help businesses make future predictions and is the basis for a form of target marketing known as generational marketing.

GENERATIONAL MARKETING

As with basic target marketing, generational marketing entails gathering as much information as possible about current and potential customers for any given product. How old are the users? How much money do they make? What are their hobbies? Where do they live? What are their career goals? Do they have children? What magazines do they subscribe to? What are the key events that have shaped their world?

Generational marketing involves two key terms: generation and cohort. A generation is defined by dates of birth, while a cohort is defined by the key events that occur during early years of a person's life. For example, people born from 1967 to 1972 might be termed the Vietnam generation, because they were born during the height of the conflict in Southeast Asia, while people born between 1949 and 1954 would be called the Vietnam cohort because their formative years occurred during the peak years of the war.

Markets today are most commonly divided by age brackets. Radio ratings, for example, are divided into very broad categories: a station might be trying to capture the 25- to 54-year-old market for example. Television executives might tell their programming departments to give them a new show that appeals to 18- to 49-year-old males.

Generational marketing puts less stock into age breakdowns and instead emphasizes life events that have shaped the generation or cohort that is being targeted. As Steve Goldstein, director of marketing for Levi Strauss, told *Fortune,* ''Instead of looking at the typical age breaks, like 18 to 49, we want to lay a more sophisticated layer of generational information. We tell [media buyers] to find quintessential programs that resonate with the values of the generation we are targeting. The show must relate to their lifestyles and attitudes.''

Targeting specific groups to market products or services means a shift in advertising as well. Instead of large-scale, mass market campaigns, direct mail pieces sent to carefully screened prospective customers are used. Many people think this is more expensive than mass market campaigns, but that is not true. For example, one small company studied by *Fortune* that switched to direct mail based on generational marketing reduced its advertising budget from 7.8 percent of sales to 4.8 percent in three years; sales increased 40 percent during that time.

Psychographics play a more important role in generational marketing than in mass marketing. To gather the specific information that is needed for this type of marketing, companies often supplant traditional demographic data with telephone interviews, in-home visits, mail intercepts, and focus groups. Generational marketing requires far more sophistication than traditional mass marketing.

SOURCES OF DEMOGRAPHIC DATA

Many companies now make demographic data available on diskette or CD-ROM. In addition, the U.S. Census Bureau maintains a World Wide Web site that provides access to raw data. The site can be found at http://www.census.gov.

FURTHER READING:

Boutilier, Robert. *Targeting Families: Marketing To and Through the New Family.* American Demographics Books, 1993.

Campanelli, Melissa. ''It's All in the Family.'' *Sales & Marketing Management.* April 1994.

Miller, Berna. ''A Beginner's Guide to Demographics.'' *Marketing Tools.* October 1995.

Rice, Faye. ''Making Generational Marketing Come of Age.'' *Fortune.* June 26, 1995.

Russell, Cheryl. *The Official Guide to the American Marketplace.* 2d ed. New Strategist Books, 1995.

SEE ALSO: Advertising Strategy; Market Analysis; Market Research

DEPRECIATION

The cost of **assets** that are totally consumed within an accounting period will be recognized as an expense within that period. When an asset is not totally consumed within a single accounting period, the cost of the asset must be allocated as an expense over the periods in which the asset is consumed. Depreciation arises from this attempt to assign asset cost to the periods of asset consumption. The depreciation for an asset in a period is simply an estimate of the portion of the original cost to be assigned as an expense to the period. A similar concept is depletion, which is applied to the extraction of natural resources in recognition of the fact that a certain part of the natural resource has been consumed during a given period.

MISCONCEPTIONS ABOUT DEPRECIATION

Since depreciation is an allocation of cost over accounting periods, it is not directly connected to market value—or the amount that the asset would be worth if it were sold. The book value of an asset, computed as the actual cost minus the accumulated depreciation, is simply the unallocated cost of the item. The pattern of depreciation is fixed, and does not respond to changing market conditions.

Depreciation does not involve any cash flow. This is clearest in the simple case of an asset acquired entirely by cash payment. Although the initial purchase is a cash flow, the subsequent allocation of part of the cost as a period expense involves only an accounting entry. Depreciation is not intended as a mechanism to provide for replacement of the asset. There are no cash flows associated with depreciation, and there is no connection with any cash accumulated for replacement of the asset. The asset may or may not be replaced—this is a capital budgeting decision that is immaterial to the recognition of expense.

Because depreciation is an expense but has no associated cash flow, it is sometimes described as being ''added back'' to arrive at cash flow for the firm. This gives the impression that depreciation is somehow a source of cash flow. The ''adding back,'' however, is simply a recognition that no cash flow occurred, and depreciation cannot supply cash.

METHODS OF DEPRECIATION

The concept and relevance of allocating the portion of the original cost of an asset ''used up'' in a period as an expense of the period is clear. In many practical cases, however, the proportion of cost to be allocated as an expense of a particular accounting period can only be estimated. Allocating cost as an expense requires estimation of the useful lifetime of the asset (which may be expressed in terms of time or in terms of units of production), and any residual or salvage value. These estimates must reflect obsolescence, and may be dependent on maintenance, rate of use, or other conditions. While some guidelines exist, they are in the form of suggested ranges, and the estimate may be strongly influenced by industry practice. The choice of depreciation parameters and methods is made by management. For a given type of asset, the estimates may differ widely among firms or industries.

In recognition of the difficulties of such estimation, generally accepted accounting principles (GAAP) allow wide discretion in the depreciation method used. Where the productive life of an asset can be expressed in terms of units of production, the units-of-production method can be applied. Under this approach, the amount of depreciation for an accounting period is the depreciable value of the asset (actual cost minus any residual value), divided by the (unit) lifetime, and multiplied by the units produced in the period; depreciation in a period will thus be a function of production in the period.

Straight-line depreciation is the allocation of equal depreciation amounts to accounting periods over the life of the asset. The straight-line depreciation amount is the depreciable value divided by the lifetime in accounting periods. For example, for an asset with a four-year useful life, yearly depreciation would be 25 percent of its depreciable value. An argument against this procedure is that obsolescence and other factors are not linear over time, but rather reduce the usefulness or productivity of an asset by larger amounts in early years.

Accelerated depreciation methods recognize this nonlinear decrease in productivity by assigning more depreciation to early periods, and less depreciation to later periods. The double-declining balance accelerated method allocates depreciation as a constant percent equivalent to twice the straight-line rate, but applies this to the book value of the asset. For an asset with a four-year useful life, yearly depreciation would be two times 25 percent or 50 percent of book value. The final year of double-declining balance depreciation, however, is the amount necessary to equate book value to residual value. Sum-of-years' digits accelerated depreciation is computed by multiplying depreciable value by the remaining periods of useful life at the start of the period divided by the sum of the digits in the original useful life. For an asset with a four-year useful life, depreciation in the first year would be $4/(4+3+2+1)$ or 40 percent of depreciable value.

DEPRECIATION AND TAXES

Depreciation is an expense, and it affects taxes by reducing taxable income. A firm may use different depreciation treatments for tax purposes and for **financial statements**. Typically, straight-line depreciation would be used for financial reporting because it produces more consistent earnings and is easily understood. An accelerated depreciation treatment would be chosen for tax accounting because the higher depreciation in early periods results in lower taxable income, and shifts tax payment to later periods when lower depreciation results in higher taxable income. This is solely a timing advantage. The total amount of taxes paid is not reduced, but a portion of the payments is shifted to later periods.

The Tax Reform Act of 1986 created a modified accelerated cost recovery system (MACRS) that may be used for tax accounting purposes. This system groups assets into eight classes of estimated useful life, and most classes are depreciated using some form of double-declining balance (rental property, however, is depreciated using straight-line depreciation).

FURTHER READING:

Bernstein, L. A. *Financial Statement Analysis: Theory, Application and Interpretation.* 4th ed. Homewood, IL: Irwin, 1989.

Harrison, Jr., W. T., and C.T. Horngren. *Financial Accounting.* 2nd ed. Englewood Cliffs, NJ: Prentice Hall, 1995.

Kieso, Donald E., and J. G. Weygandt. *Financial Accounting.* New York: Wiley, 1995.

Marullo, Gloria Gibbs. ''Catching Up on Depreciation.'' *Nation's Business.* October 1996.

White, G. I., A. C. Sondhi, and D. Fried. *The Analysis and Use of Financial Statements.* New York: Wiley, 1994.

SEE ALSO: Tax Planning

DESKTOP PUBLISHING

Desktop publishing is the process of using computers and software to design, prepare, and typeset a variety of documents (business cards, fliers, brochures, manuals, resumes, newsletters, in-store signage). This technology, which continues to change with sometimes dizzying speed, has been embraced by all levels of the business world, from giant corporations to small, independently-owned enterprises.

PREPARING FOR DESKTOPPING IN YOUR BUSINESS

Small businesses need to take a number of different factors under consideration when pondering how to introduce a desktop publishing system into their operations. Writing in *Association Management,* Dennis F. Pierman cited a number of areas to examine when evaluating the proliferating number of desktopping systems now available in the marketplace. First, he suggested that business owners should not only understand their business needs, but also study how new systems can help them meet those needs. Business owners and managers should take all aspects of the company's operation into consideration, said Pierman, including personnel, training, **management information systems** supervision, system software and future upgrades, initial capital acquisition, and equipment depreciation. In addition, managers should "isolate and analyze the real cost associated with the mix of in-house and vendor resources you are currently using, and use the cost as a benchmark against which to measure your needs analysis." Pierman also recommended that businesses consult with companies that currently take care of their publishing needs to 1) see if future expansion of their services or capabilities might lessen your need to purchase a desktopping system; 2) determine if pricing changes can be negotiated; and 3) ensure that you do not inadvertently invest in "equipment, software, and technical redundancies." Finally, Pierman recommended that companies "poll staff who would be affected directly by going desktop publishing about their 'feel' for its impact."

IN-HOUSE APPLICATIONS

Many small business owners have reaped the benefits of desktop technology in recent years. "Desktop publishing software has made substantial advances in the past few years," wrote *Nation's Business* writer Ripley Hotch, "and many programs really can save your business time and money—if you learn to use them correctly." Indeed, countless small businesses have been able to parlay desktop publishing into improvements in marketing, advertising, and bottom-line profitability.

But while desktop publishing has many passionate defenders, even proponents of the technology's usefulness for business purposes admit that problems can crop up when it is used. Complaints about desktop publishing that small business owners should bear in mind include:

LOST PRODUCTIVITY Ironically, some businesses actually report declines in **productivity** after turning to desktop publishing, as business owners, managers, and communications personnel fall into the trap of excessive experimentation with fonts, formatting, graphics, etc. Small business owners need to show restraint when using desktop applications, and they should monitor employee use to ensure that the company's desktop projects do not become a black hole of lost hours and productivity.

In addition, owners have to recognize that the purchase of a desktop publishing system is going to require an investment of hours of studying, training, and practice on the part of the owner himself and/or one or more of the company's employees. Indeed, one business executive indicated to *Association Management* that the human factors associated with turning to desktop publishing were as important as the economic implications of doing so: "Make changes as gradually or as quickly as the entire staff will allow."

POOR QUALITY Many business analysts and consultants have lamented that the emergence of desktop publishing has also brought with it an upswing in the amount of poorly prepared and presented brochures, newsletters, and guides dotting the business landscape, particularly from in-house staff (whether owner or employees). As one desktop publishing professional told Glenn Jochum for *LI Business News,* design quality can be compromised because people have a tendency to adopt the attitude, "I did it, ain't it great." In reality, however, some booklets, newsletters, signage, and other materials that are created via desktop publishing are little more than a blizzard of mismatched formats and typefaces, while others reveal a distressing over-reliance on spell-checking programs. Publishing professionals urge users to practice basic rules of presentation when desktopping, just as they would in using any other communication media. "Knowing desktop publishing technology is just the beginning," stated Tim O'Brien in *Communication World.* "No computer can replace your own design sense or writing ability." As desktop publishing continues to increase in popularity, he added, "it is more important than ever to take the time to actually read the material from a critical perspective prior to printing. Make sure that the writing follows a logical sequence; that there are no typos; that the layout supports the writing; that type, format and spacing work together to provide a clean look that communicates effectively."

APPLICABILITY Consultants caution business owners and managers to recognize that desktop publishing systems, while quite useful for many organizations, have varying levels of application for companies depending on their size, industry area, and future business plans. After all, some businesses may have a far greater need for brochures, newsletters, and advertising materials (grocery stores, retail outlets, manufacturers, resorts, hospitals, etc.) than gas stations and other businesses that are less reliant on advertising/public relations.

OTHER EXPENSES Pierman noted that when a company invests in a desktop publishing system, ''a variety of traditional tools are required to make 'electronic' publishing work. Even independent studios and service bureaus still use drafting tables, special lighting, light tables, waxers, paper cutters, flat files, artist's tape, flow markers, colored pencils, rulers, triangles, knives, and reams of paper.''

CHOOSING AN OUTSIDE VENDOR

Desktop publishing vendors typically offer a broad spectrum of services, and they can provide clients with printed material in practically any form desired, from advertising fliers to dense training manuals or annual reports. And while all desktop publishing services are not created equal, most of them are armed with a fair amount of experience and technical knowledge. This leads many consultants to echo the words of Hotch, who remarked that ''when the publishing is really complex, it usually makes sense to obtain the services of a professional.'' This is especially true when the material that is being prepared is intended for an audience outside the company's walls. Many entrepreneurs and long-time publishing veterans have taken advantage of this continued need. In addition to desktop publishers that make a living by providing their services for clients, *LI Business News* noted that by the mid-1990s, the ''desktop revolution'' had created a whole new business niche: the service bureau that serves as an intermediary between the customer and the high-end printer.

FURTHER READING:

Bjelland, Harley. *Create Your Own Desktop Publishing System.* Blue Ridge Summit, PA: Windcrest/McGraw-Hill, 1994.

Cavuoto, James, and Stephen Beale. *Guide to Desktop Publishing.* Pittsburgh, PA: Graphic Arts Technical Foundation, 1992.

Harper, Doug. ''Desktop Publishing Has Become Easy and Inexpensive.'' *Journal of Commerce and Commercial.* December 7, 1992.

Hotch, Ripley. ''Refined Desktop Publishing.'' *Nation's Business.* August 1994.

Jochum, Glenn. ''Ups and Downs of Desktop Revolution.'' *LI Business News.* January 16, 1995.

McGoon, Cliff. ''Desktop Publishing: Communicators' Best Friend or Worst Enemy?'' *Communication World.* November 1993.

O'Brien, Tim. ''Ride Hard on Quality: Don't Let Desktop Publishing Lower Your Standards.'' *Communication World.* November 1990.

Pierman, Dennis F. ''Myths and Realities of Desktop Publishing.'' *Association Management.* October 1993.

Stonely, Dorothy. ''Desktop Publishing Industry Evolves with Demand.'' *The Business Journal.* March 17, 1997.

SEE ALSO: Communication Systems; Computers and Computer Systems

DIFFICULT CUSTOMERS

Successful small business owners recognize that customer satisfaction is one of the essential elements of organizational prosperity. After all, providing quality service that clients appreciate not only ensures repeat business from them, but also encourages future ''word-of-mouth'' sales. But virtually all small business operations will sooner or later encounter customers who prove troublesome in one respect or another, sometimes even if you believe that the service that they have received is exemplary. **Customer service** experts counsel small business owners who encounter this situation to: 1) determine whether the difficult customer actually has a legitimate complaint; 2) determine whether the business can take steps to mollify the client's concerns (regardless of their legitimacy) and improve the relationship; and 3) in cases where the customer is being unreasonable, decide whether the customer's value is sufficient to warrant continuance of service. ''No business wants to lose customers,'' confirmed *Nation's Business* contributor Jenny McCune. ''But you need to recognize why the customer is difficult and to figure out how—and whether—to save the relationship.''

In most industry sectors, the vast majority of customers are fairly easy to work with. They understand the basic rules of commerce, in which they pay your business an agreed-upon amount to render a service or provide a product to them under certain terms that are also mutually agreed upon. But a minority of customers—experts place the number at anywhere from 5 to 10 percent—qualify as difficult. Sometimes these customers seem more prevalent, however, simply because they can take up so much of a business's time and energy.

Nonetheless, small businesses need to learn to differentiate between truly difficult customers that are ultimately of questionable value to their operations and those customers that may be annoying for one reason or another but who are basically solid clients who appear to be comfortable with the arrangement. Often, the difficult customer is someone who has simply taken an annoying habit to an extreme. For example, Richard F. Gerson, author of *Great Customer Service for Your Small Business,* listed ten types of customer behaviors, only one of which—The Perfect Customer—was wholly desirable to the small business owner. But the others—customers that are ''know-it-alls,'' unduly dependent, argumentative, indecisive, chronic complainers, or monopolizers of time—sometimes comprise the majority of customer types. These are the individuals who your establishment depends on for long-term success, and as long as their quirks do not develop into a formidable obstacle to business transactions, your business should continue to do its best to satisfy them. It is when these and other characteristics show themselves in full-blown form that the small business owner needs to intercede and decide how his or her business will interact with that customer—if at all—in the future.

DETERMINING IF THE DIFFICULT CUSTOMER HAS A LEGITIMATE GRIPE Customer service experts contend that many difficult customers are behaving in that manner because they have a legitimate gripe with the product or service that they have received. Indeed, Oren Harari commented in an article in *Management Review* that ''businesses often automatically label customers who complain as customers from hell, which is about as stupid a business decision as one can imagine.'' McCune agreed: ''Many 'bad' customers are the result of a bad situation. A salesclerk is surly; your company doesn't respond quickly enough to a request; a product defect ruins the customer's day; or an order promised for Wednesday doesn't arrive until Friday.'' (Indeed, the chances are very good that a poorly run business operation is apt to encounter a far greater number of so-called ''difficult'' customers than will an establishment that is efficient, competent, and dedicated to ideals of customer service.)

Small business owners and managers, then, need to determine whether the customer has a legitimate complaint before taking any other action. The client is obviously the individual that is best equipped to explain the reasons for his dissatisfaction, so he or she should have a full opportunity to express the grievance. From there—provided that it is determined that the customer was poorly served in one respect or another—the small business manager should gather all the pertinent facts from his or her staff to determine where the error occurred and to figure out how best to correct the problem and/or ensure that future transactions will not suffer a similar fate. The manager should then address the client's concerns appropriately and sincerely, including a full apology. If the customer—who, after all, may have provided a service to your company by alerting it to an operational weakness or personnel problem—is convinced that you are genuinely sorry for the slip-up and genuinely interested in solving the problem to his satisfaction, the chances are good that your company will do business with that client in the future.

ANTICIPATING CUSTOMER CONCERNS In addition to making apologies and moving to address problems in performance, small business owners can take several other steps to improve their relationships with difficult customers. For example, consultants believe that firms that take preventive measures—such as regular inquiries into customer satisfaction—are often able to address minor grievances before they erupt into major spots of contention. Instituting such an arrangement, say proponents, actually gives businesses the opportunity to prevent attitudes that eventually grow into problem attitudes from ever taking root.

Similarly, small businesses should make sure that their employees are empathetic with customers. ''Complaining customers are often further alienated by what they perceive as legally 'correct,' but nevertheless unempathic, insensitive, by-the-book, bureaucratic responses they receive when they are angry or distressed,'' wrote Harari. ''Customers will tolerate even the most intense foul-ups as long as they believe that the company really cares about their feelings. And as any lawyer will tell you, the big-time lawsuits come when people feel that they've been ignored or bureaucratically jerked around by impersonal, uncaring organizations.''

LETTING DIFFICULT CUSTOMERS GO There are occasions, however, when even a company's best efforts to address or anticipate customer complaints are fruitless. In other words, a small but significant percentage of customers who your business deals with will likely prove to be extremely unpleasant no matter how you try to please them. Few businesses are exempt from this reality. After all, the convenience store owner confronted with a disruptive customer is essentially grappling with the same problem as the owner of a small manufacturing company who is treated shabbily by a corporate buyer. In both cases, the business owner is dealing with a customer/client who makes conducting business a distinctly unpleasant experience.

When confronted with difficult customers who appear unlikely to change their stripes, small business owners have to decide whether their business is worth the aggravation. Several factors should be considered:

1) Impact on Business—This is generally the single most important consideration in weighing whether to continue doing business with a difficult customer. Is the customer one of your major clients? How difficult would it likely be to replace the revenue from that customer? Is the client a possible conduit to other potentially valuable customers? What is the nature of the difficulty? This latter consideration is an important one, say customer service experts. For example, a customer that is an indecisive or impossible-to-please sort, and whose demands result in extensive drains on your business's resources, may be far more problematic than a client who is difficult simply because he is woefully lacking in interpersonal skills. If your business can handle the loss, it is per-

fectly acceptable to sever ties with a difficult customer. But small business owners should do their best to end the relationship decisively and as civilly as possible. "It is impossible to please unreasonable or marginal customers on all occasions, and it's best to consider leaving them to other vendors," summarized Jack Falvey in *Sales and Marketing Management*. "It's far better to expend your efforts in further satisfying already satisfied accounts. The return on investment is almost always far greater."

2) Impact on Staff—This consideration is sometimes overlooked by small business owners, to their detriment. Unhappy employees are far more likely to secure employment elsewhere than those that are content, and few things can make an employee unhappy more quickly than the spectre of regularly dealing with unpleasant customers. As Harari indicated, "there is no excuse for tolerating individuals who are ugly, abusive, destructive, or potentially violent with your staff. Customers from hell exist, and they must be dealt with firmly, fairly, quickly, and unapologetically. Any other response is an insult to your employees and a double insult to the vast majority of customers who are decent human beings."

3) Impact on Business Owner—Small business owners are more likely to be personally affected by difficult customers than are corporate executives, who are often fairly insulated from such unpleasantness. And since small businesses tend to rely on their founders for a sizable share of their direction and management, the feelings of those founders need to be considered. A small business owner who approaches encounters with a given customer with dread needs to carefully consider whether such meetings are having an adverse impact on his or her ability to attend to other needs of the business. "It can take as long as 24 hours for your heart rate to return to normal after episodes of severe stress," wrote Mitch Schneider in *Motor Age*. "It can take even longer to achieve a psychological state balanced and secure enough to function normally."

4) Mitigating Circumstances—Finally, in some instances there may be reasons for difficult behavior that are not immediately apparent. "Most difficult customer situations are complicated by all kinds of subjective judgements and seemingly mitigating circumstances," said Falvey. For example, changes in personnel at a client company can have a dramatic impact on inter-company relations. If the new representative is insecure about his or her capabilities and knowledge, that may manifest itself in a variety of undesirable ways. If the small business owner takes the time to figure out why the customer has suddenly become a problematic one, he or she may be able to devise a strategy to repair the relationship rather than end it.

FURTHER READING:

Bell, Chip. *Customers as Partners*. Barrett-Koehler, 1994.

Falvey, Jack. "Dealing with Difficult Customers: When Customers Become Unreasonable in Their Demands, It may be Time to Cut Them Loose." *Sales and Marketing Management*. April 1995.

Gerson, Richard F. *Great Customer Service for Your Small Business*. Crisp, 1996.

Harari, Oren. "To Hell and Back: Learn to Discriminate Between Customers From Hell and Customers Who Have Gone Through Hell." *July 1996*.

Kroskey, Carol Meres. "It's Okay to Fire a Customer." *Bakery Production and Marketing*. October 15, 1997.

McCune, Jenny C. "When Customers Are Bad Apples." *Nation's Business*. February 1998.

Paajanen, George. "Customer Service: Training, Sound Practices, and the Right Employee." *Discount Store News*. September 15, 1997.

Plagakis, Jim. "Persona Non Grata." *Drug Topics*. September 15, 1997.

Schneider, Jim. "High Maintenance." *Motor Age*. July 1997.

Sewell, Carl. *Customers for Life*. New York: Doubleday, 1990.

SEE ALSO: Customer Retention; Decision Making

DIRECT MAIL

Direct mail is a type of advertising media in which messages are sent to target customers through the mail. The Direct Marketing Association estimates that direct mail generated approximately $390 billion in sales in 1996, a staggering figure.

Newcomers to the field of direct mail often use the terms "direct mail," "direct marketing," and "mail order" interchangeably. Perhaps the best way to distinguish these three similar, yet different, terms is to remember that direct mail is simply an advertising medium, like print or broadcast media. Print media messages are delivered through the printed word, usually in newspapers or magazines, while broadcast media messages are delivered through the airwaves, on television or radio. In direct mail, advertising and other types of messages are delivered through the mail.

By way of contrast, mail order is a way of doing business, like retail or personal selling. A mail order business delivers its products through the mail. It may also use direct mail to send out advertising messages, but many other businesses use direct mail without being in the mail order business. Direct marketing is a broader term that refers to a type of marketing that utilizes a variety of advertising media to appeal directly to the consumer. **Direct marketing** is distinct from other types of marketing in that it makes an offer and solicits a direct response. Direct mail is simply one advertising medium that direct marketers employ, although it is the one most frequently used.

Direct mail is a particularly attractive option for small business owners, as it can communicate complete information about a product or service and reach almost any conceivable target group, all for a relatively low cost. Direct mail can provide the basis for a business, or it can be used to supplement a company's traditional sales efforts. For example, a small business could use direct mail to inform potential customers about its offerings, then follow up with a phone call or a visit from a salesperson. Owners of start-up businesses may find direct mail an effective method of creating awareness and interest in a new product, while owners of existing companies may find it useful in generating new business outside of their usual customers or geographic area. Another advantage of direct mail is that it is testable, so that entrepreneurs can try out different sales messages on various audiences in order to find the most profitable market for a new product or service.

USES OF DIRECT MAIL

Direct mail is the most heavily used direct marketing medium, and its popularity continues to grow despite postage increases. While most advertisers use third class mail, a significant number of mailings are sent first class, making it difficult to arrive at accurate statistics about the volume of advertising mail being sent. In his book *Profitable Direct Marketing,* Jim Kobs noted that 714,000 businesses held bulk mail permits and sent out more than 63 billion pieces of advertising mail a year.

The primary application of direct mail is to reach consumers with offers of traditional goods and services. Some of the earliest examples of direct mail were seed catalogs sent to American colonists before the Revolutionary War. More recently, direct mail has been used to offer consumers a range of financial services, **coupons** for discounts on packaged goods, and requests for donations to a variety of nonprofit organizations.

Direct mail is also an effective medium in business-to-business marketing. Since business orders are usually of larger value than consumer purchases, it often takes more than one mailing to make a sale. Imaginative packages are often used to get through to hard-to-reach executives whose mail is screened by their secretaries. In addition to making sales, business-to-business direct mail can be used to generate sales leads and reinforce the personal selling effort.

ELEMENTS OF DIRECT MAIL

THE OFFER There are three key elements of successful direct mail: making an offer, selecting the target audience among customer lists and databases, and creating the direct mail package. Making an offer is one element that distinguishes direct marketing from general advertising and other types of marketing. Offers are designed to motivate the reader to take action: place an order, request more information, etc. Writing in *Successful Direct Marketing Methods,* Bob Stone gave the following example of how the same offer could be presented in three different ways: 1) Half-price! 2) Buy one—get one free! 3) 50% off! All three convey the same offer, but statement number two pulled a 40 percent higher response than statements one or three because consumers perceived it to be the most attractive offer.

In direct mail the offer can be tailored to fit the characteristics of the individual recipients. Direct mail allows marketers to target individuals with known purchase histories or particular psychographic or demographic characteristics, all of which affect how an offer should be made. Some basic types of offers include: optional features; a special introductory price or quantity discount; free trial or bill me later; order by mail, phone, or fax; premiums or sweepstakes; and special conditions of sale and types of guarantees.

MAILING LISTS AND DATABASES **Mailing lists** and databases offer direct mail marketers the opportunity for more selectivity and personalization than any other advertising medium. The two basic types of lists are in-house lists and external lists. In-house lists—sometimes called response lists—are those compiled by the company based on responses to its previous mailings or to its advertising in other media. These lists, which represent prime repeat business opportunities, are among a small business's most important assets. They are usually not available to competitors for rental, though they are sometimes exchanged with other companies that offer similar products. In contrast, external lists are typically compiled for rental by sources outside the company. There are thousands of different lists available that classify consumers according to a variety of demographic criteria. External lists may be rented by competitors as well.

Depending on the product being sold through direct mail, lists may consist of the names of consumers or businesses. Some examples of compiled consumer lists available for rental include: buyers of certain vehicle models, collectors of different items, subscribers to various periodicals, organic gardeners, or golf enthusiasts. Business lists are typically categorized according to the Standard Industrial Classification (SIC) system, which assigns different types of businesses two-, three-, or four-digit codes. The two-digit codes designate major business groups, while the three- and four-digit codes indicate more specialized business types.

In direct mail, lists are often rented from a list source for one-time use. When multiple lists are rented, a technique known as merge/purge is used to eliminate duplications. The transaction between a direct mailer hoping to obtain a list and a compiler hoping to rent a list may be facilitated by a list broker or list manager. The list broker's job is to match the list buyer with the most appropriate list for its offerings. Although brokers technically represent both the list buyer and the list owner, they are usually paid by the list owner. Whereas a list broker helps a direct mailer find the right list, a list manager is more like an agent who represents one or more specific lists. List managers handle the rental and billing procedures for the list owners, and also work with list brokers and list compilers as well as with direct mailers to arrange usage for the list. List costs tend to vary with specificity. That is, a list of subscribers to a particular magazine may rent for $50 per thousand (lists are typically rented on a ''per thousand'' basis), while a list of women subscribers who live in certain zip codes may rent for $100 per thousand.

Direct mailers employ a variety of selectivity techniques to better target their mailings. Traditional segmentation techniques look at past behavior, including time since most recent purchase, frequency of purchase, and amounts of purchases. More advanced segmentation techniques employ formulas that help predict future behavior. One such technique is list enhancement, or the process of overlaying social, economic, demographic, or psychographic data obtained from other sources on a mailing list. Adding such data to an in-house list allows mailers to develop a customer profile based on such factors as age, gender, car ownership, dwelling type, and lifestyle factors. Once that process is undertaken, the in-house list becomes an in-house database, or a collection of information about customers and prospects that can be used for marketing purposes. Modeling techniques can then be applied to the in-house database to help predict response rates from externally compiled lists whose individuals share some of the characteristics of the company's customer profile.

THE DIRECT MAIL PACKAGE Direct mail packages come in all shapes and sizes, which makes direct mail one of the most flexible of the direct marketing media. A standard direct mail package includes an envelope, a letter, a brochure, and a response device. A variation

on the classic format is the multi-mailer—a package with a number of flyers each selling a different product. Another popular format is the self-mailer, or any piece that is mailed without an outer envelope. More complex direct mail packages are three-dimensional; that is, they include an object such as a gift or product sample. These three-dimensional mailings can be effective in reaching top executives whose mail is screened by a secretary, and they are practically guaranteed to be opened by consumers at home.

Catalogs ranging from six to more than 100 pages are used to sell a variety of goods. They are also used to sell services, such as seminars. A variation of the catalog is called a magalog, which combines a certain amount of editorial content along with sales content to give the catalog the appearance of a magazine. A specialized field of direct marketing, catalog marketing is a discipline unto itself and accounts for a significant part of all direct mail activity.

Looking more closely at the classic direct mail package, the envelope's job is to motivate the recipient to open the package. The recipient's decision whether to open, set aside, or discard the mailing piece takes just one or two seconds. Regardless of the volume of mail a person receives, whether at home or a place of business, the envelope must distinguish itself from other mail by its size, appearance, and any copy that might be written on it. Envelopes that take on the appearance of an invitation or telegram might grab someone's attention faster than a plain envelope, for example. Other choices that are made concerning envelopes include color and texture, window or closed face, and whether to use a preprinted indicia or a postage stamp.

The letter is a sales letter and provides the opportunity to directly address the interests and concerns of the recipient. In a sense the letter replaces the salesperson in face-to-face selling. The letter typically spells out the benefits of the offer in detail. The more personal the sales letter, the more effective it generally is. The letter writer must be intimately familiar with not only the product or service and its benefits, but also the concerns and needs of the person to whom the letter is addressed. While the letter tells the recipient about the benefits of the offer, the brochure illustrates them. Illustrated brochures are used to sell services as well as products. Brochures come in a range of sizes and different folds. While the use of color may increase response, the brochure's look should fit the product or service it is selling.

Finally, the package must include a response device, such as a business reply card or coupon, that the recipient can send back. Response rates are generally higher when the response device is separate from, rather than part of, the brochure or letter. **Toll-free telephone numbers** are often prominently displayed to allow the recipient to respond via telephone. However, since some customers will not use the phone to place an order, a response device should be included in addition to a toll-free number. The key to a successful response device is to keep it simple and easy to fill out. A ''lift letter'' is often added to the package to ''lift'' the response rate. The lift letter usually carries a message such as, ''Read this only if you've decided not to accept our offer,'' to grab the recipient's attention one more time.

Other enclosures that may be added to the direct mail package include gift or premium slips, article reprints, a business reply envelope, and a variety of involvement devices. Involvement devices such as stamps, stickers, pencils, and rub-off messages motivate the recipient to become involved with the response device and, hopefully, continue to take the action required to make a purchase.

TESTING DIRECT MAIL

Since large expenditures are involved in mailing to lists of thousands, most direct mailers take advantage of the medium's testing capabilities. Every element of direct mail—the offer, the list, and the package—can easily be tested to avoid committing major resources to unproductive mailings. In *Successful Direct Marketing Methods,* Stone recommended testing in six major areas: products and services, media, propositions made, copy platforms, formats, and timing. The point is that tests should concentrate on meaningful components.

For products and services being sold by mail, pricing and payment options are often tested. A test may reveal that a higher price actually produces a better response. While the product and the price are considered the main offer, premiums and other incentives that enhance the offer are also subject to testing.

List testing is basic to direct mail. Experts recommend testing different segments of a particular list, preferably testing the best segment first. The appropriate size of a test sample is dependent on the anticipated response. The smaller the anticipated response rate, the larger the necessary list sample should be. A rule of thumb is that the list sample should be large enough to generate thirty to forty anticipated responses. While list testing may clearly identify winners and losers, it will also reveal that some lists are marginal, or near break-even. In that case, the list may be discarded, or another test may be conducted using different selection criteria on the list to make it pay out better.

The direct mail package is subject to a variety of tests focusing on format and copy. If the mailer has established a control package, then one element at a time is tested to see if it lifts the response to the package. Another type of creative testing is sometimes called breakthrough testing, where an entirely new approach is developed to sell a product or service.

Lists, offers, and packages can all be tested in one mailing when done properly. A test matrix consisting of individual test cells is constructed. Each test cell contains a unique combination of elements being tested and makes up a portion of the overall mailing. After the entire mailing is dropped, responses from each test cell are tracked to determine the performance of the tested elements.

WHEN DIRECT MAIL WORKS BEST

Direct mail offers marketers several advantages over other advertising media. It provides a high degree of measurability, for example, which in turn allows for extensive testing. Of course, for direct mail to work well the direct marketer must be able to identify the target audience and create or rent the appropriate mailing lists to reach them. Direct mail also gives marketers control over the sales message and allows them to present a great deal of information about a product or service in the sales letter and brochure. Repeat mailings can be done to take advantage of the product's or service's potential for repeat sales as well as to sell related goods and services to the same lists. While direct marketing has grown over the years to employ a variety of advertising media as they became available, such as the telephone, broadcast media, and print media, it is direct mail that remains the most heavily used medium in direct marketing today.

FURTHER READING:

Bly, Robert W. *Business-to-Business Direct Marketing.* Lincolnwood, IL: NTC Business Books, 1993.

Direct Mail List Rates and Data. Wilmette, IL: Standard Rate & Data Services, 1994.

Jones, Susan K. *Creative Strategy in Direct Marketing.* Lincolnwood, IL: NTC Business Books, 1991.

Jutkins, ''Rocket'' Ray. *Direct Marketing: How You Can Really Do It Right.* 2nd ed. Rockingham Jutkins Marketing, 1990.

Kobs, Jim. *Profitable Direct Marketing.* 2nd ed. Lincolnwood, IL: NTC Business Books, 1992.

Lewis, Herschell Gordon. *Direct Marketing Strategies and Tactics.* Chicago, IL: Dartnell, 1992.

Stone, Bob. *Successful Direct Marketing Methods.* 4th ed. Lincolnwood, IL: NTC Business Books, 1989.

Scott, Howard. ''Targeting Prospects with Direct Mail.'' *Nation's Business.* September 1997.

SEE ALSO: Advertising Media, Print; Mail Order Business

DIRECT MARKETING

According to the official definition of the Direct Marketing Association (DMA), direct marketing is an ''interactive system of marketing which uses one or more advertising media to effect a measurable response and/or transaction at any location.'' While there are many other possible definitions, the DMA captures the four basic concepts that set direct marketing apart from traditional marketing.

The notion of interactivity, or one-to-one communication between the marketer and the prospect or customer, is one factor that distinguishes direct marketing from general advertising and other types of marketing. Direct marketing makes an offer and asks for a response. By developing a history of offers and responses, direct marketers acquire knowledge of their prospects and customers, resulting in more effective targeting.

Measurability also sets direct marketing apart from general advertising and other forms of marketing. Direct marketers can measure the response to any offer. Measurability allows direct marketers to test a variety of lists, offers, media—virtually any aspect of a campaign—in order to allocate marketing resources to the most effective combination of elements.

Direct marketing uses a variety of media, including mail, magazine ads, newspaper ads, television and radio spots, infomercials (also television but longer format), free standing inserts (FSIs), and card decks. This flexibility allows direct marketing to provide interactivity and measurability and still take advantage of new technologies. By being adaptable to virtually any media, direct marketing will lead marketers into the twenty-first century as interactive television, the information superhighway, and other new technologies become a reality.

Finally, in direct marketing, the transaction may take place at any location and is not limited to retail stores or fixed places of business. The transaction may take place in the consumer's home or office via mail, over the phone, or through interactive television. It may also occur away from the home or office, as at a kiosk, for example.

It is necessary to distinguish direct marketing from **direct mail** or **mail-order businesses**, although direct marketing encompasses those two concepts. Direct mail is an advertising medium, one of several media that direct marketers utilize. Mail order is a **distribution channel**, as are retail outlets and **personal selling**.

GROWTH OF DIRECT MARKETING

Jim Kobs, author of *Profitable Direct Marketing,* identified several factors contributing to the rapid growth of direct marketing in the 1990s. First, changing lifestyles were an important factor in the acceptance of direct marketing among consumers. The number of women working outside the home jumped from 42 percent to 58 percent between 1980 and 1990. Given less time to go shopping, many of these women found it convenient to select and examine merchandise in their own homes. Direct marketing extends this convenience beyond mail-order shopping to consumers receiving all kinds of offers in the home—via mail or commercial television, as is common today, or via home-shopping networks and interactive television.

Another factor contributing to the growth of direct marketing was the increased cost associated with personal sales calls. By the end of the 1970s, the average cost of a single sales call was estimated to be about $137. By the end of the 1980s, the cost had risen to more than $250 per call. An interesting application of direct marketing now is to generate qualified sales leads that can be followed up with a personal sales call. Thus direct marketing can make personal selling more cost-effective.

The growth of technology in general, and of computer-based technologies in particular, has also played an important role in many areas of direct marketing. New computer technologies have allowed direct marketers to be more precise in the analysis of results, in the targeting of messages based on more complex psychographics and demographics, in developing more sophisticated customer and prospect databases, and even in the creative execution of direct mail packages.

Increased consumer acceptance of the telephone as a way to place orders has also helped direct marketing achieve phenomenal growth. Coupled with telephone-based ordering are faster order fulfillment and the elimination of delays previously associated with mail order. Today, placing an order by phone offers almost the same ''instant gratification'' as picking up a piece of merchandise at the store.

Other socioeconomic factors contributing to the growth and acceptance of direct marketing include a population growing older, rising discretionary income, more single households, and the emergence of the ''me'' generation. External factors include the rising cost of gasoline (at-home shoppers use less gasoline and reduce environmental pollution), the availability of toll-free telephone numbers, the expanded use of credit cards, the low cost of data processing, and the widespread availability of mailing lists.

DIRECT MARKETING MEDIA

While many people associate direct marketing with direct mail, direct mail is only one of several **advertising media** utilized by direct marketers. Other major direct marketing media include the telephone, magazines, newspapers, television, and radio. Alternative media include card decks, package and bill inserts, and matchbooks. Within the major media, new technological developments are giving direct marketers an expanded range of choices from videocassettes (possibly advertised on television, requested by telephone or interactive computer, and delivered via mail or alternate delivery services) to home-shopping networks and interactive television.

DIRECT MAIL Direct mail is the most heavily used direct marketing medium and the one most direct marketers learn first. Direct mail has been used to sell a wide variety of goods and services to consumers as well as businesses, and it continues to grow despite postage increases. Direct mail offers several advantages over other media, including selectivity, personalization, flexibility, and testability. It allows businesses to target individuals with known purchase histories or particular psychographic or demographic characteristics that match the marketer's customer profile. Direct mail can be targeted to a specific geographic area based on zip codes or other geographic factors. Personalization in direct mail means not only addressing the envelope to a person or family by name, but also perhaps including the recipient's name inside the envelope.

Direct mail packages come in all shapes and sizes, making it one of the most flexible of the direct marketing media. A standard direct mail package includes an envelope, a letter, a brochure, and a response device. The envelope's job is to motivate the recipient to open the package. Regardless of the volume of mail a person receives, the envelope must distinguish itself from other mail by its size, appearance, and any copy that might be written on it. The letter is a sales letter and provides the opportunity to directly address the interests and concerns of the recipient. The letter typically spells out the benefits of the offer in detail. While the letter tells the recipient about the benefits of the offer, the brochure illustrates them. Illustrated brochures are used to sell services as well as products. Finally, the package must include a response device, such as a business reply card, that the recipient can send back. Response rates are generally higher when the response device is separate from, rather than part of, the brochure or letter. Toll-free numbers are often prominently displayed to allow the recipient to respond via telephone.

Direct mail is the most easily tested advertising medium. Every factor in successful direct marketing—the right offer, the right person, the right format, and the right timing—can be tested in direct mail. Computer technologies have made it easier to select a randomized name sample from any list, so that mailers can run a test mailing to determine the response from a list before ''rolling out,'' or mailing, the entire list. Different packages containing different offers can also be tested. Other media allow some degree of testing, but direct mail is the most sophisticated. In relation to the other direct marketing media, direct mail is considered to offer the most cost-effective way of achieving the highest possible response. Telemarketing usually produces a higher response rate, but at a much higher cost per response.

TELEPHONE-BASED DIRECT MARKETING (TELE-MARKETING) The use of the telephone in direct marketing has grown dramatically over the past two decades. Expenditures now may equal, or even surpass, those of direct mail. Telephone-based direct marketing may be outbound and/or inbound. Inbound telemarketing is also known as teleservicing and usually involves taking orders and responding to inquiries. Outbound telemarketing for consumers may be used for one-step selling, lead generation, lead qualification or follow-up, and selling and servicing larger and more active customers. In business, telemarketing can be used to reach smaller accounts that do not warrant a personal sales call as well as to generate, qualify, and follow up leads.

Telemarketing has the advantages of being personal and interactive. It is an effective two-way communications medium that enables company representatives to listen to customers. Telephone salespeople typically work from a script, but the medium allows the flexibility of revising the script as needed. It also allows for up- and cross-selling. While customers are on the phone it is possible to increase the size of their orders by offering them additional choices—something that tends to lead to confusion in other direct marketing media.

Telemarketing also has its disadvantages. For example, it is more expensive than direct mail. It also lacks a permanent response device that the prospect can set aside or use later. It is not a visual medium—though the technology to make it one may soon be available. Finally, it is perceived as intrusive, generating consumer complaints that have led to legislative actions to regulate the telemarketing industry.

MAGAZINES Direct response print ads in magazines must make a definite offer or request that asks the reader to do something. Typically, such ads require a reader to send in a coupon or reply card, or call a toll-free number. With well over 2,000 consumer magazines now being published, magazine ads allow direct marketers to reach audiences with identifiable interests. In addition to advertising heavily in special interest magazines, direct marketers utilize mass consumer magazines and take advantage of regional advertising space to target specific audiences.

Unlike general advertisers, who measure the effectiveness of their print ads in terms of reach and frequency, direct marketers measure the effectiveness of their print ads in terms of cost effectiveness— either cost-per-inquiry or cost-per-order. Magazine ads offer the advantages of good color reproduction, a relatively long ad life (especially compared to daily newspapers), and a lower cost. Creative costs for magazine ads are also usually lower than for direct mail. But direct marketers find magazines' long lead times, slower response, and scarcer space than direct mail to be disadvantages.

NEWSPAPERS While direct marketers advertise in magazines more than newspapers, newspapers have some distinct advantages. These include the variety of sections offered within a newspaper, shorter closing dates, an immediate response, and broad coverage of a large and diverse audience. Disadvantages include poor ad reproduction and the limited availability of color. Editorial content can also have more of an adverse effect on ad response than in magazines. In addition to advertising in the regular pages of a newspaper, direct marketers also advertise in free-standing inserts (FSIs) that are usually distributed with the Sunday editions of newspapers.

TELEVISION Direct marketing on television is increasing. Early examples of direct response advertisements on television that should be familiar to viewers include those for knives, garden tools, exercise equipment, records, and books, which ask viewers to call in and order a specific product. More recent developments in direct response television advertising include a return to a lengthier format, commonly known as the infomercial, where a product or other offer is explained in some detail over a time period extending to 30 minutes or more. Advocates of this format point out that the greater length gives the advertiser the opportunity to build a relationship with the viewer and overcome initial viewer skepticism, and at the same time present a convincing story spelling out product features and benefits in detail.

Not all direct response television involves asking for an order. Long-distance telephone companies and automobile manufacturers, among other advertisers, have included 800 telephone numbers with their television ads to get viewers to call and request more information about their product or service. Any television ad that includes an 800 number is asking for a response and qualifies as a direct response advertisement.

With the prospect of interactive television looming on the horizon, together with developments in the delivery of more cable channels that offer audiences with identifiable interests and demographics, direct response television promises to be a dynamic area in the future of direct marketing.

DIRECT MARKETING LISTS AND DATABASES

Lists are commonly used in direct mail and telemarketing. The two basic types of lists are response lists and compiled lists. Response lists contain the names of all the prospects who have responded to the same offer. These individuals typically share a common interest. Names on a response list may include buyers, inquirers, subscribers, continuity club members, or sweepstakes entrants. They may have responded to an offer from one of several media, including direct mail, television, or a print ad. Response lists are not usually rented; rather, they are an in-house list compiled by a particular business. Compiled lists are often rented by direct marketers. Compiled mass consumer, specialized consumer, and business lists are available for a wide range of interests.

Direct marketing databases are similar to **mailing lists** in that they contain names and addresses, but they go much further. They are the repository of a wide range of customer information and may also contain psychographic, demographic, and census data compiled from external sources. They form the basis of direct marketing programs whereby companies establish closer ties with their customers.

In the 1980s, database marketing became one of the buzzwords of the direct marketing industry. Whether it is called relationship marketing, relevance marketing, or bonding, the common theme of database marketing is strengthening relationships with existing customers and building relationships with new ones. Databases allow direct marketers to uncover a wealth of relevant information about individual consumers and apply that knowledge to increase the probability of a desired response or purchase.

As with mailing lists, there are two basic types of marketing databases, customer databases and external databases. Customer databases are compiled internally and contain information about a company's customers taken from the relationship-building process. External databases are collections of specific individuals and their characteristics. These external databases may be mass-compiled from public data sources; they may contain financial data based on confidential credit files; they may be compiled from questionnaires; or they may be a combination of all three sources.

Database marketing, and especially the prospect of using confidential information for marketing purposes, has made privacy an important issue in the direct marketing industry. Some states have passed legislation limiting access to previously public data or limiting the use of such data as automobile registrations, credit histories, and medical information. In order to avoid excessive government regulation, the direct marketing industry has attempted to be self-policing with regard to the use of sensitive data. However, the struggle between industry self-regulation and government regulation will probably continue for some time.

SUCCESSFUL DIRECT MARKETING FOR SMALL BUSINESSES

Thanks to its relatively low cost, its ability to reach specialized target markets, and its ability to provide immediate and measurable results, direct marketing can be an important tool for start-up businesses. It can also be used effectively as a supplement to a small business's traditional sales efforts. Entrepreneurs interested in starting a direct marketing program can consult with advertising and direct marketing agencies for help in evaluating their sales potential and preparing materials for a campaign.

In the *Macmillan Small Business Handbook,* Mark Stevens identified three steps for a small business owner to take in initiating a direct marketing effort: 1) create promotional tools (such as catalogs, advertisements, or direct mail pieces) that emphasize the benefits of the product or service; 2) identify the target market and select mailing lists and advertising media to reach it; and 3) monitor the results of each campaign and revise the tactics as needed to find the optimum mix of price, copy, and audience. Stevens noted that entrepreneurs might also find it helpful to give consumers an incentive to act, such as a free gift or special price; promote to existing customers—who usually provide the highest response rate—as well as new prospects; and build on successful promotions by broadening the product line.

There are certain situations where direct marketing is more likely to work than others. First, the direct marketer must be able to identify the target audience in terms of shared characteristics. Are they likely to read a particular magazine? Live in a certain geographic area? Have a certain minimum income? Be a certain age or gender? The more characteristics of the target audience that can be identified, the more likely it is that a direct marketing campaign targeted to those individuals will work.

Since direct marketing relies on one-to-one communications and motivating the recipient to act, it is essential to be able to reach the target audience. It is no use identifying a target market if there is no mailing list or print or broadcast medium available to reach them. Some other situations in which direct marketing works well are when there is a lot to say about a product or service; when the product or service has the potential for repeat sales; and when there is a need to have greater control over the sales message.

The success of a direct marketing program depends on delivering the right offer at the right time to the right person in the right way. Direct marketing is a complex discipline that requires expertise in several areas to achieve success. It involves identifying the target market correctly and selecting the appropriate media and/or lists to reach it. The offer must be presented in the best way, and direct marketers must use the most effective creative execution to successfully motivate customers and prospects. At its most effective, direct marketing is an ongoing process of communication to maintain relationships with existing customers and build relationships with new ones.

FURTHER READING:

Jutkins, "Rocket" Ray. *Direct Marketing: How You Can Really Do It Right,* 2nd ed. Rockingham Jutkins Marketing, 1990.

Kobs, Jim. *Profitable Direct Marketing,* 2nd ed. Lincolnwood, IL: NTC Business Books, 1992.

Lewis, Herschell Gordon. *Direct Marketing Strategies and Tactics.* Chicago, IL: Dartnell, 1992.

Nash, Edward L., ed. *The Direct Marketing Handbook,* 2nd ed. New York: McGraw-Hill, 1992.

David Shepard Associates. *The New Direct Marketing: How to Implement a Profit-Driven Database Marketing Strategy.* Business One Irwin, 1990.

Stevens, Mark. *The Macmillan Small Business Handbook.* Macmillan, 1988.

Stone, Bob. *Successful Direct Marketing Methods,* 4th ed. Lincolnwood, IL: NTC Business Books, 1989.

DIRECT PUBLIC OFFERINGS

A direct public offering (DPO) is a financial tool that enables a company to issue **stocks** directly to investors—without using a broker or underwriter as an intermediary—and avoid many of the costs associated with "going public" through an initial public offering (IPO). DPOs are a form of exempt securities offering, which means that companies choosing this form of offering are exempt from many of the registration and reporting requirements of the Securities and Exchange Commission (SEC). DPOs first became available to small businesses in 1976, but they only gained popularity beginning in 1989, when the rules were simplified. In 1992, the SEC established its Small Business Initiatives program, which eliminated even more of the barriers that had limited the ability of small companies to raise **capital** by selling stock.

Prior to the establishment of DPOs, selling stock to the public through **initial public offerings (IPOs)** was often the only alternative available to private companies that needed funds for expansion and growth. But staging an IPO is a very time-consuming and expensive process. A small business interested in going public must apply to the SEC for permission to sell stock to the public. The SEC registration process is quite complex and requires the company to disclose a variety of information to potential investors. The IPO process can take as little as six months or as long as two years, during which time management's attention is distracted away from day-to-day operations. It can also cost a company between $50,000 and $250,000 in underwriting fees, legal and accounting expenses, and printing costs. Furthermore, the public ownership of the company has a significant impact on the amount of control that rests in the hands of its management.

Although many small businesses need the capital that an IPO can provide, they often lack the financial strength and reputation to appeal to a broad range of investors—necessary ingredients for a successful IPO. For other small businesses, the loss of control, the strict reporting requirements, or the expense of staging an IPO are prohibitive factors. "Under certain circumstances, though, federal law allows companies to issue stock without registering with the SEC in the normal manner or filing periodic reports. These direct public offerings—direct because the company can market them without a broker—are often registered only with state securities commissions," according to Robert L. Lowes in *Medical Economics.*

ADVANTAGES AND DISADVANTAGES

DPOs, private placements of stock, and other exempt offerings provide small businesses with a quicker, less expensive way to raise capital. The primary advantage of DPOs over IPOs is a dramatic reduction in cost. IPO underwriters typically charge a commission of 13 percent of the proceeds of the sale of securities, whereas the costs associated with a DPO are closer to 3 percent. DPOs also can be completed within a shorter time frame and without extensive disclosure of confidential information. Finally, since the stock sold through a DPO goes to a limited number of investors who tend to have a long-term orientation, there is often less pressure on the company's management to deliver short-term results.

DPOs also involve disadvantages, however. For example, the amount that a company can raise through a DPO within any 12-month period is limited. In addition, the stock is usually sold at a lower price than it might command through an IPO. Stock sold through exempt offerings is not usually freely traded, so no market price is established for the shares or for the overall company. This lack of a market price may make it difficult for the company to use equity as loan collateral. Finally, DPO investors are likely to demand a larger share of ownership in the company to offset the lack of liquidity in their position. Investors

eventually may pressure the company to go public through an IPO so that they can realize their profits.

TYPES OF DPOS

Companies interested in raising capital through a DPO have several options from which to choose. The most common type of DPO is known as a Small Corporate Offering Registration, or SCOR. The SEC provided this option to small businesses in 1982, through an amendment to federal securities law known as Regulation D, Rule 504. SCOR gives an exemption to private companies that raise no more than $1 million in any 12-month period through the sale of stock. There are no restrictions on the number or types of investors, and the securities can be freely traded. The SCOR process is easy enough for a small business owner to complete with the assistance of a knowledgeable accountant and attorney. It is available in all states except Delaware, Florida, Hawaii, and Nebraska.

A related type of DPO is outlined in SEC Regulation D, Rule 505. This option enables a small business to sell up to $5 million in stock during a 12-month period to an unlimited number of investors, provided that no more than 35 of them are non-accredited. To be accredited, an investor must have sufficient assets or income to make such an investment. According to the SEC rules, individual investors must have either $1 million in assets (other than their home and car) or $200,000 in net annual personal income, while institutions must hold $5 million in assets. A DPO registered through Regulation D, Rule 506, allows a company to sell unlimited securities to an unlimited number of investors, provided that no more than 35 of them are non-accredited. Under Rule 506, investors must be sophisticated, or able to evaluate the merits and understand the risks of the transaction. In both of these options, the securities cannot be freely traded.

Another type of DPO is outlined in SEC Regulation A. This option is frequently referred to as a "mini public offering," because it follows many of the same procedures as an IPO and the securities may be freely traded. However, companies choosing this option may only offer up to $5 million in securities in any 12-month period. Regulation A offerings are allowed to bypass federal SEC registration and instead are filed with the Small Business Office of the SEC.

Two further types of DPOs are available to businesses with less than $25 million in annual revenues. A Small Business Type 1 (SB-1) offering enables a company to sell up to $10 million in securities in a 12-month period and has simpler paperwork. A Small Business Type 2 (SB-2) filing enables a company to sell an unlimited amount of securities and has more difficult paperwork. In an article for *Corporate Cashflow Magazine,* Gary D. Zeune and Timothy R. Baer suggested that it might make sense for some public companies to ''step down'' to SB status in order to reduce their registration and reporting costs.

A final type of DPO is available through the SEC's intrastate filing exemption, Rule 147. This option allows companies to raise unlimited funds through the sale of securities as long as the stock is sold only in the primary state in which they do business. Both the company and all the investors must be residents of the same state. This exemption is intended to provide local businesses with a means of raising capital within their locale.

PROCEEDING WITH A DPO REQUIRES CAUTION

Though DPOs can simplify the process of raising capital for small business growth, there is no guarantee that an offering will be successful. ''In all types of DPOs, the companies usually declare a minimum amount needed to carry out the business plan. Seven of every ten SCORs fail to reach that target—to 'break escrow,' in the parlance,'' Lowes noted. Small business owners considering a DPO need to realize that there is hard work involved. In fact, the business may suffer during the offering period, because management often does not have time to promote the offering and run the company simultaneously. For this reason, DPOs are most likely to be successful in companies that are not overly dependent on their top management and that have a sound business plan in place.

DPOs are also more likely to be successful for companies that have an established and loyal customer base. Customers are often the best source of potential investors for growing businesses. Companies that initiate DPOs can advertise their stock to customers on product packaging, through mailing lists, with posted messages in offices or other facilities, or by making the prospectus available on an Internet site. ''Experts suggest that any company gauge investor enthusiasm before launching a DPO—because costs for attorneys, accountants, and marketing materials can add up,'' Carol Steinberg wrote in an article for *Success.*

Finally, companies can improve their chances for a successful DPO by availing themselves of expert securities advice. ''Whether an offering is properly exempt from registration with the SEC is a matter for competent legal counsel and careful structuring of the offering. Errors must be avoided, since a faulty offering generally gives investors the right to get their money back,'' according to Zeune and Baer. The fact that a DPO does not have to be registered with the SEC does not release a company from compliance with the antifraud provisions of U.S. securities laws. Potential investors must have ample, accurate information to make an informed decision about whether

or not to buy stock in the company. Finally, securities laws vary by state, so it is important that small business owners interested in pursuing a DPO consider the laws applicable to their companies.

FURTHER READING:

Arkebauer, James B., and Ronald M. Schultz. *Cashing Out: The Entrepreneur's Guide to Going Public.* New York: HarperBusiness, 1991.

Field, Drew. ''Raising Equity through a Direct Public Offering.'' *Bankers Magazine.* March-April 1991.

Lindsey, Jennifer. *The Entrepreneur's Guide to Capital: The Techniques for Capitalizing and Refinancing New and Growing Businesses.* Chicago, IL: Probus, 1986.

Lowes, Robert L. ''Try a Do-It-Yourself Public Offering.'' *Medical Economics.* April 14, 1997.

Saxlehner, Andrew C. ''Equity Made Easy.'' *Inc.* July 1983.

Sherman, Andrew J. *The Complete Guide to Running and Growing Your Business.* New York: Random House, 1997.

Steinberg, Carol. ''The DPO Revolution: Direct Public Offerings Turn Customers into Investors.'' *Success.* March 1997.

Sutton, David P., and M. William Benedetto. *Initial Public Offerings: A Strategic Planner for Raising Equity Capital.* Chicago, IL: Probus, 1988.

Zeune, Gary D., and Timothy R. Baer. ''Floating a Stock Offering: New Buoyancy from the SEC.'' *Corporate Cashflow Magazine.* August 1993.

SEE ALSO: Investor Relations and Reporting

DISABILITY INSURANCE

Disability insurance provides policyholders with coverage that replaces a portion of an employer's or employee's income if he or she becomes too sick or disabled to return to the job. While many small business owners carry a variety of other insurance plans (health, fire, theft, and life), a smaller percentage maintain plans that cover themselves or their employees in the event of long-term disabilities. Many business experts state, however, that small businesses that do not carry such coverage are courting disaster. They note, for instance, that according to the National Association of Insurance Commissioners, a 35-year-old person has a 50 percent chance of being struck down by a disability of three months or longer before he or she turns 65, and that in a partnership of two 35-year-olds, the odds of a long (three months or more) disability striking one of them before they turn 65 jumps to 75 percent. Moreover, Bob D'Angelo noted in *San Diego Business Journal* that people in their early 30s are three times more likely to suffer a disability lasting three months or longer than to die, and people in their early 50s are twice as likely to be on the disabled list than to die, yet disability insurance coverage continues to lag behind other forms of business insurance. "While most employers recognize the need for health and life insurance," wrote D'Angelo, "relatively few are aware that the greatest threat to their own and their employees' livelihood is long-term disability. Indeed, the viability of a business could be at stake if a disabling illness or injury strikes a key executive."

TYPES OF DISABILITY POLICIES

Small business owners seeking to purchase long-term disability insurance (DI) coverage for themselves and their workers have two basic policies to choose from, each tailored to a specific target.

GROUP LONG-TERM-DISABILITY PACKAGES Group coverage generally replaces 40 to 60 percent of the insured person's income, usually up to about $5,000 a month. This compensation is fully taxable if the premium is paid by the employer, but the company is permitted to deduct the premium as a business expense. Comparatively inexpensive (an average of $180 per employee per year) when compared with other business insurances, it nonetheless is not widely used by small businesses (the U.S. Bureau of Labor Statistics indicated that only 23 percent of companies with fewer than 100 employees offered such coverage in the mid-1990s). Small business consultants contend, however, that firms that do offer this coverage have often found that it increases their attractiveness to potential employees, provided that the company pays for the policy.

INDIVIDUAL LONG-TERM-DISABILITY PACKAGES "Individual policies," wrote *Nation's Business* contributor Abby Livington, "are costlier but come with better coverage, namely a higher percentage of replacement income (up to 70 percent), portability from job to job, and noncancelable coverage. Individual policies are sold solo or to individuals within a group. The latter are called employer-sponsored individual policies." Livington goes on to note that while sole proprietors who seek individual policies may be put off by the cost of the policy, "the cost drops considerably when individual policies are sponsored by an employer and at least three people purchase a plan. Individual coverage under an employer-sponsored LTD [Long-Term-Disability] plan costs about $1500 annually. . . . Employer-sponsored individual LTD policies provide what is in effect a higher percentage of income replacement primarily because the income is not taxable. That's because the individual—and not the company—pays the premium with after-tax dollars, which exempts benefits from taxation."

KEY DISABILITY INSURANCE BENEFITS

Many disability insurance policies carry provisions that are particularly appealing to small business owners. Demarais discussed several specific aspects that can be of significant benefit:

- Rehabilitation—Many policies provide for retraining of employees (or business owners) who prove unable to resume their previous job duties. As Demarais noted, "most people who are on long-term disability don't want to be there; they want to be productive again, even if it means pursuing another occupation."

- Waiving of Premium Payments—In some instances, policyholders who remain disabled past the time specified in their policy may be able to have their premiums paid for the duration of their disability.

- Tax Deductions—Premiums often qualify as a deductible business expense.

- Return of Premium—Some policies provide for policyholders to receive all or part of their accumulated premium payments at age 65, provided that have never fallen victim to disability.

- Hospital Indemnity Waiver—Under this arrangement, policyholders who are hospitalized for a certain period of time will have their benefits paid.

FINDING THE RIGHT DISABILITY POLICY

"Given the changing landscape, it's important to understand some basics before you buy any group or individual policy," counseled Livington. "Generally, the cost of a policy is driven by the definition of disability, the level of income replacement, the length of the waiting period before coverage takes effect, and the length of time that benefits are payable."

Factors to consider in weighing the advantages and disadvantages of a long-term-disability policy include:

- Cost of Policy—"Although business owners are attracted to—and see the need for—DI, affordability is the ultimate factor in determining whether they buy or not," wrote Steve Demarais in *National Underwriter Life and Health.*

- Length and Amount of Coverage—Demarais noted that some business owners have difficulty purchasing the amount of coverage that they desire. "In terms of underwriting and determining the amount of coverage a person is eligible for, the owner's last year net (not gross) income is a key factor. And, because business owners have many expenses, their net income may be lower and not reflect the amount of DI they feel they truly need.''

- Insurer Options—Can the insurer increase the premium or cancel the policy? Group policies generally provide less protection to the policyholder than individual policies in this area.

- ''Key Person'' Policy Option—Some insurers offer ''key person'' disability insurance wherein a company would receive compensation, either through a lump sum or a schedule of regular payments, in the event that an essential member of the business (often an owner or co-owner) becomes disabled.

- Riders—Individual long-term-disability policies can be adjusted in many ways via riders. Livington noted that one of the most common riders to appear in individual plans is the cost-of-living rider, which increases the size of disability benefits to cover inflation once payment on a claim has begun.

- Percentage of Salary to be Paid.

- Policy's Definition of ''Disability''—Two broad definitions of disability exist, observed Livington, ''and their differences are significant. 'Own-occupation' coverage pays benefits if you can't perform the important duties of your occupation. 'Any-occupation' coverage pays benefits only if you can't work in an occupation that is consistent with your education, training, or experience. . . . Although most existing individual policies are written with own-occupation coverage for the entire benefit period, such coverage is becoming harder to find'' due to the high level of payments that the insurance industry has come to associate with such policies.

Both insurance agents and business consultants can be most helpful in sorting through the many variables of disability insurance plans that must be studied before settling on a final plan.

AFTER A CLAIM HAS BEEN FILED

The specifics of disability plans vary from policy to policy, depending on the policyholders priorities when he or she signed up. Most group long-term-disability policies have a 180-day waiting period for a disability, said Livington, while ''Individual policies' premiums decline as the waiting period for the start of benefits increases. A policy with a 90-day waiting period costs about 20 percent less than one with a 30-day waiting period, and a policy with a 180-day wait-ing period is about 30 percent less than one with a 90-day waiting period.''

Duration of coverage varies from policy to policy as well. Individual policies can be shaped so that beneficiaries will receive compensation until they reach age 65, but insurance companies often limit the duration of group policies to three to five years.

DISABILITY INSURANCE AND "BUY-SELL" AGREEMENTS

D'Angelo pointed out that disability insurance also can be wielded for purposes other than simple disability compensation. Indeed, business partners can shape disability insurance plans to finance ''buy-sell'' agreements: ''This arrangement guarantees that the disabled partner's interest in the business will be sold to the remaining partner(s) at a price that has been agreed on in advance. The insurance policy provides the cash at the time of the buy out, eliminating the need for the business to deplete its assets or to incur long-term debt to make the purchase. The disabled partner gets a fair price for his equity in the business—and receives monies at a time when he has lost his earning power and is likely grappling with increased health care costs.''

FURTHER READING:

Anastasio, Susan. *Small Business Insurance and Risk Management Guide.* Washington: U.S. Small Business Administration, n.d.

Bury, Don. *The Buyer's Guide to Business Insurance.* Grants Pass, OR: Oasis Press, 1994.

D'Angelo, Bob. ''Disability can be Greatest Threat to Livelihood.'' *San Diego Business Journal.* January 24, 1994.

Demarais, Steve. ''Many Business Owners Showing Wish to Own DI.'' *National Underwriter Life and Health.* February 17, 1997.

''How to Choose the Right Disability Coverage.'' *The Business Owner.* January-February 1997.

Janecek, Lenore. *Health Insurance: A Guide for Artists, Consultants, Entrepreneurs, and Other Self-Employed.* New York: Allworth Press, 1993.

Livington, Abby. ''Insuring Your Earning Power.'' *Nation's Business.* April 1997.

Lynn, Jacquelyn. ''A Quick Guide to Insurance.'' *Entrepreneur.* June 1997.

Williams, C. Arthur Jr., and Richard M. Heins. *Risk Management and Insurance.* New York: McGraw-Hill, 1989.

SEE ALSO: Business Insurance; Employee Benefits; Health Insurance Options; Life Insurance

DISABLED CUSTOMERS

Disabled customers comprise a huge market of more than 43 million people in the United States alone, with millions more in other international markets. Yet until relatively recently, many businesses operated in a manner that was seemingly oblivious to their needs and their considerable purchasing power. The passage of the **Americans with Disabilities Act (ADA)** in 1990 was perhaps the single biggest factor in jarring U.S. businesses into a recognition that they were overlooking a huge segment of the American population (and one that is expected to continue to grow as the "baby boomer" generation enters retirement age). Certainly, some businesses garnered healthy profits by concentrating their efforts on meeting the needs of disabled people in the "pre-ADA" business world, but it was not until the early 1990s, when the ADA became law, that many other companies suddenly realized that a considerable number of their goods and services—while acceptably designed and packaged for their primary non-disabled customers—were unfriendly to disabled customers. Thus the requirements contained in the ADA forced businesses to revisit the usefulness of their products and services to disabled customers at the same time that publicity about the law stirred a dawning realization that disabled people amounted to a largely untapped target market of significant size. Since that time, however, businesses of varying sizes have endeavored to reach disabled customers with a combination of improved service and improved product design and **packaging**.

The portion of the Americans with Disabilities Act that most directly relates to customer service issues for disabled people is Title III (other sections cover issues such as ensuring that disabled people are not discriminated against in hiring, promotions, and other internal operational areas). Title III requires that private businesses that are open to the public—including retail establishments, restaurants, and hotels and motels—give individuals with disabilities the same access to their goods and services that non-disabled customers enjoy. This section of the ADA also required that all future construction of commercial facilities, including office buildings, factories, and warehouses, as well as places of public accommodation, be constructed so that the building is accessible to individuals with disabilities.

The regulations contained in the ADA, coupled with new looks at product designs, packaging, and **marketing** have spurred a revolution in how some goods are made and marketed. For example, many manufacturers of milk, juices, and other liquids have turned to new design alternatives so that receptacles can be more easily opened and closed (manufacturers belatedly realized that some designs, such as cartons and screwtop covers, served to turn away large numbers of customers with arthritis and other maladies that affected their grip and strength). "The physically elite can easily overcome design flaws simply by working a bit harder at the task," said one design researcher in an interview with *Appliance Manufacturer.* But for disabled people, minor design shortcomings can prove problematic. Manufacturers who do not take adequate steps to ensure that their products can be used by disabled people, then, are likely to alienate a big part of the total market that will continue to grow in the coming years. "As the demographic profile of the American marketplace changes, a growing segment of consumers will find it difficult to compensate for the less-than-optimal design in many products," wrote Norman C. Remich Jr. in *Appliance Manufacturer.*

Finally, business observers note that the growing numbers of disabled people in the general population, combined with the access-related mandates contained in the ADA, have made disabled customers a much more visible presence in stores and business offices. Small business owners and managers should thus make certain that they have adequate employee training and insurance safeguards in place for interactions with this customer group. Writing in *Discount Store News,* Thomas Georgouses made an observation about convenience store owners that is also true of many business owners in a wide range of industry occupations: "Most discount store owners are well aware of the importance of job training for their employees, and some may even recognize the importance of complying with statutes, regulations, and ordinances as they apply to physical access to premises. However, only a few truly appreciate the importance of good employee training when it comes to conducting relations with disabled customers, especially in today's litigious climate." Business owners are thus encouraged to require training and education to employees on disability issues and consult with an attorney to make sure that their insurance policies provide adequate protection. Finally, business advisors and advocates for the disabled agree that disabled customers simply want to be treated fairly; small business owners that are able to accomplish that will thus position themselves to garner a healthy share of this growing market.

FURTHER READING:

The Americans with Disabilities Act—Title II Technical Assistance Manual. Office on the Americans with Disabilities Act, Civil Rights Division, U.S. Department of Justice.

Duffy, Yvonne. "14 Ways to Attract Disabled Customers." *Bottomline.* June 1988.

Georgouses, Thomas. "Treat Disabled Customers Like All the Rest of Us: Use Common Sense." *Discount Store News.* February 9, 1998.

Goerne, Carrie. "Marketing to the Disabled: New Workplace Law Stirs Interest in Largely Untapped Market." *Marketing News.* September 14, 1992.

Gofton, Ken. "Opening Up to Disability." *Marketing.* May 19, 1994.

Lunt, Penny. "Reaching People with Disabilities." *ABA Banking Journal.* December 1994.

Remich, Norman C., Jr. "Designing for the Disabled." *Appliance Manufacturer.* July 1991.

SEE ALSO: Customer Service; Facility Layout and Design; Product Development; Training and Development

DISASTER ASSISTANCE LOANS

Disaster assistance loans are utilized by businesses to recover from floods, fires, earthquakes, tornadoes, etc. that damage their operation, from physical structure to inventory to lost business. Of course, adequate insurance policies offer the best protection for small business owners, but many businesses do not maintain adequate coverage. Small businesses are particularly reliant on disaster loans since they can not draw on the corporate coffers to which larger firms often turn. Some small business owners solicit loans from banks and other lending institutions, but many others turn to loan programs offered by the **U.S. Small Business Administration (SBA)** and other federal agencies. Indeed, the SBA is a primary source of funding for businesses seeking to rebuild after a disaster strikes.

Any business that qualifies under SBA definitions as a "small business," is located in a major disaster area, and has suffered damage as a consequence of that disaster may apply for a disaster assistance loan to: 1) help repair or replace damaged property; or 2) help it meet those financial obligations that it would have been able to honor had a disaster not taken place. The SBA maintains separate programs for each of these eventualities. The agency notes, however, that qualification for an SBA disaster relief loan is not a given. "The SBA disaster relief program is not an immediate emergency relief program such as Red Cross assistance, temporary housing assistance, etc.," stated the agency "It is a loan program to help you in your long-term rebuilding and repairing. To make a loan. We have to know the cost of repairing the damage, be satisfied that you can repay the loan, and take reasonable safeguards to help make sure the loan is paid."

PHYSICAL DISASTER BUSINESS LOANS The SBA makes physical disaster loans of up to $1.5 million to qualified businesses, provided that the businesses use this money for the repair or replacement of real property, equipment, machinery, fixtures, inventory, and leasehold improvements. This property may have been insured or uninsured prior to the disaster. "In addition," noted the SBA, "disaster loans to repair or replace real property or leasehold improvements may be increased by as much as 20 percent to protect the damaged real property against possible future disasters of the same type." This latter allowance can be particularly attractive to victims of natural disasters that tend to occur on a cyclical basis. Finally, some businesses can use this money to relocate, although the SBA cautions business owners not to formally commit to such plans before gaining loan approval.

Applications for these loans require the business to file a variety of financial and other records, including an itemized list of losses (with estimated replacement/repair cost), federal income tax information, history of the business, personal financial statements, and business financial statements. Whereas loans of less than $10,000 require no collateral, loans of amounts greater than that require the pledging of collateral to the extent that it is available. The SBA notes that while it will not decline a loan solely for lack of collateral, it does require businesses to pledge collateral when it is available.

Interest rates on physical disaster loans vary, depending on whether or not the applicant is able to obtain credit with other financial institutions. In instances where the business is not able to obtain credit elsewhere, U.S. law sets a maximum interest rate of 4 percent per year on these loans, with a maximum maturity of 30 years. Businesses that would be able to secure credit elsewhere, however, do not get quite so advantageous terms. For these latter enterprises, the interest rate is either 8 percent or whatever is being charged in the private sector at the time, whichever is less. The maturity of these loans cannot exceed three years. (Please note, however, that nonprofit organizations can secure better interest rates and maturity terms through the SBA than can for-profit businesses.)

ECONOMIC INJURY DISASTER LOANS The EIDL loan program is available to small businesses and small agricultural cooperatives that have suffered substantial economic injury resulting from a physical disaster or an agricultural production disaster. The SBA defines "substantial economic injury" as "the inability of a business to meet its obligations as they mature and to pay its ordinary and necessary operating expenses." In essence, it gives companies an opportunity to catch their breath in the wake of a disaster.

EIDL assistance is available only to those entities that are unable to secure credit from other private sources (banks, etc.). It is used less often than the physical disaster loan option for several other reasons as well: 1) The SBA limits its total assistance to any one company to $1.5 million, no matter how many programs are utilized. This means that a business that secures a $1.5 million loan for facility repair through the SBA's physical disaster business loan would not be eligible for any monies through EIDL. 2) The SBA puts limitations on how EIDL funds can be used. For instance, these funds can not be used to pay cash bonuses or dividends, or for disbursements to owners, partners, officers, or stockholders who are not directly related to the performance of services for the business. 3) Finally, EIDL loans do not give the borrower any leeway in the realms of relocation or physical improvements, both of which are sometimes possible through the SBA's physical disaster loan program.

In many other respects, however—determination of interest rates, penalties for misuse of funds, use of collateral, procedures for securing a loan, etc.—the procedures for economic injury disaster loans are largely the same as those for physical disaster business loans.

SBA LOANS AND FLOOD INSURANCE According to the SBA, if damage is caused by flooding, or the business is in a special flood hazard area, the business seeking the SBA loan must have flood insurance before the agency will disburse the loan.

DISASTER LOANS FOR PERSONAL PROPERTY AND HOMES Finally, the SBA also maintains loan programs for homeowners, renters, and/or personal property owners who are victimized by a disaster. Personal property loans of up to $40,000 are available to individual homeowners or renters to help repair or replace personal goods (boats, automobiles, clothes, appliances, furniture, etc.). Real property loans of up to $200,000, meanwhile, are available to homeowners for replacement or repair of actual homes. "The loan may not be used to upgrade the home or make additions to it," stated the SBA. "If, however, city or county building codes require structural improvements, the loan may be used to meet these requirements." Secondary homes and vacation homes are not eligible for these loans.

Critics of the SBA have charged that the majority of the agency's disaster loans have actually been granted to homeowners and renters through this latter program, rather than to the small business owners that are supposedly the primary reason for the agency's existence. Critics have faulted both the SBA's priorities and an overly bureaucratic application process. These and other criticisms led the SBA to adopt a series of internal reforms in the mid-1990s that were designed to make it easier for small business owners to secure assistance in a broad range of areas.

FURTHER READING:

Attard, Janet. *The Home Office and Small Business Answer Book.* New York: Henry Holt, 1993.

Breuer, George, and George Spencer. "Codes Push Expenses of Recovery Up." *National Underwriter Property & Casualty— Risk and Benefits Management.* July 18, 1994.

The Facts About . . . Disaster Assistance Loans for Homes & Personal Property. Washington: U.S. Small Business Administration, 1996.

The Facts About . . . Economic Injury Disaster Loans for Small Businesses. Washington: U.S. Small Business Administration, 1997.

The Facts About . . . Physical Disaster Business Loans. Washington: U.S. Small Business Administration, 1997.

Hogan, Bill. "Double Whammy." *D & B Reports.* March/April 1994.

Levitt, Alan M. *Disaster Planning and Recovery: A Guide for Facility Professionals.* New York: John Wiley and Sons, 1997.

SEE ALSO: Disaster Planning and Recovery; Loans

DISASTER PLANNING AND RECOVERY

Small business owners are strongly encouraged to make contingency plans for responding to and recovering from disasters that may befall them. Analysts note that disasters—whether they take the form of floods, corporate espionage, fires, or power outages—can have a devastating affect on a business's viability, and that disaster insurance, while valuable, is often only of limited usefulness.

Kenneth N. Myers, author of *Total Contingency Planning for Disasters,* confirmed that disaster insurance is only one element of a comprehensive disaster contingency plan. "The role of insurance in protecting against loss of physical assets, such as buildings and equipment, is clear," wrote Myers. "However, using insurance policies to protect against the loss of cash flow, the ability to service customers, or the ability to maintain market share is often not practical. . . . The primary function of business insurance is to provide a hedge against loss or damage. A disaster recovery and business continuation plan, however, has three objectives: 1) Prevent disasters from happening; 2) Provide an organized response to a disaster situation; 3) Ensure business continuity until normal business operations can be resumed."

Business experts also insist that the importance of a good disaster and recovery plan has never been as acute as it is today, in large part because so many businesses rely on vulnerable technology (communication networks, management information systems, process control systems, etc.) to execute fundamental business operations.

Yet as Alan M. Levitt reported in *Disaster Planning and Recovery*, "various studies and surveys instruct us that most organizations have not established a comprehensive strategy for disaster planning and recovery. The percentage of organizations that lack any semblance of a plan is, simply put, frighteningly large." Levitt also noted that many disaster contingency plans that do exist are "applicable only to certain specific business processes (put another way, it is designed only to rescue specific bits and pieces of the business, not to save the entire organization!)." On the other hand, consultants indicate that small businesses that take the time and effort to construct comprehensive disaster and recovery plans will be far more likely to weather the unwelcome event in good financial and market condition. "Some call it Crisis Management," reported *Building Design & Construction* magazine. "Others call it Disaster Management, Emergency Preparedness, Business Resumption, or Contingency Planning. The newest 'buzz word' is Business Continuity Planning. It really doesn't matter what it's called as long as your company does it."

TYPES OF DISASTERS

"It is not easy to recognize the hundreds of hazards or perils that can lead to an unexpected loss," wrote Susan Anastasio in the SBA's *Small Business Insurance and Risk Management Guide*. "For example, unless you've experienced a fire, you may not realize how extensive fire losses can be. Damage to the building and its contents are obvious, but you should also consider: smoke and water damage; damage to employees' personal property and to others' property (e.g., data-processing equipment you lease or customers' property left with you for inspection or repair) left on the premises; the amount of business you'll lose during the time it takes to return your business to normal; the potential permanent loss of customers to competitors."

Of course, many other types of disasters can strike a business as well, ranging from those triggered by natural events such as floods, tornadoes, earthquakes, or hurricanes, to those that come about as a result of localized environmental problems, like water main breaks, work force strikes, power outages, hazardous materials spills, explosions, and major transportation mishaps (aircraft crashes, train derailments, etc.). In addition, damage that is the direct result of premeditated human actions such as vandalism, sabotage, and arson can also be classified as a disaster.

CREATING A DISASTER AND RECOVERY PLAN

"The process of creating a disaster planning and recovery strategy is, in reality, the result of determin-

ing the organization's goals and objectives for business continuation—the ability to deliver its goods and services in the as-intended manner, utilizing its as-intended processes, methods, and procedures—whenever any out-of-course event might impair, impact, impede, interrupt, or halt the as-intended workings and operations," stated Levitt. "*A disaster planning and recovery strategy* is not a method; it is a medium to sustain . . . the organization."

The first step in creating such a strategy (or reviewing existing contingency plans) involves mustering the necessary business will to undertake the challenges associated with the task. Business observers contend that many companies fail in this regard. "The fact is that the majority of private-sector management is still reluctant to allocate the necessary time, staff, or funds to prepare and plan for the possibility of a disaster that may put them out of business," according to *Building Design & Construction*. Myers agreed that this tendency to give short shrift to disaster planning is a common one, observing that "when the economic climate is favorable, contingency planning is last on the list of things to do; when profits are down, contingency planning is the first item to be cut from the budget."

Small business owners, then, need to make sure that they devote adequate resources to disaster preparedness and recovery planning before beginning the process. Indeed, Levitt said that contingency planning efforts are ultimately doomed if they are undertaken without top management commitment, involvement, and support; participation of front line managers and staff teams in both planning and implementation; and ongoing communication with all constituencies of the business.

Once a business's leadership has decided to invest the necessary time and effort into the creation of a good disaster preparedness and recovery plan, it can proceed with the following steps.

DETERMINING VULNERABILITIES "Begin the process of identifying exposures by taking a close look at each of your business operations and asking yourself what could cause a loss," counseled Anastasio. "If there are dozens of exposures you may find dozens of answers. . . . Many business owners use a risk analysis questionnaire or survey, available from insurance agents, as a checklist." These questionnaires will typically address the business's vulnerability to losses in the areas of property, business interruption, liability, and key personnel, among others.

Obviously, this component of disaster preparedness planning—often referred to as risk management—needs to be comprehensive, covering all aspects of business operations, including telecommunications, computer systems, infrastructure, equipment, and the facility itself.

GATHERING INFORMATION Businesses should make an extra effort to solicit the opinions of all functional areas when putting together a disaster and recovery plan. Facility management areas may be most knowledgeable when it comes to the vulnerabilities of computer systems, office areas, etc., but other areas can often provide helpful information about the areas of the business that most need protection or fall-back plans so that the business can continue to operate in the case of a disaster.

RECONCILING FINDINGS WITH PRINCIPLE OBJECTIVES All businesses should be concerned with meeting certain fundamental goals of disaster prevention, safety, and fiscal well-being when working on contingency plans. Analysts offer similar assessments of priorities in this regard, although minor differences in nuance and emphasis are inevitable, depending on the industry, the size of the business, and the viewpoint of the analyst. Most experts agree, however, that the primary objectives of a good disaster response plan should include:

- Preventing disasters from occurring whenever possible (through use of annual reviews, disaster prevention devices such as fire detectors and alarm systems, and physical access control procedures).

- Containment of disasters when they do occur.

- Protecting the lives, safety, and health of employees and customers.

- Protecting property and assets.

- Establishing priorities for utilization of internal resources (such as staffing, talent, and materials).

- Providing an organized response to a disaster/incident.

- Minimizing risk exposure and financial loss (disruptions to cash flow as a result of canceled orders, etc.) through alternate procedures and practices.

- Preventing a significant long-term loss of market share.

Disaster response strategies will vary from business to business, but in the final analysis, they should all be structured in ways that will ensure that essential business functions can be maintained until operations can be returned to normal.

COMMUNICATION OF PLAN Disaster contingency plans should be widely disseminated throughout the company. All employees should be cognizant of the business's basic disaster plan, but this is particularly important for managers, who are often called upon to make important operational decisions in the aftermath of crises.

RECOVERY This final stage of contingency planning is concerned with returning the business to its pre-disaster competitive position (or at least returning it as close to the position as is possible) and normal business operations in the event that a crisis does take place. According to *Industry Week*'s Karen G. Strouse, this entails restoring productivity in three primary areas: people, information, and facilities. ''People are the priority,'' stated Strouse. ''You need to account for them physically and emotionally, and enlist them in your recovery efforts. . . . Contact each employee personally; don't be satisfied with an answering-machine connection. Restoring technology is critical for two reasons. First, most companies rely on technology to conduct day-to-day business. Second, technology may represent your only means of giving your employees, customers, and the media important information as soon as they need it.'' Finally, Strouse observed that while information and employees are portable, ''facilities are not. Your central facilities—mailroom, copy center, file room—need to be restored immediately. Office space is often on the critical path to people and information; without it, nothing else can happen.'' She also warned business owners to ensure that safe practices are followed when searching for and conducting operations in temporary locations.

Levitt, meanwhile, broke the recovery stage down into two elements: ''First is the aspect of planning concerned with providing the resources for recovery. This encompasses the resources of a workplace, equipment, facilities, power, communication capabilities, information and data, forms and other supplies, people, food, lodging, transport, and all else that enables to the business processes to continue or to be re-established—within the planned time-line basis—after being impeded, impaired, interrupted, or halted.'' The other aspect of the recovery phase, wrote Levitt, is ''concerned with impact, consequence and affect mitigation, and damage restoration requisite for the return to as-intended functioning.''

EVALUATING EXISTING PLANS

Experts warn that some companies can become complacent about contingency planning if they already have a plan. But such a plan will be of little or no use if it is obsolete or flawed. The only way to ensure that existing plans meet changing business needs is through continual evaluation and updating. ''Contingency plans should be reassessed annually in order to ensure compatibility with business practices and to integrate lessons learned in plan maintenance and testing into more cost-effective solutions,'' said Myers, who warned that many existing plans are either unnecessarily detailed (a particularly prevalent problem when consultants are involved), sketchy on alternate procedures, or focused "on keeping the computer running rather than on keeping the business running."

FURTHER READING:

Anastasio, Susan. *Small Business Insurance and Risk Management Guide.* Washington: U.S. Small Business Administration.

Arend, Mark. "Time to Dust Off Your Contingency Plan." *ABA Banking Journal.* February 1994.

Crichlow, Douglas. "Taking a Comprehensive Approach to Handling Disasters." *American City & County.* June 1997.

"Dealing with Disasters Takes Careful Planning Ahead of Time." *Building Design & Construction.* September 1996.

DeBompa, Barbara. "Date with Disaster." *Informationweek.* May 2, 1994.

Head, George L., and Stephen Horn, II. *Essentials of Risk Management.* Insurance Institute of America, 1991.

Karpiloff, Douglas G. "When Disaster Strikes . . . How to Manage a Successful Comeback." *Site Selection.* August/September 1997.

Levitt, Alan M. *Disaster Planning and Recovery: A Guide for Facility Professionals.* New York: John Wiley & Sons, 1997.

Myers, Kenneth N. *Total Contingency Planning for Disasters.* New York: John Wiley & Sons, 1993.

Naff, Kevin C. "Can You Plan For Disasters?" *Business Credit.* October 1995.

Strouse, Karen G. "What If Your Office Vanishes? Practical Advice on What to Do if Disaster Strikes." *Industry Week.* July 3, 1995.

Sullivan, Kristina B. "Disaster-Recovery Planning: Pricey, But Worth It." *PC Week.* July 26, 1993.

SEE ALSO: Crisis Management

DISCLOSURE LAWS AND REGULATIONS

Companies that are privately owned are not required by law to disclose detailed financial and operating information. They have a wide latitude in deciding what types of information to make available to the public. Small businesses and other enterprises that are privately owned may shield information from public knowledge and determine for themselves who needs to know specific types of information. Companies that are publicly owned, on the other hand, are subject to detailed disclosure laws about their financial condition, operating results, management compensation, and other areas of their business. While these disclosure obligations are primarily linked with large publicly traded companies, many smaller companies choose to raise capital by making shares in the company available to investors. In such instances, the small business is subject to many of the same disclosure laws that apply to large corporations. These regulations are monitored and enforced by the U.S. **Securities and Exchange Commission (SEC)**.

Disclosure laws are designed to protect investors through the disclosure of business and financial information that could be considered relevant to making an investment decision. Since private companies do not raise money from the investing public, they are not subject to the same disclosure laws as public companies. Investors in private companies are considered to be sufficiently well informed about their investment decisions so as not to require the protection of disclosure laws. Congress and the SEC balance a concern for investor safety with a concern for business's ability to raise capital. They recognize that disclosure laws should not be so burdensome on companies that they discourage capital formation through the offering of stock and other securities to the public. Nonetheless, it is generally recognized that registration requirements for new securities issues and the ongoing reporting requirements for public companies are more burdensome on smaller businesses and stock issues than on big ones.

All of the SEC's disclosure requirements have statutory authority, and these rules and regulations are subject to changes and amendments over time. Some changes are made as the result of new accounting rules adopted by the principal rule-making bodies of the accounting profession. In other cases changes in accounting rules follow changes in SEC guidelines. In any event, SEC regulations have a direct impact on what are known as generally accepted accounting principles (GAAP). The rule-making bodies of the accounting profession, most notably the Financial Accounting Standards Board (FASB) and the American Institute of Certified Public Accountants (AICPA), must rely on "acceptance" of their statements. While FASB and AICPA statements do not have the force of law, they are widely accepted in the accounting profession and in some cases influence subsequent SEC rules on disclosure.

REQUIRED DISCLOSURES

SEC regulations require publicly owned companies to disclose certain types of business and financial data on a regular basis to the SEC and to the company's stockholders. The SEC also requires disclosure of relevant business and financial information to potential investors when new securities, such as stocks and bonds, are issued to the public, although exceptions are made for small issues and private placements. The current system of mandatory corporate disclosure is known as the integrated disclosure system. By amending some of its regulations, the SEC has attempted to make this system less burdensome on corporations by standardizing various forms and eliminating some differences in reporting requirements to the SEC and to shareholders.

Publicly owned companies prepare two annual reports, one for the SEC and one for their shareholders. Form 10-K is the annual report made to the SEC, and its content and form are strictly governed by federal statutes. It contains detailed financial and operating information, as well as a management response to specific questions about the company's operations.

Historically, companies have had more leeway in what they include in their annual reports to stockholders. Over the years, however, the SEC has gained more influence over the content of such annual reports, primarily through its statutory power concerning proxy statements. By amending its rules covering proxy statements, the SEC has been able to increase its authority over the content of corporate annual reports. Since most companies mail annual reports along with their proxy statements, they must make their annual stockholder reports comply with SEC requirements.

SEC regulations require that annual reports to stockholders contain certified financial statements and other specific items. The certified financial statement must include a two-year audited balance sheet and a three-year audited statement of income and cash flows. In addition, annual reports must contain five years of selected financial data, including net sales or operating revenues, income or loss from continuing operations, total assets, long-term obligations and redeemable preferred stock, and cash dividends declared per common share.

Annual reports to stockholders must also contain management's discussion and analysis of the firm's financial condition and results of operations. This section should disclose or discuss the firm's liquidity, capital resources, results of operations, any favorable or unfavorable trends in the industry, and any significant events or uncertainties. Other information to be included in annual reports to stockholders includes a brief description of the business covering such matters as main products and services, sources of materials, and status of new products. Directors and officers of the corporation must be identified. Specific market data on common stock must also be supplied.

REGISTRATION OF NEW SECURITIES

Private companies that wish to become publicly owned must comply with the registration requirements of the SEC. In addition, companies floating new securities must follow similar disclosure requirements. The required disclosures are made in a two-part registration statement that consists of a prospectus as one part and a second section containing additional information. The prospectus contains all of the information that is to be presented to potential investors. It should be noted that SEC rules and regulations governing registration statements are subject to change.

In order to meet the disclosure requirements of new issue registration, companies prepare a basic information package similar to that used by publicly owned companies for their annual reporting. The prospectus, which contains all information to be presented to potential investors, must include such items as audited financial statements, a summary of selected financial data, and management's description of the company's business and financial condition. The statement should also include a summary of the company's material business contracts and list all forms of cash and noncash compensation given to the chief executive officer (CEO) and the top five officers making more than $100,000 a year. Compensation paid to all officers and directors as a group must also be disclosed. Basically, a company seeking to go public must disclose its entire business plan.

SECURITIES INDUSTRY REGULATIONS

Additional disclosure laws apply to the securities industry and to the ownership of securities. Officers, directors, and principal stockholders (defined as holding 10 percent or more of the company's stock) of publicly owned companies must submit two reports to the SEC. These are Form 3 and Form 4. Form 3 is a personal statement of beneficial ownership of securities of their company. Form 4 records changes in such ownership. These reporting requirements also apply to the immediate families of the company's officers, directors, and principal stockholders. Individuals who acquire 5 percent or more of the voting stock of a SEC-registered company, meanwhile, must also submit notification of that fact to the SEC.

Securities broker-dealers must provide their customers with a confirmation form as soon as possible after the execution of an order. These forms provide customers with minimum basic information required for every trade. Broker-dealers are also responsible for presenting the prospectus to each customer for new securities issues. Finally, members of the securities industry are subject to reporting requirements of their own self-regulating organizations. These organizations include the New York Stock Exchange (for listed securities transactions) and the National Association of Securities Dealers (for over-the-counter traded securities).

One area of the securities industry in which new disclosure rules are being developed by the SEC is that of mutual funds. While mutual funds must issue a prospectus for potential investors, the pospectus does not have to disclose what specific stocks and bonds the fund owns. The language of some prospectuses as they are currently written also does not clearly indicate the risks and potential rewards of investing in the mutual fund. More information about the compensation paid to the fund's director and other fees may also be required, along with information about the effect of such fees and compensation on the performance of the fund.

DISCLOSURE RULES OF THE ACCOUNTING PROFESSION

Generally accepted accounting principles (GAAP) and specific rules of the accounting profession require that certain types of information be disclosed in a business's audited financial statements. As noted above, these rules and principles do not have the same force of law as SEC rules and regulations. Once adopted, however, they are widely accepted and followed by the accounting profession. Indeed, in some instances, disclosures required by the rules and regulations of the accounting profession may exceed those required by the SEC.

It is a GAAP that financial statements must disclose all significant information that would be of interest to a concerned investor or creditor. The relevant information may be disclosed in a footnote, a separate schedule, or another part of the financial statement. Among the types of information that accountants must disclose are accounting policies employed, litigation in progress, lease information, and details of pension plan funding. Generally, full disclosure is required when alternative accounting policies are available, as with inventory valuation, depreciation, and long-term contract accounting. In addition, accounting practices applicable to a particular industry and other unusual applications of accounting principles are usually disclosed.

Certified financial statements contain a statement of opinion from an auditor, in which the auditor states that it is his or her opinion that the financial statements were prepared in accordance with GAAP and that no material information was left undisclosed. If the auditor has any doubts, then a qualified or adverse opinion statement is written.

FURTHER READING:

Diamond, Michael R., and Julie L. Williams. *How to Incorporate: A Handbook for Entrepreneurs and Professionals.* 3d ed. New York: John Wiley, 1996.

Fulkerson, Jennifer. "How Investors Use Annual Reports." *American Demographics.* May 1996.

Seligman, Joel. *The SEC and the Future of Finance.* Praeger, 1985.

Skousen, K. Fred. *An Introduction to the SEC.* 5th ed. South-Western Publishing, 1991.

SEE ALSO: Financial Statements; Initial Public Offering; Investor Relations and Reporting

DISCOUNT SALES

Discounts are reductions that are made from the regular price of a product or service in order to obtain or increase sales. These discounts—also commonly referred to as sales or markdowns—are utilized in a wide range of industries by both retailers and manufacturers. The merits of discount pricing, however, have been a subject of considerable debate over the past several years, as analysts argue about their effects on short-term sales, longer term profits, brand loyalty, and total supply chain costs for retailers and manufacturers.

RETAILER AND MANUFACTURER VIEWS OF DISCOUNTING Discounts are a staple of business strategy for many retail firms. As Tom Hartley noted in *Business First of Buffalo,* sales remain "the fuel that drives the retail engine." He cited the views of several retail experts who flatly insist that sales promotions are integral to most retailers' success. "The name of the game is promotion," one expert told Hartley. "Sales are the only way to drive the business and retailers have to have them, even if they seem to be going on all the time. Discounting in America has been built into the retail cycle. It is no longer a big deal."

But small retail firms should make sure that they go about the discounting process in an intelligent fashion. Business consultants cite several considerations that small retailers should weigh when putting together their overall marketing strategy. For example, retailers should beware of overuse. "Sales are useful and we don't know how we'd replace them," said one business executive in an interview with *Business First.* "But their effectiveness is diminished by having too many." Indeed, according to many economists and business owners, discount periods increase sales volume, but they also deepen sales troughs in between sales. Other analysts contend that frequent sales tend to numb customer response over time, and Hartley pointed out that "many retail experts think consumer have become less trustful of retailers who they see running weekly sales, or marking up items so high that they make a profit even after slashing prices 20, 30, or 50 percent."

In addition, retailers should study historic customer response, inventory levels, competitor pricing, seasonal cycles, and other factors in determining the level of discount. Some businesses are able to dramatically increase sales volume through discounts of 20 percent or less, which in many instances enables them to maintain a decent profit margin on sales. Other businesses, though, may have to offer discounts of 40–50 percent (because of seasonal considerations, industry trends, etc.) in order to see meaningful increases in traffic. Of course, some retailers employ a price philosophy that emphasizes every-day low prices in the hopes that the increased volume will make up for the small profit margin on individual sales.

Manufacturers, meanwhile, should be very careful in establishing discounts for their goods. Recent studies have indicated that price promotions offered by manufacturers often set a dangerous precedent and condition customers to make purchases based on price rather than brand loyalty. "Over the long term," claimed *Management Today* contributor Alan Mitchell, "[discount pricing initiatives] do precious little to improve base-line sales, increase the incidence of repeat buying or attract new customers. They do, however, undermine other marketing initiatives by sensitizing consumers to price." A top manufacturing executive agreed with this analysis, noting that "[manufacturers] are actually training consumers to hunt around, to look for high-value offers. We're either encouraging them to shop up heavily when the offer appears and distort the supply chain, or we're really annoying them if they miss the offer because it's just stopped. Net, we're undermining their loyalty." Finally, ill-considered discount sales can lead to price wars with other competitors and can tarnish the image of the brand in question.

There are other drawbacks often associated with discount sales as well, and these can quickly get an unsuspecting small business owner in serious trouble. *Sales & Marketing Management* contributor Minda Zetlin noted, for example, that "discounts have a way of taking on a life of their own." Indeed, the customer that receives a 15 percent discount for one purchase may well feel entitled to an even greater discount the following year. Moreover, news of a discount extended to one client is often difficult to keep under wraps, and when one client finds out that his deal is not as good as the one that another client is getting, he is apt to react in ways that are not good for business. "What happens is customers talk," one executive told Zetlin. "You get a call from Fred, who thought he was getting your best deal, and found out last night at the bar that he isn't and is now unhappy with you." One way of minimizing the likelihood of running into such complications, say experts, is to make sure that you adhere to a uniform set of discount rules. Of course, some small business owners have to give customers different deals as part of their efforts to establish and grow their enterprises. Nonetheless, as one businessman recounted to *Sales & Marketing Management,* "[with] indiscriminant discounting . . . you wind up giving different deals to different customers based on their negotiating ability rather than some more rational technique."

DISCOUNT SALES AND THE COMPANY SALES FORCE

Almost all businesses utilize sales representatives to deal with customers and close deals. But whereas sales personnel employed by retail outlets typically do not have the power to offer discounts, many representatives in the manufacturing and service sectors are provided with some leeway by their employers in this area. Both existing and prospective customers on whom they call are well aware of this state of affairs. Small business owners, then, need to pay extra attention to this reality as they build their sales force. For as business experts in all industry areas will attest, many sales representatives are so eager to secure a sale—and thus a commission—that they will offer a discount on a sale at the first hint of a price objection. "Salespeople offer discounts too quickly because they get flustered and fear losing a deal, or because it's easier than making the customer understand why this product is worth more," wrote Zetlin.

To head off scenarios in which salespeople might unnecessarily fritter away profits on a sale with an unnecessary discount offer, business consultants and successful salespeople recommend that entrepreneurs consider the following:

1) Informed salespeople are formidable salespeople—Many requests for discounts are based on ignorance (feigned or not) of the difference between your company's goods and/or services and those of the competition, which may be dangling a lower price. The challenge for the small business owner, then, is to make sure that sales representatives can talk about non-price benefits authoritatively. "A rep with a thorough knowledge of his product has a greater ability to offer creative solutions to his customers' problems," wrote Barry J. Farber in *Sales & Marketing Management.* "Similarly, a rep must be able to articulate what makes his company different from the competition, and better suited to work with a customer. When a customer asks, 'Why should I pay six dollars for your product when your competitor is selling it to me for three?' the rep had better be prepared to answer: 'I understand your concern. My competitor is a fine company, but let me tell you a few things about our organization that makes us unique.' By going immediately to the company's strengths, the rep automatically colors the competition to look weak."

2) Knowledge of client issues—Of course, knowledge includes not only representative awareness of his or her employer's circum-

stances (inventory, profit margin, etc.), but also an understanding of the challenges facing current and potential customers. ''The only way you can build value for a customer is to find out his needs and concerns, and that's done by asking questions,'' said Farber. By taking a proactive approach that seeks out answers to customer hopes, strategies, and concerns, many representatives can head off attempts to secure a discount by highlighting customer service advantages that they can secure through your company. In addition, small business owners who are knowledgeable about key customers are better able to offer discounts that ultimately benefit their companies. For example, offering a small discount can be a good way to curry favor with a client that is on the verge of significant growth.

3) Provide guidelines and training to sales staff—Sales personnel should be provided with firm guidelines regarding their authority to negotiate discount prices to customers. Moreover, many business experts counsel entrepreneurs—who often serve as their own sales representatives, especially during a business's formative years—and their sales staff to receive training in negotiation tactics so that they can better differentiate between customers who truly are unhappy with the price and those who are merely angling for a discount.

4) Recognize industry dynamics—Some industries allow participants to adhere to set price guidelines fairly closely, while others—whether because of intense competition, economic problems experienced by target markets, or some other factor—may have to be considerably more flexible in providing discount sales to clients.

5) Talk to the right personnel—Negotiations over price can vary considerably, depending on the personnel that are involved on the customer's side of the table. ''There are a lot of people who impact a large purchasing decision, and some are charged with getting the best price,'' admitted one consultant in an interview with *Sales & Marketing Management*. But she also added that ''some are charged with doing what's good for the organization, and some have to work directly with the results of that decision every day. Who you're talking to will determine how much emphasis there is on price. . . . A lot of people say that if you can show value the customer won't care about the price. But if you're talking to a buy whose job is to get the best price, he or she won't care about value. If you want to show better value, you had better also talk to someone more senior, whose job is to find value for the company's bottom line.''

6) Recognize sales representative priorities—Zetlin pointed out that ''one of the chief problems with giving salespeople leeway to negotiate prices or offer discounts is that it creates a conflict of interest between many salespeople and their employers. After all, it's to the salesperson's advantage to close every deal—no matter how unprofitable—if she will always earn a commission by doing so.'' Small business owners who closely monitor the performance of sales personnel can curb such abuses to some degree, as can those who firmly communicate sales margin expectations to their sales force. But consultant Al Hahn suggested to *Sales & Marketing Management* that a better solution might be to tie the salesperson's compensation to the profitability of the sale. ''In my experience, salespeople . . . respond very strongly to the incentive systems they're given, and they'll do what the commission plan tells them to do to make money.'' By linking compensation to the profitability of the sale, representatives are thus rewarded for making *good* deals for the company, not just by the number of sales they make irrespective of incentives that are handed out to the client.

7) Know when to look elsewhere for business—Some customers simply will not agree to terms without unreasonable discounts that cut too great a swath into your profit margin (or obliterate it altogether). In such instances, it is usually better to move on in search of other customers rather than continually butt heads with a single client. Certainly, individual business realities can color an entrepreneur's ability to do this. If the entrepreneur's business is predicating a big marketing push on marketplace legitimacy that it owes to its relationship with the client, for instance, then it may be forced to accede to the client's discount demands. But as Farber indicated, if a customer is unable to get beyond the price issue, it may be time to look elsewhere for business. ''Salespeople waste a lot of time on prospects who are not qualified, don't have the decision-making ability, or are stalling them.''

ALTERNATIVES TO TRADITIONAL DISCOUNT STRUCTURES

In addition to traditional discounts, wherein individual goods or services are offered at a given percentage below the original asking price, small business owners also have the option of instituting several different discounting variations, such as "earned" discounts, early-payment discounts, and multi-buy promotions.

"EARNED" DISCOUNTS Some companies offer their customers discounts if they meet certain requirements. Under this scenario, customers that agree to make large purchases, provide repeat business, or sign multi-year contracts are in essence rewarded for their business by receiving a discount on the price of the goods or services they have purchased.

EARLY-PAYMENT DISCOUNTS Some small business owners offer discounts to customers who pay promptly (within 10 days is a common stipulation). Small businesses that do this are often relatively new firms that are operating under tight financial constraints. Unlike established business owners, who may have a financial cushion from which to draw to meet various business and/or personal obligations, entrepreneurs are often in greater need of securing prompt payment from customers. An early-payment discount provides customers with an incentive for them to make payment quickly. Businesses that utilize this discount option range from manufacturers to freelance writers.

Business consultants warn, however, that some customers may abuse this option by taking the early-payment discount, only to pay off the bill after the discount period has ended. Christopher Caggiano noted in *Inc.* that small business owners can institute a couple of different policies that can do a lot to curb such abuses. One device that entrepreneurs can use is to make it clear that the early-payment discount will be offered only if collection can be made in person by the entrepreneur himself or a member of his staff. Another option is to charge customers for the difference on the next invoice that they submit. In most cases, the customer will pay the amount without complaint since it did not meet the previously agreed-upon terms.

MULTI-BUY PROMOTIONS Multi-buy promotions are an increasingly popular alternative to the standard discount pricing strategies, especially for retailers. Rather than knock 25 percent off the price of a product, some companies are choosing to offer "buy one, get one free" or "buy three for the price of two" promotions to consumers. This strategy is driven by statistics that indicate that such promotions are often so tremendously popular that the volume of sales outweighs the cost of the discount given. Business observers point out that many multi-buy promotions are made economical by the hidden savings that can be realized through them. "Supermarkets now have computer systems which recognize a second or third pack and automatically adjust the bill at the till, thereby eliminating most of the administrative hassle," wrote Alan Mitchell in *Management Today*. "And the fact that the goods being promoted come in standard packs eradicates many of the design, manufacture, and transport costs associated with other types of promotional offers."

FURTHER READING:

Caggiano, Christopher. "Customers Take Our Early-Payment Discount—But Pay Late." *Inc.* October 1997.

The Facts About Pricing Your Products and Services. Washington: U.S. Small Business Administration, 1996.

Farber, Barry J. "The High Cost of Discounting." *Sales & Marketing Management.* November 1996.

Fraccastoro, Katherine, Scot Burton, and Abhijit Biswas. "Effective Use of Advertisements Promoting Sale Prices." *Journal of Consumer Marketing.*

Hartley, Tom. "You Always Hear the Word 'Sale'—But Does It Work?" *Business First of Buffalo.* March 23, 1992.

Hayes, Mary. "Discount is Name of the Game in Retail: Some Wonder, However, Is Big Better?" *The Business Journal.* December 30, 1991.

Marn, M.V., and R.L. Rosiello. "Managing Price, Gaining Profit." *Harvard Business Review.* September-October 1992.

Mitchell, Alan. "Multibuys that Wash." *Management Today.* May 1996.

Peppers, Don, and Martha Rogers. "Avoid Price Dilution By Making Yourself Valuable to Loyal Customers." *Business Marketing.* December 1997.

Rasmussen, Erika. "Leading Edge: The Pitfalls of Price-Cutting." *Sales & Marketing Management.* May 1997.

Walker, Bruce J. *A Pricing Checklist for Small Retailers.* Washington: U.S. Small Business Administration.

Winninger, Thomas J. *Price Wars: How to Win the Battle for Your Customer.* St. Thomas Press, 1994.

Zetlin, Minda. "Kicking the Discount Habit: Teach Your Salespeople to Stop Leaving Money on the Table." *Sales & Marketing Management.* May 1994.

SEE ALSO: Sales Force

DISCOUNTED CASH FLOW

Discounted cash flow (DCF) is the sum of a series of future cash transactions, on a present value basis. DCF analysis is a capital budgeting technique used to quantify and assess the receipts and disbursements from a particular activity, project, or business venture in terms of constant dollars at the outset, considering risk-return relationships and timing of the cash flows. Under DCF, each successive year's cash flow is discounted to a greater extent than the prior year, due to the fact that it is received further out in time. Discounted cash flow analysis is utilized in a wide variety of business and financial applications; a common example is a mortgage loan.

One of the most useful applications of DCF analysis is for business **valuation** purposes. Here the analyst calculates the present value of the company's future cash flows. The most common form of this analysis involves using company-produced forecasts of cash flow for the next five years, along with a ''steady state'' cash flow for year six and beyond. The analyst will calculate the present value of the first five years' cash flows, plus the present value of the capitalized residual value from the steady state cash flow. Under this methodology, all years of the company's future cash flows are impounded in the measure of value. Of course, it is critical that the cash flows are reasonably estimated, with due care given to the various factors than can affect future results of operations. The analyst must work with knowledgeable company management, and gain a thorough understanding of the business, its competitors, and the marketplace in general. Collateral affects of various decisions must be quantified and entered into the calculus of the overall cash flows.

CORNERSTONES OF DISCOUNTED CASH FLOW ANALYSIS According to Ronald W. Hilton, author of *Managerial Accounting,* there are two primary methods of discounted cash flow analysis: net-present-value method (NPV) and internal-rate-of-return (IRR) method. Hilton noted, however, that both of these methods are based on the same four assumptions:

1) All cash flows are treated as though they occur at the end of the year. ''The additional computational complexity that would be required to reflect the exact timing of all cash flows would complicate an investment analysis considerably,'' said Hilton. ''The error introduced by the year-end cash-flow assumption generally is not large enough to cause any concern.''

2) DCF methods treat cash flows associated with investment projects as though they were known with certainty, although Hilton noted that ''risk adjustments can be made in an NPV analysis to partially account for uncertainty about the cash flows.''

3) Both methods assume that all cash inflows are reinvested in other projects that earn monies for the company.

4) DCF analysis assumes a perfect capital market.

Hilton admitted that ''in practice, these four assumptions rarely are satisfied. Nevertheless, discounted cash flow models provide an effective and widely used method of investment analysis. The improved decision making that would result from using more complicated models seldom is worth the additional cost of information and analysis.''

DETERMINING DISCOUNT RATES An important element of discounted cash flow analysis is the determination of the proper discount rate that should be applied to bring the cash flows back to their present value. Generally, the discount rate should be determined in accordance with the following factors:

- Riskiness of the business or project—The higher the risk, the higher the required rate of return.

- Size of the company—Studies indicate that returns are also related inversely to the size of the entity. That is, a larger company will provide lower rates of return than a smaller company of otherwise similar nature.

- Time horizon—Generally, yield curves are upward sloping (longer term investments command a higher interest rate); therefore, cash flows to be received over longer periods may require a slight premium in interest, or discount, rate.

- Debt/equity ratio—The leverage of the company drives the mix of debt and equity rates in the overall cost of capital equation. This is a factor that can be of considerable importance, since rates of return on debt and equity within a company can vary considerably.

- Real or nominal basis—Market rates of interest or return are on a nominal basis. If the cash flow projections are done on a real basis (non-inflation adjusted), then the discount rate must be converted to real terms.

- Income tax considerations—If the cash flows under consideration are on an after-tax basis, then the discount rate should be calculated using an after-tax cost of debt in the cost of capital equation.

FURTHER READING:

Bangs, David H., Jr., with Robert Gruber. *Finance: Mastering Your Small Business.* Upstart, 1996.

Financial Accounting Standards Board. *Statements of Financial Accounting Concepts.* Irwin, 1987.

Hilton, Ronald W. *Managerial Accounting.* New York: McGraw-Hill, 1991.

Woelfel, C. J. *Financial Statement Analysis.* Probus, 1994.

SEE ALSO: Cash Flow Statements

DISCRETIONARY INCOME

Discretionary income is the amount of income consumers have left over after paying their necessary expenses, such as food, rent or mortgage payments, utilities, and insurance. A similar concept is disposable income, which is the amount of income consumers have left over after paying their taxes. Disposable income is then used to pay necessary expenses. Many consumers do not spend all of their disposable income; instead, they may save or invest some of it. The amount that remains can be spent on luxuries, as opposed to necessities, at the consumers' discretion, and so is known as discretionary income. It is important to note that what qualifies as discretionary income may vary for different individuals and different income levels, as well as over time. For example, a color television set may be a discretionary purchase for a lower-income family, but it may be considered a necessity by a wealthy senior citizen.

The U.S. Bureau of Labor Statistics and the U.S. Census Bureau collaborate to publish ongoing studies of discretionary income and consumer spending. Census Bureau statisticians rank a number of American households according to age, size, and geographic area of residence. They then track the income levels of these households as well as their level of spending in various expense categories, including necessities (such as food, housing, clothing, transportation, and health care) as well as luxuries (such as alcohol, tobacco, entertainment, and education). These studies are used to determine how much money a household typically needs to maintain its standard of living. Many private firms in the country undertake their own studies of discretionary income, but their analyses are also based on the publicly available (online as well as on CD-ROM) census data.

Knowing the pertinent facts about discretionary income is of vital importance to both business and government. Business managers are interested in discretionary income levels of consumers in various geographic areas and age brackets because consumers with larger levels are more likely to spend their money on luxury items. The statistics also provide information about consumer spending habits that can be useful in targeting marketing campaigns. Although the data alone cannot predict how a certain consumer will choose to spend his or her discretionary income, it can provide useful information to help marketers make sound planning decisions.

ANALYZING THE DATA

Based on 1990 census data, approximately 26 million households in the U.S. were determined to have discretionary income. Since a household typically consists of more than one individual, this 26 million figure translates into the majority of the population having some kind of disposable income, totaling in the hundreds of billions of dollars. Such enormous sums of potential buying power make it worthwhile for business and industry to know as much as they can about discretionary income.

Discretionary incomes of people in certain age groups are of particular value to business and marketing specialists. For example, those over the age of 50 have half of the total amount of discretionary income in their control, making the 50-plus age category the wealthiest group in the nation. This group also corners three-quarters of the bank deposits in the nation, and accounts for 80 percent of all savings accounts. In short, the ''over 50s'' have enormous financial clout.

Marketers can also glean a great deal of useful information from studies of the discretionary income levels of different social and ethnic groups. Discretionary income studies reveal that—in general—the higher a consumer's level of education, the greater the amount of disposable income. Gays and lesbians in general have an unusually high level of education and a corresponding high level of income. A little more than half of gay couples have household incomes of at least $50,000 per year, a fact that translates into high discretionary income, particularly since most of these couples often do not have children. This is a fact that many businesses are noticing.

There are a wide range of businesses that depend entirely on consumers having discretionary income, such as florists, arts and crafts shops, jewelry stores, gambling casinos, symphony orchestras, and many non-profit organizations. Knowing where the most discretionary income is located and who has most of it is important for these and many other businesses.

FURTHER READING:

A Marketer's Guide to Discretionary Income: A Joint Study. Conference Board, 1983.

McCarthy, E. Jerome, and William D. Perreault, Jr. *Basic Marketing: A Managerial Approach.* 10th ed. Homewood, IL: Irwin, 1990.

Russell, Cheryl. *The Official Guide to American Incomes: A Comprehensive Look at How Much Americans Have to Spend: With a Special Section on Discretionary Income.* New Strategist Publications and Consulting, 1993.

SEE ALSO: Demographics

DISTRIBUTION CHANNELS

Distribution channels move products and services from businesses to consumers and to other businesses. Also known as marketing channels, channels of distribution consist of a set of interdependent organizations—such as wholesalers, retailers, and sales agents—involved in making a product or service available for use or consumption. Distribution channels are just one component of the overall concept of distribution, which also includes storage, transportation, and allocation of inventories. In short, distribution describes all the logistics involved in delivering a company's products or services to the right place, at the right time, for the lowest cost. The channels of distribution selected by a business play a vital role in successful distribution. In fact, well-chosen channels can provide a competitive advantage, while poorly chosen channels can doom even a superior product or service to failure in the market.

For many products and services, their manufacturers or providers use multiple channels of distribution. A personal computer, for example, might be bought directly from the manufacturer, either over the telephone or via direct mail, or through several kinds of retailers, including independent computer stores, franchised computer stores, and department stores. In addition, large and small businesses may make their purchases through other outlets.

Channel structures range from two to five levels. The simplest is a two-level structure in which goods and services move directly from the manufacturer or provider to the consumer. Two-level structures occur in some industries where consumers are able to order products directly from the manufacturer and the manufacturer fulfills those orders through its own **physical distribution** system.

In a three-level channel structure retailers serve as intermediaries between consumers and manufacturers. Retailers order products directly from the manufacturer, then sell those products directly to the consumer. A fourth level is added when manufacturers sell to wholesalers rather than to retailers. In a four-level structure retailers order goods from wholesalers rather than manufacturers. Finally, a manufacturer's agent can serve as an intermediary between the manufacturer and its wholesalers, making a five-level channel structure consisting of the manufacturer, agent, wholesale, retail, and consumer levels. A five-level channel structure might also consist of the manufacturer, wholesale, jobber, retail, and consumer levels, whereby jobbers service smaller retailers not covered by the large wholesalers in the industry.

BENEFITS OF INTERMEDIARIES

If selling directly from the manufacturer to the consumer were always the most efficient way, there would be no need for channels of distribution. Intermediaries, however, provide several benefits to both manufacturers and consumers: improved efficiency, a better assortment of products, routinization of transactions, and easier searching for goods as well as customers.

The improved efficiency that results from adding intermediaries in the channels of distribution can easily be grasped with the help of a few examples. In the first example there are five manufacturers and 20 retailers. If each manufacturer sells directly to each retailer, there are 100 contact lines—one line from each manufacturer to each retailer. The complexity of this distribution arrangement can be reduced by adding wholesalers as intermediaries between manufacturers and retailers. If a single wholesaler serves as the intermediary, the number of contacts is reduced from 100 to 25: five contact lines between the manufacturers and the wholesaler, and 20 contact lines between the wholesaler and the retailers. Reducing the number of necessary contacts brings more efficiency into the distribution system by eliminating duplicate efforts in ordering, processing, shipping, etc.

In terms of efficiency there is an effect of diminishing returns as more intermediaries are added to the channels of distribution. If, in the example above, there were three wholesalers instead of only one, the number of essential contacts increases to 75: 15 contacts between five manufacturers and three wholesalers, plus 60 contacts between three wholesalers and 20 retailers. Of course this example assumes that each retailer would order from each wholesaler and that each manufacturer would supply each wholesaler. In fact geographic and other constraints might eliminate some lines of contact, making the channels of distribution more efficient.

Intermediaries provide a second benefit by bridging the gap between the assortment of goods and services generated by producers and those in demand from consumers. Manufacturers typically produce large quantities of a few similar products, while consumers want small quantities of many different products. In order to smooth the flow of goods and services, intermediaries perform such functions as sorting, accumulation, allocation, and creating assortments. In sorting, intermediaries take a supply of different items and sort them into similar groupings, as exemplified by graded agricultural products. Accumulation means that intermediaries bring together items from a number of different sources to create a larger supply for their customers. Intermediaries allocate products by breaking down a homogeneous supply into smaller units for resale. Finally, they build up an assortment of products to give their customers a wider selection.

A third benefit provided by intermediaries is that they help reduce the cost of distribution by making transactions routine. Exchange relationships can be standardized in terms of lot size, frequency of delivery and payment, and communications. Seller and buyer no longer have to bargain over every transaction. As transactions become more routine, the costs associated with those transactions are reduced.

The use of intermediaries also aids the search processes of both buyers and sellers. Producers are searching to determine their customers' needs, while customers are searching for certain products and services. A degree of uncertainty in both search processes can be reduced by using channels of distribution. For example, consumers are more likely to find what they are looking for when they shop at wholesale or retail institutions organized by separate lines of trade, such as grocery, hardware, and clothing stores. In addition, producers can make some of their commonly used products more widely available by placing them in many different retail outlets, so that consumers are more likely to find them at the right time.

WHAT FLOWS THROUGH THE CHANNELS

Members of channels of distribution typically buy, sell, and transfer title to goods. There are, however, many other flows between channel members in addition to physical possession and ownership of goods. These include promotion flows, negotiation flows, financing, assuming risk, ordering, and payment. In some cases the flow is in one direction, from the manufacturer to the consumer. Physical possession, ownership, and promotion flow in one direction through the channels of distribution from the manufacturer to the consumer. In other cases there is a two-way flow. Negotiation, financing, and the assumption of risk flow in both directions between the manufacturer and the consumer. Ordering and payment are channel flows that go in one direction from the consumer to the manufacturer.

There are also a number of support functions that help channel members perform their distribution tasks. Transportation, storage, insurance, financing, and advertising are tasks that can be performed by facilitating agencies that may or may not be considered part of the marketing channel. From a channel management point of view, it may be more effective to consider only those institutions and agencies that are involved in the transfer of title as channel members. The other agencies involved in supporting tasks can then be described as an ancillary or support structure. The rationale for separating these two types of organizations is that they each require different types

of management decisions and have different levels of involvement in channel membership.

Effective management of the channels of distribution involves forging better relationships among channel members. With respect to the task of distribution, all of the channel members are interdependent. Relationships between channel members can be influenced by how the channels are structured. Improved performance of the overall distribution system is achieved through managing such variables as channel structure and channel flows.

SELECTING CHANNELS FOR SMALL BUSINESSES

Given the importance of distribution channels—along with the limited resources generally available to small businesses—it is particularly important for entrepreneurs to make a careful assessment of their channel alternatives. In evaluating possible channels, it may be helpful first to analyze the distribution channels used by competitors. This analysis may reveal that using the same channels would provide the best option, or it may show that choosing an alternative channel structure would give the small business a competitive advantage. Other factors to consider include the company's pricing strategy and internal resources. As a general rule, the more intermediaries are included in a channel, the less control producers have over the product and the more it costs to compensate each channel level for their participation. At the same time, however, more intermediaries can also provide greater market coverage.

Among the many channels a small business owner can choose from are: direct sales (which provides the advantage of direct contact with the consumer); original equipment manufacturer (OEM) sales (in which a small business's product is sold to another company that incorporates it into a finished product); manufacturer's representatives (salespeople operating out of agencies that handle an assortment of complimentary products); wholesalers (which generally buy goods in large quantities, warehouse them, then break them down into smaller shipments for their customers—usually retailers); brokers (who act as intermediaries between producers and wholesalers or retailers); retailers (which include independent stores as well as regional and national chains); and direct mail. Ideally, the distribution channels selected by a small business owner should be close to the desired market, able to provide necessary services to buyers, able to handle local advertising and promotion, experienced in selling compatible product lines, solid financially, cooperative, and reputable.

Since many small businesses lack the resources to hire, train, and supervise their own sales forces, sales agents and brokers are a common distribution channel. Many small businesses consign their output to an agent, who might sell it to various wholesalers, one large distributor, or a number of retail outlets. In this way, an agent might provide the small business with access to channels it would not otherwise have had. Moreover, since most agents work on a commission basis, the cost of sales drops when the level of sales drops, which provides small businesses with some measure of protection against economic downturns. When selecting an agent, an entrepreneur should look for one who has experience with desired channels as well as with closely related—but not competitive—products.

Other channel alternatives can also offer benefits to small businesses. For example, by warehousing goods, wholesalers can reduce the amount of storage space needed by small manufacturers. They can also provide national distribution that might otherwise be out of reach for an entrepreneur. Selling directly to retailers can be a challenge for small business owners. Independent retailers tend to be the easiest market for entrepreneurs to penetrate. The merchandise buyers for independent retailers are most likely to get their supplies from local distributors, can order new items on the spot, and can make adjustments to inventory themselves. Likewise, buyers for small groups of retail stores also tend to hold decision-making power, and they are able to try out new items by writing small orders. However, these buyers are more likely to seek discounts, advertising allowances, and return guarantees.

Medium-sized retail chains often do their buying through a central office. In order to convince the chain to carry a new product, an entrepreneur must usually make a formal sales presentation with brochures and samples. Once an item makes it onto the shelf, it is required to produce a certain amount of revenue to justify the space it occupies, or else it will be dropped in favor of a more profitable item. National retail chains, too, handle their merchandise buying out of centralized offices and are unlikely to see entrepreneurs making cold sales calls. Instead, they usually request a complete marketing program, with anticipated returns, before they will consider carrying a new product. Once an item becomes successful, however, these larger chains often establish direct computer links with producers for replenishment.

FURTHER READING:

J. K. Lasser Institute. *How to Run a Small Business.* 7th ed. New York: McGraw-Hill, 1994.

Rosenbloom, Bert. *Marketing Channels*, 4th ed. Fort Worth, TX: Dryden, 1991.

Stern, Louis W., and Adel I. El-Ansary. *Marketing Channels.* 3rd ed. Upper Saddle River, NJ: Prentice-Hall, 1988.

SEE ALSO: Distribution Networks; Manufacturers' Agents; Transportation

DISTRIBUTION NETWORKS

A distribution network is a system of interconnected sources and destinations through which products pass on their way to final consumers. According to Howard J. Weiss and Mark E. Gershon in their text *Production and Operations Management,* a basic distribution network consists of two parts: 1) a set of locations that store, ship, or receive materials; and 2) a set of routes that connect these locations. The locations may include factories, **suppliers**, warehouses, local distributors, and retail outlets. The connecting **transportation** routes may include land (train, truck, pipeline), sea, and air, as well as satellite or cable systems that are used to transmit data between computer systems.

Distribution networks may be classified as either simple or complex. A simple distribution network is one that consists of only a single source of supply, a single source of demand, or both, along with fixed transportation routes connecting that source with other parts of the network. In a simple distribution network, the major decisions for managers to make include when and how much to order and ship, based on internal purchasing and inventory considerations.

Weiss and Gershon described three different types of simple distribution networks: arborescent, coalescent, and series. An arborescent network gets its name from the fact that it spreads out from a single source like a tree. An example might be a factory that produces goods and ships them to two regional warehouses. Then each of the warehouses ship the goods to three local distributors, each of which supply four retail outlets.

A coalescent network is very similar, except that it flows in the opposite direction—materials start out at a number of different locations and all end up in the same place. An example might be a factory that assembles a complex product from a number of different subcomponents. In this case, raw materials from four different sources are shipped to each of three subcomponent assembly plants. After processing, the completed subcomponents are shipped to one final assembly plant.

A series network is sort of a combination of the other two types. Rather than proceeding from one source to many destinations or from many sources to one destination, goods in a series network are shipped from one location, to the next, to the next. Each location in the series performs further processing operations on the materials. An example might be a paper manufacturing operation, in which raw lumber is transported to a mill, and then processed lumber is transported from the mill to a paper plant.

In contrast to simple distribution networks, complex distribution networks consist of multiple sources of supply, multiple sources of demand, and a variety of possible routes of shipment. Of course, the multiple locations involved mean that managers must make many more decisions in designing and operating complex networks. For example, it is often not necessary to use all possible transportation routes in a complex distribution network, so managers must choose the most economical way of shipping materials. ''The goal is to minimize the total transportation cost that accrues between all sources and destinations subject to meeting the supply (capacity) and demand restrictions for the product,'' Weiss and Gershon explained.

Distribution management, or logistics, is the function concerned with designing and operating distribution networks. Thanks to the complicated interrelationship of various decisions relating to distribution, it is a highly specialized function. Available distribution networks have implications for the optimal location of new facilities, for example, as well as the capacity of facilities, the storage mechanisms involved, the ideal size and frequency of shipments, the types of transportation used, the routes selected, and the form of packaging for shipments.

FURTHER READING:

Weiss, Howard J., and Mark E. Gershon. *Production and Operations Management.* Boston: Allyn and Bacon, 1989.

SEE ALSO: Distribution Channels

DIVERSIFICATION

For businesses, diversification is the process of entering new markets with new products. Such efforts may be undertaken either through acquisitions or through extension of the company's existing capabilities and resources.

RELATED AND UNRELATED DIVERSIFICATION

Analysts of diversification generally break such efforts down into two categories: 1) related or concentric diversification, and 2) unrelated or conglomerate diversification. ''In related diversification,'' wrote Henry Mintzberg and James Brian Quinn, authors of *The Strategy Process: Concepts and Contexts,* ''there is evident potential synergy between the new business and the core one, based on a common facility, asset, channel, skill, even opportunity.'' But they also noted that ''no matter what its bases, every related diversification is also fundamentally an unrelated one, as many diversifying organizations have discovered to their re-

gret. That is, no matter what *is* common between two different businesses, many other things are not.''

''The range of success [of diversification efforts] varies considerably,'' observed the editors of the *Complete MBA Companion.* ''Although it is agreed that most acquisitions fail to meet expectations, the odds of success decline precipitously the further the firm strays from existing competencies. Kodak's foray into health care via its acquisition of Sterling Drug was far removed from its core business. By contrast, its move into digital imaging (while risky) may be a logical business decision, building on its commitment to picture-taking via whatever technology.''

DIVERSIFICATION THROUGH ACQUISITION AND EXPANSION

Companies diversify either by acquiring already existing businesses or by expanding their own businesses into new markets and new areas of production or service. Acquisition is generally used more frequently by big companies than smaller ones, since most business acquisitions require a degree of financial leverage and health that only larger firms can bring to bear. Indeed, Mintzberg and Quinn remarked that ''as organizations grow large, they become inclined to diversify and then to divisionalize. One reason is protection: large organizations tend to be risk averse—they have too much to lose—and diversification spreads the risk. Another is that as firms grow large, they come to dominate their traditional market, and so must often find growth opportunities elsewhere, through diversification. Moreover, diversification feeds on itself. It creates a cadre of aggressive general managers, each running his or her own division, who push for further diversification and further growth. Thus, most of the giant corporations . . . not only were able to reach their status by diversifying but also feel great pressures to continue doing so.''

Controversy has swirled around some high-profile business transactions in recent years, as critics have pointed to hostile takeovers and antitrust concerns. But another, less-noticed complaint has also been leveled at the practice in general, and not just those acquisitions that are painted as predatory or monopolistic. ''Acquisition has been criticized as sometimes stifling innovation,'' noted the *Complete MBA Companion.* ''A company deploys its resources to take over an existing business rather than to pursue innovation.'' But the editors contend that acquisition can actually liberate creativity if executed for the right reasons: ''If driven by visions of diversification, acquisition can be an innovative impetus for that company in pursuing new opportunities and moving in directions that might otherwise be blocked and which might have greater incremental potential than its existing business opportunities.''

Diversification-by-expansion, on the other hand, is much more likely to be utilized by small- and mid-sized companies. A **business expansion** strategy typically requires smaller—though often still hefty—up-front financial obligations, and often involves moving into a market or service/product with which the business already has at least some passing acquaintance.

FACTORS TO CONSIDER WHEN WEIGHING DIVERSIFICATION

Although diversification into new markets and production areas can be an exciting and profitable step for small business owners, consultants caution them to ''look before they leap.'' As entrepreneur Steven L. Marks remarked in *Inc.,* when presented with opportunities to diversify, ''we view them against our focus criteria: Is the idea consistent with our mission statement? Will it dilute our current efforts? How will it affect our operations?'' Indeed, many factors should be considered before a small company launches a course of diversification:

FINANCIAL HEALTH This is the most basic consideration of all. Business owners should undertake a comprehensive and clinical review of their present fiscal standing—and future prospects—before expanding a business into a new area.

COST OF ENTRY This factor is closely linked to a business's examination of its fundamental financial health. Diversification, whether through expansion or acquisition, typically requires financial outlays of significant size. Does your company have the means to meet those requirements while simultaneously keeping the existing business running smoothly?

ATTRACTIVENESS OF THE INDUSTRY AND/OR MARKET Analysts attach varying level of importance to this factor. Obviously, diversification into an industry or market that is flagging, whether because of general economic conditions or local problems, can result in a significant loss of income and security. As Mintzberg and Quinn observed, though, some businesses attach little significance to this, relying instead on vague beliefs that the industry or market is a good fit with its existing operations, or that the industry or market is headed for an upturn. ''Another common reason for ignoring the attractiveness test is a low entry cost,'' they added. ''Sometimes the buyer has an inside track or the owner is anxious to sell. Even if the price is actually low, however, a one-shot gain will not offset a perpetually poor business.'' Finally, some businesses mistakenly interpret recent market or industry trends as indications of long term health. Many companies that ''rushed into fast-growing industries (personal computers, video games, and robotics, for example), were burned because they mistook early growth for long-term profit potential,'' wrote Mintz-

berg and Quinn. ''Industries are profitable not because they are sexy or high tech; they are profitable only if their structures are attractive.''

WORK FORCE RESOURCES When considering diversification, companies need to analyze the ways in which such a step could impact their current employee work forces. Are you counting on some of those employees to take on added duties with little or no change in their compensation? Will you ask any of your workers to relocate their families or their place of work as a consequence of your business expansion? Does your current work force possess the skills and knowledge to handle the requirements of the new business, or will your company need to initiate a concerted effort to attract new employees? Business owners need to know the answers to such questions before diversifying.

ACCESS TO DISTRIBUTION CHANNELS A company engaged in introducing a new product or service into the marketplace should first ensure that it will have adequate access to **distribution channels** within the targeted market. ''The more limited the wholesale or retail channels for a product are and the more existing competitors have these tied up, obviously the tougher entry into the industry will be,'' wrote Michael E. Porter in *Competitive Strategy: Techniques for Analyzing Industries and Competitors.* ''Existing competitors may have ties with channels based on long relationships, high-quality service, or even exclusive relationships in which the channel is solely identified with a particular manufacturer. Sometimes this barrier to entry is so high that to surmount it a new firm must create an entirely new distribution channel.''

REGULATORY ISSUES Governmental regulatory policies at the local, state, and national level can also have an impact on the diversification decision. For instance, a successful restauranteur may want to open a bar and grille in a certain area, only to learn that the city council has imposed an indefinite moratorium on granting liquor licenses in the area in question. ''Government can limit or even foreclose entry into industries with such controls as licensing requirements and limits on access to raw materials,'' confirmed Porter, who added that regulatory controls on air and water pollution standards and product safety and efficacy should also be weighed. ''For example, pollution control requirements can increase the capital needed for entry and the required technological sophistication and even the optimal scale of facilities. Standards for product testing, common in industries like food and other health-related products, can impose substantial lead times, which not only raise the capital cost of entry but also give established firms ample notice of impending entry and sometimes full knowledge of the new competitor's product with which to formulate retaliatory strategies.'' Many of these regulations,

DIVIDENDS

while enormously beneficial to society, can have a bearing on the ultimate wisdom of a diversification strategy.

FURTHER READING:

Byrd, John, Kent Hickman, and Hugh Hunter. "Diversification: A Broader Perspective." *Business Horizons.* March-April 1997.

Caulkin, Simon. "Focus is for the Wimps." *Management Today.* December 1996.

The Complete MBA Companion. Lanham, MD: Pitman Publishing, 1997.

Heller, Robert. "Concentrate on Keeping Control." *Management Today.* September 1995.

Louk, Steve. "Diversify and Survive." *Industrial Distribution.* September 1995.

Marks, Steven L. "Say When." *Inc.* February 1995.

McCallum, John S. "Dusting Off Diversification." *Business Quarterly.* Spring 1997.

Mintzberg, Henry, and James Brian Quinn. *The Strategy Process: Concepts and Contexts.* Englewood Cliffs, NJ: Prentice-Hall, 1992.

Porter, Michael E. *Competitive Strategy: Techniques for Analyzing Industries and Competitors.* New York: The Free Press, 1980.

DIVIDENDS

Dividends and stock repurchases are the two major ways that corporations can distribute cash to their shareholders. Dividends may also be distributed in the form of stock (stock dividends and stock splits), scrip (a promise to pay at a future date), or property (typically commodities or goods from inventory). By law dividends must be paid from profits; dividends may not be paid from a corporation's capital. This law, which is designed to protect the corporation's creditors, is known as the impairment of capital rule. This law stipulates that dividend payments may not exceed the corporation's retained earnings as shown on its balance sheet.

Companies usually pay dividends on a quarterly basis. When the company is about to pay a dividend, the company's board of directors makes a dividend announcement that includes the amount of the dividend, the date of record, and the date of payment. The date on which the dividend announcement is made is known as the declaration date.

The date of record is significant for the company's shareholders. All shareholders on the date of record are entitled to receive the dividend. The ex-dividend date is the first day on which the stock is traded without the right to receive the declared dividend. All shares traded before the ex-dividend date are bought and sold with rights to receive the dividend

(also known as the cum dividend). Since it usually takes a few business days to settle a stock transaction, the ex-dividend date is usually a few business days before the record date. On the ex-dividend date the trading price of the stock usually falls to account for the fact that the seller rather than the purchaser is entitled to the declared dividend.

When a company puts together its dividend policy, it must decide whether to distribute a certain amount of earnings to the company's shareholders or retain those earnings for reinvestment. Dividend policy is influenced by a number of factors that include various legal constraints on declaring dividends (bond indentures, impairment of capital rule, availability of cash, and penalty tax on accumulated earnings) as well as the nature of the company's investment opportunities and the effect of dividend policy on the cost of capital of common stock. Most firms have chosen to follow a dividend policy of issuing a stable or continuously increasing dividend. Relatively few firms issue a low regular dividend and declare special dividends when annual earnings are sufficient.

The effect of a company's dividend policy on the value of the company is a field of ongoing investigation and study. In 1961 Modigliani and Miller published a classic study that demonstrated that a company's dividend policy has no effect on its value under a certain set of assumptions: there are no taxes on dividends or capital gains; there are no transaction costs associated with buying or selling securities; all investors have the same information as the managers of the firm; and the firm's investment policies are fixed and known by investors. With those assumptions the authors analyzed the dividend policies of various firms and concluded that investors could simply create their own dividends by selling shares of stock instead of holding them.

Subsequent research into dividend policies has focused on removing one or more of Modigliani and Miller's assumptions. In the real world, of course, there are taxes and transaction costs associated with buying and selling securities and receiving dividends or capital gains. It is also evident that financial managers and stock analysts appear to be concerned about dividends and their effect on stock prices. After more than 30 years of research and study, though, there is little or no agreement as to the effect of dividend policy on the value of the firm.

DIVIDENDS AND TAXATION Opinions vary regarding the relationship between dividend policy and corporate taxation as well. "The usual argument is that since dividends are taxed as income, they have a tax disadvantage with respect to capital gains in a relatively light capital gains tax regime, especially for recipients in high tax brackets," wrote Francesca Cornelli in *The Complete MBA Companion.* "Therefore,

298

ENCYCLOPEDIA OF SMALL BUSINESS

other things being equal, companies that pay out high dividends should be valued less than companies that pay out low dividends. In response to this argument, however, economists have argued that the increasing domination of the market by tax-exempt institutions, the reduction of personal marginal income tax rates, the moves in both the UK and US to tax dividends and capital gains at the same rate and the abundance of tax shelters have all combined largely to neutralize the potential tax disadvantage of dividend payments.''

FURTHER READING:

Allen, F., and R. Michaely. *Dividend Policy*. N. Holland Handbooks.

Cornelli, Francesca. ''The Thinking Behind Dividends.'' In *The Complete MBA Companion*. Edited by George Bickerstaffe. Lanham, MD: Pitman Publishing, 1997.

Lazo, Shirley A. ''The Dividends of Dividends: How Significant are Boosts and Cuts?'' *Barron's*. July 1, 1996.

SEE ALSO: Stocks; Tax Planning

DOUBLE TAXATION

Double taxation is a situation that affects **C corporations** when business profits are taxed at both the corporate and personal levels. The corporation must pay income tax at the corporate rate before any profits can be paid to shareholders. Then any profits that are distributed to shareholders through **dividends** are subject to income tax again at the individual rate. In this way, the corporate profits are subject to income taxes twice. Double taxation does not affect **S corporations**, which are able to ''pass through'' earnings directly to shareholders without the intermediate step of paying dividends. In addition, many smaller corporations are able to avoid double taxation by distributing earnings to employee/shareholders as wages. Still, double taxation has long been subject to criticism from accountants, lawyers, and economists.

Critics of double taxation would prefer to integrate the corporate and personal tax systems, arguing that taxes should not affect business and investment decisions. They claim that double taxation places corporations at a disadvantage in comparison with unincorporated businesses, influences corporations to use **debt financing** rather than **equity financing** (because interest payments can be deducted and dividend payments cannot), and provides incentives for corporations to retain earnings rather than distributing them to shareholders. Furthermore, critics of the current corporate taxation system argue that integration would simplify the tax code significantly.

AVOIDING DOUBLE TAXATION

There are many ways for corporations to avoid double taxation. For many smaller corporations, all of the major shareholders are also employees of the firm. These corporations are able to avoid double taxation by distributing earnings to employees as wages and fringe benefits. Although the individual employees must pay taxes on their income, the corporation is able to deduct the wages and benefits paid to employees as a business expense, and thus is not required to pay corporate taxes on that amount. For many small businesses, distributions to employee/owners account for all of the corporation's income, and there is nothing left over that is subject to corporate taxes. In cases where income is left in the business, it is usually retained in order to finance future growth. Although this amount is subject to corporate taxes, these tax rates are usually lower than those paid by individuals.

Larger corporations—which are more likely to have shareholders who are not employed by the business and who thus cannot have corporate profits distributed to them in the form of salaries and fringe benefits—are often able to avoid double taxation as well. For example, a non-active shareholder may be called a ''consultant,'' since payments to consultants are considered tax-deductible business expenses rather than dividends. Of course, the shareholder/consultant must pay taxes on his or her compensation. It is also possible to add shareholders to the payroll as members of the board of directors. Finally, tax-exempt investors such as pension funds and charities are often significant shareholders in large corporations. The tax-exempt status of these groups enables them to avoid paying taxes on corporate dividends received.

FURTHER READING:

Dailey, Frederick W. *Tax Savvy for Small Business*. Berkeley, CA: Nolo Press, 1997.

Gelband, Joseph F. ''Far from Letter Perfect.'' *Barron's*. January 6, 1997.

Thomas, Deborah W., and Keith F. Sellers. ''Eliminate the Double Tax on Dividends.'' *Journal of Accountancy*. November 1994.

SEE ALSO: Tax Deductible Business Expenses; Tax Planning

DOWNSIZING

Downsizing—also known as work force reduction, right-sizing, restructuring, re-engineering, and reorganization—occurs when a company reduces the size of its work force in order to cut costs, streamline operations, or become more competitive. Downsizing became a buzzword during the late 1980s and early 1990s, as more and more companies made drastic reductions in staff levels. In fact, a study published in *Fortune* magazine reported that 30 percent of all jobs that had existed in 1989 no longer existed by the end of 1993. These downsizing efforts differed from the work force reductions of previous eras because they took place even at highly profitable firms, and because they affected a much larger proportion of managerial positions.

Employee terminations that take place during downsizing are usually the result of surplus labor caused by economic factors, changing markets, poor management, or some other consideration unrelated to worker behavior. But because work force reductions make a company vulnerable to many of the same legal risks inherent in behavior-related terminations, companies usually downsize workers by means of a carefully planned and documented process.

Selecting the employees to be terminated during a downsizing effort and actually letting them go are handled carefully because organizations are obviously concerned about losing talent, diluting the effectiveness of the company, or harming the firm's public image. But care must also be taken to ensure that the reductions do not violate state and federal laws. As with behavior-related terminations, downsizing terminations cannot be based on bias against protected minorities, or even unintentionally result in an inequitable outcome for a protected group. In fact, extensive legislation exists to protect disabled workers, racial minorities, workers over the age of forty, women, and other groups.

In addition to bias-related laws, moreover, companies must comply with a battery of laws specifically directed at corporate layoffs. For example, the federal Worker Adjustment and Retraining Notification (WARN) Act of 1988 requires companies with 100 or more employees to file at least sixty days prior notice before conducting mass layoffs or work force reductions. Among other stipulations, the notice must be in writing and addressed to employees and specified government workers.

STEPS INVOLVED IN DOWNSIZING

The actual termination of employees as a result of downsizing should follow the same general procedures used in terminating employees for behavioral reasons. That is, the situation should be reviewed carefully ahead of time and a plan established; the criteria for dismissal should be well documented; the employees should be informed of their termination during a personal, face-to-face meeting that is not scheduled on a Friday afternoon or just before a holiday; the employees should be presented with a letter outlining the assistance and benefits they will receive;

and then other employees and customers should be notified. ''The exiting process is contingent on a variety of factors,'' said Richard Bunning in *Personnel Journal*, ''including whether employees have volunteered to exit, the potential danger of sabotage (such as in the computer area), the potential for vandalism and the importance of the employees' continued presence in the organization. With a partial downsizing, quicker usually is better. . . . With a complete plant closure, a phased exit process may be necessary.''

According to Richard S. Deems in his book *How to Fire Your Friends,* there are a number of additional considerations that apply specifically to downsizing situations. For example, the company must formulate a strategic plan or vision, establish a time frame for the downsizing, decide on a criteria for job elimination, perform a demographic analysis of the work force, prepare in-house communications, deal with the media, and provide outplacement services.

Formulating a strategic plan or vision of the company as it will function after the downsizing takes place, including the number of employees needed in various areas or departments, helps managers to make objective rather than subjective decisions about which employees to let go. The time frame for the downsizing should be as short as possible in order to minimize the negative effects on employee morale and productivity. Developing a criteria for job elimination helps a company avoid discrimination against certain classes of employees. Some options include eliminating positions by job title or classification, reducing each area or department by a certain percentage or number of employees, and determining which resources will be needed to handle future work. It is vital that the criteria selected does not target members of a protected minority group. Many companies find it helpful to compile a demographic profile of the work force before and after the downsizing to be sure that no discrimination is involved.

Finally, Bunning cited several other important factors that need to be considered before embarking on a course of work force reduction: ''1) The impact of turnover in the months following the reduction. Even though a downsizing has occurred, there will continue to be turnover, although perhaps at a reduced level. It will be more cost-effective to run a bit heavy with head count than to hire and train new employees a few months after outplacing experienced employees. 2) The possible effects of early retirement inducements or so-called golden handshakes. 3) The feasibility of limiting or even eliminating the need to downsize by moving to reduced work weeks, job sharing, leaves of absence, pay cuts, and/or reductions in paid time off. These alternatives may be particularly effective if there's a seasoned and supportive work force and there appears to be a probability of a business turnaround within a few months. 4) The option of bringing subcontracted work in-house and assigning it to employees who might be displaced. 5) The possibility of transferring employees to other work sites within the organization.''

DOWNSIZING AND INTERNAL COMMUNICATION

Downsizing, which may eliminate the jobs of many employees all at once, requires a more extensive communication effort on the part of management than does a single employee termination. Deems suggested that managers announce the changes to remaining employees personally, explaining the company's reasoning and the job-placement assistance provided to the employees who left. Indeed, Richard Bunning recommended that ''as the necessity to downsize becomes clear, management should openly acknowledge the difficulty it had making this decision, which is required to restore (or maintain) the organization's health.''

The personal announcement should be followed with written communication, such as newsletters and bulletin-board postings, to help keep employees informed, eliminate rumors, and maintain morale and productivity. Dealing with the media is another consideration in downsizing, since the loss of jobs may be of interest to the community. Deems noted that companies might find it helpful to prepare press releases ahead of time and choose one person as a contact.

The final stage of the downsizing process, outplacement, helps maintain the morale of remaining employees, enhance the public image of the company, and reduce the amount of unemployment compensation owed. Deems suggested that companies offer a comprehensive program, conducted by professional counselors in a neutral location, beginning as soon as possible after the downsizing occurs. Outplacement usually includes two activities: counseling and job search assistance. Both are necessary to help the displaced workers: 1) develop a positive attitude; 2) assess their career potential and direction, including background and skills, personality traits, financial requirements, geographic constraints, and aspirations; 3) develop job search skills, such as resume writing, interviewing, networking, and negotiating; and 4) adjust to life in transition or with a new employer. ''The outplacement process often can be coordinated with local governmental and social service agencies,'' noted Bunning. ''That way, employees may sign up for unemployment benefits, receive information about retraining programs, hear about other employment opportunities, receive financial planning tips and so on when they're told about benefits and receive severance pay.''

FURTHER READING:

Bunning, Richard L. ''The Dynamics of Downsizing.'' *Personnel Journal.* September 1990.

Cameron, Kim. ''Downsizing Can Be Hazardous to Your Future.'' *HR Magazine.* July 1991.

Crofts, Pauline. ''Outplacement: A Way of Never Having to Say You're Sorry?'' *Personnel Management.* May 1992.

Deems, Richard S. *How to Fire Your Friends: A Win-Win Approach to Effective Termination.* Kansas City, MO: Media Publishing, 1989.

''Job Insecurity,'' *Fortune.* May 30, 1994.

Leana, C.R., and D.C. Feldman. ''Layoffs: How Employees and Companies Cope.'' *Personnel Journal.* May 1988.

Meyer, Harvey. ''Avoiding Pink Slips.'' *Nation's Business.* June 1997.

''No End in Sight for Downsizing.'' *Human Resources Briefing.* September 1993.

''Rightsizing and Its Impact on Employees.'' *Human Resources Briefing.* March 1993.

''Strong Companies Are Joining Trend to Eliminate Jobs.'' *New York Times.* July 26, 1993.

''Study: Layoffs Haven't Boosted Profits, Productivity.'' *Washington Post.* September 26, 1993.

''U.S. Companies Speed Pace of Downsizing.'' *Washington Post.* February 9, 1994.

SEE ALSO: Managing Organizational Change; Layoffs

DRUG TESTING

Drug testing is the process wherein companies utilize the resources of scientific laboratories to determine whether any of their employees use illegal drugs. This practice, which most commonly requires workers to submit urine samples for analysis, is a controversial one in the United States. Proponents argue that it has been an effective deterrent, and that employers have the right to know if their employees are engaging in behavior that can damage the company. Opponents contend, however, that the practice violates fundamental individual rights and can have a corrosive effect on workplace morale.

Over the last 30 years or so, America has seen a significant rise in drug use among its citizens, and this increase spilled over into U.S. offices, retail outlets, and factory floors as well. As awareness of the serious impact that **substance abuse** can have on company productivity and profitability, companies of all shapes and sizes began to turn to drug testing as a method of curbing substance abuse among the members of their workforce. Large corporations were by and large the leaders in this trend, but in recent years, increasing numbers of small- and mid-sized companies have turned to drug testing as well.

POSITIVE ASPECTS Supporters of workplace drug testing note that over the past several years, as drug testing has become more prevalent in American businesses, cases of workplace substance abuse have undergone a significant drop. Indeed, *Security Management* reported in mid-1996 that according to federal government statistics, illicit drug use among full-time workers in America dropped from 16.7 percent of the work force in 1985 to 7.3 percent in 1993, a decline of better than 50 percent. Proponents of the practice argue that there is a clear correlation between these two trends.

Moreover, some researchers and business owners claim that the introduction of drug testing in the work environment has actually *improved* the morale of the larger workforce, since the majority of employees are more interested in ensuring that their workplace is a safe and productive one. And of course, proponents of drug testing note that studies clearly show that companies are far more likely to enjoy financial health if they are able to establish and maintain an environment in which substance abuse is not tolerated.

NEGATIVE ASPECTS Nonetheless, even as use of drug testing continues to increase throughout nearly all geographic regions and industries in the nation, detractors claim that the practice is not all that it is cracked up to be. "Despite the fact that the constitutional right to privacy does not apply to private-sector employees, many people feel strongly that drug testing is too 'invasive' and violates an important right," wrote George R. Gray and Darrel R. Brown in *HR Focus*. In addition, they charged that, whatever the protestations of drug testing supporters, "testing current employees seems to promote a statement that employers do not trust their workers to behave responsibly regarding drug use," although they also stated that businesses can take steps to minimize this impression: "Careful education efforts about the need for testing can help prepare workers for a new program. A program directed toward sensitive positions or departments, tailored to a company's specific problems, and carefully designed to avoid communicating a feeling of mistrust among all employees appears to be the company's best approach in drug testing."

Critics also argue that the findings of many drug-testing laboratories, which operate according to varying levels of regulation around the country, are simply not reliable. More detailed testing has proven effective in significantly reducing the number of errors made by testing laboratories, but observers note that additional testing is more expensive, and that this added cost could prove prohibitive to smaller companies in particular.

FURTHER READING:

Armbruster, David A. "On-Site Drug Testing: On the Rise and Growing Strong." *Medical Laboratory Observer*. April 1997.

"Drug Trends: A Shot in the Arm?" *Security Management*. August 1996.

Gray, George R., and Darrel R. Brown. "Issues in Drug Testing for the Private Sector." *HR Focus*. November 1992.

Moss, Leonard. "Partners for a Drug-Free Workplace." *Across the Board*. December 1989.

Peters, Tom. "Why Workplace Drug tests Send Workers Bad Message." *Washington Business Journal*. October 21, 1994.

Solomon, Robert M., and Sydney J. Usprich. "Employment Drug Testing." *Business Quarterly*. Winter 1993.

"Substance Abuse in the Workplace." *HR Focus*. February 1997.

SEE ALSO: Employee Rights; Workplace Safety

E

The Economic Order Quantity (EOQ) is the number of units that a company should add to **inventory** with each order to minimize the total costs of inventory—such as holding costs, order costs, and shortage costs. The EOQ is used as part of a continuous review inventory system, in which the level of inventory is monitored at all times, and a fixed quantity is ordered each time the inventory level reaches a specific reorder point. The EOQ provides a model for calculating the appropriate reorder point and the optimal reorder quantity to ensure the instantaneous replenishment of inventory with no shortages. It can be a valuable tool for small business owners who need to make decisions about how much inventory to keep on hand, how many items to order each time, and how often to reorder to incur the lowest possible costs.

The EOQ model assumes that demand is constant, and that inventory is depleted at a fixed rate until it reaches zero. At that point, a specific number of items arrive to return the inventory to its beginning level. Since the model assumes instantaneous replenishment, there are no inventory shortages or associated costs. Therefore, the cost of inventory under the EOQ model involves a tradeoff between inventory holding costs (the cost of storage, as well as the cost of tying up capital in inventory rather than investing it or using it for other purposes) and order costs (any fees associated with placing orders, such as delivery charges). Ordering a large amount at one time will increase a small business's holding costs, while making more frequent orders of fewer items will reduce holding costs but increase order costs. The EOQ model finds the quantity that minimizes the sum of these costs.

The basic EOQ formula is as follows:

$$TC = PD + \frac{HQ}{2} + \frac{SD}{Q}$$

where TC is the total inventory cost per year, PD is the inventory purchase cost per year (price P multiplied by demand D in units per year), H is the holding cost, Q is the order quantity, and S is the order cost (in dollars per order). Breaking down the elements of the formula further, the yearly holding cost of inventory is H multiplied by the average number of units in inventory. Since the model assumes that inventory is depleted at a constant rate, the average number of units is equal to Q/2. The total order cost per year is S multiplied by the number of orders per year, which is equal to the annual demand divided by the number of orders, or D/Q. Finally, PD is constant, regardless of the order quantity.

Taking these factors into consideration, solving for the optimal order quantity gives a formula of:

$$\frac{HQ}{2} = \frac{SD}{Q}, \quad \text{or} \quad Q = \text{the square root of } \frac{2DS}{H}.$$

The latter formula can be used to find the EOQ. For example, say that a painter uses 10 gallons of paint per day at $5 per gallon, and works 350 days per year. Under this scenario, the painter's annual paint consumption (or demand) is 3,500 gallons. Also assume that the painter incurs holding costs of $3 per gallon per year, and order costs of $15 per order. In this case, the painter's optimal order quantity can be found as follows: EOQ = the square root of (2 ×

3,500 × 15) / 3 = 187 gallons. The number of orders is equal to D/Q, or 3,500 / 187. Thus the painter should order 187 gallons about 19 times per year, or every three weeks or so, in order to minimize his inventory costs.

The EOQ will sometimes change as a result of quantity discounts, which are provided by some suppliers as an incentive for customers to place larger orders. For example, a certain supplier may charge $20 per unit on orders of less than 100 units and only $18 per unit on orders over 100 units. To determine whether it makes sense to take advantage of a quantity discount when reordering inventory, a small business owner must compute the EOQ using the formula (Q = the square root of 2DS/H), compute the total cost of inventory for the EOQ and for all price break points above it, and then select the order quantity that provides the minimum total cost.

For example, say that the painter can order 200 gallons or more for $4.75 per gallon, with all other factors in the computation remaining the same. He must compare the total costs of taking this approach to the total costs under the EOQ. Using the total cost formula outlined above, the painter would find TC = PD + HQ/2 + SD/Q = (5 × 3,500) + (3 × 187)/2 + (15 × 3,500)/187 = $18,062 for the EOQ. Ordering the higher quantity and receiving the price discount would yield a total cost of (4.75 × 3,500) + (3 × 200)/2 + (15 × 3,500)/200 = $17,187. In other words, the painter can save $875 per year by taking advantage of the price break and making 17.5 orders per year of 200 units each.

FURTHER READING:

Weiss, Howard J., and Mark E. Gershon. *Production and Operations Management.* Boston, MA: Allyn and Bacon, 1989.

SEE ALSO: Inventory Control Systems

ECONOMIES OF SCALE

Economies of scale refer to economic efficiencies that result from carrying out a process (such as production or sales) on a larger and larger scale. The resulting economic efficiencies are usually measured in terms of the unit costs incurred as the volume of the relevant operation increases. "Scale economies can be present in nearly every function of a business, including manufacturing, purchasing, research and development, marketing, service network, sales force utilization, and distribution," wrote Michael E. Porter, author of *Competitive Strategy.* "Scale economies may relate to an entirely functional area, as in the case of a sales force, or they may stem from particular operations or activities that are part of a functional area."

Many small business operations are of insufficient size to utilize economies of scale to major strategic advantage, though there are instances in which even smaller businesses can use such economic efficiencies to gain an edge over startup competitors. Indeed, John Pearson and Joel Wisner noted in *Industrial Management* that "since company productivity is generally defined as a ratio of output to input (for example, revenues divided by costs) management strategies for improving productivity have usually included some form of cost-reduction effort," of which economies of scale is often an essential element. In other words, even the smallest company can make itself healthier by improving its economy of scale. In competitive terms, however, small businesses often find that economies of scale are most visible as a weapon utilized by their larger competitors as a barrier to market entry. As Porter noted, "economies of scale deter entry by forcing the entrant to come in at large scale and risk strong reaction from existing firms or come in at a small scale and accept a cost disadvantage, both undesirable options."

As noted above, the concept of economies of scale has been used in a wide range of business operations, including sales and marketing, Most often, however, discussions of economies of scale have centered around manufacturing, equipment, and **facility management** areas. For instance, Howard J. Weiss and Mark E. Gershon, authors of *Production and Operations Management,* separated economies of scale into two types—construction and operations. "The construction economy of scale is that construction costs rise less than proportionately to building size," they wrote. The operating economy of scale, meanwhile, is based on the idea that "for any given facility size, there is an optimal operating level that minimizes the cost per unit. . . . Consider the fact that two plants will require a duplication of resources, whereas one large plant may not. This is the operating economy of scale."

But researchers have also distinguished economies of scale by other criteria. Pearson and Wisner, for example, separated economies of scale into "learning" and "volume" segments. "Learning economies of scale include labor and organizational production and planning advancements that accrue with time throughout the company's transformation process," they explained. "A company's learning curve provides an opportunity to identify and forecast supply costs, transformation costs, and finished product costs. Learning curves identify the rate a business has historically reduced the real, value-added, per-unit cost of its products. The ability of a company to continue this cost-reduction trend gives an indication of the adequacy of existing production cost-cutting or value-enhancing procedures and proposals. If a company cannot continue to cut product costs or increase value sufficiently over the long run while maintaining satisfactory levels of quality, it stands a good chance of being priced out of the industry by competitors.''

Volume economies of scale, meanwhile, are described by Pearson and Wisner as episodes wherein ''increases in product capacity cause lower unit costs (achieved in absence of any learning or technical innovation) by making additions to plant, equipment, labor and/or other facilities. While these additions to capacity tend to increase fixed costs, the added production can cause unit costs to decline.'' This latter example is the most commonly understood form of economies of scale.

FURTHER READING:

Ludwig, Dean C. ''Size Versus Sustainability: The Environmental, Social, and Competitive Diseconomies of Scale.'' *Mid-American Journal of Business*. Fall 1994.

Pearson, John N., and Joel D. Wisner. ''Using Volume and Economies of Scale to Benefit Long-Term Productivity.'' *Industrial Management*. November-December 1993.

Porter, Michael E. *Competitive Strategy: Techniques for Analyzing Industries and Competitors*. New York: Free Press, 1980.

Reynolds, R. L. ''Policy Choices and Economies of Scale.'' *Journal of Economic Issues*. December 1983.

Weiss, Howard J., and Mark E. Gershon. *Production and Operations Management*. Boston, MA: Allyn and Bacon, 1989.

SEE ALSO: Cost Control and Reduction; Operations Management

8(A) PROGRAM

The 8(a) Program is a **U.S. Small Business Administration (SBA)** program intended to provide assistance to economically and/or socially disadvantaged business owners. The initiative, which originated out of Section 8(a) of the Small Business Act provides participants with access to a variety of business development services, including the opportunity to receive federal contracts on a sole-source or limited competition basis. The program has been an important one for thousands of minority entrepreneurs over the past few years, but persistent criticisms that the program's eligibility parameters were too narrow led the SBA to announce a revamp of some features of the program in 1997. As of 1997, approximately 6,000 small businesses were enrolled in the 8(a) program. These enterprises employed approximately 150,000 workers.

8(A) PROGRAM ELIGIBILITY REQUIREMENTS

Entrepreneurs seeking to gain entrance into the SBA's 8(a) program must meet a number of criteria in such areas as ownership, management, and likelihood of success.

- An applicant must qualify as a small business enterprise as defined by the U.S. Small Business Administration's rules and regulations.

- An applicant firm must be majority-owned (51 percent or more) by American citizen(s). If the business is a corporation, stated the U.S. Small Business Administration, ''at least 51 percent of each class of voting stock and 51 percent of the aggregate of all outstanding shares of stock must be unconditionally owned by an individual(s) determined by SBA to be socially and economically disadvantaged.''

- Majority owners of the applicant firm have to meet the SBA definition of a socially and economically disadvantaged group. Socially disadvantaged individuals are defined by the SBA as those who have been subjected to racial or ethnic prejudice or cultural bias because of their identification of members of groups without regard to their individual qualities. Economically disadvantaged individuals, meanwhile, are defined by the SBA as socially disadvantaged people whose ability to compete in the free enterprise system has been diminished as a result of lesser capital and credit opportunities. Individuals from a broad array of social/ethnic groups have been found eligible for the 8(a) program under the above criteria, including African Americans, Hispanic Americans, Native Americans, Pacific Americans, and members of other ethnic groups. Individuals who are not members of recognized socially disadvantaged groups may also apply, but the SBA notes that such applicants ''must establish social disadvantage on the basis of clear and convincing evidence.''

- Stock status is also considered. For example, a business may not claim to be unconditionally owned by socially/economically disadvantaged individuals if they make that claim on the basis of unexercised stock options. Similarly, the SBA considers options to purchase stock held by non-disadvantaged entities when determining ownership.

- One 8(a) firm may not hold more than a 10 percent equity ownership interest in any other 8(a) firm. Moreover, no individual owner of an 8(a) firm, even if he or she qualifies as disadvantaged, may hold an equity ownership interest of more than 10 percent in another firm involved in the 8(a) program.

- According to the SBA, "the management and daily business operations of a firm must be controlled by an owner(s) of the firm who has (have) been determined to be socially and economically disadvantaged. For a disadvantaged individual to control the firm, that individual must have managerial or technical experience and competency directly related to the primary industry in which the firm is seeking 8(a) certification. . . . for those industries requiring professional licenses, SBA determines that the firm or individuals employed by the firm hold(s) the requisite license(s)."

- At least one full-time manager who qualifies under SBA definitions as a disadvantaged person must hold the position of president or CEO in the company.

- The individual or individuals claiming disadvantage must demonstrate that they personally suffered disadvantage, not just that the group of which they are a member has historically been considered to be disadvantaged. Moreover, the SBA stipulates that social disadvantage must be: 1) rooted in treatment received in American society, not other countries; 2) chronic and substantial; 3) and hindered their entrance or progress in the world of business. Applicants can point to several kinds of experiences to demonstrate the above, including denial of equal access to institutions of higher education; exclusion from social and professional associations; denial of educational honors; social pressures that discouraged the individual from pursuing education; and discrimination in efforts to secure employment or secure professional advancement.

- Individuals claiming economic disadvantage can not have a personal net worth in excess of $250,000, no matter what their origins are.

- Applicants have to show that they have been in business in the industry area to which they are applying for at least two years prior to the date of their 8(a) application. They can do this by submitting income tax returns showing revenues for those years.

- Applicants have to be deemed by the SBA to have a good probability of success in the

industry in which they are involved. In making this determination, the U.S. Small Business Administration considers many factors, including the technical and managerial abilities and experiences of the owners, the financial situation of the applicant firm, and the company's record of performance on prior federal and private sector contracts.

Businesses owned by white women may also be eligible for the program. In the past, white **women entrepreneurs** had to demonstrate in strong terms that they had been discriminated against in the past because of gender, and that this discrimination had been sufficiently egregious to hinder their success in the business world. In 1997, however, the SBA indicated that they intended to make it easier for white women-owned businesses to gain entrance into the 8(a) program.

Certain kinds of businesses are ineligible for inclusion in the 8(a) program. These include franchises of any kind, nonprofit organizations, brokers and packagers, and businesses owned by other disadvantaged firms.

WAIVERS OF THE "TWO-YEARS-IN-BUSINESS" REQUIREMENT Under certain circumstances, the SBA permits small businesses that have not yet been in operation for two years to participate in the 8(a) program. These mitigating circumstances include:

- Individual or individuals making the application have "substantially demonstrated business management experience."

- Applicant has sufficient technical expertise in their chosen area of business to make it very likely that they will be able to launch and maintain a successful business.

- Applicant had enough capital to carry out his or her business plan.

- Applicant shows that he or she has the ability to obtain the necessary personnel, facilities, equipment, and other requirements to perform all duties and obligations associated with contracts available through the 8(a) program.

- Individual or individuals making the application have a record of successful performance of contract work in the past, provided that those contracts (which may be from either government or private clients) are in the primary industry category in which the applicant is seeking program certification.

APPLYING TO THE 8(A) PROGRAM

Applications to the SBA's 8(a) program can be made through local SBA district offices. Small business owners will be asked to provide a wide range of materials, ranging from personal and business financial statements to organization charts, licenses, and schedules of business insurance. Rulings on completed applications are generally made within 90 days. Not all applicants are accepted into the 8(a) program, which has been a very popular one since its inception. If an application is turned down, the owner has the right to resubmit the application to the SBA with additional or changed information, but if the resubmitted application is again turned down, the owner may not present a new application until 12 months have passed from the date of the reconsideration decision. Finally, in cases where the applicant has been denied enrollment in the program solely because of questions about the applicant's social or economic disadvantage or majority ownership, then the owner may appeal the SBA's decision to that agency's Office of Hearings and Appeals (OHA). In this case, however, the applicant may not change the application in any way.

If a disadvantaged individual acquires a business that is enrolled in the 8(a) program, he or she may be able to continue to maintain the firm's participation in the program, provided that prior approval was obtained by the SBA.

Companies that are accepted into the 8(a) program are not eligible for 8(a) contracts until they submit and receive approval from the SBA for their business plan. "After the firm has an approved plan, the length of time before the first 8(a) contract is awarded will vary based on the success of the firm's marketing efforts," said the SBA. "While SBA will make every effort to assist a firm with its marketing efforts, the 8(a) program is a self-marketing program and SBA cannot guarantee 8(a) contract awards."

In addition to marketing assistance, participants in the 8(a) program receive help in the following areas during both the developmental stage (first four years) and transitional stage (next five years) of their involvement. During the developmental stage, enrollees can look forward to sole source and competitive 8(a) program support, transfer via grants of technology or surplus property owned by the U.S., and training to enhance entrepreneurial skills in a variety of areas. During the transitional period, meanwhile, small business owners can look forward to continued aid in the above areas, as well as assistance from procuring agents in forming joint ventures and technical assistance in planning for graduation from the 8(a) program.

PROPOSED CHANGES

Several changes to the program are expected to be phased in over the next few years. In mid-1997 the U.S. Small Business Administration announced a number of ways in which it planned to adjust the program, including changing the rules so that greater numbers of white female business owners can enjoy its benefits and so that enrollees are prevented from excessive reliance on business contracts secured through 8(a). Noting that only nine of the program's 6,000 participants were white women in 1997, the SBA proposed changes that would give these entrepreneurs greater access to federal contracts available through the program. Women's business groups have understandably been more receptive to this proposal than organizations representing minority businesspeople, who fear a dilution in their contract values because of the expansion of eligibility requirements.

Changes in the 8(a) program that are most likely to impact minority participants, meanwhile, are SBA proposals to place restrictions on the total value of contracts that can be received by an 8(a) firm. Sougata Mukherjee noted in the *San Antonio Business Journal* that under the proposed changes, "8(a) companies could receive up to $100 million in special, non-competition contract awards. Once they exceed this threshold, they would be forced to compete against other large 8(a) companies for any additional 8(a) contracts," although businesses that have been a part of the 8(a) program for a certain period of time may enjoy some exemptions in this regard. Mukherjee also reported that the SBA hopes to "tighten enforcement and push 8(a) firms to pursue non-8(a) contracts. The SBA wants 8(a) firms in their fifth year of participation to have at least 15 percent of their revenue from non-8(a) work. By the ninth year, when companies are required to exit the program, the non 8(a) work should reach 75 percent."

Finally, The SBA announced that it was investigating the possibility of instituting a mentor-protégé element to the 8(a) program to help small business owners. "The SBA plans to offer firms in their early years of participation a chance to pair up with older 8(a) firms who already have graduated from the program," explained Mukherjee. Under this system, new firms would be able to establish joint ventures with graduates of the program and apply for 8(a) contracts and subcontracts. The minimum duration of the relationship would be one year, and the arrangement would include an escape clause for proteges who find themselves mismatched with their mentor.

FURTHER READING:

Bowles, Erskine. "Bite-Sized Loans." *Entrepreneur.* December 1993.

Caplan, Suzanne. *A Piece of the Action: How Women and Minorities Can Launch Their Own Successful Businesses.* New York: AMACOM, 1994.

Mukherjee, Sougata. "SBA Planning Major Overhaul of 8(a) Program." *San Antonio Business Journal.* August 25, 1997.

SEE ALSO: Government Procurement; Minority-owned Businesses

Eldercare is an important issue for many members of today's **work force**, and is thus a relevant matter for employers to study as well. Analysts contend that businesses often lose valuable production from employees who have to contend with the needs of elderly parents and other relatives, and they point out that America's changing **demographics** are likely to make this an even more important issue for employers and employees in the coming years. Indeed, people age 65 and older are the fastest-growing segment of the nation's population.

According to *Small Business Reports* contributor Elise Feuerstein Karras, approximately one in four employees in the United States fit the profile of a caregiver to the elderly in the mid-1990s. This is obviously a significant percentage of many companies' work forces, and analysts note that the percentage is likely to be even higher in firms that have a high percentage of women employees (studies indicate that as much as 75 percent of elderly caregiving is done by women). Eldercare receives far less publicity than does **child care**, another very important issue to workers. But as Karras noted, "in many ways, eldercare is more complex than childcare because it covers such a wide range of needs. Many elderly people need assistance with routine tasks such as eating, dressing, bathing and obtaining medical care. But as adults, they also need to pay their bills, access Social Security benefits and deal with legal matters such as estate planning. Employees may have to help with these tasks or arrange for others to do it—sometimes for relatives who live far away." Karras added that the level of dependency that older relatives have for caregivers also increases with time, while the opposite is true of childcare. Finally, she pointed out that caregivers for elderly parents and relatives often have to tread a fine, and sometimes exhausting line between diplomacy and control: "The balance of authority between employees and their parents can make the [eldercare] arrangements awkward. An employee with children can simply make any necessary arrangements because he or she has the authority to do so. But the grown son or daughter of an elderly person must obtain the parent's consent before arranging for care."

IMPACT OF ELDERCARE OBLIGATIONS ON EMPLOYEE PERFORMANCE

In many instances, obligations associated with providing eldercare can become a considerable drain on an employee's **productivity**. A small percentage of caregiving employees quit their jobs entirely in order to meet the needs of elderly parents (again, the likelihood of this rises in businesses that have a high percentage of female employees). When this happens, small business owners and other employers are faced with the loss of a productive, trained employee and additional costs associated with finding and training a replacement.

But the obligations associated with eldercare are felt in other ways, too. Workers who provide assistance to their elderly parents or other relatives are likely to take off several days each year to attend to routine care issues, and while employers might comfort themselves by pointing out that those lost days are often taken out of vacation time, they should note that losing vacation time for this reason can have a negative impact on employee morale and, ultimately, performance. Moreover, partial **absenteeism**—late arrivals, long lunch breaks, early departures, etc.—can take a heavy toll as well. But Tibbet L. Speer contended in *American Demographics* that an even bigger problem for employers are "the workday interruptions faced by caregivers who talk on the phone with loved ones and service providers. This situation can arise even with employees who don't physically care for parents or whose parents live elsewhere. Estimated at one hour per week per caregiver, this factor is the biggest drain of all on employee productivity."

SMALL BUSINESS AND ELDERCARE BENEFITS

Many small business owners operate under the assumption that they can provide little assistance to employees who are grappling with eldercare issues. In reality, however, business experts say that both small and large companies can take several relatively inexpensive measures to help their staffers out and, in the long run, help them reach or return to high levels of productivity.

PROVIDE INFORMATION A very inexpensive way in which employers can help employees with eldercare problems is to offer resource and referral hotlines for such services and subjects as adult day care, nursing home evaluation, insurance issues, and "meals on wheels." Finding such information can be a time-consuming process for employees, and the establishment of a small in-house library that contains contact information can save workers significant hassles. In addition, many resource and referral services offer one-on-one counseling and/or seminars, many of which can be arranged to take place at the business's facilities. These seminars and counseling sessions can provide employees with important information on diverse issues such as nursing home care, Medicare and Medicaid, legal issues, and Alzheimer's disease.

FLEXIBLE WORK SCHEDULES Employers have a variety of options from which to choose here, including job sharing, compressed work weeks, and work-at-home arrangements. Karras noted, meanwhile, that small business owners "can resolve many eldercare problems simply be allowing employees to work flexible hours, within reasonable limits set by your company. Suppose that a worker needs to stay with an elderly parent until a home care worker arrives each morning. Your flex-time policy could permit the staffer to both begin and finish work later than usual, thereby minimizing the stress of being late."

USE OF PAID LEAVE TIME FOR ELDERCARE
Employees would obviously rather not use vacation time to attend to the needs of an elderly parent, but sometimes that is their only option. To help them out in this regard, Karras urged small business owners to make paid vacation time "even more flexible by allowing [workers] to use it in half-day increments." This would make it easier for employees to save some of their vacation time for themselves rather than allocate it all on appointments, etc. to which they have to accompany their parents. Sick day policies could be adjusted as well, so that employees can take sick time to attend to needs of elderly relatives as well as themselves (many workers do this, anyway, so it is an imminently practical change).

FINANCIAL BENEFITS Employers should consider setting up dependent care assistance programs (DCAPs) for their employees. Under this plan, employees who have elderly dependents live with them can gain assistance in paying for various eldercare expenses. "Employees who join the program may be able to set aside up to $5,000 a year in wages—before taxes—to cover their dependent care expenses," said Karras. A plan in which funds are regularly withheld for employee paychecks is put in place; employees bill the plan and receive reimbursements for eldercare expenses. "The result," noted Karras, "is that employees don't pay income or Social Security taxes on the DCAP funds. Your company saves as well because it won't owe Social Security and unemployment taxes on the money they set aside." Business consultants note, however, that businesses that set up DCAP plans do run into administration expenses, whether they choose to administer the program themselves or hire an outside firm to do so.

INTERGENERATIONAL CARE

Another trend that is shaping the way in which employees and employers approach eldercare is the increased popularity of intergenerational care facilities. These programs allow working parents who also have obligations to care for their own parents to place both children and elderly relatives in a single facility. Given the steady growth of women in the work place and the success that many hospitals, child care centers, and nursing homes have had with intergenerational care programs, many analysts believe that the

availability of such facilities will continue to grow over the next number of years, especially in regions in which competition for labor talent is intense. Indeed, demographic trends would seem to guarantee the continued growth of intergenerational care facilities. A study in the early 1990s by the National Council on Aging, for example, determined that approximately 40 percent of the American work force was providing care for both children and elders. Such statistics indicate that businesses seeking to attract and retain top talent will not only examine child care assistance options in greater depth, but will also factor the elder care issue into their analysis of options with increasing frequency.

ELDERCARE RESOURCES

Employees and employers can turn to a variety of sources for information on dealing with the many financial, medical, and personal aspects of eldercare. Local hospitals, churches, and agencies on aging are often good sources of information on eldercare issues. In addition, several national organizations maintain a variety of services and information on the subject. Notable organizations include the American Association of Retired Persons (202-434-3525), the Alzheimer's Association (800-272-3900), and the American Association of Homes and Services for the Aging (202-783-2242).

FURTHER READING:

Caldwell, Bernice. "Support is Key to Employers' LTC Initiatives." *Employee Benefit Plan Review.* October 1995.

Chambers, Nancy. "Where to Turn for Help." *Working Woman.* June 1995.

Goodstein, Jerry. "Employer Involvement in Eldercare: An Organizational Adaptation Perspective." *Academy of Management Journal.* December 1995.

Karras, Elise Feuerstein. "Affordable Eldercare Benefits." *Small Business Reports.* November 1994.

Levin, Nora Jean. *How to Care for Your Parents: A Handbook for Adult Children.*

Matthes, Karen. "A Coming of Age for Intergenerational Care." *HR Focus.* June 1993.

Reece, Barry L., and Rhonda Brandt. *Effective Human Relations in Organizations.* Boston, MA: Houghton Mifflin, 1993.

Sandroff, Ronni. "Helping Your Company Become Family-Friendly." *Working Woman.* November 1989.

Speer, Tibbett L. "The Unseen Costs of Eldercare: Employers Can Help Employees Help Their Aging Parents, and Save Money in the Process." *American Demographics.* June 1996.

SEE ALSO: Career and Family; Flexible Work Programs

ELECTRONIC DATA INTERCHANGE

Electronic data interchange (EDI) is the electronic movement of data between or within organizations in a structured, computer-retrievable data format that permits information to be transferred from a computer program in one location to a computer program in another location without rekeying. EDI includes the direct transmission of data between locations; transmission using an intermediary such as a communication network; and the exchange of computer tapes, disks, or other digital storage devices. In many cases, content-related error checking and some degree of processing of the information are also involved. EDI differs from **electronic mail** in that an actual transaction is transmitted electronically, rather than a simple message consisting primarily of text.

EDI is used for electronic funds transfer (EFT) between financial institutions, which facilitates such common transactions as the direct deposit of payroll checks by employers, the direct debit of consumer accounts to make mortgage or utility payments, and the electronic payment of federal taxes by businesses. Another common application of EDI involves the direct exchange of standard business transaction documents—such as purchase orders, invoices, and bills of lading—from one business to another via computer. EDI is also used by retail businesses as part of their electronic scanning and **point-of-sale (POS) systems**. Overall, EDI offers a number of benefits to businesses and—thanks to the rapid evolution of the related technology—is becoming more readily available to small businesses all the time.

BENEFITS OF EDI

''EDI saves money and time because transactions can be transmitted from one information system to another through a telecommunications network, eliminating the printing and handling of paper on one end and the inputting of data at the other,'' Kenneth C. Laudon and Jane Price Laudon wrote in their book *Management Information Systems: A Contemporary Perspective.* ''EDI may also provide strategic benefits by helping a firm 'lock in' customers, making it easier for customers or distributors to order from them rather than from competitors.'' EDI was developed to solve the problems inherent in paper-based transaction processing and in other forms of electronic communication. In solving these problems, EDI is a tool that enables organizations to reengineer information flows and business processes. It directly addresses several problems long associated with paper-based transaction systems:

- Time delays—Paper documents may take days to transport from one location to another, while manual processing methodologies necessitate steps like keying and filing that are rendered unnecessary through EDI.

- Labor costs—In non-EDI systems, manual processing is required for data keying, document storage and retrieval, sorting, matching, reconciling, envelope stuffing, stamping, and signing. While automated equipment can help with some of these processes, most managers will agree that labor costs for document processing represent a significant proportion of their overhead. In general, labor-based processes are much more expensive in the long term EDI alternatives.

- Accuracy—EDI systems are more accurate than their manual processing counterparts, in part because there are simply fewer points at which errors can be introduced into the system.

- Information Access—EDI systems permit myriad users access to a vast amount of detailed transaction data in a timely fashion. In a non-EDI environment, in which information is held in offices and file cabinets, such dissemination of information is possible only with great effort, and it cannot hope to match an EDI system's timeliness. Because EDI data is already in computer-retrievable form, it is subject to automated processing and analysis. It also requires far less storage space.

INFRASTRUCTURE FOR EDI

Several elements of infrastructure must exist in order to introduce an EDI system, including: 1) format standards to facilitate automated processing by all users; 2) translation software to translate from a user's proprietary format for internal data storage into the generic external format and back again; 3) value-added networks to solve the technical problems of sending information between computers; 4) inexpensive microcomputers to bring all potential users—even small ones—into the market; and 5) procedures for complying with legal rules. It has only been in the past several years that all of these factors have fallen into place.

FORMAT STANDARDS To permit the efficient use of computers, information must be highly organized into a consistent data format. A format defines how information in a message is organized: what data goes where, what data is mandatory, what is optional, how many characters are permitted for each data field, how data fields are ordered, and what codes or abbreviations are permitted.

Early EDI efforts in the 1960s used proprietary formats developed by one firm for exclusive use by its trading partners. This worked well until a firm wanted to exchange EDI documents with other firms who wanted to use their own formats. Since the different formats were not compatible, data exchange was difficult if not impossible. To facilitate the widespread use of EDI, standard formats were developed so that an electronic message sent by one party could be understood by any receiver that subscribes to that format standard. In the United States the Transportation Data Coordinating Committee began in 1968 to design format standards for transportation documents. The first document was approved in 1975. This group pioneered the ideas that are used by all standards organizations today.

North American standards are currently developed and maintained by a volunteer organization called ANSI (American National Standards Institute) X12 Accredited Standards Committee (or simply ANSI X12). The format for a document defined by ANSI X12 is broad enough to satisfy the needs of many different industries. Electronic documents (called transaction sets by ANSI X12) are typically of variable length and most of the information is optional. When a firm sends a standard EDI purchase order to another firm, it is possible for the receiving firm to pass the purchase order data through an EDI translation program directly to a business application without manual intervention.

Under the auspices of the United Nations, a format standard has been developed to reach a worldwide audience. These standards are called EDI for Administration, Commerce, and Transport (EDIFACT). They are similar in many respects to ANSI X12 standards but they are accepted by a larger number of countries. Beginning in 1996, all new ANSI X12 EDI documents have been developed using the EDIFACT format.

TRANSLATION SOFTWARE Translation software makes EDI work by translating data from the sending firm's internal format into a generic EDI format. Translation software also receives a sender's EDI message and translates it from the generic standard into the receiver's internal format. There are currently translation software packages for almost all types of computers and operating systems.

VALUE-ADDED NETWORKS When firms first began using EDI, most communications of EDI documents were directly between trading partners. Unfortunately, direct computer-to-computer communications requires that both firms: 1) use similar communication protocols; 2) have the same transmission speed; 3) have phone lines available at the same time; and

4) have compatible computer hardware. If these conditions are not met, then communication becomes difficult if not impossible. A value-added network (VAN) can solve these problems by providing an electronic mailbox service. By using a VAN, an EDI sender need only learn to send and receive messages to or from one party: the VAN. Since a VAN provides a very flexible computer interface, it can talk to virtually any type of computer. This means that to conduct EDI with hundreds of trading partners, an organization only has to talk to one party.

VANs also provide a security interface between trading partners. Since trading partners send EDI messages only through a VAN, there is no fear that a trading partner may dip into sensitive information stored on the computer system nor that a trading partner may send a computer virus to the other partners.

INEXPENSIVE COMPUTERS The fourth building block of EDI is inexpensive computers that permit even small firms to implement EDI. Since relatively inexpensive microcomputers are now so prevalent, it is possible for firms of all sizes to deal with each other using EDI.

PROCEDURES FOR COMPLYING WITH LEGAL RULES Legal rules apply to the documents that accompany a wide variety of business transactions. For example, some contracts must include a signature or must be an original in order to be legal. If documents are to be transmitted via EDI, companies must establish procedures to verify that messages are authentic and that they comply with the agreed-upon protocol. In addition, EDI requires companies to institute error-checking procedures as well as security measures to prevent unauthorized use of their computer systems. Still, it is important to note that some sorts of business documents—such as warranties or limitations of liability—are difficult to transmit legally using EDI.

FURTHER READING:

Emmelhainz, Margaret A. *EDI: A Total Management Guide.* 2nd ed. New York: Van Nostrand Reinhold, 1993.

Hill, Ned C., and Daniel M. Ferguson. "Electronic Data Interchange: A Definition and Perspective." *EDI FORUM: The Journal of Electronic Data Interchange.* March 1989.

Laudon, Kenneth C., and Jane Price Laudon. *Management Information Systems: A Contemporary Perspective.* New York: Macmillan, 1991.

SEE ALSO: Computer Applications; Computers and Computer Systems

ELECTRONIC MAIL

"Electronic mail"—or "E-mail," as it is commonly called, is the process of sending or receiving a computer file or message by computer modem over telephone wires to a preselected "mail box" or "address" on another computer. E-mail can also be sent automatically to a large number of electronic addresses via **mailing lists**. E-mail messages can range from the simplest correspondence to book chapters or detailed contracts. Graphics files of artwork or photography can be transmitted via this technology as well, though text messages comprise the vast majority of E-mail transmissions. Today, E-mail stands as a central component of business communication, both within businesses and between business enterprises, because of the many advantages that it offers over regular mail. Electronic mail reaches its destination instantly, and can be delivered 24 hours a day at low cost.

E-mail is available through a number of different arrangements. Small business owners should choose the option that best suits their business needs. Some companies are primarily E-mail providers, offering E-mail and services such as E-mail-to-fax conversion and **electronic data interchange**. Other companies provide access to online services such as research databases and real-time chat lines, with access to an E-mail address bestowed as an additional benefit. These companies have been experiencing rapid growth through the mid-1990s as more home computer owners purchase modems and software companies unveil new and easier programs. The major online services in the mid-1990s included America Online (AOL), Prodigy, and CompuServe. In addition to E-mail and Internet access, these outfits typically provide clients with access to "bulletin board systems" and "real-time chat lines" where users can discuss virtually any subject that interests them.

SMALL BUSINESSES AND E-MAIL Since E-mail has emerged as an important method of business communication in recent years, it is important for small business owners to know how to use this technology effectively. Toward that end, consultants such as Calvin Sun generally recommend that small business owners and entrepreneurs select and shape E-mail packages that emphasize convenience and ease of use. "Look for an E-mail package that lets you select specific settings and preferences that affect all your E-mail activity," Sun wrote in *Entrepreneur*. He also counseled business owners to take steps to ensure that recipients of their E-mail can easily determine their identity by including their real name in their E-mail addresses and including telephone number and mailing address information as a standard part of any E-mail. "Most e-mail packages allow you to include

this information through a 'signature file,'" Sun said. "To do so, you simply use word processing software to create and save the address information you want to appear on every E-mail message you send."

Small business consultants also note that, for whatever reason, the messages of many E-mail users reflect a casual attitude toward appearance that would never be tolerated in regular correspondence. They encourage users of E-mail to adopt the same standards of professionalism that dictate the tone and appearance of postal correspondence when putting together electronic mail communication. Proper spelling and the ability to frame correspondence in suitably diplomatic language are essential components of electronic mail. Consultants also caution small business owners to be circumspect in their use of "emoticons," a set of symbols that have been developed by E-mail users to denote various non-verbal reactions, such as smiles, winks, and laughs, to supplement the included text. While use of these symbols is fine in some settings, inclusion of a flurry of such symbols is apt to confuse E-mail recipients who are unfamiliar with the meaning behind them.

E-MAIL HAZARDS "The process of sending and replying to message is rife with opportunities for error," wrote Sun, but most pitfalls can be avoided if you take the time to learn the nuances of electronic mail. For instance, said Sun, "if you wish to avoid embarrassment (or worse), pay attention when sending a reply. Do you disagree with a message that was sent to you and dozens of others? Then be sure to 'reply to sender' rather than 'reply all.' Otherwise, your reply will go to *all* the original recipients, making your private disagreement public." Other recommendations made by Sun include:

- Use E-mail in appropriate circumstances— Standard mail correspondence remains preferable in instances where someone's employment is being terminated or legal squabbles have erupted.

- Compose E-mail messages in a professional manner—E-mail can conceivably reach the eyes of people that it was not meant to reach (incorrect addresses, etc.), so correspondence should be shaped accordingly.

- Recognize Presence of Back-up Tapes— Some computer systems have the ability to back up messages—even deleted ones—on tapes for security reasons.

- Promptly Respond to E-Mail—Small businesses and employees that do not promptly reply to electronic mail send the signal that they are either disinterested, incompetent, or disorganized. The business world is an often hectic one, and most people who participate in it recognize that delays in response do occur for a variety of legitimate reasons. But people who let E-mail messages go unacknowledged for several days or more are in essence informing the sender that delivering a response is not a priority for them.

SPAMMING In recent years, a practice known as "spamming" has become commonplace on the Internet. Spamming is a method of bulk E-mail advertising in which thousands (and sometimes millions) of marketing letters are sent to online addresses with the use of software that extracts the addresses from online services. Also known as UCE (unsolicited commercial E-mail), spamming has attracted a deluge of negative publicity for a variety of reasons. Most critics rail that the practice is in essence an online version of junk mail, and many others complain that spamming detracts from over-all system performance. Recipients of these advertisements for various goods and services, meanwhile, have expressed outrage over the blizzard of unsolicited E-mail messages that await them every morning. In recognition of the general unpopularity of the practice, federal legislation has been drafted that would do much to neutralize the practice, and some industry experts predict that spamming will become less evident in the future. In the immediate future, however, spamming shows no signs of abating. As companies that engage in the practice have noted, it is a relatively cost-efficient method of advertising that, despite its poor public image, seems to produce results.

FURTHER READING:

Fisher, Jerry. "E-Mail Feedback." *Entrepreneur.* October 1997.

Sun, Calvin. "E-Mail Etiquette: Minding Your Manners When Using E-Mail Pays Off." *Entrepreneur.* September 1997.

SEE ALSO: Computers and Computer Systems; Internet Commerce; Written Communication

ELECTRONIC TAX FILING

Electronic tax filing refers to various systems that enable individuals and small businesses to file their **tax returns** and make tax payments through electronic data transfer. In 1996, the **Internal Revenue Service** began requiring businesses that owed more than $47 million in payroll taxes annually to make their monthly payments via telephone or computer through the Electronic Federal Tax Payment System (EFTPS). The threshold for electronic filing was scheduled to drop to $50,000 in annual payroll taxes by January 1, 1997, but the deadline was pushed back

to June 30, 1998. In addition, two bills were introduced in Congress that would make electronic payments of payroll taxes voluntary for small businesses with few employees. When this system is eventually phased in, there will be a five percent penalty for late payments and an additional 10 percent penalty for non-electronic payments, which will still be accepted.

To enroll in EFTPS, a small business must fill out IRS Form 9799, the Electronic Federal Tax Payment System Business Enrollment Form. Experts recommend completing the necessary paperwork well in advance, because it can take more than 10 weeks to process. At the time Form 9799 is filled out, the business owner must choose from two payment options: an Automated Clearinghouse (ACH) debit or an ACH credit. For the debit option, funds are automatically withdrawn from the taxpayer's bank account by an IRS-appointed bank. For the credit option, the taxpayer's bank initiates the transfer of funds to the IRS-appointed bank. When it comes time to pay taxes, the small business simply needs to call a toll-free number to the appropriate bank, and provide information such as the business's tax ID number, the amount and type of taxes owned, and the period to which the payment applies. Afterward, the business receives a confirmation number from the bank indicating that the electronic transfer has taken place.

It is possible for individuals and home-based businesses to file their taxes electronically as well. To do this, the business owner prepares his or her taxes on the computer using a tax preparation software package, then transmits the completed return to an online service, such as Compuserve. The online service converts the file to meet IRS specifications and passes it along. The IRS then notifies the taxpayer electronically whether the return has been accepted, or whether corrections must be made. Once the electronic return has been accepted, the business owner must mail a signed form 8453-OL, as well as any W-2 forms, to the IRS.

PROS AND CONS

The IRS prefers businesses to submit their taxes via electronic means because the costs and error rates for electronic tax filing are dramatically lower than those for paper filing. But critics worry that converting 1.2 million businesses to an electronic tax filing system is such an enormous undertaking that it will create a significant potential for error. "While the amount of paperwork will be reduced under the new system, so will the number of IRS personnel, or at least that's the intention," Mike Dries wrote in the *Milwaukee Business Journal.* "Computers will have to work flawlessly to achieve a zero-defect system." Others feel that the system places an undue burden on the nation's small business owners. "For small-business owners who approach emerging technologies with wonder and suspicion, the Internal Revenue Service is about to give you another reason to dread paying taxes,'' Dries stated.

In reality, however, new electronic tax filing systems probably seem scarier than they will actually be. The IRS is offering companies free software to help them meet electronic filing requirements, and has also issued specifications for companies that wish to develop their own software. In addition, private software vendors are entering the electronic tax filing software market. Some private versions of the software come packaged with financial applications, so that companies can draw data directly from their financial systems and put it into the ACH file format required by the IRS. Tax professionals, payroll services, and banks are also developing a wide variety of systems to help small businesses with electronic tax filing. For more specific information on the requirements, see the IRS site on the Internet at www.irs.ustreas.gov.

FURTHER READING:

Barlas, Stephen. ''Electronic Avenue: A New Deadline for Electronic Tax Filing Gives Small Businesses a Break—For Now.'' *Nation's Business.* October 1997.

Dailey, Frederick W. *Tax Savvy for Small Business.* 2nd ed. Berkeley, CA: Nolo Press, 1997.

Dries, Mike. ''Dialing for Dollars.'' *Milwaukee Business Journal.* September 7, 1996.

''E-filing Myths and Facts.'' *Byte.* March 1997.

''Electronic Filing Can Be All Gain, No Pain.'' *ABA Banking Journal.* April 1995.

''File from Your Home Computer.'' *Journal of Accountancy.* May 1996.

Foust, Dean. ''Online Help: Need a Tax Break? Surf the Net.'' *Business Week.* February 3, 1997.

Machlis, Sharon. ''Study: Boost E-filing to Cut Error Rates.'' *Computerworld.* June 30, 1997.

Weston, Randy. ''Tax Software Vendors Compete against the IRS.'' *Computerworld.* January 13, 1997.

EMERGING MARKETS

Emerging markets are those countries or geographic regions in which a previously untapped potential for U.S. exports or investment might be anticipated. Nations typically characterized under this banner are often developing countries, but they may also be economically formidable countries with markets that are increasingly open to exports. ''The BEMs [big emerging markets] share certain characteristics,'' wrote Mark Tran in *Working Woman.* ''They have large territories and populations, and they are undertaking extraordinary development projects that call for new infrastructure, such as power-generating

plants and telecommunications systems. And, of course, with development comes increased demand for consumer goods, like computers and washing machines. These countries have pursued economic policies leading to faster growth and expanding trade and investment with the rest of the world. They aspire to be technological leaders. Their economic growth would have enormous spillover into their respective regions, and they all have political clout.'' In 1996, the International Trade Administration cited ten emerging markets as particularly important to U.S. companies with overseas ambitions: Argentina, Mexico, Brazil, Turkey, Poland, South Africa, India, South Korea, the Association of South East Asian Nations (ASEAN), and the Chinese Economic Area (China, Hong Kong, and Taiwan).

International trade analysts note, however, that the above-mentioned areas are by no means the only developing markets on the planet. Other nations commonly mentioned as key emerging markets for various U.S. exporting sectors include Chile, Vietnam, Malaysia, Thailand, the Czech Republic, Hungary, Uruguay, and Paraguay. In addition, Russia and several of the newly independent states of the former Soviet Union—though riddled with political instability, economic confusion, a weak technological infrastructure, and a lack of business expertise—are regarded as intriguing potential markets. This is because Russia and the newly independent states are all markets receptive to U.S. products that have never before been tapped by U.S. exporters.

In previous eras, international business activity in the ITA's BEMs and other promising areas was primarily the province of large companies with millions of dollars in investment resources and, often, a multinational presence in Europe and other economically powerful areas. In the 1990s, however, small- and mid-sized businesses staked out a sizable piece of the emerging market action for themselves. ''Fortune 500 companies are no longer the only ones doing business beyond our borders,'' said the U.S. Secretary of Commerce in 1997. ''Small- and medium-sized firms—manufacturing, telecom, high-tech, and information systems, among others—are positioning themselves to become global economic players. We will help them do that by assisting them in reaching promising new markets.''

FACTORS IN BEM DESIGNATION

Countries and regions that come to be known as promising, largely untapped markets often reach that status only after making changes in their internal political and economic structure. Indeed, liberalization of trade regulations between an emerging nation and America, which is an important factor in any analysis of emerging markets, typically reflects changes in U.S. policy toward the emerging market that take place only because of fundamental political changes within that market. For example, the lifting of various U.S. trade embargoes against South Africa over the past several years dramatically increased the region's potential for U.S. exports. Similarly, U.S. interest in Vietnam as a market jumped significantly after that nation and the United States formally opened relations in 1995. A particularly dramatic example of this trend could be seen with the emergence of the post-Communist governments of eastern European nations and the former Soviet Union, the populations of which had been previously walled off from most U.S. exports.

Political factors from abroad have also helped some nations emerge as U.S. export and investment destinations. Turkey's active role as an alternative Moslem economic system to such fundamentalist Islamic models of Iran has been vital in helping it establish itself as a major regional player in the Islamic states of the former Soviet Union, such as Kazakhstan and Turkmenistan. The mutual lifting of restrictions in trade simultaneously from both the United States and from another nation could also earmark that nation as an emerging market for U.S. goods. Certainly, the passage of the **North American Free Trade Agreement (NAFTA)** marked a significant change in Mexico's status as a trading partner of the United States.

Some countries or regions, meanwhile, come to be regarded as promising markets by dint of internal economic reforms. For instance, the massive economic reform program begun in the early 1990s in India, which included planks of privatization, deregulation, tariff reduction, and foreign investment regulation reform, created strong economic growth that was further encouraged with increased U.S. investment.

The list of top emerging markets is an ever-changing one, subject to economic, political, military, and environmental influences. Some nations lose their footing, scaring away investors and exporters because of political instability, unfair trade practices, and other factors. Some emerging markets do so well, however, that they eventually graduate to "established market" status.

BUSINESS CHALLENGES IN EMERGING MARKETS

The potential rewards of making a successful entry into an emerging market are considerable, and analysts contend that many U.S. companies—large and small—have the capacity to dramatically strengthen businesses that devise effective strategies. "We expect that the BEMs will double their share of world imports, rising to 38 percent by 2010, from 19 percent in 1994," said the ITA in its report, *The Big*

Emerging Markets. "No other category of market shows such dramatic growth potential. From Seoul to Bombay, plans call for well over $1 trillion of infrastructure projects in the next ten years—in energy exploration and power generation, airports and air traffic control, auto parts production, banking and insurance, and environmental cleanup. At least half that much is projected for Latin America. These mega-deals portend massive trade and investment opportunities for American companies."

But business consultants and trade observers acknowledge that establishing a presence in an emerging market is a process that typically has its share of trials and tribulations. Small business owners considering an entrance into one of these markets—whether that entrance takes the form of opening an office or trying to sell a product—should weigh several factors before making the move.

First, companies thinking about doing business in emerging markets should recognize that such efforts are almost certainly doomed to fail if the firm's affairs are a mess back home. "There is a myth passed from entrepreneur to entrepreneur," stated Jane Applegate in *Strategies for Small Business Success.* "If your business isn't doing so well at home, think globally. That's where all the money is, and millions of consumers are hungry for American goods. The problem is, it's a myth. If your business is faltering domestically, you won't have the time, money, or resources to crack the global market."

Even if the firm's domestic business is a sound one that provides a good foundation for international expansion, emerging markets present certain problems. "Relationships take longer to develop, and businesses in these countries rarely commit to your terms unless they're certain they can meet them," wrote Charlotte Mulhern in *Entrepreneur.* "They also may be unable to respond to sudden increases in product demand, due to frequent lapses in electrical power or unreliable transportation. And of course, fax and phone lines are often nonfunctional." Some countries are also bedeviled with high crime rates, political instability, and other unattractive features.

But Applegate noted several steps that small business owners can take to increase their odds of success in emerging market ventures:

- Conduct comprehensive research to learn everything possible about the country that you are considering.

- Find smart, ethical business partners in the country.

- Commit adequate time and resources to establishing a presence in the country.

- Take advantage of the many information resources that exist for small businesses seeking to expand into emerging markets, from the U.S. Chamber of Commerce to various private and nonprofit export information services.

- Utilize state economic development agencies in forging international business relationships.

Small business owners that follow the above guidelines will be well-equipped to make their mark in emerging markets, provided, of course, that their products or services are desired by the targeted populace. But as one small business owner who successfully expanded into a number of new markets told *Working Woman*, ''There is so much demand for virtually everything, everywhere's an opportunity. The world is moving much closer together, and if you want to do business today, you had better become an international person even if you're fixing skateboards on the street corner.''

FURTHER READING:

Applegate, Jane. *Strategies for Small Business Success*. New York: Plume, 1995.

Baird, Inga S., Marjorie A. Lyles, and J. B. Orris. ''The Choice of International Strategies by Small Businesses.'' *Journal of Small Business Management*. January 1994.

The Big Emerging Markets: 1996 Outlook and Sourcebook. International Trade Administration, 1995.

Mulhern, Charlotte. ''The Road Less Traveled: Don't Disregard the Potential of Developing Nations.'' *Entrepreneur*. February 1998.

Reynolds, Rhonda. ''New Ground: Emerging Nations Offer Sales Opportunities to Small U.S. Companies.'' *Black Enterprise*. October 1995.

Tran, Mark. ''The World is Your Market.'' *Working Woman*. December-January 1998.

''The World Will Beat a Path to Your Door.'' *Inc*. May 15, 1996.

SEE ALSO: Exporting; International Marketing

EMPLOYEE ASSISTANCE PROGRAMS

An employee assistance program (EAP) is an increasingly popular element of total benefits packages for small and large businesses alike. First created in response to business concerns about the affect of employee alcohol and **drug abuse** on bottom-line productivity, employee assistance programs are now designed to deal with a wide range of issues confronting workers today. ''Employee assistance programs are, in general, becoming more and more catch-alls'' for a variety of personal programs, confirmed one EAP executive in an interview with the *Pittsburgh Business Times*. Most business consultants now be-

lieve that EAPs can have a positive affect on employee mental and physical health—and thus their performance in the workplace. Analysts note that the characteristics and benefits of programs often vary. For example, some companies maintain internal employee assistance programs, while others choose to secure the services of an outside counseling provider. Most smaller businesses choose the latter option, in large part because of the cost savings that are usually realized.

Employee assistance programs were developed to help employees who had problems with various forms of substance abuse (alcohol, cocaine, etc.) But modern EAP systems are designed to help workers with other problems as well, such as family and/or marriage counseling, depression, stress, gambling addiction, financial difficulties, crisis planning, illness among family or co-workers, and pre-retirement planning. Many EAPs have expanded the scope of their counseling to help workers grapple with **eldercare** issues, natural disasters, and workplace violence. In addition, many employee assistance programs have added proactive elements to their offerings. For example, a number of employee assistance programs have actively promoted AIDS/HIV workplace policies and education efforts.

This expansion in the scope of EAP counseling is commonly attributed to changes in America's larger social fabric. ''The prevalence of two-wage-earner families, single parent households, mobility and career change patterns, demographic shifts, and technological change have helped to create new and different types of stress and mental health crises, which affect the health and productivity of many employees,'' wrote Jody Osterweil in *Pension World*. ''Where individuals formerly sought advice and counsel from a respected cleric, a personal physician, a close family member or a friend, those relationships are increasingly rare and cannot fulfill individuals' needs for crisis intervention. Thus, individuals experiencing a personal or family crisis, or who are under chronic stress, may have no place to turn for advice other than to the benefits [the EAP] offered through their workplace.''

In addition, companies have become aware of the link between employee well-being and employee **productivity**, and that the difference in value between happy and unhappy employees can often be quite profound. ''Despite continuing technological advances, today's companies rely on their employees to improve productivity and increase the bottom line,'' wrote Brian W. Gill in *American Printer*. ''Therefore, the relationship between employees' well-being and productivity cannot be ignored. Personal and work-related problems may manifest themselves in poor job performance, which adversely affects the firm's overall productivity.'' Indeed, consultants contend that few staffers are able to wholly shield their work performance from the negative residue of personal difficulties. Increased **absenteeism**, higher accident rates, substandard performance, **employee theft**, and poor morale are just some of the symptoms that may appear if an employee is struggling to handle a problem in his or her personal or professional life.

KEY ADVANTAGES OF EAP IMPLEMENTATION
Benefits experts and businesses alike cite several important benefits associated with employee assistance programs. Business owners are, of course, concerned with the utility of an EAP as a cost-management tool. To an entrepreneur with a small business, the most important advantage associated with an EAP is likely to be its positive impact on employee productivity and its use in controlling health care costs. But according to many businesses that have adopted employee assistance programs, there are other benefits that may accrue as well. For example, companies that provide for an EAP may be viewed as more employee-supportive in the community in which they operate than will competitors for workers who do not provide such a program. In addition, employee assistance programs have been cited as an effective element in employee retention efforts.

But a less publicized advantage associated with EAP implementation is that it frees up the company to do what it does best—provide its goods or services to its customers—instead of devoting work time to issues that may not be directly related to meeting production deadlines, etc. Basically, putting together an EAP allows business owners and managers to concentrate on their internal operations. ''We have to focus on the job and the ability to do the job,'' one business executive told the *Pittsburgh Business Times*. ''We don't want to play counselor and dive into areas we're not qualified for.''

CHOOSING AN EMPLOYEE ASSISTANCE PROGRAM

''Many employers who want to set up an EAP may hesitate because they fear the cost will outweigh the benefits,'' wrote Gill. ''Are they too small to support such a program? Will their employees utilize the services? These are important issues that must be addressed before implementing an EAP. It also is important for management to establish clear program objectives in order to evaluate the program's effectiveness.''

Perceived **costs** associated with implementation and maintenance of an employee assistance program is perhaps the biggest concern for small business owners. Many owners of small businesses recognize that EAPs can be helpful to the members of their work force, but the spectre of yet another operating expenditure may dissuade them. Analysts report that small business owners can institute an employee assistance program for their employees at relatively small expense. Gill noted in 1997 that ''while each program is different, depending on the services offered and the size of the program, EAPs have been estimated to cost $100 per individual covered per year,'' and he pointed out that smaller employers have several options from which they can choose when putting together an EAP. In addition to taking on the expense themselves, ''they can contract out services with a local EAP provider, join with other small businesses to form a consortium, or contact trade and business associations to set up a service. Some of these services may be offered through a company health plan, so it is important to research the best possible service available within your company's budget.'' Benefits experts also recommend that small business owners make sure that materials and administration costs incurred by EAP providers are included in their base fee. Writing in *Inc.,* Karen E. Carney cited a number of other considerations that small business owners should weigh as well when choosing an EAP:

Value-added Services—EAP training programs vary widely, with the best of them providing managers with assistance in confronting troubled employees, developing wellness policies, and arranging seminars on health issues.

Appropriate Credentials—Employee assistance programs should be operated by professionally licensed staff; ideally, these staffers will have solid relations with local health groups and/or national self-help organizations.

Convenience—Carney noted that small business owners should look for EAP providers that are in the same geographic region as the company, so that employees can visit the facilities before, during, or after work. The EAP that is ultimately selected should also have a toll-free telephone line that is operational around the clock, since difficulties do not always strike employees during traditional working hours.

Communication—''Most providers issue monthly updates,'' said Carney. ''But they should also record their own effectiveness in helping you reach agreed-upon productivity goals or implement safety programs. Some providers also supply payroll stuffers on subjects like practical parenting.''

NOURISHING YOUR EMPLOYEE ASSISTANCE PROGRAM

Training of managers and other supervisory personnel (including the owner, if he or she is actively involved in supervision) is a vital component of instituting a successful EAP. ''Managers who have the most contact with employees will be the first line of defense in recognizing potential problems and correcting them before they reach the termination stage," stated Gill. "Therefore, it is imperative that managers understand the objectives of the EAP to ensure the program's success and reduce any potential employer liability." In addition, management personnel have to be adequately instructed about what Gill termed "the do's and don'ts of EAPs. They can refer employees to the assistance program, but no one can be forced to seek assistance. Supervisors and employees must understand that these services are strictly confidential and using them will not be cause for disciplinary action. However, being involved in an EAP service does not exempt employees from disciplinary action when company rules are violated. This is a very fine line that must be addressed in supervisory training."

Promotion of the program is another important element for small businesses seeking to maximize the effectiveness of their EAP. "All too often, plan sponsors assume that employees are fully cognizant of the EAP and the services it offers," stated Osterweil. "Employees and dependents must become more aware of the programs' existence, the nature of its resources and coverages, and the means of accessing such programs. Employees must develop confidence in the abilities of those providing such services, trust that confidentiality will be assured, and obtain knowledge that their specific needs can be addressed through the resources available from the EAP. Simply publishing an '800' telephone number in a summary plan description, or posting a notice in the workplace, is not likely to effectively communicate the existence of this valuable resource."

Osterweil noted, though, that a coordinated approach that is non-threatening in tone and that indicates that "the sponsor truly desires to meaningfully assist and retain employees and sees them as a valuable resource" can help significantly in reassuring employees about the program's character and purpose. For that reason, benefits experts counsel small businesses to establish a plan in which workers are provided with regular, timely (around the holidays, for instance) reminders of the availability and offerings of their employee assistance program.

EVALUATING ESTABLISHED EAPS

Once an employee assistance program has been put in place, it is up to the sponsor to make certain that it is an effective addition to their overall benefits package. After all, an EAP that does not address the primary needs and concerns of a company's employees is essentially a waste of money. Admittedly, determining the effectiveness of an employee assistance program can sometimes be a difficult task, since employee problems like family strife, substance abuse, and workplace stress are impossible to quantify. For example, an EAP provider will not be able to provide statistics to a client stating that over the previous six months, workplace stress dropped by 27 percent and family strife declined by 14 percent. In addition, the confidentiality restrictions associated with employee assistance programs place further limitations on tracking EAP use and effectiveness. Small business owners looking for information on the effectiveness of their EAP do have other options, however. "Attention to trends in utilization and expenditures by type of service (such as in- or out-patient detoxification, rehabilitation, and aftercare) can help plan sponsors evaluate the cost-effectiveness of their EAP and the efficacy of the vendors providing these services," said Osterweil. "For example, a successful EAP should show a positive influence on expenditures under the employer's health plan. It should also show towards lessening absenteeism, tardiness, and disability and improving productivity. And, the evaluation process gives plan sponsors an opportunity to design a system that can capture data that will more readily assess the ongoing cost-effectiveness of the program." Osterweil pointed out that anecdotal information can also be helpful in determining whether an EAP is doing what it is supposed to do. Such data should not be excessively relied upon when evaluating an employee assistance program, but it can provide employers with solid insights into how the program performed in certain instances. For example, if a staffer volunteers as to how the EAP helped him or her deal with an unsettling incident of workplace violence, that information should be weighed. Conversely, weight should also be given to employee complaints that the program is too narrowly focused on one issue such as substance abuse. If confronted with the latter data, a smart employer will commence an inquiry into whether or not the EAP should be broadened to expand treatment and provide resources for dealing with other problems, such as childcare, eldercare, workplace stress, marital problems, and financial difficulties.

Benefits experts also encourage sponsors of employment assistance programs to look at their EAP within the overall context of its total benefits structure. *Pension World* pointed out that in many instances, employee assistance programs are regarded by workers as being "peripherally attached to the rest of the employee benefits package. This is certainly understandable as the need for employee confidentiality must be preserved, so that a certain degree of arms-length delivery of services is desirable. Because of privacy issues, EAPs may be managed by professional, outside vendors, with services provided at sites away from the workplace." But as much as possible, company sponsors of EAPs should try to integrate their programs with their other efforts to promote wellness for employees and their dependents.

SIGNS OF A FLAWED EMPLOYEE ASSISTANCE PROGRAM Employee assistance programs are commonly touted as a valuable cost-management tool, but if the implementation or design of an EAP is flawed, then much of the cost savings associated with the program will not be realized. Benefits experts counsel small business owners to look out for the following indications that an employee assistance program may need revision:

- General dissatisfaction with the program expressed by employees

- Only a small percentage (less than five percent) of eligible employees use the program

- Issues that prompted the initial use of the EAP are not resolved within three or four sessions

- EAP referrals indicate a bias toward one type of care

- Employees view the EAP with distrust, seeing it as a possible management tool for doling out punishment or justifying termination

- EAP staff have potential conflicts of interest (for example, a staffer who is found to have financial ties to a provider to whom referrals are made)

All of these warning signs can be addressed, but companies should make sure that they conduct adequate research into the needs and desires of their employees before attempting any sort of shake-up. And when revision of an EAP does occur, employers should take every precaution to ensure that any employees who did benefit from the previous program are not left behind.

FURTHER READING:

Carney, Karen E. ''Choosing an EAP.'' *Inc.* July 1994.

''Counsel for the Depressed.'' *IRS Employment Trends.* September 1995.

''Does Counseling Work?'' *Small Business Reports.* June 1992.

Gill, Brian W. ''Employee Assistance Programs.'' *American Printer.* June 1997.

Goldstein, Taryn F. ''Employee Assistance Programs.'' *Journal of Compensation and Benefits.* September-October 1997.

Haskins, Sharon A., and Brian H. Kleiner. ''Employee Assistance Programs Take New Directions.'' *HR Focus,* January 1994.

Herlihy, Patricia. ''Employee Assistance Programs and Work/ Family Programs: Obstacles and Opportunities for Organizational Integration.'' *Compensation & Benefits Management.* Spring 1997.

Hurley, Susan. ''Measuring the Value of Employee Assistance Programs.'' *Risk Management.* June 1986.

Osterweil, Jody. ''Evaluating and Revising EAPs.'' *Pension World.* June 1991.

Robinet, Jane-Ellen. ''Employee Assistance Programs Gain Popularity as Benefit.'' *Pittsburgh Business Times,* November 11, 1996.

Spragins, Ellyn E. ''Dry Shoulder for Hire.'' *Inc.* December 1991.

SEE ALSO: Employee Benefits

EMPLOYEE BENEFITS

Employee benefits encompass a broad range of benefits—other than salary—that companies provide to their employees. Some of these benefits, such as **workers' compensation**, social security, and unemployment insurance, are required by law. The majority of benefits offered to employees, however, are bestowed at the discretion of the business owner. Such benefits, which are commonly called ''fringe'' benefits, range from such major expenditures as paid holidays, health insurance, paid vacations, **employee stock ownership plans** (ESOPs), and **profit sharing** to more modest ''extras'' like bestowing performance awards and prizes, providing an employee lunchroom, or paying for a company picnic.

Employee benefits are an indirect means of compensating workers, but they can be quite important in fostering economic security and stability within the work force. Insurance coverage, for instance, is often terribly expensive, so the company that offers medical and/or **life insurance** to employees as part of its benefits package is bestowing significant savings on those employees and their families. Companies, however, must be careful when putting together a compensation package for their work forces, and prudence is especially important for the small business owner. As Irving Burstiner remarked in 1989 in *The Small Business Handbook,* ''all the 'extras' that firms have added to the basic compensation of their employees over the years amount to a sizable cost factor today.'' Noting that financial 'fringe benefits' can often add up to a startling amount of money, Burstiner added that ''small firms are cautioned against adopting these fringe benefits too quickly and too freely. Some are almost mandatory if an organization is to compete effectively for personnel against other firms in the industry. Other fringe benefits, while perhaps desirable, should be postponed until the company is in a strong, healthy position.''

Employee benefits are any kind of compensation provided in a form other than direct wages and paid for in whole or in part by an employer, even when they are provided by a third party such as the government, which disburses social security benefits that have been paid for by employers. Employee benefits can be most easily divided into two categories: mandatory and optional.

MANDATORY BENEFITS Mandatory benefits are required by law. They serve to provide economic security for employees (and their dependents) who have ceased working because of retirement, unemployment, disability, poor health, or other factors. Notable mandatory benefits include: Medicaid; basic Medicare; Public Assistance; Social Security retirement; Social Security disability; Supplemental Security income; unemployment insurance; and workers compensation.

OPTIONAL BENEFITS Optional benefits are those that an employer has the option of providing. These optional, or supplementary, benefits include such major compensation areas as insurance and tax-qualified plans of deferred compensation. Such compensation programs are designed for the exclusive benefit of employees and their beneficiaries and are subject to specific Internal Revenue Service (IRS) regulations. Primary deferred compensation plans include: 1) **Pension plans**—established and maintained by employers and paid out to employees over a period of years after retirement; 2) Annuity plans—paid out of annuity or insurance contracts; 3) Stock bonus plans—arrangement wherein employees are given stock in the company and receive money from appreciation in the value of shares and/or the dividends or income from that stock; 4) Profit-sharing programs—plan in which business profits earned by the employer are shared with employees; 5) **401(k) Plans**—option that allows employees to deduct a portion of their pre-tax salary and invest it in a profit-sharing, fixed contribution, or stock bonus plan.

Optional benefits are handled in a variety of ways under the tax code. Some are fully taxable, but others are tax-preferred, tax-exempt, or tax-deferred, meaning that taxes are not incurred on the benefit until it is used. Optional benefits serve many of the same basic functions as mandatory benefits, but also include perquisites—known as ''perks''—only tangentially related to actual business. These perks, which can range from country club membership to use of a company car, are designed primarily to attract and please workers.

Fully taxable optional benefits include cash bonuses and awards; non-qualifying stock bonuses; non-qualifying stock ownership and profit-sharing programs; and severance pay. Tax-preferred benefits include life insurance; long-term disability insurance; and sickness and accident insurance.

Tax-deferred benefits include 401(k) retirement plans; deferred profit-sharing plans; employee stock ownership plans (ESOPs); most types of qualified pension plans; stock bonus plans; and thrift savings plans.

Finally, tax-exempt benefits that companies may offer include cafeteria facilities and meals; dental and vision insurance; dependent care; flexible spending accounts; free or discount club memberships; health insurance for employees and retirees; legal assistance; free parking or parking subsidies; supplementary Medicare premiums; tuition reimbursement; and use of company car.

In addition, most companies offer time-oriented compensation packages that encompass paid vacations and holidays; paid sick days; **flexible work programs**; maternity and paternity leave; bereavement leave; jury duty; overtime; paid lunch; and sabbaticals. These time-oriented benefits, while optional, are among the most popular and widely used of the various non-salary compensation options.

A comprehensive benefits package, while expensive, can be an important and useful asset for a company. Indeed, while salary considerations remain paramount for many workers, an attractive benefits package can be a major factor when a prospective employee is weighing his or her options. A parent with two small children, for example, might well be willing to choose a lower-paying position with a company that offers a superior family health insurance package over a significantly higher paying one that does not provide good health insurance benefits for its employees and their dependents.

One option that some companies have turned to is known as the ''cafeteria plan'' or ''flexible benefit program.'' Under this type of arrangement, employees are given a certain number of ''credits'' which they can use to choose, from a menu of possible benefits, the benefits that they most desire for themselves and their families. Each worker thus puts together his or her own individualized package of employee benefits.

INCOME PROTECTION BENEFITS

Indeed, a chief role of employee benefits is to provide various types of income protection to groups of workers. Five principal types of income protection delivered by benefits are: disability income replacement; medical expense reimbursement; retirement income replacement; involuntary unemployment income replacement; and replacement income for survivors. Different mandatory and voluntary elements of each of these categories are typically combined to deliver a benefits package to a group of workers that complements the resources and goals of the organization supplying the benefits.

DISABILITY BENEFITS Benefits that provide disability income replacement include programs such as Social Security and worker compensation. The bulk of these benefits are mandatory, although numerous supplementary plans, most of which are tax-favored, exist. Most organizations seek to assemble a disability package that will provide an adequate safety net, yet not act as a disincentive to return to work. A common objective is long-term income reimbursement of 60 percent of pay, which is preceded by higher levels of reimbursement, usually as much as 100 percent during the first six months of disability. Long-term disability pay typically ends at retirement age (when pension payments begin), or when the worker recovers or finds another job.

Another disability-related benefit incentive is sick pay, although companies handle this category in a variety of ways. Some organizations have instituted policies that provide cash awards for unused sick days at the end of the year. Others opt to combine separate leave policies for vacation, illness, and ''personal time'' into a single policy for paid time off. (Such a policy provides employees with an allotment of days off each year that can be used at the employee's discretion.) Employers may vary the quality of their disability package with different co-payment options, limits on payments for voluntary coverage, and extended coverage for health insurance, life insurance, and medical benefits related to the disability.

MEDICAL BENEFITS Medical expense reimbursements are typically one of the most expensive and important elements of a company's compensation package. The two primary types of voluntary medical coverage options are fee-for-service plans and prepaid plans. In addition to voluntary plans, government-backed health care plans, such as Medicare and Medicaid, serve as safety nets to furnish medical coverage to select groups of society and to those least able to afford other types of health insurance.

Under traditional fee-for-service plans, the insurer pays the insured directly for any hospital or physician costs for which the insured is covered. Under a prepaid plan, insurance companies arrange to pay health care providers for any service for which an enrollee has coverage. The insurer effectively agrees to provide the insured with health care services, rather than reimbursement dollars. Typical features of prepaid plans are reduced administrative expenses and a greater emphasis on cost control. The most common type of prepaid plan is the health maintenance organization (HMO).

Most plans cover basic costs related to: hospitalization, including room and board, drugs, and emergency room care; professional care, such as physician visits; and surgery, including any procedures performed by surgeons, radiologists, or other specialists. More comprehensive plans provide higher dollar limits for coverage or cover miscellaneous services not encompassed in some basic plans, such as medical appliances and psychiatric care. The most inclusive plans eliminate deductible and coinsurance requirements, and may even cover dental, vision, or hearing care.

Companies have many options that they can pursue in shaping their medical benefits packages. Indeed, a dizzying array of co-insurance, co-payment, and coverage limit options are available today. Some companies pick comprehensive medical benefits packages that handle all health care costs incurred by employees and their dependents, while others select less expensive plans that call for employee co-payment of insurance coverage and/ or high deductibles (the deductible is a set amount that an individual must pay before insurance coverage begins). The plan that a company ultimately selects is predicated on any number of factors, from its own financial well-being to the benefits packages offered by its industry competitors.

RETIREMENT BENEFITS Companies provide retirement-related employee benefits through three avenues: Social Security, pension plans, and individual savings. The Social Security system is a federal government program paid for by a tax on earnings; this tax is shared equally by both employee and employer. The system, which is administered primarily through the Social Security Administration, provides payments to qualified individuals; it is designed to defray income lost by people as a result of old age, unemployment, or sickness.

Pension plans are primarily financed by employers. Unlike the financially troubled U.S. Social Security system, pension plans, which are created by private employers, are subject to strict government controls designed to ensure their long-term existence. The two major categories of pension funds are defined benefit and defined contribution. Under the former arrangement, workers are assured a specified level of regular payments (given expected Social Security disbursements) upon retirement, and the company is responsible for managing the account. In contrast, defined contribution plans utilize such savings techniques as money purchase plans, stock ownership plans, and profit sharing. Companies make regular contributions to workers' accounts through those different instruments, and may also integrate employee contributions. The beneficiary simply receives the value of the contributions, with interest, at retirement. The latter methodology is preferred by some because of its comparative flexibility and the fact that taxes on earnings are deferred.

The third type of retirement benefit offered by many employers is the supplementary individual savings plan. These plans include various tax-favored savings and investment options. Employers may also provide retirement benefits such as retirement counseling, credit unions, investment counseling, and sponsorship of retiree clubs and organizations.

UNEMPLOYMENT BENEFITS Many employers offer some form of protection against termination as a benefit to employees. This is due in part to the fact that termination benefits are required under various circumstances by collective bargaining agreements and state and federal laws. A common unemployment benefit is severance pay. Under this arrangement, a worker whose employment is terminated may be compensated financially with a lump sum or a series of payments. Length of employment is generally an important factor in determining severance pay. It is important to note, however, that an employee who is discharged because of legitimate misconduct is not entitled to receive unemployment benefits. ''The unemployment office will note the precise language you used when they determine if an ex-employee is entitled to receive unemployment insurance benefits,'' noted Mark A. Peterson in *The Complete Entrepreneur.* ''If your employee quit without good cause, he cannot receive any benefits. If you fire him for misconduct connected with work, he cannot receive any benefits. If he fails to accept other suitable work that you may have offered him, he cannot receive any benefits.'' Peterson and other small business consultants thus encourage small business owners to contest unemployment claims that have been unfairly lodged against them, for they can ultimately result in higher premium payments for the business.

Some industries provide supplemental unemployment pay plans. These are employer-funded accounts designed to ensure adequate and regular payments to workers, usually members of labor unions, during periods of inactivity. Other companies, meanwhile, provide placement assistance to workers who have been laid off.

SURVIVOR BENEFITS Like disability compensation, benefits for the survivors of deceased employees are comprised primarily of mandatory Social Security and workers compensation benefits. Eligibility for these benefits is determined by such factors as age, marital status, and parental responsibilities. In addition, a plethora of different privately financed benefit packages are available; many of these enjoy favored tax status. Most plans are set up to make payments to a beneficiary designated by the employee. Payment levels are usually contingent on the cause of death. For example, a worker killed while on the job would likely receive much more than an employee who died at home or on vacation. A common survivorship benefit is some form of term life insurance that takes advantage of tax preferences and exemptions. Those plans often allow employees to make financial contributions as well.

EMPLOYEE BENEFITS AND SMALL BUSINESS

The entrepreneur who is launching a new business faces a daunting array of options when the time arrives to design a compensation package for his or her employees. As Michael Armstrong observed in *A Handbook of Human Resource Management,* benefits ''are no longer merely the icing on the cake of cash remuneration, but a considerable part of it.'' But before making any decisions as to the character and scope of an employee benefits package, the new small business owner needs to gain a familiarity with the various laws and regulations that apply to employee benefits. ''There are numerous federal and state laws which regulate the administration of wages and benefits,'' wrote Jill A. Rossiter in *Human Resources: Mastering Your Small Business.* ''For example, the Federal Fair Labor Standards Act stipulates the **minimum wage** and regulated **overtime** pay.'' In addition to withholding various federal, state, and local taxes from payroll checks, employers are responsible for adhering to ''other laws [that] specifically regulate the administration of retirement programs, withholdings for child care, etc. Finally, there are tax laws regarding what payments are and are not deductible as normal business expenses and what benefits might be taxable to the employees.'' Given these myriad factors, small business consultants commonly recommend that the owner(s) of a fledgling small business enterprise utilize the services of legal and accounting professionals when putting together their company's benefits packages.

The small business owner should work to put together a fair and equitable package, but he or she should also remain mindful of business realities and the ultimate need to be a profitable enterprise. The intelligent entrepreneur, then, will undertake research on the issue before making any decisions. In addition to investigating legal aspects, he or she should research typical compensation packages both in the geographic region and in the industry in which they will be operating. Newspapers, associations, libraries, and various municipal and state agencies all can be helpful sources of information in this regard. Successful entrepreneurs also need to gauge their own expenses and business expectations (in terms of profitability, growth, debt, etc.) when pondering the character of the benefits package they will offer. Employee benefits can be a significant business cost, and if your profit margin is slim—or if you expect to operate in the red for your first few years of operation—then you need to be cautious. Some fringe benefits—vacation days, for example—are practically mandatory in today's business environment. But others, such as health insurance or pensions, can create an unacceptable burden on a new company. In addition, there are also some industries whose membership simply does not offer much in the way of fringe benefits for its workers, either because of narrow profit margins or the laws of supply and demand within the labor market.

In the final analysis, the benefits package that a new or growing company puts together should be predicated on a few very important factors: company size and financial health, regional standards, industry standards, employee benefits offered by competitors, and work force needs.

FURTHER READING:

Briggs, Virginia L., Michael G. Kushner and Michael J. Schinabeck. *Employee Benefits Dictionary*. Washington: The Bureau of National Affairs, Inc., 1992.

Burstiner, Irving. *The Small Business Handbook*. Upper Saddle River, NJ: Prentice Hall, 1989.

Fundamentals of Employee Benefit Programs. Washington: Employee Benefit Research Institute, 1990.

Gomez-Mejia, Luis R., ed. *Compensation and Benefits*. Washington: The Bureau of National Affairs, Inc., 1989.

Jenks, James M. and Brian L.P. Zevnik. *Employee Benefits Plain and Simple*. Collier Books, 1993.

Peterson, Mark A. *The Complete Entrepreneur*. Barron's Educational Series, 1996.

Rossiter, Jill A. *Mastering Your Small Business Human Resources*. Chicago, IL: Upstart Publishing, 1996.

Williams, Stephen J., and Sandra Guerra. *Health Care Services in the 1990s*. Westport, CT: Praeger Publishers, 1991.

SEE ALSO: Employee Reward Systems; Health Insurance Options

EMPLOYEE COMPENSATION

Compensation is a primary motivator for employees. People look for jobs that not only suit their creativity and talents, but compensate them—both in terms of salary and other benefits—accordingly. Compensation is also one of the fastest changing fields in Human Resources, as companies continue to investigate various ways of rewarding employees for performance.

DETERMINING WAGES AND SALARIES

WAGE VS. SALARY It is important for small business owners to understand the difference between wages and salaries. A wage is based on hours worked. Employees who receive a wage are often called "nonexempt." A salary is an amount paid for a particular job, regardless of hours worked, and these employees are called "exempt." The difference between the two is carefully defined by the type of position and the kinds of tasks that employees perform. In general, exempt employees include executives, administrative and professional employees, and others as defined by the Fair Labor Standards Act of 1938. These groups are not covered by **minimum wage** provisions. Non-exempt employees are covered by minimum wage as well as other provisions.

It is important to pay careful attention to these definitions when determining whether an individual is to receive a wage or a salary. Improper classification of a position can not only pose legal problems, but often results in employee dissatisfaction, especially if the employee believes that execution of the responsibilities and duties of the position warrant greater compensation than is currently awarded.

CONDUCTING AN EVALUATION AND SETTING THE STRUCTURE When setting the level of an employee's monetary compensation, several factors must be considered. First and foremost, wages must be set high enough to motivate and attract good employees. They must also be equitable—that is, the wage must accurately reflect the value of the labor performed. As the authors of *Compensation Theory and Practice* point out, "management cannot hope to influence employee behavior and performance toward company objectives unless the compensation system is perceived as fair or equitable by employees."

In order to determine salaries or wages that are both equitable for employees and sustainable for companies, businesses must first make certain that they understand the responsibilities and requirements of the position under review. The next step is to review prevailing rates and classifications for similar jobs. This process requires research of the competitive rate for a particular job within a given geographical area. Wage surveys can be helpful in defining wage and salary structures, but these should be undertaken by a professional (when possible) to achieve the most accurate results. In addition, professional wage surveys can sometimes be found through local employment bureaus or in the pages of trade publications. Job analysis not only helps to set wages and salaries, but ties into several other Human Resource functions such as hiring, training, and performance appraisal. As the job is defined, a wage can be determined and the needs for hiring and training can be evaluated. The evaluation criteria for performance appraisal can also be constructed as the specific responsibilities of a position are defined.

Other factors to consider when settling on a salary for a position include:

- Availability of people capable of fulfilling the obligations and responsibilities of the job.

- Level of demand elsewhere in the community and/or industry for prospective employees.

- Cost of living in the area.

- Attractiveness of the community in which the company operates.

- Compensations levels already in existence elsewhere in the company.

COMPENSATION LAWS

There are many federal, state and local employment and tax laws that impact compensation. These laws define certain aspects of pay, influence how much pay a person may receive, and shape general benefits plans.

The Fair Labor Standards Act (FLSA) is probably the most important piece of compensation legislation. Small business owners should be thoroughly familiar with it. This act contains five major compensation laws governing minimum wage, overtime pay, equal pay, recordkeeping requirement, and child labor, and it has been amended on several occasions over the years. Most of the regulations set out in the FLSA impact non-exempt employees, but this is not true across the board.

The Equal Pay Act of 1963 is an amendment to FLSA, which prohibits differences in compensation based on sex for men and women in the same workplace whose jobs are similar. It does not prohibit seniority systems, merit systems, or systems that pay for performance, and it does not consider exempt or non-exempt status.

In addition, the United States government has passed several other laws that have had an impact, in one way or another, on compensation issues. These include the Consumer Credit Protection Act of 1968, which deals with wage garnishments; the Employee Retirement Income Security Act of 1974 (ERISA), which regulates pension programs; the Old Age, Survivors, Disability and Health Insurance Program (OASDHI), which forms the basis for most benefits programs; and implementation of unemployment insurance, equal employment, worker's comp, Social Security, Medicare, and Medicaid programs and laws.

TRADITIONAL COMPENSATION

For the most part, traditional methods of compensation involve set pay levels (wage or salary) with regular increases. Increases can be given for a variety of reasons, but are typically given for promotions, merit increases, or cost of living increases. The Hay Group points out that there is less distinction today between merit increases and cost of living increases: "Because of the low levels (three to four percent) of salary budget funding, most merit raises are perceived as little more than cost of living increases. Employees have come to expect them." This "base pay" system is one that most people are familiar with. Often, it includes a set salary or wage, a set schedule for merit increases, and a set benefits package.

BENEFITS

Benefits are an important part of an employee's total compensation package. Benefits packages became popular after World War II, when wage controls made it more difficult to give competitive salaries. Benefits were added to monetary compensation to attract, retain, and motivate employees, and they still perform that function today. They are not cash rewards, but they do have monetary value (today, spiraling health care costs make health benefits particularly essential to families). Many of these benefits are nontaxable to the employee and deductible by the employer.

Many benefits are not required by law, but are nonetheless common in total compensation packages. These include health insurance, accidental death and dismemberment insurance, some form of retirement plan (including profit-sharing, stock option programs, 401(k) plans and employee stock ownership plans), vacation and holiday pay, and sick leave. Companies may also offer various services, such as day care, to employees, either free or at a reduced cost. It is also common to provide employees with discounted services or products offered by the company itself. In addition, there are also certain benefits that *are* required by either state or federal law. Federal law, for example, requires the employer to pay into Social Security, and unemployment insurance is mandated under OASDHI. State laws govern worker's compensation.

CHANGES IN COMPENSATION SYSTEMS

As businesses change their focus, their approach to compensation must change as well. Traditional compensation methods may hold a company back from rewarding its best workers. When compensation is tied to a base salary and a position, there is little flexibility in the reward system. Some new compensation systems, on the other hand, focus on reward for skills and performance, with the work force sharing in company profit or loss. One core belief of new compensation policies is that as employees become employee owners, they are likely to work harder to ensure the success of the company. Indeed, programs that promote employee ownership—and thus employee responsibility and emotional investment—are becoming increasingly popular. Examples of these types of programs include gain sharing, in which employees earn bonuses by finding ways to save the company money; pay for knowledge, in which compensation is based on job knowledge and skill rather than on position (and in which employees can increase base pay by learning a variety of jobs); and incentive plans such as employee stock options plans (ESOPs).

PAY FOR PERFORMANCE Probably the most popular of the newer concepts in compensation is the easiest to understand—compensation based on performance. These programs generally offer compensation incentives based on employee performance or on the performance of a team. Pay for performance rewards high performance and does not reward mediocre or low performance, and is the definition of the "merit" system.

In a true merit based system, there are a few conditions which must be satisfied for it to be meaningful:

- Employees must have control over their performance. If employees are overly dependent on the actions and output of other employees or processes, they may have little control over their own performance.

- Differences in performance must mean something to the business. If there is little difference between a high performer and a mediocre one, merit pay won't work.

- Performance must be measured regularly and reliably. A clear system of performance appraisal, with defined criteria that are understood by the employee and regularly scheduled meetings must be in place.

ADMINISTERING COMPENSATION PROGRAMS

Compensation programs and policies must be communicated clearly and thoroughly to employees. Employees naturally want to have a clear understanding of what they can reasonably expect in terms of compensation (both in terms of monetary compensation and benefits) and performance appraisal. To ensure that this takes place, consultants urge business owners to detail all aspects of their compensation programs in writing. Taking this step not only helps reassure employees, but also provides the owner with additional legal protection from unfair labor practices accusations.

FURTHER READING:

Boyett, Joseph H., and Henry P. Conn. *Workplace 2000: The Revolution Reshaping American Business.* Plume, 1992.

Hay Group. *People, Performance, & Pay: Dynamic Compensation for Changing Organizations.* New York: The Free Press, 1996.

Milkovich, George T., and Alexandra K. Wigdor. *Pay for Performance: Evaluating Performance Appraisal and Merit Pay.* Washington: National Academy Press, 1991.

Tate, Curtis E., Leon C. Megginson, Charles R. Scott Jr., and Lyle R. Trueblood. *Successful Small Business Management.* Business Publications, Inc., 1985.

Wallace, Marc J., and Charles H. Fay. *Compensation Theory and Practice.* Kent Publishing Company, 1983.

SEE ALSO: Employee Benefits; Employee Reward Systems; Human Resource Policies

EMPLOYEE HIRING

Hiring employees is a process crucial to the success of a business, and as most successful small business owners know, the hiring process does not begin with the interview and end with the job offer. Rather, it involves planning and considering the job prior to an interview, recruiting and interviewing wisely to bring in the right person, and providing new workers with an orientation that enables them to get off to a strong start with the company.

WHEN AND WHO TO HIRE

Prior to advertising a position, interviewing, or making a selection, the manager must consider several key aspects of the open position and the person they will seek to fill that job.

CONSIDER THE JOB Any employee selection process must take place within the context of the larger business enterprise. An open position is an invitation to make positive changes in workforce structure. Does the job need to be created or filled? Does it need to be reorganized? These are questions that should be considered before beginning the hiring process.

First, consider the position itself. Prior to the employee hiring process, business owners should determine what tasks need to be addressed by the work force, and gauge how many people will be needed to accomplish that task. Consider the ideal functions and responsibilities of the job itself, not the person or persons who last held the position. At this point, it is beneficial to compose a **job description** and a job specification. The job description lists the duties and responsibilities of the job, and can include a ranking of the importance of each of these tasks. A job specification includes a listing of critical skills—those skills that are necessary for an individual to perform the job effectively. The job description and specification are tools which can not only aid the employer in finding the appropriate person to fill a job opening, but can also help guide the employee during his or her time with the business.

If the job exists and has been adequately defined, there is still opportunity to make changes to the position. Consider whether the position needs to be restructured. Are you asking that the job encompass too much responsibility? Are you asking too little? Small business owners might also want to consider whether the tasks associated with a position can be incorporated into one or more already existing positions. Often, it is not necessary to hire another employee, but only to re-evaluate present positions and re-design the work flow.

CONSIDER THE CANDIDATE After making sure that the position is thoroughly defined, consider the person that you want to fill the position. What skills, knowledge base, and personal traits will allow someone to successfully perform these tasks? Should the candidate have an advanced degree? What kind of personality would compliment the team? By consulting the critical skills in the job description, the manager will be able to get a solid idea of the type of candidate who will be most likely to successfully meet the challenges of the position.

A hiring manager should be careful, however, that they not become unduly idealistic in determining employment criteria. Few small businesses have the luxury of biding their time until the perfect prospective employee comes along. A would-be employee may not embody every single desirable trait on a business owner's wish list, yet still provide a fundamentally sound performance. Ultimately, each business owner needs to determine for him or herself whether a prospect's positives are sufficient to outweigh any negatives (in lack of experience, personality, or training) that they may carry with them.

RECRUITING

Finding good employees is an increasingly difficult task for many small business owners today. "The national jobless rate continues to hover at about 5 percent, with unemployment in some states dipping below 3 percent," observed *Entrepreneur*'s Jacquelyn Lynn. "While this may be good news for workers, it's another challenge for employers. When you combine low unemployment with the need for greater job skills, it's easy to understand why competition for qualified workers is stronger than ever." When creating a bank of candidates for the position, small business owners and entrepreneurs can look either within or without the company. There are advantages and disadvantages to both methods.

HIRING FROM WITHIN The advantages to hiring employees from within the company are a greater company knowledge base, continuity, and improved morale. An employee already in a business is likely to know more about the company's needs and will be able to approach a new position with the added perspective of his or her previous position. Hiring from within also brings continuity to a company—the talent of the individuals remains within the company, and therefore is "re-invested." Finally, employees generally feel good about a company which promotes from within. It signals a company's belief in their people and in the quality of work that they do, and

provides them with tangible evidence that their own efforts can bring about career advancement.

The disadvantage of hiring from the existing employee base is that it means a limited pool of qualified candidates. Within the current employee bank, especially if that bank is relatively small, there may not be a person qualified to fill the position, or there may not be a person who wants to fill the position.

HIRING FROM OUTSIDE Ultimately, every employee comes from outside the company at some time. Sometimes, bringing someone in from outside of the company is difficult because of the high learning curve. Often, though, external sources are necessary and desirable. People within the organization may not have a specialized skill or a specific level of education that is necessary for a position. Moreover, when hiring from within is practiced to exclusion, any company runs the risk of growing stagnant in its ideas and methods. Though they might be challenged by a new position, people from inside a company approach things in a way that has always worked for them. Sometimes, a fresh outlook can bring new vitality to an enterprise.

METHODS OF RECRUITING A small business can turn to several different methods of recruiting to secure external applicants. Newspaper advertising is by far the most popular and well-known of these methods. A well-written advertisement can bring in many candidates. Generally, the more specific the advertisement about the job and qualifications sought, the better qualified the applicants will be. But as Peggy Isaacson, a Florida-based human resources consultant told Lynn, "[Small business employers] can't just place a help-wanted ad in the newspaper and expect to be flooded with top-notch candidates. While advertising has its place in the hiring process, it's not enough. In this market, good people won't just come to you; you have to aggressively look for them."

In recognition of this reality, Isaacson recommended to Lynn that companies consider the following methods of recruitment:

- Utilize personal and professional networks—This encompasses everything from neighbors to fellow community/business association members.

- Establish an employee referral program—Companies that offer cash bonuses for referrals that result in hirings sometimes enjoy success with these programs.

- Utilize school placement offices

- Establish a presence at job fairs.

- Post notices at senior citizen centers.

- Contact area employment agencies.

- Post job openings with job banks—Many professional associations maintain job banks for their members.

- Offer competitive compensation packages.

- Instill a positive, attractive work environment.

Any or all of these methods may be used simultaneously to draw the best selection of applicants.

CANDIDATE SELECTION

Once a bank of potential candidates is established, the manager must select candidates and begin the interview process.

CHECKING REFERENCES Checking references, though time consuming, is an important step in the hiring process. Prospective employees will often provide professional references, if not on the resume itself, then at least on request. A manager may choose to check references before the interview with a candidate if they are provided, or may opt to check references between a first and second interview. In any event, a manager should always request references and make the calls.

Chances are good that a previous employer will not provide more information about the employee than their name, the dates of employment and the positions the person held. This is because a company, or any person within a company, which provides false information can be held legally liable for that misinformation. This potential liability does not, however, prevent a hiring manager from asking about the employee's work habits, performance or attitude. It is possible that someone may comment further on the employee, especially if the person is not a member of the Human Resources Department, but is a former manager.

If this kind of additional information about the employee is made available, never discuss it with the employee directly, saying, for example, ''Mrs. Smith at XYZ Corporation said that you were. . . .'' Rather, use it as a guide for probing questions about the person's previous work experience with that company.

EMPLOYMENT TESTING According to Lester Bittel and John Newstrom in *What Every Supervisor Should Know,* over 50,000 companies use employment testing of some kind to evaluate candidates prior to employment. Employment testing is a very touchy area, however, and can produce results that are questionable at best. It is often best to seek the advice of a professional employment testing service or of the state employment agency before making such a requirement of candidates. If testing, be sure that the test is skills oriented and designed and administered ob-

jectively. Its sole purpose should be to show how much a candidate knows with regard to the job's critical skills as defined in the job description. Also be sure that tests do not unfairly discriminate against the person being tested. Tests which measure a client's psychological characteristics, attitude, or personality are often questionable.

To prevent the appearance of discrimination, it is also important to ask for the same type of test from of every candidate. For example, if a job requirement is that the candidate must be able to lift a 50-pound box, you may ask this question or consider this a test for employment, but must ask the question and test every candidate for the position—men and women, slight and muscular. If you do not, you may be accused of discrimination.

MAKING A DECISION AND AN OFFER

After the interviewing process has taken place, it is not always easy to come to a final hiring decision. Sometimes a business may be forced to choose among a number of highly qualified, attractive applicants. This is obviously a nice problem to have. Conversely, on other occasions a business may undertake a time-consuming search, only to find themselves with candidates who are notably flawed in one respect or another. In such instances, the company leadership needs to determine whether the business can afford to extend the search, or whether business realities require that they fill the position with the best of the candidates before them.

THE OFFER The hiring manager should personally extend an offer of employment to the selected candidate as soon as possible after the interview. This begins the employee/manager relationship. Define the amount of time the candidate has to consider the offer—a few days to one week is usually enough. The offer can be extended in person or over the phone. It is important to note that an offer, even verbal, may be construed as a contract between the employee and the company. Therefore, construct the offer carefully.

An offer should include the following:

- Confirmation that you are speaking with the right person.

- Offer of the position, including title and reporting relationship.

- Starting salary for the position.

- A suggested date for the candidate's response

- Proposed starting date for the position.

- Indicate necessary follow through by you and/or the candidate

A manager should note that the position itself may dictate how to offer the starting salary. If the person is being offered an exempt (salaried) position, consider offering the salary in terms of bi-weekly earnings, or the smallest possible increment in which they are paid. If you are offering a person a non-exempt (hourly) position, you might offer the salary as an hourly wage. This could be important because the offer may be construed as a contractual agreement. If a yearly salary is offered, this may imply employment for one year. If the person is employed for a shorter period of time they could conceivably sue for the full, offered salary. By offering the salary in smaller increments, you avoid the possibility of any misunderstanding.

NEGOTIATING TERMS Every candidate offered a position has the option to either accept or reject the job offer and may want to negotiate terms, usually salary or benefits. Though the company may not be able to consider alternate terms of employment, it is often wise to hear a candidate's proposal. If the candidate is truly the best qualified person for the job, there may be some room for compromise on both the part of the candidate and on the part of the company. Listening to a proposal also establishes the manager's willingness to hear out other suggestions, a practice which is well received by any employee.

LAWS IMPACTING THE HIRING PROCESS

The hiring process is subject to legal guidelines set out by both federal and state government defining the boundaries for discriminatory hiring practices. Companies may not discriminate in hiring on the basis of sex, age, race, national origin, religion, physical disability, or veteran status. These are called protected classes. A hiring manager may not screen out any applicant because of membership in a protected class, nor may any interview questions address topics pertaining to the protected class. The main acts and laws which define these classes and the hiring practices based on them are:

- The Civil Rights Act of 1964 (Title VII);
- Age Discrimination in Employment Act of 1967(ADEA);
- **Americans with Disabilities Act** of 1990 (ADA);
- The Uniformed Services Employment Reemployment Rights Act of 1994 (USERRA);
- Immigration Reform and Control Act.

Anti-discrimination laws do not require any company to hire an applicant because of membership in a protected class. A manager is not required to hire applicants from any protected class in proportion to their numbers in the community. A manager is required to select the best qualified applicant for the position, based on the critical skills of the job, and is required to make that selection irrespective of whether or not that applicant belongs to a protected class. To be sure that hiring practices do not violate any of these laws, focus on the candidate's capabilities based on the critical skills of the job. Any questions about the legal aspects of hiring should be directed to a capable employment lawyer.

NEW EMPLOYEE ORIENTATION

Once the hiring decision is made and the offer is accepted, a manager needs to prepare to welcome a new employee. An employee orientation program helps introduce carefully selected, enthusiastic employees to the company. An orientation program should produce good will and provide education about the company; a poorly planned program can increase confusion and even hasten turnover. Employee orientation is more than a paperwork session—it is the new employee's first impression of the company.

One of the first things the manager should review is the job description, along with the specifics of the position, its goals, and the critical skills. After this has been accomplished, the new employee can be introduced to the company at large.

REQUIRED FORMS All new employees are required to fill out specific forms on the first day of employment. These include federal and state forms such as:

- Federal Tax Withholding Form (W-4);
- State and/or Local Tax Withholding Forms;
- Employment Eligibility Verification Form (I-9).

The company may also have specific forms for emergency notification and other critical information. Be sure each form and its purpose is explained to the employee and that the employee is given sufficient time to complete them.

COMPANY SPECIFICS New employees need to know more than where their desk is. They need to know the way to operate on a daily basis within the company. An orientation session should address any of the following topics pertinent to the workplace:

- Areas for public information (bulletin boards, etc.) and private information (mailboxes, etc.);
- Entrance and exit for the building;
- Introduction to managers and co-workers;
- Location of departments;
- Location of restrooms and breakroom;

- Location of secured area for personal belongings;

- Operation of the phone system;

- Parking;

- Training schedule.

COMPANY POLICIES Specific company policies should be thoroughly reviewed with every new employee, so that all employees understand the guidelines under which they work. Though these might be discussed during the interview, they should be reiterated in an employee's orientation. Policies to review can include the following:

- Company Mission Statement, history and future;

- Company benefits and payroll policies;

- Company dress code, office hours;

- Company communications and open door policies;

- Company policies against harassment and discrimination.

Often, this kind of information is found in the company's Employee Handbook. If a handbook is available, it should be provided to the employee immediately on the employee's first day of employment.

FURTHER READING:

Bittel, Lester, and John Newstrom. *What Every Supervisor Should Know,* 6th ed. New York: McGraw Hill, 1990.

Boyett, Joseph H., and Henry P. Conn. *Workplace 2000: The Revolution Reshaping American Business.* Plume, 1992.

Cadwell, Charles M. *New Employee Orientation: A Practical Guide for Supervisors.* Menlo Park, CA: Crisp Publications, 1988.

Half, Robert. *Finding, Hiring & Keeping the Best Employees.* New York: John Wiley & Sons, 1993.

Lynn, Lacquelyn. "Hire Power: How to Find the Best Employees in Today's Dwindling Market." *Entrepreneur.* September 1997.

Morgan, Ronald B., and Jack E. Smith. *Staffing the New Workplace: Selecting and Promoting for Quality Improvement.* Milwaukee, WI: ASQC Quality Press, 1996.

Tate, Curtis E., et al. *Successful Small Business Management.* Business Publications, Inc., 1985.

Weiss, Donald. *Fair, Square & Legal: Safe Hiring, Managing & Firing Practices.* New York: Amacom, 1993.

SEE ALSO: Employee Manuals; Employee Screening; Employment Applications; Employment Interviewing; Human Resource Policies

EMPLOYEE LEASING PROGRAMS

Employee leasing programs are arrangements in which businesses lease their employees through an outside contractor that attends to the various personnel-related activities commonly associated with human resources management. Employee leasing programs have become particularly popular among small- and mid-sized companies, who view leasing as: 1) a viable option for increasing the benefits that their work force receives, and 2) an effective strategy for getting rid of burdensome and time-consuming paperwork. "Small businesses often have one person wearing four or five different hats," confirmed one leasing company executive in an interview with *Personnel.* "Many businesses simply don't have the internal personnel to handle all the administrative tasks" associated with human resources management.

Writing in *Inc.,* Jay Finegan offered a succinct summary of the employee leasing process as it is practiced in the mid-1990s: "An employee-leasing company, also known as a professional employer organization (PEO), 'leases' the employees of the business that's hired it. That means the PEO serves as a co-employer, taking control of the personnel administration and paperwork that drive small business owners to distraction. Most PEOs offer a wide range of services and benefits packages, including payroll administration, medical benefits, workers' compensation and unemployment insurance, retirement plans, and compliance assistance with labor laws. In return, the PEO charges an administrative fee of roughly 2 percent to 8 percent of total payroll."

GROWTH OF EMPLOYEE LEASING Employee leasing surged in popularity in the 1980s, when observers tracked annual increases of anywhere from 20 to 40 percent in the total number of employees involved in the programs. This pace showed no sign of slowing during the early 1990s. Indeed, the National Association of Professional Employer Organizations (NAPEO) reported that the number of employees being managed by PEOs rose from one million in 1992 to 1.6 million in 1993, an astounding increase in only 12 months. In 1995 NAPEO reported that the industry was growing at an annual rate of 30 percent, and in 1997 *Inc.* reported that according to one analysis, the industry could involve $185 billion in revenues and more than 9 million employees by the year 2005.

ADVANTAGES OF EMPLOYEE LEASING

Supporters of employee leasing programs point to a variety of advantages associated with such arrangements:

- Since leasing firms handle more than one company payroll, they can wield their greater buying power to get discounts on group health insurance, life insurance, and dental insurance that smaller companies simply would not be able to get. The small company is thus able to provide its workers with better benefits, which in turn help it to keep valuable current employees and attract promising new employees.

- Leasing companies can handle chores associated with workers' compensation and unemployment insurance. Indeed, mid-1990s studies undertaken by various governmental and industry groups suggest that small businesses with 1-25 employees can save as much as 40 percent on the cost of unemployment and workers' compensation with a PEO, while businesses with 25-100 employees can save 25-35 percent.

- Leasing companies assume risk and responsibility for preparing a client company's payroll and for paying payroll taxes, along with state and federal reporting requirements.

- Employee leasing programs allow small business owners and managers to spend their time doing what they do best, rather than struggling in swamps of paperwork. "A good 35-40 percent of my time, which could have been used more efficiently, was being used to evaluate health policies and benefits packages for my staff," recalled one executive in *Association Management.* "Plus, my controller was spending an enormous amount of time on payroll, taxes, and so forth." Once the organization turned to an employee leasing program, however, the firm's leadership was able to devote much more of its time and energy to more appropriate tasks.

- PEOs can often lend significant human resources expertise. "Because of the numbers of employees they represent (hundreds, if not thousands), [leasing companies] can hire in-house experts in areas of human resources management that small companies rarely have," noted Bruce G. Posner in *Inc.* Other analysts confirm that many PEOs offer a wealth of knowledge that can be utilized by client companies for everything from rewriting job descriptions to helping with recruiting. "The better PEOs are much more than dressed-up payroll services," wrote Sammi Soutar in *Association Management.* "They assume the role of your off-site hu-

man resource professional, performing the sometimes perplexing, often complicated, and time-consuming duties of that office."

- Companies still wield ultimate control over how their business is run. Leasing companies take care of payroll and benefits administration functions, but this does not give them a voice in their clients' other business decisions. "Under a leasing arrangement, the employees still report to the same bosses, who remain in charge of how the business is managed," stated Posner.

- Leasing companies can also provide legal assistance to their clients in various aspects of personnel law. There is some self-interest involved here, since in the event of a lawsuit, both the leasing company and its client could be targeted as co-employers.

DISADVANTAGES OF EMPLOYEE LEASING PROGRAMS

Employee leasing programs obviously have many well-documented advantages, as evidenced by the ever-growing popularity of the practice. But as Posner observed, "however appealing leasing may be, it isn't without risks. Essentially . . . you're delegating a vital area of your business to outsiders." And as Finegan noted, "the employee-leasing industry has seen spectacular flameouts, owing to everything from bad risks and poor management to outright fraud. When a PEO goes under, its clients often discover that their payroll cash and insurance coverage vanish with it."

Many business observers blame the presence of unscrupulous leasing companies in the industry on the lack of regulation that exists. Indeed, more than half of the states in the United States have no licensing requirements for employee leasing companies. Fortunately, associations such as the National Association of Professional Employer Organizations (NAPEO) keep a close eye on the industry, and they can sometimes provide assistance in determining whether an area PEO will adequately fill your needs (NAPEO accredits firms that meet its standards).

FINDING A GOOD PROFESSIONAL EMPLOYER ORGANIZATION

Small business owners looking into the possibility of establishing an employee-leasing environment in their workplace, then, should make sure that they select a solid leasing company. To help ensure that they secure one, they should consider the following:

- Services—small businesses need to make sure that the PEO under consideration can meet the business's human resources administration needs, including reasonable program customization desires.

- Financial Strength—This is a vital aspect of any PEO, for an organization that is standing on faulty financial footing could conceivably leave its clients with a crippling debt load if it ultimately folds as a result of incompetent or criminal management. "Ask for banking and credit references and proof that payroll taxes and insurance premiums have been paid," wrote Soutar. "NAPEO-accredited members must complete a quarterly audit. Make sure PEOs under serious consideration have been certified for at least a couple of years." Finegan agreed, commenting in *Inc.* that small business owners should "demand to see audited financial statements and have an accountant dissect them with you." Small businesses should also check out the financial standing of the banks and insurance companies with which the PEO works.

- References—Ask for a good-sized list of PEO clients, and then take the time to follow up. "A lengthy list of clients helps ensure that you won't get only references who are well schooled in the 'right' answers, and it also offers a look at the PEO's customer base," noted Finegan. Conversely, small businesses should be prepared for some scrutinization as well. As Pamela Sherrid pointed out in *U.S. News and World Report,* "a reputable leasing firm will respond to your scrutiny by scrutinizing you. It should want to inspect your workplace and look at your workers'-compensation experience and at the claims history of your group health plan. It might not want as a client a company with serious workplace hazards, for instance, since it could be sued by an injured employee. The cost of its health premiums could go up if your employees are often sick."

- Fee Structure—Small business owners and managers should examine the fee structure closely to make sure that it is appropriate for all services. Companies looking to secure the services of a PEO should avoid companies that offer excessively expensive rates, but they should also beware of those that offer "bargain basement" terms. "Be on the lookout for companies that either don't charge fees or charge rates significantly lower than the national average," wrote Soutar. "This is a warning sign that the leasing company's intention may be to get in the market, make a quick buck from the client's cash flow, and then get out."

- Personal Comfort—Industry analysts note that a good working relationship is an important component in making any PEO arrangement work. Small business owners and managers, then, need to make certain that they get along with the PEO representatives with whom they will interact. Other observers note that PEO attitudes can sometimes tip prospective clients off to problems that might lurk beneath the surface. "Some PEOs, in rushing to lock up as many clients as possible, take on risky accounts that can undermine their financial stability. The soundest PEOs are picky in accepting new business," wrote Finegan.

- Contractual Details—Contracts should spell out every detail of the arrangement that is being made. After all, human resources management is a complex area that is rife with complicated rules and regulations in the realms of payroll, benefits, etc. Moreover, human resources management has seen increased lawsuit activity in recent years, a trend that has led some PEOs to ask for varying levels of input in the realms of hiring and firing of workers in their clients' workforce. "Even when a leasing firm only supplies help with paper work and benefits, some firms demand the hire-and-fire prerogative to ensure they won't be in legal trouble because you've discriminated against a job candidate or an employee," explained Sherrid. Small business consultants also encourage their clients to insist on a contract that includes a termination clause. This clause should allow the business to terminate the agreement with the leasing company with 30 or 60 days' notice (90 days is the absolute maximum that should be accepted). "The more specific your contract about the leasing firm's responsibilities, the better," concluded Sherrid. "It should be clear, for example, that your partner will be liable for any mistakes made in the activities it carries out. If it errs in calculating your taxes, for example, it should be responsible for any fines or penalties."

FURTHER READING:

Belinsky, Ronald G. "Employee Leasing: A Viable Method to Reduce Personnel Costs for the Small Business." *Michigan CPA.* Spring 1987.

Feldman, Stuart. "Companies Buy Into Employee Leasing Plans." *Personnel.* October 1990.

Finegan, Jay. "Look Before You Lease: Employee Leasing Can Be a Boon—Or a Nightmare." *Inc.* February 1997.

"If You're Considering Employee Leasing, Heed the Latest Warnings." *Profit-Building Strategies for Business Owners.* November 1992.

Murthy, B., and Suzanne K. Murrmann. "Employee Leasing: An Alternative Staffing Strategy." *Cornell Hotel and Restaurant Administration Quarterly.* June 1993.

Posner, Bruce G. "The Joy of Leasing." *Inc.* May 1990.

Sherrid, Pamela. "More Time for Business: Owners can Avoid the Paper Work and Buy Benefits Cheaper, too." *U.S. News and World Report.* November 5, 1990.

Soutar, Sammi. "Leasing Your Staff." *Association Management.* October 1995.

Traynor, Kenneth, and James G. Pesek. "Implications of Employee Leasing for Small Businesses." *Journal of Small Business Management.* October 1987.

SEE ALSO: Employee Benefits; Work Force

EMPLOYEE MANUALS

The employee manual (or employee handbook) is critical for every organization. It spells out guidelines for the employment relationship, documenting company policies and procedures for the benefit of both employer and employee. Not only a descriptive document, the employee manual is a necessity since it can provide a foundation for settling potential legal disputes between employers and employees. Because of its importance, it is crucial for the employee manual to be carefully crafted.

THE PURPOSE OF THE MANUAL Employee manuals fulfill many functions in an organization. They can:

- Define an employer's legal responsibilities by putting policy on record.

- Make employees aware of rights, benefits, and policy and thus protect the employer against claims that an employee was not informed of these rules if a legal dispute arises.

- Describe the organization in detail.

- Serve as a employee reference tool when an answer is sought for a frequently asked question.

- Protect the employee from inconsistencies in an employer's policies or practices.

CONTENTS OF THE MANUAL When constructing an Employee Manual, it is worthwhile to consider using a team approach, bringing in people from all areas of the company who are impacted by the policies embodied in the manual. This group insures that policies are not developed solely by Human Resources representatives (although their input can certainly be valuable) but by a representative cross-section of the entire company. If this technique is used, it is critical to assign trustworthy people to manage the project and see to its completion.

Most employee manuals contain these basic sections:

- A welcome from the president, the company's mission or vision statement, and a brief history of the company.

- The company's harassment policy. By incorporating a harassment policy in the manual, an employee understands that there is no tolerance for harassment. It can also protect the company from liability for harassment charges.

- Employee classifications and an explanation of them.

- General pay and overtime provisions. Often, there are state laws that must be reflected with regard to pay, so this section should be thoroughly reviewed.

- Hiring and recruiting policy, including a statement regarding equal employment opportunity.

- Sections on general procedures such as work hours, dress code, and other office-specific policies.

- Sections describing benefits, including vacation, leaves of absence, insurance, pensions, sick time, etc. Again, because many of these are covered by state as well as federal regulations, it is important to review these carefully before publication.

- Statement of disciplinary procedure, including a clear list of behaviors that can result in immediate termination.

- Outline of grievance procedures.

- An acknowledgment, to be signed and returned to the employer, stating that an employee has received, read, and understood the information contained in the manual.

- An employment-at-will statement, defining the rights of the employer to terminate an employee at any time. This right is also granted the employee, who may resign at any time for any reason.

Disclaimers may also be added, such as a disclaimer stating that the manual does not represent a contract made with the employee, or a disclaimer stating that the list of company rules and procedures is not exhaustive. Disclaimers protect the company from potential legal action in these areas.

LEGAL REVIEW Because the employee manual is often seen as a legal contract, it is important that its contents be carefully reviewed by legal counsel before publication. A lawyer will look for legally contestable or problematic statements in both policy and disclaimers. Is this really important? Yes. As Cecily Waterman observed in *HRMagazine*, "employee handbooks have become the springboard for employees' successful lawsuits against their employers. In 1992, employee handbooks played a major role in the outcome of more than 200 reported decisions in the United States."

DISTRIBUTION AND REVISIONS An employee manual should be distributed at the time of hire to all incoming employees. This does not mean that the manual does not ever change, however. If revisions are to be made, a manual must first state that the employer has the right to revise the policies in it at any time. It should then be re-distributed (in whole or in part, depending on its format) to all employees, with a detailed description of the revisions made. Generally, the manual should be reviewed once per year to see if revisions are necessary.

FURTHER READING:

Cooke, Rhonda. "Becoming Book Smart." *Credit Union Management.* October 1994.

Jenner, Lisa. "Employee Communications: How to Effectively use Disclaimers." *HR Focus.* February 1994.

Ramey, Ardella, and Carl R. J. Sniffen. *A Company Policy and Personnel Handbook.* Grants Pass, OR: The Oasis Press/PSI Research, 1991.

Theye, Larry D., Larry G. Carsetnson, and Betty Becker-Theye. "Translating the Employee Handbook: Potentially Hazardous Duty." *ATA Chronicle.* August 1997.

Waterman, Cecily A. "Update Handbooks to Avoid Risk." *HRMagazine.* November 1992.

SEE ALSO: Employee Hiring; Employee Benefits; Human Resource Policies

EMPLOYEE MOTIVATION

Employee motivation describes the level of energy, commitment, and creativity that a company's workers apply to their jobs. In the increasingly competitive business environment of recent years, finding ways to motivate employees has become a pressing concern for many managers. In fact, a number of different theories and methods of employee motivation have emerged, ranging from monetary incentives to increased involvement and empowerment.

Employee motivation can sometimes be problematic in small businesses, because the owner often tries to maintain too much control over employees. But the effects of low employee motivation on small businesses can be devastating. "As much as 30 percent of an uninspired employee's potential energy is left on the table, untapped," said motivation consultant John Thompson in *Entrepreneur.* Some of the problems associated with unmotivated workers include complacency, declining morale, and widespread discouragement. If allowed to continue, these problems can reduce productivity, earnings, and competitiveness in a small business.

On the other hand, small businesses can also provide an ideal atmosphere for fostering employee motivation, because employees are able to see the results of their contributions in a more immediate way than in large firms. Besides increasing productivity and competitiveness, a highly motivated work force can allow a small business owner to relinquish day-to-day, operational control and instead concentrate on long-term strategies to grow the business. "Workers really do want to be inspired about their work, and when they are, they work better, smarter, and harder," business coach Don Maruska told *Entrepreneur.*

WHAT MOTIVATES?

One approach to employee motivation has been to view "add-ins" to an individual's job as the primary factors in improving performance. Endless mixes of **employee benefits**—such as health care, life insurance, profit sharing, employee stock ownership plans, exercise facilities, subsidized meal plans, child care availability, company cars, and more—have been used by companies in their efforts to maintain happy employees in the belief that happy employees are motivated employees.

Many modern theorists, however, propose that the motivation an employee feels toward his or her job has less to do with material rewards than with the design of the job itself. Studies as far back as 1924 show that simplified, repetitive jobs, for instance, fostered boredom and the taking of frequent, unauthorized breaks by those who performed them. In 1950 a series of attitude surveys found that highly segmented and simplified jobs resulted in lower employee morale and output. Other consequences of low employee motivation include absenteeism and high turnover, both of which are very costly for any company. As a result, "job enlargement" initiatives began to crop up in major companies in the 1950s.

On the academic front, Turner and Lawrence suggested that there are three basic characteristics of a "motivating" job: 1) It must allow a worker to feel personally responsible for a meaningful portion of the work accomplished. An employee must feel ownership of and connection with the work he or she performs. Even in team situations, a successful effort will foster an awareness in an individual that his or her contributions were important in accomplishing the group's tasks.

2) It must provide outcomes which have intrinsic meaning to the individual. Effective work that does not lead a worker to feel that his or her efforts matter will not be maintained. The outcome of an employee's work must have value to himself or herself and to others in the organization.

3) It must provide the employee with feedback about his or her accomplishments. A constructive, believable critique of the work performed is crucial to a worker's motivation to improve.

While terminology changes, the tenets of employee motivation remain relatively unchanged from findings over half a century ago. Today's buzzwords include ''empowerment,'' ''quality circles,'' and ''teamwork.'' All of these terms demonstrate the three characteristics of motivating jobs set forth in the theory of Turner and Lawrence. Employee empowerment gives autonomy and allows an employee to have ownership of ideas and accomplishments, whether acting alone or in teams. **Quality circles** and the increasing occurrence of teams in today's work environments give employees opportunities to reinforce the importance of the work accomplished by members as well as receive feedback on the efficacy of that work.

In small businesses, which may lack the resources to enact formal employee motivation programs, managers can nonetheless accomplish the same basic principles. In order to help employees feel like their jobs are meaningful and that their contributions are valuable to the company, the small business owner needs to communicate the company's purpose to employees. This communication should take the form of words as well as actions. In addition, the small business owner should set high standards for employees, but also remain supportive of their efforts when goals cannot be reached. It may also be helpful to allow employees as much autonomy and flexibility as possible in how their jobs are performed. Creativity will be encouraged if honest mistakes are corrected but not punished. Finally, the small business owner should take steps to incorporate the vision of employees for the company with his or her own vision. This will motivate employees to contribute to the small business's goals, as well as help prevent stagnation in its direction and purpose.

MOTIVATION METHODS

There are as many different methods of motivating employees today as there are companies operating in the global business environment. Still, some strategies are prevalent across all organizations striving to improve employee motivation. The best employee motivation efforts will focus on what the employees deem to be important. It may be that employees within the same department of the same organization will have different motivators. Many organizations today find that flexibility in job design and reward systems has resulted in employees' increased longevity with the company, improved productivity, and better morale.

EMPOWERMENT Giving employees more responsibility and decision-making authority increases their realm of control over the tasks for which they are held responsible and better equips them to carry out those tasks. As a result, feelings of frustration arising from being held accountable for something one does not have the resources to carry out are diminished. Energy is diverted from self-preservation to improved task accomplishment. Empowerment brings the job enlargement of the 1950s and the job enrichment that began in the 1960s to a higher level by giving the employees some of the power to expand their own jobs and create new, personally identified challenges.

CREATIVITY AND INNOVATION At many companies, employees with creative ideas do not express them to management for fear of jeopardizing their jobs. Company approval and toeing the company line have become so ingrained in some working environments that both the employee and the organization suffer. When the power to create in the organization is pushed down from the top to line personnel, employees who know a job, product, or service best are given the opportunity to use their ideas to improve it. The power to create motivates employees and benefits the organization in having a more flexible work force, using more wisely the experience of its employees, and increasing the exchange of ideas and information among employees and departments. These improvements also create an openness to change that can give a company the ability to respond quickly to market changes and sustain a first mover advantage in the marketplace.

LEARNING If employees are given the tools and the opportunities to accomplish more, most will take on the challenge. Companies can motivate employees to achieve more by committing to perpetual enhancement of employee skills. Accreditation and licensing programs for employees are an increasingly popular and effective way to bring about growth in employee knowledge and motivation. Often, these programs improve employees' attitudes toward the client and the company, while bolstering self-confidence. Supporting this assertion, an analysis of factors which influence motivation-to-learn found that it is directly related to the extent to which training participants believe that such participation will affect their job or career utility. In other words, if the body of knowledge gained can be applied to the work to be accomplished, then the acquisition of that knowledge will be a worthwhile event for the employee and employer.

QUALITY OF LIFE The number of hours worked each week by American workers is on the rise, and many families have two adults working those increased hours. Under these circumstances, many workers are left wondering how to meet the demands of their lives beyond the workplace. Often, this concern occurs while at work and may reduce an employee's productivity and morale. Companies that have instituted flexible employee arrangements have gained motivated employees whose productivity has increased. Programs incorporating flextime, condensed workweeks, or job sharing, for example, have been successful in focusing overwhelmed employees toward the work to be done and away from the demands of their private lives.

MONETARY INCENTIVE For all the championing of alternative motivators, money still occupies a rightful place in the mix of motivators. The sharing of a company's profits gives incentive to employees to produce a quality product, perform a quality service, or improve the quality of a process within the company. What benefits the company directly benefits the employee. Monetary and other rewards are being given to employees for generating cost-savings or process-improving ideas, to boost productivity and reduce absenteeism. Money is effective when it is directly tied to an employee's ideas or accomplishments. Nevertheless, if not coupled with other, nonmonetary motivators, its motivating effects are short-lived. Further, monetary incentives can prove counterproductive if not made available to all members of the organization.

OTHER INCENTIVES Study after study has found that the most effective motivators of workers are nonmonetary. Monetary systems are insufficient motivators, in part because expectations often exceed results and because disparity between salaried individuals may divide rather than unite employees. Proven nonmonetary positive motivators foster team spirit and include recognition, responsibility, and advancement. Managers who recognize the ''small wins'' of employees, promote participatory environments, and treat employees with fairness and respect will find their employees to be more highly motivated. One company's managers brainstormed to come up with 30 powerful rewards that cost little or nothing to implement. The most effective rewards, such as letters of commendation and time off from work, enhanced personal fulfillment and self-respect. Over the longer term, sincere praise and personal gestures are far more effective and more economical than awards of money alone. In the end, a program that combines monetary reward systems and satisfies intrinsic, self-actualizing needs may be the most potent employee motivator.

FURTHER READING:

Clark, Catherine S., Gregory H. Dobbins, and Robert T. Ladd. ''Exploratory Field Study of Training Motivation.'' *Group & Organization Management*. September 1993.

Coates, Joseph F., and Jarrett, Jennifer. ''Workplace Creativity.'' *Employment Relations Today*. Spring 1994.

Herzberg, Frederick. ''One More Time: How Do You Motivate Employees?'' *Harvard Business Review*. January-February 1968.

Kennish, John W. ''Motivating with a Positive, Participatory Policy.'' *Security Management*. August 1994.

Kinni, Theodore B. ''The Empowered Workforce.'' *Industry Week*. September 19, 1994.

McGarvey, Robert. ''Inspiration Points: Unmotivated Employees Could Cost You Your Business.'' *Entrepreneur*. September 1997.

Peters, Tom. ''Get Innovative or Get Dead, Part II.'' *California Management Review*. Winter 1991.

SEE ALSO: Corporate Culture; Employee Reward Systems

EMPLOYEE PERFORMANCE APPRAISALS

A high-performing employee can help a small business owner surpass her goals while a low-performing employee can undermine a business' ability to reach even the most basic objectives. Since small businesses by definition have fewer employees, poor performing employees can have a major bearing on the success of a company. All employees want to know how they are performing in a job. Documenting performance provides a basis for pay increases and promotions. Feedback is also important to help staff members improve their performance or to be rewarded or recognized for a job well done. Whether feedback is provided formally or informally, small businesses need to appraise employee performance on a regular basis.

PERFORMANCE APPRAISAL AND DEVELOPMENT

While the term *performance appraisal* has meaning for most small business owners, it might be helpful to consider the goals of an appraisal system. They are as follows:

1) To improve the company's productivity

2) To make informed personnel decisions regarding promotion, job changes, and termination

3) To identify what is required to perform a job (goals and responsibilities of the job)

4) To assess an employee's performance against these goals

5) To work to improve the employee's performance by naming specific areas for improvement, developing a plan aimed at improving these areas, supporting the employee's efforts at improvement via feedback and assistance, and ensuring the employee's involvement and commitment to improving her performance.

DEVELOPING AN APPRAISAL SYSTEM

A small business with few employees or one that is just starting to appraise its staff may choose to use a pre-packaged appraisal system, consisting of either printed forms or software. These software packages can be customized either by using a firm's existing appraisal methods or by selecting elements from a list of attributes that describe successful employee's work habits such as effective communication, timeliness, and ability to perform work requested. Eventually, many companies choose to develop their own appraisal form and system in order to accurately reflect an employee's performance in light of the business's goals. In developing an appraisal system for a small business, an entrepreneur needs to consider the following:

1) Size of staff

2) Employees on an alternative work schedule

3) Goals of company and desired employee behaviors to help achieve goals

4) Measuring performance/work

5) Pay increases and promotions

6) Communication of appraisal system and individual performance

7) Performance planning

SIZE OF STAFF A small business with few employees may choose to use an informal approach with employees. This would entail meeting with each employee every six months or every year and discussing his or her work performance and progress since the last discussion. Feedback could be provided verbally, without developing or using a standard appraisal form, but in many cases, legal experts counsel employers to maintain written records in order to provide themselves with greater legal protections. As a company increases its staff, a more formal system using a written appraisal form developed internally or externally should always be used, with the results of the appraisal being tied to salary increases or bonuses. Whether the appraisal is provided verbally or in writing, a small business owner needs to provide consistent feedback on a regular basis so that employees can improve their work performance.

ALTERNATIVE WORK SCHEDULES Employees working alternative work schedules—such as working at home, working part-time, or job-sharing—will most likely need to have their performance appraised differently than regular full-time staffs in order to be fairly evaluated. A **flexible work program** may require different duties to perform a job and these new responsibilities should be incorporated into the appraisal. A small business owner should also be careful to ensure that these employees are treated fairly with regard to both the appraisal and resulting promotions. As Leslie Hammer and Karen Barbera noted in *Human Resource Planning*, ''There is no conclusive evidence demonstrating that individuals who work reduced hours perform less effectively than those who work full-time.'' In addition, they warned that ''because more women and elderly people occupy part-time and job sharing positions, using work status when making promotion decisions may result in adverse impact.''

COMPANY GOALS AND DESIRED PERFORMANCE The performance of employees, especially in a smaller firm, has a definite impact on a company's goals. In a one-person business, goal-setting and achieving is a matter of transforming words into action, but moving the business toward its goals in a larger firm means that the employer has to determine each person's role in the success of the business, communicate that role to them, and reward or correct their performance. Before developing a formal appraisal form or using one developed by others, an entrepreneur should first consider the company's business goals and how an individual or group's performance impacts these. Although an appraisal by its nature is subjective—interpreting a person's ability to perform certain tasks—setting down these tasks as a function of achieving company goals can make it less so. Obviously, a job description would have some of this information contained within it. However, as a company's goals change from year to year, an employee's tasks will most likely change to reflect these goals.

MEASURING/ASSESSING PERFORMANCE Once a list of tasks and attributes is developed, a small business owner or manager needs to determine how to measure an employee's performance on these tasks. Measurement provides another objective element to the appraisal. Ideally, measurement would be taken against previous performance, whether of the individual employee, the group, or the company at large. If a company is just developing its appraisal system or does not have a baseline performance to measure against, it should develop realistic goals based on business needs or on the similar performance of competitors.

PAY INCREASES AND PROMOTIONS When developing an appraisal system, a small business owner needs to consider the connection between the appraisal and pay increases or promotions. While performance feedback for development/improvement purposes may be given verbally, a written summary of the individual's work performance must accompany a pay increase or promotion (or demotion or termination). It is crucial, therefore, that a manager or small business owner regularly document an employee's job performance.

The method of pay increases impacts the appraisal as well. If a small business uses merit-based increases, the appraisal form would include a rating of the employee on certain tasks. If skill-based pay is used, the appraisal would list skills acquired and level of competency. Appraisals and resulting salary increases that take into account group or company performance should include the individual's contributions to those goals.

COMMUNICATING THE SYSTEM A performance appraisal system is only effective if it is properly communicated and understood by employees. When devising an appraisal system for his or her company, an entrepreneur may want to consider involving staff in its development. Supporters contend that this promotes buy-in and understanding of the plan, as well as ensuring that the appraisal takes into account all tasks at the company. If the small business owner is unable to involve her staff, she should walk through the system with each employee or manager and have the manager do the same, requesting feedback and making adjustments as necessary.

COMMUNICATING PERFORMANCE AND PLANNING Part of the appraisal system is the actual communication of the performance assessment. While this assessment may be written, it should always be provided verbally as well. This provides an opportunity to answer any questions the employee may have on the assessment, as well as to provide context or further detail for brief assessments. Finally, the employee and the entrepreneur or manager should make plans to meet again to develop a plan aimed at improving performance and reaching agreed-upon goals for the following review period. This planning session should relate company and/or group goals to the individual's tasks and goals for the review period and provide a basis for the next scheduled review.

TYPES OF APPRAISALS AND ASSESSMENT TERMS

TRADITIONAL In a traditional appraisal, a manager sits down with an employee and discusses performance for the previous performance period, usually one year. The discussion is based on the manager's observations of the employee's abilities and performance of tasks as noted in a job description. The performance is

rated, with the ratings tied to salary percentage increases. However, as David Antonioni notes in *Compensation & Benefits*, "The traditional merit raise process grants even poor performers an automatic cost of living increase, thereby creating perceived inequity. . . . In addition, most traditional performance appraisal forms use too many rating categories and distribute ratings using a forced-distribution format." Antonioni suggests the appraisal form use just three rating categories—outstanding, fully competent, and unsatisfactory—as most managers can assess her best and worst employees, with the rest falling in between.

SELF-APPRAISAL Somewhat self-explanatory, the self-appraisal is used in the performance appraisal process to encourage staffs to take responsibility for their own performance by assessing their own achievements or failures and promoting self-management of development goals. It also prepares employees to discuss these points with their manager. It may be used in conjunction with or as a part of other appraisal processes, but does not substitute for an assessment of the employee's performance by a manager.

EMPLOYEE-INITIATED REVIEWS In an employee-initiated review system, employees are informed that they can ask for a review from their manager. However, cautions Ellyn E. Spragins in *Inc.*, "The on-demand appraisal isn't meant to replace a conventional semiannual review, but it promotes an attitude of self-management among workers and often makes critiques more honest." This type of review would also promote regular communication between staff and managers, but would obviously be dependent on employees' initiative.

360 DEGREE FEEDBACK 360 degree feedback in the performance appraisal process refers to feedback on an employee's performance being provided by the manager, different people or departments an employee interacts with (peer evaluation), external customers, and the employee herself. This type of feedback would also include staffs providing feedback on a manager's performance (also known as upward appraisals). As a company grows in size, a small business owner should consider using 360 degree feedback to appraise employees. Communication in a business of ten people varies wildly from that of a company of 100 persons and 360 degree feedback would ensure that an employee's performance is observed by those who work most closely with her. Small business owners or managers could either include the feedback in the performance review or choose to provide it informally for development purposes.

LEGAL ISSUES

Given that the results of a performance appraisal are often used to support a promotion, termination, salary increase, or job change, they are looked at very closely in employee discrimination suits. Besides providing a written summary of the appraisal to the employee, a small business owner would be well-advised to ensure the following with regards to the system at large:

- Job expectations as well as appraisal system and its impact on employee's work status are adequately communicated to all employees.

- Performance measures are related to the job being performed.

- Managers or co-workers providing input into the appraisal must be sufficiently trained as to be able to provide objective input.

- Employees are given timely feedback on performance and reasonable amount of time and support in improving their performance.

Assistance in developing a system is available through a variety of sources including consultants, periodicals and books, and software. In addition, given the legal implications of appraisals, a small business owner would be well-advised to have her counsel review the company's performance assessment process, including training of managers and employees. While performance appraisal systems require a substantial amount of thought and work on the part of the entrepreneur, they are an important key to unlocking a growing company's potential.

FURTHER READING:

Antonioni, David. "Improve the Performance Management Process Before Discontinuing Performance Appraisals." *Compensation & Benefits*, Vol. 26.

Chapman, Elwood N. *Human Relations in Small Business.* Crisp Publications, 1994.

Church, Allen H., and David W. Bracken. "Advancing the State of the Art of 360-Degree Feedback." *Group & Organization Management.* June, 1997.

Edwards, Mark. R., and Ann J. Ewen. *360 Degree Feedback: The Powerful New Model for Employee Assessment & Performance Improvement.* AMACOM, 1996.

Hammer, Leslie B., and Karen M. Barbera. "Toward an Integration of Alternative Work." *Human Resource Planning.* June, 1997.

Olson, Richard F. *Performance Appraisal: A Guide to Greater Productivity.* Wiley, 1991.

Spragins, Ellyn E. "Encouraging Open Communication and Motivating Employees Through Employee-Initiated Reviews." *Inc.* July 1991.

SEE ALSO: Employee Compensation

EMPLOYEE PRIVACY

Employee privacy issues have surged to the forefront of the business press in recent years, spurred on by changing workplace dynamics and a litigation-conscious business environment. Observers say that advances in **telecommunications**—such as **e-mail** and the Internet—have exacerbated management concerns about appropriate employee behavior, while an explosion of lawsuits have been aimed not only at employees, but at the companies that employ them, which has led many businesses to embrace elevated personnel monitoring practices. Indeed, employee privacy is already fairly restricted in many respects in many of America's large corporations. Studies indicate that small business owners have increased their monitoring practices as well, and many experts expect that trend to continue in the near future. But analysts note that the close owner-employee interaction that typifies many small business enterprises often makes monitoring a delicate issue.

FUNDAMENTALS OF WORKPLACE PRIVACY

While stipulations on employee privacy parameters vary from state to state, legal experts state that private sector employees have fewer rights than they commonly believe. "There is no general federal or state law creating or protecting a 'zone of privacy' in the workplace," wrote George Webster in *Association Management.* "The U.S. Constitution's First Amendment free-speech clause and the Fourth Amendment protection against 'unreasonable searches and seizures' apply only to action by the government, not to private-sector employers. . . . By and large, employees leave their constitutional rights at the workplace door. A few state constitutions do extend speech and search protection to private-sector employees."

According to Webster, the central legal issue in the area of workplace privacy boils down to once question: "Did the employer, by what it did or failed to do, create a reasonable expectation of privacy by the employee? If the answer is yes and the employer did not meet that expectation, then it may be held liable for invasion of privacy." He went on to delineate basic employer and **employee rights** in a variety of areas:

Searches and seizures—An employer has the right to inspect personal belongings (bags, purses, briefcases, cars, lockers, desks, etc.), except when the employer "has created a reasonable expectation of privacy," said Webster. These expectations can be raised if the employee is given a key to a desk, or if the employer has disseminated a written policy explicitly stating that it will not make such inspections.

Monitoring computer, e-mail, Internet, and fax use—Although businesses have some significant rights in this regard, since they own the equipment, Webster noted that ''if the employer allows employees to use corporate computers for their personal work or business, then it has created a reasonable expectation of privacy and the organization would not be allowed access to employees' personal files.''

Monitoring telephone calls—Companies are allowed to monitor calls to make sure that they are business-related, but according to Webster, ''listening to or recording calls beyond that point may violate federal law,'' especially in the area of recording. ''The best practice is to prohibit excessive personal use of the phones and then discipline employees who violate the policy.''

Surveillance and Investigation—Many surveillance methods (cameras, ID checkpoints, etc.) are legal, as are investigations of employees, provided that they are ''reasonable'' and undertaken for work-related purposes.

Testing—Embraced by increasing numbers of companies, many **drug testing** policies have stood up to legal scrutiny.

TRENDS IN COMPANY MONITORING

Countless studies and reports indicate that monitoring of employee behavior, both in and out of the workplace, has undergone a dramatic increase in recent years. Such monitoring may range from checking on the business relevance of Internet sites that an employee visits to ''midnight raids'' on an employee's locker or cubicle to see if the person is stealing equipment or information from the company. ''Companies not only have stepped up midnight raids but no longer hesitate to seek information on what was once assumed to be the private side of workers' lives,'' wrote Dana Hawkins in *U.S. News and World Report*, who noted that according to a 1997 study, ''more than one third of the members of the American Management Association, the nation's largest management development and training organization, tape phone conversations, videotape employees, review voice mail, and check computer files and E-mail. . . . Scrutiny of job applicants has intensified, and this has fueled a boom in companies that do database searches of applicants' credit reports, driving and court records, and even workers' compensation claims. Personal behavior is no longer off limits: Some firms have adopted rules that limit co-workers' dating. Others ban off-the-clock smoking and drinking. Many companies regularly test for drugs. Much of this is done without the workers' knowledge.'' Indeed, according to the *Labor Law Journal,* in 1997 less than one-third of employers notified their employees when they engaged in electronic monitoring practices in the workplace.

This latter element of company monitoring has been a particular sore spot for employees and civil liberties advocates alike. They note that even if one were to set aside the ethical issues of such monitoring for the moment, errors in monitoring practice can have devastating repercussions on workers. ''Careers may be damaged when investigators overreach, when mistakes are made, or when managers are too aggressive in enforcing company rules,'' said Hawkins.

Nonetheless, three major factors—increased litigation, rising medical costs, and technological change—have pushed many companies into increasingly proactive investigations into the activities of current and prospective employees, both in and out of the office.

INCREASED LITIGATION ''Why has the worker's sphere of privacy shrunk?'' wrote Hawkins. ''Employers say they feel intense pressure from lawsuits of every sort.'' Indeed, businesses have seen an increase in lawsuit activity in nearly every conceivable area. As one attorney told *U.S. News & World Report,* ''If [companies] are going to be held liable, they'd better monitor.''

RISING MEDICAL COSTS Rising medical costs have encouraged many businesses to check into the medical history of prospective employees, especially if the business is one that self-insures. For example, rising medical costs have been cited by advocates of workplace drug testing as an important factor in its usefulness. In addition, access to previously private medical information has increased dramatically in recent years. ''Technology now makes it possible to store medical records in electronic form in a central database, providing an easily accessible 'cradle-to-grave' look at an individual's health history,'' reported Maureen Minehan in *HR Magazine*. ''Medical information on approximately 15 million U.S. and Canadian citizens is already on file with the Medical Information Bureau (MIB), a database of medical information that more than 750 insurance firms subscribe to.'' Minehan also pointed out that recent developments in genetic testing have focused attention on medical privacy issues. Noting that ''tests can now determine whether an individual carries the gene mutation for certain illnesses,'' which indicates a greater risk for contracting a particular disease, Minehan stated that a number of employee advocacy groups have expressed concern that this technology could be used by employers to discriminate against both potential and current workers.

TECHNOLOGICAL ADVANCES Amazing advances in computer and other technological capabilities have dramatically increased the abilities of employers to monitor the activities of those workers. As Kathy Compton stated in *HRMagazine,* technological advances have provided employers with the ability to access information on current and potential employees to an unprecedented degree. Hawkins agreed, writing that "technology—particularly new software that can track and record everything workers do on their computers—is making it easier to peek over a worker's shoulder."

BALANCING EMPLOYEE AND EMPLOYER RIGHTS

Given the threat of litigation, the impact of worker performance on bottom line financial performance, and the wide assortment of monitoring technology available, it is hardly surprising that employee privacy has suffered setbacks in recent years. But observers note that many companies are trying to strike a balance between self-protection and sensitivity to the feelings of their workers. This is particularly true in the small business world. Observers note that small business environments typically feature working arrangements where owners operate in close proximity to their employees. Friendships often blossom in such cases, but the likelihood of developing close personal relationships with an employer or employee is severely curtailed if the company insists on maintaining policies that are regarded as intrusive on employee privacy. Of course, many small businesses are family-owned businesses as well, another factor that can complicate employee monitoring efforts considerably. Some analysts would argue that family businesses that feel a need to implement monitoring strategies on family members within the business is likely to be a distressingly dysfunctional one on several levels.

But even if friendships or family relations are not issues for a small business owner, he or she should still approach employee privacy issues with some care. Certainly, small business owners have every right to protect themselves and their businesses, and many of them encounter situations in which monitoring practices become a viable option. But some analysts think that small business owners who practice active monitoring of employees run a greater risk of undercutting morale. After all, whereas employee monitoring has become a recognized reality in many sectors of the often impersonal "Fortune 500" world, it is viewed as a practice that is at odds with the atmosphere at many small business establishments. And of course, some small businesses operate in niche industries in which the opportunity/need to engage in employee monitoring is less evident. The activities of employees in a small outdoor landscaping firm, for example, would probably be less likely to be monitored than those of employees in a small market research company or other firm that makes extensive use of computer technology. In addition, legal experts point out that small businesses that are found liable for excesses in this area are far more likely to be irrevocably crippled than are larger corporations with deeper pockets.

Finally, each business owner has to decide or his or her self how much privacy employees are entitled to on an ethical level. Writing in his essay "Discrimination and Privacy," Jack Mahoney argued that while companies naturally compose policies that are based on self-interest, they should recognize that "there are limits to the information a company is entitled to seek about its members in such areas as their personal lifestyle, sexual preferences, affiliations, use of alcohol, drugs, and so on. What is at stake here is the psychic as well as physical privacy of individuals and the respecting and safeguarding of their personal autonomy and freedom. This seems to imply that is a company wishes to acquire personal information about individual employees, then the burden of proof to justify such a wish is on the company." Still, Mahoney granted that in instances "when performance is adversely affected, then the company is ethically justified in enquiring into the reason for such behavior."

Finally, Decker added that "To ensure that employee privacy procedures and policies are understood by managers, supervisors, and employees, communication is important. Through communication, employee privacy procedures and policies are disseminated within the employer's organization. Communication assures knowledge, understanding, and consistent application of privacy procedures and policies."

FURTHER READING:

Cappel, James J. "Closing the E-Mail Privacy Gap." *Journal of Systems Management.* December 1993.

Compton, Kathy. "How to Handle Privacy in the Workplace." *HRMagazine.* June 1997.

Conlon, Kevin J. "Privacy in the Workplace." *Labor Law Journal.* August 1997.

Decker, Kurt H. *A Manager's Guide to Employee Privacy: Laws, Policies, and Procedures.* New York: John Wiley & Sons, 1989.

Edwards, Richard. *Rights at Work: Employment Relations in the Post-Union Era.* Washington: Brookings Institution, 1993.

Guffey, Cynthia J., and Judy F. West. "Employee Privacy: Legal Implications for Managers." *Labor Law Journal.* November 1996.

Hawkins, Dana. "Who's Watching Now? Hassled by Lawsuits, Firms Probe Workers' Privacy." *U.S. News & World Report.* September 15, 1997.

Jacobs, Deborah L. "The Perils of Policing Employees." *Small Business Reports.* February 1994.

Lang, Kathy J., and Elaine Davis. "Personal E-Mail: An Employee Benefit Causing Increasing Privacy Concerns." *Employee Benefits Journal.* June 1996.

Lotito, Michael J., and Lynn C. Outwater. *Minding Your Business: Legal Issues and Practical Answers for Managing Workplace Privacy.* Alexandria, VA: Society for Human Resource Management, 1997.

Mahoney, Jack. "Discrimination and Privacy." In *The Complete MBA Companion.* Lanham, MD: Pitman Publishing, 1997.

Minehan, Maureen. "The Right to Medical Privacy." *HRMagazine.* March 1997.

Webster, George D. "Respecting Employee Privacy." *Association Management.* January 1994.

Weiss, Donald H. *Fair, Square, and Legal: Safe Hiring, Managing & Firing Practices to Keep You & Your Company Out of Court.* New York: Amacom, 1991.

SEE ALSO: Human Resource Management

EMPLOYEE REGISTRATION PROCEDURES

When a business hires a new employee, it is legally obligated to make sure that certain information about these new hires is provided to relevant government agencies. This information, which is provided by having the employee fill out specific forms on their first day of employment, is used for tax purposes and to ensure that they are legally eligible to work in the United States.

The primary documents that are necessary for employee registration with the government are the following:

- Federal Tax Withholding Form (W-4)
- State and/or Local Tax Withholding Forms
- Employment Eligibility Verification Form (I-9).

The company may also have specific forms for emergency notification and other critical information. The content of each form, as well as its purpose, should be fully explained to each employee.

TAX WITHHOLDING FORMS "As an employer you have a tremendous fiduciary responsibility to collect and withhold taxes from employees on virtually every paycheck you issue," wrote Bob Adams in his *Adams Streetwise Small Business Start-Up.* "Throughout the United States, you must withhold an appropriate amount for federal income and other earnings-related taxes. Many states and some municipalities also require the payment of an income or other tax on earnings."

A cornerstone of the federal tax-gathering system is the federal W-4 form. This form, also known as the Employee's Withholding Allowance Certificate, provides the Internal Revenue Service with the filing status and withholding allowances of each employee. Once a new hire has determined his or her filing status and number of withholding allowances, the employer uses IRS tables to determine how much federal income tax should be withheld from the employee's wages. Employers should understand that under this arrangement, they are essentially acting as agents for the taxing authority; the money that is withheld belongs to the taxing authority, even if possession has not been formally transferred.

Where applicable, employers also have to withhold state and local income taxes from worker paychecks. States and municipalities have dramatically different arrangements in this regard; some states for instance, have no state income tax, while others have fairly sizable ones. Employers who wish to keep up to speed on their requirements, if any, in this area should contact their local and state tax agencies for information on specific employee registration procedures, etc.

EMPLOYEE ELIGIBILITY The other major employee registration procedure that small business owners need to pay attention to is the completion of the federal Form I-9. This document assures the U.S. Immigration and Naturalization Service (INS) that the employee is legally eligible to work in America. The Form I-9 is filled out by both the employee and the employer. For further information, contact the INS at 800-755-0777.

FURTHER READING:

Adams, Bob. *Adams Streetwise Small Business Start-Up: Your Comprehensive Guide to Starting and Managing a Business.* Holbrook, MA: Adams Media, 1996.

"Employer's Supplemental Tax Guide." Washington: Internal Revenue Service, 1997.

Morgan, Ronald B., and Jack E. Smith. *Staffing the New Workplace: Selecting and Promoting for Quality Improvement.* ASQC Quality Press, 1996.

Tate, Curtis E., et al. *Successful Small Business Management.* Business Publications, Inc., 1985.

Weiss, Donald. *Fair, Square & Legal: Safe Hiring, Managing & Firing Practices.* AMACOM, 1993.

SEE ALSO: Employee Hiring; Tax Withholding

EMPLOYEE REWARD SYSTEMS

In a competitive business climate, business owners want to improve quality while reducing costs. Meanwhile, a strong economy has resulted in a tight job market. So while small businesses need to get more from their employees, their employees are looking for more out of them. Employee reward and recognition programs are one method of motivating employees to change work habits to benefit a small business.

REWARD VS. RECOGNITION

Although these terms are often used interchangeably, reward and recognition systems should be considered separately. Employee reward systems refer to programs set up by a company to reward performance and motivate employees on individual and/or group levels. They are normally considered separate from salary but may be monetary in nature or otherwise incur a cost to the company. While previously considered the domain of large companies, small businesses have also begun employing them as a tool to lure top employees in a competitive job market as well as to increase employee performance.

As noted, although employee recognition programs are often combined with reward programs they retain a different purpose altogether. Recognition programs are generally not monetary in nature though they may have a cost to the company. Sue Glasscock and Kimberly Gram in *Productivity Today* differentiate the terms by noting that recognition elicits a psychological benefit whereas reward indicates a financial or physical benefit. Although many elements of designing and maintaining reward and recognition systems are the same, it is useful to keep this difference in mind, especially for small business owners interested in motivating staffs while keeping costs low.

DIFFERENTIATING REWARDS FROM MERIT PAY AND THE PERFORMANCE APPRAISAL

In designing a reward program, a small business owner needs to separate the salary or merit pay system from the reward system. Financial rewards, especially those given on a regular basis such as bonuses or gainsharing should be tied to an employee's or a group's accomplishments and should be considered ''pay at risk'' in order to distance them from salary. By doing so, a manager can avoid a sense of entitlement on the part of the employee and ensure that the reward emphasizes excellence or achievement rather than basic competency.

Merit pay increases, then, are not part of an employee reward system. Normally, they are an increase for inflation with additional percentages separating employees by competency. They are not particularly motivating since the distinction that is usually made between a good employee and an average one is relatively small. In addition, they increase the fixed costs of a company whereas variable pay increases (such as bonuses) have to be ''re-earned'' each year. Finally, in many small businesses teamwork is a crucial element of a successful employee's job. Merit increases generally review an individual's job performance, without adequately taking into account the performance within the context of the group or business.

DESIGNING A REWARD PROGRAM

The keys to developing a reward program are as follows:

1) Identification of company or group goals that the reward program will support

2) Identification of the desired employee performance or behaviors that will reinforce the company's goals

3) Determination of key measurements of the performance or behavior, based on the individual or group's previous achievements

4) Determination of appropriate rewards

5) Communication of program to employees.

In order to reap benefits such as increased **productivity**, the entrepreneur designing a reward program must identify company or group goals to be reached and the behaviors or performance that will contribute to this. While this may seem obvious, companies frequently make the mistake of rewarding behaviors or achievements that either fail to further business goals or actually sabotage them. If teamwork is a business goal, a bonus system rewarding individuals who improve their productivity by themselves or at the expense of another does not make sense. Likewise, if quality is an important issue for an entrepreneur, the reward system that he or she designs should not emphasize rewarding the *quantity* of work accomplished by a business unit.

Properly measuring performance ensures the program pays off in terms of business goals. Since rewards have a real cost in terms of time or money, small business owners need to confirm that performance has actually improved before rewarding it. Once again, the measures need to relate to a small business's goals. As Linda Thornburg noted in *HR Magazine*, ''Performance measures in a rewards program have to be linked to an overall business strategy. . . . Most reward programs use multiple measures which can include such variables as improved financial performance along with improved customer service, improved customer satisfaction, and reduced defects.''

When developing a rewards program, an entrepreneur should consider matching rewards to the end result for the company. Perfect attendance might merit a different reward than saving the company $10,000 through improved contract negotiation. It is also important to consider rewarding both individual and group accomplishments in order to promote both individual initiative and group cooperation and performance.

Lastly, in order for a rewards program to be successful, the specifics need to be clearly spelled out for every employee. Motivation depends on the individual's ability to understand what is being asked of her. Once this has been done, reinforce the original communication with regular meetings or memos promoting the program. Keep your communications simple but frequent to ensure staff are kept abreast of changes to the system.

TYPES OF REWARD PROGRAMS

There are a number of different types of reward programs aimed at both individual and team performance.

VARIABLE PAY **Variable pay** or pay-for-performance is a compensation program in which a portion of a person's pay is considered "at risk." Variable pay can be tied to the performance of the company, the results of a business unit, an individual's accomplishments, or any combination of these. It can take many forms, including bonus programs, stock options, and one-time awards for significant accomplishments. Some companies choose to pay their employees less than competitors but attempt to motivate and reward employees using a variable pay program instead. According to Shawn Tully in *Fortune*, "The test of a good pay-for-performance plan is simple: It must motivate managers to produce earnings growth that far exceeds the extra cost of [the program]. Though employees should be made to stretch, the goals must be within reach."

BONUSES Bonus programs have been used in American business for some time. They usually reward individual accomplishment and are frequently used in sales organizations to encourage salespersons to generate additional business or higher profits. They can also be used, however, to recognize group accomplishments. Indeed, increasing numbers of businesses have switched from individual bonus programs to one which reward contributions to corporate performance at group, departmental, or company-wide levels.

According to some experts, small businesses interested in long-term benefits should probably consider another type of reward. Bonuses are generally short-term motivators. By rewarding an employee's performance for the previous year, say critics, they encourage a short-term perspective rather than future-oriented accomplishments. In addition, these programs need to be carefully structured to ensure they are rewarding accomplishments above and beyond an individual or group's basic functions. Otherwise, they run the risk of being perceived as entitlements or regular merit pay, rather than a reward for outstanding work. Proponents, however, contend that bonuses are a perfectly legitimate means of rewarding outstanding performance, and they argue that such compensation can actually be a powerful tool to encourage future top-level efforts.

PROFIT SHARING **Profit sharing** refers to the strategy of creating a pool of monies to be disbursed to employees by taking a stated percentage of a company's profits. The amount given to an employee is usually equal to a percentage of the employee's salary and is disbursed after a business closes its books for the year. The benefits can be provided either in actual cash or via contributions to employee's **401(k) plans**. A benefit for a company offering this type of reward is that it can keep fixed costs low.

The idea behind profit-sharing is to reward employees for their contributions to a company's achieved profit goal. It encourages employees to stay put because it is usually structured to reward employees who stay with the company; most profit-sharing programs require an employee to be vested in the program over a number of years before receiving any monies. Unfortunately, since it is awarded to all employees, it tends to dilute individual contributions. In addition, while profit is important, it is only one of many goals a company may have and is, according to Jack Stack in *Inc.*, "an accumulation of everything that happens in the business over a given period of time." Stack argued that "[employees] have to be able to see the connection between their actions, decisions, and participation, and changes in [a company's goals]." Like bonuses, profit sharing can eventually be viewed as an entitlement program if the correlation between an employee's actions and his or her reward becomes murky.

STOCK OPTIONS Previously the territory of upper management and large companies, stock options have become an increasingly popular method of rewarding middle management and other employees in both mature companies and start-ups. Employee stock-option programs give employees the right to buy a specified number of a company's shares at a fixed price for a specified period of time (usually around ten years). They are generally authorized by a company's board of directors and approved by its shareholders. The number of options a company can award to employees is usually equal to a certain percentage of the company's shares outstanding.

Like profit-sharing plans, stock options usually reward employees for remaining with the company, serving as a long-term motivator. Once an employee has been with a company for a certain period of time (usually around four years), he or she is fully vested in the program. If the employee leaves the company prior to being fully vested, those options are canceled. After an employee becomes fully vested in the program, he or she can purchase from the company an allotted number of shares at the strike price (or the fixed price originally agreed to). This purchase is known as "exercising" stock options. After purchasing the stock, the employee can either retain it or sell it on the open market with the difference in strike price and market price being the employee's gain in the value of the shares.

Offering additional stock in this manner presents risks for both the company and the employee. If the option's strike price is higher than the market price of the stock, the employee's option is worthless. When an employee exercises an option, the company is required to issue a new share of stock that can be publicly traded. The company's market capitalization grows by the market price of the share, rather than the strike price at which the employee purchases the stocks. The possibility of reduction of company earnings (impacting both the company and shareholders) arises when the company has a greater number of shares outstanding. To keep ahead of this possibility, earnings must increase at a rate equal to the rate at which outstanding shares increase. Otherwise, the company must repurchase shares on the open market to reduce the number of outstanding shares.

One benefit to offering stock options is a company's ability to take a tax deduction for compensation expense when it issues shares to employees. Another benefit to offering options is that while they could be considered a portion of compensation, current accounting methods do not require businesses to show options as an expense on their books. This tends to inflate the value of a company. Companies should think carefully about this as a benefit, however. If accounting rules were to become more conservative, corporate earnings could be affected.

GROUP-BASED REWARD SYSTEMS

As more small businesses use team structures to reach their goals, many entrepreneurs look for ways to reward cooperation between departments and individuals. Bonuses, profit sharing, and stock options can all be used to reward team and group accomplishments. An entrepreneur can choose to reward individual or group contributions or a combination of the two. Group-based reward systems are based on a measurement of team performance, with individual rewards received on the basis of this performance. While these systems encourage individual efforts toward common business goals, they also tend to reward underperforming employees along with average and above-average employees. A reward program which recognizes individual achievements in addition to team performance can provide extra incentive for employees.

RECOGNITION PROGRAMS

For small business owners and other managers, a recognition program may appear to be merely extra effort on their part with few tangible returns in terms of employee performance. While most employees certainly appreciate monetary awards for a job well done, many people merely seek recognition of their hard work. For an entrepreneur with more ingenuity than cash available, this presents an opportunity to motivate employees.

In order to develop a successful recognition program, a small business owner must be sure to separate it from the company's reward program. This ensures a focus on recognizing the efforts of employees. To this end, although the recognition may have a monetary value (such as a luncheon, gift certificates, or plaques), money itself is not given to recognize performance. Glasscock and Gram noted in *National Productivity Review* that effective recognition methods should be sincere; fair and consistent; timely and frequent; flexible; appropriate; and specific. They go on to explain that it is important that every action which supports a company's goals is recognized, whether through informal feedback or formal company-wide recognition. Likewise, every employee should have the same opportunity to receive recognition for their work. Recognition also needs to occur in a timely fashion and on a frequent basis so that an employee's action does not go overlooked and so that it is reinforced to spur additional high performance. Like rewards, the method of recognition needs to be appropriate for the achievement. This also ensures that those actions which go farthest in supporting corporate goals receive the most attention. However, an entrepreneur should remain flexible in the methods of recognition, as employees are motivated by different forms of recognition. Finally, employees need to clearly understand the behavior or action being recognized. A small business owner can ensure this by being specific in what actions will be recognized and then reinforcing this by communicating exactly what an employee did to be recognized.

Recognition can take a variety of forms. Structured programs can include regular recognition events such as banquets or breakfasts, employee of the month or year recognition, an annual report or yearbook which features the accomplishments of employees, and department or company recognition boards. Informal or spontaneous recognition can take the form of privileges such as working at home, starting late/leaving early, or long lunch breaks. A job well done can also be recognized by providing additional support or empowering the employee in ways such as greater choice of assignments, increased authority, or naming the employee as an internal consultant to other staff. An article in *Small Business Reports* recommends establishing an award after the name of an employee as a way of recognizing extra effort and performance. Symbolic recognition such as plaques or coffee mugs with inscriptions can provide longer-term recognition of a job well done. There are a number of books with additional ideas on rewarding performance that small business owners can investigate. It is most important that the entrepreneur be sincere in their appreciation for their employee's hard work.

Both reward and recognition programs have their place in small business. Small business owners should first determine desired employee behaviors, skills, and accomplishments that will support their business goals. By rewarding and recognizing outstanding performance, entrepreneurs will have an edge in a competitive corporate climate.

FURTHER READING:

Caggiano, Christopher. ''Perks You Can Afford.'' *Inc.* November 1997.

Deeprose, Donna. *How to Recognize and Reward Employees.* AMACOM, 1994.

Glasscock, Sue, and Kimberly Gram. ''Winning Ways: Establishing an Effective Workplace Recognition System.'' *National Productivity Review.* Summer 1996.

Henemen, Robert L., and Courtney Von Hippel. ''Balancing Group and Individual Rewards: Rewarding Individual Contributions to the Team.'' *Compensation and Benefits Review.* July 17, 1995.

Imberman, Woodruff. ''Pay for Performance Boosts Quality Output.'' *IIE Solutions.* October 1996.

Lyons, Nancy J. ''Managing the Volunteer Workforce.'' *Inc.* December 1997.

Siegel, William L. *People Management for Small Business.* Wiley, 1978.

Spitzer, Dean R. ''Power Rewards: Rewards That Really Motivate (Employee Incentives).'' *Management Review.* May 1, 1996.

Stack, Jack. ''The Problem with Profit Sharing.'' *Inc.* November 1996.

Thornburg, Linda. ''Pay for Performance: What You Should Know.'' *HR Magazine.* June 1992.

Tully, Shawn ''Your Paycheck Gets Exciting.'' *Fortune.* November 1, 1993.

Weber, Joseph. ''Offering Employees Stock Options They Can't Refuse.'' *Business Week.* October 7, 1991.

Welles, Edward O. ''Motherhood, Apple Pie & Stock Options.'' *Inc.* February 1998.

SEE ALSO: Employee Compensation; Employee Motivation

EMPLOYEE RIGHTS

Employee rights is a broad term used to describe the range of legal protections that are afforded to individuals and groups that are in the employ of business organizations. Employee rights can be broken down into four primary categories: rights relating to **labor union** organizing and collective bargaining; rights relating to working hours and pay; rights relating to **workplace safety** and **workers' compensation**; and rights relating to discrimination in hiring or in the workplace. Fundamental employee rights are thus a significant factor in a wide range of **human resource management** issues that small business

owners and supervisors face today, including questions concerning employee privacy, promotion policies, drug and alcohol testing and investigations, compilation and upkeep of personnel records and files, monitoring of employee performance, and dealing with labor unions.

Contemporary employee rights were established primarily through legislation, much of which was itself triggered by societal pressures. Workers also secured rights through collective bargaining, but these rights were themselves established largely through legislation. Joseph D. Levesque, writing in *The Human Resource Problem-Solver's Handbook,* contended that individual privacy rights in the workplace have seen their greatest growth over the last century or so in three primary legal areas: federal and state constitutional law, state statutory law, and various forms of related tort law. ''Most courts applying provisions of the U.S. Constitution [to employee rights in the workplace] have focused on two primary issues: autonomy and confidentiality. Autonomy has been normally limited to matters of free choice involving such personal and sensitive issues as marriage, sexual affiliations and practices, and contraception. More recently it has touched on such employer policy issues as nepotism and extramarital relations. . . . Confidentiality has usually been a more straightforward issue involving the disclosure of information known or believed to be of a confidential nature.''

Some observers—and particularly those whose sympathies lie with business owners and management—have criticized the growth in protections that have been extended to employees over the last several decades, but others argue that many of these affirmations of individual rights—such as the right to equal treatment in the workplace, regardless of race, religion, or gender—are common-sense changes that do not threaten the ability of companies to operate in a proficient or profitable manner. Indeed, some critics contend that legally, corporate entities continue to hold too much power over their employees. Employers ''still retain the fundamental and important rights to operate their enterprise and make business decisions,'' stated Levesque. ''The manager who sees the challenge [of dealing with employee rights] will be the one who finds a solution when problems arise. This manager knows that both employee and organizational rights must be protected for the mutual benefit of both; that objectivity in the actions and decisions of managers is tantamount to judicious problem solving; and that managers must practice humane and precise methods of dealing with a more complex, informed, and idealistic workforce.''

FUNDAMENTAL EMPLOYEE RIGHTS State and federal law is full of statutes that extend rights to workers in one area or another, but essentially, all of those statutes provide the following basic rights:

- Employees have the right to affiliate with or become a member of a recognized labor union or employee organization.

- Employees have the right to work in a safe environment.

- Employees have the right to file legal complaints against their employer without being punished in any way by their employer.

- Personal information about employees will be treated with extreme confidentiality.

- Employees will not be subject to what Levesque termed ''arbitrary or capricious decisions that affect their employment or life in an adverse fashion.''

- Employees have the right to work in an environment where they receive fair and reasonable treatment.

- Employees will not be required to perform any illegal or unethical act on behalf of their employer.

Employee rights is a sometimes-blurry term in today's business environment, as changing **demographics**, increased emphasis on individual rights in other areas of society, increased demand for educated workers, and changes in corporate management philosophies have all contributed to uncertainties about its exact dimensions. For example, many workers believe, as Andrea Gross noted in *Ladies Home Journal,* that ''a full-time employee is entitled to a paid vacation and a certain number of paid sick days.'' In reality, however, this is ''false. Sick days and vacation leave with pay are benefits, not rights, and employers may provide or withhold them as they wish.'' Yet paid vacation and sick days are so commonplace in many industries—as companies work to offer competitive benefit packages for prospective employees—that managers and employees come to see such benefits as staples of employee rights. Small business owners, then, would do well to research the major laws that serve as the cornerstones of employee rights and communicate the relevant aspects of those laws to their employees.

FURTHER READING:

Brown, Tom. ''Defining a 'New Social Contract:' GTE's Emerging Employee-Partnership Philosophy Reflects New Market Realities.'' *Industry Week.* August 15, 1994.

Ewing, David. *Justice on the Job: Resolving Grievances in the Nonunion Workplace.* Harvard Business School Press, 1989.

Gross, Andrea. ''What Rights Do You Have?'' *Ladies Home Journal.* October 1995.

Kinni, Theodore B. ''The Empowered Workforce.'' *Industry Week.* September 19, 1994.

Levesque, Joseph D. *The Human Resource Problem-Solver's Handbook.* New York: McGraw-Hill, 1992.

McWhirter, Darien A. *Your Rights at Work.* New York: Wiley, 1992.

SEE ALSO: Employee Benefits; Labor Unions and Small Business

EMPLOYEE SCREENING

Trustworthy, qualified employees are an essential part of any business. This is especially true of small businesses, where every employee counts. The time to ensure an employee is trustworthy and qualified is during the hiring process, rather than on the job. Therefore, employee screening is a crucial part of any small business's hiring process.

Screening may include reference and credit checks, verification of employment, investigations into any criminal activity (where allowed by law), and psychological, physical, and **drug testing**. These programs can be managed by the small business owner, but some businesses prefer to hire out at least portions of them to companies specializing in screening. When hiring a firm to check out prospective employees, it is important that the company itself be trustworthy. A small business would be well advised to find out what services the company offers, how the company goes about getting its information, and whether or not the company uses its own services. It may also be helpful to speak with some of the company's long-time clients.

LEGAL ISSUES Many companies will engage in at least a portion of the screening process themselves. Before doing so, it is important that they have a thorough knowledge of local, state, and federal laws against discrimination. These may impact both the questions asked of prospective employees as well as additional investigations of them. Many local and state governments have laws on the books which prevent an employer from inquiring about criminal convictions. A business should note the difference between an arrest and a conviction; merely being arrested proves nothing.

In addition to ensuring qualifications, proper screening of prospective employees supports a business's hiring practices in the face of possible lawsuits. Courts may hold companies responsible for injuries their employees inflict on others while on the job. Companies found liable in a negligent hiring suit may be held responsible for punitive damages, medical bills, or lost wages. For a small business, such a suit could be potentially devastating.

ELEMENTS OF A SCREENING PROGRAM

PREVIOUS EMPLOYMENT AND REFERENCES Employers should review resumes and employment histories for gaps in employment. The employer should also be sure to contact specific business references as opposed to merely friends and family of the prospective employee. Finally, companies may choose to contact other individuals not listed as references, such as previous co-workers, who may provide additional background on the employee. This check may be subject to local or state laws or require the consent of the applicant.

CREDIT AND VEHICLE CHECKS These may be done through credit agencies. While checking an applicant's credit and vehicle records is not conclusive regarding qualifications for employment, these records may give an indication of an applicant's dependability or honesty.

CRIMINAL RECORDS As noted, these may be subject to local or state laws against discrimination. It is also important to consider whether the applicant's previous arrest or crime would have a direct bearing on the work that he or she would be doing.

IQ OR PERSONALITY TESTS More and more businesses are choosing to use personality tests or IQ tests in addition to interviewing, in order to round out or verify their impressions of a prospective employee. Outside agencies can run a battery of tests on applicants, providing employers with profiles on each of them. A small business can also take advantage of current software or standardized tests to handle at least a portion of these, which can be more labor-intensive. Many companies choose to outsource testing and narrow down the number of applicants, reserving valuable time for personal interviews with candidates deemed most suitable.

PHYSICAL SCREENING OR DRUG TESTS These are often handled by a qualified clinic or laboratory. Prospective employees provide blood or urine samples to the contracted agency. The company is then sent results and can make a determination regarding employment.

Given the tight job market as well as the intimate atmosphere of a small business, it is crucial that companies hire qualified, dependable people. Screening programs can assist in ensuring a proper fit between employer and employee.

FURTHER READING:

Chapman, Elwood N. *Human Relations in Small Business.* Crisp Publications, 1994.

Gruber, Stephanie. "Once Burned." *Inc.* October 15, 1995.

Manley, Marisa. "The Employer's Burden: Avoid Negligent-Hiring Suits by Thoroughly Checking the Backgrounds of Your Job Applicants." *Inc.* September 1989.

Spragins, Ellyn E. "Screening New Hires: Employee-Screening Companies Offer One of the Cheapest and Fastest Ways to Help You Hire Successfully." *Inc.* August 1992.

SEE ALSO: Employee Hiring; Employment Interviewing; Liabilities

EMPLOYEE STOCK OWNERSHIP PLANS

An Employee Stock Ownership Plan, or ESOP, is a qualified retirement program through which employees receive shares of the corporation's stock. Like cash-based retirement plans, ESOPs are subject to eligibility and vesting requirements and provide employees with monetary benefits upon retirement, death, or disability. But unlike other programs, the funds held in ESOPs are invested primarily in employer securities (shares of the employer's stock) rather than in a stock portfolio, mutual fund, or other type of financial instrument.

ESOPs offer several advantages to employers. First and foremost, federal laws accord significant tax breaks to such plans. For example, the company can borrow money through the ESOP for expansion or other purposes, and then repay the loan by making fully tax-deductible contributions to the ESOP (in ordinary loans, only interest payments are tax deductible). In addition, business owners who sell their stake in the company to the ESOP are often able to defer or even avoid capital-gains taxes associated with the sale of the business. In this way, ESOPs have become an important tool in succession planning for business owners preparing for retirement.

A less tangible advantage many employers experience upon establishing an ESOP is an increase in employee loyalty and productivity. In addition to providing an employee benefit in terms of increased compensation, like cash-based profit sharing arrangements do, ESOPs give employees an incentive to improve their performance because they have a tangible stake in the company. "Under an ESOP, you treat employees with the same respect you would accord a partner. Then they start behaving like owners. That's the real magic of an ESOP," explained Don Way, CEO of a California commercial insurance firm, in *Nation's Business.*

In fact, in a 1995 survey of companies that had recently instituted ESOPs quoted in *Nation's Business,* 68 percent of respondents said that their financial numbers had improved, while 60 percent reported increases in employee productivity. Some experts also claim that ESOPs—more so than regular **profit sharing** plans—make it easier for small businesses to recruit, retain, and motivate their employees. "An ESOP creates a vision for every employee and gets everybody pulling in the same direction," said Joe Cabral, CEO of a

California-based producer of computer network support equipment, in *Nation's Business.*

GROWTH OF ESOPS

The first ESOP was created in 1957, but the idea did not attract much attention until 1974, when plan details were laid out in the Employee Retirement Income Security Act (ERISA). The number of businesses sponsoring ESOPs expanded steadily during the 1980s, as changes in the tax code made them more attractive for business owners. Though the popularity of ESOPs declined during the recession of the early 1990s, it has rebounded since then. According to the National Center for Employee Ownership, the number of companies with ESOPs grew from 9,000 in 1990 to 10,000 in 1997, but 60 percent of that increase took place in 1996 alone, causing many observers to predict the beginning of a steep upward trend. The growth stems not only from the strength of the economy, but also from small business owners' recognition that ESOPs can provide them with a competitive advantage in terms of increased loyalty and productivity.

ESOP SPECIFICS

In order to establish an ESOP, a company must have been in business and shown a profit for at least three years. One of the main factors limiting the growth of ESOPs is that they are relatively complicated and require strict reporting, and thus can be quite expensive to establish and administer. According to *Nation's Business,* ESOP set up costs range from $20,000 to $50,000, plus there may be additional fees involved if the company chooses to hire an outside administrator. For closely held corporations—whose stock is not publicly traded and thus does not have a readily discernable market value—federal law requires an independent evaluation of the ESOP each year, which may cost $10,000. On the plus side, many plan costs are tax deductible.

Employers can choose between two main types of ESOPs, loosely known as basic ESOPs and leveraged ESOPs. They differ primarily in the ways in which the ESOP obtains the company's stock. In a basic ESOP, the employer simply contributes securities or cash to the plan each year—like an ordinary profit-sharing plan—so that the ESOP can purchase stock. Such contributions are tax-deductible for the employer to a limit of 15 percent of payroll. In contrast, leveraged ESOPs obtain bank loans to purchase the company's stock. The employer can then use the proceeds of the stock purchase to expand the business, or to fund the business owner's retirement nest egg. The business can repay the loans through contributions to the ESOP that are tax-deductible for the employer to a limit of 25 percent of payroll.

An ESOP can also be a useful tool in facilitating the buying and selling of small businesses. For example, a business owner nearing retirement age can sell his or her stake in the company to the ESOP in order to gain tax advantages and provide for the continuation of the business. Some experts claim that transferring ownership to the employees in this way is preferable to third-party sales, which entail negative tax implications as well as the uncertainty of finding a buyer and collecting installment payments from them. Instead, the ESOP can borrow money to buy out the owner's stake in the company. If, after the stock purchase, the ESOP holds over 30 percent of the company's shares, then the owner can defer capital-gains taxes by investing the proceeds in a Qualified Replacement Property (QRP). QRPs can include stocks, bonds, and certain retirement accounts. The income stream generated by the QRP can help provide the business owner with income during retirement.

ESOPs can also prove helpful to those interested in buying a small business. Many individuals and companies choose to raise capital to finance such a purchase by selling nonvoting stock in the business to its employees. This strategy allows the purchaser to retain the voting shares in order to maintain control of the business. At one time, banks favored this sort of purchase arrangement because they were entitled to deduct 50 percent of the interest payments as long as the ESOP loan was used to purchase a majority stake in the company. However, this tax incentive for banks was eliminated with the passage of the **Small Business Jobs Protection Act**.

In addition to the various advantages that ESOPs can provide to business owners, sellers, and buyers, they also offer several benefits to employees. Like other types of retirement plans, the employer's contributions to an ESOP on behalf of employees are allowed to grow tax-free until the funds are distributed upon an employee's retirement. At the time an employee retires or leaves the company, he or she simply sells the stock back to the company. The proceeds of the stock sale can then be rolled over into another qualified retirement plan, like an Individual Retirement Account (IRA) or a plan sponsored by another employer. Another provision of ESOPs gives participants—upon reaching the age of 55 and putting in at least ten years of service—the option of diversifying their ESOP investment away from company stock and toward more traditional investments.

The financial rewards associated with ESOPs can be particularly impressive for long-term employees who have participated in the growth of a company. Of course, employees encounter some risks with ESOPs, too, since much of their retirement funds are invested in the stock of one small company. In fact, an ESOP may become worthless if the sponsoring company goes bankrupt. But history has shown that this scenario is unlikely to occur: only 1 percent of ESOP firms have gone under financially in last 20 years.

WHO SHOULD ESTABLISH AN ESOP

Although 1996 legislation opened the door for S corporations to establish ESOPs, the plans continue to be much more attractive for C corporations. In general, ESOPs are likely to prove too costly for very small companies, those with high employee turnover, or those that rely heavily on contract workers. ESOPs might also be problematic for businesses that have uncertain cash flow, since companies are contractually obligated to repurchase stock from employees when they retire or leave the company. Finally, ESOPs are most appropriate for companies that are committed to allowing employees to participate in the management of the business. Otherwise, an ESOP might tend to create resentment among employees who become part-owners of the company and then are not treated in accordance with their status.

FURTHER READING:

The Entrepreneur Magazine Small Business Advisor. Wiley, 1995.

Kaufman, Steve. "ESOPs' Appeal on the Increase." *Nation's Business.* June 1997.

Shanney-Saborsky, Regina. "Why It Pays to Use an ESOP in a Business Succession Plan." *The Practical Accountant.* September 1996.

SEE ALSO: Buying an Existing Business; Employee Motivation; Equity Financing; Retirement Planning; Succession Plans

EMPLOYEE STRIKES

An employee strike is an episode wherein a company's **work force** engages in a work stoppage in an effort to elicit changes from its employer in such areas as wages, benefits, job security, and management practices. Strikes are typically engineered by labor unions, whose memberships accounted for approximately 15 percent of all employees in the United States in the mid-1990s (about 10 percent of all private sector employees). Union strikes are usually associated with large companies, but they can be implemented against smaller employers as well. Given the enormous financial stakes of such actions, small business owners need to be prepared in the event that an employee strike is called against them.

TYPES OF STRIKES

The **National Labor Relations Board (NLRB)** provides legal protections for two kinds of strikes, economic strikes and unfair labor practices strikes. The former is a strike that is undertaken by workers in order to garner improvements in their wages, benefits, hours, or working conditions. An unfair labor practices strike is an action that has far more serious legal implications for small business owners. An unfair labor practices strike occurs in instances where the employer violates NLRB rules that protect workers during collective bargaining. "Typical violations that prompt an unfair labor practices strike include refusing to pay benefits when they're due, discharging an employee for engaging in union activities, and refusing to bargain in good faith," reported J. D. Thorne in *Small Business Reports.* "An unfair labor practices strike not only threatens a loss of business, but also requires that you return picketing workers to their jobs when the strike ends. Therefore, you must fire loyal replacement workers who crossed the picket line to work—and helped keep your business afloat." Businesses that do not do so are liable for back pay starting on the date that striking workers made their unconditional offer to return to work.

Given the added risks associated with an unfair labor practices strike, then, Thorne contended that "the most important aspect of managing an economic strike—the most common type—is to prevent it from becoming an unfair labor practices strike." Thorne noted that employer actions that could trigger this transformation include blatant ones, such as discharging an employee for engaging in his or her right to strike or withholding benefits (earned vacation time, pension-plan eligibility, etc.) as well as more subtle ones that nonetheless violate the National Labor Relations Act. The issue of communications with union members, for instance, is rife with rules that can ensnare the unknowing small business owner. These communication rules apply both to the pre-strike and strike periods. Following are specific guidelines that small businesses should adhere to in negotiations:

1) Continue to bargain in good faith throughout the process. "Both sides have a continuing responsibility to engage in good faith collective bargaining," wrote Thorne, "which means that you must meet with the union with the intent of reaching an agreement about the workers' demands." Failure to do so also could convert the nature of a strike.

2) Provide unions with all information to which they are legally entitled. Under U.S. labor law, unions can request information about management's plans regarding various operational aspects of the business during the strike. For example, the union can ask for information about where the business plans to get replacement workers and the wages that they will be paid.

3) Know management rights. Many legal protections are in place to protect workers from unfair management practices, but business owners have rights, too. Thorne noted, for instance, that businesses can discuss and clarify with striking employees how their proposal differs from that of the union leadership, and they can "ask employees to vote to accept your final offer when it's presented for ratification." Many strike situations also give them the option of utilizing replacement workers without penalty. Nonetheless, businesses should be aware that there are many legal "do's and don'ts" associated with management-union interactions during collective bargaining and strike periods, and they should make sure that they have adequate legal representation to assist them in this area.

MANAGING A STRIKE

The beginning of an employee strike is almost always a difficult period for small business owners. The adversarial nature of such actions can be jarring for company leaders who are unfamiliar with strikes, and the walk-out itself can threaten small- and mid-sized business owners with devastating economic consequences (large companies can be hurt by strikes, too, of course, but their very existence is not usually called into question). Given this reality, small business owners and their management teams must take steps to ensure that their companies will be able to continue their operations during the strike. As Brenda Paik Sunoo wrote in *Personnel Journal,* "A strike will inevitably pose challenges in many areas: managing contingent workers; setting up communication between management and all employees; maintaining **customer service**; establishing interim policies regarding benefits, overtime, vacations, and sick leave; and bolstering non-striking employees' morale. Clearly, those that prepare well in advance will suffer the least trauma during and after a labor dispute."

Indeed, business experts universally agree that advance planning is key to managing a strike. They note that few companies can claim that they were caught flat-footed by a work stoppage. Most strikes occur when labor contracts expire, and even those that do not take place on a specific date typically provide management with plenty of warning signs. Businesses that prepare for contract expirations and other potential strike periods by drawing up detailed contingency plans in advance will be much better equipped to weather a strike than will those firms that wait until the last minute. In recognition of this reality, *Risk Management* noted in 1998 that increasing numbers of companies have created management teams—sometimes called strike contingency planning teams (SCPTs)—to address potential strike issues.

Advance preparation efforts should cover a broad spectrum of operational areas. For example, businesses should have a plan in place to put together a contingent work force, whether comprised of replacements, non-striking employees (often supervisory personnel), or a combination of the two. A company that maintains information on recent job applicants, for example, may find itself better positioned to form a contingent work force than a firm that neglects to do so. Contingent work forces will also need training on a variety of issues, from duties to customer relations to legal matters (non-striking personnel already employed by the company may well need this training as well, since they will in many cases be undertaking unfamiliar tasks and interacting with customers and suppliers with whom they may not be familiar). Appropriate training programs should be in place well before a strike, not cobbled together after a strike actually occurs. Employers will also have to prepare interim policies governing various human resource issues for both striking and non-striking workers.

Companies facing strike actions should also make sure that their customers and suppliers are notified at appropriate times of that possibility. If your company suddenly announces to a major customer that your facility has been hit with a strike without providing that customer without any prior warning, you are likely to lose that customer for good, even after the labor dispute has been resolved. "Maintain their good will by keeping them up to date on the strike negotiations and the projected outcome," counseled Thorne. Businesses facing strikes should also make preparations for alternative service to valued clients and customers. This may necessitate arranging shipping alternatives, wrote Thorne, "since unionized employees who work for your regular transportation provider may refuse to cross your workers' picket line."

Another key to successful strike management, say labor experts, is for management to try to understand why the strike took place. Many labor disputes disintegrate into intensely negative clashes, with repercussions that are felt long after the strike itself has been settled. Small business owners should do their best to prevent negotiations from becoming acrimonious. Owners who are capable of empathy with their striking employees will be better able to manage than those who automatically dismiss all work stoppages as solely an outgrowth of union greed.

"With increased downsizings, global competition, deregulation, technological changes, and subcontracting of work, unionized employees are understandably concerned about their futures," wrote Sunoo.

Finally, business owners should plan ahead to make sure that they have adequate security if a strike takes place. ''Strikes, by their very nature, are adversarial,'' stated Sunoo. ''They often are accompanied by disruptions in service and product delivery, and sometimes even violence.'' Savvy businesses will contact local legal and governmental authorities in advance to discuss issues such as picket lines, responses to disturbances, etc. In addition, businesses at risk of being the target of a work stoppage will often need to hire security forces to monitor the premises and protect their contingent work force. The role of security is twofold, said one security expert in an interview with *Personnel Journal:* 1) providing managers and non-striking employees with assurances that they can go to work without being injured, and 2) gathering evidence of any strike-related misconduct on the part of strikers for later use in legal proceedings.

Companies seeking security service have a number of options from which to choose, including their own personnel, local off-duty law enforcement personnel, and local security firms that provide security guards. Experts recommend that companies seeking security help look to firms with previous strike experience and avoid local security firms unless they can get assurances that none of their guards have any meaningful social or familial relationship to any of the strikers.

FURTHER READING:

Gould, William B., IV. *Agenda for Reform: The Future of Employment Relations and the Law.* The MIT Press, 1993.

Lane, Marc J. *Legal Handbook for Small Business.* Rev. ed. New York: AMACOM, 1989.

Mills, Daniel Quinn. *Labor-Management Relations.* 5th ed., New York: McGraw-Hill, 1994.

Sunoo, Brenda Paik. ''Managing Strikes, Minimizing Loss.'' *Personnel Journal.* January 1995.

Taylor, B.J., and F. Witney. *Labor Relations Law.* Englewood-Cliffs, NJ: Prentice-Hall, 1987.

Thorne, J. D. ''Don't Strike Out.'' *Small Business Reports.* June 1994.

''Unions and Strikers: A Huge Nonproblem.'' *Fortune.* May 31, 1993.

Waidelich, Eric. ''Controlling the Strike Zone.'' *Risk Management.* February 1998.

Worsham, James. ''Labor's New Assault.'' *Nation's Business.* June 1997.

SEE ALSO: Labor Unions

EMPLOYEE TERMINATION

Employee termination, or firing, describes the process by which an organization ends an individual's employment against his or her will. Termination may occur due to an employee's poor job performance, lack of ''fit'' with the organization, or gross misconduct, as well as a company's restructuring, **downsizing**, or acquisition (known as a reduction in force). In states that promote ''employment at will,'' employees may be terminated for no reason whatsoever, but the legal risks involved make such dismissals the exception.

It is important for small businesses, perhaps even more so than large ones, to terminate employees when such action is warranted. Small firms cannot afford to keep unproductive employees because of the effect their poor performance can have on the company's results, as well as on the motivation level of more talented workers. ''If you fail to purge chronic poor performers, the best [performers] will either believe that you condone lackluster performance, or assume that you don't know the difference. Being the best, they will only want to associate with the best,'' according to Martin Yate in his book *Keeping the Best.*

When firing is necessary, small businesses must handle the situation properly to avoid numerous possible pitfalls, including a reduction in morale and productivity among remaining employees, a decline in the company's public image, and difficulty in recruiting new employees. ''Do it the right way, and there's no lasting negative effect on the company or the person who is exiting. Do it the wrong way, and the fired employee may have a very difficult time finding a new job and you and your company may end up in court,'' Richard S. Deems explained in his book *How to Fire Your Friends.* There are numerous steps a small business can take to reduce the negative impacts of employee termination.

BACKGROUND

An employment-at-will doctrine emerged in the United States in the mid-nineteenth century and was applied in both state and federal courts throughout the late 1800s and early 1900s. Among the most concise interpretations of the creed was that penned by the California Supreme Court in 1910: ''Precisely as may the employee cease labor at his whim or pleasure, and, whatever be his reason, good, bad, or indifferent, leave no one a legal right to complain; so, upon the other hand, may the employer discharge, and whatever be his reason, good, bad, or indifferent, no one has suffered a legal wrong.''

Although employees retained their employment-at-will rights, employers' rights to terminate workers at their discretion began to erode in the 1930s. The federal Wagner Act of 1935 made it illegal for companies to fire employees because of union activity. Subsequent laws and court decisions during the mid-twentieth century reflected increasing concern about "wrongful discharge," implying that circumstances do exist in which it is legally wrong for a company to fire a worker. During the 1960s and 1970s, particularly, a number of new laws and regulations were enacted to protect workers from wrongful discharge in all types of cases, including those related to bias, whistle blowing, and trait-related factors.

Employment-at-will remained theoretically intact during the 1980s and early 1990s. A company could legally fire an employee without any reason whatsoever, or even for some arbitrary reason that had nothing to do with the worker's performance. Doing so, however, would likely leave the company open to legal action on the grounds of age, disability, race, or sex discrimination (or some other type of discrimination against a legally protected minority), or for defamation of character, breaking an implied contract, or some other infraction that could be construed by the courts as constituting wrongful discharge. As a result, the employee termination process has become more complex and more formalized in most organizations.

BEHAVIOR-RELATED TERMINATIONS

Behavior-related dismissals involve a termination of an employer-worker relationship by the employer as a result of the actions of the employee. Common behaviors that lead to terminations, in rough order of prevalence, include: **absenteeism** and tardiness; unsatisfactory performance; lack of qualifications or ability; changed job requirements; and gross misconduct, which might involve **substance abuse**, stealing, or other breaches of company or public policy. The term "behavior-related" distinguishes this type of termination from trait-related dismissals, which are based on immutable characteristics of the employee, such as color of skin or physical disability. Trait-related terminations may be legal if the employer can prove that the trait keeps the employee from performing a job satisfactorily. However, they are uncommon.

Employers are generally allowed by law to terminate workers based on any type of behavior they deem unacceptable (or, technically, for no reason at all). However, laws and court decisions have protected some types of behavior when the employer's retaliatory action is deemed: 1) a violation of public policy; 2) a violation of an implied contract between the employer and the employee; or 3) an act of bad faith. An act of bad faith is vaguely defined, and is simply a recognition of an employer's duty to treat employees fairly. For example, it might be considered illegal for a company to fire a worker because he refused to engage in an activity that a reasonable person would consider excessively dangerous or hazardous.

One illustration of a public policy violation would be a company that fired a worker because she refused to engage in an unlawful act, such as falsifying public financial documents or giving false testimony in court. Another public policy violation would be the firing of an employee because he exercised a statutory right, such as voting in an election or worshiping at a church. A third type of infraction in this category would be dismissal of an employee for reasons stemming from her exercising a right to perform an important public obligation. Known as "whistle-blower" laws, legislation passed during the late 1900s serves to protect workers who expose corporate wrongdoing for public, not personal, interests. For instance, it would be illegal for a company to fire an employee that alerted authorities to the illegal dumping of toxic wastes.

Violations of implied contracts occur when a company dismisses a worker despite the existence of an insinuated promise. For example, if an employer conveys to a worker that he will receive long-term employment in an effort to get the employee to take a job, it could be liable if it fired the worker without what the courts deem just cause or due process. As another example, one court ruled that an employer had broken an implied contract when it terminated a poorly performing employee after eighteen years of good service because it deprived the worker of pension benefits. Implied contracts often emanate from interviews, policy manuals, or long-term patterns of behavior by the employer in a relationship with an employee.

Even when an employer acts in good faith and does not violate the public trust or an implied contract, it can be legally liable for dismissing a worker for other reasons. Specifically, a business may be found liable if it cannot prove that: 1) its decision to dismiss an employee is not founded on bias against a protected minority; or 2) the firing does not produce inequitable results. Suppose, for instance, that a company decided to fire all managers who did not have a college degree. Doing so, however, resulted in the dismissal of a disproportionate number of legally protected minorities from its work force. The company could be held liable if it could not show that having a college degree was necessary to effectively execute the duties of the position.

STEPS IN A BEHAVIOR-RELATED TERMINATION
Partially because of the legal risks inherent in dismissing employees, most companies terminate workers for behavior-related causes only after administering a progressive disciplinary and counseling process. Besides legal reasons, studies show that most companies try to correct behavior out of a perceived moral obligation to the employee. Furthermore, many employers benefit economically from correcting employee behavior, rather than terminating workers, because of the high costs of employee turnover.

In *How to Fire Your Friends,* Richard S. Deems provides a list of general guidelines designed to help everyone who is involved in a termination. These include:

1) determining the final decision maker;

2) documenting the reasons for termination;

3) scheduling a meeting with the employee to discuss the termination;

4) conducting the meeting in a professional manner;

5) preparing a letter confirming termination and outlining assistance and benefits;

6) enabling the employee to leave without embarrassment;

7) notifying other employees and customers; and

8) developing and following established policies.

The first step involves bringing management's attention to the fact that an employee may need to be terminated. Then the situation should be reviewed in order to slow down the process, examine other options, and plan the termination if it indeed seems necessary. Such reviews might include the employee's direct supervisor, the manager of the employee's work unit, and a human resources manager. At the conclusion of the meeting, a process should be in place through which the final decision will be made.

The second step is important in protecting the company against lawsuits stemming from discrimination. The performance or behavioral problem should be documented in specific, quantifiable terms, and the employee should be informed about the problem and be made to understand the steps necessary to correct it. A memo summarizing the discussion and the timetable for correction should be prepared and signed by the supervisor, the employee, and a witness. Follow-up discussions should be held as needed to chart progress or provide reminders of expectations. If these discussions fail, the supervisor then issues some form of final written warning to the worker. The written warning may include: copies and summaries of previous admonishments; specific behaviors that need to be corrected; a time limit to make corrections; and a formal statement that specifies the actions that will be taken if the worker fails to reform. If the final warning does not produce the desired results, the manager or some other authority officially terminates employment.

The termination should take place during a private, face-to-face meeting between the employee and the decision makers. Ideally, the meeting will take place early in the week to give the employee time to adjust and begin searching for a new job, and to reduce the stress and uncertainty for remaining em-ployees. In addition, the meeting should take place early in the day so that the remaining employees will have ample opportunity to ask questions and air concerns. Finally, managers should be sure that the meeting is not scheduled on the employee's birthday or just before a holiday.

The meeting should be conducted in a professional manner by the person who had direct responsibility for the decision to terminate the employee. It is best to have another manager present to provide an objective viewpoint. The managers should plan what will be said ahead of time, stick to the script, avoid arguing or making small talk, and make it clear that the decision is final. It is important for the manager to have some understanding of the range of emotions that an employee might go through upon learning of the termination—including fear, frustration, shock, anger, denial, self-doubt, depression, and acceptance—and be prepared to deal with them.

At the end of the meeting, the employee should be presented with a memo confirming the termination and outlining the benefits to which he or she is entitled. Depending on laws and company policies, the company may provide severance pay, unemployment compensation, career and placement counseling, ongoing health insurance, or other post-termination benefits. Then the employee should be allowed to leave the premises without embarrassment. Rather than asking the employee to pack up their possessions and be escorted from the building, Deems recommends allowing an unobtrusive exit and scheduling a later time for retrieval of personal belongings. This strategy reduces the disruption for remaining employees and lessens the employee's anger toward the company. The final step in the termination process involves notifying other employees and clients with a simple announcement.

To make the entire process easier for everyone involved, Deems recommends developing policies and procedures relating to terminations. The company's policies should be in formal, written form and readily accessible to employees in an employee handbook. The termination guidelines should include definitions of poor performance and gross misconduct, detailed descriptions of the review procedures that may lead to termination, and policies regarding severance, future employment references, and the return of company property.

REDUCTIONS IN FORCE (RIF)

Reductions in force (RIF)—also known as work force reductions, downsizing, right-sizing, restructuring, and reorganization—may include a number of methods of eliminating worker hours, including **layoffs**. Employee terminations in such cases are usually the result of surplus labor caused by economic factors, changing markets, poor management, or some other factor unrelated to worker behavior. Because work force reductions make a company vulnerable to many of the same legal risks inherent in behavior-related terminations, companies usually terminate workers by means of a carefully planned and documented process. The process is typically conducted in two stages: 1) selecting the workers to be dismissed and then terminating them according to the above process; and 2) providing benefits to ease the transition, including severance packages, unemployment compensation, and outplacement services.

Selecting and terminating employees is handled carefully because most profit-maximizing organizations are obviously concerned about losing talent or diluting the effectiveness of the company. But care must also be taken to ensure that the reductions do not violate state and federal laws. As with behavior-related terminations, downsizing terminations cannot be based on bias against protected minorities, or even unintentionally result in an inequitable outcome for a protected group. In fact, extensive legislation exists to protect disabled workers, racial minorities, workers over the age of forty, women, and other groups.

In addition to bias-related laws, moreover, companies must comply with a battery of laws specifically directed at corporate layoffs. For example, the federal Worker Adjustment and Retraining Notification (WARN) Act of 1988 requires companies with 100 or more employees to file at least sixty days prior notice before conducting mass layoffs or work force reductions. Among other stipulations, the notice must be in writing and addressed to employees and specified government workers.

The second stage of the downsizing process, outplacement, is also heavily influenced by legislation aimed at protecting employees. But it is also used to maintain the morale of the work force and to enhance the public image of the company conducting the work force reduction. Outplacement usually includes two activities: counseling and job search assistance. Counseling occurs on both the individual and group levels. Both are necessary to help the displaced worker 1) develop a positive attitude; 2) correctly assess career potential and direction, including background and skills, personality traits, financial requirements, geographic constraints, and aspirations; 3) develop job search skills, such as resume writing, interviewing, networking, and negotiating; and 4) adjust to life in transition or with a new employer.

Many companies assist with the job search by hiring a job-search firm to help their fired employees find new work. In addition to providing some or all of the counseling services described above, job-search companies act as brokers, bringing together job hunters and companies looking for employees. Job-search companies can expedite the job hunting process by eliminating mismatches from the interview process and by helping both parties to negotiate employment terms. In some cases, the former employer will reimburse job hunting costs as part of the severance package of benefits.

FURTHER READING:

Coulson, Robert. *The Termination Handbook.* Macmillan, 1981.

Deems, Richard S. *How to Fire Your Friends: A Win-Win Approach to Effective Termination.* Kansas City, MO: Media Publishing, 1989.

Fischer, Judith. "Firing with Confidence." *Management World.* December 1988.

Frierson, James G. "How to Fire without Getting Burned." *Personnel.* September 1990.

Macklin, Phyllis, and Lester Minsuk. "Ten Ways to Ease Dismissal Dread." *HR Magazine.* November 1991.

Michal-Johnson, Paula. *Saying Good-bye: A Manager's Guide to Employee Dismissal.* Glenview, IL: Scott Foresman, 1985.

Morin, William J., and Lyle Yorks. "Good News about Firing: It Can Benefit Everyone." *Success.* June 1990.

Spragins, Ellyn E. "How to Fire." *Inc.* May 1992.

Yate, Martin. *Keeping the Best: And Other Thoughts on Building a Super Competitive Workforce.* Adams, 1991.

SEE ALSO: Constructive Discharge; Employee Manuals; Human Resource Policies

EMPLOYEE THEFT

Employee theft is a problem of considerable size for many companies. Many corporate security experts estimate that 25 to 40 percent of all employees steal from their employers, and the U.S. Department of Commerce (DOC) estimates that employee theft of cash, property, and merchandise may cost American businesses as much as $50 billion on an annual basis. Small business owners are not immune to this scourge; indeed, many analysts believe that internal theft of money or goods from employees is a primary cause of a significant percentage of small business failures. In the early 1990s, the DOC estimated that employee theft and embezzlement activities accounted for one out of five business failures, many of which were smaller firms that were unable to weather the erosion that those activities brought to their bottom lines.

Security experts also contend that small business enterprises may be particularly vulnerable to internal theft because of a set of assumptions that their owners—who are often less experienced businesspeople than their big-company brethren—have about: 1) the nature of their relationship with employees, and 2) their ability to effectively combat employee theft.

Business consultants point out that owners of small firms that have 50 or fewer employees may well view the work force as a ''family'' of sorts that operates in a more personable, friendly atmosphere than those that proliferate in the office corridors of multinational companies. Owners of such businesses may place too much faith on this ''first-name-basis'' atmosphere as an effective deterrent against internal theft. Moreover, business consultants point out people can have widely divergent views of the basic character qualities of the same company culture. For example, one employee may wholeheartedly agree with the owner that the company environment is friendly and open, while a fellow co-worker may feel that owner-employee relations are characterized by condescension and meaningless gestures. Indeed, many employees who steal rationalize their illegal behavior away with aspersions on their employers. ''Stealing may be considered by many to be unofficial compensation—and a justifiable payback for what is assumed to be employer greed,'' wrote Bob Ingram in *Supermarket News*. Finally, owners are sometimes too willing to rely on self-policing among employees when it comes to internal theft. Workers who do not steal from their employers may not approve of the actions of those that do, but studies indicate that in most cases, they will not report such thefts either, since their light-fingered colleagues are also, in many instances, members of their family or social circle.

Some small business owners, meanwhile, adopt a remarkably fatalistic attitude toward employee theft. Everyone agrees that employee theft is difficult to detect, but security experts contend that much of it can be curtailed if the employer makes deterrence of such theft a business goal. ''Some companies view employee theft as something that can't be controlled,'' wrote Joan Delaney in *Small Business Reports*. ''[but] this attitude only leads to ever-increasing losses that can seriously drain profits. Minimizing theft should receive the same attention you devote to cutting costs, improving operating efficiencies, and optimizing earnings. Deterrents include pre-employment screening techniques and strong internal controls.''

Many analysts believe that a more proactive approach to employee theft could be detected among business owners in the mid-1990s. Indeed, some studies indicate that both small and large businesses are increasingly cognizant of their need to put anti-theft strategies and programs in place, even if employee theft is not currently regarded as a serious problem. As Ingram observed in *Supermarket Business,* ''with bottom line enhancement objectives touching virtually every aspect of store operation, indications are more companies will invest accordingly [in anti-theft programs and equipment]—replacing embarrassment over internal theft problems with determination to solve them and recover lost profits.''

FORMS OF EMPLOYEE THEFT

Employee theft can take many forms. Some of these may involve the swiping of items of relatively small face value—a couple of candy bars, for example, or a box of ballpoint pens—but experts warn small business owners that thefts of individually inexpensive items such as office supplies or small retail items can add up to significant sums over time, and security consultants add that such thefts can help erode employee performance and loyalty in other areas. Other kinds of employee theft, meanwhile, can form a far more immediate threat to a company's financial well-being. Embezzlement, for instance, can devastate small businesses, wrecking owners' personal and business finances at the same time. Other specific examples of employee theft include the following:

- Forgery of company checks for personal gain.

- Using a ''ghost payroll,'' which occurs when one or more employees create ''phantom'' employees, submit time cards for those employees, and then cash their paychecks themselves.

- Theft of raw materials or inventory items.

- Outright theft of cash from a register drawer.

- ''Sweethearting.'' This term refers to an unethical practice wherein an employee will grant a friend or other person a discount at the register when they pay, undercharge them, or ring up fewer items than the person has actually bought.

- Theft of information. As countless feature stories in various media have attested, internal theft of information has become an increasingly serious problem for employers, especially since huge amounts of meaningful information are commonly stored in computer files. In fact, security consultants point out that employees often are more computer literate than their bosses, which may strengthen the temptation to abscond with proprietary information or otherwise engage in illicit activities.

SIGNS OF EMPLOYEE THEFT Small business owners should be aware of several common warning signs of employee theft, and of the types of employee that are most likely to steal from their employers. According to Delaney, common tangible signs that an employee may be stealing include missing records (such as shipping and receiving bills), company checks that bounce, customer complaints about missing or late deliveries, hefty payments made for ''miscellaneous'' purposes in employee expense claims, and managers who insist on performing clerical duties. But as Gary

Ward noted in *Developing and Enforcing a Code of Business Ethics,* employers may also be tipped off by behavioral signs, such as maintaining a lifestyle beyond his or her apparent means, acting differently with co-workers and managers, signs of alcohol or drug abuse, changes in emotional behavior, and physical ailments (such as digestive ailments or headaches). "If an employee shows several of these signs," stated *Profit-Building Strategies for Business Owners,* "talk to him or her. It may well be a problem . . . that has nothing to do with your business." On the other hand, if the employee is engaging in larcenous behavior, the meeting may well convince them that they are not being as successful with their activities as they had hoped. This cold realization is often sufficient to put an end to further incidents of theft on their part.

Studies also indicate that certain types of employees are more likely to steal than others. Perhaps the single biggest factor here is whether or not the employee has a problem with drug abuse. "Many drug users hold legitimate jobs and a substantial number either deal or steal," wrote Delaney. Some studies also show that employees who plan on quitting their jobs are much more likely to engage in stealing than are those who have no plans to leave. Other characteristics of employees who steal include the following: they are more likely to harbor complaints—whether legitimate or illegitimate—about their employer; they believe that their co-workers accept, or at least do not actively oppose, employee theft; and they believe that it is relatively easy to steal from their employer without getting caught.

STOPPING EMPLOYEE THEFT

Since employee theft is both commonplace and costly, small business owners can take several steps to curb it. Some of these steps are inexpensive and easy to impose, while others require greater investments of time and money. All should be weighed by entrepreneurs interested in shoring up their internal security systems.

1) Ensure that appropriate business ethics are practiced at the top levels of the company. Business owners and supervisors are role models for their employees, and if they want their work force to behave honestly, they will have to do so in both their internal and external dealings. "Despite the widespread existence of official corporate ethics policies," the impression that management will bend certain rules or look the other way in the name of expediency has an undeniable trickle-down effect," wrote Ingram.

2) Establish a clear policy on theft and security and distribute it to all employees. This policy should make it clear that the company has a zero-tolerance policy on theft and that any employee—including executives and managers—who violates it will be terminated. In addition, many consultants believe that written policy statements on drug and alcohol use can be effective in curbing internal theft, since abuse of those substances is a leading cause of employee stealing.

3) Hiring policies should be shored up to better ensure that honest employees are brought on board. Employers should ask prospective workers to submit to an honesty test, in which they are asked about past behaviors and responses to hypothetical questions. "When job applicants are asked directly about theft and drug use, they tend to admit to such behavior both on and off the job," confirmed one researcher in an interview with *Small Business Reports.* But while a surprising percentage of applicants will admit to dishonest behavior on such tests, others will lie. This reality makes it very important for small business owners to conduct thorough checks on the references of prospective new hires as well as checks on their educational credentials and criminal history. The latter can be conducted through public court records.

4) Examine and update financial controls. "The more financial controls you implement and enforce, the less opportunity for theft errant employees will have," stated Delaney. Indeed, there are many steps that businesses can take in this realm, including:

- Keep checkbooks locked up, restricting access to cash and checks to authorized employees.

- Limit the number of people with authority to write checks, etc.

- Segregate financial responsibilities among several people.

- Control cash flow and have good documentation on where money is spent.

- Audit internal financial documents frequently using independent auditors.

- Make regular deposits of cash in banks rather than allowing them to pile up in cash registers.

- Check all invoices to make sure they match what was delivered and to ensure that vendors were paid.

5) Offer financial support. Some business experts contend that employers can prevent some forms of employee theft by establish-

ing a policy in which financially troubled employees can get financial counseling or short-term loans. Small business owners should consult with legal and accounting professionals before launching any such sort of program like this, however.

6) Maintain uniform policies. Employers who do not treat everyone the same are far more likely to encounter incidents of theft than will those businesses that are consistent in their application of rules and guidelines. Delaney noted that this can be particularly problematic for business owners who have spouses, children, or other relations on their payroll: ''Take expense accounts. The owner's son may be allowed to wine and dine clients on an unlimited expense account, while a non-related employee is limited to one client lunch a week. Such unfair treatment can fan resentment among employees who may then retaliate by stealing.''

7) Consider fidelity bonds. Under this type of insurance coverage, employers can insure one employee or a group of employees. ''Then, if an employee steals merchandise or money and you have the evidence to prove it, the insurance company has to cover the loss and assume responsibility for recovering the goods from the employee,'' wrote Delaney.

8) Act decisively when confronted with employee theft. Dishonest workers should not be tolerated, and if a business obtains proof that an employee has stolen from the company he or she should be immediately dismissed. This not only removes a drain on financial resources, but also sends a message to the rest of the work force. Legal experts note that while most employees that are confronted with evidence of unethical behavior will leave without a big fuss, they should still be asked to sign a statement releasing the employer from all liability. This document will provide the employer with legal protection should the fired worker subsequently decide to pursue a lawsuit for wrongful termination.

FURTHER READING:

Bliss, Edwin C., with Isamu S. Aoki. *Are Your Employees Robbing You Blind?* Pfeiffer and Co. 1993.

Coates, Joseph F. ''Emerging HR Issues for the Twenty-First Century.'' *Employment Relations Today.* Winter 1997.

Delaney, Joan. ''Handcuffing Employee Theft.'' *Small Business Reports.* July 1993.

Greiner, Lynn. ''Small Business: Managing Your System.'' *CMA - The Management Accounting Magazine.* September 1996.

''Hints that an Employee may be Stealing from You.'' *Profit-Building Strategies for Business Owners.* May 1992.

Ingram, Bob. ''Honesty: Just a Policy?'' *Supermarket Business.* April 1994.

Kinni, Theodore B. ''Lock the Door Before the Horse is Stolen.'' *Industry Week.* May 4, 1992.

Poling, Travis E. ''A Thief Among Us: Employee Sabotage and Theft Leave Businesses Holding Hefty Tab.'' *San Antonio Business Journal.* January 2, 1993.

Schierhorn, Carolyn. ''A Breach of Trust.'' *Building Supply Home Centers.* March 1992.

Snyder, Neil H., O. Whitfield Broome, and Karen Zimmerman. ''Using Internal Controls to Reduce Employee Theft in Small Businesses.'' *Journal of Small Business Management.* July 1989.

Ward, Gary. *Developing and Enforcing a Code of Business Ethics.* Pilot Industries, 1992.

''Ways to Control Employee Theft.'' *The Business Owner.* September-October 1997.

SEE ALSO: Computer Crime; Drug Testing; Employee Screening; Employee Termination; Facility Management; Office Security

EMPLOYER IDENTIFICATION NUMBER

A federal employer identification number (EIN), also sometimes referred to as a tax identification number, is a nine-digit code that businesses use to identify themselves for tax reporting, banking, and other purposes. **Sole proprietorships** without employees are allowed to use the owner's Social Security number for tax reporting purposes. But any company that has employees other than the owner—in addition to all **partnerships**, **limited liability companies**, and corporations—must instead apply for and use an EIN. The EIN is specific to a certain business, like a Social Security number is specific to a certain person. Therefore, if an individual or group owns more than one business, a separate EIN is required for each one.

There are several situations in which a business person should apply for an EIN. For example, an EIN may be needed in order to start a new business (other than a sole proprietorship with no employees) or upon the purchase of an ongoing business. An EIN is also needed when a business undergoes a change in its organization type (i.e., from a sole proprietorship to partnership or corporation) or when it hires employees for the first time. Some businesses may require an EIN in order to create a **pension plan** or form a trust. Still others find that they must have an EIN for banking purposes (many banks hold commercial accounts under EINs and personal accounts under Social Security numbers).

Businesses are required to file for an EIN as soon as it is needed for one of the above-mentioned reasons. In order to be assigned an EIN, the company must file Form SS-4, the Application for Employer Identification Number, with the **Internal Revenue Service (IRS)**. The forms are available at all IRS and Social Security offices, or they can be downloaded from the IRS site on the Internet or ordered by telephone at 800-829-1040. No application fee applies, but the form can take several weeks to process. If any business tax forms are due in the meantime, the small business owner should simply write "applied for" in the space for the company's EIN. In addition to the federal EIN, states that charge their own income tax often require businesses to file for a state EIN.

FURTHER READING:

Dailey, Frederick W. *Tax Savvy for Small Business: Year-Round Tax Advice for Small Businesses.* Berkeley, CA: Nolo Press, 1997.

The Entrepreneur Magazine Small Business Advisor. New York: Wiley, 1995.

EMPLOYING MINORS

Businesses in some industries rarely utilize minors as employees, but in many other industries, teenagers comprise a large component of the total work force; indeed, some businesses engaged in retail and food service sectors rely on minors to a considerable degree. The primary advantage associated with employing minors is that compensation is far less costly than if the employer decided to hire adults as staff. But employers should be aware of the various legal restrictions that state and federal agencies have placed on the employment of minors, as well as the particular challenges and rewards that often accompany the decision to hire teenagers.

LEGAL CONSIDERATIONS

In addition to state laws, which have rules regarding child labor and compulsory school attendance, employers should be familiar with the federal government's Fair Labor Standards Act (FLSA). The rules in the FLSA differ from individual states in some respects; in cases where differences exist, the stricter law prevails.

Ignorance of state and federal child labor laws will not save employers from fines, some of which can be quite substantial. "Many companies have discovered that there are two sides to the child labor issue,"

wrote Steven Slutsky in *Journal of Business Strategy.* "On the one hand, minors can be a cost-effective and flexible supplement to your core work force. But on the other hand, the penalties for violating the child labor laws can be steep." Indeed, the U.S. Department of Labor (DOL) imposes fines of up to $10,000 per minor on those businesses that violate the child labor provisions detailed in the FLSA, and in the mid-1990s the DOL upped the stakes for employers who flout or remain ignorant of American child labor law by adding fines of $10,000 per *infraction*—not per minor—and eliminating the cap on the total amount of fines that could be imposed. These latter measures were taken for the purpose of punishing employers whose violations contributed to the death or significant injury of a minor.

Slutsky admitted that the likelihood of an employer being singled out by the U.S. Department of Labor for a random compliance audit is remote unless the company is active in a high-risk industry. "But don't assume that the DOL won't find out about child labor law violations," he warned. "Word usually gets back to the agency in the form of complaints from underage employees or their parents or even unions. The publicity factor is involved here as well, since violations that result in injuries or death often are picked up by the media."

Small business owners, then, should make sure that they their supervisory personnel are fully aware of what minor employees are permitted to do. First, it is important to recognize that employees can basically be broken down into three age groups: workers who are 18 years old or older, and thus regarded as adults in the eyes of the law; youngsters who are 16 or 17 years old; and minors who are 14 or 15 years old (employment of children under the age of 14 is severely restricted, although parents who employ their children enjoy greater leeway).

RESTRICTIONS ON MINORS UNDER AGE 18 According to the Department of Labor, minors under the age of 18 are not allowed to perform jobs that the department has classified as detrimental to their physical safety, mental safety, and health. As the *Journal of Business Strategy* noted, minors are not permitted to operate, set up, repair, adjust, or clean any power-driven machines, including woodworking machinery, metal forming machines, punching and shearing machines, paper products machines, circular and band saws, bakery machines, meat-processing equipment, or hoisting apparatus (forklifts, cranes, derricks, and freight elevators). In addition, minors are prohibited from engaging in the following activities at their place of employment:

- Operating motor vehicles or assisting as outside help on those vehicles.

- Working in any capacity on roofing, wrecking, or demolition jobs.

- Working in mining operations, unless in office, maintenance, or repair capacities away from the mine site.

- Working in areas where explosives (such as fireworks, dynamite, and ammunition) are manufactured or stored.

- Working in logging or sawmilling operations.

- Assisting in the manufacture of brick, tile, and kindred products.

- Working at tasks that require exposure to radioactive substances.

- Undertaking excavation work (exceptions are made for manual excavation in trenches and building excavations, provided the dig does not exceed four feet in depth).

It should be noted that exceptions to some of these rules may be made for minors who are participating in recognized **apprenticeship programs**. On a practical basis, however, these restrictions mean that minors are of limited use in non-office settings to businesses engaged in construction and manufacturing. But as many human resource consultants point out, manufacturers and construction firms maintain staff devoted to clerical work and custodial duties. Moreover, the above restrictions generally have little impact on businesses looking for cashiers, salespersons, stocking personnel, and other positions that do not require handling of motor-driven equipment.

RESTRICTIONS ON MINORS AGED 14 AND 15
Additional restrictions have been put in place by both federal and state agencies concerning the employment of 14- and 15-year-old minors. "This is where it gets tricky," cautioned Slutsky, "since the environment in which 14-year-olds and 15-year-olds do their work also plays an important role in determining whether the duties are permissible. For example, although workers in this age group may clean, wrap, seal, label, weigh, price, and stock produce, they can't perform these tasks in a freezer. And while they may assemble, pack, and shelve merchandise—as can 16-year-olds and 17-year-olds—they can't do it in a warehouse or rooms where manufacturing and processing work takes place." Moreover, owners of construction and transportation companies should be aware that minors under age 16 may not perform any kind of work (including office work) on the construction site or transportation medium. Other environments in which 14- and 15-year-olds are restricted from working include boiler/engine rooms, meat coolers, and places where products are being loaded or unloaded from conveyors or railroad cars.

In addition, 14- and 15-year-old teens are not allowed to work before 7:00 a.m. and after 7:00 pm during the school year. They also are not permitted to work during school hours. Finally, these minors may only work certain numbers of hours. When school is in session, 14- and 15-year-old minors may work no more than three hours a day on school days, no more than 18 hours total a week, no more than eight hours a day on non-school days, and no more than 40 hours total during weeks in which school is not in session (during summer and vacation breaks).

EFFECTIVE EMPLOYMENT OF MINORS

Small business owners and employment analysts agree that the key to securing skilled and motivated minors as employees lies at the very beginning, with the application and interview. In order to find top-notch minor employees, small business owners are encouraged to pay close attention to the information provided in the job application form. Are the students high academic achievers in high school? Do they participate in extracurricular activities? Do they provide good references, such as former employers or school teachers/administrators?

Employers who hire minors also need to recognize that, as Bess Ritter May said in *Supervision,* "adolescence is a transitional period. Those who are in this age group are forming their personalities and identities." This sometimes awkward period of development will likely manifest itself in all phases of the teen's life—including work. But while employers may experience some frustration dealing with teens who are buffeted by school, societal, and peer pressures, they can take comfort in the fact "that it's easy to train these kids since they have little or no prior work experience and have consequently acquired little or no work-related bad habits," said May. "Most intelligent youngsters can also be instructed quickly concerning specific business systems and procedures, pick up and remember new things easily and have few or no preconceived ideas concerning how specific workplace tasks should be handled. Such aptitudes have surprised and astonished many supervisors." Observers also note that younger people often have considerable aptitude for office work that is done on computers, since a much greater emphasis is placed on that area in today's school environment.

Minor employees may require closer supervision than other employees. Often, they are unfamiliar with various facets of the workplace, and they may be so intimidated that they will be reluctant to ask questions about issues or tasks that they do not fully understand. Employers should anticipate this and 1) fully explain projects and tasks, and 2) maintain an office environment that is clearly receptive to their questions. In addition, May counsels employers to "communicate with the young people you hire in clear, caring, constructive and respectful ways in order to build a positive working relationship with them. . . . Emphasize the positive.'' This includes communication that may be necessary to correct errors. Adopting a tactful, reasonable, but firm approach in such instances is important, wrote May, because ''adolescents who are starting out on their first or second jobs are often more sensitive to corrections concerning their work by those who are older and (presumably) wiser. Such youngsters do not always understand that it is only their skills that are being faulted and not their innate characters and consequently are often very defensive.''

Small business owners who employ minors should also consider giving their top workers opportunities to show their abilities. Young employees are fully capable of contributing to your business's success in ways other than filing paperwork or sweeping floors. As one supervisor told May, ''It's an investment in your company's future since such youngsters often become its longest term employees.''

Finally, employers should at all times remain cognizant of the importance of adhering to state and federal laws. ''Conduct periodic check-ups of your compliance with child labor law,'' Slutsky counseled business owners. ''Be sure to keep your managers up to date on the child labor issue. Make sure they are not hiring new employees without obtaining proper age documentation, and then key them into which employers are minors and what type of job duties they may perform. After all, it won't do your company much good if you are well-versed in the laws, but the managers who directly oversee workers are unaware of the requirements.'' In addition, small business experts recommend that owners or managers establish a regular practice of reviewing underage employees' schedules to catch violations before they occur.

FURTHER READING:

Bartram, Dave, Patricia A. Lindley, Linda Marshall, and Julie Foster. ''The Recruitment and Selection of Young People by Small Businesses.'' *Journal of Occupational and Organizational Psychology.* December 1995.

Grossman, Robert J. ''Summer Jobs Mold Tomorrow's Workforce.'' *HRMagazine.* April 1997.

May, Beth Ritter. ''Youthful Problems—Adult Solutions.'' *Supervision.* September 1993.

Sanders, Lisa. ''Revenge of the Nerds.'' *Business Week.* June 16, 1997.

Slutsky, Steven H. ''No Minor Asset.'' *Journal of Business Strategy.* May-June 1995.

Williams, Nicolas. ''Regional Effects of the Minimum Wage on Teenage Employment.'' *Applied Economics.* December 1993.

SEE ALSO: Employee Hiring; Employment Interviewing

EMPLOYMENT APPLICATIONS

Most businesses consider the employment application to be an important part of the hiring process, for it provides employers with clear and relevant information about applicants. An application is also a legal document and it becomes a part of a person's permanent file once they are hired. For this reason, the employment application must be thoroughly and carefully reviewed before it is used.

APPLICATION CONTENTS Applications contain questions designed to help the employer make a hiring decision. In essence, they reorganize the information the employer typically finds on a resume while also furnishing additional information that can be helpful in making hiring decisions. Application contents typically include the following:

- Name, address, phone number, and other relevant contact information.

- Position the applicant is seeking within the company.

- Hours of availability.

- Expected salary.

- Past experience—This will make up the majority of the application form, for it is common for companies to request a listing of all positions that an applicant has held over the past three to five years. This section may include a request for supervisor names and reasons for leaving previous positions.

- Educational background—This typically includes schools attended, years attended and degrees attained.

- Other information—This might include questions about the applicant's experience with computer software programs and other office equipment, or it might ask the person to describe hobbies and other interests. This section of the application can be a tricky one for employers, as some questions may violate legal parameters. A good rule of thumb for small business owners weighing whether to include questions of this type is to always make sure that the responses could be pertinent to making a hiring decision.

- Closing statement—The statement at the end of an application usually includes legally worded information for the applicant about the application, including permissible uses of the information contained therein. The employer should mention that they are an equal opportunity employer on the document, and legal experts recommend that employment applications include a statement regarding the right of the hiring company to check references and verify information on the application. The employer should state clearly that falsifying any information on an application can be considered grounds for dismissal.

• Signature of applicant.

Because there are many other types of information that a company may want to ask on its application, depending on the business which is designing the form, it is always advisable to have legal counsel review the form before using it for applicants.

POTENTIAL PITFALLS There are several possible pitfalls in designing an application form. On an application form, it is not permissible to ask the following types of questions:

• Questions about the applicant's age, race, sex, religion, national origin, physical characteristics, or other personal information that violates **Equal Employment Opportunity Commission** (EEOC) guidelines.

• Questions about the applicant's health history or handicaps (if any) that violate the **Americans with Disabilities Act** (ADA).

• Questions that violating any state regulations (individual states may have regulations concerning employer rights to inquire about past salary history, referral sources, credit, access to transportation, or personal emergency information.) It is important to check for state guidelines in employment applications before putting together a business application.

USING THE APPLICATION The application should be given to every person applying for a position from outside the company. It should be required regardless of level of position, so that all potential employees have a similar experience and receive similar treatment. Normally, a separate, abbreviated application form is used for people who are already employed by the company who wish to apply for positions elsewhere within the company.

Some laws require employers to retain applications—whether the person is hired or not—for up to one year after the date the application is made. The employer is not usually required to reconsider the applications on file as new positions become available, but they must have record of the applications made to the company. Applications become a part of the permanent record of the employee once hired. For some companies, the Human Resource Information System (HRIS) can make storage of numerous appli-

cations and employee files more efficient by holding employee records in electronic files. There are also software packages which allow a user to fill out a form electronically, allowing the form to be printed as needed. If storage space is a concern in the small office, it might be worthwhile to look into electronic versions of the employment application.

The well designed employment application is an aid in hiring the right people for the right position. Care should always be taken, however, to ask questions that are within the legal boundaries of the company and that respect the rights of the applicant. For this reason, all applications should be reviewed by legal counsel before they are used.

FURTHER READING:

Bittel, Lester, and John Newstrom. *What Every Supervisor Should Know,* 6th ed. New York: McGraw Hill, 1990.

Frierson, James G., and James P. Jolly. ''Developing a Safe Job Application Form.'' *Employment Relations Today.* Winter 1988/1989.

Frierson, James G., and James P. Jolly. ''Problems in Employment Application Forms (Part 1).'' *Employment Relations Today.* Autumn 1988.

Mandell, Mel. ''Software Fights Corporate Form Flood.'' *Computerworld.* June 15, 1992.

Meisinger, Susan. ''Putting the ADA to Work.'' *Association Management.* July 1992.

Schmitt, Diane Festino. ''The HR Files.'' *Credit Union Management.* February 1996.

SEE ALSO: Employee Hiring; Human Resource Policies

EMPLOYMENT INTERVIEWING

Interviewing is an integral part of the hiring process. It provides small business owners with their primary opportunity to learn about a candidate's work experience, education, and interpersonal abilities, as well as characteristics—such as enthusiasm—that are rarely conveyed in **resumes**; similarly, the interview process often provides would-be employees with their best opportunity to inquire about various aspects of company operations and expectations.

BEFORE THE INTERVIEW

Before beginning the interview, the manager must define the skills needed to fill the position. This, along with careful applicant research and candidate selection, helps to ensure a smooth interview process.

CRITICAL SKILLS To secure the right person for a job, the manager must define the necessary skills for the job, often called the critical skills. These describe exactly the skills a person needs to successfully perform the tasks. Sample critical skills could be phrased as "facility with communication," "high degree of organization," or "ability to work well independently." Critical skills are expanded upon in the **job description** and help guide the manager during the selection process and then provide structure for the position throughout employment.

APPLICANT RESEARCH Applicants must be researched before the interview. The most common methods of receiving candidate information are the resume and cover letter, generated by the applicant, or the **employment application**, generated by the company. Though they describe much about a person, these vehicles cannot describe everything. It is important to know what to look for when reading resumes, cover letters, and applications.

A manager should watch for such problems as typographical errors, spelling errors, or incomplete information about the applicant. Likewise, pay attention to the length of time an applicant has spent at a position, the responsibilities they were given in successive positions, and the chronological information on the resume. Frequent job changes, declining responsibility, or gaps in employment are all items that should be pursued for clarification. None of these call for immediate rejection of a candidate, but any could signal a potential area of exploration.

SELECTING CANDIDATES Not all people who apply will be qualified for the position. The manager selects candidates for the position from the entire group of applicants, choosing individuals who demonstrate the best skills for the open position in their written presentation.

When putting together an interview schedule, a manager needs to balance the desire to interview all qualified people with the practical necessity of concluding the search in a timely fashion. Consider the time frame for the hiring decision, the amount of time available to interview, and select candidates carefully. A good rule of thumb is to allow from thirty to sixty minutes per interview; then add fifteen minutes in between interviews, to prevent back-to-back interviews. Small business consultants caution that a day of back-to-back interviews can exhaust the interviewer, and ultimately hinder his or her ability to make a well-reasoned decision.

THE INTERVIEW

Time well spent in the interviewing process can prevent a poor hiring decision. Preparation is the key to a successful interview. Don't scrimp on time during the interview, and be sure to let the candidate do the majority of the talking. The space for the interview should be ready, and the interviewer should have already prepared questions for the discussion.

ENVIRONMENT The interviewer can make the candidate feel at ease or an interviewer can make the candidate uncomfortable. In short, the interviewer sets the tone for the meeting. To insure a successful interview, be sure that the space is free of distractions and interruptions such as telephones or other employees; allow for minimal barriers between you and the candidate (desks or tables); and always offer the candidate coffee, soda, or water. Be courteous and professional without presenting an environment which is too formal.

BEHAVIORAL INTERVIEWING Though there are many kinds of interviewing techniques, behavioral interviewing allows the interviewer to focus on future performance based in large part on past behavior. This is one of the most popular interviewing techniques, and it is effective precisely because it focuses on specific situations and examples, not hypothetical situations. It requires that candidates draw on past experience to describe what they actually did in specific work situations, and this discourages "made up" answers or hypothetical exaggerations.

TYPES OF QUESTIONS Interview questions are designed to explore the candidate's previous work experience, education, and other areas which will enable the interviewer to determine if the candidate has the best match of critical skills for the position. There are many types of questions.

The biggest mistake interviewers make is to ask only factual questions during an interview. Often, an interviewer asks "closed ended questions" which illicit a yes or no or other single response answer. "When did you join the company?" or "How long were you in the position?" are closed ended questions which limit the candidate's response options because they do not require the candidate to consider or analyze any specific problem or situation.

Open ended questions allow the candidate to expand on a topic, describing experiences and actual situations. They keep the candidate talking and the interviewer listening. The focus of open ended questions is always on past performance, using wording such as "Give me an example of ...," "Tell me about a time when you ...." Such questions are the basis of behavioral interviewing and focus on specific examples of past behavior—how a candidate performed in a specific circumstance.

Probing questions are used to uncover more information than the original answer given. If a candidate answers with "yes / no" or a very general response, the interviewer can probe by encouraging the candidate to elaborate on a point within the answer. Ask very specific questions when probing. Specific questions encourage a candidate to expand on a general answer.

Avoid leading questions which direct the candidate to a specific answer and do not encourage an honest, spontaneous response. If leading, the interviewer may nod or to encourage a particular response, or may stack two or more questions which are guaranteed to produce a desired answer. This biases the interviewer to the candidate who responds most easily with the correct answer.

CLOSING THE INTERVIEW When closing the interview, first offer to answer any questions the candidate may have. Have basic factual information about the company and position readily available. Make the follow-up process clear to the candidate. If there are other candidates to interview, be sure that the candidate knows this and knows when to expect your decision. Always thank the candidate for interviewing, and try to leave the candidate with the most favorable impression possible of the company, regardless of whether or not the person is offered the job.

NOTE TAKING There are different schools of thought on note taking. Some feel that notes during the interview distract the interviewer; others say that notes should be made both during and after the interview. Whatever system is used, notes must be specific enough to help the interviewer reconstruct the details of the interview, particularly when a number of candidates are being interviewed for the same position. Notes should never be made about the appearance or other physical aspects of the candidate or about anything that might be legally questionable. Note taking should be reserved to commentary about the applicant's qualifications and skills suitable to the job.

TEAM INTERVIEWING In the current atmosphere of work teams and group decision making, it may be desirable to have a group interview the candidate. When this is deemed appropriate, be sure that every member of the team has all of the information about the candidate prior to the interview, including copies of the person's resume, cover letter, and application. Plan the interview questions that each member of the team will ask, so that the candidate is not asked the same question by more than one member of the team.

LEGAL ASPECTS OF INTERVIEWING

Interviewing is subject to both state and federal laws which define employment discrimination in all aspects of employment. It is worthwhile to check for any state hiring regulations that might apply. The main federal regulations for hiring include:

- The Civil Rights Act of 1964 (Title VII);

- The Age Discrimination in Employment Act of 1967 (ADEA);

- The **Americans with Disabilities Act** of 1990 (ADA);

- The Uniformed Services Employment Reemployment Rights Act of 1994 (USERRA);

- The Immigration Reform and Control Act.

Together, these acts forbid a company to discriminate in hiring on the basis of sex, age, race, national origin, religion, physical disability or veteran status. These are called protected classes and questions about any aspect of these topics during an interview is illegal.

The interviewer must avoid all questions that could seem legally questionable, such as those about height, weight, age, marital status, religious or political beliefs, dependents, birth control, birthplace, race, and national origin. Generally, it is a good rule to measure a question's necessity by the role it plays in the determination of a candidate's ability to perform a job. If the question has nothing to do with the job, don't ask it.

TURNING SOMEONE DOWN

Once the job is accepted by the chosen candidate, immediately notify other candidates that they have not been selected for the position. A rejection is best done by phone—it is immediate, and it allows the manager to personally thank the candidate for taking the time to interview. When unable to phone, a letter of rejection is suitable. Although the candidate may ask, it is not necessary to be extremely specific about the types of qualities that the person lacks. An exact description of what was lacking in the candidate may open the manager to lawsuits for unfair hiring practices and discrimination.

The importance of making the right hiring decision is crucial in staffing a business. It means nothing short of selecting the right person for the right job at the right time. Since the interview is often the most decisive factor in determining who is hired for a specific position, business consultants contend that the importance of mastering the interview process should be appreciated; indeed, the interview process is ultimately an important factor in determining workforce quality and satisfaction.

FURTHER READING:

Allen, Jeffrey. *Complying with the ADA: A Small Business Guide to Hiring.* New York: Wiley, 1993.

Bell, Arthur. *Complete Manager's Guide to Interviewing.* New York: Dow Jones Irwin, 1989.

Drake Beam Morin, Inc. *Seven Imperatives for Fair, Legal & Productive Interviewing.* New York: DBM Publishing, 1993.

Drake, John. *Effective Interviewing.* New York: Amacom, 1982.

Half, Robert. *Finding, Hiring & Keeping the Best Employees.* New York: Wiley, 1993.

Weiss, Donald. *Fair, Square & Legal: Safe Hiring, Managing & Firing Practices.* New York: Amacom, 1993.

Yate, Martin. *Hiring the Best.* Bob Adams, Inc., 1988.

SEE ALSO: Employee Hiring; Employee Screening; Recruiting

EMPLOYMENT PRACTICES LIABILITY INSURANCE

Employment practices liability (EPL) insurance is a type of coverage that protects businesses from the financial consequences associated with a variety of employment-related lawsuits. Some of the events that may be covered by EPL insurance include liability lawsuits involving a company's directors and officers, negligence lawsuits affecting a company's human resources department, and liability lawsuits over fiduciary duty. Some of the types of covered lawsuits that may be initiated by employees or former employees include racial or age discrimination, **sexual harassment**, wrongful termination, or noncompliance with the **Americans with Disabilities Act**.

The market for EPL insurance coverage began to develop with large companies in 1991. But between that year and 1994, according to Michael Schachner in an article for *Business Insurance,* the number of employment-related lawsuits increased by over 2,000 percent. As a result, the need for EPL insurance coverage has expanded to businesses of all sizes. "The growing number of employment-practices suits directed against not only prominent companies but also small- to medium-sized ones is creating a new market," Charles Luchs noted in an article for *Best's Review.* "EPL insurance has become a standard risk management purchase for many companies," Stephanie D. Esters added in an article for *National Underwriter Property and Casualty—Risk and Benefits Management.*

Despite the growing need for such coverage, however, insurance industry surveys indicate that a majority of small businesses think that they are already covered for such events under their regular liability insurance. In fact, most standard liability policies do not provide adequate coverage. All businesses need to insure against the risk of lawsuits, but it is especially important for small businesses. Oftentimes, the life savings of the small business owner are tied up in the company, so the owner must take steps to protect his or her family from the financial consequences of events that could disrupt operations, reduce profits, or even cause the business to go bankrupt. EPL insurance, like other types of coverage, can help a small business be successful by reducing the uncertainties under which it operates. It places the economic burden of risk elsewhere so that managers can focus their attention on running the business. In

addition, the premiums paid for EPL and many other types of insurance are usually considered tax deductible business expenses.

One popular option for small businesses that require EPL insurance is a Business Opportunity Plan (BOP). A BOP provides basic property coverage for computers and other office equipment, plus liability protection for work-related accidents. In some cases, a BOP might also include business interruption coverage that will maintain the company's income stream for up to a year if a catastrophe disrupts business. Many BOPs also offer optional coverage against power failures and mechanical breakdowns, liability for workplace practices (including discrimination, sexual harassment, and compliance with the Americans with Disabilities Act), professional liability, and other risks.

FURTHER READING:

Betterley, Richard S., and Sandra Jane Meindersma. "Evaluating Employment Practices Liability Insurance Policies." *Risk Management.* December 1993.

Blakely, Stephen. "Finding Coverage for Small Offices." *Nation's Business.* June 1997.

Esters, Stephanie D. "Customer Sophistication Fuels EPL Market." *National Underwriter Property and Casualty—Risk and Benefits Management.* November 10, 1997.

Luchs, Charles. "Small Companies, Large Exposures." *Best's Review—Property/Casualty Insurance Edition.* January 1997.

Schachner, Michael. "Suits Send Employers Running for Cover." *Business Insurance.* November 21, 1994.

Stanway, Bill. "Smaller Companies Need Employment Protection." *Best's Review—Property/Casualty Insurance Edition.* December 1996.

Trexler, Stephen H. "Extra Insurance." *HR Magazine.* September 1996.

Wojcik, Joanne. "Majority of Firms Hit by EPL Suits." *Business Insurance.* July 7, 1997.

EMPOWERMENT ZONES

An empowerment zone is an economically distressed American community that receives tax incentives and grants from the federal government under the Empowerment Zones and Enterprise Communities Act of 1993. The act provided for the designation of nine empowerment zones nationwide—six urban and three rural—as well as 95 enterprise communities, which receive similar benefits on a smaller scale. A second round of designations was proposed in 1996 that would create 20 new empowerment zones and 80 new enterprise communities. The term "empowerment zone" comes from the program's goal of providing resources and opportunities that will empower poor persons to become self-sufficient.

In order to be designated as an empowerment zone, a community had to meet a series of eligibility criteria based on its economic distress and its development potential. It then had to apply for consideration by submitting a detailed strategic plan outlining the coordinated public and private efforts that would contribute to its renewal and growth. The nine empowerment zones receive a number of tax incentives designed to stimulate employment and business investment in the region. In addition, each zone receives a block grant of $100 million over two years toward social service and economic development programs. Under the 1996 proposal to create 20 new empowerment zones, each zone would receive $75 million in grants over three years.

About 500 communities applied for a coveted spot in the $3.8 billion empowerment zone program by the June 1994 deadline. The six urban U.S. empowerment zones, which were announced in December 1994, are Atlanta, Georgia; Baltimore, Maryland; Chicago, Illinois; Detroit, Michigan; New York City, and a joint effort between Philadelphia, Pennsylvania and Camden, New Jersey. The three rural empowerment zones are in the Kentucky highlands, the mid-delta region of Mississippi, and the Rio Grande valley in Texas. The designation lasts for ten years.

IDEA EVOLVED OVER 15 YEARS

The main ideas behind empowerment zones—using tax incentives to encourage business investment, improve employment opportunities, and stimulate economic growth in certain geographical areas—originated in the late 1970s. Sir Geoffrey Howe, a member of the British Parliament, announced the first ''enterprise zones'' in 1978 to help improve economic conditions in the dock districts of London. The system implemented in England reduced government restrictions in order to encourage the formation of new businesses in impoverished areas. It met with limited success, however, because it did not include provisions for improving the infrastructure of the urban areas, which was found to be necessary for the new businesses to succeed.

In the United States, the zone concept gained its first supporters among leaders of the Republican party, which advocated an overall reduction of government influence. In the early 1980s, Ronald Reagan included enterprise zones in the urban policy platform for his presidential campaign, and Senator Jack Kemp introduced the first bill featuring enterprise zones in Congress. The idea gradually expanded its base of supporters to include more liberal members of Congress, like Democrats Robert Garcia and Charles Rangel of New York, as well as the leaders of prominent minority organizations, such as the National Ur-

ban League and the National Association for the Advancement of Colored People (NAACP).

The first enterprise zone legislation enacted in the United States came in 1987, with the passage of Title VII of the Housing and Community Development Act. Rather than providing tax incentives, the act was intended to relax federal regulations and coordinate the efforts of existing programs in the designated zones. Although the Department of Housing and Urban Development (HUD) received applications from 270 distressed communities for assistance under the program, it never designated any enterprise zones. When George Bush became president, he also voiced his support for the idea of creating enterprise zones to revitalize urban areas. Several bills were introduced during his administration, but Bush vetoed the two that passed because they included tax increases. This development meant that no federal enterprise or empowerment zones were created in the United States during the 1980s, despite widespread support for the idea.

In the meantime, many states adopted the enterprise zone idea and started their own programs. According to Marilyn Marks Rubin in *Public Administration Review,* 37 states had enacted some variation of the enterprise zone concept by July 1993, and 25 of these states claimed that their programs had created jobs. The state programs all differed in their eligibility criteria, types of incentives, and methods for measuring success or failure. Consequently, evaluating and comparing the state programs was problematic.

President Bill Clinton supported the idea of empowerment zones during his campaign, but he proposed several changes to the plans put forth by previous administrations. Most significantly, the Clinton plan combined tax incentives, to lure new businesses to the zones, with grants—or ''targeted government investment''—to help improve the zones' social and economic infrastructure. The Clinton plan also differed in that it provided for two tiers of assistance by designating nine empowerment zones and 95 enterprise communities. The Democrat-controlled Congress passed the Empowerment Zones and Enterprise Communities Act in May 1993.

SPECIFICS OF THE CLINTON PLAN

For a community to be considered for designation as an empowerment zone under the act, it had to demonstrate economic distress. Some of the measures of economic distress include high levels of unemployment, a poverty rate of at least 20 percent, a declining population, and a pattern of disinvestment by businesses. In addition, an empowerment zone community had to show the potential for economic development. Communities could meet this requirement by having public and private resources available to aid in the renewal process, and by involving various community groups and other interested parties in developing and implementing the strategic plan.

Once a community met the economic distress and development potential criteria, it had to apply for the program with the help of its local and state governments. The application for the empowerment zone designation required communities to submit a strategic development plan—incorporating the input of all affected members of the community, from business and government to church groups and community organizations—and identify sources of private funds and support for the renewal effort. Finally, the community had to develop baseline measurements and benchmark goals to evaluate the success of the program.

The nine communities that were designated as empowerment zones receive a number of tax incentives to help stimulate business activity. In order to create jobs for area residents, employers receive a 20 percent wage credit for the first $15,000 paid to a resident of the empowerment zone, in addition to tax breaks for any expenses incurred to train these workers. The credits can be applied to full- or part-time workers, but not to workers who are closely related to the business owner, who own part of the business themselves, or who work for golf courses, massage parlors, liquor stores, gambling facilities, or a number of other types of businesses.

In order to encourage investment in the zones, the act allows businesses to exclude from taxation 50 percent of any capital gains from such investments. It also provides tax-exempt bond financing for the purchase of certain properties within the zones, and increases the allowance for depreciating such properties by $10,000 to $20,000 in the first year (which has the effect of reducing taxes). In contrast to empowerment zones, which receive all of these benefits, enterprise communities are eligible only for tax-exempt bond financing.

Each empowerment zone also receives a block grant of $100 million over two years toward the economic development programs included in its strategic plan. Such programs might focus on reducing drug abuse and crime or providing affordable housing. Each enterprise community receives a block grant of $2.8 million. Another provision of the act was to establish a Specialized Small Business Investment Company (SSBIC) in each empowerment zone. An SSBIC is a private lender that receives matching funds from the **U.S. Small Business Administration (SBA)** for its investments in empowerment zone businesses. The SSBICs are intended to become "one-stop capital shops" and distribute $300 to $400 million in loans and equity investments to zone businesses over a five-year period. Considering the various tax and financing advantages, locating in empowerment zones would

seem to provide an attractive alternative for entrepreneurs and small business owners.

FURTHER READING:

Bates, Timothy. "A Bad Investment." *Inc.* January 1995.

"Empowerment Zone Applications Being Taken." *Practical Accountant.* March 1994.

James, Jeffrey K. "Empowerment Zones, Enterprise Communities, and Rural Development Investment Areas." *CPA Journal.* July 1994.

Lloyd, Fonda Marie. "Time to Live Up to the Hype." *Black Enterprise.* June 1994.

McCoy, Frank. "Can Clinton's Urban Policies Really Work?" *Black Enterprise.* June 1994.

Rubin, Marilyn Marks. "Can Reorchestration of Historical Themes Reinvent Government? A Case Study of the Empowerment Zones and Enterprise Communities Act of 1993" *Public Administration Review.* March/April 1994.

SEE ALSO: Community Development Corporations; Targeted Jobs Tax Credit

ENTREPRENEURIAL COUPLES

Many of today's small business enterprises are co-owned and co-managed by entrepreneurs who are also partners in their personal lives. These partnerships can be immensely positive experiences, strengthening each person's commitment to and enjoyment of both the business and personal sides of the partnership. Indeed, accounts of husband-wife teams and other romantic partnerships that built thriving companies together are ubiquitous. But business experts and entrepreneurs who have built successful firms via this route warn that entrepreneurial couples often face additional hurdles that solo business builders do not encounter, and they note that when businesses founded by couples fail, their union is often placed in jeopardy as well.

"More and more married couples are going into business together," wrote Echo Montgomery Garrett in *Small Business Reports.* "You might call it the new American dream. When it clicks, working elbow-to-elbow is emotionally and financially rewarding." Indeed, tax returns turned in during the 1980s and 1990s indicate that the number of businesses jointly owned by married couples far outpaced the growth of proprietorships in general, and that the trend toward so-called "co-preneurships" was a sustained one that shows no signs of slowing in the latter part of the 1990s. Analysts cite several reasons for this growth. During the 1980s and early 1990s, observers pointed to corporate downsizing and anemic economic conditions as significant factors in the increase in entrepreneurial couples, although ironically, the great economic conditions of the mid-1990s have also been cited as key to the growth in small business start-ups during that period as well. In fact, experts agree that entrepreneurial couples of the mid-1990s have benefited from the same positive environmental factors that have helped so many other entrepreneurs, such as access to capital, low interest rates, consumer confidence, technology advancements, increased quality of life concerns, and a variety of other factors. "The lure of unlimited possibilities if you're successful and the security of having a trustworthy and caring partner to share the load tempt many couples to take the marital as well as financial risk," noted *Profit-Building Strategies for Business Owners.*

CONSIDERATIONS THAT FACE THE ENTREPRENEURIAL COUPLE

Couples that are considering launching a business enterprise together, however, need to weigh many aspects of that effort before taking the plunge. As *Profit-Building Strategies for Business Owners* observed, "many couples understand what they're getting into: long hours, a life that's often too shared, tough sledding till the business shows a profit. But veteran couples-in-business-together say that knowing about it still doesn't prepare you for living through it. The daily pressures of working side by side, frequently hassled, with no time left for any other life and taking few or no vacations, can put a heavy strain on any marriage." Entrepreneurial couples and business consultants alike cite the following as important factors in creating a successful business with a spouse or partner:

1) Both partners need to bring significant value to the business. As Dennis Jaffe observed in *Working With the Ones You Love,* each spouse should have a clear skill to contribute to the business. Spouses that are unable to make meaningful contributions in one or more areas of a business's operation should not be partners in that company. Such people are unlikely to be happy, since they are usually well aware that they are not "pulling their weight," and also because efforts to give them responsibilities in areas in which they are ill-equipped often end in failure, if not outright disaster for the company. Moreover, arrangements in which one spouse is basically doing all the work of both "partners" often generate resentment on the part of the spouse doing all the work. This problem can be particularly acute in instances where one spouse gets a business up and running, and then has to introduce his or her partner to the intricacies of the business. Consultants note, however, that the value split does not necessarily have to be 50-50.

After all, a spouse whose duties run exclusively toward taking care of the company's bookkeeping needs or serving as a restaurant's host/general troubleshooter during main traffic periods may not be taking care of half of the business's management requirements, but their execution of those duties can go far toward giving them a feeling of self-worth and assuring spouses that they are not shouldering the full weight of the business by themselves.

Ideally, partners in a couple-owned business will have separate, complementary skills. When partners handle different responsibilities of the business, it tends to minimize disagreements over day-to-day matters and creates an environment in which both partners are able to exercise some autonomy and develop respect for the talents that the other brings to the enterprise.

2) Partners should not be competitive with one another. Successful couple-owned business are willing to accept blame for business problems rather than simply point fingers at one another.

3) Newlyweds should exercise caution before partnering up for business. "The newness of both ventures causes uncertainties that can hamper growth in the business and cause problems in the marriage," stated *Profit-Building Strategies for Business Owners.*

4) Good communication is essential. "Couples sometimes have trouble making the transition to a working relationship," one consultant pointed out in *Travel Weekly.* "The way they communicate as couples may not work in an office setting." Experts note that the keys to good communication in dialogue with a spouse are the same as they would be for any other business partner—listening, focusing on the issue at hand, and not taking criticism personally —and that entrepreneurial couples have to recognize business disagreements have nothing to do with their personal relationship.

5) Adapt to changing roles. "Some spouses have difficulty seeing the person they married in a totally different light," wrote Garrett. "If, for instance, your spouse has always been the more passive one, it may be disconcerting when he or she suddenly becomes an aggressive CEO." Experts say that this adjustment is often particularly hard to make for husbands who are accustomed to calling the shots in their marriage, only to find their wives tapping into previously un-

known reserves of independence and purpose in the work environment.

6) Separate work life and home life. Many entrepreneurial couples warn that it is easy for husband-wife and other romantically involved business partnerships to lose sight of the personal side of their relationship in a flurry of business issues. In such cases, the romantic spark that first drew the partners together can be snuffed out by payroll concerns, worries about the landlord, proposed regulatory changes, and a plethora of other issues that are always swirling outside the doors of small business enterprises. In such instances, warned Garrett, "the business swallows up their home life to the degree that a work crisis quickly escalates into a marital one as well."

Entrepreneurial couples can take several steps to curb this threat, however. Some couples agree to never discuss work at home or in bed, while others actively seek out non-work activities that they can do together. Other couples, meanwhile, agree to have one or the other take time away from the business, so that both partners can take a step back, regain their perspective, and rekindle their personal relationship. "Usually the marriage existed before the business, and if it falls apart, the business falls apart," said consultant Kathy Engstrom in an interview with *Travel Weekly*. "Both have to be nurtured and protected." This is particularly important in instances where children are involved.

7) Set aside time away from your spouse or partner. Entrepreneurial couples spend enormous amounts of time together, and many successful husband-wife teams agree that one of the keys to their success is their decision to establish solo time in which each person can do his or her own thing. Even if the activity (community work, a class, or a sport league) is only one evening a week, this time can do a lot to recharge the partnership batteries of both people.

8) Objectively assess whether you and your partner would work well together in a business. Some couples enjoy good personal relationships, only to see their eagerly embarked-on business partnership quickly deteriorate into an unsightly welter of hurt feelings and financial losses. "Basic personality traits have a lot to do with how couples fare together in business," stated *Profit-Building Strategies for Business Owners*. "One researcher found that spouses who

plan vacations easily and enjoy doing home renovations are the kinds of personalties that tend to make good business partners. For couples who communicate and share their business ups and downs on an open, equal basis, experts predict that the marriage can thrive and grow more healthy as partners learn to work out conflicts and differences."

FURTHER READING:

Benson, Benjamin. *Your Family Business*. Irwin, 1990.

Bowman-Upton, Nancy. *Challenges in Managing a Family Business*. Washington: U.S. Small Business Administration, 1991.

Fraser, Jill Andresky. "The New American Dream: Building a Business Together." *Inc.* April 1990.

Garrett, Echo Montgomery. "And Business Makes Three." *Small Business Reports*. September 1993.

Granfield, Mary. "Till Debt Do Us Part." *Working Woman*. June 1993.

Jaffe, Dennis. *Working with the Ones You Love*. Conari, 1990.

Long, Felicity. "Sleeping With the Enemy: How to Work With a Spouse." *Travel Weekly*. February 3, 1994.

"Married to the Job." *Oregon Business*. January 1992.

Shook, Carrie. "Partners in Business—And in Life." *Business First—Columbus*. September 25, 1995.

Thompson, Kevin D. "Married . . . With Business." *Black Enterprise*. April 1990.

Ward, John L. *Keeping the Family Business Healthy*. Jossey Bass, 1988.

"What a Couple Needs to Know Before Plunging Into Business Together." *Profit-Building Strategies for Business Owners*. July 1992.

Wiley, Jenny. "Making Husband and Wife Partnerships Work." *Custom Builder*. May-June 1997.

SEE ALSO: Career and Family; Family-owned Business

ENTREPRENEURSHIP

An entrepreneur is one who organizes a new business venture in the hopes of making a profit. Entrepreneurship is the process of being an entrepreneur, of gathering and allocating the resources—financial, creative, managerial, or technological—necessary for a new venture's success. One engages in entrepreneurship when one begins to plan an organization that uses diverse resources in an effort to take advantage of the newly found opportunity. It usually involves hard work, long hours, and, usually, the hope of significant financial return. More importantly, entrepreneurship is characterized by creative solutions to old or overlooked problems; ingenuity and innovation are the entrepreneur's stock in trade. By taking a new look at difficult situations, the entrepreneur discerns an opportunity where others might have seen a dead end.

Entrepreneurship is also a source of more entrepreneurship. Societies around the world have always been fueled by the innovations and new products that entrepreneurs bring to the market. All big businesses started out small, usually as one man or woman with a good idea and the willingness to work hard and risk everything. While it is true that many new businesses fail, the ones that succeed contribute a great deal to the creation of other new ventures which leads, in turn, to a dynamic national economy. Indeed, today's economists and business researchers cite entrepreneurship as a key component of future economic growth in North America and around the world. "Entrepreneurship is viewed as the catalyst to transfer a segment of our new generation of [downsized] people into self-employed business owners who will, in turn, provide jobs for the rest," wrote Mitch Lenko in *CMA*. "It is viewed as the necessary component to the creation of new wealth; and hopefully represents the fountainhead from which will spawn innovative management techniques for the design, manufacture and marketing of products that will compete globally."

Successful entrepreneurship depends on many factors. Of primary importance is a dedicated, talented, creative entrepreneur. The person who has the ideas, the energy and the vision to create a new business is the cornerstone to any start-up. He or she is the glue that holds the pieces together. But the individual must have ready access to a variety of important resources in order to make the new venture more than just a good idea. He or she needs to develop a plan of action, a road map that will take the venture from the idea stage to a state of growth and institutionalization. He or she needs to put together a team of talented, experienced individuals to help manage the new venture's operations. Entrepreneurship also depends on access to **capital**, whether it be human, technological, or financial. In short, entrepreneurship is a process that involves preparation and the involvement of others in order to exploit an opportunity for profit.

ENTREPRENEURSHIP DEFINED

The multiplicity of the entrepreneur's motivations and goals leads to questions aimed at distilling the essence of entrepreneurship. To what or to whom does one refer when one uses the word? Is there any difference between a person who opens yet another dry cleaning establishment, sandwich shop, or bookstore and the entrepreneur? If so, what is it that separates the two? What characteristics define an entrepreneur and entrepreneurship itself? Historians and business writers have struggled with providing the answers. Even today, there is no widely accepted definition, but the variety of possibilities provides important clues as to what makes entrepreneurship special.

Harvard professor Joseph Schumpeter, for example, argued that the defining characteristic of entrepreneurial ventures was **innovation**. By finding a new "production function" in an existing resource—a previously unknown means through which a resource could produce value—the entrepreneur was innovating. The innovation was broadly understood; an innovation could take place in product design, organization of the firm, marketing devices, or process design. Nevertheless, innovation was what separated the entrepreneur from others who undertook closely related endeavors. Other researchers, such as professor Arthur Cole, defined entrepreneurship as purposeful activity to initiate, maintain, and develop a profit-oriented business. The important part of this definition is the requirement that individuals must create a new business organization in order to be considered entrepreneurial. Cole's entrepreneur was a builder of profit-minded organizations.

Still other observers, such as Shapero and Sokol, have argued that all organizations and individuals have the potential to be entrepreneurial. These researchers focus on activities rather than organizational make-up in examining entrepreneurship. They contend that entrepreneurship is characterized by an individual or group's initiative taking, resource gathering, autonomy, and risk taking. Their definition could theoretically include all types and sizes of organizations with a wide variety of functions and goals. By defining an "entrepreneurial event" instead of entrepreneurship itself, Shapero and Sokol avoid the pitfalls inherent in trying to delineate what types of organizations can or cannot be entrepreneurial.

In his book *Innovation and Entrepreneurship*, Peter F. Drucker took the ideas set forth by Schumpeter one step further. He argued that Schumpeter's type of innovation can be systematically undertaken by managers to revitalize business *and* nonbusiness organizations. By combining managerial practices with the acts of innovation, Drucker argued, business can create a methodology of entrepreneurship that will result in the institutionalization of entrepreneurial values and practice. Drucker's definition of entrepreneurship—a systematic, professional discipline available to anyone in an organization—brings our understanding of the topic to a new level. He demystified the topic, contending that entrepreneurship is something that can be strategically employed by any organization at any point in their existence, whether it be a start-up or a firm with a long history. Drucker understood entrepreneurship as a tool to be implemented by managers and organizational leaders as a means of growing a business.

THE ENTREPRENEURIAL PERSONALITY

Writing in his book *The Entrepreneurial Mind,* Jeffry Timmons defined entrepreneurship as ''the ability to create and build something from practically nothing.'' His definition captures the spirit of the word, the sense that entrepreneurs are like magicians, creating thriving organizations out of good ideas by virtue of hard work, canny business dealing, and personal skills. Timmons's words hint at the myths inherent in the common understanding of entrepreneurship. They bring to mind the great entrepreneurs who have become icons of American business mythology.

Many businesspeople believe that entrepreneurs have a personality that is different than those of ''normal'' people. Entrepreneurs are seen as having ''the right stuff.'' But defining the various characteristics and qualities that embody entrepreneurial success can be an elusive task, for as Lanko indicated, ''today's entrepreneurs are big and tall, and short and small. They come from every walk of life, every race and ethnic setting, all age groups, male and female, and from every educational background. There is no mould for the entrepreneur. Entrepreneurs make their own mold.''

But while it is hard to generalize about what it takes to be a successful entrepreneur, some personality traits seem to be more important than others. ''While many authors and researchers have disagreed on the relative significance of individual entrepreneurial traits, all agree on one quality that is essential to all entrepreneurs, regardless of definition,'' wrote Lanko. ''That quality is 'commitment'; it is self-motivation that distinguishes successful entrepreneurs from those that fail. It is the common thread in the lives and biographies of those that have succeeded in new enterprises. It is the one quality which entrepreneurs themselves admit is critical to the success of their initiatives.''

Other traits commonly cited as important components of entrepreneurial success include business knowledge (for example, business planning, marketing strategies, and asset management), self-confidence, technical and other skills, communication abilities, and courage. But there are other, less obvious, personality characteristics that an entrepreneur should develop as a means of further ensuring their success. In his book *Entrepreneurship: Texts, Cases, Notes,* Robert C. Ronstadt indicated some additional traits that help entrepreneurs build thriving organizations, including creativity and the ability to tolerate ambiguous situations.

Creative solutions to difficult problems may make or break the young and growing business; the ability of an entrepreneur to find unique solutions could be the key to his or her success. One of the most vexing situations entrepreneurs face is the allocation of scarce resources. For instance, owners of new ventures need to be able to decide how to best use a small advertising budget or how best to use their limited computer resources. Furthermore, they must be creative in their ability to find capital, team members, or markets. Entrepreneurial success is often directly predicated on the business owner's ability to make do with the limited resources available to him or her.

In addition to being creative, an entrepreneur must be able to tolerate the ambiguity and uncertainty that characterize the first years of a new organization. In nearly all cases, business or market conditions are bound to change during the first few years of a new business's life, causing uncertainty for the venture and for the entrepreneur. Being creative enables entrepreneurs to more successfully manage businesses in new and ambiguous situations, but without the ability to handle the pressure that uncertainty brings upon an organization, the entrepreneur may lose sight of his or her purpose.

Finally, environmental factors often play a significant part in influencing would-be entrepreneurs.

Often, personal or work history has led individuals to be more open to taking the risks involved with undertaking a new venture. For instance, individuals who know successful entrepreneurs may be stimulated to try their hand at running their own business. The successful entrepreneurs act as role models for those thinking about undertaking a new venture, providing proof that entrepreneurship does not always end in bankruptcy.

In addition, work experience can provide entrepreneurs with invaluable experience and knowledge from which to draw. ''First and foremost, entrepreneurs should have experience in the same industry or a similar one,'' insisted the *Portable MBA in Entrepreneurship.* ''Starting a business is a very demanding undertaking indeed. It is no time for on-the-job training. If would-be entrepreneurs do not have the right experience, they should either go out and get it before starting their new venture or find partners who have it.''

THE PROCESS OF ENTREPRENEURSHIP

The myths that have grown up around the great entrepreneurs in America have focused more on the personality of the individual than on the work that he or she did to create a prosperous organization. What sticks in our memories are the qualities of a great entrepreneur, those personality traits that ''make'' a great businessperson. Successful entrepreneurs, however, work hard to build their organizations, starting from little and undertaking a process that results in a thriving business. Even the best ideas become profitable only because the entrepreneur went through the steps necessary to build a company from the ground up. Successful new ventures do not appear magically out of the swirl of the marketplace; they are planned, created, and managed.

It is important to understand some of the stages a businessperson must go through in order to create a successful entrepreneurial venture. All entrepreneurs go through three very general stages in the process of creating their ventures: a concept formation stage where ideas are generated, the innovation and opportunity are identified, and the business begins to take shape; a resource gathering stage where necessary resources are brought together to launch the new business; and a stage where the organization is actually created.

CONCEPT FORMATION Before any business opens its doors, it must make crucial decisions about the way the business will be run. This first step in the entrepreneurial process is where the entrepreneur determines what kind of potential market exists for the business and forms a rough idea of how to penetrate the existing market. During the concept formation stage, the entrepreneur must answer hard questions about the potential business as well as his or her own motivations for starting his or her own business. The answers to these questions will provide the framework for future planning, growth, and innovation.

There is a great deal that is unknown to the entrepreneur before he or she starts out. The viability of the venture depends on the individual's ability to lessen that which is unknown and maximize that which is known. The central question an entrepreneur should ask him or herself during the idea generation stage is whether there is actually an opportunity for a successful venture. That is, will starting a new business enable the entrepreneur to accomplish things or meet personal and professional goals that he or she might not otherwise meet? Some entrepreneurs want to make a certain return on their efforts and investment or are looking to run a business that will afford them a certain lifestyle. Others are looking to capture a certain percentage of the market and thus increase their wealth. Still others go into business for themselves because it would afford them the independence and freedom that working for someone else would not. Before taking the plunge, prospective entrepreneurs should investigate the extent to which their envisioned business will give them an opportunity to meet their goals.

A new business can be opened by anyone with the capital and time to do it. Nevertheless, businesses that will be successful for years to come must maintain a certain level of financial soundness. Among the first questions an entrepreneur should ask are those that explore the potential profitability of the venture. The entrepreneur should be able to estimate sales and selling expenses as well as other costs of doing business. In order to develop a sense of the economic feasibility of a venture, the entrepreneur should investigate the size and other characteristics of the potential market for the product or service, including competitive pressures and capital start-up requirements. Quantitative analysis of the opportunity is a vital part of the conceptualization of the business. The results of "running the numbers" and creating a set of figures with which the future can be planned will enable the entrepreneur to determine whether the potential business will be profitable. "There is no more luck in becoming successful at entrepreneurship than in becoming successful at anything else," wrote William D. Bygraves in *The Portable MBA in Entrepreneurship.* "In entrepreneurship, it is a question of recognizing a good opportunity when you see one and having the skills to convert that opportunity into a thriving business. To do that, you must be prepared. So in entrepreneurship, just like any other profession, *luck is where preparation and opportunity meet.*"

RESOURCE GATHERING The first stage of the entrepreneurship process should give the individual enough information to decide whether or not the business has the capacity to meet the individual's personal and professional goals. Once the decision has been made, the entrepreneur may: 1) continue to work in his or her present employment capacity; 2) begin looking for a new entrepreneurial opportunity that is a better fit; or 3) beings the second step in the entrepreneurial process, that of gathering the necessary resources.

Without a sufficient supply of resources the opportunity might never be turned into a business that makes money for the entrepreneur. In the resource gathering stage the entrepreneur begins to assemble the tools that he or she will need to make the business idea a successful one. In general, a person has to gather three types of primary resources: capital, human/managerial, and time. Capital can be financial (in the form of cash, stock ownership, or loans), intellectual (patents, trademarks, brand names and copyrights), and technical (innovations in design or production that competitors can not or will not duplicate). Human resources refers to the individuals who will help the entrepreneur take advantage of the opportunity, either as employees of the new organization or as paid and unpaid counselors. In order to create a viable organization, an entrepreneur has to be ready and able to manage the resources at his or her disposal, bringing them together in advantageous, efficient ways that meet the needs of the fledgling organization.

An often-overlooked consideration in the resource gathering stage is time. Many entrepreneurial ventures that manage to succeed do so in part because they were launched at an opportune time, and because their founders were able to carve out an adequate amount of time—a most valuable resource, after all—

to attend to the myriad start-up needs of the business. For instance, a business based on a patented technological innovation has a certain amount of time to operate before the patent expires and competitors can duplicate the innovation. When the patent expires, the competitive advantage held by the business is diminished or gone. Other businesses may be based on selling to an emerging market. The entrepreneur who runs the business has a certain amount of time before potential competitors notice that the business is (or will be) profitable. In that time frame—the window of opportunity—the entrepreneur who found the opportunity must manage resources so that the business is established and protected from the threat of competition. Bygraves warned, however, that entrepreneurs should "avoid fads or any window of opportunity that they believe will only be open for a very brief time, because it inevitably means that they will rush to open their business, sometimes before they have time to gather the resources they will need. Rushing to open a business without adequate planning can lead to costly mistakes."

ORGANIZATION CREATION AND DEVELOPMENT
This stage of the entrepreneurial process is the actual establishment and opening of the business. During this stage, the entrepreneur goes from being just a visionary to a visionary with a business to run. One way to examine the changing managerial activities of the entrepreneur is to look at the different roles filled by the entrepreneur as the business develops. In her book *Entrepreneurial Behavior*, Barbara J. Bird examined entrepreneurial roles and their place in the management of ventures. The first role most entrepreneurs fill is that of the organization creator. As the founder of the organization, the entrepreneur sets the philosophy of the organization, establishes the strategic focus, and educates new employees. In this role, the entrepreneur lays the groundwork for the emerging **corporate culture**. In addition, most entrepreneurs serve as the primary promoters for their new start-ups. They must act as the new venture's chief spokesperson in contacts with financial backers, prospective clients, employees, suppliers, and others. In many cases, the entrepreneur acts as a role model or a mentor to others in the organization. As founders (or founding team members) of organizations, entrepreneurs are often called upon to provide counsel or advice to community members or employees. The roles that an entrepreneur must fill demand flexibility and creativity. In order to successfully manage a new venture, an entrepreneur must be comfortable in all the roles.

ENTREPRENEURSHIP AND LEADERSHIP

Entrepreneurs must also be able to balance their managerial duties with leadership activities. In other

words, they have to be able to handle both the day-to-day operations of the business as well as decision making obligations that determine the organization's long-term direction, philosophy, and future. It is a precarious relationship, but entrepreneurs must be both managers and visionaries in order to build their organizations. Indeed, researchers contend that many otherwise talented entrepreneurs have failed because they were unable to strike an appropriate balance between details of management and the larger mission that guides the new venture. Many entrepreneurs eventually reach a point where they realize that these twin obligations cannot be fully met alone. It is at this point that staffing decisions can become a critical component of long-term business success. In general, entrepreneurs should search for ways to delegate some of their management tasks rather than their leadership tasks. After all, in most cases the new business has long been far more dependent on its founder's leadership and vision than on his or her ability to monitor product quality or select new computers.

The mission of the new venture can only be fulfilled if the entrepreneur remains entrepreneurial throughout the life of the organization. That is, innovation has to be a primary strategy of the venture. Drucker pointed out that the venture must be receptive to innovation and open to the possibilities inherent in change. Change must be seen as a positive for a business to remain entrepreneurial. Therefore, management of an entrepreneurial organization requires policies that encourage innovation and rewards those who innovate. If the venture is to remain dedicated to entrepreneurship, management has to take the lead in establishing the patterns that will lead to a dynamic, flexible, and vital organization.

FURTHER READING:

Bird, Barbara J. *Entrepreneurial Behavior*. Glenview, IL: Scott, Foresman and Co., 1989.

Brockhaus, Robert H., Sr. "The Psychology of the Entrepreneur." In *Encyclopedia of Entrepreneurship*, edited by Calvin A. Kent, Donald L. Sexton, and Karl H. Vesper. Englewood Cliffs, NJ: Prentice-Hall, 1982.

Bygrave, William D., ed. *The Portable MBA in Entrepreneurship*. 2d ed. New York: John Wiley & Sons, 1997.

Casson, Mark, ed. *Entrepreneurship*. Brookfield, VT: Edward Elgar Publishing, 1990.

Drucker, Peter F. *Innovation and Entrepreneurship: Practice and Principles*. New York: Harper & Row, 1986.

Jones, Seymour, M. Bruce Cohen, and Victor V. Coppola. *The Coopers & Lybrand Guide to Growing Your Business*. New York: John Wiley & Sons, 1988.

Kent, Calvin A., Donald L. Sexton, and Karl H. Vesper, eds. *Encyclopedia of Entrepreneurship*. Englewood Cliffs, NJ: Prentice-Hall, 1982.

Lenko, Mitch. "Entrepreneurship: The New Tradition." *CMA—The Management Accounting Magazine*. July-August 1995.

Ronstadt, Robert. *Entrepreneurship: Texts, Cases & Notes.* Dana Point, CA: Lord Publishing, 1985.

Timmons, Jeffry A. *The Entrepreneurial Mind.* Andover, MA: Brick House Pub. Co., 1989.

SEE ALSO: Business Planning; Choosing a Small Business; Organizational Growth; Organizational Development

ENVIRONMENTAL LAW AND BUSINESS

Environmental laws and regulations deal with myriad pollution problems, including the contamination of our air, surface waters, drinking water, ground waters, and land. Pollution or contamination of the environment is found inside as well as outside the walls of factories and other business facilities Those affected include workers and their families as well as other members of their communities. In addition, as U.S. businesses increase their participation in a global marketplace, it is becoming increasingly clear that environmental contamination extends beyond local and regional concerns; its effects are international and even global.

Every business in this country is affected by environmental laws. In fact, most businesses deal with one or more environmental laws and the administrative agencies that enforce them on a daily basis. For example, businesses must inform and educate their employees about hazardous materials in the workplace as required by the **Occupational Safety and Health Administration (OSHA)**, and they must inform their communities about such materials on their premises pursuant to the Comprehensive Environmental Response, Clean Up, and Liability Act (CERCLA—the Superfund Program). Businesses must apply for and adhere to permits from the federal **Environmental Protection Agency (EPA)** for their air emissions and their effluents discharged into waterways. Businesses generating hazardous wastes must comply with the EPA's manifest system (a record-keeping system), and the disposal of both hazardous and non-hazardous waste is regulated extensively. Businesses are increasingly being required to clean up or pay for clean up of environmental contamination caused by their past acts and practices. Further, businesses are now being required to monitor their production methods and seek ways to prevent pollution. The list of the ways in which environmental law affects the daily operations of business goes on.

Environmental regulations are constantly changing and, as J. Stephen Shi and Jane M. Kane noted in *Business Horizons,* "businesses, especially small- to mid-sized businesses, understandably have a hard time staying abreast of all rules and regulations,"

which are typically enforced in fairly strict fashion. "This means that whether or not a firm knowingly violated a regulation or was not aware of the violation is irrelevant. Businesses, in the eyes of the law, have a duty to find out what regulations apply to their industry and comply with them." Therefore, for any business person, it is helpful to be familiar with the problems addressed by our environmental laws, the provisions of those laws, and the kinds of mechanisms and administrative agencies through which those laws are enforced.

EVOLVING APPROACHES TO ENVIRONMENTAL PROTECTION

A great deal of the environmental legislation affecting small businesses today originated in the 1970s. In fact, 1970 has been called the "year of the environment." On April 22, 1970, the first celebration of "Earth Day" took place. Also that year, the National Environmental Policy Act was passed by the U.S. Congress, the EPA was created, and OSHA was established. Various U.S. environmental laws predate 1970, but those laws have been developed extensively since that year, and the enforcement of those laws has changed the way business "does business."

Individuals and groups of concerned citizens have long relied upon the legal system to compensate individuals who suffered harm due to exposure to environmental contamination (toxic substances), to provide a mechanism for clean up of environmental contamination, to protect citizens from exposure to toxic (hazardous) substances, and to prevent further contamination of the environment. One well-known early example is the community of Love Canal, New York, where beginning around 1970 families realized that they were suffering from unusually high rates of cancer and other illnesses as well as birth defects. Investigation revealed that the families' homes and even an elementary school for their children had been built on top of tons of chemical wastes that had been deposited in a ditch and covered over. In one of various legal responses to the disaster, the residents sued the Occidental Petroleum Corp. based on tort law and recovered millions of dollars in damages. Since then, thousands of cases have been brought against businesses based on similar, if less extensive, contamination at hazardous waste disposal sites and industrial facilities throughout the United States.

In recent times, the United States has moved away from the "reactive" approach of tort law—which is used to compensate victims after harm has occurred—to a more proactive statutory approach—through which future contamination is prevented and existing contaminated sites are cleaned up. Administrative (or regulatory) agencies have been set up by Congress to deal with environmental problems.

Through a statute (or statutes) called "enabling legislation," each agency is charged with planning, creation of regulations (or standards), and enforcement of those standards relating to a specific set of environmental problems.

ADMINISTRATIVE AGENCIES

The federal Environmental Protection Agency (EPA) and its state counterparts are the primary enforcers of environmental laws in the United States. Each of the fifty states has an administrative agency which serves as a counterpart to the federal EPA. The state agency is often the primary environmental law-enforcing agency with which businesses deal on a daily basis. However, it must be recognized that environmental law is not exclusively the domain of the EPA. Various other administrative agencies, both state and federal, enforce laws that are related to the environment. Further, the EPA often coordinates its enforcement efforts with those of other administrative agencies whose missions complement or even overlap with those of the EPA. Some of the federal administrative agencies which are engaged in such environmentally related missions include:

- Occupational Safety and Health Administration—Regulates to protect the health and safety of workers within workplaces (excluding mining).

- Mine Safety and Health Administration—Regulates to protect the health and safety of workers in mines and to protect the public from hazards associated with mining.

- Bureau of Land Management—Manages federally owned lands, which total over 350 million acres, as well as the resources on those lands, including timber; oil, gas and minerals; rivers and lakes; plants, animals, and fish and their habitats.

- U.S. Fish and Wildlife Service—Manages the National Wildlife Refuge System, which was created in 1983 and now includes at least 472 national wildlife refuge areas.

- National Park Service—Administers the U.S. National Parks, which cover over 80 million acres.

- U.S. Forest Service—Manages wilderness areas covering 33.6 million acres, controlling decisions regarding the use of public forest resources for lumbering, mining, farming, and grazing.

- Council on Environmental Quality (CEQ)—Oversees compliance with the National Environmental Policy Act (NEPA) by agencies throughout federal government.

- **Consumer Product Safety Commission**—Charged with enforcement of various enabling acts designed to protect consumers, including responsibility for protecting consumers from toxic (hazardous) chemicals.

- Food and Drug Administration—Charged with enforcement of statutes designed to protect the public from harmful food or drugs. Also works with the EPA to protect the public from hazards associated with pesticide residues in food.

- Nuclear Regulatory Commission—Regulates nuclear facilities and handling and disposal of nuclear materials.

- Federal Energy Regulatory Commission—Regulates dams and hydroelectric power.

- Federal Maritime Commission—Certifies that ships carrying oil and hazardous materials have the ability to cover the cost of any spills.

- Army Corps of Engineers—Regulates construction projects on navigable waters; coordinates administration of Superfund cleanups; engages in construction projects to protect wildlife on shorelines and in navigable waters; and other projects.

- National Institute for Occupational Safety and Health (NIOSH)—Under jurisdiction of the Centers for Disease Control (CDC), conducts research on the effects of toxic substances on humans, the results of which are used by OSHA, EPA, and other agencies.

TYPES OF ENVIRONMENTAL REGULATIONS

One of the nation's first environmental laws was the National Environmental Policy Act (NEPA) of 1970, which requires that all federal administrative agencies prepare an Environmental Impact Statement (EIS) before undertaking any major action which is likely to have a significant effect on the environment. Although the utility of the EIS in protecting the environment has been debated by scholars in law and economics, the high ideals represented by NEPA have earned the statute the label "Environmental Magna Carta." Since then, various kinds of regulation have been developed to deal with varying environmental concerns, ranging from cleanup of past mistakes, to record-keeping detailing where toxic wastes are being placed, to efforts to protect citizens from exposure to toxic materials being used daily in industry.

REGULATIONS PROTECTING CITIZENS One major area of regulatory concern is to protect workers and other citizens from toxic materials used by industry.

In the 1970s, the majority of environmental regulation applied to business facilities could be described as "command and control" regulation. Such regulation, most of which is still in effect, consists of detailed standards set down by an administrative agency. For example, if a business applies for an emissions permit pursuant to the Clean Air Act, the EPA will base the terms of that permit on EPA regulations (standards) for that chemical. The permit will specify what chemicals can be emitted and in what amounts. If a business exceeds the limits of its permit, it is subject to civil or criminal penalties.

Closely related to "command and control" regulation is the concept of "end of pipe" regulation. "End of pipe" regulation requires treatment of waste or pollutant just before it is emitted. For example, companies use "scrubbers" on smokestacks to reduce the amount of a pollutant emitted. "End of pipe" regulation was relied on heavily during the 1970s and continues to be used extensively today.

During the 1980s, "command and control" regulations began to be supplemented by a new kind of regulation of known as "Right to Know" (RTK). In the early 1980s, workers advocated the adoption of Worker Right to Know laws, which were designed to give workers access to information about the presence and identities of toxic chemicals in the workplace. OSHA formalized Worker RTK laws across the nation under its Hazard Communication Standard (HCS) in 1984, and by 1989 coverage had been extended to protect workers in all public businesses. Following the example of workers, environmentalists began to advocate Community Right to Know laws during the 1980s. Community RTK on the federal level was created through the 1986 Superfund Amendments and Reauthorization Act. Such laws give citizens access to information about chemicals located on the premises of businesses in their communities.

Worker RTK and Community RTK laws place duties on employers and businesses to provide information to workers and communities through documents called Material Safety Data Sheets (MSDS), which describe chemicals, their properties, and the hazards associated with their use. Further, the Community RTK program requires that a business inventory toxic materials on its premises and document all releases into the environment of such materials. That information, in turn, is made available to citizens and various committees and regulatory bodies. Thus, RTK is primarily an information policy that allows citizens, including workers, to make better-informed decisions about dealing with toxic (hazardous) materials in their workplaces and communities.

As a result of greater citizen awareness of the presence of toxic materials and the hazards they create, citizens in the 1990s are demanding that more be done to reduce those hazards. In response to citizens' concerns, a third type of environmental laws regulating businesses' activities is being advocated and enacted in various states and on the federal level. Pollution Prevention Laws, which are also known as Toxics Use Reduction Laws, have been enacted in at least twenty-six states. In addition, Congress passed the Pollution Prevention Act of 1990, which is not as stringent as most of the state laws but takes some important steps to require pollution prevention.

Pollution prevention statutes are designed to prompt business facilities to examine their production processes and change those processes to reduce their use of toxic chemicals. Some comprehensive statutes impose planning and reporting requirements on business facilities with respect to toxic chemicals used. Such statutes also cover: 1) protection of the business' proprietary interests; 2) worker and community involvement in planning processes; 3) technical assistance and research to assist business facilities and funding for such programs; and 4) enforcement mechanisms and penalties for non-compliance. The Federal Pollution Prevention Act of 1990 provides matching grant money for state programs to assist businesses in reducing their use of toxic substances. Some companies have found that the elimination of wastes saves money both immediately and in the long run, as the costs of meeting the increasingly more stringent requirements of "command and control" regulations rise.

REGULATIONS RELATING TO DISPOSAL AND CLEANUP OF TOXIC SUBSTANCES A variety of other environmental laws and statutes regulate businesses' handling of toxic substances. Laws such as the Federal Insecticide, Fungicide, and Rodenticide Act (FIFRA) and the Toxic Substance Control Act (TSCA), for example, regulate the manufacture of economic poisons and other chemicals. Such laws require approval and licensing by the EPA before a chemical product can be produced and marketed.

The Comprehensive Environmental Response, Clean Up, and Liability Act (CERCLA—the Superfund program) involves programs to identify hazardous waste sites, evaluate and prioritize them, and clean up or contain hazardous wastes at such sites. The program relies on public funds, taxation of the chemical industry, and a "polluter pays" principle (collection of cleanup costs from those who contributed hazardous wastes to the site) as funding sources. To prevent the creation of future "Superfund" sites, the Resource Conservation and Recovery Act (RCRA) requires licensing and close monitoring of hazardous waste generators, transporters, and disposal or treatment sites. The program creates a "cradle to grave" written record of each and every batch of hazardous waste produced by a business facility in the United States.

LOOKING AHEAD

As businesses enter the twenty-first century, they will deal increasingly with the environmental laws of other countries and with the ramifications of international treaties dealing with both trade and the environment. For example, the environment is one of the major areas of public debate regarding the **North American Free Trade Agreement (NAFTA)**. Expanded industrialization in underdeveloped countries resulting from such trade pacts is accompanied by serious concerns about the environmental effects of such industrialization. In 1994, such concerns were included in what are known as the ''Uruguay Round'' of negotiations regarding the **General Agreement on Tariffs and Trade (GATT)**. Further, President Clinton's administration has already called for a future ''Green Round'' of the GATT at which various environmental concerns would be addressed. Such concerns include the need for upward harmonization of health, safety, and environmental standards as well as the need to adopt dispute resolution processes that will result in rulings that are more protective of the environment than those currently in effect.

Overall, consideration of the environment and adherence to environmental laws and regulations have become important in the day-to-day conduct of business in the United States and throughout the world. Many businesses today conduct ''environmental audits'' to determine whether their facilities and operations meet the requirements of all applicable environmental laws and regulations. One of the main lessons that has been learned is that businesses, workers, environmentalists, and government officials need to work together to find economically sound ways of reducing the amounts of toxic substances released into the environment.

FURTHER READING:

Eblen, Ruth A., and William R. Eblen, eds. *The Encyclopedia of the Environment.* Boston, MA: Houghton Mifflin, 1994.

Kubasek, Nancy K., and Gary S. Silverman. *Environmental Law.* Upper Saddle River, NJ: Prentice-Hall, 1994.

Stenzel, Paulette L. ''The Crucial, Yet Difficult, Partnership Between Science and Law in Litigation and Regulation Related to Toxic Substances.'' In *Selected Readings on Business and the Law,* 1994.

——. ''Right to Act: Advancing the Common Interests of Labor and Environmentalists.'' In *Albany Law Review* 57.

Shi, J. Stephen, and Jane M. Kane. ''Green Issues.'' *Business Horizons.* January-February 1996.

SEE ALSO: Green Production

ENVIRONMENTAL PROTECTION AGENCY

The U.S. Environmental Protection Agency (EPA) was created on December 2, 1970, by executive order of President Richard Nixon to ''permit coordinated and effective government action on behalf of the environment.'' Fifteen different environmental programs from various federal offices were combined and placed under the jurisdiction of the newly created EPA. The EPA was designed to serve as an ''umbrella agency'' through which most federal environmental laws, regulations, and policies would be administered.

EPA'S ORGANIZATION

The administrator of the EPA is appointed by the President of the United States and approved by the Senate, along with a deputy administrator, nine assistant administrators, an inspector general, and a general counsel. The inspector general is responsible for investigating environmental crimes, and the general counsel provides legal advice. Within the EPA are four ''program'' offices. They are 1) Air and Radiation; 2) Water; 3) Pesticides and Toxic Substances; and 4) Solid Waste and Emergency Response. There is also an office for Research and Development which works in coordination with each of the four program offices.

The main office of the EPA, which is located in Washington, D.C., oversees implementation of national environmental laws and programs, directs the EPA's regional offices and laboratories, and submits budget requests to Congress. Research is conducted through the EPA's main office and at its regional field laboratories. There are ten regional EPA offices and field laboratories which work directly with state and local governments to coordinate pollution control efforts. The EPA uses a portion of its federal funding to provide grants and technical assistance to states and local governmental units that seek to prevent pollution.

OBJECTIVES, POWERS AND PROGRAMS

The EPA's powers and programs are established through legislation passed by Congress. (Such legislation delegating powers to an agency is known as ''enabling'' legislation.) Today the EPA is charged with the administration of a myriad of federal environmental laws dealing with air and water pollution, drinking water quality, radioactive wastes, pesticides, solid wastes, and noise pollution. Those environmental statutes include, for example, the Clean Air Act, the Clean Water Act, the Resource Conservation and Recovery Act (RCRA), the Comprehensive Environmental Response, Compensation, and Liability Act

(CERCLA)—also known as the "Superfund" Program—the Toxic Substances Control Act (TOSCA), and the Nuclear Waste Policy Act (NWPA). In general, the EPA develops standards or regulations pursuant to environmental statutes; enforces those standards, regulations, and statutes; monitors pollutants in the environment; conducts research; and promotes public environmental education.

The EPA has five main objectives, which are called "core functions." These include: 1) Pollution Prevention, which is also know as "source reduction"; 2) Risk Assessment and Risk Reduction, which is the task of identifying those issues which pose the greatest risks to human health and the environment and taking action to reduce those risks; 3) Science, Research, and Technology, which involves research designed to develop innovative technologies to deal with environmental problems; 4) Regulatory Development, which involves developing standards for operations of industrial facilities—including, for example, standards for air emissions of pollutants pursuant to Clean Air Act permits and standards for discharge of effluents under Clean Water Act permits; and 5) Environmental Education, which involves developing educational materials and providing grants to educational institutions.

COORDINATION WITH OTHER ENVIRONMENTAL PROGRAMS

The EPA works closely with state and local governments in their pollution control efforts. During the early 1980s, efforts to "downsize" federal government led the EPA to hand over more responsibility for enforcement of regulatory programs to state and local governments. States are encouraged to pass their own statutes and regulations which meet or exceed the requirements of federal statutes such as the Clean Air Act, the Clean Water Act, RCRA, and CERCLA. Upon certification by the federal EPA, such states take over day-to-day enforcement of a specific statutory program and of the regulations pertaining to that program.

As a result, business people in many states find that their day-to-day contact with enforcement officials regarding environmental statutes and regulations is with a state counterpart to the EPA rather than with the federal EPA itself. For example, in Michigan a business applies to the Michigan Department of Natural Resources (MDNR—Michigan's counterpart to the EPA) for emissions permits under the Clean Air Act and effluent permits under the Clean Water Act; files its "hazardous waste manifests" required by RCRA with the MDNR; and deals with the MDNR with regard to identification and clean-up of a contaminated site under the Superfund program. However, even when a state has been certified to administer such a program, the federal EPA continues to oversee the state's enforcement activities. It provides assistance to state officials and sometimes participates directly in major enforcement actions against violators of environmental laws.

The EPA also works closely with other federal environmental control agencies, such as the National Oceanic and Atmospheric Administration and the United States Coast Guard. The National Oceanic and Atmospheric Administration engages in long-range research on pollution problems, especially problems affecting the ocean and the atmosphere. The EPA works with the Coast Guard on flood control, dredging activities, and shoreline protection. Since 1970, the EPA has worked closely with the Council on Environmental Quality (CEQ), a relatively small executive agency which was created pursuant to the National Environmental Policy Act. Its mission is to advise the president on federal policy and action in the environmental area and to ensure that other federal agencies comply with NEPA. Compliance with NEPA requires all federal agencies to pursue environmentally sound policies and prepare an Environmental Impact Statement (EIS) before undertaking any major action which might significantly affect the environment.

EPA IN THE 1990S

The current chief administrator of the EPA, who was chosen by President Clinton in December 1992, is Carol Browner. Browner is considered to be prominent among a new group of environmentalists who view environmental protection and economic development as compatible objectives. Thus, her views fit in with the Pollution Prevention Act of 1990, which directs the administrator of the EPA to develop and implement strategies to promote "source reduction." "Source reduction" refers to pollution prevention practices designed to reduce the amount of hazardous substances entering the environment. Browner strongly supports pollution prevention as an alternative to the EPA's former emphasis on "command and control" methods of regulation, which focus on regulating only that which comes from the "end of the pipe," such as the emissions coming from a smokestack.

Leading the EPA in another departure from its past practices, Ms. Browner instituted a plan in 1993 to strengthen the EPA's Office of Enforcement by reconsolidating it and adding some staff. The Office has been directed to target entire industries rather than focus only on individual companies breaking environmental laws. Because the EPA has been criticized in recent years for failing to enforce anti-pollution laws, Browner's moves to revamp the EPA's Enforcement Office are viewed by environmentalists as a positive step toward making the EPA more effective.

But the EPA faces tremendous challenges as it moves into the twenty-first century, particularly with regards to revising the Superfund program and the Clean Air and Water Acts, dealing with the constitutional issues that arise when property owners are denied permission to develop land due to federal wetlands-protection policies, and working with foreign governments to study and develop mechanisms to deal with global warming. The Superfund program, in particular, has come under criticism in recent years for being too slow and expensive in cleaning up hazardous waste sites. Although 15,000 sites have been identified as requiring federal action since 1980, cleanup had been completed on only 150 sites by the end of 1992.

In 1997, many small business groups sought to block enactment of strict new EPA air-quality standards. Although proponents noted that the standards would cut down on respiratory illnesses and deaths, small business interests feared that the lower allowable emission levels would require states to target smaller sources of pollution that they had previously ignored. In any case, it is widely agreed that although the EPA has achieved some notable successes over the years, it must find more efficient and cost-effective ways to clean up the environment and protect the public from contamination in the future.

FURTHER READING:

Barlas, Stephen. "Clearing the Air: New EPA Clean Air Standards Have Some Small Businesses Fuming." *Entrepreneur.* November 1997.

Bukro, Casey. "EPA Chief Ties Ecology to Economy." *Chicago Tribune.* February 13, 1993.

Eblen, Ruth A., and William R. Eblen. *The Encyclopedia of the Environment.* Boston, MA: Houghton Mifflin, 1994.

Environmental Protection Agency. *Securing Our Legacy.* 1992.

SEE ALSO: Environmental Law and Business; Green Production

EQUAL EMPLOYMENT OPPORTUNITY COMMISSION

The Equal Employment Opportunity Commission (EEOC) was established to enforce provisions of Title VII of the Civil Rights Act of 1964. Title VII forbids discrimination in the workplace based on race, age, handicap, religion, sex, or national origin. Title VII covers all phases and aspects of employment including but not necessarily restricted to hiring, termination of employment, layoffs, promotions, wages, on-the-job training, and disciplinary action. Businesses covered by Title VII include employers in the private sector with 15 or more employees, educational institutions, state and local governments, labor unions

with 15 or more members, employment agencies, and, under certain circumstances, labor-management committees.

Originally, government-owned corporations, Indian tribes, and federal employees were not covered under the provisions of Title VII; the latter group was protected from discriminatory practices by Executive Order 11478, which was administered and enforced by the U.S. Civil Service Commission. In 1978, however, federal equal employment functions were transferred to the EEOC. Title VII—which, along with the rest of the 1964 Civil Rights Act, became operational on July 2, 1965—has since been amended several times over the years. Key amendments include the Equal Opportunity Act of 1972, the Pregnancy Discrimination Act of 1978, and the Civil Rights Act of 1991. The EEOC is also responsible for enforcing the Equal Pay Act of 1963, the Age Discrimination in Employment Act of 1967, the Rehabilitation Act of 1973, and the **Americans with Disabilities Act** of 1990. Today, the EEOC provides oversight and coordination of all federal regulations, practices, and policies affecting equal employment opportunity.

ORIGINS OF THE EEOC Title VII and the EEOC trace their beginnings to World War II federal defense contracts. Faced with the threat of a "Negro march" on Washington to protest discrimination in hiring of defense contract workers, President Roosevelt issued Executive Order 8802 in 1941. This order called for the participation of all U.S. citizens in defense programs regardless of race, creed, color, or national origin. The order also established the Fair Employment Practices Committee (FEPC), which by 1943 was processing 8,000 employment discrimination complaints annually. The powers of the FEPC were decidedly limited. While the committee discouraged discrimination within the defense industry, it lacked the legal clout to enforce its desires. Over the next several years, both Presidents Truman and Eisenhower established committees on government contract compliance, but again enforcement power was absent. Only when President Kennedy created the President's Committee on Equal Employment Opportunity were one of these groups given enforcement powers. Even in this case, however, the committee's legal authority was limited. Moreover, Kennedy's Committee on Equal Employment Opportunity, like its predecessors, dealt only with discrimination within businesses that had government contracts, not workplace discrimination in the overall private sector. The Civil Rights Act of 1964 changed this by addressing discrimination in all areas of employment.

FILING A COMPLAINT WITH THE EEOC Anyone who feels that he or she has suffered workplace discrimination because of his or her race, age, physical disability, religion, sex, or national origin is eligible to file a complaint with the EEOC. Complaints or charges are generally filed at an EEOC office by the aggrieved party or by his or her designated agent. All charges must be filed in writing, preferably but not necessarily on the appropriate EEOC form, within 180 days of the occurrence of the act that is the reason the complaint is being filed. Complaints may be filed at any one of 50 district, area, local, and field EEOC offices throughout the United States.

Upon receiving a discrimination charge the EEOC defers that charge to a state or local fair employment practices agency. This agency has either 60 or 120 days to act on the complaint (the allotted time depends on several factors). If no action is taken on the state or local level within that time the charge reverts back to the EEOC, which processes the charge on the 61st or 121st day. This becomes the official filing day of the complaint. Within 10 days of the filing date the EEOC notifies those parties charged with discrimination. The EEOC subsequently undertakes an investigation of the charge. If the investigation shows reasonable cause to believe that discrimination occurred, the Commission launches conciliation efforts. The reaching of an agreement between the two parties signals closure of the case. If such an agreement cannot be reached, the EEOC has the option of filing suit in court or the aggrieved party may file suit on his or her own. If no violation of Title VII is found, the EEOC removes itself from the case, though the party charging discrimination is still free to file suit in court within a specified time.

EEOC PROGRAMS The Equal Employment Opportunity Commission has established numerous programs designed to inform the public of EEOC activities and responsibilities. The Voluntary Assistance Program is a one-day educational seminar for unions and small and mid-size employers. This program highlights the rights of employers and employees under Title VII. The Expanded Presence Program sends contact teams to areas that would otherwise have little immediate accessibility to the EEOC. The EEOC also sponsors a Federal Dispute Resolution Conference, aids state and local fair practices employment agencies, and maintains liaison programs with unions, civil rights organizations, and various federal, state and local government agencies.

To contact the EEOC, write the Commission at the following address: U.S. Equal Employment Opportunity Commission, 1801 L Street, N.W., Washington, DC 20507.

FURTHER READING:

U.S. Equal Employment Opportunity Commission. *The First Decade*. Equal Employment Opportunity Commission, 1974.

SEE ALSO: Affirmative Action

EQUITY FINANCING

Equity financing is a strategy for obtaining **capital** that involves selling a partial interest in the company to investors. The equity, or ownership position, that investors receive in exchange for their funds usually takes the form of stock in the company. In contrast to **debt financing**, which includes loans and other forms of credit, equity financing does not involve a direct obligation to repay the funds. Instead, equity investors become part-owners and partners in the business, and thus are able to exercise some degree of control over how it is run.

Since creditors are usually paid before owners in the event of business failure, equity investors accept more risk than debt financiers. As a result, they also expect to earn a higher return on their investment. But because the only way for equity investors to recover their investment is to sell the stock at a higher value later, they are generally committed to furthering the long-term success and profitability of the company. In fact, many equity investors in startup ventures and very young companies also provide managerial assistance to the entrepreneurs.

ADVANTAGES AND DISADVANTAGES

The main advantage of equity financing for small businesses, which are likely to struggle with cash flow initially, is that there is no obligation to repay the money. In contrast, bank loans and other forms of debt financing provide severe penalties for businesses that fail to make monthly principal and interest payments. Equity financing is also more likely to be available to concept and early stage businesses than debt financing. Equity investors primarily seek growth opportunities, so they are often willing to take a chance on a good idea. But debt financiers primarily seek security, so they usually require the business to have some sort of track record before they will consider making a loan. Another advantage of equity financing is that investors often prove to be good sources of advice and contacts for small business owners.

The main disadvantage of equity financing is that the founders must give up some control of the business. If investors have different ideas about the company's strategic direction or day-to-day operations, they can pose problems for the entrepreneur. In addition, some sales of equity, such as initial public offerings, can be very complex and expensive to administer. Such equity financing may require complicated legal filings and a great deal of paperwork to comply with various regulations. For many small businesses, therefore, equity financing may necessitate enlisting the help of attorneys and accountants.

In the Small Business Administration publication *Financing for the Small Business,* Brian Hamilton listed several factors entrepreneurs should consider when choosing a method of financing. First, the entrepreneur must consider how much ownership and control he or she is willing to give up, not only at present but also in future financing rounds. Second, the entrepreneur should decide how leveraged the company can comfortably be, or its optimal ratio of debt to equity. Third, the entrepreneur should determine what types of financing are available to the company, given its stage of development and capital needs, and compare the requirements of the different types. Finally, as a practical consideration, the entrepreneur should ascertain whether or not the company is in a position to make set monthly payments on a loan.

As W. Keith Schilit pointed out in his book *The Entrepreneur's Guide to Preparing a Winning Business Plan and Raising Venture Capital,* small business owners must keep in mind that the more equity they give up to investors, the more they are working for someone else rather than themselves. Some entrepreneurs tend to think of equity financing as a free loan, but in fact it can be quite an expensive way to raise capital. For a small business to make equity financing cost-effective, it must be able to command a fair price for its stock. This entails convincing potential investors that the business has a high current valuation and a strong potential for future earnings growth. Schilit recommended that entrepreneurs proceed cautiously and try to use more than one form of financing to ensure business growth. They should also compare the cost of equity financing to that of other financing options, as well as consider the ramifications of equity financing on company's current and future capital structure.

SOURCES OF EQUITY FINANCING

Equity financing for small businesses is available from a wide variety of sources. Some possible sources of equity financing include the entrepreneur's friends and family, private investors (from the family physician to groups of local business owners to wealthy entrepreneurs known as "angels"), employees, customers and suppliers, former employers, venture capital firms, investment banking firms, insurance companies, large corporations, and government-backed **Small Business Investment Companies (SBICs)**.

Venture capital firms are professionally managed funds that exist to invest in new and young companies. Since their investments are highly risky, they expect a large return, which they usually realize by selling stock back to the company or on a public stock exchange at some point in the future. In general, venture capital firms are most interested in rapidly growing, new technology companies. They usually set stringent policies and standards about what types of companies they will consider for investments, based on industries, technical areas, development stages, and capital requirements. As a result, formal **venture capital** is not available to a large percentage of small businesses.

Closed-end investment companies are similar to venture capital firms but have smaller, fixed (or closed) amounts of money to invest. These companies themselves sell shares to investors, then use this money to invest in other companies. Closed-end investment companies usually concentrate on high-growth companies with good track records rather than startup companies. Similarly, investment clubs consist of groups of private investors that pool their resources to invest in new and existing businesses within their communities. These clubs are less formal in their investment criteria than venture capital firms, but they also are more limited in the amount of capital they can provide.

Large corporations often establish investment arms very similar to venture capital firms. However, such corporations are usually more interested in gaining access to new markets and technology through their investments than in strictly realizing financial gains. Partnering with a large corporation through an equity financing arrangement can be an attractive option for a small business. The association with a larger company can increase a small business's credibility in the marketplace, help it to obtain additional capital, and also provide it with a source of expertise that might not otherwise be available. Equity investments made by large corporations may take the form of a complete sale, a partial purchase, a joint venture, or a licensing agreement.

The most common method of using employees as a source of equity financing is an **Employee Stock Ownership Plan (ESOP)**. Basically a type of retirement plan, an ESOP involves selling stock in the company to employees in order to share control with them rather than with outside investors. ESOPs offer small businesses a number of tax advantages, as well as the ability to borrow money through the ESOP rather than from a bank. They can also serve to improve employee performance and motivation, since employees have a greater stake in the company's success. However, ESOPs can be very expensive to establish and maintain. They are also not an option for companies in the very early stages of development. In order to establish an ESOP, a small business must have employees and must be in business for three years.

Private investors are another possible source of equity financing. A number of computer databases and venture capital networks have been developed in recent years to help link entrepreneurs to potential private investors. A number of government sources also exist to fund small businesses through equity financing and other arrangements. Small Business Investment Companies (SBICs) are privately owned investment companies, chartered by the states in which they operate, that make equity investments in small businesses that meet certain conditions. There are also many "hybrid" forms of financing available that combine features of debt and equity financing.

METHODS OF EQUITY FINANCING

There are two primary methods that small businesses use to obtain equity financing: the private placement of stock with investors or venture capital firms; and public stock offerings. Private placement is simpler and more common for young companies or startup firms. Although the private placement of stock still involves compliance with several federal and state securities laws, it does not require formal registration with Securities and Exchange Commission. The main requirements for private placement of stock are that the company cannot advertise the offering and must make the transaction directly with the purchaser.

In contrast, public stock offerings entail a lengthy and expensive registration process. In fact, the costs associated with a public stock offering can account for more than 20 percent of the amount of capital raised. As a result, public stock offerings are generally a better option for mature companies than for startup firms. Public stock offerings may offer advantages in terms of maintaining control of a small business, however, by spreading ownership over a diverse group of investors rather than concentrating it in the hands of a venture capital firm.

Entrepreneurs interested in obtaining equity financing must prepare a formal business plan, including complete financial projections. Like other forms of financing, equity financing requires an entrepreneur to sell his or her ideas to people who have money to invest. Careful planning can help convince potential investors that the entrepreneur is a competent manager who will have an advantage over the competition. Overall, equity financing can be an attractive option for many small businesses. But experts suggest that the best strategy is to combine equity financing with other types, including the entrepreneur's own funds and debt financing, in order to spread the business's risks and ensure that enough options will be available for later financing needs. Entrepreneurs must approach equity financing cautiously in order to remain the main beneficiaries of their own hard work and long-term business growth.

FURTHER READING:

Gladstone, David. *Venture Capital Handbook.* Englewood Cliffs, NJ: Prentice Hall, 1988.

Hamilton, Brian. *Financing for the Small Business.* Washington, D.C.: U.S. Small Business Administration, 1990.

Lindsey, Jennifer. *The Entrepreneur's Guide to Capital.* Chicago: Probus, 1986.

Schilit, W. Keith. *The Entrepreneur's Guide to Preparing a Winning Business Plan and Raising Venture Capital.* Englewood Cliffs, NJ: Prentice Hall, 1990.

Silver, A. David. *Up Front Financing: The Entrepreneur's Guide.* New York: Wiley, 1982.

Timmons, Jeffrey A. *Planning and Financing the New Venture.* Amherst, NH: Brick House Publishing Company, 1990.

SEE ALSO: Initial Public Offering; Investor Relations and Reporting; Stocks

ERGONOMICS

Ergonomics is the process of changing the work environment (equipment, furniture, pace of work, etc.) to fit the physical requirements and limitations of employees, rather than forcing workers to adapt to jobs that can, over time, have a debilitating effect on their physical well-being. Companies of all shapes and sizes have increasingly recognized that establishing an ergonomically sensitive work environment for employees can produce bottom-line benefits in cutting **absenteeism**, reducing health care costs, and increasing **productivity**. The most progressive of these firms have—after careful analysis of the workplace environment and the tasks that their employees have to perform—taken steps to modify that environment (whether in a shop floor or an office) to better fit the physical needs and abilities of workers.

The **Occupational Safety and Health Administration (OSHA)** of the Department of Labor defines ergonomic disorders (EDs) as a range of health ailments arising from repeated stress to the body. These disorders—which are sometimes also called repetitive strain injuries (RSIs) or cumulative trauma disorders—may affect the musculoskeletal, nervous, or neurovascular systems. They typically strike workers involved in repetitious tasks, or those whose jobs require heavy lifting or awkward postures or movements. These ailments often occur in the upper body of workers, causing injuries in the back, neck, hands, wrists, shoulders, and/or elbows. Carpal tunnel syndrome is the most well-known of these maladies, but thousands of employees have also fallen victim to tendinitis and back injuries over the years. Ergonomics experts say that EDs are particularly prevalent in certain industries. Cashiers, nurses, assembly line workers, computer users, dishwashers, truck drivers, stock handlers, construction workers, meat cutters, and sewing machine operators are among those cited as being most at risk of falling victim to EDs.

In the mid-1990s, the issue of ergonomics has become a subject of considerable debate between unions and industries. The AFL-CIO, for instance, has called RSIs and job-related back injuries "the nation's biggest job safety problem," contending that more than 700,000 workers miss work each year because of these ailments. Certainly, for workers who are debilitated by carpal tunnel syndrome or some other injury, the consequences can be dire. Long-term disability (with its attendant diminishment of financial well-being) is a real possibility for many workers who fall victim to RSIs. Some unions have subsequently called for the Occupational Safety and Health Administration (OSHA) to impose minimum ergonomic standards, and OSHA has responded by beginning work on a standard on economics that could be ready for public comment in 1998. Industry groups have resisted these calls, though individual companies in a wide variety of industries have made efforts to consider ergonomics in their operations.

It is obviously in the best interests of workers to labor in an ergonomically sensitive environment. Many business consultants, however, contend that such an environment is also beneficial to the business itself. They point out that businesses boasting such environments often see a lower rate of absenteeism, lower health care expenses, lower turnover rates, and higher productivity than do other businesses in the same industry. OSHA estimates that the average cost to business is $29,000 per musculoskeletal disorder, and notes that 60 percent of new occupational illnesses reported to the Bureau of Labor Statistics in 1992 were disorders associated with repeated trauma. Such evidence led Greg Watchman, acting director of OSHA in 1997, to say that "repetitive-stress injuries are the biggest workplace health problem in the country today." But opponents of proposed OSHA regulations contend that the agency is overstating the impact of ergonomic disorders in the workplace, and *Nation's Business* contributor David Warner noted that the U.S. Labor Department's Bureau of Labor Statistics, which bases its findings on OSHA statistics, found that only four percent of injuries and illnesses that resulted in work absence in 1995 were reported to be a result of repetitive motions.

For small business owners, building an ergonomically sensitive work environment can depend on a number of different factors. While instituting an additional work break or two during the workday (a simple step that is sometimes cited as a deterrent to development of carpal tunnel syndrome and other repetition-related injuries) does not require the business owner to make any additional capital expenditures, instituting physical changes can be significantly more expensive, especially for established businesses that are small. Buying ergonomic furniture or making significant changes in assembly line layout can be quite expensive, and while the owner of a new business may choose to take ergonomics into account with

his or her initial investment, it may be more difficult for the already-established small business owner to replace still-functional equipment and furniture. Each small business owner must determine for himself or herself whether the long-term gains that can be realized from establishing an ergonomically sound workplace (employee retention, productivity, diminished health costs, etc.) make up for the added financial investment (and possible debt) that such expenditures entail.

RISK FACTORS In the mid-1990s OSHA cited a set of risk factors—along with corresponding limits—that businesses should consider when considering ergonomics issues in their workplace. Primary risk factors and limits cited by OSHA, wrote Warner, included:

- Performing the same motion or pattern of motions for more than two hours at a time.

- Using tools or machines that cause vibrations for more than two hours a day.

- Handling objects that weigh more than 25 pounds more than one time in a work shift.

- Working in fixed or awkward positions for more than two hours a day.

- Performing work that is mechanically or electronically paced for more than four hours at a time.

FURTHER READING:

Warner, David. "OSHA is Moving on Ergonomics Rule." *Nation's Business.* August 1997.

SEE ALSO: Workplace Safety

ESTATE TAXES

Estate taxes are taxes due to the federal government upon the death of the owner of a business or estate. At first glance, IRS figures indicate that the tax has a far greater impact on wealthy individuals than on small business owners, but representatives of the latter group insist that it has long been a dreaded levy that packs a deceptive punch among small businesses. They charge that some companies have purposefully stunted their growth in order to avoid ringing up an overwhelming estate tax debt, while others have minimized the impact only through canny—and time-consuming—estate planning. Given such sentiments, recent changes in estate tax law have been warmly received by the nation's small business community.

Federal estate taxes were first established by Congress more than 80 years ago. Since 1976, estate taxes have ranged from 37 percent to 55 percent, depending on the value of the estate, but each citizen had a one-time exemption of $600,000—dubbed the "unified credit"—that may be used against the estate tax or another federal tax known as the gift tax. In 1997, however, this one-time exemption underwent a significant change for the better for small business owners, as the balanced budget deal included a major piece of estate tax relief. Under the agreement, the exemption was increased from $600,000 to $1.3 million, provided the heirs have been involved in operating the business for at least 10 years. "This [change]," commented Janean Chun in *Entrepreneur,* "will be a relief to family business owners, who may have been limiting their growth to avoid paying estate taxes. It will likely allow family-owned businesses to be passed from one generation to the next, rather than having to be sold to pay inheritance taxes."

ESTATE TAX PAYMENT OPTIONS

Usually, taxes on an estate are due nine months after the death of an individual. However, estates involving closely held businesses have the option of making installment payments instead. These installment payments, which include interest, can be spread out over as long as 14 years, and the first $1 million of the business's value is eligible for a low 4 percent interest rate.

MINIMIZING LIABILITY In addition, small business owners worried about looming estate taxes can take several steps to minimize its impact. "One of the principal steps that companies take in preparing for an expected estate-tax bill is to buy life insurance on the owner or owners," wrote *Nation's Business* contributor Joan Pryde, "making certain that the policy is owned by the company or a life-insurance trust and that the proceeds are kept out of the owner's taxable estate. Another popular estate-planning technique involves the annual gift giving that is tax-free as long as it doesn't exceed $10,000 per recipient. The gifts can be in the form of stock or other assets." Pryde points out that businesses can also use tax-exempt charitable bequests of business interests and trusts to minimize estate tax liability. In addition, "transferring ownership of a business through buy-sell agreements, partnerships, trusts, or outright gifts is a key component in many of the planning strategies available to minimize or eliminate estate-tax liability." Business experts caution that taking such steps may be even more important—and also even more complicated—when a small business is owned by two or more family members, since the business can potentially be hit with estate taxes every time one of the owners passes away.

Small business consultants note, however, that establishment of various estate planning initiatives generally involves a fairly significant outlay of cash in and of itself. "You can create trusts, and you can create other vehicles, but they're very costly to administer, and they're very prone to being overturned by the IRS if you don't dot every 'i' and cross every 't,' an owner of an accounting firm told Pryde. Avoiding the estate tax, said the accountant, "creates wonderful work for accountants and lawyers, but that's not really to the benefit of the small business."

A final option for small business owners hoping to avoid estate taxes is to sell the business before he or she dies. While such a step brings other tax issues to life, it does provide the owner with cash to pay the estate tax. But as Pryde pointed out, "often the whole point of maintaining a business is to be able to pass it on to the next generation. So selling a business is usually the last resort."

FURTHER READING:

Chun, Janean. "The New Deal." *Entrepreneur.* October 1997.

Pryde, Joan. "The Estate-Tax Toll on Small Firms." *Nation's Business.* August 1997.

"Reform Plans on Congress' Agenda." *Nation's Business.* August 1997.

SEE ALSO: Retirement Planning; Succession Plans; Tax Planning

EXPENSE ACCOUNTS

Expense accounts, also called expense allowances, are plans under which companies reimburse employees for business-related expenses. These expenses include travel, entertainment, gifts, and other expenses related to the employer's business activity. Of particular interest to businesses and their employees is the tax treatment of business-related expenses, the types of expenses for which employees will be reimbursed, and the manner in which those reimbursements are made.

For tax purposes a company's expense account plan is either accountable or nonaccountable. An accountable plan must meet the following requirements of the **Internal Revenue Service**: there must be a business connection; expenses must be substantiated (usually through a receipt); and any amount received by an employee in excess of actual expenses must be returned to the employer. Substantiation means that the employer must be able to identify the specific nature of each expense and determine that the expense was business-related. Expenses may not be aggregated into broad categories, and they may not be reported using vague terminology. If the company's plan is in fact an accountable plan, then all money received by an employee under the plan is excluded from the employee's gross income. It is not reported as wages or other compensation, and it is exempt from withholding.

Companies that fail to require employees to substantiate their expenses or allow employees to retain amounts in excess of substantiated expenses are considered by the IRS to have nonaccountable plans. Funds that employees receive under nonaccountable plans are treated as income, subject to withholding, and such expenses are deductible by the employee only as a miscellaneous itemized deduction. Even then, the expenses are deductible only if they exceed two percent of the employee's adjusted gross income.

The tax laws affecting business-related expenses change from time to time. Starting in 1994, for example, allowable meal expenses were reduced from 80 percent to 50 percent. Other types of business-related expenses affected by changing tax laws include deductions for spousal business travel and dues, deductions for memberships in certain types of clubs, and deductions for gifts.

It is in the best interests of both employer and employee that all affected parties have a complete understanding of expense accounts and reimbursable expenses. Employees who find that they are incurring business-related expenses need to determine from their employer exactly what types of expenses are reimbursable, and companies—and especially small business owners—need to make sure that employees do not take advantage of expense account policies with excessive spending on lodging, food, and entertainment. In an effort to control spiraling travel and other business-related expenses, some companies have developed reimbursement policies that spell out in detail the various travel expenses qualify for reimbursement. For example, companies may require employees to book their travel in a certain way or from certain vendors.

Because of the IRS's substantiation requirement, employees need to carefully document all business-related expenses. Receipts are normally required for all expenses. If it is not possible to obtain a receipt, the amount of the expense should be noted along with the date, place, and reason for the expense.

SEE ALSO: Record Retention; Tax-Deductible Business Expenses

EXPERIENCE AND LEARNING CURVES

Learning curves graphically portray the costs and benefits of experience when performing routine or repetitive tasks. Also known as experience curves, cost curves, efficiency curves, and productivity curves, they illustrate how the cost per unit of output decreases over time as the result of learning and experience. That is, as cumulative output increases, learning and experience cause the cost per unit to decrease. Experience and learning curves are used by businesses in production planning, cost forecasting, and setting delivery schedules, among other applications.

Learning curves are geometric curves that can be graphed on the basis of a formula. Typically the X (horizontal) axis measures cumulative output, and the Y (vertical) axis measures the cost per unit. The curve starts with a high cost per unit at the beginning of output, decreases quickly at first, then levels out as cumulative output increases. The slope of the learning curve is an indication of the rate at which learning becomes transformed into cost savings.

An 80 percent learning curve is standard for many activities and is sometimes used as an average in cost forecasting and production planning. An 80 percent learning curve means that, for every doubling of output, the cost of new output is 80 percent of prior output. As output doubles from one unit to two units to four units, etc., the learning curve descends quite sharply as costs decrease dramatically. As output increases, it takes longer to double previous output, and the learning curve flattens out. Thus, costs decrease at a slower pace when cumulative output is higher.

One can explain the shape of learning curves another way. When a new task or production operation begins, a person or system learns quickly, and the learning curve is steep. With each additional repetition, less learning occurs and the curve flattens out. At the beginning of production or learning, individuals or systems are said to be ''high'' on the learning curve. That means that costs per unit are high, and cumulative output is low. Individuals and systems ''move down'' the experience or learning curve by learning to complete repetitive tasks more efficiently, eliminating hesitation and mistakes, automating certain tasks, and making adjustments to procedures or systems.

Some theorists believe that learning curves are not actually curves, but more like jagged lines that follow a curving pattern. They assert that learning occurs in brief spurts of progress, followed by small fallbacks to previous levels, rather than in a smooth progressive curve. Such a model of learning, however, does not affect the usefulness of learning curves in business and production applications.

System changes that affect how tasks are accomplished cause disruptions in learning curves. Every change has costs and, presumably, benefits that can be graphed by overlaying the learning curve based on the new way of doing things with the old learning curve. When the change is introduced, a new learning curve starts at a point above the current learning curve. The new learning curve soon intersects the old learning curve as cumulative output increases. The graphic area above the old learning curve and under the new learning curve represents costs associated with the change. Once the new learning curve intersects the old learning curve, the area under the old learning curve and above the new learning curve represents benefits associated with the change. Optimally, no new changes would be introduced until change benefits exceed change costs.

FURTHER READING:

Henry, Jane, ed. *Creative Management.* London: Sage Publications, 1992.

Weiss, Howard J., and Mark E. Gershon. *Production and Operations Management.* Boston: Allyn and Bacon, 1989.

EXPORT-IMPORT BANK

The United States Export-Import (Ex-Im) Bank, originally established in 1945, is an independent agency that was created to help finance U.S. exports, provide credit to purchasers of U.S. goods outside the United States, and guarantee export loans by commercial banks. In 1996, more than 80 percent of the Export-Import Bank's transactions involved establishments classified as small businesses. Moreover, small businesses accounted for a particularly large percentage (87 percent) of the Ex-Im Bank's insurance authorizations, the total of which was valued at $3.8 billion.

Given such statistics—and the U.S. Congress's 1997 authorization of an extension of the bank's charter into the next century—it is not surprising that small business consultants and analysts tout the institution as one of the most viable sources of financing for small- and mid-sized exporters. This viability is underscored by the continued reluctance of many banks to make loans for international trade purposes, despite the growing consensus that international markets are a potentially lucrative new area for many small businesses to explore. "You've seen the statistics on the economic benefits of exporting," wrote Jan Alexander in *Working Woman.* "You've read the success stories about small companies that quadrupled their revenues through international sales. All you need is a little extra cash to get things started." But since "loan officers in the U.S. have a tendency to see nearly all foreign markets as unpredictable and all loans associated with foreign expansion as very risky," said Alexander, organizations like the Export-Import Bank and the **U.S. Small Business Administration (SBA)**"have a mandate to help American businesses each step of the way, offering instruction

and support in everything from identifying viable foreign markets to closing and financing the deal."

The Export-Import Bank confirms as much in its own words. "Small business is big business at the Export-Import Bank of the United States," stated bank representative Angela M. Phifer in *Business America.* "Ex-Im Bank provides financing for U.S. export sales that would not happen otherwise. Ex-Im Bank only steps in where U.S. exports and jobs are endangered by foreign trade practices, contrary to a free market system. Ex-Im Bank levels the playing field for U.S. companies facing subsidized foreign competition." Added Maria Luisa Haley, one of the bank's directors: "We want to ensure that no innovative small company loses the opportunity to make a foreign sale because it lacks working capital or competitive export financing."

Indeed, organizations such as the Ex-Im Bank are widely recognized as a valuable resource for small businesses that might otherwise be wholly muscled out of international markets by larger competitors. "Small business and middle market companies must be aware of the existence of export financing programs that can help them increase their export sales by providing access to competitively priced working capital financing," said William Easton in *Business Credit.* "Historically, small businesses and middle market companies have experienced a significant competitive disadvantage in obtaining working capital financing versus larger Fortune 500 companies." Easton noted that lenders' usual exclusion of foreign accounts receivable and inventory that will be exported from a borrower's collateral base "penalizes both smaller and more highly leveraged businesses that are more dependent upon their assets' value than larger, more highly capitalized companies." The programs maintained by the Ex-Im Bank are designed to address these competitive disadvantages.

PRIMARY EX-IM PROGRAMS

The primary way in which the Ex-Im Bank aids small- and medium-sized U.S. exporters is through one or more of its financing programs. These are summarized as follows:

WORKING CAPITAL GUARANTEE PROGRAM The Working Capital Guarantee Program (WCGP), which is operated in conjunction with the SBA's Export Working Capital Program, assists small business exporters in obtaining the capital they need to purchase inventory or raw materials, market exports, or engage in manufacturing activities. "Under the WCGP," said Phifer, "Ex-Im Bank provides repayment guarantees to lenders on secured, short-term working capital loans made to qualified exporters. The guarantee may be approved for a single loan to a revolving line of credit. If the exporter defaults on the loan, Ex-Im

Bank will cover 90 percent of the loan and interest up to the date of claim payment at the stated rate on the loan.'' Moreover, according to Alexander, if you are a small business owner hoping to export to Russia or another high-risk country, ''the Export-Import Bank will issue insurance policies that assume up to 98 percent of the commercial risk and 100 percent of the political risk in extending credit to your foreign customer.''

The WCGP program is the largest of the Ex-Im Bank's lending programs. In fiscal year 1996, the Bank approved a record $378 million in financing under the WCGP. But small business owners thinking of applying for a WCGP loan should be aware of the various stipulations and conditions that are attached. Easton pointed out that the program (and the SBA's Export Working Capital Program) require the lender to obtain collateral covering 100 percent of any export and 25 percent of any related letter of credit, including bids or performance bond letters of credit that are issued to support an export sale. ''The collateral must be covered by a perfected, first priority security interest through a UCC filing, and can consist of readily identifiable export inventory and receivables. Both agencies permit advance rates on export related inventory to exceed rates that asset-based lenders permit, and allow work-in-process inventory to be included in a borrowing base. The guarantee will cover either a loan financing a single export sale or multiple export sales occurring over a period of up to one year.'' Finally, small- and mid-sized exporters can not qualify for a WCGP loan unless they have been in operation for at least one year and have a positive net worth.

In addition, WCGP loans can only be used for the following business purposes:

- Financing the purchase of raw materials for export

- Financing the purchase of finished goods for export

- Paying the cost of labor, overhead, and other materials for export

- Covering the cost of engineering, legal, and other services for export.

Finally, small business owners should be aware that there are differences between the working capital programs offered by the SBA and the Ex-Im Bank that should be weighed when deciding where to seek help. Larger loan applications—those in excess of $833,333—should be directed to the Ex-Im Bank, while those for smaller amounts should be placed with the SBA. In addition, the Export-Import Bank charges a higher front-end guarantee fee for assuming the exporter's credit risk. ''The other difference [between the two organizations],'' wrote Easton, ''relate to legislative and charter prohibitions on Ex-Im Bank's ability to support sales to buyers in certain countries, to support the sale of military equipment, or to support the sale of goods and services having less than 50 percent U.S. content.''

DELEGATED AUTHORITY LENDER PROGRAM The Delegated Authority Lender Program (DALP) was created to give qualified lenders the freedom to approve loans—and Ex-Im Bank coverage of the loan—without prior approval from the Ex-Im Bank. According to Phifer, 50 percent of the institution's transactions were undertaken under this program in its very first year of existence (1994), and that percentage has continued to rise in subsequent years. ''The Delegated Authority Lender Program empowers commercial and community banks, as well as non-bank lenders, to make decisions quickly at the local level,'' stated Phifer. ''By 'cutting red tape,' the program allows lenders to work within their own time frame.''

CITY/STATE PARTNERS PROGRAM This program is a joint effort that was launched by the Export-Import Bank and various state and local agencies and organizations to provide exporters with yet another avenue to secure financing. ''Ex-Im Bank trains the staff of its City/State Partners to market Ex-Im Bank's programs to local businesses and commercial banks, to teach seminars, to counsel exporters and banks, and to package transactions. Packaging a transaction is often too expensive for a bank to do on its own. By providing this service, City/State Partners facilitate many commercial loans that otherwise would not go forward.'' As with all of the Ex-Im Bank's lending programs, the City/State Partners Program has grown dramatically in recent years. From fiscal years 1991 to 1996, the dollar volume of loans through this program increased from $119 million to more than $270 million.

The Export-Import Bank maintains five regional trade resource centers in the United States. For more information on these centers, or on any of the institution's other programs and services, call 1-800-565-EXIM or access their Web site at http://www.exim.gov.

FURTHER READING:

Alexander, Jan. ''Where the Money Is.'' *Working Woman.* December-January 1998.

Barnes, Melinda. ''How to Select Your International Bank.'' *Business America.* October 1997.

The Big Emerging Markets: 1996 Outlook and Sourcebook. International Trade Administration, 1995.

Breaking into the Trade Game: A Small Business Guide. Washington: U.S. Small Business Administration.

Easton, William. ''SBA and Ex-Im Bank Working Capital Guarantee Program.'' *Business Credit.* July-August 1997.

Greenberger, Robert S. ''Ex-Im Bank's Head Expects Guarantees and Loans to Rise.'' *Wall Street Journal.* November 20, 1997.

Kraus, James R. ''House Extends Export-Import Bank Charter.'' *American Banker.* November 13, 1997.

Phifer, Angela M. ''Ex-Im Bank's Support for Small Business.'' *Business America.* October 1997.

Sletten, Eric. *How to Succeed in Exporting and Doing Business Internationally.* New York: John Wiley, 1994.

SEE ALSO: Emerging Markets; Exporting; Exporting—Financing and Pricing Issues

---

EXPORTING

Exporting is the practice of sending or carrying merchandise to a foreign country for trade or sale. International business is a potentially lucrative area for many businesses, but the small business owner should be aware that establishing oneself in a foreign market is a complex, time-consuming task. Many small businesses in the United States have dramatically improved their financial fortunes by pursuing exporting opportunities, but the vast majority of enterprises that have been successful in this regard did not enter the world of international trade until they had fully researched both their own exporting capabilities and various business conditions in the target market(s) abroad. Indeed, consultants point to a wide range of factors to consider when assessing your company's readiness to expand its business beyond America's borders. These include company export readiness, potential foreign markets, product **distribution** options, legal factors, operating costs and **profit margin**, financing resources, and exporting alternatives (such as joint ventures or off-shore manufacturing facilities).

Exporting is sometimes thought of as a practice that is largely the province of large businesses and international corporations, but exporting can also be helpful to a small business in a variety of ways. A small business that establishes its products in the international marketplace can increase sales and profitability, enhance its domestic reputation, reduce its dependence on domestic markets, reinvigorate the sales potential of existing products, stabilize seasonal market fluctuations, sell excess production capacity, and increase awareness of possible foreign competitors.

Of course, exporting is not a risk-free venture. Expanding a small business's operations into foreign markets may require the development of new promotional materials, assumption of increased short-term debt as a result of new operational and administrative costs, re-assignment of personnel, and adjustments in product functionality and appearance to meet the commercial and social standards of the environment in which the business hopes to establish itself. But many business analysts contend that, as the lines between domestic and international markets continue to blur, those small businesses that remain ignorant of exporting do so at their peril.

PREPARING FOR THE WORLD OF EXPORTING

Small business consultants counsel their clients to undertake a stringent regimen of research and self-analysis before committing time and resources to breaking into international markets. Indeed, consultants stress that a small business should be able to answer affirmatively to the following questions before considering expanding its business to include exporting:

- Is the business currently successful in its domestic operations?

- Does the business owner understand the types and amounts of investments—in the realms of time, capital, and people— he or she will have to make to establish the business's product in the targeted market?

- Is the business sensitive to the cultural implications of doing business in the targeted market?

- Is the business willing to commit needed resources to make the exporting effort work?

In order to arrive at an informed answer to the above questions, consultants recommend that business owners with an eye to international markets take the time to complete an international **business plan**. This document can highlight potential trouble spots and business areas that need further research. Exporting factors that should be considered in any international business plan include:

- Identification of potential market

- Demographic and political environment of potential market

- Economic status of potential market

- Social and cultural environment of potential market

- Access to potential market (includes research on tariffs and other trade barriers, treaties, trade regulations, patent and trademark protection)

- Demand for product

- Possible competition within potential market

- Possible distribution channels

- Local distribution and production environment within potential market

- Exporting methodology

- Any necessary adjustments to product or packaging

- Marketing strategy

- Cost of exporting operation
- Pricing strategy
- Projected sales
- Projected fortunes of domestic operation

SOURCES OF INFORMATION ON EXPORTING

A wide range of sources are available to help the small business owner research these issues. Trade associations, exporters' associations, state and federal government agencies, and foreign governments are all potential sources of valuable information.

Relevant trade associations include the Small Business Exporter's Association, the American Association of Exporters and Importers, the National Association of Export Companies (NEXCO), the National Federation of Export Associations (NFEA), and the National Federation of International Trade Associations (NFITA), which lists more than 150 U.S. organizations that can help small businesses enter international markets. In addition, the United States houses more than 5,000 trade and professional organizations with a wide range of industry specializations, many of which actively promote exporting among their members. The federal government, meanwhile, maintains a number of agencies that can be tremendously helpful to the small business owner who is pondering expansion into international markets. These include the United States and Foreign Commercial Service (US&FCS), the **U.S. Small Business Administration** (SBA) and its various programs (Service Corps of Retired Executives-SCORE, Small Business Development Centers-SBDCs, Small Business Institute-SBI), and the International Trade Administration (ITA), which is an arm of the **U.S. Department of Commerce** (DOC). Resources available through the ITA include international trade specialists and District Export Councils (DECs). The latter groups, which are scattered around the country, are comprised of nearly 2,000 executives with experience in international trade who have volunteered their time to help small businesses.

Finally, the U.S. government maintains three databases that can provide small business owners with important data on various exporting factors. These are the SBA's Automated Trade Locator Assistance System (SBAtlas), the National Trade Data Bank (NTDB), and Foreign Trade Report FT925. SBAtlas provides current market information to SBA clients on world markets suitable for their products and services. Foreign Trade Report FT925, meanwhile, provides users with a monthly breakdown of imports and exports by Standard Industrial Trade Classification (SITC) number for each country. The National Trade Data Bank, which is maintained by the Department of Commerce, includes more than 100,000 government documents on various aspects of export promotion and international economics.

CHANGING YOUR PRODUCT FOR THE INTERNATIONAL MARKET

Before entering a foreign market, a small business needs to make certain that the product that it is selling is suitable in its current form. As the Small Business Administration has cautioned, "when entering a foreign market, the manufacturer should consider the tastes and preferences in each market as part of marketing strategy. Frequently, only a small change may be required to successfully market the product. The color of the product, the design of the package, the size of the product all may need adjustment."

Sometimes the name of the product itself has to be changed. Horror stories abound of businesses that have launched products in foreign markets, only to belatedly discover that the product name has a negative connotation in the local language. More often, however, an exporter will find it necessary to make labeling changes (changing size measurements to the Metric system, for example, or providing instructions in three languages, as required in the European Community). Finally, the would-be exporter might have to make changes to the product itself in order to meet standards of the market in which he or she hopes to become established. Many nations, for example, have different electrical power systems; an American manufacturer that neglects to outfit its product with plugs that will fit into the target market's electrical outlets is doomed from the start.

In order to avert such disastrous scenarios, small business consultants recommend that exporters familiarize themselves with **ISO 9000**, a series of documents that provide guidance on the selection and implementation of appropriate quality management programs for international operations. Produced by the International Organization of Standardization (ISO), the ISO 9000 series is intended to document various quality assurance systems utilized by companies engaged in international trade. ISO standards are reviewed every five years to ensure that they are kept up-to-date with ever-changing international regulations and standards.

Many small business consultants also recommend that their clients not move too quickly in launching an exporting arm to their business. Instead, they suggest that entrepreneurs and small business owners take their product lines on "test drives" of one or two selected foreign markets. By conducting such testing, companies can uncover unanticipated factors that can hinder product acceptance in a given market. Indeed, test marketing allows manufacturers to check on the viability of much of their business forecasting and strategy.

METHODS OF EXPORTING

Businesses have several options to choose from when entering foreign markets. One method commonly employed is to enter into a joint business venture with a company based in the targeted market. Such arrangements often take the form of licensing agreements—wherein the business assigns the rights to distribute or manufacture its product or service to the foreign company—or off-shore production—in which a business either establishes its own facility or contracts with an off-shore facility operator to manufacture the product. Most small businesses, however, choose to introduce their products or services to foreign markets via a variety of exporting arrangements. But while there are many nuances and options associated with exporting, these various practices are commonly divided into two areas: direct exporting and indirect exporting.

DIRECT EXPORTING Direct exporting practices generally require greater initial outlays of funds, personnel, and other resources, and they are generally regarded as riskier in nature than indirect exporting options. But direct exporting can also be a tremendously profitable practice. It basically requires businesses to find a foreign buyer for its products and make all arrangements to deliver those goods to the buyer.

There are four primary methods of direct exporting, each of which entails doing business with a different element of the international business world. The simplest option if you are a small business owner is simply to export your product line directly to the end-user. End-users that may make purchases in this manner range from foreign governments and major businesses to individual consumers.

Some businesses, though, choose to sell their goods directly to foreign retailers. Firms that employ this kind of direct exporting either hire sales representatives to work in the target market or introduce themselves and their products to retailers via direct mail campaigns. The latter approach is less expensive, for it eliminates commission fees and travel expenses associated with maintaining a sales force, but it also curtails opportunities to engage in one-on-one communication with potentially valuable clients. Some business owners, of course, employ both direct mail and sales representatives to establish themselves in new markets.

Another way of direct exporting is to secure the services of a sales representative or agent who conducts business in the target market. Representatives work on a commission basis to secure buyers for the exported product; they often handle other non-competing product lines as well. Agents, meanwhile, are often empowered to make legal commitments on behalf of client businesses, so small business owners should make certain that any agreement they sign with an agent specifies whether the agent will have legal authority to represent the company.

A commonly utilized method of direct exporting is to turn to distributors, who purchase goods from U.S. companies and re-sell them for profit in international markets. Listings of distributors can be found through the Department of Commerce's Agent/Distributor Service program, trade associations, and U.S. and foreign chambers of commerce located in targeted foreign markets. Again, the legal agreement between a company and a distributor is very important, so many business analysts recommend that small business owners consult with a legal and/ or accounting professional when putting one together.

The Small Business Administration recommends several different approaches for the small business entrepreneur who wants to find foreign buyers for his or her product line. Advertising in trade journals—especially the DOC's widely read *Commercial News USA*—is commonly cited as an effective way of publicizing a small business product line to overseas markets, as are catalog and video/catalog exhibitions. Trade shows and trade missions are other potentially valuable avenues to explore, but the SBA also encourages small business owners to be proactive in their approach to finding buyers for their products. ''Rather than wait for potential foreign customers to contact you,'' suggests the SBA, ''another option is to search out foreign companies looking for the particular product you produce'' by investigating information held on the DOC's Economic Bulletin Board, the World Trade Centers Network, and other government and business sources.

INDIRECT EXPORTING Small businesses that wish to enter international markets also have the option of pursuing a variety of indirect exporting options. Many of these options involve the use of intermediaries. Export intermediaries include commissioned agents, export management companies (EMCs), export trading companies (ETCs), ETC cooperatives, and foreign trading companies.

The SBA characterizes commissioned agents as brokers who serve businesses by linking their product or service with foreign purchasers. Export management companies, meanwhile, are firms that represent the interests of a range of companies; acting as representatives for their client companies, EMCs solicit and transact business with prospective foreign buyers. They are not, however, responsible for ensuring that foreign buyers meet their payment obligations once a transaction has been made. Specific services offered by EMC generally include: undertaking market research, assessing viability of various distribution channels, arranging financing, handling export logistics (preparing invoices, arranging insurance, etc.), and providing legal advice on trade matters. Some EMCs also provide help in negotiating export contracts and after-sales support.

Export trading companies are similar to EMCs in many functional respects, but their standing is more neutral. ETCs act as agents between buyers and sellers, directly paying manufacturers for goods that they subsequently sell to purchasers. Since a small business does not have to rely on the end purchaser to receive compensation under this arrangement, an ETC is seen as a fairly risk-free indirect exporting option. ETC cooperatives, meanwhile, are described by the SBA as U.S. government-sanctioned cooperatives of companies with similar product lines who are interested in securing increased foreign market share. Agricultural interests and trade associations have enjoyed notable success with such cooperatives over the years.

Finally, small companies that choose not to enter into any of the above agreements may still explore foreign markets through agreements with export merchants or via a practice commonly known as ''piggyback exporting.'' Export merchants or agents are businessmen who will purchase and repackage products for export. They assume all risks associated with selling the goods, but analysts caution that such arrangements can also compromise a business's control over the pricing and marketing of its product in key markets. Piggyback exporting, meanwhile, is a practice wherein another company armed with an already-established export distribution system sells both its own products and those of other, often smaller enterprises who are not similarly equipped.

Business consultants view indirect exporting options such as EMCs and ETCs as sensible alternatives for small companies because they provide greater financial protection to businesses than do direct exporting avenues. Moreover, these indirect exporting options still allow an entrepreneur to publicize his or her product in international markets in relatively inexpensive fashion. Finally, they give small businesses an opportunity to gain knowledge from outfits that are both well-connected and experienced in various nuances of international trade. Analysts caution, however, that there are also possible drawbacks to casting one's lot with such organizations. Use of an intermediary in reaching and dealing with customers inevitably means that a business loses some control over the manner in which it and its products are presented. As the Small Business Administration noted in *The Trade Game: A Small Business Guide to Exporting,* this is no small matter: ''Your company's image and name are at stake. You will want to incorporate any concerns you may have into your contract, and you

will want to monitor closely the activities and progress of your intermediary.'' The small business owner also needs to gauge whether the increased sales realized through use of an intermediary compensate for the discounts that he or she has to offer to secure that intermediary's services.

Small businesses interested in securing these indirect exporting options can find further information through a number of sources, ranging from trade fairs and trade journals to organizations such as NEXCO and NFEA and government agencies such as the DOC's Office of Export Trading Company Affairs (OETCA).

FURTHER READING:

Barrett, Amy. ''It's a Small (Business) World.'' *Business Week.* April 17, 1995.

Branch, Alan E. *Elements of Export Marketing and Management.* 2d ed. New York: Chapman and Hall, 1990.

Breaking into the Trade Game: A Small Business Guide. Washington, DC: U.S. Small Business Administration, n.a.

Chan-Herur, K.C. *Communicating with Customers Around the World: A Practical Guide to Effective Cross-Cultural Business Communication.* San Francisco: AuMonde International, 1994.

Sandhusen, Richard L. *Global Marketing.* Hauppauge, NY: Barron's Educational Series, 1994.

Sletten, Eric. *How to Succeed in Exporting and Doing Business Internationally.* New York: Wiley, 1994.

''Special Report: Going Global.'' *Working Woman.* December 1997-January 1998.

SEE ALSO: Exporting—Financing and Pricing Issues; International Marketing

EXPORTING—FINANCING AND PRICING ISSUES

One of the most important elements in establishing a successful exporting business is understanding financing and pricing issues associated with international trade. Production costs and product pricing are profoundly interrelated aspects of any business venture; an enterprise has to fully understand its marketing, production, distribution, and other operating costs if it hopes to make an informed decision regarding pricing strategies for its product line. These factors are complicated enough in the domestic arena. For a company to successfully expand into foreign markets, it needs to gather even more information—often on a market or markets with which it is largely unfamiliar. This market research is essential to any company hoping to make informed decisions regarding pricing strategies—the cornerstone of any push into a new market—and secure financing. As the Small Business Administration (SBA) has noted, ''setting proper export prices is crucial to a successful international sales program; prices must be high enough to generate a reasonable profit, yet low enough to be competitive in overseas markets.''

FINANCING EXPORT SALES

Whereas large corporations are usually able to easily secure financing for exporting initiatives, either internally or through venture capitalists or lenders, small businesses often have difficulty getting financing for such plans. This is a significant obstacle, for small business owners are far more likely to need such outside financing in order to execute their exporting strategy. Analysts thus recommend that small businesses have their financial arrangements firmly in place before launching their exporting business.

Before hunting down financing for their exporting business, prospective exporters need to understanding the differences between the two general financing options that are available through commercial lenders: working capital financing and trade financing. With working capital financing, a small business can get money for long-term development. Trade financing, however, is aimed only at financing a specific business transaction, sale, or event. These loans, which are easier to qualify for than working capital financing, generally have several notable stipulations attached. Principal among these is its ''self-liquidating'' character. This means that the bank structures the loan so that it receives payment directly from the foreign company that is purchasing the borrower's goods. The bank subsequently applies the sales proceeds to the loan before crediting whatever money is left to the borrower's account. Small business analysts note that trade financing is often utilized by small and/or undercapitalized companies who have no choice but to accept the more stringent conditions associated with those loans. This does not mean that a trade financing arrangement should necessarily be avoided; it simply reflects: 1) the limited bargaining power possessed by many small businesses; and 2) the caution with which many lending institutions approach exporting financing arrangements.

Small businesses may choose from several types of institutions when seeking financing for exporting. The first of these is the local bank with which they already do business. Banks that are active in small business lending or maintain an international department are more likely to be agreeable to providing a loan than will banks without those characteristics. Since many banking institutions do not focus on export financing, it may be necessary to go elsewhere. During this search, however, the small business owner should be mindful of the differences between international trade lending and international trade services. Some banks offer international trade services, such as negotiating letters of intent, but these services do not include financing. To secure financing, the owner must make arrangements with an international lender. He or she is more likely to be successful in securing financing with such a lender if he or she can show that repayment can be made through a secondary source if necessary. The small business owner who negotiates with a bank for financing should also be prepared to provide a variety of documentation on the business, including domestic and export **business plans**; purpose of loan; export transaction-related documentation; **tax returns** (usually for the past three years); **financial statements** (again, for previous three years); projections of income, expenses, and cash flow; schedule of term debts; and signed personal financial statements.

If these financing avenues prove fruitless, the small business owner still has other places to turn. These include factoring houses, export trading companies, private trade finance companies, export management companies, and U.S. government agencies.

Factoring houses purchase export receivables on a discounted basis. These companies, which are also known as ''factors,'' agree to purchase exported materials at a certain percentage below invoice value (the percentage rate is dependent on, among other things the intended market and the type of buyer). Under this arrangement, the exporter does not receive full value for its goods, but it does receive payment immediately, and does not have to worry about future collection hassles with foreign customers who are tardy with their payments.

Private trade finance companies provide a range of financing options to small businesses in exchange for fees, commissions, or outright involvement in the transactions under consideration.

Export trading companies (ETCs) and export management companies (EMCs) are popular with some small exporters as well. In addition to providing assistance in arranging financing for exporters, ETCs and EMCs may offer a wide range of potentially helpful other services, including international market research, legal assistance, insurance, administration, warehousing and distribution, and product design. As small business consultants note, a small business that utilizes these services intelligently can productively leverage its resources.

Finally, small business owners may choose to seek assistance from the government. Several federal agencies—and some state agencies—maintain programs that offer financial aid to small enterprises seeking to expand or consolidate their businesses in foreign markets. Loan programs offered by the **U.S. Small Business Administration**, for example, include the International Trade Loan Program, a long-term financing option; the ERLC (Export Revolving Line of Credit) Program, which lasts for up to 36 months; regular SBA business loans. Businesses may also seek loans through the **Small Business Investment Company** (SBIC), the Department of Agriculture's Commodity Credit Corporation (CCC), or the Export-Import Bank of the United States (Ex-Im Bank). The latter is an independent federal agency charged with assisting U.S. exporters of goods and services through a wide range of programs. Some of these export assistance programs are maintained in cooperation with various state governments. Lastly, some small business owners choose to secure financing for deals in moderate- to high-risk emerging markets through the Overseas Private Investment Corporation (OPIC), an organization that guarantees and/or provides project loans to American companies in 140 developing nations, or the U.S. Agency for International Development (USAID). The latter agency, said *Working Woman's* Jan Alexander, "commits loans and awards grants to eligible countries, with the requirement that the country use the money for projects that buy commodities or services from U.S. suppliers. If [an American small business] can address a market need in any one of four areas—the environment, agribusiness, the health sciences, or information technology—[the business] might be able to get a so-called procurement opportunity, paid for by USAID."

EVALUATING COST FACTORS

A business that seeks to determine its total operating expenses for export products—whether doing so for its own internal records or to secure export financing—needs to make certain that it includes only those costs that are pertinent to its international efforts. For example, a company that has incorporated the total annual cost of raw materials that are used in products sold in both domestic and international markets into calculations of exporting expenses is unintentionally inflating the cost of its forays into the foreign market. Myriad other operating cost factors can be misconstrued or misinterpreted as well.

To arrive at an accurate understanding of total exporting costs, then, many businesses utilize "marginal cost pricing." This method calculates the direct operating expenses of producing and selling products for export as a way of establishing a bottom-line figure below which a company cannot set a price without incurring a loss. In order to tabulate this figure accurately, businesses first determine the fixed costs (production costs, overhead, administration, research and development) of producing an additional unit for export. They then incorporate any product modification expenses that are necessary into the equation. Once this "floor price" has been established, businesses should deduct any operating expenses that are not attributable to international operations. Moreover, they should prorate other operating costs—including insurance, rental or leasing obligations, factory over-head costs, taxes, administration, communications, patent and trademark fees, legal expenses, and office supplies—that cover a business's combined domestic and foreign operations. Finally, companies need to calculate the various costs involved in manufacturing the product or products for export.

The primary **costs** associated with producing a good for export are usually direct materials and labor costs. Other cost factors associated with exporting can include promotional materials (including brochures, magazines, catalogs, slide shows, and videos), sales commissions, travel expenses, export advertising, packing materials, market research, translation costs, product modification expenses, consultancy fees, and distribution expenses (from freight fees to tariffs to customs duties). These cost factors can be extremely variable, depending on the nature of the product, the exporting company's business philosophy, and its chosen channels of distribution. They can also be fundamentally altered by political, economic, and environmental changes within a target market, and legal and/or regulatory developments in the world of international commerce.

Currency value fluctuations, for instance, can dramatically alter a company's profit margin. The SBA recommends that small businesses new to exporting arrange transactions in U.S. dollars; that is, they should both price their goods and request payment for those goods in U.S. dollars. This precaution provides a company with significant protection against such fluctuations. If a buyer balks at conducting the transaction in U.S. dollars, an exporter can still protect him or herself through **factoring** or hedging. In factoring, the exporter transfers title to its foreign accounts receivable on a discounted basis to a factoring house, which will subsequently assume take care of the client's credit, collection, and accounting needs. Hedging, meanwhile, guarantees a set exchange rate through the use of option and forward contracts.

A second international pricing method that is sometimes utilized is called the "cost-plus" method. This is arrived at by taking a company's domestic price for a product and adding all exporting costs, including documentation expenses, freight charges, customs duties, and international marketing costs. Trade experts note that this method allows a business to maintain its domestic profit margin percentage, but it does not factor in local market conditions that might make introduction of the product a questionable endeavor.

PRICING GOODS AND SERVICES FOR FOREIGN MARKETS

"Pricing products to be competitive in international markets can be a challenge," cautioned the

SBA in its exporting guidebook, *Breaking into the Trade Game: A Small Business Guide.* "Pricing that works in one market may be totally uncompetitive in another." A well-considered pricing strategy, then, is regarded as an essential component of any business's exporting plan.

Any business, large or small, needs to ponder several factors when putting together a pricing strategy for foreign markets. In addition to considering operating and marketing expenses, businesses should weigh both competition and product demand within the targeted country. Finally, a business owner pondering entry into the world of international trade needs to establish practices that are in concert with his or her ultimate goals. "Your goals will vary depending on the target overseas market," noted the SBA. "Are you entering the market with a new or unique product? Are you selling excess or obsolete products? Can your product demand a higher price because of brand recognition or superior quality? Maybe you are willing to reduce profits to gain market share for long-term growth. Your pricing decisions will be affected by your company's goals."

Very few exporters are able to set prices for their goods and services without carefully evaluating their competitor's pricing policies. In a crowded foreign market that features a number of competitors, an exporter may have little choice but to match the going price or even go below it to establish a market share. Conversely, an exporter armed with a product or service that is new to a particular foreign market may be able to set a higher price than normally charged domestically. Of course, sometimes a company introduces a brand new product or service into a foreign market, only to discover to its great distress that nobody is interested in the product or service. Businesses that find themselves in such situations almost invariably did not devote sufficient time or resources to assessing market demand.

PAYMENT MECHANISMS IN INTERNATIONAL TRADE

There are five principal arrangements that exporters use in securing payment for their products or services. The most popular method of payment among exporters is, understandably, one in which they receive payment for their goods in advance. Indeed, many small businesses refuse to make exporting arrangements with a buyer who is unwilling to agree to this transaction method.

PAYMENT IN ADVANCE This protects exporters from buyers who prove unwilling or unable to make full payment once they have received the ordered goods. Some business analysts contend, however, that this insistence on such advantageous (for the exporter) terms may cost a company business over time if it is

not careful. They point out that some importers of their goods might interpret this stipulation as a suggestion that they do not conduct their business honorably. Well-established and respected buyers with good credit histories—exactly the sort of customers that small businesses should court—are even more likely to take offense at such a requirement. Consultants thus encourage some small business clients to be somewhat malleable regarding payment mechanisms instead of insisting on strict adherence to up-front payments on all occasions.

LETTER OF CREDIT Another payment method is known as the letter of credit (LC). The LC payment mechanism is a complex transaction that can seem somewhat cumbersome, but its safeguards make it quite attractive to many businesses involved in international trade. In this situation, a bank in essence insures that the importer's credit is good by bestowing upon it an LC. Under this arrangement, the bank makes payment to the importer. Financial experts note that if a letter of credit comes from a U.S. bank, it virtually eliminates the commercial credit risk of an export sale. In other words, the exporter is assured of receiving his or her due compensation for the sale. The terms of an irrevocable letter of credit cannot be changed without the express permission of the exporter once it has been opened. The letter of credit also extends some protection to importers, for it includes steps that ensure that the exporter has fully complied with the terms of sale discussed in the LC. But some importers balk at the added costs that LC arrangements bring on them.

Letters of credit can be shaped in accordance with a number of different payment schedules. For instance, some LCs call for payment within 72 hours, while others call for payment a certain number of days after export materials have been received. Most exporters, however, prefer to have a specified date of payment included in the letter of credit.

DOCUMENTARY COLLECTION This payment mechanism, which is also known as a draft, is roughly equivalent to COD (cash on delivery) or payment by check terms. Under this system of payment, a draft is drawn that requires the buyer to make payment either on sight (sight draft) or by a specified date (time draft). Legal possession of the products does not pass from the exporter to the importer until the draft has been paid or accepted. Analysts note that this arrangement serves to protect both parties (although an exporter may still have to pursue legal options to secure payment if the buyer defaults).

CONSIGNMENT Under terms of consignment, an exporter receives no revenue for his or her sale until the buyer of the goods has sold the products. Exporters run a greater risk of being burned financially under this arrangement than under any of the above-mentioned payment systems. If the importer proves unable to sell all the goods that he or she has received, the exporter's profits, already compromised, can be lost completely because of the cost of recovering the unsold products. Indeed, even if the goods are all sold, the exporter has no way of predicting the amount of time that will be required to do so.

OPEN ACCOUNT Among exporters, this is the most unpopular of the various international payment mechanisms that are available. It should be avoided by small businesses except in circumstances when you have an established, secure relationship with a healthy buyer who is operating in a stable country. With this arrangement, goods are manufactured and delivered to the buyer before payment is required. In some cases, payment is not required until as long as 60 days after delivery.

FURTHER READING:

Alexander, Jan. "Where the Money Is." *Working Woman*. December 1997-January 1998.

Branch, Alan E. *Elements of Export Marketing and Management*. 2d ed. New York: Chapman and Hall, 1990.

Breaking into the Trade Game: A Small Business Guide. Washington, DC: U.S. Small Business Administration, n.a.

Sandhusen, Richard L. *Global Marketing*. Hauppauge, NY: Barron's Educational Series, 1994.

Sletten, Eric. *How to Succeed in Exporting and Doing Business Internationally*. New York: Wiley, 1994.

SEE ALSO: International Exchange Rate; International Marketing; Pricing

EXTERNAL AUDITS

An audit is a systematic process of objectively obtaining and evaluating the accounts or financial records of a governmental, business, or other entity. Whereas some businesses rely on audits conducted by employees—these are called **internal audits**—others utilize so-called external or independent auditors to handle this task (some businesses rely on both types of audits). "The primary objective of the external audit is to add credibility to the financial statements of management," said Leonard Savoie in *What Every Manager Needs to Know About Finance*. "The role of the external auditor is to render an independent professional opinion on the fairness of financial statements to the extent that is required by generally accepted auditing standards." External audits are often used by smaller businesses that do not have the resources or inclination to maintain internal audit systems.

INTERNAL AND EXTERNAL AUDITORS

Internal auditors are employees of the organization whose activities are being examined and evaluated. The primary goal of internal auditing is to determine the extent to which the organization adheres to managerial policies, procedures, and requirements.

The independent or external auditor, on the other hand, is not an employee of the organization. He or she performs an examination with the objective of issuing a report containing an opinion on a client's financial statements. The attest function of external auditing refers to the auditor's expression of an opinion on a company's financial statements. The typical independent audit leads to an attestation regarding the fairness and dependability of the statements. This is communicated to the officials of the audited entity in the form of a written report accompanying the statements (an oral presentation of findings may sometimes be requested as well). In addition, Savoie pointed out that "the independent auditor has the professional competence to provide many additional services not required in performing the audit. Frequently during the course of the audit, he may become aware of opportunities to improve the efficiency or effectiveness of the client's accounting procedures. Recommendations of this nature are often included in the auditor's report to management on internal controls."

The audit committee of an enterprise is a major committee of the board of directors or the board of trustees. The committee is often composed of outside directors who nominate the independent auditors and react to the auditor's report and findings. Matters that the auditor believes should be brought to the attention of the shareholders are usually first brought before the audit committee.

TYPES OF EXTERNAL AUDITS

Major types of audits conducted by external auditors include the financial statements audit, the operational audit, and the compliance audit. A financial statement audit (or attest audit) examines financial statements, records, and related operations to ascertain adherence to generally accepted accounting principles. An operational audit examines an organization's activities in order to assess performances and develop recommendations for improvements, or further action. A compliance audit has as its objective the determination of whether an organization is following established procedures or rules. Auditors also perform statutory audits, which are performed to comply with the requirements of a governing body, such as a federal, state, or city government or agency.

INDEPENDENT AUDITING STANDARDS

The auditing process is based on standards, concepts, procedures, and reporting practices that are primarily imposed by the American Institute of Certified Public Accountants (AICPA). The auditing process relies on evidence, analysis, conventions, and informed professional judgment. General standards are brief statements relating to such matters as training, independence, and professional care. AICPA general standards declare that:

- External audits should be performed by a person or persons having adequate technical training and proficiency as an auditor.

- In all matters relating to the assignment, complete independence should be maintained by the auditor or auditors.

- The independent auditor or auditors should make sure that all aspects of the performance of the examination and the preparation of the audit report are carried out with a high standard of professionalism.

Standards of fieldwork provide basic planning standards to be followed during audits. AICPA standards of field work stipulate that:

The work is to be adequately planned and assistants, if any, are to be properly supervised.

Independent auditors will carry out proper study and evaluation of the existing internal controls to determine their reliability and suitability for conducting all necessary auditing procedures.

External auditors will make certain that they are able to review all relevant evidential materials, whether obtained through inspection, observation, inquiries, and confirmation, so that they can form an informed and reasonable opinion regarding the financial statements under examination.

Standards of reporting describe auditing standards relating to the audit report and its requirements. AICPA standards of reporting stipulate that the auditor indicate whether the financial statements examined were presented in accordance with generally-accepted accounting principles; whether such principles were consistently observed in the current period in relation to the preceding period; and whether informative disclosures to the financial statements were adequate. Finally, the external auditor's report should include 1) an opinion about the financial statements/records that were examined, or 2) a disclaimer of opinion, which typically is included in instances where, for one reason or another, the auditor is unable to render an opinion on the state of the business's records.

THE EXTERNAL AUDITING PROCESS

The independent auditor generally proceeds with an audit according to a set process with three steps: planning, gathering evidence, and issuing a report.

In planning the audit, the auditor develops an audit program that identifies and schedules audit procedures that are to be performed to obtain the evidence. Audit evidence is proof obtained to support the audit's conclusions. Audit procedures include those activities undertaken by the auditor to obtain the evidence. Evidence-gathering procedures include observation, confirmation, calculations, analysis, inquiry, inspection, and comparison. An audit trail is a chronological record of economic events or transactions that have been experienced by an organization. The audit trail enables an auditor to evaluate the strengths and weaknesses of internal controls, system designs, and company policies and procedures.

THE AUDIT REPORT

The independent audit report sets forth the independent auditor's findings about the business's financial statements and their level of conformity with generally accepted accounting principles, applied on a basis consistent with that of the preceding year (or in conformity with some other comprehensive basis of accounting that is appropriate for the organization). A fair presentation of financial statements is generally understood by accountants to refer to whether: The accounting principles used in the statements have general acceptability; the accounting principles are appropriate in the circumstances; the financial statements are prepared so they can be used, understood, and interpreted; the information presented in the financial statements is classified and summarized in a reasonable manner; and the financial statements reflect the underlying events and transactions in a way that presents the financial position, results of operations, and cash flows within reasonable and practical limits.

The auditor's unqualified report contains three paragraphs. The introductory paragraph identifies the financial statements audited, states that management is responsible for those statements, and asserts that the auditor is responsible for expressing an opinion on them. The scope paragraph describes what the auditor has done and specifically states that the auditor has examined the financial statements in accordance with generally accepted auditing standards and has performed appropriate tests. The opinion paragraph expresses the auditor's opinion (or formally announces his or her lack of opinion and why) on whether the statements are in accordance with generally accepted accounting principles.

Various audit opinions are defined by the AICPA's Auditing Standards Board as follows:

1) Unqualified opinion—According to Jeffrey Davidson and Charles Dean, authors of *Cash Traps,* this opinion "means that all criteria were used and no restrictions prevented the disclosure of any information. This is, of course, the most favorable opinion that can be given by an auditor."

2) Explanatory language added—Circumstances may require that the auditor add an explanatory paragraph (or other explanatory language) to his or her report.

3) Qualified opinion—This type of opinion states that most of the materials were in order, except for a disparity in a certain account or transaction. In these instances, noted Davidson and Dean, the disparity is deemed "not significant enough to qualify the entire financial statement as misrepresented."

4) Adverse opinion—An adverse opinion states that the financial statements do not represent fairly the financial position, results of operations, or cash flows of the entity in conformity with generally accepted accounting principles. Such an opinion is obviously not good news for the business being audited.

5) Disclaimer of opinion—A disclaimer of opinion states that the auditor does not express an opinion on the financial statements, generally because he or she feels that the company did not present sufficient informa-tion. Again, this opinion casts an unfavorable light on the business being audited.

The fair presentation of financial statements does not mean that the statements are fraud-proof. The independent auditor has the responsibility to search for errors or irregularities within the recognized limitations of the auditing process. An auditor is subject to risks that material errors or irregularities, if they exist, will not be detected.

Investors should examine the auditor's report for citations of problems such as debt-agreement violations or unresolved lawsuits. "Going-concern" references can suggest that the company may not be able to survive as a functioning operation. If an "except for" statement appears in the report, the investor should understand that there are certain problems or departures from generally accepted accounting principles in the statements, and that these problems may cast into question whether the statements fairly depict the company's financial situation. These statements typically require the company to resolve the problem or somehow make the accounting treatment acceptable.

FURTHER READING:

American Institute of Certified Public Accountants. *AICPA Professional Standards*. Chicago, IL: Commerce Clearing House, Inc.

Davidson, Jeffrey P., and Charles W. Dean. *Cash Traps: Small Business Secrets for Reducing Costs and Improving Cash Flow*. New York: John Wiley & Sons, 1992.

Delaney, P. R. *CPA Examination Review: Auditing*. New York, NY: John Wiley & Sons, 1994.

Savoie, Leonard M. "The External Audit." In *What Every Manager Needs to Know About Finance*. Hubert D. Vos, ed. New York: Amacom, 1986.

Taylor, D. H., and G. W. Glazen. *Auditing: Integrated Concepts and Procedures*. New York, NY: John Wiley & Sons.

F

Facility layout and design is an important component of a business's overall operations, both in terms of maximizing the effectiveness of production processes and meeting employee needs and/or desires. Writing in *Production and Operations Management,* Howard J. Weiss and Mark E. Gershon defined facility layout as ''the physical arrangement of everything needed for the product or service, including machines, personnel, raw materials, and finished goods. The criteria for a good layout necessarily relate to people (personnel and customers), materials (raw, finished, and in process), machines, and their interactions.''

FACTORS IN DETERMINING LAYOUT AND DESIGN

Small business owners need to consider many operational factors when building or renovating a facility for maximum layout effectiveness. These criteria include the following:

1) Ease of future expansion or change—Facilities should be designed so that they can be easily expanded or adjusted to meet changing production needs. ''Although redesigning a facility is a major, expensive undertaking not to be done lightly, there is always the possibility that a redesign will be necessary,'' said Weiss and Gershon. ''Therefore, any design should be flexible. . . . Flexible manufacturing systems most often are highly automated facilities having intermediate-volume production of a variety of products. Their goal is to minimize changeover or setup times for producing the different products while still achieving close to assembly line (single-product) production rates.''

2) Flow of movement—The facility design should reflect a recognition of the importance of smooth process flow. In the case of factory facilities, the editors of *How to Run a Small Business* state that ''ideally, the plan will show the raw materials entering your plant at one end and the finished product emerging at the other. The flow need not be a straight line. Parallel flows, U-shaped patterns, or even a zig-zag that ends up with the finished product back at the shipping and receiving bays can be functional. However, backtracking is to be avoided in whatever pattern is chosen. When parts and materials move against or across the overall flow, personnel and paperwork become confused, parts become lost, and the attainment of coordination becomes complicated.''

3) Materials handling—Small business owners should make certain that the facility layout makes it possible to handle materials (products, equipment, containers, etc.) In an orderly, efficient—and preferably simple—manner.

4) Output needs—The facility should be laid out in a way that is conducive to helping the business meet its production needs.

5) Space utilization—This aspect of facility design includes everything from making sure that traffic lanes are wide enough to making certain that inventory storage ware-

houses or rooms utilize as much vertical space as possible.

6) Shipping and receiving—The J. K. Lasser Institute counseled small business owners to leave ample room for this aspect of operations. ''While space does tend to fill itself up, receiving and shipping rarely get enough space for the work to be done effectively,'' it said in *How to Run a Small Business.*

7) Ease of communication and support—Facilities should be laid out so that communication within various areas of the business and interactions with vendors and customers can be done in an easy and effective manner. Similarly, support areas should be stationed in areas that help them to serve operating areas.

8) Impact on employee morale and job satisfaction—Since countless studies have indicated that employee morale has a major impact on productivity, Weiss and Gershon counsel owners and managers to heed this factor when pondering facility design alternatives: ''Some ways layout design can increase morale are obvious, such as providing for light-colored walls, windows, space. Other ways are less obvious and not directly related to the production process. Some examples are including a cafeteria or even a gymnasium in the facility design. Again, though, there are costs to be traded off. That is, does the increase in morale due to a cafeteria increase productivity to the extent that the increased productivity covers the cost of building and staffing the cafeteria.''

9) Promotional value—If the business commonly receives visitors in the form of customers, vendors, investors, etc., the small business owner may want to make sure that the facility layout is an attractive one that further burnishes the company's reputation. Design factors that can influence the degree of attractiveness of a facility include not only the design of the production area itself, but the impact that it has on, for instance, ease of fulfilling maintenance/cleaning tasks.

10) Safety—The facility layout should enable the business to effectively operate in accordance with Occupational Safety and Health Assocation guideliness and other legal restrictions.

''Facility layout must be considered very carefully because we do not want to constantly redesign the facility,'' summarized Weiss and Gershon. ''Some of the goals in designing the facility are to ensure a minimum amount of materials handling, to avoid bottlenecks, to minimize machine interference,

to ensure high employee morale and safety, and to ensure flexibility. Essentially, there are two distinct types of layout. *Product layout* is synonymous with assembly line and is oriented toward the products that are being made. *Process layout* is oriented around the processes that are used to make the products. Generally, product layout is applicable for high-volume repetitive operations, while process layout is applicable for low-volume custom-made goods.''

DIFFERENCES BETWEEN OFFICE AND FACTORY LAYOUTS

Offices and manufacturing facilities are typically designed in much different ways—a reflection of the disparate products that the two entities make. ''A factory produces things,'' wrote Stephan Konz in *Facility Design.* ''These things are moved with conveyors and lift trucks; factory utilities include gas, water, compressed air, waste disposal, and large amounts of power as well as telephones and computer networks. A layout criterion is minimization of transportation cost.'' Konz pointed out, however, that the mandate of business offices is to produce information, whether disseminated in physical (reports, memos, and other documents), electronic (computer files), or oral (telephone, face-to-face encounters) form. ''Office layout criteria, although hard to quantify, are minimization of communication cost and maximization of employee productivity,'' wrote Konz.

Layout requirements can also differ dramatically by industry. The needs of service-oriented businesses, for instance, are often predicated on whether customers receive their services at the physical location of the business (such as at a bank or pet grooming shop, for instance) or whether the business goes to the customer's home or place of business to provide the service (as with exterminators, home repair businesses, plumbing services, etc.) In the latter instances, these businesses will likely have facility layouts that emphasize storage space for equipment, chemicals, and paperwork rather than spacious customer waiting areas. Manufacturers may also have significantly different facility layouts, depending on the unique needs that they have. After all, the production challenges associated with producing jars of varnish or mountaineering equipment are apt to be considerably different than those of making truck chassis or foam beach toys. Retail outlets comprise yet another business sector that have unique facility layout needs. Such establishments typically emphasize sales floor space, inventory logistics, foot traffic issues, and overall store attractiveness when studying facility layout issues.

Konz also observed that differences in factory and office layouts can often be traced to user expectations. ''Historically, office workers have been much more concerned with status and aesthetics than factory workers. A key consideration in many office layouts is 'Who will get the best window location?' To show their status, executives expect, in addition to preferred locations, to have larger amounts of space. Rank expects more privacy and more plush physical surroundings.'' In addition, ''offices are designed to be 'tasteful' and to 'reflect the organization's approach to business dealings.' '' Conversely, in the factory setting, aesthetic elements take a back seat to utility.

Given these emphases, it is not surprising that, as a general rule, office workers will enjoy advantages over their material production brethren in such areas as ventilation, lighting, acoustics, and climate control.

FURTHER READING:

Cornacchia, Anthony J. ''Facility Management: Life in the Fast Lane.'' *The Office.* June 1994.

Groover, M. P. *Automation, Production Systems, and Computer-Integrated Manufacturing.* Englewood Cliffs, NJ: Prentice-Hall, 1987.

J. K. Lasser Institute. *How to Run a Small Business.* 7th ed. New York: McGraw-Hill, 1994.

Konz, Stephen. *Facility Design.* New York: John Wiley and Sons, 1985.

Myers, John. ''Fundamentals of Production that Influence Industrial Facility Designs.'' *Appraisal Journal.* April 1994.

Weiss, Howard J., and Mark E. Gershon. *Production and Operations Management.* Boston: Allyn and Bacon, 1989.

SEE ALSO: Construction; Facility Management; Renovation

FACILITY MANAGEMENT

Facility management encompasses all activities related to keeping a complex operating. Facilities include grocery stores, auto shops, sports complexes, jails, office buildings, hospitals, hotels, retail establishments, and all other revenue-generating or government institutions. Responsibilities associated with facility management typically include a wide range of function and support services, including janitorial services; facility and office **security**; property or building management; engineering services; space planning and accounting; mail and messenger services; records management; computing, telecommunications and information systems; safety; and other support duties. It is the job of the facility manager to create an environment that encourages productivity, is safe, is pleasing to clients and customers, meets government mandates, and is efficient.

DIFFERENT BUSINESSES AND THEIR DIFFERENT FACILITY NEEDS

The term ''facility'' is used to refer to a broad spectrum of buildings, complexes, and other physical entities. ''The only thread common among these entities is the fact that they are all *places,* wrote Alan M. Levitt in *Disaster Planning and Recovery: A Guide for Facility Professionals.* ''A 'facility' may be a space or an office or suite of offices; a floor or group of floors within a building; a single building or a group of buildings or structures. These structures may be in an urban setting or freestanding in a suburban or rural setting. The structures or buildings may be a part of a complex or office park or campus.'' The key is to define the facility as a physical place where business activities are done, and to make facility management plans in accordance with the needs and demands of those business activities. After all, the facility needs of a movie theatre, a museum, a delicatessen, a plastics manufacturer, and a bank are apt to be considerably different, even though there will likely be certain basic needs that all will share (furniture, office space, air conditioning systems, light fixtures, etc.). Good facility management is concerned with addressing those needs in the best and most cost-effective ways possible. Indeed, facility management encompasses a wide range of responsibilities, including the following:

- Monitoring organization efficiency, since, as the J.K. Lasser Institute noted in *How to Run a Small Business,* ''personnel, machines, supplies, work in progress, finished products, and deliveries must all be coordinated if your plant is to be successful. Production efforts must be judged by time, cost, quantity, and quality.''

- Ensuring that the business receives the most it can for its facility-related expenditures (this is often done through standardization of company-wide needs so that high-volume purchases of necessary products can be made).

- Real estate procurement, leasing, and disposal (or facility construction, renovation, and relocation).

- Ensuring that the divergent processes, procedures, and standards present in a business complement rather than interfere with one another.

- Monitoring all aspects of facility maintenance and upkeep so that the business can operate at highest capacity.

- Tracking and responding to environmental, health, safety, and security issues.

- Ensuring facility compliance with relevant codes and regulations

- Anticipating future facility needs in areas as diverse as fluorescent light procurement, new space for expanded assembly lines, automation, and wiring for new computer networks.

- Educating work force about all manner of standards and procedures, from ordering office supplies to acting in the event of a disaster.

THE EVOLVING CHARACTER OF FACILITY MANAGEMENT

Facility management has traditionally been associated with janitorial services, mailrooms, and security. Since the mid-1900s, though, facility management has evolved into a demanding discipline. Factors driving the complexity of the facility manager's job are numerous. For example, facilities have become much larger and more complicated, often relying on computerized and electronic support systems that require expertise to operate and repair. As Randy Brown observed in *Buildings,* "personal computer networks, telecommunications systems and other technological tools have significantly increased office tenant requirements in the past 15 years." This trend is evident in manufacturing sectors as well.

Of course, many other factors have impacted on the challenges of facility management as well in recent years. For example, the newfound corporate cost-consciousness that emerged during the 1980s has generated an emphasis on operational efficiency. Writing in *IIE Solutions,* Steven M. Price summarized the facility manager's situation thusly: "Facilities professionals are being asked to contain costs while achieving maximum beneficial use—that is, to achieve more with less." In addition, philosophical changes such as increased reliance on teamwork, cross-functional teams, and telecommuting have created new spacing and infrastructure demands. Finally, the responsibilities of facility managers have continued to broaden into all areas of facility upkeep, including insuring that the business adheres to regulatory requirements in such areas as handicapped access, hazardous material handling and disposal, and other "safe workplace" issues.

The end result of new technology, efficiency pressures, and government regulations has been an expansion of the facility management role. Facility managers in the 1990s are often highly trained and educated and must wear several hats. Depending on the size of the complex, the manager will likely be responsible for directing a facility management and maintenance staffs. In addition to overseeing the im-

portant duties related to standard maintenance, mailroom, and security activities, he may also be responsible for providing engineering and architectural services, hiring subcontractors, maintaining computer and telecommunications systems, and even buying, selling, or leasing real estate or office space.

For example, suppose that a company has decided to consolidate five branch offices into a central computerized facility. It may be the facility manager's job to plan, coordinate, and manage the move. He may have to find the new space and negotiate a purchase. And he will likely have to determine which furniture and equipment can be moved to the new office, and when and how to do so with a minimal disruption of the operation. This may include negotiating prices for new furniture and equipment or balancing needs with a limited budget. The facility management department may also furnish engineering and architectural design services for the new space, and even provide input for the selection of new computer and information systems. Of import will be the design and implementation of various security measures and systems that reduce the risk of theft and ensure worker safety. The manager will also be responsible for considering federal, state, and local regulations. For example, he will need to ensure that the complex conforms with mandates associated with the **Americans with Disabilities Act (ADA)**, clean air and other environmental protection regulations, and other rules. The ADA dictates a list of requirements related to disabled employee and patron access with which most facilities must comply, while clean air laws impose standards for indoor air quality and hazardous emissions. Similarly, other laws regulate energy consumption, safety, smoking, and other factors that fall under the facility manager's umbrella of responsibility.

FACILITY MANAGEMENT IN THE FUTURE Price and other analysts have suggested that evolving business realities in the realms of process improvement, cost containment, speed-to-market accelerations, quality control, and workplace arrangements and concepts will all have a big impact on future notions of facility management. Price argued that "the challenge for facilities planning will be to integrate knowledge workers into a dynamic business environment of global competition, technological developments, and changing values," and he laid out four primary precepts that will likely form the underpinnings of future financial management planning:

1) Understanding the evolving nature of knowledge-based business—"The new workforce and the content of its work is migrating from a bureaucratic control of resources and the movement of materials through a process toward a highly flexible and networked organization whose added value is exploiting specialized knowledge

and information to solve complex problems,'' wrote Price.

2) Understanding workspace trends—Price and other business analysts believe that computing and communications technologies are fundamentally transforming the workplace landscape. As shared jobs, telecommuting, home-based businesses, flexible work hours and other trends make further inroads in the business world, facility management philosophies will have to keep pace.

3) Understanding how new technologies have removed old restrictions on conducting business—This, said Price, basically entails recognizing that ''the removal of physical limitations caused by transportation and communications technology has changed the scope, strategy, and structure of the business world.''

4) Understanding ''Job Factor'' basics—Price noted that IBM and other companies have developed facility management philosophies that study the interaction of all job factors, including those of physical environment and job content.

CONTRACT FACILITY MANAGEMENT

Increasing numbers of business owners are choosing to contract out their facility management tasks to specialized facility management companies that operate the complex for the owner on a contract basis. This arrangement has become more common in part because of the increasing scope and complexity of facility management. Companies that hire contract managers prefer to focus on other goals, such as producing a product or providing a service. Many of those firms find that outsourcing facility management duties to a specialist reduces costs and improves operations.

Contract facility managers may be hired to manage an entire complex or just one part of a large operation. For example, some companies hire contract managers that specialize in operating mailrooms or providing janitorial services. In any case, the company expects to benefit from the expertise of the manager it hires. A contractor that manages data processing systems, for example, may bring technical know-how that its employer would have great difficulty cultivating in-house. Likewise, a recreation facility owner that employs a facility manager specializing in the operation of sport complexes may benefit from the contractor's mix of knowledge related to groundskeeping, accounting and reporting, and sports marketing, among other functions.

Besides expertise and efficiency, several other benefits are provided by contract facility managers. For example, they reduce the owner's or occupant's liability related to personnel. By contracting a firm to manage one of its factories, an organization can substantially reduce its involvement in staffing, training, worker's compensation expenses and litigation, employee benefits, and worker grievances. It also eliminates general management and payroll responsibilities—rather than tracking hours and writing checks for an entire staff, it simply pays the facility management company. In addition, a company that hires a facility management firm can quickly reduce or increase its staff as it chooses without worrying about hiring or severance legalities.

Whether a small business chooses to outsource or maintain internal control of its facility management processes, however, the ultimate goals are the same. As Raymond O'Brien commented in *Managing Office Technology,* ''both the in-house facility management department and outsourced services must recognize that the facility management business is changing. While, traditionally, interior planning has been driven by preconceived notions of what is appropriate, business today increasingly is not being conducted in a traditional manner or in traditional locations. . . . Changing roles, combined with changing technology, drives the environment of the future.'' But although he concurred that the field of facility management is in a state of flux at the moment, O'Brien argued that quality facility management could became an even greater advantage for attentive businesses in the future: ''[Facility management] offers those with entrepreneurial spirit enormous opportunity. Whether working within a corporation or as an outsourced service provider, imaginative facility managers can find myriad ways to improve service to the company or the client while creating an interesting, challenging position for themselves.''

FURTHER READING:

Becker, Franklin. *The Total Workplace: Facilities Management and the Elastic Organization.* New York: Van Nostrand, 1990.

Brown, Malcolm. ''Rulers of the New Frontier.'' *Management Today.* March 1996.

Cornacchia, Anthony J. ''Facility Management: Life in the Fast Lane.'' *The Office.* June 1994.

Gregory, William L. ''Roll Up Your Sleeves: Here's Your Next Challenge.'' *Managing Office Technology.* June 1994.

J. K. Lasser Institute. *How to Run a Small Business.* 7th ed. New York: McGraw-Hill, 1994.

Kaiser, Harvey H. *The Facilities Manager's Reference: Management, Planning, Building Audits, Estimating.* Kingston, MA: R.S. Means Co., 1989.

Kruk, Leonard B. ''Facilities Planning Supports Changing Office Technologies.'' *Managing Office Technology.* December 1996.

Levitt, Alan M. *Disaster Planning and Recovery: A Guide for Facility Professionals.* New York: John Wiley and Sons, 1997.

Macknight, Diane. "Facility Management in the '90s." *The Office.* January 1993.

O'Brien, Raymond. "Facility Managers Provide Invaluable Services." *Managing Office Technology.* September 1995.

Price, Steven M. "Facilities Planning: A Perspective for the Information Age." *IIE Solutions.* August 1997.

Sopko, Sandy. "Smaller Staffs and Budgets Boost FM Outsourcing." *The Office.* August 1993.

SEE ALSO: Facility Layout and Design

FACSIMILE TRANSMISSION

The facsimile machine has become a staple item in the offices of small and large businesses alike. Fax usage increased at the rate of 20 percent in 1996 alone, according to *PC Week.* Indeed, the ubiquity of fax technology, coupled with price reductions that have dropped fax machines to levels that are imminently affordable for even the smallest businesses, have created an environment in which 99 percent of all businesses with more than five employees have a fax machine. Small business owners, then, are generally faced with questions about the kind of fax machines they will buy, not whether to buy them at all. According to *What to Buy for Business,* if your business sends a small number of faxes each day, it can probably get by with a less expensive thermal paper fax machine. For those businesses willing to pay a slightly higher amount for a clearer image and better quality, it will probably be beneficial to purchase a plain paper fax machine.

INNOVATIVE USES FOR YOUR FAX MACHINE

Fax machines have traditionally been used to transfer single or small numbers of documents from one location to another. Within the past couple of years, new uses have been found for the fax machine. In addition to a stand-alone fax machine, most entry-level personal computers sold today have a fax modem installed. As *Target Marketing* observed, the addition of advanced software programs have revolutionized the use of fax machines in some industries. The magazine noted that fax machines armed with the appropriate software can be used to generate large volumes of pre-programmed transmissions. A personal computer can be used effectively to distribute faxes to about 50 different locations utilizing a single phone line. If your target group is greater than 50 locations, contracting with a service bureau that disperses mass faxes might be your best bet. Be sure to shop around, but a service bureau can be a cost-effective way to reach thousands of customers in about an hour. Advertising and marketing firms can easily test new offers and turn around projects in a day utilizing a high-speed fax service bureau.

ENHANCED SERVICES ENCOURAGE YOUR FAX BUSINESS

Although your fax needs might be simple in the beginning, as your business grows your fax demands probably will as well. One of the most common problems your business may encounter is a busy signal when trying to connect with another fax machine. In addition, fax transmissions destined for your business might encounter the same problem. With this in mind, *PC Week* reports that companies like Ameritech are offering a number of fax services to business accounts. Companies offering these services are able to store outgoing documents for later delivery if they cannot be delivered at the receiving end. In addition, they can store your incoming faxes if your machine is bogged down or out of service. When your machine becomes available, your faxes will be delivered. Companies offering these services can also arrange to notify you by pager or voice mail if your line has received an incoming fax.

REDUCING FAX COSTS THROUGH THE INTERNET

Small business owners engaged in efforts to streamline their business expenses have been urged by some consultants to consider using the Internet to send their faxes. *American Salesman* reported that business can expect to save up to 50 percent on telecommunications costs by using the Internet for transmitting faxes. The most economical and convenient way to utilize the Internet for fax needs is to hire an Internet fax service bureau. Although similar to distributing an **e-mail** message, Internet faxing will allow you to send a fully formatted document instead of simply text. This technology is not yet in widespread use, but *The Financial Times* and other observers predict that improving technology will continue to encourage growth in fax transmission via the Internet.

Still, even though using the Internet can reduce facsimile transmission costs, it is important for small business owners to remember the following points to maximize their financial savings:

- Fax at night when rates are traditionally lower

- Avoid using a cover page, unless absolutely necessary

- If possible, avoid graphics or photographs in your faxes.

The ability to communicate instantly, both verbally and by document, has become a standard in the business world. Lower prices for quality fax machines have given even the smallest business the opportunity to purchase and use a this technology. In addition to utilizing a fax for your business necessities, desktop computer fax software and contract fax bureaus make it possible for you to reach large customer bases via fax. Coupled with the enhanced faxing capabilities possible by using the Internet, few businesses can afford to ignore the role a fax machine can play in improving their bottom line.

FURTHER READING:

"Make Smart Fax Connections: Ameritech Launches Handful of Fax Management
Services in Chicago." *PC Week*, June 16, 1997.

Mummert, Hallie. "Getting There by Fax." *Target Marketing*, September 1997.

"Plain-Paper Facts." *What to Buy for Business*, July 1995.

"Pitney Bowes Survey Shows Fax Usage is On the Rise." *PC Week*, September
22, 1997.

Shillingford, Joia. "Fax Faces Up to Cut-Price Competitor." September 17,
1997.

"Use the Internet!" *American Salesman*, April 1997.

SEE ALSO: Written Communication

FACTORING

Factoring is a form of financing in which a business sells its receivables to a third party or "factor company" at a discounted price. Under this arrangement, the factor agrees to provide financing and other services to the selling business in return for interest and fees on the money that they advanced against receivables invoices. Businesses in need of cash can thus secure up to 80 percent of the receivables' face value (a higher percentage can sometimes be secured, but in most instances, 20 percent is held in reserve until the account balances are paid off). This is a favorite **capital** raising choice for established small business owners. "A factor company can be a useful source of funds if you are already in business and have made sales to customers," indicated the U.S. Small Business Administration publication *Financing for the Small Business*. "Factor companies purchase your **accounts receivable** at a discount, thereby freeing cash for you sooner than if you had to collect the money yourself." Factor companies can either provide recourse financing, in which the small business is ultimately responsible if its customers do not pay, or nonrecourse financing, in which the factor company

bears that risk. Factor companies can be a useful source of funds for existing businesses, but they are not a realistic "seed money" option for startups because such businesses do not yet have a base of customers—or accounts receivable—to offer.

In some respects, the factoring process is roughly comparable to credit card arrangements. "Just as MasterCard buys a retailer's receivables, paying the store as soon as a sale is made, factors do much the same on the wholesale level," one executive told Mark Stevens, author of *The Macmillan Small Business Handbook*. "Assume a manufacturer of wool hats ships a $50,000 order to one of its customers. Rather than waiting for the account to pay, the manufacturer can sell the receivables to a factor, receiving up to 85 percent of the total as soon as the goods leave the shipping dock. This speeds the collection process. The balance is paid when the factor collects from the customer."

Small business owners should be aware that factoring is different in several fundamental respects from bank financing. For one thing, noted Mike Willis in the *Tampa Bay Business Journal,* it is more expensive. "Costs usually represent 2 percent to 10 percent of sales," he reported. "Fees deducted from the balances paid to you [the small business owner] include a finance charge, which may run 1 percent to 5 percent above the current prime rate, and a service charge that is often a function of the daily balance outstanding, increasing as the balances age. Arrangements for fees vary widely, depending on the credit quality of your customer account balances and the range of services that you are purchasing from the factor." In addition, small business owners should recognize that utilizing a factor company is a sort of all or nothing proposition. As Mark Stevens noted in *The Macmillan Small Business Handbook,* "factors demand 100 percent of a client's receivables. They will not limit their efforts to those receivables considered marginal or high risk."

Factor companies are an increasingly mainstream choice for small business owners seeking capital. In 1993, for instance, factor companies financed more than $60 billion in receivables. Indeed, even though it carries some risks for small enterprises, it is regarded as a viable short-term cash management tool. "If you take into account the costs associated with maintaining accounts receivable, such as bookkeeping, collections, and credit verifications, and compare those expenses against the discount rate you'll have to apply when selling them, sometimes it even pays to utilize this financing method," said the *Entrepreneur Magazine Guide to Raising Money.* "In addition to reduced internal costs, factoring also frees up money that would otherwise be tied to receivables, especially for businesses that sell to other businesses or to the government where there are often prolonged delays in payment that factoring could easily offset. You can then turn around and use the money to generate profit through other avenues of the company.'' But factor companies should be selected with care; some factor companies have been known to alienate customers through excessively aggressive collection policies.

SELECTING A FACTOR ''Selecting a factor is much the same as selecting any other service provider,'' said Willis. ''Find the best price for the services provided.'' He pointed to several considerations that should be weighed by the small business owner in making fee arrangements with a factor:

- Recourse—Small business enterprises that elect to go with a recourse factor (in which they bear final responsibility for collecting monies owed) over nonrecourse factors (where the factor company bears that responsibility) will find that they may gain lower fees and more money from the factor in return for increasing their risk.

- Customer Base—''The larger the number of customers, the more cost advantages the factor can provide,'' Willis stated. ''Automation gives factors significant economies of scale in this area. Creditworthiness of customers is a fundamental element in factor pricing. Factors will not purchase substandard customer balances.''

- Size and Age of the Average Invoice—Smaller receivables that have been on the books for a while will result in less advantageous factoring arrangements for small business owners than will large, current receivables.

- Factor Preferences—Some factors tend to work with larger businesses, while others concentrate their efforts on smaller enterprises. *Tampa Bay Business Journal* reported that large factor companies tend to focus their attentions on companies that have at least $10 million in annual sales, while smaller factor companies—sometimes known as ''re-factors''—may provide services to companies with annual sales as low as $300,000.

- Industry Knowledge—Most factors that reach agreements with small businesses will have a fairly solid understanding of the industry and competitive environment in which those businesses operate. Such factor companies can provide help to small businesses in determining who they should (and should not) extend credit to. In addition, factor companies can be helpful in settling upon credit limits for both new and existing customers. ''Assess the factor's understanding

of your industry to get the most for your money,'' counseled Willis.

- System Compatibility—Willis noted that most businesses in today's environment have implemented automated processes to calculate and monitor accounts receivable and cash applications of cash received. Small business owners should make sure that their systems are compatible with those of the factor before agreeing to a factoring arrangement.

- Collections—As indicated above, this can be a tricky area for the small business owner. Handing over collection duties to a factor company is more expensive, and over-aggressive collection efforts on their part can damage a small business's relations with legitimate clients. But Willis pointed out that factor companies also often have better luck in collecting monies owed than do small business enterprises, which have limited resources that they can allocate to the collections process. Business owners should recognize, however, that the factor is only interested in business transactions in which their client is owed money. Factors will not be responsible for non-payment that is attributed to other factors, such as vendor disputes or defective merchandise.

A variety of institutions, including bank subsidiaries and finance companies, provide factoring services. These companies can be found via several different methodologies. The *Edwards Directory of American Factors* provides information on many factors, but these businesses also advertise in local yellow pages under such headings as ''factors,'' ''financing commercial,'' ''accounts receivable financing,'' or ''billing service.''

FURTHER READING:

Andresky Fraser, Jill. ''Show Me the Money: You Can Look for Money in All the Wrong Places.'' *Inc.* March 1997.

Banchero, Paola. ''Financing Fight: Nonbank Lenders Want Nothing More Than to Take Business Away from Traditional Banks.'' *Kansas City Business Journal.* October 10, 1997.

Entrepreneur Magazine Guide To Raising Money. New York: John Wiley & Sons, 1998.

Financing for the Small Business. Washington: U.S. Small Business Administration, 1990.

Gupta, Udayan. ''Factoring and Venture Firms' Roles in Financing Growth.'' *Wall Street Journal.* June 1994.

''How to Make Them Give You the Money.'' *Money.* June 1995.

Sherman, Andrew J. *The Complete Guide to Running and Growing Your Business.* New York: Times Books, 1997.

Stevens, Mark. ''Financing: When Your Bank Says No.'' *Executive Female.* July-August 1994.

Stevens, Mark. *The Macmillan Small Business Handbook.* New York: Macmillan, 1988.

Whittemore, Meg. "Creative Financing that Succeeds." *Nation's Business.* April 1995.

Willis, Mike. "How to Select a Factoring Company." *Tampa Bay Business Journal.* July 28, 1995.

FAMILY LIMITED PARTNERSHIP

Family limited partnerships (sometimes known as FLPs) are an increasingly popular succession planning alternative utilized by owners of family businesses who want to pass the establishment on to their children without being hit by heavy federal taxes. Neil Alexander, writing in *Best's Review,* described the family limited partnership as "a legal agreement that allows business owners and their children to address several tax, business-succession, and estate-planning needs all at once. This vehicle allows parents to gift assets to their children at highly discounted rates while still maintaining lifetime control of those assets. In addition, eventual estate taxes are reduced by virtue of reducing the total estate." This reduced taxation, said *Nation's Business* contributor Marsha Bertrand, "has propelled family limited partnerships to the forefront of estate-planning techniques."

ESTATE PLANNING IN THE FAMILY-OWNED BUSINESS

When considered in the context of family-owned businesses, estate planning is basically the practice of transferring ownership of the family business to the next generation. Families must plan to minimize their tax burden at the time of the owner's death so that the resources can stay within the company and the family. The complexity of American tax law, however, makes it necessary for most estate planning to be undertaken with the assistance of professionals in the realms of accounting and law.

Since estate planning is such a vital element of long-term family business strategies, consultants encourage business owners to establish them as soon as their enterprise becomes successful, and to make sure that they update them as necessary as business or family circumstances change. A variety of options are available that can help a business owner defer or otherwise minimize the transfer taxes associated with handing down a family business. A marital deduction trust, for example, passes property along to a surviving spouse in the event of the owner's death, and no taxes are owed until the spouse dies. It is also possible to pay the **estate taxes** associated with the transfer of a family business on an installment basis, so that no taxes are owed for five years and the remainder are paid in annual installments over a ten-year period. Other techniques exist that allow business owners to exclude some or all of their assets from estate taxes as well, but few have been as popular in recent years as the family limited partnership.

ADVANTAGES OF FAMILY LIMITED PARTNERSHIPS

The primary purpose of family limited partnerships is to blunt the impact of estate taxes. "Estate taxes can hit family businesses hard because the full value of a parent's business can be included in the parent's estate when he or she dies," explained Joan Szabo in *Entrepreneur.* "Estate tax is one of the highest taxes levied on individuals. The first $600,000 of a person's estate is exempt from federal estate tax, but amounts above the exempt portion are subject to a graduated tax ranging from 37 percent to a whopping 55 percent." One way to dampen the impact of this tax, noted Szabo, is to make use of an IRS rule that allows individuals to make annual gifts of up to $10,000 ($20,000 if joined by your spouse) to other individuals without incurring gift taxes. The other way to elude the full brunt of this tax is via an FLP.

A basic family limited partnership operates in fairly simple fashion. "Under a typical family limited partnership," wrote Bertrand, "the parents (or a single parent) retain a general partnership interest in the property—as little as 1 percent—and give limited-partnership interests to their children over a number of years. The general partners retain complete control over the assets in the partnership, and no management authority is given to the limited partner or partners."

"A family limited partnership allows the business to be transferred to the younger generation at substantially less than its value, thus reducing the size of the estate and the federal tax bite," noted Szabo. Indeed, observers indicate that these discounts can amount to as much as 50 percent of a business's value. The discounted valuation occurs because the shares can not be easily sold or otherwise transferred and because such partnership interests do not carry any voting rights or control in the business in question. "Since the gifted shares are discounted, the partnership pays lower gift taxes on those shares," explained Alexander. "For example, if a $15,000 limited partnership share is appraised at $7,500, the parents can transfer that share to a child plus $2,500 worth of something else that year and still stay within their $10,000 annual exclusion. Second, this reevaluation also applies to the shares the parents continue to hold. Third, because the parents are transferring shares out of their estate, they're reducing the value of the estate for tax purposes."

OTHER CONSIDERATIONS

Many estate planners and business consultants encourage their clients to look into FLPs, but they do note that family business owners should weigh some other non-tax factors as well. These include:

TIMING OF THE FORMATION OF THE LIMITED PARTNERSHIP Estate planners and business consultants warn that the Internal Revenue Service will not necessarily approve a family limited partnership if it is transparently obvious that the step has been taken simply to skirt paying taxes. Family business owners who attempt to institute an FLP a few weeks before their death from some foreseeable illness will likely find their efforts blocked.

DIVORCE In most instances, a child's ownership of limited partnership shares will not be impacted by a divorce action between that child and his or her spouse, but business owners seeking to ensure protection for their child can take a couple steps to provide additional insurance. Writing in *Best's Review,* Neil Alexander explained that since limited partners (children) receive their shares as a gift and are not permitted to vote or "otherwise exercise any authority in the partnership," the child's shares will not be considered part of the marital assets. Instead, they will remain the sole and separate property of the child. The key, say legal experts, is to make sure that the shares were never formally made part of the marital property. In addition, Alexander wrote that "in the event that a spouse can persuade a court that the family limited partnership shares are marital assets, the general partners can still exercise their option not to distribute income to their limited partners. In that situation, the limited partners assume the tax liability without receiving the income—a situation known as phantom income. It is a good idea to communicate to the in-law at the time the family partnership is established that it is the separate property of the recipient of the gifted shares. This will avoid any future misunderstanding if the marriage ends in divorce."

EXPENSE OF SETTING UP AN FLP Establishing a family limited partnership can be somewhat expensive, although the price tag depends in large part on the size of the company, the value of its assets, the number of intended minority owners, and other factors.

COMPATABILITY WITH BUSINESS According to Bertrand, the FLP plan is better suited to some businesses than others. "It's effective for real estate or companies in which capital assets are the essence of the business, but it isn't suited to personal-services companies whose income depends on the activity of the owner, such as consulting firms," she said.

FUNDING THROUGH LIFE INSURANCE Writing in the *Journal of the American Society of CLU & ChFC,* James Allen and Thomas Bilello pointed out that family limited partnerships can also be funded through life insurance policies. According to Allen and Bilello, even though life insurance has traditionally been used to fund irrevocable life insurance trusts, they can fund FLPs as well.

INCREASED RISK OF IRS AUDITS Although family limited partnerships can be very valuable, and their use is increasing, accountants and estate planning attorneys do caution family business owners that using FLPs to transfer ownership of a company does tend to draw the attention of the IRS, which pays particular attention to whether the owners are deemed to have tried to take too great a discount on the value of the business in question. To minimize the risk of an **Internal Revenue Service audit**, estate planners urge family business owners to have the business appraised by an experienced, respected professional who can provide a solid valuation. For information on securing the services of an established appraiser, contact the American Society of Appraisers at (800) 272-8258.

DISSATISFACTION AMONG MINORITY OWNERS Ironically, some family businesses find that FLPs actually spark difficulties between parents and their children, despite the formidable savings that such a plan can provide and the ultimate aim—succession—of the partnership. This is certainly not always the case; many families put together family limited partnerships that garner significant tax savings without a ripple of internal dissension or dissatisfaction. But it is a factor that can crop up, depending on the personalities and financial situations of the persons involved. Writing in *Agency Sales Magazine,* Leon Danco contended that the financial restraints imposed on minority owners in FLPs—who, after all, do not receive actual salaries from the family business—are usually the cause of this ill will: "Because of the tax laws and the fact that the growing business needs all of the pretax cash it can get its hands on, there are seldom, if ever, any dividends. Because there is no 'market' for a minority share in such a business, the poor minority owner can't even sell his or her shares to convert them into some kind of useable wealth. . . . This situation is almost guaranteed to encourage the minority owners to see their own self-interest in harassing the management, criticizing decisions, lobbying for dividends, opposing corporate investments, and generally fomenting trouble."

NEED FOR PROFESSIONAL GUIDANCE Establishing a family limited partnership is a complex estate-planning strategy festooned with regulations. Subsequently, business owners are strongly encouraged to secure qualified legal and/or accounting help in setting up such plans.

FURTHER READING:

Alexander, Neil. "Limited Partnerships Keep It All in the Family." *Best's Review—Life-Health Insurance Edition.* November 1995.

Allen, James R., and Thomas C. Bilello. "Life Insurance and the Family Limited Partnership." *Journal of the American Society of CLU & ChFC.* January 1997.

Ambler, Aldonna R. "The Legacy: Family Businesses Struggle with Succession." *Business Journal of New Jersey.* October 1991.

Bertrand, Marsha. "Keeping Assets in the Family." *Nation's Business.* July 1997.

Danco, Leon A. "The 'Prisoners' of Family Business." *Agency Sales Magazine.* August 1991.

Harrison, Ellen. "FLIPs: It's Your Choice, Uncle Sam or Your Family." *The CPA Journal.* October 1996.

Heidelberger, Suzanne. "Family Limited Partnership." *National Real Estate Investor.* June 1996.

"Passing IRS Scrutiny of a Family Limited Partnership." *Taxes: The Tax Magazine.* August 1997.

Szabo, Joan. "Spreading the Wealth: Transferring Part of Your Business to Your Children Now Could Lower Their Taxes Later." *Entrepreneur.* July 1997.

Vogelsang, Stephen G., and James B. Bertles. "Effective Drafting Strategies for Family Limited Partnerships." *Estate Planning.* November 1996.

Ward, John L., and Craig E. Aronoff. "Overcoming a Major Obstacle to Succession." *Nation's Business.* September 1996.

Washelesky, Frank L. "When is a Family Limited Partnership an Appropriate Tax Savings Vehicle?" *The Tax Advisor.* October 1997.

SEE ALSO: Family-owned Business; Partnerships; Succession Plans

FAMILY AND MEDICAL LEAVE ACT

The Family and Medical Leave Act (FMLA) provides employees who qualify with up to 12 workweeks of unpaid, job-protected leave in a 12-month period for specified family and medical reasons, and requires group health benefits to be maintained during the leave as if employees continued to work instead of taking leave. The employer can elect to use the calendar year, a fixed 12-month fiscal year, or a 12-month period prior to or after the commencement of leave as the 12-month period. The Act, which became effective on August 5, 1993, for most employers, is primarily administered and enforced by the U.S. Department of Labor's Employment Standards Division, Wage and Hour Division.

ELIGIBILITY FOR FMLA

To qualify for FMLA benefits, an employee must 1) work for an employer subject to FMLA rules; 2) have worked for that employer for a total of 12 months; 3) have worked at least 1,250 hours over the previous 12 months; 4) work at a location in the United States or in any territory or possession of the United States where at least 50 employees are employed by the employer within 75 miles. This latter stipulation exempts many small business owners from FMLA rules and guidelines.

But while FMLA does not apply to small businesses that employ fewer than 50 people, it does apply to small and mid-size companies that employed 50 or more employees in 20 or more workweeks in the current or preceding calendar year. FMLA also applies to all public agencies, including local, state, and federal employers; large companies; and school administrations.

LEAVE ENTITLEMENT There are several different situations under which employers covered under FMLA must grant eligible employees unpaid leave from work without penalty. Reasons include:

- Situations in which the employee is unable to work because of illness or other health difficulties;

- Placement with the employee or a child for adoption or foster care;

- Birth and care of the newborn child of the employee;

- Caring for an immediate family member with serious health difficulties (immediate family members are defined as spouse, child, or parent).

In addition, spouses employed by the same company or agency are jointly entitled to a combined total of 12 workweeks of family leave for the birth and care of a newborn child, for placement of a child for adoption or foster care, or to care for a parent suffering from a serious health condition.

Finally, depending on the circumstances, some employees may be able to take leave in blocks of time or by scaling back their normal work schedule. In addition, employers or employees are sometimes may choose to use accrued paid leave to cover some or all of the FMLA leave.

ILLNESSES AND OTHER CONDITIONS COVERED UNDER FMLA The FMLA was written so that employees who have family members in "serious health condition"—or who themselves are in such condition—can use the law to protect their job during the time that they are on leave. The Department of Labor defines "serious health condition" as an illness, injury, impairment, or physical or mental conditions that involves any of the following:

- Any period of incapacity or treatment connected with overnight stays in a hospital or other residential medical care facility, and any period of incapacity or subsequent treatment in connection with such inpatient care

- Continuing treatment by a health care provider that includes any period of incapacity due to: 1) a health condition (including treatment of, or recovery from) lasting more than three consecutive days, and any subsequent treatment or period of incapacity relating to the same condition; 2) pregnancy or prenatal care; 3) a chronic serious health conditions which continues over an extended period of time, requires periodic visits to a doctor or other health care professional, and may involve occasional episodes of incapacity (diabetes, asthma); 4) permanent or long-term conditions for which treatment may not work (cancer, stroke); 5) absences to receive treatments for restorative surgery or for a condition which would likely result in incapacitation for more than three days if not treated (radiation or chemotherapy treatments for cancer).

EMPLOYER REQUIREMENTS UNDER FMLA

Under FMLA law, employers who are subject to its regulations must maintain group health insurance coverage for any employee taking FMLA leave whenever that employee already had that insurance. The employer is not allowed to make any changes in the terms of that insurance coverage, either. There are some situations, however, where an employer may be able to recover any insurance premiums that it paid out to maintain health coverage for an employee if that worker fails to return to work from FMLA leave.

In instances where the employee does return from FMLA leave, that employee is entitled to be restored to his or her original job, or to an equivalent job, complete with equivalent pay, benefits, and other terms of employment. Moreover, FMLA stipulates that an employee cannot lose any employment benefit that he or she earned prior to using FMLA leave once the employee returns to work. There are exceptions to the above rules, but they come into play only in extreme circumstances wherein returning an employee to his or her previous station will cause ''substantial and grievous economic injury'' to the business. Obviously, such circumstances arise only when the company is in deep financial jeopardy.

Employers who are subject to FMLA law are required to post notices that explain the Family and Medical Leave Act in the workplace. These notices are approved by the Secretary of Labor. Companies that willfully violate this requirement are subject to fines. This requirement is part of a general mandate that directs employers to inform employees of all pertinent aspects of FMLA, including employee responsibilities.

STEPS TO SECURING FMLA LEAVE

Employees who wish to take advantage of the Family and Medical Leave Act must adhere to certain steps so as to soften the impact on the businesses where they are employed. Workers using FMLA must first provide 30-day advance notice of their intention to take leave in all instances where the need is foreseeable. In addition, some employers require employees using FMLA to do some or all of the following:

- Provide medical certification supporting the need for leave;
- Second or third medical opinions (at the employer's expense);
- Periodic recertification of health status;
- Periodic reports on employee status and intentions regarding returning to work;
- Adhere to limitations on intermittent leave.

FURTHER READING:

Compliance Guide to the Family and Medical Leave Act. Washington: U.S. Department of Labor, 1996.

The HR Focus Guide to the Family and Medical Leave Act. New York: American Management Association, n.d.

SEE ALSO: Health Insurance Options

FAMILY-OWNED BUSINESSES

A family-owned business is any business in which two or more family members are involved and the majority of ownership or control lies within a family. Family-owned businesses may be the oldest form of business organization, and today they are recognized as important and distinct participants in the world economy. According to Nancy Bowman-Upton in the Small Business Administration publication *Transferring Management in the Family-Owned Business,* about 90 percent of American businesses are family owned or controlled. Ranging in size from two-person partnerships to *Fortune 500* firms, these businesses generate about half of the nation's **Gross National Product**. Family businesses may have some advantages over other business entities in their focus on the long term, their commitment to quality (which is often associated with the family name), and their care and concern for employees. But family businesses also face a unique set of management challenges stemming from the overlap of family and business issues.

ISSUES IN FAMILY BUSINESSES

A family business can be described as an interaction between two separate but connected systems—the business and the family—with uncertain boundaries and different rules. Graphically, this concept can be presented as two intersecting circles. Family businesses may include numerous combinations of family members in various business roles, including husbands and wives, parents and children, extended families, and multiple generations playing the roles of stockholders, board members, working partners, advisors, and employees. Conflicts often arise due to the overlap of these roles. The ways in which individuals typically communicate within a family, for example, may be inappropriate in business situations. Likewise, personal concerns or rivalries may carry over into the work place to the detriment of the firm. In order to succeed, a family business must keep lines of communication open, make use of strategic planning tools, and engage the assistance of outside advisors as needed.

Bowman-Upton listed a number of common issues that most family businesses face. Attracting and retaining nonfamily employees can be problematic, for example, because such employees may find it difficult to deal with family conflicts on the job, limited opportunities for advancement, and the special treatment sometimes accorded family members. In addition, some family members may resent outsiders being brought into the firm and purposely make things unpleasant for nonfamily employees. But outsiders can provide a stabilizing force in a family business by offering a fair and impartial perspective on business issues. Family business leaders can conduct exit interviews with departing nonfamily employees to determine the cause of turnover and develop a course of action to prevent it. If the problem is a troublemaking family member, Bowman-Upton suggests counseling them on their responsibilities to the business, transferring them to another part of the company, finding them a job with another firm, or encouraging them to start their own, noncompeting company.

Many family businesses also have trouble determining guidelines and qualifications for family members hoping to participate in the business. Some companies try to limit the participation of people with certain relationships to the family, such as in-laws, in order to minimize the potential for conflicts. Family businesses often face pressure to hire relatives or close friends who may lack the talent or skill to make a useful contribution to the business. Once hired, such people can be difficult to fire, even if they cost the company money or reduce the motivation of other employees by exhibiting a poor attitude. A strict policy of only hiring people with legitimate qualifications to fill existing openings can help a company avoid such problems, but only if the policy is applied without exception. If a company is forced to hire a less-than-desirable employee, Bowman-Upton suggests providing special training to develop a useful talent, enlisting the help of a nonfamily employee in training and supervising, and assigning special projects that minimize negative contact with other employees.

Another challenge frequently encountered by family businesses involves paying salaries to and dividing the profits among the family members who participate in the firm. In order to grow, a small business must be able to use a relatively large percentage of profits for expansion. But some family members, especially those that are owners but not employees of the company, may not see the value of expenditures that reduce the amount of current dividends they receive. In order to convince such people of the value of investments in the company's future, Bowman-Upton suggests that the leader of the family business use nonfamily employees to gather facts and figures to support the argument, demonstrate the bottom-line effect of the expenditure, and enlist the help of outside advisors such as an accountant, banker, or attorney. To ensure that salaries are distributed fairly among family and nonfamily employees, business leaders should match them to industry guidelines for each job description. When additional compensation is needed to reward certain employees for their contributions to the company, fringe benefits or equity distributions can be used.

Another important issue relating to family businesses is succession—determining who will take over leadership and/or ownership of the company when the current generation retires or dies. Bowman-Upton recommends that families take steps to prepare for succession long before the need arises. A family retreat, or a meeting on neutral ground without distractions or interruptions, can be an ideal setting to open discussions on family goals and future plans, the timing of expected transitions, and the preparation of the current generation for stepping down and the future generation for taking over. When succession is postponed, older relatives who remain involved in the family firm may develop a preference for maintaining the status quo. These people may resist change and refuse to take risks, even though such an attitude can inhibit business growth. The business leaders should take steps to gradually remove these relatives from the daily operations of the firm, including encouraging them to become involved in outside activities, arranging for them to sell some of their stock or convert it to preferred shares, or possibly restructuring the company to dilute their influence.

Family business leaders can take a number of steps in order to avoid becoming caught up in these issues and their negative consequences. Bowman-Upton noted that having a clear statement of goals, an organized plan to accomplish the goals, a defined hierarchy for decision-making, an established **succession plan**, and strong lines of communication can help prevent many possible problems from arising. All family members involved in the business must understand that their rights and responsibilities are different at home and at work. While family relationships and goals take precedence at home, the success of the business comes first at work.

When emotion intrudes upon work relationships and the inevitable conflicts between family members arise, the business leader must intervene and make the objective decisions necessary to protect the interests of the firm. Rather than taking sides in a dispute, the leader must make it clear to all employees that personal disagreements will not be allowed to interfere with work. This approach should discourage employees from jockeying for position or playing politics. The business leader may also find it useful to have regular meetings with family members, engage the services of outside advisors who have no connection to family members as needed, and put all business agreements and policy guidelines in writing.

THE PLANNING PROCESS

Strategic planning—centering around both business and family goals—is vital to successful family businesses. In fact, planning may be more crucial to family businesses than to other types of business entities, because in many cases families have a majority of their assets tied up in the business. Since much conflict arises due to a disparity between family and business goals, planning is required to align these goals and formulate a strategy for reaching them. The ideal plan will allow the company to balance family and business needs to everyone's advantage. Unfortunately, *Nation's Business* reported that only 31 percent of family businesses surveyed in 1997 had written strategic plans. There are four main types of planning that should be conducted by family businesses: family planning, **business planning**, succession planning, and estate planning.

FAMILY PLANNING In family planning, all interested members of the family get together to develop a mission statement that describes why they are committed to the business. In allowing family members to share their goals, needs, priorities, strengths, weaknesses, and ability to contribute, family planning helps create a unified vision of the company that will guide future dealings.

A special meeting called a family retreat or family council can guide the communication process and encourage involvement by providing family members with a venue to voice their opinions and plan for the future in a structured way. By participating in the family retreat, children can gain a better understanding of the opportunities in the business, learn about managing resources, and inherit values and traditions. It also provides an opportunity for conflicts to be discussed and settled. Topics brought to family councils can include: rules for joining the business, treatment of family members working and not working in the business, role of in-laws, evaluations and pay scales, stock ownership, ways to provide financial security for the senior generation, training and development of the junior generation, the company's image in the community, philanthropy, opportunities for new businesses, and diverse interests among family members. Leadership of the family council can be on a rotating basis, or an outside family business consultant may be hired as a facilitator.

BUSINESS PLANNING Business planning begins with the long-term goals and objectives the family holds for themselves and for the business. The business leaders then integrate these goals into the business strategy. In business planning, management analyzes the strengths and weaknesses of the company in relation to its environment, including its organizational structure, culture, and resources. The next stage involves identifying opportunities for the company to pursue, given its strengths, and threats for the company to manage, given its weaknesses. Finally, the planning process concludes with the creation of a mission statement, a set of objectives, and a set of general strategies and specific action steps to meet the objectives and support the mission. This process is often overseen by a board of directors, an advisory board, or professional advisors.

SUCCESSION PLANNING Succession planning involves deciding who will lead the company in the next generation. Unfortunately, less than one-third of family-owned businesses survive the transition from the first generation of ownership to the second, and only 13 percent of family businesses remain in the family over 60 years. Problems making the transition can occur because the business was no longer viable or because the owner or his or her children did not want it to occur, but usually result from a lack of planning. At any given time, a full 40 percent of American firms are facing the succession issue, yet relatively few make succession plans. Business owners may be reluctant to face the issue because they do not want to relinquish control, feel their successor is not ready, have few interests outside the business, or wish to maintain the sense of identity work provides.

But it is vital that the succession process be carefully planned before it becomes necessary due to the owner's illness or death. Bowman-Upton recommends that family businesses follow a four-stage process in planning for succession: initiation, selection, education, and transition. In the initiation phase, possible successors are introduced to the business and guided through a variety of work experiences of increasing responsibility. In the selection phase, a successor is chosen and a schedule is developed for the transition. During the education phase, the business owner gradually hands over the reigns to the successor, one task at a time, so that he or she may learn the requirements of the position. Finally, the transition is made and the business owner removes himself or herself from the daily operations of the firm. This final stage can be the most difficult, as many entrepreneurs experience great difficulty in letting go of the family business. It may help if the business owner establishes outside interests, creates a sound financial base for retirement, and gains confidence in the abilities of the successor.

ESTATE PLANNING Estate planning involves the financial and tax aspects of transferring ownership of the family business to the next generation. Families must plan to minimize their tax burden at the time of the owner's death so that the resources can stay within the company and the family. Unfortunately, tax laws today provide disincentives for families wishing to continue the business. Heirs are taxed upon the value of the business at a high rate when ownership is transferred. Due to its complexity, estate planning is normally handled by a team of professional advisors which includes a lawyer, accountant, financial planner, insurance agent, and perhaps a family business consultant. An estate plan should be established as soon as the business becomes successful and then updated as business or family circumstances change.

One technique available to family business owners in planning their estate is known as "estate freeze." This technique enables the business owner to "freeze" the value of the business at a particular point in time by creating preferred stock, which does not appreciate in value, and then transferring the common stock to his or her heirs. Since the majority of shares in the firm are preferred and do not appreciate, estate taxes are reduced. The heirs are required to pay gift taxes, however, when the preferred stock is transferred to them.

A variety of tools are available that can help a business owner defer the transfer taxes associated with handing down a family business. A basic will outlines the owner's wishes regarding the distribution of property upon his or her death. A living trust creates a trustee to manage the owner's property not covered by the will, for example during a long illness. A marital deduction trust passes property along to a surviving spouse in the event of the owner's death, and no taxes are owed until the spouse dies. It is also possible to pay the **estate taxes** associated with the transfer of a family business on an installment basis, so that no taxes are owed for five years and the remainder are paid in annual installments over a ten-year period. Other techniques exist that allow business owners to exclude some or all of their assets from estate taxes, including a unified credit/exemption trust, a dynamic trust, and an annual exclusion gift. Since laws change frequently, retaining legal assistance is highly advisable.

ASSISTANCE IN PLANNING

A professional family business **consultant** can be a tremendous asset when confronting planning issues. The consultant is a neutral party who can stabilize the emotional forces within the family and bring the expertise of working with numerous families across many industries. Most families believe theirs is the only company facing these difficult issues, and a family business consultant brings a refreshing perspective. In addition, the family business consultant can establish a family council and advisory board and serve as a facilitator to those two groups.

Advisory boards can be established to advise the company's president or board of directors. These boards consist of five to nine nonfamily members who meet regularly to provide advice and direction to the company. They too can take the emotions out of the planning process and provide objective input. Advisory board members should have business experience and be capable of helping the business to get to the next level of growth. In most cases, the advisory board is compensated in some manner.

As the family business grows, the family business consultant may suggest different options for the family. Often professional nonfamily managers or an outside CEO are recruited to play a role in the future growth of the business. Some families simply retain ownership of the business and allow it to operate with few or no family members involved.

THE FUTURE OF FAMILY BUSINESSES

According to *Nation's Business,* the leadership of more than 40 percent of America's family-owned businesses will either change or begin to shift by the year 2002. Such large-scale changes will bring both challenges and opportunities to these businesses. One expert worried that with so many companies facing succession issues in the near future, disagreements between family members over estates and wills may become more common.

The vast majority of firms that planned a change in leadership (92 percent) expected that ownership of the family business would remain within the family. But the nature of that leadership may change in other ways. One-fourth of the firms said that it was likely their next CEO would be a woman, while 42 percent thought it likely that their company would name co-CEOs. Ross W. Nager, executive director of the Arthur Anderson Center for Family Business, warned that parents should avoid naming co-CEOs just to placate their children who want the job: "Only qualified, competent, capable, motivated people should be in the CEO spot."

Finally, some leaders of family-owned businesses near retirement age, only to find that the list of candidates to carry on the business is a distressingly short one. "As many disappointed family business owners learn too late, it's dangerous to assume that a son or daughter will follow you into the business," wrote Sharon Nelton in *Nation's Business*. "Just because you, without question, followed your parents into the family firm doesn't mean your children will do the same. Today's young people have more options than ever before—more to lure them away from the family enterprise."

James Lea, author of *Keeping It In the Family,* recommended five ways in which current leaders of family-owned enterprises can attract future generations to keep the business afloat after their retirement or death.

- Expose family members to all aspects of the business, including employees, customers, products, and services.

- Define the business's attractive qualities in terms that will appeal to the listener.

- Recognize those factors that have the potential to dissuade family members from staying involved in the business. These factors can range from personal interests that lie in other areas to conflicts with other family members.

- Reward family members who decide to join or stay with the family business. "The 'price' successors pay to join and operate your business may include giving up career options that are financially and personally attractive," noted Nelton. "It may mean loss of privacy, or the tension that occurs between parent and child when their management styles conflict. Lea says a business may make compromises—such as making it possible for the successor to spend more time with his or her family or hiring an interim senior manager to buffer conflicts between parent and child. But the company's 'cost' and the successor's 'price' must be affordable to both."

- Give family members outlets to explore their ideas, interests, and concerns.

Finally, Nelton said, "marketing doesn't end once you have successfully brought your children aboard. You have to continue selling them—and their families—on the challenges and rewards of your company."

FURTHER READING:

Ambler, Aldonna R. "The Legacy: Family Business Struggle with Succession." *Business Journal of New Jersey.* October 1991.

Benson, Benjamin. *Your Family Business.* Homewood, IL: Irwin, 1990.

Bowman-Upton, Nancy. *Challenges in Managing a Family Business.* Washington: U.S. Small Business Administration, 1991.

Bowman-Upton. *Transferring Ownership in the Family-Owned Business.* Washington: U.S. Small Business Administration, 1991.

Cohn, Mike. *Passing the Torch.* New York: McGraw Hill, 1992.

Danco, Leon. "The Prisoners of Family Business." *Agency Sales Magazine.* August 1991.

Jaffe, Dennis. *Working with the Ones You Love.* Conari, 1990.

Lea, James. "The Best Way to Teach Responsibility is to Delegate It." *South Florida Business Journal.* July 25, 1997.

Lea, James. *Keeping it in the Family: Successful Succession of the Family Business.* New York: Wiley, 1991.

Nelton, Sharon. "Family Business: Major Shifts in Leadership Lie Ahead." *Nation's Business.* June 1997.

Poza, Ernesto. *Smart Growth.* San Francisco: Jossey Bass, 1989.

Rowland, Mary. "Putting Your Kids on the Payroll." *Nation's Business.* January 1996.

Ward, John L. *Keeping the Family Business Healthy.* San Francisco: Jossey Bass, 1988.

SEE ALSO: Career and Family; Family Limited Partnership; Nepotism

FEASIBILITY STUDY

A feasibility study is a detailed analysis of a company and its operations that is conducted in order to predict the results of a specific future course of action. Small business owners may find it helpful to conduct a feasibility study whenever they anticipate making an important strategic decision. For example, a company might perform a feasibility study to evaluate a proposed change in location, the acquisition of another company, a purchase of major equipment or a new computer system, the introduction of a new product or service, or the hiring of additional employees. In such situations, a feasibility study can help a small business's managers understand the impact of any major changes they might contemplate.

"Conduct a feasibility study to start your course of action," consultants Judy Capko and Rebecca Anwar suggested in an article for *American Medical News*. "It will provide you with objective information to evaluate existing services and strengths. You will gain an understanding of the competition and marketplace indicators that affect your [business]. This is the best way for you to grasp the impact of future decisions you may be considering. The feasibility study will help you accurately anticipate what will and will not work in varied situations. You will be able to determine what resources are essential to complete varied situations and gain an understanding of how to draw on your strengths.''

The main objective of a feasibility study is to determine whether a certain plan of action is feasible—that is, whether or not it will work, and whether or not it is worth doing economically. Although the core of the study is dedicated to showing the outcomes of specific actions, it should begin with an evaluation of the entire operation. For example, a good feasibility study would review a company's strengths and weaknesses, its position in the marketplace, and its financial situation. It would also include information on a company's major competitors, primary customers, and any relevant industry trends. This sort of overview provides small business owners and managers with an objective view of the company's current situation and opportunities. By providing information on consumer needs and how best to meet them, a feasibility study can also lead to new ideas for strategic changes.

The second part of a good feasibility study should focus on the proposed plan of action and provide a detailed estimate of its costs and benefits. In some cases, a feasibility study may lead management to determine that the company could achieve the same benefits through easier or cheaper means. For example, it may be possible to improve a manual filing system rather than purchase an expensive new computerized database. If the proposed project is determined to be both feasible and desirable, the information provided in the feasibility study can prove valuable in implementation. It can be used to develop a strategic plan for the project, translating general ideas into measurable goals. The goals can then be broken down further to create a series of concrete steps and outline how the steps can be implemented. Throughout the process, the feasibility study will show the various consequences and impacts associated with the plan of action.

In most cases, a feasibility study should be performed by a qualified consultant in order to ensure its accuracy and objectivity. To be able to provide a meaningful analysis of the data, the consultant should have expertise in the industry. It is also important for small businesses to assign an internal person to help gather information for the feasibility study. The small business owner must be sure that those conducting the study have full access to the company and the specific information they need.

FURTHER READING:

Capko, Judy, and Rebecca Anwar. ''Feasibility Studies Can Help You Control Your Destiny.'' *American Medical News.* September 23, 1996.

Jones, Seymour, M. Bruce Cohen, and Victor V. Coppola. *The Coopers and Lybrand Guide to Growing Your Business.* New York: Wiley, 1988.

SEE ALSO: Business Planning

FEDERAL TRADE COMMISSION

The Federal Trade Commission (FTC) was established as an independent administrative agency pursuant to the Federal Trade Commission Act of 1914. The purpose of the FTC is to enforce the provisions of the Federal Trade Commission Act, which prohibits ''unfair or deceptive acts or practices in commerce.'' The Clayton Antitrust Act (1914) also granted the FTC the authority to act against specific and unfair monopolistic practices. The FTC is considered to be a law enforcement agency, and like other such agencies it lacks punitive authority. Although the FTC cannot punish violators—that is the responsibility of the judicial system—it can issue cease and desist orders and argue cases in federal and administrative courts.

Today, the Federal Trade Commission serves an important function as a protector of both consumer and business rights. While the restrictions that it imposes on business practices often receive the most attention, other laws enforced by the FTC—such as the 1979 Franchise Rule, which directed franchisors to provide full disclosure of franchise information to prospective franchisees—have been of great benefit to entrepreneurs and small business owners. Basically, all business owners should educate themselves about the guidelines set forth by the FTC on various business practices. Some of its rules can be helpful to small businesses and entrepreneurs. Conversely, businesses that flout or remain ignorant of the FTC's operating guidelines are apt to regret it.

CREATION OF THE FTC

The FTC was created in response to a public outcry against the abuses of monopolistic trusts during the late 19th and early 20th centuries. The Sherman Antitrust Act of 1890 had proven inadequate in limiting trusts, and the widespread misuse of economic power by companies became so problematic that it became a significant factor in the election of Woodrow Wilson to the White House in 1912. Once Wilson assumed the office of the Presidency, he followed through on his campaign promises to address the excesses of America's trusts. Wilson's State of the Union Message of 1913 included a call for extensive antitrust legislation. Wilson's push, combined with public displeasure with the situation, resulted in the passage of two acts. The first was the Federal Trade

Commission Act, which created and empowered the FTC to define and halt "unfair practice" in trade and commerce. It was followed by the Clayton Antitrust Act, which covered specific activities of corporations that were deemed to be not in the public interest. Activities covered by this act included those mergers which inhibited trade by creating monopolies. The FTC began operating in 1915; the Bureau of Operations, which had previously monitored corporate activity for the federal government, was folded into the FTC.

The FTC is empowered to enforce provisions of both acts following specific guidelines. The offense must fall under the jurisdiction of the various acts and must affect interstate commerce. The violations must also affect the public good; the FTC does not intervene in disputes between private parties. As noted, the FTC lacks authority to punish or fine violators, but if an FTC ruling—such as a cease and desist order—is ignored, the FTC can seek civil penalties in federal court and seek compensation for those harmed by the unfair or deceptive practices.

Since 1914 both the Federal Trade Commission Act and the Clayton Act have been amended numerous times, thus expanding the legal responsibilities of the FTC. Some of the more notable amendments are:

- Webb-Pomerene Export Trade Act of 1918—This act promoted exports by encouraging cooperative activities.

- Robinson-Patman Act of 1936—This act strengthened the Clayton Act and addressed pricing practices of suppliers and wholesalers.

- Wool Products Labeling Act of 1939—This act ensured the purity of wool products.

- Lanham Trademark Act of 1946—This act required the registration and protection of trademarks used in commerce.

- Fair Packaging and Labeling Act of 1966—This act legislated against unfair or deceptive labeling and packaging.

- Truth in Lending Act of 1969—This legislation offered increased protection to consumers by requiring that companies provide full disclosure of credit terms and limit consumer liability concerning stolen credit cards; it also established regulations for advertising for credit services.

- Fair Credit Reporting Act of 1970—This act established regulations and fair operating practices for credit reporting agencies.

- Magnuson-Moss Warranty-Federal Trade Commission Improvement Act of 1975— This legislation expanded the authority of

the FTC by allowing it to seek redress for consumers and civil penalties for repeat offenders. It also increased the FTC's authorization to pursue violations "affecting commerce" rather than violations "in commerce." This was an important distinction. Under the terms of the act, manufacturers are not required to warrant their products but if they do they must specify whether their warranties are "full" or "limited." The law also introduced rules requiring businesses to explain any limitations on warranties in writing.

- FTC Franchise Rule of 1979—This rule requires franchisors to provide prospective franchisees with a full disclosure of relevant information about the franchise.

- Telemarketing and Consumer Fraud and Abuse Prevention Act of 1994—This law, commonly referred to as the "Telemarketing Sales Rule," was put together in response to widespread consumer complaints about fraudulent and/or bothersome **telemarketing** practices. The act imposed meaningful curbs on such activities. Among the restrictions imposed by the legislation were specific identity disclosure requirements, prohibitions on misrepresentations, limitations on time during which telemarketers can make their calls, prohibitions on making calls to consumers who specifically ask not to be called, restrictions on sales of certain goods and services, and new record-keeping requirements.

FTC BUREAUS

The FTC is administered by a five-member commission. Each commissioner is appointed by the President for a seven-year term with the advice and consent of the Senate. The commission must represent at least three political parties and the President chooses from its ranks one commissioner to be chairperson. The chairperson appoints an executive director with the consent of the full commission; the executive director is responsible for general staff operations.

Three bureaus of the FTC interpret and enforce jurisdictional legislation: the Bureau of Consumer Protection, the Bureau of Competition, and the Bureau of Economics.

BUREAU OF CONSUMER PROTECTION The Bureau of Consumer Protection is charged with protecting the consumer from unfair, deceptive, and fraudulent practices. It enforces congressional consumer protection laws and regulations issued by the Commission. In order to meet its various responsibilities, the Bureau often becomes involved in federal litigation, consumer, and business education, and conducts various investigations under its jurisdiction. The Bureau has divisions of advertising, marketing practices, credit, and enforcement.

BUREAU OF COMPETITION The FTC's Bureau of Competition is responsible for antitrust activity and investigations involving restraint of trade. The Bureau of Competition works with the Antitrust Division of the U.S. Department of Justice, but while the Justice Department concentrates on criminal violations, the Bureau of Competition deals with the technical and civil aspects of competition in the marketplace.

BUREAU OF ECONOMICS The Bureau of Economics predicts and analyzes the economic impact of FTC activities, especially as these activities relate to competition, interstate commerce, and consumer welfare. The Bureau provides Congress and the Executive Branch with the results of its investigations and undertakes special studies on their behalf when requested.

APPLICATIONS FOR COMPLAINTS

The FTC becomes aware of alleged unfair or deceptive trade practices as a result of its own investigations or complaints from consumers, business people, trade associations, other federal agencies, or local and state governmental agencies. These complaints become known as ''applications for complaints'' and are reviewed to determine whether or not they fall under FTC jurisdiction. If the application does fall under FTC jurisdiction, the case can be settled if the violator agrees to a consent order. This is a document issued by the FTC after a formal—and in some cases—public hearing to hear the complaint. Consent orders are handed down in situations where the offending company or person agrees to discontinue or correct the challenged practices. If an agreement is not reached via a consent order, the case is litigated before an FTC Administrative Law Judge. After the judge has handed down his or her decision, either the FTC counsel or the respondent can appeal the decision to the Commission. The Commission may either dismiss the case or issue a cease and desist order. If a cease and desist order is issued, the respondent has sixty days to take all necessary steps to obey the order or launch an appeal process through the federal court system.

For further information on the FTC, its various responsibilities, and its impact on small business owners, contact the agency at the following address: Federal Trade Commission, Pennsylvania Avenue at Sixth Street NW, Washington, D.C. 20580; phone: (202) 326-2222.

FURTHER READING:

A Guide to the Federal Trade Commission. Washington: Federal Trade Commission, 1987.

Rosch, J. Thomas. *Manual of Federal Trade Commission Practice*. Washington: Bureau of National Affairs, 1989.

United States Federal Trade Commission Annual Report. Washington: Federal Trade Commission, U.S. Government Printing Office.

SEE ALSO: Consumer Advocacy

FICA TAXES

Federal Insurance Contribution Act (FICA) taxes, which include contributions to federal Social Security and Medicare programs, must be paid by all American workers, whether they are employed by a company or are self-employed. Small businesses that employ persons other than the owner or partners are required to withhold FICA taxes—along with regular income taxes—from the wages paid to employees, remit these taxes to the **Internal Revenue Service**, and make regularly scheduled reports to the IRS about the amount of taxes owed and paid. Businesses are not required to withhold FICA taxes on wages paid to independent contractors, and self-employed persons must pay their own FICA taxes.

Employers are required to withhold 7.65 percent of the first $62,700 of an employee's income for FICA taxes. Social Security (also known as OldAge Survivors and Disability Insurance or OASDI) accounts for 6.2 percent of the FICA tax, while Medicare accounts for 1.45 percent (the Medicare percentage is applicable to unlimited amounts of income, rather than just the first $62,700). Employers are also required to match the 7.65 percent contributed by every employee, so that the total FICA contribution is 15.3 percent. Self-employed persons are required to pay both the employer and employee portions of the FICA tax.

In addition to withholding FICA taxes for employees, employers must remit these taxes to the IRS in a timely manner. The regular income taxes and the portion of the FICA taxes that are withheld from employees' wages each pay period must be remitted to the IRS monthly, along with a Federal Tax Deposit Coupon (Form 8109-B). If the total withheld is less than $500, however, the business is allowed to make the payments quarterly. FICA tax payments also must be reported on Form W-2, the Annual Statement of Taxes Withheld, which must be sent to all employees and to the Social Security Administration before January 31 of the following year.

Small businesses also must maintain specific employment records regarding FICA tax withholding and remittance in order to meet federal requirements. These records, which must be kept for every employee, include the amount of each payment subject to FICA taxes, the amount of FICA tax collected from each payment, along with the date, and an explanation for any difference between the amount subject to FICA taxes and the amount of tax collected.

Many small businesses fall behind in paying their FICA taxes or filing the associated reports at some time during their existence. A company struggling with cash flow may opt to pay suppliers and worker salaries in order to stay in business, rather than remitting its FICA tax withholdings on time. This is a very bad practice, however, because significant interest and penalties apply for late payment or nonpayment of FICA taxes. In fact, the Trust Fund Recovery Penalty allows the IRS to hold a small business owner or accountant personally liable for 100 percent of the amount owed, even in cases where the business has gone bankrupt.

There are certain situations in which small businesses can avoid owing FICA taxes. For example, special rules apply to **sole proprietorships** and husband-and-wife **partnerships** that pay their minor (under 18) children for work performed in the business. These small businesses receive an exemption from withholding FICA taxes from their children's paychecks, and are also not required to pay the employer portion of the FICA taxes. In this way, the parent and child each save 7.65 percent, for a total of 15.3 percent. In addition, the child's wages can still be deducted from the parents' income taxes as a business expense.

There is no limit on how much children can earn under this FICA tax exemption. However, it is important that the wages paid to the child are reasonable for the job performed, and that the hours worked by the child are carefully documented, so it will be clear to the IRS that the child has not been paid for nothing. In addition, parents should note that their child's financial aid for college may be reduced if they earn more than $1,750 per year.

FURTHER READING:

Dailey, Frederick W. *Tax Savvy for Small Business.* 2nd ed. Berkeley, CA: Nolo Press, 1997.

DeJong, David S., and Ann Gray Jakabcin. *J.K. Lasser's Year-Round Tax Strategies.* New York: Macmillan, 1997.

Ellentuck, Albert B. *Laventhol and Horwath Small Business Tax Planning Guide.* New York: Avon Books, 1988.

The Entrepreneur Magazine Small Business Advisor. New York: Wiley, 1995.

Glen, Heidi. "Young Americans Face Higher FICA Taxes or Lower Benefits." *Tax Notes.* March 18, 1996.

Marullo, Gloria Gibbs. "Hiring Your Child: Tax Breaks and Trade-Offs." *Nation's Business.* June 1997.

Robertson, Cliff. *The Small Business Tax Advisor: Understanding the New Tax Law.* Blue Ridge Summit, PA: Liberty House, 1987.

SEE ALSO: Employing Minors; Medicare and Medicaid; Self-Employment Contributions Act; Tax Withholding

FIDUCIARY DUTY

Fiduciary duty is a legal requirement of loyalty and care that applies to any person or organization that has a fiduciary relationship with another person or organization. A fiduciary is a person, committee, or organization that has agreed to accept legal ownership or control and management of an asset or group of assets belonging to someone else. Some examples of fiduciary relationships might include an investment manager to participants in a pension plan, a majority stockholder in a corporation to minority investors, the members of a partnership to one another, a banker to customers, an attorney to a client, or even a parent to a child.

A fiduciary duty is one of complete trust and utmost good faith. While fiduciaries take legal title to assets, the assets do not belong to them. Rather, legal title allows fiduciaries to administer and manage the assets for a temporary period and for a specific purpose. In taking control of another's assets, fiduciaries also agree to manage those assets in accordance with the wishes of the individual who established the fiduciary relationship. The powers and duties of fiduciaries are often established in a document that formally establishes the fiduciary relationship. The conduct of fiduciaries is governed by common law as well as by specific federal and state laws. The Uniform Fiduciary Act and the Uniform Trustees' Powers Act serve as models for state legislation.

Fiduciaries owe two main duties to their clients: a duty of loyalty and a duty of care. The duty of loyalty requires that fiduciaries act solely in the interest of their clients, rather than in their own interest. Thus fiduciaries must not derive any direct or indirect profit from their position, and must avoid potential conflicts of interest. The duty of care requires that fiduciaries perform their functions with a high level of competence and thoroughness, in accordance with industry standards.

Corporate directors have a special fiduciary duty to their shareholders. They are accountable not only for the safekeeping of assets but also for their efficient and effective use. Directors may not profit personally at the expense of, or contrary to, the corporation's shareholders. In other words, corporate directors must place the interests of shareholders above their own interests. The concept of fiduciary duty has a wide variety of other applications in the business world. But a particular area of concern for small businesses is the expanded definition of fiduciary duty that applies to employers that offer certain types of benefit plans to their employees.

EMPLOYEE BENEFIT PLANS

Employers that offer employee benefit plans—such as 401(k) plans or other types of pension plans—are bound by the definition of fiduciary duty set forth in the Employee Retirement Income Security Act of 1974 (ERISA). ERISA, in regulating employee benefit plans, established higher standards of fiduciary duty for individuals who have control over a plan's assets than had existed for other types of fiduciaries under common law.

In spelling out fiduciary duties with regard to employee benefit plans, ERISA covers the duty of loyalty, the duty to use prudence, and the duty to comply with the plan. The duty of loyalty means that fiduciaries must act in the best interests of the plan and its participants. If fiduciaries are also plan participants, they must subordinate their own interests to those of the plan. In cases where plan participants form a diverse group with different interests, it may be difficult to balance the interests of all concerned.

ERISA expands the concept of care beyond that found in common law. Section 404(a)(1) of ERISA states that a fiduciary shall discharge his duties with respect to a plan "with the care, skill, prudence, and diligence under the circumstances then prevailing that a prudent man acting in a like capacity and familiar with such matters would use in the conduct of an enterprise of a like character and with like aims." Thus, fiduciaries of employee benefit plans must discharge their duties with adequate expertise. The courts have found that fiduciary duties were breached when nonexpert laypersons failed to seek independent qualified counsel when making decisions affecting plan assets. Plan fiduciaries are under an obligation not only to use their special skills and expertise, but also to engage qualified advisers and managers if they lack the expertise themselves.

The prudent person standard, as expressed in ERISA, also requires that fiduciaries "diversify the investments of the plan so as to minimize the risk of large losses, unless under the circumstances it is clearly prudent not to do so." ERISA also makes note of prohibited transactions. Additional specific duties of plan fiduciaries may be set forth in the plan document, and fiduciaries have a duty to administer the plan "in accordance with the documents and instru-

ments governing the plan." Fiduciary duties outlined in the plan document must be consistent with ERISA.

A much-discussed aspect of ERISA is that it established personal liability for breaches of fiduciary duty. That is, fiduciaries of employee benefit plans can be held personally liable for any breaches of their duties as spelled out in ERISA. ERISA expanded the concept of fiduciary duty to cover named fiduciaries as well as anyone else who has the power to manage, acquire, or dispose of any assets of a plan. Thus, even if they are not named specifically as fiduciaries, small business owners, chief financial officers, controllers, and management accountants can be held to ERISA's standards of fiduciary duty if they have the power to manage, acquire, or dispose of the plan's assets. As a result, small businesses that offer employee pension plans must be careful to manage plan assets in accordance with ERISA.

FURTHER READING:

Hofmann, Mark A. "Fiduciary Liability in Review." *Business Insurance.* October 9, 1995.

Karol, Bernard. "Fiduciaries Must Beware of Potential Conflicts." *American Banker.* June 26, 1997.

FINANCE COMPANIES

Commercial finance companies have in recent years become a favorite option for entrepreneurs seeking small business **loans**. These institutions generally charge higher **interest rates** than banks and credit unions, but they also are more likely to approve a loan request. Most loans obtained through finance companies are secured by a specific asset as **collateral**, and that asset can be seized if the entrepreneur defaults on the loan. Consumer finance companies make small loans against personal assets and provide an option for individuals with poor **credit** ratings. Commercial finance companies provide small businesses with loans for inventory and equipment purchases and are a good resource for manufacturing enterprises. Insurance companies often make commercial loans as a way of reinvesting their income. They usually provide payment terms and interest rates comparable to a commercial bank, but require a business to have more assets available as collateral. "In general, finance companies want to see strong assets to back up a loan and will monitor those assets much more carefully," one expert told *Entrepreneur*. "For that reason, they can loan more against the assets. So chances are a smaller business might get a larger loan from a finance company" than from a bank. Paola Banchero of *Kansas City Business Journal* noted that commercial finance companies have also grown because that are more flexible in arranging loan repayment schedules than are banks. Whereas banks typically require a seven-year repayment schedule on term loans and 15-year schedules for loans on commercial property, finance companies may extend payment schedules up to 10 years for term loans and up to 25 years for loans on commercial real estate.

Reasons for the growth of finance companies in the world of small business are myriad. For example, the U.S. Small Business Administration (SBA) reported that two of the top three lenders for its 7(a) loan program for fiscal year 1996 were nonbank lenders. A recent SBA-sponsored study entitled *Finance Companies and Small Business Borrowers,* meanwhile, indicated that from 1980 to 1992, nonbank financing companies enjoyed a tremendous period of growth, increasing the amount of their loans to business enterprises from about $85 billion to nearly $300 billion. This sustained growth places finance companies as America's second largest source of business credit, behind banking institutions.

Larger commercial finance companies often offer small business owners a variety of lending options from which to choose. These include **factoring**, working capital loans, equipment financing and leasing, specialized equity investments, collateral-based financing, and cash-flow financing. Some also offer additional services in connection with those loans, such as assistance with **collections**.

BIG AND SMALL NONBANK LENDERS Commercial finance companies, though, come in all shapes and sizes, and the breadth of their services often has some bearing on their exact services. The nation's largest finance firms (The Money Store, AT&T Small Business Lending Corp.) have established networks of offices across the country, and they sometimes offer lending services that even banks do not. For example, The Money Store—which made more than 1,700 loans worth $635 million in fiscal year 1996—offers loans to entrepreneurs looking to take ownership of a franchise, an option that is not available at all banks. But as *Entrepreneur*'s Cynthia Griffin noted, ''in addition to the mega players, the commercial finance industry is populated by hundreds of smaller firms.'' These firms generally make asset-based loans, providing services to small business owners who are unable to secure loans from their banks.

FURTHER READING:

Andresky Fraser, Jill. ''Show Me the Money: You Can Look for Money in All the Wrong Places.'' *Inc.* March 1997.

Banchero, Paola. ''Financing Fight: Nonbank Lenders Want Nothing More Than to Take Business Away from Traditional Banks.'' *Kansas City Business Journal.* October 10, 1997.

Financing for the Small Business. Washington: U.S. Small Business Administration, 1990.

Griffin, Cynthia E. ''Breaking the Bank.'' *Entrepreneur.* March 1998.

''How to Make Them Give You the Money.'' *Money.* June 1995.

Prins, Ruth. ''From the Frying Pan to the Fire?'' *U.S. Banker.* December 1997.

Sherman, Andrew J. *The Complete Guide to Running and Growing Your Business.* New York: Times Books, 1997.

Whittemore, Meg. ''Creative Financing that Succeeds.'' *Nation's Business.* April 1995.

Wolf, F. David. ''How to Select a Commercial Bank Vs. A Non-Bank Lender.'' *Tampa Bay Business Journal.* July 28, 1995.

FINANCE AND FINANCIAL MANAGEMENT

Finance and financial management encompass numerous business and governmental activities. In the most basic sense, the term *finance* can be used to describe the activities of a firm attempting to raise **capital** through the sale of stocks, bonds, or other promissory notes. Similarly, *public finance* is a term used to describe government capital-raising activities through the issuance of bonds or the imposition of taxes. Financial management, in the broadest sense, can be defined as business activities undertaken with the goal of maximizing shareholder wealth, utilizing the principles of the time value of money, leverage, diversification, and an investment's expected rate of return versus its risk.

Within the discipline of finance, there are three basic components. First, there are financial instruments. These instruments—stocks and bonds—are recorded evidence of obligations on which exchanges of resources are founded. Effective investment management of these financial instruments is a vital part of any organization's financing activities. Second, there are financial markets, which are the mechanisms used to trade the financial instruments. Finally, there are banking and financial institutions, which facilitate the transfer of resources among those buying and selling the financial instruments.

In today's business environment, corporate finance addresses issues relating to individual firms. Specifically, the field of corporate finance seeks to determine the optimal investments that firms should make, the best methods of paying for those investments, and the best ways of managing daily financial activities to ensure that firms have adequate cash flow. Financial management influences all segments of corporate activity, for both profit-oriented firms and non-profit firms. Through the acquisition of funds, the allocation of resources, and the tracking of financial performance, financial management provides a vital function for any organization's activities. Furthermore, finance provides stockholders and other interested parties with a tool with which to assess management activities.

Large corporations usually employ managers who specialize in finance as treasurers, controllers, and a chief financial officer (CFO). In a small business, many of the functions that would be performed by these specialists fall upon the small business owner or manager. He or she would likely be responsible for obtaining financing, maintaining the company's relationship with banks and other financial institutions, ensuring that the company meets its obligations to investors and creditors, analyzing and deciding upon capital investment projects, and conducting overall financial policymaking and planning. For this reason, a basic understanding of financial management can be very helpful for a small business owner.

The discipline of finance, which was originally part of economics, has undergone significant changes over the years. In the mid-1950s, it evolved from a purely descriptive discipline to a proactive field allowing managers to make choices regarding their firms' financial operations. Much of these changes can be attributed to the work of Joel Dean, who furthered the understanding of the area of capital budgeting and sought to make it a major discipline within the field of finance. With this advancement, there was increased understanding of the cost of capital and the valuation of financial assets. Furthermore, these changes led to more interest in the theory of capital structure, security analysis, and portfolio management. The field of finance continues to evolve even today; it is constantly reacting to activities in the economy and to new theoretical ideas. For instance, because of today's volatile, global business climate, managers must be able to react swiftly to economic downturns and to better understand the operations of firms abroad.

FURTHER READING:

Brealey, Richard A., and Stewart C. Myers. *Principles of Corporate Finance.* 4th ed. New York: McGraw-Hill, 1991.

Brigham, Eugene F. *Fundamentals of Financial Management.* 5th ed. Chicago: Dryden Press, 1989.

Cooper, S. Kerry, and Donald R. Fraser. *The Financial Marketplace.* Reading, MA: Addison-Wesley, 1986.

Gallinger, George W., and Jerry B. Poe. *Essentials of Finance: An Integrated Approach.* Englewood Cliffs, NJ: Prentice Hall, 1995.

Petty, J. William, Arthur J. Keown, David F. Scott, Jr., and John D. Martin. *Basic Financial Management.* 6th ed. Englewood Cliffs, NJ: Prentice Hall, 1993.

Spiro, Herbert T. *Finance for the Nonfinancial Manager.* 3rd ed. New York: Wiley, 1988.

FINANCIAL ANALYSIS

Financial analysis is an aspect of the overall business finance function that involves examining historical data to gain information about the current and future financial health of a company. Financial analysis can be applied in a wide variety of situations to give business managers the information they need to make critical decisions. ''The inability to understand and deal with financial data is a severe handicap in the corporate world,'' Alan S. Donnahoe wrote in his book *What Every Manager Should Know about Financial Analysis.* ''In a very real sense, finance is the language of business. Goals are set and performance is measured in financial terms. Plants are built, equipment ordered, and new projects undertaken based on clear investment return criteria. Financial analysis is required in every such case.''

The finance function in business organizations involves evaluating economic trends, setting financial policy, and creating long-range plans for business activities. It also involves applying a system of internal controls for the handling of cash, the recognition of sales, the disbursement of expenses, the valuation of **inventory**, and the approval of **capital** expenditures. In addition, the finance function reports on these internal control systems through the preparation of **financial statements**, such as **income statements**, **balance sheets**, and **cash flow statements**.

Finally, finance involves analyzing the data contained in financial statements in order to provide valuable information for management decisions. In this way, financial analysis is only one part of the overall function of finance, but a very important one. ''The mathematical tools produce data, not explanations; information, not interpretation; measurement, not meaning,'' according to James E. Kristy and Susan Z. Diamond in their book *Finance without Fear.* ''To these tools you must add judgment, which develops slowly—mostly out of experience.''

DOCUMENTS USED IN FINANCIAL ANALYSIS

The two main sources of data for financial analysis are a company's balance sheet and income statement. The balance sheet outlines the financial and physical resources that a company has available for business activities in the future. It is important to note, however, that the balance sheet only lists these resources, and makes no judgment about how well they will be used by management. For this reason, the balance sheet is more useful in analyzing a company's current financial position than its expected performance.

The main elements of the balance sheet are **assets** and **liabilities**. Assets generally include both current assets (cash or equivalents that will be converted to cash within one year, such as accounts receivable, inventory, and prepaid expenses) and noncurrent assets (assets that are held for more than one year and are used in running the business, including fixed assets like property, plant, and equipment; long-term investments; and intangible assets like patents, copyrights, and goodwill). Both the total amount of assets and the makeup of asset accounts are of interest to financial analysts.

The balance sheet also includes two categories of liabilities, current liabilities (debts that will come due within one year, such as accounts payable, short-term loans, and taxes) and long-term debts (debts that are due more than one year from the date of the statement). Liabilities are important to financial analysts because businesses have same obligation to pay their bills regularly as individuals, while business income tends to be less certain. Long-term liabilities are less important to analysts, since they lack the urgency of short-term debts, though their presence does indicate that a company is strong enough to be allowed to borrow money.

The balance sheet also commonly includes stockholders' equity accounts, which detail the permanent capital of the business. The total equity usually consists of two parts: the money that has been invested by shareholders, and the money that has been retained from profits and reinvested in the business. In general, the more equity that is held by a business, the better the ability of the business to borrow additional funds.

In contrast to the balance sheet, the income statement provides information about a company's performance over a certain period of time. Although it does not reveal much about the company's current financial condition, it does provide indications of its future viability. The main elements of the income statement are revenues earned, expenses incurred, and net profit or loss. Revenues consist mainly of sales, though financial analysts may also note the inclusion of royalties, interest, and extraordinary items. Likewise, operating expenses usually consists primarily of the cost of goods sold, but can also include some unusual items. Net income is the "bottom line" of the income statement. This figure is the main indicator of a company's accomplishments over the statement period.

ELEMENTS OF FINANCIAL HEALTH

As Kristy and Diamond noted, a company's overall financial health can be assessed by examining three major factors: its liquidity, leverage, and profitability. All three of these factors are internal measures that are largely within the control of a company's management. It is important to note, however, that they may also be affected by other conditions—such as overall trends in the economy—that are beyond management's control.

LIQUIDITY Liquidity refers to a company's ability to pay its current bills and expenses. In other words, liquidity relates to the availability of cash and other assets to cover accounts payable, short-term debt, and other liabilities. All small businesses require a certain degree of liquidity in order to pay their bills on time, though start-up and very young companies are often not very liquid. In mature companies, low levels of liquidity can indicate poor management or a need for additional capital. Of course, any company's liquidity may vary due to seasonality, the timing of sales, and the state of the economy.

Companies tend to run into problems with liquidity because cash outflows are not flexible, while income is often uncertain. "Creditors expect their money when promised, just as employees expect regular paychecks. However, the cash being generated does not follow a set schedule. Sales of inventory vary, as do collections from customers," Kristy and Diamond explained. "Because of this difference between cash generation and cash payments, businesses must maintain a certain ratio of current assets to current liabilities in order to ensure adequate liquidity."

LEVERAGE Leverage refers to the proportion of a company's capital that has been contributed by investors as compared to creditors. In other words, leverage is the extent to which a company has depended upon borrowing to finance its operations A company that has a high proportion of debt in relation to its equity would be considered highly leveraged. Leverage is an important aspect of financial analysis because it is reviewed closely by both bankers and investors. A high leverage ratio may increase a company's exposure to risk and business downturns, but along with this higher risk also comes the potential for higher returns.

PROFITABILITY Profitability refers to management's performance in using the resources of a business. Many measures of profitability involve calculating the financial return that the company earns on the money that has been invested. As James O. Gill stated in his book *Financial Basics of Small Business Success,* most entrepreneurs decide to start their own businesses in order to earn a better return on their money than would be available through a bank or other low-risk investments. If profitability measures demonstrate that this is not occurring—particularly once a small business has moved beyond the start-up phase—then the entrepreneur should consider selling the business and reinvesting his or her money elsewhere. However, it is important to note that many factors can influence profitability measures, including changes in price, volume, or expenses, as well the purchase of assets or the borrowing of money.

PERFORMING ANALYSES WITH FINANCIAL RATIOS

"Measuring the liquidity, leverage, and profitability of a company is not a matter of how many dollars in assets, liabilities, and equity it has, but of the proportions in which such items occur in relation to one another," Kristy and Diamond wrote. "We analyze a company, therefore, by looking at ratios rather than just dollar amounts." **Financial ratios** are determined by dividing one number by another, and are usually expressed as a percentage. They enable business owners to examine the relationships between seemingly unrelated items and thus gain useful information for **decision making**. "They are simple to calculate, easy to use, and provide a wealth of information that cannot be gotten anywhere else," Gill noted. But, he added, "Ratios are aids to judgment and cannot take the place of experience. They will not replace good management, but they will make a good manager better. They help to pinpoint areas that need investigation and assist in developing an operating strategy for the future."

Virtually any financial statistics can be compared using a ratio. In fact, Kristy and Diamond claimed that there are over 150 recognized financial ratios that can be computed in a financial analysis. In reality, however, small business owners and managers only need to be concerned with a small set of ratios in order to identify where improvements are needed. Determining which ratios to compute depends on the type of business, the age of the business, the point in the business cycle, and any specific information sought. For example, if a small business depends on a large number of fixed assets, ratios that measure how efficiently these assets are being used may be the most significant.

There are a few general ratios that can be very useful in an overall financial analysis, however. To assess a company's liquidity, Kristy and Diamond recommend using the current, quick, and liquidity ratios. The current ratio can be defined as Current Assets divided by Current Liabilities. It measures the ability of an entity to pay its near-term obligations. Though the ideal current ratio depends to some extent on the type of business, a general rule of thumb is that it should be at least 2:1. A lower current ratio means that the company may not be able to pay its bills on time, while a higher ratio means that the company has money in cash or safe investments that could be put to better use in the business.

The quick ratio, also known as the "acid test," can be defined as Quick Assets (cash, marketable securities, and receivables) divided by Current Liabil-

ities. This ratio provides a stricter definition of the company's ability to make payments on current obligations. Ideally, this ratio should be 1:1. If it is higher, the company may keep too much cash on hand or have a poor collection program for accounts receivable. If it is lower, it may indicate that the company relies too heavily on inventory to meet its obligations. The liquidity ratio, also known as the cash ratio, can be defined as Cash divided by Current Liabilities. This measure eliminates all current assets except cash from the calculation of liquidity. Ideally, the ratio should be approximately .40:1.

To measure a company's leverage, Kristy and Diamond recommend using the debt/equity ratio. Defined as Debt divided by Owners' Equity, this ratio indicates the relative mix of the company's investor-supplied capital. A company is generally considered safer if it has a low debt to equity ratio—that is, a higher proportion of owner-supplied capital—though a very low ratio can indicate excessive caution. In general, debt should be between 50 and 80 percent of equity.

Finally, to measure a company's level of profitability, Kristy and Diamond recommend using the **return on equity (ROE)** ratio, which can be defined as Net Income / Owners' Equity. This ratio indicates how well the company is utilizing its equity investment. ROE is considered to be one of the best indicators of profitability. It is also a good figure to compare against competitors or an industry average. Experts suggest that companies usually need at least 10 to 14 percent ROE in order to fund future growth. If this ratio is too low, it can indicate poor management performance or a highly conservative business approach. On the other hand, a high ROE can mean that management is doing a good job, or that the firm is undercapitalized.

In conclusion, financial analysis can be an important tool for small business owners and managers to measure their progress toward reaching company goals, as well as toward competing with larger companies within an industry. When performed regularly over time, financial analysis also can help small businesses recognize and adapt to trends affecting their operations. It is also important for small business owners to understand and use financial analysis because it provides one of the main measures of a company's success from the perspective of bankers, investors, and outside analysts.

FURTHER READING:

Bangs, David H., Jr. *Managing by the Numbers: Financial Essentials for the Growing Business.* Dover, NH: Upstart Publishing, 1992.

Casteuble, Tracy. "Using Financial Ratios to Assess Performance." *Association Management.* July 1997.

Donnahoe, Alan S. *What Every Manager Should Know about Financial Analysis.* New York: Simon and Schuster, 1989.

Gill, James O. *Financial Basics of Small Business Success.* Menlo Park, CA: Crisp Publications, 1994.

Jones, Allen N. "Financial Statements: When Properly Read, They Share a Wealth of Information." *Memphis Business Journal.* February 5, 1996.

Kristy, James E., and Susan Z. Diamond. *Finance without Fear.* New York: American Management Association, 1984.

Larkin, Howard. "How to Read a Financial Statement." *American Medical News.* March 11, 1996.

Vos, Hubert D., ed. *What Every Manager Needs to Know about Finance.* New York: AMACOM, 1983.

SEE ALSO: Finance and Financial Management

FINANCIAL PLANNERS

Financial planners provide individuals and small businesses with investment advice and, in some cases, also manage their clients' assets. Financial planners can be particularly valuable in helping small business owners to make decisions about both their personal and business finances. "A good financial planner can double the profits of a small firm or help save a company from bankruptcy," according to Robert J. Klein in *Dun and Bradstreet Reports.* Since virtually anyone can call themselves a financial planner, small business owners must be diligent in obtaining referrals, checking qualifications and licenses, and inquiring about fees. "The real pros can help you map out a route to goals like retirement and estate planning, asset allocation, and tax and cash-flow planning," Laura Koss-Feder wrote in an article for *Money.*

A good financial planner will conduct an in-depth interview to gather information about the client's income, expenses, assets, liabilities, future goals, and risk tolerance. Then the planner will use this information to develop a detailed, written financial plan specifically for the client. Financial planners may steer their clients into a wide range of investment products, including stocks, bonds, mutual funds, **money market instruments**, **independent retirement accounts (IRAs)**, and insurance. In most cases, clients receive monthly or quarterly reports detailing the progress of their investment portfolios.

FINDING A GOOD FINANCIAL PLANNER

"There is no shortage of good financial planners, but the challenge is to identify them among as many as 450,000 stockbrokers, insurance salespeople, and outright cranks who claim to be effective planners. Unlike, say, a plumber, hairdresser, or neurosurgeon, a financial planner does not necessarily have to open a book, take an exam, or otherwise demonstrate any competence before hanging out a shingle," Koss-Feder explained.

The first step in finding a good financial planner is obtaining referrals from friends and business associates, preferably those who are in similar financial situations and have similar financial needs. If personal recommendations are not available, trade groups such as the National Association of Personal Financial Advisors, the International Association for Financial Planning, and the Institute of Certified Financial Planners provide referrals for their members. After obtaining referrals, experts recommend that small business owners interview at least three potential planners before making a decision. It may be helpful to examine financial plans that each planner has prepared for clients with similar circumstances, and to gather information about the problems the planners have solved for other clients. Though it may not be necessary if the referral came from a trusted friend, the small business owner may wish to contact some of these clients directly and ask about the planners' strengths and weaknesses, responsiveness to phone calls, and willingness to explain things. Since financial planners often work with other professionals—such as attorneys and accountants—the small business owner may wish to ask for professional references as well.

The next step in hiring a financial planner is to conduct a thorough examination of their qualifications and experience. Experts recommend that financial planners have a strong background in finance, accounting, banking, stock brokerage, or a related field, as well as five years experience. Potential financial planners should also be able to show proof that they are licensed with regulatory bodies. In order to obtain a credential such as Certified Financial Planner (CFP) or Chartered Financial Consultant (ChFC), a planner must pass a series of tests, take continuing education courses, and comply with a code of ethics. In addition, financial planners who provide advice about securities must file a disclosure document known as an ADV with the **Securities and Exchange Commission (SEC)**. They are required to show potential clients part II of this document upon request, which gives information on their educational background, qualifications, fees charged for services, and any business affiliations that could cause a conflict of interest. Although financial planners are not obliged to show clients part I of their ADVs, small business owners may want to avoid any planner who is unwilling to do so, as part I outlines any disciplinary problems the planner has experienced.

FEE-BASED OR COMMISSION-BASED PLANNERS

The final step in hiring a financial planner is to find out how the planner will be compensated—through client fees or brokerage commissions. Fee-based planners charge their clients various fees depending on the type of work they perform. In contrast, commission-based planners do not charge their clients up-front fees, but instead take a commission on the investments they recommend. Commission-based planners generally work with their clients to create an investment plan for free, then charge commissions ranging from 1 percent on money-market accounts to 90 percent of first-year insurance premiums. In some ways, choosing a fee-based planner may seem preferable because it promotes objectivity and eliminates the potential for conflict of interest. But the fees charged can be expensive; according to Koss-Feder, the average fee to create a basic financial plan was over $1,100. "As long as you have confidence in the planner, it really doesn't matter which type you choose—as long as you know how he is making his money," Koss-Feder concluded. The fee structure should always be spelled out in a written agreement.

Until an atmosphere of trust develops between the small business owner and the financial planner, it may be best to start slowly, by investing around 25 percent of assets. The amount can then increase over time if the client is satisfied with the planner's performance. In order to establish a strong relationship with a financial planner, Lorayne Fiorillo of *Entrepreneur* recommended that small business owners "treat your financial advisor and his or her staff with respect. Don't call your advisor with paperwork questions; that's a job for his or her assistant. If you have a complex question, call when the stock market is closed—your advisor will have more time to talk. Most of all, keep the lines of communication open."

FURTHER READING:

Fairley, Juliette. "The Right Choice: Choosing a Financial Planner You Can Trust." *Black Enterprise*. March 1996.

Fiorillo, Lorayne. "Rope One In: How to Spot the Good, the Bad, and the Ugly When Looking for a Financial Advisor." *Entrepreneur*. December 1997.

Hamilton, Patricia W. "How to Choose a Financial Planner." *Dun and Bradstreet Reports*. May-June 1990.

Kahn, Virginia Munger. "Defining, and Finding, a Fee-Only Planner." *New York Times*. January 12, 1997.

Klein, Robert J. "The Very Model of a Financial Planner." *Dun and Bradstreet Reports*. May-June 1988.

Koss-Feder, Laura. "Smart Ways to Find a Financial Planner." *Money*. March 1997.

Williams, Fred O. "Managing Your Money: Services Provided by Certified Financial Planners." *Washington Business Journal*. May 3, 1996.

FINANCIAL RATIOS

Financial ratios illustrate relationships between different aspects of a small business's operations. They involve the comparison of elements from **balance sheets** or **income statements**, and are crafted with particular points of focus in mind. Financial ratios can provide small business owners and managers with a valuable tool to measure their progress against predetermined internal goals, a certain competitor, or the overall industry. In addition, tracking various ratios over time is a powerful way to identify trends as they develop. Ratios are also used by bankers, investors, and business analysts to assess various attributes of a company's financial strength or operating results.

Ratios are determined by dividing one number by another, and are usually expressed as a percentage. They enable business owners to examine the relationships between seemingly unrelated items and thus gain useful information for decision-making. "They are simple to calculate, easy to use, and provide a wealth of information that cannot be gotten anywhere else," James O. Gill noted in his book *Financial Basics of Small Business Success*. But, he added, "Ratios are aids to judgment and cannot take the place of experience. They will not replace good management, but they will make a good manager better. They help to pinpoint areas that need investigation and assist in developing an operating strategy for the future." Virtually any financial statistics can be compared using a ratio. In reality, however, small business owners and managers only need to be concerned with a small set of ratios in order to identify where improvements are needed. "As you run your business you juggle dozens of different variables," David H. Bangs, Jr. wrote in his book *Managing by the Numbers*. "Ratio analysis is designed to help you identify those variables which are out of balance."

It is important to keep in mind that financial ratios are time sensitive; they can only present a picture of the business at the time that the underlying figures were prepared. For example, a retailer calculating ratios before and after the Christmas season would get very different results. In addition, ratios can be misleading when taken singly, though they can be quite valuable when a small business tracks them over time or uses them as a basis for comparison against company goals or industry standards. As a result, business owners should compute a variety of applicable ratios and attempt to discern a pattern, rather than relying on the information provided by only one or two ratios. Gill also noted that small business owners should be certain to view ratios objectively, rather than using them to confirm a particular strategy or point of view.

Perhaps the best way for small business owners to use financial ratios is to conduct a formal ratio analysis on a regular basis. The raw data used to compute the ratios should be recorded on a special form monthly. Then the relevant ratios should be computed, reviewed, and saved for future comparisons. Determining which ratios to compute depends on the type of business, the age of the business, the point in the business cycle, and any specific information sought. For example, if a small business depends on a large number of fixed assets, ratios that measure how efficiently these assets are being used may be the most significant. In general, financial ratios can be broken down into four main categories—profitability or return on investment, liquidity, leverage, and operating or efficiency—with several specific ratio calculations prescribed within each.

PROFITABILITY OR RETURN ON INVESTMENT RATIOS

Profitability ratios provide information about management's performance in using the resources of the small business. As Gill noted, most entrepreneurs decide to start their own businesses in order to earn a better return on their money than would be available through a bank or other low-risk investments. If profitability ratios demonstrate that this is not occurring—particularly once a small business has moved beyond the start-up phase—then the entrepreneur should consider selling the business and reinvesting his or her money elsewhere. However, it is important to note that many factors can influence profitability ratios, including changes in price, volume, or expenses, as well the purchase of assets or the borrowing of money. Some specific profitability ratios follow, along with the means of calculating them and their meaning to a small business owner or manager.

Gross profitability: Gross Profits / Net Sales—measures the margin on sales the company is achieving. It can be an indication of manufacturing efficiency, or marketing effectiveness.

Net profitability: Net Income / Net Sales—measures the overall profitability of the company, or how much is being brought to the bottom line. Strong gross profitability combined with weak net profitability may indicate a problem with indirect operating expenses or non-operating items, such as interest expense. In general terms, net profitability shows the effectiveness of management. Though the optimal level depends on the type of business, the ratios can be compared for firms in the same industry.

Return on assets: Net Income / Total Assets—indicates how effectively the company is deploying its assets. A very low ROA usually indicates inefficient management, whereas a high ROA means efficient management. However, this ratio can be distorted by depreciation or any unusual expenses.

Return on investment 1: Net Income / Owners' Equity—indicates how well the company is utilizing its equity investment. Due to leverage, this measure will generally be higher than return on assets. ROI is considered to be one of the best indicators of profitability. It is also a good figure to compare against competitors or an industry average. Experts suggest that companies usually need at least 10–14 percent ROI in order to fund future growth. If this ratio is too low, it can indicate poor management performance or a highly conservative business approach. On the other hand, a high ROI can mean that management is doing a good job, or that the firm is undercapitalized.

Return on investment 2: Dividends $+/-$ Stock Price Change / Stock Price Paid—from the investor's point of view, this calculation of ROI measures the gain (or loss) achieved by placing an investment over a period of time.

Earnings per share: Net Income / Number of Shares Outstanding—states a corporation's profits on a per share basis. It can be helpful in further comparison to the market price of the stock.

Investment turnover: Net Sales / Total Assets—measures a company's ability to use assets to generate sales. Although the ideal level for this ratio varies greatly, a very low figure may mean that the company maintains too many assets or has not deployed its assets well, whereas a high figure means that the assets have been used to produce good sales numbers.

Sales per employee: Total Sales / Number of Employees—can provide a measure of productivity, though a high figure can indicate either good personnel management or good equipment.

LIQUIDITY RATIOS

Liquidity ratios demonstrate a company's ability to pay its current obligations. In other words, they relate to the availability of cash and other assets to cover accounts payable, short-term debt, and other liabilities. All small businesses require a certain degree of liquidity in order to pay their bills on time, though start-up and very young companies are often not very liquid. In mature companies, low levels of liquidity can indicate poor management or a need for additional capital. Any company's liquidity may vary due to seasonality, the timing of sales, and the state of the economy. But liquidity ratios can provide small business owners with useful limits to help them regulate borrowing and spending. Some of the best-known measures of a company's liquidity include:

Current ratio: Current Assets / Current Liabilities—measures the ability of an entity to pay its near-term obligations. ''Current'' usually is defined as within one year. Though the ideal current ratio depends to some extent on the type of business, a general rule of thumb is that it should be at least 2:1. A lower current ratio means that the company may not be able to pay its bills on time, while a higher ratio means that the company has money in cash or safe investments that could be put to better use in the business.

Quick ratio (or ''acid test''): Quick Assets (cash, marketable securities, and receivables) / Current Liabilities—provides a stricter definition of the company's ability to make payments on current obligations. Ideally, this ratio should be 1:1. If it is higher, the company may keep too much cash on hand or have a poor collection program for accounts receivable. If it is lower, it may indicate that the company relies too heavily on inventory to meet its obligations.

Cash to total assets: Cash / Total Assets—measures the portion of a company's assets held in cash or marketable securities. Although a high ratio may indicate some degree of safety from a creditor's viewpoint, excess amounts of cash may be viewed as inefficient.

Sales to receivables (or turnover ratio): Net Sales / Accounts Receivable—measures the annual turnover of accounts receivable. A high number reflects a short lapse of time between sales and the collection of cash, while a low number means collections take longer. It is best to use average accounts receivable to avoid seasonality effects.

Days' receivables ratio: 365 / Sales to receivables ratio—measures the average number of days that accounts receivable are outstanding. This number should be the same or lower than the company's expressed credit terms. Other ratios can also be converted to days, such as the cost of sales to payables ratio.

Cost of sales to payables: Cost of Sales / Trade Payables—measures the annual turnover of accounts payable. Lower numbers tend to indicate good performance, though the ratio should be close to the industry standard.

Cash turnover: Net Sales / Net Working Capital (current assets less current liabilities)—reflects the company's ability to finance current operations, the efficiency of its working capital employment, and the margin of protection for its creditors. A high cash turnover ratio may leave the company vulnerable to creditors, while a low ratio may indicate an inefficient use of working capital. In general, sales five to six times greater than working capital are needed to maintain a positive cash flow and finance sales.

LEVERAGE RATIOS

Leverage ratios look at the extent that a company has depended upon borrowing to finance its operations. As a result, these ratios are reviewed closely by bankers and investors. Most leverage ratios compare assets or net worth with liabilities. A high leverage ratio may increase a company's exposure to risk and business downturns, but along with this higher risk also comes the potential for higher returns. Some of the major measurements of leverage include:

Debt to equity ratio: Debt / Owners' Equity—indicates the relative mix of the company's investor-supplied capital. A company is generally considered safer if it has a low debt to equity ratio—that is, a higher proportion of owner-supplied capital—though a very low ratio can indicate excessive caution. In general, debt should be between 50 and 80 percent of equity.

Debt ratio: Debt / Total Assets—measures the portion of a company's capital that is provided by borrowing. A debt ratio greater than 1.0 means the company has negative net worth, and is technically bankrupt. This ratio is similar, and can easily be converted to, the debt to equity ratio.

Fixed to worth ratio: Net Fixed Assets / Tangible Net Worth—indicates how much of the owner's equity has been invested in fixed assets, i.e., plant and equipment. It is important to note that only tangible assets are included in the calculation, and that they are valued less depreciation. Creditors usually like to see this ratio very low, but the large-scale leasing of assets can artificially lower it.

Interest coverage: Earnings before Interest and Taxes / Interest Expense—indicates how comfortably the company can handle its interest payments. In general, a higher interest coverage ratio means that the small business is able to take on additional debt. This ratio is closely examined by bankers and other creditors.

EFFICIENCY RATIOS

By assessing a company's use of credit, inventory, and assets, efficiency ratios can help small business owners and managers conduct business better. These ratios can show how quickly the company is collecting money for its credit sales or how many times inventory turns over in a given time period. This information can help management decide whether the company's credit terms are appropriate and whether its purchasing efforts are handled in an efficient manner. The following are some of the main indicators of efficiency:

Annual inventory turnover: Cost of Goods Sold for the Year / Average Inventory—shows how efficiently the company is managing its production, warehousing, and distribution of product, considering its volume of sales. Higher ratios—over six or seven times per year—are generally thought to be better, although extremely high inventory turnover may indicate a narrow selection and possibly lost sales. A low inventory turnover rate, on the other hand, means that the company is paying to keep a large inventory, and may be overstocking or carrying obsolete items.

Inventory holding period: 365 / Annual Inventory Turnover—calculates the number of days, on average, that elapse between finished goods production and sale of product.

Inventory to assets ratio: Inventory / Total Assets—shows the portion of assets tied up in inventory. Generally, a lower ratio is considered better.

Accounts receivable turnover: Net (credit) Sales / Average Accounts Receivable—gives a measure of how quickly credit sales are turned into cash. Alternatively, the reciprocal of this ratio indicates the portion of a year's credit sales that are outstanding at a particular point in time.

Collection period: 365 / Accounts Receivable Turnover—measures the average number of days the company's receivables are outstanding, between the date of credit sale and collection of cash.

SUMMARY

Although they may seem intimidating at first glance, all of the aforementioned financial ratios can be derived by simply comparing numbers that appear on a small business's income statement and balance sheet. As Gill noted, small business owners would be well-served to "think of ratios as one of your best friends when scrutinizing your business."

Financial ratios can be an important tool for small business owners and managers to measure their progress toward reaching company goals, as well as toward competing with larger companies within an industry. Ratio analysis, when performed regularly over time, can also give help small businesses recognize and adapt to trends affecting their operations. Yet another reason small business owners need to understand financial ratios is that they provide one of the main measures of a company's success from the perspective of bankers, investors, and business analysts. Often, a small business's ability to obtain debt or equity financing will depend on the company's financial ratios.

Despite all the positive uses of financial ratios, however, small business managers are still encouraged to know the limitations of ratios and approach ratio analysis with a degree of caution. As Gill explained, "[Ratios] do not make decisions for you, but will provide information from which decisions may be made."

FURTHER READING:

Bangs, David H., Jr. *Managing by the Numbers: Financial Essentials for the Growing Business.* Dover, NH: Upstart Publishing, 1992.

Casteuble, Tracy. "Using Financial Ratios to Assess Performance." *Association Management.* July 1997.

Gill, James O. *Financial Basics of Small Business Success.* Menlo Park, CA: Crisp Publications, 1994.

Jones, Allen N. "Financial Statements: When Properly Read, They Share a Wealth of Information." *Memphis Business Journal.* February 5, 1996.

Larkin, Howard. "How to Read a Financial Statement." *American Medical News.* March 11, 1996.

Parrish, Deidra Ann. "Getting the Cash to Flow Your Way." *Black Enterprise.* July 1997.

SEE ALSO: Financial Analysis

FINANCIAL STATEMENTS

Financial statements are written records of business finances, including **balance sheets** and profit and loss statements. They stand as one of the most essential components of business information, and as the principal method of communicating financial information about an entity to outside parties. In a technical sense, financial statements are a summation of the financial position of an entity at a given point in time. General purpose financial statements are designed to meet the needs of many diverse users, particularly present and potential owners and creditors. Financial statements result from simplifying, condensing, and aggregating masses of data obtained primarily from a company's (or individual's) accounting system.

FINANCIAL REPORTING

The Financial Accounting Standards Board, in its *Statements of Financial Accounting Concepts*, remarked that financial reporting includes not only financial statements but also other means of communicating financial information about an enterprise to its external users. Financial statements provide information useful in investment and credit decisions and in assessing cash flow prospects. They provide information about an enterprise's resources, claims to those resources, and changes in the resources.

Financial reporting is a broad concept encompassing financial statements, notes to financial statements and parenthetical disclosures, supplementary information (such as changing prices), and other means of financial reporting (such as management discussions and analysis, and letters to stockholders). Financial reporting is but one source of information needed by those who make economic decisions about business enterprises.

The primary focus of financial reporting is information about earnings and its components. Information about earnings based on accrual accounting usually provides a better indication of an enterprise's present and continuing ability to generate positive cash flows than that provided by cash receipts and payments.

MAJOR FINANCIAL STATEMENTS

The basic financial statements of an enterprise include the 1) balance sheet (or statement of financial position), 2) income statement, 3) cash flow statement, and 4) statement of changes in owners' equity or stockholders' equity. The balance sheet lists all the assets, liabilities, and stockholders' equity (for a corporation) of an entity as of a specific date. The balance sheet is essentially a financial snapshot of the entity. The income statement presents a summary of the revenues, gains, expenses, losses, and net income or net loss of an entity for a specific period. This statement is similar to a moving picture of the entity's operations during a period. The cash flow statement summarizes an entity's cash receipts and cash payments relating to its operating, investing, and financing activities during a particular period. A statement of changes in owners' equity or stockholders' equity reconciles the beginning of the period equity of an enterprise with its ending balance.

For an item to be recognized in the financial statements, it should meet four fundamental recognition criteria:

- Definitions: The item meets the definition of an element of financial statements.

- Materiality: It has a relevant attribute measurable with sufficient reliability.

- Relevance: The information about it is capable of making a difference in user decisions.

- Reliability: The information is representational, faithful, verifiable, and neutral.

Items currently reported in financial statements are measured by different attributes (for example, historical cost, current cost, current market value, net reliable value, and present value of future cash flows). While historical cost has traditionally been the major attribute assigned to assets and liabilities, the Financial Accounting Standards Board expects to continue to use different attributes.

Notes to financial statements are informative disclosures appended to financial statements. They provide information concerning such matters as deprecia-

tion and inventory methods used, details of long-term debt, pensions, leases, income taxes, contingent liabilities, method of consolidation, and other matters. Notes are considered an integral part of the financial statements. Schedules and parenthetical disclosures are also used to present information not provided elsewhere in the financial statements.

Each financial statement has a heading, which gives the name of the entity, the name of the statement, and the date or time covered by the statement. The information provided in financial statements is primarily financial in nature and expressed in units of money. The information relates to an individual business enterprise. The information often is the product of approximations and estimates, rather than exact measurements. The financial statements typically reflect the financial effects of transactions and events that have already happened (i.e., historical).

Financial statements presenting financial data for two or more periods are called comparative statements. Comparative financial statements usually give similar reports for the current period and for one or more preceding periods. They provide analysts with significant information about trends and relationships over two or more years. Comparative statements are considerably more significant than are single-year statements. Comparative statements emphasize the fact that financial statements for a single accounting period are only one part of the continuous history of the company.

Interim financial statements are reports for periods of less than a year. The purpose of interim financial statements is to improve the timeliness of accounting information. Some companies issue comprehensive financial statements while others issue summary statements. Each interim period should be viewed primarily as an integral part of an annual period and should generally continue to use the generally accepted accounting principles (GAAP) that were used in the preparation of the company's latest annual report. Financial statements are usually audited by independent accountants for the purpose of improving the level of confidence in their reliability.

Every financial statement is prepared on the basis of several accounting assumptions: that all transactions can be expressed or measured in dollars; that the enterprise will continue in business indefinitely; and that statements will be prepared at regular intervals. These assumptions provide the foundation for the structure of financial accounting theory and practice, and explain why financial information is presented in a given manner. Financial statements also must be prepared in accordance with generally accepted accounting principles, and must include an explanation of the company's accounting procedures and policies. Pervasive accounting principles include the recording of assets and liabilities at cost, the recognition of revenue when it is realized and when a transaction has taken place (generally at the point of sale), and the recognition of expenses according to the matching principle (costs to revenues). The convention of conservatism requires that uncertainties and risks related to a company be reflected in its accounting reports. The convention of materiality requires that anything that would be of interest to an informed investor should be fully disclosed in the financial statements.

Accounting procedures are those rules and practices that are associated with the operations of an accounting system and that lead to the development of financial statements. Accounting procedures include the methods, practices, and techniques used to carry out accounting objectives and to implement accounting principles. Accounting policies are those accounting principles followed by a specific entity. Information about the accounting policies adopted by a reporting enterprise is essential for financial statement users and should be disclosed in the financial statements. Accounting principles and their method of application in the following areas are considered particularly important: 1) a selection from existing alternatives; 2) areas that are peculiar to a particular industry in which the company operates; and 3) unusual and innovative applications of GAAP. Significant accounting policies are usually disclosed as the initial note or as a summary preceding the notes to the financial statements.

ELEMENTS OF FINANCIAL STATEMENTS

The Financial Accounting Standards Board (FASB) has defined the following elements of financial statements of business enterprises: assets, liabilities, equity, revenues, expenses, gains, losses, investment by owners, distribution to owners, and comprehensive income. According to FASB, the elements of financial statements are the building blocks with which financial statements are constructed—the broad classes of items that financial statements comprise. FASB concepts statement No. 3, ''Elements of Financial Statements of Business Enterprises,'' defined the interrelated elements that are directly involved in measuring the performance and the financial position of a business enterprise:

- Assets are probable future economic benefits obtained or controlled by a particular entity as a result of past transactions or events.

- Comprehensive income is the change in equity (net assets) of an entity during a period from transactions and other events and circumstances from nonowner sources. It includes all changes in equity during a period except those resulting from investments by owners and distributions to owners.

- Distributions to owners are decreases in net assets of a particular enterprise resulting from transferring assets, rendering services, or incurring liabilities to owners. Distributions to owners decrease ownership interest or equity in an enterprise.

- Equity is the residual interest in the assets of an entity that remains after deducting its liabilities. In a business entity, equity is the ownership interest.

- Expenses are outflows or other uses of assets or incurring of liabilities during a period from delivering or producing goods or rendering services, or carrying out other activities that constitute the entity's ongoing major or central operation.

- Gains are increases in equity (net assets) from peripheral or incidental transactions of an entity and from all other transactions and other events and circumstances affecting the entity during a period except those that result from revenues or investments by owner.

- Investments by owners are increases in net assets of a particular enterprise resulting from transfers to it from other entities of something of value to obtain or increase ownership interest (or equity) in it.

- Liabilities are probable future sacrifices of economic benefits arising from present obligations of a particular entity to transfer assets or provide services to other entities in the future as a result of past transactions or events.

- Losses are decreases in equity (net assets) from peripheral or incidental transactions of an entity and from all other transactions and other events and circumstances affecting the entity during a period except those that result from expenses or distributions to owners.

- Revenues are inflows or other enhancements of assets of an entity or settlement of its liabilities (or a combination of both) during a period from delivering or producing goods, rendering services, or other activities that constitute the entity's ongoing major or central operations.

SUBSEQUENT EVENTS

A subsequent event is an important event that occurs between the balance sheet date and the date of issuance of the annual report. Subsequent events must have a material effect on the financial statements. A subsequent event does not include the recurring economic fluctuations associated with the economy and with free enterprise, such as a strike or management change. A subsequent event is considered to be important enough that without such information the statement would be misleading if the event were not disclosed. The recognition and recording of these events requires the professional judgment of an accountant or external auditor.

Events that effect the financial statements at the date of the balance sheet might reveal an unknown condition or provide additional information regarding estimates or judgments. These events must be reported by adjusting the financial statements to recognize the new evidence. Events that relate to conditions that did not exist on the balance sheet date but arose subsequent to that date do not require an adjustment to the financial statements. The effect of the event on the future period, however, may be of such importance that it should be disclosed in a footnote or elsewhere.

PERSONAL FINANCIAL STATEMENTS

The reporting entity of personal financial statements is an individual, a husband and wife, or a group of related individuals. Personal financial statements are often prepared to deal with obtaining bank loans, income tax planning, retirement planning, gift and estate planning, and the public disclosure of financial affairs.

For each reporting entity, a statement of financial position is required. The statement presents assets at estimated current values, liabilities at the lesser of the discounted amount of cash to be paid or the current cash settlement amount, and net worth. A provision should also be made for estimated income taxes on the differences between the estimated current value of assets. Comparative statements for one or more periods should be presented. A statement of changes in net worth is optional.

Personal financial statements should be presented on the accrual basis. A classified balance sheet is not used. Assets and liabilities are presented in the order of their liquidity and maturity, respectively (not on a current/noncurrent basis). A business interest that constitutes a large part of an individual's total assets should be shown separate from other assets. Such an interest would be presented as a net amount and not as a pro rata allocation of the business's assets and liabilities. A statement of changes in net worth would disclose the major sources of increases and decrease in net worth. Increases in personal net worth arise from income, increases in estimated current value of assets, decreases in estimated current amount of liabilities, and decreases in the provision for estimated income taxes. Decreases in personal net worth arise from expenses, decreases in estimated current value of

assets, increases in estimated current amount of liabilities, and increases in the provision for income taxes.

DEVELOPMENT STAGE COMPANIES

An enterprise is a development stage company if substantially all of its efforts are devoted to establishing a new business and either of the following is present: 1) principal operations have not begun, or 2) principal operations have begun but revenue is insignificant. Activities of a development state enterprise frequently include financial planning, raising capital, research and development, personnel recruiting and training, and market development.

A development stage company must follow generally accepted accounting principles applicable to operating enterprises in the preparation of financial statements. In its balance sheet, the company must report cumulative net losses separately in the equity section. In its income statement it must report cumulative revenues and expenses from the inception of the enterprise. Likewise, in its cash flow statement, it must report cumulative cash flows from the inception of the enterprise. Its statement of stockholders' equity should include the number of shares issued and the date of their issuance as well as the dollar amounts received. The statement should identify the entity as a development stage enterprise and describe the nature of development stage activities. During the first period of normal operations, the enterprise must disclose in notes to the financial statements that the enterprise was but is no longer in the development stage.

COMPANIES IN FINANCIAL DISTRESS

Businesses may experience increasing financial distress as a result of financing and/or operating problems. Financing problems can be identified in situations where the company experiences liquidity deficiency, equity deficiency, debt default, and funds shortage. Operating problems are expressed in terms of continued operating losses, doubtful prospective revenues, jeopardization of the ability to operate, incapable management, and poor control over operations. An examination of the financial statements along with evidence obtained from management and other sources can provide a person with a basis for evaluating the going-concern condition of an enterprise. As a general rule, the assumption is made that the entity is a going concern in the absence of evidence to the contrary.

During the auditing process, the auditor may raise questions concerning the going-concern possibilities of the company. The auditor considers whether management's plans for dealing with the conditions and events concerning the uncertainty are likely to negate the problem. If, after evaluating management's plans, substantial doubt still exists, the auditor should either add explanatory language to his or her qualified report or disclaim an opinion. The audit report must explicitly include the phrase ''substantial doubt about the entity's ability to continue as a going concern.''

FRAUDULENT FINANCIAL REPORTING

Fraudulent financial reporting is defined as intentional or reckless reporting, whether by act or by omission, that results in materially misleading financial statements. Fraudulent financial reporting can usually be traced to the existence of conditions in either the internal environment of the firm (e.g., inadequate internal control), or in the external environment (e.g., poor industry or overall business conditions). Excessive pressure on management, such as unrealistic profit or other performance goods, can lead to fraudulent financial reporting.

The accounting profession generally is of the opinion that it is not the responsibility of the auditor to detect fraud, beyond what can be determined with the diligent application of generally accepted auditing standards. Because of the nature of irregularities, particularly those involving forgery and collusion, a properly designed and executed audit may not detect a material irregularity. The auditor is not an insurer and the auditor's report does not constitute a guarantee that material misstatements do not exist in the financial statement. The legal system generally defines the auditor's responsibilities associated with the detect of fraudulent reporting by a company.

AUDITING

The preparation and presentation of a company's financial statements are the responsibility of the management of the company. Published financial statements are audited by an independent certified public accountant. During audits, the auditor conducts an examination of the accounting system, records, internal controls, and financial statements in accordance with generally accepted auditing standards. The auditor then expresses an opinion concerning the fairness of the financial statements in conformity with generally accepted accounting principles. The auditor's standard opinion typically includes the following statements: the auditor is independent; the audit was performed on specified financial statements; the financial statements are the responsibility of the company's management; the opinion of the auditor is the auditor's responsibility; the audit was conducted according to generally accepted auditing standards; the audit was planned and performed to obtain reasonable assurance about whether the financial statements are free of material misstatements; the audit included examination, assessment, and evaluation stages; the audit provided a reasonable basis for an expression of an opinion concerning the fair presentation of the audit; and the signature and date by the auditing firm.

An unqualified opinion contains three paragraphs: an introductory paragraph, a scope paragraph, and the opinion paragraph. In addition to the unqualified opinion, an auditor may issue a qualified opinion, an adverse opinion, or a disclaimer of opinion.

FURTHER READING:

Beams, F. A. *Advanced Accounting*. 5th ed. Englewood Cliffs, NJ: Prentice Hall, 1992.

Financial Accounting Standards Board. *Statements of Financial Accounting Concepts*. Homewood, IL: Irwin, 1987.

——. *FASB No. 14: Financial Reporting for Segments of a Business Enterprise*. Stamford, CT.: FASB, 1976.

Harrison, W. T., Jr., and C. T. Horngren. *Financial Accounting*. 2nd ed. Englewood Cliffs, NJ: Prentice Hall, 1995.

Hendriksen, E. S., and M. F. Van Breda. *Accounting Theory*. 5th ed. Homewood, IL: Irwin, 1992.

Jarnagin, B. D. *Financial Accounting Standards*. Chicago, IL: Commerce Clearing House, 1992.

Jones, Allen N. ''Financial Statements: When Properly Read, They Share a Wealth of Information.'' *Memphis Business Journal*. February 5, 1996.

Kieso, D. E., and J. J. Weyugandt. *Intermediate Accounting*. New York: Wiley, 1995.

Larkin, Howard. ''How to Read a Financial Statement.'' *American Medical News*. March 11, 1996.

Nikolai, L. A., and J. D. Bazley. *Intermediate Accounting*. 5th ed. Boston: PSW-KENT, 1988.

Parrish, Deidra Ann. ''Getting the Cash to Flow Your Way.'' *Black Enterprise*. July 1997.

Woelfel, C. J. *Financial Statement Analysis*. Chicago, IL: Probus, 1994.

Wolk, H. I. *Accounting Theory: A Conceptual and Institutional Approach*. Cincinnati, OH: South-Western, 1992.

SEE ALSO: Financial Analysis

FIXED AND VARIABLE EXPENSES

Fixed and variable expenses are the two main components of a company's total **overhead expense**. Fixed costs are those that do not fluctuate with changes in production activity level or sales volume, such as rent, insurance, dues and subscriptions, equipment leases, payments on loans, **depreciation**, management salaries, and advertising. Variable costs are those that respond directly and proportionately to changes in activity level or volume, such as raw materials, hourly wages and commissions, utilities, inventory, office supplies, and **packaging**, mailing, and shipping costs.

Although fixed costs do not vary with changes in production or sales volume, they may change over time. As a result, fixed costs are sometimes called period costs. Some fixed costs are incurred at the discretion of a company's management, such as advertising and promotional expense, while others are not. It is important to remember that all non-discretionary fixed costs will be incurred even if production or sales volume falls to zero. Although production and sales volume are the main factors determining the level of variable costs incurred by a company, these costs also may fluctuate in relation to other factors, such as changes in suppliers' prices or seasonal promotional efforts. Some expenses may have both fixed and variable elements. For example, a company may pay a sales person a monthly salary (a fixed cost) plus a percentage commission for every unit sold above a certain level (a variable cost).

It is important to understand the behavior of the different types of expenses as production or sales volume increases. Total fixed costs remain unchanged as volume increases, while fixed costs per unit decline. For example, if a bicycle business had total fixed costs of $1,000 and only produced one bike, then the full $1,000 in fixed costs must be applied to that bike. On the other hand, if the same business produced 10 bikes, then the fixed costs per unit decline to $100. Variable costs behave differently. Total variable costs increase proportionately as volume increases, while variable costs per unit remain unchanged. For example, if the bicycle company incurred variable costs of $200 per unit, total variable costs would be $200 if only one bike was produced and $2,000 if 10 bikes were produced. However, variable costs applied per unit would be $200 for both the first and the tenth bike. The company's total costs are a combination of the fixed and variable costs. If the bicycle company produced 10 bikes, its total costs would be $1,000 fixed plus $2,000 variable equals $3,000, or $300 per unit.

It is very important for small business owners to understand how their various costs respond to changes in the volume of goods or services produced. The breakdown of a company's underlying expenses determines the profitable price level for its products or services, as well as many aspects of its overall business strategy. A small business owner can use a knowledge of fixed and variable expenses to determine the company's break-even point (the number of units or dollars at which total revenues equal total costs), and in making decisions related to pricing goods and services.

Determining the fixed and variable expenses is the first step in performing a **break-even analysis**. The number of units needed to break even = fixed costs / (price − variable costs per unit). This equation provides a small business owner with a great deal of valuable information by itself, and it can also be changed around to answer a number of important questions, like whether a planned expansion will be profitable. Knowing how to work with information about fixed and variable expenses can be particularly helpful for individuals who are considering buying a small business. Many businesses, particularly franchises, are reluctant to give out information about projected profits, but will provide information about costs and unit prices. The potential purchaser can then use this information to calculate the number of units and the dollar volume that would be needed to make a profit, and determine whether these numbers seem realistic.

FURTHER READING:

Duncan, Ian. "Controlling Expenses: The Key to Profitability in a Recession." *CMA—The Management Accounting Magazine.* November 1992.

Hilton, Ronald W. *Managerial Accounting.* New York: McGraw-Hill, 1991.

Livingstone, John Leslie. *The Portable MBA in Finance and Accounting.* New York: Wiley, 1992.

"Numbers You Should Know to Keep in Touch with Your Business." *Profit-Building Strategies for Business Owners.* May 1993.

Thompson, Kevin D. "Business Management: Planning for Profit." *Black Enterprise.* April 1993.

FLEXIBLE BENEFIT PLAN

Health and child care costs have risen tremendously over the past several decades. This has had a major effect on a business's ability to offer benefits, yet most employees still expect to receive benefits as a result of employment. Small businesses in particular are often unable to take advantage of the **economies of scale** that larger companies can use in securing benefits programs. Companies both large and small, have subsequently sought palatable means by which their employees can contribute to the cost of benefits. One option is a flexible benefit plan. Indeed, many businesses have begun to offer flexible benefits in order to retain a competitive benefits package for employees.

In a flexible benefit plan, employees choose the benefits they want or need. They contribute to the cost of these benefits through a payroll deduction of their before-tax income, reducing the employer's contribution. In addition, the ability to pay for benefits with pre-tax income lowers an employee's taxable income while raising the amount of their take-home pay—an added "benefit." In the short term, companies obviously benefit from sharing costs with employees. But a business may also choose to cap their future contributions to benefits by passing along increased costs to employees through these plans.

Flexible benefit plans may include health insurance, other benefits such as **401(k) plans**, and reimbursement accounts that employees can use to reimburse themselves for health or dependent care expenses. These plans have proven increasingly popular with a majority of employers. According to an annual survey conducted by KPMG Peat Marwick in early 1996, 60 percent of all employers offered a flexible benefit plan in 1996, increasing from 47 percent in 1993.

CAFETERIA PLANS A type of flexible benefit plan known as a cafeteria plan enables employees to choose between receiving some or all of an employer's nontaxable benefits, or receiving cash or other taxable benefits such as stock. These plans were established by the Revenue Act of 1978 and are regulated by Section 125 of the Internal Revenue Code. As a result, only certain benefits can be offered under a cafeteria plan, though employers may offer any or all of these benefits. These include: health and group life insurance as well as medical reimbursement plans for non-insured expenses; disability, dental, and vision coverage; daycare or eldercare; 401(k) plans; and vacation days. **Tuition assistance programs** and other fringe benefits are exempt from the plans, even if they aren't taxable. Funding for cafeteria plans may come from the employer, employee or both. Often, the employee receives a spending credit, with which she may choose to ''buy'' benefits from a list of options such as health or life insurance. The benefits themselves may be provided in cash or via actual coverage.

In order to ensure these plans are fair to all employees and to limit the number of changes employees can make to their plan, the IRS has set up a number of restrictions. Employees are unable to change their selections to the plan after the start of the plan year unless they have had a change in family status such as marriage, birth, or change in spouse's employment status. They are also unable to carry over unused credits or benefits to the next plan year. Employers need to be sure that no more than 25 percent of the tax-favored benefits can go to ''highly compensated'' employees. These employees could be officers making beyond a certain salary range or those who have a percentage of ownership in the company greater than one percent (if they earn over $150,000) or greater than five percent (for others).

FLEXIBLE SPENDING ACCOUNTS With a type of cafeteria plan known as a flexible spending account, an employee decides between receiving taxable cash or before-tax reimbursement of expenses such as medical bills. These spending accounts establish a nest egg for health and dependent care expenses and may be funded by employees through money de-

ducted from their paycheck on a pre-tax basis. For example, if an employee makes a regular contribution to the company's health plan, this money can be deposited in the flexible spending account, reducing the amount contributed since the money is taken on a pre-tax basis. If an employee has expenses beyond the plan's coverage, she may decide to have an amount regularly deducted from her paycheck and deposited in the flexible spending account in order to cover these. As expenses arise, she submits a claim or bill and is reimbursed for that expense via the account.

Flexible spending accounts must be specific in the type of expense reimbursed. That is, a daycare spending account can't be used to reimburse health care costs and vice versa. Also, employees must prove they have a legitimate expense in order to be reimbursed from these accounts. Invoices from health care professionals or daycare facilities would serve this purpose. However, employees must also prove that the claim has not been reimbursed by other coverage, such as a spouse's.

It should also be noted companies must still cover fund shortages to an extent. For example, if an employee does not have enough funds in his account to cover a large medical bill incurred early in the plan year, the company must still reimburse the employee up to his annual scheduled contribution. Cash-poor small businesses may find this hard to fund.

SET-UP AND TAX IMPLICATIONS A small business can manage its own flexible benefit plan with the proper software. Since these plans are under the watchful eye of the IRS, it is important that record keeping and benefit payments be accurate and timely. Many companies hire an outside firm to manage their plan, which reduces internal headaches but at a higher cost to the company. Some insurance companies also provide administrative services for flexible plans as well.

Employer contributions to cafeteria plans are tax deductible for the employer and are not subject to income tax for the employee. The contributions are taken before taxes, as mentioned, and therefore are not subject to Social Security (FICA) or federal unemployment (FUTA) taxes unless the monies are contributed to 401(k) plans. Many states follow the same guidelines regarding state taxes but companies should check with their accountant or the state's Tax Department to be sure.

Obviously, flexible benefit plans are not without their drawbacks. But for small businesses looking to attract and retain key personnel with competitive benefit packages while keeping their own costs low, they can be an attractive alternative to standard benefit plans.

FURTHER READING:

Albin, Mel, and Noel A. Johnson. *Financial Planning With Employee Benefits.* Crisp Publications, Inc., 1990.

Hunt, Kelly A. "Survey Finds Flexible Benefits on the Rise, Particularly Among Public Employers." *Government Finance Review.* August 1997.

Solomon, Stephen D. "Help Wanted: How Small Companies Can Lower Their Health Care Costs." *Inc.* December 1989.

White, Jane, and Bruce Pyenson. *Employee Benefits for Small Business.* Prentice Hall, 1991.

Williams, Phillip. *Five Easy Steps to Setting Up an IRS-Approved Plan for Your Small Business (Incorporated or Unincorporated), With Forms.* The P. Gaines Co., 1989.

SEE ALSO: Employee Benefits

FLEXIBLE WORK PROGRAMS

Flexible work programs are work arrangements wherein employees are given greater scheduling freedom in how they fulfill the obligations of their positions. The most commonplace of these programs is flextime, which gives workers far greater leeway in terms of the hours when they begin and end work, provided they put in the total amount of hours that they are supposed to. Other common flexible working arrangements involve **telecommuting**, job-sharing, and compressed work-weeks. Supporters of flexible work programs hail them as important recognition of the difficulties that many employees have in balancing their family obligations and their work duties, and they note that such programs can make a company more attractive to prospective employees. Critics contend, however, that while flexible employment initiatives do attempt to redress some long-time inequities in the work life-family life balance, ill-considered plans can have a deleterious impact on a company when they are implemented.

PRIMARY FLEXIBLE WORK PROGRAMS

Flexible work arrangements can take any number of forms, from basic flex time programs to innovative **child care** and **eldercare** programs.

- Flex Time—This is a system wherein employees choose their starting and quitting times from a range of available hours. These periods are usually at either end of a "core" time during which most company business takes place. Formerly regarded as a rare, cutting-edge workplace arrangement, flex time is now commonly practiced in a wide variety of industries.

- Compressed Work Week—Under this arrangement, the standard work week is compressed into fewer than five days. The most common incarnation of the compressed work week is one of four 10-hour days. Other options include three 12-hour days or arrangements in which employees work 9- or 10-hour days over two weeks and are compensated with an extra day or two of time off during that time.

- Flexplace—This term encompasses various arrangements in which an employee works from home or some other non-office location. Telecommuting is the most commonly practiced example of this.

- Job Sharing—Under these arrangements, two people voluntarily share the duties and responsibilities of one full-time position, with both salary and benefits of that position prorated between the two individuals.

- Work Sharing—These programs are increasingly used by companies that wish to avoid layoffs. It allows businesses to temporarily reduce hours and salary for a portion of their workforce.

- Expanded Leave—This option gives employees greater flexibility in terms of requesting extended periods of time away from work without losing their rights as employees. Expanded leave, which can be granted on either a paid or unpaid basis, is used for a variety of reasons, including sabbaticals, education, community service, family problems, and medical care (the latter two reasons are now largely covered by the terms of the Family and Medical Leave Act).

- Phased Retirement—Under these arrangements, the employee and employer agree to a schedule wherein the employee's full-time work commitments are gradually reduced over a period of months or years.

- Partial Retirement—These programs allow older employees to continue working on a part time basis, with no established end date.

- Work and Family Programs—These programs are still relatively rare, although some larger companies have reported good results with pilot initiatives in this area. These programs are ones in which employers provide some degree of assistance to their employees in the realms of child care and elder care. The best-known of these programs are in-house facilities providing care for the children of employees, but even basic flex time programs can ease child-care logistics for employees. "Employers see that the availability, affordability, and accessability of good child care have a bottom line impact," wrote Diane E. Kirrane in *Association Management*. "Lack of quality child care leads to employees' absenteeism, tardiness, distraction, and stress-related health problems. Conversely, employees' reliability, good morale, and motivation are positive results that derive from safe, stable, developmentally sound child care arrangements."

ADVANTAGES OF FLEXIBLE WORK PROGRAMS

Defenders of flexible work initiatives point to the competitive advantages that such programs bring to companies that move in that direction. Perhaps the single most cited reason for introducing a flexible work environment is employee retention. Indeed, many businesses contend that the recent trend toward flextime and other programs has made it necessary for them to introduce their own programs or risk losing valued employees. "Another business argument for flexible work arrangements is that they allow companies to match the peaks and valleys of activity," wrote Elizabeth Sheley in *HRMagazine*. "More organizations have shifted their focus to how potential changes in schedule will affect the product. Reduced absenteeism, though often overlooked, is also a legitimate business rationale; flexible options not only strengthen commitment, but also give employees more time to handle the very situations that sometimes lead to **absenteeism**."

Proponents also note that in many respects, flexible work programs provide a way for businesses to increase employee loyalty to the organization without resorting to making fundamental changes in its operations. Indeed, Sheley observed that "the most popular flexible work options are those that involve the least change. Flex time and compressed work weeks, for example, call for the same number of hours, at the same workplace, as in traditional work arrangements."

In addition, some supporters of flexible work arrangements argue that such programs can actually have a positive impact on the **productivity** of employees. They contend that employees who are better able to attend to family needs through flex time are more likely to be contented and productive, while good employees who telecommute may get even more work done if they are freed up from office interruptions.

Business can also use flexible programs to address institutional problems. For instance, a small- or mid-sized business that is crammed into a small facility or office may want to explore telecommuting programs in order to relieve the situation without resorting to an expensive relocation or expansion. Finally, proponents say the flexible work programs can be beneficial to companies by enhancing their public image and expanding the number of hours during which customers can be serviced.

DISADVANTAGES OF FLEXIBLE WORK PROGRAMS

Flexible work programs have many apparent advantages, but critics point out that ill-conceived programs can have a negative impact on businesses, and they add that even good programs often present challenges that a business has to address.

First of all, business owners and managers need to recognize that flexible work arrangements are not always appropriate for all people, jobs, or industries. Telecommuting and other "flexplace" arrangements, for example, can be disastrous (or at the very least a productivity drain) if used by employees who are unwilling or unable to put in a full day of work amid the non-work temptations (television, pleasure reading, housecleaning, etc.) of a home setting. Other companies, meanwhile, find that employees "flex" in and out of the business at such different hours that overhead costs increase, customer service suffers (i.e., no one comes in until 9:30 a.m., a state of affairs that forces customers and vendors to cool their heels until then), and manufacturing output suffers. This latter factor makes flex time a difficult fit for many manufacturing facilities. "Many of the factory operations depend on each other being there," said human resources consulting executive Terry McGeorge in an interview with *The Milwaukee Business Journal*. "Especially when you talk about the concept of work-cell team manufacturing, they really all have to be there at the same time."

Critics also contend that flex programs often leave managers in exceedingly difficult situations. "Far too often, flex is embraced . . . for its 'family-friendly' aspects long before the corporate support needed to manage it takes root," wrote Martha H. Peak in *Management Review*. "In these companies, flex policies are outlined in the employee manual but implementation is left up to individual managers. Then, when managers try to implement these programs, they discover that to be fair, flex requires them to treat different employees differently."

Finally, many observers argue that businesses launch flexible work plans without adequate preparation. "I know that flex is a basic element of family-friendly and that family-friendly is a requisite for competitive companies," stated Peak. "But it takes more than a statement in the policy manual to institutionalize flex. It takes new methodologies to measure job success and investment in technologies to keep employees in constant communication."

INSTITUTING A FLEXIBLE WORK ENVIRONMENT

Business experts and companies that have instituted flexible work programs offer a variety of recommendations to businesses that are pondering a move to a "flex" environment.

RESEARCH Research the pros and cons of instituting a flexible work program in your company. Every company's needs and operating environment is different; just because a flex program worked for a neighboring business, that does not necessarily mean that it will work for your company. Conversely, a program that fails in another firm may work in yours. Detailed research into the needs and pressures of both the operations and the employees of each business, then, is a necessary component of any decision. So is an honest assessment of the qualities of the business's work force. Obviously, a company that is blessed with a work force of dedicated and conscientious employees is far more likely to be productive in a flex environment than is one that is saddled with a heavy sprinkling of unmotivated employees. Kirane recommended that businesses "assess current work-home issues affecting the [company] and its staff. If feasible, also assess the future needs of the work force and labor pool. Defuse concerns about invasion of privacy. Structure a needs assessment survey—for example, as a checklist that doesn't require respondents to show their handwriting or give their names. Or, within guidelines related to business needs, allow staffers to propose flexible arrangements for themselves."

GUIDELINES Create guidelines and systems of flex program administration that: 1) address all business needs, and 2) stand up to tests of fairness and comprehensiveness. Barney Olmstead and Suzanne Smith, co-authors of the book *Creating a Flexible Workplace: How to Select and Manage Alternative Work Options,* recommended that the creation process include steps to ensure that new policies are compatible with existing company objectives. They also noted that such issues as eligibility, application processes, reversibility, and changes to employee status should be plainly addressed. Finally, companies should formalize guidelines to head off complaints about favoritism or unfair treatment. "Partly to avoid polarizing staffers who have school-aged children and those who don't, more general terms (such as work-life and flexible work arrangements) are gaining favor," noted Kirrane. "In the workplace there is concern about equity."

TRAINING Employees should be educated about policies and feel comfortable using them. This can only happen, stated Olmstead and Smith, if the company actively promotes the program. Employees need to know that participation in such initiatives will not hurt their career. Indeed, *HRMagazine* noted that a mid-1990s report by the Catalyst research organization indicated that this can be a significant deterrent: "Many of the options for flexible scheduling are perceived as being bad for one's career by management and by co-workers who have more traditional working arrangements. A job-share partner or part-time employee cannot be as committed, the thinking goes. A positive experience with less than full-time work depends on the cultural values of the employee's organization. In some organizations, people who have taken less traditional schedules have been perceived as committing career suicide."

Employees are not the only workers who need to be reassured. Companies instituting flex work plans must also develop resource materials and training programs for managers. In fact, in many respects, managers of personnel and projects are the people who must make the biggest adjustment to a flexible work environment. "Workplace flexibility requires managers to develop a new set of skills," wrote Sheley. "Managers used to manage by sight, and defined work by hours on site. If a worker was in the office for eight hours, the boss assumed that person did eight hours of work." With flex time and other developments, however, managers need to develop new skills that emphasize work flow and productivity. "Managers may need to learn about new thinking on employee motivation and performance standards," wrote Kirrane. "Employees may need to be cross-trained for greater flexibility in assignments."

CONTROL Ultimately, a flexible work program is only worth keeping if it benefits your company's financial, strategic, and production goals. A key to making sure that those needs are met is to maintain control of the program. Employees and work teams can be very helpful in shaping flexible work guidelines, but business owners and managers should be wary of handing over too much control. Indeed, they need to make sure that business considerations remain paramount in any discussion of flex time and other options, and that ultimate control over flexible work programs rests with them. Dysfunctional work teams, for example, will reduce flex time to a shambles if they are left to institute and supervise it themselves.

EVALUATION Businesses should evaluate their flex work programs on a regular basis. Too many businesses introduce workplace flexibility programs that are flawed, but rather than review the program and make the necessary corrections, they throw up their arms and ask their personnel (managers and eligible employees alike) to reshape their responsibilities, priorities, and planning to match the flawed program. Other companies, meanwhile, launch good programs that lose their effectiveness over time because of neglect. Instead, business managers and owners need to practice continuous improvement in their workplace flexibility programs, just as they do in other aspects of their operations. ''Fine-tune the program,'' wrote Sheley. ''The evaluation process will provide at least some of the information necessary to make the adjustments that will make a workplace flexibility program of optimum benefit to both the company and its employees.''

CONTINUED CHANGE IN FLEXIBLE WORK PROGRAMS

In today's business world, flexible employment staples such as flextime and telecommuting continue to grow, in large measure because businesses that introduce them continue to prosper while simultaneously improving the quality of life of their employees. And as Kirrane noted, other familiar practices and benefits continue to contribute to flexibility and strengthened families as well, including **employee assistance programs**, seminars, and counseling; assistance and subsidies for work-related moves; and leaves and subsidies for education of employees and family members. ''Looking ahead, as more American workplaces and homes become networked electronically, it is to be expected that some of today's newfangled arrangements will become familiar, too,'' she added.

FURTHER READING:

''Flexible Working Practices Boost Business Success.'' *Leadership & Organization Development Journal.* February-March 1997.

Graham, Baxter W. ''The Business Argument for Flexibility.'' *HRMagazine.* May 1996.

Kirrane, Diane E. ''Wanted: Flexible Work Arrangements.'' *Association Management.* November 1994.

Leveen-Sher, Margery. ''Flexibility is the Key to Small Business Benefits.'' *Washington Business Journal.* February 16, 1996.

Marinelli, Marilyn, and Kathy Berman. ''Divide and Conquer—Everything!'' *Supervision.* April 1991.

Mullins, Robert. ''Flex Time—and Frustrations with It—Continue to Grow.'' *The Business Journal-Milwaukee.* May 7, 1994.

Olmstead, Barney, and Suzanne Smith. *Creating a Flexible Workplace: How to Select and Manage Alternative Work Options.* AMACOM.

Peak, Martha H. ''Why I Hate Flextime.'' *Management Review.* February 1994.

Sheley, Elizabeth. ''Flexible Work Options.'' *HRMagazine.* February 1996.

Skyrme, David J. ''Flexible Working: Building a Lean and Responsive Organization.'' *Long Range Planning.* October 1994.

Thornburg, Linda, Leon Rubis, and Alice M. Starcke. ''Change Comes Slowly.'' *HRMagazine.* February 1994.

SEE ALSO: Employee Motivation

FLOW CHARTS

A flow chart, or flow diagram, is a graphical representation of a process or system that details the sequencing of steps required to create output. A typical flow chart uses a set of basic symbols to represent various functions, and shows the sequence and interconnection of functions with lines and arrows. Flow charts can be used to document virtually any type of business system, from the movement of materials through machinery in a manufacturing operation to the flow of applicant information through the hiring process in a human resources department.

Each flow chart is concerned with one particular process or system. It begins with the input of data or materials into the system and traces all the procedures needed to convert the input into its final output form. Specialized flow chart symbols show the processes that take place, the actions that are performed in each step, and the relationship between various steps. Flow charts can include different levels of detail as needed, from a high-level overview of an entire system to a detailed diagram of one component process within a larger system. In any case, the flow chart shows the overall structure of the process or system, traces the flow of information and work through it, and highlights key processing and decision points.

Flow charts are an important tool for the improvement of processes. By providing a graphical representation, they help project teams to identify the different elements of a process and understand the interrelationships among the various steps. Flow charts may also be used to gather information and data about a process as an aid to decision making or performance evaluation. For example, the owner of a small advertising agency who hopes to reduce the time involved in creating a print ad might be able to use a flow chart of the process to identify and eliminate unnecessary steps. Though flow charts are relatively old design tools, they remain popular among computer programmers working on systems analysis and design. In recent years, many software programs have been developed to assist business people in creating flow charts.

CONSTRUCTING FLOW CHARTS

Creating flow charts requires the use of specialized symbols. Some of the main symbols that are used to construct flow charts include:

- A round-edged rectangle to represent starting and ending activities, which are sometimes referred to as terminal activities.

- A rectangle to represent an activity or step. Each step or activity within a process is indicated by a single rectangle, which is known as an activity or process symbol.

- A diamond to signify a decision point. The question to be answered or decision to be made is written inside the diamond, which is known as a decision symbol. The answer determines the path that will be taken as a next step.

- Flow lines show the progression or transition from one step to another.

Constructing a flow chart involves the following main steps: 1) Define the process and identify the scope of the flow diagram; 2) Identify project team members that are to be involved in the construction of the process flow diagram; 3) Define the different steps involved in the process and the interrelationships between the different steps (all team members should help develop and agree upon the different steps for the process); 4) Finalize the diagram, involving other concerned individuals as needed and making any modifications necessary; and 5) Use the flow diagram and continuously update it as needed.

FURTHER READING:

Laudon, Kenneth C., and Jane Price Laudon. *Management Information Systems: A Contemporary Perspective.* Macmillan, 1991.

SEE ALSO: Management Information Systems

FOCUS GROUPS

A focus group is a marketing research tool which involves interviewing a small group of people in an informal setting. The leader, or moderator, of a focus group usually guides the discussion in order to obtain the group's opinions about or reactions to specific products or marketing-oriented issues, known as test concepts. While focus groups can provide marketing managers, product managers, and market researchers with a great deal of helpful information, their use as a research tool is limited in that it is difficult to measure the results objectively. Nonetheless, many small businesses find focus groups to be useful means of staying close to consumers and their ever-changing attitudes and feelings. By providing qualitative information from well-defined target audiences, focus groups can aid businesses in decision making and in the development of marketing strategies and promotional campaigns.

APPLICATIONS

Traditionally, focus groups have been used by makers of consumer products to gather qualitative data from target groups of consumers. They are often used in the new product development process, for example, to test consumer reaction to new product concepts and **prototypes**. Focus groups are also used to test marketing programs, as they can provide an indication of how consumers will react to specific advertising messages and other types of marketing communications. In this way, focus groups can help advertising and promotion managers position a particular product, service, or institution with respect to their target audience. Reactions to new types of product packaging can also be determined.

In addition, many companies use focus groups to discover more about consumer habits and product usage. Quality of service can also be evaluated through the use of focus groups. Idea generation is another area in which focus groups are useful to businesses. When participants are encouraged to talk about their problems and unfulfilled needs, their discussion may help a company to generate ideas concerning possible new products and services.

As focus groups increased in popularity during the 1980s and 1990s, their applications expanded beyond the traditional uses. For example, pharmaceutical companies have convened focus groups consisting of medical professionals to test concepts related to new drug products. The legal profession has used focus groups to improve the quality of their cases. Nonprofit organizations have used focus groups to test fundraising campaigns. Focus groups have been used in industrial settings by business-to-business marketers. Some companies have even set up employee focus groups to learn more about **employee motivation**.

CHARACTERISTICS

A key factor in determining the success of focus groups is the composition of the group in terms of the participants' age, gender, and product usage. Product usage, or nonusage in some cases, means that participants are selected on the basis of their use, knowledge, attitudes, or feelings about the products, services, or other test concepts that are the subject of the focus group. In selecting participants, the objective is to find individuals who can discuss the topics at hand and provide quality output that meets the specified research objectives.

The most common method of selecting participants for focus groups is from some type of database that contains demographic, psychographic, and lifestyle information about a large number of consumers. Such databases are available from a variety of commercial vendors. A list of desired characteristics is drawn up and matched with the database to select participants for focus groups. These characteristics may include purchase behavior, attitudes, and demographic data such as age and gender. The goal is to select participants who would likely be in the target audience for the products, services, or concepts being tested.

There is no absolute ideal in terms of the number of participants. Different moderators are comfortable with different sizes of focus groups. A full group usually includes from eight to ten participants. Minigroups consist of four to six individuals. Full groups offer several advantages over smaller groups, but in some cases it is not possible to convene a full group. Full groups of eight to ten participants provide a sufficient amount of output that smaller groups may not be able to offer, especially if one or two individuals either dominate the discussion or tend to be withdrawn and shy. There is usually better interaction, or group dynamics, in full groups. Participants in full groups are not made to feel like experts, as may be the case in minigroups; instead, they participate as average consumers and provide more reliable output. Groups that include more than ten participants are usually more difficult for moderators to control. Group interaction is also more difficult, and moderators have a harder time stimulating discussion. Similarly, it is more difficult for a moderator to spend time probing one individual when there are too many participants.

Focus groups that are relatively homogeneous in terms of age, gender, and product usage generally work better than mixed groups. When it is desirable to obtain data from different age and gender groups, most experts recommend scheduling a series of focus groups using homogeneous participants. There are several reasons homogeneous groups work better than mixed groups. One is that it is easier to evaluate output from homogeneous groups. It would not be possible in a mixed-gender group, for example, to distinguish between male and female attitudes toward a certain topic. To do so would require two separate, homogeneous groups, one consisting of males and one of females. Another reason homogeneous groups work better is that group dynamics tend to become inhibited in mixed-gender or age focus groups. In addition, specific topics can be explored in greater depth when there is homogeneity among the participants with regard to usage of or attitudes toward the products being tested.

MODERATORS

Moderators play an important role in determining the success of focus groups. Well-trained moderators can provide a great deal of added value in terms of their past experience, skills, and techniques. On the other hand, poorly trained moderators are likely to fail to generate quality output from their focus groups. In addition to professional, full-time focus group moderators, other types of individuals who often serve as moderators include professional researchers, academicians, marketing consultants, psychologists or psychiatrists, and company representatives.

Focus group moderators serve as discussion leaders. They try to stimulate discussion while saying as little as possible. They are not interviewers. They usually work from a guide that provides them with an outlined plan of how the discussion should flow. The guide includes topics to be covered together with probes that can be used to stimulate further discussion. Moderators try to include everyone in the discussion. They allocate available time to make sure the required topics are covered. When the discussion digresses, it is up to the moderator to refocus the group on the topic at hand.

SESSIONS

When setting up a focus group session, it is important to give careful consideration to the physical setting where it will take place. The location be one that encourages relaxed participation and informal, spontaneous comments. The focus group facility must be of adequate size and have comfortable seating for all of the participants. Living room and conference room settings both provide good locations for focus groups, but public places—such as restaurants and auditoriums—generally do not. In selecting a focus group site it is also important to make it geographically convenient for the participants. Locations that are hard to find or located in out of the way places may cause delays and scheduling problems.

The facility should also be relatively soundproof, to minimize outside noises and distractions. While focus group sessions are almost always audiotaped and many are videotaped, client company representatives usually like to observe their focus groups firsthand. The ideal focus group facility would be equipped with a one-way mirror that allows company representatives to observe without intruding. An alternative viewing arrangement would be to use a remote video hookup that would allow company representatives to view the proceedings on a video screen. Having company representatives in the same room as the focus group is the least desirable arrangement.

Once the facility, moderator, and participants have been selected, typical focus group sessions begin with an introduction. During the introductory part of the session the moderator welcomes the participants, informs them of what will take place during the session, and generally sets the stage for the discussion to follow. Prior to the main discussion there is usually a warm-up phase. The warm-up is designed to make the participants feel at ease. During the warm-up participants generally introduce themselves to the group.

General topic discussions, usually related to the specific topics that will be covered later, also form part of the warm-up stage. These general discussions help participants focus their attention. They also provide the moderator with some insight into the different participants and allow the moderator to disguise the specific objectives of the focus group.

Gradually the moderator moves the level of discussion from general topics to more specific ones. The moderator may present different concepts for discussion. These include the test concepts for which the group was convened. The moderator may choose to use props to focus the group's attention. Typical props include product samples, actual or concept ads, concept statements that participants read together, photographs, and television commercials.

Once all of the test concepts have been discussed and evaluated by the group, the moderator moves the discussion into a wrap-up phase. During this phase the best concepts are identified and their strengths and weaknesses discussed. Participants may be asked to write down their reactions to what they have seen and discussed. During this final phase, any outstanding issues that were omitted are covered. When all of the substantive discussions have been completed, the moderator closes the session by thanking the participants and giving them any final instructions. Participants should leave with a positive feeling about the experience and the company, if the company that arranged the focus group has been identified. After the participants have left, it is standard practice for the moderator and the client company observers to have a post-group discussion.

Following the conclusion of the focus group or series of focus group sessions, the moderator may prepare a report for the client company. The report generally provides a written summary of the results of the session or sessions as interpreted by the moderator. Focus group reports may be summary in nature or more detailed. In some cases the client company may not require a written report.

ADVANTAGES

Focus groups have become a widely used **market research** tool because of the advantages they offer. With respect to other qualitative research methods—such as in-depth interviews with one or two individuals at a time—focus groups are much faster and more cost effective. Focus groups also allow companies to participate by viewing the discussions, something which is usually not possible with in-depth interviews.

The group dynamics of focus group discussions also provide many benefits. The synergy, or combined effect, of group interactions results in more output than would be obtained individually. Group discussions often snowball, or build on previous statements, to reach a level of output that does not usually occur individually. Participants are likely to be more spontaneous in focus groups than in one-to-one interviews, and their informal comments may produce unexpected results.

FURTHER READING:

Greenbaum, Thomas L. *The Handbook for Focus Group Research*. Lexington Books, 1993.

——. *The Practical Handbook and Guide to Focus Group Research*. D.C. Heath, 1988.

Krueger, Richard A. *Focus Groups: A Practical Guide for Applied Research*. Thousand Oaks, CA: Sage Publications, 1988.

SEE ALSO: Marketing; Market Research; Product Positioning

FORECASTING

Forecasting can be broadly considered as a method or a technique for estimating many future aspects of a business or other operation. Planning for the future is a critical aspect of managing any organization, and small business enterprises are no exception. Indeed, their typically modest capital resources make such planning particularly important. In fact, the long-term success of both small and large organizations is closely tied to how well the management of the organization is able to foresee its future and to develop appropriate strategies to deal with likely future scenarios. Intuition, good judgment, and an awareness of how well the economy is doing may give the manager of a business firm a sense of future market and economic trends. Nevertheless, it is not easy to convert a feeling about the future into a precise and useful number, such as next year's sales volume or the raw material cost per unit of output. Forecasting methods can help estimate many such future aspects of a business operation.

''Perfect accuracy [in forecasting] is not obtainable,'' warned Richard Brealey and Stewart Myers in *Principles of Corporate Finance.* ''If it were, the need for planning would be much less. Still the firm must do the best it can. Forecasting cannot be reduced to a mechanical exercise. Naive extrapolation or fitting trends to past data is of limited value. It is because the future is *not* likely to resemble the past that planning is needed. To supplement their judgement, forecasters rely on a variety of data sources and forecasting methods. For example, forecasts of the economic and industry environment may involve use of econometric models which take account of interactions between economic variables. In other cases the forecaster may employ statistical techniques for analyzing and projecting time series. Forecasts of demand will partly reflect these projections of the economic environment, but they may also be based on formal models that marketing specialists have developed for predicting buyer behavior or on recent consumer surveys to which the firm has access.''

FORECASTING AND ITS PRACTICAL APPLICATIONS

Forecasting methods have many practically applications for business establishments. For example, a number of important business decisions could conceivably be affected by the forecasted sales of a given product. Production schedules, raw material purchasing plans, policies regarding inventories, and sales quotas will be affected by such forecasts. Given these stakes, it is vitally important for the business to utilize accurate forecasting methodologies.

How should the business go about preparing the quarterly sales volume forecasts for the product in question, then? The firm will certainly want to review the actual sales data for the product in question for past periods. Suppose that the forecaster has access to actual sales data for each quarter over the 25-year period the firm has been in business. Using these historical data, the forecaster can identify the general level of sales. He or she can also determine whether there is a pattern or trend, such as an increase or decrease in sales volume over time. A further review of the data may reveal some type of seasonal pattern, such as peak sales occurring before a holiday. Thus by reviewing historical data over time, the forecaster can often develop an accurate understanding of the previous pattern of sales. Understanding such a pattern can often lead to better forecasts of future sales of the product. In addition, if the forecaster is able to identify the factors that influence sales, historical data on these factors (or variables) can also be used to generate forecasts of future sales volumes.

FORECASTING METHODS

All forecasting methods can be divided into two broad categories: qualitative and quantitative. Many forecasting techniques use past or historical data in the form of time series. A time series is simply a set of observations measured at successive points in time or over successive periods of time. Forecasts essentially provide future values of the time series on a specific variable such as sales volume. Division of forecasting methods into qualitative and quantitative categories is based on the availability of historical time series data.

QUALITATIVE FORECASTING METHODS Qualitative forecasting techniques generally employ the judgment of experts to generate forecasts. A key advantage of these procedures is that they can be applied in situations where historical data are simply not available. Moreover, even when historical data are available, significant changes in environmental conditions affecting the relevant time series may make the use of past data irrelevant and questionable in forecasting future values of the time series. For example, historical data on gasoline prices would likely be of questionable value in determining future gasoline prices if other factors (oil boycotts, gasoline rationing programs, scientific breakthroughs in alternative energy use, etc.) suddenly assumed increased importance. Qualitative forecasting methods offer a way to generate forecasts in such cases. Three important qualitative forecasting methods are: the Delphi technique, scenario writing, and the subject approach.

In the Delphi technique, an attempt is made to develop forecasts through ''group consensus.'' Usually, a panel of experienced people are asked to respond to a series of questionnaires. These people, who should ideally come from a variety of backgrounds (marketing, production, management, finance, purchasing, etc.) are asked to respond to an initial questionnaire. Sometimes, a second questionnaire that incorporates information and opinions of the whole group is distributed for further discussion or study. Each expert is asked to reconsider and revise his or her initial response to the questions. This process is continued until some degree of consensus among experts is reached. It should be noted that the objective of the Delphi technique is not to produce a single answer at the end. Instead, it attempts to produce a relatively narrow spread of opinions—the range in which opinions of the majority of experts lie.

Under the scenario writing approach, the forecaster starts with different sets of assumptions. For each set of assumptions, a likely scenario of the business outcome is charted out. Thus, the forecaster generates several different future scenarios (corresponding to the different sets of assumptions). The decision maker or business person is presented with the different scenarios, and has to decide which scenario is most likely to prevail.

The subjective approach allows individuals participating in the forecasting decision to arrive at a forecast based on their feelings, ideas, and personal experiences. Many corporations in the United States have started to increasingly use the subjective approach. Internally, these subjective approaches sometimes take the form of ''brainstorming sessions,'' in which managers, executives, and employees work together to develop new ideas or to solve complex problems. At other times, the subjective approach may take the form of a survey of the company's sales people. This approach, which is known as the sales force composite or grass roots method, is relied on because, as Howard Weiss and Mark Gershon stated in *Production and Operations Management,* "presumably, because salespeople interact directly with purchasers, they have a good feel for which products will or will not sell and the quantity of sales for the various products. . . . The advantage of using the salespeople's forecasts is that (in theory) salespeople are most qualified to explain the demand for products, especially in their own territories. The disadvantage is that salespeople may tend to be optimistic in their estimates if they believe that a low estimate might lead to the unemployment line." Moreover, the opinions of salespeople should not be relied on to the exclusion of all else because they may not be aware of impending changes in other areas, such as availability of raw materials, national economic developments, or the arrival of a formidable new competitor.

A final subjective approach that is also sometimes used is known as the "user expectations" approach. This method of forecasting is essentially an exercise in market research, for it involves extracting information from prospective buyers. "Essentially, user expectations provide better forecasts than the (optimistic) sales force composite," wrote Weiss and Gershon. "Unfortunately, typically it is easier and less costly to obtain the sales force composite than it is to obtain the user expectations."

QUANTITATIVE FORECASTING METHODS Quantitative forecasting methods are used when historical data on variables of interest are available—these methods are based on an analysis of historical data concerning the time series of the specific variable of interest. There are two major categories of quantitative forecasting methods. The first type uses the past trend of a particular variable in order to make a future forecast of the variable. In recognition of this method's reliance on time series of past data of the variable that is being forecasted, it is commonly called the "time series method." The second category of quantitative forecasting techniques also uses historical data. But in forecasting future values of a variable, the forecaster examines the cause-and-effect relationships of the variable with other relevant variables such as the level of consumer confidence, changes in consumers' disposable incomes, the interest rate at which consumers can finance their spending through borrowing, and the state of the economy represented by such variables as the unemployment rate. Thus, this category of forecasting techniques uses past time series on many relevant variables to produce the forecast for the variable of interest. Forecasting techniques falling under this category are called causal methods, since such forecasting is predicated on the cause-and-effect relationship between the variable forecasted and the other selected elements.

SMALL BUSINESS FORECASTING IN THE 1990S

As Dianne Waddell and Amrik S. Sohal observed in *Management Decision,* forecasting is an increasingly turbulent—and important—element of the marketing and production picture for many businesses. Managerial success in forecasting is predicated on their understanding of the forecasting requirements of each situation, as well as an understanding of the various techniques that are available (and the limitations of each). "Forecasting is an ongoing process," added Weiss and Gershon, "which means that it is not sufficient to simply pick a technique and then continuously use that technique. Control must be exercised in order to ensure that the technique is working. If it is not, either the technique must be adjusted or a new technique must be used."

FURTHER READING:

Anderson, David P., Dennis J. Sweeney, and Thomas A. Williams. *An Introduction to Management Science: Quantitative Approaches to Decision Making.* 7th ed. West Publishing Company, 1994.

Brealey, Richard A., and Stewart C. Myers. *Principles of Corporate Finance.* 4th ed. New York: McGraw-Hill, 1991.

Gardner, Everette S. Jr. "Evaluating Forecast Performance in an Inventory Control System." *Management Science.* April 1990.

Jones, Vernon Dale, Stuart Bretschneider, and Wilpen L. Gorr. "Organization Pressures on Forecast Evaluation: Managerial, Political, and Procedural Influences." *Journal of Forecasting.* July 1997.

McMaster, Mike. "Foresight: Exploring the Structure of the Future." *Long Range Planning.* April 1996.

O'Connor, Marcus, William Remus, and Ken Griggs. "Going Up—Going Down: How Good are People at Forecasting Trends and Changes in Trends?" *Journal of Forecasting.* May 1997.

Sanders, Nada R. "Measuring Forecast Accuracy: Some Practical Suggestions." *Production and Inventory Management Journal.* Winter 1997.

Sanders, Nada R. "The Status of Forecasting in Manufacturing Firms." *Production and Inventory Management Journal.* Spring 1997.

Waddell, Dianne, and Amrik S. Sohal. "Forecasting: The Key to Managerial Decision Making." *Management Decision.* January 1994.

Weiss, Howard J., and Mark E. Gershon. *Production and Operations Management.* Boston, MA: Allyn and Bacon, 1989.

SEE ALSO: Strategy; Market Research

401(K) PLANS

A 401(k) plan is a tax-deferred, defined-contribution retirement plan. The name comes from a section of the Internal Revenue Code that permits an employer to create a retirement plan to which employees may voluntarily contribute a portion of their compensation on a pre-tax basis. This section also allows the employer to match employee contributions with tax-deductible company contributions, or to contribute additional funds to employee accounts at the company's discretion as a form of **profit-sharing**. Earnings on all contributions are allowed to accumulate tax-deferred until the employee withdraws them upon retirement. In many cases, employees are able to borrow from their 401(k) accounts prior to retirement at below-market interest rates. In addition, employees may decide to roll over funds in their 401(k) accounts to another qualified retirement plan without penalty if they change jobs. By the mid-1990s, 401(k) plans ranked among the most popular and fastest-growing types of retirement plans in America. In fact, according to Stephen Blakely in *Nation's Business,* funds held in 401(k) plans increased from $190 billion to $925 billion between 1987 and 1997.

HISTORY

The 401(k) provision was created in 1978 as part of that year's Tax Revenue Act, but went largely unnoticed for two years until Ted Benna, a Pennsylvania benefits consultant, devised a creative and rewarding application of the law. Section 401(k) stipulated that cash or deferred-bonus plans qualified for tax deferral. Most observers of tax law had assumed that contributions to such plans could be made only after income tax was withheld, but Benna noticed that the clause did not preclude pre-tax salary reduction programs.

Benna came up with his innovative interpretation of the 401(k) provision in 1980 in response to a client's proposal to transfer a cash-bonus plan to a tax-deferred profit-sharing plan. The now-familiar features he sought were an audit-inducing combination then—pre-tax salary reduction, company matches, and employee contributions. Benna called his interpretation of the 401(k) rule ''Cash-Op,'' and even tried to patent it, but most clients were wary of the plan, fearing that once the government realized its tax revenue-reducing implications, legislators would pull the plug on it.

Luckily for Benna and the millions of participants who have since utilized his idea, the concept of employee savings was gaining political ascendancy at that time. Ronald Reagan had made personal saving through tax-deferred **individual retirement accounts**, or IRAs, a component of his campaign and presidency. Payroll deductions for IRAs were allowed in 1981 and Benna hoped to extend that feature to his new plan. He establish a salary-reducing 401(k) plan even before the **Internal Revenue Service** had finished writing the regulations that would govern it. The government agency surprised many observers when it provisionally approved the plan in spring 1981 and specifically sanctioned Benna's interpretation of the law that fall.

401(k) plans quickly became a leading factor in the evolving retirement benefits business: from 1984 to 1991, the number of plans increased more than 150 percent, and the rate of participation grew from 62 percent to 72 percent. The number of employees able to participate in 401(k) plans rose to more than 48 million by 1991 from only 7 million in 1983, and Benna's breakthrough earned him the appellation ''the grandfather of 401(k)s.'' As expected, the government soon realized the volume of salary reductions it was unable to tax and tried to quash the revolution—the Reagan administration made two attempts to invalidate 401(k)s in 1986—but public outrage prevented the repeal.

The advent of 401(k) plans helped effect a philosophical shift among employers, from the provision of defined-benefit **pension plans** for employees to the administration of defined-contribution retirement plans. In the past, companies had offered true pension plans which guaranteed all individuals a predetermined retirement benefit. But after 1981, rather than providing an employer-funded pension, many companies began to give employees the opportunity to save for their own retirement through a cash or deferred arrangement such as a 401(k). This change helped level the playing field for small businesses, which were now able to offer the same type of retirement benefits as many larger employers. Small businesses thus found themselves better able to attract and retained qualified employees who may previously have opted for the security of a large company and its pension plan.

THE BASICS OF 401(K) PLANS

In benefits parlance, employers offering 401(k)s are sometimes called ''plan sponsors'' and employees are often known as ''plan participants.'' Most 401(k)s are qualified plans, meaning that they conform to criteria established in the Economic Recovery Tax Act of 1981 (ERTA). ERTA expanded upon and refined the Employee Retirement Income Security Act of 1974 (ERISA), which had been enacted to protect participants and beneficiaries from abusive employer practices and created guidelines that were intended to ensure adequate funding of retirement benefits and minimum standards for pension plans.

Basic eligibility standards were set up with this legislation, though they have changed frequently since and may vary slightly from plan to plan. As of 1996, an employee had to be at least 21 years of age and have put in at least one year of service with the company to participate in the 401(k) program. Some union employees; nonresident aliens, and part-time employees were excluded from participation.

401(k) plans incorporate many attractive features for long-term savers, including tax deferral, flexibility, and control. Taxes on both income and interest are delayed until participants begin receiving distributions from the plan. Rollovers (the direct transfer of 401(k) funds into another qualified plan, such as a new employer's 401(k), an IRA, or a self-employed pension plan)—as well as emergency or hardship loans for medical expenses, higher-education tuition, and home purchases—allayed participants' fears about tying up large sums for the long term. While there are restrictions on these loans' availability, terms, and amounts, the net cost of borrowing may be quite reasonable because the interest cost is partly offset by the investment return.

Employees may also receive lump sum distributions of their accounts upon termination. If an employee elects to take his or her distribution in cash before retirement age, however, the employer is required by law to withhold 20 percent of the distribution. If the account is rolled over into another qualified plan, nothing is withheld. Employees' self-determination of investments has allowed tailoring of accounts according to individual needs. For example, younger participants may wish to emphasize higher-risk (and potentially higher-return) investments, while employees who are closer to retirement age can focus on more secure holdings. These features have been refined over the years through legislation, especially after the government realized the tax revenue losses engendered by the popular plans.

The Tax Equity and Fiscal Responsibility Act of 1982 (TEFRA) reduced maximum contribution limits that had been set by ERISA, introduced the "top heavy" concept, and revised the rules for federal income **tax withholding** on plan distributions. Most plans allowed employees to defer 1 percent to 10 percent of current compensation, but such internal limitations have been bound by compensation and contribution ceilings enumerated in TEFRA and subsequent legislation. As of 1996, the amount an employee could defer annually under such programs was set at $9,500. In addition, the sum of employer and employee contributions was limited to 25 percent of annual compensation, or $30,000, per individual. The employer was further limited to an annual contribution of 15 percent of payroll, including both employee deferrals and employer matching and profit-sharing contributions. Finally, the amount of compensation that could be considered in determining an employee's deferral was limited to $150,000 per year under the 1993 tax law.

These limits have made senior executives and other highly paid employees the big losers under 401(k) plans. Mandatory "top heavy" tests prevent 401(k) programs from favoring highly compensated employees by restricting the amount that a company's top earners can contribute to 401(k) plans. Known as "nondiscrimination tests" in the benefits industry, top heavy rules separate employers and employees into two groups: those who are highly compensated and all others. The amount that the highly paid employees may defer is based upon what the lower-paid employees deferred during the year. If the average lower-paid employee only contributed 2 percent of his or her compensation to the corporate 401(k), for example, highly paid employees may only divert 4 percent of their pay. This test adds a second level of limitation on the amount that highly paid employees can defer, often reducing it from legally established limits. Benefits and tax specialists have, of course, devised strategies to circumvent these restrictions, such as 401(k) wrap-arounds, "rabbi trust arrangements," and other "non-qualified" plans that consciously and legally operate outside the bounds of "qualified" 401(k)s.

The Deficit Reduction Act of 1984 (DEFRA) continued the government's revenue-raising—and often 401(k)-limiting—provisions. The Retirement Equity Act (REACT or REA) of that same year helped protect spouses of plan participants by requiring that qualified plans provide numerous survivor benefits. The Tax Reform Act of 1986 (TRA 86) incorporated some of the most extensive, revenue-raising changes in 401(k) criteria since ERISA by imposing new coverage tests and accelerating vesting requirements. Although much of this legislation was intended to benefit employees, it has also been cited as the principal cause of the voluntary termination of thousands of pension plans—a total of 32,659 between July 1987 and September 1988. These terminations eliminated future pension benefits for hundreds of thousands of workers.

During the 1980s, many plan sponsors offered employees only two investment options for their 401(k) accounts: an insurance company's guaranteed income contract (GIC) and a profit-sharing plan. Insurance companies often had full-service capabilities in place and the GICs, with their high interest rates, garnered the lion's share of plan sponsors and participants. Statistics from the Employee Benefit Research Institute and the U.S. Department of Labor showed that about 40 percent of the assets in 401(k) plans were invested in GICs, which placed the burden of performance on employers and their fiduciary agents. But a rash of insurance company failures late in the decade prompted many portfolio managers to increase the number of investment alternatives.

A new provision, ERISA rule 404(c), that went into effect January 1, 1994, stipulated several changes in the way employers administered their programs.

First, plans were required to offer at least three distinctly different investment options that spanned the entire investment spectrum, in addition to the employer's stock. Qualified plans were also compelled to educate participants by providing adequate information about each investment option, thereby enabling employees to make informed choices among them. Finally, employers and their 401(k) administrators were obliged to make more frequent performance reports and allow more frequent changes in investments. These changes have shifted the responsibility for choosing investments from employer to employee, thereby limiting the potential liability of employers for investment results. Although 404(c) is not mandatory, industry observers predicted that many plan sponsors would comply with the new provisions in the interest of happier, more financially secure employees. Compliance was also expected to help employers avoid liability for losses employees suffered in their 401(k) accounts due to fluctuations in the value of their investments.

It was anticipated that the enactment of provision 404(c) would trigger an investment shift among 401(k)s from GICs and employer stocks to mutual funds. As of the end of 1992, mutual funds held about 24 percent of the then-$410 billion 401(k) market, but that percentage was expected to grow dramatically by the end of the century. Mutual funds were seen as an easy way for employers to comply with 404(c) because of the benefits and services they afforded, including access to top professional money managers, instant diversification, portfolios managed according to specified investment objectives and policies, liquidity, flexibility, and ease and economy of administration.

At the end of 1993, surveys showed that approximately 70 percent of eligible workers, or 16 million people, participated in a 401(k) plan. Defined-contribution plans overall, including 401(k), profit-sharing, and thrift savings plans, are expected to grow threefold, to more than $1 trillion, by the end of the century.

ADVANTAGES AND DISADVANTAGES OF 401(K) PLANS

The shift from defined-benefit plans to defined-contribution plans such as 401(k)s has had both positive and negative ramifications for both employees and employers. On the downside, employees have been compelled to shoulder more of the financial burden for their retirement, and employers have had a larger responsibility to report their application of pension funds. But most observers have applauded the movement. Employees have gained greater control over their retirement assets. The plans provide immediate tax advantages as the contributions are not subject to federal income taxes nor to most state and local

taxes. They also provide long-term tax advantages, as earnings accumulate tax-free until withdrawal at retirement, when withdrawals can receive favorable tax treatment. In addition, 401(k)s offer loan provisions that many other types of plans lack.

Employers have been able to share or even eliminate their pension contributions. And if employers do choose to contribute, they too get a tax deduction. 401(k)s have evolved into a valuable perk to attract and retain qualified employees. Employers can even link contributions to a profit-sharing arrangement to increase employee incentive toward higher productivity and commitment to the company. By enabling employees to become active participants in saving and investing for their retirement, 401(k) plans can raise the level of perceived benefits provided by the employer.

Small business owners can set up a 401(k) plan by filling out the necessary forms at any financial institution (a bank, mutual fund, insurance company, brokerage firm, etc.). Beginning in the mid-1990s, these types of institutions began competing to serve the small business sector, since only 25 percent of small employers (with between 50 and 100 employees) sponsored 401(k) plans, compared to 80 percent of large employers (with more than 1,000 employees).

The fees involved in establishing and administering a 401(k) plan are relatively high, since sponsors of this type of plan are required to file Form 5500 annually to disclose plan activities to the IRS. The preparation and filing of this complicated document can increase the administrative costs associated with a plan, as the business owner may require help from a tax advisor or plan administration professional. In addition, all the information reported on Form 5500 is open to public inspection. But, for many business owners, the advantages of 401(k) plans outweigh the disadvantages. It has become the most popular type of plan for businesses with more than 25 employees.

FURTHER READING:

Battle, Carl W. *Senior Counsel: Legal and Financial Strategies for Age 50 and Beyond.* New York: Alworth Press, 1993.

Blakely, Stephen. "Pension Power." *Nation's Business.* July 1997.

Burzawa, Sue. "Companies Add Funds, Educate Employees." *Employee Benefit Plan Review.* January 1994.

Connor, John B., Jr. "Pay Me Later." *Small Business Reports.* July 1994.

Crouch, Holmes F. *Decisions When Retiring.* Allyear Tax Guides, 1995.

"How a 401(K) Plan Works." *Management Accounting.* November 1993.

Martin, Ray. *Your Financial Guide: Advice for Every Stage of Your Life.* Macmillan, 1996.

Myers, Randy. "A Tax Break Probably Not Worth Taking." *Nation's Business.* June 1997.

Vosti, Curtis. "Creator Faced Long Struggle." *Pensions & Investments*. October 28, 1991.

Vosti, Curtis. "401(k) 'Clarification' a Crossroads." *Pensions & Investments*. October 28, 1991.

Wilcox, Melynda Dovel. "Why New Rules Worry the Founder of 401(k)s." *Kiplinger's Personal Finance Magazine*. December 1993.

Williams, Gordon. "Fiddling with 401(k)s." *Financial World*. February 1, 1994.

SEE ALSO: Retirement Planning; Employee Benefits; Simplified Employee Pensions

FRANCHISING

Franchising is a kind of licensing arrangement wherein a business owner, known as the "franchisor," distributes or markets a trademarked product or service through affiliated dealers, who are known as "franchisees." While these franchisees own their establishments, terms of franchising agreements typically make require them to share operational responsibilities with the franchisor.

Over the past few decades, franchising has emerged as an integral part of America's commercial landscape. Indeed, companies as diverse as McDonald's, The Gap, and Jiffy Lube owe their ubiquitous presence in the marketplace to the practice. Department of Commerce figures indicate that franchises were closing in on $300 billion in annual sales in the mid-1990s, and business analysts expect that this total will continue to climb. In fact, the International Franchising Association (IFA) estimates that within a few short years, 50 percent of all U.S. retail sales will take place in franchise outlets (currently more than one third of all retail sales take place there).

Franchising has been embraced by many entrepreneurs eager to run their own company. But the characteristics of a franchising business are dissimilar in some crucial respects from those of other start-up businesses. Some businesspeople have even gone so far as to characterize franchisees as glorified employees of the franchisor, the company that owns the trademark and business concept that the franchisees use. Other observers find this description of the relationship to be misleading and simplistic, but they also acknowledge that there are many aspects of franchising that a prospective small business owner should learn about before entering into such an agreement.

FRANCHISE TYPES

Three different kinds of franchising arrangements are commonly found in the United States today. Business format franchises are the most popular of the franchise types. Under this arrangement, the franchisee pays an initial fee and an ongoing royalty to the franchisor in exchange for a proven business operation and identity. Benefits of this package include the franchisor's name and its product line, marketing techniques, production and administration systems, and operating procedures. A second option is to pursue a product or trade name franchise in which the franchisee becomes part of a franchisor's distribution network. Still other small business owners, meanwhile, choose to combine their resources under the banner of a single operating network. These affiliate franchises are thus able to pool their assets together for purchasing, advertising, and marketing visibility purposes.

BENEFITS OF FRANCHISE OWNERSHIP

There are many significant advantages to franchise ownership. In most instances, an entrepreneur who decides to buy a franchise is purchasing a business concept with a proven track record of success. In addition, a franchise agreement provides instant name recognition for the business, which can be a huge advantage if the name enjoys a solid reputation in the marketplace. But franchising provides benefits in many other areas of business operation as well. These include:

ADVERTISING AND PROMOTION Franchisees benefit from any national advertising campaigns launched by the corporation with which they have gone into business. In addition, many franchisors provide their franchises with a wide range of point-of-sale advertising materials, ranging from posters to mobiles to brochures. Since such materials are often expensive to produce, they would otherwise be beyond the reach of some individual franchisees.

OPERATIONS Franchisors provide franchisees with a wide range of help in the areas of administration and general operations. The entrepreneur who becomes a franchise owner is instantly armed with proven products and production systems; inventory systems; financial and accounting systems; and human resources guidelines. Many franchisors also provide management training to new franchisees, and ongoing seminar workshops for established owners.

BUYING POWER Franchisees are often able to fill inventory needs at discount prices because of their alliance with the franchisor, which typically has made arrangements to buy supplies at large-volume prices. "This is an increasingly great advantage because today you have to compete with national chains, conglomerates, buying consortiums, and other large franchises," observed the editors of *The Entrepreneur Magazine Small Business Advisor*. "The small-business person who purchases in small quantities can't compete with their buying power. When you become a franchisee, you have the collective buying power of the entire franchise system.''

RESEARCH AND DEVELOPMENT Most small business owners are able to devote little time or money to **research and development** efforts. Franchising, then, can provide a huge lift in this regard, for many franchisors maintain ongoing research and development systems to develop new products and forecast market trends.

CONSULTING SERVICES It is in the franchisor's best interests to do all it can to ensure the success of all of its franchises. As a result, the entrepreneur who decides to become a franchisee can generally count on a wide range of training and consulting services from the larger company. Such services can be particularly helpful during the start-up phase of operations.

DRAWBACKS OF FRANCHISE OWNERSHIP

But while the benefits of franchising are many and varied, there are well-documented drawbacks that should be considered as well. These include:

COST The initial franchise fee, which in some cases is not refundable, can be quite expensive. Some fees are only a few thousand dollars, but others can require an up-front investment of several hundred thousand dollars. In addition, some franchisors require their franchisees to pay them regular royalty fees—a percentage of their weekly or monthly gross income—in exchange for permission to use their name. Some franchisors also require their franchise owners to help pay for their national advertising expenditures. Other costs include insurance, initial inventory purchases, and other expenses associated with equipping a new business.

LIMITED CONTROL Franchisees are subject to many franchisor regulations concerning various aspects of business operation and conduct. As the Federal Trade Commission (FTC) acknowledged to prospective franchisees in its *Consumer Guide to Buying a Franchise,* ''these controls may significantly restrict your ability to exercise your own business judgment.'' Areas in which franchisors generally wield significant control include the following:

Site Approval—Many franchise agreements include stipulations that give the franchisor final say in site selection. Some franchisors also limit franchise territories, and while such restrictions generally prevent other company franchisees from impinging on your territory, they can also act to restrict your ability to relocate once you have become established.

Operating Restrictions—Franchise agreements include many instructions on the ways in which a franchisee must conduct business. These encompass all aspects of a business's operation, from operating hours to accounting procedures to the goods or services that are offered. ''These restrictions may impede you from operating your outlet as you deem best,'' admitted the FTC. ''The franchisor also may require you to purchase supplies only from an approved supplier, even if you can buy similar goods elsewhere at a lower cost.''

APPEARANCE Many franchisors cultivate a certain readily recognizable look to their outlets, for they know that such standards, when applied consistently, contribute to national recognition of the company name and its products and services. Franchisees generally accept these regulations willingly, for these standards of appearance in the areas of decor, design, and uniforms have proven to be part of a winning formula elsewhere. This is just as well, for the franchise owner who does wish to make changes in his business's appearance often has little freedom to do so.

ASSOCIATION WITH THE FRANCHISOR For the small business owner whose franchise is attached to a highly regarded, financially robust franchisor, the association can be a powerful positive in his or her business. Business experts note, however, that a franchise outlet can suffer severe damage if its franchisor is beset with financial difficulties or public relations problems. ''If the franchisor hits hart times, you'll most likely feel them as well,'' noted the editors of the *Small Business Advisor.* ''You are inevitably tied to the franchisor, not only by contract, but by concept, name, product, and services sold.''

Prospective franchisees, then, need to weigh many factors in their decision making about entering the burgeoning world of franchising. But most small business consultants acknowledge that these factors usually boil down to a couple of fundamental concerns. As Steve Spinelli wrote in *The Portable MBA in Entrepreneurship,* ''the choice of becoming a franchisee or starting a stand-alone business hinges on your answers to two important questions: Is risk sufficiently mitigated by the trademark value, operating system, economies of scale, and support process of the franchise to justify a sharing of equity with the franchisor (vis-à-vis the franchise fee and royalty payments)? Is my personality and management style amenable to sharing decision-making responsibilities in my business with the franchisor and other franchisees?''

SELECTING A FRANCHISE

It is imperative for prospective franchise owners to make an intelligent, informed decision regarding franchise selection, for once a contract has been signed, the franchisee has committed himself to the enterprise. As Janet Attard warned in *The Home Of-*

fice and Small Business Answer Book, "A franchise isn't something you can walk away from easily if it doesn't work out." But the selection process can be a bewildering one for the unprepared entrepreneur. Franchise opportunities are available in a wide array of industries, each of which offer their own potential benefits and drawbacks. Moreover, every franchisor has its own strengths and weaknesses. Several business areas, then, need to be investigated as part of any effective franchise selection process.

ANALYSIS OF SELF Experts counsel prospective franchise owners to evaluate their own strengths and weaknesses before signing any franchise contract. Prospective franchisees should also have an understanding of their ultimate business and personal objectives before beginning the search for an appropriate franchise. The entrepreneur who is most interested in achieving financial security may want to look in an entirely different industry than the entrepreneur who hopes to land a franchise that will enable him or her to devote more time to family life.

ANALYSIS OF INDUSTRY AND MARKET Prospective franchise owners need to evaluate which industries interest them. They also need to determine whether the franchisor's principal goods or services are in demand in the community in which he or she hopes to operate. Other industry wide factors, such as the cost of raw materials used and the amount of industry competition, need to be weighed as well. The latter issue is a particularly important one, for it can be a fundamental factor in a franchisee's success or failure. The presence of some competition, for instance, often indicates a healthy demand for goods or services in that industry area. A dearth of competitors, though, might indicate that demand is low (or nonexistent). Similarly, the presence of several competitors might necessitate an examination of whether the market can support another provider in that area, or whether you might have to take meaningful market share from already existing businesses in order to survive.

ANALYSIS OF FRANCHISOR Entrepreneurs interested in franchising should be knowledgeable about the strengths and weaknesses of companies that offer such arrangements. Factors that should be considered include the franchisor's profitability, organizational structure, growth patterns, public reputation, litigation history, financial management capabilities, fee requirements, and relationship with other franchisees.

Perhaps the best source of information on these and many other issues is the franchisor's disclosure document. This important document, which must be given to prospective franchise owners at least ten business days before any contract is signed or any deposits are owed, usually takes the form of the Uniform Franchise Offering Circular (UFOC). The UFOC contains important information on key aspects of the franchisor's business and the nature of their dealings with franchisees. Information contained in the UFOC includes a franchise history; audited financial statements and other financial history documents; franchise fee and royalty structures; background on the franchise's leading executives; terms of franchise agreements; estimated start-up costs for franchisees (including equipment, inventory, operating capital, and insurance); circumstances under which the franchisor can terminate its relationship with a franchisee; franchisor training and assistance programs; franchisee advertising costs (if any); data on the success (or lack thereof) of current and former franchisee operations; and litigation history.

Some prospective franchise owners pay less attention to a company's litigation history than other information included in the UFOC, but a company's past litigation experiences can, in some cases, provide important insights into the franchisor's **business ethics** and/ or operating style. "The disclosure document tells you if the franchisor, or any of its executive officers, has been convicted of felonies involving, for example, fraud, any violation of franchise law or unfair or deceptive practices law, or are subject to any state or federal injunctions involving similar misconduct," noted the Federal Trade Commission. "It also will tell you if the franchisor, or any of its executives, has been held liable or settled a civil action involving the franchise relationship. A number of claims against the franchisor may indicate that it has not performed according to its agreements, or, at the very least, that franchisees have been dissatisfied with the franchisor's performance. Be aware that some franchisors may try to conceal an executive's litigation history by removing the individual's name from their disclosure documents."

The inclusion of other information on a franchisor's business dealings with franchisees is up to the discretion of the franchisor. For example, while franchisors are required by law to provide prospective franchisees with documentation of expected start-up costs, they are not required to provide long-term earnings projections. Those who do provide such information are obligated by the FTC's Franchise Rule to have a reasonable basis for the claims they make and provide prospective franchisees with written information substantiating their projections.

It is important, then, to utilize other sources of information in addition to the disclosure document when pondering a move into the world of franchising. For example, small business consultants often urge prospective franchisees to conduct interviews with franchisor representatives about various business issues. Other sources of information often cited include financial institutions (for financial evaluations of the franchisor), state agencies (for information on franchisee rights in the state in which the franchisee is operating), the Better Business Bureau (for news of possible complaints against the franchisor), industry surveys, and associations (such as the Franchise Consultants International Association and the International Franchise Association).

Many experts also encourage prospective small business owners to interview current and former franchisees associated with the franchisor. Would-be franchisees can thus gain first-hand information on a great many business subjects, including: likely size of total investment, hidden or unexpected costs, satisfaction with franchisor performance (in training, advertising, operating, etc.), franchisee backgrounds, and business trends in the industry. Franchisee lists can be a valuable resource, but consultants caution their clients to make certain that they receive a complete list, rather than a list of selected franchisees who are compensated by the franchisor for giving positive appraisals of the company.

FRANCHISING LAWS

The United States has developed an extensive regulatory system designed to govern franchising practices throughout the business world. Chief among the federal guidelines are the FTC's Franchising and Business Opportunity Ventures Trade Regulation Rules and Subsequent Guidelines. In addition, many state governments have fashioned pieces of legislation that directly impact on franchising operations. A good many of the laws governing franchising—both at the state and federal level—are expressly designed to protect prospective small business owners from unscrupulous franchisors who misrepresent themselves.

Franchising experts commonly urge prospective franchisees to enlist the help of an attorney during the franchise selection process. Indeed, since franchising is such a complicated business, many entrepreneurs secure an attorney's services throughout the process. Legal assistance is especially helpful when the time comes to sign the franchise or license agreement, the document that lays out the terms of the partnership between a franchisee and a franchisor. "The franchise agreement is the foundation on which your franchise is built," stated the *Entrepreneur Magazine Small Business Advisor.* "The agreement gives both parties a clear understanding of the basis on which they are going to continue to operate."

The franchise **contract** covers all aspects of the franchisee-franchisor agreement, from record keeping to site selection to quality control provisions. The contract is designed to cover both relatively minor issues—such as sign display requirements—to matters of major importance—such as the franchisee's schedule of royalty payments and required insurance provisions. Franchise agreements also include a section devoted to detailing the length of the contract,

and any possibilities for extending the terms of the contract beyond the termination date. Long term agreements (15 years or more) give franchisees more security, though this can be problematic if their relations with the franchisor take a bad turn. Since shorter terms do make it easier for franchisors to rid themselves of under-performing or troublesome franchisees, some prefer to go this route. Others, however, place a higher value on securing the franchisee royalties that often pour in under the longer agreements.

Information included in the franchise contract includes the following:

- Accounting and recordkeeping provisions;
- Existence (and terms) of any performance quotas;
- Fairness of the franchise fee;
- Fairness of the royalty arrangement;
- Franchisor's continuing services to franchisee;
- Insurance protection (if any) under franchisor's patent or liability insurance coverage;
- Operating provisions (including quality control, human resource management, and other areas);
- Restrictions (if any) on business activities outside the franchise;
- Restrictions (if any) on selling franchise;
- Start-up investment required;
- Termination or default terms (as well as arbitration clauses);
- Terms of contributions, if any, to parent company's national advertising campaigns;
- Terms of inventory and ordering practices;
- Terms of renewing the franchise agreement;
- Territorial protections.

Given the scope of its coverage—and its importance as the binding legal document between franchisee and franchisor—the franchise contract is, in its final form, an imposing and complicated document. Again, the importance of the agreement makes it imperative that prospective franchise owners consult with an attorney before signing the contract.

FURTHER READING:

Attard, Janet. *The Home Office and Small Business Answer Book.* New York: Henry Holt, 1993.

A Consumer Guide to Buying a Franchise. Washington: U.S. Federal Trade Commission, n.a.

Dicke, Thomas S. *Franchising In America.* University of North Carolina Press, 1992.

The Entrepreneur Magazine Small Business Advisor. Wiley, 1995.

Evaluating Franchise Opportunities. Washington: U.S. Small Business Administration, n.a.

International Franchise Association. *What You Need to Know to Buy a Franchise.* Washington: International Franchise Association, 1988.

Luhn, Rebecca. *Buying Your First Franchise.* Menlo Park, CA: Crisp Publications, 1993.

Spinelli, Steve. "Franchising," in *The Portable MBA in Entrepreneurship.* Edited by William D. Bygrave. New York: John Wiley & Sons, 1994.

SEE ALSO: Buying an Existing Business; Choosing a Small Business

FREELANCE EMPLOYMENT/ INDEPENDENT CONTRACTORS

Freelance employees, also known as independent contractors, are individuals who work on their own, without a long-term contractual commitment to any one employer. A freelance employee usually performs services or completes work assignments under short-term contracts with several employers, or clients, who have the right to control only the final result of the individual's work, rather than the specific means used to get the work done. Examples of positions held by independent contractors range from doctors and computer programmers to maids and farm workers. Freelance employment can offer a number of advantages to individuals, including flexible work arrangements, independence, variety, and some tax deductions. It can also hold some pitfalls, however, such as assuming risk in business dealings, paying self-employment taxes, and taking personal responsibility for health insurance, disability, and retirement coverage.

Specifically, individuals who are classified as independent contractors can deduct work-related expenses for tax purposes. In contrast, the first 2 percent of expenses are not deductible for those classified as employees, plus the deduction is phased out above $55,900 in income. In addition, independent contractors often qualify for tax deductions for using part of their home as an office and for salaries paid to other people, while employees usually do not. Independent contractors also have the benefit of sheltering 15 percent of their annual income, or up to $30,000, for retirement, while employees are limited to $9,500 annually. Finally, independent contractors must pay the full amount of Social Security and Medicare taxes and make quarterly estimated tax payments to the federal government. Employers must withhold taxes for their employees and pay half of their Social Security and Medicare taxes.

Freelance employment boomed in the United States during the 1980s, as many companies sought to reduce their payroll costs in order to remain competitive. Instead of hiring new employees and paying an additional 30 percent or more in payroll taxes and benefits, many companies chose to make "work-for-hire" arrangements with independent contractors. Businesses, and especially small businesses, can gain several advantages from such arrangements. For example, employers are not responsible for paying taxes for freelance employees, and they avoid the high costs of providing health insurance, paid vacation and sick leave, and other benefits often granted to regular, full-time employees. Instead, employers simply file Form 1099 with the government to report the total compensation paid to each independent contractor for the year.

FREELANCE TREND CAUSES CONTROVERSY

The boom in freelance employment led to increased scrutiny by the U.S. **Internal Revenue Service (IRS)** in the early 1990s. Section 1706 of the Internal Revenue Code provides a 20-part test to determine whether workers are employees or independent contractors. The IRS began using this test to reclassify many independent contractors—particularly those engaged in high-paying professions—as employees in order to eliminate tax deductions and increase tax revenues. This practice "leaves virtually everyone angry, and that includes the IRS," according to David Cay Johnston in the *New York Times.* "The agency is trying to apply tax laws that were largely written for an age of manual work and factories to an era of intellectual labor, often conducted in home offices." The IRS would argue that the law also protects individuals from unfair treatment by employers—such as being fired and then rehired as an independent contractor without benefits—but few of the reclassifications have involved exploited low-wage laborers, because they generate minimal tax revenues. Since the issue could potentially affect up to five million self-employed Americans, Johnston called it "the most contentious employment tax issue in the nation today."

Although the controversy surrounding freelance employment has received increased attention in recent years, it is not new. As early as the 1960s, the IRS started looking more closely at household employees—such as maids, nannies, and gardeners—who often received income "under the table" and thus did not pay taxes. The main cause of dissention over current application of the law, according to the *New York Times,* is that it often tends to penalize individuals who wish to be classified as independent contractors and take advantage of tax breaks (as well as the small businesses that depend on them), while it often fails to protect individuals who should be classified as employees and be eligible for benefits. For example, the IRS would be likely to review the case of a highly paid engineer who markets her services to several companies as an independent contractor and deducts various expenses of doing business. However, the IRS would be unlikely to review the case of a migrant farm worker who is employed by a large producer but, as an independent contractor, makes less than minimum wage and receives no disability or old-age benefits.

ELEMENTS OF THE IRS TEST

The IRS applies a 20-part test in order to determine whether a certain worker should be classified as an employee or an independent contractor. The main issue underpinning the test is who sets the work rules: employees must follow rules set by their bosses, while independent contractors set their own rules. The hours during which a job is performed is one determination of work rules. For example, if the employer dictates an individual's work hours or pays an individual by the hour rather than by the job, that individual is likely to be considered an employee rather than an independent contractor. Likewise, if the employer requires that an individual work full-time or not be employed by another company simultaneously, that individual would appear to be an employee. On the other hand, an individual who sets his own hours, receives payment by the job, and divides his time between work for several different employers would probably be classified as an independent contractor.

Other criteria involve who provides the tools and materials needed to complete the work. For example, an individual who works at an employer's facility and uses the employer's equipment would be considered an employee, while one who works at a separate location and provides her own equipment would be classified as an independent contractor. Another element of the IRS test involves termination of the work relationship. Employees can usually quit their jobs at will, and can also be fired by their employers. However, a freelance employee would have a contractual obligation to complete a specific amount of work for an employer, and neither party could break the agreement without cause. Finally, an independent contractor usually pays his own expenses of doing business and takes the risk of not receiving payment when work is not completed in accordance with a contract, while an employee is usually reimbursed for business-related expenses by the employer and receives a paycheck whether his work is completed or not.

Despite such specific guidelines, the IRS test has generated criticism. "This 20-factor test has frustrated both the IRS and the small-business owner," said an accountant quoted in *Crain's Small Business Detroit.* "Ten different revenue agents could review the same case, and ten different responses could result." The IRS recognized that the test was sometimes applied inconsistently, and was evaluating whether to modify or eliminate it. However, the agency had no plans to reduce its efforts to reclassify certain independent contractors as employees because of the potential gains in tax revenue. Reclassification can cost small businesses that rely on freelance employees huge sums in penalties, back taxes, and interest—and can even force some out of business. In Michigan alone, the IRS reclassified 51,000 independent contractors in 1993 and assessed a total of $100 million in back taxes. In 1997, however, the IRS agreed to provide amnesty for businesses that had erroneously classified workers as independent contractors when they were in fact employees. Those businesses that come forward, admit their mistake, and agree to treat affected workers as full-time employees in the future are not penalized for their past actions.

FREELANCE EMPLOYMENT AND SMALL BUSINESSES

The rules governing independent contractors affect small businesses in two significant ways. First, many entrepreneurs are themselves freelance employees, and they must understand and adhere to the IRS guidelines in offering services to clients. Otherwise, they risk falling into what Robert Laurance called "the employee trap" in his book *Going Freelance.* An entrepreneur who is reclassified as an employee of a major client loses a variety of tax breaks and other advantages of self-employment.

In order to be considered independent contractors, entrepreneurs must establish that they are in business for themselves for the purpose of making a profit. They might demonstrate that their enterprise is a business—rather than a hobby or the work of an employee—by registering a business name, obtaining an occupational permit or license, establishing an office, soliciting clients, and printing stationery and business cards. Even if the majority of work will be performed for one client, entrepreneurs should make clear their intention of soliciting work from other clients.

Next, the entrepreneur should subject his or her business activities to the IRS 20-step test in order to avoid the appearance of being an employee. For example, the entrepreneur should be certain that the client does not set his or her hours, determine the location where work is performed, pay withholding taxes on his or her income, or provide needed equipment, tools, supplies, or transportation. Instead, the entrepreneur should sign a contract specifying an amount of work that will be completed by a certain deadline. The contract should include a specific disclaimer stating that this work will be performed as an independent contractor. The entrepreneur should also be certain to obtain a 1099 form (a statement of miscellaneous income) from the client for tax purposes, rather than a W-2 form (a statement of income from employment).

The rules governing independent contractors affect small businesses in another significant way. Many small businesses lack the resources to hire permanent employees to provide support for short-term projects or to provide expertise in highly technical fields, so instead they enlist the services of independent contractors. In these cases, it is to the benefit of the small business owner as well as the independent contractor to spell out the details of the work arrangement in a contract. The small business owner should also choose freelance employees carefully to be sure that they present themselves as in business to make a profit.

FURTHER READING:

Brodsky, Ruthan, and Marsha Stopa. "Sneak a Tax." *Crain's Small Business Detroit.* July 1994.

"Employee vs. Independent Contractor." *IRS Publication No. 937.* Washington, D.C.: Internal Revenue Service, 1994.

Hand, Larry E. *Freelancing Made Simple.* New York: Doubleday, 1995.

Johnston, David Cay. "Are You Your Own Boss? Only if the IRS Says So." *New York Times.* March 19, 1995.

Laurance, Robert. *Going Freelance: A Guide for Professionals.* New York: Wiley, 1988.

Saunders, Laura. "Attention, Income Hiders." *Forbes.* March 2, 1992.

Spragins, Ellyn E. "Protecting Independent Contractor Status." *Inc.* March 1992.

Szabo, Joan C. "Contract Workers: A Risky Business." *Nation's Business.* August 1993.

SEE ALSO: Employee Hiring; Self-Employment; Tax-Deductible Business Expenses; Work Force

FULL-TIME AND PART-TIME EMPLOYEES

Many small business owners rely on a blend of full- and part-time employees to attend to basic operational needs, although some industries rely more heavily on one type or another. Retail sectors, for instance, utilize large percentages of part-time employees, while the work force of many manufacturers and service providers tends to be primarily composed of full-time employees.

Studies indicate, however, that there seems to be a general across-the-board trend toward part-time status in the American workplace. Small business establishments are an important component of this trend, for as Elwood N. Chapman stated in *Human Relations in Small Business,* "the majority of these part-timers

will be recruited and managed by small business organizations." Business consultants indicate that each small business needs to determine for itself how to compose its work force in these areas, weighing the benefits and drawbacks associated with each type of employee.

TYPES OF PART-TIMERS

Federal law defines a part-time employee as one who works less than 1,000 hours a year for the same firm. This annual total averages out to about 17.5 hours per week. In reality, however, part-time employees may work more than 30 hours a week without gaining designation as full-time employees. Analysts admit, however, that the distinction between full- and part-time work grows quite hazy when an employee works more than 30 hours a week, and many consultants counsel small business owners who ask workers to put in weekly time above that threshold to consider making them full-time employees, especially if they are not providing any benefits to the employees when they work under "part-time" designations.

According to the U.S. Bureau of Labor Statistics, 18.3 percent of the work force in the United States in the mid-1990s consisted of part-time workers. Studies indicate that the overwhelming majority of these employees turn to part-time work not because of their inability to secure full-time employment, but because of the scheduling flexibility that part-time work offers. Some studies, for instance, state that more than three out of four part-time employees voluntarily work on that basis.

Analysts cite four primary demographic categories into which most part-time employees fall. These are: 1) Retirees, who may want to supplement a fixed income or ensure that they maintain a certain level of involvement in the world around them; 2) Parents, who choose to have one member of their partnership work on a part-time basis so that more time can be spent raising children; 3) Students, who embrace part-time employment as a way to make money without interrupting their education, and 4) Temporary agency workers, who sometimes become part-time employees of a particular establishment over time.

ADVANTAGES OF HIRING PART-TIMERS

Writing in *Human Relations In Small Business,* Elwood Chapman cited several advantages associated with utilizing part-time help:

- Costs are lower in terms of direct monetary compensation—"Some part-timers are paid less than half of what full-timers who do the same work are paid. Many small businesses would be forced to close without part-timers." And of course, many businesses save significant amounts of money in terms of benefits by hiring part-time workers.

- Energy and enthusiasm—Chapman contended that part-timers—especially college and high school students—can give businesses a needed injection of liveliness. Analysts state that this quality is particularly evident in retail clothing establishments and other businesses that survive on the expenditures of younger customers.

- In-house candidates for full-time job openings—Chapman said that "when full-time positions open up, employers can make better choices from part-timers, whom they have had the opportunity to observe and test out."

- Willingness to learn—Chapman and others indicate that young part-timers are often willing to learn new tasks and responsibilities.

- Availability during peak periods—Researchers note that many businesses that utilize part-time help have pronounced cycles of activity (for holidays, seasonal attractions, etc.). Students are particularly useful in meeting these periods of high demand because many of these periods coincide with times when they are not in school (Christmas vacation, summertime).

- Execution of mundane or unpleasant tasks—Analysts note that many part-time employees do not have the clout to refuse certain tasks, and they indicate that many young part-timers recognize that there is a "paying your dues" quality to worklife in many early employment experiences. This also frees up full-time employees to use their time to tackle more complicated, long-term challenges facing the business.

- Availability—Chapman indicated that "some smaller and isolated communities offer a larger supply of responsible and hard-working part-timers, because fewer part-time jobs are available."

DISADVANTAGES ASSOCIATED WITH PART-TIMERS

Chapman noted, however, that there are disadvantages associated with part-time employees as well. One of the major drawbacks, he wrote, is that "part-timers are less committed to their jobs; they usually have a long-term goal that is more important. This causes them to be less stable and dependable." Indeed, it is a basic business reality that the turnover rate among part-time positions is significantly higher than the rate among full-timers.

Other disadvantages cited by Chapman included:

- Higher **absenteeism** rates.

- Inexperience, which can translate into higher training costs and/or unprofessional behavior.

- Mistakes in hiring decisions, since younger applicants for part-time positions have less of a track record.

- Excessive socializing (again, especially with younger employees).

PART-TIME EMPLOYEES AND BENEFITS

Mid-1990s studies of American business indicate that although part-time employees are more likely to receive benefits than they were even a few years before, many still are not compensated with benefits packages. These reports also indicate that small business owners are less likely to offer additional benefits in such realms as paid vacation, health insurance, etc., than their larger counterparts, largely because of their more modest financial positions. Another key factor in determining the likelihood of a part-time worker receiving benefits was the number of hours worked, according to a 1995 survey by Hewitt Associates. The survey, which garnered responses from 505 employers, including 479 establishments that utilized part-time help, indicated that the availability of benefits to employees was predicated fairly directly on the number of hours worked.

The Hewitt survey broke benefits down into several key areas: medical benefits, dental benefits, flexible benefits, life insurance, long-term disability, and paid sick leave.

- Medical Benefits—The Hewitt survey indicated that nearly 75 percent of respondent companies offered medical benefits to employees working 30 or more hours per week, but only one out of four offered medical coverage to part-timers who put in less than 20 hours per week.

- Dental Benefits—Although 69 percent of businesses surveyed offered dental insurance to part-timers working more than 30 hours a week, that percentage dropped significantly when the employees worked between 20 and 29 hours a week (56 percent) or less than 20 hours a week (23 percent).

- Flexible Benefits—Not all companies surveyed offered **flexible work programs**, but those that did overwhelmingly allowed their part-time employees to take part.

- Life Insurance—Life insurance was made available to fewer than one in four part-time workers who put in fewer than 20 hours a week, but for those employees who put in at least 30 hours a week, the percentage rose to nearly seven out of ten workers.

- Long-Term Disability—Employees working fewer than 20 hours a week rarely receive this benefit, but the Hewitt survey indicated that about half of employers were willing to provide this benefit to workers who put in more than 30 hours a week.

- Paid Sick Leave—Once again, the likelihood of receiving this benefit is directly dependent on number of hours worked; while 64 percent of respondent companies indicated that they provided paid sick leave to employees who worked 30 hours or more a week (and 57 percent of companies offered the benefit to employees working 20–29 hours a week), only 28 percent offered paid sick leave to workers who put in fewer than 20 hours a week.

THE RETAIL INDUSTRY AND PART-TIME EMPLOYMENT

Many types of businesses rely on part-time employees to one degree or another, but historically, few industry sectors have counted on part-timers to the extent that the retail sector has. Indeed, the unique operational needs of retail establishments make the part-time employee an ideal one in many respects. "For retailers, seasonal buying patterns, year-round promotional activities, and ever-changing consumers demand a flexible work force," wrote Tracy Mullen in *Chain Store Age Executive with Shopping Center Age*. Retail stores also register major savings in bene-fits because of the composition of their work force. But as Mullen indicated, the retail industry would not be able to employ an estimated seven million part-time workers if those employees did not receive some rewards in return. "For most of these employees, the inherent value in part-time retail employment is [scheduling] flexibility," said Mullen. But she goes on to note that "another big draw for part-time retail employment is the discounts on merchandise. Part-time employees don't get a part-time discount on goods. While the average retail wage is far above the minimum wage at $8 per hour, who can say how much more that hourly wage is worth when you factor in the 20 percent to 40 percent discount part-timers enjoy?"

FURTHER READING:

Chapman, Elwood N. *Human Relations in Small Business*. Crisp Publications, 1994.

Craver, Alan. "Welcome to the Full Time." *Baltimore Business Journal*. September 27, 1996.

Epstein, Gene. "A Small-Scale Revolution." *Barron's*. August 11, 1997.

Gruner, Stephanie. "The Benefits of Part-Time Work." *Inc.* December 1994.

Mullen, Tracy. "Part-Time Values Mean Full-Time Benefits." *Chain Store Age Executive with Shopping Center Age*. October 1997.

"Part-Time, Contingent Worker Benefits: Being Creative Doesn't Mean Being Expensive." *Employee Benefit Plan Review*. June 1997.

"Part Time Employees Getting More Benefits and Options." *Journal of Accountancy*. September 1995.

"Part-Timers Still Trailing on Employee Benefits." *National Underwriter Property & Casualty—Risk & Benefits Management*. April 10, 1995.

SEE ALSO: Employee Benefits; Employee Hiring; Work Force

G

The General Agreement on Tariffs and Trade (GATT) is an agreement between nations to promote international economic growth, consisting of legally binding rules by which participating economic parties trade. The GATT seeks to improve market access through the elimination of trade barriers and regional, preferential economic blocks. The most recent GATT was signed in Marrakesh, Morocco, on April 13, 1994, by 121 countries. According to Thomas A. Faulhaber in the *Business Forum,* the 1994 agreement—while generally viewed as most beneficial to large, multinational corporations—in fact "offers some surprisingly attractive benefits to the smaller business—even smaller businesses that are not engaged directly in international trade." At the beginning of 1995, the GATT organization officially ceased to exist and was replaced by the World Trade Organization (WTO).

BACKGROUND

The roots of the GATT organization are in the Bretton Woods Conference of 1944, from which emerged a supranational body, the International Trade Organization (ITO). The role of the ITO was to monitor economic policy—that is, tariffs and trade—among economic partners in the West. The GATT organization was established in 1947. In the immediate aftermath of World War II and the debilitating economic nationalism that preceded it, the United States in particular anticipated the creation of a new economic order and an international treaty and institution to monitor economic policy.

The original GATT membership consisted of 23 nations, but it soon swelled to 84. Under the GATT, trade barriers were to be torn down through multilateral negotiations. As barriers came down, international trade and production would supposedly increase. The GATT first secured these gains through reciprocity—where one country lowers its tariffs to another country's exports so that the other country will in turn lower its tariffs. Next, GATT implemented the "most-favored-nation" status, which is accorded to member countries that do not grant one member or a group of members preferential trade treatment. Trade negotiations since World War II have indeed reduced average tariffs on manufactured and semi-manufactured goods from 40 percent in 1947 to less than 10 percent by the mid-1970s. During the early 1990s, that tariff figure dropped to approximately 5 percent. These reductions helped world trade to surge from $94 billion in 1955 to over $2 trillion in 1980.

Since the late 1970s, however, global trade output has grown at a much slower pace. The early 1990s recession hindered trade cooperation between GATT member countries. During this time, three preferential trading blocks arose: the European Union, the **North American Free Trade Agreement (NAFTA)**, and ASEAN in Southeast Asia. These trading blocks indicated future foreign policy tensions. For example, the United States and Europe—original framers of the GATT—imposed protectionist measures on entire industrial sectors, like steel, chemicals, and electronics, just as formerly protectionist nations of the developing world embraced free market principles and looked to join GATT's supposedly open international trading system. Thus, despite GATT's aims and past accomplishments, anti-dumping and countervailing-duty measures adopted by member countries resulted in not less but more protectionism since the 1980s.

THE URUGUAY ROUND

The latest round of multilateral trade negotiations, launched in 1986 as the Uruguay Round, was designed in large part to reconcile the newfound protectionist principles of GATT member nations with the newfound free market principles of developing nations. These negotiations were a long, drawn-out process, in which the concerns of developing nations that wanted to join GATT and attain export-led economic growth were often ignored. Instead, the United States fought to secure significant reforms of Europe's Common Agricultural Policy, which originally aimed to protect the continent's farmers against hardship but which led in time to massive over-production of food and increasing government subsidies.

Although agriculture is only a small part of economic production among developed nations of the West, the United States saw multilateral farm trade reform—or progressively cutting support and protection of farm sectors—as the litmus test to the success of eventually liberalizing trade in services and especially in protecting intellectual property. If the West could liberalize its farm and textile sectors, the United States reasoned, developing countries would in turn open their markets to the services and capital of developed economies and offer better protection for intellectual property. If such an agreement could be negotiated, the World Bank forecast a $300 billion annual boost to global income.

As many predicted, once American and European Union negotiators reached their own private agreement on trade reform in Brussels on December 15, 1993, the GATT of April 13, 1994, was made possible. The final agreement signed in Marrakesh was voluminous, calling for a new World Trade Organization to settle trade disputes as well as tougher anti-dumping rules and sanctions. Four new areas were covered under GATT for the first time: agriculture, textiles, services, and intellectual property rights.

EFFECTS ON SMALL BUSINESSES

The main benefits of the 1994 GATT to the United States involved eliminating barriers to international trade, such as tariffs, quotas, import-licensing rules, and customs regulations. In general, since U.S. trade barriers tended to be lower than those of its major trading partners, American companies of all sizes seemed likely to become more competitive in the global marketplace as a result of the GATT. The agreement's reduction of tariffs in all countries by an average of one-third, for example, would reduce the cost of goods for small businesses dependent on im-

ports. It would also reduce the costs of American-made goods for overseas consumers, which could increase sales not only for major exporters but also for their smaller suppliers. Overall, Faulhaber noted, analysts predicted that the pact would increase in U.S. income by $100 billion within a decade.

FURTHER READING:

Faulhaber, Thomas A. "WTO and the Smaller Business." *Business Forum Online.* July 1997.

SEE ALSO: International Law; Tariffs

GOOD HOUSEKEEPING SEAL

The Good Housekeeping Seal is the symbol of the Good Housekeeping Consumers' Policy, a legal warranty that provides for a replacement or refund of purchase price for products that prove defective within two years of sale. Excluding some products and services, the warranty covers items bearing the seal or those advertised within the pages of *Good Housekeeping* magazine. The expense of refund or replacement is assumed by *Good Housekeeping,* rather than the manufacturer, and the warranty is extended to original purchasers as well as consumers given the product by the buyer.

HISTORY OF THE SEAL

Good Housekeeping published its first issue in 1885, and in 1900 established a private laboratory, the Good Housekeeping Institute, for the purpose of product evaluation. Located in the Hearst Magazines Building in New York City, the Institute reviews all products submitted for advertisement in *Good Housekeeping* magazine, with departments devoted to beauty products, chemistry, engineering, food, food appliances, home care, nutrition, and textiles. The Institute began granting the seal in 1909, originally offering the refund-or-replace warranty for a one-year period (coverage was extended to two years in 1997, coinciding with a graphic redesign of the seal itself).

A list of *Good Housekeeping*'s recognized advertisers illustrates that seal-bearing products run the gamut of consumer goods, including water filters, vitamin supplements, shampoos and other hair care products, laundry detergents, various foods, vinyl siding, and toys.

With a continuous run of more than seventy years, Jolly Time Popcorn has displayed the seal the longest. The lengthy, broad presence the seal maintains allows *Good Housekeeping* to point to research giving the symbol a 92 percent familiarity rate among American women.

OBTAINING THE SEAL

To have a product evaluated by the Institute a minimum of one full-page advertisement in *Good Housekeeping* magazine must be purchased. The cost of making such a purchase was estimated at $160,000 in 1997. Products meeting the standards of the Institute are then accepted for advertisement, with a one-year renewable seal license agreement being issued at no additional charge. Advertisers can display the seal on product packaging and in advertising elsewhere under conditions set forth in the agreement.

PRODUCTS/SERVICES INELIGIBLE FOR THE SEAL

According to the Consumers' Policy appearing in every issue of *Good Housekeeping,* the warranty the seal represents is not extended to ''insurance; realty (including housing of any kind); automotive and camping vehicles; public transportation; travel facilities; catalogs and merchandise portfolios; ''Shopping by Mail'' items; premiums; schools, hotels, summer camps, and similar organizations; prescription drugs; and institutional advertisements.'' Additionally, the warranty does not cover eligible products that have been abused or improperly installed or serviced.

BENEFITS OF THE SEAL

The foremost benefit to advertisers granted the use of the seal is the warranty it represents, specifically the monetary liability assumed by *Good Housekeeping.* While the magazine does not disclose an annual amount spent on fulfilling the warranty, it does report receiving several hundred consumer complaints each year. Indeed, the magazine admits to have refunded $70,000 to consumers in the mid-1980s for one product alone, a faulty waterbed heater.

Less tangible an advantage is consumer perception of the seal and, by association, the products deemed worthy to bear it. The Good Housekeeping Seal has long been one of the most recognizable symbols in American commerce. However, market researchers point out that familiarity can lead to a lack of meaning, especially in a time of less reliance on brand name products. As Paul Lukas observed in *Fortune* magazine, ''In an era when shopping habits are changing and most manufacturers and retailers already stand behind their products, the seal's value to today's consumers appears to be waning, which probably explains why *Good Housekeeping* is spending $2.9 million on its marketing campaign for the new seal [design].''

DISADVANTAGE OF THE SEAL

Clearly, the drawback to the seal is the associated advertising cost required in obtaining it. While *Good Housekeeping* correctly asserts that use of the seal is not available for purchase, the full-page ad requirement for testing by the Institute likely keeps the icon out of reach for many small business owners.

FURTHER READING:

Gall, Timothy L., and Susan B. Gall. *Consumers' Guide to Product Grades and Terms.* Detroit, MI: Gale Research, 1993.

Lukas, Paul. ''In Which We Bash a Baby Seal.'' *Fortune.* September 8, 1997.

Wollenberg, Skip. ''Good Housekeeping Extends Warranty on Products.'' *Detroit News.* July 31, 1997.

SEE ALSO: Warranties and Guarantees

GOODWILL

Goodwill is a type of intangible business asset. It is defined as the difference between the fair market value of a company's assets (less its liabilities) and the market price or asking price for the overall company. In other words, goodwill is the amount in excess of the company's book value that a purchaser would be willing to pay to acquire it. ''For example, a happy combination of advertising, research, management talent, and timing may give a particular company a dominant market position for which another company is willing to pay dearly,'' Charles T. Horngren and Gary L. Sundem explained in their book *Introduction to Financial Accounting.* ''This ability to command a premium price for the total business is goodwill.''

The sale of a business may involve a number of intangible assets. Some of these may be specifically identifiable intangibles—such as **trademarks**, patents, **copyrights**, licensing agreements—that can be assigned a value. The remaining intangibles—which may include the business's reputation, brand names, customer lists, unique market position, well-trained work force, good location, and special skills or operating methods—are usually lumped into the category of goodwill. Although these factors that contribute to goodwill do not necessarily have an assignable value, they nonetheless add to the overall value of the business by convincing the purchaser that the company will be able to generate abnormally high future earnings.

Although goodwill undoubtedly has value, it is still an intangible asset and as such is not recorded on a company's books. In fact, many companies use a value of one dollar for goodwill in their everyday accounting procedures. ''There are many owners who could obtain a premium price for their companies. *But such goodwill is never recorded,''* Horngren and Sundem wrote. "Only the goodwill arising from an *actual acquisition* with arm's-length bargaining is shown as an asset on the purchaser's records." The acquisition price determines the amount of goodwill that is recorded following the purchase of a company. For example, if a small business with assets of $40,000 is purchased for $50,000, then the purchaser records $10,000 of goodwill.

In general, determining the sales price of a business begins with an assessment of its equity, which includes tangible assets such as real estate, equipment, inventory, and supplies. Then an additional amount is added on for intangible assets (sometimes called a "blue sky" amount), which may include things like patent rights, a trade name, a noncompete clause, and goodwill. Experts note that in small business sales, the combined total of "blue sky" additions should rarely be more than a year's net income, because few purchasers are willing to work longer than that for free. For public companies, the amount of goodwill is often dependent on the vagaries of the stock market. Since the share price determines the purchase price, the value attributed to goodwill may fluctuate wildly during the course of an acquisition.

Standard accounting procedures state that, following an acquisition, the purchaser should amortize goodwill over a period of 15 years using the straight-line method. In other words, 1/15 of the original amount attributed to goodwill is deducted each year. Since this writeoff period is longer than that required for most tangible assets, it is usually a good idea to allocate as much of the purchase price as possible to business equipment. The shorter **depreciation** period would enable the purchaser to accelerate deductions and thus achieve earlier tax savings.

Over the years, there has been some dissatisfaction expressed with the way that goodwill is handled for **accounting** purposes. First, since goodwill is sometimes a huge component of a company's acquisition price (particularly in the case of large public companies), the amortization of goodwill can have a significant negative effect on the purchaser's **net income**. Second, the treatment of goodwill under U.S. law differs from many other countries, which sometimes puts American companies at a disadvantage in international **mergers and acquisitions**.

FURTHER READING:

Davis, Michael. "Goodwill Accounting: Time for an Overhaul." *Journal of Accountancy.* June 1992.

"The Goodwill of a Business: Valuing, Buying, and Selling." *The Business Owner.* March-April 1992.

Horngren, Charles T., and Gary L. Sundem. *Introduction to Financial Accounting.* 4th ed. Englewood Cliffs, NJ: Prentice Hall, 1990.

SEE ALSO: Buying an Existing Business; Selling a Business

GOVERNMENT PROCUREMENT

Many small businesses maintain and increase their operations through reliance on local, state, and federal government contracts. While these businesses may also secure business through the offering of competitive bids on jobs offered by the private sector, small business owners should be aware of the differences in procuring work from the public and private sectors. The most fundamental difference between the procurement process in the public and private sectors concerns the process itself. Some private companies may have fairly streamlined processes for awarding contracts to outside bidders—or may not even bother with **competitive bidding** at all, if they are comfortable with a certain contractor. Governments at the local, state, and federal level are all obligated to adhere to a significant body of law designed to ensure that: 1) taxpayer money is spent wisely; 2) contracts are not awarded for less-than-legitimate reasons; and 3) all businesses are provided with a fair opportunity to make their case for the contract in question. "Government buyers are expected to spend money wisely—in the public interest—so their purchases are usually subject to much public review," explained E. Jerome McCarthy and William D. Perreault Jr. in *Basic Marketing.* "To avoid charges of favoritism, most government customers buy by specification using a mandatory bidding procedure. Often the government buyer is required to accept the lowest bid that meets the specifications."

Submitting bids for public contracts can be a frustrating experience for businesses. The process of awarding contracts—at the local, state, or national levels—can be a cumbersome one that is still heavy on bureaucracy, despite recent streamlining. In addition, government contracts are far more exposed to public scrutiny than are private ones, although business consultants hasten to add that quality work on a contract that is fairly obtained will almost certainly not arouse any interest from outsiders. But business analysts and government procurement officers agree that the potential benefits of securing public contracts far outweigh the disadvantages. After all, local, state, and federal government offices and agencies comprise the single biggest customer block in the nation. Most small business owners recognize that government procurement is a potentially lucrative avenue to long-term organizational growth and success.

Government agencies and legislators recognize this reality as well. In recognition of the importance of federal contracts to many small business establishments, U.S. legislation requires that a certain percentage of its contracts go to companies that qualify as small businesses. These goals, which are arrived at through the combined input of the **U.S. Small Business Administration (SBA)** and individual agencies, classify bidding companies not only by their size, but also by other classifications (such as minority-owned businesses) and government purchasing agents work to fill these slots as well. In fact, some contracts are specifically set-aside for the ''exclusive participation'' of small businesses, minority- and women-owned enterprises, and businesses in high unemployment areas.

CHANGES IN GOVERNMENT PROCUREMENT RULES

The foundation of modern-day government contracting at the federal level is based on two laws—the Armed Services Procurement Act of 1947 and the Federal Property and Administrative Services Act of 1949. These laws sought to codify all the various contract laws that had sprouted up over the years and provide overarching guidelines on government procurement. The laws also resulted in the creation of two sets of regulations designed to oversee affairs in the realm of government contracts--Armed Services Procurement Regulation (ASPR) for military agencies and Federal Procurement Regulation (FPR) for civilian agencies. These voluminous guidelines, though, were rife with exceptions and alternate procurement procedures and in 1979, Congress passed the Office of Federal Procurement Policy Act Amendments. These pieces of legislation called on the federal government to develop a single set of simplified procurement regulations for all government agencies.

The result of that directive was the Federal Acquisition Regulation (FAR), which covered all federal agencies. The FAR, said Barry L. McVay, author of *Proposals That Win Federal Contracts,* ''changed no laws; it required government purchasing agents to follow the same procedures that were prescribed in the earlier regulations.'' But, he added, ''it was written in simpler language, arranged subject matter in a more logical sequence, and eliminated many of the contradictions and ambiguities that bedeviled everyone. . . . The FAR is the 'bible' for all who conduct business with the federal government. Government business is conducted in accordance with its rules, and contractors must comply with its procedures or risk being eliminated from consideration.'' That same year, Congress also passed the Competition in Contracting Act of 1984 (CICA), which opened up the doors to competitive bidding in numerous areas that had previously only allowed limited bidding practices.

Today, bidding for government contracts at all levels, but especially the state and federal levels, is intense. Many small businesses are in the thick of the battle, fighting for contracts that look to be within their financial and operational grasp. But making a bid on a government is a time-consuming process, and consultants often counsel small business enterprises to be selective in their bid choices, singling out those that they have the greatest likelihood of getting.

Federal procurement offices have recognized that the process takes a toll on small businesses as well. In 1995, Congress passed the Federal Acquisitions Reform Act, which arranged for a two-phase process of contract awarding in which the agency office selects a limited group of bidders based on their qualifications and general approach to the project, then examines detailed proposals from those ''short listed'' bidders, choosing the awardee on a ''best value'' basis. ''Best value calls for ranking proposals based on a weighted average of scores on all criteria stated in a solicitation,'' explained Markus. ''The agency may award the contract after this evaluation, or it may discuss proposals with those considered in the competitive range and then permit all short listed proposers to submit best and final offers.'' In the fall of 1997 the *Wall Street Journal* reported that government purchasing agents were pursuing new methodologies of whittling down the list of bidders earlier in the selection process, thus saving greater numbers of businesses additional time that could be spent pursuing other leads.

FAR UPDATES AND SUPPLEMENTS Small business owners currently engaged in soliciting government contracts—or weighing the possibility of doing so—should make sure that they obtain a copy of the Federal Acquisition Regulation. FAR is available through the Government Printing Office (GPO). In addition, business owners should be aware that the FAR is updated in two different ways. 1) Federal Acquisition Circulars (FACs) contain changes to the FAR as a result of federal legislation; these are easy to use, because they are distributed as replacement pages that can be instituted in place of outdated FAR regulations. 2) Each federal department also has its own materials that supplement—not supplant—FAR guidelines. These supplementary materials, which can be quite extensive, are also available through the GPO. ''Potential suppliers should focus on the government units they want to cater to and learn the bidding methods of those units,'' recommended McCarthy and Perreault. ''Then it is easier to stay informed since most government contracts are advertised.

COMMERCE BUSINESS DAILY The *Commerce Business Daily (CBD)* is the primary information source for businesses seeking federal contracts. It is through this publication that various government agencies notify the public sector of upcoming solicitations and decisions on contracts. The *Commerce Business Daily* is available through the GPO.

METHODS OF SOLICITATION

Small businesses hoping to secure a federal contract will turn to one of three methods of solicitation: **Request For Proposals (RFP)**, Invitation For Bid (IFB), or oral solicitation. RFPs are the most commonly utilized of these solicitation methods.

For smaller contracts, government purchasing agents typically use a simplified award system in order to minimize administrative costs. In such instances, a purchasing agent may simply call a few potential contractors from their bidders list and ask for a quote, awarding the contract to whoever comes in with the lowest responsible quote. ''Ninety-eight percent of all federal contractual action are made through simplified procedures,'' wrote McVay. ''While that may seem surprising, you must realize that these small purchases are the government's equivalent of buying a cup of coffee or a newspaper, something that is done routinely to meet recurring needs.''

Not surprisingly, awards for larger contracts—which can, after all, run into millions of dollars—are bestowed only after a more comprehensive process. When a government agency has a project for which it wishes to receive bids it may: 1) Ask for sealed bids through the use of an IFB, or 2) Negotiate with a bidder on specific terms of the agreement. This latter methodology is more frequently used.

KEYS TO SUCCESSFUL BIDS FOR GOVERNMENT CONTRACTS Business consultants, executives, managers, and purchasing officers alike note that there are several keys to successfully pursuing government contracts, no matter what their size or other characteristics. Writing in *Proposals That Win Federal Contracts,* McVay encapsulated several of the basics as follows:

1) Get Organized—Small business owners need to attend to a wide range of issues before delving into the world of government procurement. In addition to conducting basic research on the agencies and project areas in which you are interested, you also need to educate yourself on the nuances of bidding, the repercussions of a successful bid on company operations (workforce allocation, needed facility upgrades, etc.), and a host of other factors.

2) Gather Intelligence—McVay recommended to ''identify the contracting activities most likely to provide contracting opportunities.'' He cited individual purchasing agents as among the most valuable of contacts in this area.

3) Obtain RFPs—Small business owners should stay alert to RFPs that match their desires. Ensuring that your business is placed on the bidders list—which can be accomplished through skillful activity during the intelligence-gathering phase—is only half the battle; you should also faithfully check *CBD* and other sources to make sure that possible projects do not pass by you unnoticed.

4) Select Projects for Proposals—Small business owners should consider many factors when weighing whether to put in a bid on a project, such as current workload, delivery schedule, and expectations of the agency.

5) Decide How to Fill Contractual Requirements—McVay advised businesses to ''decide on the approach that best suits your firm's strengths and solves the government's problem.''

6) Devise a Proposal—Businesses do not always allow for sufficient time to put together an adequately researched and detailed bid. Company leadership should make sure that adequate resources—both in terms of time and effort—are allocated for this purpose.

7) Submit the Proposal in Accordance with Guidelines—Government agencies take their deadlines seriously. If a bidder submits his or her proposal after the deadline, it will simply not be considered.

8) Negotiate from a Position of Knowledge—''Study your proposal and know what is in it,'' recommended McVay. ''If you find errors, be ready with the correct information. . . . Develop your minimum, maximum, and negotiation objectives. Establish the points you want to bring up during negotiations, those you want to avoid if possible, those you can concede, and those on which you must stand firm.'' He also counseled business representatives to keep a detailed accounts of all aspects of the negotiation session.

9) Prepare for the Award of the Project—McVay noted that businesses are sometimes subjected to pre-award surveys to determine their ability to fulfill all contract obligations; this is especially true if the government office has never worked with the bidder before. ''Should the contracting officer decide that your firm is nonresponsible and your firm is a small business, apply for a Certificate of Competency and remedy your shortcomings quickly,'' he said. ''If you win the contract, celebrate and then get to work. If you lose, ask the contracting officer for a debriefing and use the information to prepare a winning proposal next time.''

INCREASED POPULARITY OF LOW BID ALTERNATIVES

In recent years, various government offices at all levels have followed the federal government's lead and pursued "low bid" alternatives when awarding contracts to the private sector. In previous eras, cities, counties, states, and federal offices all generally awarded contracts to the lowest responsible bidder, reasoning that, as Edward Markus wrote in *American City and County,* it was "the best way to prevent favoritism, collusion, and other problems. While by no means a perfect system, until fairly recently it was deemed to be the best way to assure taxpayers that their money was being spent wisely."

Both contractors and purchasing agents have observed, however, that this dynamic has undergone considerable change, especially in such high-cost areas as public works projects (building and road construction, etc.). "In recent years," wrote Markus, "more and more localities have grown frustrated with this traditional approach to procurement. Some have found that completed projects were not fully responsive to their needs, while others found that their new facilities were difficult to operate and expensive to maintain. Some local agencies have had trouble controlling the escalating costs of public works projects, including change orders and claims, at a time when jurisdictions are trying to stabilize or reduce taxes."

As a result, agencies at local levels have increasingly followed the lead of federal offices, which have encouraged "best value" and "performance-based" considerations in awarding contracts to bidders. As mentioned above, "best value" calls for ranking various proposals on a whole range of criteria and selecting the winner based on all those factors, not just price. "Performance-based" contracting, on the other hand, is an arrangement wherein the contract defines the required performance standards for the project but, as Markus said, "does not dictate how the contractor should do the work." Several procurement policy-making agencies in the federal government, including the Office of Federal Procurement Policy, have touted performance-based contracting as superior to traditional low-bid contracting in every way, including cost, service, and delivery time.

BUSINESS REQUIREMENTS WHEN BIDDING ON GOVERNMENT CONTRACTS Part of the job of government purchasing agents is ensuring that businesses that are awarded contracts are capable of doing the job for which they are bidding. "The award of a contract based solely on the lowest evaluated price is false economy if the contractor defaults, delivers late, or performs in a manner that caused additional contractual or administrative costs for the government," said McVay. "Therefore, before award, a contractor must demonstrate its responsibility to the satisfaction of the contracting officer and, when necessary, the responsibility of its subcontractors."

According to McVay, a contractor will meet all requirements in the realm of competency if it:

- Has adequate financial resources to perform the contract

- Is able to comply with the required delivery or performance schedule

- Has an acceptable prior performance record

- Has a good reputation in the business community and with prior customers

- Is possessed of the necessary organizational and operational controls to execute the requirement of the contract

- Has, or is able to obtain, the necessary technical skills to complete the job

- Has, or is able to obtain, the necessary production, construction, and technical equipment and facilities

- Keeps an accounting system that is appropriate for the contract that is being bid on

- Is fully eligible to receive an award under all relevant laws and regulations.

Contractors are often asked for extensive information by government purchasing agents, and they should be prepared to hand it over and accommodate surveys and other information-gathering activities by the government office in question. Information that may be requested from the contractor includes financial data, personnel information, and reports on all aspects of production (from technical capability to quality assurance capability), but the agent may also contact suppliers, trade and business associations, customers, financial institutions, and contract administrators of previous government jobs that your company has completed.

FURTHER READING:

Ho, Rodney. "Federal Procurement Rule Changes Streamline Bidding Process." *Wall Street Journal.* October 14, 1997.

Markus, Edward. "Low Bid Alternatives Earning Respect." *American City and County.* August 1997.

McCarthy, E. Jerome, and William D. Perreault, Jr. *Basic Marketing: A Managerial Approach.* 10th ed. Homewood, IL: Irwin, 1990.

McKenzie, Richard B. "Bidding for Business." *Society.* March-April 1996.

McVay, Barry L. *Getting Starting In Federal Contracting: A Guide Through the Federal Procurement Maze.* Woodbridge, VA: Panoptic Enterprises, 1987.

McVay, Barry L. *Proposals That Win Federal Contracts: How to Plan, Price, Write, and Negotiate to Get Your Fair Share of*

Government Business. Woodbridge, VA: Panoptic Enterprises, 1989.

Roberts, Kenneth, and Nancy Smith. "Design-Build Contracts Under State and Local Procurement Laws." *Public Contract Law Journal.* Summer 1996.

GREEN MARKETING

Environmentally-responsible or "green" marketing is a business practice that takes into account consumer concerns about promoting preservation and conservation of the natural environment. Green marketing campaigns highlight the superior environmental protection characteristics of a company's products and services, whether those benefits take the form of reduced waste in packaging, increased energy efficiency in product use, or decreased release of toxic emissions and other pollutants in production. As the *Encyclopedia of the Environment* noted, marketers have responded to growing consumer demand for environment-friendly products in several ways: "by promoting the environmental attributes of their products; by introducing new products; and by redesigning existing products—all components of environmental marketing." Indeed, marketing campaigns touting the environmental ethics of companies and the environmental advantages of their products have proliferated in recent years. The **Environmental Protection Agency (EPA)**, for example, recently reported that the percentage of new grocery store products marketed in America with environmental claims in their advertising or on their packages rose from 5.9% in 1989 to 11.4% in the first half of 1992.

Most observers agree that while some businesses engage in green marketing solely because such an emphasis will enable them to make a profit, other businesses conduct their operations in an environmentally-sensitive fashion because their owners and managers feel a responsibility to preserve the integrity of the natural environment even as they satisfy consumer needs and desires. Indeed, true green marketing emphasizes environmental stewardship. Writing in *Marketing Education Review,* Alma T. Mintu and Hector R. Lozada defined green marketing as "the application of marketing tools to facilitate exchanges that satisfy organizational and individual goals in such a way that the preservation, protection and conservation of the physical environment is upheld." *Environmental Marketing* author Walter Coddington, meanwhile, defined environmental marketing as "marketing activities that recognize environmental stewardship as a business development responsibility and business growth responsibility." Another analyst of green marketing, *Greener Marketing* editor Martin Charter, de-

fined the practice as "a holistic and responsible strategic management process that identifies, anticipates, satisfies and fulfills stakeholder needs for a reasonable reward that does not adversely affect human or natural environmental well-being." Such interpretations expand on the traditional understanding of business's responsibilities and goals.

REACTIONS TO "GREEN CONSUMERISM"

A number of factors have caused business firms in some industries to behave more responsibly towards the natural environment. The principal factor, of course, is the growing public awareness of the environmental degradation that has resulted as a consequence of the growth in population and natural resource consumption throughout the world during the last 50 years. The issue is particularly relevant in America, which accounts for fully one quarter of world consumption despite having only a small fraction of the world's population. This growing public awareness of environmental issues has brought with it a corresponding change in the buying decisions of large numbers of consumers. As the *Encyclopedia of the Environment* observed, "many consumers, and not just the most environmentally conscious, are seeking ways to lessen the environmental impacts of their personal buying decisions through the purchase and use of products and services perceived to be environmentally preferable."

Businesses took heed of this growth in "green consumerism," and new marketing campaigns were devised to reflect this new strain of thought among consumers. Companies with product lines that were created in an environmentally friendly fashion (i.e., with recycled products, comparatively low pollutant emissions, and so on) quickly learned to shape their marketing message to highlight such efforts and to reach those customers most likely to appreciate those efforts (an advertisement highlighting a company's recycling efforts, for instance, is more likely to appear in an outdoor/nature magazine than a general interest periodical). Ironically, studies have shown that the most environmentally aware consumers are also the ones most likely to view green claims of companies with skepticism. As George M. Zinkhan and Les Carlson wrote in the *Journal of Advertising,* "green consumers are the very segment most likely to distrust advertisers and are quite likely to pursue behaviors and activities that confound business people." Corporate reputation, then, has emerged as a tremendously important factor in reaching and keeping these consumers. A company that touts its sponsorship of an outdoor-oriented event or utilizes nature scenery in its advertising, but also engages in practices harmful to the environment, is unlikely to gain a significant portion of the green consumer market. (Of course, such tactics are sometimes effective in reaching less informed sectors of the marketplace.)

By the 1990s it was clear that environmental or green marketing differed from other forms of advertising in some fairly fundamental ways. The *Encyclopedia of the Environment* summarized the most striking differences effectively: "First, unlike, price, quality, and other features, the environmental impacts of a product are not always apparent and may not affect the purchaser directly. Thus environmental claims are often more abstract and offer consumers the opportunity to act on their environmental concerns. Second, unlike most advertised product attributes, environmental claims may apply to the full product life cycle, from raw material extraction to ultimate product disposal, reuse, or recycling [see the discussion of life cycle analysis below]. Third, and most important, environmental marketing provides an incentive for manufacturers to achieve significant environmental improvements, such as toxics use reduction and recycling, by competing on the basis of minimizing environmental impacts of their products.''

GREEN PRODUCTS

In their book *The Green Consumer,* John Elkington, Julia Hailes, and John Makower discussed several characteristics that a product must have to be regarded as a "green" product. They contended that a green product should not:

- Endanger the health of people or animals;

- Damage the environment at any stage of its life, including manufacture, use, and disposal;

- Consume a disproportionate amount of energy and other resources during manufacture, use, or disposal;

- Cause unnecessary waste, either as a result of excessive packaging or a short useful life;

- Involve the unnecessary use of or cruelty to animals;

- Use materials derived from threatened species or environments.

J. Stephen Shi and Jane M. Kane, meanwhile, noted in *Business Horizons* that the consulting firm FIND/SVP also judged a product's friendliness to the environment by ultimately simple measurements: "FIND/SVP considers a product to be 'green' if it runs cleaner, works better, or saves money and energy through an efficiency. Businesses practice being green when they voluntarily recycle and attempt to reduce waste in their daily operations. Practicing green is inherently proactive; it means finding ways to reduce waste and otherwise be more environmentally responsible, before being forced to do so through govern-

ment regulations. Green promotion, however, requires businesses to be honest with consumers and not mislead them by overpromising.''

LIFE CYCLE ANALYSIS Most analysts agree that the "life" of the product and its parts is one of the most important components in determining whether a product is "green" or not. Most people think only of the process of creating a product when gauging whether a product is green, but it also includes a product's impact on the environment at several additional stages of its useful life. Life cycle analysis (LCA) and/or product line analysis (PLA) studies measure the cumulative environmental impact of products over their entire life cycle—from extraction of the resources used to create the product to all aspects of production (refining, manufacturing, and transportation) to its use and ultimate disposal. These studies are sometimes referred to as "cradle to grave" studies. Since such studies track resource use, energy requirements, and waste generation in order to provide comparative benchmarks, both manufacturers and consumers can select products involving the least impact upon the natural environment. Some detractors of LCA studies, though—while granting that they do provide useful information—contend that they are subjective in setting analysis boundaries, and that it's sometimes difficult to compare the ecological impact of disparate products.

GREEN PROMOTION

Perhaps no area of green marketing has received as much attention as promotion. In fact, green advertising claims grew so rapidly during the late 1980s that the **Federal Trade Commission** (FTC) issued guidelines to help reduce consumer confusion and prevent the false or misleading use of terms such as "recyclable," "degradable," and "environmentally friendly" in environmental advertising. Within this document, titled the *Guidelines for the Use of Environmental Marketing Claims,* the FTC offers four general guidelines for environmental claims:

- Qualifications and disclosures should be sufficiently clear and prominent to prevent deception.

- Environmental claims should make clear whether they apply to the product, the package, or a component of either. Claims need to be qualified with regard to minor, incidental components of the product or package.

- Environmental claims should not overstate the environmental attribute or benefit. Marketers should avoid implying a significant environmental benefit where the benefit is, in fact, negligible.

- A claim comparing the environmental attributes of one product with those of another product should make the basis for the comparison sufficiently clear and should be substantiated.

The FTC regulations, noted Shi and Kane, "apply to labeling, advertising, promotional materials, and other forms of marketing. All claims through words, symbols, emblems, logos, depictions, or product brand names are regulated whether they are made directly or implicitly. This includes any claims of environmental attributes in connection with the sale or marketing of a product or package sold for person, commercial, institutional, or industrial use. . . . When a business makes any environmental claim, it must be able to support that claim with reliable scientific evidence. A corporation trumpeting an environmental benefit that it is unable to substantiate is treading on thin ice and leaving itself open to substantial penalties of a legal suit is brought against the company."

In addition to delineating marketing claims that might be regarded as false or misleading, the FTC report also provided guidance to businesses on how to make specific claims about environmentally-friendly aspects of their operation, in part by clarifying the definitions of such commonly used terms as "recyclable," "biodegradable," and "compostable." These guidelines were issued not only to curb businesses engaged in misleading advertising practices, but also to clarify the regulatory environment for companies. Various entities, from states and cities to industry groups and standards-setting organizations, had developed their own definitions in the years prior to the publication of the FTC report precisely because of the dearth of federal guidelines. "As a consequence," said the *Encyclopedia of the Environment,* "marketers faced a patchwork and sometimes costly marketplace where relabeling, legal actions, and negative publicity can create additional costs, can cause market share losses, and may deter some from making credible claims altogether."

ECO-SPONSORING

One avenue commonly used by companies to promote their ecological concerns (or polish their reputations as good corporate citizens) is to affiliate themselves with groups or projects engaged in environmental improvements. In eco-sponsoring's simplest form, firms contribute funds directly to an environmental organization to further the organization's objectives. Another approach is to "adopt" a particular environmental cause (community recycling programs are popular), thus demonstrating the company's interest in supporting environmental protection efforts. Sponsorships of educational programs, wildlife refuges, and park or nature area clean-up efforts also communicate concern for environmental issues. Environmental organizations charge, however, that some businesses use eco-sponsorships to hide fundamentally rapacious attitudes toward the environment.

ECO-LABELING

Another vehicle that has been used with increasing frequency in recent years to convey environmental information to consumers is "eco-labeling." Eco-labeling programs are typically voluntary, third-party expert assessments of the environmental impacts of products. "By performing a thorough evaluation of a product, but awarding only a simple logo on packages, ecolabels offer consumers clear guidance based on expert information," claimed the *Encyclopedia of the Environment,* which noted that government-sponsored ecolabeling programs have been launched with great success in many areas of the world, including Europe, Canada, and Japan. Indeed, those programs, which provide consumers with easily understandable information on the most environmentally sensitive of products and services in various market areas, can be a potent factor in guiding the purchasing decisions of consumers. Recognition may be given for several different reasons. For instance, a product may have particularly low pollutant or noise emissions, give off less waste material in its production, or be more recyclable than competing products.

In the United States, two private firms, Scientific Certification Systems and Green Seal, have developed guidelines to identify environmentally preferable products. Scientific Certification Systems, a private testing concern, awards a "Green Cross" for products meeting very specific criteria in areas like recycled content percentage, presence of pesticide residues, etc. Green Seal, a nonprofit organization, is engaged in a more ambitious effort; it uses life cycle analysis to identify a product's impact on the environment at all stages of its life.

Eco-labeling programs increase awareness of environmental issues, set high standards for firms to work towards, and help reduce consumer uncertainty regarding a product's environmental benefits. Thus far, however, the U.S. government has resisted instituting an officially-sanctioned eco-labeling program.

FURTHER READING:

Charter, Martin. "Greener Marketing Strategy." *Greener Marketing.* Greenleaf Publishing, 1992.

Coddington, Walter. *Environmental Marketing.* New York: McGraw-Hill, 1993.

Elkington, John, Julia Hailes, and Joel Makower. *The Green Consumer.* 1993.

Guidelines for the Use of Environmental Marketing Claims. Washington: Federal Trade Commission, 1995.

Mintu, Alma T., and Héctor R. Lozada. "Green Marketing Education: A Call For Action." *Marketing Education Review.* Fall 1993.

Ottman, Jacquelyn A. *Green Marketing.* Lincolnwood, IL: NTC Business Books, 1993.

Ottman, Jacquelyn A. "New and Improved Won't Do." *Marketing News.* January 30, 1995.

Rehak, Robert. *Greener Marketing and Advertising: Charting a Responsible Course.* Emmaus, PA: Rodale Press, 1993.

Shi, J. Stephen, and Jane M. Kane. "Green Issues." *Business Horizons.* January-February 1996.

Stoeckle, Andrew, et al. "Green Consumerism and Marketing." *Encyclopedia of the Environment,* Ruth A. Eblen and William R. Eblen, eds. Boston, MA: Houghton Mifflin, 1994.

Zinkhan, George M., and Les Carlson. "Green Advertising and the Reluctant Consumer." *Journal of Advertising.* Summer 1995.

SEE ALSO: Business Ethics; Corporate Sponsorship; Green Production; Product Life Cycle

GREEN PRODUCTION

Green production is a business **strategy** that seeks to secure profits through environmentally friendly operating processes. Proponents of this management philosophy contend that green production is a sensible course to follow not only because of the benefits that it bestows on the natural environment, but also because of its fundamental strategic soundness. As Stuart Hart, director of the University of Michigan's Corporate Environmental Management Program (CEMP), indicated in *Northwest Environmental Journal,* "green business strategies based on the principle of environmental sustainability may constitute a key basis for competitive advantage in the coming decades." Other business observers concur with this evaluation. Writing in *Business Horizons,* J. Stephen Shi and Jane M. Kane asserted that companies that take a proactive stance toward environmental improvements in production have a decided advantage over businesses that are indifferent to—or actively oppose—new standards: "First, they gain a 'greener' image in the public eye. Second, because adopting new standards takes time and money, they have more time to develop methods for reducing waste and can do so on their own schedule. Companies that wait until they are forced to change often find themselves in an expensive, last-minute scramble to meet the requirements. As a result, they end up throwing more money at the problem for a less effective solution than their more proactive counterparts."

SATISFYING THE GREEN CONSUMER

In 1992 the Roper Organization undertook a major poll on American attitudes toward business and the environment. Even accounting for the differences between consumer sentiment and consumer purchasing behavior that are a given in the United States, many business analysts found the poll results (and other, similar polling data) to be of considerable interest. Nearly three out of four Americans in the Roper poll said that business executives should be held personally liable in cases where their corporation causes damage to the environment, while a full 84% said that pollution and environmental damage were more serious business crimes than price fixing or insider trading. Another 78% indicated that they were willing to pay higher prices for goods sold in recyclable packaging. Supporters of green production methods have cited such statistics as hard evidence that companies that operate in a manner that is compatible with environmental protections can attract far more customers than the estimated 5–10% of consumers who make their purchasing decisions significantly/primarily on the basis of environmental concerns.

DEFINING AND INSTITUTING GREEN PRODUCTION PROCESSES

Many people think that green production simply entails instituting pollution controls or recycling programs when manufacturing goods. The reality, however, is that green production processes seek to minimize the impact of the manufacturing process on the environment at every stage. As Hart observed in *Northwest Environmental Journal,* "pollution prevention . . . can only deliver half the loaf: Green production also means that firms transform their input (raw material use) and output (product disposition) processes." George Zinkhan and Les Carlson agreed, stating in the *Journal of Advertising* that green consumers "are worried about more than just the purchase and the consumption processes. They are also concerned about the production process, in terms of scarce resources consumed." Taking all these factors into consideration, Hart and P. Shrivastava defined green production as follows in a study titled "Greening Organizations": "Green production focuses upon three fundamental goals: 1) minimize emissions, effluents, and accidents; 2) minimize the use of virgin materials and non-renewable forms of energy; and 3) minimize the life-cycle cost (cradle to grave) of products or services."

"GREEN" USE OF RAW MATERIALS "Growing concerns over depletion of forests and other natural resources, and environmental degradation created by mining and fossil fuel production," remarked Hart, "suggest that corporations may need to rethink their raw material and procurement strategies." Significant sectors of the business community—especially large corporations engaged in the lumber and energy industries—continue to take issue with such sentiments, arguing instead that resources remain plentiful. But many other businesses, citing the findings of both the scientific and environmental communities (or the internal data of their marketing arms), have begun to make changes in the ways that they gather raw materials for their products. Reliance on recyclable or renewable materials, new energy and material conservation initiatives, and "replenishment" programs (such as forest replanting programs) have all been touted as effective tools in establishing processes that do not unduly harm the environment.

GREEN MANUFACTURING/PRODUCTION PROCESSES

Information from industry studies and consumer research is being used to develop new products and to redesign existing products and services in order to reduce their impact on the environment. In its book *Green Products by Design,* the U.S. Office of Technology Assessment (OTA) advocated green design as a thoroughly viable goal. The OTA called it "a design process in which environmental attributes are treated as design objectives, rather than as constraints. . . . green design incorporates environmental objectives with minimum loss to product performance, useful life or functionality." In fact, supporters of green production assert that it makes financial sense for businesses of all sizes and shapes to undertake the process of green design. "Wasteful and polluting throughput processes lead to inefficient use of material and human resources as well as occupational and public health risks," wrote Hart in *Northwest Environmental Journal.* "Just as the 'zero-defects' goal in quality control demands preventative action and continuous improvement at every production step, a 'zero-waste' goal can focus efforts toward the virtual elimination of pollution. This preventative approach has proven far more efficient than efforts aimed at controlling discharges at the 'end of the pipe.' Corporations are realizing that pollution prevention can be a cost saving activity (e.g. by lowering compliance, waste treatment, disposal, and raw material costs)." Subsequently, some businesses have increasingly steered their product and packaging designs to use less materials or to be easily disassembled so that high-value components can be recycled or refurbished more readily.

PACKAGING

According to J. Stephen Shi and Jane M. Kane, writing in *Business Horizons,* "packaging is perhaps the most noticeable step a company can take in going green. Examples of green **packaging** include the use of recycled content in packaging materials, source reduction, refill alternatives, and aerosol replacements." Shi and Kane go on, however, to caution businesses that all environmental claims must clearly state whether they pertain to the product or to its package. "If the particular environmental quality that is lauded applies only to a portion or component of the product or packaging, this fact must also be clearly indicated. For example, a manufacturer of aluminum foil displays a 'recyclable' claim on a box of aluminum foil with no qualifications. But if only the foil and not the box is recyclable, the claim is deceptive. The manufacturer must instead distinguish between the product and the packaging in claiming such recyclability. The exception to this rule is when only a minor, incidental component of the product or packaging is not recyclable."

THE "ENVIRONMENTALLY SUSTAINABLE" COMPANY

As Shrivastava and Hart remarked in "Greening Organizations," companies that wish to embrace green production philosophies and processes usually have to redesign significant aspects of the business, including its mission and vision, competitive strategies, core technological systems, performance measurement and reward systems, and organizational processes and culture. Of the above elements of a business, perhaps none is more important than "mission and vision," for all the other aspects of the organization are fundamentally shaped by those values. But while the process of establishing a green production company can be quite daunting, proponents argue that cost savings associated with pollution prevention efforts, coupled with marketplace benefits in the realms of reputation and consumer loyalty, can make the shift a beneficial one not only for the environment, but also for the company itself.

SMALL BUSINESS AND GREEN PRODUCTION

Although most media attention on green production has been directed at the efforts of big corporations, increasing numbers of small companies have successfully established ecologically sensitive business practices as well. Indeed, some small companies operate in regions or industries that are ideally suited to green production. Many companies that provide goods (equipment and clothing manufacturers) or services (retail stores, guiding services) to backpackers, anglers, mountain bikers, canoeists, and other aficionados of the outdoors are very careful to operate in environmentally friendly ways. Similarly, companies that operate in geographical regions that are very supportive of environmental protection may well publicize their use of green production methods and philosophies. The marketplace goodwill that can be realized in such situations should not be underestimated.

Small business consultants, meanwhile, counsel their clients to carefully research the obligations that a commitment to green production entails before making any decision. Smaller businesses sometimes have difficulty securing the necessary financing to switch physical operations to a green production mode. Moreover, jumps in other operating costs as a result of changes to green production methods sometimes result in higher prices for customers, and subsequent drops in sales. While larger companies can usually shrug off such ripple effects with ease, smaller businesses are often less able to do so. But consultants acknowledge that green production methods can boost business as well, increasing sales while decreasing production costs. Indeed, proponents argue that for many small businesses—and especially new ventures, which do not have previously established modes of operation—green production can be a rewarding business philosophy.

FURTHER READING:

Environmental Behavior, North America. The Roper Organization, 1992.

Green Products by Design: Choices for a Cleaner Environment. Washington: Office of Technology Assessment, 1992.

Hart, Stuart L. ''Commentary: Sustainable Strategy in a Greening World.'' *Advances in Strategic Management.* Vol. 9. 1993.

Hart, Stuart L. ''How Green Production Might Sustain the World.'' *Northwest Environmental Journal.* 1994.

Post, J., and B. Altman. ''Corporate Environmentalism: The Challenge of Organizational Learning.'' Paper presented at Academy of Management, Miami Beach, Florida, 1991.

Prahalad, C.K., and G. Hamel. ''The Core Competence of the Corporation.'' *Harvard Business Review.* May-June 1990.

Ruckelshaus, W. ''Toward a Sustainable World.'' *Scientific American.* September 1989.

Shi, J. Stephen, and Jane M. Kane. ''Green Issues.'' *Business Horizons.* January-February 1996.

Shrivastava, P., and Stuart Hart. ''Greening Organizations.'' *Academy of Management Best Paper Proceedings.* Vol. 52. 1992.

Zinkhan, George, and Les Carlson. ''Green Advertising and the Reluctant Consumer.'' *Journal of Advertising.* Summer 1995.

SEE ALSO: Business Ethics; Environmental Law and Business; Green Marketing

GROSS DOMESTIC PRODUCT

A country's gross domestic product (GDP) is a measure of the value of its production of goods and services for a specific period, usually one year. A country's GDP is similar to its gross national product (GNP), except that GDP excludes net income from foreign sources. Comparisons of GDP or GNP from year to year, when measured in constant dollars, indicate changes in a country's overall production and the direction of its economy. In general, economic policy makers look to the size and growth of the GNP or GDP as an indication of the well-being of a country's economy. The figures can also be used to make comparisons between the productivity of different countries.

As reported by the Bureau of Economic Analysis in *Survey of Current Business*, the United States's GDP is calculated as the sum of the four components of aggregate demand: consumption, investment, government purchases, and net exports. Personal consumption expenditures are broken out for durable goods, nondurable goods, and services. Gross private domestic investment includes fixed investment and changes in business inventories. Net exports include the value of all goods produced in the United States but sold abroad, minus the value of goods produced abroad and imported into the United States. Government purchases are reported for federal, state, and local governments. All government purchases are considered as final purchases for the purpose of calculating the GDP.

Once the GDP has been calculated, the Bureau of Economic Analysis obtains the nation's GNP by adding all receipts of factor income from the rest of the world and subtracting payments of factor income to the rest of the world. Factor income refers to income received by various factors involved in the production of goods and services, such as employees, business owners, and investors. Factor income from the rest of the world consists largely of receipts by American residents of interest, dividends, and reinvested earnings of foreign affiliates of American corporations. Payments of factor income to the rest of the world consist largely of payments to foreign residents of interest, dividends, and reinvested earnings of American affiliates of foreign corporations.

The difference between the United States's GNP and GDP is ordinarily relatively small. Whereas the GDP for 1996 was reported at $7,636.0 billion, for example, the GNP was $7,637.7 billion. In other words, net income from foreign sources was only $1.7 billion in a $7 trillion economy.

SEE ALSO: Gross National Product; Gross Product Originating

GROSS NATIONAL PRODUCT

A country's gross national product (GNP) is a measure of the value of its production of goods and services for a specific time period, usually one year. Comparisons of GNP from year to year, when measured in constant dollars, indicate changes in a country's overall production and the direction of its economy. In general, economic policy makers look to the size and growth of the GNP as an indication of the health of the country's economy.

GNP can be measured in at least two different ways, both of which yield the same result. One way of measuring the GNP is from the buyer's point-of-view, or in terms of aggregate demand. Also known as the expenditure approach to measuring GNP, this method calculates the value of the GNP as the sum of the four components of national expenditures: consumption, investment, government purchases, and net exports. The expenditure method accounts for the source of the monetary demand for products and services.

The largest component of expenditures, consumption, includes the value of all the goods and services purchased by consumers during the year. (As a general rule, consumption expenditures account for approximately 65 percent of GNP in the United States.) The investment category includes the production of buildings and equipment as well as the net accumulation of inventories. Financial investments, which involve only transfer payments rather than the production of capital goods, are not counted. Government purchases include only expenditures for goods and services, not transfer payments such as social security. Net exports include the value of all goods produced in the United States but sold abroad, minus the value of goods produced abroad and imported into the United States.

Since every transaction involves a buyer and a seller, the GNP can also be calculated from the seller's point-of-view, which focuses on where money payments go. The method, also known as the income approach, measures GNP as the sum of all the incomes received by all owners of resources used in production. Such income payments are known as factor payments, because they are paid to various factors involved in the production of goods and services. These include employee compensation, rental income, proprietary income, corporate profits, interest income, depreciation, and indirect business taxes.

Employee compensation includes all payments relating to labor, including fringe benefits and taxes paid on labor. In the United States, employee compensation accounts for approximately 60 percent of GNP. Rental income is paid for the use of capital goods. Proprietary income represents payments to owners of business firms. Corporate profits are earned by the shareholders of a business. Interest income is received for lending financial resources. **Depreciation** is a charge against assets used in production. Indirect business taxes refer to sales taxes, which represent part of the payments for goods and services that are not paid to any of the income recipients.

The measurement of GNP is fairly complex and follows a set of rules that, while generally agreed upon, may nevertheless appear somewhat arbitrary. For example, housing is treated in a manner that protects GNP calculations from changes in the rate of home ownership. All occupant-owned housing, as opposed to rental housing, is treated in the GNP accounts as if rented. Thus, the rental value of occupant-owned housing is included as a service in the GNP along with the rental value of houses that are actually rented.

GNP measures the value of final products and services, so it is necessary to avoid double-counting the many intermediary products that are bought and sold in the economy. Products and services are counted as part of the GNP when they reach their final form. But some important final products are actually excluded from the GNP. Many household activities are excluded, as are all illegal goods and services. In the case of housework, the services of a hired maid are considered part of the GNP, but not if the same services are performed by a member of the household. The exclusion of domestic chores has a greater effect on the calculation of the GNP of lesser-developed countries, where households may produce their own food and clothing to a greater extent than in the United States.

The treatment of government expenditures also affects GNP calculations. All government expenditures are considered final; there is no attempt to categorize them as intermediate and final. The effect of this rule is an upward bias in the GNP. In addition, all government expenditures are considered as current consumption rather than as investments; they are only measured once, in the year in which they occur. Finally, government goods and services, which are usually not sold in the marketplace, are valued at cost in the GNP.

In the United States the GNP is reported at an annual rate every quarter by the U.S. Department of Commerce's Bureau of Economic Analysis. That is, the quarterly figures represent what the GNP would have been for the year had the same rate of production continued for the entire year. GNP is usually reported in current dollars. To obtain a comparison with past GNPs, the real GNP is calculated in constant dollars using what is known as the GNP deflator. The difference between reported GNP and real GNP is due to price increases rather than increases in the production of goods and services.

FURTHER READING:

Carson, Carol. "The History of the United States National Income and Product Accounts: The Development of an Analytical Tool." *Review of Income and Wealth.* June 1975.

SEE ALSO: Gross Domestic Product; Gross Product Originating

GROSS PRODUCT ORIGINATING

Gross Product Originating (GPO)—also known as gross product by industry—is a numerical measure of the contribution made by each separate industry to an overall nation's **Gross Domestic Product (GDP)**. According to Robert E. Yuskavage in an article for the

Survey of Current Business, "An industry's GPO, often referred to as its 'value added,' is equal to its gross output (sales or receipts and other operating income, commodity taxes, and inventory change) minus its intermediate inputs (consumption of goods and services purchased from other industries or imported)." GPO statistics are released annually in the United States by the Bureau of Economic Analysis.

Given the definition of GPO, GDP could be said to be equal to the sum of GPO in all industries. But GDP is not typically measured this way in practice, because it leads to a slight statistical discrepancy. Instead, GDP is usually calculated as the sum of expenditures by all groups in the economy. This figure includes consumer spending and investment, government expenditures and investment, and net exports. A similar figure, Gross Domestic Income, is calculated as the sum of all costs incurred and profits earned in the production of goods in the economy. "Because the current-dollar GPO estimates are measured as the sum of distributions by industry of the components of gross domestic income, the sum of the current-dollar GPO estimates also differs from current-dollar GDP by the statistical discrepancy," Yuskavage explained.

In general, estimates of GPO are not considered to be as accurate as estimates of GDP. This is largely due to the fact that the underlying data for the former measure comes from private industries and must be adjusted to account for a variety of factors. "The amount of detailed expenditures data that are available for weighting the price indexes used in calculating GDP is greater than that for gross outputs and intermediate inputs used in calculating GPO, and little information is collected annually on the composition of inputs or of nonmanufacturing outputs," Yuskavage noted. "For some industries, no source data are available to measure gross output, and the resulting GPO estimates are prepared using less reliable methodologies." Still, GPO is an important measure for assessing the growth and vitality of various industries. GPO figures can be used to compare different industries to each other or to track developments in a single industry over time.

FURTHER READING:

Yuskavage, Robert E. "Gross Product Originating: Definition and Relationship to Gross Domestic Product." *Survey of Current Business.* August 1996.

GROUPTHINK

Groupthink occurs when the pressure to conform within a group interferes with that group's analysis of a problem and causes poor group **decision making**.

Individual creativity, uniqueness, and independent thinking are lost in the pursuit of group cohesiveness, as are the advantages that can sometimes be obtained by making a decision as a group—bringing different sources of ideas, knowledge, and experience together to solve a problem. Psychologist Irving Janis defines groupthink as: "a mode of thinking people engage in when they are deeply involved in a cohesive in-group, when the members' striving for unanimity override their motivation to realistically appraise alternative courses of action. Groupthink refers to a deterioration of mental efficiency, reality testing, and moral judgment that results from in-group pressures." It can also refer to the tendency of groups to agree with powerful, intimidating bosses.

The concept of groupthink provides a summary explanation of reasons groups sometimes make poor decisions. Indeed, groups are supposed to be better than individuals at making complex decisions, because, through the membership, a variety of differing perspectives are brought to bear. Group members not only serve to bring new ideas into the discussion but also act as error-correcting mechanisms. Groups also provide social support, which is especially critical for new ideas. But when new perspectives are rejected (as in the "not invented here" syndrome), it is hard to correct errors. And if the social support is geared toward supporting the group's "accepted wisdom," the elements that can make groups better decision makers than individuals become inverted, and instead make them worse. Just as groups can work to promote effective thinking/decision making, the same processes which enhance the group's operation can backfire and lead to disastrous results.

HOW GROUPTHINK WORKS

Janis identified seven points on how groupthink works. First, the group's discussions are limited to a few alternative courses of action (often only two), without a survey of the full range of alternatives. Second, the group does not survey the objectives to be fulfilled and the values implicated by the choice. Third, the group fails to reexamine the course of action initially preferred by the majority of members from the standpoint of the nonobvious risks and drawbacks that had not been considered when it was originally evaluated. Fourth, the members neglect courses of action initially evaluated as unsatisfactory—they spend little or no time discussing whether they have overlooked nonobvious gain. Fifth, the members make little or no attempt to obtain information from experts who can supply sound estimates of gains and losses to be expected from alternative courses of action. Sixth, selective bias is shown in the way the group reacts to factual information and relevant judgments from experts. Seventh, the members spend little time deliberating about how the chosen policy might be hindered by bureaucratic inertia or sabotaged by political opponents; consequently, they fail to work out contingency plans.

Three general problems seem to be at work: overestimation of group power and morality, closed mindedness, and pressures toward uniformity. Groupthink occurs when a group feels too good about itself. The group feels both invulnerable and optimistic. The group feels morally right. Linked to this attitude of perfection is a correlative close mindedness. Warnings are ignored. Messengers of difference are dismissed. Negative, stereotypical views of opponents are created and used. Finally, there is pressure for uniformity. A certain amount of self-censorship occurs. If individuals have questions, they keep them to themselves. This lack of dissent results in what Janis calls an "illusion of unanimity." If any difference does occur, group pressure is applied to bring the dissident into line. Janis also mentions "the emergence of self-appointed mindguards—members who protect the group from adverse information that might shatter their shared complacency."

If these precipitating problems support tendencies to groupthink, there are predisposing conditions as well. Janis suggests four conditions that predispose a group to groupthink: cohesiveness, group isolation/ insulation, leader intimidation, and an absence of decision-making procedures. As a group "hangs together" and members grow to like each other, there will be greater pressure not to introduce disturbing information and opinion that might tear at that cohesiveness. Maintaining the good feelings that come from such cohesion become part of the group's "hidden agenda." The insulation of the policy-making group is another factor. Frequently groupthinking groups are removed from interaction with others, perhaps because of their position within the organization. Lack of impartial leadership is a third contributing cause. When powerful leaders want to "get their way" they can overtly and covertly pressure the group into agreement. Finally, the lack of a template or protocol for decision making, or what Janis calls "norms requiring methodological procedures for dealing with decision making tasks," can also contribute to groupthink.

HOW TO AVOID GROUPTHINK

There are several things businesspeople can do to avoid groupthink: follow good meeting procedures, including the development of an agenda; aim for proper and balanced staff work; present competing views; and attend to correlative meeting problems, like exhaustion. A template for discussion might also be useful. One suggestion is to use an "options memo technique" in which information is presented as a problem statement, a list of options, and a preliminary recommendation. The group then looks at the preliminary recommendation with at least four questions in mind: 1) is the logic correct? (in selecting the preliminary recommendation from among the options); 2) is the judgment correct? (the logic may be fine, but the judgment may be poor); 3) are there any problems or errors remaining in the preliminary recommendation?; and 4) can the preliminary recommendation be improved? In order to prevent group isolation, it may be helpful to bring in new participants on a regular basis, use outside experts, and invite the group to meet off-site so that changes in settings and surroundings are a stimulant.

To avoid groupthink, it is vital for the group leader to become a statesperson or conductor instead of a partisan virtuoso. Leadership almost always involves getting work done through others. High-quality decisions are not made through intimidation, whether intentional or unintentional. Some bosses have no idea why people do not speak up, while the reason they do not is because they are likely to be attacked. Bosses encourage the best performance from groups when they can alert them to the kind of review that is expected. If the leader can be clear, and temperate, there is a great likelihood that norms of disagreement will develop.

Finally, there is the cohesion process itself. Decision making tears at the fabric of group cohesion, and it is the desire to preserve cohesion that is an underlying dynamic of groupthink. But if decisions lower group cohesion it is not necessary to avoid decisions; an alternative is to rebuild cohesion each time. One way to accomplish this rebuilding is to complete decision making by about 65 percent of the way through the meeting, then move on to brainstorming for the last 20–30 percent of the meeting. People who have differed before have a chance to continue to interact, now around less threatening, future-oriented items. This meeting technique allows for decompression, and for rebonding of the group.

Because of the flaws of individual decision making—selective perception, excessive self-interest, limited knowledge, limited time—most important decisions today are made in groups. And groups can do a spectacular job; but they often do not. Meetings, the place where groups do their decision-making work, have a bad reputation these days, largely because of processes such as groupthink. Groupthink is the result of flawed procedures, poor leadership, insulation, and an unmanaged desire for the maintenance of group cohesion and its good feelings. These factors can be addressed positively, and group decision making improved, while groupthink is kept to a minimum.

FURTHER READING:

"Creating a Team of Individuals." *Journal of Management Development.* September 1995.

Goodman, Paul S. *Designing Effective Work Groups*. San Francisco, CA: Jossey-Bass, 1986.

Janis, I. *Crucial Decisions*. Free Press, 1989.

Janis, I. *Groupthink: Psychological Studies of Policy Decisions and Fiascoes*. Boston, MA: Houghton Mifflin, 1983.

Janis, I., and L. Mann. *Decision Making: A Psychological Analysis of Conflict, Choice, and Commitment*. Free Press, 1977.

Neck, Christopher P., and Charles C. Manz. "From Groupthink to Teamthink: Toward the Creation of Effective Thought Patterns in Self-Managing Work Teams." *Human Relations*. August 1994.

Neck, Christopher P., and Gregory Moorhead. "Groupthink Remodeled: The Importance of Leadership, Time Pressure, and Methodical Decision-Making Procedures." *Human Relations*. May 1995.

Plous, Scott. *The Psychology of Judgment and Decision Making*. New York: McGraw Hill, 1993.

Tropman, John E. *Effective Meetings*. Thousand Oaks, CA: Sage Publications, 1995.

SEE ALSO: Brainstorming; Meetings

H

Health insurance continuation coverage is a benefit that employers may be required to provide to employees and their dependents who are no longer eligible for the company's health insurance program. Employees can lose eligibility for coverage by terminating their employment, reducing their working hours, becoming eligible for Medicare, or by a number of other ways. Under the terms of the Consolidated Omnibus Budget Reconciliation Act (COBRA) of 1985, all businesses that employ more than twenty people and offer a group health insurance plan must give employees the option of continuing coverage at their own expense for a limited period of time when they lose eligibility for company-provided benefits. In addition, forty-four states have their own laws regarding continuation coverage, some of which apply to smaller businesses and to benefits in addition to health insurance.

Health insurance continuation coverage laws affect small businesses in two ways. First, many entrepreneurs start their own businesses after leaving their jobs with larger companies. These entrepreneurs may wish to take advantage of continuation coverage for themselves and their dependents until they are able to arrange their own health insurance plans. Second, many small business owners must comply with COBRA or other applicable state laws and offer continuation coverage to their employees. Although workers must pay the actual cost of the insurance themselves, the administration of COBRA can be time-consuming and expensive for businesses. There are severe financial penalties for noncompliance, including a fine of $100 per day for

failure to notify an employee of his or her COBRA rights, or even the revocation of a company's tax deduction for its group health insurance plan. As a result, many companies outsource the activities associated with COBRA compliance to experienced independent administrators and management programs.

COBRA SPECIFICS

COBRA applies to nearly all businesses that have more than twenty employees and offer a group health care plan. The only exceptions are churches, church-related tax-exempt organizations, and some federal employees. Companies that are subject to COBRA are required to offer continuation coverage to all "qualified beneficiaries," a category which includes employees, spouses, dependents, and retirees who were covered under the company's group health insurance plan up until they lost eligibility for coverage through a "qualifying event." Companies are not required to offer COBRA benefits to those employees who were not eligible for or declined to participate in the group health plan, or who were eligible for Medicare benefits.

The qualifying events that activate COBRA provisions include a voluntary or involuntary termination of employment, a reduction in hours from full to part-time, a failure to return to work after taking family or medical leave, a call for active military duty, or the bankruptcy of the business. An employee's spouse or dependents can qualify for COBRA benefits—provided they were covered by the company's group health plan—upon the employee's death, the couple's separation or divorce, or a dependent's change in eligibility status (i.e., a child reaches an age at which he or she no longer qualifies for coverage under the employee's insurance). The company may deny

COBRA coverage to an employee who was involuntarily terminated from employment due to willful, job-related misconduct. But since these cases often end up in federal court, the company should weigh the expense of court costs against the expense of providing continuation coverage.

When a qualifying event occurs and COBRA is triggered, the company is required to offer a qualified beneficiary the option to continue coverage under all health care plans, medical spending accounts, dental, vision, and hearing plans, prescription drug programs, substance abuse plans, and mental health programs that are offered to regular employees. However, the company is not required to offer continuation coverage for **life insurance**, **disability insurance**, retirement plans, or vacation plans. Under normal circumstances, COBRA coverage lasts a maximum of eighteen months. This time limit is extended to twenty-nine months for dependents, or in cases where the employee becomes disabled. If the employee qualifies for COBRA for a reason other than termination of employment or reduction of hours, or experiences a second qualifying event during the regular COBRA coverage period, then the time limit may be extended to thirty-six months.

The employee pays 100 percent of the costs of health insurance coverage under COBRA, plus a 2 percent surcharge to help the employer cover administrative expenses. The employer is entitled to terminate coverage if payments are late, but must allow a thirty-day grace period. This time lag may pose a problem for some small businesses, since most insurance companies require payment for COBRA coverage in advance.

Another component of COBRA involves communication with affected employees. A company is required to explain the right to continue benefits to the each employee when they first join the company group health insurance plan, and again when a qualifying event occurs. When an employee qualifies for COBRA, the company has thirty days to notify the insurance company of that person's eligibility, and the insurance company then has fourteen days to provide the employee with information regarding the costs and benefits of their health care continuation coverage. The employee has sixty days to decide whether he or she wants to continue coverage. If so, the coverage is retroactive to the time of the qualifying event so that no lapses occur. Overall, compliance with COBRA and the various state laws governing health insurance continuation can be tricky and expensive. The U.S. Department of Labor and the U.S. Public Health Service offer free information on how the laws affect businesses.

FURTHER READING:

Anastasio, Susan. *Small Business Insurance and Risk Management Guide.* Washington: U.S. Small Business Administration, n.d.

Bury, Don. *The Buyer's Guide to Business Insurance.* Grants Pass, OR: Oasis Press, 1994.

Janecek, Lenore. *Health Insurance: A Guide for Artists, Consultants, Entrepreneurs, and Other Self-Employed.* New York: Allworth Press, 1993.

Lynn, Jacquelyn. ''A Quick Guide to Insurance.'' *Entrepreneur.* June 1997.

Williams, C. Arthur Jr., and Richard M. Heins. *Risk Management and Insurance.* New York: McGraw-Hill, 1989.

SEE ALSO: Health Insurance Options; Medicare and Medicaid

HEALTH INSURANCE OPTIONS

Health insurance is a contractual agreement between an individual or group and an insurance provider through which the insurance provider agrees to pay for some or all of the health care costs incurred by the person or group in exchange for their regular payment of a sum known as a premium. In this way, the insurance company assumes the financial risk of reimbursing health care costs, but it is able to offset that risk by collecting premiums from a large number of people, many of whom will have very low medical expenses. Traditionally, health insurance has been provided as an **employee benefit** by large companies, so many people have come to think of health insurance as part of an employment compensation package. But self-employed people and small business owners, lacking such coverage, must wade through the many available options to find plans that meet their own health insurance needs.

In recent years, many health insurance providers have begun offering affordable plans for small businesses, even those with fifteen or fewer employees. In some states, businesses are required to provide health insurance if they employ more than five workers. The type of coverage a business needs depends upon its work force. For example, a company with a work force consisting primarily of married people with dependent children will need more comprehensive coverage than a company with a mostly unmarried, childless work force. Many plans can be specifically tailored to the needs of a company's work force. For example, firms whose employees work at computers may wish to provide eye care as part of their health insurance plans, while other firms may find that employees would value a fitness program.

Many insurance companies offer computer models that enable small businesses to determine the most economical insurance plan given the previous year's health care expenses. Another option that can reduce premiums is pooling insurance with other small businesses through trade associations or other organizations. Experts note that business owners may find it helpful in comparing different plans to ask the providers for references to other small business clients. Even though health insurance coverage can be expensive for small businesses, plan costs are tax deductible. In addition, providing such benefits can help smaller companies compete with larger ones for talented employees and can act to reduce employee turnover. It is important to note that, under the terms of the Consolidated Omnibus Budget Reconciliation Act (COBRA), all businesses that employ more than twenty people and offer a group health insurance plan must give employees the option of continuing coverage at their own expense for a limited period of time when they lose eligibility for company-provided benefits.

Health insurance is also important for self-employed persons. Health care costs increase dramatically every year, and individuals need to protect themselves against the expense of an unforeseen illness, injury, or accident. But according to Lenore Janecek in her book *Health Insurance: A Guide for Artists, Consultants, Entrepreneurs, and Other Self-Employed,* between 27 and 37 million Americans have no health insurance, and another 60 million have inadequate coverage.

There are a variety of health insurance plans available from commercial insurance companies, hospital and medical service plan providers, and health maintenance organizations (HMOs). Coverage can generally be purchased on an individual or group basis. Group plans may be handled through an employer or through various organizations, including professional associations, colleges, labor unions, and health cooperatives. These plans usually have lower premiums than individual plans, cannot be canceled, and do not depend on the physical condition of individuals within the group. Most types of policies cover part of the costs of hospitalization, diseases and illnesses, surgery, and injuries from accidents, but the extent of coverage depends on the particular policy. Most policies do not cover cosmetic surgery, self-inflicted injuries, or preexisting conditions. Supplemental coverage is usually required to pay for eye and dental care, special hazards (such as football, skiing, hunting), rehabilitation services, and travel accidents. Some policies have a deductible that requires the insured to pay a certain amount out-of-pocket before benefits kick in, while others have a co-payment that requires the insured to pay a percentage of the costs after satisfying the deductible.

The most popular types of health insurance plans in the United States are: fee-for-service plans, which encompass traditional indemnity insurance; and prepaid plans, which include popular managed care options such as HMOs. Other possibilities include self-insurance, which basically involves a company or individual covering their own health care costs, and medical savings accounts (MSAs), which allow people to set aside money before taxes to be used for medical expenses. In addition, government-backed health care plans are available to federal employees, members of the military, veterans, the elderly, low-income families, Native Americans, and other societal groups.

As a result of the proliferation of health insurance options, deciding upon a plan can be a complicated process for a self-employed person or small business owner. Experts recommend that individuals and companies choose a plan that protects them against experiencing financial harm from an unexpected injury or illness, but is not prohibitively costly to maintain. In deciding on an appropriate amount of coverage, it is important to consider the amount of money available for emergencies, the unusual hazards that may exist, the family or work force health history, the extent of protection already available, and the level of health care costs in the community.

BACKGROUND

The first form of health insurance in the United States can be traced back to the 1800s, when merchant seamen could pay a modest premium and then obtain health care as they traveled from port to port. Private health insurance plans grew in popularity after World War II as a result of federal government initiatives. Health insurance premiums became tax deductible for employers and were not taxable to employees, which turned health insurance into a cost-effective form of compensation. Before long, health care benefits became a popular bargaining tool for labor unions seeking to improve their total pay package. As living standards increased throughout the world, people in industrialized nations began to view health insurance as a necessity.

During the 1960s, the health insurance industry in the United States grew tremendously in relation to other types of insurance. The main impetus for that growth was the advent of modified agreements, which shifted a greater amount of health care risk to the employers that offered insurance plans to their employees. Under these agreements, insurers, employees, and health care providers had little reason to control health care costs, because the employers, as policy holders, were paying the insurance bill. As a result, insurance company profits increased in proportion to the rise in the cost of medical care.

By the 1970s, American society began to address the dilemma of spiraling health care costs. The federal Health Maintenance Organization Act of 1973 stimulated the growth of the managed care industry by providing grants and loans that expanded existing plans and spawned new HMOs. Still, fewer than 3 percent of Americans enrolled in managed care plans during this time, and traditional fee-for-service plans remained the dominant health care option into the 1980s.

Eventually, changes in the American economy began to dictate a transformation of health insurance. As economic stagnation exerted downward pressure on company profits and a new corporate cost-consciousness developed, employers began to shift more of the insurance burden to their employees. Likewise, insurance companies were battling new economic and regulatory forces that contributed to a decline in profitability. This led the insurance companies to seek more cost-effective insurance instruments, particularly managed care.

Health care costs continued to spiral upward much faster than inflation throughout the 1980s and early 1990s. Between 1988 and 1993, aggregate U.S. health care expenditures rose 63 percent, to $889 billion. In the meantime, the average employee contribution to company-sponsored health insurance plans increased 50 percent, while the amount of services diminished and deductibles went up. Those trends resulted in fewer people having health insurance, and in a greater reliance on government-backed health care options. They also helped to open the door to managed care programs, which served nearly 30 percent of the population by 1992 and were rapidly gaining market share.

TYPES OF PLANS

The most common types of health insurance plans are prepaid (also known as managed care) and fee-for-service. Under traditional fee-for-service plans, the insurer pays the insured directly for any covered hospital or physician costs. Under a prepaid plan, insurance companies arrange to pay health care providers for any service for which an enrollee has coverage. The insurer effectively agrees to provide the insured with health care services, rather than reimbursement dollars. Prepaid plans offer the advantage of lower costs, which result from reduced administrative expenses and a greater emphasis on cost control. However, such plans also restrict enrollees' choices as to the doctors and hospitals from which they receive service.

FEE-FOR-SERVICE Fee-for-service health insurance plans waned in popularity during the late 1980s and 1990s. In fact, the percentage of insured Americans covered by such plans declined from 96 to 28 percent between 1984 and 1991, and was expected to reach 20 percent by 2000. The primary reason for this decline was that fee-for-service arrangements do not emphasize preventative care or containment of costs. Fee-for-service health insurance plans are available to both individuals and groups. By spreading the costs among a pool of enrollees, group health insurance offers benefits derived from economies of scale. Group insurance generally features lower premiums

and deductibles, more comprehensive coverage, and fewer restrictions than individual policies.

Most fee-for-service plans cover basic costs related to: hospitalization, including room and board, drugs, and emergency room care; professional care, such as physician visits; and surgery, including any procedures performed by surgeons, radiologists, or other specialists. Insured persons generally have their choice of hospitals and doctors. More inclusive health insurance plans are referred to as major medical insurance. Two types of major medical plans are: 1) supplemental, which provides higher dollar limits for coverage or covers miscellaneous services not encompassed in some basic plans, such as medical appliances and psychiatric care; and 2) comprehensive, which usually covers all costs included in basic and supplemental plans, and may also eliminate deductible and coinsurance requirements. Basic, supplemental, and comprehensive plans usually do not insure dental, vision, or hearing care.

Most health care options related to fee-for-service plans relate to different degrees of coverage. For instance, insureds may select a high deductible as a way of lowering the cost of the plan. Likewise, different levels of coinsurance are usually available. For example, the plan participant may agree to pay for 20 percent of all costs incurred after the deductible amount, up to a total of, say, $50,000 (for a total disbursement by the insured of $10,000). A more expensive plan may reduce the participant's share of those costs to 5 or 10 percent. The total limit on insurer payments can also be adjusted; an individual lifetime maximum of $1 million is not uncommon.

PREPAID PLANS The second major category of health insurance is prepaid, or managed care, plans. Managed care plans typically arrange to provide medical services for members in exchange for subscription fees paid to the plan sponsor. Members receive services from physicians or hospitals that also have a contract with the sponsor. Thus, managed care plan administrators act as middlemen by contracting with both health care providers and enrollees to deliver medical services. Subscribers benefit from reduced health care costs, and the health care providers profit from a guaranteed client base.

Although they serve the same basic function as traditional health insurance, managed care plans differ because the plan sponsors play a greater role in administering and managing the services that the health care providers furnish. For this reason, advocates of managed care believe that it provides a less expensive alternative to traditional insurance plans. For instance, plan sponsors can work with health care providers to increase outpatient care, reduce administrative costs, eliminate complicated claims forms and procedures, and minimize unnecessary tests.

Managed care sponsors accomplish these tasks by: reviewing each patient's needs before treatment, sometimes requiring a second opinion before allowing doctors to administer care; providing authorization before hospitalization; and administering prior approval of services performed by specialists. Critics of managed care claim that some techniques the sponsors use, such as giving bonuses to doctors for reducing hospitalization time, lead to undertreatment. Some plans also offer controversial bonuses to doctors for avoiding expensive tests and costly services performed by specialists.

Managed care plan sponsors also have more of an incentive to emphasize preventive maintenance procedures that help patients avoid serious future health problems and expenses. For instance, they typically provide physicals and checkups at little or no charge to their members, which helps them detect and prevent many long-term complications. Many plans offer cancer screenings, stress reduction classes, programs to help members stop smoking, and other services that save the sponsor money in the long run. Some plans also offer financial compensation to members who lose weight or achieve fitness goals. For example, one plan offers $175 to overweight members who lose 10 pounds and gives $100 to members who participate in a fitness program.

Another difference between traditional insurance and managed care is that members typically have less freedom to choose their health care providers and have less control over the quality and delivery of care in a managed system. Members of managed care plans usually must select a ''primary care physician'' from a list of doctors provided by the plan sponsor.

Managed care plans can take many forms. The most popular plans are **health maintenance organizations (HMOs) and preferred provider organizations (PPOs)**. Other services that mimic these two plans include point-of-service plans and competitive medical organizations. In addition to these established plans, many employers and organizations offer hybrid plans that combine various elements of fee-for-service and managed care options.

The most popular plan, the basic HMO, is the purest form of the managed care concept. HMOs are differentiated by four organizational models that define the relationship between plan sponsors, physicians, and subscribers. Under the first model, called individual practice associations (IPA), HMO sponsors contract with independent physicians who agree to deliver services to enrollees for a fee. Under this plan, the sponsor pays the provider on a per capita, or fee-for-service basis each time it treats a plan member. Under the second model, the group plan, HMOs contract with groups of physicians to deliver client services. The sponsor then compensates the medical group on a negotiated per capita rate. The physicians determine how they will compensate each member of their group.

A third model, the network model, is similar to the group model but the HMO contracts with various groups of physicians based on the specialty that a particular group of doctors practices. Enrollees then obtain their service from a network of providers based on their specialized needs. Under the fourth model, the staff arrangement, doctors are actually employed by the managed care plan sponsor. The HMO owns the facility and pays salaries to the doctors on its staff. This type of arrangement allows the greatest control over costs but also entails the highest start-up costs.

A PPO is a variation of the basic HMO. It combines features of both indemnity insurance and HMO plans. A PPO is typically organized by a large insurer or a group of doctors or hospitals. Under this arrangement, networks of health care providers contract with large organizations to offer their services at reduced rates. The major difference from the HMO is that PPO enrollees retain the option of seeking care outside of the network with a doctor or hospital of their choice. They are usually charged a penalty for doing so, however. Doctors and hospitals are drawn to PPOs because they provide prompt payment for services as well as access to a large client base.

OTHER OPTIONS Various other health insurance options exist for small businesses and self-employed individuals. One possibility is self-insurance, which requires a company to absorb most of the financial risk of its own health care coverage. An outside administrator may handle the paperwork, but the company pays its own claims. Self-insurance can provide a company with greater control over its health care costs and improved cash flow, but it can also be prohibitively expensive in cases of severe illness or injury. As a result, some companies choose to limit their liability by purchasing stop-loss insurance, which covers expenses after they reach a certain limit.

Another option is a medical savings account (MSA), which was approved by Congress for a four-year test in 1996. This option is available to self-employed persons or companies with fifty or fewer employees. It allows employees to fund special accounts with pre-tax dollars that can be used later to pay health care costs. Disbursements from the accounts are tax-free as long as they are used for approved medical expenses, and unused funds can earn interest and accumulate indefinitely. In most cases, the MSA option is coupled with a high-deductible insurance policy.

FURTHER READING:

Abromovitz, Les. *Family Insurance Handbook*. Tab Press, 1990.

Anastasio, Susan. *Small Business Insurance and Risk Management Guide*. Washington: U.S. Small Business Administration, n.d.

Blakely, Stephen. "Finding Coverage for Small Offices." *Nation's Business*. June 1997.

Bury, Don. *The Buyer's Guide to Business Insurance*. Grants Pass, OR: Oasis Press, 1994.

Janecek, Lenore. *Health Insurance: A Guide for Artists, Consultants, Entrepreneurs, and Other Self-Employed*. New York: Allworth Press, 1993.

Lynn, Jacquelyn. "A Quick Guide to Insurance." *Entrepreneur*. June 1997.

McIntyre, William Stokes. *101 Ways to Cut Your Business Insurance Costs without Sacrificing Protection*. McGraw-Hill, 1988.

Weiner, Edith. "The Changing Face of Health Care." *Best's Review*. January 1993.

Williams, Stephen J., and Sandra J. Guerra. *Health Care Services in the 1990s*. Westport, CT: Praeger, 1991.

Wolford, G. Rodney, Montague Brown, and Barbara P. McCool. "Getting to Go in Managed Care." *Health Care Management Review*. Winter 1993.

SEE ALSO: Business Insurance; Health Insurance Continuation Coverage

HEALTH MAINTENANCE ORGANIZATIONS AND PREFERRED PROVIDER ORGANIZATIONS

Health Maintenance Organizations (HMOs) and Preferred Provider Organizations (PPOs) administer the most common types of managed care health insurance plans. Managed care plans typically arrange to provide medical services for members in exchange for subscription fees paid to the plan sponsor—usually an HMO or PPO. Members receive services from a network of approved physicians or hospitals that also have a contract with the sponsor. Thus, managed care plan administrators act as middlemen by contracting with both health care providers and enrollees to deliver medical services. Subscribers benefit from reduced health care costs, and the health care providers profit from a guaranteed client base.

Managed care plans emerged during the 1990s as the main alternative to traditional, fee-for-service health insurance arrangements. In a fee-for-service arrangement, employees can go to the hospital or doctor of their choice. The plan reimburses costs at a set rate—for example, the insurance company might pay 80 percent and the company or individual enrollee might pay 20 percent—for all medically necessary services. Although they serve the same basic function as traditional health insurance plans, managed care plans differ because the plan sponsors play a greater role in administering and managing the services that the health care providers furnish. For this reason, advocates of managed care believe that it provides a less

expensive alternative to traditional insurance plans. For instance, plan sponsors can work with health care providers to increase outpatient care, reduce administrative costs, eliminate complicated claims forms and procedures, and minimize unnecessary tests.

Managed care sponsors accomplish these tasks by reviewing each patient's needs before treatment, requiring a second opinion before allowing doctors to administer care, providing authorization before hospitalization, and administering prior approval of services performed by specialists. Critics of managed care claim that some techniques the sponsors use—such as giving bonuses to doctors for reducing hospitalization time—lead to undertreatment. Some plans also offer controversial bonuses to doctors for avoiding expensive tests and costly services performed by specialists.

On the plus side, managed care plan sponsors also have more of an incentive to emphasize preventive maintenance procedures that can help patients avoid serious future health problems and expenses. For instance, they typically provide physicals and checkups at little or no charge to their members, which helps them detect and prevent many long-term complications. Many plans offer cancer screenings, pre-natal care, stress reduction classes, programs to help members stop smoking, and other services that save the sponsor money in the long run. Some plans also offer financial compensation to members who lose weight or achieve fitness goals.

Another difference between traditional health insurance and managed care plans is that members typically have less freedom to choose their health care providers and have less control over the quality and delivery of care in a managed system. Participants in managed care plans usually must select a "primary care physician" from a list of doctors provided by the plan sponsor. The sponsor pays the health care provider a predetermined price for each covered service. The individual participant may have to meet a deductible and make a small co-payment.

HMOS

HMOs provide a wide range of comprehensive health care services to their members in exchange for a fixed periodic payment. In most cases, participants must select a "primary care physician" from a list of approved providers which usually includes internists, pediatricians, and general practitioners. These doctors act as "gatekeepers" to coordinate all the basic health care needs for their patients. A patient with a knee injury, for example, would be required to see his or her primary care physician, who would then decide whether referral to a specialist for surgery or rehabilitation was warranted. In this way, the primary care physician helps eliminate unnecessary care that would cause an increase in plan costs. Another way in which HMOs seek to reduce costs is by providing care only within a restricted geographical area. Most HMOs provide local service and do not cover visits to doctors or hospitals outside the network except when the patient is traveling or has an emergency.

HMOs can be classified into four organizational models that define the relationship between plan sponsors, physicians, and subscribers. Under the first model, called individual practice associations (IPA), HMO sponsors contract with independent physicians who agree to deliver services to enrollees for a fee. Under this plan, the sponsor pays the provider on a per capita, or fee-for-service, basis each time it treats a plan member. Under the second model, the group plan, HMOs contract with groups of physicians to deliver client services. The sponsor then compensates the medical group on a negotiated per capita rate. The physicians determine how they will compensate each member of their group.

A third model, the network model, is similar to the group model but the HMO contracts with various groups of physicians based on the specialty that a particular group of doctors practices. Enrollees then obtain their service from a network of providers based on their specialized needs. Under the fourth model, the staff arrangement, doctors are actually employed by the managed care plan sponsor. The HMO owns the facility and pays salaries to the doctors on its staff. This type of arrangement allows the greatest control over costs but also entails the highest start-up costs.

For small businesses in the market for a health care plan, HMOs offer relatively low costs, broad coverage, and little administrative work. Many HMOs had begun establishing plans for smaller companies by the mid-1990s, although some of the larger HMOs still did not provide coverage for individuals. Experts recommend that small business owners check the financial security of an HMO before signing a contract, since many managed care providers went bankrupt in the early 1990s. In addition, employers should be aware of the possibility of facing increased liability by choosing an HMO plan for employees. Because such plans limit employees' freedom to select their own doctors and hospitals, the employer may be held liable when an employee is the victim of malpractice by a network health care provider.

Although employees have a reduced ability to choose their own doctors and limited out-of-area coverage with an HMO, they also benefit from low out-of-pocket costs, comprehensive services, preventative care, and no claim forms. In addition, there is no waiting period for coverage of preexisting conditions, and no maximum lifetime limits on benefits. Many HMOs also provide other services, like dental care and eye exams.

PPOS

A PPO is a variation of the basic HMO that combines features of traditional insurance with those of managed care. With a PPO, the plan sponsor negotiates discounts with participating doctors and hospitals, then pays them on a fee-for-service basis rather than prepaying. Patients are usually permitted to choose from a fairly extensive list of doctors and hospitals. The patient is required to pay a set amount per visit, and the insurer pays the rest. The amount of the co-payment depends on the type of plan—those with higher premiums usually feature lower out-of-pocket costs.

The major difference between PPOs and HMOs is that PPO enrollees retain the option of seeking care outside of the network with a doctor or hospital of their choice. They are usually charged a penalty for doing so, however, as the percentage of costs paid by the PPO is reduced. Doctors and hospitals are drawn to PPOs because they provide prompt payment for services as well as access to a large client base. There are still restrictions on patients that are intended to control the frequency and cost of health care services, but not as many as with a typical HMO. PPOs are a popular choice for sole proprietors or owners of very small companies, since they require employees to pay a larger percentage of their own health care costs. Most insurance agents and brokers can provide information on the various PPO plans available to small businesses.

FURTHER READING:

Health Insurance. Washington: Council of Better Business Bureaus, 1995.

Janecek, Lenore. *Health Insurance: A Guide for Artists, Consultants, Entrepreneurs, and Other Self-Employed.* New York: Allworth Press, 1993.

Lynn, Jacquelyn. ''A Quick Guide to Insurance.'' *Entrepreneur.* June 1997.

Weiner, Edith. ''The Changing Face of Health Care.'' *Best's Review.* January 1993.

White, Jane, and Bruce Pyenson. *Employee Benefits for Small Business.* Upper Saddle River, NJ: Prentice-Hall, 1991.

Williams, Stephen J., and Sandra J. Guerra. *Health Care Services in the 1990s.* Westport, CT: Praeger, 1991.

Wolford, G. Rodney, Montague Brown, and Barbara P. McCool. ''Getting to Go in Managed Care.'' *Health Care Management Review.* Winter 1993.

SEE ALSO: Business Insurance; Health Insurance Options

HIGH-TECH BUSINESS

High-technology businesses are those enterprises engaged in securing growth and revenue from industry sectors characterized by rapidly changing and advanced technology. In fact, advanced technology has come to be utilized in so many different industries that members of the business community now often regard it as its own unique industry subset, with applications across the spectrum of the world of commerce. Indeed, high-tech businesses are involved in industries as diverse as food exporting, retail product design, oil extraction, and a host of others.

Businesses immersed in the world of high technology range from huge corporations (Microsoft, Intel, and Nokia) to small enterprises of relatively short duration. The differences between these organizations are many, but it is perhaps more consequential that their leaders—whether the president of a multinational computer chip manufacturer or the owner of a ten-employee CAD/CAM outfit—share a recognition of the startling changes that technology advances are bringing to the global marketplace and the opportunities that such changes are creating. Those managers and business owners afflicted with what J. Wyman termed ''technological myopia'' in *Sloan Management Review,* on the other hand, are unlikely to establish a presence in high-tech business. According to Wyman, failure to adequately study the potential ramifications of technology can lead to two potentially harmful kinds of managerial myopia: internal myopia, in which the business fails to recognize technology's full power or uses it poorly; and external myopia, which is basically a fundamental ignorance of the implications of an emerging technology.

Successful high-tech firms, on the other hand, are adept at recognizing the possibilities associated with technological advancements, and nurture **corporate cultures** that enable them to seize on those opportunities.

CHANGE AND UNCERTAINTY IN THE GLOBAL MARKETPLACE Today's high-tech companies are operating in a business world that all observers agree is changing at a pace that often seems alternately exciting and unnerving. Economists, business executives, consultants, and entrepreneurs alike have debated fiercely about the ultimate character of these changes. Even *The Economist,* which offered a wary caution about the long-term character and direction of current economic patterns in late 1997, acknowledged that ''the belief that technology and globalization promise unbounded prosperity and render old economic rules redundant has infected American managers, investors, and politicians with remarkable speed. . . . Why has the belief in the New Economy spread so quickly? One reason is that some of its elements really do exist. Imports and exports do play a bigger role than they did a generation ago. Information technology is altering the nature of America's economic output, as well as the ways that companies operate.'' Indeed, it is this latter factor that is most often touted as the most dependable and signifi-

cant engine of economic growth in the United States and the world. After all, exciting new technologies have revolutionized huge areas of the business landscape, from manufacturing to communication to marketing, and they are less subject to the vagaries of international trade disputes, weather, and other factors that can impact exporting and importing. And Neil Gross and John Carey, writing in *Business Week,* pointed out two other important reasons why observers expect many high-tech businesses to continue to soar: 1) There is a relatively low cost associated with purchasing and implementing the necessary equipment and other infrastructure for high-tech ventures, at least when compared with many other industries; and 2) breakthrough technologies in such areas as computers and communication equipment can be rapidly designed into commodity products.

Moreover, researchers point out that unlike other growth sectors, high technology ventures are not limited to larger corporations. Indeed, small business enterprises have carved out an impressive niche in the industry, and they are expected to remain firmly entrenched in the world of high-tech for years to come (although many of the successful ones may no longer be small by that time) due to the sheer magnitude of demand for their services. ''Despite a long list of hurdles,'' wrote *Entrepreneur'* Heather Page, ''high-tech entrepreneurs can still look to the future with well-founded optimism. Thanks to a recent convergence of opportunities—namely changing market needs and the evolution of technologies to address them, ready access to capital, and a larger pool of talented technical personnel to hire or partner with—the odds have swung in favor of high-tech businesses in recent years.''

KEYS TO LAUNCHING AND MAINTAINING A SUCCESSFUL HIGH-TECH BUSINESS

In addition to adhering to common-sense entrepreneurial guidelines—don't spread your finances too thin, devise a sound marketing strategy, hire good employees, weigh the impact of your actions on your family, etc.—people hoping to start or add to a high-technology business should take into account the following key points, many of which concern taking advantage of available opportunities in such areas as education, training, and financing:

1) Keep up with industry changes—This can be a daunting task, but the entrepreneur who stays up to date on new technologies and innovations, new applications, and changing markets will be far better equipped to spot the gaps in products and services that still dot the high-tech landscape and fill that spot with their own company's offerings.

2) Make full use of technology transfer opportunities—In recent years, laboratories and research institutions operated by universities, government agencies, and corporations have all shown a much greater inclination to share their knowledge and technology with entrepreneurs and other business enterprises in commercial industries. "These types of programs are effectively placing technology in the hands of those most capable of turning it into viable ventures: entrepreneurs," claimed Page. "Moreover, not only is it now easier to identify which technologies can make the shift into the commercial sector, but more systems are being created to facilitate their transfer."

3) Use the Internet and other Information Technology (IT) markets to full advantage—Perhaps no segment of the U.S. (and international) economy has seen greater growth in opportunity than the IT sector, led by the continued robust growth of the Internet.

4) Reward employees—Workforce stability and reliability is an important factor in small business success for just about any entrepreneur, but its importance may be particularly pronounced in one of the fast-paced high-tech industries. Indeed, it is a far more serious matter to replace a software programmer three months before a new product launch than it is to replace a cashier or stockperson. For many small high-tech companies, workers are among their most valuable assets; the smart entrepreneur will compensate them accordingly, via salary, benefits, promotion, responsibility, or some combination thereof. Otherwise, they will likely find key personnel taking up residence with other high-tech businesses within a matter of months.

5) Empowerment—An issue closely related to the subject of **employee reward systems** is that of empowerment. High-tech companies that follow the so-called "Silicon Valley" model, which is characterized by fewer levels of management and higher degrees of employee empowerment—and hence, shorter product cycles—not only satisfy employee desires for advancement and autonomy, but also help companies keep pace with their competitors. In such environments, noted *Business Week*'s Ira Sager, risk-taking is embraced as a natural part of doing business and there is a genuine inclination not to penalize those who take a chance and fail. Small businesses, of course, often can not withstand failures to the same degree as their larger competitors, but the

basic message is clear: in the dynamic, ever-changing world of high technology, companies that succumb to micromanagement practices are likely to be left behind.

6) Admit mistakes—Given the rapid pace at which high-tech industries are changing, companies need to be aggressive in their implementation of new strategies and initiatives. Yet almost inevitably, a high-tech business will find itself pursuing a product or market that, for whatever reason, comes to look decidedly less appealing than it appeared when it was first targeted. The key to weathering such disappointments, say many analysts, lies not only in diligent research and detailed planning, but also in pulling the plug on plans that have gone sour rather than pouring additional money and resources into it while your competitors pursue more promising avenues. This uncertainty is perhaps most often seen in IT areas, where, as one entrepreneur told *Entrepreneur,* "nobody really knows where the Internet is going. Since there's no force pushing it in a particular direction, you may spend time working on a project and by the time you're done, the market has totally shifted in another direction."

7) Explore various funding options—High-technology companies in such areas as communications, networking, the Internet, and various other software applications have become major recipients of funding from venture capital companies, although some analysts contend that venture capital firms too often extend their cooperation only to larger firms. Another option for high-tech start-ups and small businesses, however, is one of the growing number of programs sponsored by federal, state, and regional agencies to help them secure risk capital and research and development funding.

8) Utilize education and training opportunities—Entrepreneurial programs have proliferated across the country in recent years, and many of these feature a heavy emphasis on technology.

The challenges facing entrepreneurs who decide to jump into the high-tech business fray are considerable, but so are the rewards, and most researchers believe that high technology will continue to be a major growth area both in the U.S. and around the world for years to come. "It's not really surprising so many small technology-based companies . . . are finding seemingly sudden success," stated Page. "On the contrary, myriad marketplace indicators point to the fact that all systems are go for today's start-up technology companies. An alignment of the entrepreneurial planets, if you will, is making the climate riper than ever for starting or growing a high-tech business.''

FURTHER READING:

Aronwitz, Stanley, and William DiFazio. ''High Technology and Work Tomorrow.'' *Annals of the American Academy of Political and Social Science.* March 1996.

Arthur, Brian. ''The New Rules of the Game.'' *U.S. News & World Report.* July 8, 1996.

''Assembling the New Economy: A New Economic Paradigm is Sweeping America; It Could Have Dangerous Consequences.'' *The Economist.* September 13, 1997.

Bateman, Thomas S., and Carl P. Zeithaml. *Management: Function and Strategy.* Homewood, IL: Irwin, 1990

Baum, Geoff. ''Bouncing Back: In High Tech, Failure is Rarely a Dead End; It's Just Another Opportunity.'' *Forbes,* June 2, 1997.

''Forecast: Long-Term Growth.'' *PC Magazine.* August 1997.

Gross, Neil, and John Carey. ''In the Digital Derby, There's No Inside Lane.'' *Business Week.* November 18, 1994.

Kirkpatrick, David. ''Riding the Real Trends in Technology.'' *Fortune.* February 19, 1996.

Olesen, Douglas E. ''The Top 10 Technologies for the Next 10 Years.'' *The Futurist.* September-October 1995.

Page, Heather. ''Power Play.'' *Entrepreneur.* June 1997.

Sager, Ira. ''Cloning the Best of the Valley.'' *Business Week.* August 18, 1997.

Schlender, Brent. ''Cool Companies.'' *Fortune.* July 7, 1997.

Wyman, J. ''Technological Myopia: The Need to Think Strategically about Technology.'' *Sloan Management Review.* Summer 1985.

SEE ALSO: Managing Organizational Change

HOME-BASED BUSINESS

A home-based business is any enterprise for which the principal administrative and managerial activities take place within an individual's personal residence. People start home-based business ventures for a wide variety of reasons. For example, some people are forced to leave the corporate world as a result of downsizing or early retirement, while others leave voluntarily out of a desire to be their own boss, to avoid the hassles associated with commuting, or to facilitate caring for children or elderly relatives. Whatever the reason, home-based businesses have become a significant trend in recent years. Once viewed as way for an unemployed person to make some money until a ''real'' job came along, home-based businesses are now taken much more seriously. Today, home-based businesses run the gamut from consulting firms and advertising agencies to photography studios and free-lance writing services. In fact,

such well-known companies as Amway, Ben and Jerry's, Domino's Pizza, Estee Lauder, Hallmark, and Nike all started as home-based businesses.

The main driving force behind the growth of home-based businesses is the increasing capability and availability of computer and communications technology. Powerful yet affordable home computer systems equipped with modems allow people to send and receive messages, transfer data, and conduct research from their homes, largely eliminating the need to commute to a place of employment. Similarly, sophisticated software programs offering applications in desktop publishing, database management, financial management, and word processing enable one individual to do the work formerly handled by an entire support staff. In addition, the widespread use of cellular phones, pagers, voice mail systems, and toll-free telephone numbers has enhanced the ability of home-based business owners to remain connected to the outside business world. In all, rapid improvements in technology have enabled large numbers of home-based business people to earn the same income they could at a regular jobs while also gaining a number of life-style benefits. Another important factor in the growth of home-based businesses is the transformation of the American economy from a product orientation to a service orientation. Since service businesses generally have no need to store inventory or run production machinery, they are less disruptive and more adaptable to a neighborhood environment.

As a result of these and other factors, an estimated 40 million Americans now work from their homes. Not surprisingly, the majority of home-based business owners are women, who choose this option either because of child care concerns or because of a perceived glass ceiling limiting their earnings potential in the corporate world. Running a business out of the home offers a number of advantages, including time savings, control over working hours and conditions, independence, and flexibility. Starting a home-based business is also considerably cheaper than starting a business in rented facilities. In addition to saving money on overhead expenses, commuting costs, and wardrobe expenditures, many home-based business owners can deduct a portion of their rent or mortgage interest from their personal income taxes. There are also several disadvantages to home-based businesses, however, including uncertain income, reduced benefits, isolation, and distractions. In addition, home-based business owners, like other self-employed individuals, must be able to handle all sorts of business-related tasks, like bookkeeping, billing, marketing and sales, and tax compliance. Still, home-based businesses do tend to be more successful than other types of small business ventures. According to the editors of *Income Opportunities* magazine in their *Home Business Handbook,* only 20 to 25 percent of home-based businesses fail within five years, compared to a failure rate of over 50 percent for all small business ventures.

REQUIREMENTS FOR A SUCCESSFUL HOME-BASED BUSINESS

As Paul and Sarah Edwards noted in their book *Working from Home,* successful home-based business owners are usually good at what they do and enjoy doing it. It is also helpful to be independent, self-sufficient, and flexible. Other keys to success include being able to sell oneself and the business, and staying on top of personal and business finances. Since it is often difficult to associate being at home with working, home-based business people must be able to maintain boundaries between their personal and professional lives. In addition, they require a great deal of self-discipline to overcome the sense of isolation, frequent distractions, and lack of motivation and concentration that commonly affect those working from home.

Formal planning can help ease the transition for a person starting a home-based business. By being aware of the potential pitfalls and creating a plan to overcome them, a home-based business owner can significantly increase his or her chances for success. The main planning tool recommended by experts is a business plan. A formal business plan, which is generally created in anticipation of starting a new business venture, includes a description of the business; a statement of purpose; information about the business's structure, organization, and management; a marketing plan; and a financial plan.

The process of gathering information and writing a **business plan** helps the entrepreneur take an objective, critical look at the business idea and its chances for success. A home-based business may be related to an individual's previous occupation, but may also be based upon a hobby or the discovery of a unique business opportunity. In any case, the idea should be evaluated with an eye toward market potential and competition. Once the business is up and running, the business plan sets forth goals and standards for management and serves as an operational tool to measure progress. Although there are many ways to start a home-based business—including ''moonlighting'' while employed full-time, working part-time for an employer and part-time at home, and just taking the plunge—planning is important to all of them.

After creating a plan for the home-based business, the entrepreneur is ready to put the plan in action. One of the earliest steps involves preparing family members and enlisting their support. The loss of a reliable source of income may cause some anxiety or resentment among other members of the household. In addition, the creation of a home office will probably necessitate changes in family members' schedules

or life-style. Dealing with such issues in advance can help avoid problems later. Another important step is to establish an area of the home as a business office. The most important considerations when choosing a location for a home office are that it allow the entrepreneur room to work comfortably and efficiently without too many distractions. The office should be as physically separate from the living area of the home as possible, and should project an air of professionalism to potential visitors as well as to its occupant.

Other steps in the process of forming a home-based business include selecting a legal structure, filing a fictitious name or ''doing business as'' statement, and obtaining any needed permits or licenses. The entrepreneur should also evaluate the risks associated with the business venture and make any necessary arrangements for health, life, liability, property, or business interruption insurance. Since it is sometimes difficult for a home-based business to be taken seriously by customers or creditors, it may be helpful to communicate a professional image through stationery and business cards, a separate phone line answered with a formal greeting, and distinct working hours.

OVERCOMING COMMON PROBLEMS

Many people start home-based businesses in the hopes of setting their own work schedules and increasing their free time, but few people realize the careful planning that is required to achieve these goals. In fact, time management is one of the most important challenges a home-based business owner may face. Experts recommend that home-based business owners set up a workable schedule immediately upon starting their ventures in order to establish good habits. In many cases, the limited amount of work available in the early stages of a home-based business's existence may cause the entrepreneur to establish a pattern of running personal errands or watching television during work time. In this way, lethargy and unproductive use of time becomes ingrained and perpetuates itself. Instead, downtime that has been reserved for working should be used to market and promote the business.

Once the home-based business gets off the ground, many entrepreneurs tend to go to the opposite extreme and overcommit themselves. In their need to attract clients, they become uncomfortable turning down work. But unlike people who work for a large employer in an outside office, home-based business owners cannot leave their work behind and go home, because home is where their work is. As a result, some entrepreneurs work too many hours and abandon their personal lives, resulting in stress and burnout. Instead, experts recommend that home-based business owners set up realistic work schedules in order to reinforce the boundaries between their personal and business lives. It may be helpful to establish the following day's schedule the previous afternoon and prioritize the activities. The schedule should be realistic and allow for inevitable interruptions. Some experts claim that an important factor in successful time management for home-based business owners is arising early in the morning to get a jump start on work. Others stress the importance of dressing comfortably yet professionally in order to establish a positive psychological state for working. Although these methods do not apply to everyone, it is important for home-based business people to find a pattern that maximizes their productivity and stick with it.

Another common problem faced by those who work from home is isolation. In a standard business environment, people are dealing with co-workers constantly, as well as the noise of ringing phones and running machines. There are also meetings, breaks, and lunch hours that serve to break up the day and provide opportunities for socializing. This contact with other people provides a built in system of motivation to at least appear busy at work. In contrast, many people who start a home-based business are faced with nothing but a quiet, empty house. Some find it difficult to motivate themselves and succumb to boredom and loneliness. But such isolation does have a positive side: working at home increases productivity by an average of 20 percent, so home-based business owners can often get more work done in less time. Planning is necessary to overcome the negative effects of isolation, however. Experts recommend that home-based business owners schedule interaction with other people on regular basis, using such means as business meals, outside meetings and appointments, clubs and associations, and **networking**.

Yet another common problem encountered by home-based business people is frequent distractions that reduce productivity. In fact, distractions are everywhere for people who work from home. When faced with a difficult work task, it sometimes seems far preferable to run the vacuum, clean out a closet, walk the dog, have a snack, take a nap, raid the refrigerator, pull some weeds in the garden, or do any of the myriad other things that need doing around a normal household. In addition, people who work from home lack the motivation that peer pressure can provide in a regular office. They also face spouses and children who demand time and attention, as well as friends and neighbors who call to chat or stop by to ask favors.

To be successful, home-based business owners need to be aware that time-stealing temptations exist and take steps to counteract digressions before they turn into habits. If distractions seem overwhelming, the first step is to analyze the situation. If the problem lies with household chores, eating, or the television, the solution may be to get the distractions out of sight.

If the problem involves family members or friends and neighbors, it may be necessary to have a frank discussion or family meeting concerning work time and free time. Options for resolving people conflicts include moving the office to another part of the house, hiring a baby-sitter or arranging for day care, or not taking personal calls during business hours. Ideally, an entrepreneur should set up a daily work schedule, try to work diligently for several hours at a time, and then take a break as a reward.

FINANCIAL AND TAX ASPECTS

Like other forms of **self-employment**, home-based businesses face a number of challenges relating to financial management and tax compliance. Part of the business plan that is prepared prior to forming a home-based business is a financial plan detailing how much it will cost to begin the new venture and keep it running. After the business has been established, it is vital that the entrepreneur set up a good bookkeeping system to manage cash flow and ensure compliance with tax laws. Bookkeeping systems can be manual or computer based. Experts also recommend that entrepreneurs set up a separate checking account for their home-based businesses in order to better document business expenses. Canceled checks, paid bills, invoices, sales slips, receipts, and other financial documentation should be kept on file in case of an audit. Another important aspect of financial planning for a home-based business is tracking working capital—the difference between current assets (cash, accounts receivable, and inventory) and current liabilities (operating expenses, debts, and taxes)—in order to maintain a realistic picture of where the business stands financially.

Taxes become significantly more complicated with a home-based business. Self-employed persons are allowed to deduct business-related expenses—such as wages paid to others, the cost of professional services, shipping and postage charges, advertising costs, the cost of **office supplies** and equipment, professional dues and publications, insurance premiums, automobile expenses, and some entertainment and travel costs—from their income taxes, but are also required to pay self-employment taxes. People who work from their homes may be eligible for another tax deduction known as a home office deduction. The home office deduction allows individuals who meet certain criteria to deduct a portion of mortgage interest or rent, depreciation of the space used as an office, utility bills, home insurance costs, and cleaning, repairs, and security costs from their federal income taxes. Although the **Internal Revenue Service (IRS)** has set strict regulations about who qualifies for the deduction, about 1.6 million people claim the deduction each year.

For many years, the IRS has followed a very strict interpretation of "principal place of business," which prevented some self-employed persons—such as an accountant who maintained a home office but also spent a great deal of time visiting clients—from claiming the deduction. But in July 1997 the U.S. Congress passed a tax bill that redefined an individual's "principal place of business" to include a home office that meets the following two criteria: 1) it is used to conduct the management or administrative activities of a business; and 2) it is the only place in which the small business owner conducts those management or administrative activities. When this change becomes effective on January 1, 1999, it is expected that many home-based business owners who also perform services outside of their homes will be able to take advantage of this deduction.

FURTHER READING:

Editors of *Entrepreneur* Magazine. *Complete Guide to Owning a Home-Based Business.* New York: Bantam Books, 1990.

Editors of *Income Opportunities* Magazine. *Home Business Handbook: Expert Advice for Running a Successful Business Out of Your Home.* New York: Perigee Books, 1990.

Edwards, Paul, and Sarah Edwards. *Working from Home: Everything You Need to Know about Living and Working under the Same Roof.* Los Angeles: Tarcher, 1990.

Eliason, Carol. *The Business Plan for Home-Based Business.* Washington: U.S. Small Business Administration, 1991.

Kanarek, Lisa. *Organizing Your Home Office for Success: Expert Strategies That Can Work for You.* New York: Penguin, 1993.

Marullo, Gloria Gibbs. "Redefining the Home-Office Deduction." *Nation's Business.* September 1997.

SEE ALSO: Free-lance Employment/Independent Contractors; Home Office; Tax-Deductible Business Expenses

HOME OFFICES

A home office is a space within an individual's personal residence that is used for business purposes. It may be a corner of a spare bedroom equipped with nothing more than a desk. Or, it could be one whole floor of a house filled with the latest in computer and communications devices. Whatever its size and composition, however, the home office is increasingly common in American business today. A majority of the estimated 40 million Americans who work from their homes are self-employed small business owners. In addition, many professionals maintain two offices, and a growing number are equipping their home computers with modems that allow them access to their office computer files. Many large corporations are also expanding experiments in "**telecommuting**," which enables employees to work from home, using modem-equipped computers, just as they would in the office.

Establishing a home office involves a number of important considerations. For example, individuals interested in working out of their homes must gather information on local zoning restrictions, find and set aside an appropriate work area, and gain the support of family and neighbors for the home office. Other considerations include whether the home office will offer sufficient privacy, will be convenient for customers and vendors, and will provide room for future expansion and growth. The expense involved in furnishing a home office and purchasing necessary computers, **office supplies**, and other equipment is another factor to consider.

The use of part of a home as a business office may enable an individual to qualify for significant tax deductions. The " home office deduction" allows individuals who meet certain criteria to deduct a portion of mortgage interest or rent, depreciation of the space used as an office, utility bills, home insurance costs, and cleaning, repairs, and security costs from their federal income taxes. Although the Internal Revenue Service (IRS) has set strict regulations about who qualifies for the deduction, about 1.6 million people claim the deduction each year. According to Gloria Gibbs Marullo in an article for *Nation's Business,* the savings can be considerable: a sole proprietor living in a $150,000 home stands to save about $2,500 in actual taxes annually.

HOME OFFICE TAX DEDUCTION

The most important aspects of setting up a home office are the potential tax and legal implications. Home office operators may claim a deduction for those offices on IRS Form 8829 (Expenses for Business Use of Your Home), which is filed along with Schedule C (Profit or Loss From Your Business). There are restrictions, however, which are covered in IRS Publication 587 (*Business Use of Your Home*). Failing to abide by these restrictions may put a red flag on a home office user's federal income tax return, which could result in an audit.

In general, a home office deduction is allowed if the home office meets at least one of three criteria: 1) the home office is the principal place of business; 2) the home office is the place where the business owner meets with clients and customers as part of the normal business day; or 3) the place of business is a separate structure on the property, but is not attached to the house or residence. The deduction is figured on the size of the home office as a percentage of the total house or residence. For example, if the total house size is 2,400 square feet and the home office is 240 square feet, 10 percent of the total house is considered used for business. That would allow the business owner to deduct 10 percent of the household's costs for electricity, real estate taxes, mortgage interest, insurance, repairs, etc. as business expenses.

Be warned, however, that the home office deduction cannot be used by everyone who has a home office. A 1993 United States Supreme Court decision made the home office deduction more difficult to apply outside of these very carefully worded circumstances. In the case in question, a doctor worked in three different hospitals, but did not maintain an office in any of them. Therefore, he established a home office, which he claimed was necessary to keep up with his billing and patient records, and claimed a home office deduction. But the Supreme Court ruled that since the doctor spent most of his working hours visiting patients, the hospitals were his principal place of work, and his home office deduction was denied.

This ruling, which more narrowly defined the concept of ''principal place of business'' affected a large number of people, particularly professionals such as sales agents who see customers at the customers' places of business. Since the demonstration and sale of the merchandise occurs away from the home office, the IRS ruling says that those offices are not critical to conducting that business. As a general rule, if the income-producing activity takes place away from the office, a deduction is not allowed. On the other hand, a second job conducted exclusively from the home office may qualify for the deduction. The key is that the income must be generated from the home office.

A home office deduction is still possible, however, if the space is set aside exclusively to meet with clients or customers, even if it is not always the principal place of business. The IRS uses an example of a lawyer who works three days in an office and two days at home in an office set up so that clients can come to his home. The last test for an unchallenged home office deduction is that it can be a separate structure—such as a studio or garage apartment—that is essential for running the business. For example, a floral shop owner who runs a greenhouse on her property would qualify under this rule.

In July 1997, responding to the concerns of small business advocates, the U.S. Congress passed a tax bill that effectively overturned the 1993 Supreme Court ruling. The legislation redefined an individual's ''principal place of business'' to include a home office that meets the following two criteria: 1) it is used to conduct the management or administrative activities of a business; and 2) it is the only place in which the small business owner conducts those management or administrative activities. When this change becomes effective on January 1, 1999, it is expected to enable many business owners who perform services outside of their homes to claim the home office deduction.

Even after meeting the criteria to qualify for the home office deduction, a myriad of different IRS rules apply to exactly what expenses can be deducted. These rules cover depreciation of the home, depreciation of equipment, how to recover that depreciation if the home is sold, etc. One important thing to note is that the monthly residential telephone charge cannot be deducted, even if most of the calls pertain to the business. However, long distance business related calls can be deducted. Individuals are advised to consult an accountant to stay within the law on home office deductions.

OTHER CONSIDERATIONS

Besides the IRS regulations, some municipal governments have **zoning ordinances** that restrict and/or license home offices. Originally designed to protect residential neighborhoods from becoming commercial zones, the zoning laws have sometimes been strictly interpreted to keep residents from conducting any sort of business from their home, even if it does not have a commercial impact on the rest of the neighborhood. Zoning laws and ordinances may affect such varied issues as parking for customers, access for deliveries, the number and types of employees permitted, and the use of signs or other forms of advertising. As a result, people wishing to set up home offices should check with their city's zoning office and licensing board for restrictions that may apply to the city, or even to their particular neighborhood.

If a home-based business is allowed at the site, the next step is to determine whether a home office is a workable option in the residence. For example, individuals interested in working from their homes must consider where the office should be located, how much it will cost to equip the area for business use, and what adjustments will need to be made in living arrangements. While a home office offers an entrepreneur a number of tax and life-style benefits, it can also pose problems relating to limited space, isolation, household distractions, and security concerns.

Providing that a home office is feasible, the next step is to choose a location for the office. This location may be a spare bedroom, a den or study, a basement, an attic, a garage, a kitchen table, or a corner of a living room. When choosing a location for the home office, entrepreneurs should take into consideration their own working needs, the needs of clients who may visit, and the life-style needs of other members of their family. Though it is important for the home office to be located out of the mainstream of household activities, it also should be located in a desirable spot that will offer a pleasant working environment. The location of a home office is very significant; ''in fact, almost every problem people have in working from home . . . is either aggravated or alleviated by where they put their offices,'' Paul and Sarah Edwards noted in their book *Working from Home*. At a minimum, the location chosen must be large enough to contain a desk and chair, computer and phone equipment, storage and shelf space, and contemplation or meeting space.

After a location has been determined, the work space must be clearly defined in order to eliminate potential distractions and create a good working atmosphere. ''A peaceful marriage of home and office depends on establishing effective boundaries,'' according to Paul and Sarah Edwards. If no extra room is available in the home, it is possible to use room dividers or office partitions to creatively define the office space. It is vital that the space be well-lit, as lighting is key contributor to productivity. In addition, if clients are expected to visit the home office, then ideally the office should be the only part of the home they see. Thus if clients will visit regularly, it might be helpful to have an outside entrance to the office space. Besides defining the work space, it is important for an individual working out of his or her home to establish specific working hours and stick to them. Home-based business owners should let family, friends, and neighbors know when they are available for socializing and when they will be working. Otherwise, family members may interrupt business activities, or friends and neighbors may impinge upon work time with visits or requests for favors or baby-sitting services.

After a home office space has been defined, that space needs to be outfitted with the necessary equipment to conduct business activities. In her book *Organizing Your Home Office for Success,* Lisa Kanarek recommended plotting the available office space on a grid in order to help select and organize appropriate furniture and equipment. It may also be helpful to think in terms of vertical space as well as horizontal. For example, it may be possible to install storage shelves above a desk, or to use office walls for bulletin boards, dry-erase boards, or planning calendars. The most important consideration in selecting office furniture, besides fit with the available space, is ergonomics. After all, an average person spends 75 percent of his or her day sitting at a desk. If that desk is the wrong height, or the chair is uncomfortable, the entrepreneur may experience back pain, fatigue, carpal tunnel syndrome, or a variety of other productivity-reducing problems. In addition, Kanarek noted that individuals shopping for home office furniture avoid the temptation simply to seek out bargains. Poorly designed or constructed furniture will only need to be replaced, which may make it more expensive than selecting high-quality materials in the first place.

Some of the most costly equipment commonly purchased for home offices includes computers, printers, and other technological devices. According to Mike Brennan in an article for the *Detroit Free Press,* the first step in buying computer equipment for a home office is to evaluate what tasks it will need to accomplish. For example, a business that depends upon professional presentations may require a computer system capable of handling complex desktop publishing programs. The next step is to decide whether to buy the best computer model available to meet these needs, or to spend less money for an older, yet servicable model. In general, experts recommend that entrepreneurs buy the best computer that they can afford. Renting or leasing computer equipment may be an attractive option for small business owners who anticipate that they will not be able to afford top-of-the-line equipment, or who want to keep up with the rapid changes in technology prevalent in today's market.

In addition to the computer itself, home office workers today usually need to invest in a modem to connect their business computer to the Internet, to communicate with customers, and to facilitate e-mail and fax capabilities. The majority of home offices also purchase one or more peripheral devices—such as a printer, scanner, copier, or fax machine—depending on their needs. Brennan noted that a multiple function machine encompassing several of these peripherals may be a good way for home offices to save space, although such machines generally entail a tradeoff in the quality of any one function. Finally, a home office must also invest in software to perform work on the computer. Many new computers come with a variety of useful software already installed. One good general option for small businesses is Microsoft Office 97, which includes word processing and spreadsheet programs, as well as a variety of other business applications.

When establishing the physical layout of the home office space, it is also important to provide for storage of **office supplies** and business records. Most home-based businesses require at least one filing cabinet, shelves for books or manuals, and space to store paper and other office supplies. Office superstores, mail-order office supply companies, and computer shopping are all convenient options for home business owners in restocking their office supplies. Home-based businesses also need to provide the means for customer contact. Experts recommend establishing a separate phone line for business contacts, and equipping it with a reliable answering machine or voice mail system to handle calls during non-business hours. A separate phone line, which can be answered in a professional manner, gives more credibility and control to the small business owner, and also acts to solidify boundaries between an individual's business and personal life. Finally, some entrepreneurs choose not to use their home address in business dealings, either because of the image it projects or to protect their privacy and security. Home-based business owners may want to consider obtaining a post office box, renting an address from an office suite service, or using a mail receiving service as alternatives to using a home address for business correspondence.

Finally, individuals investing in a home office often need to make significant changes in their insurance coverage to ensure that their business is protected. For example, fire and theft coverage must be expanded to include business equipment, and liability coverage needs to include customers, vendors, and delivery persons visiting the premises. Depending on the type of home-based business, additional coverage may be needed to protect against business interruption, product or workmanship liability, and business use of a vehicle.

FURTHER READING:

Brennan, Mike. "Do Your Homework: Setting Up an Office in Your House Can Be a Disaster if You're Not Computer Literate." *Detroit Free Press.* November 24, 1997.

Editors of *Income Opportunities* Magazine. *Home Business Handbook: Expert Advice for Running a Successful Business Out of Your Home.* New York: Perigee Books, 1990.

Edwards, Paul, and Sarah Edwards. *Working from Home: Everything You Need to Know about Living and Working under the Same Roof.* Los Angeles: Tarcher, 1990.

Eliason, Carol. *The Business Plan for Home-Based Business.* Washington: U.S. Small Business Administration, 1991.

Kanarek, Lisa. *Organizing Your Home Office for Success: Expert Strategies That Can Work for You.* New York: Penguin, 1993.

Marullo, Gloria Gibbs. "Redefining the Home-Office Deduction." *Nation's Business.* September 1997.

SEE ALSO: Facility Layout and Design; Home-Based Business; Tax-Deductible Business Expenses

HUMAN RESOURCE MANAGEMENT

Human Resource Management (HRM) is the term used to describe formal systems devised for the management of people within an organization. These human resources responsibilities are generally divided into three major areas of management: staffing, **employee compensation**, and defining/designing work. Essentially, the purpose of HRM is to maximize the **productivity** of an organization by optimizing the effectiveness of its employees. This mandate is unlikely to change in any fundamental way, despite the ever-increasing pace of change in the business world. As Edward L. Gubman observed in the *Journal of Business Strategy,* "the basic mission of human resources will always be to acquire, develop, and retain talent; align the workforce with the business; and be an excellent contributor to the business. Those three challenges will never change."

Until fairly recently, an organization's human resources department was often consigned to lower rungs of the corporate hierarchy, despite the fact that its mandate is to replenish and nourish the company's **work force**, which is often cited—legitimately—as an organization's greatest resource. But in recent years recognition of the importance of human resources management to a company's overall health has grown dramatically. This recognition of the importance of HRM extends to small businesses, for while they do not generally have the same volume of human resources requirements as do larger organizations, they too face personnel management issues that can have a decisive impact on business health. As Irving Burstiner commented in *The Small Business Handbook,* "Hiring the right people—and training them well—can often mean the difference between scratching out the barest of livelihoods and steady business growth. . . . Personnel problems do not discriminate between small and big business. You find them in all businesses, regardless of size."

PRINCIPLES OF HUMAN RESOURCE MANAGEMENT

Business consultants note that modern human resource management is guided by several overriding principles. Perhaps the paramount principle is a simple recognition that human resources are the most important assets of an organization; a business cannot be successful without effectively managing this resource. Another important principle, articulated by Michael Armstrong in his book *A Handbook of Human Resource Management,* is that business success "is most likely to be achieved if the personnel policies and procedures of the enterprise are closely linked with, and make a major contribution to, the achievement of corporate objectives and strategic plans." A third guiding principle, similar in scope, holds that it is HR's responsibility to find, secure, guide, and develop employees whose talents and desires are compatible with the operating needs and future goals of the company. Other HRM factors that shape corporate culture—whether by encouraging integration and cooperation across the company, instituting quantitative performance measurements, or taking some other action—are also commonly cited as key components in business success. HRM, summarized Armstrong, "is a strategic approach to the acquisition, motivation, development and management of the organization's human resources. It is devoted to shaping an appropriate corporate culture, and introducing programs which reflect and support the core values of the enterprise and ensure its success."

POSITION AND STRUCTURE OF HUMAN RESOURCE MANAGEMENT

Writing in *Personnel Management,* Paul S. Greenlaw and John P. Kohl described three distinct, interrelated fields of interest addressed by the HRM discipline: human relations, organization theory, and decision areas. Human relations encompasses matters such as individual motivation, leadership, and group relationships. Organization theory refers to job design, managerial control, and work flow through the organization. Decision areas encompass interests related to the acquisition, development, rewarding, and maintenance of human resources. Although the method and degree to which those areas of interest are handled vary among different human resource management entities, a few general rules characterize the responsibilities, positioning, and structure of most HRM divisions.

HRM department responsibilities, other than related legal and clerical duties, can be classified by individual, organizational, and career areas. Individual management entails helping employees identify their strengths and weaknesses; correct their shortcomings; and make their best contribution to the enterprise. These duties are carried out through a variety of activities such as performance reviews, training, and testing. Organizational development, meanwhile, focuses on fostering a successful system that maximizes human (and other) resources as part of larger business strategies. This important duty also includes the creation and maintenance of a change program, which allows the organization to respond to evolving outside and internal influences. The third responsibility, career development, entails matching individuals with the most suitable jobs and career paths within the organization.

Human resource management functions are ideally positioned near the theoretic center of the organization, with access to all areas of the business. Since the HRM department or manager is charged with managing the productivity and development of workers at all levels, human resource personnel should have access to—and the support of—key decision makers. In addition, the HRM department should be situated in such a way that it is able to effectively communicate with all areas of the company.

HRM structures vary widely from business to business, shaped by the type, size, and governing philosophies of the organization that they serve. But most organizations organize HRM functions around the clusters of people to be helped—they conduct recruiting, administrative, and other duties in a central location. Different employee development groups for each department are necessary to train and develop employees in specialized areas, such as sales, engineering, marketing, or executive education. In contrast, some HRM departments are completely independent and are organized purely by function. The same training department, for example, serves all divisions of the organization.

In recent years, however, observers have cited a decided trend toward fundamental reassessments of human resources structures and positions. "A cascade of changing business conditions, changing organizational structures, and changing leadership has been forcing human resource departments to alter their perspectives on their role and function almost overnight," wrote John Johnston in *Business Quarterly.* "Previously, companies structured themselves on a centralized and compartmentalized basis—head office, marketing, manufacturing, shipping, etc. They now seek to decentralize and to integrate their operations, developing cross-functional teams. . . . Today, senior management expects HR to move beyond its traditional, compartmentalized 'bunker' approach to a more integrated, decentralized support function." Given this change in expectations, Johnston noted that "an increasingly common trend in human resources is to decentralize the HR function and make it accountable to specific line management. This increases the likelihood that HR is viewed and included as an integral part of the business process, similar to its marketing, finance, and operations counterparts. However, HR will retain a centralized functional relationship in areas where specialized expertise is truly required," such as compensation and recruitment responsibilities.

HUMAN RESOURCE MANAGEMENT—KEY RESPONSIBILITIES

Human resource management is concerned with the development of both individuals and the organization in which they operate. HRM, then, is engaged not only in securing and developing the talents of individual workers, but also in implementing programs that enhance communication and cooperation between those individual workers in order to nurture organizational development.

The primary responsibilities associated with human resource management include: job analysis and staffing, organization and utilization of work force, measurement and appraisal of work force performance, implementation of reward systems for employees, professional development of workers, and maintenance of work force.

JOB ANALYSIS Job analysis consists of determining—often with the help of other company areas—the nature and responsibilities of various employment positions. This can encompass determination of the skills and experiences necessary to adequately perform in a position, identification of job and industry trends, and anticipation of future employment levels and skill requirements. "Job analysis is the cornerstone of HRM practice because it provides valid information about jobs that is used to hire and promote people, establish wages, determine training needs, and make other important HRM decisions,'' stated Thomas S. Bateman and Carl P. Zeithaml in *Management: Function and Strategy*. Staffing, meanwhile, is the actual process of managing the flow of personnel into, within (through transfers and promotions), and out of an organization. Once the recruiting part of the staffing process has been completed, selection is accomplished through job postings, interviews, reference checks, testing, and other tools.

ORGANIZATION OF PERSONNEL Organization and utilization of a company's work force is another key function of HRM. This involves designing an organizational framework that makes maximum use of an enterprise's human resources and establishing systems of communication that help the organization operate in a unified manner.

PERFORMANCE MEASUREMENT Performance appraisal is the practice of assessing employee job performance and providing feedback to those employees about both positive and negative aspects of their performance. Performance measurements are very important both for the organization and the individual, for they are the primary data used in determining salary increases, promotions, and, in the case of workers who perform unsatisfactorily, dismissal. As Bateman and Zeithaml noted, information that is often incorporated into performance appraisals include production data (such as sales posted by a salesman or number of goods produced by a line worker), personnel data (such as absenteeism or misuse of organization resources, like the telephone), meeting of performance goals, and input from other sources, such as supervisors. Performance goals for the future are often formed from these appraisals as well.

REWARD SYSTEMS Once performance measurement of an employee has been completed, rewards (in the form of promotions, raises, or other expressions of recognition) and punishments (in the form of probationary arrangements or outright dismissal) are arrived at. This aspect of human resource management is very important, for it is the mechanism by which organizations provide their workers with rewards for past achievements and incentives for high performance in the future. It is also the mechanism by which organizations address problems within their work force, through institution of disciplinary measures. Aligning the work force with company goals, stated Gubman, ''requires offering workers an employment relationship that motivates them to take ownership of the business plan.''

EMPLOYEE DEVELOPMENT AND TRAINING Human resource management personnel are responsible for researching an organization's training needs, and for initiating and evaluating employee development programs designed to address those needs. These training programs can range from orientation programs, which are designed to acclimate new hires to the company, to ambitious education programs intended to familiarize workers with a new software system.

''After getting the right talent into the organization,'' wrote Gubman, ''the second traditional challenge to human resources is to align the workforce with the business—to constantly build the capacity of the workforce to execute the business plan.'' This is done through performance appraisals, training, and other activities. In the realm of performance appraisal, HRM professionals must devise uniform appraisal standards, develop review techniques, train managers to administer the appraisals, and then evaluate and follow up on the effectiveness of performance reviews. They must also tie the appraisal process into compensation and incentive strategies, and work to ensure that federal regulations are observed.

Responsibilities associated with **training and development** activities, meanwhile, include the determination, design, execution, and analysis of educational programs. The HRM professional should be aware of the fundamentals of learning and motivation, and must carefully design and monitor training and development programs that benefit the overall organization as well as the individual. The importance of this aspect of a business's operation can hardly be overstated. As Roberts, Seldon, and Roberts indicated in *Human Resources Management*, ''the quality of employees and their development through training and education are major factors in determining long-term profitability of a small business. . . . Research has shown specific benefits that a small business receives from training and developing its workers, including: increased productivity; reduced employee turnover; increased efficiency resulting in financial gains; [and] decreased need for supervision.''

MAINTENANCE OF HUMAN RESOURCES Responsibilities in this area include **employee benefits**, safety and health, and worker-management relations. Human resource maintenance activities related to safety and health usually entail compliance with federal laws that protect employees from hazards in the workplace. These regulations are handed down from several federal agencies, including the **Occupational Safety and Health Administration (OSHA)** and the **Environmental Protection Agency (EPA)**, and various state agencies, which implement laws in the realms of worker's compensation, employee protection, and other areas. Maintenance tasks related to worker-management relations primarily entail: working with labor unions; handling grievances related to misconduct, such as theft or sexual harassment; and devising communication systems to foster cooperation and a shared sense of mission among employees.

CONTRIBUTING TO BUSINESS PROCESSES "The final challenge to human resources departments is to be an excellent contributor to the business," wrote Gubman. "The road to success is the road to greater, value-added contribution and partnership in the enterprise." Of course, human resource managers have always contributed to overall business processes in certain respects—by disseminating guidelines for and monitoring employee behavior, for instance, or ensuring that the organization is obeying worker-related regulatory guidelines—but increasing numbers of businesses are incorporating human resource managers into other business processes as well. In the past, human resource managers were cast in a support role in which their thoughts on cost/benefit justifications and other operational aspects of the business were rarely solicited. But as Johnston noted, HR managers who participate as "businesspeople" rather than "HR people" can make a valuable contribution to corporate performance. Moreover, Johnston contended that the changing character of business structures and the marketplace are making it increasingly necessary for business owners and executives to pay greater attention to the human resource aspects of operation: "Tasks that were once neatly slotted into well-defined and narrow job descriptions have given way to broad job descriptions or role definitions. In some cases, completely new work relationships have developed; telecommuting, permanent part-time roles and outsourcing major non-strategic functions are becoming more frequent." All of these changes, which human resource managers are heavily involved in, are important factors in shaping business performance.

FACTORS THAT INFLUENCE HRM ACTIVITIES

The principal obligations of human resource management are fixed, but the methodologies employed in HRM can be dramatically altered by a number of different business and societal factors, including general economic health, unions, labor markets, legal guidelines, and business strategies.

- General economic conditions—whether in a town, region, or nation—are important because they directly impact on an organization's financial outlook, which in turn influence human resource management decisions in the realms of payroll, work force size, and career development.

- Business **strategy** can also be an important factor in dictating the shape and direction of human resource management decisions and initiatives. Some business strategies are predicated, albeit indirectly, on general economic conditions. For instance, a strategic decision to suspend production of a certain good that is selling poorly because of a region-wide recession can directly impact work force size, compensation, and development. Other business strategies simply reflect guiding management philosophy.

- The labor market can affect HRM activities in a variety of ways. The business world's increased reliance on technology, for example, has created a demand for continuing education and training initiatives within many organizations. Indeed, implementation of such programs has become an increasingly important part of human resources management in many industries.

- **Labor unions** can have a pronounced effect on all aspects of employee-management relations; a labor union, wrote Bateman and Zeithaml, "may affect [a company's] staffing system (by requiring seniority to play a role in promotions), the reward system (by negotiating the terms and amounts of pay), and the work system (by playing a role with management in developing the content of jobs)."

- **Labor laws and legislation**—both at the state and federal level—can greatly influence human resource management as well. Much of this legislation is designed to protect workers from unfair labor practices. Landmark workplace laws include the Fair Labor Standards Act of 1938, the Equal Pay Act of 1963, Title VII of the Civil Rights Act of 1964, the Occupational Safety and Health Act of 1970, and the Family and Medical Leave Act of 1993, but there are hundreds of others that impact on HRM as well.

THE CHANGING FIELD OF HUMAN RESOURCE MANAGEMENT

In the 1990s several forces had a significant impact on the broad field of HRM. Chief among them were new technologies. These new technologies, particularly in the areas of electronic communication and information dissemination and retrieval, have dramatically altered the business landscape. Satellite communications, computers and networking systems, fax machines, and other devices have all facilitated change in the ways in which businesses interact with each other and their workers. **Telecommuting**, for instance, has become a very popular option for many workers, and HRM professionals have had to develop new guidelines for this emerging subset of employees.

Changes in organizational structure have also influenced the changing face of human resource management. Continued erosion in manufacturing industries in the United States and other nations, coupled with the rise in service industries in those countries, have changed the workplace, as has the decline in union representation in many industries (these two trends, in fact, are commonly viewed as interrelated). In addition, organizational philosophies have undergone change. Many companies have scrapped or adjusted their traditional, hierarchical organizations structures in favor of flatter management structures. HRM experts note that this shift in responsibility brought with it a need to reassess job descriptions, appraisal systems, and other elements of personnel management.

A third change factor was accelerating market globalization. This phenomenon served to increase competition for both customers and jobs. The latter development enabled some businesses to demand higher performances from their employees while holding the line on compensation. Other factors that have changed the nature of HRM in recent years include new management and operational theories like **Total Quality Management (TQM)**; rapidly changing **demographics**; and changes in health insurance and federal and state employment legislation.

SMALL BUSINESS AND HUMAN RESOURCE MANAGEMENT

A small business's human resource management needs are not of the same size or complexity of those of a large firm. Nonetheless, even a business that carries only two or three employees faces important personnel management issues. Indeed, the stakes are very high in the world of small business when it comes to employee recruitment and management. No business wants an employee who is lazy or incompetent or dishonest. But a small business with a work force of half a dozen people will be hurt far more badly by such an employee than will a company with a work force that numbers in the hundreds (or thousands). Nonetheless, "most small business employers have no formal training in how to make hiring decisions," noted Jill A. Rossiter in *Mastering Your Small Business Human Resources*. "Most have no real sense of the time it takes nor the costs involved. All they know is that they need help in the form of a 'good' sales manager, a 'good' secretary, a 'good' welder, or whatever. And they know they need someone they can work with, who's willing to put in the time to learn the business and do the job. It sounds simple, but it isn't."

Before hiring a new employee, the small business owner should weigh several considerations. After all, said Rossiter, "in essence, the people you hire become the company, and the company becomes whatever the people make it." The first step the small business owner should take when pondering an expansion of employee payroll is to honestly assess the status of the organization itself. Are current employees being uti-

lized appropriately? Are current production methods effective? Can the needs of the business be met through an arrangement with an outside contractor or some other means? Are you, as the owner, spending your time appropriately? As Rossiter noted, "any personnel change should be considered an opportunity for rethinking your organizational structure."

Small businesses also need to match the talents of prospective employees with the company's needs. Efforts to manage this can be accomplished in a much more effective fashion if the small business owner devotes energy to defining the job and actively taking part in the recruitment process. But the human resource management task does not end with the creation of a detailed job description and the selection of a suitable employee. Indeed, the hiring process marks the beginning of HRM for the small business owner.

Small business consultants strongly urge even the most modest of business enterprises to implement and document policies regarding human resource issues. "Few small enterprises can afford even a fledgling personnel department during the first few years of business operation," acknowledged Burstiner. "Nevertheless, a large mass of personnel forms and data generally accumulates rather rapidly from the very beginning. To hold problems to a minimum, specific personnel policies should be established as early as possible. These become useful guides in all areas: recruitment and selection, compensation plan and employee benefits, training, promotions and terminations, and the like." Depending on the nature of the business enterprise (and the owner's own comfort zone), the owner can even involve his employees in this endeavor. In any case, a carefully considered employee handbook or personnel manual can be an invaluable tool in ensuring that the small business owner and his or her employees are on the same page. Moreover, a written record can lend a small business some protection in the event that its management or operating procedures are questioned in the legal arena.

Some small business owners also need to consider training and other development needs in managing their enterprise's employees. The need for such educational supplements can range dramatically. A bakery owner, for instance, may not need to devote much of his resources to employee training, but a firm that provides electrical wiring services to commercial clients may need to implement a system of continuing education for its workers in order to remain viable. "Small businesses realize that they, not the government, must take responsibility for training workers," wrote Ronald Henkoff in *Fortune* in 1993. "Nearly four in ten members of the National Association of Manufacturers say that deficiencies in math, reading, and technical skills are causing 'serious problems' in upgrading factories and increasing productivity. Companies cannot wait for the schools to solve America's education crisis. The Bureau of Labor Statistics estimates that nearly two-thirds of the workers who will be in the labor force in the year 2005 are already on the job. . . . Effective training is concise and interactive, interspersed with group projects, role-playing, and hands-on experiments. . . . Concepts like empowerment, accountability, and total quality management can come off as corporate bunk if they aren't accompanied by training.''

Finally, the small business owner needs to establish and maintain a productive working atmosphere for his or her work force. Employees are far more likely to be productive assets to your company if they feel that they are treated fairly. The small business owner who clearly communicates personal expectations and company goals, provides adequate compensation, offers meaningful opportunities for career advancement, anticipates work force training and developmental needs, and provides meaningful feedback to his or her employees is far more likely to be successful than the owner who is neglectful in any of these areas.

FURTHER READING:

Armstrong, Michael. *A Handbook of Human Resource Management.* Kogan Page Limited, 1988.

Bateman, Thomas S., and Carl P. Zeithaml. *Management: Function and Strategy.* Homewood, IL: Irwin, 1990.

Beer, Michael, Bert Specter, Paul R. Lawrence, D. Quinn Mills, and Richard E. Walton. *Human Resource Management.* New York: The Free Press, 1985.

Burstiner, Irving. *The Small Business Handbook.* Rev. ed. Englewood Cliffs, NJ: Prentice Hall, 1988.

Chapman, Elwood N. *Human Relations in Small Business.* Menlo Park, CA: Crisp Publications, 1994.

Greenlaw, Paul S., and John P. Kohl. *Personnel Management: Managing Human Resources.* New York: Harper & Row, 1986.

Gubman, Edward L. ''The Gauntlet is Down.'' *Journal of Business Strategy.* November-December 1996.

Henkoff, Ronald. ''Companies that Train Best.'' *Fortune,* March 22, 1993.

Johnston, John. ''Time to Rebuild Human Resources.'' *Business Quarterly.* Winter 1996.

Pace, R. Wayne. *Human Resource Development: The Field.* Englewood Cliffs, NJ: Prentice Hall, 1991.

Reece, Barry L., and Rhonda Brandt. *Effective Human Relations in Organizations.* Boston: Houghton Mifflin, 1993.

Roberts, Gary, Gary Seldon, and Carlotta Roberts. *Human Resources Management.* Washington, D.C.: Small Business Administration, n.a.

Solomon, Charlene Marmer. ''Working Smarter: How HR Can Help.'' *Personnel Journal.* June 1993.

SEE ALSO: Employee Hiring; Employee Performance Appraisal; Employee Reward Systems; Human Resource Management and the Law; Human Resource Policies

HUMAN RESOURCE POLICIES

Human resource policies are the formal rules and guidelines that businesses put in place to hire, train, assess, and reward the members of their work force. These policies, when organized and disseminated in an easily used form—such as in **employee manuals** or large postings—can go far toward eliminating any misunderstandings between employees and employers about their rights and obligations in the business environment. ''Sound human resource policy is a necessity in the growth of any business or company,'' wrote Ardella Ramey and Carl R. J. Sniffen in *A Company Policy and Personnel Workbook.* ''Recognition of this necessity may occur when management realizes that an increasing amount of time is being devoted to human resource issues: time that could be devoted to production, marketing, and planning for growth. Effective, consistent, and fair human resource decisions are often made more time consuming by a lack of written, standardized policies and procedures. Moreover, when issues concerning **employee rights** and company policies come before federal and state courts, the decisions generally regard company policies, whether written or verbal, as being a part of an employment contract between the employee and the company. Without clearly written policies, the company is at a disadvantage.''

It is particularly important for small business establishments to implement and maintain fairly applied human resource policies in their everyday operations. Small businesses—and especially business start-ups—can not afford to fritter away valuable time and resources on drawn-out policy disputes or potentially expensive lawsuits. The business owner who takes the time to establish sound, comprehensive human resource management policies will be far better equipped to succeed over the long run than will the business owner who deals with each policy decision as it erupts; the latter ad hoc style is much more likely to produce inconsistent, uninformed, and legally questionable decisions that will cripple—or even kill—an otherwise prosperous business. For as many small business consultants state, human resource policies that are inconsistently applied or based on faulty or incomplete data will almost inevitably result in declines in worker morale, deterioration in employee loyalty, and increased vulnerability to legal penalties (*Nation's Restaurant News,* for example, noted that employment litigation increased 2,000 percent between 1970 and 1990; of these cases, about three out of four concerned wrongful termination accusations). To help ensure that personnel management policies are fairly applied, business owners and consultants alike recommend that small business enterprises produce and maintain a written record of its HR policies and of instances in which those policies came into play. "To ensure evenhanded and fair treatment of employees, an important interpretation of a policy should be documented, including the facts giving rise to the issue," said Ramey and Sniffen. "These interpretations are valuable as precedents for future use."

SUBJECTS COVERED BY COMPANY HUMAN RESOURCE POLICIES

Small business owners should make sure that they address basic human resource issues when putting together their personnel policies. Ramey and Sniffen highlighted the following subjects as ones of particular importance to employers and employees alike:

- Equal Employment Opportunity policies

- Employee classifications

- Workdays, paydays, and pay advances

- Overtime compensation

- Meal periods and break periods

- Payroll deductions

- Vacation policies

- Holidays

- Sick days and personal leave (for bereavement, jury duty, voting, etc.)

- Performance evaluations and salary increases

- Performance improvement

- Termination policies.

In addition, a broad spectrum of other issues can be addressed via human resource policies, depending on the nature of the business in question. Examples of such issues include promotion policies; medical/dental benefits provided to employees; use of company equipment/resources (access to Internet, personal use of fax machines and telephones, etc.); continuity of policies; **sexual harassment**; **substance abuse** and/or **drug testing**; smoking; flextime and **telecommuting** policies; pension, profit-sharing, and retirement plans; reimbursement of employee expenses through **expense accounts** (for traveling expenses and other expenses associated with conducting company business); **child care** or **eldercare**; **tuition assistance programs**; grievance procedures; **employee privacy**; dress codes; parking; mail and shipping; and sponsorship of recreational activities.

ADVANTAGES OF FORMAL HUMAN RESOURCE POLICIES

Small business owners who have prepared and updated good personnel management policies have cited several important ways in which they contribute to the success of business enterprises. Many observers have pointed out that even the best policies will falter if the business owners or managers who are charged with administering those policies are careless or incompetent in doing so. As Sniffen and Ramey indicated, "if managers and supervisors are not capable of uniformly and consistently applying the policies or if they lack good interpersonal skills, the policy manual will fail in its essential purposes." But for those businesses that are able to administer their HR policies in an intelligent and consistent manner, benefits can accrue in several areas:

- Curbing litigation—Members of the legal and business communities agree that organizations can do a lot to cut off legal threats from disgruntled current or ex-employees simply by creating—and applying—a fair and comprehensive set of personnel policies. "Updated and comprehensive human resources policies are an employer's best defense against the growing number of costly employment-related lawsuits," Robin Lee Allen flatly stated in *Nation's Restaurant News.*

- Communication with employees—A good, written human resource policy manual can be an enormously effective tool in disseminating employer expectations regarding worker performance and behavior.

- Communication with managers and supervisors—Formal policies can be helpful to managers and other supervisory personnel faced with hiring, promotion, and reward decisions concerning people who work under them.

- Promotion of company philosophy—Ramey and Sniffen contended that HR policies can "reflect the company's philosophy of business and employee relations as they demonstrate: Your creativity in solving policy issues; the competitive position of the company in providing a variety of employee benefits; and the respect and appreciation for human resource management."

- Time Savings—Prudent and comprehensive human resource management policies can save companies significant amounts of management time that can then be spent on other business activities, such as new product development, competitive analysis, marketing campaigns, etc.

Comprehensive human resource policies, then, can be very helpful to a company's operation. Observers note, however, that human resource policy-making is a task that never ends. "As the company grows and the work force becomes larger and more diverse, new issues will have to be faced and new policies developed to cover them," commented Ramey and Sniffen. "Similarly, changes in laws, regulations, employee benefits, and other areas will necessitate revisions."

MAKING CHANGES TO EXISTING HUMAN RESOURCE POLICIES

Companies typically have to make changes to established HR policies at one point or another, but it is important for small businesses to make sure that they do not make such changes prematurely or without adequate information. For example, if an employee asks the owner of a small business if he might telecommute from his home one day a week, the owner may view the request as a reasonable, relatively innocuous one. But even minor variations in personnel policy can have repercussions that extend far beyond the initially visible parameters of the request. If the employee is granted permission to work from home one day a week, will other employees ask for the same benefit? Does the employee expect the business to foot the bill for any aspect of the telecommuting endeavor (purchase of computer, modem, etc.?) Do customers or vendors rely on the employee (or employees) to be in the office five days a week? Do other employees need that worker to be in the office to answer questions? Is the nature of the employee's workload such that he can take meaningful work home? Can you implement the telecommuting variation on a probationary basis?

Small business owners need to recognize that changes in HR policy have the potential to impact, in one way or another, every person in the company, *including* the owner. Proposed changes should be examined carefully and in consultation with others within the business who may recognize potential pitfalls that other managers, or the business owner himself, might not detect. Once a change in policy is made, it should be disseminated widely and effectively so that all employees are made aware of it. A decision to make the lunchroom a smoke-free environment, for instance, should be well-publicized to minimize misunderstandings and the likelihood of unpleasantness—and possible declines in morale—between non-smokers who might be aware of the new policy and smokers who were not informed of the change. "Give prompt and reasonable notice of any such changes to avoid the problems caused by some-

one's reliance on a discontinued or modified policy," said Ramey and Sniffen.

FURTHER READING:

Allen, Robin Lee. "Human-Resource Policies Offer Best Defense Against Lawsuits." *Nation's Restaurant News.* October 12, 1992.

Armstrong, Michael. *A Handbook of Human Resource Management.* Kogan Page Limited, 1988.

Beer, Michael, Bert Specter, Paul R. Lawrence, D. Quinn Mills, and Richard E. Walton. *Human Resource Management.* New York: The Free Press, 1985.

Greenlaw, Paul S., and John P. Kohl. *Personnel Management: Managing Human Resources.* New York: Harper & Row, 1986.

Johnston, John. "Time to Rebuild Human Resources." *Business Quarterly.* Winter 1996.

Koch, Marianne J., and Rita Gunther McGrath. "Improving Labor Productivity: Human Resource Management Policies Do Matter." *Strategic Management Journal.* May 1996.

Pace, R. Wayne. *Human Resource Development: The Field.* Englewood Cliffs, NJ: Prentice Hall, 1991.

Ramey, Ardella, and Carl R. J. Sniffen. *A Company Policy and Personnel Workbook.* Grants Pass, OR: The Oasis Press/PSI Research, 1991.

Reece, Barry L., and Rhonda Brandt. *Effective Human Relations in Organizations.* Boston: Houghton Mifflin, 1993.

Theye, Larry D., Larry G. Carsentson, and Betty Becker-Theye. "Translating the Employee Handbook: Potentially Hazardous Duty." *ATA Chronicle.* August 1997.

SEE ALSO: Human Resource Management; Human Resource Management and the Law

HUMAN RESOURCES MANAGEMENT AND THE LAW

The field of human resources management is greatly influenced and shaped by state and federal employment legislation. Indeed, regulations and laws govern all aspects of human resource management, including recruitment, placement, development, and compensation areas.

The most important piece of HRM legislation, which affects all of the functional areas, is Title VII of the Civil Rights Act of 1964 and subsequent amendments, including the Civil Rights Act of 1991. These acts made illegal the discrimination against employees or potential recruits for reasons of race, color, religion, sex, and national origin. It forces employers to follow—and often document—fairness practices related to hiring, training, pay, benefits, and virtually all other activities and responsibilities related to HRM. The 1964 act established the **Equal Employment Opportunity Commission** to enforce the act, and provides for civil penalties in the event of discrimination. The net result of the all-encompassing civil rights acts is that businesses must carefully design and document numerous procedures to ensure compliance, or face potentially significant penalties. Another important piece of legislation that complements the civil rights laws discussed above is the Equal Pay Act of 1963. This act forbids wage or salary discrimination based on sex, and mandates equal pay for equal work with few exceptions. Subsequent court rulings augmented the act by promoting the concept of comparable worth, or equal pay for unequal jobs of equal value or worth.

Other important laws that govern significant aspects of human resource management include the following:

- Age Discrimination in Employment Act of 1967—This legislation, which was strengthened by amendments in the early 1990s, essentially protects workers 40 years of age and older from discrimination.

- Davis-Bacon Act of 1931—This law requires the payment of minimum wages to nonfederal employees.

- The Walsh-Healy Public Contracts Act of 1936—This law was designed to ensure that employees working as contractors for the federal government would be compensated fairly.

- Fair Labor Standards Act of 1938—this important law mandated employer compliance with restrictions related to minimum wages, overtime provisions, child labor, and workplace safety.

- Occupational Safety and Health Act of 1970—This act, which established the **Occupational Safety and Health Administration**, was designed to force employers to provide safe and healthy work environments and to make organizations liable for workers' safety. Today, thousands of regulations, backed by civil and criminal penalties, have been implemented in various industries to help ensure that employees are not subjected to unnecessarily hazardous working conditions.

- The Wagner Act of 1935—This law, also known as the National Labor Relations Act, is the main piece of legislation governing union/management relations, and is a chief source of regulation for HRM departments.

- The Norris-Laguardia Act of 1932—This law protects the rights of unions to organize, and prohibits employers from forcing job applicants to promise not to join a union in exchange for employment.

Other important laws related to human resource management include the Social Security Act of 1935, the Taft-Hartley Act of 1947, and the Landrum-Griffin Act of 1959.

FURTHER READING:

Chapman, Elwood N. *Human Relations in Small Business.* Menlo Park, CA: Crisp Publications, 1994.

Coates, Joseph F. ''Emerging HR Issues for the Twenty-First Century.'' *Employment Relations Today.* Winter 1997.

Greenlaw, Paul S., and John P. Kohl. *Personnel Management: Managing Human Resources.* New York: Harper & Row, 1986.

SEE ALSO: Human Resource Management

I

An income statement presents the results of a company's operations for a given reporting period. Along with the **balance sheet**, the statement of cash flows, and the statement of changes in owners' equity, the income statement is one of the primary means of financial reporting. It is prepared by accountants in accordance with accepted principles. The income statement presents the revenues and expenses incurred by an entity during a specific time period, culminating in a figure known as **net income**. A company's net income for an accounting period is measured as follows: Net income = Revenues − Expenses + Gains − Losses.

The income statement provides information concerning return on investment, risk, financial flexibility, and operating capabilities. Return on investment is a measure of a firm's overall performance. Risk is the uncertainty associated with the future of the enterprise. Financial flexibility is the firm's ability to adapt to problems and opportunities. Operating capability relates to the firm's ability to maintain a given level of operations.

The current view of the income statement is that income should reflect all items of profit and loss recognized during the accounting period, except for a few items that would be entered directly under retained earnings on the balance sheet, notably prior period adjustments (i.e., correction of errors). The main area of transaction that is not included in the income statement involves changes in the equity of owners. The following summary income statement

illustrates the format under generally accepted accounting principles:

Revenues	$1,000,000
Expenses	(400,000)
Gains (losses) that are not extraordinary	(100,000)
Other gains (losses)	20,000
Income from continuing operations	520,000
Gains (losses) from discontinued operations	75,000
Extraordinary gains (losses)	20,000
Cum. effect of changes in accounting principles	10,000
Net income	$625,000
Pre-tax earnings per share (2,000 shares)	$3.13

TERMS ON THE INCOME STATEMENT

The Financial Accounting Standards Board provides broad definitions of revenues, expenses, gains, losses, and other terms that appear on the income statement in its Statement of Concepts No. 6. Revenues are inflows or other enhancements of assets of an entity or settlement of its liabilities (or both) during a period, based on production and delivery of goods, provisions of services, and other activities that constitute the entity's major operations. Examples of revenues are sales revenue, interest revenue, and rent revenue.

Expenses are outflows or other uses of assets or incurrence of liabilities (or both) during a period as a result of delivering or producing goods, rendering services, or carrying out other activities that constitute the entity's ongoing major or central operations. Examples are cost of goods sold, salaries expense, and interest expense.

Gains are increases in owners' equity (net assets) from peripheral or incidental transactions of an entity and from all other transactions and events affecting the entity during the accounting period, except those that result from revenues or investments by owners. Examples are a gain on the sale of a building and a gain on the early retirement of long-term debt.

Losses are decreases in owners' equity (net assets) from peripheral or incidental transactions of an entity and from all other transactions and events affecting the entity during the accounting period except those that result from expenses or distributions to owners. Examples are losses on the sale of investments and losses from litigations.

Discontinued operations are those operations of an enterprise that have been sold, abandoned, or otherwise disposed. The results of continuing operations must be reported separately in the income statement from discontinued operations, and any gain or loss from the disposal of a segment must be reported along with the operating results of the discontinued separate major line of business or class of customer. Results from discontinued operations are reported net of income taxes.

Extraordinary gains or losses are material events and transactions that are both unusual in nature and infrequent in occurrence. Both of these criteria must be met for an item to be classified as an extraordinary gain or loss. To be considered unusual in nature, the underlying event or transaction should possess a high degree of abnormality and be clearly unrelated to, or only incidentally related to, the ordinary and typical activities of the entity, taking into account the environment in which the entity operates. To be considered infrequent in occurrence, the underlying event or transaction should be of a type that would not reasonably be expected to recur in the foreseeable future, taking into account the environment in which the entity operates.

Extraordinary items could result if gains or losses were the direct result of any of the following events or circumstances: 1) a major casualty, such as an earthquake, 2) an expropriation of property by a foreign government, or 3) a prohibition under a new act or regulation. Extraordinary items are reported net of income taxes.

Gains and losses that are not extraordinary refer to material items which are unusual or infrequent, but not both. Such items must be disclosed separately and would be not be reported net of tax.

An accounting change refers to a change in accounting principle, accounting estimate, or reporting entity. Changes in **accounting methods** result when an accounting principle is adopted that is different from the one previously used. Changes in estimate involve revisions of estimates, such as the useful lives or residual value of depreciable assets, the loss for bad debts, and warranty costs. A change in reporting entity occurs when a company changes its composition from the prior period, as occurs when a new subsidiary is acquired.

Net income is the excess of all revenues and gains for a period over all expenses and losses of the period. Net loss is the excess of expenses and losses over revenues and gains for a period.

Generally accepted accounting principles require disclosing earnings per share amounts on the income statement of all public reporting entities. Earnings per share data provides a measure of the enterprise's management and past performance and enables users of financial statements to evaluate future prospects of the enterprise and assess dividend distributions to shareholders. Disclosure of earnings per share for effects of discontinued operations and extraordinary items is optional, but it is required for income from continuing operations, income before extraordinary items, cumulative effects of a change in accounting principles, and net income.

Primary earnings per share and fully diluted earnings per share may also be required. Primary earnings per share is a presentation based on the outstanding common shares and those securities that are in substance equivalent to common shares and have a diluting effect on earnings per share. Convertible bonds, convertible preferred stock, stock options, and warrants are examples of common stock equivalents. The fully diluted earnings per share presentation is a pro forma presentation that shows the dilution of earnings per share that would have occurred if all contingent issuances of common stock that would individually reduce earnings per share had taken place at the beginning of the period.

PRINCIPLES FOR RECOGNIZING REVENUES AND EXPENSES

The revenue recognition principle provides guidelines for reporting revenue in the income statement. The principle generally requires that revenue be recognized in the financial statements when: 1) realized or realizable, and 2) earned. Revenues are realized when products or other assets are exchanged for cash or claims to cash or when services are rendered. Revenues are realizable when assets received or held are readily convertible into cash or claims to cash. Revenues are considered earned when the entity has substantially accomplished what it must do to be entitled to the benefits represented by the revenues. Recognition through sales or the providing (performance) of services provides a uniform and reasonable test of realization. Limited exceptions to the basic revenue principle include recognizing revenue during production (on long-term construction contracts), at the completion of production (for many commodities), and subsequent to the sale at the time of cash collection (on installment sales).

In recognizing expenses, accountants rely on the matching principle because it requires that efforts (expenses) be matched with accomplishments (revenues) whenever it is reasonable and practical to do so. For example, matching (associating) cost of goods sold with revenues from the interrelated sales that resulted directly and jointly from the same transaction as the expense is reasonable and practical. To recognize costs for which it is difficult to adopt some association with revenues, accountants use a rational and systematic allocation policy that assigns expenses to the periods during which the related assets are expected to provide benefits, such as depreciation, amortization, and insurance. Some costs are charged to the current period as expenses (or losses) merely because no future benefit is anticipated, no connection with revenue is apparent, or no allocation is rational and systematic under the circumstances, i.e., an immediate recognition principle.

The current operating concept of income would include only those value changes and events that are controllable by management and that are incurred in the current period from ordinary, normal, and recurring operations. Any unusual and nonrecurring items of income or loss would be recognized directly in the statement of retained earnings. Under this concept, investors are primarily interested in continuing income from operations.

The all-inclusive concept of income includes the total changes in equity recognized during a specific period, except for dividend distributions and capital transactions. Under this concept, unusual and nonrecurring income or loss items are part of the earning history of a company and should not be overlooked. Currently, the all-inclusive concept is generally recognized; however, certain material prior period adjustments should be reflected adjustments of the opening retained earnings balance.

FORMATS OF THE INCOME STATEMENT

The income statement can be prepared using either the single-step or the multiple-step format. The single-step format lists and totals all revenue and gain items at the beginning of the statement. All expense and loss items are then fixed and the total is deducted from the total revenue to give the net income. The multiple-step income statement presents operating revenue at the beginning of the statement and nonoperating gains, expenses, and losses near the end of the statement. However, various items of expenses are deducted throughout the statement at intermediate levels. The statement is arranged to show explicitly several important amounts, such as gross margin on sales, operating income, income before taxes, and net income. Extraordinary items, gains and losses, accounting changes, and discontinued operations are always shown separately at the bottom of the income statement ahead of net income, regardless of which format is used.

Each format of the income statement has its advantages. The advantage of the multiple-step income statement is that it explicitly displays important financial and managerial information that the user would have to calculate from a single-step income statement. The single-step format has the advantage of being relatively simple to prepare and to understand.

FURTHER READING:

Horngren, Charles T., and Gary L. Sundem. *Introduction to Financial Accounting.* 4th ed. Englewood Cliffs, NJ: Prentice Hall, 1990.

Welsch, Glen A., Robert N. Anthony, and Daniel G. Short. *Fundamentals of Financial Accounting.* 4th ed. Homewood, IL: Irwin, 1984.

SEE ALSO: Cash Flow Statements; Financial Statements

INCORPORATION

Corporate ownership is one of three broad categories of legal ownership of a business, along with **sole proprietorship** and **partnership**. In a sole proprietorship, the owner is personally liable for his or her business's debts and losses, there is little distinction made between personal and business income, and the business terminates upon the death of the owner or the owner's decision to change the legal character of the firm (by relinquishing part or all of his or her ownership in the enterprise). A partnership is merely joint ownership, and in terms of personal liability, is similar to a sole proprietorship. Both of these categories of business ownership are simple arrangements that can be entered into and dissolved fairly easily. Incorporation, on the other hand, is a more complex process for it involves the creation of a legal entity that serves as a sort of ''person'' that can enter into and dissolve contracts; incur debts; initiate or be the recipient of legal action; and own, acquire, and sell goods and property. A corporation, which must be chartered by a state or the federal government, is recognized as having rights, privileges, assets, and liabilities distinct from those of its owners.

Prospective entrepreneurs and established businesspeople operating sole proprietorships and partnerships are encouraged to weigh several factors when considering incorporating. Indeed, incorporation can have a fundamental impact on many aspects of business operation, from taxes to raising capital to owner liability.

ADVANTAGES OF INCORPORATION

- Raising Capital—Incorporation is generally regarded as an indication that the owners are serious about their business enterprise, and intend to devote time and resources to the venture for a significant period of time. This factor, as well as the reporting requirements of incorporation and—in some cases—the owners' more formidable financial resources—make corporations more attractive to some lending institutions. In addition, corporations have the option of raising capital by selling shares in their business to investors. Stockholders know that if the business they are investing in is a corporation, their personal assets are safe if the company gets into litigation or debt trouble.

- Ease of Ownership Transfer—Ownership of the company can be transferred fairly easily by simply selling stock (though some corporations attach restrictions in this regard).

- Tax Advantages—Some businesses enjoy lower tax rates under the incorporated designation than they would if they operated as a partnership or sole proprietorship. For instance, business owners can adjust the salaries they pay themselves in ways that impact on the corporation's profits and, subsequently, its tax obligations. It can also be easier for a business to invest in pension plans and other fringe benefits as a corporation because the cost of these benefits can be counted as tax-deductible business expenses.

- Liability—This factor is often cited as far and away the most important advantage to incorporation. When a company incorporates, ''the shareholders, the owners of a corporation, are liable only up to the amount of money they contribute to the firm, basically equal to their shares of stock,'' wrote Todd Buchholz in *From Here to Economy: A Shortcut to Economic Literacy.* ''In contrast, partners are legally liable for all debts and unpaid bills of the partnership. Because investors in a corporation do not risk their personal assets if the firm goes belly-up, the corporate system encourages people to invest.'' Moreover, while a corporation can be targeted in legal actions such as lawsuits, the personal assets of the company's owners cannot be touched if a judgement is rendered against their establishment since it is recognized as a legal entity separate from the owners/shareholders.

Still, while incorporation provides business owners with far greater liability protection than they would enjoy if they operated as a partnership or sole proprietorship, business experts note that certain instances remain wherein the personal assets of business owners may be vulnerable:

- Many small business owners who approach banks to secure financing for a new corporation are asked to sign a personal guarantee that assures the lending institution that they will pay back the loan if the corporation is unable to do so. Banks sometimes require similar guarantees from entrepreneurs and small business owners seeking financial assistance to lease equipment or facilities. Owners are also held personally responsible for ensuring that the corporation makes its required tax payments.

- Protection from liability can also be compromised in situations in which legal action is brought against a director or officer who is alleged to have committed some transgression outside the parameters of his or her job description. In other words, a business owner or shareholder can still be sued for personal actions.

- In some cases, key personnel of a corporation—such as board members or officers—can be held personally liable if the establishment that they operate has been found criminally negligent or guilty of willful criminal acts.

- The personal assets of business owners operating a corporation can also be threatened if it is determined that the business has not been properly established and adequately maintained. In such instances, noted the *Entrepreneur Magazine Small Business Advisor,* ''a plaintiff may claim that the corporation and you [the owner] are one and the same, and therefore your personal assets can be used to satisfy the judgement. This is called 'piercing the corporate veil.' '' The *Small Business Advisor* added, however, that there are several steps that business owners can take to ensure that their corporation protection is maintained. These include: 1) Keeping up with taxes and regulatory requirements; 2) Staying in full compliance with guidelines regarding corporate minutes and various organizational bylaws; 3) Keeping personal and corporate accounts completely separated from one another; and 4) Showing proper capitalization by maintaining a satisfactory debt-to-equity ratio;

DISADVANTAGES OF INCORPORATION

- Regulatory and Record keeping Requirements—Corporate operations are governed by local, state, and federal regulations to a greater degree than are other businesses.

- Added Cost of Doing Business—Regulatory and Record keeping guidelines and requirements often make it necessary for corporations to make additional investments (in accounting staffing, etc.) devoted to seeing that those legal requirements are met. In addition, there are fees associated with incorporating that do not have to be paid for business partnerships and sole proprietorships.

- **Double Taxation**—People who are owners of a corporation, and who also work as an employee of the business, can receive financial compensation in two different ways. In addition to receiving a salary or wages for work performed, the owner may also receive a dividend or distribution on the stock that he or she owns. Any distribution of income to stockholders via dividends is taxable, however, if the corporation is organized as a **C corporation**. This is sometimes called ''double taxation'' in recognition of the fact that such income has in reality been taxed twice, first when the corporation paid taxes on its profits, and secondly when the dividends were distributed. Companies that register as an **S corporation**, however, are able to avoid this added tax.

- Separation of Finances—While incorporation provides significant protection of owners' personal assets from repercussions of business downturns, it also means that a business owner is not allowed to tap into the corporation's account for assistance in meeting personal debts.

S CORPORATIONS AND C CORPORATIONS

Small business owners can choose from two basic types of corporations. The C corporation is the more traditional of the arrangements, and is more frequently employed by large companies. With a regular corporation, the business's profits or losses are absorbed directly into the company. With the alternative corporate arrangement—the S corporation (also sometimes known as the Subchapter S corporation)—profits and losses pass through to the company's shareholders.

The S corporation option was actually put together by the federal government in recognition of the fact that the operating challenges faced by small businesses and large businesses can often be quite different. Indeed, the S corporation was shaped specifically to accommodate small business owners. S corporations give their owners the limited liability protections provided by corporate status, while also providing them with a more advantageous tax environment. In fact, S corporation status puts companies in the same basic tax situation as partnerships and sole proprietorships. Whereas C corporations are subject to the above-mentioned double taxation, profits registered by an S corporation is taxed only once, when it reaches the company's shareholders.

To qualify as an S corporation, a business must meet the following requirements: 1) It must be a U.S. corporation; 2) It can have only a limited number of shareholders (35 in the mid-1990s); 3) It may not offer more than one class of outstanding stock. Seekers of S corporation status should also be aware that the government has additional stipulations regarding the citizenship of owners/shareholders and affiliations with other business entities. Prospective S corporations must be in accordance with all these restrictions.

THE PROCESS OF INCORPORATION

The actual fees required to incorporate generally amount to several hundred dollars, although the total cost differs from state to state (corporations usually pay both an initial filing fee and an annual fee to the states in which they operate). But while the actual cost of incorporating is nominal, the Small Business Administration has noted that the owners of a business that is going to be incorporated must agree on several important issues, including the nature of the business; the total number of shares of stock the corporation will make available; the stock that the owners will be able to purchase; the amount of financial investment that each of the owners will make; the bylaws by which the corporation will operate; the management structure of the corporation; and the name under which the business will operate.

Indeed, it is a good idea to reserve the proposed name of the corporation with the state before filing articles of incorporation. The owners of the business must make sure that they have a clear right to that name, since only one corporation may possess any given name in each state. If a business owner files articles of incorporation using a name that already belongs to another corporation, the application will be rejected. The name of the business must also include either 'corporation,' 'company,' 'limited,' or 'incorporated' as part of its legal name; such terms serve notice to people and businesses outside the company that it is a legal entity unto itself and thus subject to different laws than other business types.

Since the corporation will be a legal entity separate from its owners, separate financial accounts and record keeping practices also need to be established. Once the shareholders have reached agreement on these issues, they must prepare and file articles of incorporation or a certificate of incorporation with the corporate office of the state in which they have decided to incorporate. Any corporation—with the exception of banks and insurance companies—can incorporate under Section 3 of the Model Business Corporation Act.

Business experts also counsel organizers of a corporation to put together a preincorporation agreement that specifies the various roles and responsibilities that each owner will take on in the corporation once it has come into being. Preincorporation agreements typically cover many of the above-mentioned issues, and can be supplemented with other legal documents governing various business operations, such as inventory purchases and lease agreements. Preincorporation agreements are also sometimes drawn up with third parties. The editors of *The Entrepreneur Magazine Small Business Advisor* noted that such contracts generally address: 1) Scope of potential liability; 2) Rights and obligations for both the corporation and its organizers once it has been formed; 3) Provisions to address business issues if incorporation never occurs for some reason; and 4) Provisions for declining the contract once the corporation has been formed. The services of an attorney should be employed when putting together such a contract.

Once a company has incorporated, stock can be distributed and the shareholders can elect a board of directors to take formal control of the business. Small corporations often institute buy-sell agreements for its shareholders. Under this agreement, stock that is given up by a shareholder—either because of death or a desire to sell—must first be made available to the business's other established shareholders. Stock issues and shareholder responsibilities are, generally speaking, fairly straightforward in smaller companies, but larger corporations with large numbers of shareholders generally have to register with state regulatory agencies or the federal **Securities and Exchange Commission (SEC)**.

In addition, incorporation requires the adoption of corporate bylaws. The bylaws, which are not public record, include more specific information about how the corporation will be run. These are the rules and regulations that govern the internal affairs of the corporation, although they may not conflict with the **Articles of Incorporation** or the corporate laws of your state. The bylaws are adopted by the board or the corporation's shareholders and may be amended or repealed at a later date. When preparing bylaws, it is sometimes easiest to start with the model bylaws that typically arrive with corporate kits or incorporation guides, although these may be altered. The bylaws should specify such information as:

- The location of corporate offices;
- The names and powers of shareholders and directors;
- The date and time for regular shareholders' and board of directors' meetings;
- The content of such meetings;
- The period of notice required before such meetings;
- Voting eligibility;
- Voting procedures;
- Election procedures for seating directors and officers;
- The names and duties of officers;
- How financial transactions will be conducted;
- The procedures for amending or repealing bylaws;
- Stipulations as to whether powers or duties of board of directors may be relegated to ad hoc committees;
- Procedures to be followed in the event of a merger with another company or the dissolution of the corporation itself.

CORPORATE OWNERSHIP AND CONTROL

The owners of a corporation remain the ultimate controllers of that business's operations, but exercising that control is a more complicated process than it is for owners of partnerships or sole proprietorships. Control depends in part on whether the owners decide to make the corporation a public company—in which shares in the company are available to the general public—or a private or closely held corporation, where shares are concentrated in the hands of a few owners.

In most cases, small businesses have a modest number of shareholders or owners. As noted in *The Small Business Advisor,* ''the shareholders generally have very few powers in regard to the day-to-day operations of the corporation but are responsible for electing the board of directors and removing them from office. In smaller corporations, the shareholders can give themselves more operational powers by including provisions in the articles and bylaws of the corporation.'' In most cases, however, it is the share-holder-appointed board of directors that runs the company. Directors are responsible for all aspects of the company's operation, and it is the board that appoints the key personnel responsible for overseeing the business's daily operations. The officers (president, vice-president, treasurer, etc.), though appointed by the board of directors, often wield the greatest power in a corporation; indeed, in some corporations, officers are also members of the board of directors. Of course, in situations where only one person owns the incorporated company, he or she will bear many of the above responsibilities. As Janet Attard, author of *The Home Office and Small Business Answer Book,* commented, ''if you are the only stockholder, you might appoint yourself director, then, as director, appoint yourself, or whoever else you choose, to each of the corporate officer positions required by law in your state . . . unless your state requires different people hold those positions or requires corporations to have more than one director.''

INCORPORATING IN DELAWARE AND NEVADA

Over the years, many companies have chosen to incorporate in Delaware or Nevada because of those states' business-friendly environment regarding taxation and liability issues. But some business experts caution small businesses from automatically casting their lots with these states. As Attard noted, small businesses with a small number of shareholder-employees should probably incorporate within their own state of operation: ''Although Delaware may offer some tax breaks and potentially more statutory protection from liability for corporate directors than your own state, for a small corporation the advantages are likely to be outweighed by the disadvantages. For instance, you will have to appoint someone in Delaware to be an agent for your corporation (there are companies in Delaware that do this) [and] you will have to pay an annual franchise (corporate) tax to the state of Delaware.'' Finally, Attard pointed out that companies that incorporate in Delaware but do business in another state have to file an application in its home state to do business as a foreign corporation. This designation will require them to pay a franchise fee in addition to their usual state income taxes.

FURTHER READING:

Adams, Bob. *Adams' Streetwise Small Business Start-Up: Your Comprehensive Guide to Starting and Managing a Business.* Adams, 1996.

Allen, Kathleen R. *Launching New Ventures: An Entrepreneurial Approach.* Chicago, IL: Upstart, 1995.

Anastasio, Susan. *Small Business Insurance and Risk Management Guide.* Washington: U.S. Small Business Administration, n.a.

Attard, Janet. *The Home Office and Small Business Answer Book.* Holt, 1993.

Brittin, Jocelyn West. *Selecting the Legal Structure for Your Business.* Washington: U.S. Small Business Administration, n.a.

Buchholz, Todd G. *From Here to Economy: A Shortcut to Economic Literacy.* Dutton, 1995.

The Entrepreneur Magazine Small Business Advisor. Wiley, 1995.

Diamond, Michael R., and Julie L. Williams. *How to Incorporate: A Handbook for Entrepreneurs and Professionals.* 3d ed. Wiley, 1996.

Kirk, John. *Incorporating Your Business.* Chicago, IL: Contemporary Books, 1994.

Lewis, Ruth. ''Why Incorporate a Small Business?'' *National Public Accountant.* November 1994.

Moses, Paul W. II. ''Is Incorporating the Best Thing, Really?'' *Orlando Business Journal.* January 17, 1997.

SEE ALSO: Limited Liability Corporation; Professional Corporation

INDIVIDUAL RETIREMENT ACCOUNTS

An individual retirement account (IRA) is a tax-deferred retirement program in which any employed person can participate, including self-employed persons and small business owners. In most cases, the money placed in an IRA is deducted from the worker's income before taxes and is allowed to grow tax-deferred until the worker retires. IRA funds can be invested in a variety of ways, including stocks and bonds, money market accounts, Treasury bills, mutual funds, and **certificates of deposit**. Intended to make it easier for individuals to save money for their own retirement, IRAs are nonetheless subject to a number of complex government regulations and restrictions. The extent of annual contributions, and the tax deductibility thereof, are dependent on the individual worker's situation.

The main difference between IRAs and employer-sponsored retirement plans is that IRA funds—although held by a trust or annuity—are under the complete discretion of the account holder as far as withdrawals and choice of investments. For this reason, IRAs are known as self-sponsored and self-directed retirement accounts. Even combination plans that allow employers to make contributions, like **Simplified Employee Pension (SEP)** IRAs, are considered self-sponsored since they require the employee to set up his or her own IRA account. A special provision of IRAs allows individuals to roll over funds from an employer-sponsored retirement plan to an IRA without penalty.

IRAs were authorized by Congress in 1974 as part of a broader effort to reform laws governing pensions.

Recognizing that employers facing intense competition might decide to cut costs by reducing the retirement benefits provided to employees—and that government programs such as Social Security would not be enough to fill in the gaps—Congress sought to encourage individual taxpayers to undertake long-term savings programs for their own retirement. The **Internal Revenue Service** responded by making provisions for individual retirement accounts in section 408 of the tax code. IRAs quickly became recognized as one of the most opportunistic and flexible retirement options available, enabling workers to control their own preparations for the conclusion of their working lives.

IRA PROVISIONS

In the original provisions, elective pre-tax contributions to IRAs were limited to $1,500 per year. The maximum annual contribution increased to $2,000 in 1982, but new restrictions were imposed upon workers who were covered under an employer's retirement plan. For example, such workers were not eligible to deduct their total IRA contributions unless their adjusted gross income was less than $25,000 if unmarried, or less than $40,000 if married. A partial deduction was available for single workers who earned up to $35,000 and married workers who earned up to $50,000, but no deductions were allowed for people with higher income levels. These restrictions did not apply to self-employed individuals and others who did not participate in an employer's plan.

The way the tax code was written, individuals were intended to begin making regular withdrawals from their IRAs upon retirement. These withdrawals would be considered income and subjected to income tax, but the individual was presumed to be in a lower tax bracket by this time than they had been during their working years. "Ordinary" distributions from an IRA are those taken when a worker is between the ages of 59½ and 70½. Though workers are not required to begin receiving distributions until they reach age 70½, most establish a regular schedule of distributions to supplement their income during this time. The total annual distributions cannot exceed $150,000 per year, or they are subject to a 15 percent penalty in addition to the regular income tax. "Early" withdrawals, or those taken before a worker reaches age 59½, are subject to a 10 percent penalty on top of the regular income tax, except in cases of death or disability of the account holder. This penalty is intended to discourage younger people from viewing an IRA as a tax-deferred savings account. "Late" withdrawals, or those beginning after a worker reaches age 70½, are subject to a whopping 50 percent penalty. Since IRAs are supposed to provide income for the worker during retirement rather than inheritance for others after the worker's death, the government imposed an especially stiff penalty to ensure timely distributions.

Subsequent legislation—in particular, the Tax Reform Act of 1986—has refined the scope, provisions, and requirements of IRAs so that other forms are available besides the basic, individual "contributory" IRA. As outlined by W. Kent Moore in *The Guide to Tax-Saving Investing,* the different IRA variations include: 1) spousal IRAs, which enable a working spouse to contribute to an IRA opened for a nonworking partner; 2) third-party-sponsored IRAs, which are used by employee organizations, labor unions, and others wishing to contribute on workers' behalf; 3) Simplified Employee Pensions (SEPs), which enable employers to provide retirement benefits by contributing to workers' IRAs; 4) Savings Incentive Match Plan for Employees (SIMPLE) IRAs, which require employers to match up to 3 percent of an employee's salary, or $6,000 annually, plus allow employees to contribute another $6,000 per year to their own accounts; 5) rollover contribution accounts, which allow distributions from an IRA or an employer's qualified retirement plan to be reinvested in another IRA without penalty; and 6) nondeductible IRAs, which enable people of all income levels to contribute $2,000 per year after taxes, whether they are covered by an employer's plan or not. Though money placed in nondeductible IRAs is subject to taxes when invested, the earnings grow tax-deferred and the distributions are not taxed later.

FACTORS TO CONSIDER

Those interested in opening an IRA should familiarize themselves with the current regulations governing the amounts that may be contributed, the timing of contributions, the criteria for tax deductibility, and the penalties for making early withdrawals. They should also shop around when investigating financial institutions that offer IRAs—such as banks, credit unions, mutual funds, brokerage firms, and insurance companies—inasmuch as fees vary from institution to institution, ranging from no charge to a one-time fee for opening the account to an annual fee for maintaining the IRA. Financial institutions also differ in the amount of minimum investment, how often interest is compounded, and the type and frequency of account statement provided. There is no limit to the number of IRAs an individual can open, as long as he or she does not exceed the maximum allowable annual contribution.

Another important factor to consider, in addition to the trustee of the account, is where the IRA funds should be invested. Individuals have a wide range of investment options available to choose from—including bank accounts, certificates of deposit, stocks, bonds, annuities, mutual funds, or a combination thereof—each offering different levels of risk and rates of growth. According to the *Entrepreneur Magazine Small Business Advisor,* the ideal IRA investment is one that is reasonably stable, can be held for the long term, and provides a level of comfort for the individual investor. Most financial advisors advise against playing the stock market or investing in a single security with funds that have been earmarked for retirement, due to the risk involved. Instead, they recommend that individuals take a more diversified approach with their IRAs, such as investing in a growth-income mutual fund, in order to protect themselves against **inflation** and the inevitable swings of the stock market.

The decision about where IRA funds should be invested can be changed at any time, as often as the individual deems necessary. Switching to a different type of investment or to a mutual fund with a different objective usually only requires filling out a transfer form from the sponsoring financial institution. Since the IRA simply changes custodians in this type of transaction, and never passes through the hands of the individual investor, it is not subject to any sort of penalty or tax, and it is not considered a rollover.

Despite the number of decisions involved, IRAs nonetheless provide an important means for people to save for their retirement. "The advantages of IRAs far outweigh the disadvantages," as Moore noted. "Earnings for either deductible or nondeductible IRAs grow faster than ordinary savings accounts, because IRA earnings are tax deferred, allowing all earnings to be reinvested. Even when withdrawals are made, the remaining funds continue to grow as tax-deferred assets."

FURTHER READING:

Blakely, Stephen. "Pension Power." *Nation's Business.* July 1997.

Crouch, Holmes F. *Decisions When Retiring.* Allyear Tax Guides, 1995.

Downes, John, and Jordan Elliot Goodman. *Barron's Finance and Investment Handbook.* Barron's, 1986.

The Entrepreneur Magazine Small Business Advisor. Wiley, 1995.

Gitman, Lawrence J., and Michael D. Joehnk. *Fundamentals of Investing.* 5th ed. Scranton, PA: HarperCollins, 1993.

Moore, W. Kent. "Deferring Taxes with Retirement Accounts." In *The Guide to Tax-Saving Investing*, by David L. Scott. Old Saybrook, CT: Globe Pequot Press, 1995.

SEE ALSO: Retirement Planning

INDUSTRIAL SAFETY

The issue of industrial safety evolved concurrently with industrial development in the United States. Of central importance was the establishment of protective legislation, most significantly the **workers' compensation** laws, enacted at the start of the twenti-

eth century, and the Occupational Safety and Health Act, enacted in 1970. The issue of industrial safety was marked by a shift from compensation to prevention as well as toward an increasing emphasis on addressing the long-term effects of occupational hazards. This emphasis was helped along by insurance companies who, in order to protect themselves from workers' compensation expenses, found that it made good business sense for them to promote industrial safety programs and research industrial safety issues. Today, industrial safety is widely regarded as one of the most important factors that any business, large or small, must consider in its operations.

Worker's compensation laws vary widely from state to state but have key objectives in common. Employers are required to compensate employees for work-related injuries or sickness by paying medical expenses, disability benefits, and compensation for lost work time. In return, workers are barred in many instances from suing their employers, a provision that protects employers from large liability settlements (of course, employers may still be found liable in instances where they are found guilty of neglect or other legal violations). In his *Industrial Safety: Management and Technology,* David Colling contended that "workmen's compensation laws have done more to promote safety than all other measures collectively, because employers found it more cost-effective to concentrate on safety than to compensate employees for injury or loss of life."

THE CREATION OF OSHA

One of the key developments in industrial safety legislation was the Occupational Safety and Health Act of 1970. The Act, which was the first comprehensive industrial safety legislation passed at the federal level, passed nearly unanimously through both houses of Congress. One of the factors contributing to strong support for the act was the rise in the number of work-related fatalities in the 1960s and particularly the Farmington, West Virginia, mine disaster of 1968, in which 78 miners were killed. The Occupational Safety and Health Act was distinguished by its emphasis on the prevention of—rather than compensation for—industrial accidents and illnesses. The legislation provided for the establishment of the **Occupational Safety and Health Administration (OSHA)** and the National Institute of Occupational Safety and Health (NIOSH). Among the key provisions of the act were the development of mandatory safety and health standards, the enforcement of these standards, and standardized record-keeping and reporting procedures for businesses.

OSHA issues regulations governing a wide range of worker safety areas, all intended to meet OSHA's overriding principle that "each employer shall furnish to each of his employees employment and a place of employment which are free from recognized hazards that are causing or are likely to cause death or serious physical harm to his [or her] employees.'' OSHA regulations include both safety standards, designed to prevent accidents, and health standards, designed to protect against exposure to toxins and to address the more long-term effects of occupational hazards. So-called ''horizontal'' standards apply to all industries whereas ''vertical'' standards apply to specific industries or occupations. Some of OSHA's standards were adopted from private national organizations, such as the American National Standards Institute, the National Fire Protection Association, and the American Society of Mechanical Engineers. Other standards are developed by OSHA itself, often based on recommendations from NIOSH.

When OSHA drafts a proposal for a permanent standard, it first consults with industry and labor representatives and collects whatever scientific, medical, and engineering data is necessary to ensure that the standard adequately reflects workplace realities. Proposed standards are published in the *Federal Register.* A comment period is then held, during which input is received from interested parties including, but not limited to, representatives of industry and labor. At the close of the comment period, the proposal may be withdrawn and set aside, withdrawn and re-proposed with modifications, or approved as a final standard that is legally enforceable. All standards that become legally binding are first published in the *Federal Register* and then compiled and published in the *Code of Federal Regulations.*

OSHA's effectiveness in reducing industrial injury and illness has been debated since its earliest years. There was a 27 percent decline in the actual number of workplace fatalities from 1974 to 1986 and a 40 percent decline in the rate of fatalities over these same years. However, in his *Cooperation and Conflict in Occupational Safety and Health*, Richard Wokutch cites several studies that argue that these declines are not readily attributable to OSHA's actions. Consistent with the anti-regulatory agenda of the Reagan Administration, OSHA suffered substantial cutbacks in the areas of budget and workforce in the 1980s.

Despite the anti-regulatory trend among lawmakers in Washington, D.C., however, proponents of industrial safety measures were heartened by the passage of significant legislation during the 1980s as well. Indeed, so-called ''Right-to-Know'' laws were an important development in industrial safety legislation. The first of these laws was OSHA's Hazard Communication Standard, enacted in 1983. The **Environmental Protection Agency (EPA)** is also engaged in the administration of Right-to-Know laws as a result of the Superfund Amendments and Reauthorization Act of 1986. Right-to-Know laws require

that dangerous materials in the workplace be identified and that workers be informed of these dangers as well as trained in their safe use.

In the 1990s, increases in funding for OSHA programs under the Clinton Administration enabled the agency to increase its watchdog role in the realm of worker safety, and findings of ''willful violations'' of industrial safety laws have increased in recent years as a result. But while OSHA's enforcement actions garner the bulk of attention, especially from anti-regulatory business groups and lawmakers, the agency emphasizes its efforts to convince businesses that quite aside from moral issues, insuring worker safety makes good business sense. In the mid-1990s OSHA estimated that deaths and injuries in the workplace were costing American businesses well over $100 billion annually. The agency contends that workplace safety is particularly problematic among some smaller businesses. OSHA reported, for instance, that an analysis of 500,000 federal and state inspection records from 1988 to 1992 revealed that while more than 4,300 employees died while working for firms with fewer than 20 employees, only 127 died in the employ of firms with more than 2,500 employees.

STATE WORKER SAFETY LAWS In addition to federal worker health and safety laws, individual states are permitted to develop and operate their own job safety and health programs. If the state can show that its job safety and health standards are ''at least as effective as'' comparable federal standards, the state can be certified to assume OSH Act administration and enforcement in that state. OSHA approves and monitors state plans, and provides up to 50 percent of operating costs for approved plans. As of the mid-1990s, 23 states and jurisdictions operated complete state plans covering not only the private sector, but also state and local government employees.

INDUSTRIAL HAZARDS

One of the important aspects of industrial safety programs is the identification of hazards. Managers typically determine hazards by the examination of accident records, interviews with engineers and equipment operators, and the advice of safety specialists, such as OSHA or insurance companies. Industrial health hazards are typically categorized into three classes: chemical hazards, in which the body absorbs toxins; ergonomic hazards, such as those resulting from improper lifting or repetitive stress; and physical hazards, in which the worker is exposed to temperature extremes, atmospheric pressure, dangerous conditions, or excessive noise.

About one-tenth of industrial accidents result from operating machinery, and these accidents often result in severe injury. Among the most dangerous types of machinery are power presses and woodworking tools, which most commonly cause injury to the hands. A number of mechanisms have been developed to safeguard against such injuries. The simplest of these are barrier guards, in which the moving parts of machinery are enclosed in a protective housing. These safeguards are typically used in conjunction with sensors so that the machine cannot be operated without them. Other types of safeguards include those which prevent a machine from operating unless a worker has both hands properly in place, automated material feeding devices, warning labels, and color coding.

Toxins are most commonly ingested through inhalation, and the most commonly inhaled substances are dust, fumes, and smoke. Toxins are also commonly absorbed through the skin, and this is a bigger problem than many business owners and managers realize. Indeed, some studies indicate that skin disorders result in approximately 200,000 lost working days each year. The most common of these disorders is dermatitis, which is particularly problematic in the food preparation and chemical industries.

Among the most commonly-used toxins are industrial solvents. The toxicity of solvents varies widely by type, but the most toxic of these are carcinogens and can cause permanent damage to the nervous system through prolonged occupational overexposure. In addition, organic solvents, such as those made from petroleum, are often highly flammable. Tightly-fitted respirators with activated charcoal filters are used to protect against inhalation of organic solvents, particularly in spraying applications in which solvents are atomized. Ventilation systems comprised of fans and ducts are also used to control airborne toxins of all types. Rubber gloves are commonly used to prevent skin absorption of organic solvents.

One of the most rapidly-growing types of reported occupational injury is what the U.S. Bureau of Labor Statistics refers to as ''disorders associated with repeated trauma.'' These conditions result from repeatedly performing the same tasks over a prolonged period of time. For the manufacturing sector, they accounted for 47 percent of worker's compensation claims in 1986, up from just 20 percent in 1976. By 1994, repetitive stress disorders accounted for fully 60 percent of all workplace injuries. This increase results at least in part from the fact that a number of these disorders, such as carpal tunnel syndrome, have only recently been diagnosed.

SMALL BUSINESSES AND INDUSTRIAL SAFETY

All companies, including small businesses, are required to keep records on various aspects of their operations that are relevant to employee safety and health. All employers covered by the OSH Act are required to keep records regarding enforcement of OSHA standards; research records; job-related injury, illness, and death records; and job hazard records.

But while small businesses must adhere to many of the same regulations that govern the operations or larger companies, there also are several federal industrial safety programs available exclusively to smaller business enterprises, and OSHA and state regulatory agencies both enjoy some discretion in adjusting penalties for industrial safety violations for small companies. For example, OSHA has discretion to grant monetary penalty reductions of up to 60 percent for businesses that qualify as small firms. Other breaks that may be available to small business owners include:

1) Flexibility—OSHA gives smaller firms greater flexibility in certain safety areas (i.e., lead in construction, emergency evacuation plans, process safety management) in recognition of their limited resources.

2) Grants—Non-profit groups often receive funding from federal and state sources for the development of programs designed to help entrepreneurs and small business owners establish safety and health guidelines for their companies.

3) Mentoring—OSHA and the Voluntary Protection Programs Participants Association (VPPA) operate a mentoring program to help small firms applying for entry into VPP refine their health and safety programs. The VPP is an OSHA program that is intended to recognize a firm's safety and health achievements.

Given the importance of industrial safety both for worker health and business vitality, experts counsel small business owners to solicit the knowledge of a consultant or an attorney to ensure that they are in compliance with regulatory requirements.

FURTHER READING:

''Clinton Plan Boosts MSHA and OSHA Funding.'' *Pit and Quarry,* March 1994.

Colling, David A. *Industrial Safety: Management and Technology.* Upper Saddle River, NJ: Prentice Hall, 1990.

Dallabrida, Dale. ''OSHA Targets Injury from Repeated Motion.'' *USA Today,* November 23, 1993.

Marsh, Barbara. ''Workers at Risk: Chance of Getting Hurt is Generally Far Higher at Small Companies.'' *Wall Street Journal,* February 3, 1994.

''OSHA: Injuries, Deaths Cost Firms $115 Billion a Year.'' *Journal of Commerce and Commercial,* May 3, 1994.

''Small-Business Owners Get Cleanup Tips from OSHA.'' *Wall Street Journal,* July 12, 1994.

Stenzel, Paulette L. ''Right to Act: Advancing the Common Interests of Labor and Environmentalists,'' *Albany Law Review.* Vol. 57, no. 1, 1993.

Wokutch, Richard E. *Cooperation and Conflict in Occupational Safety and Health: A Multination Study of the Automotive Industry.* Westport, CT: Praeger, 1990.

Yohay, Stephen C. ''Recent Court Decisions on Important OSHA Enforcement Issues.'' *Employee Relations Law Journal.* Spring 1997.

SEE ALSO: Risk Management; Workplace Safety

INDUSTRY ANALYSIS

Industry analysis is a tool that facilitates a company's understanding of its position relative to other companies that produce similar products or services. Understanding the forces at work in the overall industry is an important component of effective strategic planning. Industry analysis enables small business owners to identify the threats and opportunities facing their businesses, and to focus their resources on developing unique capabilities that could lead to a competitive advantage.

''Many small business owners and executives consider themselves at worst victims, and at best observers of what goes on in their industry. They sometimes fail to perceive that understanding your industry directly impacts your ability to succeed. Understanding your industry and anticipating its future trends and directions gives you the knowledge you need to react and control your portion of that industry,'' Kenneth J. Cook wrote in his book *The AMA Complete Guide to Strategic Planning for Small Business.* ''However, your analysis of this is significant only in a relative sense. Since both you and your competitors are in the same industry, the key is in finding the differing abilities between you and the competition in dealing with the industry forces that impact you. If you can identify abilities you have that are superior to competitors, you can use that ability to establish a competitive advantage.''

An industry analysis consists of three major elements: the underlying forces at work in the industry; the overall attractiveness of the industry; and the critical factors that determine a company's success within the industry. The premier model for analyzing the structure of industries was developed by Michael E. Porter in his 1980 book *Competitive Strategy: Techniques for Analyzing Industries and Competitors.* Porter's model shows that rivalry among firms in industry depends upon five forces: the potential for new competitors to enter the market; the bargaining power of buyers and suppliers; the availability of substitute goods; and the competitors and nature of competition. These factors are outlined below.

INDUSTRY FORCES

The first step in performing an industry analysis is to assess the impact of Porter's five forces. ''The collective strength of these forces determines the ultimate profit potential in the industry, where profit potential is measured in terms of long term return on invested capital,'' Porter stated. ''The goal of competitive strategy for a business unit in an industry is to find a position in the industry where the company can best defend itself against these competitive forces or can influence them in its favor.'' Understanding the underlying forces determining the structure of the industry can highlight the strengths and weaknesses of a small business, show where strategic changes can make the greatest difference, and illuminate areas where industry trends may turn into opportunities or threats.

EASE OF ENTRY Ease of entry refers to how easy or difficult it is for a new firm to begin competing in the industry. The ease of entry into an industry is important because it determines the likelihood that a company will face new competitors. In industries that are easy to enter, sources of competitive advantage tend to wane quickly. On the other hand, in industries that are difficult to enter, sources of competitive advantage last longer, and firms also tend to benefit from having a constant set of competitors.

The ease of entry into an industry depends upon two factors: the reaction of existing competitors to new entrants; and the barriers to market entry that prevail in the industry. Existing competitors are most likely to react strongly against new entrants when there is a history of such behavior, when the competitors have invested substantial resources in the industry, and when the industry is characterized by slow growth. Some of the major barriers to market entry include economies of scale, high capital requirements, switching costs for the customer, limited access to the channels of distribution, a high degree of product differentiation, and restrictive government policies.

POWER OF SUPPLIERS Suppliers can gain bargaining power within an industry through a number of different situations. For example, suppliers gain power when an industry relies on just a few suppliers, when there are no substitutes available for the suppliers' product, when there are switching costs associated with changing suppliers, when each purchaser accounts for just a small portion of the suppliers' business, and when suppliers have the resources to move forward in the chain of distribution and take on the role of their customers. Supplier power can affect the relationship between a small business and its customers by influencing the quality and price of the final product. ''All of these factors combined will affect your ability to compete,'' Cook noted. ''They will impact your ability to use your supplier relationship to establish competitive advantages with your customers.''

POWER OF BUYERS The reverse situation occurs when bargaining power rests in the hands of buyers. Powerful buyers can exert pressure on small businesses by demanding lower prices, higher quality, or additional services, or by playing competitors off one another. The power of buyers tends to increase when single customers account for large volumes of the business's product, when a substitutes are available for the product, when the costs associated with switching suppliers are low, and when buyers possess the resources to move backward in the chain of distribution.

AVAILABILITY OF SUBSTITUTES ''All firms in an industry are competing, in a broad sense, with industries producing substitute products. Substitutes limit the potential returns of an industry by placing a ceiling on the prices firms in the industry can profitably charge,'' Porter explained. Product substitution occurs when a small business's customer comes to believe that a similar product can perform the same function at a better price. Substitution can be subtle—for example, insurance agents have gradually moved into the investment field formerly controlled by financial planners—or sudden—for example, compact disc technology has taken the place of vinyl record albums. The main defense available against substitution is product differentiation. By forming a deep understanding of the customer, some companies are able to create demand specifically for their products.

COMPETITORS ''The battle you wage against competitors is one of the strongest industry forces with which you contend,'' according to Cook. Competitive battles can take the form of price wars, advertising campaigns, new product introductions, or expanded service offerings—all of which can reduce the profitability of firms within an industry. The intensity of competition tends to increase when an industry is characterized by a number of well-balanced competitors, a slow rate of industry growth, high fixed costs, or a lack of differentiation between products. Another factor increasing the intensity of competition is high exit barriers—including specialized assets, emotional ties, government or social restrictions, strategic interrelationships with other business units, labor agreements, or other fixed costs—which make competitors stay and fight even when they find the industry unprofitable.

INDUSTRY ATTRACTIVENESS

''Industry attractiveness is the presence of absence of threats exhibited by each of the industry forces,'' Cook explained. ''The greater the threat posed by an industry force, the less attractive the industry becomes.'' Small businesses, in particular, should attempt to seek out markets in which the threats are low and the

attractiveness is high. Understanding what industry forces are at work enables small business owners to develop strategies to deal with them. These strategies, in turn, can help small businesses to find unique ways to satisfy their customers in order to develop a competitive advantage over industry rivals.

INDUSTRY SUCCESS FACTORS

Success factors are those elements that determine whether a company succeeds or fails in a given industry. They vary greatly by industry. Some examples of possible success factors include quick response to market changes, a complete product line, fair prices, excellent product quality or performance, knowledgeable sales support, a good record for deliveries, solid financial standing, or a strong management team. ''The reason for identifying success factors is that it will help lead you to areas where you can establish competitive advantages,'' Cook noted. The first step is to determine whether or not the company possesses each success factor identified. Then the small business owner can decide whether the company can and should develop additional success factors.

CONCLUSION

A comprehensive industry analysis requires a small business owner to take an objective view of the underlying forces, attractiveness, and success factors that determine the structure of the industry. Understanding the company's operating environment in this way can help the small business owner to formulate an effective strategy, position the company for success, and make the most efficient use of the limited resources of the small business. ''Once the forces affecting competition in an industry and their underlying causes have been diagnosed, the firm is in a position to identify its strengths and weaknesses relative to the industry,'' Porter wrote. ''An effective competitive strategy takes offensive or defensive action in order to create a *defendable* position against the five competitive forces.'' Some of the possible strategies include positioning the firm to use its unique capabilities as defense, influencing the balance of outside forces in the firm's favor, or anticipating shifts in the underlying industry factors and adapting before competitors do in order to gain a competitive advantage.

FURTHER READING:

Cook, Kenneth J. *The AMA Complete Guide to Strategic Planning for Small Business.* Chicago, IL: American Marketing Association, 1995.

Porter, Michael E. *Competitive Strategy: Techniques for Analyzing Industries and Competitors.* New York: Free Press, 1980.

SEE ALSO: Business Planning; Competitive Analysis; Barriers to Market Entry; Product Placement

INFLATION

Inflation is commonly understood as a steady (and usually sizable) increase in the general price level of goods and services in an economy. Inflation results from an increase in the amount of circulating currency beyond the needs of business trade. This surplus of currency is, like everything else, subject to the laws of supply and demand. When an excess is present, then, the value of the currency is decreased and on a practical level, the prices of goods and services increase. Inflation is formally defined as the rate of change in the price level, so an inflation rate of five percent per annum means that the price level is increasing at the rate of five percent annually.

INFLATION AND STANDARD OF LIVING If the inflation rate is positive and an individual's income remains constant, his or her real standard of living will fall as the individual's income will be worth less and less in successive periods. For instance, a small business owner who earns $65,000 in two successive years will likely see a drop in his or her standard of living during that second year, since even economies in excellent shape usually post mild inflation from year to year. If the inflation rate for the period in question was ten percent, then the ultimate purchasing power of that small business owner would decline at the rate of ten percent as well, unless he or she can boost earnings above the $65,000 figure.

KEY ELEMENTS IN DETERMINING THE INFLATION RATE The rate of inflation is derived by calculating the rate of change in a price index. A price index, in turn, measures the level of prices of goods and services at any point of time. The number of items included in a price index vary depending on the objective of the index.

Generally, the federal government tracks three primary price indices. These indices are closely studied by business executives, investors, and other members of the business community when they are released to the public, for they all have their particular advantages and uses for gauging economic trends. The first index is called the **consumer price index (CPI)**, which measures the average retail prices paid by consumers for goods and services bought by them. About 400 items are included in this index.

The second price index used to measure the inflation rate is called the producer price index (PPI). It is a much broader measure than the consumer price index because it measures the wholesale prices of approximately 3000 items. The items included in this index are those that are typically used by producers (manufacturers and businesses) and thus contain many raw materials and semifinished goods.

The third measure of inflation is called the implicit price deflator. This index measures the prices of all goods and services included in the calculation of the current output of goods and services in the economy, known as **gross domestic product (GDP)**. It is the broadest measure of the price level. These three measurements of the inflation rate are most likely to move in the same direction, although they usually do not do so to the same extent. Differences can arise due to the differing number of goods and services included for the purpose of compiling the three indexes.

FURTHER READING:

Brealey, Richard A., and Stewart C. Myers. *Principles of Corporate Finance.* 4th ed. New York: McGraw-Hill, 1994.

Froyen, Richard T. *Macroeconomics: Theories and Policies.* 4th ed. Macmillan Publishing Company, 1993.

Gordon, Robert J. *Macroeconomics.* 6th ed. HarperCollins College Publishers, 1993.

Sommers, Albert T. *The U.S. Economy Demystified.* Lexington Books, 1985.

INFORMATION BROKERS

Information brokers provide, for a fee, information retrieval from publicly accessible data sources, most often online databases. Information brokering first emerged as a business opportunity for individuals in the mid-1950s. Also known as independent information specialists, brokers often do much more than gather the information. In this day and age, when almost anyone can access huge amounts of data over the Internet, brokers provide a number of special services, including: writing reports that analyze the data they obtain, creating internal databases for clients to manage their in-house information, maintaining current awareness services that update a client whenever new information on a given topic becomes available, and more.

A good broker can save a client time and money. While it may be tempting to try to jump on the Internet and do the research yourself (especially for a small businessperson with limited financial resources), searching for data can be an arduous and time-consuming process, especially if you are not an expert in the realm of online searching. In addition, most brokers subscribe to online databases that are not available to the public, even on the Internet. Subscriptions to these databases, which often contain high-level professional, business, and/or scientific information, can cost up to several thousand dollars a year. Clearly, that cost is prohibitive for many small businesses, especially when a one-time information search is all that is needed.

Finding a good broker is important. A good broker will tell you when you actually can find the information yourself for free, but will also make it clear when his or her services are needed. Check to see what online services the broker subscribes to, and how long they have been in business. The growth of the Internet and commercial services such as America Online and CompuServe have led to an explosion in the number of people who call themselves information brokers or specialists, but not all of these businesses are legitimate. Relatively new information broker businesses may be perfectly legitimate, but business consultants still urge small business owners to be careful about selecting a specialist without first conducting adequate research into the company's history and other clients. Analysts indicate that the best information brokers in the field often have a background in library science (many brokers have been employed at public or corporate libraries) or have started out actually working for one of the large database provider companies. Other factors to consider include education, rates, specialty areas, subcontracting capability, and business practices.

Be aware that information brokers can do more than collect online data. They can search public records, conduct competition checks when you are starting a new business, or visit a local library to comb through materials there. Perhaps most importantly, they can, if needed, conduct phone research by interviewing people and then preparing a report based on those interviews. As one broker said in *Searcher* magazine, "The most desired information is, and will continue to be, in people's heads."

HOUSEBROKERS If a one-time search is needed, one should also keep in mind that many of the online services maintain their own in-house information brokering services. Sometimes known as "housebrokers," these in-house retrieval specialists work for one of the data providers. These data providers maintains staffs of information retrieval specialists for customers. A businessperson can call a specific data provider, explain that they need a one-time search (as opposed to a full-time subscription to their databases, which again, can cost thousands of dollars), and the company will hand the job off to one of their housebrokers, who will conduct the search and provide the clients with the results for a fee. Using a housebroker can be advantageous if the information you need is limited to one topic and will not require extensive searches of numerous databases from several vendors. In the latter instance, however, it may be preferable to secure the services of a private broker who can take advantage of many sources.

FURTHER READING:

Detwiler, Susan M. "How to Choose an Information Broker." *Bulletin of the American Society for Information Science.* February-March 1995.

Gullickson, Cindy T. "Information Brokering: Sailing the Sea of Change." *Searcher.* January 1997.

Haswell, Holli. "A Customer's Perspective." *Searcher.* March 1996.

Laver, Ross. "The Next Frontier." *Macleans.* January 22, 1996.

Levine, Marilyn M. "A Brief History of Information Brokering." *Bulletin of the American Society for Information Science.* February-March 1995.

Ojala, Marydee. "Housebrokers: Home Alone No More." *Searcher.* September 1993.

INITIAL PUBLIC OFFERINGS

An initial public offering (IPO) is the process through which a privately held company issues shares of stock to the public for the first time. Also known as "going public," an IPO transforms a small business from a privately owned and operated entity into one that is owned by public stockholders. An IPO is a significant stage in the growth of many small businesses, as it provides them with access to the public capital market and also increases their credibility and exposure. Becoming a public entity involves significant changes for a small business, though, including a loss of flexibility and control for management. In many cases, however, an IPO may be the only means left of financing growth and expansion. The decision to go public is sometimes influenced by venture capitalists or founders who wish to cash in on their early investment.

Staging an IPO is also a very time-consuming and expensive process. A small business interested in going public must apply to the **Securities and Exchange Commission (SEC)** for permission to sell stock to the public. The SEC registration process is quite complex and requires the company to disclose a variety of information to potential investors. The IPO process can take as little as six months or as long as two years, during which time management's attention is distracted away from day-to-day operations. It can also cost a company between $50,000 and $250,000 in underwriting fees, legal and accounting expenses, and printing costs.

Overall, going public is a complex decision that requires careful consideration and planning. Experts recommend that small business owners consider all the alternatives first (such as securing venture capital, forming a limited partnership or joint venture, or selling shares through private placement, self-underwriting, or a direct public offering), examine their current and future capital needs, and be aware of how an IPO will affect the availability of future financing.

According to Jennifer Lindsey in her book *The Entrepreneur's Guide to Capital,* the ideal candidate for an IPO is a small- to medium-sized company in an emerging industry, with annual revenues of at least $10 million and a profit margin of over 10 percent of revenues. It is also important that the company have a stable management group, growth of at least 10 percent annually, and capitalization featuring no more than 25 percent debt. Companies that meet these basic criteria still need to time their IPO carefully in order to gain the maximum benefits. Lindsey suggested going public when the stock markets are receptive to new offerings, the industry is growing rapidly, and the company needs access to more **capital** and public recognition to support its strategies for expansion and growth.

ADVANTAGES OF GOING PUBLIC

The primary advantage a small business stands to gain through an initial public stock offering is access to capital. In addition, the capital does not have to be repaid and does not involve an interest charge. The only reward that IPO investors seek is an appreciation of their investment and possibly dividends. Besides the immediate infusion of capital provided by an IPO, a small business that goes public may also find it easier to obtain capital for future needs through new stock offerings or public debt offerings. A related advantage of an IPO is that it provides the small business's founders and venture capitalists with an opportunity to cash out on their early investment. Those shares of equity can be sold as part of the IPO, in a special offering, or on the open market some time after the IPO. However, it is important to avoid the perception that the owners are seeking to bail out of a sinking ship, or the IPO is unlikely to be a success.

Another advantage IPOs hold for small businesses is increased public awareness, which may lead to new opportunities and new customers. As part of the IPO process, information about the company is printed in newspapers across the country. The excitement surrounding an IPO may also generate increased attention in the **business press**. There are a number of laws covering the disclosure of information during the IPO process, however, some small business owners must be careful not to get carried away with the publicity. A related advantage is that the public company may have enhanced credibility with its suppliers, customers, and lenders, which may lead to improved credit terms.

Yet another advantage of going public involves the ability to use stock in creative incentive packages for management and employees. Offering shares of stock and stock options as part of **employee compensation** may enable a small business to attract better management talent, and to provide them with an incentive to perform well. Employees who become part-owners through a stock plan may be motivated by sharing in the company's success. Finally, an initial public offering provides a public valuation of a small business. This means that it will be easier for the company to enter into **mergers and acquisitions**, because it can offer stock rather than cash.

DISADVANTAGES OF GOING PUBLIC

The biggest disadvantages involved in going public are the costs and time involved. Experts note that a company's management is likely to be occupied with little else during the entire IPO process, which may last as long as two years. The small business owner and other top managers must prepare registration statements for the SEC, consult with investment bankers, attorneys, and accountants, and take part in the personal marketing of the stock. Many people find this to be an exhaustive process and would prefer to simply run their company.

Another disadvantage is that an IPO is extremely expensive. In fact, it is not unusual for a small business to pay between $50,000 and $250,000 to prepare and publicize an offering. In his article for *The Portable MBA in Finance and Accounting,* Paul G. Joubert noted that a small business owner should not be surprised if the cost of an IPO claims between 15 and 20 percent of the proceeds of the sale of stock. Some of the major costs include the lead underwriter's commission; out-of-pocket expenses for legal services, accounting services, printing costs, and the personal marketing ''road show'' by managers; .02 percent filing costs with the SEC; fees for public relations to bolster the company's image; plus ongoing legal, accounting, filing, and mailing expenses. Despite such expense, it is always possible that an unforeseen problem will derail the IPO before the sale of stock takes place. Even when the sale does take place, most underwriters offer IPO shares at a discounted price in order to ensure an upward movement in the stock during the period immediately following the offering. The effect of this discount is to transfer wealth from the initial investors to new shareholders.

Other disadvantages involve the public company's loss of confidentiality, flexibility, and control. SEC regulations require public companies to release all operating details to the public, including sensitive information about their markets, profit margins, and future plans. An untold number of problems and conflicts may arise when everyone from competitors to employees know all about the inner workings of the company. By diluting the holdings of the company's original owners, going public also gives management less control over day-to-day operations. Large shareholders may seek representation on the board and a say in how the company is run. If enough shareholders become disgruntled with the company's stock value or future plans, they can stage a takeover and oust management. The dilution of ownership also reduces management's flexibility. It is not possible to make decisions as quickly and efficiently when the board must approve all decisions. In addition, SEC regulations restrict the ability of a public company's management to trade their stock and to discuss company business with outsiders.

Public entities also face added pressure to show strong short-term performance. Earnings are reported quarterly, and shareholders and financial markets always want to see good results. Unfortunately, long-term strategic investment decisions may tend to have a lower priority than making current numbers look good. The additional reporting requirements for public companies also add expense, as the small business will likely need to improve accounting systems and add staff. Public entities also encounter added costs associated with handling shareholder relations.

THE PROCESS OF GOING PUBLIC

Once a small business has decided to go public, the first step in the IPO process is to select an underwriter to act as an intermediary between the company and the capital markets. Joubert recommended that small business owners solicit proposals from a number of investment banks, then evaluate the bidders on the basis of their reputation, experience with similar offerings, experience in the industry, distribution network, record of post-offering support, and type of underwriting arrangement. Other considerations include the bidders' valuation of the company and recommended share price.

There are three basic types of underwriting arrangements: best efforts, which means that the investment bank does not commit to buying any shares but agrees to put forth its best effort to sell as many as possible; all or none, which is similar to best efforts except that the offering is canceled if all the shares are not sold; and firm commitment, which means that the investment bank purchases all the shares itself. The firm commitment arrangement is probably best for the small business, since the underwriter holds the risk of not selling the shares. Once a lead underwriter has been selected, that firm will form a team of other underwriters and brokers to assist it in achieving a broad distribution of the stock.

The next step in the IPO process is to assemble an underwriting team consisting of attorneys, independent accountants, and a financial printer. The attorneys for the underwriter draft all the agreements, while the attorneys for the company advise management about meeting all SEC regulations. The accountants issue opinions about the company's financial statements in order to reassure potential investors. The financial printer handles preparation of the prospectus and other written tools involved in marketing the offering.

After putting together a team to handle the IPO, the small business must then prepare an initial registration statement according to SEC regulations. The main body of the registration statement is a prospectus containing detailed information about the company, including its financial statements and a management analysis. The management analysis is perhaps the most important and time-consuming part of the IPO process. In it, the small business owners must simultaneously disclose all of the potential risks faced by the business and convince investors that it is a good investment. This section is typically worded very carefully and reviewed by the company's attorneys to ensure compliance with SEC rules about truthful disclosure.

The SEC rules regarding public stock offerings are contained in two main acts: the Securities Act of 1933 and the Securities Act of 1934. The former concerns the registration of IPOs with the SEC in order to protect the public against fraud, while the latter regulates companies after they have gone public, outlines registration and reporting procedures, and sets forth insider trading laws. Upon completion of the initial registration statement, it is sent to the SEC for review. During the review process, which can take up to two months, the company's attorneys remain in contact with the SEC in order to learn of any necessary changes. Also during this time, the company's financial statements must be audited by independent accountants in accordance with SEC rules. This audit is more formal than the usual accounting review and provides investors with a much higher degree of assurance about the company's financial position.

Throughout the SEC review period—which is sometimes called the ''cooling off'' or ''quiet'' period—the company also begins making controlled efforts to market the offering. The company distributes a preliminary prospectus to potential investors, and the small business owners and top managers travel around to make personal presentations of the material in what are known as ''road shows.'' It is important to note, however, that management cannot disclose any further information beyond that contained in the prospectus during the SEC review period. Other activities taking place during this time include filing various forms with different states in which the stock will be sold (the differing state requirements are known as ''blue sky laws'') and holding a due diligence meeting to review financial statements one last time.

At the end of the cooling off period, the SEC provides comments on the initial registration statement. The company then must address the comments, agree to a final offering price for the shares, and file a final amendment to the registration statement. Technically, the actual sale of stock is supposed to become effective 20 days after the final amendment is filed, but the SEC usually grants companies an acceleration so that it becomes effective immediately. This acceleration grows out of the SEC's recognition that the stock market can change dramatically over a 20-day period. The actual selling of shares then takes place, beginning on the official offering date and continuing for seven days. The lead investment banker supervises the public sale of the security. During the offering period, the investment bankers are permitted to "stabilize" the price of the security by purchasing shares in the secondary market. This process is called pegging, and it is permitted to continue for up to ten days after the official offering date. The investment bankers may also support the offering through over-allotment, or selling up to 15 percent more stock when demand is high.

After a successful offering, the underwriter meets with all parties to distribute the funds and settle all expenses. At that time the transfer agent is given authorization to forward the securities to the new owners. An IPO closes with the transfer of the stock, but the terms of the offering are not yet completed. The SEC requires the filing of a number of reports pertaining to the appropriate use of the funds as described in the prospectus. If the offering is terminated for any reason, the underwriter returns the funds to the investors.

IMPROVING THE PROSPECTS FOR A SUCCESSFUL IPO

For most small businesses, the decision to go public is made gradually over time as changes in the company's performance and capital needs make an IPO seem more desirable and necessary. But many companies still fail to bring their plans to sell stock to completion due to a lack of planning. In an article for *Entrepreneur,* David R. Evanson outlined a number of steps small business owners can take to improve the prospects of an IPO long before their company formally considers going public. One step involves assessing and taking action to improve the company's image, which will be scrutinized by investors when the time comes for an IPO. It is also necessary to reorganize as a corporation and begin keeping detailed financial records.

Another step small business owners can take in advance to prepare their companies to go public is to supplement management with experienced professionals. Investors like to see a management team that generates confidence and respect within the industry, and that can be a source of innovative ideas for future growth. Forming this sort of management team may require a small business owner to hire outside of his or her own local network of business associates. It may also involve setting up lucrative benefit plans to help attract and retain top talent. Similarly, the small business owner should set about building a solid board of directors that will be able to help the company maximize shareholder value once it has become a public entity. It is also helpful for the small business owner to begin making contacts with investment banks, attorneys, and accountants in advance of planning an IPO. Evanson recommended using a Big Six accounting firm, since they have earned the trust of investors nationwide.

Finally, Evanson recommended that small businesses interested in eventually going public begin acting like a large corporation in their relationships with customers, suppliers, employees, and the government. Although many deals involving small businesses are sealed with an informal handshake, investors like to see formal, professional contracts with customers, suppliers, and independent contractors. They also favor formal human resource programs, including hiring procedures, performance reviews, and benefit plans. It is also important for small businesses to protect their unique products and ideas by applying for patents and trademarks as needed. All of these steps, when taken in advance, can help to smooth a small business's passage to becoming a public entity.

FURTHER READING:

Arkebauer, James B., and Ronald M. Schultz. *Cashing Out: The Entrepreneur's Guide to Going Public.* New York: HarperBusiness, 1991.

Evanson, David R. "Public School: Learning How to Prepare for an IPO." *Entrepreneur.* October 1997.

Joubert, Paul G. "Going Public." In *The Portable MBA in Finance and Accounting.* Edited by John Leslie Livingstone. New York: Wiley, 1992.

Lindsey, Jennifer. *The Entrepreneur's Guide to Capital: The Techniques for Capitalizing and Refinancing New and Growing Businesses.* Chicago: Probus, 1986.

Roberts, Holme, and Harold A. S. Bloomenthal. *Going Public Handbook.* New York: Clark Boardman, 1991.

Sutton, David P., and M. William Benedetto. *Initial Public Offerings: A Strategic Planner for Raising Equity Capital.* Chicago: Probus, 1988.

SEE ALSO: Business Expansion; Stocks

INNOVATION

According to Jane Henry in her book *Creative Management,* innovation is "the process whereby creative ideas are developed into something tangible, like a new product or practice." Innovation is the basic driving force behind entrepreneurship and the creation of small businesses. When an individual comes up with an idea that has not previously been explored, or a niche that larger businesses have not been able to exploit, he or she may be able to turn that idea into a successful business venture. "Ideas are the fuel that keep entrepreneurial fires blazing," I. Satya Sreenivas wrote in an article for *The Business Journal.* "Savvy entrepreneurs realize the fact that ideas can originate from anywhere at anytime, and a random idea could be more worthwhile than a well-researched project."

Of course, not every new idea has the potential to become a successful business. And in many cases, individuals with good, marketable ideas fail to come up with the capital needed to turn their ideas into reality. But innovation is still a necessary first step for small business success. "Small business experts advise that a businessperson should be open-minded and grab an opportunity that comes his or her way," Sreenivas noted. "While recognizing which one of the hundreds of ideas may turn into a success is an art rather than a science, there are still some rules of thumb to keep the stream of ideas flowing and evaluate them for their potential." Sreenivas went on to explain that the ideas with the best potential are usually obvious, appeal to the gut instincts, and involve a leap forward in thinking.

Entrepreneurs cannot afford to stop innovating once they have established a successful business. Innovation applies not only to new business and product ideas, but also to the internal workings of a company. Successful business owners continually innovate with regards to internal systems and processes in order to create and sustain a source of competitive advantage. "The global economy requires that companies generate an unending stream of new products, systems, technologies, and services," Claus Weyrich wrote in an article for *Electronic News.* "And innovation has to be applied to things other than products."

According to Weyrich, sustaining innovation in a business organization requires an understanding of the company's core competencies, an innovative **corporate culture**, and a systematic approach. He described three phases in the innovation process: 1) the invention phase, in which ideas are generated; 2) the implementation phase, in which the best ideas are selected and developed further; and 3) the market penetration phase, in which ideas are exploited for commercial gain. This process is an ongoing one, with feedback used to close the loop.

In an article for *Chemical Week,* Ken Cottrill claimed that companies of all sizes need to place innovation in a broader context than just traditional research and development and manage the process of innovation in a structured way. "Companies need to establish a seamless innovation process—an enterprise-wide exchange of ideas that will ensure that the information and expertise required to create, market, and service breakthrough products is available and accessible to those who need it," he explained. "If all the people able to extract value from a new product or technology are in the information loop, there is a smaller chance that opportunities will be squandered." Making use of the information resources available within a company allows employees to benefit from "corporate memory." They are better able to focus on innovation because they know where others have been before them.

It is important to include the whole company in the innovation process, because the germ of idea can come from anywhere, and the best ideas often grow out of a combination of functional areas. Cottrill recommended establishing a network structure in order to provide a framework for innovation. A network structure includes cross-functional groups within the company, cross-links between the various groups, and also links involving external organizations such as customers and **suppliers**. "Companies of all sizes can adopt this approach to innovation. The basic requirement is the development of networks that act as agents for innovation within the company," Cottrill noted. "There is no standard blueprint for these networks, because they are shaped by a company's business goals and organizational structure. However, the individuals who make up these groups are unified by a common mission and are in regular communication." A network structure can be overlaid on a hierarchy and thus does not necessarily require a major overhaul.

Small businesses face a number of obstacles to effective innovation, including a shortage of resources. But studies suggest that a lack of strategic alignment and well-defined processes can be greater obstacles to innovation. In fact, one of the most important factors in promoting company-wide innovation is the support of the small business owner. "A corporation's synapses may be buzzing with creative ideas and initiatives, but without support from the top echelons, this effort can lose momentum, and innovation becomes stifled," Cottrill stated.

FURTHER READING:

Cottrill, Ken. "Networking for Innovation." *Chemical Week.* February 25, 1998.

Henry, Jane, ed. *Creative Management.* London: Sage Publications, 1991.

Michalko, Michael. *Thinkertoys: A Handbook of Business Creativity for the 1990s.* Berkeley, CA: Ten Speed Press, 1991.

Sreenivas, I. Satya. "First Idea May Not Be the Best." *The Business Journal.* November 3, 1997.

Weyrich, Claus. "The Meaning of Innovation." *Electronic News.* February 16, 1998.

SEE ALSO: Cross-Functional Teams; Entrepreneurship

INSURANCE POOLING

Insurance pooling is a practice, rapidly gaining popularity in the small business community, wherein a group of small firms join together to secure better insurance rates and coverage plans by virtue of their increased buying power as a bloc. This practice is primarily used for securing health and **disability insurance** coverage.

Small business enterprises have long complained that insurers hand out discounts to big clients, who have substantial purchasing power and large numbers of employees, and that those insurers too often try to make up those discount losses by hiking rates for their smaller clients. Unable to buy good coverage on their own, smaller companies were forced to rely on pooling plans created and managed by trade associations or other affiliated business groups. In recent years, however, another alternative, in which private businesses band together and organize their own pools, has emerged. Distinct entities have been created to address both health and disability coverage needs, and these two types differ in several significant respects in their respective approaches.

HEALTH INSURANCE POOLS Health insurance pools, which are also sometimes called insurance purchasing alliances or health-insurance purchasing co-ops, provide group health policies exclusively to small businesses. Rules governing these alliances vary from state to state, with some states offering eligibility to sole proprietorships and others providing coverage to businesses with up to 100 employees. On average, however, these health insurance pools target employers of three to 50 people.

Small businesses that join one of these pools can typically count on the following benefits: 1) A community premium rate that is significantly lower than any individual rate it could demand; 2) In many cases, premium increases are capped for the first several years of the policy; 3) Centralized administration of the policy among all of companies covered under it, which results in savings in work hours and paperwork; and 4) Standard rates that do not fluctuate according to company size or work force health history. Most importantly, these policies provide coverage that is comparable to that offered in more expensive packages.

First tried in California in the early 1990s, these types of pools could be found in 15 states by 1997. In addition, several more states are slated to open their doors to such pooling strategies over the next few years. Analysts warn, however, that the rules and regulations governing health insurance pools vary considerably from state to state, and note that the laws of a number of states make it unlikely that these alliances will make an appearance within their borders any time soon. "Because they are usually locally based and privately operated, health co-ops or alliances have evolved quite differently in the 15 states where they are functioning," explained Stephen Blakely in *Nation's Business*. "For instance, California's co-op plan is run by an independent state agency that defines the benefits and negotiates with insurers. Florida and Texas have less state control and permit more autonomy among alliances. In New York and some other states, local business-sponsored health alliances operate on their own. . . . Some states have long-standing laws expressly prohibiting businesses from coming together to obtain insurance. Other states have not enacted laws that would enable small firms to buy health insurance regardless of their workers' health status, that would limit insurance-rate variability between companies of similar size and labor characteristics, and that would prohibit insurers from canceling small groups' coverage without cause."

DISABILITY INSURANCE POOLS Disability insurance pools, also called risk-purchasing groups, operate under the same guiding principles as health insurance alliances—by joining together into one single negotiating group, small businesses can increase their bargaining power when dealing with insurers. These groups, noted *Nation's Business* contributor Roberta Reynes, are usually composed of companies that hail from the same industry sector, and thus face many of the same disability risks.

These disability insurance pools arose in the aftermath of the 1986 Risk Retention Act, which was passed by Congress in an effort to address the growing inability of small business owners to obtain liability insurance because of its rapidly growing cost. "Risk-retention groups enable companies in the same industry, such as plastics or chemicals, to cut insurance costs by forming what are, in effect, mini insurance companies to self-insure against liability claims," explained Lynn Woods in *Nation's Business*. "Risk-purchasing groups, on the other hand, permit group purchasing of liability coverage."

Interestingly, insurance companies have been among the biggest boosters of this new type of disability coverage arrangement. Woods pointed out that "insurance companies find risk-purchasing groups attractive prospects because the companies can save costs in two ways—by using a single agent or broker for multiple states and by tailoring a policy for a group based on a similar level of risk."

FURTHER READING:

Anastasio, Susan. *Small Business Insurance and Risk Management Guide.* Small Business Administration, n.a.

Blakely, Stephen. "An Update on Health-Care Pools." *Nation's Business.* May 1997.

Reynes, Roberta. ''Do-It-Yourself Workers Comp.'' *Nation's Business.* April 1995.

Woods, Lynn. ''Gaining an Edge on Liability.'' *Nation's Business.* June 1996.

SEE ALSO: Health Insurance Options; Multiple Employer Trust; Risk Management

INTELLECTUAL PROPERTY

Intellectual property is an intangible creation of the human mind, usually expressed or translated into a tangible form, that is assigned certain rights of property. Examples of intellectual property include an author's **copyright** on a book or article, a distinctive logo design representing a soft drink company and its products, or a patent on the process to manufacture chewing gum. Intellectual property law covers the protection of copyrights, patents, **trademarks**, and trade secrets, as well as other legal areas, such as unfair competition. In effect, intellectual property laws give the creator of a new and unique product or idea a temporary monopoly on its use. The value of intellectual property to an individual or company is not based on physical properties, such as size and structure. Instead, intellectual property is valuable because it represents ownership and an exclusive right to use, manufacture, reproduce, or promote a unique creation or idea. In this way, it is perhaps the most valuable asset a person or small business can own.

DEVELOPMENT OF INTELLECTUAL PROPERTY LAWS

The laws protecting intellectual property in the United States exist at both the state and federal levels. State laws cover a broad spectrum of intellectual property fields, from trade secrets to the right of publicity. The laws differ somewhat from state to state. At the federal level, the Constitution and legislation authorized under the Constitution deal exclusively with patents and copyrights, and partially with trademarks and related areas of unfair competition.

Intellectual property protection first became an important issue at an international level during trade and tariff negotiations in the nineteenth century, and has remained so ever since. One of the first international treaties relating to intellectual property in the broadest sense was the International Convention for the Protection of Industrial Property, or the Paris Convention. Written in 1883, the treaty created under the Paris Convention provided protection for such properties as patents, industrial models and designs, trademarks, and trade names. Over 100 countries have signed the Paris Convention treaty, and it has been modified several times. Two of the most important provisions of the treaty relate to the rights of national treatment and priority.

The right of national treatment ensures that those individuals seeking a patent or trademark in a foreign country will not be discriminated against and will receive the same rights as a citizen of that country. The right of priority provides an inventor one year from the date of filing a patent application in his or her home country (six months for a trademark or design application) to file an application in a foreign country. The legal, effective date of application in the foreign country is then retroactively the legal, effective filing date in the home country, provided the application is made within the protection period. If the invention is made public prior to filing the home country application, however, the right of priority in a foreign country is no longer applicable.

Enforcement and protection of intellectual property at the international level has historically been extremely complex. Laws have varied significantly from country to country, and the political climate within each country has influenced the extent of protection available. Separate legislation and treaties specifically addressed relevant procedures, conventions, and standards for each area within the scope of intellectual property, such as copyright or trade secrets.

Many U.S. and international laws relating to intellectual property were significantly altered with the 1994 passage of the **General Agreement on Tariffs and Trade (GATT)**. In fact, the member nations that signed the GATT committed themselves to a higher degree of intellectual property protection than had been provided under any earlier multinational treaties. Under the guidance of the World Trade Organization (WTO), all member nations were required to adopt specific provisions for the enforcement of rights and settlement of disputes relating to intellectual property. Under these provisions, trademark counterfeiting and commercial copyright piracy are subject to criminal penalties.

INTELLECTUAL PROPERTY AND SMALL BUSINESSES

The protection of intellectual property—such as new products, processes, designs, and writings—is one of the cornerstones encouraging the formation and growth of small businesses in the United States. It allows individuals who come up with a new idea to enjoy the exclusive use of that idea for a certain period of time. Of course, those rights can be assigned to others via a contract if the individual is not in a position to exploit his or her invention. Since intellectual property law is so complex, small business owners will usually need to consult an attorney in order to protect themselves to the full extent of the law. It is also important for would-be entrepreneurs to be aware of the legal rights of others as they prepare to engage in business activities. For example, intellectual property created by another person or company cannot be used without first obtaining a written release.

FURTHER READING:

Foster, Frank H., and Robert L. Shook. *Patents, Copyrights & Trademarks*. Wiley, 1993.

Lickson, Charles P. *A Legal Guide for Small Business*. Crisp Publications, 1994.

McCarthy, J. Thomas. *McCarthy's Desk Encyclopedia of Intellectual Property*. Washington: Bureau of National Affairs, 1991.

Miller, Arthur R., and Michael H. Davis. *Intellectual Property: Patents, Trademarks, and Copyright in a Nutshell*. West, 1990.

"Protecting Intellectual Property: An Introductory Guide for U.S. Businesses on Protecting Intellectual Property Abroad." *Business America*. July 1991.

Tabalujan, Benny. "Keeping the Fruits of Your Intellectual Pursuit to Yourself." *Business Times*. July 1993.

SEE ALSO: Corporate Logo; Inventions and Patents; Proprietary Information

INTERCULTURAL COMMUNICATION

The term "intercultural communication" is often used to refer to the wide range of communication issues that often arise within an organization composed of individuals from a variety of religious, social, ethnic, and technical backgrounds. Each of these individuals brings a unique set of experiences and values to the workplace, many of which can be traced to the culture in which they grew up and now operate. Businesses that are able to facilitate effective communication—both written and verbal—between the members of these various cultural groups will be far better equipped to succeed in the competitive business world than will those organizations that allow problems from internal cultural differences to fester and harden, for such developments inevitably have a negative impact on overall performance.

The importance of effective intercultural communication can hardly be overstated. Indeed, as Trudy Milburn pointed out in *Management Review,* communication serves not only as an expression of cultural background, but as a *shaper* of cultural identity. "Cultural identities, like meaning, are socially negotiated," she wrote. "Ethnic identities, class identities, and professional identities are formed and enacted through the process of communication. What it means to be white, Jewish, or gay is based on a communication process that constructs those identities. It is more than just how one labels oneself, but how one acts in the presence of like and different others, that constructs a sense of identity and membership."

LANGUAGE—CORNERSTONE OF INTERCULTURAL COMMUNICATION

Differences in culture reflect themselves in a variety of ways. For instance, one cultural norm may have a significantly different conception of time than another, or a different idea of what constitutes appropriate body language and physical space when engaged in conversation. But most researchers, employees, and business owners agree that the most important element in effective intercultural communication concerns language. "A great deal of ethnocentrism is centered around language," said John P. Fernandez in *Managing a Diverse Work Force: Regaining the Competitive Edge.* "Language issues are becoming a considerable source of conflict and inefficiency in the increasingly diverse work force throughout the world. . . . No corporation can be competitive if co-workers avoid, don't listen to, perceive as incompetent, or are intolerant of employees who have problems with the language. In addition, these attitudes could be carried over into their interactions with customers who speak English as a second language, resulting in disastrous effects on customer relations and, thus, the corporate bottom line."

Small business owners, then, should make sure that they do not make assumptions about the abilities of another person—either a vendor, employee, or partner—that are based on ethnocentric assumptions of their own culture's superiority in the realm of communication. "Each time you hold up your standards of what is good when judging written or oral communication from another culture, you must be careful," cautioned Herta A. Murphy and Herbert W. Hildebrandt in *Effective Business Communications.* "To say, as did an American manager, 'German reports begin with Adam and Eve' misses the point: German are more thorough in submitting reports than we are. Withhold evaluative statements on foreign communication styles until you recognize that different cultures use different communication methods."

CULTURAL DIFFERENCES IN LISTENING Often overlooked in discussion of intercultural communication are the sometimes significant cultural differences that exist concerning the practice of listening. Tips about establishing culturally sensitive verbal and **written communication** practices within an organization are plentiful, but in many cases, relatively short shrift is given to cultural differences in listening, the flip side of the communication coin. "Codes of conduct that specify how listening should be demonstrated are based upon certain cultural assumptions about what counts as listening," said Milburn. But while the prevailing norms of communication in American business may call for the listener to be quiet and offer body language (steady eye contact, for instance) intended to assure the speaker that his or her words are being heeded, many cultures have different standards that may strike the uninitiated as rude or disorienting. "A person who communicates by leaning forward and getting close may be very threatening to someone who values personal space," pointed out *Oregon Business*'s Megan Monson. "And that person could be perceived as hostile and unfriendly, simply because of poor eye contact." The key, say analysts, is to make certain that your organization recognizes that cultural differences abound in listening as well as speaking practices, and to establish intercultural communication practices accordingly.

DIVERSITY/INTERCULTURAL COMMUNICATION POLICIES

In recent years, many companies of various shapes, sizes, and industry sectors have embraced programs designed to celebrate diversity and encourage communication between individuals and groups from different cultural backgrounds. But according to Milburn, "diversity is one of those concepts that is very context-bound. It does not have a singular meaning for everyone. Companies that try to institute diversity programs without understanding the cultural assumptions upon which these programs are based may find it difficult to enact meaningful diversity policies. . . . Many companies believe that through sharing they can promote diverse cultural values. Yet, how a company defines sharing may actually hinder its diversity initiatives since some cultures have specific rules about sharing. These rules are enacted in everyday communication practices."

Milburn cautioned business owners and managers to keep in mind that every act of communication is based on certain cultural guidelines, and that efforts to increase intercultural communication are doomed to failure if they ignore or otherwise do not take into account that reality. She also noted that many organizations fall victim to one or more of the following traps:

1) Failure to recognize that people from different cultural backgrounds often have varying attitudes toward the very act of communication: "When organizational members act as if communication is merely the sending and receiving of messages, they become fixated by the message rather than recognizing the significance of the process."

2) Insistence on establishing a single standard of appropriate communication that does not allow for culturally based variances.

INTERCULTURAL COMMUNICATION AND JOB FUNCTION

Most business owners recognize that their companies are far more likely to be successful if they are able to establish effective systems of intercultural communication between employees of different religious, social, and ethnic backgrounds. But profound differences in communication styles can also be found within functional areas of a company as well, and these too need to be addressed to ensure that the organization is able to operate at its highest level of efficiency. For example, employees engaged in technical fields (computers, mechanical engineering, etc.) often have educational and work backgrounds that are considerably different from workers who are engaged in "creative" areas of the company (marketing, public relations, etc.). Writing in *Oregon Business,* Megan Monson contended that these differences often manifest themselves in the modes of communication that the respective parties favor. "Engineers tend to be introverted and analytical with very logical ways of solving problems," observed one software industry veteran in an interview with Monson. "Those in marketing tend to be extroverted and intuitive. It's a perennial source of possible contention, and really, it's just a matter of style." A Portland-area software engineer concurred with that evaluation, adding that "the people and cultures of marketing and engineering are so different that communication gets misinterpreted."

Consultants and researchers agree, though, that many differences between these distinct functional cultures can be addressed through proactive policies that recognize that such differences exist and work to educate everyone about the legitimacy of each culture. "Today's dynamic marketplace demands that high-tech companies be able to move quickly, which in turn needs accurate communication, both with customers and among employees. Poor communication can mean loss of morale, production plunges, and perhaps even a failed start-up," said Monson.

FURTHER READING:

Beeth, Gunnar. "Multicultural Managers Wanted." *Management Review.* May 1997.

Cox, Taylor, Jr. *Cultural Diversity in Organizations.* San Francisco, CA: Berrett-Koehler Publishers, 1993.

Cox, Taylor, Jr. "The Multicultural Organization." *Academy of Management Executive.* Vol. 5, no. 2, 1991.

Dresser, Norine. *Multicultural Manners: New Rules of Etiquette for a Changing Society.* New York: John Wiley, 1996.

Faird, Elashmawia, and Philip Harris. *Multicultural Management.* Houston, TX: Gulf Publishing Company, 1993.

Fernandez, John P. *Managing a Diverse Work Force: Regaining the Competitive Edge.* Lexington, MA: Lexington Books, 1991.

Galagan, Patricia. "Tapping the Power of a Diverse Workforce." *Training and Development Journal.* March 1991.

Levesque, Joseph D. *The Human Resource Problem-Solver's Handbook.* New York: McGraw-Hill, 1992.

Milburn, Trudy. "Bridging Cultural Gaps." *Management Review.* January 1997.

Monson, Megan. "Talking to Techweenies." *Oregon Business.* February 1997.

Murphy, Herta A., and Herbert W. Hildebrandt. *Effective Business Communications.* New York: McGraw-Hill, 1991.

Singer, Marshall R. *Intercultural Communication: A Perceptual Approach.* Englewood Cliffs, NJ: Prentice-Hall, 1987.

Stamps, David. "Welcome to America: Watch Out for Culture Shock." *Training.* November 1996.

Young Yun Kim, and Gudykunst, William B., eds. *Theories in Intercultural Communication.* Newbury Park, CA: Sage, 1988.

SEE ALSO: Communication Systems; Interpersonal Communication; Multicultural Work Force

INTEREST RATES

Lenders of money profit from such transactions by arranging for the borrower to pay back an additional amount of money over and above the sum that they borrow. This difference between what is lent and what is returned is known as interest. The interest on a loan is determined through the establishment of an interest rate, which is expressed as a percentage of the amount of the loan.

Borrowing is a staple in many arenas of the U.S. economy. This has resulted in a dizzying array of borrowing arrangements, many of which feature unique wrinkles in the realm of interest rates. Common borrowing and lending arrangements include business and personal loans (from government agencies, banks, and commercial finance companies), credit cards (from corporations), mortgages, various federal and municipal government obligations, and corporate bonds. In addition, interest is used to reward investors and others who place money in savings accounts, **individual retirement accounts (IRAs)**, **certificates of deposit (CDs)**, and many other financial vehicles.

TYPES OF INTEREST RATES

The prime rate is the best known of the various interest rates that are utilized. This non-fluctuating rate is the one usually employed by banks when it makes short-term loans to large borrowers such as corporations. Established by the banks themselves, the prime rate is adjusted on a periodic basis to reflect changes in the larger market. The prime rate, said Art DeThomas in *Financing Your Small Business,* "serves as the floor for bank loans, and the base rate to which premiums are added as perceived customer risk increases." Lawrence W. Tuller noted in *Finance for Non-Financial Managers and Small Business Owners* that banks commonly attribute their prime rate to a complex cost-of-operation formula, and that "theoretically, this cost, plus a reasonable profit margin, equals the prime rate." Economists like Tuller, however, contend that in reality, banks simply base their prime rate on what the market will bear. "All correspondent banks around the country . . . follow suit," wrote Tuller, "regardless of what their specific cost structure may be. Obviously it doesn't cost a bank in rural Wyoming as much to operate as a bank in midtown Manhattan. Yet they both use the same prime measure to establish interest rates. It should be clearly understood that the Federal Reserve Bank does *not* set the prime rate. . . . The prime rate is established by money-center banks as a measuring base against which to calculate customer interest charges."

Other important interest rates that are used in making capital investment decisions include:

- Discount Rate—The rate at which the Federal Reserve charges on loans made to commercial banking institutions is known as the discount rate.

- Commercial Paper Rate—These are short-term discount bonds issued by established corporate borrowers. These bonds mature in six months or less.

- Treasury Bill Rate—A Treasury bill is a short-term (one year or less) risk-free bond issued by the U.S. government. Treasury bills are made available to buyers at a price that is less than its redemption value upon maturity.

- Treasury Bond Rate—Unlike the short-term Treasury bills, Treasury bonds are bonds that do not mature for at least one year, and most of them have a duration of 10 to 30 years. The interest rates on these bonds vary depending on their maturity.

- Corporate Bond Rate—The interest rate on long-term corporate bonds can vary depending on a number of factors, including the time to maturity (20 years is the norm for corporate bonds) and risk classification.

Economic variables set the interest rate as a rate of increase (or decrease) in borrowers' ability to make purchases—whether of homes, farm machinery, or manufacturing equipment—based on changes in the economy. This rate of increase is called the "real" rate of interest. The "nominal" or dollar rate of interest, meanwhile, measures the increase in terms of dollar amounts, but economists point out that this latter measurement can sometimes be misleading because of the impact of inflation and other economic factors on the dollar's buying power.

TERM STRUCTURE OF INTEREST RATES

The actual interest on a loan is not fully known until the duration of the borrowing arrangement has been specified. Interest rates on loans are typically figured on an annual basis, though other periods are sometimes specified. This does not mean that the loan is supposed to be paid back in a year; indeed, many loans—especially in the realm of small business—do not mature for five or ten years, or even longer. Rather, it refers to the frequency with which the interest and "principal owed"—the original amount borrowed—are refigured according to the terms of the loan.

Interest is normally assumed to be "compounded." For small business owners and other borrowers, this means that the unpaid interest due on the principal is added to that base figure in determining interest for future payments. Most loans are arranged so that interest is compounded on an annual basis, but in some instances, shorter periods are used. These latter arrangements are more beneficial to the loaner than to the borrower, for they require the borrower to pay more money in the long run.

While annual compound interest is the accepted normal measure of interest rates, other equations are sometimes used. The yield or interest rate on bonds, for instance, is normally computed on a semiannual basis, and then converted to an annual rate by multiplying by two. This is called simple interest. Another form of interest arrangement is one in which the interest is "discounted in advance." In such instances, the interest is deducted from the principal, and the borrower receives the net amount. The borrower thus ends up paying off the interest on the loan at the very beginning of the transaction. A third interest payment method is known as a floating- or variable-rate agreement. Under this common type of business loan, the interest rate is not fixed. Instead, it moves with the bank's prime rate in accordance with the terms of the loan agreement. A small business owner might, for instance, agree to a loan in which the interest on the loan would be the prime rate plus 3 percent. Since the prime rate is subject to change over the life of the loan, interest would be calculated and adjusted on a daily basis.

FACTORS THAT INFLUENCE INTEREST RATES

Interest rate levels are in essence determined by the laws of **supply and demand**. In an economic environment in which demand for loans is high, lending institutions are able to command more lucrative lending arrangements. Conversely, when banks and other institutions find that the market for loans is a tepid one (or worse), interest rates are typically lowered accordingly to encourage businesses and individuals to take out loans.

Interest rates are a key instrument of American fiscal policy. The Federal Reserve Board determines the interest rate at which the federal government will bestow loans, and banks and other financial institutions, which establish their own interest rates to parallel those of the "Fed," typically follow suit. This ripple effect can have dramatic impact on the U.S. economy. In a recessionary climate, for instance, the Federal Reserve might lower interest rates in order to create an environment that encourages spending. Conversely, the Federal Reserve often implements interest rate hikes when its board members become concerned that the economy is "overheating" and prone to **inflation**.

By raising or lowering their discount interest rate on loans, summarized Robert Heilbroner and Lester Thurow in *Economics Explained,* "The Federal Reserve can make it attractive or unattractive for member banks to borrow or augment their reserves. . . . In addition, changes in the discount rate tend to influence the whole structure of interest rates, either tightening or loosening money. When interest rates are high, we have what we call tight money. This means not only that borrowers have to pay higher rates, but that banks are more selective in judging the credit worthiness of business applications for loans. Conversely, when interest rates decline, money is called easy, meaning that it is not only cheaper but also easier to borrow." The monetary tools of the Federal Reserve work most directly on short-term interest rates. Interest rates for longer maturities are indirectly affected through the market's perception of government policy and its impact on the economy.

Another key factor in determining interest rates is the lending agency's confidence that the money—and the interest on that money—will be paid in full and in a timely fashion. Default risk encompasses a wide range of circumstances, from borrowers who completely fail to fulfill their obligations to those that are merely late with a scheduled payment. If lenders are uncertain about the borrower's ability to adhere to the specifications of the loan arrangement, they will often demand a higher rate of return or risk premium. Borrowers with an established credit history, on the other hand, qualify for what is known as the prime interest rate, which is a low interest rate.

THE INTEREST RATE AND SMALL BUSINESSES

Entrepreneurs and small business owners often turn to **loans** in order to establish or expand their business ventures. Business enterprises that choose this method of securing funding, which is commonly called **debt financing**, need to be aware of all components of those loan agreements, including the interest.

Business consultants point out that interest paid on debt financing is tax deductible. This can save entrepreneurs and small business owners thousands of dollars at tax time, and analysts urge business owners to factor those savings in when weighing their company's capacity to accrue debt. But other interest rate elements can cut into those tax savings if borrowers are not careful. As DeThomas remarked, "lenders often use different methods to calculate the proceeds of a loan, the interest on a loan, and the amount and timing of the repayment schedule. These inconsistencies may result in a significant difference between the loan's stated or nominal rate of interest and the true cost to the borrower."

Commercial banks remain the primary source of loans for small business firms in America, especially for short-term loans. Small business enterprises who are able to secure loans from these lenders must also be prepared to negotiate several important aspects of the loan agreement which directly impact on interest rate payments. Both the interest rate itself and the schedule under which the loan will be repaid are, of course, integral factors in determining the ultimate cost of the loan to the borrower, but a third important subject of negotiation between the borrowing firm and the bank concerns the *manner* in which the interest on a loan is actually paid. There are three primary methods by which the borrowing company can pay back interest on a loan to a bank: a simple- or ordinary-interest plan, a discounted-interest plan, or a floating interest rate plan.

Securing long-term financing is more problematic for many entrepreneurs and small business owners, and this is reflected in the interest rate arrangements that they must accept in order to secure such financing. As DeThomas remarked in *Financing Your Small Business,* "small businesses are often viewed by most creditors as having a highly uncertain future, and making an extended-term loan to such a business means being locked into a high-risk agreement for a prolonged period. To make this type of loan, therefore, a lender must feel comfortable with your business and the quality of its management, be compensated for the additional risk exposure, and take precautions to minimize risk and potential loss." This compensation, as DeThomas and other economists have observed, usually includes imposition of interest rates that are considerably higher than those charged for short-term financing. As with short-term financing arrangements, interest on long-term agreements can range from floating interest plans to those tied to a fixed rate. The actual cost of the interest rate method that is ultimately chosen appears in interest rate disclosures (which are required by law) as a figure known as the **annual percentage rate (APR)**.

FURTHER READING:

DeThomas, Art. *Financing Your Small Business: Techniques for Planning, Acquiring & Managing Debt.* Grants Pass, OR: Oasis Press, 1992.

Heilbroner, Robert, and Lester Thurow. *Economics Explained: Everything You Need to Know About How the Economy Works and Where It's Going.* Revised ed. Touchstone, 1994.

Pindyck, Robert S., and Daniel L. Rubinfeld. *Microeconomics.* 2d ed. Macmillan, 1992.

Seglin, Jeffrey L. *Financing Your Small Business.* New York: McGraw-Hill, 1990.

Tuller, Lawrence W. *Finance for Non-Financial Managers and Small Business Owners.* Holbrook, MA: Adams Media, 1997.

SEE ALSO: Banks and Banking; Risk and Return

INTERNAL AUDITS

Internal auditing, an independent appraisal function, is performed in a wide variety of companies, institutions, and governments. What distinguishes internal auditors from governmental auditors and public accountants is the fact that they are employees of the same organizations they audit. Their allegiance is to their organization, not to an external authority. Titles other than "internal auditor" are sometimes used for those performing an internal audit function. Internal auditors have been named control analysts, systems analysts, business analysts, internal consultants, evaluators, or operations analysts. Regardless of the position title, it is the characteristics of the service being performed that classify it as internal auditing.

Because internal auditing has evolved only within the last few decades, the roles and responsibilities of internal auditors vary greatly from one organization to another. Internal audit functions have been structured based on the differing perceptions and objectives of owners, directors, and managers. While some companies have very sophisticated internal audit functions providing a broad array of services, other organizations have only one or two internal auditors performing routine inspections. "The scope and emphasis [of internal auditing practices] depend to a great extent on the size of company, type of business, philosophy of management, and interest or concern of the chief executive and the board of directors," summarized Nicholas C. Gilles in *What Every Manager Needs to Know About Finance.* "In a very small business, the owner-manager, to a limited extent, performs the role of internal auditor through continuing surveillance of all activities."

Despite the diversity in roles and responsibilities of practicing internal auditors, the Institute of Internal Auditors (IIA) is a governing body for internal auditors that brings some uniformity and consistency to the practice. An international association, the IIA by 1995 had grown to 52,000 members and 210 chapters operating in more than 100 countries. The IIA provides general standards for performing internal audits and serves as a source for education and information.

In its *Standards for the Professional Practice of Internal Auditing*, the IIA defines the internal auditing function in the following way: ''Internal auditing is an independent appraisal function established within an organization to examine and evaluate its activities as a service to the organization. The objective of internal auditing is to assist members of the organization in the effective discharge of their responsibilities. To this end, internal auditing furnishes them analysis, appraisals, recommendations, counsel, and information concerning activities reviewed.''

There is theoretically no restriction on what internal auditors can review and report about within an organization or its components. In practice, internal auditors work within an approved plan. In this way internal auditing resources are coordinated with the goals and objectives of the organization. Internal auditors perform a variety of audits, including compliance audits, operational audits, program audits, financial audits, and information systems audits. Internal audit reports provide management with advice and information for making decisions or improving operations. When problems are discovered, the internal auditor serves the organization by finding ways to prevent them from recurring. Internal audits can also be used in a preventative fashion. For example, if the internal auditor evaluates a situation, noting potential risks and notifying management of those possible problems, management could presumably take preemptive action to prevent the problem from occurring in the first place.

DEVELOPMENT AND CURRENT STATUS OF INTERNAL AUDITING PRACTICES

Prior to the twentieth century, companies and other institutions relied on **external audits** for financial and other information on their operations. The growing complexity of American companies after World War I, however, required better techniques for planning, directing, and evaluating business activities. These needs, coupled with the Stock Market Crash of 1929 and increased evidence of questionable accounting practices by corporations, led to the creation of the Securities Exchange Act of 1934, which established the Securities and Exchange Commission (SEC) as a monitor of corporate financial reporting. In the wake of these developments, wrote Gilles, ''the new thrust for internal auditing was the verification of financial statements, as well as the continued testing of transactions. World War II led internal auditors into the assurance of compliance with government regulations. The boom that followed, with the growth of

conglomerates and international subsidiaries, required auditors to review the adequacy of corporate procedures and practices in operational evaluations, along with performing the financial audit.'' This growth in internal auditing was further fueled by the advent of the computer age in the 1970s.

The importance of quality internal auditing was further underlined with the passage of the Foreign Corrupt Practices Act and the establishment of the Financial Accounting Standards Board. While these developments did not specifically call for an internal auditing function, internal auditors were poised to help management fulfill the additional requirements implicit therein. In the 1980s, highly publicized business failures, and fraudulent financial statements that went undetected by external auditing firms, gave further merit to the concept of internal auditing. Today, supported by a variety of private sector accounting organizations, including the American Institute of Certified Public Accountants (AICPA), the American Accounting Association (AAA), the Financial Executives Institute (FEI), the Institute of Internal Auditors (IIA), and the National Association of Accountants (NAA), internal audit functions have become an important component of many business's operations management system.

INTERNAL AUDITING AND INTERNAL CONTROL

The manner in which internal auditing has evolved has linked it directly to the concepts and objectives of internal control. The IIA clearly advocates an internal control focus when it defines the scope of internal auditing: ''The scope of internal auditing should encompass the examination and evaluation of the adequacy and effectiveness of the organization's system of internal control and the quality of performance in carrying out assigned responsibilities.'' At the most basic level, internal controls can be identified as individual preventive, detective, corrective, or directive actions that keep operations functioning as intended. These basic controls are aggregated to create whole networks and systems of control procedures which are known as the organization's overall system of internal control.

The IIA's *Standards of Professional Practice* outlines five key objectives for an organization's system of internal control: 1) reliability and integrity of information; 2) compliance with policies, plans, procedures, laws and regulations; 3) safeguarding of assets; 4) economical and efficient use of resources; and 5) accomplishment of established objectives and goals for operations or programs. It is these five internal control objectives that provide the internal auditing function with its conceptual foundation and focus for evaluating an organization's diverse operations and programs.

KEY ASSUMPTIONS ABOUT THE INTERNAL AUDIT FUNCTION

There are three important assumptions implicit in the definition, objectives, and scope of internal auditing: independence, competence, and confidentiality.

INDEPENDENCE Internal auditors have to be independent from the activities they audit so that they can evaluate them objectively. Internal auditing is an advisory function, not an operational one. Therefore, internal auditors should not be given responsibility or authority over any activities they audit. They should not be positioned in the organization where they would be subject to political or monetary pressures that could inhibit their audit process, sway their opinions, or compromise their recommendations. Independence and objectivity of internal auditors must exist in both appearance and in fact; otherwise the credibility of the internal auditing work product is jeopardized.

Related to independence is the assumption that internal auditors have unrestricted access to whatever they might need to complete an appraisal. That includes unrestricted access to plans, forecasts, people, data, products, facilities, and records necessary to perform their independent evaluations.

COMPETENCE A business's internal auditors have to be people who possess the necessary education, experience, and proficiency to complete their work competently, in accordance with internal auditing standards. An understanding of good business practices is essential for internal auditors. They must have the capability to apply broad knowledge to new situations, to recognize and evaluate the impact of actual or potential problems, and to perform adequate research as a basis for judgments. They must also be skilled communicators and be able to deal with people at various levels throughout the organization.

CONFIDENTIALITY Evaluations and conclusions contained in internal auditing reports are directed internally to management and the board, not to stockholders, regulators, or the public. Presumably, management and the board can resolve issues that have surfaced through internal auditing and implement solutions privately, before problems get out of hand. Management is expected to acknowledge facts as stated in reports, but has no obligation to agree with an internal auditor's evaluations, conclusions, or recommendations. After internal auditors report their conclusions, management and the board have responsibility for subsequent operating decisions—to act or not to act. If action is taken, management has responsibility to ensure that satisfactory progress is made and

internal auditors later can determine whether the actions taken have the desired results. If no action is taken, internal auditors have responsibility to determine that management and the board understand and have assumed any risks of inaction. Under all circumstances, internal auditors have the direct responsibility to apprise management and the board of any significant developments that the auditors believe warrant ownership/management consideration or action.

Internal auditors should not be confused with industrial engineers. The industrial engineer analyzes and measures methods of performing work, suggests improvements, designs and installs work systems, and evaluates the results of those systems. Internal auditors do use some of the analytical techniques belonging to industrial engineers, but do not focus on them. Further, internal auditors do not design and install systems.

DIFFERENCES BETWEEN INTERNAL AND EXTERNAL AUDITING

Internal auditors and external auditors both audit, but have different objectives and a different focus. Internal auditors generally consider operations as a whole with respect to the five key internal control objectives, not just the financial aspects. External auditors focus primarily on financial control systems that have a direct, significant effect on the figures reported in financial statements. Internal auditors are generally concerned with even small amounts of fraud, waste, and abuse as symptoms of underlying operational issues. But the external auditor may not be concerned if the incidents do not materially affect the financial statements—which is reasonable given the fact that external auditors are engaged to form an opinion only on the organization's financial statements. Internal auditors are concerned with such practices as ill-conceived business expansions, management override of internal controls, mismanaged contracts, and employee unrest, which can cause far greater loss and not be immediately reflected in financial data. Lawrence B. Sawyer summarized the differences in focus succinctly and emphatically in his *Sawyer's Internal Auditing* : ''Management controls over financial activities have been greatly strengthened throughout the years. The same cannot always be said of controls elsewhere in the enterprise. Embezzlement can hurt a corporation; the poor management of resources can bankrupt it. Therein lies the basic difference between external auditing and modern internal auditing; the first is narrowly focused and the second is comprehensive in scope.'' The external auditor does perform services for management, including making recommendations for improvement in systems and controls. By and large, however, these are financially oriented, and often are not based on the same level of understanding of an organization's systems, people, and objectives that an internal auditor would have.

This comparison of internal auditing to external auditing considers only the external auditors' traditional role of attesting to financial statements. During the 1990s a number of the large public accounting firms began establishing divisions offering ''internal auditing'' services in additional to existing tax, actuarial, external auditing, and management consulting services. Predictably, the event has caused a flurry of debate among auditors about independence, objectivity, depth of organizational knowledge, operational effectiveness, and true costs to the organization.

TYPES OF INTERNAL AUDITS

Various types of audits are used to achieve particular objectives. The types of audits briefly described below illustrate a few approaches internal auditing may take. The examples are not to be considered all-inclusive.

OPERATIONAL AUDIT An operational audit is a systematic review and evaluation of an organizational unit to determine whether it is functioning effectively and efficiently, whether it is accomplishing established objectives and goals, and whether it is using all of its resources appropriately. Resources in this context include funds, personnel, property, equipment, materials, information, space, and whatever else may be used by that unit. Operational audits can include evaluations of the work flow and propriety of performance measurements. These audits are tailored to fit the nature of the operations being reviewed. ''Carefully done, operational auditing is a cost-effective way of getting a higher return from the audit function by making it helpful to operating management,'' wrote Hubert D.Vos in *What Every Manager Needs to Know About Finance.*

SYSTEM AUDIT A system analysis and internal control review is an analysis of systems and procedures for an entire function such as information services or purchasing. Those systems and procedures are appraised with respect to one or more or the five key internal control objectives already mentioned.

ETHICAL PRACTICES AUDIT An ethical business practices audit assesses to what extent employees follow established codes of conduct, policies, and standards of ethical practices. Policies that may fall within the scope of such an audit include procurement policies, conflicts of interest, gifts and gratuities, entertainment, political lobbying, patents and licenses, use of organization name, speaking engagements, fair trade practices, and private use of the organization's facilities.

COMPLIANCE AUDIT A compliance audit determines whether the organizational unit or function is following particular rules or directives. Such rules or directives can originate internally or externally and can include one or more of the following: organizational policies; performance plans; established procedures; required authorizations; applicable external regulations; relevant contractual provisions; and federal, state, and local laws. Characteristic of compliance audits is the yes/no aspect of the evaluation—for each event or transaction examined, either it follows the rule or it does not.

FINANCIAL AUDIT A financial audit is an examination of the financial planning and reporting process, the conduct of financial operations, the reliability and integrity of financial records, and the preparation of financial statements. Such a review includes an appraisal of the system of internal controls related to financial functions.

INFORMATION SYSTEMS AUDIT A systems development and life cycle review is a unique type of information systems audit conducted in partnership with operating personnel who are designing and installing new information systems. The objective is to appraise the new system from an internal control perspective and independently test the system at various stages throughout its design, development, and implementation. The approach intends to identify and correct internal control problems before systems are actually put in place because modifications made during the developmental stages are less costly. Sometimes problems can be avoided altogether. There is risk in this approach that the internal auditor could lose objectivity and independence with considerable participation in the design and installation process.

PROGRAM AUDIT A program audit evaluates whether the stated goals or objectives of a certain program or project have been achieved. It may include an appraisal of whether an alternative approach can achieve the desired results at a lower cost. These types of audits are also called performance audits, project audits, or management audits.

FRAUD AUDIT A fraud audit investigates whether the organization has suffered a loss through misappropriation of assets, manipulation of data, omission of information, or any illegal or irregular acts. It assumes that intentional deception has occurred.

PARTICIPATIVE AUDIT A participative audit enlists the auditee to perform a self-assessment and otherwise assist in the audit process. In effect this become a problem-solving partnership between the internal auditor and auditee. This can be cost-effective but is not without risk. The internal auditor must retain the right to independently test any positions taken by the auditee.

INTERNAL AUDIT PLANNING

Business consultants strongly encourage small business owners to establish self-auditing practices. "Not many years ago a company measured its success by how much of its product it was able to sell," stated Jeffrey Davidson and Charles Dean in *Cash Traps: Small Business Secrets for Reducing Costs and Improving Cash Flow.* "Today success is heavily influenced by the ability to keep costs under control and, of course, to maintain a healthy cash flow. Volatile interest rates, shrinking profit margins, and increasing operational costs are causing many businesses to reassess and upgrade their internal control procedures."

For a small business owner, knowing what areas to audit and where to commit resources is an integral part of the internal audit function. A long-range audit plan provides a complete view of audit strategy and coverage in relation to the relative significance of functions to be audited. The goal is to plan an audit strategy that is cost-effective and emphasizes audit projects that have high impact or address areas of significant risk.

An in-depth understanding of the organization and how it operates is a prerequisite for the audit planning process. Developing the plan first requires identifying and listing all auditable units or functions. (This is frequently called the "audit universe.") Next, a rational system must be devised to assign significance and risk to each auditable unit or function. Based on perceived significance and estimated risk, the audit priorities and strategies are documented in the audit plan. The planning process is not fixed, however. Departure of key people, changes in markets, new demographics, and other factors can dramatically affect small businesses and other organizations. Drastic upheavals in the business environment are possible, changing the total character of operations. Organizational processes and existing internal control systems may become obsolete with new technology. Laws and regulations may change, as do attitudes about the degree of enforcement that is necessary. Consequently, risks and significance rankings, the audit universe, and audit strategies will change. The successful small business owner, though, will learn to anticipate such changes, and adjust his or her internal auditing strategies accordingly.

FURTHER READING:

Albrecht, W. Steve, James D. Slice, and Kevin D. Stocks. *A Common Body of Knowledge for the Practice of Internal Auditing.* Alamonte Springs, FL: Institute of Internal Auditors, 1992.

Davidson, Jeffrey P., and Charles W. Dean. *Cash Traps: Small Business Secrets for Reducing Costs and Improving Cash Flow.* New York: John Wiley, 1992.

Gilles, Nicholas C. "Internal Auditing" In *What Every Manager Needs to Know About Finance.* Hubert D. Vos, ed. New York: Amacom, 1986.

Institute of Internal Auditors. *Professional Internal Auditing Standards Volume. Standards for the Professional Practice of Internal Auditing.* Alamonte Springs, FL: Institute of Internal Auditors, 1992.

Price Waterhouse. *Improving Audit Committee Performance: What Works Best.* Alamonte Springs, FL: Institute of Internal Auditors Research Foundation, 1993.

Sawyer, Lawrence B. *Sawyer's Internal Auditing.* Alamonte Springs, FL: Institute of Internal Auditors Research Foundation, 1988.

Schiff, Jonathan. "A Report from the Conference Board and KPMG Peat Marwick." *In New Directions in Internal Auditing.* Research Report no. 946. New York: 1990.

Willson, James D., and Steven J. Root. *Internal Auditing Manual.* Boston, MA: Warren, Gorham, & Lamont, 1989.

INTERNAL REVENUE SERVICE (IRS)

The Internal Revenue Service (IRS) is the agency of the U.S. Department of the Treasury responsible for collecting income taxes from individuals and businesses within the country. In addition to tax on income, the IRS collects several other kinds of taxes for the government, including Social Security, estate, excise, and gift taxes (they are not responsible for collecting revenue derived from the sale of alcohol, tobacco, or firearms). The agency's other responsibilities include enforcement of U.S. tax laws, distribution of forms and instructions necessary for the filing of **tax returns**, and provision of counseling for businesses and individuals subject to its regulations.

The IRS, which is a part of the U.S. Department of the Treasury, was first created by Congress in 1862. In the first years of the IRS, its money-gathering activities were very modest. Until the Civil War, the United States gathered approximately as much money from customs duties as it did from taxation, and the federal government's financial needs were slight because it offered few programs for its citizens. In 1913 IRS responsibilities increased with the introduction of the federal income tax system. Since that time, the government has imposed steadily higher taxes on its citizenry to pay for national defense, social programs, transportation and other infrastructure, and other aspects of modern American society. As internal revenue gathering increased in scope during the past century, the Internal Revenue Service saw similar growth. The IRS, which employed approximately 86,000 workers in the mid-1990s, is currently organized into eight functional areas: resources management, taxpayer service and returns processing, compliance, data services, employee plans and exempt organizations, inspection, planning and research, and technical.

The Internal Revenue Service processes more than 180 million tax returns on an annual basis. On a small percentage of these returns, the IRS performs a more detailed tax return examination called an "audit." If an individual or business is audited, the IRS representative conducting the examination typically asks for proof of the various deductions and exemptions claimed on the tax return. Depending on how the audit unfolds, the IRS agent may ultimately decide that additional taxes are owed (or, less frequently, that the taxpayer actually paid too much). Taxpayers who object to these audit findings have the option of appealing to an independent division within the IRS specifically created to deal with such cases. If negotiations still do not satisfy the taxpayer, appeals can be filed in U.S. Tax Court or other federal courts, depending on the nature of the case.

SMALL BUSINESS AND THE IRS The Internal Revenue Service sponsors several different programs designed to help entrepreneurs and small business owners fulfill their revenue reporting and taxpaying obligations. These include the Small Business Tax Education Program (STEP), which is designed to help small business owners maneuver through the plethora of business tax issues that they face.

Other recent IRS initiatives have met with opposition from small business groups, however. For example, IRS regulations requiring businesses that paid more than $50,000 in employment taxes in 1995 to file federal payments electronically—and implementing heavy penalties for those not in compliance—deeply angered many small business owners. The IRS's new Market Segment Specialization Program (MSSP) has also been a subject of some controversy within the small business community. The MSSP is described as a research initiative intended to provide the IRS with a greater understanding of the typical structure and operation of several dozen kinds of small businesses. The initiative, which arose as a result of studies that indicated that independent business owners had a relatively high rate of noncompliance with tax laws, is designed to ultimately provide auditors with greater understanding of how each business is conducted and the compliance problems that they sometimes have. While supporters argue that the MSSP will give the IRS greater insights into the tax difficulties that small businesses face, critics contend that the program could ultimately result in tougher audits for small businesses.

THE CHANGING IRS

The rapidly changing face of technology and communications has presented small businesses and multinational corporations alike with a wide array of challenges. The Internal Revenue Service has not been immune to these changes. Indeed, the agency has struggled to modernize its operations, especially in the realm of computers. The IRS recently announced that it is considering outsourcing of its tax-return data entry after replacing some aging computers. According to *Computerworld,* IRS priorities now include finding an interim solution to the data input situation, solving remittance processing problems, and addressing Year 2000 compliance.

FURTHER READING:

Griffin, Cynthia E. "Audit Alert: The Key to Surviving an IRS Audit, Know the Rules." *Entrepreneur.* July 1997.

Hodges, Susan. "Getting Wired for the IRS." *Nation's Business.* October 1996.

Machlis, Sharon. "Newly Candid IRS Has Year 2000 Fix, Mulls Outsourcing." *Computerworld.* February 10, 1997.

Stern, Linda. "The IRS's New Focus on Small Business." *Home Office Computing.* April 1994.

Tax Guide for Small Business. Washington: Internal Revenue Service, n.a.

SEE ALSO: Electronic Tax Filing; Estate Taxes; Internal Revenue Service Audits; Tax Deductible Business Expenses; Tax Planning

INTERNAL REVENUE SERVICE AUDITS

Each year, the **Internal Revenue Service (IRS)** conducts audits on individuals and businesses to ensure that they are in compliance with U.S. tax law. The percentage of people and businesses subject to these audits is relatively small—in 1996, for instance, the IRS audited only 1 percent of tax returns filed by partnerships, 2.3 percent of returns filed by corporations, and 4 percent of individual returns—but the prospect of being targeted does provoke dread among a certain portion of the American public. Indeed, many business analysts believe that smaller businesses in certain industries are at greater risk of being subjected to an audit because of historically higher levels of noncompliance in those industries, many of which are primarily composed of small firms. Home-based businesses that are characterized by cash-based transactions are particularly likely to undergo formal IRS review. Many business and tax experts, however, contend that small businesses that conduct their operations honestly and maintain good record keeping practices should be able to weather an IRS audit without too much difficulty. Indeed, some small business owners have been known to actually request an audit in instances where they have a dispute with the IRS over tax obligations.

When providing advice on IRS audits, tax advisors counsel small business owners to adhere to the following:

- Be honest in business operations and in claiming deductions.

- If you prepare your own returns, be familiar with IRS rules regarding deductions and other tax matters; if not, make certain that you hire an accountant or tax advisor who is knowledgeable in these areas.

- Keep all receipts and maintain sound and thorough record keeping practices.

- Keep expenses in line with industry norms.

- Make sure that the auditing agent is knowledgeable about the industry in which you operate.

- Be cooperative; promptly answer all communications from the IRS and make every effort to provide the auditing agent with all requested information.

- If you are unhappy with the results of an IRS audit, consider making a written appeal; the Internal Revenue service maintains an independent division specifically designed to hear such appeals (such appeals may not work, but the small business owner will never know unless he or she makes an attempt).

MARKET SEGMENT SPECIALIZATION PROGRAM
The Market Segment Specialization Program (MSSP), established in 1992, is an IRS initiative that "was designed to improve the quality of examinations by publishing audit guides and to boost tax-law compliance," said Joan Pryde in *Nation's Business.* The Program, noted Pryde, was set up to targeted 100 industries and professional areas, although as of mid-1997 only one third of the guides had been released to the public.

Some observers have expressed disappointment at the pace with which the audit guides have been released, but they also note that for small business operators engaged in those industries that have been covered, the audit guides can be a valuable resource. The guides that are currently available cover many diverse industries that have a strong small business element, including artists and art galleries, auto body repair shops, bars and restaurants, bed and breakfast operations, commercial fishing businesses, garment manufacturers, grain farms, independent used car dealerships, ministers, reforestation projects, taxicab businesses, trucking, and the wine making industry. Some of these guides can be downloaded from the Internet at the IRS's World Wide Web site (www.irs.ustreas.gov), and all are available through the U.S. Government Printing Office.

FURTHER READING:

Baran, Dan, and Gerald Bernard. *The IRS Audit Protection and Survival Guide Series.* 6 vols. New York: John Wiley.

Goldberg, Seymour. *How to Handle an IRS Audit.* Garden City, NY: IRG Publications.

Griffin, Cynthia E. "Audit Alert: The Key to Surviving an IRS Audit; Know the Rules." *Entrepreneur.* July 1997.

Pryde, Joan. "When the IRS Comes to Check." *Nation's Business.* October 1997.

Stern, Linda. "The IRS's New Focus on Small Business." *Home Office Computing.* April 1994.

Tax Guide for Small Business. Washington: Internal Revenue Service, n.a.

SEE ALSO: Tax Returns

INTERNATIONAL EXCHANGE RATE

A international exchange rate, also known as a foreign exchange (FX) rate, is the price of one country's currency in terms of another country's currency. Prior to 1971, exchange rates were fixed by an agreement among the world's central banks. Since then, however, currencies have floated, or moved up and down, based on supply and demand.

A number of factors influence exchange rates, including: relative rates of **inflation**; comparative **interest rates**; growth of domestic money supply; size and trend of balance of payments; economic growth (as measured by the **gross national product**); dependency on outside energy sources; central bank intervention; government policy and political stability; and the world's perception of the strength of the foreign currency.

THE FOREIGN EXCHANGE MARKET

As nations and their economies have become increasingly interdependent, the FX market has emerged as a global focal point. With an estimated daily FX turnover exceeding $1 trillion, this is by far the world's largest market. In order to remain competitive in the world economy, it is vital to manage the risk of adverse currency fluctuations. In recent times, the worldwide trend has been toward the consolidation of markets and currencies, as in the case of the European Economic Union.

The largest users of the FX market are commercial banks, which serve as intermediaries between currency buyers and sellers. Corporations and financial institutions also trade currencies, primarily to safeguard their foreign currency-denominated assets and liabilities against adverse FX rate movement. Banks and fund managers trade currencies to profit from FX rate movements. Individuals also are subject to fluctuating FX rates, most commonly when a traveler exchanges his/her native currency for a foreign one before embarking on a business trip or vacation.

When the Chicago Mercantile Exchange introduced trading in foreign currency futures in 1972, it enabled all currency market participants, including individual investors, to capitalize on FX rate fluctuations without having to make or take delivery of the actual currencies. Foreign currency futures offer risk management and profit opportunities to individual investors, as well as to small firms and large companies.

There are two types of potential users of foreign currency futures: the hedger and the speculator. The hedger seeks to reduce and manage the risk of financial losses that can arise from transacting business in currencies other than one's native currency. Speculators provide risk capital and assume the risk the hedger is seeking to transfer in the hope of making a profit by correctly forecasting future price movement.

THE EFFECT OF EXCHANGE RATE CHANGES ON BUSINESS

The results of companies that operate in more than one nation often must be "translated" from foreign currencies into U.S. dollars. Exchange rate fluctuations make financial forecasting more difficult for these companies, and also have a marked effect on unit sales, prices, and costs. For example, assume that current market conditions dictate that one American dollar can be exchanged for 125 Japanese yen. In this business environment, an American auto dealer plans to import a Japanese car with a price of 2.5 million yen, which translates to a price in dollars of $20,000. If that dealer also incurred $2,000 in transportation costs and decided to mark up the price of the car by another $3,000, then the vehicle would sell for $25,000 and provide the dealer with a profit margin of 12 percent.

But if the exchange rate changed before the deal was made so that one dollar was worth 100 yen—in other words, if the dollar weakened or depreciated compared to the yen—it would have a dramatic effect on the business transaction. The dealer would then have to pay the Japanese manufacturer $25,000 for the car. Adding in the same costs and mark up, the dealer would have to sell the car for $30,000, yet would only receive a 10 percent profit margin. The dealer would either have to negotiate a lower price from the Japanese manufacturer or cut his profit margin further to be able to sell the vehicle.

Under this FX scenario, the price of American goods would compare favorably to that of Japanese goods in both domestic and foreign markets. The opposite would be true if the dollar strengthened or appreciated against the yen, so that it would take more

yen to buy one dollar. This type of exchange rate change would lower the price of foreign goods in the U.S. market and hurt the sales of U.S. goods both domestically and overseas.

FURTHER READING:

Brigham, Eugene F. *Fundamentals of Financial Management.* 5th ed. Chicago, IL: Dryden Press, 1989.

An Introduction to Currency Futures and Options. Chicago Mercantile Exchange. January 1994.

MidAm Foreign Currency Futures. MidAmerica Commodity Exchange. August 1993.

Rolling Spot. Chicago Mercantile Exchange. August 1993.

INTERNATIONAL FRANCHISE ASSOCIATION

Founded in 1960, the International Franchise Association (IFA) is the world's largest and oldest association in the realm of franchising. It represents franchisors, franchisees, and suppliers. The association has grown tremendously in recent years, and it now has more than 30,000 members, including such franchising giants as Century 21 and McDonald's. But the IFA also includes thousands of small franchise owners and hundreds of consultants and suppliers who are heavily involved in the franchising industry.

Until the early 1990s the IFA only represented the interests of franchisors. Its membership, comprised exclusively of franchisors, did not allow franchisees to join, despite the fact that William Rosenberg, the IFA's original founder, had insisted that the association's bylaws include provisions that would permit franchisees as members. For its first few decades of existence, then, the IFA was known as a champion of franchisors rather than the franchising industry as a whole. Since disputes inevitably arose between franchisors and franchisees over various aspects of operation, franchisees generally came to see the IFA as a foe rather than a friend. "Hostility flared between franchisors and the excluded franchisees," wrote Charles Bernstein in *Restaurants & Institutions,* "with franchisees forming associations within chains and thus resisting enforced conformity."

By the early 1990s, however deteriorating relationships between the IFA and franchisees, coupled with Congressional concerns about ensuring a good environment for small business owners, had sparked a wave of talk about imposing additional franchising regulations. Recognizing that most of the proposed regulations would not strengthen the hand of their longstanding membership, the IFA began to explore the possibility of adding franchisees and other industry members to their ranks; the association hoped that this change, as well as several others, would convince

Congress that the industry remained capable of self-regulation. This decision to open the membership gates to franchisees was not without controversy— some franchisors argued that the IFA would become a sluggish creature incapable of swift action, while others feared that the association would become primarily a tool of franchisees—but the IFA did so in October 1993, in great part because of the efforts of some of its younger leadership. Proponents argued that the IFA needed to take some dramatic steps to improve relations between franchisees and franchisors, and they further contended that the combined might of the two camps—which, after all, had many interests in common—would make for a potent lobbying force.

The IFA organized a category of membership specifically for franchisees, and tens of thousands of franchisees quickly joined. The association also established a Franchisee Advisory Council specifically designed to 1) provide programs and services to franchisee members and 2) work to improve communication between franchisees and franchisors. In addition, the IFA established a membership category for franchise suppliers. These members include accounting firms, consultants, public relations firms, and trade show operators.

In addition to dramatically expanding its membership, the IFA and its franchisor members took several other steps to improve its relations with both franchisees and the government. It integrated franchisee representatives onto its various business committees, fostered a national mediation program to settle fights between franchisees and franchisors, and established a new "Code of Ethics" for franchisors to heed when conducting business with franchisees.

Today, the International Franchise Association includes franchisors and franchisees engaged in a broad array of industries, from fast food restaurants to home furnishings stores to automotive retail outlets. Franchisors and franchisees interested in learning more about the IFA can contact the association at 1350 New York Avenue NW, Suite 900, Washington, DC 20005.

FURTHER READING:

Bernstein, Charles. "The Franchising Wars: Time for Peace." *Restaurants & Institutions.* May 1, 1993.

"IFA Sets the Standard." *Success.* April 1993.

Oleck, Joan. "The 200,000 Club." *Restaurant Business.* April 10, 1994.

SEE ALSO: Exporting; Franchising

INTERNATIONAL LAW

International law comes from a variety of sources, including international organizations and nations. Since there is no unified "world government," there are multiple sources of rules and customs governing relations among nation-states, relations among individuals (including corporations) and foreign nations, and relations among individuals from different nations. The many rules that have evolved for these three different areas encompass most of what is generally known as international law. Given the increased "globalization" of commerce due to technological advances, new trade agreements, and the growth of emerging markets, it is incumbent upon any business entity—whether large or small—that hopes to do business beyond its borders to have a working familiarity with the basic principles and precepts of international law.

Historically, international law began as the "law of nations." The recognition of separate nations and their reciprocal rights and duties toward one another has, at its core, the notion of national sovereignty. Each recognized government in the international community of nations is considered the political and legal ruler (sovereign) over a defined territory, economy, and population, and is entitled to self-determination in its political and economic affairs. Activities internal to the nation are governed by the laws and values legitimated by the national government; international law recognizes that each sovereign has the power to prescribe and enforce laws within its boundaries.

RELATIONS AMONG NATION-STATES Much of the law governing relations among nation-states developed from history, customs, and traditions that found their way into legal precedents. In cases where nations disagreed over their rights and duties toward one another, consensus developed slowly. For example, when a citizen attempted to bring a lawsuit in his home country against a foreign sovereign, the court would typically deny relief on the ground of foreign sovereign immunity as a generally recognized principle of customary international law.

Customary international law, however, could not serve all the needs of nation-states and their citizens. Agreements between nations were needed to improve alliances in pursuit of war, or to encourage trading relations in more peaceful times. A typical agreement for the United States is a treaty of "friendship, commerce, and navigation" (FCN). The purpose of such agreements is to define the reciprocal rights and duties of each nation in furtherance of each nation's self-interest. Most FCN treaties cover issues such as the entry of individuals, goods, ships, and capital into the other nation's territory; acquisition of property; repatriation of funds; and protection of each nation's persons and their property in the treaty-partner's nation. At one time, when most nations discriminated in trade against other nations (by setting steep tariff barriers or enacting total embargoes on foreign goods), bilateral FCN treaties began the process of removing trade barriers.

Many treaties have more than two nations as signatories. These are "conventions," such as the United Nations-sponsored Convention on Contracts for the International Sale of Goods, or the Treaty of Rome which began the Common Market (which eventually led to the European Community). Not all conventions are under the auspices of the United Nations, but the U.N. has sponsored and continues to encourage multi-lateral agreements among nation-states.

One organization within the United Nations has also encouraged the growth of international law: the International Court of Justice (ICJ). The ICJ hears and rules on disputes between nation-states but usually does so only where the respective nations agree that the ICJ should have jurisdiction. The ICJ also issues advisory opinions requested by agencies of the United Nations. The ICJ relies on customary international law, treaties, and conventions in making its decisions.

After World War II, when the United Nations was organized, it was envisioned that a World Bank and International Trade Organization (ITO) would also be established. The World Bank came into being as an international lending and development agency to which industrialized nations make contributions for the ostensible purpose of promoting global development. But in 1948 the U.S. Congress had serious reservations about the wisdom of surrendering any of its sovereignty or discretion over trade matters to an international organization. Under powers delegated to the President in the Reciprocal Trade Agreement Act of 1934, the United States joined in the **General Agreement on Tariffs and Trade (GATT)**, which had been drafted in 1947 in Geneva. The basic purpose of GATT was to encourage free trade practices around the world.

Under GATT, member nations obligated themselves to give "most favored nation" treatment to all goods originating in member countries. That is, trade concessions to one member nation would automatically be extended to all others. A series of negotiating "rounds" since 1947 has progressively lowered tariff barriers among GATT signatory nations. In the most recently concluded "Uruguay Round," both tariff and non-tariff barriers were further reduced. Moreover, the original vision of a global trade organization such as the ITO has been at least partially realized in agreement on a World Trade Organization (WTO) to replace the GATT. The WTO would have considerably more power to set and enforce standards than the current GATT secretariat in Geneva.

The institutionalization of free trade principles has been furthered by regional free trade arrangements, such as the European Community and the **North American Free Trade Agreement (NAFTA)**. Nations who belong to either group are also members of the GATT, whose provisions allow that concessions given to other members of a regional trading block do not have to be given to other GATT-member nations.

RELATIONS AMONG INDIVIDUALS AND NATION STATES

One of the traditional principles of international law is that rights granted under international law are given to nations, not individuals. Violations of international law by nations which affect individuals (or corporations) must be raised, if at all, by a nation on behalf of its citizen.

A citizen of a country may mean either an individual or a corporation. While many corporations doing business globally tend to think of themselves as international in character, they nonetheless must depend on their native governments to protect their rights. For example, if an entrepreneur find that his or her patented or trademarked products have been counterfeited, the entrepreneur will typically seek legal remedies through the legal system of the country in which the transgression took place. If that protection is not forthcoming, however, the entrepreneur may request that his or her home government advocate the business's interests in treaty or convention negotiations. (Protection of intellectual property was one of the principal areas of concern for industrialized nations in the recently concluded Uruguay Round of the GATT.)

Similarly, where a corporation chooses to engage in foreign direct investment in a foreign country, political uncertainties and legal risk have frequently resulted in a loss of assets through expropriation or nationalization. In such cases, diplomatic efforts of the home country have been enlisted to recover adequate compensation. Or, if a corporation with a large number of employees in the United States experiences a serious competitive threat from products originating in another country, one time-honored strategy has been to seek protective legislation from the home country government.

The free trade movement has at least partially limited the success (or validity) of such efforts, but even the GATT has allowed exceptions for member nations to impose anti-dumping duties or countervailing duties where the country of origin has provided unfair subsidies for the product, or the product is being sold at below home country cost to establish a foothold in a new market.

Companies seeking to do business outside their home country have encountered many legal difficulties other than **tariffs**, anti-dumping duties, or countervailing duties. Technical and non-tariff barriers to trade often exist in the export market, including government procurement rules (requirements that a certain percentage of business must be given to home countries), byzantine licensing and procedural requirements, and restrictions on the mobility of key personnel. In addition, Andrew Sherman noted in *The Complete Guide to Running and Growing Your Business* that "a country's laws may not be conducive to the establishment of certain types of distributor arrangements," which smaller businesses typically depend on. "Any one of a body of laws—governing taxes, customs, imports, and liability of corporate organizations and agencies—may prove to be a significant stumbling block," he added. "For example, laws covering technology transfer and foreign investment may 'force' a given business relationship to be essentially a joint venture, when it was originally intended as a master franchise or license."

Exports may also be limited by political and strategic considerations: since the 1950s, for example, the United States has had various statutes and executive orders establishing export controls for political reasons. Some of the export control laws include the Export Administration Act, the International Emergency Economic Powers Act, the Trading with the Enemy Act, and various executive orders under each. When U.S. Embassy personnel were held hostage in Iran, President Carter ordered a cessation of all trade with Iran. A number of U.S. companies with contracts pending in Iran were adversely affected. Similarly, when President Bush ordered cessation of all business with Iraq after its invasion of Kuwait, a number of U.S. companies were affected.

When the Soviets invaded Afghanistan in 1980, U.S. companies with subsidiaries abroad were ordered by President Carter to cease doing business on the Soviet oil pipeline that was to serve Europe and bring much-needed hard currency to the Soviets. A French subsidiary of the U.S. company, Dresser Industries, had a pending contract with the U.S.S.R. Dresser U.S. was informed by the U.S. government that it must act to prevent its subsidiary from dealing with the Soviets. Dresser, its French subsidiary, and the government of France all resisted the application of U.S. law to a French company, and ultimately their resistance succeeded after the subsidiary was restructured to reduce formal control by Dresser U.S. This incident illustrates a principal difficulty of international law: much of it is made by national legislatures and courts, and one nation's laws may reach beyond its own boundaries—or attempt to. When, for example, the

U.S. public learned that many "U.S." corporations were obtaining and retaining business in foreign countries by means of bribes or kickbacks, the U.S. Congress enacted the Foreign Corrupt Practices Act (FCPA). The FCPA criminalized the act of making payments to foreign officials for the purpose of getting or keeping business. A U.S. company found to have made such payments could be prosecuted in the United States for actions taken outside U.S. territory; thus, the FCPA is an example of extra-territorial application of U.S. law.

Under customary international law, the basic principle of sovereign jurisdiction to prescribe and enforce law is territorial. International law also recognizes the nationality principle, the right of a sovereign to make and enforce law with respect to its citizens (nationals). Not only the FCPA, but also U.S. antitrust law, securities law, and employment discrimination law may apply to actions of U.S. companies outside U.S. territory. In the case of U.S. antitrust law, the action alleged to be a violation of the Sherman Act or the Clayton Act must have a "direct effect" on the United States for extra-territorial application to be upheld. For employment discrimination cases, a U.S. company must adhere to the provisions of Title VII of the Civil Rights Act of 1964 (as amended) with respect to a U.S. citizen employed by that company overseas.

Conflicts between U.S. law and the law of foreign states has led to certain nations blocking the application of U.S. law by statute. Blocking statutes typically limit the extent to which U.S. plaintiffs can obtain evidence through discovery and make it difficult to enforce a U.S. judgment outside of the United States. Even where Congress clearly intends U.S. law to have extra-territorial application, U.S. courts are reluctant to apply it where doing so would raise a clear conflict or implicate foreign policy concerns in any way.

Where U.S. companies and individuals actually have an adversarial relationship with a foreign nation, either sovereign immunity and the Act of State Doctrine may apply. In the case of a claim in U.S. courts against a foreign sovereign, plaintiffs must show that the case fits one of the exceptions to sovereign immunity listed in the Foreign Sovereign Immunities Act of 1976 (FSIA). Under the FSIA, which adopts the restrictive theory of sovereign immunity (rather than the absolute theory), governmental activities are generally immune, whereas private or commercial kinds of activities are not. Under the FSIA, a foreign sovereign that engages in commercial activities in the United States or having a direct effect in the United States cannot avail itself of the sovereign immunity defense in U.S. courts. Most other industrialized nations follow the restrictive theory of sovereign immunity, either by statute or judicial precedents.

In certain cases, deciding a lawsuit in U.S. courts may require that the public act of a foreign sovereign (on its own territory) be declared invalid by the court. In such cases, the Act of State Doctrine may be invoked by the court to avoid coming to a decision on the merits in a way that would discredit the public act of the foreign sovereign. The Supreme Court has declared in numerous cases that it is not constitutionally proper for a U.S. court to decide a case in a way that would invalidate the public act of a foreign sovereign; this, it believes, would tread upon the proper prerogatives of the executive and legislative branches of U.S. government. For the Act of State Doctrine to apply, it is not necessary that the foreign sovereign be a named defendant; it is only necessary that the court be unable to find for a certain party without questioning the lawfulness of a public act of a foreign sovereign on its own territory.

RELATIONS BETWEEN INDIVIDUALS FROM DIFFERENT NATIONS

One of the common problems that arises in international commercial transactions concerns where a dispute between citizens of different countries shall be heard. Without a contractual choice of forum, issues of personal jurisdiction often arise. For example, a Japanese company may find itself sued in a U.S. court for a small valve that was incorporated in a wheel by a Taiwanese manufacturer, then incorporated in a motorcycle by a different Japanese company. If the motorcycle is sold in the United States, and the wheel malfunctions, the tire valve manufacturer may find itself in a U.S. court. The U.S. Supreme Court has declared that, in fairness, a company must deliberately target the U.S. market to be held legally accountable in the United States. Mere predictability that its product may wind up in a certain market is insufficient to give the court valid personal jurisdiction over the non-resident corporation. Of course, if a company goes to another country to do business (either directly or through agents) and is sued there, courts generally will assume personal jurisdiction over the non-resident company.

For disputes between parties to a contract, the parties may have chosen to avoid any questions of personal jurisdiction by specifying the judicial forum where any disputes arising between them will be settled. Courts have typically upheld these "choice of forum" clauses in commercial contracts, as well as clauses that specify which law (e.g. German law, U.S. law, or Mexican law) will be applied in resolving the dispute.

International companies may entirely avoid judicial settlement of their dispute by choosing arbitration. This can be done prior to any disagreement—by including a pre-dispute arbitration clause in the contract—or after a dispute arises. In this way, a more neutral forum is often selected, so that the "home court" advantage does not favor either disputant. Often, the parties will have pre-selected a set of procedural rules to follow, such as those of the International Chamber of Commerce, or those of United Nations Commission on International Trade Law (UNCITRAL). This process is aided by the U.N.-sponsored United Nations Convention on Recognition and Enforcement of Arbitral Awards (sometimes known as the New York Convention), which has been ratified by most major trading nations. If a Japanese and German firm agree to arbitrate their dispute in New York state, for example, either party may proceed under the agreed-upon rules (even without the cooperation of the other party), obtain an arbitral award, and have it enforced in any signatory nation without the need to re-hear the facts and issues of the dispute. Companies dealing internationally with agencies of a national government may wish to include an arbitration clause in contracts with the foreign sovereign so as to secure a clear waiver of sovereign immunity.

Because international dispute settlement is often fraught with such considerations, sellers of goods may well choose to secure payment for full performance under a contract by securing a letter of credit from the buyer. A buyer must establish a line of credit with a bank (the issuing bank), and the bank issues a letter of credit in favor of the seller, who often specifies a corresponding bank in its own country. The letter of credit will specify that the seller will be paid by the corresponding bank upon presentation of certain documents, such as a clean bill of lading. If the entries on the documents correspond to the requirements of the letter of credit, the seller is promptly paid by the corresponding bank, regardless of whether the goods are delivered to the buyer in a timely fashion. Goods may be held up by forces of nature, acts of war, or may be damaged in transit due to no fault of the seller. The logic of the letter of credit is that the seller, having performed its transactional duties, is itself entitled to prompt payment.

RECENT TRENDS

During the 1990s, an increasing number of countries have expressed increased commitment to unifying business law around the world. More than two dozen international organizations have worked on this goal, but analysts note that the issue is a complex one, and that legislation will undoubtedly be slow in passing, if at all. Observers, however, believe that a hybrid of American and British law may well dominate if a single canon of international business law is devised. "Big British law firms know all about globalization," noted The Economist, "mainly because English law has been so widely used. As a system of common law . . . it has more flexibility than a civil code that sets general principles from which specific judgments are derived, which is what exists in most European countries.'' The magazine also noted the considerable legacy of the British Empire, ''which installed English legal systems around the world,'' and the English laws that have served as the foundation for huge international construction projects in Latin America, Africa, and elsewhere. But legal experts note that the use of New York law (America's laws are codified by state) has expanded dramatically in many parts of the globe over the past 50 years thanks in large measure to the international expansion of American firms.

FURTHER READING:

August, Ray. *International Business Law: Text, Cases, and Readings.* Prentice Hall, 1993.

Hermann, A. H. ''Sweet Sound of Harmony: Unifying Business Law is No Simple Matter.'' *Financial Times.* July 27, 1993.

Hotchkiss, Carolyn. *International Law for Business.* McGraw-Hill, Inc., 1994.

Pooler, Victor H. ''Know the Laws of the Lands When You Start Global Sourcing.'' *Purchasing.* January 28, 1988.

''Red Tape Around the World: The Globalization of Corporation Law.'' *Economist.* November 23, 1996.

Richards, Eric L. *Law for Global Business.* Richard D. Irwin, Inc., 1994.

Schaffer, Richard, Beverley Earle, and Filiberto Agusti. *International Business Law and Its Environment.* West Publishing Co., 1993.

Sherman, Andrew J. *The Complete Guide to Running and Growing Your Business.* New York: Times Business, 1997.

SEE ALSO: Exporting; Environmental Law and Business; Legal Advice and Services

INTERNATIONAL MARKETING

International marketing takes place when a business directs its products and services toward consumers in a country other than the one in which it is located. While the overall concept of marketing is the same worldwide, the environment within which the marketing plan is implemented can be dramatically different from region to region. Common marketing concerns—such as input costs, price, advertising, and **distribution**—are likely to differ dramatically in the countries in which a firm elects to market its goods or services. Business consultants thus contend that the key to successful international marketing for any business—whether a multinational corporation or a small entrepreneurial venture—is the ability to adapt, manage, and coordinate an intelligent plan in an unfamiliar (and sometimes unstable) foreign environment.

Businesses choose to explore foreign markets for a host of sound reasons. In some instances, firms initiate foreign market exploration in response to unsolicited orders from consumers in those markets. Many others, meanwhile, seek to establish a business to absorb overhead costs at home, diversify their corporate holdings, take advantage of domestic or international political or economic changes, or tap into new or growing markets. The overriding factor spurring international marketing efforts is, of course, to make money, and as the systems that comprise the global economy become ever more interrelated, many companies have recognized that international opportunities can ultimately spell the difference between success and failure. ''The world is getting smaller,'' concluded E. Jerome McCarthy and William D. Perreault Jr. in *Basic Marketing.* ''Advances in communications and transportation are making it easier to reach international customers. Product-market opportunities are often no more limited by national boundaries than they are by state lines within the United States. Around the world there are potential customers with needs and money to spend. Ignoring those customers doesn't make any more sense than ignoring potential customers in the same town.''

While companies choosing to market internationally do not share an overall profile, they seem to have two specific characteristics in common. First, the products that they market abroad, usually patented, are believed to have high earnings potential in foreign markets. Second, the management of companies marketing internationally must be ready to make a commitment to these markets. This entails far more than simply throwing money at a new exporting venture. Indeed, a business that is genuinely committed to establishing an international presence must be willing to educate itself thoroughly on the particular countries it chooses to enter through a course of market research.

DEVELOPING FOREIGN MARKETS

There are several general ways to develop markets on foreign soil. They include: **exporting** products and services from the country of origin; entering into **joint venture** arrangements; licensing patent rights, trademark rights, etc. to companies abroad; **franchising**; contract manufacturing; and establishing subsidiaries in foreign countries. A company can commit itself to one or more of the above arrangements at any time during its efforts to develop foreign markets. Each method has its own distinct advantages and disadvantages.

New companies, or those that are taking their first steps into the realm of international commerce, often begin to explore international markets through exporting (though they often struggle with financing). Achieving export sales can be accomplished in numerous ways. Sales can be made directly, via mail order, or through offices established abroad. Companies can also undertake indirect exporting, which involves selling to domestic intermediaries who locate the specific markets for the firm's products or services. Many companies are able to establish a healthy presence in foreign markets without ever expanding beyond exporting practices.

International licensing occurs when a country grants the right to manufacture and distribute a product or service under the licenser's trade name in a specified country or market. Although large companies often grant licenses, this practice is also frequently used by small and medium-sized companies. Often seen as a supplement to manufacturing and exporting activities, licensing may be the least profitable way of entering a market. Nonetheless, it is sometimes an attractive option when an exporter is short of money, when foreign government import restrictions forbid other ways of entering a market, or when a host country is apprehensive about foreign ownership. A method similar to licensing, called franchising, is also increasingly common.

A fourth way to enter a foreign market is through a joint venture arrangement, whereby a company trying to enter a foreign market forms a partnership with one or more companies already established in the host country. Often, the local firm provides expertise on the intended market, while the exporting firm tends to general management and marketing tasks. Use of this method of international investing has accelerated dramatically in the past 20 years. The biggest incentive to entering this type of arrangement is that it reduces the company's risk by the amount of investment made by the host-country partner. A joint venture arrangement allows firms with limited capital to expand into international arenas, and provides the marketer with access to its partner's distribution channels. Contract manufacturing, meanwhile, is an arrangement wherein an exporter turns over the production reins to another company, but maintains control of the marketing process.

A company can also expand abroad by setting up its own manufacturing operations in a foreign country, but capital requirements associated with this method generally preclude small companies from pursuing this option. Large corporations are far more likely to embrace this alternative, which often allows them to avoid high import taxes, reduce transportation costs, utilize cheap labor, and gain increased access to raw materials.

INTERNATIONAL MARKETING FACTORS

Although firms marketing abroad face many of the same challenges as firms marketing domestically, international environments present added uncertainties which must be accurately interpreted. Indeed, there are a host of factors that need to be researched and evaluated when preparing an international marketing strat-

egy. Key aspects of any potential foreign market include: demographic and physical environment; political environment; economic environment; social and cultural environment; and legal environment.

DEMOGRAPHIC AND PHYSICAL ENVIRONMENT Elements that needs to be assessed that fit under this category include population size, growth, and distribution; climate factors that could impact on business; shipping distances; time zones; and natural resources (or lack thereof).

ECONOMIC ENVIRONMENT Factors in this area include disposable income and expenditure patterns; per capita income and distribution; currency stability; inflation; level of acceptance of foreign businesses in economy; **Gross National Product (GNP)**; industrial and technological development; available channels of distribution; and general economic growth. Obviously, the greater a nation's wealth, the more likely it will be that a new product or service can be introduced successfully. Conversely, a market in which economic circumstances provide only a tiny minority of citizens with the resources to buy televisions may not be an ideal one for a television-based marketing campaign.

SOCIAL AND CULTURAL ENVIRONMENT This category encompasses a wide range of considerations, many of which can—if misunderstood or unanticipated—significantly undermine a business's marketing efforts. These include literacy rates; general education levels; language; religion; ethics; social values; and social organization. "The ability of a country's people to read and write has a direct influence on the development of the economy—and on marketing strategy planning," observed McCarthy and Perreault. "The degree of literacy affects the way information is delivered—which in marketing means promotion." Writing in *The Portable MBA in Marketing,* Alexander Hiam and Charles D.Schewe showed how literacy rates in a given market often dramatically impact on a company's promotional choices: "A company marketing baby food in Sweden, which has a 99-percent literacy rate, could advertise the product in various magazines and newspapers, perhaps including information about the product's nutritional content. In Yemen, however, where the literacy rate is about 30 percent, an approach based on the use of visual media, such as posters, would be more appropriate." Attitudes based on religious beliefs or cultural norms often shape marketing choices in fundamental ways as well. As Hiam and Schewe noted, "cultures differ in their values and attitudes toward work, success, clothing, food, music, sex, social status, honesty, the rights of others, and much else." They observed that even business practices can vary tremendously from people to people. "For instance, haggling is never done by the Dutch, often by Brazilians, and always by the Chinese." The company that does not take the time to make itself aware of these differences runs the risk of putting together an international marketing venture that can fail at any number of points.

LEGAL ENVIRONMENT This includes limitations on trade through **tariffs** or quotas; documentation and import regulations; various investment, tax, and employment laws; patent and trademark protection; and preferential treaties. These factors range from huge treaties—such as the **North American Free Trade Agreement (NAFTA)** and the **General Agreement on Tariffs and Trade (GATT)**—that profoundly shape the international transactions of many nations to trade barriers erected by a single country.

POLITICAL ENVIRONMENT Factors here include system of government in targeted market; political stability; dominant ideology; and national economic priorities. This aspect of an international market is often the single most important one, for it can be so influential in shaping other factors. For example, a government that is distrustful of foreigners or intent on maintaining domestic control of an industry or industries might erect legal barriers designed to severely curtail the business opportunities of foreign firms.

MARKETING STRATEGIES International market efforts take many forms. Companies that conduct international business in several nations often favor what is known as an "individualized" marketing strategy. This approach, which also is often utilized by smaller businesses involved in only one or two foreign markets, typically involves a comprehensive market research component and a significant effort to tailor a product or service to each individual target market. Under this approach, political, social, and economic factors are important components of the marketing process.

Another strategy that is sometimes used is commonly called the Global Marketing Strategy (GMS). This controversial approach largely ignores differences between nations. Instead, its proponents claim that while a business that sells its products in the same way in every market may suffer losses in isolated instances, it will reap compensatory savings elsewhere. "GMS is based on the notion that consumers around the world are growing more and more similar and that a standardized product and marketing mix can achieve enormous economies, especially in advertising, packing, and distribution because they would not be changed," summarized Hiam and Schewe. "Proponents of this strategy believe that modern technology has created a commonalty among people around the world. Global travel and communication have exposed more and more people to products and services that they have heard about, actually seen, or even experienced—and now want. Although differences exist in consumer preferences, shopping behavior, cultural institutions, and promotional media, those who support GMS believe that these preferences and

practices can and will change to be more similar." Of course, many companies have embraced a hybrid of the GMS and individualized marketing strategies. This approach is sometimes summed up in the phrase, "Think globally, act locally."

Small businesses are discouraged from relying on the GMS strategy. Analysts note that whereas large multinational companies can afford to take a hit on a poorly marketed product on occasion, most small businesses are not so strong. For small enterprises, then, market research becomes an essential component of operations. After all, a single misstep in the international market can cripple a young company, or at least make it apprehensive about future forays. This can be damaging in and of itself, for as the SBA warned, "your business cannot ignore international realities if you intend to maintain your market share and keep pace with your competitors."

FURTHER READING:

Breaking Into the Trade Game: A Small Business Guide to Exporting. Washington: U.S. Small Business Administration, n.a.

Gowa, Joanne. *Allies, Adversaries, and International Trade.* Princeton, NJ: Princeton University Press, 1994.

Hiam, Alexander, and Charles D. Schewe. *The Portable MBA in Marketing.* Wiley, 1992.

McCarthy, E. Jerome, and William D. Perreault Jr. *Basic Marketing.* 10th ed. Irwin, 1990.

Paliwoda, Stan. *The Essence of International Marketing.* Upper Saddle River, NJ: Prentice-Hall, 1994.

Phillips, Chris, Isobel Doole, and Robin Lowe. *International Marketing Strategy: Analysis, Development, and Implementation.* Routledge, 1994.

Sletten, Eric. *How to Succeed in Exporting and Doing Business Internationally.* Wiley, 1994.

SEE ALSO: Marketing

INTERNET COMMERCE

Internet commerce refers to the buying and selling of goods on the Internet, primarily the World Wide Web. In the broadest sense it can refer to anything purchased from a Web site, even if the product is ordered by phone or by mail-order, but the term most accurately refers to transactions made electronically.

In that sense, Internet commerce is poised on the brink of explosive growth. One estimate by International Data Corporation states that global electronic commerce is expected to be worth $220 billion in the year 2001, a nearly hundred-fold increase from the $2.6 billion recorded in 1996. Another computer think-tank, Forester Research, pegs the growth even higher—$327 billion by 2002.

"Most companies have realized they must have a net commerce presence," said Ezra Gottheil, of the Hurwitz Group in *InfoWorld*. "Whatever it is you do, you have to do that business on the Web as well." And for good reason—computer users are one of the wealthiest target markets around. Surveys show that Internet users have a medium income of $60,000, while those who actually shop online and make purchases electronically earn even more at $75,000 annually.

At the Internet World '97 trade show, huge computer companies such as Hewlett-Packard, IBM, Microsoft, and Intel were stressing their commitment to Internet commerce (or I-commerce, as it is sometimes called), ensuring its continued growth. IBM, for example, announced the formation of the Institute for Advanced Commerce, to which it will commit $10 million and 50 researchers. The institute will draw its members from the worlds of business, the analyst community, and academia.

Despite the involvement of such large industry players, not all is rosy on the I-commerce front. It is very much a work in progress that has a long way to go before it clears major technical hurdles and reaches broad acceptance. People started out with a "build it and they will come" attitude, but even a company as big as IBM saw how fickle consumers were when its highly touted World Avenue Web shopping mall went bust. Today, expectations in the realm of Internet commerce have lessened somewhat, although as mentioned above, many analysts expect continued rapid growth in the medium as a whole.

The companies that are already succeeding on the Web are those that have developed new business models or services directly tailored for the Web, such as the bookseller amazon.com, which features a service that specializes in locating hard-to-find books, or Auto-by-Tel, which links automobile buyers and sellers online. Traditional retailers like Lands' End and Dell Computers have also found success selling to computer savvy consumers who are comfortable with the Internet. To succeed, companies taking the Internet plunge must understand both traditional marketing concepts and Internet-specific marketing concepts.

One common criticism of consumer sites is that companies are not being aggressive enough to close the sale. Those companies that are doing the best are those who say "buy now and receive this discount" or offer a "special for Internet customer only." Companies should post price comparisons and show through numbers that their site is the best, or that buying off the Internet is cheaper and easier than going to the store.

The other main problem with I-commerce in the late 1990s is fear. Many consumers do not trust the Internet. They worry about the security of online transactions, which involve giving out address and credit card information. For that reason, the hottest growth area of I-commerce is not the consumer marketplace (although hopes are high there), but rather the business-to-business market, such as a company ordering directly from its suppliers through a Web site that is accessible only by the company and the supplier, not the public.

CREATING AN INTERNET COMMERCE SITE

Despite the consumer fears, most companies are realizing they need to have some kind of business presence on the World Wide Web. For small businesses, the Web can actually be a great way to broaden a customer base and increase sales. However, creating a commerce site is technologically challenging and can be costly. Basically, there are three routes a company can choose when creating a commerce site:

1) Select a "turnkey" firm (i.e., a consultant) to create the site for you—This is the most expensive method, but it also the easiest. The contractor attends to all aspects of site construction, including conducting market analysis, designing and developing the site, implementing electronic payment processing, and conducting overall site management, including troubleshooting and security.

2) Develop your own Web page, then select a major Internet service provider (ISP) to act as middle man and handle the commerce portions of the site—This is still a fairly easy route to take, but far cheaper than the turnkey option. Some ISPs will handle the design and order processing, but others will help you turn your existing site into a commerce site by adding credit card processing and ordering capability. Most ISPs are not extensively involved in commerce sites, but they do offer the basics. The key is to shop around and check on the reliability of each ISP. Ask about their security methods. Check out other sites they built or manage. For business-to-business commerce sites, select an ISP that specializes in developing commerce for "extranets," which are company web sites that are only accessible to suppliers and partners and not to the general public.

3) Do-it-yourself—If you are very good with computers, understand Web design, have some programming skills, and understand Internet commerce and security issues, then you can build the entire site yourself using hardware and software that can be purchased at any major computer store. There are many software programs aimed specifically at small businesses interested in starting a

commerce site that have become available over the past few years. These range from very simple programs—templates for online catalogs and software for sales reporting and inventory management—to complex programs that can match a customer's database with your inventory list to create sales incentives and promotions that directly target customer needs. Costs can range from the low hundreds to thousands of dollars.

SECURITY ISSUES

No matter how you decide to build your site, the single most important issue you face will be security. Most consumers are still wary about buying online, so companies are striving to address this. "Security is a [concern] that everyone shares," said Rebecca Duncan of Datapro Information Services in *Entrepreneur* magazine. "We are seeing a lot more interest from commercial vendors to work with security vendors." Companies are even running print and television ads trying to convince consumers that the Internet is a safe place to shop

The National Computer Security Association has listed five keys for secure electronic commerce: privacy, integrity, authenticity, nonfabrication, and nonrepudiation. First, transmissions must be private between the merchant and the customer. There must be data integrity to ensure that someone has not intercepted the data and tampered with it. Authenticity and nonfabrication assure the merchant and the customer that each is who he or she says they are. Nonrepudiation means the customer cannot deny he or she made the purchase.

Currently, there are two primary methods of payment on the Internet, and both have their drawbacks. The first, credit card payment, is the most common, but the one that causes most consumer fear in regards to security. The second, electronic cash, is more secure, but more cumbersome and less accepted than credit cards.

CREDIT CARDS With credit card theft of all types a common occurrence these days, it is not surprising that consumers are concerned about sending such sensitive information through cyberspace. Companies are trying to address those fears.

A credit card transaction most often works in the following manner when conducted on the Web: the merchant or his ISP sets up an HTML form where buyers enter the item they want to buy, their shipping information, and a credit card number and expiration date. When the form is submitted, a form of encryption called Secure Sockets Layer (SSL) that is in place on the customer's browser and the merchant's computer server ensures that the credit card number and

all the other information can be read only by the merchant. Information can be stolen as it is on its way to and from the merchant's computer, but with the SSL protection, no one but the merchant can decipher it. When the merchant receives the order, he manually verifies the credit card, then ships the goods. If a company has high sales volume at its Web site, or customers do not want to wait for verification, there is software available that instantly verifies credit cards. Such software means the merchant has to have a direct line or satellite connection to the credit card processing company open at all times.

Credit cards can also be handled in other ways. Third party vendors are springing up to handle credit card transactions. The merchant who uses these vendors puts a "buy" button on his Web page. When the customer hits that button, control over the process temporarily switches to the third party vendor's server, which processes the transaction, then sends the user back to the merchant's site. This frees the merchant from having to deal with credit card companies. Examples of such systems include the Internet Mall's OrderEasy (www.ordereasy.com) system and Internet Commerce Systems' MerchantTrax (www.icomms.com).

Another way to ensure credit card secrecy is to use an intermediary between the customer and merchant, so that the merchant never sees the customer's credit card number. Two examples are CyberCash and First Virtual. With both, you apply for an account with those companies using your credit card. Then, when you visit a merchant who accepts CyberCash or First Virtual, you give them your access codes for that service, instead of your credit card. The merchant then sends the transaction information to the intermediary, who verifies the account, approves the credit card transaction, and notifies the merchant to ship the product. The only difference between First Virtual and CyberCash is that with CyberCash, the customer sends his or her credit card number to them over the Web via SSL, while with First Virtual, the customer makes a voice phone call and provides his number over the phone.

In 1997, a new technology for handling credit card transactions was announced. Called Secure Electronic Transaction (SET), it was created by the major credit card companies with the help of most of the major technology companies active on the Web. SET utilizes "digital certificates" to verify that both the merchant and the customer is who they say they are. Under this arrangement, the credit card company will issue a digital certificate to the card-issuing financial institution, which will then issue a separate certificate to each cardholder. The same process will be undertaken for each merchant. These certificates are a form of electronic signature—they are unique to that person or merchant and act as proof of identification. Transactions using these certificates will work this way: At the time of the transaction, each party's SET-compliant software validates both merchant and cardholder before any information is exchanged. The validation takes place by checking the digital certificates which were both issued by the credit card company or bank.

The certificates will operate with a level of encryption known as "public key" encryption. Public key encryption works this way: two digital "keys" are encoded into a message. One, the private key, is used by the sender to "lock" his or her message by encrypting it. Each private key is unique, and only the person issuing the message has access to it. When the person receives the message, it is still locked and undecipherable. The recipient of the message only has access to the public key if the sender gives it to him or her. To read the message, they use the other half of the key, known as the "public key" to unlock the message. When special software joins the two keys, the message is decoded and returned to its original state. Both portions of the key have to be present, or the message remains coded forever.

Thus, with digital certificates, each cardholder who is issued a card will be issued his or her own private and public keys. When a person wishes to make a purchase over the Internet, he or she will encrypt the order with the private key portion of the digital certificate. The public key portion of the digital certificate will automatically be sent to the merchant along with the order, and the merchant will use the public key provided in the certificate to unlock the order. Because each certificate is unique, the merchant can rest assured that the order was really placed by the cardholder, and not someone fraudulently impersonating the cardholder. The certificate process creates what cryptographers call a "digital signature." A digital signature provides a way to associate the message with the sender, and is the cyberspace form of "signing" for your purchases. In this way, you and only you will be able to use your credit card account over the Internet.

While there is a growing move to make SET the new credit card standard, it remained in its early stages in the late 1990s. As of the end of 1997, a pilot program had just been extended to allow for more testing. As a result, very few merchants and customers are taking advantage of SET in early 1998.

ELECTRONIC CASH The second most popular form of Internet commerce involves electronic cash. Electronic cash was created for two main reasons. First, transactions of less than $5.00 are not profitable for credit card companies or merchants because it costs more than that to actually process the transaction. Second, credit card transactions are highly traceable—some consumers want more privacy than credit cards offer.

For those customers, there is electronic cash, or ecash. Ecash is fairly complicated. Internet banks, such as CyberCash and DigiCash, allow customers to open "accounts" by exchanging real money (with payment made by check, money order, or credit card) for ecash, which is held in "purse" software by the consumer. When the consumer visits a website that allows payment by ecash, they give the merchant their ecash number when they purchase something. The merchant then turns the transaction over to the Internet bank, which pays him or her in real money. The bank then deducts the correct amount of ecash from the consumer's account. Intricate serial numbers must be used to make sure each "ecoin" is only used once, and merchants must pay a fairly hefty price for the privilege of using the ecash services, plus pay a per transaction fees. In the late 1990s, digital money is accepted in very few places.

THE FUTURE

While consumer acceptance of I-commerce is expected to grow steadily, business-to-business transactions are rapidly gaining popularity and are considered the real future of I-commerce. This form of I-commerce promises to lower costs, reduce order processing time, and improve information flow.

Business-to-business will be driven by EDI—**electronic data interchange**. This means creating a set of computerized forms for commonly processed transactions, including purchase orders, invoices, shipping notices, and requests for proposals. Companies tried to set this up in the past with private networks created just for one company and its suppliers, but that proved to be far too expensive. With the Internet, the network is already in place. Small companies that want to become new partners with a larger firm no longer have to invest in that firm's computer system. EDI via the Internet makes it cost-effective to:

- Exchange documents at any time, even during non-business hours

- Lower business costs and eliminate paper

- Reduce information float

- Enhance customer service

- Replenish inventory faster

- Provide advance notification of shortages, cuts, and substitutions

- Improve forecasting by vendors and suppliers

- Improve shipping, receiving, and product tracking.

Using the web for EDI means companies can take advantage of the other things that make the web so attractive, like multimedia capabilities. A company can, for example, include pictures or even movies of each product in its online catalog. Real-time can be added to the service by providing online assistants who can answer questions as they are asked.

Most companies launch their business-to-business I-commerce efforts in stages. First, a company might provide product literature, software updates or patches, and answers to frequently asked questions online. Customers can then receive answers to questions immediately, and the company can save thousands on printing and postage costs. Then the company can move into advanced EDI functions, such as online ordering and other transaction-based systems. Electronic commerce can increase productivity, improve data accuracy, promote vendor loyalty, and improve inventory management.

THE BACKLASH TO BUSINESS-TO-BUSINESS I-COMMERCE

One unexpected backlash has occurred with Internet commerce. Many companies are choosing to move to the Internet because this allows them to directly interact with their customers, eliminating distributors and resellers from the process for those transactions. This has angered some resellers, who have retaliated by taking their business to other companies. This can still be done effectively today because most business is still conducted off-line. As more and more companies move online, however, the effectiveness of this tactic may dwindle.

Of course, some observers contend that the widespread assumption of a future Internet-dominated business world may not ever come to pass. This possibility is a grim one for many companies. After all, many companies have already taken the Internet plunge, losing large sums of money now with the expectation that, by being there first and being the best, they will make money eventually as more and more people migrate to the Internet. But even some celebrated Internet success stories, such as the bookseller amazon.com, are still not posting a profit. (However, its mere existence forced competitor and traditional bookstore Barnes and Noble to create its own extensive website, and now both are losing money.) Uncertainty over what the future holds, then, continues to make Internet commerce a scary proposition in some respects.

Finally, analysts point to other Internet commerce issues that will have to be addressed in the coming years. For example, some computer consultants estimate that it will be 10 years before a full-featured, scalable electronic commerce system will be available. The biggest problem is integrating archaic back-end systems to flashy new Internet systems. For example, a company's inventory is likely to be managed with an outdated computer system that would be astronomically expensive to replace, yet is utterly incompatible with new Internet systems.

FURTHER READING:

Etzel, Klaus. "E-Commerce Heads for the 'Net." *Communications News.* November 1997.

Lundquist, Eric. "The Web's Not Dead: It's Under Construction." *PC World.* November 17, 1997.

Mulqueen, John T. "The Sense (and Cents) of Money On the Net." *InternetWeek.* September 1, 1997.

Nelson, Matthew. "Enter I-Commerce." *InfoWorld.* December 8, 1997.

Page, Heather. "Open for Business." *Entrepreneur.* December 1997.

Paquet, Cheri. "Officials Discuss I-Commerce Tactics." *InfoWorld.* December 1, 1997.

Ryan, Pat. "Ringing Up Sales On the Internet." *InfoWorld.* December 8, 1997.

Seymour, Jim. "Making Online Commerce Work." *PC Magazine.* June 10, 1997.

Stewart, Alan. "Easier Access to World Markets." *Financial Times.* December 3, 1997.

Sullivan, Eamonn. "Outsource the Commerce in Electronic Commerce." *PC Week.* December 8, 1997.

Tebbe, Mark. "New I-Commerce Plans May Make 1998 the Year Business Booms." *InfoWorld.* December 8, 1997.

Vizard, Michael. "I-Commerce May Be a Tough Sell After All." *InfoWorld.* September 15, 1997.

SEE ALSO: Advertising Media, World Wide Web; Web Page Design

INTERNSHIPS

Internships are arrangements in which college students lend their talents to companies in return for an opportunity to develop business skills and gain exposure to the work environment. Many internship programs do not compensate interns financially—though some companies make exceptions to this general rule, either voluntarily or to meet state guidelines—but such positions are nonetheless often quite beneficial to the students who participate, for they receive "real world" business experience and an early opportunity to impress potential employers.

BENEFITS OF INTERNSHIP PROGRAMS

FOR STUDENTS "Internships are now seen by the majority of college students as an essential prerequisite for any job search," wrote Bibi Watson in *Management Review.* Such arrangements can provide them with valuable work experience (both practical and for résumé enhancement) and an opportunity to line up a job before graduation. Of course, not all internships are created equal. But whereas some companies still view interns as little more than a free source of labor to catch up on filing and other tedious office tasks, Watson notes that "companies have now come to realize that top students would rather spend their time studying than showing up every day for an internship they find meaningless." Moreover, colleges and universities have, in recent years, begun to hold company internship programs to a higher standard as well.

In addition to securing good work experience, students also may be able to gain academic credit and financial compensation (albeit modest in size) for internships. As Steven Bahls and Jane Easter Bahls observed in *Entrepreneur,* "when an internship is set up through a local college or university, students can often obtain academic credit for their effort. The fact that they're receiving credit, though, doesn't mean they're not also entitled to minimum wage if your business derives immediate benefit from their labor."

FOR COMPANIES Internship programs can be a valuable asset for large companies, who have traditionally maintained some of the country's best and largest internship initiatives. But small companies can realize significant benefits as well. In many respects, interns can be ideal workers for small and mid-sized companies. They are typically hungry to gain experience, willing to perform less-desirable tasks (although a steady diet of it is apt to wilt their enthusiasm), and eager to perform well. In addition, internship programs enable businesses to sort through a pool of potential employees. As the weeks pass, intern performances can be evaluated, and the pool can be culled down to good workers who are already familiar with the company. Moreover, Watson points out that "there are some strong financial incentives to a strong internship program. One study estimates that companies save about $15,000 per person by hiring from the intern pool. The study computes, among other benefits, lower turnover rates and well-trained employees."

SETTING UP INTERNSHIPS

Small businesses can benefit enormously when they establish an internship program, but such initiatives should not be launched in haphazard fashion. "Before you bombard colleges with leaflets announcing the availability of internships, decide what it is you want to achieve," counseled Deborah Brightman in *Public Relations Journal.* "These goals will help you determine the length of your program (two months should be a minimum) and the number of interns you should hire. The latter will also depend on your experience in managing an internship program, the available budget and space, and the number of people on staff who are available to supervise and train interns." In addition, companies should have a full understanding of the specific tasks to which in-

terns will be assigned, and make plans to ensure that interns will have an opportunity to receive meaningful feedback on their performance.

A written plan providing details of the plan should then be prepared. This plan serves to educate potential interns and internship directors at colleges and universities, and can serve as a blueprint and guide for the company after the program is launched. "The plan," wrote Brightman, "should cover the program's purpose, recruitment, activities and responsibilities, evaluation, and follow-up steps. Be sure to make those employees who will be involved in the program aware of their parts before the interns arrive." Once these materials have been created, companies can go about the process of contacting appropriate colleges and universities, many of whom have established internship centers in recent years.

The interviewing process for internships is not unlike the regular interview process in many respects. Factors such as attitude, academic achievement, and suitability for the job are paramount. Small business consultants also counsel their clients to set up summer internship programs in the winter when possible, since the pool of both full- and part-time students available for internships is deepest at that time of the year.

MONITORING INTERNSHIPS

Internships naturally need to be supervised, and the choice of supervisors is often essential in determining whether the company's program will be successful, mediocre, or downright lousy. Business experts recommend that interns be monitored by enthusiastic people who have time to tackle the responsibilities associated with the job. "The internship director should have regular contact with both the interns and their . . . supervisors, monitoring the quality of work that's being performed, the experience the interns are gaining, and how happy they and their supervisors are with the program," wrote Brightman. "The supervisor must also be available to mediate any problems, oversee the recruitment process, and handle administrative details such as salary, office space, and evaluations." Finally, the director should be able to handle necessary communications with the intern's university.

DISTINGUISHING INTERNS FROM EMPLOYEES

Internship programs can be tremendously helpful to small businesses, but there are legal hazards associated with such programs of which employers should be aware. "Unless your internship program is essentially educational," caution *Entrepreneur* contributors Steven Bahls and Jane Easter Bahls, "your interns may look suspiciously like employees, who are entitled to the federal **minimum wage**.'' Companies that operate internship programs that are found to be *not* primarily educational may run the risk of being found in violation of the Fair Labor Standards Act (FLSA), which applies to all companies with two or more employees and annual sales of at least $500,000.

Bahls and Bahls note that the U.S. Labor Department's *Wage and Hour Field Operations Manual* establishes six criteria for distinguishing interns from employees:

1) Interns may be trained using equipment and procedures specific to the employer, but internship experiences must be akin to experiences that they would be able to gain in a vocational school.

2) Regular employees cannot be displaced by interns, who should be closely supervised. ''Farming work out to unpaid interns after a regular employee quits would raise a red flag,'' said Bahls and Bahls.

3) Interns are not guaranteed jobs at the completion of their internship. ''If they are,'' wrote Bahls and Bahls, ''the experience looks more like the training period at the start of a new job, for which they'd be entitled to fair wages.''

4) Both employer and intern need to understand that training time does not entitle interns to wages.

5) Training should be primarily for the benefit of the intern.

6) Companies providing training to interns, noted Bahls and Bahls, ''must derive no immediate advantage from the activities of the intern. . . . Although an internship program will benefit your business over the long term by providing a pool of trained applicants with familiar work habits, it's not meant to be a source of free labor.''

Most business consultants offer soothing advice to small companies that might be scared off by such criteria. They point out that the overwhelming majority of firms that establish internship programs are pleased with them, and as Bahls and Bahls wrote, ''while the Labor Department closely adheres to its six criteria, courts tend to look at the spirit of the internship program as a whole.''

Business owners and managers also need to be aware that, generally speaking, even unpaid interns have the same legal rights as employees when it comes to protection against discrimination or harassment. ''It's best to cover them for **workers' compensation**, too,'' said Bahls and Bahls, ''because if they're injured on the job and not covered, they can

sue your business for medical expenses and possibly for negligence, which can subject your business to unlimited damages.'' However, interns do not have the same rights as employees in the realms of unemployment compensation or termination procedures.

FURTHER READING:

Aldrich, Michael. ''Breathing New Life into a Small-College Internship Program.'' *Journal of Career Planning.* Spring, 1993.

Bahls, Steven C., and Jane Easter Bahls. ''Internal Affairs.'' *Entrepreneur.* November 1997.

Bell, Justine. ''Marketing Academic Internships in the Public Sector.'' *Public Personnel Management.* Fall 1994.

Brightman, Deborah E. ''How to Build an Internship Program.'' *Public Relations Journal.* January 1989.

Burkins, Glenn. ''Summer Jobs Go Begging as Unemployment Stays Very Low.'' *Wall Street Journal.* May 20, 1997.

Edleson, Harriet. ''Expanding the Talent Search.'' *HR Magazine.* July 1991.

Gornstein, Leslie. ''Heard at Downsized Firms: 'Hey! Let the Intern Do It!' '' *Crain's Chicago Business.* September 5, 1994.

Kaplan, Rochelle. ''Hiring Student Interns.'' *Small Business Reports.* May 1994.

Pedersen, Laura. ''Minding Your Business: Apprenticeships Abound for Students.'' *New York Times.* June 18, 1995.

Ruiz, Jon, and Steve VanderMeer. ''Internships: High Return on Low Investments.'' *Public Management.* February 1989.

Watson, Bibi S. ''The Intern Turnaround.'' *Management Review.* June 1995.

SEE ALSO: Apprenticeship Programs; Employee Screening; Recruiting

INTERPERSONAL COMMUNICATION

Although interpersonal communication can encompass oral, written, and nonverbal forms of communication, the term is usually applied to spoken communication that takes place between two or more individuals on a direct, face-to-face level. Interpersonal communication is a vital part of the business world. ''Giving and receiving information, or *communicating,* is the most fundamental component of the manager's job,'' according to Thomas S. Bateman and Carl P. Zeithaml in their book *Management: Function and Strategy.* Some of the types of interpersonal communication that are commonly used within a business organization include staff **meetings**, formal project discussions, employee performance reviews, or informal chats. Interpersonal communication with those outside of the business organization might take the form of client meetings, employment interviews, or sales visits. In order to understand the principles of effective interpersonal communication, it is helpful to look at the basic process of communication.

THE COMMUNICATION PROCESS

The basic process of communication begins when a fact is observed or an idea formulated by one person. That person (the sender) decides to translate the observation into a message, and then transmits the message through some communication medium to another person (the receiver). The receiver then must interpret the message and provide feedback to the sender indicating that the message has been understood and appropriate action taken.

Unfortunately, errors can be introduced during any phase of the communication process. For example, misunderstandings can occur when the sender does not possess a clear idea of the message he or she is trying to communicate, or has a clear idea but is not able to express it well. Errors in the process can also occur when the receiver does not listen carefully, infers a different meaning than what was intended by the sender, or fails to provide feedback. Since effective communication is so important in business, managers should take any necessary steps to eliminate sources of errors in the process.

According to Herta A. Murphy and Herbert W. Hildebrandt in their book *Effective Business Communications,* good communication should be complete, concise, clear, concrete, correct, considerate, and courteous. More specifically, this means that communication should: answer basic questions like who, what, when, and where; be relevant and not overly wordy; focus on the receiver and his or her interests; use specific facts and figures and active verbs; employ a conversational tone; include examples and visual aids when needed; be tactful and good natured; and be accurate and nondiscriminatory. Unclear, inaccurate, or inconsiderate business communication can waste valuable time, alienate employees or customers, and destroy goodwill toward management or the overall business.

Perhaps the most important part of business communication is taking the time to prepare an effective and understandable message. According to Murphy and Hildebrandt, the first step is to know the main purpose of the message. For example, a message to a supplier might have the purpose of obtaining a replacement for a defective part. The next step is to analyze the audience so that the message can be adapted to fit their views and needs. It may be helpful to picture the recipient and think about which areas of the message they might find positive or negative, interesting or boring, pleasing or displeasing. After that, the sender needs to choose the ideas to include and collect all the necessary facts. The next step involves organizing the message, since a poorly organized message will fail to elicit the required response. It may be helpful to prepare an outline beforehand, paying particular attention to the beginning and end-ing portions. Finally, before transmitting the message it is important to edit and revise.

INTERPERSONAL COMMUNICATION STYLES

In general terms, interpersonal communication can be classified as either one-way or two-way. One-way communication occurs when the sender transmits information in the form of direction, without any expectation of discussion or feedback. For example, a manager may stop by an employee's desk to inform him that a certain project will be due the following day. One-way communication is faster and easier for the sender—because he or she does not have to deal with potential questions or disagreement from the receiver—but tends to be overused in business situations.

In contrast, two-way communication involves the sharing of information between two or more parties in a constructive exchange. For example, a manager may hold a staff meeting in order to establish the due dates for a number of projects. Engaging in two-way communication indicates that the sender is receptive to feedback and willing to provide a response. Although it is more difficult and time-consuming for the sender than one-way communication, it is also ensures a more accurate understanding of the message.

In addition to being classified as one-way or two-way, interpersonal communication can also be broken down into a variety of styles, or specialized sets of behaviors. Bateman and Zeithaml identified six main styles of interpersonal communication that are used in business settings: controlling, egalitarian, structuring, dynamic, relinquishing, and withdrawal. ''Different individuals use different communication styles,'' the authors noted. ''A communicator should realize that some styles are more effective than others in certain situations.''

The controlling style is a form of one-way communication that is used to direct others and gain their compliance. Managers using this style usually do not want feedback, and they tend to employ power and even manipulation to reinforce their message. Although the controlling style can be effective when it is used on occasion by respected individuals, particularly in times of crisis, it can also alienate workers. In contrast, the egalitarian style is a form two-way communication that involves sharing information rather than directing behavior. It is used to stimulate others to express their ideas and opinions in order to reach a mutual understanding. In most situations—particularly when cooperation is needed—it is more effective than the controlling style.

The structuring style of interpersonal communication is used to establish schedules or impose organization. Managers using this style would be likely to cite company standards or rules. Though the structuring style may be necessary to inform others of goals or procedures when complex tasks must be performed by a group, it should usually be counterbalanced with the egalitarian style. The dynamic style is a high-energy approach that uses inspirational pleas to motivate another person to take action. This style can be effective in crisis situations, but it is generally ineffective when the receivers do not have enough knowledge or experience to take the required action.

The relinquishing style of interpersonal communication is deferential rather than directive. It is highly receptive to the ideas of others, to the point of shifting responsibility for communication to the receiver. For example, a manager employing this style might allow her staff to discuss and develop the final solution to a problem while making little comment. This style is particularly effective when the receivers have the knowledge, experience, and willingness to assume responsibility. The withdrawal style is more like a lack of communication. Managers using this style try to avoid using their influence and may indicate a disinterest or unwillingness to participate in the discussion.

Finally, an often overlooked element of interpersonal communication is being a good receiver, which involves developing listening skills. Good listening skills can be vital in finding a solution to grievances or even in making sales calls. Listening involves showing an interest in the speaker, concentrating on the message, and asking questions to ensure understanding. One useful listening technique is reflection, or attempting to repeat and clarify the other person's message rather than immediately responding to it with a message of your own. Used correctly, reflection can allow managers to view issues from their employees' point of view. Some other keys to effective listening include: keeping an open mind rather than allowing emotions to intervene; finding a part of the subject that may have application to your own experience; and resisting distractions such as the speaker's mannerisms or clothing. It also helps to be prepared for the discussion, to take notes as needed, and to summarize the speaker's statements.

Strong interpersonal communication skills, utilizing a variety of styles and techniques, are particularly important for small business owners who must supervise the work of others. Bateman and Zeithaml described some of the characteristics of supervisors who receive high marks from their employees. First, these managers tend to communicate more than other managers, explaining the reasons behind decisions and providing advance warning of changes. Second, they tend to employ an egalitarian rather than controlling style when communicating with subordinates, asking for instead of demanding their compliance. Third, they tend to take others' needs and feelings into account when communicating. Finally, most effective managers are good listeners, giving careful consideration to employee concerns and taking the time to respond to questions and complaints.

FURTHER READING:

Bateman, Thomas S., and Carl P. Zeithaml. *Management: Function and Strategy.* Homewood, IL: Irwin, 1990.

Golen, Steven. *Effective Business Communication.* Washington: U.S. Small Business Administration, 1989.

Murphy, Herta A., and Herbert W. Hildebrandt. *Effective Business Communications.* 6th ed. New York: McGraw-Hill, 1991.

Townsend, Robert. *Up the Organization.* New York: Knopf, 1984.

SEE ALSO: Oral Communication

INTRAPRENEURSHIP

Intrapreneurs are employees who work within a business in an entrepreneurial capacity, creating innovative new products and processes for the organization. Intrapreneurship is often associated with larger companies that have taken notice of the rise in entrepreneurial activity in recent years; these firms endeavor to create an environment wherein creative employees can pursue new ways of doing things and new product ideas within the context of the corporation. But smaller firms can instill a commitment to intrapreneurship within its work force as well. In fact, small businesses, which originate as entrepreneurial ventures, are often ideally suited to foster an intrapreneurial environment, since their owners have first-hand knowledge of the opportunities and perils that accompany new business initiatives. "For larger companies, intrapreneuring is a way to recapture the spirit that put them on the road to success in the first place," observed *Nation's Business*. "For smaller companies, it can be a way of maintaining the entrepreneurial drive that gave them birth."

Intrapreneurship practices have developed in response to the modern world's rapidly changing marketplace. "While businesses of varying sizes have long had internal units for development of new products, many found such arrangements were inadequate in today's business environment," contended *Nation's Business*. "Creative young people chafed under corporate bureaucracies and frequently left to develop their ideas as entrepreneurs. Their former employers lost not only highly promising talent, but also a chance for profitable new lines. Intrapreneuring in its current form represents the determination of such employers to solve their particular brain drain problem. They are doing so by creating the environment—and providing the incentives—for **entrepreneurship** within their existing business operations."

ORGANIZATIONAL CHARACTERISTICS THAT ENCOURAGE INTRAPRENEURSHIP

The single most important factor in establishing an "intrapreneur-friendly" organization is making sure that your employees are placed in an innovative working environment. Rigid and conservative organizational structures often have a stifling effect on intrapreneurial efforts. Conservatively managed firms are capable of operating at a high level of efficiency and profitability, but they generally do not provide an environment that is conducive to intrapreneurial activity (and organizations that do not encourage creativity and leadership often alienate talented employees). But as Erik Rule and Donald Irwin stated in *Journal of Business Strategy,* companies that establish a culture of innovation through: 1) formation of intrapreneurial teams and task forces; 2) recruitment of new staff with new ideas; 3) application of strategic plans that focus on achieving innovation; and 4) establishment of internal research and development programs are likely to see tangible results.

Other keys to instilling an intrapreneurial environment in your business include the following:

1) Support from ownership or top management. Researchers point out, however, that this support should not simply consist of passive approval of innovative ways of thinking. Ideally, it should also take the form of active support, such as can be seen in mentoring relationships. Indeed, the small business owner's own entrepreneurial experiences can be valuable to his firm's intrapreneurial employees if he makes himself available to them.

2) Recognition that the style of intrapreneurialism that is encouraged needs to be compatible with business operations and the organization's overall culture.

3) Make sure that communication systems within the company are strong so that intrapreneurs who have new ideas for products or processes can be heard.

4) Intelligent allocation of resources to pursue intrapreneurial ideas.

5) Reward intrapreneurs. All in all, intrapreneurs tend to be creative, dedicated, and talented in a variety of areas. They are thus of significant value even to companies that do not feature particularly innovative environments. Their importance is heightened, then, to firms that do rely on intrapreneurial initiatives for growth. Since they are such important resources, they should be rewarded accordingly (both in financial and emotional terms). For while intrapreneurs may not want to go into business for themselves, they still have a hunger to make use of their talents and a wish to be compensated for their contributions. If your small business is unable or unwilling to provide sufficient rewards, then it should be prepared to lose that intrapreneur to another organization.

6) Allow intrapreneurs to follow through. Intrapreneurs who think of a new approach or process deserve to be allowed to maintain their involvement on the project, rather than have it be handed off to some other person or task force. Ensuring that the individual stays involved with the initiative makes sense for several important reasons. The intrapreneur's creativity and emotional investment in the project can be tremendously helpful in further developing the process or product for future use. Even more importantly, however, the small business enterprise should make sure that its talented and creative employees have continued input because not allowing them to do so can have a profoundly morale-bruising impact.

FURTHER READING:

Carrier, Camille. "Intrapreneurship in Large Firms and SMEs: A Comparative Study." *International Small Business Journal.* April-June 1994.

Carrier, Camille. "Intrapreneurship in Small Businesses: An Exploratory Study." *Entrepreneurship: Theory and Practice.* Fall 1996.

De Chambeau, Franck A., and Fredericka Mackenzie. "Intrapreneurship." *Personnel Journal.* July 1986.

Feinberg, Mortimer. "On Intrapreneurship." *Restaurant Business.* March 1, 1989.

"Intrapreneurship: A Welcome Trend in the Business World." *Nation's Business.* June 1986.

"Intrapreneurship Pros and Cons." *Chain Store Age Executive.* October 1987.

Matkins, Pamela. "Making Entrepreneurship an Inside Job." *Black Enterprise.* February 1989.

Oliver, Carol, et al. "Intrapreneurship and Entrepreneurship Amongst MBA Graduates." *Management Decision.* September 1991.

Pinchot, Gifford. *Intrapreneuring.* New York: Harper & Row, 1985.

Pryor, Austin K., and E. Michael Shays. "Growing the Business with Intrapreneurs." *Business Quarterly.* Spring 1993.

Rule, Erik G., and Donald W. Irwin. "Fostering Intrapreneurship: The New Competitive Edge." *Journal of Business Strategy.* May-June 1988.

Shatzer, Lisa, and Linda Schwartz. "Managing Intrapreneurship." *Management Decision.* Annual 1991.

SEE ALSO: Innovation

INVENTIONS AND PATENTS

A patent is a document that secures to an inventor the exclusive right to sell, make, or otherwise use his or her invention for a specified number of years. The document details the terms under which the government has granted the inventor full possession of the invention. These terms of possession or "intellectual property right" include specifications designed to exclude all others from making, using, or selling the invention in the United States for the life of the patent. The patent also provides rightful patentholders with specific legal steps that can be taken to stop (or be compensated for) instances in which others have infringed on the patent.

Patented inventions have spawned thousands of small businesses over the years. Not all of these businesses have succeeded, of course; some were predicated on new products or designs that were fundamentally flawed, while others faded because of operational problems, economic trends, or personal frailties. But countless successful entrepreneurs have launched their businesses on the strength of a single invention, and patents continue to stand as among the most valuable assets of thousands of small business owners across the nation.

TYPES OF PATENTS

Inventors may apply for patents on inventions in three major categories: utility patents, design patents, and plant patents.

UTILITY PATENTS Utility Patents are the most common kind of patents. They are granted to inventors who, according to the U.S. Patent and Trademark Office (PTO), invent or discover any new and useful process, machine, manufacture, or compositions of matter (mixtures of ingredients, chemical compounds), or any new and useful variations of existing products, processes, or compositions. The legal definition of "process" in this instance includes new industrial or technical methods. Utility patents are the most complex of the three kinds of patents, for they require the patent applicant to provide a full description of the invention's functional and/or structural features (often including detailed drawings) as well as the inventor's explanation of what he or she feels is "patentable." Inventors filing utility patents subsequently are more likely to secure legal help in making certain that all details of the patent are adequately addressed.

DESIGN PATENTS Inventors can also obtain patents on the appearance of a product, provided that it is a new and original design. As Richard C. Levy noted in his *Inventor's Desktop Companion,* "if you've invented any new, original, and ornamental designs for an article of manufacture, a design patent may be appropriate. A design patent protects only the appearance of an article and not its structure or utilitarian features." Thomas Field, author of the Small Business Administration's *Avoiding Patent, Trademark and Copyright Problems,* pointed out that both design patents and utility patents "do more than prevent copying; they forbid the making, using or selling of an invention similar to or the same as the protected invention," even in situations where the second invention was independently created.

PLANT PATENTS This kind of patent is granted to anyone who invents or discovers and asexually reproduces any distinct and new variety of plant, including cultivated sports, mutants, hybrids, and newly found seedlings. The PTO does not grant plant patents, however, for tuber-propagated plants or plants found in an uncultivated state. Asexually propagated plants, noted Levy, are those that are reproduced by means other than from seeds, such as rooting of cuttings, layering, budding, grafting, and inarching. Plant patents comprise only a small minority of the total number of patents that have been bestowed by the PTO.

Although millions of patents have been granted in the United States and other countries over the years, there are many things that are not eligible to receive patent protection. These include general business ideas and strategies, printed material, scientific theories, mathematical formulas, and obvious changes to existing items, although some of the above can be legally protected in other ways. Printed material, for instance, can be protected through **copyrights**.

FILING A PATENT

Patents are arranged according to a massive classification system encompassing more than 400 subject classes and 115,000 subject subclasses. The *Index to the U.S. Patent Classification System,* an alphabetical subject listing of these various classes and subclasses, is produced by the PTO to aid searchers of the system. "The Classifications," wrote Levy, "are to searching a patent what the card catalog is to looking for a library book. It is the only way to discover what exists in the field of prior art [prior patents]. The Classifications are a star to steer by, without which no meaningful patent search can be completed." The *Index,* coupled with the *Official Gazette of the United States Patent and Trademark Office,* the *Manual of Classification,* are among the most important tools available to patent searchers.

Another important cog in the PTO's efforts to disseminate information about patents to the public is the Patent and Trademark Depository Library (PTDL), a national network of academic, research, and public libraries. Many inventors are frequent users of often-extensive PTDL resources.

CONDUCTING A PATENT SEARCH Inventors, lawyers, and patent experts all advise inventors armed with a possible new product or design to undertake a comprehensive patent search before taking any other steps. ''You cannot avoid doing a search,'' Levy flatly stated. ''The [Patent and Trademark Office] examiner will do one anyway and if your application is rejected based upon prior art (patents that have previously issued), you'll have lost the application cost not to mention the significant time and energy you invested.''

Patent searches can be mounted in one of three ways. Some inventors choose to undertake the task themselves, but the majority choose to secure the services of a patent attorney or a professional patent search firm. Patent attorneys typically hire professional researchers to do the actual patent search; the turnaround time with lawyers who specialize in handling such searches is usually fast, but they are also expensive because of the mark-up charge that attorneys impose. ''If you want to save the lawyer's mark-up,'' wrote Levy, ''consider going directly to a patent search firm. Searchers are best found through inventor grapevines, inventor associations, or university intellectual property departments.'' Patent search companies can also be found in local yellow pages, but inventors need to be careful in making agreements with such firms. Some are perfectly legitimate, but others prey on unsuspecting inventors, saddling them with service contracts or other bad business arrangements. Given this reality, inventors should ask for references, evidence that the search firm has prior experience in the field in which their inventions are classified, and a signed letter of non-disclosure before agreeing to any arrangement with a search firm.

The cost of a search can vary substantially, depending on the nature of the search. As Levy remarked, ''there are different charges for different assignments (for example, searching utility patents versus design patents). Electronic, chemical, biological, botanical, and medical searches are often more expensive. And, in most cases, there will be incidental charges for copies, phone and fax, online fees, and shipping and handling of your materials. This is all standard.'' Another fact that can influence the final cost is turnaround time. Some patent search services now offer same-day service, but at higher prices than their usual searches.

Once a patent search has been completed, the inventor can proceed accordingly. In instances where the invention is in the public domain (a patent on the invention has expired), the inventor is, according to Field, ''free to manufacture and market it without concern for the patent laws. Also, even if the inventor didn't find exactly what he or she originally had in mind, a host of good and freely used ideas that are even better might have been discovered. These alone could be worth several times the price of the search in saving research and development time.''

If the inventor finds that any part of his or her proposed product or design is covered by a current patent, then the inventor can either drop the idea or approach the patent holder about securing a license to use it. ''Infringing on a current patent exposes one to a suit for damages as well as an injunction against future use,'' warned Field. ''Even an injunction might mean substantial costs, including the loss of current inventory, and a patent covering even a small feature of the new [product] might give rise to the need to retool. Although deliberate infringement is more serious, ignorance of others' patents is no defense.''

If one or more elements of the proposed product or design appear to be new, with notable advantages over prior patents, then the inventor can submit a patent application. Inventors should be sure that they not let their enthusiasm get the better of them in such instances. If he or she begins selling the product or design without first filing an application for patent, then he or she forfeits any possibility of securing patent rights in the United States after one year. In addition, the inventor loses all possible protection in most other countries.

APPLYING FOR A PATENT

Most experts counsel inventors to retain patent counsel to handle utility patents (although they are permitted to make utility patent applications themselves if they so desire). Utility patent applications are complex documents with myriad requirements, and as Levy indicated, ''smart inventors use experienced patent counsel to assure that they obtain the strongest patent protection available on their inventions. There is too much at stake. Smart inventors do not rely on patent-it-yourself books.'' Design patent applications, however, are far less complicated, so many inventors take care of those documents themselves.

PATENT ATTORNEYS Before making an arrangement with a patent attorney, savvy inventors take steps to ensure that they have found competent, responsible legal counsel. The first step is to make sure that the lawyer is registered with the Patent and Trademark Office. ''To be listed,'' said Levy, ''a person must comply with the regulations prescribed by the PTO, which require proof that the person is of good moral character and of good repute and that he or she has the legal, scientific, and technical qualifications necessary to give inventors valuable service.'' In addition, attorneys listed with the PTO are required to have minimum academic and professional qualifications, and must pass a PTO examination.

Inventors should also make certain that their legal counsel is familiar with the field or industry in which the invention would be used. In addition, they should do their best to insure that their attorney has all relevant information needed to make the best possible patent application. Finally, experts counsel inventors to shop around to find the best combination of price and value, and they encourage them to secure written agreements on attorney fees.

PATENT DRAWINGS Patent experts advise inventors to secure the services of an experienced patent draftsmen when the time comes to make patent drawings. "The requirements for drawings are strictly enforced," warned Levy. "Professional draftsmen will stand behind their work and guarantee revisions if requested by the PTO due to inconsistencies in the drawings. . . . Because the design patent is granted for the appearance of the article, the drawing in the design patent is more critical than the drawing in a utility patent. The design drawing is the disclosure of the claimed design, whereas the utility drawing is intended to provide only an exemplary illustration of some aspects of the mechanism described in the specification and claims."

PATENTS AND THE PTO It generally takes the Patent and Trademark Office a little over 18 months to process patent applications and issue approved patents. Examinations of patent applications, which are undertaken in the order in which they are received, are arduous exercises. "The application examination inspects for compliance with the legal requirements and includes a search through U.S. patents, prior foreign patent documents which are available in the PTO, and available literature to ensure that the invention is new," explained Levy. "A decision is reached by the examiner in light of the study and the result of the search."

If an application is approved, then the inventor can proceed with his business plan, whether that involved launching a small business or seeking buyers for the invention. Many applications, however, are rejected when they are first submitted. Even applications for genuinely new products or designs sometimes need changes to meet PTO requirements. In instances in which the application is rejected, the inventor has limited options. The inventor can prepare a response to the examiner's stated grounds for rejection, explaining why he or she believes that the examiner erred; this is a viable step, and one which sometimes convinces examiners to reconsider. The inventor can also offer amendments to the application designed to assuage the examiner's objections.

On many occasions, however, the examiner will remain unswayed and will reject the inventor's claims. If this happens, the inventor can lodge appeals with the PTO commissioner and, after that, the Board of Patent Appeals and Interferences. If the application is still deemed unacceptable, and the inventor remains determined to pursue the issue, he or she can then turn to the U.S. court system. The Court of Appeals for the Federal Circuit and the U.S. District Court for the District of Columbia have both heard such cases.

FEES Receivers of patents must pay fees to the PTO for services rendered when a patent is reviewed. In 1982 a law was passed that cut some of these fees (patent application, extension of time, revival, appeal, patent issues, statutory disclaimer, maintenance on patents) for "small entities." Small entities were held to include independent inventors, small businesses, and nonprofit organizations. In addition, all utility patents are subject to the payment of maintenance fees which must be paid to keep the patent going. These payments are made at several different points of the patent's life. Inventors need to heed this payment schedule closely, for nonpayment may result in the premature expiration of the patent (a six-month grace period is typically provided during which the fee can be paid, albeit with a surcharge). Inventors who secure the services of a patent attorney generally do not have to worry about this scenario as much, since a competent attorney will notify them of impending maintenance fee payments.

In recent years, the government's decision to retool the PTO so that it could operate without federal funding has triggered significant increases in PTO fees. In 1991 Congress dramatically raised patent application fees to cover the Office's operating costs, but by the mid-1990s this income was being redistributed to pay for other government programs or address the federal budget deficit, and the PTO was being forced to mull additional fee increases. The situation deeply angers many members of the small business community, who note that such increases disproportionately impact individual inventors and entrepreneurs. "Our economy is based on new products and new technologies, many of which come from the independent inventor," Inventors Awareness Group founder Robert Lougher told *Entrepreneur*. "If you interrupt that process, we're going to have fewer new products. Everyone [will feel] it down the line."

U.S. PATENTS AND GATT The 1994 **General Agreement on Tariffs and Trade (GATT)** also brought significant changes to U.S. patent law. The biggest one changed the duration of patent protection. Prior to GATT, patents lasted for 17 years (14 years for design patents) from the date that the patent was granted. After GATT, patent terms were extended to 20 years *from the date at which the patent application was first filed*. This is a significant change, for as Levy noted, under the new arrangement, a competitor could conceivably file a long stream of fraudulent interference objections (claims that it had developed a similar product or design at the same time) in order to delay the issuance of a patent, "thereby reducing the patent's life when it does issue." Many observers fear that entrepreneurs and small businesses could be hurt by this arrangement.

GATT does provide some patent rules of potential advantage to small inventors. For example, it provides for the issuance of "provisional patent applications," which in effect allows inventors to file a preliminary application that establishes the data of invention. The provisional application does not replace the regular PTO application, but it gives inventors additional time to prepare for that step. Other GATT rules changed import/export rules regarding intellectual property and expanded the number of scenarios under which interference proceedings could be launched.

FILING PATENTS IN THE U.S. AND ABROAD Most experienced inventors and patent experts counsel inventors to file for a patent as soon as possible. In the United States you have to apply for a patent within one year of the time you first disclose the device or start selling it. At the conclusion of that year, a valid patent may not be obtained. Inventors should also note that a U.S. patent will not provide him or her with protection in other countries; patent applications need to be made in every country in which protection is desired. Moreover, in other countries, inventors have to apply for the patent before it is publicly disclosed. Finally, the PTO notes that in most instances, American inventors seeking to secure a patent in another country must first get a license from the Commissioner of Patents and Trademarks. This requirement is waived, however, if the filing in the foreign country takes place more than six months after the U.S. filing took place.

There are two major international patent treaties that should be studied by inventors hoping to market their products abroad. The Paris Convention for the Protection of Industrial Property, which was signed by the United States and nearly 100 other nations, stipulates that each signing nation provide the same rights in patents and trademarks to citizens of other participating nations that it does to its own. The Patent Cooperation Treaty, meanwhile, is a patent agreement that includes more than 50 nations.

FURTHER READING:

Attard, Janet. *The Home Office and Small Business Answer Book.* New York: Henry Holt, 1993.

Chun, Janean. "Patent Lather." *Entrepreneur.* June 1997.

Field, Thomas. *Avoiding Patent, Trademark and Copyright Problems.* Washington: U.S. Small Business Administration, 1992.

GATT Implementing Legislation. Washington: Intellectual Property Owners Association, 1994.

Levy, Richard C. *The Inventor's Desktop Companion.* Detroit, MI: Visible Ink Press, 1995.

SEE ALSO: Innovation; Legal Advice and Services

INVENTORY

An inventory is a detailed, itemized list or record of goods and materials in a company's possession. "The main components of inventory," wrote *Transportation and Distribution* contributors David Waller and Barbara Rosenbaum, "are cycle stock: the order quantity or lot size received from the plant or vendor; in-transit stock: inventory in shipment from the plant or vendor or between distribution centers; [and] safety stock: each distribution center's inventory buffer against forecast error and lead time variability."

Writing in *Production and Operations Management,* Howard J. Weiss and Mark E. Gershon observed that, historically, there have been two basic inventory systems: the continuous review system and the periodic review system. With continuous review systems, the level of a company's inventory is monitored at all times. Under these arrangements, businesses typically track inventory until it reaches a predetermined point of "low" holdings, whereupon the company makes an order (also of a generally predetermined level) to push its holdings back up to a desirable level. Since the same amount is ordered on each occasion, continuous review systems are sometimes also referred to as event-triggered systems, fixed order size systems (FOSS), or economic order quantity systems (EOQ). Periodic review systems, on the other hand, check inventory levels at fixed intervals rather than through continuous monitoring. These periodic reviews (weekly, biweekly, or monthly checks are common) are also known as time-triggered systems, fixed order interval systems (FOIS), or economic order interval systems (EOI).

INVENTORY AND THE GROWING COMPANY

Most successful small companies find that as their economic fortunes rise, so too do the complexity of inventory logistics. Weiss and Gershon noted that this rise in inventory work is primarily due to two factors: 1) greater volume and variety of products, and 2) increased allocation of company resources (such as physical space and financial capital) to accomodate that growth in inventory. "The transition from seat-of-the-pants ordering policies and little or no record keeping to a formal inventory system that includes specific ordering policies and a formalized inventory record file is a difficult one for most companies to make," stated Weiss and Gershon. "It is but one of the many sources of growing pains that emerging companies experience, especially those in the fast-growing industries, such as fast food or high technology. This transition requires the creation of new job functions to identify the costs (holding, shortage) associated with inventory and to implement the inventory analysis. The inventory record file also must be maintained by someone, and, on a periodic basis, it must be audited by someone. In addition, the transition requires more coordination between different company functions." This transition, they note, often leads into computerization of inventory management [which may or may not be a daunting prospect, depending on the background of key business personnel]. Implementation of a computerized recordkeeping system, wrote Weiss and Gershon, "necessitates the involvement of data processing in the inventory system, requiring further interdepartmental coordination. The motivation for computerizing the system may be that growth has created so many new inventory items that the card system is no longer an adequate monitor. Very often, however, the motivation is to keep in line with the computerization of other company functions, such as payroll and billing. No other major transitions occur during the life cycle of an inventory system unless a conversion is made to the just-in-time philosophy."

JUST-IN-TIME INVENTORY CONTROL " Just-in-time production is a simple idea that may be difficult to implement," wrote Gershon and Weiss. "The basic concept is that finished goods should be produced just in time for delivery, and raw materials should be delivered just in time for production. When this occurs, materials or goods never sit idle, which means that a minimum amount of money is tied up in raw materials, semifinished goods, and finished goods. . . . The just-in-time approach calls for slashing production and purchase lot sizes and also buffer stocks—but incrementally, a little at a time, month after month, year after year. The result is sustained productivity and quality improvement with greater flexibility and delivery responsiveness." This production concept, which originated in Japan and became immensely popular in American industries in the early and mid-1990s, continues to be hailed by proponents as a viable alternative for businesses looking for a competitive edge. Just-in-time strategies provide direct savings in inventory carrying costs, wrote Gershon and Weiss, but they contend that even greater benefits accrue from enforced problem solving: "Without extra inventory, small ripples in the rate of production or delivery at one stage of manufacture appear as large waves; all hands rally to correct the problems causing the ripple because the next stages of production are being starved of parts. The idea is to induce parts starvation deliberately in order to get the

underlying problems attended to. Many of the problems are quality problems, so quality improves. And each solved quality problem contributes to improved productivity (not to mention marketability) through reductions in scrap and rework."

SETTING AN INVENTORY STRATEGY

No single inventory strategy is equally effective for all businesses. Indeed, there are many different factors that can impact on the usefulness of a given inventory strategy, including positioning of inventory, rationalization, segmentation, and continuous improvement efforts. Moreover, small businesses in particular often face financial and logistical limitations when erecting their inventory systems. And of course, different industries have different inventory needs. Consumer goods producers, for instance, need to have well-balanced inventories at the point of sale, while producers of industrial and commercial products typically do not have clients that require the same degree of delivery lead time.

When a company is faced with a need to establish or reevaluate its **inventory control systems**, business experts often counsel their corporate clients to engage in a practice commonly known as "inventory segmenting" or "inventory partitioning." This practice is in essence a breakdown and review of total inventory by classifications, inventory stages (raw materials, intermediate inventories, finished products), sales and operations groupings, and excess inventories. Proponents of this method of study say that such segmentation break the company's total inventory into much more manageable parts for analysis.

KEY CONSIDERATIONS Inventory management is a key factor in the successful operation of fledgling businesses and long-time industry veterans alike. For both kinds of companies, determining whether their inventory systems are successful or not is predicated on one fundamental question: Does the inventory strategy insure that the company has adequate stock for production and goods shipments while at the same time minimizing inventory costs? If the answer is yes, then the company in question is far more likely to be a successful one. Conversely, if the answer is no, then the business is operating under twin burdens that can be of considerable consequence to its ability to survive, let alone flourish.

According to business experts, perhaps no factor is more important in ensuring successful inventory management than regular analysis of policies, practices, and results. Companies that hope to establish or maintain an effective inventory system should make sure that they do the following on a regular basis:

- Regularly review product offerings, including the breadth of the product line and the impact that peripheral products have on inventory.

- Ensure that inventory strategies are in place for each product and reviewed on a regular basis.

- Review transportation alternatives and their impact on inventory/warehouse capacities.

- Undertake periodic reviews to ensure that inventory is held at the level that best meets customer needs; this applies to all levels of business, including raw materials, intermediate assembly, and finished products.

- Regularly canvas key employees for information that can inform future inventory control plans.

- Determine what level of service (lead time, etc.) is necessary to meet the demands of customers.

- Establish and regularly review a system for effectively identifying and managing excess or obsolete inventory, and determining why these goods reached such status.

- Devise a workable system wherein ''safety'' inventory stocks can be reached and distributed on a timely basis when the company sees an unexpected rise in product demand.

- Calculate the impact of seasonal inventory fluctuations and incorporate them into inventory management strategies.

- Review the company's forecasting mechanisms and the volatility of the marketplace, both of which can (and do) have a big impact on inventory decisions.

- Institute ''continuous improvement'' philosophy in inventory management.

- Make inventory management decisions that reflect a recognition that inventory is deeply interrelated with many other areas of business operation.

To summarize, inventory management systems should be regularly reviewed from top to bottom as an essential part of the annual strategic and business planning processes.

Indeed, even cursory examinations of inventory statistics can sometimes provide business owners with valuable insights into the company's foundations. Business consultants and managers alike note that if an individual business has an inventory turnover ratio that is low in relation to the average for the industry in which it operates, or if it is low in comparison with the average ratio for the business, it is pretty likely that the business is carrying a surplus of obsolete or otherwise unsalable stock inventory. Conversely, they note

that if a business is experiencing unusually high inventory turnover when compared with industry or business averages, then the company may be losing out on sales because of a lack of adequate stock on hand. ''It will be helpful to determine the turnover rate of each stock item so that you can evaluate how well each is moving,'' noted *The Entrepreneur Magazine Small Business Advisor.* ''You may even want to base your inventory turnover on more frequent periods than a year. For perishable items, calculating turnover periods based on daily, weekly, or monthly periods may be necessary to ensure the freshness of the product. This is especially important for food-service operations.''

INVENTORY ACCOUNTING

The way in which a company accounts for its inventory can have a dramatic affect on its financial statements. Inventory is a current asset on the balance sheet. Therefore, the valuation of inventory directly affects the inventory, total current asset, and total asset balances. Companies intend to sell their inventory, and when they do, it increases the cost of goods sold, which is often a significant expense on the income statement. Therefore, how a company values its inventory will determine the cost of goods sold amount, which in turn affects gross profit (margin), net income before taxes, taxes owed, and ultimately net income. It is clear, then, that a company's inventory valuation approach can cause a ripple effect throughout its financial picture.

One may think that inventory valuation is relatively simple. For a retailer, inventory should be valued for what it cost to acquire that inventory. When an inventory item is sold, the inventory account should be reduced (credited) and cost of goods sold should be increased (debited) for the amount paid for each inventory item. This works if a company is operating under the Specific Identification Method. That is, a company knows the cost of every individual item that is sold. This method works well when the amount of inventory a company has is limited and each inventory item is unique. Examples would include car dealerships, jewelers, and art galleries.

The Specific Identification Method, however, is cumbersome in situations where a company owns a great deal of inventory and each specific inventory item is relatively indistinguishable from each other. As a result, other inventory valuation methods have been developed. The best known of these are the FIFO (first-in, first out) and LIFO (last-in, first-out) methods.

FIFO First-in, first-out is a method of inventory accounting in which the oldest stock items in a company's inventory are assumed to have been the first items sold. Therefore, the inventory that remains is from the most recent purchases. In a period of rising prices, this accounting method yields a higher ending inventory, a lower cost of goods sold, a higher gross profit, and a higher taxable income.

The FIFO Method may come the closest to matching the actual physical flow of inventory. Since FIFO assumes that the oldest inventory is always sold first, the valuation of inventory still on hand is at the most recent price. Assuming inflation, this will mean that cost of goods sold will be at its lowest possible amount. Therefore, a major advantage of FIFO is that it has the effect of maximizing net income within an inflationary environment. The downside of that effect is that income taxes will be at their greatest.

LIFO Last-in, first-out, on the other hand, is an accounting approach that assumes that the most recently acquired items are the first ones sold. Therefore, the inventory that remains is always the oldest inventory. During economic periods in which prices are rising, this inventory accounting method yields a lower ending inventory, a higher cost of goods sold, a lower gross profit, and a lower taxable income. The LIFO Method is preferred by many companies because it has the effect of reducing a company's taxes, thus increasing cash flow. However, these attributes of LIFO are only present in an inflationary environment.

The other major advantage of LIFO is that it can have an income smoothing effect. Again, assuming inflation and a company that is doing well, one would expect inventory levels to expand. Therefore, a company is purchasing inventory, but under LIFO, the majority of the cost of these purchases will be on the income statement as part of cost of goods sold. Thus, the most recent and most expensive purchases will increase cost of goods sold, thus lowering net income before taxes, and hence net income. Net income is still high, but it does not reach the levels that it would if the company used the FIFO method.

Given the importance differences that exist between the various inventory accounting methodologies, it is imperative that the inventory footnote be read carefully in financial statements, for this part of the document will inform the reader of the method of inventory valuation chosen by a company. Assuming inflation, FIFO will result in higher net income during growth periods and a higher, and more realistic inventory balance. In periods of growth, LIFO will result in lower net income and lower income tax payments, thus enhancing a company's cash flow. During periods of contraction, LIFO will result in higher income levels, but it will also undervalue inventory over time.

Small business owners weighing a switch to a LIFO inventory valuation method should note that while making the change is a relatively simple process (the company files IRS Form 970 with its tax return), switching away from LIFO is not so easy. Once a company adopts the LIFO method, it can not switch to FIFO without securing IRS approval.

FURTHER READING:

"Companies Count on Inventory Management for Accuracy, Convenience, Piece of Mind." *Chain Store Age Executive with Shopping Center Age.* May 1997.

Finkin, Eugene F. "How to Limit Inventory Expenses." *Journal of Business Strategy.* January-February 1989.

Gleckman, Howard. "A Tonic for the Business Cycle." *Business Week.* April 4, 1994.

"Good Business Ushers in More Inventory Problems." *Purchasing.* April 3, 1997.

Haire, Kevlin C. "Keeping the Merchandise Moving." *Baltimore Business Journal.* August 2, 1996.

Karmarker, Uday. "Getting Control of Just-In-Time." *Harvard Business Review.* September-October 1989.

Krupp, James A. "Measuring Inventory Management Performance." *Production and Inventory Management Journal.* Fall 1994.

"Manage Your Space." *Transportation and Distribution.* May 1996.

Ross, Julie Ritzer. "Inventory Management Systems Cut Costs While Keeping Store Shelves Full." *Stores.* July 1997.

Scanlon, Patrick C. "Controlling Your Inventory Dollars." *Production and Inventory Management Journal.* Fall 1993.

Valero, Greg. "Minimize Inventory for Maximum Success." *U.S. Distribution Journal.* July-August 1997.

Waller, David G., and Barbara A. Rosenbaum. "Plan Inventory Decisions to Cut Costs." *Transportation and Distribution.* November 1990.

Weiss, Howard J., and Mark E. Gershon. *Production and Operations Management.* Boston: Allyn and Bacon, 1989.

SEE ALSO: Inventory Control Systems

INVENTORY CONTROL SYSTEMS

Inventory control systems maintain information about activities within firms that ensure the delivery of products to customers. The subsystems that perform these functions include sales, manufacturing, warehousing, ordering, and receiving. In different firms the activities associated with each of these areas may not be strictly contained within separate subsystems, but these functions must be performed in sequence in order to have a well-run inventory control system.

In today's business environment, even many smaller businesses have come to rely on computerized inventory management systems. Certainly, there are plenty of small retail outlets, manufacturers, and other businesses that still rely on manual means of inventory tracking. Indeed, for some small businesses, like convenience stores, shoe stores, or nurseries, purchase of an electronic inventory tracking system might constitute a wasteful use of financial resources. But for other firms operating in industries that feature high volume turnover of raw materials and/or finished products, computerized tracking systems have emerged as a key component of business strategies aimed at increasing productivity and maintaining competitiveness. Moreover, the recent development of powerful computer programs capable of addressing a wide variety of record keeping needs—including inventory management—in one integrated system have also contributed to the growing popularity of electronic inventory control options.

Given such developments, it is little wonder that business experts commonly cite inventory management as a vital element that can spell the difference between success and failure in today's keenly competitive business world. Writing in *Production and Inventory Management Journal,* Godwin Udo described telecommunications technology as a critical organizational asset that can help a company realize important competitive gains in the area of inventory management. According to Udo, companies that make good use of this technology are far better equipped to succeed than those who rely on outdated or unwieldy methods of inventory control.

COMPUTERS AND INVENTORY

Automation can dramatically impact all phases of inventory management, including counting and monitoring of inventory items; recording and retrieval of item storage location; recording changes to inventory; and anticipating inventory needs, including inventory handling requirements. This is true even of stand-alone systems that are not integrated with other areas of the business, but many analysts indicate that productivity—and hence profitability—gains that are garnered through use of automated systems can be increased even more when a business integrates its inventory control systems with other systems such as accounting and sales to better control inventory levels. According to Dennis Eskow in *PC Week,* business executives are "increasingly integrating financial data, such as accounts receivable, with sales information that includes customer histories. The goal: to control inventory quarter to quarter, so it doesn't come back to bite the bottom line. Key components of an integrated system . . . are general ledger, electronic data interchange, database connectivity, and connections to a range of vertical business applications." David Cahn, a director of product strategy for business applications at a firm in New York, confirmed this view in an interview with Eskow: "What drives business is optimization of working capital. The amount of control you have on inventory equals the optimization of the capital. That's why it's so important to integrate the inventory data with everything else."

THE FUTURE OF INVENTORY CONTROL SYSTEMS
In the latter part of the 1990s, many businesses are

investing heavily in integrated order and inventory systems designed to keep inventories at a minimum and replenish stock quickly. But as Eskow noted, business owners have a variety of system integration options from which to choose, based on their needs and financial liquidity. "Integrated inventory systems may range in platform and complexity," he noted.

At the same time that these integrated systems have increased in popularity, business observers have suggested that "stand-alone" systems are falling into disfavor. Tom Andel and Daniel A. Kind, for instance, cited a 1996 study by the International Mass Retail Association (IMRA) in *Transportation and Distribution:* "The study concludes that stand alone Warehouse Management System (WMS) packages acquired today to perform individual functions will probably be abandoned in just a few years because they do not integrate well with other systems. Systems investments must be considered in context of future systems objectives."

Another development of which small business vendors should be aware is a recent trend wherein powerful retailers ask their suppliers to implement vendor-managed inventory systems. These arrangements place the responsibility for inventory management squarely on the shoulders of the vendors. Under such an agreement, the vendors obtain warehouse or point of sale information from the retailer and use that information to make inventory restocking decisions.

WAREHOUSE LAYOUT AND OPERATION

The move toward automation in inventory management naturally has moved into the warehouse as well. Citing various warehousing experts, Sarah Bergin contended in *Transportation and Distribution* magazine that "the key to getting productivity gains from inventory management . . . is placing real-time intelligent information processing in the warehouse. This empowers employees to take actions that achieve immediate results. Real-time processing in the warehouse uses combinations of hardware including material handling and data collection technologies. But according to these executives, the intelligent part of the system is sophisticated software which automates and controls all aspects of warehouse operations."

Another important component of good inventory management is creation and maintenance of a sensible, effective warehousing design. A well-organized, user-friendly warehouse layout can be of enormous benefit to small business owners, especially if they are involved in processing large volumes of goods and materials. Conversely, an inefficient warehouse system can cost businesses dearly in terms of efficiency, customer service, and, ultimately, profitability.

Transportation and Distribution magazine cited several steps that businesses that utilize warehouse storage systems can take to help ensure that they get the most out of their facilities. It recommended that companies utilize the following tools:

Stock locator database—"The stock locator database required for proactive decision making will be an adjunct of the inventory file in a state-of-the-art space management system. A running record will be maintained of the stock number, lot number, and number of pallet loads in each storage location. Grid coordinates of the reserve area, including individual rack tier positions, must therefore be established, and the pallet load capacity of all storage locations must be incorporated into the database."

Grid coordinate numbering system—Warehouse numbering system should be developed in conjunction with the storage layout, and should be user-friendly so that workers can quickly locate currently stocked items and open storage spaces alike.

Communication systems—Again, this can be a valuable investment if the business's warehouse requirements are significant. Such facilities often utilize fork lift machinery that can be used more effectively if their operators are not required to periodically return to a central assignment area. Current technology, however, makes it possible for the warehouse computer system to interact with terminal displays on the fork lifts themselves. "Task assignment can then be made by visual display or printout, and task completion can be confirmed by scanning, keyboard entry, or voice recognition," observed *Transportation and Distribution.*

Maximization of storage capacity—Warehouses that adhere to rigid "storage by incoming lot size" storage arrangements do not always make the best use of their space. Instead, businesses should settle on a strategy that eases traffic congestion and best eases problems associated with ongoing turnover in inventory.

OUTSOURCING WAREHOUSE RESPONSIBILITIES

Some companies choose to outsource their warehouse functions. "This allows a company that isn't as confident in running their own warehousing operations to concentrate on their core business and let the experts worry about keeping track of their inventory," wrote Bergin. "There are third party services available for managing warehouse operations. SonicAir, for one, provides companies with an analysis of products and spare parts, evaluations of their time sensitivity, and current installations and locations of vendor's distribution centers." Inventory control systems such as the one utilized by SonicAir, said Bergin, provide them with the ability to do real-time updating of inventory, cross-docking and dispatch, verification, and up to the minute tracking of inventory item location. Such systems are also capable of providing "a strategic stocking analysis which looks at the customer's equipment locations to determine which strategic stocking locations should be used, the expected transit time, and projected fill rate," added Bergin. Of course, businesses weighing whether to outsource such a key component of their operation need to consider the expense of such a course of action, as well as their feelings about relinquishing that level of control.

FURTHER READING:

Andel, Tom, and Daniel A. Kind. "Flow It, Don't Stow It." *Transportation and Distribution.* May 1996.

Bergin, Sarah. "Make Your Warehouse Deliver: New Developments in Warehouse Management Systems Inspire New Productivity in Needy Operations." *Transportation and Distribution.* February 1997.

Betts, Mitch. "Manage My Inventory or Else!" *Computerworld.* January 31, 1994.

Eskow, Dennis. "Rising Stock: Integrated Inventory Systems Help Companies Shoot Economic Rapids." *PC Week.* June 5, 1995.

Gleckman, Howard. "A Tonic for the Business Cycle." *Business Week.* April 4, 1994.

Haire, Kevlin C. "Keeping the Merchandise Moving." *Baltimore Business Journal.* August 2, 1996.

Udo, Godwin J. "The Impact of Telecommunications on Inventory Management." *Production and Inventory Management Journal.* Spring 1993.

Weiss, Howard J., and Mark E. Gershon. *Production and Operations Management.* Boston: Allyn and Bacon, 1989.

Weisfeld, Barry. "Automated Ordering Puts Profits in Sight." *Transportation and Distribution.* February 1997.

SEE ALSO: Inventory

INVESTOR PRESENTATIONS

Investor presentations are an important but often overlooked aspect of entrepreneurial efforts to secure financing for their businesses. Presentations are particularly important to small business owners hoping to raise money from private investors. Whereas institutional investors such as banks rely primarily on financial statements, business plans, etc., in making their lending decisions (though presentations to loan officers can also be important), private investors are more likely to be swayed by other factors, such as the owner's vision of a new product's appeal, knowledge of the marketplace, or ability to present a compelling picture of future profits for both the owner and the investor.

Business advisors note, however, that poor investor presentations can also close the door on potential avenues of financing as well, even if the entrepreneur's idea for a new business or product is a good one.

"Putting together a winning presentation isn't as easy as it might seem," said David R. Evanson in *Nation's Business.* "Whatever the forum—a formal dog-and-pony show before a roomful or institutional investors, a clubby luncheon with 10 to 15 wealthy individuals, or a one-on-one meeting with a venture capitalist—founders . . . have often shown they can shoot themselves in the foot with deadly accuracy." Entrepreneurs and small business owners seeking expansion **capital**, then, need to make certain that their presentations grab the attention of investors in a favorable way.

KEYS TO SUCCESSFUL INVESTOR PRESENTATIONS

Business experts point to several considerations that small businesspeople should keep in mind when planning their presentations to potential investors. These range from tips on public speaking to recommendations on presentation content.

TAILOR PRESENTATION TO AUDIENCE Some business owners make investor presentations that are only negligibly different from presentations that they make to internal salespeople or to customers. This choice—which is often a byproduct of laziness more than anything else—can have a negative impact on the owner's chances of landing an investor. "Topics such as product features, new technology and customer service—the things that matter to customers—are of interest to investors only as part of an overall menu of competitive advantages that will help drive sales," said Evanson. Moreover, no two investors are alike; one individual may have a reputation for daring business initiatives; another may be predisposed toward (or away from) involvement in a specific industry; still another may be most interested in receiving assurances about the competence of the enterprise's management team. Entrepreneurs preparing to make a pitch toward private investors should find out as much as possible about their audience's interests and investment philosophies beforehand.

JUDICIOUS USE OF VISUAL AIDS Visual aids should augment the presentation, not dominate it. Slides and overheads can be valuable tools in a presentation, but their use contains a number of potential pitfalls for entrepreneurs. Some people place so much importance on the visual component of their presentation that they flounder in situations where they have to deviate from their script. Others cram their visual aids so full of information that viewers are unable to digest it all, which merely triggers resentment or annoyance from potential investors. However, visual support—when intelligently utilized—can be most helpful in providing context and illustrating key points.

Presentation-graphics computer programs are utilized frequently today for such purposes. Such pro-grams have several advantages. They can compose impressive displays and their content can be altered quickly to reflect needed changes. Moreover, their portability is a big improvement over big slide carousels, overhead projectors, and display boards. But many of the advantages associated with computer displays hinge on a certain level of program mastery. Given this reality, *Los Angeles Business Journal* contributors John Greer and Francie Murphy counseled presenters not to make any changes in the 24 hours before a presentation. "The more sophisticated the equipment, the more time it takes to make changes and be sure they will work," they warned.

LIVE DEMONSTRATIONS It may be tempting for an entrepreneur to make a live demonstration or his or her product as part of the total presentation package, but demonstrations have a pretty hefty downside. This is especially true of technology products, which can end up looking hopeless because of some minor glitch. "As people with sales experience will tell you, the customer has a picture in mind of what the product is and what it's supposed to do," wrote Evanson. "Any uncontrolled situation that distorts that image is ultimately counterproductive to closing the sale." Of course, there may be situations wherein the presenter is pointedly asked for a live demonstration by a potential investor. Not granting such a request may throw prospects for financial assistance in jeopardy as well, so entrepreneurs should be prepared to make such a demonstration if it seems necessary. Finally, there are certain categories of products (generally involving simpler, non-technological designs) that can be more safely demonstrated than others. Each presenter has to weigh the potential risks of a live demonstration.

RELEVANCE Presentations that spend excessive amounts of time on relatively unimportant points are unlikely to attract investors. Instead, presentations should remain focused on the basic information that investors are likely to want to hear, such as company background, ownership/management background, key employees, product development, market opportunities, existing competition, present and future marketing plans, and financial analysis.

COMMUNICATION ABILITIES This element of presentation encompasses several different areas. First of all, the presenter should ideally be able to speak in an authoritative, confident, and smooth manner. Fairly or not, public speaking ability can make a profound difference in an entrepreneur's success in securing investors for his or her business or product. "There are a number of golden rules in making a presentation and plenty of speakers break them all," observed Sue Bryant in *Marketing.* "No eye contact. No pauses. Patronizing the audience by putting text on screen and reading it out loud. Writing a speech, failing to rehearse and reading it woodenly. Fumbling with equipment and muttering: 'Now, how do I work this thing. . . .'" Indeed, Bryant pointed out that excessive use of visual aids can often be traced to a presenter's discomfort with public speaking. Given the importance of a good delivery, then, entrepreneurs who are uncomfortable with speaking in public should consider investing in one of the many courses that are available to help people with such difficulties.

Presenters also need to make sure that the presentation itself is appropriately focused and understandable. Karen Kalish, author of *How to Give a Terrific Presentation,* stated that effective presentations have seven key organizational elements:

- Audience-grabbing opening
- Well-organized information (including examples, analogies, and anecdotes where appropriate)
- Logical transitions
- Short sentences
- Understandable language
- Good closing
- Appropriate responses to questions.

Entrepreneurs seeking funding for high-tech products are particularly prone to straying off track. They have to beware of paying excessive attention to relatively esoteric subjects that may bore the prospective investors. "Yes, the technical aspects of your company's product or service are important," wrote Evanson and Art Beroff in *Entrepreneur,* "inasmuch as they deliver competitive advantages, open new markets or change the balance of power in an existing market—but to investors, technology is not important in and of itself."

HONEST PRESENTATION Presenting projected financial performance for a company or product is an important and delicate part of the investor presentation process. Entrepreneurs naturally want to put their prospects in a good light, but consultants warn that private investors are wary of overly optimistic numbers, and view misleading data in this area as a clear sign that they should withhold assistance. "With so many exciting opportunities in the marketplace, you've got to walk a very fine line between numbers that are exciting enough to attract investors and those that will turn them off because they're simply unrealistic," one successful business founder told *Entrepreneur.*

LENGTH OF PRESENTATION Most experts advise entrepreneurs to limit their presentation to 20-30 minutes. It may be tempting to devote more time than that—and in some cases it may be warranted (the potential investor has already indicated that he or she wants a full accounting, the entrepreneur's idea is a complex one)—but for the most part, entrepreneurs should limit themselves as indicated above. Whereas excessively long presentations can bore investors and unduly short ones can leave investors wondering if they are being told everything, presentations of 20-30 minutes can usually provide an adequate overview and leave sufficient time to answer investor questions.

QUESTION-AND-ANSWER SESSIONS Questions from investors are an inevitable part of investor presentations. Entrepreneurs who avoid answering certain questions, answer with rambling sermons in "tech-speak," or respond in an arrogant, "know it all" fashion are unlikely to favorably impress their audience. "It's dissatisfying to an investor when he or she asks a question and the answer isn't even relevant," one investor told *Entrepreneur.* "In fact, it's as close to the kiss of death as there is. By not listening to an investor's question carefully, you reduce your chances of success."

FOLLOW-UP Entrepreneurs should follow up with investors within a few days of the presentation, but they should be careful not to badger him or her with multiple queries. "When raising capital, particularly from individual investors, the old rule is that yes comes fast, and no takes forever," commented Evanson and Beroff. "Still, many investors test the mettle of the business owner by seeing how long it take him or her to follow up. If it's not forthcoming, even for reasons of perceived courtesy, many investors get turned off. On the other side of the coin, calling every day doesn't work, either."

FURTHER READING:

Arthur, Audrey. "Keeping Up Public Appearances: Master the Fine Art of Public Speaking and Give a Great Presentation Every Time." *Black Enterprise.* July 1997.

Bryant, Sue. "Speak for Yourself." *Marketing.* October 31, 1996.

"Elements of a Great Speech." *Industry Week.* February 17, 1997.

Evanson, David R. "Capital Pitches that Succeed." *Nation's Business.* May 1997.

Evanson, David R., and Art Beroff. "Perfect Pitch." *Entrepreneur.* March 1998.

Greer, John, and Francie Murphy. "Be Prepared When Making Multimedia Presentations." *Los Angeles Business Journal.* September 22, 1997.

Greising, David. "Hunting Investors Who Will Go the Distance." *Business Week.* November 9, 1992.

Kalish, Karen. *How to Give a Terrific Presentation.* New York: AMACOM, 1997.

"Lights, Camera, Action!" *What to Buy for Business.* May 1997.

Mahoney, William F., and Charles K. Wessendorf. "How to Get Investors Online." *Financial Executive.* January-February 1996.

Malouf, Doug, Carolyn Dickson, and Paula DePasquale. "The Seven Deadly Sins of Speakers." *Training & Development.* November 1995.

Martin, Larry. "The Fate of Business Often Comes Down to the Quality of the Presentation." *Public Relations Quarterly.* Spring 1995.

McCollum, Tim. "The New Face of Presentations." *Nation's Business.* July 1997.

Rosen, Robert M. "How Smaller Companies Can Get Bank Loans." *Corporate Cashflow Magazine.* December 1991.

INVESTOR RELATIONS AND REPORTING

Once a privately held company issues shares of stock to the public—through an **initial public offering (IPO)**, for example—it incurs a number of new responsibilities related to investor relations and reporting requirements. Also known as "going public," an IPO transforms a small business from a privately owned and operated entity into one that is owned by public stockholders. An IPO is a significant stage in the growth of many small businesses, as it provides them with access to the public capital market and also increases their credibility and exposure. Becoming a public entity involves significant changes for a small business, though, including a loss of flexibility and control for management.

"Along with fresh infusions of **capital** come the shareholders who invest in them. Now the company has a large number of new owners who want to see *their* CEO and *their* company perform," David P. Sutton and M. William Benedetto wrote in their book *Initial Public Offerings: A Strategic Planner for Raising Equity Capital.* "The CEO may have 1,000 or more new bosses overnight."

REPORTING REQUIREMENTS

Public companies must comply with all the rules and regulations set forth by the Securities Act of 1934, not only during the IPO process, but also afterward. Small business owners who take their companies public must comply with regular reporting procedures required by the **Securities and Exchange Commission (SEC)**. "Suddenly, management must see that these new owners are kept up-to-date on all material company events," according to Sutton and Benedetto. In addition to the periodic reports known as 8A, 10K, and 10Q, public companies also must issue **annual reports**, quarterly reports, proxy statements, and press releases in order to keep shareholders, financial analysts, and regulatory agencies informed of their actions.

Form 8A is the main form for registering a stock issue with the SEC. It must be filed if the shares will be traded on a major stock exchange (NYSE, AMEX, or NASDAQ), if the firm will have more than 500 shareholders, or if it has more than $3 million in assets. Companies that register their stock offerings using Form 8A must also file periodic reports until they no longer meet the aforementioned requirements. These updates are an important means of communication with shareholders, who use the information in making investment decisions.

All public companies are required to file Form 10K annually within 90 days of end of their fiscal year. This form requires disclosure of the company's audited financial statements, a summary of operations, a description of the overall business and its physical property, identification of any subsidiaries or affiliates, disclosure of the revenues contributed by major products or departments, and information on the number of shareholders, the management team and their salaries, and the interests of management and shareholders in certain transactions. The idea of Form 10K is to update on an annual basis the information that the company provided for its initial filing.

Form 10Q, which must be filed within 45 days of the end of each of the first three quarters in a company's fiscal year, includes audited financial statements with management discussion, as well as details of any corporate events that had a significant impact on the company. Another important reporting requirement is Form 8K, which discloses major changes in corporate control or assets due to such events as mergers, acquisitions, or bankruptcy. Several other types of filings are required for specific events, such as a significant increase or decrease in the amount of outstanding stock, or distributions to shareholders in the form of stock splits or dividends. In addition, public companies are required to inform stockholders of impending meetings or votes and send out proxy statements. Finally, insider trading laws require that public companies disclose any changes in the holdings of managers or directors who own more than 10 percent of the company's stock.

INVESTOR RELATIONS

In addition to SEC reporting requirements, public companies also face the responsibility of maintaining good investor relations. Although it is not legally required, it is nonetheless important for public companies to establish systems to deal with stockholders, financial analysts, the media, and the overall community. "A key responsibility of management, over and above filing all necessary reports, is to keep the company name in front of investors," Sutton and Benedetto noted. "Remember, the only way to have a rising stock price is to have more buyers than sellers. That means more than just increased earnings. It means investors, both current and prospective ones, must know about the company.''

It is therefore vital that interested outsiders are presented with a complete and accurate picture of what is happening within the company. In some cases, this may entail obtaining the services of a public relations firm that specializes in investor relations. Such firms can guide newly public companies through the maze of information that they must disseminate. Though investor relations can be expensive, ''Getting the word out about the company and its stock is critical to the company's stock price,'' as Sutton and Benedetto stated.

FURTHER READING:

Arkebauer, James B., and Ronald M. Schultz. *Cashing Out: The Entrepreneur's Guide to Going Public.* New York: HarperBusiness, 1991.

Lindsey, Jennifer. *The Entrepreneur's Guide to Capital: The Techniques for Capitalizing and Refinancing New and Growing Businesses.* Chicago, IL: Probus, 1986.

Roberts, Holme, and Harold A. S. Bloomenthal. *Going Public Handbook.* New York: Clark Boardman, 1991.

Sutton, David P., and M. William Benedetto. *Initial Public Offerings: A Strategic Planner for Raising Equity Capital.* Chicago, IL: Probus, 1988.

SEE ALSO: Stocks

ISO 9000

ISO 9000 is a set of international standards of quality management that have become increasingly popular for large and small companies alike. ''ISO is grounded on the 'conformance to specification' definition of quality,'' wrote Francis Buttle in the *International Journal of Quality and Reliability Management.* ''The standards specify how management operations shall be conducted. ISO 9000's purpose is to ensure that suppliers design, create, and deliver products and services which meet predetermined standards; in other words, its goal is to prevent nonconformity.'' Used by both manufacturing and service firms, ISO 9000 had been adopted by more than 100 nations as their national quality management/quality assurance standard by the end of 1997.

This quality standard was first introduced in 1987 by the International Organization for Standards (ISO) in hopes of establishing an international definition of the essential characteristics and language of a quality system for all businesses, irrespective of industry or geographic location. Initially, it was used almost exclusively by large companies, but by the mid-1990s, increasing numbers of small- and mid-sized companies had embraced ISO 9000 as well. In fact, small and

moderate-sized companies account for much of the growth in ISO 9000 registration over the past several years. The total number of ISO 9000 registrations in the United States increased from a little more than 2,200 in 1993 to more than 17,000 early in 1998; of those 17,000 registrations, nearly 60 percent were held by companies with annual sales of $100 million or less.

The increased involvement of small and mid-sized firms in seeking ISO 9000 registration is generally attributed to several factors. Many small businesses have decided to seek ISO 9000 certification because of their corporate customers, who began to insist on it as a method of ensuring that their suppliers were paying adequate attention to quality. Other small business owners, meanwhile, have pursued ISO 9000 certification in order to increase their chances of securing new business or simply as a means of improving the quality of their processes. ''The pressure for companies to become ISO 9000-certified is absolutely increasing and will continue to increase,'' predicted one management consultant in an interview with *Nation's Business.* ''The question many smaller companies have to ask is when, not if, they [will] get ISO 9000-registered.''

ELEMENTS OF ISO 9000 QUALITY MANAGEMENT SYSTEMS The standards of ISO 9000 detail 20 requirements for an organization's quality management system in the following areas:

- Management Responsibility
- Quality System
- Order Entry
- Design Control
- Document and Data Control
- Purchasing
- Control of Customer Supplied Products
- Product Identification and Tractability
- Process Control
- Inspection and Testing
- Control of Inspection, Measuring, and Test Equipment
- Inspection and Test Status
- Control of Nonconforming Products
- Corrective and Preventive Action
- Handling, Storage, Packaging, and Delivery
- Control of Quality Records
- Internal Quality Audits
- Training
- Servicing
- Statistical Techniques

MODELS OF ISO 9000

The ISO 9000 quality standards are broken down into three model sets—ISO 9001, ISO 9002, and ISO 9003. Each of these models, noted *Industrial Management* contributors Stanislav Karapetrovic, Divakar Rajamani, and Walter Willborn, "stipulate a number of requirements on which an organization's quality system can be assessed by an external party (registrar)" in accordance with the ISO's quality system audits standard. "A quality system," they added, "involves organizational structure, processes, and documented procedures constituted towards achieving quality objectives."

Each of the three sets concentrates on a different quality area. ISO 9001 is the most wide-ranging, for it specifies the various operating requirements in areas such as product design and development, production, installation, and servicing. ISO 9002 is concerned with quality assurance at the production and installation stages. ISO 9003 covers testing and inspections. As Karapetrovic, Rajamani, and Willborn noted, "if the minimum requirements are met [for the above operating areas], a registrar accredited by a national accreditation institution issues a certificate of compliance and the organization's quality system becomes ISO 9001, 9002, or 9003 registered." It is worth noting that certification is handed out for individual quality systems, not companies; this means that one company may hold more than one ISO 9000 registration. Moreover, Harvey R. Meyer pointed out in *Nation's Business* that "the standards do not certify the quality of a product or service. Rather, they attest that a company has fully documented its quality-control processes and consistently adheres to them. If that's done, quality products and services generally follow."

ADVANTAGES OF ISO 9000

The advantages associated with ISO 9000 certification are numerous, as both business analysts and business owners will attest. These benefits, which can impact nearly all corners of a company, range from increased stature to bottom-line operational savings:

- Increased marketability—Nearly all observers agree that ISO 9000 registration provides businesses with markedly heightened credibility with current and prospective clients alike. Basically, it proves that the company is dedicated to providing quality to its customers, which is no small advantage whether the company is negotiating with a long-time customer or endeavoring to pry away a potentially lucrative customer from a competitor. Indeed, a 1991 survey published in the *International Journal of Quality and Reliability Management* indicated that 70 percent of the small and mid-sized compa-

nies that responded cited **marketing** as the principle area in which ISO 9000 registration proved most advantageous. This benefit manifested itself not only in increased **customer retention**, but also in increased customer acquisition and heightened ability to enter into new markets; indeed, ISO 9000 registration has been cited as being of particular value for small and mid-sized businesses hoping to establish a presence in international markets.

- Reduced operational expenses—Sometimes lost in the many discussions of ISO 9000's public relations cache is the fact that the rigorous registration process often exposes significant shortcomings in various operational areas. When these problems are brought to light, the company can take the appropriate steps to improve its processes. These improved efficiencies can help companies garner savings in both time and money. "The cost of scrap, rework, returns, and the employee time spent analyzing and troubleshooting various products are all considerably reduced by initiating the discipline of ISO 9000," confirmed Richard B. Wright in *Industrial Distribution.*

- Better management control—The ISO 9000 registration process requires so much documentation and self-assessment that many businesses that undergo its rigors cite increased understanding of the company's overall direction and processes as a significant benefit.

- Increased customer satisfaction—Since the ISO 9000 certification process almost inevitably uncovers areas in which final product quality can be improved, such efforts often bring about higher levels of customer satisfaction. In addition, by seeking and securing ISO 9000 certification, companies can provide their clients with the opportunity to tout their suppliers' dedication to quality in their own business dealings.

- Improved internal communication—The ISO 9000 certification process's emphasis on self-analysis and operations management issues encourages various internal areas or departments of companies to interact with one another in hopes of gaining a more complete understanding of the needs and desires of their internal customers.

- Improved **customer service**—The process of securing ISO 9000 registration often serves to refocus company priorities on pleasing their customers in all respects, in-

ISO 9000

cluding customer service areas. It also helps heighten awareness of quality issues among employees.

- Reduction of product-liability risks—Many business experts contend that companies that achieve ISO 9000 certification are less likely to be hit with product liability lawsuits, for example, because of the quality of their processes.

- Attraction to investors—Business consultants and small business owners alike agree that ISO-9000 certification can be a potent tool in securing funding from venture capital firms.

DISADVANTAGES OF ISO 9000

Despite the many advantages associated with ISO 9000, however, business owners and consultants caution companies to research the rigorous certification process before committing resources to it. Following is a list of potential hurdles for entrepreneurs to study before committing to an initiative to gain ISO 9000 certification:

- Owners and managers do not have an adequate understanding of the ISO 9000 certification process or of the quality standards themselves—Some business owners have been known to direct their company's resources toward ISO 9000 registration, only to find that their incomplete understanding of the process and its requirements results in wasted time and effort.

- Funding for establishing the quality system is inadequate—Critics of ISO 9000 contend that achieving certification can be a very costly process, especially for smaller firms. Indeed, according to a 1996 *Quality Systems Update* survey, the average cost of ISO certification for small firms (those registering less than $11 million in annual sales) was $71,000.

- Heavy emphasis on documentation—The ISO 9000 certification process relies heavily on documentation of internal operating procedures in many areas, and as Meyer stated, "many say ISO's exacting documentation requirements gobble up time. Indeed, there are horror stories about companies losing substantial business because a documentation obsession redirected their priorities." According to *Nation's Business,* small business owners need to find an appropriate balance between ISO documentation requirements, which are admittedly "one of ISO 9000's hallmarks," and attending to the fundamental business of running a company: "Strike a balance among obsessively writing down every employee's task, offering training for the work, and letting common sense dictate how a task is to be performed."

- Length of the process—Business executives and owners familiar with the ISO 9000 registration process warn that it is a process that takes many months to complete. The 1996 *Quality Systems Update* survey indicated that it took businesses an average of 15 months to move from the early stages of the process to passage of the final audit, and that processes of 18-20 months or even longer were not that uncommon.

SELECTING A LEADER FOR THE ISO 9000 REGISTRATION PROCESS

ISO 9000 experts and businesses that have gone through the rigorous process of certification agree that businesses that appoint someone to guide the process are much more likely to be able to undergo the process in a healthy, productive manner than are firms that have murky reporting relationships. Hiring an outside consultant is one option for businesses. "An ISO 9000 advisor could give you a rough sketch of the registration process and help you get started," stated *Nation's Business.* "Or the consultant could counsel you through the entire process, writing the company's quality policy statement and even specific operating procedures." In addition, firms should hire an ISO-9000 registrar with a background in their industry, legitimacy with international customers, and knowledge of small business issues.

Some small firms choose to appoint an employee as their ISO 9000 representative rather than hire an outside consultant. Many companies have done this successfully, but small business owners should take great care in making this decision. "The ISO 9000 representative [should be] a person who encompasses a genuine and passionate commitment to quality and success, knowledge of processes and systems within the company, and power to influence employees at all levels," wrote Karapetrovic, Rajamani, and Willborn. "He should be familiar with the standards. If this is not the case, there are ample training opportunities available to acquire sufficient expertise."

For more information on ISO 9000 registration, small business owners can contact several organizations, including the American Society for Quality (611 E. Wisconsin Ave., Milwaukee, WI 53202, phone 800-248-1946) and American National Standards Institute (11 W. 42nd St., New York, NY 10036, phone 212-642-4900).

FURTHER READING:

Buttle, Francis. "ISO 9000: Marketing Motivations and Benefits." *International Journal of Quality and Reliability Management.* July 1997.

Johnson, P. L. *ISO 9000: Meeting the New International Standards.* New York: McGraw-Hill, 1993.

Karapetrovic, Stanislav, Divakar Rajamani, and Walter Willborn. "ISO 9000 for Small Business: Do It Yourself." *Industrial Management.* May-June 1997.

Meyer, Harvey R. "Small Firms Flock to Quality System." *Nation's Business.* March 1998.

Rabbit, J. T. *The ISO 9000 Book: A Global Competitor's Guide to Compliance and Registration.* Quality Resources, 1993.

Randall, Richard C. *Randall's Practical Guide to ISO 9000 Implementation, Registration, and Beyond.* Reading, MA: Addison-Wesley.

Rayner, P., and L. J. Porter. "BS 5750/ISO 9000: The Experience of Small and Medium-Sized Firms." *International Journal of Quality and Reliability Management.* Vol. 8, no. 6, 1991.

Voehl, F., P. Jackson, and D. Ashton. *ISO 9000: An Implementation Guide for Small to Mid-Sized Businesses.* St. Lucie Press, 1994.

Wilson, L. A. "Eight-Step Process to Successful ISO 9000 Implementation: A Quality Management System Approach." *Quality Progress.* January 1996.

Wright, Richard B. "Why We Need ISO 9000." *Industrial Distribution.* January 1997.

SEE ALSO: Market Share; Operations Management; Quality Control